The 2010 World Book

YEAR BOOK

A REVIEW OF THE EVENTS OF 2009

The Annual
Supplement to
The World Book
Encyclopedia

World Book, Inc.
a Scott Fetzer company
Chicago
www.worldbook.com

To request cross-reference tabs to associate *Year Book* content with your set of *The World Book Encyclopedia,* please phone 1-888-626-5362 or 1-800-975-3250. The tabs will be sent to you free of charge.

Thank you.
The Publisher

World Book, Inc.
233 N. Michigan Ave.
Chicago, IL 60601

ISBN: 978-0-7166-0503-4 (Year Book binding)
ISBN: 978-0-7166-0504-1 (Year in Review binding)
ISSN: 0084-1439
Library of Congress Control Number: 62004818

Printed in the United States of America by RR Donnelley, Willard, Ohio
1st Printing February 2010

STAFF

EXECUTIVE COMMITTEE

President
Paul A. Gazzolo

Vice President and Chief Financial Officer
Donald D. Keller

Vice President and Editor in Chief
Paul A. Kobasa

Vice President and Chief Marketing Officer
Patricia Ginnis

Vice President, Licensing & Business Development
Richard Flower

Chief Technology Officer
Tim Hardy

Managing Director, International
Benjamin Hinton

Director, Human Resources
Bev Ecker

EDITORIAL

Associate Director, Supplementary Publications
Scott Thomas

Managing Editor, Supplementary Publications
Barbara A. Mayes

Associate Manager, Supplementary Publications
Cassie Mayer

Senior Editor, Supplementary Publications
Kristina A. Vaicikonis

Manager, Research, Supplementary Publications
Cheryl Graham

Administrative Assistant
Ethel Matthews

Editors
Shawn Brennan
Jake Bumgardner
Jeff De La Rosa
Michael DuRoss
Brian Johnson
Daniel Kenis
Nicholas Kilzer
Dawn Krajcik
Mike Lewis
S. Thomas Richardson
Kenneth J. Shenkman
Christine Sullivan
Daniel O. Zeff

Contributing Editors
Sara Dreyfuss
Robert Knight
Alfred J. Smuskiewicz

Statistics Editor
William M. Harrod

Manager, Contracts & Compliance (Rights & Permissions)
Loranne K. Shields

EDITORIAL ADMINISTRATION

Director, Systems and Projects
Tony Tills

Senior Manager, Publishing Operations
Timothy Falk

Associate Manager, Publishing Operations
Audrey Casey

Manager, Indexing Services
David Pofelski

Associate Manager, Indexing Services
Aamir Burki

GRAPHICS AND DESIGN

Manager
Tom Evans

Coordinator, Design Development and Production
Brenda B. Tropinski

Senior Designers
Don Di Sante
Isaiah W. Sheppard, Jr.

Associate Designer
Matthew Carrington

Photographs Editor
Kathryn Creech

Manager, Cartographic Services
Wayne K. Pichler

Senior Cartographer
John M. Rejba

PRODUCTION

Director, Manufacturing and Pre-Press
Carma Fazio

Manufacturing Manager
Barbara Podczerwinski

Production/Technology Manager
Anne Fritzinger

Proofreading
Emilie Schrage

MARKETING

Director, Direct Marketing
Mark R. Willy

Marketing Analyst
Zofia Kulik

CONTRIBUTORS

Contributors not listed on these pages are members of the editorial staff.

ANDREWS, PETER J., B.A., M.S.; free-lance writer. **[Chemistry]**

BAYNHAM, SIMON, B.A., M.A., Ph.D.; senior research associate, Centre for Defence & International Security Studies, University of Lancaster, U.K. **[Africa and African country articles]**

BECK, STEFAN, B.A.; associate editor, *The New Criterion* magazine. **[Literature]**

BERGER, ERIC R., B.A, M.A.; science writer, *Houston Chronicle.* **[Houston]**

BOYD, JOHN D., B.S.; economics writer. **[Economics, United States Special Report: Economic Crisis, Then and Now; Economics, U.S.; Economics, World; International trade]**

BRADSHER, HENRY S., A.B., B.J.; foreign affairs analyst. **[Asia and Asian country articles]**

BRETT, CARLTON E., B.A., M.S., Ph.D.; Professor of Geology, University of Cincinnati. **[Paleontology]**

CASEY, MIKE, B.S., M.A.; former assistant editor, *Kansas City Star.* **[Automobile]**

CITRIN, ADRIENNE, B.A.; Manager of Public Relations, Toy Industry Association, Incorporated. **[Toys and games]**

DEEB, MARIUS K., B.A., Ph.D.; Professor, School of Advanced International Studies, Johns Hopkins University. **[Middle East and Middle Eastern country articles; North African country articles]**

DEEB, MARY-JANE, B.A., Ph.D.; Chief of the African and Middle Eastern Division, Library of Congress. **[Middle Eastern country articles; North African country articles]**

DeFRANK, THOMAS M., B.A., M.A.; Washington Bureau Chief, *New York Daily News.* **[Armed forces]**

DILLON, DAVID, B.A., M.A., Ph.D.; architecture and design editor, *The Dallas Morning News.* **[Architecture]**

ELLIS, GAVIN, former Editor in Chief, *The New Zealand Herald & Weekend Herald.* **[New Zealand]**

FISHER, ROBERT W., B.A., M.A.; free-lance writer. **[Labor and employment]**

FITZGERALD, THOMAS, A.B., S.T.M, Ph.D.; Dean and Professor of Church History and Historical Theology, Holy Cross Greek Orthodox School of Theology. **[Eastern Orthodox Churches]**

FRIEDMAN, EMILY, B.A.; health policy and ethics analyst. **[United States, Government of the Special Report: Food and Drug Safety and the FDA; Health care issues]**

GADOMSKI, FRED, B.S., M.S.; meteorologist, Pennsylvania State University. **[Weather]**

GOLDBERG, BEVERLY, B.A.; senior editor, American Library Association. **[Library]**

GOLDEN, JONATHAN J., B.A., M.J.Ed.; Chair, History Department at the Gann Academy, New Jewish High School of Greater Boston. **[Judaism]**

HAVERSTOCK, NATHAN A., A.B.; affiliate scholar, Oberlin College. **[Latin America and Latin American country articles]**

HELMS, CHRISTINE MOSS, B.A. D.Phil; free-lance writer/political analyst. **[Middle East Special Report: Iran's Long, Hot Summer]**

HOGAN, ERIN, B.A.; Director of Public Affairs, Art Institute of Chicago. **[Art Special Report: Bright Idea: The Art Institute of Chicago's New Modern Wing]**

JOHANSON, DONALD C., B.S., M.A., Ph.D.; Director and Professor, Institute of Human Origins, Arizona State University. **[Anthropology]**

JOHNSON, JULIET, A.B., M.A., Ph.D.; Associate Professor of Political Science, McGill University. **[Russia and other former Soviet republic articles]**

KATES, MICHAEL, B.S.J.; associate sports editor, *Chicago Tribune.* **[Sports articles]**

KENNEDY, BRIAN, M.A.; free-lance writer. **[Australia; Australia, Prime Minister of; Australian rules football]**

KILGORE, MARGARET, B.A., M.B.A.; free-lance writer, Kilgore and Associates. **[Los Angeles]**

KING, MIKE, reporter, *The (Montreal) Gazette.* **[Montreal]**

KLINTBERG, PATRICIA PEAK, B.A.; agricultural journalist. **[Agriculture]**

KNIGHT, ROBERT N., B.A., M.M.; free-lance writer. **[Deaths Special Report: Edward M. Kennedy, Lion of the Senate; Bank; People in the news]**

KOPSTEIN, JEFFREY, B.A., M.A., Ph.D; Professor of Political Science and Director, Centre for European, Russian, and Eur-asian Studies, University of Toronto. **[Europe and Western European country articles]**

LAWRENCE, ALBERT, B.A., M.A., M.Ed.; Executive Director, World Chess Hall of Fame. **[Chess]**

MANZO, KATHLEEN KENNEDY, B.A., M.Ed; associate editor, *Education Week.* **[Education]**

MARCH, ROBERT H., A.B., M.S., Ph.D.; Professor Emeritus of Physics and Liberal Studies, University of Wisconsin at Madison. **[Physics]**

MARKSJARVIS, GAIL, B.A.; personal finance columnist, *Chicago Tribune.* **[Stocks and bonds]**

MARSCHALL, LAURENCE A., B.S., Ph.D.; W.K.T. Sahm Professor of Physics, Gettysburg College. **[Astronomy]**

MARTY, MARTIN E., Ph.D.; Fairfax M. Cone Distinguished Service Professor Emeritus, University of Chicago. **[Protestantism]**

MAY, SALLY RUTH, B.A, M.A.; free-lance art writer. **[Art]**

McDONALD, ELAINE STUART, B.A.; free-lance public policy writer and editor. **[State government]**

McWILLIAM, ROHAN, B.A., M.A., D.Phil; Senior Lecturer in History, Anglia Polytechnic University, Cambridge, U.K. **[Ireland; Northern Ireland; United Kingdom; United Kingdom, Prime Minister of]**

MINER, TODD J., B.S., M.S.; Meteorologist, Pennsylvania State University. **[Weather]**

MORITZ, OWEN, B.A.; urban affairs editor, *New York Daily News.* **[New York City]**

MORRING, FRANK, Jr., B.A.; senior space technology editor, *Aviation Week & Space Technology* magazine. **[Space exploration]**

MORRIS, BERNADINE, B.A., M.A.; free-lance fashion writer. **[Fashion]**

MULLINS, HENRY T., B.S., M.S., Ph.D.; Professor of Geology, Syracuse University. **[Geology]**

4

NGUYEN, J. TUYET, M.A.; United Nations correspondent, Deutsche Presse-Agentur. **[Population; United Nations]**

OGAN, EUGENE, B.A., Ph.D.; Professor Emeritus of Anthropology, University of Minnesota. **[Pacific Islands]**

REINHART, A. KEVIN, B.A., M.A., Ph.D.; Associate Professor of Religious Studies, Dartmouth College. **[Islam]**

REITER, SUSAN, B.A.; free-lance performing arts journalist. **[Dance]**

RICCIUTI, EDWARD, B.A.; free-lance writer. **[Public health** Special Report: **Influenza: A New Threat from an Old Foe; Biology; Conservation; Zoos]**

ROBERTS, THOMAS W., Editor, *The National Catholic Reporter*. **[Roman Catholic Church]**

ROSE, MARK J., B.A., M.A., Ph.D.; Executive editor, *Archaeology* magazine. **[Archaeology]**

RUBENSTEIN, RICHARD E., B.A., M.A., J.D.; Professor of Conflict Resolution and Public Affairs, George Mason University. **[Terrorism]**

RUBENSTONE, JEFFREY, B.A.; Editor, *Engineering News-Record* magazine. **[Building and construction]**

RUSSELL, MARY HARRIS, B.A., M.A, Ph.D.; Professor of English, Indiana University. **[Literature for children]**

SARNA, JONATHAN D., Ph.D.; Joseph H. & Belle R. Braun Professor of American Jewish History, Brandeis University. **[Judaism]**

SHAPIRO, HOWARD, B.S.; staff writer and travel columnist, *The Philadelphia Inquirer*. **[Philadelphia; Washington, D.C.]**

SMUSKIEWICZ, ALFRED J., B.S., M.S.; free-lance writer. **[AIDS; City; Crime; Drug abuse; Drugs; Medicine; Mental health; Prison; Public health; Safety]**

STEIN, DAVID LEWIS, B.A., M.S.; former urban affairs columnist, *The Toronto Star*. **[Toronto]**

STOS, WILLIAM, B.A., M.A.; free-lance writer. **[Canada; Canada, Prime Minister of; Canadian provinces; Canadian territories]**

TANNER, JAMES C., B.J.; former news editor—energy, *The Wall Street Journal*. **[Energy supply]**

TATUM, HENRY K., B.A.; retired associate editor, *The Dallas Morning News*. **[Dallas]**

von RHEIN, JOHN, B.A.; classical music critic, *Chicago Tribune*. **[Classical music]**

WILLIAMS, BRIAN, B.A.; free-lance writer. **[Cricket; Soccer]**

WOLCHIK, SHARON L., B.A., M.A., Ph.D.; Professor of Political Science and International Affairs, George Washington University. **[Eastern European country articles]**

YEZZI, DAVID, B.F.A., M.F.A.; Executive editor, *The New Criterion* magazine. **[Poetry; Theater]**

ADVISERS

Mary Alice Anderson, B.S., M.A. Lead Media Specialist, Winona Area Public Schools, Winona, Minnesota, United States

Ali Banuazizi, B.S., M.A., Ph.D. Professor of Political Science and Co-Director of Middle Eastern & Islamic Studies Program, Boston College, Chestnut Hill, Massachusetts, United States

David J. Bercuson, O.C., B.A., M.A., Ph.D. Professor of History and Director, Centre for Military and Strategic Studies, University of Calgary, Calgary, Alberta, Canada

Marianna Anderson Busch, B.A., Ph.D. Professor of Chemistry and Biochemistry and Co-Director, Center for Analytical Spectroscopy, Baylor University, Waco, Texas, United States

Jesus Garcia, M.A., Ed.D. Professor of Social Studies Education, Department of Curriculum and Instruction, University of Nevada, Las Vegas, Nevada, United States

Marc B. Garnick, M.D. Clinical Professor of Medicine, Harvard Medical School, Harvard University; Physician, Beth Israel Deaconess Medical Center, Boston, Massachusetts, United States

Michael F. Graves, B.A., M.A., Ph.D. Professor Emeritus of Literacy Education, University of Minnesota, Twin Cities Campus, Minneapolis, Minnesota, United States

John T. Greene, B.A., M.A., Ph.D. Professor Emeritus of Religious Studies, Michigan State University, East Lansing, Michigan, United States

Robert Hodierne, B.A. Associate Professor of Journalism, University of Richmond, Richmond, Virginia, United States

Alan E. Mann, B.A., M.A., Ph.D. Professor of Anthropology, Princeton University, Princeton, New Jersey, United States

William McKeen, B.A., M.A., Ph.D. Professor and Chair, Department of Journalism, College of Journalism and Communication, University of Florida, Gainesville, Florida, United States

Jay M. Pasachoff, A.B., A.M., Ph.D. Field Memorial Professor of Astronomy and Director, Hopkins Observatory of Williams College, Williamstown, Massachusetts, United States

Michael Plante, B.A., M.A., Ph.D. Jessie J. Poesch Professor in Art, Newcomb Art Department, Tulane University, New Orleans, Louisiana, United States

Robert B. Prigo, B.S., M.S., Ph.D. Director of Teacher Education and Professor of Physics, Middlebury College, Middlebury, Vermont, United States

Michael Seidel, B.A., M.A., Ph.D. Jesse and George Siegel Professor of Humanities, Columbia University, New York City, New York, United States

Whitney Smith, A.B., A.M., Ph.D. Director, The Flag Research Center, Winchester, Massachusetts, United States

Scott L. Waugh, B.A., Ph.D. Executive Vice Chancellor and Provost, University of California, Los Angeles, United States

CONTENTS

SPECIAL REPORTS

FOCUS ON

PORTRAITS

417 WORLD BOOK
SUPPLEMENT

Four new or revised articles
are reprinted from the 2010
edition of *The World Book
Encyclopedia.*

481 INDEX

A 14-page cumulative
index covers the contents
of the 2008, 2009, and
2010 editions of *The
Year Book.*

From the worldwide economic downturn to the swine flu pandemic, 2009 was a year of extraordinary events. On these three pages are stories that the editors picked as some of the most important of the year, along with details on where to find more information about them in this volume.

The Editors

2009

FLU PANDEMIC

Thousands of people throughout the world become ill in 2009 as a disease popularly known as "swine flu" sweeps the globe. In June, the World Health Organization officially declares the outbreak, caused by the H1N1 virus, a pandemic. The governments of many nations adopt public health measures and rush to vaccinate their populations amid concerns that the new variety of flu may prove as deadly as the Spanish flu of 1918. See **Medicine,** page 263; **Mexico,** page 264; **Public Health: A Special Report,** page 326.

TYPHOONS KILL THOUSANDS

A series of typhoons, which began in August, drop massive amounts of rain on parts of Asia, triggering landslides and the worst flooding in decades. The storms leave some 2,000 people dead in Cambodia, China, Laos, the Philippines, Taiwan, and Vietnam. Pummeled by four typhoons in 2009, the Philippines are particularly hard hit. See **Asia,** page 68; **Disasters,** page 163; **Philippines**, page 316; **Taiwan,** page 367; **Weather,** page 410.

WILDFIRES IN AUSTRALIA

The worst wildfires in Australia's history burn across some 500,000 acres (200,000 hectares) in the state of Victoria in September. The product of years of drought, the fires level whole towns and leave 173 people dead. On September 23, an enormous dust storm shrouds hundreds of miles of Australia's east coast, including the city of Sydney, in red dust. According to the New South Wales Department of the Environment, air pollution levels are the highest since record keeping began in the 1970's. To the north in Queensland, the hot, dry weather is triggering more wildfires. See **Australia,** page 76; **Disasters,** page 163; **Weather,** page 410.

A NEW PRESIDENT

Barack Obama is inaugurated on Jan. 20, 2009, as the 44th president of the United States—and the nation's first African American president—before a crowd of more than 1 million people in Washington, D.C. He spends much of his first year in office responding to an economic recession, lobbying for health care reform, and overseeing U.S. military efforts overseas. On October 9, he wins the Nobel Peace Prize. See **Cabinet, U.S.**, page 105; **Congress of the United States**, page 130; **Nobel Prizes**, page 297; **United States, Government of the**, page 390; **United States, President of the**, page 406.

ECONOMIC STIMULUS

Even before taking office in January, President-elect Barack Obama asks Congress to pass a massive stimulus package to jump-start the economy, which had fallen deeply into recession. Congress responds with $787-billion legislation that conservatives condemn as a waste of taxpayer money and some liberals complain is too small to be effective. The Federal Reserve, the nation's central bank, cuts interest rates to historic lows and—with the U.S. Treasury Department—continues to pump massive amounts of bailout money into some of the nation's biggest banks and an insurance company. In the spring of 2009, the federal government provides multibillion-dollar loans to General Motors and Chrysler to stave off their financial collapse. With government help, both companies quickly go into and out of bankruptcy reorganization, resulting in the loss of thousands of jobs and the shut-down of hundreds of auto dealerships. By fall, economists point out that the financial sector, which stood on the brink of collapse in late 2008, had stabilized and that the economy appears to be slowly recovering. However, there is no sign that the economy would soon generate the millions of jobs lost to the "Great Recession." At year's end, the U.S. unemployment rate stubbornly remains above 10 percent. See **Automobile,** page 82; **Congress of the United States**, page 130; **Economics, U.S.**, page 168; **Economics, U.S.: A Special Report**, page 170; **International trade**, page 221; **Labor and employment**, page 246.

WAR IN AFGHANISTAN

The pace of war in Afghanistan escalates again in 2009. Upon taking command of NATO operations and U.S. forces in Afghanistan, General Stanley A. McChrystal asks President Obama for 30,000 to 40,000 more troops. On November 2, Afghan election officials declare Hamid Karzai the winner of the presidential election. His closest challenger, Abdullah Abdullah, had withdrawn from the runoff, alleging that the vote would be as corrupt as the previous round. See **Afghanistan,** page 37; **Armed forces,** page 54; **Asia,** page 68; **Pakistan,** page 302; **United States, Government of the**, page 390.

continued

IRAN ELECTION

On June 12, Mahmoud Ahmadinejad is declared the winner of the presidential election in Iran. Widespread protests and violence erupt in reaction to the election, which many believe had been stolen from Ahmadinejad's chief rival, Mir Hussein Moussavi. Ayatollah Ali Khamenei, Iran's supreme leader, defends the validity of the election as the protests are brutally put down by government forces. See **Iran**, page 234; **Middle East**, page 266; **Middle East: A Special Report**, page 270.

SURPRISING ANCIENT HUMAN ANCESTOR

The long-awaited description of *Ardipithecus ramidus,* a 4.4-million-year-old human ancestor, was published in September by a team of scientists. The team took more than 15 years to prepare and restore the fragile bones, which include a partial fossil skeleton of an adult female, nick-named "Ardi." What emerges is a view of a creature that lived shortly after hominids split from a common ancestor that gave rise to both chimpanzees and human beings between 6 and 10 million years ago. Surprisingly, she does not closely resemble human beings or modern apes. See **Anthropology,** page 49.

ISLAMIC MILITANTS IN PAKISTAN

The Pakistani Army launches two major military offensives in 2009—in the Swat Valley in May and in South Waziristan in October—in an effort to root out Islamic militants, particularly the Pakistani Taliban. Militants retaliate with dozens of bomb attacks—generally suicide attacks—that kill hundreds of Pakistani security forces as well as civilians. See **Afghanistan,** page 37; **Asia,** page 68; **Pakistan,** page 302.

2009

YEAR IN BRIEF

A month-by-month listing of the most significant world events that occurred during 2009.

JANUARY

2009

Barack Obama takes the oath of office as the 44th president of the United States on January 20 in Washington, D.C. His wife, Michelle, stands with him. President Obama's left hand rests on the same Bible used for the swearing-in of President Abraham Lincoln in 1861.

1 Gazprom, Russia's state-owned energy company, cuts delivery of natural gas to customers in Ukraine after the countries fail to settle a dispute over price and unpaid bills.

3 Israel sends tanks, gunships, and thousands of troops into the Gaza Strip to try to cripple Hamas, the Palestinian militant organization that controls the territory. The land offensive follows a week of Israeli air strikes. Israel began its campaign in response to Hamas rocket attacks on southern Israel. The violence has left hundreds of Palestinians and a handful of Israelis dead.

6 Israeli mortar fire kills at least 43 people, including a number of children, near a United Nations-run school in the Gaza Strip.

7 Russia's state-owned energy company, Gazprom, halts all natural gas exports to Europe via Ukrainian pipelines. Gazprom began reducing its gas shipments to Ukraine on January 1 because of a dispute over prices and unpaid bills. The gas supply disruptions have left millions of homes in central and eastern Europe without heat.

9 The nation's employers cut more than 2.5 million jobs in 2008, including an estimated 524,000 jobs in December, announces the U.S. Department of Labor. It was the largest yearly job loss since 1945. The department reports that the country's unemployment rate rose from 6.8 percent in November 2008 to 7.2 percent in December.

9 The Illinois House of Representatives votes 114-1 to impeach Governor Rod Blagojevich on grounds that he abused his power as the state's chief executive.

11 More than 300 people drown when a crowded ferry sinks during a storm west of the Indonesian island of Sulawesi.

15 Responding to lobbying efforts by U.S. President-elect Barack Obama, the U.S. Senate votes 52-42 to allow the release of the second half of a $700-billion financial rescue fund for use by the Obama administration. The first half was released when the fund was established in October 2008. The intent of the fund is to stabilize troubled financial markets.

15 A US Airways jet splashes down in the Hudson River off Manhattan after losing power in both engines shortly after take-off. Boats quickly surround the plane and rescue the 150 passengers and 5 crew members, all of whom survive the crash without serious injury.

16 The U.S. government agrees to provide Bank of America with a $20-billion capital injection, making taxpayers the largest single stockholder in the bank, with a stake that now totals $45 billion. The government also agrees to partially guarantee some $118 billion worth of the bank's troubled assets.

17 Israel announces a cease-fire in the Gaza Strip, ending a three-week air and ground offensive that left more than 1,300 Palestinians dead and thousands of buildings destroyed. On January 18, Hamas, the Palestinian militant group that controls the Gaza Strip, indicates that it will also observe a cease-fire. Israeli troops complete their withdrawal from the Gaza Strip by January 21.

19 Russian Prime Minister Vladimir Putin and Ukrainian Prime Minister Yulia Tymoshenko sign a 10-year natural gas agreement, ending a price dispute that left millions of Europeans without heat for days. Russian gas shipments to Europe resume on January 20.

20 Barack Obama takes the oath of office as the 44th president of the United States before a crowd of more than 1 million people on the National Mall in Washington, D.C. Obama, a Democrat, becomes the nation's first African American president. In his inaugural address, he calls on the country's citizens to begin the work of "remaking America" and to enter "a new era of responsibility."

21 The U.S. Senate confirms Hillary Rodham Clinton as U.S. secretary of state.

22 United States President Barack Obama orders the U.S. military prison at Guantánamo Bay, Cuba, closed by January 2010. Obama also bans the use of harsh interrogation techniques on terrorism suspects by the Central Intelligence Agency.

26 The U.S. pharmaceutical giant Pfizer announces that it will buy another huge U.S. drug maker, Wyeth, for $68 billion.

26 Iceland's coalition government resigns, three months after the collapse of the country's currency and its three major banks. Prime Minister Geir Haarde is the first world leader to leave office as a direct result of the world financial crisis.

26 The U.S. Senate confirms Timothy Geithner as secretary of the U.S. Treasury.

28 The global economy is expected to grow by just 0.5 percent in 2009, the lowest rate since World War II, announces the International Monetary Fund (IMF). The IMF's forecast is much lower than its November 2008 projection of a 2.2-percent global growth rate in 2009.

28 The U.S. House of Representatives votes 244-188 to approve an $819-billion economic stimulus bill supported by President Barack Obama. The U.S. Senate is considering a similarly huge bill aimed at reviving the U.S. economy.

29 United States President Barack Obama signs a bill that makes it easier for workers to file claims of pay discrimination based on gender, race, or other factors. It is the first bill he has signed into law.

29 The Illinois Senate votes 59-0 to remove Governor Rod Blagojevich from office and to permanently bar him from holding public office in Illinois. The vote convicts Blagojevich on an article of impeachment alleging abuse of power. Federal corruption charges were brought against Blagojevich in December 2008.

30 The U.S. economy shrank at a 3.8-percent annual rate in the fourth quarter of 2008, based on advance estimates, reports the U.S. Commerce Department. It was the sharpest contraction since 1982. Economists blame the steep decline on large cutbacks in consumer and business spending, a global credit crunch, and a crippled domestic real-estate market.

31 Elections for Iraq's provincial councils are held. Relatively little violence occurs.

1 The Pittsburgh Steelers defeat the Arizona Cardinals 27-23 in Super Bowl XLIII to claim the National Football League championship.

2 The U.S. Senate confirms Eric Holder as U.S. attorney general. He becomes the first African American to hold that position.

3 Kyrgyz President Kurmanbek Bakiev announces his government's plan to close an important U.S. base in Kyrgyzstan. Manas Air Base is a key transit point for U.S. and coalition troops and supplies en route to Afghanistan. The closure could severely hamper the U.S.-led military effort in the region.

4 United States President Barack Obama signs a bill to provide $33 billion in additional funding for the State Children's Health Insurance Program. The program provides insurance for children whose families earn too much to qualify for Medicaid but not enough to afford private health coverage.

6 The U.S. unemployment rate rose from 7.2 percent in December 2008 to 7.6 percent in January 2009, and the country's employers cut an estimated 598,000 jobs in January, reports the U.S. Labor Department.

7 Bushfires driven by high winds begin in the Australian state of Victoria. Over the following weeks, fires burn across about 1 million acres (430,000 hectares), leaving more than 170 people dead and destroying hundreds of homes. The fires are the deadliest in Australia's history. Police blame some of them on arsonists.

10 United States Treasury Secretary Timothy Geithner announces a $2-trillion plan intended to rescue the U.S. banking system and thaw frozen credit markets. The plan includes joint public-private funds to buy troubled assets from financial institutions; injection of more capital into banks; and expansion of a financing program designed to encourage consumer loans.

10 The U.S. Senate votes 61-37 to approve an $838-billion economic stimulus bill supported by President Barack Obama. The U.S. House of Representatives passed an $819-billion stimulus bill on January 28. A House-Senate conference will need to resolve the differences between the two bills.

10 Parliamentary elections are held in Israel. The centrist Kadima party wins 28 seats in the 120-seat Knesset, and the conservative Likud party wins 27. Neither party secures enough seats to govern alone. President Shimon Peres must ask one of the party leaders to try to form a coalition government.

11 Taliban militants assault three government buildings in Afghanistan's capital, Kabul. The attacks leave at least 20 people dead.

11 Morgan Tsvangirai, leader of the political opposition in Zimbabwe, is sworn in as the country's prime minister as part of a tenuous power-sharing deal with long-time President Robert Mugabe. The deal is an attempt to resolve a political crisis sparked by Zimbabwe's disputed 2008 presidential election.

12 A commuter plane crashes into a house in a suburb of Buffalo, New York. All 49 people on board are killed, as is a man inside the house.

13 Both houses of the U.S. Congress vote to approve a compromise economic stimulus package that includes $212 billion in tax cuts for businesses and individuals and $575 billion in new spending on education, health care, energy, transportation infrastructure, and aid to the unemployed and needy.

17 United States President Barack Obama signs the economic stimulus legislation that Congress approved on February 13.

17 The struggling U.S. automakers General Motors and Chrysler submit restructuring plans to the U.S. government and ask for another $21.6 billion in federal loans. The government extended $17.4 billion in loans to the companies in December 2008.

17 United States President Barack Obama announces that 17,000

Members of the U.S. Senate and House of Representatives meet in conference at the U.S. Capitol on February 11 to hash out differences between the Senate and House economic stimulus bills. The negotiations produced a $787-billion package that President Barack Obama signed on February 17.

extra U.S. troops will be deployed to Afghanistan later in 2009, raising the number of U.S. troops there to about 55,000.

18 A program intended to keep millions of Americans from losing their homes is announced by U.S. President Barack Obama. Under the plan, $75 billion will be used to subsidize lenders who agree to reduce mortgage payments for homeowners at risk of foreclosure. Another $200 billion will be given to the giant mortgage finance companies Fannie Mae and Freddie Mac to help homeowners refinance their mortgages.

19 The Kyrgyz parliament votes to close Manas Air Base, a key U.S. military installation in Kyrgyzstan. The next day, Kyrgyzstan delivers a formal air base eviction notice to the U.S. embassy in Bishkek. The United States and its allies have relied on the air base since 2001 to send troops and supplies to Afghanistan.

20 Israeli President Shimon Peres invites Benjamin Netanyahu, leader of the conservative Likud party, to try to form the country's next government.

26 United States President Barack Obama delivers to Congress a $3.6-trillion budget plan for fiscal year (FY) 2010. It proposes higher taxes on the wealthy and vast new investments in health care, education, and energy. The plan projects a record $1.75-trillion deficit for FY 2009.

27 According to revised estimates, the U.S. economy shrank at a 6.2-percent annual rate in the fourth quarter of 2008, the U.S. Commerce Department reports. It was the worst decline since 1982. The department had earlier estimated the contraction to be 3.8 percent.

27 The U.S. government will increase its ownership of Citigroup, one of the nation's largest and most troubled financial firms, from 8 percent to 36 percent, announce U.S. Treasury Department officials. The government will convert up to $25 billion of its preferred stock in Citigroup into common stock.

27 United States President Barack Obama says that he plans to withdraw U.S. combat forces from Iraq by August 2010 and remaining troops by December 2011.

15

MARCH

2009

On March 19, a demonstrator outside the American International Group (AIG) building in Los Angeles protests AIG paying its financial products division employees $165 million in bonuses after the giant insurance company received $180 billion in federal bailout money. On March 2, AIG had reported a record $61.7-billion deficit in the fourth quarter of 2008, primarily due to losses sustained by the financial products division.

2 The U.S. insurance giant American International Group (AIG) reports a loss of $61.7 billion in the fourth quarter of 2008—by far the largest quarterly loss in corporate history. The same day, federal officials announce a revised bailout plan for AIG that commits another $30 billion in government aid—on top of $150 billion already allocated in 2008—to keep the company afloat.

2 The Dow Jones Industrial Average drops 300 points to close at 6,763, falling below 7,000 for the first time since 1997.

3 Gunmen in Lahore, Pakistan, attack a bus convoy carrying Sri Lanka's national cricket team. Six police officers and a driver are killed, and several players are injured.

4 The International Criminal Court issues an arrest warrant for Sudan's president, Umar al-Bashir, on charges of war crimes and crimes against humanity in Sudan's Darfur region. In response, Bashir's government orders several foreign aid agencies to leave Sudan.

6 The U.S. unemployment rate rose from 7.6 percent in January to 8.1 percent in February, and the nation's employers cut an estimated 651,000 jobs in February, the U.S. Labor Department announces.

9 United States President Barack Obama signs an executive order rescinding former President George W. Bush's restrictions on federal funding for embryonic stem cell research.

10 A gunman kills 10 people, including his mother, during an hourlong shooting rampage in southern Alabama. He then kills himself.

10 After weeks of sliding, the Dow Jones Industrial Average jumps 379 points on the announcement that struggling U.S. banking corporation Citigroup was profitable in the first two months of 2009. Stocks continue to gain through the rest of the week. By March 13, the Dow hits 7,224, up 9 percent for the week.

11 A 17-year-old boy goes on a shooting rampage at his former secondary school in Winnenden, a suburb of Stuttgart, Germany. He kills nine students and three teachers, then flees the school and kills three more people. After a shoot-out with police, he kills himself.

12 The disgraced financier Bernard Madoff pleads guilty in a U.S. district court to bilking investors out of as much as $65 billion. The judge revokes Madoff's bail and sends him to jail to await sentencing. Madoff ran a giant Ponzi scheme in which returns were paid to investors from the principal contributed by later investors rather than from profits.

14 A political outcry erupts in response to news that the U.S. insurance firm American International Group (AIG)—the recipient of a $180-billion government bailout—is paying $165 million in bonuses to employees of its financial products division. The division specialized in exotic financial products that nearly drove the company to bankruptcy in 2008. In the following days, members of Congress and President Barack Obama express outrage over the bonuses.

16 Iftikhar Muhammad Chaudhry will be restored as chief justice of Pakistan's Supreme Court, announces Prime Minister Yousaf Raza Gilani. Chaudhry was ousted from the position in 2007 by former President Pervez Musharraf. Gilani's announcement follows days of protests across the country calling for the reinstatement of Chaudhry and other ousted judges. Protesters were angry about President Asif Ali Zardari's failure to reinstate the judges after Zardari succeeded Musharraf in 2008.

18 In its latest dramatic bid to unfreeze credit markets, the U.S. Federal Reserve System announces that it will buy up to $300 billion in long-term U.S. Treasury securities—a departure from its usual practice of buying short-term debt—and will increase its purchases of mortgage-backed assets by up to $750 billion.

19 The U.S. House of Representatives votes 328-93 for a bill that would place a 90-percent income tax on bonuses paid by financial firms that have received large government bailout packages.

23 The U.S. Treasury Department releases details of its plan for helping major U.S. banks sell mortgage-backed assets that have collapsed in value and crippled the financial sector. The plan's intent is to encourage private investors to buy the assets by providing the investors with extensive government financing. Stock markets respond positively to the plan. The Dow Jones Industrial Average shoots up 497 points to close at 7,776.

23 New York Attorney General Andrew Cuomo announces that some employees of the U.S. insurance giant American International Group (AIG) will return bonus money that they received earlier in the month. Cuomo says that of the $165 million in bonuses that was paid, $50 million will be returned.

26 According to final estimates, the U.S. economy shrank at a 6.3-percent annual rate in the fourth quarter of 2008, reports the U.S. Commerce Department.

27 About 50 people die in a suicide bombing at a mosque in Pakistan's northwest.

30 Gunmen attack a police academy near Lahore, Pakistan, killing 8 people and wounding over 100. After an eight-hour siege, security forces retake the facility and kill or capture the attackers.

30 The administration of U.S. President Barack Obama rejects the restructuring plans submitted in February by the ailing U.S. automakers General Motors (GM) and Chrysler. Both companies are currently dependent on federal loans to fund operations. The administration gives GM 60 days to develop a new plan and gives Chrysler 30 days to merge with Fiat, an Italian automaker. On March 29, the administration forced Rick Wagoner, the head of GM, to resign.

31 A new Israeli coalition government is sworn in, with Benjamin Netanyahu, leader of the right-wing Likud party, as prime minister.

APRIL

2009

2 At a Group of 20 (G-20) summit in London, leaders of the world's major economic powers pledge $1.1 trillion to ease the global economic crisis. Most of the money will go to the International Monetary Fund for the purpose of issuing loans to crisis-stricken countries. The rest will be used to boost global trade.

3 The U.S. unemployment rate jumped from 8.1 percent in February to 8.5 percent in March, and U.S. employers cut an estimated 663,000 jobs in March, reports the U.S. Department of Labor.

3 The Iowa Supreme Court declares unconstitutional a state law that limited marriage to opposite-sex couples. Iowa becomes the third U.S. state with legal gay marriage.

3 A gunman shoots and kills 13 people at an immigrant services center in Binghamton, New York, before killing himself.

4 European allies of the United States, attending a NATO summit in France, back U.S. President Barack Obama's new strategy for NATO's campaign in Afghanistan but agree to provide only up to 5,000 new troops, 3,000 of which are to be deployed only briefly.

5 North Korea launches a rocket that flies over Japan before falling into the Pacific Ocean. North Korea claims the rocket was for carrying a satellite into space. But many countries condemn the launch as an illicit long-range missile test.

6 A 6.3-magnitude earthquake strikes Italy's Abruzzo region. Nearly 300 people are killed. Most of the deaths and damage occur in L'Aquila, the region's capital.

7 The Vermont Legislature overrides Governor Jim Douglas's veto of a bill allowing same-sex marriage. Vermont becomes the first state to legalize gay marriage through legislation rather than a court ruling.

8 Somali pirates hijack a U.S.-flagged container vessel, the *Maersk Alabama,* in the Indian Ocean east of Somalia. The American crew members soon regain control of the ship, but the pirates take the ship's captain, Richard Phillips, aboard a lifeboat and hold him hostage.

12 After a five-day stand-off, U.S. Navy SEAL forces rescue an American merchant ship captain, Richard Phillips, from Somali pirates holding him hostage on a boat in the Indian Ocean. The rescue occurs when SEAL snipers on a U.S. destroyer shoot and kill the pirates.

13 Pakistani President Asif Ali Zardari signs a bill allowing Shari`ah (Islamic law) in the Swat Valley region of northwestern Pakistan. The establishment of Shari`ah was part of a cease-fire deal reached in February between the Pakistani army and Taliban militants.

13 The United Nations Security Council unanimously condemns North Korea for its April 5 rocket launch. In response, on April 14, North Korea orders international nuclear monitors out of the country and announces that it will restart its nuclear program and never again take part in denuclearization talks.

15 The U.S. Consumer Price Index declined by 0.4 percent from March 2008 to March 2009, reports the U.S. Department of Labor. It was the country's first one-year deflationary period since 1955.

16 Russia officially ends its campaign against separatist rebels in Chechnya and lifts curfews, roadblocks, and travel restrictions there. Russian troops invaded Chechnya in 1999 to regain control of the republic, which had won de facto independence in a 1994-1996 war.

16 The U.S. Department of Justice releases four memos, written by department lawyers in 2002 and 2005, that outlined several harsh interrogation techniques, including waterboarding, approved for use by the Central Intelligence Agency (CIA) on terrorism detainees. President Barack Obama says that CIA agents who followed the guidelines in the memos will not face prosecution. However, he also later indicates that the officials who formulated the guidelines may face legal consequences.

The cathedral in L'Aquila, Italy, was one of hundreds of buildings damaged by a 6.3-magnitude earthquake that struck the country's Abruzzo region on April 6. Nearly 300 people were killed as a result of the earthquake.

22 The International Monetary Fund (IMF) projects that the global economy will fall by 1.3 percent in 2009—a sizeable downward revision from its January projection of a 0.5-percent growth rate in 2009.

22 In South Africa, the ruling African National Congress party wins 66 percent of the vote in National Assembly elections.

23 In Iraq, separate suicide bombings in Baghdad and Al Miqdadiyah leave about 75 people dead.

24 A suicide bombing kills about 70 people near a Shi`ite shrine in Baghdad, Iraq.

24 A swine flu outbreak prompts Mexico's government to close schools and public buildings in Mexico City. In the following days, health officials confirm dozens of swine flu cases in Mexico and other countries, with hundreds more cases suspected. On April 26, the U.S. government declares a public health emergency. Mexico orders schools to close nationwide starting April 28 and orders nonessential businesses to close starting May 1. On April 29, the World Health Organization raises its pandemic alert level to Phase 5, the next-to-highest level.

28 Senator Arlen Specter of Pennsylvania declares that he is switching from the Republican Party to the Democratic Party, giving the Democrats 59 seats in the U.S. Senate, just 1 seat short of the 60 needed to stop Republican filibusters.

29 The U.S. economy shrank at a 6.1-percent annual rate in the first quarter of 2009, according to advance estimates, the U.S. Commerce Department reports.

29 Several car and roadside bombs in Baghdad, Iraq, leave nearly 60 people dead.

30 The U.S. automaker Chrysler files for bankruptcy. Chrysler will reorganize its finances and will proceed with a planned merger with Fiat, an Italian automaker.

30 The United Kingdom officially ends its military operations in Iraq, shutting down a six-year mission that cost the lives of 179 British soldiers.

19

MAY

2009

The U.S. automaker General Motors (GM), once the largest and richest corporation in the world, in May announced the elimination of nearly one-fifth of its dealerships and secured agreements with union workers and bondholders in anticipation of filing for bankruptcy on June 1.

1 Justice David Souter announces that he will retire from the U.S. Supreme Court when the court goes into recess at the end of June.

4 Dozens of villagers are killed by U.S. air strikes in western Afghanistan's Farah province. Afghan officials claim that the air strikes killed about 140 civilians and 25 Taliban insurgents. The U.S. military later claims that the death toll was 26 civilians and 78 insurgents.

6 South Africa's National Assembly elects Jacob Zuma as the country's president. He is sworn in on May 9. Zuma's party, the African National Congress, won a majority in parliamentary elections on April 22.

6 The Maine Legislature approves a bill legalizing same-sex marriage in the state, and Governor John Baldacci signs the bill into law.

7 Pakistani Prime Minister Yousaf Raza Gilani announces the start of a major army offensive against Taliban militants in the Swat Valley region of northwestern Pakistan. Many thousands of civilians have already fled the region. The offensive signals the collapse of a peace deal reached in February between the government and the militants.

7 The U.S. government releases the results of its "stress tests" of 19 of the nation's largest banks. The tests show that 9 of the banks have enough capital to withstand losses and sustain lending if the economy deteriorates further. The other 10 banks need to raise a combined $75 billion in capital to weather a worsening of the recession. Bank of America needs to raise $33.9 billion; Wells Fargo and GMAC need to raise $13.7 billion and $11.5 billion, respectively.

8 The U.S. unemployment rate rose from 8.5 percent in March to 8.9 percent in April, and U.S. employers eliminated an estimated 539,000 jobs in April, the U.S. Department of Labor announces.

11 An American soldier opens fire on fellow troops at a U.S. base in Baghdad, Iraq, killing five soldiers and wounding three others. The attack takes place at a clinic for soldiers suffering from war stress.

11 General David McKiernan, the top U.S. and NATO commander in Afghanistan, has been asked to resign after less than a year in the role, announces U.S. Defense Secretary Robert Gates. Citing the need for a "fresh approach," Gates also states that he has chosen Lieutenant General Stanley McChrystal to replace McKiernan.

14 The bankrupt U.S. automaker Chrysler informs 789 of its dealers that their franchises will be revoked. On May 15, another ailing U.S. automaker, General Motors, notifies about 1,100 of its dealers that their contracts will not be renewed. Both companies are undergoing government-mandated restructuring.

17 India's Election Commission releases the results of parliamentary elections held in five stages from April 16 to May 13. An alliance led by Prime Minister Manmohan Singh's Indian National Congress party won 262 seats in the 543-member Lok Sabha. On May 22, Singh is sworn in for his second term as prime minister.

19 Sri Lankan President Mahinda Rajapakse formally declares victory in the government's 26-year civil war against the rebel Liberation Tigers of Tamil Eelam (LTTE), also known as the Tamil Tigers. On May 18, the army killed LTTE chief Velupillai Prabhakaran in its final offensive against the rebels. The Tamil Tigers were fighting for a separate state for the ethnic Tamil minority in northeastern Sri Lanka.

20 About 100 people are killed when a military transport plane crashes on the island of Java in Indonesia.

22 President Barack Obama signs a bill that restricts the ability of U.S. credit card companies to raise interest rates and impose fees. The bill includes an amendment allowing people to carry firearms in national parks and wildlife refuges.

23 Former South Korean President Roh Moo-hyun commits suicide by leaping into a ravine near his home in the country's southeast. In April, he became implicated in an unfolding bribery investigation.

25 North Korea conducts its second nuclear test, in violation of an international ban, and test-fires a few short-range missiles. The incidents draw widespread international condemnation. On May 27, North Korea threatens to attack South Korea if any of the North's ships are searched as part of a U.S.-led initiative to intercept shipments of banned weapons. North Korea also announces that it is no longer bound by the 1953 armistice that ended the Korean War. North Korea's first nuclear test was in October 2006.

26 President Barack Obama names Sonia Sotomayor, a judge of the U.S. Second Circuit Court of Appeals, to replace retiring Justice David Souter on the U.S. Supreme Court. If confirmed, Sotomayor would be the first Hispanic and the third female judge in the court's history.

27 Attackers fire guns and detonate a car bomb outside a police station and an intelligence agency building in Lahore, Pakistan. More than 20 people are killed.

28 The U.S. media giant Time Warner announces its plan to spin off AOL, an Internet services subsidiary, by the end of 2009. AOL bought Time Warner in 2001 for more than $100 billion, but AOL revenues have declined greatly since then.

29 According to revised estimates, the U.S. economy shrank at a 5.7-percent annual rate in the first quarter of 2009, the U.S. Commerce Department reports.

29 The U.S. automaker General Motors (GM) takes its last steps ahead of an expected bankruptcy filing on June 1. On May 29, the company's unionized workers vote to approve major contract concessions. On May 31, a majority of GM's bondholders agree to swap their debt for a 10-percent stake in the reorganized company.

30 Pakistani military officials announce that, after a monthlong offensive, the army has retaken Mingaora, the largest city in the country's Swat Valley region, from Taliban militants. The Swat fighting has displaced as many as 3 million civilians.

31 George Tiller, one of the few physicians in the United States who performed late-term abortions, is shot and killed at his Lutheran church in Wichita, Kansas.

JUNE

2009

1 An Air France jet en route from Rio de Janeiro, Brazil, to Paris crashes in the Atlantic, killing all 216 passengers and 12 crew members.

1 After a decades-long slide, and at the behest of the U.S. government, General Motors (GM), once the world's dominant automaker, files for bankruptcy. The company will restructure into a pared-down "new GM," with the U.S. government taking 61-percent ownership. The government will also invest an extra $30 billion in GM on top of $19.4 billion in loans already made.

3 New Hampshire's legislature passes a bill legalizing same-sex marriage in the state, and Governor John Lynch signs the bill into law.

5 The U.S. unemployment rate rose from 8.9 percent in April to 9.4 percent in May, and employers cut an estimated 345,000 jobs in May, reports the U.S. Labor Department.

9 A truck bomb explodes outside a luxury hotel in Peshawar, Pakistan, leaving up to 18 people dead.

9 The U.S. Treasury Department determines that 10 of the nation's largest financial companies are sufficiently capitalized and can be allowed to repay a total of $68 billion in federal aid that they received from the Troubled Asset Relief Program (TARP), a $700-billion fund created in 2008 to bail out struggling financial firms.

10 The U.S. automaker Chrysler finalizes its alliance with Fiat, an Italian automaker, and emerges from bankruptcy as a smaller company called Chrysler Group LLC, headed by Fiat's chief executive officer. The U.S. government lends the new company $6.6 billion.

11 The World Health Organization declares an H1N1 swine flu pandemic, raising its alert level to Phase 6, the highest level, for the first time since 1968. The agency reports that nearly 30,000 swine flu cases have been confirmed in 74 countries, with over 140 deaths.

12 Huge numbers of people vote in Iran's presidential election.

13 Iranian officials announce that the conservative incumbent, Mahmoud Ahmadinejad, won 63 percent of the June 12 presidential election vote compared with 34 percent for reformist candidate Mir Hussein Moussavi. The announcement triggers protests by hundreds of thousands of Moussavi supporters, who allege election rigging. Several violent clashes occur between protesters and security forces. On June 16, Iran's Guardian Council agrees to a partial vote recount.

17 United States President Barack Obama proposes a huge overhaul of the nation's financial regulatory system. His recommendations include creating a new agency to oversee consumer financial products and increasing the government's power to supervise—and if necessary, seize and dismantle—any financial firm that poses a risk to the financial system as a whole.

19 After days of mass protests in Iran over the disputed presidential election, Iran's supreme leader, Ayatollah Ali Khamenei, gives a sermon in Tehran in which he defends the results and demands an end to the protests. In the following days, security forces intensify their crackdown on protests, thus reducing their size. Thousands of protesters have been arrested since June 13, and several have been killed.

20 More than 80 people die when a truck bomb detonates in Taza, a town in northern Iraq near Kirkuk.

22 United States President Barack Obama signs a bill giving the Food and Drug Administration wide-ranging regulatory power over tobacco products for the first time.

22 Kyrgyz and U.S. officials sign an agreement to allow a U.S. air base in Kyrgyzstan to remain open, thus reversing Kyrgyzstan's February decision to close the base. The Manas base has been a key transit point for troops and supplies en route to Afghanistan. Kyrgyzstan's parliament ratifies the deal on June 24.

24 A bomb detonates at a market in the Sadr City area of Baghdad, Iraq, killing nearly 80 people.

25 According to final estimates, the U.S. economy shrank at a 5.5-percent annual rate in the first quarter of 2009, reports the U.S. Department of Commerce.

25 The pop superstar Michael Jackson dies at age 50 after going into cardiac arrest.

26 The U.S. House of Representatives votes 219-212 for a bill that would place caps on emissions of man-made greenhouse gases and create a market in which companies could trade emissions permits.

28 Honduras's president, Manuel Zelaya, is ousted by the military and sent into exile in Costa Rica, after a dispute between Zelaya and the National Congress and Supreme Court over his efforts to hold a referendum on revising the Constitution.

29 Iran's Guardian Council certifies the disputed results of the country's June 12 presidential election, declaring incumbent President Mahmoud Ahmadinejad the winner over reformist candidate Mir Hussein Moussavi. Council members claim that a partial vote recount revealed no major election irregularities.

29 A U.S. district judge sentences the financier Bernard Madoff to 150 years in prison for running a scheme that defrauded investors of as much as $65 billion.

29 The U.S. Supreme Court rules that the city of New Haven, Connecticut, unfairly denied promotions to a group of mostly white firefighters by discarding the results of promotion exams after no blacks and only two Hispanics did well on them.

30 A Yemenia Airways jet with 153 people aboard crashes in the Indian Ocean as it tries to land in Moroni, Comoros. Only 1 passenger, a 12-year-old girl, survives.

30 In compliance with a 2008 U.S.-Iraqi security deal, U.S. troops complete their withdrawal from Iraqi cities and towns.

30 After a long legal battle, the Minnesota Supreme Court rules that Democratic candidate Al Franken won the state's 2008 U.S. Senate election by a razor-thin margin. The Republican incumbent, Norm Coleman, concedes defeat. Democrats now hold 60 U.S. Senate seats, enough to block Republican filibusters.

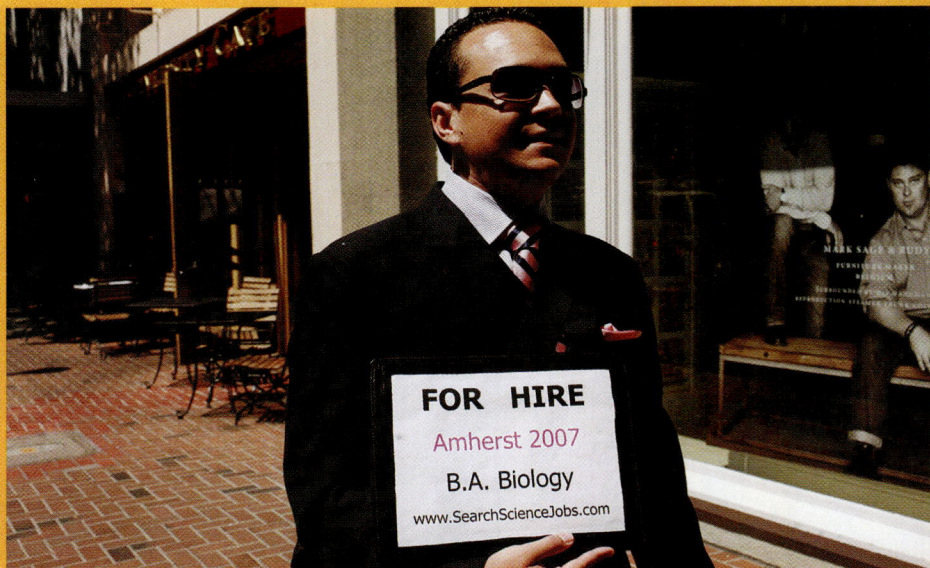

JULY

2009

An unemployed college graduate walks around downtown Palo Alto, California, on July 22, offering himself for hire. The U.S. unemployment rate reached 9.5 percent in the summer of 2009, up from 5 percent in late 2007, when the country entered a recession.

2 Around 4,000 U.S. Marines launch a major operation against Taliban insurgents in southern Afghanistan's Helmand province.

2 The U.S. economy lost an estimated 467,000 jobs in June, pushing the unemployment rate to 9.5 percent, about what it was in May, reports the U.S. Department of Labor.

3 Alaska Governor Sarah Palin, the 2008 Republican nominee for U.S. vice president, unexpectedly announces that she will resign as governor, effective July 26.

5 Ethnic violence erupts in Ürümqi, the capital of the Xinjiang region in western China, when a protest march by Uygurs escalates into rioting and attacks on Han Chinese. On July 7, Han groups carry out reprisal attacks. The violence leaves about 200 people dead, according to the Chinese government.

5 At the Wimbledon tennis championships in England, the Swiss star Roger Federer wins his 15th grand slam tournament title, breaking the record of 14 titles held by Pete Sampras of the United States.

6 At a summit in Moscow, U.S. President Barack Obama and Russian President Dmitry Medvedev sign a preliminary deal on reducing the countries' nuclear stockpiles. They also announce an accord that will allow the U.S. military to fly troops and supplies through Russian airspace en route to Afghanistan.

6 Seven U.S. soldiers are killed in different areas of Afghanistan.

8 Susilo Bambang Yudhoyono is reelected president of Indonesia.

8 The global economy is expected to drop by 1.4 percent in 2009 but then expand by 2.5 percent in 2010, reports the International Monetary Fund.

8 The leaders of the world's major developed and developing economies, meeting in Italy, fail to agree on cuts in global greenhouse gas emissions. The Group of Eight (G-8) industrialized countries embrace a goal of reducing their own emissions by 80 percent by 2050. But a larger group of 17 economies—the G-8 plus 9 others—tables a proposal to reduce global emissions by 50 percent by 2050.

9 In Iraq, multiple bombings in Baghdad and in the northern city of Tall Afar leave more than 50 people dead.

10 Eight British soldiers are killed in a 24-hour period in Afghanistan. It is the deadliest day for British forces since the war in Afghanistan began in 2001.

10 After racing through the restructuring process, the U.S. automaker General Motors (GM) emerges from bankruptcy as a leaner company. It will focus on just four core brands—Buick, Cadillac, Chevrolet, and GMC. The U.S. government owns 61 percent of the "new GM." The Canadian government, the United Auto Workers, and bondholders hold minority stakes. GM is in the process of closing several plants and cutting thousands of jobs.

11 The U.S. Central Intelligence Agency (CIA) was ordered in 2001 by then-Vice President Dick Cheney to conceal from Congress information about a secret counterterrorism project, reports *The New York Times.* The project—which was shut down by CIA Director Leon Panetta after he learned about it on June 23, 2009—was an initiative to capture or assassinate members of the international terrorist network al-Qa`ida, reports *The Wall Street Journal* on July 12. The project never became fully operational.

14 The bodies of 12 Mexican federal police officers—tortured and murdered by drug gangs—have been found in the state of Michoacán, announce Mexican officials. It is the largest one-day death toll for Mexican police since December 2006, when the government began dispatching tens of thousands of soldiers and police across Mexico to combat the drug trade. More than 11,000 people have died in drug-related violence since then.

14 Several of the biggest U.S. banks report larger-than-expected profits for the second quarter of 2009. On July 14, Goldman Sachs reports a $3.4-billion profit. On July 16, JPMorgan Chase reports a $2.7-billion profit. On July 17, Bank of America and Citigroup report profits of $3.2 billion and $4.3 billion, respectively.

15 A Caspian Airlines plane crashes near Qazvin, Iran, 16 minutes after taking off from Tehran. All 153 passengers and 15 crew members are killed.

17 Suicide bombings at two hotels in Jakarta, Indonesia, leave nine people dead.

17 Former Iranian President Ali Akbar Hashemi Rafsanjani, speaking in Tehran, warns that the government's handling of the June 12 presidential election and its crackdown on postelection protests has caused it to lose the trust of many Iranians, and he calls for the release of jailed protesters. Nearby, thousands of people demonstrate against the election results.

23 The Dow Jones Industrial Average closes at 9,069, climbing above 9,000 for the first time since January. The Dow has leapt more than 2,500 points, or nearly 39 percent, since mid-March.

26 Boko Haram, a militant group that seeks to impose Shari`ah (Islamic law) throughout Nigeria, attacks a police station in the northern city of Bauchi after the arrest of some group members. The attack triggers a wave of violence between the militants and Nigerian security forces that spreads to other northern cities and lasts for five days, leaving over 700 people dead. Police shoot and kill the leader of Boko Haram on July 30 in Maiduguri.

30 All $1 billion that Congress appropriated for the "cash for clunkers" program has been used up, announce U.S. officials. The program, launched on July 24, offers credits of $3,500 to $4,500 to people who trade in an old vehicle for one with better fuel economy. On July 31, the House of Representatives votes 316-109 to add $2 billion to the program.

31 The U.S. gross domestic product (GDP) shrank at a 1-percent annual rate in the second quarter of 2009, based on advance estimates, the U.S. Department of Commerce reports. In addition, the department releases a comprehensive revision of historical GDP data. According to the revised data, GDP grew by only 0.4 percent in 2008, much less than the 1.1-percent growth previously estimated for the year. Also, GDP declined at a 5.4-percent annual rate in the fourth quarter of 2008 and fell at a 6.4-percent annual rate in the first quarter of 2009.

AUGUST

2009

4 Former U.S. President Bill Clinton meets with North Korea's leader, Kim Jong-il, in Pyongyang for the purpose of securing the release of two American reporters who were arrested in March along the North Korean-Chinese border and sentenced in June to 12 years of hard labor. After the meeting, Kim pardons the two women. They return with Clinton to the United States.

5 Mahmoud Ahmadinejad is sworn in for a second term as president of Iran, two months after a disputed presidential election that sparked massive protests by the opposition. Several Iranian legislators and other officials boycott the ceremony.

6 The U.S. Senate, in a 68-31 vote, confirms Judge Sonia Sotomayor as a justice of the U.S. Supreme Court. She is sworn in on August 8, becoming the first Hispanic and the third woman to sit on the court.

6 The U.S. Senate votes 60-37 to add $2 billion to the "cash for clunkers" program, which offers credits of $3,500 to $4,500 to people who trade in an old vehicle for a new one with better fuel economy. The program proved so popular with consumers that it burned through its initial $1 billion in funding in a single week in July. On August 7, President Barack Obama signs the $2-billion extension into law.

7 Pakistani officials claim that the leader of the Pakistani Taliban, Baitullah Mehsud, was killed on August 5 by a U.S. drone air strike in northwestern Pakistan. Mehsud has been blamed for dozens of terrorist attacks in Pakistan, including the one that killed former Prime Minister Benazir Bhutto in 2007.

7 A truck bomb explosion near a mosque in Mosul, Iraq, leaves 41 people dead. Another 14 people are killed in bombings in Baghdad.

7 The U.S. unemployment rate was 9.4 percent in July, about what it was in June, and around 247,000 jobs were cut in July, reports the U.S. Department of Labor.

7 Typhoon Morakot makes landfall in Taiwan. Over the next two days, the storm dumps more than 80 inches (200 centimeters) of rain on the island and causes huge mudslides and severe flooding. Some 700 people are killed in Taiwan as a result of the storm.

10 Two truck bombs destroy an entire village east of Mosul, Iraq, leaving about 35 people dead. Meanwhile, more than 20 people are killed in various bombings in Baghdad.

11 A court controlled by Myanmar's military rulers convicts prodemocracy leader Aung San Suu Kyi of violating the terms of her house arrest. She is sentenced to another 18 months of house arrest. Many world leaders condemn the conviction as a political move designed to keep her from participating in elections planned for 2010.

14 The U.S. Consumer Price Index fell by 2.1 percent from July 2008 to July 2009, the U.S. Department of Labor reports. It was the sharpest price decline since the 12-month period ending in January 1950.

19 Bomb and mortar attacks in Baghdad, Iraq—including two massive car bomb blasts near the country's finance and foreign ministry buildings—leave some 130 people dead.

20 Presidential and local elections are held in Afghanistan, with incumbent President Hamid Karzai facing a strong challenge from former Foreign Minister Abdullah Abdullah. Numerous threats and attacks by the Taliban suppress voter turnout, especially in the south.

20 The Scottish government releases Abdel Basset Ali al-Megrahi, a Libyan who was convicted of the 1988 bombing of a Pan Am passenger jet over Lockerbie, Scotland, that killed 270 people. He is freed on compassionate grounds because he is terminally ill. Upon his return to Libya, several hundred people give him a hero's welcome. Megrahi's release and his reception in Libya are strongly condemned by U.S. officials and by families of victims of the Lockerbie bombing.

24 The U.S. Justice Department releases a 2004 report by the Central In-

Cash For Clunkers!

Consumers flocked to auto dealerships in July and August to take advantage of the "cash for clunkers" program, which offered credits to people who traded in an old vehicle for a more fuel-efficient one. Congress authorized another $2 billion in funding when the program's initial $1 billion was used up within days.

telligence Agency (CIA) inspector general on the CIA's terrorism detention and interrogation program. The report found that unauthorized and inhumane techniques were used on detainees. Later that day, Attorney General Eric Holder appoints a special prosecutor, John Durham, to review several cases of alleged CIA mistreatment or abuse of detainees.

24 The successful $3-billion "cash for clunkers" program is shut down by the U.S. Department of Transportation. Under the program, nearly 700,000 old vehicles were traded in for more fuel-efficient ones, and dealers submitted rebate applications worth nearly $2.9 billion.

25 Members of the Pakistani Taliban confirm that their leader, Baitullah Mehsud, died as the result of a U.S. drone strike on August 5, though they claim that he survived until August 23.

25 President Barack Obama nominates Ben Bernanke to a second four-year term as U.S. Federal Reserve System chairman.

25 Edward M. Kennedy (D., Massachusetts), a U.S. senator since 1962, dies of brain cancer at age 77. Long a dominant force in U.S. politics, Kennedy was often called the "liberal lion" of the Senate.

27 According to revised estimates, the U.S. economy shrank at a 1-percent annual rate in the second quarter of 2009, the U.S. Commerce Department reports.

27 Sudan's Darfur region is no longer in a state of war, though low-level fighting and banditry are continuing, announces General Martin Agwai, the outgoing head of the joint African Union-United Nations peacekeeping force in Darfur.

30 Japan's Liberal Democratic Party—which has ruled the country since 1955 with only an 11-month break—is decisively defeated in parliamentary elections by the Democratic Party of Japan.

30 General Stanley McChrystal, the top U.S. and NATO commander in Afghanistan, delivers to his superiors a widely anticipated assessment of the Afghan conflict. Military experts believe that the classified report emphasizes the need to protect Afghan civilians from the Taliban, a move that could require more troops.

SEPTEMBER

A wall of fire in the mountains north of Los Angeles threatens a house and utility lines near Acton, California, on August 31. The Station Fire burned across 160,000 acres (65,000 hectares) of Angeles National Forest in August and September.

2009

1 A fast-moving wildfire in Angeles National Forest north of Los Angeles forces thousands of area residents to flee. The Station Fire, so named because it began near a ranger station on August 26, has burned across some 120,000 acres (50,000 hectares). On September 3, the U.S. Forest Service declares that the fire was started deliberately.

4 A NATO air strike on two hijacked fuel tankers in northern Afghanistan's Qonduz province leaves scores of people dead, including many civilians as well as militants.

4 The U.S. economy lost an estimated 216,000 jobs in August, driving the unemployment rate to 9.7 percent, up from 9.4 percent in July, reports the U.S. Department of Labor.

7 Taiwanese Premier Liu Chao-shiuan announces that he and his Cabinet will resign on September 10 in response to criticism about his government's slow response to Typhoon Morakot in August.

8 With 92 percent of polling stations declared, the preliminary results of Afghanistan's August 20 presidential election give incumbent Hamid Karzai 54 percent of the vote, compared with rival Abdullah Abdullah's 28 percent. However, the United Nations-backed Electoral Complaints Commission reports that it has found evidence of vote fraud and orders a partial recount.

9 Hoping to rekindle support for comprehensive health care reform among lawmakers and the public, U.S. President Barack Obama gives a special prime-time-televised speech on the subject before a joint session of Congress. He outlines his proposal to provide more security to Americans who already have health insurance, extend health insurance to Americans who do not already have it, and slow the growth of health care costs.

11 Former Taiwanese President Chen Shui-bian and his wife are convicted of corruption charges and sentenced to life in prison. Chen has denied any wrongdoing.

15 The U.S. House of Representatives votes 240-179, mostly along party lines, to formally rebuke one of its members, Joe Wilson (R., South Carolina), for having shouted "You lie!" at President Barack Obama during the president's September 9 address to Congress on health care reform.

16 Yukio Hatoyama takes office as prime minister of Japan. His Democratic Party of Japan won a major victory in parliamentary elections on August 30, ending over 50 years of almost unbroken Liberal Democratic Party rule.

17 President Barack Obama announces that the United States will abandon a plan introduced by former President George W. Bush to set up a radar station in the Czech Republic and 10 missile interceptors in Poland for defense against long-range Iranian missiles. Instead, a system of land- and sea-based sensors and interceptors will be implemented to stop shorter-range Iranian missiles.

21 General Stanley McChrystal, the top U.S. and NATO commander in Afghanistan, warned in a confidential August 30 assessment to his superiors that the war in Afghanistan "will likely result in failure" unless additional troops are deployed there over the next 12 months, reports *The Washington Post.*

22 Some 100 heads of state and government, including President Hu Jintao of China and President Barack Obama of the United States, meet in New York City for a United Nations conference on climate change. President Hu pledges that China will cut carbon dioxide emissions by "a notable margin."

23 An enormous dust storm blows across hundreds of miles of Australia's east coast, including the city of Sydney. The shroud of red dust limits visibility so much that Sydney Harbour ferry traffic is disrupted, planes are grounded, flights into the city are diverted, and auto traffic is bumper to bumper on major roads.

24 The United Nations (UN) Security Council unanimously adopts a U.S.-drafted resolution that provides significant international support for U.S. President Barack Obama's agenda of stopping the proliferation of nuclear weapons.

25 Iran is building a new uranium enrichment plant near Qom, announce U.S. President Barack Obama, French President Nicolas Sarkozy, and British Prime

Minister Gordon Brown during a Group of 20 (G-20) summit in Pittsburgh. The three leaders strongly criticize Iran for failing to tell the International Atomic Energy Agency about this nuclear facility until September 21, several years after starting construction.

26 More than 16 inches (42 centimeters) of rain in 12 hours from Tropical Storm Ketsana leaves 80 percent of Manila, capital of the Philippines, flooded. Over 400 people in the Philippines are killed and hundreds of thousands are left homeless as a result of the storm. On September 29, Typhoon Ketsana slams into central Vietnam, leaving more than 160 people dead.

27 German Chancellor Angela Merkel's center-right CDU/CSU bloc wins 34 percent of the vote in parliamentary elections, giving her a clear path to form a coalition with the probusiness Free Democratic Party, which wins 15 percent.

27 Amid heightened tension between Iran and the major international powers over Iran's nuclear ambitions, Iran test-fires several short-, medium-, and long-range missiles on September 27 and 28.

28 Troops in Guinea's capital, Conakry, open fire on demonstrators protesting the country's military government. At least 157 people are killed, and more than 1,200 people are wounded.

29 A roadside bomb blast destroys a bus en route from Herat, Afghanistan, to Kandahar. At least 30 civilians, including 10 children, are killed in the explosion.

29 An 8.0-magnitude earthquake in the South Pacific triggers towering tsunami waves that hit the island countries of Samoa and Tonga and the U.S. territory of American Samoa. Around 190 people are killed, mostly in Samoa.

30 A 7.6-magnitude earthquake off the coast of the Indonesian island of Sumatra leaves over 1,100 people dead and damages thousands of buildings. The quake's epicenter is about 35 miles (60 kilometers) west of the city of Padang. Another quake, of 6.6 magnitude, strikes on October 1, hindering rescue efforts.

30 According to final estimates, the U.S. economy contracted at a 0.7-percent annual rate in the second quarter of 2009, the U.S. Commerce Department reports.

OCTOBER

2009

1 The global economy will contract by 1.1 percent in 2009 but grow by 3.1 percent in 2010, projects the International Monetary Fund.

1 The journal *Science* publishes the research of an international team of scientists on a 4.4-million-year-old skeleton of *Ardipithecus ramidus.* Nicknamed "Ardi," it is the oldest known skeleton of an ancient human ancestor. The skeletal remains were discovered in the 1990's in the Ethiopian desert.

2 The American economy eliminated an estimated 263,000 jobs in September, pushing the unemployment rate to 9.8 percent, up from 9.7 percent in August, announces the U.S. Department of Labor.

2 The International Olympic Committee, meeting in Copenhagen, Denmark, chooses Rio de Janeiro, Brazil, to host the 2016 Summer Olympic Games, making Rio the first South American city to stage an Olympics. Rio was chosen over Madrid, Spain; Tokyo; and Chicago.

2 Voters in Ireland approve the Lisbon Treaty in a referendum, reversing their earlier rejection of the treaty in June 2008. The intent of the treaty is to reform the institutions of the European Union (EU) to make them more efficient. To take effect, the treaty still requires the signatures of the presidents of Poland and the Czech Republic.

3 Taliban militants stage an attack on a small U.S. outpost in eastern Afghanistan's Nuristan province. Eight U.S. soldiers and four Afghan security officers are killed.

3 Typhoon Parma strikes the main island of the Philippines, Luzon, which is already water-logged as a result of Tropical Storm Ketsana in late September. Parma dumps rain on Luzon for a week, triggering floods and landslides that leave some 500 people dead.

9 A suicide bomber blows up a car in a crowded bazaar in Peshawar, Pakistan, killing over 50 people.

9 United States President Barack Obama wins the Nobel Peace Prize.

10 The foreign ministers of Armenia and Turkey sign an accord to establish normal diplomatic relations and open their shared border. Armenian-Turkish relations have long been strained because of a dispute over the mass killings of Armenians in the Ottoman Empire during and after World War I.

11 Thirty-nine hostages are freed by commandos after being held for 22 hours by Taliban militants at the Pakistani army headquarters in Rawalpindi. The militants stormed the army base on October 10 and took 42 civilians and soldiers captive. The attack and subsequent rescue mission leave 9 militants, 12 soldiers, and 2 civilians dead.

12 A suicide attack on an army convoy in the Swat Valley region of northwestern Pakistan kills 41 people.

14 Buoyed by announcements of better-than-expected earnings at the computer chip maker Intel and the banking giant JPMorgan Chase, the Dow Jones Industrial Average closes at 10,016, its first close above 10,000 since October 2008.

15 In Pakistan, militants attack three law enforcement buildings in Lahore and one in Kohat. About 40 people are killed. The next day, a suicide attack on a police station in Peshawar leaves 13 people dead.

17 The Pakistani army sends about 30,000 troops into South Waziristan, a largely tribal area along the Afghan border, to launch a major offensive against mountain strongholds of the Taliban and al-Qa`ida.

18 A suicide bombing in southeastern Iran kills more than 40 people, including several top leaders of the Revolutionary Guard Corps, an elite branch of Iran's military.

19 The United Nations-backed Electoral Complaints Commission, which audited Afghanistan's August 20 presidential election, confirms that there was fraud at many polling sites and concludes that incumbent President Hamid Karzai did not get enough valid votes to pass the 50-percent threshold. On October 20, Karzai accepts the commission's

findings and agrees to a November 7 runoff against rival Abdullah Abdullah.

22 The U.S. Federal Reserve System announces that it will begin closely regulating pay packages at banks to discourage excessive risk-taking. Also, the U.S. Treasury Department orders steep pay cuts for the 25 top employees at seven firms that received large federal bailouts after the 2008 financial meltdown—Citigroup, Bank of America, American International Group, General Motors, Chrysler, GMAC, and Chrysler Financial.

23 President Barack Obama declares the H1N1 swine flu epidemic a national emergency in the United States. The declaration allows hospitals and local governments to set up alternate treatment sites and establish triage procedures to handle a potential patient surge.

25 Two coordinated suicide vehicle bombings devastate three government buildings in Baghdad, Iraq, and leave 160 people dead and over 700 others injured.

26 A total of 14 Americans—11 soldiers and 3 civilians—are killed in two separate helicopter crashes in Afghanistan.

27 Improvised explosive device (IED) attacks in southern Afghanistan's Kandahar province leave eight U.S. soldiers dead.

28 A huge car bomb is detonated in a busy market in Peshawar, Pakistan. At least 118 people, mostly women and children, are killed. Some 200 others are injured.

28 President Barack Obama signs legislation broadening the definition of federal hate crimes to include attacks motivated by the victim's sexual orientation.

29 The U.S. economy grew at a 3.5-percent annual rate in the third quarter of 2009, according to advance estimates, reports the U.S. Department of Commerce. It was the first expansion in over a year.

30 Former French President Jacques Chirac is indicted on charges of embezzling funds when he was mayor of Paris (1977-1995).

NOVEMBER

2009

Floodwaters fill the high street in Workington, United Kingdom, on November 20. A record 12.4 inches (31.4 centimeters) fell in one area of Cumbria in 24 hours, triggering flooding in areas of the county in northwestern England.

1 Afghan politician Abdullah Abdullah withdraws from Afghanistan's presidential runoff election scheduled for November 7, arguing that election officials are biased in favor of incumbent President Hamid Karzai. On November 2, election officials cancel the runoff and declare Karzai the election winner.

1 CIT Group, a large U.S. business finance firm, declares bankruptcy.

3 An Afghan policeman opens fire on British troops in Afghanistan's Helmand province, killing five.

3 The president of the Czech Republic, Vaclav Klaus, signs the European Union's Lisbon Treaty, the final step in its ratification. The treaty, intended to streamline the organization's decision making, could go into effect as early as December.

3 Republican candidates win gubernatorial races in New Jersey and Virginia, and Michael Bloomberg wins a third term as mayor of New York City. In Maine, voters repeal a law that was enacted in May to allow same-sex marriage.

4 The New York Yankees beat the defending champion Philadelphia Phillies in Major League Baseball's World Series, four games to two. It is the Yankees' 27th title.

5 An Army psychiatrist opens fire inside a medical processing center at Fort Hood, Texas, killing 12 soldiers and 1 civilian and wounding dozens of others. The gunman, identified as Major Nidal Malik Hasan, is shot by civilian police officers and hospitalized. On November 12, military prosecutors charge Hasan with 13 counts of murder.

6 The U.S. economy shed an estimated 190,000 jobs in October, pushing the unemployment rate from 9.8 percent in September to 10.2 percent in October—the highest rate since 1983, announces the U.S. Department of Labor.

7 The U.S. House of Representatives votes 220-215 to pass sweeping health care reform legislation. The $1.1-trillion bill would extend health coverage to millions of Americans who currently lack it.

13 There is water on the moon, announces NASA. The discovery is based on data collected when NASA's Lunar Crater Observation and Sensing Satellite (LCROSS) crashed into a crater near the moon's south pole on October 9.

13 Khalid Shaikh Mohammed—believed to be the mastermind of the Sept. 11, 2001, terrorist attacks on the United States—and four suspected co-conspirators will be transferred from the military prison at Guantánamo Bay, Cuba, to New York City to stand trial in a U.S. federal court, announces Attorney General Eric Holder.

16 Most women should start having routine mammograms to screen for breast cancer at age 50 rather than age 40, and the mammograms should be every two years rather than every year, recommends the U.S. Preventive Services Task Force, a government-sponsored panel of private-sector experts. The new guidelines spark controversy, with many physicians and health groups in disagreement. The American Cancer Society announces that it will continue to recommend annual mammograms starting at age 40.

18 United States President Barack Obama acknowledges that his administration will miss a self-imposed January 2010 deadline to close the U.S. military prison at Guantánamo Bay, Cuba.

19 Hamid Karzai is sworn in as president of Afghanistan for a second five-year term.

19 Leaders of the European Union (EU) member nations, meeting in Brussels, Belgium, choose Belgian Prime Minister Herman Van Rompuy to be the first permanent president of the European Council under the Lisbon Treaty. They select Catherine Ashton of the United Kingdom to be head of foreign affairs.

20 Emergency workers in military helicopters and inflatable boats rescue scores of people from flooding in northwestern England following extremely heavy rains. In one area of the county of Cumbria, 12.4 inches (31.4 centimeters) fell in 24 hours, a United Kingdom record. Flooding continues for days in several parts of the United Kingdom and Ireland.

23 Fifty-seven people are stopped at a roadblock and murdered in Maguindanao province on the island of Mindanao in the Philippines. They were traveling in a convoy to file nomination papers for a candidate in local elections. The victims include family members and supporters of the candidate as well as at least 30 members of the media.

24 The U.S. economy grew at an annual rate of 2.8 percent in the third quarter of 2009, according to revised estimates, the U.S. Commerce Department announces. The department had earlier estimated the expansion to be 3.5 percent.

24 The federal insurance fund that protects depositors fell $8.2 billion into the red in the third quarter of 2009 as bank failures accelerated, announces the U.S. Federal Deposit Insurance Corporation (FDIC). The FDIC has seized and sold more than 120 banks in 2009. To replenish the fund, the agency has ordered banks to prepay three years of annual assessments.

25 The emirate of Dubai, part of the United Arab Emirates, asks to delay payment on billions of dollars of debt owed by Dubai World, a government-owned conglomerate, and Nakheel, Dubai World's main real estate subsidiary. In the following days, investors around the world dump stocks and move into safer assets. Economists fear that Dubai World's debt issues will hinder the global economic recovery.

27 A bomb explosion causes the Nevsky Express, a luxury high-speed train en route between Moscow and St. Petersburg, Russia, to derail. At least 26 people are killed, including at least two high-ranking government officials, and nearly 100 people are injured.

29 Iranian officials announce plans to build 10 new plants to enrich uranium for nuclear fuel. The announcement comes two days after the International Atomic Energy Agency passed a resolution condemning Iran for its failure to cooperate with the agency and demanding that Iran stop construction on a recently revealed nuclear facility near Qom.

DECEMBER

2009

1 The European Union's Lisbon Treaty goes into force.

1 President Barack Obama announces that 30,000 more U.S. troops will be sent to Afghanistan in the first half of 2010. He also states that U.S. forces will begin to withdraw from Afghanistan in July 2011. On Dec. 4, 2009, NATO countries agree to send 7,000 additional troops.

2 Bank of America announces that it will repay all of the $45 billion in federal bailout aid it received during the 2008-2009 financial crisis.

3 The U.S. conglomerate General Electric (GE) and the U.S. cable operator Comcast announce a joint venture under which Comcast will acquire 51 percent of GE's TV and film subsidiary, NBC Universal.

4 Militants attack a mosque in Rawalpindi, home base of Pakistan's military, killing more than 40 people.

4 The U.S. unemployment rate fell in November to 10 percent from 10.2 percent in October, announces the U.S. Department of Labor. An estimated 11,000 jobs were cut in November, far fewer than had been predicted by most analysts.

7 About 50 people die as a result of two bomb blasts in a crowded market of Lahore, Pakistan.

7 The U.S. Environmental Protection Agency officially finds that greenhouse gases threaten public health and that vehicle emissions contribute to greenhouse gas pollution. The United Nations Climate Change Conference opens in Copenhagen, Denmark.

7 On Student Day, a holiday in Iran, antigovernment protests erupt at several Iranian universities. Police clash with the demonstrators and dozens are arrested. Protests continue on December 8.

8 More than 120 people are killed and some 500 others are wounded in five nearly simultaneous car bombings in Baghdad, Iraq.

10 Accepting the Nobel Peace Prize in Oslo, Norway, U.S. President Barack Obama defends the right of the United States to wage "just wars."

11 The U.S. Central Intelligence Agency (CIA) has canceled a contract with the private security firm Xe Services, formerly known as Blackwater, to load bombs onto drone aircraft in Pakistan and Afghanistan, announce CIA officials. The secret contract was first revealed in August by *The New York Times.* In early 2009, the Iraqi government refused to renew Blackwater's license to operate in Iraq, accusing the company of inappropriate use of force. The *Times* reported on December 10 that Blackwater employees had often participated in secret CIA raids against suspected militants in Iraq and Afghanistan.

14 The Dubai government announces that the Abu Dhabi government has provided $10 billion to help meet the debts of Dubai World, a government-owned conglomerate. Dubai and Abu Dhabi are both part of the United Arab Emirates.

14 The U.S. banks Citigroup and Wells Fargo announce deals to pay back the federal bailout aid they received in 2008 and 2009.

18 On the last day of the Copenhagen climate conference, U.S. President Barack Obama—meeting with representatives from a small group of countries, including China—brokers a nonbinding statement of intention to begin taking action on global warming. Conference delegates agree to "take note" of the accord.

21 Tens of thousands of Iranians take part in a funeral procession in Qom for Grand Ayatollah Hoseyn Ali Montazeri, a dissident cleric who died on December 19. After the funeral, clashes erupt between antigovernment protesters and police.

22 According to final estimates, the U.S. economy grew at an annual rate of 2.2 percent in the third quarter of 2009, reports the U.S. Department of Commerce.

23 Subzero temperatures and days of snowstorms across Europe have disrupted air, road, and train travel and caused the deaths of more

United States Army troops patrol an area of Afghanistan's Kandahar province on December 3. With violence escalating in Afghanistan, President Barack Obama announced on December 1 that 30,000 additional U.S. troops would be deployed there in early 2010.

than 100 people, mostly in Poland and Ukraine, report news sources.

24 The U.S. Senate, in a strictly party-line 60-39 vote, passes an $871-billion bill to extend health care coverage to nearly all Americans. The bill's passage sets the stage for reconciliation with a similar, $1.1-trillion bill passed by the House of Representatives on November 7.

24 The U.S. Treasury Department announces that it will, over the next three years, cover an unlimited amount of losses at the mortgage finance giants Fannie Mae and Freddie Mac. The department took over the companies in 2008. Previously, there was a cap of $200 billion in government aid available to each company.

25 A Nigerian man attempts to detonate a plastic explosive aboard a transatlantic Northwest Airlines flight as the plane prepares to land in Detroit. The device fails to go off properly, and passengers subdue the man, who is believed to have connections to al-Qa`ida.

27 At least eight people are killed and hundreds of others are arrested during huge antigovernment demonstrations in Tehran, Iran, on the Shi`ite holiday of Ashura. Among the dead is a nephew of the opposition leader Mir Hussein Moussavi, who was defeated in Iran's disputed presidential election in June.

28 An attack on Shi`ite pilgrims in Karachi, Pakistan, kills more than 40 people.

29 Wildfires in Western Australia level some 40 homes on December 29 and 30.

30 A suicide bomb attack at a U.S. intelligence base in eastern Afghanistan's Khowst province kills seven agents of the U.S. Central Intelligence Agency and leaves six others wounded.

2009 UPDATE

The major events of 2009 are covered in more than 250 alphabetically arranged articles, from "Afghanistan" to "Zoos." Included are Special Reports that offer in-depth looks at the continuing economic crisis and the H1N1 influenza pandemic. Special Reports are found on the following pages.

SPECIAL REPORTS

FOCUS ON

PORTRAITS

Afghanistan. A disputed presidential election amid widespread corruption darkened shadows over Afghanistan's government in 2009 while the Islamic militant Taliban intensified its battle against the government. The International Security Assistance Force (ISAF) in Afghanistan, mostly American troops led by the North Atlantic Treaty Organization (NATO), grew more worried about long-term prospects of success.

Election. On November 2, election officials declared that President Hamid Karzai had been elected to a second term. His first elected term had ended on May 21, but the Afghan Supreme Court extended it until the election, which was held on August 20. Voter turnout was low amid Taliban intimidation and reports of violent attacks and polling stations set ablaze.

Running against 40 other candidates, Karzai was initially reported by the national election commission to have gotten 3.09 million votes, a winning 54.6 percent of the total. A former foreign minister, Abdullah Abdullah, placed second with 1.57 million votes, or 27.8 percent of the total. Afghan and international election observers reported extensive voter fraud and ballot stuffing, however. After prolonged controversy over the legitimacy of the election, the United Nations (UN) mission head in Kabul, the capital, acknowledged on October 11 that the election had involved "widespread fraud." The UN-led Electoral Complaints Commission ordered some 1.3 million votes thrown out, dropping Karzai's share below the 50 percent he needed to win.

Because of strong Western pressure on Karzai, who did not acknowledge the scale of fraud, a runoff election between Karzai and Abdullah was set for November 7. Abdullah called for the removal of top officials of the national election commission, who were Karzai appointees, but the officials remained in office. Abdullah accused Karzai's government of profound corruption and said the runoff would be at least as fraudulent as the first round. On November 1, Abdullah withdrew from the runoff. The next day, the election commission declared Karzai reelected because he was the only remaining contender in the runoff and he had won the most votes in the first round.

Tarnished. The outcome left a cloud over Karzai, whose administration and election campaign had depended on regional warlords and people accused of trafficking narcotics. Muhammad Qasim Fahim, one of the two vice presidents elected with Karzai, was a former warlord accused of corruption, trafficking, and other crimes. Critics also focused on Karzai's brother, Ahmed Wali Karzai, who was accused of involvement with Afghanistan's booming narcotics business, which financed the Taliban.

In congratulating Karzai on his reelection, United States President Barack Obama urged him to tackle the drug trade and corruption. On November 3, Karzai said, "Afghanistan has been tarnished by administrative corruption, and I will launch a campaign to clean the government of corruption." Three days later, British Prime Minister Gordon Brown warned Karzai that he might lose international support against the Taliban if this campaign failed.

On November 7, Afghanistan's foreign ministry struck back at a list of reforms requested by the top UN official in Kabul. The ministry said his comments "violated respect for Afghanistan's national sovereignty." The European Union increased civilian aid despite finding that, amid a critical security situation, "Progress on political reform, governance, and state-building is too slow, and in some parts of the country almost non-existent."

Fighting intensified in 2009 as ISAF forces with only limited Afghan military and police support tried to root out Taliban militants, but ISAF lacked manpower to keep them from returning to cleared areas. Militants increasingly relied on roadside bombs, the number of which had nearly doubled from 2006 to 2009. Air strikes against militants to support NATO troops in 2009 often hit civilians, causing bitter villagers to demand that NATO forces leave.

The deteriorating military situation, combined with faults of Karzai's regime, caused NATO governments to reevaluate prospects for a peaceful, well-governed Afghanistan. American military deaths in Afghanistan for 2009 exceeded 300, roughly double the number in 2008. Deaths among British troops also more than doubled, from 51 in 2008 to 106 in 2009.

On February 17, President Obama authorized an additional 17,000 U.S. troops for ISAF, raising the U.S. total to 68,000 in an ISAF of more than 100,000 soldiers. In June, Obama replaced General David McKiernan as the senior commander in Afghanistan with General Stanley McChrystal, a specialist in counterinsurgency. McChrystal said it would take at least four years for Afghanistan's own army and police to improve enough to replace ISAF, and he asked the Obama administration for some 40,000 additional U.S. troops. This led U.S. officials to conduct a detailed examination of the whole situation.

As a result of the review, President Obama announced on December 1 that he would send an additional 30,000 U.S. troops to Afghanistan and that American forces would begin to pull out in mid-2011. NATO officials announced that they would send at least 7,000 more non-U.S. troops to Afghanistan in 2010. ■ Henry S. Bradsher

See also **Armed forces; Asia.**

Election workers (above) count votes following Afghanistan's presidential election in August. A runoff was scheduled after allegations of massive fraud forced some 1.3 million votes to be invalidated. However, incumbent President Hamid Karzai was declared to have won another term after his main challenger withdrew from the runoff, claiming it would not be any fairer than the first round.

Corruption, oppression, and militant attacks continued to plague efforts to rid Afghanistan of Taliban influence in 2009.

In April, Afghan women protest a new family law that they claimed could be used to justify rape. Supporters said the law defended Islamic justice. Opponents warned that the law was a return to the same oppression of women instituted under the militant Taliban, who were overthrown in 2001.

U.S. soldiers fire mortars at Taliban militants in northeastern Afghanistan, along the country's border with Pakistan. Throughout the year, U.S. military leaders expressed concern that militants based in Pakistan were launching attacks in Afghanistan and then retreating across the border.

AFRICA

According to figures released by the United Nations (UN) in July 2009, the number of people in Africa getting poor nutrition could triple over the coming four decades. The number could rise from some 200 million in 2009 to around 600 million in 2050. The UN's analysis indicated that the world's population would grow by more than a third during this time. Africa's population growth, however, would likely be much higher. For instance, the United Nations estimated that Ethiopia's population would more than double from 83 million to 183 million and that Nigeria's population would expand from 148 million to almost 289 million.

The UN released its figures as leaders of the Group of Eight (G-8) leading industrialized nations met in Italy. The G-8 leaders pledged $20 billion (all monetary amounts in United States dollars) over three years to boost the capacity of developing countries to grow and store more food. In 2009, 34 of the world's 49 least developed countries (LDC's) were in Africa.

Obama visit. On his first trip to sub-Saharan Africa as president of the United States, President Barack Obama delivered a challenging speech to Ghana's Parliament on July 11, 2009. The speech condemned corrupt African politicians for creating what Obama called "brutality and bribery" amid the continent's chronic poverty. Obama, the first African American U.S. president, promised "fresh partnerships" with nations that were well governed. He singled out Ghana as an example of progressive democracy.

Pope Benedict XVI provoked widespread controversy during his seven-day trip to Africa in March when he said in Cameroon that distributing condoms would not solve the HIV/AIDS crisis. On the contrary, he said, condoms would actually make the problem worse by encouraging irresponsible sexual behavior. The solution, he said, lay in resisting the desire to have sexual intercourse and in remaining faithful to one partner. AIDS educators denounced the pope's claims as unscientific and demanded that he withdraw his comments. Since HIV/AIDS was first identified in the early 1980's, an estimated 25 million Africans have died from the disease. Two-thirds of the 33 million people infected in 2009 with HIV, the virus that causes AIDS, live in sub-Saharan Africa.

"Witchcraft" arrests. Four Tanzanians were sentenced to death in early November for the killing of an albino man. Albinism is a genetic condition that produces milky-white skin, white hair, and light-colored eyes. Some traditional African healers claim albino body parts have special powers to bring wealth and good luck. More than 50 albinos had been murdered in Tanzania over the previous two years. In neighboring Burundi, the police arrested eight people on murder charges in mid-March after finding in their houses human bones that may have come from albinos.

On March 18, Amnesty International, a London-based human rights organization, revealed that Gambian authorities had rounded up as many as 1,000 villagers and held them for days as part of a "witch-hunting" campaign. Police officers and army soldiers took the villagers to detention centers and forced them to take *hallucinogens* (drugs that produce delusions or visions). Some villagers were badly beaten. Amnesty International said that Gambia's President Yahya A. J. J. Jammeh ordered the roundup because he blamed sorcery for his aunt's death earlier in 2009. Jammeh reportedly had invited "witch doctors" from nearby Guinea to help Gambian officials in the campaign.

African elephants. According to an October 2009 report in the journal *Scientific American,* African elephants are threatened with extinction because of the illegal ivory trade. Biologist Samuel K. Wasser of the Center for Conservation Biology at the University of Washington in Seattle warned that the current population of 600,000 elephants is diminishing by 38,000 each year. Wasser predicted that the animals could face extinction in

A team from the U.S.S. *Gettysburg,* carrying assault rifles, arrests suspected Somali pirates in the Gulf of Aden on May 13. The Somalis were accused of attacking an Egyptian ship. Pirates based in Somalia regularly robbed and ransomed ships in the Gulf of Aden and the Indian Ocean during 2009.

Africa within 15 years. The International Fund for Animal Welfare (IFAW) in Yarmouth Port, Massachusetts, an organization that works to protect animals throughout the world, called for an immediate ban on ivory sales. The IFAW urged the global community to back Kenya's proposal to extend the current "resting period" on ivory sales from 9 years to 20 years.

Elections in 2009 brought new leaders to power in some African countries and extended the rule of current leaders in others. On May 9, Jacob Zuma took office for a five-year term as South Africa's president. Zuma's African National Congress won parliamentary elections on April 22 with 65.9 percent of the vote.

On May 19, President Bingu wa Mutharika won a second term in Malawi's presidential election with 66 percent of the vote. International observers said, however, that his party misused state resources to tilt the election in his favor.

On July 12, President Denis Sassou-Nguesso of Congo (Brazzaville) won another seven-year term in office with more than 78 percent of the vote. However, human rights groups said that the former military ruler, who had led the country for much of the previous three decades, had won the election by fraud.

Gabon's president, El Hadj Omar Bongo, died on June 8 at the age of 73. President Bongo had ruled the oil-rich country almost as a dictator since 1967 and ranked as Africa's longest-serving leader. He was believed to have become wealthy by treating Gabon's riches as his personal property. His son, Defense Minister Ali Ben Bongo, replaced him, winning presidential elections on Aug. 30, 2009.

President Ian Khama's ruling Botswana Democratic Party won a landslide victory on October 16, confirming him as Botswana's president for the next five years. Khama—the son of the country's

FACTS IN BRIEF ON AFRICAN COUNTRIES

Country	Population	Government	Monetary unit*	Foreign trade (million U.S.$) Exports†	Imports†
Algeria	35,415,000	President Abdelaziz Bouteflika; Prime Minister Ahmed Ouyahia	dinar (72.14 = $1)	78,230	39,160
Angola	18,484,000	President José Eduardo dos Santos	kwanza (75.00 = $1)	67,200	17,080
Benin	9,056,000	President Thomas Yayi Boni	CFA franc (456.95 = $1)	894	1,399
Botswana	1,893,000	President Ian Khama	pula (6.58 = $1)	4,904	4,463
Burkina Faso	15,454,000	President Blaise Compaoré; Prime Minister Tertius Zongo	CFA franc (456.95 = $1)	544	1,343
Burundi	9,417,000	President Pierre Nkurunziza	franc (1,200.00 = $1)	79	350
Cameroon	19,331,000	President Paul Biya; Prime Minister Philemon Yang	CFA franc (456.95 = $1)	4,816	4,303
Cape Verde	566,000	President Pedro Pires; Prime Minister José Maria Pereira Neves	escudo (76.17 = $1)	99	866
Central African Republic	4,574,000	President François Bozizé; Prime Minister Faustin-Archange Touadéra	CFA franc (456.95 = $1)	147	237
Chad	11,678,000	President Idriss Déby; Prime Minister Youssouf Saleh Abbas	CFA franc (456.95 = $1)	4,502	1,862
Comoros	773,000	President Ahmed Abdallah Mohamed Sambi	franc (361.35 = $1)	32	143
Congo (Brazzaville)	4,012,000	President Denis Sassou-Nguesso	CFA franc (456.95 = $1)	10,850	2,988
Congo (Kinshasa)	69,963,000	President Joseph Kabila; Prime Minister Adolphe Muzito	franc (823.00 = $1)	6,100	5,200
Côte d'Ivoire (Ivory Coast)	21,059,000	President Laurent Gbagbo; Prime Minister Guillaume Soro	CFA franc (456.95 = $1)	10,410	7,155
Djibouti	877,000	President Ismail Omar Guelleh; Prime Minister Dileita Mohamed Dileita	franc (177.00 = $1)	340	1,555
Egypt	81,495,000	President Mohammed Hosni Mubarak; Prime Minister Ahmed Nazif	pound (5.53 = $1)	29,850	56,620
Equatorial Guinea	598,000	President Teodoro Obiang Nguema; Prime Minister Ignacio Milam Tang	CFA franc (456.95 = $1)	13,040	3,156
Eritrea	5,338,000	President Issaias Afewerki	nakfa (15.00 = $1)	13	601
Ethiopia	88,013,000	President Girma Woldegiorgis; Prime Minister Meles Zenawi	birr (12.50 = $1)	1,550	6,901
Gabon	1,394,000	President Ali Ben Bongo; Prime Minister Paul Biyoghé Mba	CFA franc (456.95 = $1)	9,333	2,577
Gambia	1,847,000	President Yahya A. J. J. Jammeh	dalasi (27.00 = $1)	85	299
Ghana	24,842,000	President John Atta Mills	new cedi (1.46 = $1)	5,245	10,240
Guinea	10,088,000	President Moussa Dadis Camara; Prime Minister Kabiné Komara	franc (4,740.00 = $1)	1,392	1,388
Guinea-Bissau	1,803,000	President Malam Bacai Sanhá; Prime Minister Carlos Gomes Júnior	CFA franc (456.95 = $1)	133	200
Kenya	40,602,000	President Mwai Kibaki	shilling (76.05 = $1)	4,958	11,070
Lesotho	2,046,000	King Letsie III; Prime Minister Pakalitha Mosisili	loti (7.78 = $1)	953	1,882

*Exchange rates as of Sept. 30, 2009.   †Latest available data.

Country	Population	Government	Monetary unit*	Foreign trade (million U.S.$)	
				Exports†	Imports†
Liberia	4,177,000	President Ellen Johnson-Sirleaf	dollar (49.00 = $1)	1,197	7,143
Libya	6,518,000	Leader Mu'ammar Muhammad al-Qadhafi; General People's Committee Secretary (Prime Minister) al-Baghdadi Ali al-Mahmudi	dinar (1.23 = $1)	60,260	25,310
Madagascar	21,200,000	President Andry Rajoelina; Prime Minister Colonel Vital Albert Camille	ariary (1,926.24 = $1)	1,155	2,419
Malawi	14,735,000	President Bingu wa Mutharika	kwacha (142.01 = $1)	830	1,587
Mali	13,489,000	President Amadou Toumani Touré; Prime Minister Mobido Sidibé	CFA franc (456.95 = $1)	294	2,358
Mauritania	3,384,000	President Mohamed Ould Abdel Aziz; Prime Minister Moulaye Ould Mohamed Laghdaf	ouguiya (270.00 = $1)	1,395	1,475
Mauritius	1,292,000	President Sir Anerood Jugnauth; Prime Minister Navinchandra Ramgoolam	rupee (31.40 = $1)	2,404	4,391
Morocco	32,554,000	King Mohammed VI; Prime Minister Abbas El Fassi	dirham (7.90 = $1)	20,600	39,160
Mozambique	22,351,000	President Armando Guebuza	new metical (27.46 = $1)	2,653	3,458
Namibia	2,137,000	President Hifikepunye Pohamba	dollar (7.78 = $1)	2,791	3,502
Niger	15,768,000	President Mamadou Tandja	CFA franc (456.95 = $1)	428	800
Nigeria	155,142,000	President Umaru Yar'Adua	naira (154.05 = $1)	76,800	45,490
Rwanda	10,534,000	President Paul Kagame; Prime Minister Bernard Makuza	franc (567.51 = $1)	213	809
São Tomé and Príncipe	166,000	President Fradique de Menezes; Prime Minister Rafael Branco	dobra (15,657.06 = $1)	8	88
Senegal	13,315,000	President Abdoulaye Wade; Prime Minister Souleymane Ndéné Ndiaye	CFA franc (456.95 = $1)	1,983	4,313
Seychelles	88,000	President James Michel	rupee (12.57 = $1)	475	882
Sierra Leone	6,276,000	President Ernest Bai Koroma	leone (3,475.00 = $1)	216	560
Somalia	9,484,000	President Sheik Sharif Sheik Ahmed; Prime Minister Omar Abdirashid Ali Sharmarke	shilling (1,450.75 = $1)	300	798
South Africa	49,237,000	President Jacob Zuma	rand (7.78 = $1)	86,120	90,570
Sudan	41,186,000	President Umar Hassan Ahmad al-Bashir	pound (2.45 = $1)	12,150	9,339
Swaziland	1,141,000	King Mswati III; Prime Minister Barnabas Sibusiso Dlamini	lilangeni (7.78 = $1)	1,759	1,858
Tanzania	43,526,000	President Jakaya Kikwete	shilling (1,311.00 = $1)	2,413	6,259
Togo	7,091,000	President Faure Gnassingbé; Prime Minister Gilbert Houngbo	CFA franc (456.95 = $1)	782	1,549
Tunisia	10,640,000	President Zine El-Abidine Ben Ali; Prime Minister Mohamed Ghannouchi	dinar (1.32 = $1)	19,220	23,230
Uganda	33,984,000	President Yoweri Museveni	shilling (2,040.00 = $1)	2,017	3,594
Zambia	12,689,000	President Rupiah Banda	kwacha (4,625.00 = $1)	4,818	4,694
Zimbabwe	13,733,000	President Robert Gabriel Mugabe; Prime Minister Morgan Tsvangirai	dollar spot (322.36 = $1)	1,321	1.915

founding father, Sir Seretse Khama—had taken over from former President Festus Mogae in April 2008.

Mozambique's Liberation Front of Mozambique (Frelimo), the party that has ruled the nation since independence from Portugal in 1975, won presidential and parliamentary elections on Oct. 28, 2009. The victory gave Frelimo President Armando Guebuza 75.6 percent of the vote. Frelimo also won 191 of the 250 seats in parliament.

West Africa. Ghana achieved a peaceful transfer of power on January 7, when John Atta Mills of the National Democratic Congress took office as president. Atta Mills had won a runoff election on Dec. 28, 2008, by a narrow margin, receiving 50.23 percent of the vote. He beat Nana Addo Akufo-Addo of the New Patriotic Party, who won 49.77 percent.

In the early hours of March 2, 2009, a group of soldiers brutally murdered President João Bernardo Vieira of Guinea-Bissau. The assassination appeared to be revenge for the killing of Vieira's principal political rival, army chief General Batista Tagme Na Wai. Na Wai had died in a bomb explosion only hours before.

On September 28, soldiers opened fire on crowds demonstrating in Conakry, the capital of Guinea. The gunfire killed at least 157 people and wounded over 1,250. The demonstrations protested the military regime of Captain Moussa Dadis Camara, who had seized power in a *coup* (overthrow of the government) in December 2008. Witnesses reported soldiers beating and raping protesters. On December 3, Camara survived an assassination attempt by the head of his presidential guard.

President Teodoro Obiang Nguema of Equatorial Guinea granted a pardon in November to Simon Mann, a British *mercenary* (hired soldier). In July 2008, Mann had received a 34-year prison sentence for plotting Obiang's overthrow. Four South Africans convicted in the plot were released along with Mann, who returned to the United Kingdom after his release. He said that he would testify against Sir Mark Thatcher and other people whom he accused of taking part in the failed plot. Sir Mark is the son of former British Prime Minister Margaret Thatcher.

On Feb. 25, 2009, the Special Court for Sierra Leone found three former rebel leaders guilty of crimes against humanity. The court was set up jointly by the government of Sierra Leone and the United Nations (UN) in Sierra Leone's capital, Freetown. The Special Court convicted the men of war crimes, including murder, rape, and sexual enslavement, during the country's brutal 11-year civil war (1991-2002).

Charles Taylor, the former president of Liberia who was overthrown in 2003, became the first former African head of state to stand trial before an international tribunal. On July 13, 2009, Taylor appeared before the Special Court for Sierra Leone in The Hague, the Netherlands, and denied committing war crimes. The prosecutors accused Taylor of ordering acts of brutality in Sierra Leone and Liberia during Sierra Leone's civil war. They said he sought control over Sierra Leone's mineral wealth, especially diamonds.

Eastern Africa and the Horn of Africa. In September, the relief agency Oxfam, based in Oxford, United Kingdom, warned that more than 23 million people faced severe food shortages across East Africa. Oxfam cited a drought that affected seven countries, including Ethiopia, Kenya, Somalia, and Uganda. Economists also blamed the increase in global food prices since 2007.

International navies captured or killed more than 340 suspected Somali pirates during 2009. Pirates hijacked ships in the Indian Ocean, the Gulf of Aden, and other busy shipping lanes. Kenya, Mauritius, Seychelles, and Tanzania expressed concerns about pirates in their waters.

On January 9, Somali pirates released the Saudi supertanker *Sirius Star,* which they had captured in November 2008. The Saudis reportedly paid a ransom of about $3 million. In February 2009, pirates released the Ukrainian military ship M.V. *Faina,* seized in September 2008, also after reportedly receiving a ransom. Somalia has not had an effective central government since 1991, allowing pirates to use Somalia as a base.

In August 2009, U.S. Secretary of State Hillary Clinton warned that the United States would "take action" against Eritrea if it continued to support Islamist rebels in Somalia. The rebels oppose Somalia's President Sheik Sharif Sheik Ahmed and have attacked African Union peacekeeping forces. About 4,300 African Union peacekeepers had replaced Ethiopian troops in Somalia in January.

Central Africa. During 2009, the UN-backed International Criminal Tribunal for Rwanda in Arusha, Tanzania, convicted a number of Rwandans on charges of *genocide* (the extermination of an ethnic group). Those convicted included Emmanuel Rukundo, a Roman Catholic priest and former military chaplain, and Anne-Marie Nyirahakizimana, a physician. Rukundo was sentenced to 25 years in prison, and Nyirahakizimana received a life sentence. Their convictions and those of some 30 other Hutus related to a conflict that broke out in 1994 between Rwanda's two largest ethnic groups, the Hutu and the Tutsi. Hutu extremists massacred up to 1 million Tutsis and moderate Hutus.

In April 2009, the government of Burundi recognized the country's last remaining rebel group, the National Liberation Forces (FNL), as a political party after years of civil war. The FNL took up arms in 1993 to free Burundi's Hutu majority from domination by the Tutsi minority. According to a timetable issued by a South African mediation team, Burundi's army and police would absorb some 3,500 FNL fighters.

On Jan. 14, 2009, the UN Security Council unanimously approved sending some 5,500 UN peacekeepers to replace European Union troops in strife-torn areas of Chad and the Central African Republic. Chad and the Central African Republic faced challenges caring for refugees who had fled an armed conflict in Sudan's Darfur region.

Southern Africa. Events in southern Africa in 2009 were dominated once again by the continuing crisis in neighboring Zimbabwe. A power-sharing government that came into being in February virtually collapsed in October after Prime Minister Morgan Tsvangirai accused President Robert Mugabe of refusing to carry out key provisions of the agreement. President Zuma and the Southern African Development Community, a group devoted to improving economic conditions and political cooperation among the nations of southern Africa, set a deadline for the two sides to make progress on reform by December 6. By the end of 2009, however, there had been little progress.

Following weeks of political violence in which at least 135 people died, military leaders in Madagascar seized power from President Marc Ravalomanana on March 17. The military handed the office four days later to the opposition leader, Andry Rajoelina. Critics accused Ravalomanana of undermining democracy and agreeing to lease vast tracts of land to a South Korean corporation. Rajoelina canceled the deal on March 18. The African Union condemned the coup and suspended Madagascar from membership.

Citizens of the tiny island of Mayotte, an overseas possession of France, voted on March 29 for closer ties with France. The island will become an overseas department of France in 2011. Nearly 96 percent of Mayotte's mainly Muslim population voted in favor of the change, even though it will mean the end of the local tradition of *polygamy,* the practice of having more than one wife or husband at the same time. The African Union opposed Mayotte's decision.

Zambia's former president, Frederick Chiluba, was cleared of theft charges on August 17 after a five-year trial. He had been accused of embezzling $500,000 during his 10 years in office beginning in 1991. His acquittal in the criminal case contrasted sharply with a civil court ruling in London in 2007, when a British judge ordered Chiluba to repay 23 million pounds (about $38 million) that he was convicted of stealing from Zambia's government.

Simon Baynham

See also **Disasters; South Africa; Zimbabwe;** various African country articles.

Agriculture. In 2009, the global recession caused crop prices to decline, farmland values in the United States to erode, and U.S. farm income to fall 34 percent to $57 billion from the record $87 billion in 2008. Nonetheless, increases in food prices by 2.5 percent, following an overall 5.5-percent increase in 2008, put basic food staples out of the reach of many of the world's poor, expanding the ranks of the chronically hungry.

World crop production. World wheat production totaled 675 million metric tons in 2009, down about 1 percent from 2008, according to a report released by the U.S. Department of Agriculture (USDA) in December 2009. Reduced production in the United States and Canada—due chiefly to rainy weather at harvest time—as well as in Ukraine offset increased production in Kazakhstan and Australia. Analysts estimated the U.S. crop at 60 million metric tons (2.2 million bushels), down 11 percent from 2008. China, India, and Syria harvested slightly larger wheat crops in 2009 than in 2008.

Production of coarse grains—corn, barley, oats, and sorghum—totaled 1.089 billion metric tons in 2009. USDA experts projected a 2009 corn crop in the United States, the world's largest corn producer, of 328 million metric tons (12.9 billion bushels), a 7-percent increase over the 2008 crop. Experts emphasized that U.S. yields—the amount of corn harvested per unit of land—increased by 6 percent in 2009 to a record 163 bushels per acre (403 bushels per hectare). The largest corn producers outside the United States were China with 155 million metric tons; the European Union (EU) with 56 million metric tons; and Brazil with 51 million metric tons.

Production of oilseeds—soybeans, sunflower seeds, cottonseed, and rapeseed—totaled 429 million metric tons in 2009. More than half of that amount—250 million metric tons—was the soybean crop. Global soybean production was up due to a record U.S. crop of 90 million metric tons (3.32 billion bushels) and Brazil's crop of 63 million metric tons (2.5 billion bushels). Both countries posted an 11-percent increase over their 2008 crops. Argentina, Paraguay, and Uruguay also had bigger soybean harvests in 2009. In Argentina, excessively dry weather prevented sunflower seed planting, and many farmers switched to soybean crops. As a result, the soybean harvest in Argentina totaled 53 million tons in 2009, a 66-percent increase over the 2008 crop of 32 million metric tons. China, which harvested a mere 15 million metric tons of soybeans, found it necessary to import 41 million metric tons to feed its massive population, trade analysts noted.

The global rice harvest in 2009 was 434 million metric tons. Brazil, India, the Philippines, and the United States all harvested smaller crops than

Norman E. Borlaug
Agricultural Revolutionary

Norman Ernest Borlaug was a renowned agricultural scientist whose work with plant breeding was credited with saving the lives of hundreds of millions of people around the world, earning him the Nobel Peace Prize in 1970. Borlaug was often called the "father of the Green Revolution," the term used to describe the improvement in world food supply resulting from the high-yield, disease-resistant varieties of grain that he developed. The hardy wheat, rice, and other crops derived from Borlaug's research allowed many countries in which food shortages and famine had been common to become self-sufficient in food production and to change from grain importers to grain exporters. Borlaug died in Dallas at age 95 on Sept. 12, 2009, from complications of cancer.

Borlaug was born on March 25, 1914, in Cresco, Iowa. He grew up on a farm and became interested at an early age in why some crops grow well while others do not. In 1942, he earned his doctorate in plant *pathology* (diseases) from the University of Minnesota at St. Paul.

In 1944, Borlaug went to Mexico to help improve crop yields that were extremely low because of plant diseases, poor soil conditions, and other factors. Borlaug's research in Mexico was supported by the Rockefeller Foundation, a philanthropic organization based in New York City.

The focus of Borlaug's early research was crossing different strains of wheat to create new varieties that were resistant to disease and better adapted to the hot, dry climate of Mexico. The results of this research allowed Mexico to substantially increase its wheat production.

In the 1950's, Borlaug cross-bred wheat strains to introduce an unusual gene into tropical wheat plants that allowed the plants to grow in sturdy semidwarf forms with huge heads of grain. These new forms were ideally suited to thrive with the use of nitrogen-based fertilizers, which caused "normal" wheat plants to grow so large and heavy that they fell over and rotted on the ground. The combination of the short, productive wheat varieties with chemical fertilizers and pesticides became a key milestone of the Green Revolution. The breeding techniques developed by Borlaug for wheat were soon applied to rice—the main diet staple of half the world's population—greatly extending the agricultural revolution.

During the 1960's, India and Pakistan began using the high-yield wheat varieties developed by Borlaug, along with fertilizers and pesticides. As a result, crop yields soared. Borlaug's techniques were next applied in the Philippines, China, and Central and South America.

In 1984, Borlaug joined the faculty of Texas A&M University in College Station and continued his agricultural research into plant diseases. He remained at that institution for the rest of his professional life.

Thanks to Norman Borlaug and the Green Revolution, food became more abundant for countless people who might otherwise have starved. However, the agricultural techniques that made this bounty possible also fostered reliance on chemical fertilizers and pesticides that environmentalists eventually criticized.

Borlaug maintained that the real problem behind these environmental concerns was "the population monster"—overpopulation that made increasingly higher agricultural yields necessary—and called for lower birth rates. He also noted that much of the criticism came from people in rich nations who did not have to worry about their own food supplies. Because of Borlaug and the agricultural advancements that his work inspired, fewer and fewer people in poorer countries have this worry either.

■ Alfred J. Smuskiewicz

in 2008. India's projected crop of 83 million metric tons, reduced because of a poor monsoon season, was the smallest since 1997-1998. China, however, produced a record harvest of 137 million metric tons in 2009, followed by Indonesia with 38 million, Vietnam with 24 million, and Thailand with 20 million. The U.S. crop came in at 6.9 million metric tons.

World cotton production in 2009 was 102 million bales, down 4 percent from 2008. China harvested 32 million bales in 2009, a 14-percent decline from the previous year. The U.S. harvest was 12.6 million bales, the smallest crop since 1989.

World hunger. In 2009, the number of hungry and undernourished people in the world exceeded 1 billion, according to "The State of Food Insecurity in the World 2009," the annual report of the United Nations (UN) Food and Agriculture Organization (FAO). Not since 1970 had so many of the world's people been hungry, according to the report. FAO experts attributed the increase in hunger to escalating prices for such staple foods as wheat, rice, and corn. Although 2009 food prices were down from the historic highs of 2008, they were still 17 percent above 2006 levels. Officials with the FAO and the UN World Food Programme reiterated their commitment to increasing food production by 50 percent by 2020.

Biotech crops. The acreage of farmland planted to biotech (BT) crops—also known as genetically modified (GM) crops—expanded by 9 percent in 2008 (the last year for which statistics were available), comprising 309 million acres (125 million hectares). In its annual report, released in February 2009, the International Service for the Acquisition of Agri-Biotech Applications (ISAAA), an organization that promotes the use of biotechnology in developing nations, reported that 13.3 million farmers in a record 25 countries planted BT crops in 2008.

The United States, Argentina, Brazil, and Canada lead the world in biotech planting. China and India have also adopted the technology. Across the globe, many experts regard BT plantings as the best way to increase yields and attain a real chance of reducing world hunger.

In much of Europe, however, BT crops, especially food crops, have been controversial. Some member nations of the European Union (EU) impose a ban on the use of BT crops and feed. As a result of the controversy surrounding these products, analysts note, EU farmers produce far fewer BT crops than those in North America, Latin America, and some parts of Asia. Despite EU reticence, Europe's key suppliers continue to increase BT plantings. About 65 percent of Brazil's soybean crop, for example, and 50 percent of the corn crop are biotech varieties.

In 2009, ISAAA experts predicted that

drought-resistant BT corn seeds would become commercially available in the United States by 2012 and in Africa by 2017. BT research on genes for drought tolerance is expected to yield crops capable of thriving in regions afflicted by persistent drought, such as some parts of Africa.

Organic food. Despite high food prices and a weak economy, U.S. sales of organic food and drink increased 17 percent in 2008 (the latest date for which statistics were available). Sales totaled $24.6 billion, according to the Organic Trade Association's 2009 Organic Industry Survey. Expenditures for all food consumed in the United States in 2008 totaled $1.165 trillion, according to a USDA report. Thus, organic foods claimed a tiny 2-percent share of the total U.S. food market.

Pork scare. Herds of swine were credited with spreading H1N1, a new strain of flu that broke out among human populations in Mexico in early 2009 and quickly spread to the United States and many other countries. The origin of H1N1 in pigs prompted 27 countries to ban imports of U.S. pork, resulting in a price slump for pork. However, officials of the U.S. Centers for Disease Control and Prevention asserted that the H1N1 flu virus is found only in the respiratory tracts of pigs and cannot be contracted by eating pork.

Renewable fuels. In October, the International Energy Agency (IEA)—the Paris-based energy watchdog for the industrialized nations—reported that global investment in renewable energy declined 25 to 40 percent among its member countries in 2009 due to the global financial downturn. Despite tight money, however, ethanol production in the United States increased steadily throughout 2008 and 2009.

American producers of ethanol distilled 221.6 million barrels, or 9.3 billion gallons, of the biofuel in 2008 (the last year for which complete statistics were available), according to the U.S. Energy Information Administration (EIA). Ethanol production in every month of 2009 surpassed production in the corresponding month of 2008 (based on 2009 data available as of December).

Every barrel of ethanol is equivalent in energy content to two barrels of crude oil. Given that ratio, U.S. ethanol output in 2008 displaced almost 450 million barrels of crude oil. It would require about 225 supertankers to ship that much crude to the United States.

The EIA projected that the United States would use 34 percent of its 2009 corn crop for ethanol production. Each bushel of corn generates about 2.8 gallons of ethanol and about 19 pounds (8.6 kilograms) of a useful, high-protein by-product that can be fed to livestock.

■ Patricia Peak Klintberg

See also **Economics, World; Energy supply; Food.**

AIDS. Scientists reported in August 2009 that they had decoded the structure of the *genome* (set of genetic information) of the human immunodeficiency virus (HIV, the virus that causes AIDS). The report—from a team at the University of North Carolina at Chapel Hill—was expected to help researchers better understand how HIV affects the body. The researchers said that analysis of the genome might speed the development of new antiviral drugs.

Increasing virulence. HIV may be increasing in *virulence* (the ability to harm the body), according to a study published in May. The study was led by Nancy Crum-Cianflone, an expert in infectious disease at the Naval Medical Center in San Diego.

HIV kills immune system cells called CD4 cells, reducing their number and weakening the immune system, which protects the body against disease. Crum-Cianflone's team analyzed the CD4 counts reported at diagnosis for 2,174 patients infected with HIV, dating from 1985 to 2007. The researchers found that the average initial CD4 count—that is, the CD4 count at diagnosis—in these patients decreased substantially during this period.

The scientists said that, because HIV had apparently increased in virulence, treatment of patients with antiviral drugs should probably begin earlier in the course of the disease than had previously been the case.

AIDS apathy. In April 2009, survey results reported by the Kaiser Family Foundation, a health policy organization based in Menlo Park, California, showed that 17 percent of United States respondents aged 18 to 29 described themselves as "very concerned" about contracting HIV. This was a decrease from the 30 percent who expressed such concern in 1997.

In June 2009, similar survey results on AIDS attitudes among people aged 16 to 24 in the United Kingdom were reported by the Staying Alive Foundation, a charitable health organization in London. Nearly 60 percent of respondents believed that they were not at risk of contracting HIV after having unprotected sex, and 14 percent incorrectly thought that not being homosexual ensured that they could not contract HIV.

Also in June, the Centers for Disease Control and Prevention in Atlanta reported that from 2006 to 2007, cases of AIDS increased 16 percent among U.S. teenagers and more than 20 percent among U.S. adults aged 20 to 24. Experts noted that these statistics suggested that the growing lack of concern about HIV infection among young people was leading to more risky sexual behaviors in this population group.

New way to block HIV. A new contraceptive device for women may also prevent transmission of HIV to users, researchers at Weill Cornell Medical College in New York City reported in May 2009. The vaginal ring undergoing laboratory tests at the college was designed to release a combination of anticonception and antiviral compounds over a 28-day period. In lab tests, this drug combination prevented infection in human cells exposed to HIV. The researchers noted, however, that clinical trials were needed to prove the ring's effectiveness against HIV in women.

Vaccine results questioned. Positive results from a trial of an AIDS vaccine that had been reported to much media fanfare in September were questioned by scientists in October. Researchers in Thailand working on a study funded by the U.S. government had reported that an experimental vaccine—for the first time—prevented HIV infection in a group of volunteers. However, more complete analysis of the trial data later revealed that the results were not statistically significant.

Joel D. Weisman, one of the first physicians to detect AIDS, died in July. In 1981, Weisman co-wrote a report describing an array of symptoms in homosexual men in Los Angeles that signaled the beginning of the epidemic later identified as AIDS.   ■ Alfred J. Smuskiewicz

See also **Drugs; Medicine; Public health.**

Air pollution. See **Environmental pollution.**

Albania. Parliamentary elections in June 2009 failed to produce a clear winner. The ruling Democratic Party of Prime Minister Sali Berisha barely edged out the main opposition Socialist Party. In the absence of a majority, Berisha's Democratic Party formed a government with a small party that held four parliamentary seats.

The Socialists, led by Edi Rama, mayor of Tiranë, Albania's capital, alleged fraud in the June elections and boycotted parliament after it convened in September. European observers of the parliamentary elections acknowledged that the polling failed to meet international standards but urged the Socialists to return to parliament.

In April, Albania achieved one of its chief foreign policy goals when it became a member of NATO. Albania continued in 2009 to contribute troops to the NATO mission in Afghanistan.

In November, the member states of the European Union (EU) referred Albania's application for EU candidacy to the European Commission, the EU's executive arm. Approval of the application would initiate a series of talks toward eventual membership. EU officials continued to urge Albania to combat organized crime and corruption and to carry out judicial and administrative reforms.   ■ Sharon L. Wolchik

See also **Europe.**

Alberta. See **Canadian provinces.**

Algeria. President Abdelaziz Bouteflika was elected to a third term on April 9, 2009. Six months earlier, the Council of Ministers had amended the Algerian Constitution to remove the two-term limit on the presidency. Rally for Culture and Democracy, a Berber party, did not participate in the election, claiming it to be "a pathetic and dangerous circus." Official results showed a 75-percent voter turnout, with President Bouteflika handily defeating the five other candidates by winning more than 90 percent of the vote. Many expert observers, however, estimated that those figures were greatly inflated.

On June 17, members of al-Qa`ida in the Islamic Maghreb attacked a convoy of paramilitary police vehicles east of Algiers, the capital. The police were escorting Chinese workers to the site of a highway under construction. Eighteen police officers and one Chinese worker were killed.

Sonatrach, Algeria's state-owned oil company, had an estimated $17 billion in savings that could be used to shield Algerians from the international financial crisis, according to an April report by the International Monetary Fund, a United Nations credit agency.   ■ Mary-Jane Deeb

See also **Africa; Terrorism.**

Andorra. See **Europe.**

Angola. See **Africa.**

Animal. See **Biology; Conservation; Zoos.**

Anthropology. In February 2009, Swedish biologist Svante Pääbo of the Max Planck Institute for Evolutionary Anthropology in Leipzig, Germany, announced that his research team had completed a first draft of the entire Neandertal genome. A genome is a complete set of all of the hereditary information for a particular organism. Genes are encoded in the structure of DNA (deoxyribonucleic acid) that makes up chromosomes. The four molecular units of DNA, called bases, are attached in pairs along the two-stranded DNA molecule. Scientists work with DNA to *sequence* (determine the order of) the base pairs and the genes they encode. Pääbo was able to sequence about 3 billion base pairs of DNA from genetic material extracted from a 38,000-year-old Neandertal fossil excavated in Croatia, with additional material from Neandertal fossils excavated in Russia and Spain.

Most anthropologists consider Neandertals, *Homo neanderthalensis,* and modern human beings, *Homo sapiens,* as two distinct species. The evidence for this rests largely on the long list of anatomical differences between the two species in their teeth and bones. Earlier work by Pääbo established that Neandertals were distant cousins of modern human beings but probably not a direct ancestor. His new results promise to greatly expand our knowledge of the specific differences

An artist's reconstruction of *Ardipithecus ramidus,* a 4.4-million-year-old human ancestor from Ethiopia, is based on the description of a partially complete adult female skeleton published in October. The apelike creature appears to have been equally adept at climbing in trees and walking upright on the ground.

between modern people and Neandertals.

Research by geneticist Edward Rubin of the Lawrence Berkeley National Laboratory in Berkeley, California, has shown that human and Neandertal genomes overlap as much as 99.5 percent. The 0.5-percent difference in the DNA may reveal insights into the basis for the anatomical, and possibly behavioral, differences between Neandertals and modern human beings. For example, the gene FOXP2 allows human beings to control their lips, tongue, and mouth to a much greater degree than other primates. If the Neandertal version of this gene is the same, it would suggest that Neandertals had much the same language abilities as modern human beings. The analysis of the Neandertal genome may also help substantiate claims by some that Neandertals and modern humans were so distinct that they could not have interbred and produced offspring.

Ancient human ancestor unveiled. American paleoanthropologist Tim White of the University of California at Berkeley and a team of Ethiopian and American scientists unveiled long-awaited 4.4-million-year-old fossils of *Ardipithecus ramidus,* an ancient human ancestor, in the Oct. 2, 2009, issue of the journal *Science.* The fossils were first discovered between 1992 and 1994 at a site called Aramis, Ethiopia, about 140 miles (225 kilometers) northeast of the capital, Addis Ababa. However, it took the team 15 years to clean, piece together, and analyze the fragile fossil remains. The 110 fragmentary fossils represent 36 individuals, including much of the skull, pelvis, lower arms, and feet from one female. The fossils are important because scientists believe that the last common ancestor shared by human beings and chimpanzees lived about 6 million years ago. *Ardipithecus* is on the human line, but likely shared many of the common ancestor's characteristics. However, the fossils show that *Ardipithecus* did not resemble a chimpanzee or any living ape.

According to the researchers, the pelvis shows a mix of ape and human traits. For example, the large flaring bones of the upper hips were positioned so that *Ardipithecus* could walk on two legs like a human being. But the lower hipbones are built more like an ape's, to anchor huge hind limb muscles used in climbing trees. In addition, the big toe splays out from the foot like an ape's, to grasp tree limbs.

However, the fossils also lack any features that indicate *suspension* (hanging from tree limbs), vertical tree-climbing, or knuckle-walking, seen in modern chimpanzees—evidence that human beings and chimpanzees have each evolved along much different pathways since their last common ancestor. ■ Donald C. Johanson

Antigua and Barbuda. See **Latin America; West Indies.**

Archaeology. In March 2009, Idaho State University archaeologist Richard Hansen published evidence on the fall of El Mirador, one of the largest cities built by the ancient Maya in northern Guatemala. Excavators at the site uncovered hundreds of spear points and arrowheads, human bones, and smashed pottery that date to the destruction of the city around A.D. 150 by unknown invaders. However, the victors left graffiti at the site, providing a clue to their identity. The graffiti included drawings of the war god Tlaloc, known from Teotihuacán, a city in central Mexico near present-day Mexico City. The rulers of Teotihuacán were allied with Tikal, another powerful Mayan city in northern Guatemala, which was an economic and political rival of El Mirador. The findings provide evidence about the alliances and conflicts between rulers that preceded the Classic Period beginning about A.D. 250, when the Maya built their greatest cities.

Anglo-Saxon gold. In July 2009, Terry Herbert, an unemployed metal detector enthusiast, discovered a buried hoard of magnificent gold and silver artifacts, dating to about A.D. 725, in a field near Burntwood, Staffordshire, in the United Kingdom. Archaeologists believe that the collection will revolutionize their understanding of the Anglo-Saxons, who ruled England from the A.D. 400's until the Norman invasion in 1066. The hoard is the largest collection of Anglo-Saxon items ever found. The approximately 1,500 objects were unearthed in what was once the Anglo-Saxon kingdom of Mercia.

Most of the gold and silver artifacts are fittings and decorations for swords and armor. None are jewelry or items associated with women, such as dress fittings or brooches. Two gold crosses with inlaid gemstones are the only items in the hoard that are not related to weapons, leading experts to conclude that the hoard represents a collection of battle trophies amassed by a ruler in wars with neighboring kingdoms. The quality of the objects indicates that they were made for noblemen or royalty. Experts believe that the items were buried during a time of danger by their owner, who probably planned to return and dig them up when the danger passed. A coroner has declared that the hoard is "treasure"and must be declared and valued by the government's Treasure Valuation Committee. Once experts determine the value of the collection, it will be offered for sale to a museum. The proceeds will go to Herbert, who will share his fortune with the landowner.

Paleolithic innovations. In August 2009, archaeologist Nicholas Conard of the University of Tübingen, Germany, and colleagues published a description of three bone and ivory flutes that represent the oldest known evidence for music in

The Iraq National Museum, repository of artifacts from ancient Sumer, Assyria, and Babylonia, reopened in February six years after the U.S.-led invasion. The museum was looted during the chaos that followed the fall of Saddam Hussein's Baathist regime.

human prehistory. The artifacts were excavated at Hohle Fels Cave, near Ulm, Germany, and date to the Upper Paleolithic, about 35,000 years ago. The instruments were likely made by people of the Aurignacian culture, one of the earliest distinctive human cultures in Europe. The best-preserved flute is about 8.5 inches (21 centimeters) long, carved from the hollow limb bone of a vulture. It preserves two V-shaped notches at one end where the musician would blow into the instrument and four finger holes used to play musical notes. Other prehistoric musical instruments are known from Paleolithic sites in Europe, but all are more recent than 35,000 years.

In September, an international team led by archaeologist Ofer Bar-Yosef of Harvard University in Cambridge, Massachusetts, and Eliso Kvavadze of the National Museum of Georgia in Tbilisi, reported the discovery of 34,000-year-old flax fibers at Dzudzuana Cave, in the Republic of Georgia. The fibers were discovered when archaeologists examined clay from cave deposits in which the fibers were imbedded. The flax fibers, from wild plants that were common in the area, had been cut, twisted, and dyed gray, black, turquoise, and pink with pigments obtained from natural sources. The archaeologists believe they were the remains of such manufactured items as clothing, ropes, and

baskets that disintegrated long ago. Before this discovery, the oldest evidence of fiber technology was from a 28,000-year-old site in the Czech Republic.

Oldest pottery. In June, archaeologists led by Elisabetta Boaretto of Bar Ilan University in Ramat Gan, Israel, published results of precise excavation and carbon dating that show pottery from Yuchanyan Cave in southern China was made there between 17,500 and 18,300 years ago. The team was able to reassemble the pottery fragments into a cone-shaped pot, about 11 inches (28 centimeters) tall, which was probably used for cooking or storing food. Until this discovery, the earliest known pottery was from Japan, dated at 16,000 to 17,000 years ago, and several sites in eastern Russian that are nearly as old.

Yuchanyan Cave provides strong evidence that nomadic groups of hunter-gatherers in the region invented pottery long before they developed farming and settled into permanent villages. In 2005, archaeologists found the oldest preserved kernels of wild rice at the same cave. The findings at this cave site are helping archaeologists understand the transition human beings made from cave-dwelling hunter-gatherers to the settled farming communities that occurred in this region around the Yangtze River more than 10,000 years ago.   ■ Mark Rose

Architect Thom Mayne's new classroom building for Cooper Union, New York City's famed free university, is clad in crimped and cut stainless steel panels that express the raw energy of its East Village neighborhood.

Architecture.

One of the most compelling architectural projects of 2009 was not a building but an elevated railroad track transformed into an urban promenade. Designed by New York City-based Diller, Scofidio & Renfro Architects, the High Line glides 30 feet (9 meters) above New York's West Village for approximately nine blocks between Gansevoort and 20th streets, with a 10-block extension planned for 2010. Laid out along the old elevated tracks, the High Line winds through and around warehouses and abandoned meat packing plants, with sections of rusted rail popping through the pavement like relics of a vanished civilization. Landscape architect James Corner enriched the composition with native grasses and wild flowers typically found along rail lines, thereby connecting past and present, place and memory, in clear, unforced ways.

Cooper Union classroom. Across town, in the East Village, Los Angeles architect Thom Mayne designed a tough, "take that" classroom building for Cooper Union, the celebrated free university founded in 1859 by industrialist Peter Cooper. Supported on massive V-shaped concrete columns, 41 Cooper Square is clad in crimped and cut stainless steel panels that express the raw energy of the surrounding neighborhood. The architectural centerpiece is a swirling atrium with a vertiginous grand staircase rising from the lobby to classrooms and offices above. Students have embraced it as a social space; some administrators and faculty complain that, while dramatic, the staircase makes navigating the building unnecessarily complicated.

Art Institute of Chicago. Renzo Piano's $294-million addition to the Art Institute of Chicago engages the city in many ways: floor-to-ceiling windows; a long bridge connecting the museum to Millennium Park, Chicago's new living room; and a floating glass roof that brings natural light into the modern and contemporary galleries below. The addition, known simply as "The Modern Wing," increases the size of the museum by one-third and gives its extraordinary collection of post-World War II (1939-1945) paintings and sculpture a prominence it never had before.

The August Wilson Center for African American Culture finally opened in downtown Pittsburgh in 2009, nearly a decade after it was first announced. Designed by Allison Williams of Chicago-based Perkins & Will and named for the renowned Pittsburgh playwright, the Wilson is a blend of museum and performing arts center. Except for a single curving facade, like a spinnaker on a sail boat, the building is a long rectangle, welcoming but restrained. Inside are galleries, classrooms, meeting spaces, and a 485-seat theater, all focused on telling the story of African

American culture in Pittsburgh and around the world.

Dallas performing arts center. The most spectacular cultural project of the year was the $355-million AT&T Performing Arts Center in Dallas. The center features an opera house by London-based Foster + Partners; a theater by Dutch architect Rem Koolhaas and Joshua Prince-Ramus; and a civic plaza by French landscape architect Michel Desvigne. The center completes a downtown Arts District that was begun 30 years ago and has experienced numerous false starts and financial setbacks. The Winspear Opera House is a traditional horseshoe hall for 2,100 people enclosed in a concrete drum covered in red glass panels. The cubic Wyly Theatre contains 600 seats that can be reconfigured in numerous ways by means of an elaborate system of winches, pulleys, and hydraulic lifts. The exterior of this performance machine is covered in aluminum tubes that resemble a folded theater curtain.

Dallas Cowboys. At the other end of the cultural spectrum, the new Dallas Cowboys Stadium (HKS Architects of Dallas) in neighboring Arlington is a streamlined steel-and-glass oval that is part spaceship, part abstracted football, and at $1.2 billion the most expensive stadium in National Football League history. It is also sophisticated entertainment architecture, with monumental steel trusses, sloping glass walls, a retractable roof, and a hovering 168 x 74-foot (51 x 22.5-meter) video scoreboard that provides everything viewers need to know about professional sports in the digital age. The stadium can accommodate 80,000 spectators for regular games and 100,000 for the Super Bowl, which Dallas is scheduled to host in 2010.

Awards. The 2009 Pritzker Prize went to reclusive Swiss architect Peter Zumthor, whose small but exquisite body of work displays a mastery of simple geometries and a deep love of materials and craftsmanship. "Architecture is about that," he has said. "It's not about paper [or] form; it's about space and materials."

Another reclusive architect, Glenn Murcutt, won the 2009 Gold Medal from the American Institute of Architects. A solo practitioner working exclusively in his native Australia, Murcutt designs simple, understated vernacular houses that respond to the country's richly varied climate and geography. Murcutt was a "green" architect 20 years before "green" became fashionable.

The Praemium Imperiale, the Japan Art Association's award for lifetime achievement, was presented in 2009 to American architect Zaha Hadid, best known for her Cincinnati Museum of Art. The prize includes a stipend of approximately $160,000. ■ David Dillon

See also **Art: A Special Report; Dallas.**

Argentina. On Jan. 26, 2009, President Cristina Fernández de Kirchner declared a state of emergency as Argentina suffered its worst drought in decades. The most affected provinces included Buenos Aires, Chaco, Córdoba, Entre Ríos, La Pampa, Santa Fé, and Santiago del Estero. Seeds planted in the fertile soils of the Pampas died before breaking the surface of the ground in 2009. An estimated 1.5 million head of cattle, upon which Argentina depended for much of its export earnings, succumbed to heat and hunger following the loss of the country's wheat and corn crops. The measure exempted thousands of farmers from paying various taxes for one year, helping them offset an estimated $5 billion in losses in 2009.

Kirchner defeated. On June 28, former President Néstor Kirchner resigned as leader of the Peronist Party following its defeat in national congressional elections. Kirchner, the husband of President Fernández, lost his bid for a seat in the lower house in the province of Buenos Aires. Congressional candidates backed by the Kirchners lost in all of the country's main provinces. The election results meant that Fernández would face a Congress dominated by opposition parties and dissident blocks of senators and deputies within her own party for the rest of her term after the new Congress was installed on December 10.

In July, Argentines were disillusioned to learn that the Kirchners, since coming to power in 2003, had increased their personal wealth sixfold. The couple made millions of dollars through land speculation and investments even while the Argentine economy suffered.

New minister. On July 1, 2009, Juan Luis Manzur was sworn in as minister of health following the resignation of his predecessor over charges of covering up the severity of a swine flu outbreak in a failed attempt to influence the congressional elections in June. By then, more than 60 Argentines had died from the H1N1 virus—the third highest national toll after the United States and Mexico.

Controversial press law. On October 10, the Argentine Congress approved a law giving the government more control over broadcast media. The law included an article granting presidential authority to appoint a majority of the members of a new broadcast regulatory body.

Currency trade. In March, Argentina announced a currency swap of $14.5 billion with China—the first such arrangement between China and a Latin American nation. In May, Argentina concluded a similar deal worth $1.5 billion with Brazil. The exchanges of currency were designed to reduce Argentina's dependency on the United States dollar in international trade.

Human rights center. On February 13, President Fernández and Koïchiro Matsuura, director general of the United Nations Educational, Scientific, and Cultural Organization (UNESCO), inaugurated the International Center for the Promotion of Human Rights. The center is on the grounds of the notorious former Navy Mechanics' School in Buenos Aires, the scene of atrocities during the "dirty war" against dissidents by the Argentine military dictatorship from 1976 to 1983. The new center was to collect and disseminate reports of human rights abuses from around the world.

General convicted. On Aug. 12, 2009, a federal Argentine court sentenced retired General Santiago Riveros, 86, to life in prison. Santiago commanded the Campo de Mayo military barracks outside Buenos Aires and was found guilty of involvement in the 1976 torture killing of a 15-year-old Communist activist, Floreal Avellaneda. Four other former servicemen received lesser sentences for their involvement in the crime.

Death of a president. Former Argentine President Raúl Alfonsín, 82, died on March 31, 2009. In 1983, Alfonsín won Argentina's first presidential election following the end of military rule. He presided over the convictions of some of Argentina's former military junta—including two former presidents—on charges of human rights abuses.   ■ Nathan A. Haverstock
    See also **Latin America.**

Armed forces. United States military affairs were dominated in 2009 by the wars in Afghanistan and Iraq, where U.S.-led combat operations began in 2001 and 2003, respectively. In Iraq, a precarious governmental status quo held in 2009, with American combat forces retreating from cities to interior bases. In Afghanistan, however, the situation deteriorated, as guerrilla fighters fielded by a resurgent Taliban penetrated deep into the country and launched attacks against troops and civilians.

Afghanistan. On December 1, U.S. President Barack Obama called for deployment of an additional 30,000 U.S. troops in Afghanistan, supplementing the 17,000 additional soldiers the administration had already deployed in early 2009. The new troops, scheduled to enter the field in early 2010, were expected to bring U.S. troop totals in Afghanistan to around 100,000. Obama emphasized the mission's priority of training Afghan soldiers and police, and he pledged to begin withdrawing U.S. forces from Afghanistan after 18 months—in July 2011.

Command change. On May 11, 2009, Secretary of Defense Robert M. Gates relieved Army General David D. McKiernan as the U.S. military commander in Afghanistan, replacing him with Lieutenant General Stanley A. McChrystal. A specialist in unconventional warfare, McChrystal was

promoted to general and also assumed command of NATO forces in Afghanistan.

In an August report, McChrystal offered a stark assessment of the situation in Afghanistan and warned that failure was the likely outcome of the war effort unless more troops and resources were forthcoming. The commander's request for an additional 40,000 combat troops prompted President Obama to reassess Afghanistan policy and contributed to the president's December decision to increase troop levels.

On December 1, about 71,000 U.S. troops were stationed in Afghanistan. As of December 29, 508 coalition troops, including 311 U.S. troops, had died since January 1. The casualties incurred in 2009 were by far the highest of any year of the war.

Iraq. The war in Iraq entered its seventh year in 2009 with an improved security situation and the start of a U.S. military drawdown. Implementing an agreement approved by the Iraqi parliament in December 2008, U.S. combat troops left major cities by June 30, 2009, and relocated to outlying military bases.

In a February speech, President Obama said that about two-thirds of the 142,000 American troops then in Iraq would be withdrawn by the summer of 2010, leaving a residual force of 50,000 to train Iraqis. Obama pledged that all U.S. forces would leave Iraq by the end of 2011.

On Dec. 1, 2009, 120,000 U.S. troops were stationed in Iraq. As of December 29, 151 coalition troops, almost all of them U.S. servicepersons, had died since January 1.

Guantánamo. President Obama announced in early 2009 that he would close the military prison at Guantánamo Bay, Cuba, by January 2010. The facility housed terrorism suspects captured since the Sept. 11, 2001, terrorist attacks on the United States. Obama

Soldiers lead a caisson carrying the flag-draped coffin of Major Libardo Caraveo for burial in Arlington National Cemetery on Nov. 25, 2009. Major Caraveo, an army psychologist, was shot and killed in the mass shooting at Fort Hood, Texas, on November 5.

banned the torture of prisoners at Guantánamo and ordered a review of the policy of trial by military tribunals. In late 2009, President Obama acknowledged that the military would not meet his January 2010 target of closing Guantánamo, but he reiterated his commitment to its eventual closure.

Weapons systems. In 2009, the Department of Defense (DOD) continued to develop a variety of weapons systems, including a high-tech, multi-role jet fighter called a joint strike fighter; new classes of aircraft carriers and destroyers; a new generation of armored fighting vehicles; and the littoral combat ship (LCS), a small, shallow-draft vessel capable of close-in fighting along coasts.

Work also proceeded on the so-called "Star Wars" initiative, which sought to develop the capability of destroying intercontinental ballistic missiles in outer space. The DOD requested $9.3 billion for the program in the fiscal 2010 budget, the largest single weapons request, but 15 percent less than the fiscal 2009 appropriation.

In a strategic policy shift, the DOD requested more spending on weapons to fight counterinsurgency campaigns. The DOD budget included $3.8 billion to fund 1,300 unpiloted aerial vehicles, or drones, as well as increased funding for mine-resistant armored vehicles designed to reduce fatalities from roadside bombs.

At Secretary Gates's urging, the Senate on July 21 canceled funding for additional F-22 Raptor jet fighters. Gates said the 187 Raptors already on order were sufficient to maintain air superiority until the less expensive F-35 joint strike fighter became operational. DOD also recommended scrapping the costly VH-71 helicopter, which was to replace the aging helicopters that transport U.S. presidents.

Defense budget. United States President Barack Obama signed a $636-billion defense budget for fiscal year 2010 on Dec. 19, 2009, just hours after the measure won final approval in the Senate. (The 2010-2011 fiscal year runs from Oct. 1, 2009, to Sept. 30, 2010.) Adjusted for inflation, the allocation represented the most modest spending increase since the early 1980's. The budget included funding for a 3.4-percent pay raise for military personnel, expanded troop levels, and expanded medical care for wounded war veterans.

The DOD budget package, which had been approved by the House of Representatives on Dec. 16, 2009, included $128 billion in new spending for the wars in Afghanistan and Iraq. That amount brought the total war spending for fiscal 2009 and 2010 to $270 billion.

Shooting rampage. On Nov. 5, 2009, a lone gunman entered a crowded waiting room of a military processing center at Fort Hood, Texas, and opened fire. After discharging more than 100 rounds, the gunman, later identified as Major Nidal Malik Hasan, an army psychiatrist, left more than 40 people dead or wounded, before he himself was shot by police. On November 12, military officials charged Hasan with 13 counts of murder.

Hasan, a Muslim, had been scheduled to deploy to Afghanistan on November 28. He allegedly had said that the wars in Iraq and Afghanistan were directed against Muslims and, for several months leading up to the shootings, had corresponded with Anwar al-Awlaki, a radical Muslim cleric in Yemen. Senator Carl Levin (D., Michigan), chair of the Senate Armed Services Committee, characterized Hasan's attack as "terrorism," a judgment echoed by other members of Congress.

President Obama and Congress subsequently launched separate investigations into the Hasan shooting. On November 19, Secretary Gates announced a wide-ranging review to determine whether security breaches provide loopholes through which a disturbed individual or terrorist can attack military installations.

Deadly mental strains. The stress of extended and multiple combat deployments in Afghanistan and Iraq continued to produce serious mental strains in soldiers. Although many servicepersons responded positively to treatment for stress-related conditions, a few broke down. On May 11, a soldier being treated for stress at a clinic in Iraq shot and killed five fellow Americans. Army officials charged the soldier, Sergeant John M. Russell, with five counts of murder. Russell was on his third tour of duty in Iraq.

Military suicides continued to rise. On November 16, the Army reported 211 confirmed or suspected suicides for the year so far, a new record.

Personnel developments. In 2009, the U.S. military met all its recruiting objectives for the first time since the all-volunteer force was created in 1973. For the fiscal year ending Sept. 30, 2009, the services recruited 168,968 active-duty troops, or 103 percent of the annual goal. Reserve and National Guard recruitment hit 91,348, or 104 percent of the target. DOD officials attributed the recruiting success to scarcity of civilian employment in the recession that gripped the United States in 2009.

On June 8, the U.S. Supreme Court declined to review the military's controversial "don't ask, don't tell" policy prohibiting gay men and women from serving openly in the armed forces. According to the Servicemembers Legal Defense Network, a nonprofit organization that provides legal assistance to servicepersons discharged on the basis of "don't ask, don't tell," approximately 13,500 members of the various branches of the U.S. military had been discharged because of their sexual orientation since implementation of the policy in 1994. In October 2009, President Obama vowed to end the policy but did not propose a date for its elimination.

On February 26, Defense Secretary Gates announced the end of an 18-year ban on news coverage of the return of bodies of soldiers killed in combat. Critics of the ban claimed that it was designed to conceal the human cost of the Iraq and Afghan wars.

Command changes. The Senate confirmed President Obama's choice for deputy secretary of defense, William J. Lynn III, on Feb. 11, 2009. The Senate also approved a second two-year term, beginning on October 1, for Admiral Michael Mullen as chair of the Joint Chiefs of Staff.

On June 30, Admiral James G. Stavridis, commander of the U.S. Southern Command, assumed command of all U.S. and NATO military forces in Europe. He was the first naval officer appointed to the position.

John M. McHugh, a Republican congressman from New York, was sworn in as secretary of the Army on September 21, replacing Pete Geren. Former Mississippi Governor Raymond E. Mabus, Jr., became secretary of the Navy on May 19, replacing Donald C. Winter. Michele Flournoy was appointed undersecretary of defense for policy, the first woman to hold the DOD's third-highest position.

Gulf War casualty buried. The remains of Navy Captain Michael Scott Speicher were buried on August 14 in his hometown of Jacksonville, Florida. Speicher was the first casualty, and the only U.S. combatant declared missing in action, in the 1991 Persian Gulf War. His jet was shot down on Jan. 17, 1991. Navy officials said that Speicher was killed in action and buried by Bedouin tribesmen in a remote area of western Iraq.

The U.S.S. New York. On Nov. 2, 2009, the Navy ship U.S.S. *New York* glided into New York Harbor. On its way to dock at a west-side Manhattan pier, the ship paused in salute opposite Ground Zero. Before the terrorist attacks of Sept. 11, 2001, the twin towers of the World Trade Center had stood at that spot. Shipbuilders used 7.5 tons (6.8 metric tons) of steel from the wreckage of the towers to construct a section of the hull of the U.S.S. *New York*. ■ Thomas M. DeFrank

See also **Afghanistan; Iraq; United States, Government of the.**

Armenia and Turkey on Oct. 10, 2009, agreed to pacts that would allow the countries to resume diplomatic relations and to open the Armenian-Turkish border after nearly a century of diplomatic hostilities. Armenian Foreign Minister Edward Nalbandian and Turkish Foreign Minister Ahmet Davutoglu signed the protocols in Switzerland, which had hosted mediation talks for more than a year.

Armenia and Turkey have long clashed over Armenia's claim that Turks engaged in the *genocide* (systematic extermination of a cultural or racial group) of about 1.5 million Armenians from 1915 to 1917 during the collapse of the Ottoman Empire, a charge denied by Turkey. More recently, Turkey has supported Azerbaijan in its dispute with Armenia over control over Nagorno-Karabakh, a region located within Azerbaijan but primarily populated by Armenians.

Both the Armenian and Turkish parliaments must ratify the pacts before they go into effect. Armenia's ruling coalition announced that it would support ratification. Opposition leader and former President Levon Ter-Petrosian denounced a clause in the agreements that would establish a joint Turkish-Armenian commission to study the genocide. He and other critics expressed concern that Turkey would use the study to further denounce charges of genocide.   ■ Juliet Johnson

See also **Asia; Turkey.**

Art. In 2009, the art world, particularly art museums, suffered from the gravest financial crisis since the Great Depression of the 1930's. Shrinking endowments, decreased donations, reduced tourism, and cutbacks in state and local funding led to budget deficits in museums throughout the United States and the world. North American museums, which rely more on private sponsorship and endowments, were particularly hard hit. European institutions receive more government funding. Museums reacted by laying off staff, canceling exhibitions, and raising admission fees. Some museums even closed.

Museum cutbacks. One of the largest endowments of any arts organization—that of the J. Paul Getty Trust in Los Angeles—fell to $4.2 billion in March 2009, down from a high of $6.4 billion in 2007. To cut its budget, the Getty Trust eliminated 14 percent of its work force, or 205 jobs, by laying off 97 people and not filling 108 vacant positions. The trust also reduced its number of exhibitions and slashed its budget for acquisitions, imposed pay cuts for its senior staff and salary freezes for other employees, and increased parking fees for visitors. The trust operates the Getty Museum as well as conservation, research, and grant-making programs.

The endowment of the largest museum in the United States—the Metropolitan Museum of Art

(Met) in New York City—fell about 25 percent since June 2008 to $2.1 billion. The museum suffered additional losses from a drop in attendance and a $1.7-million reduction in city financing during 2009. As a result, the Met reduced its staff by 14 percent, laying off 74 workers and giving retirement packages to 95 others by the end of its fiscal year on June 30. The Met's retail business sustained major cuts, with the elimination of more than one-fourth of its sales staff and the closing of about 15 stores nationwide. In addition, the museum imposed a hiring freeze, stopped merit raises, and cut back on staff travel.

Many other museums across the United States cut staff to reduce their operating budgets. Both the Detroit Institute of Arts in Michigan and the Los Angeles Museum of Contemporary Art in California laid off approximately 20 percent of their workers. The Asia Society in New York City eliminated about 11 percent of its staff, and the Indianapolis Museum of Art cut about 10 percent of its work force. The Philadelphia Museum of Art eliminated 30 staff positions, and the High Museum in Atlanta laid off about 7 percent of its staff. A number of other museums cut staff in 2009 without making public announcements of the cuts.

Museums also economized in other ways. In Boston, the Isabella Stewart Gardner Museum cut the pay of its senior staff and imposed a salary freeze on other employees. The Boston Museum of Fine Arts enacted a salary freeze. The Baltimore Museum of Art ordered about half of its staff to take two weeks of unpaid leave, and the Brooklyn Museum of Art in New York City did the same for one week. The Brooklyn Museum and the Art Institute of Chicago raised entrance fees.

The Las Vegas Art Museum closed until further notice in February 2009. The museum began 59 years ago as an art league supporting visual arts in the city. The Minnesota Museum of American Art in St. Paul also closed.

Auction sales. Cautious bidding at the spring 2009 art auctions reflected the uncertain economy. A 1938 portrait of his daughter by the Modern Spanish master Pablo Picasso and a 1951 sculpture of a cat by the Swiss-born artist Alberto Giacometti failed to sell at Sotheby's auction house in New York City on May 5, 2009. The next day, however, two other works by the same artists sold for good prices at Christie's New York auction house. At Christie's, Picasso's brightly colored oil painting *Musketeer with a Pipe* (1968) went for $14.6 million. Giacometti's 1958 bronze sculpture *Bust of Diego (Stele III),* portraying the head of the artist's brother Diego on a tall pedestal, brought $7.6 million.

Some of the artworks offered at auction came from victims of one of the largest frauds in Wall

Street history—a $65-billion swindle by Bernard Madoff, a New York City businessman. Madoff pleaded guilty to all the federal charges filed against him in March 2009.

Christie's sale of contemporary art in May set a record for a work by the British artist David Hockney. Hockney's *Beverly Hills Housewife* (1966-1967) sold for $7.9 million. The 12-foot (3.7-meter) painting portrays an art patron standing on the patio of her Los Angeles home.

New NEA head. In May 2009, U.S. President Obama appointed the Broadway theatrical producer and theater owner Rocco Landesman as chairman of the National Endowment for the Arts (NEA). Congress confirmed Landesman's appointment in August. The NEA, which is the most important arts agency in the United States, is a major source of money for arts organizations. Despite the economic downturn, the NEA received an additional $10 million in 2009, bringing its annual budget to $155 million. Congress also approved giving another $50 million to the NEA under the American Recovery and Reinvestment Act of 2009, an economic stimulus package designed to revive the U.S. economy. Hundreds of arts groups applied for a portion of the stimulus funds.

Museum expansions. Despite the poor economy, several museums unveiled expansions or renovations in 2009. In May, the Art Institute of Chicago opened its new $294-million Modern Wing by the Italian architect Renzo Piano. The elegant three-story glass, steel, and limestone structure adds 264,000 square feet (24,500 square meters) of gallery space, making the Art Institute the second largest art museum in the United States, after the Met.

Also in May 2009, the Met unveiled the second of three stages that will renovate the museum's entire American Wing by 2011. Highlighting the second stage of the renovation was the transformed sculpture garden of the glass-enclosed Charles Engelhard Court. The Engelhard Court displays some 60 examples of large-scale sculpture, mosaics, stained glass, and *architectural elements* (parts of buildings), such as friezes and columns. On the balconies above the courtyard, the Met reinstalled approximately 1,000 pieces of ceramics, glass, silver, and pewter in chronological order. A new mezzanine-level balcony showcases decorative arts of the early 1900's, including jewelry and about 250 examples of American art pottery acquired in 2009. The art pottery movement, which began in the 1870's in the United Kingdom and the United States, created teapots, vases, and other pieces that were more decorative than everyday pottery. Most art pottery was signed by the artist and produced in limited numbers.

The Met also renovated 12 of its 20 period rooms in the American Wing, historic interiors dating from 1680 to 1810. Computer touch screens provide museumgoers with information about the rooms and their furnishings.

In June 2009, the Cleveland Museum of Art opened its new East Wing, the first of three planned additions designed by Rafael Viñoly, a Uruguayan-born and Argentine-educated architect living in the United States. Viñoly's new wing connects the museum's original 1916 building in the Neoclassical Beaux-Arts style with a Modern 1971 addition by the Hungarian-born architect Marcel Breuer. The East Wing's 139,200 square feet (12,930 square meters) houses the Cleveland Museum's collections of European, Modern, and contemporary art and photography of the 1800's and 1900's. Those collections had been removed from public view since 2005, when the renovations began. The complete three-phase expansion, which will add an additional 200,000 square feet (19,000 square meters) to the Cleveland Museum, is scheduled for completion in 2012.

Major exhibitions. "Art of Two Germanys/ Cold War Cultures" opened in January 2009 at the Los Angeles County Museum of Art. The exhibition examined art produced in East and West Germany during the Cold War, an era of international friction from the mid-1940's to the early 1990's. During the Cold War, the Western democracy of the Federal Republic of Germany and the Eastern Communist dictatorship of the German Democratic Republic produced distinctive styles of art. On view were approximately 300 paintings, sculptures, photographs, videos, and *installations* (large-scale works created for a specific site) by 120 artists. Featured artists included the installation artist Hans Haacke, the painters Sigmar Polke and Gerhard Richter, and the sculptor Dieter Roth.

Also opening in January 2009 was "Georgia O'Keeffe and Ansel Adams: Natural Affinities" at the Norton Museum of Art in West Palm Beach, Florida. The show explored how two Modern American artists, the painter O'Keeffe and the photographer Adams, celebrated and transformed the American landscape. The exhibit featured 40 O'Keeffe paintings and 54 Adams photographs, including a selection of previously unseen photos taken by Adams during a 1938 trip to Yosemite National Park in California.

"Cézanne and Beyond," which opened at the Philadelphia Museum of Art in February 2009, examined the artistic legacy of the French Postimpressionist master Paul Cézanne. The exhibition placed some 50 works by Cézanne side by side with more than 100 paintings, drawings, photographs, and sculptures by 18 other artists. These artists, who continued to revere Cézanne for generations, included the Dutch painter Piet Mondrian; the Swiss-born sculptor Alberto Giacometti; the French painters Pablo Picasso and Henri Matisse; the American painters Jasper Johns, Ellsworth Kelly, and Brice Marden; and the Canadian photographer Jeff Wall.

The first major exhibition devoted to the artistic rivalry of three of the greatest Venetian painters of the 1500's opened at the Museum of Fine Arts in Boston in March 2009. "Titian, Tintoretto, Veronese: Rivals in Renaissance Venice" displayed more than 50 paintings, many of them costly loans from European museums. On view were religious images, portraits, and female nudes with the loose technique and rich coloring that came to define the Venetian style.

In May, the Solomon R. Guggenheim Museum celebrated the 50th anniversary of its landmark New York City building with an homage to its creator. "Frank Lloyd Wright: From Within Outward" featured more than 60 projects designed by Wright, one of the leading architects of the 1900's. The projects included private residences, civic and government buildings, religious structures, and performance spaces. On view were more than 200 original drawings, models, and digital animations. The artworks were displayed on the Guggenheim's famous circular ramp, designed by Wright, that spirals up the museum's rotunda. ■ Sally-Ruth May

See also **Architecture; Art: A Special Report.**

Visitors to the Art Institute of Chicago's new Modern Wing (above) gaze out onto architect Frank Gehry's Prizker Pavillion, a performance stage in the city's lakefront Millennium Park. A computerized system monitors and filters natural light to keep the art from being damaged by harmful rays. The Art Institute's original structure (above, right) was completed in 1893 by architects Shepley, Rutan, and Coolidge.

The Art Institute of Chicago opened the Modern Wing, the eighth building project in its 130-year history, on May 16, 2009. Nearly 50,000 local, national, and international visitors came to the Modern Wing during its opening weekend to see not only the new building but also the 1,000 works of modern and contemporary art it holds. Designed by famed Italian architect Renzo Piano, the Modern Wing added 264,000 square feet (24,524 square meters) to the museum, making the Art Institute the largest art museum in the United States after the Metropolitan Museum of Art in New York City.

Founded in 1879, the Art Institute is an encyclopedic museum, meaning that it collects and displays art and artifacts from all over the world and from all periods: from ancient Egyptian, Greek, and Roman objects to Southeast Asian sculpture and from suits of armor from the 1400's to contemporary art. Like many leading museums that maintain active acquisitions programs, the Art Institute is always in need of space to store and display its objects. With a collection of approximately 300,000 objects, the museum decided in 1999 to build the largest addition in its history.

The Art Institute moved into its current location on Michigan Avenue in 1893. The art collection has grown continuously since, requiring ever more space. The additions made to the original classical Beaux-Arts

BRIGHT IDEA

The Art Institute of Chicago's New Modern Wing

By Erin Hogan

building, designed by Boston architects Shepley, Rutan, and Coolidge, form the Art Institute known today. They include Gunsaulus Hall, built in 1916 over railroad tracks in downtown Grant Park; McKinlock Court, built in the 1920's with an open court used for summer dining; the 1958 Benjamin F. Ferguson Memorial Building, which houses administrative and curatorial offices; the Morton Wing, gallery space completed in 1962; an eastern flank of studios, classrooms, and a film center dedicated in 1976; and the Rice Building, gallery space that opened in 1988.

The newly completed Modern Wing rivals the museum's original 1893 building in size. It has two perpendicular, three-story pavilions for galleries. They are connected by a central two-story "main street" atrium that also links the building to the existing Art Institute. The "main street" also provides a new north-south axis to the museum's original east-west

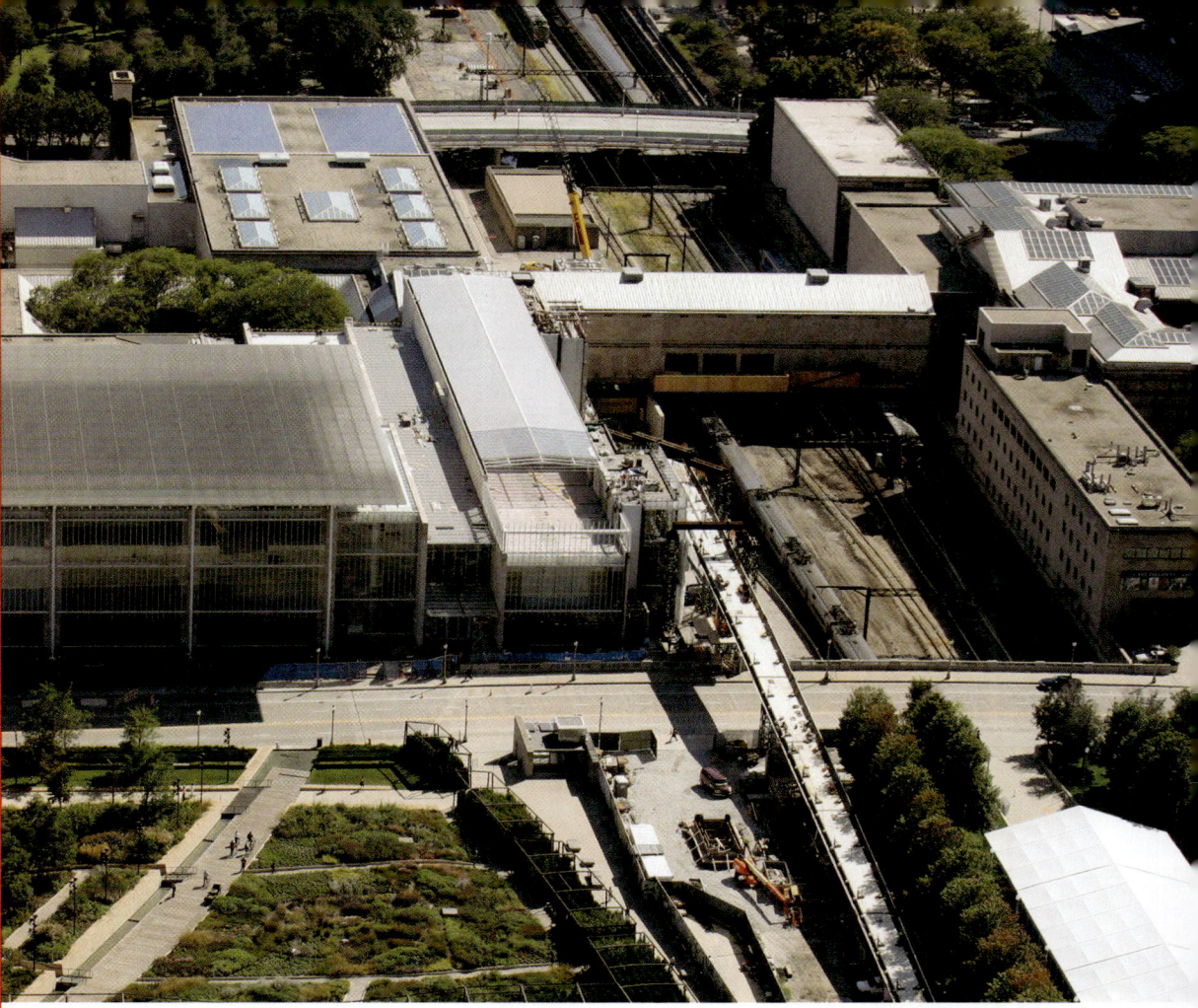

orientation. The Modern Wing holds the Art Institute's collections of 20th- and 21st-century art, architecture, design, and photography and also includes new and expanded education facilities, a public sculpture terrace, and a restaurant. The new addition increases the amount of space the museum can devote to the display of art by approximately 35 percent.

The Modern Wing and Millennium Park

The museum selected Renzo Piano as the architect soon after the decision to build was made in 1999. As originally planned, a 75,000-square-foot (6,967-square-meter) addition was to face south and be constructed over the same railroad tracks bridged by Gunsaulus Hall in 1916. As these plans took shape, construction got under way on Millennium Park, which was being built adjacent to the Art Institute over the same set of tracks, and it soon became clear that the architecturally ambitious park project was to be a public space unprecedented in its innovation. In 2001, Piano and museum leaders decided to resite the planned expansion from the south to the north side of the museum campus to face the new park. Ultimately, this reorientation placed Renzo Piano's classically restrained Modern Wing in an architectural "dialogue" with architect Frank Gehry's wildly exuberant Pritzker Pavilion, built primarily as a performance stage.

Given that the new site was larger than the one planned for the south, the addition itself grew in size, and plans for the building went through a number of revisions. With the addition of a third floor and a pedestrian bridge into Millennium Park, the design of the building was complete, and in 2005 the museum broke ground at Monroe Street and Columbus Drive, directly across from Millennium Park, which had opened in 2004 to both critical and popular acclaim.

The new Modern Wing (far left, foreground), by architect Renzo Piano, is one of eight structures, built in stages between 1893 and 2009, that make the Art Institute the second largest art museum in the United States. The museum spans railroad tracks in Chicago's lakefront Grant Park.

A pedestrian bridge offers unique vistas of the park, Lake Michigan, and the city skyline. It connects the Modern Wing with Millennium Park, which covers a functioning rail yard.

A two-story atrium serves as a "main street" between two perpendicular, three-story pavilions of gallery space. The atrium also forms a new north-south axis that links the Modern Wing to the other Art Institute structures.

The planning and construction of the Modern Wing were accompanied by the largest fund-raising campaign in the museum's history and in the history of Chicago cultural institutions. The "Building of the Century" campaign, led by chairman Louis B. Susman, had raised more than $410 million by the time the Modern Wing opened in May 2009. Gifts to the campaign ranged from $50 to $50 million, and they came primarily from individual donors and corporations. Government sources provided less than 1 percent of the funding.

Planning and renovation

The design and construction of the Modern Wing cost $294 million. The remainder of the money raised went into reorganization and reinstallation of the collections that did not move into the Modern Wing and into an endowment that would pay for the Modern Wing's operation. The reorganization project began in 2007 and will be completed by 2011. It includes the renovation of the European painting and sculpture galleries; new galleries for the prints and drawings collection; new galleries for European decorative arts; and the new Alsdorf Galleries of Indian, Southeast Asian, Himalayan, and Islamic art. Further work includes new galleries for African and Indian art of the Americas; the renovation of the galleries of Asian art; and new galleries for objects such as textiles, decorative arts, and suits of armor.

In planning the Modern Wing, the Art Institute had several priorities. First, the building needed to have ample gallery space for the museum's large modern and contemporary art collections. Second, museum leaders wanted to create more open public space within the Art Institute—non-gallery spaces accessible to the public to be enjoyed much as Millennium Park is enjoyed. These spaces include a third-floor sculpture terrace that offers views out onto Millennium Park and the pedestrian bridge with its unique vistas of the park, Lake Michigan, and the city skyline.

The Modern Wing also needed to provide updated educational facilities for students and families. The previous education center was housed on the lower level of the museum's original 1893 building. This earlier space, accessible only to those who had already paid admission to the museum, had no natural light and was not equipped for up-to-date technology.

Piano devoted the entire first floor of the Modern Wing's east pavilion to a new education center. At 20,000 square feet (1,858 square meters), it is more than twice the size of the previous center and holds studios, classrooms, a resource library for teachers, and a family orientation room with toys, books, computer games, and special exhibitions. The center has floor-to-ceiling windows that offer views of the park or an interior garden.

The education center is the most technologically advanced of any of the museum areas, with wireless Internet and new computers with specially designed programs about the museum's collection. Video technology in the classrooms and studios provides learning and teaching opportunities through multiple media.

The more than 1,000 modern and contemporary works of art displayed in the Modern Wing are bathed in filtered light from skylights above and a wall of glass facing the park to the north.

The Modern Wing's front facade and every window is made of two sets of double-thick glass that are set two feet (1.2 meters) apart. The space between insulates between the exterior and interior for enery efficiency.

A "green" museum

Another priority for the building was that it be as "green," that is as energy-saving, as possible. Museums are generally very large in square footage and have strict requirements for light, humidity, and temperature to preserve the art they display and store. As a result, running a museum requires a great deal of energy, particularly in a city like Chicago with extremes in temperature throughout the year. Architect Renzo Piano specializes in sustainable museum building, and he designed many aspects of the Modern Wing to reduce energy consumption while still keeping the art safe.

The most noticeable green aspect of the building is its "flying carpet" over-roof. The flying carpet consists of a set of approximately 2,500 aluminum blades that sit approximately 8 feet (2.4 meters) above the glass ceiling of the third-floor galleries. The blades are designed to bring natural northern light into the galleries and shield the galleries from harsh, southern light. Modeled by computers, the blades sit at a very exact angle calculated to maximize the safest light.

Inside the galleries, artificial light is determined by the amount of natural light filtered by the flying carpet. When bright sunlight from the skylights floods the galleries, computers automatically dim the interior lights. On gray, rainy, or snowy days, the computers brighten interior lights

A "flying carpet, " sitting above the roof of skylights (left), consists of approximately 2,500 aluminum blades that are designed to bring natural northern light into the galleries while shielding the art from harsh, southern light. Motorized retractable shades (below) moderate light on bright days.

to compensate for the lack of natural light. The system allows the museum to use less electricity and lower operating costs.

Museums also expend a great deal of energy heating, cooling, and maintaining safe humidity levels in the galleries. Temperature and humidity need to be carefully calibrated in areas that hold art. The Modern Wing's curtain-wall construction addresses this need. The front facade of the Modern Wing and every window in the galleries is actually made of two sets of double-thick glass that are about four feet (1.2 meters) apart. Temperature and humidity levels are adjusted in the space between the two glass sheets, which forms an insulating buffer between exterior and interior that saves energy.

As a further "green" measure, the architect specified building materials—for example, Indiana limestone—that were manufactured, milled, or quarried within fairly short distances from Chicago. This cut down on energy use and transportation costs. The architect also increased the amount of trees and other landscaping by 20 percent. Because of these measures, the Art Institute has applied to the Phoenix-based U.S. Green Building Council for silver LEED certification, a recognition of these energy-saving and green features of the building.

Ten years in the making, the Modern Wing demonstrates the Art Institute's commitment to making the visual arts a vital part of the cultural life of Chicago and maintaining a world-class art collection for the education and enjoyment of the millions of people who visit annually. Architect Renzo Piano and the director, staff, and supporters of the Art Institute all contributed to this historic effort. The result is a classic yet innovative building that will adapt and grow in the future as the Art Institute itself has for more than a century.

ASIA

By the end of 2009, many Asian nations had recovered more than countries in other parts of the world from the worldwide economic downturn that began in 2008. The region's vibrant economies were, however, negatively affected by weather problems and earthquakes. In addition, terrorism plagued several countries.

Economy. Ben S. Bernanke, the chairman of the United States Federal Reserve System, the nation's central banking network, said on October 19 that impressive economic growth in Asian nations was pulling the global economy out of the downturn. China, India, and Indonesia showed the greatest economic expansion. Such smaller countries as Malaysia, Singapore, South Korea, Taiwan, and Thailand suffered average declines of 13 percent of their gross domestic product from September 2008 to March 2009. (Gross domestic product is the value of goods and services produced in a country in a year.) Most Asian nations began to bounce back by mid-2009, however.

In 2009, China's economy became the world's second largest, after the United States, and it rivaled Germany for the world lead in the value of exports. By allowing the value of its currency to depreciate 10 percent compared with currencies of its main trading partners, China made its exports more competitive. This created some hostility abroad, especially among European countries that were slower than Asian countries to recover economically.

Climate worries. Asian countries gave greater attention in 2009 to preventing future problems from climate change. These included such factors as higher temperatures, droughts, the rise of sea levels, and reduced amounts of water for irriga-tion as rainfall became more irregular and Himalayan glaciers shrank. The United Nations (UN) Food and Agriculture Organization reported in June that the Asia-Pacific region already had 642 million people living in hunger. Predicting that Asia's demand for food would double by 2050, the organization issued a report in August 2009 urging the modernization of Asia's irrigation systems.

The Asian Development Bank reported on April 27 that global warming could reduce regional harvests. The report warned that rising levels of salty seawater could ruin rice-growing coastal areas in many countries, noting that Vietnam's Mekong River delta was already having flooding problems and other low-lying delta areas could soon become flooded. The U.S. secretary of energy, Steven Chu, warned in a visit to China in July that rising sea levels would displace even more people from coastal China than from river delta areas of Bangladesh.

China had by 2009 surpassed the United States in the emission of gases that were blamed

Maoist supporters of Nepal's former prime minister, Pushpa Kamal Dahal, protest against the government's May 2009 reinstating of the chief of Nepal's army after Dahal had fired him. Dahal stepped down as prime minister to avoid further conflict within the government.

for global warming, especially carbon dioxide. Recognizing the problem created by its rapidly expanding economy, especially the building of numerous coal-fired electric power-generating plants, China promised to reduce emissions. It also expanded efforts to generate electricity by building the world's largest arrays of wind turbines and solar panels.

The Maldives, a nation of Indian Ocean atolls whose highest point is just 8 feet (2.4 meters) above sea level, dramatized its danger of being submerged by rising sea levels. Wearing scuba gear, its government held a Cabinet meeting underwater on October 17. Officials signed a document asking all countries to cut carbon dioxide emissions.

Disasters ravaged Asia in 2009 as typhoons and earthquakes killed people in many countries. An international insurance company estimated that Asia's weather-related catastrophes had risen from about 75 incidents per year in 1980 to more than 250 in 2009.

In early August, Typhoon Morakot caused landslides and flooding in Taiwan that left at least 700 people dead or missing before causing further damage along China's coast. In late September, Tropical Storm Ketsana flooded the Philippines' capital, Manila. A week later, as rescue workers tended to survivors, Typhoon Parma struck the region, causing additional flooding and landslides. More than 920 people in the Philippines were killed by the two storms. Ketsana gained strength as it crossed the South China Sea, becoming a typhoon. It struck Vietnam, killing more than 160 people, before moving on to cause damage in Cambodia and Laos. In early October, days of heavy rain in southern India caused flooding that left at least 300 people dead.

Earthquakes rocked countries from Japan to Indonesia in 2009. These countries lie in an earthquake-prone region stretching around the Pacific Rim that is known as the Ring of Fire, where a number of Earth's tectonic plates are continually jolting against each other. The most

FACTS IN BRIEF ON ASIAN COUNTRIES

Country	Population	Government	Monetary unit*	Foreign trade (million U.S.$) Exports†	Imports†
Afghanistan	34,443,000	President Hamid Karzai	afghani (48.93 = $1)	327	4,850
Armenia	2,983,000	President Serzh Sargsyan; Prime Minister Tigran Sargsyan	dram (375.00 = $1)	1,124	3,763
Azerbaijan	8,726,000	President Ilham Aliyev; Prime Minister Artur Rasizade	manat new spot (0.82 = $1)	30,590	7,575
Bangladesh	161,315,000	President Zillur Rahman; Prime Minister Sheik Hasina Wajed	taka (68.00 = $1)	13,970	19,590
Bhutan	696,000	King Jigme Khesar Namgyel Wangchuck; Prime Minister Jigme Thinley	ngultrum (46.34 = $1)	350	320
Brunei	411,000	Sultan and Prime Minister Haji Hassanal Bolkiah	dollar (1.44 = $1)	8,250	2,055
Cambodia (Kampuchea)	15,211,000	King Norodom Sihamoni; Prime Minister Hun Sen	riel (4,154.00 = $1)	4,312	6,370
China	1,355,350,000	President Hu Jintao; Premier Wen Jiabao	yuan (6.83 = $1)	1,800,200 (includes Hong Kong)	1,162,400
East Timor	1,192,000	President José Ramos-Horta; Prime Minister Xanana Gusmão	U.S. dollar (1.00 = $1)	10	202
Georgia	4,292,000	President Mikheil Saakashvili; Prime Minister Nika Gilauri	lari (1.69 = $1)	2,428	6,261
India	1,202,135,000	President Pratibha Patil; Prime Minister Manmohan Singh	rupee (48.60 = $1)	176,400	305,500
Indonesia	239,781,000	President Susilo Bambang Yudhoyono	rupiah (9,975.00 = $1)	139,300	116,000
Iran	74,131,000	Supreme Leader Ayatollah Ali Khamenei; President Mahmoud Ahmadinejad	rial (8,229.00 = $1)	95,090	67,250
Japan	127,669,000	Emperor Akihito; Prime Minister Yukio Hatoyama	yen (92.79 = $1)	746,500	708,300
Kazakhstan	15,889,000	President Nursultan A. Nazarbayev; Prime Minister Karim Masimov	tenge (150.80 = $1)	71,970	38,450
Korea, North	24,033,000	Chairman of National Defense Commission Kim Jong-il; Premier Kim Yong-il	won (2.20 = $1)	1,684	3,055
Korea, South	48,653,000	President Lee Myung-bak; Prime Minister Chung Un-chan	won (1,167.00 = $1)	433,500	427,400
Kyrgyzstan	5,494,000	President Kurmanbek Bakiev; Prime Minister Daniyar Usenov	som (43.90 = $1)	1,847	3,754

*Exchange rates as of Sept. 30, 2009.   †Latest available data.

deadly earthquake in 2009 hit Indonesia's Sumatra island on September 30. Another quake shook the island the following day, and more than 1,100 people were reported dead from the two quakes. Other earthquakes in 2009 shook Japan, China, and the Himalayan kingdom of Bhutan.

Terrorism stalked Asia in 2009. The worst attacks occurred in Pakistan and Afghanistan, where radical Islamists used suicide attacks and other violence against police, soldiers, government officials, and civilians, killing hundreds of people in their attempts to destabilize governments.

Suicide bombings in Pakistan were part of a growing challenge by what was vaguely identified as the Pakistani Taliban. In February, radicals seized control of the northwestern Swat region before Pakistan's army drove them from main towns. In April and October, the army launched offensives into areas near the Afghan border that had been under rebel control. Some of the insurgents used Pakistani territory for bases to fight the Afghan government and its foreign supporters.

Inside Afghanistan, terrorist attacks in towns and along roads increased in number during

Country	Population	Government	Monetary unit[*]	Foreign trade (million U.S.$) Exports[†]	Imports[†]
Laos	6,167,000	President Choummaly Sayasone; Prime Minister Bouasone Bouphavanh	kip (8,502.00 = $1)	1,163	1,384
Malaysia	27,942,000	Paramount Ruler Mizan Zainal Abidin, the Sultan of Terengganu; Prime Minister Najib Razak	ringgit (3.52 = $1)	198,900	154,700
Maldives	322,000	President Mohamed Nasheed	rufiyaa (12.80 = $1)	113	1,276
Mongolia	2,748,000	President Tsakhiagiin Elbegdorj; Prime Minister Sukhbaatar Batbold	tugrik (1,441.78 = $1)	2,539	3,615
Myanmar (Burma)	50,053,000	Chairman of the State Peace and Development Council Than Shwe; Prime Minister Thein Sein	kyat (450.00 = $1)	6,348	3,427
Nepal	29,922,000	President Ram Baran Yadav; Prime Minister Madhav Kumar Nepal	rupee (77.60 = $1)	868	3,229
Pakistan	173,117,000	President Asif Ali Zardari; Prime Minister Yousaf Raza Gilani	rupee (82.85 = $1)	21,900	38,300
Philippines	93,715,000	President Gloria Macapagal-Arroyo	peso (48.78 = $1)	48,200	60,780
Russia	140,542,000	President Dmitry Medvedev; Prime Minister Vladimir Putin	ruble (31.77 = $1)	471,600	302,000
Singapore	4,701,000	President Sellapan Rama Nathan; Prime Minister Lee Hsien Loong	dollar (1.44 = $1)	342,700	219,500
Sri Lanka	20,644,000	President Mahinda Rajapakse	rupee (114.70 = $1)	7,899	12,260
Taiwan	23,166,000	President Ma Ying-jeou; Premier (President of the Executive Yuan) Wu Den-yih	dollar (32.91 = $1)	254,900	236,700
Tajikistan	7,389,000	President Emomali Rahmon; Prime Minister Oqil Oqilov	somoni (4.43 = $1)	1,493	4,122
Thailand	65,157,000	King Bhumibol Adulyadej (Rama IX); Prime Minister Abhisit Vejjajiva	baht (34.01 = $1)	174,800	157,300
Turkmenistan	5,170,000	President Gurbanguly Berdimuhammedov	manat (2.84 = $1)	11,920	5,666
Uzbekistan	28,133,000	President Islam A. Karimov; Prime Minister Shavkat Mirziyayev	som (1,507.00 = $1)	10,370	7,070
Vietnam	88,257,000	Communist Party Secretary-General Nong Duc Manh; President Nguyen Minh Triet; Prime Minister Nguyen Tan Dung	dong (17,115.00 = $1)	61,600	77,610

2009. Forces from NATO, led by 68,000 American troops, found the Taliban in Afghanistan an elusive target.

A Hindu group that had used suicide bombings before such terrorism became common in the Islamic world was defeated in Sri Lanka in 2009 after 26 years of civil war that left from 80,000 to 100,000 people dead. The group, known as the Tamil Tigers, lost the war for an independent state. After the Sri Lankan army crushed the Tamil Tigers in May, questions remained about war atrocities by both sides, and up to 300,000 people remained detained in government camps.

In other Asian nations, terrorist attacks were more sporadic. In July, suicide bombers killed nine people during attacks on luxury hotels in Jakarta, Indonesia's capital. On September 17, police killed the man believed to have masterminded the July attacks and numerous other bombings.

Several bombings occurred in urban areas of the southern Philippines, but government troops attacked jungle camps and killed some 40 members of a group tied to the international terrorist group al-Qa`ida.

Laos, along with Cambodia, was declared by the United States on June 12 to have "ceased to be a Marxist-Leninist country." American officials said Laos, where a Vietnamese-backed Communist Party took power in 1975, was still a one-party state, but its economy was no longer state-controlled. It therefore became eligible for loans from the U.S. Export-Import Bank. Nonetheless, the president of Laos and head of the Lao People's Revolutionary Party (LPRP), Choummaly Sayasone, said in 2009 that "Marxist-Leninist theory is practical and is suitable for the current situation in Laos."

In 2006, the government of Laos declared the country to be free of production of the narcotic drug opium. In 2009, however, the growing of profitable opium poppies revived in remote mountains, where farmers were unable to survive by producing other crops.

On September 18, the United States dropped an accusation that exiled General Vang Pao—a leader of the Hmong ethnic hill people who fought with the United States against the LPRP before 1975—was plotting to overthrow the Lao government. A dozen other Hmong living in California remained accused of supporting insurgents in Laos.

Mongolia. In a presidential election on May 24, 2009, opposition leader Tsakhiagiin Elbegdorj defeated incumbent President Nambaryn Enkhbayar. Elbegdorj won 51.21 percent of the 1.1 million votes cast; Enkhbayar took 47.41 percent. Elbegdorj took office on June 18.

Elbegdorj was a former prime minister with a master's degree in public administration from the John F. Kennedy School of Government at Harvard University in Cambridge, Massachusetts. He became the country's first president who had never belonged to the Mongolian People's Revolutionary Party, the Communist party that administered the nation under direction from the Soviet Union from 1921 to 1990. A leader of the democratic revolution that led to Mongolia's first multiparty elections in 1990, Elbegdorj was an author and parliamentary sponsor for a 1992 constitution guaranteeing democracy, human rights, and a free-market economy.

Elbegdorj and Enkhbayar's presidential campaigns focused on how Mongolia's mineral wealth should be used. Both supported foreign investment to expand mining industries in an economy historically based on livestock. One major project, the Oyu Tolgoi mine in the desert known as the Gobi, is being developed with foreign participation into one of the world's largest copper and gold mines. ■ Henry S. Bradsher

See also **Disasters; Middle East; Terrorism;** various Asian country articles.

Astronomy. Astronomers in 2009 renewed observations with the Hubble Space Telescope after a long-awaited repair mission. They also discovered water on the moon, observed the effects of an asteroid or comet crashing into Jupiter, identified the first rocky planet found outside our solar system, and viewed the most distant celestial object yet discovered.

Hubble's new eyes. During a 13-day mission in May, astronauts aboard the space shuttle Atlantis repaired the Hubble Space Telescope, adding some new instruments and replacing defective parts. The mission extended the life of the orbiting observatory to at least 2014 and left it more powerful. The first images from the refurbished telescope were released in September 2009. These images included photographs taken by the new Wide Field Camera 3 and the repaired Advanced Camera for Surveys, as well as *spectra* (bands of electromagnetic radiation) generated by the new Cosmic Origins Spectrograph.

Water on the moon. Astronomer Jessica Sunshine of the University of Maryland at College Park and an international group of collaborators announced in September that water ice had been discovered over much of the lunar surface. The finding contradicted the previous scientific consensus that the moon was arid. The astronomers reported that the water is present only in a thin surface layer a few molecules thick.

Sunshine and her colleagues made their observations with a battery of spacecraft instruments, including NASA's Moon Mineralogy Mapper, a *spectrometer* aboard India's Chandrayaan 1 moon-orbiting spacecraft. (A spectrometer is an instrument that analyzes light from objects to reveal such information as their chemical makeup.) Other instruments were on NASA's Cassini, Deep Impact, and EPOXI spacecraft.

In early October—to explore the possibility that substantial deposits of water may exist on the permanently shadowed floors of craters near the moon's south pole—NASA launched a rocket from its Lunar Crater Observation and Sensing Satellite into a collision course with a crater near the pole. The satellite was then directed to fly through the plume of debris cast up by the rocket impact to analyze the debris for the presence of water. The analysis revealed about 25 gallons (95 liters) of water vapor and ice.

Collision with Jupiter. Skywatchers were both surprised and delighted when a passing asteroid or comet struck Jupiter in July. Amateur astronomer Anthony Wesley, observing with his homemade telescope in New South Wales, Australia, discovered a black spot, nearly as big as Earth, in the southern hemisphere of Jupiter on July 19. He surmised that the spot might be a scar from a collision, because it resembled the dark

Hundreds of thousands of stars shine through clouds of dust and gas in a composite image of the center of the Milky Way Galaxy released by NASA in November to commemorate the 400th anniversary of Galileo's use of the telescope to observe the heavens.

spots made in 1994 when fragments of Comet Shoemaker-Levy 9 plummeted into Jupiter.

Follow-up observations by professional astronomers revealed that the spot was probably the result of a collision with an asteroid or comet no more than a few hundred yards across. The astronomers estimated that the colliding object smashed into the far side of the planet only a few hours before Wesley noticed the spot. Because this event was the second observed collision with Jupiter in only 15 years, astronomers noted that objects must strike Jupiter more frequently than previously believed.

Rocky planet beyond solar system. In February 2009, astronomers detected the first rocky planet found outside our solar system. Since 1995, approximately 350 *extrasolar planets* (planets orbiting stars other than the sun) had been discovered. However, all of these planets were gaseous objects, similar to Jupiter, or icy objects, similar to Neptune. Such planets have *densities* (amount of matter in a given unit) close to that of water. By contrast, the newly found planet—dubbed CoRoT 7b—has a rocky density, similar to that of Earth.

An international team of astronomers from Europe discovered the rocky world using the CoRoT orbiting telescope, which is designed to find small extrasolar planets by detecting the dip in starlight produced when an orbiting planet passes in front of a star, as viewed from Earth. Scientists next determined the density of the planet by analyzing the spectra of the star and planet produced by the High Accuracy Radial velocity Planet Searcher spectrograph in Chile.

The scientists also determined that CoRoT 7b has a diameter that is 80 percent greater than that of our planet. Every 20.4 hours, the planet completes an orbit around its host star, which is slightly smaller and cooler than the sun. The star is about 500 light-years away. (A light-year is the distance traveled in one year by a pulse of light—about 5.88 trillion miles [9.46 trillion kilometers]). The investigators reported that CoRoT 7b is much too close to its host star to have temperatures suitable for sustaining life.

Breaking the cosmic distance record. In April, astronomers recorded radiation from the most distant object yet observed—a dying star 13 billion light-years away that emitted an outburst as it collapsed to form a black hole. (A black hole is a region of space in which the gravitational pull is so strong that nothing, not even light, can escape.) The stellar explosion was classified as a gamma-ray burst, named GRB 090423, and it was detected by NASA's Swift Gamma Ray Burst Mission orbiting telescope.   ■ Laurence A. Marschall

See also **Space exploration.**

Saturn's rings virtually disappear as sunlight hits them edge-on in an image taken by the Cassini space probe in October. The phenomenon, called the ring plane crossing, occurs twice during each of Saturn's 29.7-year orbits around the sun. The crossing lasts for about six months. On September 4, the rings became nearly invisible to telescopes on Earth. They gradually reappeared during the following three months.

The apparent disappearance and reappearance of Saturn's rings and the discovery of a new ring highlighted observations of Saturn in 2009.

The rugged, icy surface of Enceladus, Saturn's sixth largest moon, is captured from a distance of about 6,000 miles (10,000 kilometers) in November during one of several fly-bys by the Cassini space probe. At its closest, the probe flew about 1,000 miles (1,600 kilometers) above the surface. On another fly-by, Cassini passed through giant plumes of ice erupting near the moon's south pole.

An enormous ring around Saturn, revealed in October by the Spitzer Space Telescope, is the largest by far of all the planet's fabled rings. The ring, shown in *infrared light* (heat energy) in an artist's illustration, consists of a very thin belt of ice and dust particles. The ring is 1.5 million miles (2.4 million kilometers) high. Its densest section extends from 3.7 million to 7.4 million miles (6 million to 12 million kilometers) from Saturn. Astronomers think Phoebe, Saturn's most distant moon, is probably the source of the ring's material. Phoebe is also likely the long-sought source of the dusty material covering the dark side of Saturn's moon Iapetus, about 5.8 million miles (9.3 million kilometers) from Phoebe.

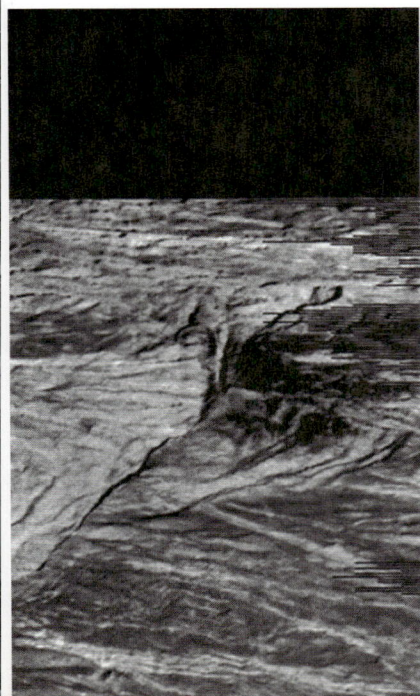

Saturn's rings, which are generally paper-thin, contain surprisingly large chunks of ice, according to new images taken by the Cassini space probe during September. Some of the chunks, which extend above and below the rings, are as high as the Rocky Mountains.

Australia suffered less from the global financial crisis than most developed countries in 2009. Observers expected that the year would be remembered mainly for the Black Saturday fires, the worst natural disaster in the country's history.

Fires. The forest, shrub, and grass wildfires known in Australia as bushfires affect many parts of the continent every summer. But on February 7, exceptionally dry conditions caused by a decade-long drought combined with strong winds and heat wave temperatures of more than 105 °F (40 °C) to create extreme fire conditions that were unprecedented in Australia's history. Fire storms swept through many towns and villages in the southeastern state of Victoria. The worst affected areas in 2009 were small townships in heavily wooded areas northeast of Melbourne, the state capital.

The official death toll for Black Saturday was 173. Previously, Australia's worst bushfire had been the Ash Wednesday fires of 1983 that left 75 people dead. Authorities estimated that some 1,060,000 acres (430,000 hectares) were burned, and property damages totaled more than $1 billion (all amounts in Australian dollars). More than 500 people were injured; at least 7,000 people were left homeless; and some 2,000 houses were destroyed. The 78 communities affected by the fires included the small townships of Marysville and Kinglake, which were almost entirely destroyed.

Queen Elizabeth II of the United Kingdom, who is the Australian head of state, sent her daughter, Princess Anne, to Australia to attend a national memorial service in Melbourne on Feb. 22, 2009, marking a national day of mourning. Queen Elizabeth was also among the thousands of people who made generous donations to the Australian Red Cross Victorian Bushfire Appeal, which raised more than $375 million.

Floods and drought. While Victoria suffered continuing drought and heat waves, northern Queensland was inundated by flooding in 2009. By mid-February, flood damages were in excess of $200 million, and more than 60 percent of the state was declared a disaster area. New South Wales was also affected by floods in February and March. Parts of southeastern Queensland and northern New South Wales were declared disaster areas after further widespread flooding began on May 20, with floodwaters reaching 32

Smoke billows from one of several hundred bushfires that burned across the Australian state of Victoria in February 2009. The fires left 173 people dead and thousands of others homeless.

feet (9.8 meters) deep in some areas. The mid-north coast of New South Wales was flooded again in November.

Australia experienced the warmest winter on record in 2009, with some areas recording their year's highest temperatures in the winter month of August. Despite the high rainfall in some parts of the continent, drought conditions continued in other areas. In May, the drought was declared to be over in Brisbane because the Queensland capital had plenty of water in its reservoirs. Northern New South Wales experienced floods, but the south and west remained dry. In October, more than 65 percent of the state was declared still affected by drought. Victoria also continued to suffer from drought. In October, work began on a desalination plant

that was designed to provide 40 billion gallons (150 billion liters) of water a year for Melbourne when it opens in 2011. (Desalination is the process of removing salt from seawater.)

Economy. Australia entered 2009 with a reasonably strong economy. However, because of the global financial crisis and a decrease in Chinese demand for Australian minerals, the Labor government took early steps to keep the economy on an even keel. In February, Prime Minister Kevin Rudd announced a $42-billion economic stimulus package to be spent on schools as well as roads and other infrastructure projects. The package also included a cash payment to low- and middle-income taxpayers. The opposition Liberal-National coalition criticized the package and voted against it in both houses of Federal Parliament. In the Senate, Australia's upper house, where Labor lacked a majority, the bill was finally passed with the help of the Australian Greens Party and two independent senators.

Treasurer Wayne Swan introduced his second budget to Parliament on May 12. Swan announced that pension payments would be increased and a maternity leave plan would be introduced. His budget predicted that the record cash deficit of $32 billion for fiscal 2008-2009 would nearly double to $57 billion for fiscal 2009-2010. This amount was equal to nearly 5 percent of Australia's gross domestic product (GDP) and would be the country's largest deficit since World War II (1939-1945). (GDP is the total value of goods and services produced in a country in a given year.)

Swan forecast that the economy would shrink for the first time since 1990-1991 but claimed that this drop of 0.5 percent was modest by international standards. Even so, unemployment was expected to exceed 8 percent and remain higher than current levels for several years. Later in the year, however, the treasury revised these figures and estimated that the economy was faring better than expected.

On April 7, 2009, the Reserve Bank of Australia cut the cash interest rate to a 49-

FACTS IN BRIEF ON AUSTRALIA

Population	21,865,000
Government	Governor General Quentin Bryce; Prime Minister Kevin Rudd
Monetary unit*	dollar (1.18 = $1 U.S.)
Foreign trade (million U.S.$)	
Exports†	190,200
Imports†	193,300

*Exchange rate as of Sept. 30, 2009.
†Latest available data.

year low of 3 percent. (The cash rate is the interest rate banks pay for overnight loans.) The bank increased the cash rate to 3.25 percent on October 6. By mid-October, unemployment had dropped to 5.8 percent, and in November, as the United States dollar declined, the Australian dollar soared to a 12-month high of more than 90 U.S. cents.

Climate change. In the May budget, Swan detailed the government's $4.5-billion Clean Energy Initiative, which was designed to provide the infrastructure needed for lower-emissions technologies. These measures were designed to decrease the greenhouse gas emissions that most scientists believe cause climate change. However, in August, the Senate defeated the Labor government's attempt to introduce a carbon emissions trading plan designed to allow polluting companies to buy permits to emit greenhouse gases.

The Greens voted down the Carbon Pollution Reduction Scheme bill because they considered the proposed reduction of carbon emissions by 5 percent by 2020 too small a target. The Liberal-National coalition opposed the bill because they claimed it would cost Australian jobs and would not achieve its purpose. Minister for Climate Change Penny Wong threatened that the Labor Party would arrange to dissolve both houses of Parliament and call a general election if the Senate did not pass the bill.

The Liberal Party was deeply divided over the issue, and its leader, Malcolm Turnbull, threatened to resign his leadership if members did not support him on emissions trading legislation. The government and the opposition then discussed a number of changes to the bill that the opposition wanted to make. Turnbull eventually agreed to support the legislation, but at a Liberal Party meeting on Dec. 1, 2009, he was ousted as party head. He was replaced by Tony Abbott, who refused to support the bill. The Senate voted on the bill the following day, and it was defeated by 41 votes to 33. Deputy Prime Minister Julia Gillard vowed to resubmit the bill in 2010.

State politics. On March 21, 2009, Queensland voters reelected the state Labor Party government. Premier Anna Bligh had been handed the leadership when Peter Beattie resigned in 2007, but in 2009 she made history by becoming the first woman to lead her party to victory in a state election. On December 3, New South Wales Premier Nathan Rees was ousted in a vote of no confidence by the state parliament. He was replaced by American-born Kristine Keneally, who became the state's first female premier.

Defense and security. The bravery of Australian soldier Mark Donaldson, who rescued a coalition interpreter during fighting in Afghanistan, was recognized at a ceremony at Government House in Canberra, the capital, on January 16. Donaldson became the first person to be awarded the Victoria Cross for Australia, the country's highest military honor. This medal, established in 1991, replaced the old Imperial Victoria Cross. No Australian had been awarded a Victoria Cross since 1969.

On May 2, 2009, Prime Minister Kevin Rudd released a 20-year defense blueprint. The multibillion-dollar plan called for a build-up of naval and air forces to ensure that Australia would be able to defend its northern borders and its sea approaches. The rationale was the possibility that the United States would decrease its forces in the Asia-Pacific region and that several emerging economic powers—particularly China—would expand their militaries. The plan envisaged a range of large-scale purchases: 100 F-35 jet fighters, additional combat helicopters, frigates, destroyers, and a doubling of Australia's submarine fleet. The plan also called for Australia to acquire its first arsenal of sea-based long-range cruise missiles.

On July 17, nine people, including three Australians, died in coordinated attacks by suicide bombers on two luxury hotels in Jakarta, the capital of Indonesia. On September 17, Indonesian police shot dead the man believed to be the mastermind behind the July attack and a number of other bombings.

On February 3, radical Muslim leader Abdul Nacer Benbrika was sentenced to 15 years in prison for heading a terrorist cell in Melbourne and for plotting attacks in Australia. Six of his followers were sentenced for shorter terms. On October 16, five of Benbrika's Sydney accomplices were found guilty of conspiring to perform terrorist acts. On September 24, Justice Megan Latham, a New South Wales Supreme Court judge, sentenced Belal Khazaal, a Lebanon-born Sydney resident, to prison for 12 years for publishing a book on the Internet explaining how to perform terrorist acts.

Immigration. In 2009, the Australian Treasury

MEMBERS OF THE AUSTRALIAN HOUSE OF REPRESENTATIVES

The House of Representatives of the 42nd Parliament first met on Feb. 12, 2008. As of Dec. 4, 2009, the House of Representatives consisted of the following members: 83 Australian Labor Party, 53 Liberal Party of Australia, 9 National Party of Australia, 3 Independents, and 2 vacancies. This table shows each legislator and party affiliation. An asterisk (*) denotes those who served in the 41st Parliament.

Australian Capital Territory
Annette Ellis, A.L.P.*
Bob McMullan, A.L.P.*

New South Wales
Tony Abbott, L.P.*
Anthony Albanese, A.L.P.*
Bob Baldwin, L.P.*
Sharon Bird, A.L.P.*
Bronwyn Bishop, L.P.*
Chris Bowen, A.L.P.*
David Bradbury, A.L.P.
Tony Burke, A.L.P.*
Jason Clare, A.L.P.
John Cobb, N.P.*
Greg Combet, A.L.P.
Mark Coulton, N.P.*
Bob Debus, A.L.P.
Justine Elliot, A.L.P.*
Pat Farmer, L.P.*
Laurie Ferguson, A.L.P.*
Joel Fitzgibbon, A.L.P.*
Peter Garrett, A.L.P.*
Joanna Gash, L.P.*
Jennie George, A.L.P.*
Sharon Grierson, A.L.P.*
Jill Hall, A.L.P.*
Luke Hartsuyker, N.P.*
Alex Hawke, L.P.
Chris Hayes, A.L.P.
Joe Hockey, L.P.*
Kay Hull, N.P.*
Julia Irwin, A.L.P.*
Mike Kelly, A.L.P.
Sussan Ley, L.P.*
Louise Markus, L.P.*
Robert McClelland, A.L.P.*
Maxine McKew, A.L.P.
Daryl Melham, A.L.P.*
Scott Morrison, L.P.
John Murphy, A.L.P.*
Belinda Neal, A.L.P.
Robert Oakeshott, Ind.
Julie Owens, A.L.P.*
Tanya Plibersek, A.L.P.*
Roger Price, A.L.P.*
Philip Ruddock, L.P.*
Janelle Saffin, A.L.P.
Alby Schultz, L.P.*
Craig Thomson, A.L.P.
Malcolm Turnbull, L.P.*
Danna Vale, L.P.*
Tony Windsor, Ind.*

Northern Territory
Damian Hale, A.L.P.
Warren Snowdon, A.L.P.*

Queensland
Arch Bevis, A.L.P.*
James Bidgood, A.L.P.
Steven Ciobo, L.P.*
Yvette D'Ath, A.L.P.
Peter Dutton, L.P.*
Craig Emerson, A.L.P.*
Michael Johnson, L.P.*
Bob Katter, Ind.*
Andrew Laming, L.P.*
Peter Lindsay, L.P.*
Kirsten Livermore, A.L.P.*
Ian Macfarlane, L.P.*
Margaret May, L.P.*
Shayne Neumann, A.L.P.
Paul Neville, N.P.*
Graham Perrett, A.L.P.
Brett Raguse, A.L.P.
Kerry Rea, A.L.P.
Bernie Ripoll, A.L.P.*
Stuart Robert, L.P.
Kevin Rudd, A.L.P.*
Bruce Scott, N.P.*
Peter Slipper, L.P.*
Alexander Somlyay, L.P.*
Jon Sullivan, A.L.P.
Wayne Swan, A.L.P.*
Chris Trevor, A.L.P.
Warren Truss, N.P.*
Jim Turnour, A.L.P.

South Australia
Jamie Briggs, L.P.
Mark Butler, A.L.P.
Nick Champion, A.L.P.
Kate Ellis, A.L.P.*
Steve Georganas, A.L.P.*
Christopher Pyne, L.P.*
Rowan Ramsey, L.P.
Amanda Rishworth, A.L.P.
Patrick Secker, L.P.*
Andrew Southcott, L.P.*
Tony Zappia, A.L.P.

Tasmania
Dick Adams, A.L.P.*
Jodie Campbell, A.L.P.
Julie Collins, A.L.P.
Duncan Kerr, A.L.P.*
Sid Sidebottom, A.L.P.

Victoria
Kevin Andrews, L.P.*
Fran Bailey, L.P.*
Bruce Billson, L.P.*
Russell Broadbent, L.P.*
Anna Burke, A.L.P.*
Anthony Byrne, A.L.P.*
Darren Cheeseman, A.L.P.
Darren Chester, N.P.
Simon Crean, A.L.P.*
Michael Danby, A.L.P.*
Marc Dreyfus, A.L.P.
Martin Ferguson, A.L.P.*
John Forrest, N.P.*
Petro Georgiou, L.P.*
Steve Gibbons, A.L.P.*
Julia Gillard, A.L.P.*
Alan Griffin, A.L.P.*
David Hawker, L.P.*
Greg Hunt, L.P.*
Harry Jenkins, A.L.P.*
Catherine King, A.L.P.*
Jenny Macklin, A.L.P.*
Richard Marles, A.L.P.
Sophie Mirabella, A.L.P.*
Brendan O'Connor, A.L.P.*
Chris Pearce, L.P.*
Andrew Robb, L.P.*
Nicola Roxon, A.L.P.*
Bill Shorten, A.L.P.
Tony Smith, L.P.*
Sharman Stone, L.P.*
Mike Symon, A.L.P.
Lindsay Tanner, A.L.P.*
Kelvin Thomson, A.L.P.*
Maria Vamvakinou, A.L.P.*
Jason Wood, L.P.*

Western Australia
Julie Bishop, L.P.*
Gary Gray, A.L.P.
Barry Haase, L.P.*
Steve Irons, L.P.
Sharryn Jackson, A.L.P.
Dennis Jensen, L.P.*
Michael Keenan, L.P.*
Nola Marino, L.P.
Judi Moylan, L.P.*
Melissa Parke, A.L.P.
Don Randall, L.P.*
Luke Simpkins, L.P.
Stephen Smith, A.L.P.*
Wilson Tuckey, L.P.*
Mal Washer, L.P.*

A thick haze of dust obscures Sydney's iconic Opera House on Sept. 23, 2009. An enormous dust storm swept across the outback, stripping topsoil from thousands of acres of valuable land, and blanketed much of eastern Australia, forcing people indoors and disrupting transportation.

estimated that more than 180,000 new settlers arrived in the country over the past year. Most of these immigrants, including an increasing number of Chinese, arrived legally by air with little or no controversy. However, when a surge in the number of people attempting to reach Australia by boat from Indonesia increased to more than 2,000, border protection once more became a political issue. Most of the immigrants were seeking political asylum from their homelands of Sri Lanka and Afghanistan. Opposition politicians blamed the increase on the government's softer policy toward such migrants.

In mid-October, the Australian customs ship *Oceanic Viking* rescued 78 Sri Lankans from a sinking boat off Indonesia's coast. The asylum seekers refused to return to Indonesia, sparking a heated public debate over Australia's immigration policies. In November, the Sri Lankan refugees agreed to be taken to a detention center in Indonesia to have their asylum claims processed.

Aborigines. As part of Australia Day celebrations on January 26, which marked the first British landing in Australia in 1788, the federal government chose Aboriginal lawyer and activist Mick Dodson as Australian of the Year. Dodson, a Yawuru man and the director of the National Centre for Indigenous Studies at the Australian

National University in Canberra, called for Australia Day to be moved because January 26 was viewed as "invasion day" by many Aboriginal people. He suggested that a more appropriate date to celebrate Australia Day would be February 13, to mark the day in 2008 that the Rudd government formally apologized to the stolen generations of Aboriginal children who had been separated from their parents by government officials.

In April 2009, the government officially adopted the United Nations (UN) Declaration on the Rights of Indigenous Peoples, a nonbinding document stressing the rights of native people. Australia's previous government, headed by Prime Minister John Howard, had voted against the declaration when the UN General Assembly adopted it in 2007.

Arts and sciences. On Feb. 22, 2009, members of the family of the late Australian actor Heath Ledger accepted a posthumous Academy Award on his behalf. Ledger, who died in 2008, won the best supporting actor Oscar for his portrayal of Batman's nemesis, the Joker, in the 2008 film *The Dark Knight.*

On March 6, 2009, Sydney artist Guy Maestri won the Archibald Prize, Australia's most prestigious award for painting. His winning work was a

THE CABINET OF AUSTRALIA*

Kevin Rudd—prime minister
Julia Gillard—minister for education, employment and workplace relations, and social inclusion; deputy prime minister
Anthony Albanese—minister for infrastructure, transport, regional development, and local government
Wayne Swan—treasurer
Simon Crean—minister for trade
John Faulkner—minister for defence
Stephen Conroy—minister for broadband, communications, and the digital economy
Stephen Smith—minister for foreign affairs
Chris Evans—minister for immigration and citizenship
Peter Garrett—minister for the environment, heritage, and the arts
Robert McClelland—attorney general
Lindsay Tanner—minister for finance and deregulation
Tony Burke—minister for agriculture, fisheries, and forestry
Jenny Macklin—minister for families, housing, community services, and indigenous affairs
Chris Bowen—minister for human services, financial services, superannuation, and corporate law
Joseph Ludwig—special minister of state; cabinet secretary
Penny Wong—minister for climate change and water
Kim Carr—minister for innovation, industry, science, and research
Nicola Roxon—minister for health and aging
Martin Ferguson—minister for resources, energy, and tourism

*As of Dec. 4, 2009.

PREMIERS OF AUSTRALIAN STATES

State	Premier
New South Wales	Kristine Keneally
Queensland	Anna Bligh
South Australia	Mike Rann
Tasmania	David Bartlett
Victoria	John Brumby
Western Australia	Colin Barnett

CHIEF MINISTERS OF AUSTRALIAN MAINLAND TERRITORIES

Australian Capital Territory	Jon Stanhope
Northern Territory	Paul Henderson

portrait of Geoffrey Gurrumul Yunupingu, a blind Aboriginal singer.

On June 18, renowned West Australian author Tim Winton won his fourth Miles Franklin Award for his novel *Breath*. The award, Australia's most prestigious literary prize, is bestowed annually for a work portraying Australian life. *Breath* is the story of a young surfer growing up in the 1970's.

On Sept. 21, 2009, Australian actress Toni Collette was named best actress in a comedy series at the 61st annual Primetime Emmy Awards ceremony in Los Angeles. She was recognized for her performance as a mother with multiple personalities in the series "The United States of Tara."

On October 5, Tasmanian-born molecular biologist Elizabeth Blackburn became Australia's first female Nobel laureate when she was named one of three recipients of the 2009 Nobel Prize in physiology or medicine. Blackburn, who teaches at the University of California, San Francisco, shared the prize with one of her former graduate students and another researcher. The three received the award for the discovery of telomerase, an enzyme critical to the reproduction of cells.

On October 28, the 2009 Prime Minister's Prize for Science was awarded to John O'Sullivan, a scientist known for his work on government telescopes. In 1977, O'Sullivan published a paper detailing how the use of particular mathematical formulas could reduce interference and sharpen images from optical telescopes. In 1992, O'Sullivan applied a similar technique to computer networks, helping to usher in the age of wireless computing.   ■ Brian Kennedy

See also **China; Disasters; Global warming; Indonesia; Nobel Prizes; Weather.**

Australia, Prime Minister of.

Australian Labor Party leader Kevin Rudd continued to maintain an approval rating of up to 70 percent with the Australian electorate in 2009. During the year, Rudd played host to a number of world leaders. He also traveled widely, visiting the United States and the United Kingdom in March to discuss the global financial crisis with U.S. President Barack Obama and British Prime Minister Gordon Brown.

In London in April, Rudd participated in a summit meeting of the Group of 20 (G-20), an informal organization of industrialized nations. The London meeting was intended to formulate an international approach to the economic downturn. At another G-20 meeting, held in Pittsburgh in September, Rudd played a leading role in having the G-20 replace the smaller Group of 8 as the world's primary economic forum. While in the United States in September, Rudd addressed the United Nations General Assembly in New York City, calling for worldwide action on global warming and the financial crisis.

On November 11, recognized as Remembrance Day in Australia, Rudd made a surprise visit to Australian troops in Afghanistan. In 2009, some 1,500 Australian soldiers served in the war in Afghanistan.   ■ Brian Kennedy

See also **Australia.**

Australian rules football.

Australian rules football. The Geelong Cats defeated the Saint Kilda Saints by 12 goals 8 behinds (80 points) to 9 goals 14 behinds (68 points) to win the Australian Football League (AFL) premiership in Melbourne on Sept. 26, 2009. The Saints led by seven points at three-quarter time and looked as if they might win their first premiership since 1966. The scores were even with five minutes left to play when Paul Chapman scored for the Cats. They kept the lead to win their second premiership in three years. Chapman was awarded the Norm Smith Medal for the best player on the ground in the grand final. Geelong's Gary Ablett won the Brownlow Medal for the best and fairest player during the season.

In the AFL Queensland grand final on Sept. 20, 2009, the Morningside Panthers beat the Mount Gravatt Vultures 14.10 (94) to 8.15 (63). On the same day, the South Fremantle Bulldogs defeated the Subiaco Lions 17.11 (113) to 13.17 (95) to win the West Australian Football League premiership. On September 25, the North Ballarat Roosters won the Victorian Football League grand final over the Northern Bullants by 14.7 (91) to 10.6 (68). The Central District Bulldogs defeated the Sturt Double Blues 13.14 (92) to 7.12 (54) to win the 2009 South Australian National Football League grand final on October 4. ■ Brian Kennedy

Austria.

Austria. The "grand coalition" of Austria's two largest parties, the center-left Social Democratic Party and the center-right Austrian People's Party, remained stable during 2009. The coalition was formed after legislative elections in September 2008, and social democrat Werner Faymann became chancellor. Analysts observed that in confronting the global economic crisis, Austrian politics returned to its traditional style of consensus building between big business and the country's heavily unionized labor force, which had dominated political life in previous decades.

Both right-wing radical parties—the Freedom Party and the Alliance for the Future of Austria—remained a force in 2009. The parties run on an anti-immigration platform and also oppose deeper integration into the European Union (EU). In March, the Alliance won the provincial election in Carinthia by a landslide. Some political analysts credited the victory to the legacy of the party's local leader, Jörg Haider, who died in an automobile accident in October 2008.

Economic crisis. The government scrambled in the first half of 2009 to ensure that overextended banks in Eastern Europe, including Austria's, were protected by loans from international financial institutions. With the international financial crisis threatening to spill over into the country's financial system, Austria's government also implemented a fiscal stimulus package and wage reforms to counteract the downturn. Nevertheless, tax receipts fell, and the budget deficit rose to 4.3 percent of GDP, above the 3-percent limit agreed upon by EU members that use the euro. (GDP—gross domestic product—is the amount of goods and services produced in a country in a year.) Several other EU countries also exceeded deficit limits during the crisis. EU economists forecast that the Austrian economy would contract by 3.7 percent in 2009. Unemployment was projected to increase from 3.8 percent in 2008 to 5.5 percent in 2009.

Foreign affairs. Austria began a two-year term as a member of the United Nations (UN) Security Council in 2009. The country also participated in the NATO-led mission in Afghanistan—though Austria does not belong to NATO—and contributed troops to UN peacekeeping missions. Nevertheless, the country's official neutrality remained a popular policy.

Trial. Josef Fritzl was sentenced to life in prison in March for imprisoning his then-18-year-old daughter in a basement for 24 years, raping her, and denying medical treatment to one of the seven children he fathered with her. The infant subsequently died. The case shocked the nation when the daughter gained her freedom in 2008 and revealed the details. ■ Jeffrey Kopstein

See also **Europe.**

Automobile.

Automobile. The auto industry in the United States, in the midst of its lowest sales in decades, suffered through historic and wrenching changes in 2009. Two of the famous Big Three car companies—General Motors Corporation (GM) of Detroit and Chrysler LLC of Auburn Hills, Michigan—entered and emerged from bankruptcy. They survived only with the aid of a multibillion-dollar taxpayer bailout that gave the federal government ownership interests in both automakers. The government took this unprecedented action to prevent their collapse.

The industry's turmoil occurred against the backdrop of a deep economic recession. Analysts predicted that 2009's auto and light truck sales would total about 10.3 million—22 percent lower than 2008's total and the lowest since 1970.

The falling sales occurred despite a 13-percent increase in incentives that averaged $2,857 per vehicle for the first nine months of 2009. The incentive program that received the most attention, "cash for clunkers," came from the federal government. It provided consumers with credits of up to $4,500 for replacing their gas guzzlers with newer, more fuel-efficient vehicles.

The program, officially called the Car Allowance Rebate System, first took effect in July and ended in late August. Nearly 700,000 vehicles were sold, generating nearly $3 billion in rebates.

Besides boosting sales, the program put more fuel-efficient vehicles on the road. The average fuel economy for the vehicles purchased was 24.9 miles per gallon (10.6 kilometers per liter), a 58-percent improvement over trade-ins.

In September, the Big Three's combined market share was 43.9 percent—compared with 47.4 percent for the same period in 2008. The Ford F-series truck was the most popular vehicle with sales of 295,426 units in the first nine months of 2009, and the Toyota Camry took the auto title with sales of 264,357.

Ford Motor Company of Dearborn, Michigan, slightly increased its market share in 2009, despite a 23-percent drop in sales. In previous years, the company had positioned itself to better withstand the economic downturn than GM and Chrysler had and did not need federal funds.

In the spring of 2009, members of the United Auto Workers (UAW) at GM and Chrysler approved concessions in their contracts in light of those companies' struggles. However, Ford's UAW workers rejected similar concessions.

Ford moved to sell its Volvo line in October. The company announced that a consortium led by China's Zhejiang Geely Holding Group won a bid for Volvo's possible sale.

General Motors' fortunes fell even further in 2009 than in the previous year, when Tokyo-based Toyota surpassed it as the world's number one automaker. By September, GM's domestic market share had fallen by 2.7 percent. Its sales had declined by 36 percent to 1.5 million units. By year's end, GM had dropped four vehicle lines.

In 2008, GM's finances had become so shaky that it sought the federal government's aid. In all, the government provided GM with $50 billion in loans and investments. To get the initial money, GM submitted a restructuring plan to the government in early 2009. However, GM's plan did not go far enough to satisfy the administration of President Barack Obama. Under government pressure, GM Chairman and CEO Rick Wagoner resigned in March. Wagoner's replacement, GM President Fritz Henderson, resigned in December.

Faced with mounting financial problems, GM filed for bankruptcy on June 1. The company reorganized and left bankruptcy on July 10 with a new name—General Motors Company. The federal government held a 61-percent interest in the new GM, with the UAW's Retiree Medical Benefits Trust, the Canadian and Ontario governments, and the old GM owning the rest.

As part of its restructuring, GM planned to cut its U.S. work force to 64,000, down from 91,000 in late 2008. The carmaker also planned to shutter 13 U.S. plants by the end of 2010.

GM sought to reduce its number of brands by selling them. In October, GM agreed to sell its Hummer division to Sichuan Tengzhong Heavy Industrial Machinery Company of China. But deals to sell its Saab and Saturn lines collapsed, and both divisions were to be shut down. GM also reneged on plans to sell Opel in November.

Along with other brands, GM discontinued its Pontiac line. Pontiac had begun operations in 1926. Buick, Cadillac, Chevrolet, and GMC were all that remained of GM's brands.

Chrysler, like GM, had sought government help to remain in business in 2008 and ended 2009 a much-changed company. The government provided Chrysler with $12 billion in loans and investments. Chrysler filed for bankruptcy reorganization on April 30 and emerged on June 10 with new owners, new leadership, and a new name: Chrysler Group LLC.

The UAW's Retiree Medical Benefits Trust owned 55 percent of the company. Fiat took a 20-percent stake with a possibility of increasing its ownership to 35 percent. The U.S. government owned 8 percent, and the Canadian government, 2 percent of the company. Fiat CEO Sergio Marchionne became the new Chrysler CEO, and Fiat pledged to provide Chrysler with technology for small- and medium-sized cars.

Through September, Chrysler sold 715,500 units—40 percent below the same period a year earlier. Chrysler held a 9.2-percent market share, or nearly 2 percentage points below its 2008 market share. With the decline, the company became the nation's number five automaker.

Other manufacturers. From September 2008 to September 2009, Japanese automakers' market share rose from 39.7 to 40.4 percent. European automakers' market share rose to 8.3 percent, from 7.6 percent in 2008. Korean automakers' market share increased by 2.1 percentage points to 7.4 percent.

Toyota, number two in U.S. sales, maintained its 16.6-percent market share, despite sales that had fallen by 28 percent to 1.3 million units as of September 2009. The company announced in March that it would close its plant in Fremont, California, shifting some of the factory's production to other plants.

Honda, the number four in U.S. sales, saw its nine-month sales fall to 884,100 units for a decline of 25 percent. However, the company's market share grew to 11.3 percent, from 11 percent in 2008.

On Dec. 9, 2009, German automaker Volkswagen announced plans to merge with Suzuki Motor of Japan. Analysts characterized the move as an aggressive bid to become the world's largest automaker. ■ Mike Casey

See also **Economics, United States; Economics, U.S.: A Special Report; Labor and employment; Transportation.**

1950 Catalina

General Motors, facing financial collapse, discontinued its venerable but sporty Pontiac line in 2009.

1976 Firebird Trans Am

The Pontiac brand, known for its stylish muscle cars, grew out of the Oakland Motor Car Company of Pontiac, Michigan, which General Motors Corporation (GM) acquired in 1909. Oakland introduced the first Pontiac in 1926 at an auto show in New York City. The Pontiac brand became so successful that it eventually displaced the Oakland name. By 1936, GM had produced 1 million Pontiacs. Models popular in the 1950's included the Bonneville, Catalina Coupe, and Star Chief Custom Safari. During the 1960's, Pontiac's muscle cars—the GTO and Firebird—made the brand synonymous with the throaty roar of a big V-8 engine. In the 1990's, GM added the Trans Sport minivan and Sunfire GT Coupe to the Pontiac lineup, reflecting changing customer demands. New models were introduced, but with market share in continuous decline, GM announced in 2009 that the Pontiac would be phased out completely by the end of 2010.

1959 Bonneville

1968 GTO

Automobile racing.

Jimmie Johnson in 2009 became the first driver to capture four straight NASCAR Sprint Cup championships. In 36 races, he won 7 and finished in the top five a total of 16 times. Seven-time Formula One champion Michael Schumacher came out of retirement in 2009 to replace Felipe Massa. Massa was hit in the helmet by a loose part and crashed at 120 miles (193 kilometers) per hour during qualifying in Budapest, Hungary, in July, fracturing his skull.

NASCAR. Jimmie Johnson captured the Nextel Sprint Cup championship on November 22 at Homestead, Florida, with a fifth-place finish in the Ford 400. He ended with 6,652 points to finish 141 points ahead of Mark Martin.

Teenager Joey Logano became the youngest driver to win a NASCAR Sprint Cup series race with his victory on June 28, 2009, in Loudon, New Hampshire. Logano, 19, broke the record that Kyle Busch set four years earlier. Despite his victory, Logano did not qualify for NASCAR's "Chase for the Championship." Tony Stewart, Jimmie Johnson, Kurt Busch, and Jeff Gordon jockeyed for position at the top of the driver standings for much of the season.

In other major developments in 2009, Matt Kenseth became the first driver since 1997 to win the opening two Sprint Cup point races. On May 20, 2009, NASCAR suspended driver Carl Long for 12 Cup championship events and penalized him 200 points. NASCAR fined his crew chief a record $200,000 for using an engine that was too large.

Driver-owner Jeremy Mayfield was suspended indefinitely by NASCAR on May 9 after allegedly testing positive for methamphetamine. The driver denied he ever took the drug and won a temporary reprieve from a federal judge to return to racing. But NASCAR claimed he tested positive a second time, and the suspension was reinstated. Mayfield vowed to fight the suspension.

Indianapolis 500. Helio Castroneves captured the 93rd running of the Indianapolis 500 on May 24, just five weeks after being acquitted on tax evasion charges that could have ended his racing career. Castroneves became the ninth driver to win at least three Indy 500's, and his 1.98-second margin of victory over Dan Wheldon was the biggest since 2000. The winning speed was 150.318 miles (241.913 kilometers) per hour, and only three other drivers led in the race: Ryan Briscoe, Scott Dixon, and Dario Franchitti. Dixon led for the most laps, 73, while Castroneves, who took the lead for good with 59 laps to go, led for 66 total laps. Danica Patrick topped her fourth-place finish as a rookie in 2005 by taking third.

Formula One. England's Jenson Button won six of the first seven races and finished in the top 10 in the first nine races of the 2009 season, building up a huge lead in a bid for his first drivers'

championship. Despite some struggles, Button held on and clinched the title with his fifth-place finish in the Brazilian Grand Prix on October 18.

IRL. With their three wins each in the first 11 races, Scott Dixon and Dario Franchitti were locked in a tight duel with Ryan Briscoe for the driver's title. Franchitti captured the championship with his first-place finish in the Firestone Indy 300 in Miami on October 10. Dixon finished second, followed by Briscoe, Helio Castroneves, and Danica Patrick. IRL president and chief executive officer Tony George stepped down midseason.

Endurance. David Donohue passed Juan Pablo Montoya with 39 minutes remaining and held on to win the Rolex 24 on January 25 by 0.167 seconds, the closest margin in the race's 47-year history. Donohue, who teamed with Antonio Garcia, Darren Law, and Buddy Rice for Brumos Racing, denied Chip Ganassi Racing a fourth straight title in the Daytona endurance race. On June 14, Spanish driver Marc Gene of Peugeot broke Audi's five-year stranglehold on the 24 Hours of Le Mans. Gene, along with David Brabham of the United Kingdom and Alexander Wurz of Austria, finished 382 laps, one lap ahead of another Peugeot team.

Dragsters. Tony Schumacher won the 2009 NHRA top fuel championship, Robert Hight won the funny car division, and Mike Edwards won the pro stock division. ■ Michael Kates

Aviation. On Dec. 25, 2009, a Nigerian man attempted to detonate an explosive aboard a trans-Atlantic Northwest Airlines flight as the plane prepared to land in Detroit. The device, which the man had sneaked onto the aircraft in his underwear, failed to detonate but started a fire. Passengers aboard the Airbus A330 jet, which had originated in Nigeria with a stop in Amsterdam, subdued the man and put out the fire. The incident, which received worldwide attention, caused officials with various United States agencies and departments to reexamine aviation security measures, particularly the effectiveness of the current No-Fly List of persons prohibited from boarding an aircraft and the Selectee List of individuals who must undergo additional security screening before being permitted to board an aircraft. The father of the Nigerian man had warned the U.S. Department of State that his son might be involved in terrorist activities.

Miracle on the Hudson. In a year with a large number of deadly air disasters, one crash in 2009 involved a pilot who was proclaimed a hero after making a difficult, forced landing through which all on board survived. US Airways Flight 1549 took off from New York City's La Guardia Airport on January 15. About a minute later, pilot Chesley "Sully" Sullenberger informed air-traffic controllers that the plane, an Airbus A320, needed to make an emergency landing. Birds had been sucked into the jet's engines, and both had failed. Sullenberger, a former pilot with the U.S. Air Force, did not have enough power to reach an airport. Instead, he crash-landed the plane in the Hudson River off midtown Manhattan.

Air temperatures were at around 18 °F (–8 °C), and the water temperature was 35 °F (2 °C) at the time of the crash. Fortunately, the plane stayed afloat long enough to allow the passengers to escape. Many passengers stood on the plane's wings awaiting rescue. Less fortunate passengers were immersed in the river. A flotilla of commuter ferries and water taxis was on the scene in minutes and moved passengers to safety. The skill with which Sullenberger, who was also a licensed glider pilot, landed the powerless jet was credited for the survival of all 155 aboard.

U.S. air disaster. The crash on February 2 of a commuter plane traveling from Newark, New Jersey, to Buffalo, New York, was the first fatal crash of a commercial airliner in the United States since 2006. According to the National Transportation Safety Board investigation, the likely cause of the crash was pilot error. All 49 people on the plane and 1 person on the ground were killed.

Other disasters. An Indonesian military transport crashed on May 20, 2009. The plane

Passengers stand on the wings of their downed US Airways jet waiting to be rescued after crash-landing on the Hudson River on January 15. Captain Chesley "Sully" Sullenberger was lauded for his skillful landing shortly after taking off from La Guardia Airport in New York City.

was landing at a military base on eastern Java. Most of the 101 people killed, including 2 people on the ground, were soldiers and their families.

On June 1, Air France Flight 447 en route from Rio de Janeiro to Paris crashed in the Atlantic Ocean. All 228 persons aboard were lost. The Brazilian military later found bodies and pieces of the plane, an Airbus A330, floating in the ocean. Medical examiners stated that autopsies on bodies recovered indicated the plane had likely broken up in midair. The debris field was large—bodies were recovered from areas more than 50 miles (80 kilometers) apart. The plane's flight data recorder, or black box, was not found. One theory about the cause of the crash focused on the failure of a part called a pitot, which measures air speed. Other Airbus A330's had experienced problems with pitots. On September 3, the U.S. Federal Aviation Administration (FAA) ordered that these air-speed sensors be replaced on all Airbus A330's and A340's owned by U.S. carriers.

On June 30, Yemenia Airways Flight 626 crashed into the Indian Ocean en route from Sanaa, Yemen's capital, to Comoros, a group of islands between the African mainland and Madagascar. Of the 153 passengers aboard the Airbus A310, only one survived. Twelve-year-old Bahia Bakari of France was in the ocean for more than 10 hours, part of the time in darkness, floating on a piece of debris before being rescued.

Caspian Airlines Flight 7908 crashed on July 15. The plane, a Russian-built Tupolev Tu-154, was traveling from Iran to Armenia when it crashed and exploded near Tehran. All 168 aboard were killed.

Pilots disciplined. The FAA revoked the licenses of two Northwest Airlines pilots after they missed the airport to which they were flying. On October 21, the pilots were flying from San Diego to Minneapolis when they became absorbed in information on their laptop computers. They lost track of time and overshot the airport by around 150 miles (240 kilometers).

Boeing's woes. The 787 Dreamliner, a new jet built by Chicago-based Boeing Co., was given its first test flight on December 15, more than two years behind schedule. The delay had been caused by production problems. To save on production costs, Boeing had outsourced not only the manufacturing of parts but also design and engineering work. Suppliers sometimes failed to meet deadlines. When the outsourced parts and work came in to Everett, Washington, to be assembled by Boeing workers, the pieces often failed to meet standards. In addition, parts manufactured around the world were incompatible in some cases.   ■ Christine Sullivan

See also **Disasters; Terrorism; Transportation.**

Azerbaijan. Voters approved 41 amendments to Azerbaijan's Constitution in a referendum on March 18, 2009. The Azerbaijani Central Election Commission (CEC) reported that all the amendments overwhelmingly passed and that turnout was nearly 71 percent of registered voters despite opposition calls for an election boycott.

One controversial amendment removed a two-term limit on Azerbaijan's presidency. This would permit President Ilham Aliyev, who was reelected in October 2008 for a second five-year term, to run again. Other key amendments allow the suspension of presidential and parliamentary elections during wartime and grant financial benefits to former Azerbaijani presidents.

Opposition politicians denounced the referendum as tainted. They claimed that the turnout had not reached the 25 percent required to ratify the amendments. However, observers from the Parliamentary Assembly of the Council of Europe reported no serious violations in the poll's conduct. Formal protest claims against the results by opposition groups were rejected by the CEC and the Supreme Court.   ■ Juliet Johnson

See also **Asia.**

Bahamas. See Latin America; West Indies.
Bahrain. See Middle East.
Ballet. See Dancing.
Baltic States. See Europe; Latvia; Lithuania.

Bangladesh. On Jan. 6, 2009, Sheik Hasina Wajed returned to the post of prime minister that she had held from 1996 to 2001. Her Awami League and its allies had won 263 out of 300 seats in parliamentary elections held on Dec. 29, 2008.

Politics. The League won a second landslide victory on Jan. 22, 2009, taking more than two-thirds of the seats in local elections. The opposition Bangladesh Nationalist Party, which had governed from 2001 to 2007, protested that this vote was unfair. Political observers said both parties were guilty of voter intimidation and stuffing ballot boxes.

Sheik Hasina's government promised to reduce the number of people in Bangladesh living in poverty to 45 million by 2013. The World Bank, a United Nations affiliate, estimated that as of 2005, about 56 million Bangladeshis lived in poverty. The goal was made difficult in 2009 by a decline in world demand for garments, which provided nearly 75 percent of Bangladesh's export earnings. In addition, a decline in the demand for labor abroad cut remittances that had provided some 10 percent of the country's overall income. Some 5.5 million Bangladeshis worked abroad in 2008.

Mutiny. On Feb. 25, 2009, members of the Bangladesh Rifles (BDR), a paramilitary force of 45,000 troops primarily responsible for guarding the nation's borders, mutinied at their headquarters in Dhaka, the capital. BDR troops in other towns around the country followed suit. The mutiny lasted for nearly two days and left more than 70 people dead, including 57 officers as well as civilians. The mutineers surrendered after army troops surrounded their barracks with tanks.

Some international observers suspected that the mutiny was connected to the impending trial of people accused of war crimes during the 1971 conflict that resulted in the independence of Bangladesh from Pakistan. During her 2008 election campaign, Sheik Hasina had promised to prosecute those accused of war crimes, some of whom remained politically active. The trials were due to start in early 2009, and some observers thought that fear of prosecution might have sparked the mutiny. However, a government inquiry into the mutiny found that the revolt stemmed from BDR troops' frustrations with low pay and poor working conditions, especially in contrast with the regular army. The Rifles were also said to be envious of benefits that the army got while working foreign assignments as United Nations peacekeepers.

Beginning in late 2009, army Major General Moinul Islam led a three-person military court that put some 4,000 BDR members on trial for their roles in the mutiny. Proceedings were expected to take several years. ■ Henry S. Bradsher

See also **Asia; Disasters.**

Bank. The banking industry in 2009 continued to cope with effects from the near collapse of the global financial industry in 2008 and its rescue by the federal government of the United States and central governments of other nations. In 2008, a succession of crises involving major U.S. banks had led to unprecedented federal intervention. The Federal Reserve System (the Fed)—the nation's central bank—and the U.S. Department of the Treasury arranged for bailout packages, bank mergers, and other means to avert collapse of giant financial firms, eventually requesting—and receiving—a congressional grant of $700 billion in emergency funding in the Troubled Asset Relief Program (TARP) legislation, approved in October.

TARP controversy. During the tenure of Secretary of the Treasury Henry Paulson—prior to the transition from the presidential administration of George W. Bush to that of Barack Obama on Jan. 20, 2009—the federal government distributed about $300 billion in TARP funds. Some members of Congress alleged that Paulson distributed the money without any strings attached, making it impossible to track use of the funds. Other members decried the intrusion of government agencies into the private economy, in some cases questioning the necessity of any rescue of the financial sector. Nevertheless, Paulson's replacement as secretary of the treasury, Timothy

Geithner, and Fed Chairman Ben Bernanke continued to assert that failure to act would have brought down the entire global financial edifice.

Revelations of the distribution of bonuses running into the billions by the very firms that were receiving federal bailout packages sharply intensified controversy over TARP. According to critics, the chief offenders were New York City-based Merrill Lynch (bought out by Charlotte, North Carolina-based Bank of America [BOA] in January 2009), which dispensed $3.6 billion in bonuses in late 2008; and New York City-based American International Group (AIG), a giant insurance company and investment bank department, which handed out $165 million in March 2009.

TARP paybacks. Treasury officials reported that about $160 billion in TARP funds were paid back in 2009. The insitutions returning funds included New York City-based JPMorgan Chase & Co., Goldman Sachs Group Inc., Morgan Stanley, Citigroup, North Carolina-based Bank of America, and San Francisco-based Wells Fargo.

Stress tests. In February, the Treasury Department announced that it would submit the nation's 19 largest banks—those with more than $100 billion in assets—to a "stress test," an analysis of the banks' available capital. The results, released in May, revealed that 9 of the 19 big banks were sufficiently capitalized. Ten big banks needed additional capital. The most cash-strapped of the big banks, BOA, needed to raise about $35 billion. All of the banks except Detroit-based GMAC Financial Services successfully raised the funds.

The FDIC and failing banks. As most of the big banks apparently stabilized during 2009, a growing number of small and medium-sized banks failed. According to the Federal Deposit Insurance Corporation (FDIC), 133 had failed by December. The FDIC also reported in late November that its Deposit Insurance Fund, which pays out funds to depositors at failed banks, had a negative balance. Expressing reluctance to draw on a line of credit with the U.S. Treasury, FDIC officials instead implemented a plan to have banks prepay their FDIC member fees through 2012.

The Merrill Lynch scandal. In early 2009, allegations surfaced that former Secretary of the Treasury Paulson and Fed chief Bernanke had exercised inappropriate influence in a merger of Bank of America with Merrill Lynch. The companies agreed to merge in September 2008, with the deal finalized on Jan. 1, 2009. Later in January, the federal government extended $20 billion in TARP funds to Bank of America.

Panic had been in the air in September 2008, as financial institutions teetered on the edge of collapse. Merrill Lynch, like a number of troubled "big banks," was known to have large holdings of "toxic assets"—securities based on the U.S. mortgage market, then in free fall. Paulson and Bernanke, eager to stave off a domino effect in bank failures, facilitated the merger.

Ken Lewis, BOA's chief executive officer, claimed that Paulson and Bernanke had strong-armed him. The alleged threat had been made in December 2008 when BOA executives expressed reservations about the merger upon learning of steep fourth-quarter losses at Merrill Lynch. In testimony before the House Committee on Over-sight and Government Reform in June 2009, Fed chief Bernanke categorically denied threatening Lewis and his fellow board members.

Mortgage delinquencies. Nearly 10 in 100 homeowners were behind in mortgage pay-ments in the third quarter of 2009, the Mortgage Bankers Association announced in November, up from about 7 in 100 in the third quarter of 2008. The figure did not include people whose homes were actually in foreclosure. The combined per-centage of mortgage holders in foreclosure and delinquent in payments was 14.41 percent, or about one in seven. According to the association, the largest share of new foreclosures was no longer on subprime loans but rather on fixed-rate mortgages. ■ Robert Knight

See also **Economics, U.S.: A Special Report.**

Barbados. See **Latin America; West Indies.**

Baseball. The New York Yankees captured the storied franchise's 27th World Series title on Nov. 4, 2009, with a resounding 7-3 victory over the defending champion Philadelphia Phillies. New York's Hideki Matsui knocked in a record-tying six runs in the decisive game, finishing the series with a .615 batting average, three home runs, and eight runs batted in (RBI's). Matsui became the first Japanese-born player to win the World Series Most Valuable Player award.

The Yankees had invested big money in the 2009 season, and not just in the new $1.5-billion Yankee Stadium, a home-run-friendly park with a short right-field porch. Before the season, New York signed three top free agents—pitchers C. C. Sabathia and A. J. Burnett and slugger Mark Teixeira—to $423 million in contracts.

Performance-enhancing drug use contin-ued to plague baseball in 2009. On May 7, domi-nant hitter Manny Ramirez of the Los Angeles Dodgers was suspended for 50 games after test-ing positive for a female fertility drug commonly used in conjunction with steroids.

Ramirez and Boston Red Sox power-hitter David Ortiz, both stars of the 2004 and 2007 championship Red Sox teams, were among 104 players who tested positive for steroids in 2003, according to multiple published reports. Major League Baseball (MLB) first tested players for

steroids in 2003. It did not issue suspensions, how-ever, because the survey was conducted only to assess the need for regular steroid testing. The results were supposed to be confidential—and destroyed—but they were seized in a federal investigation into steroid distribution by the Bay Area Laboratory Co-Operative (BALCO). Other names on the list included former Chicago Cubs outfielder Sammy Sosa, sixth on the all-time home run list with 609, and Yankee slugger Alex Rodriguez. Following the release of this informa-tion, Rodriguez admitted in February 2009 to using performance-enhancing drugs from 2001 to 2003 while with the Texas Rangers.

World Series. After the Phillies won Game 1 in New York City on Oct. 28, 2009, the Yankees took the next three games—two in Philadelphia—to build a commanding 3 games to 1 lead. The Phillies won Game 5 in Philadelphia 8-6 on November 2. Philadelphia's Chase Utley hit two home runs, bringing his World Series total to five. This total tied the record for most homers in a single World Series, set by Yankee slugger Reggie Jackson in 1977. The Yankees never trailed in Game 6 on Nov. 4, 2009, thanks to Matsui's two-run homer in the second inning. Andy Pettitte, at age 37, started and won the clinching game for the Yankees in all three rounds of the play-offs.

Play-offs. The Phillies became the first team to play in back-to-back World Series since the Yankees in 2000 and 2001, beating the Dodgers 10-4 on Oct. 21, 2009, to win the National League Championship Series (NLCS) 4 games to 1. In that series, Phillies slugger Ryan Howard tied legendary Yankee Lou Gehrig's record of eight consecutive post-season games with a run batted in. Philadelphia had beaten the Colorado Rockies 3 games to 1 in the first round. The Dodgers swept the St. Louis Cardinals 3 games to none to reach the NLCS.

The Yankees beat the Los Angeles Angels of Anaheim 4 games to 2 in the American League Championship Series (ALCS) to get to the World Series. New York had swept the Minnesota Twins 3 games to none in the first round. The Angels had swept the Boston Red Sox in the first round. Like Howard, Rodriguez tied Gehrig's eight-game RBI streak. Rodriguez batted .438 with five home runs and 12 RBI's in the first two rounds.

Regular season. The Yankees rebounded from a slow start to post the best record in 2009, 103-59. They won the American League (AL) East over Boston, the wild-card team, by eight games to return to the play-offs after a one-year absence. The Twins captured the AL Central in a one-game play-off with the Detroit Tigers, win-ning 6-5 on October 6 to finish with an 87-76 record. The Tigers had held or shared the division lead since May 10, blowing a seven-game lead in

FINAL STANDINGS IN MAJOR LEAGUE BASEBALL

AMERICAN LEAGUE

American League champions—
New York Yankees
(defeated Los Angeles Angels, 4 games to 2)

World Series champions—
New York Yankees (defeated Philadelphia Phillies, 4 games to 2)

Eastern Division	W.	L.	Pct.	G.B.
New York Yankees	103	59	.636	—
Boston Red Sox*	95	67	.586	8
Tampa Bay Rays	84	78	.519	19
Toronto Blue Jays	75	87	.463	28
Baltimore Orioles	64	98	.395	39

Central Division	W.	L.	Pct.	G.B.
Minnesota Twins	87	76	.534	—
Detroit Tigers	86	77	.528	1
Chicago White Sox	79	83	.488	7.5
Cleveland Indians	65	97	.401	21.5
Kansas City Royals	65	97	.401	21.5

Western Division	W.	L.	Pct.	G.B.
Los Angeles Angels	97	65	.599	—
Texas Rangers	87	75	.537	10
Seattle Mariners	85	77	.525	12
Oakland Athletics	75	87	.463	22

Offensive leaders

Batting average	Joe Mauer, Minnesota	.365
Runs scored	Dustin Pedroia, Boston	115
Home runs	Carlos Pena, Tampa Bay	39
	Mark Teixeira, New York	39
Runs batted in	Mark Teixeira, New York	122
Hits	Ichiro Suzuki, Seattle	225
Stolen bases	Jacoby Ellsbury, Boston	70
Slugging percentage	Joe Mauer, Minnesota	.587

Leading pitchers

Games won	Felix Hernandez, Seattle	19
	C. C. Sabathia, New York	19
	Justin Verlander, Detroit	19
Earned run average (162 or more innings)	Zack Greinke, Kansas City	2.16
Strikeouts	Justin Verlander, Detroit	269
Saves	Brian Fuentes, Los Angeles	48
Shut-outs	Roy Halladay, Toronto	4
Complete games	Roy Halladay, Toronto	9

Awards†

Most Valuable Player	Joe Mauer, Minnesota
Cy Young	Zack Greinke, Kansas City
Rookie of the Year	Andrew Bailey, Oakland
Manager of the Year	Mike Scioscia, Los Angeles

*Qualified for wild-card play-off spot.
†Selected by the Baseball Writers Association of America.

NATIONAL LEAGUE

National League champions—
Philadelphia Phillies
(defeated Los Angeles Dodgers, 4 games to 1)

Eastern Division	W.	L.	Pct.	G.B.
Philadelphia Phillies	93	69	.574	—
Florida Marlins	87	75	.537	6
Atlanta Braves	86	76	.531	7
New York Mets	70	92	.432	23
Washington Nationals	59	103	.364	34

Central Division	W.	L.	Pct.	G.B.
St. Louis Cardinals	91	71	.562	—
Chicago Cubs	83	78	.516	7.5
Milwaukee Brewers	80	82	.494	11
Cincinnati Reds	78	84	.481	13
Houston Astros	74	88	.457	17
Pittsburgh Pirates	62	99	.385	28.5

Western Division	W.	L.	Pct.	G.B.
Los Angeles Dodgers	95	67	.586	—
Colorado Rockies*	92	70	.568	3
San Francisco Giants	88	74	.543	7
San Diego Padres	75	87	.463	20
Arizona Diamondbacks	70	92	.432	25

Offensive leaders

Batting average	Hanley Ramirez, Florida	.342
Runs scored	Albert Pujols, St. Louis	124
Home runs	Albert Pujols, St. Louis	47
Runs batted in	Prince Fielder, Milwaukee	141
	Ryan Howard, Philadelphia	141
Hits	Ryan Braun, Milwaukee	203
Stolen bases	Michael Bourn, Houston	61
Slugging percentage	Albert Pujols, St. Louis	.658

Leading pitchers

Games won	Adam Wainwright, St. Louis	19
Earned run average (162 or more innings)	Chris Carpenter, St. Louis	2.24
Strikeouts	Tim Lincecum, San Francisco	261
Saves	Heath Bell, San Diego	42
Shut-outs	Bronson Arroyo, Cincinnati	2
	Cole Hamels, Philadelphia	2
	J. A. Happ, Philadelphia	2
	Tim Lincecum, San Francisco	2
	Joel Piniero, St. Louis	2
Complete games	Matt Cain, San Francisco	4
	Tim Lincecum, San Francisco	4

Awards†

Most Valuable Player	Albert Pujols, St. Louis
Cy Young	Tim Lincecum, San Francisco
Rookie of the Year	Chris Coghlan, Florida
Manager of the Year	Jim Tracy, Colorado

the final month of the season and a two-game lead with three games to play. The Angels won the AL West by 10 games with a record of 97-65.

In the National League (NL), the Dodgers captured the West with a league-leading 95-67 mark. The Phillies won the NL East at 93-69, and the Cardinals won the NL Central at 91-71.

With its 62-99 finish, the Pittsburgh Pirates became the first major North American profes-sional sports franchise in baseball, basketball, foot-ball, or hockey to have 17 straight losing seasons. The Dodgers broke the modern MLB record for a season-starting home win streak, capturing their first 13 games at home. The Tampa Bay Rays became the fastest team to reach 100 homers and 100 steals on June 28, succeeding in just 77 games.

Pitching feats. Chicago White Sox pitcher Mark Buehrle tossed a perfect game at home on

New York Yankees slugger Hideki Matsui blasts a two-run homer on Nov. 4, 2009, propelling his team toward a World Series championship over the Philadelphia Phillies. Matsui, the series MVP, drove in a record-tying six runs during the decisive game.

July 23, retiring all 27 of the Rays he faced. Buehrle's gem was the first perfect game in the majors since 2004 and just the 18th in major-league history. It was also Buehrle's second career no-hitter. The left-hander retired the first 17 batters he faced in his next outing. Together with 1 batter from his previous start, this set a record for most batters retired in a row at 45. On July 10, San Francisco Giants pitcher Jonathan Sanchez, a 26-year-old lefty, pitched the other no-hitter of 2009, an 8-0 victory over the San Diego Padres.

Milestones. Randy Johnson of the Giants became the 24th pitcher and just the 6th left-hander to win 300 games, with a 5-1 victory on June 4 in Washington, D.C. The 45-year-old became the second oldest to win 300. Seattle Mariner Ichiro Suzuki reached 2,000 hits in the

second fewest games in MLB history, reaching the milestone on September 6 in just 1,402 games. Only Al Simmons, who played from 1924 to 1944, did it faster, at 1,390 games. One week later, Ichiro became the first player in MLB history with at least 200 hits in nine straight seasons. Arizona Diamondback Mark Reynolds broke his own record, striking out 223 times in 2009.

Deaths. Nick Adenhart, a promising 22-year-old pitcher for the Angels, was killed on April 10 in Fullerton, California. The car he was riding in was struck by an alleged drunk driver who police believe ran a red light. Two other people were killed in the accident. Adenhart's death came only a few hours after his fourth major league start, and the team dedicated the season to him.

On April 13, long-time Phillies broadcaster

Harry Kalas, 73, died after collapsing in the broadcast booth at Nationals Park in Washington. Kalas was also known as a voice-over narrator for NFL (National Football League) Films. That same day, former Tigers pitcher Mark "The Bird" Fidrych, a sensation in the mid-1970's, was found dead on his farm in Massachusetts. He was 54.

Cubs sold. On October 6, the MLB owners unanimously approved the sale of the Cubs by the bankrupt Tribune Company to the wealthy Ricketts family of Chicago.

International. Japan won its second World Baseball Classic in a row with a 5-3 victory over Korea on March 23 in Los Angeles. Japan's Daisuke Matsuzaka went 3-0 and won the Most Valuable Player award.

College. Louisiana State University captured its sixth National Collegiate Athletic Association (NCAA) tournament with an 11-4 rout of the University of Texas at Austin on June 24 in Omaha, Nebraska.

Youth. A team from Chula Vista, California, rallied from a 3-0 deficit to beat a team from Taoyuan, Taiwan, 6-3 to win the Little League World Series on August 30 in South Williamsport, Pennsylvania.

■ Michael Kates

Basketball. The Los Angeles Lakers captured the franchise's 15th National Basketball Association (NBA) title in 2009, rolling past the surprising Orlando Magic. Lakers star Kobe Bryant, named the finals' Most Valuable Player, scored 30 or more points in four of the five games, including 30 in the clincher, a 99-86 victory on June 14, in Orlando, Florida.

Los Angeles Coach Phil Jackson, who had won six titles with the Chicago Bulls in the 1990's, captured his fourth with the Lakers. The 10 total titles were an all-time record for an NBA coach. Jackson had been tied with legendary Boston Celtics coach Arnold "Red" Auerbach. The title was also Bryant's fourth but the first without Shaquille O'Neal as a teammate.

In college basketball in 2009, the University of North Carolina men and the University of Connecticut women rolled through their respective National Collegiate Athletic Association (NCAA) tournaments virtually unchallenged, neither school winning a game by less than 10 points. For North Carolina, the championship was the school's fifth, and its six wins by double digits matched a feat last accomplished by Duke University in 2001.

NATIONAL BASKETBALL ASSOCIATION STANDINGS

EASTERN CONFERENCE

Atlantic Division	W.	L.	Pct.	G.B.
Boston Celtics*	62	20	.756	—
Philadelphia 76ers*	41	41	.500	21
New Jersey Nets	34	48	.415	28
Toronto Raptors	33	49	.402	29
New York Knicks	32	50	.390	30
Central Division				
Cleveland Cavaliers*	66	16	.805	—
Chicago Bulls*	41	41	.500	25
Detroit Pistons*	39	43	.476	27
Indiana Pacers	36	46	.439	30
Milwaukee Bucks	34	48	.415	32
Southeast Division				
Orlando Magic*	59	23	.720	—
Atlanta Hawks*	47	35	.573	12
Miami Heat*	43	39	.524	16
Charlotte Bobcats	35	47	.427	24
Washington Wizards	19	63	.232	40

WESTERN CONFERENCE

Northwest Division	W.	L.	Pct.	G.B.
Denver Nuggets*	54	28	.659	—
Portland Trail Blazers*	54	28	.659	—
Utah Jazz*	48	34	.585	6
Minnesota T'wolves	24	58	.268	30
Oklahoma City Thunder	23	59	.244	31
Pacific Division				
Los Angeles Lakers*	65	17	.793	—
Phoenix Suns	46	36	.561	19
Golden State Warriors	29	53	.354	36
Los Angeles Clippers	19	63	.232	46
Sacramento Kings	17	65	.207	48
Southwest Division				
San Antonio Spurs*	54	28	.659	—
Houston Rockets*	53	29	.646	1
Dallas Mavericks*	50	32	.610	4
New Orleans Hornets*	49	33	.598	5
Memphis Grizzlies	24	58	.293	30

INDIVIDUAL LEADERS

Scoring (minimum 70 games or 1,400 points)

	G.	F.G.M.	F.T.M.	Pts.	Avg.
Dwyane Wade, Miami	79	854	590	2,386	30.2
LeBron James, Cleveland	81	789	594	2,304	28.4
Kobe Bryant, Los Angeles L	82	800	483	2,201	26.8
Dirk Nowitzki, Dallas	81	774	485	2,094	25.9
Danny Granger, Indiana	67	571	404	1,728	25.8
Kevin Durant, Okl. City	74	661	452	1,871	25.3
Chris Paul, New Orleans	78	631	455	1,781	22.8
Carmelo Anthony, Denver	66	535	371	1,504	22.8
Chris Bosh, Toronto	77	615	504	1,746	22.7
Brandon Roy, Portland	78	633	416	1,765	22.6

Rebounding (minimum 70 games or 800 rebounds)

	G.	Off.	Def.	Tot.	Avg.
Dwight Howard, Orlando	79	336	757	1,093	13.8
Troy Murphy, Indiana	73	146	715	861	11.8
David Lee, New York	81	256	695	951	11.7
Tim Duncan, San Antonio	75	201	599	800	10.7
Emeka Okafor, Charlotte	82	275	552	827	10.1
Chris Bosh, Toronto	77	215	556	771	10.0
Yao Ming, Houston	77	204	557	761	9.9
Pau Gasol, Los Angeles L	81	262	518	780	9.6
Kevin Love, Minnesota	81	274	460	734	9.1
Antwan Jamison, Wash.	81	196	525	721	8.9

NBA champions—Los Angeles Lakers
(defeated Orlando Magic, 4 games to 1)

*Made play-offs.

94 Basketball

Not only did Connecticut win every women's tournament game by double digits, the school captured all 39 of its games during the 2008-2009 season, including all postseason tournaments by at least 10 points. The season was the third that the school's women had finished unbeaten (1995 and 2002).

Professional men. In the NBA finals, Bryant averaged 32.4 points per game. Although the final result was lopsided, Orlando had several chances to make it a tighter series. After Los Angeles rolled to a 25-point victory in Game 1 in Los Angeles, Orlando had a chance to steal Game 2 on June 7, 2009, in Los Angeles. But rookie Courtney Lee missed an off-balance lay-

THE 2008-2009 COLLEGE

COLLEGE TOURNAMENT CHAMPIONS

NCAA	(Men)	Division I:	North Carolina
		Division II:	Findlay
		Division III:	Washington-St. Louis
	(Women)	Division I:	Connecticut
		Division II:	Minnesota State-Mankato
		Division III:	George Fox
NAIA	(Men)	Division I:	Rocky Mountain
		Division II:	Oklahoma Wesleyan
	(Women)	Division I:	Union
		Division II:	Morningside
NIT	(Men)	Penn State	
	(Women)	South Florida	

Pat Summitt is showered with confetti after her University of Tennessee team defeated the University of Georgia for her 1,000th victory as a coach on Feb. 5, 2009. Summitt is the first basketball coach in NCAA history to win 1,000 games.

BASKETBALL SEASON

MEN'S COLLEGE CHAMPIONS

CONFERENCE	SCHOOL
America East	Binghamton–Vermont (tie) Binghamton (tournament)
Atlantic 10	Xavier Temple (tournament)
Atlantic Coast	North Carolina Duke (tournament)
Atlantic Sun	Jacksonville East Tennessee State (tournament)
Big 12	Kansas Missouri (tournament)
Big East	Louisville*
Big Sky	Weber State Portland State (tournament)
Big South	Radford*
Big Ten	Michigan State Purdue (tournament)
Big West	Cal State-Northridge*
Colonial	Virginia Commonwealth*
Conference USA	Memphis*
Horizon League	Butler Cleveland State (tournament)
Ivy League	Cornell (no tournament)
Metro Atlantic	Siena*
Mid-American East Division West Division	Akron (tournament) Buffalo–Bowling Green (tie) Ball State–Central Michigan–Western Michigan (3-way tie)
Mid-Eastern	Morgan State*
Missouri Valley	Creighton–Northern Iowa (tie) Northern Iowa (tournament)
Mountain West	BYU–New Mexico–Utah (3-way tie) Utah (tournament)
Northeast	Robert Morris*
Ohio Valley	Tennessee-Martin Morehead State (tournament)
Pacific 10	Washington USC (tournament)
Patriot League	American*
Southeastern East Division West Division	Mississippi State (tournament) South Carolina–Tennessee (tie) LSU
Southern North Division South Division	Chattanooga (tournament) Chattanooga–Western Carolina (tie) Davidson
Southland East Division West Division	Stephen F. Austin (tournament) Stephen F. Austin Sam Houston State
Southwestern	Alabama State*
Summit League	North Dakota State*
Sun Belt East Division West Division	Western Kentucky (tournament) Western Kentucky Arkansas-Little Rock
West Coast	Gonzaga*
Western Athletic	Utah State*

WOMEN'S COLLEGE CHAMPIONS

CONFERENCE	SCHOOL
America East	Boston University Vermont (tournament)
Atlantic 10	Xavier Charlotte (tournament)
Atlantic Coast	Florida State–Maryland (tie) Maryland (tournament)
Atlantic Sun	Florida Gulf Coast East Tennessee State (tournament)
Big 12	Oklahoma Baylor (tournament)
Big East	Connecticut*
Big Sky	Montana*
Big South	Liberty*
Big Ten	Ohio State*
Big West	UC-Santa Barbara*
Colonial	Drexel*
Conference USA	Southern Methodist Central Florida (tournament)
Horizon League	UW-Green Bay*
Ivy League	Dartmouth (no tournament)
Metro Atlantic	Marist*
Mid-American East Division West Division	Ball State (tournament) Bowling Green Ball State
Mid-Eastern	North Carolina A&T*
Missouri Valley	Illinois State Evansville (tournament)
Mountain West	San Diego State–Utah (tie) Utah (tournament)
Northeast	Sacred Heart*
Ohio Valley	Murray State Austin Peay (tournament)
Pacific 10	Stanford*
Patriot League	Lehigh*
Southeastern	Auburn Vanderbilt (tournament)
Southern	Chattanooga Western Carolina (tournament)
Southland East Division West Division	Texas-San Antonio (tournament) Southeastern Louisiana Texas-Arlington–Texas-San Antonio (tie)
Southwestern	Prairie View A&M*
Summit League	South Dakota State*
Sun Belt East Division West Division	Middle Tennessee State Middle Tennessee State Arkansas-Little Rock
West Coast	Gonzaga*
Western Athletic	Fresno State–Louisiana Tech (tie) Fresno State (tournament)

*Regular season and conference tournament champion.

Sources: National Collegiate Athletic Association (NCAA);
National Association of Intercollegiate Athletics (NAIA);
National Invitation Tournament (NIT); Conference Web sites.

up off an inbounds pass as time expired, and the game went into overtime, which the Lakers won 101-96.

Orlando shot a record 63 percent from the field to win Game 3 in Orlando 108-104 on June 10 and led Game 4 until the closing seconds two days later. But Los Angeles veteran guard Derek Fisher forced overtime with an open three-pointer with 4.6 left, and the Lakers won in overtime 99-91 to move within a game of the title. It was the first time in 25 years that two finals games had gone to overtime.

The Lakers, the top seed in the Western Conference, advanced to the league finals for the second straight season by eliminating the Denver Nuggets 4 games to 2 in the conference finals. The Lakers had needed seven games to eliminate the Houston Rockets in the semifinals but had rolled over the Utah Jazz 4 games to 1 in the first round. The Magic had upset the top seed in the Eastern Conference, the Cleveland Cavaliers, 4 games to 2 in the conference finals. The Cavaliers had not lost a game through the first two rounds of the play-offs.

In the conference semifinals, the Magic stunned the defending champion Boston Celtics, playing without star forward Kevin Garnett, winning a decisive Game 7 in Boston. Orlando had beaten the Philadelphia 76ers 4 games to 2 in the first round. The Celtics-Chicago Bulls first-round series featured four overtime games (including a double-OT and a triple-OT game), an NBA play-off first.

In the regular season, Cleveland's LeBron James won his first Most Valuable Player award as the Cavaliers posted the league's top record at 66-16 to win the Central Division. Boston (62-20) won the Atlantic Division, and Orlando (59-23) won the Southeast Division. In the Western Conference, the Lakers (65-17) won the Pacific, the Nuggets (54-28) won the Northwest, and the San Antonio Spurs (54-28) won the Southwest.

Professional women. The Phoenix Mercury won their second Women's National Basketball Association (WNBA) championship in three seasons, defeating the Indiana Fever in the fifth and deciding game October 9 in Phoenix. Mercury guard Diana Taurasi was named the Most Valuable Player for the finals. Taurasi had previously been selected as the league MVP for the regular season. Indiana was making its first appearance in the WNBA Finals.

College men. North Carolina (34-4) jumped all over Michigan State University in the first half of their April 6 title game in Detroit, opening up a 36-13 lead en route to a 55-34 half-time lead. The 21-point margin broke a 42-year-old record for largest advantage at the half, and the 55 points also established a new mark. North Car-

olina, led by Tyler Hansbrough's 18 points, Wayne Ellington's 19 points, and Ty Lawson's 21 points and title-game-record eight steals, coasted in the second half to an 89-72 victory.

The Tar Heels, the top seed out of the South Regional, had rolled over upstart Villanova (30-8), the third seed out of the East Regional, 83-69, on April 4. In the other national semifinal, Michigan State (31-7), the second seed out of the Midwest Regional, had stunned a favored Connecticut (31-5) 82-73 on the strength of Kalin Lucas's 21 points. Connecticut was the top seed in the West Regional.

Prior to the NCAA tournament, Connecticut had been on the losing end of one of the most memorable games in recent history. In an epic six-overtime game on March 12 in New York City in the quarterfinals of the Big East tournament, Syracuse University outlasted Connecticut 127-117. The NCAA record for the most overtimes in a game is seven.

College women. Tina Charles, a junior center, scored 25 points, grabbed 19 rebounds and hit 11 of 13 shots as Connecticut throttled the University of Louisville 76-54 on April 7 in St. Louis. It was the Huskies' sixth title, but its first since 2004. UConn, the top seed out of the Trenton Regional, had beaten Stanford (33-5), the second seed in the Berkeley Regional, 83-64, in the national semifinals on April 5, 2009. That 19-point margin was as close as any team got to Connecticut throughout the tournament. Louisville (34-5), the third seed from the Raleigh Regional, had gained the university's first women's final appearance with a 61-59 come-from-behind victory over Oklahoma (32-5), the top seed in the Oklahoma City Regional.

Notable deaths. Utah Jazz owner Larry H. Miller died on Feb. 20, 2009, at age 64, and Detroit Pistons owner William Davidson died on March 13 at age 86. On May 9, Hall of Fame head coach Chuck Daly, who had guided the Pistons to back-to-back titles in 1989 and 1990 and coached the original American "Dream Team" to gold in the 1992 Olympics, died at the age of 78.

On June 4, 2009, Randy Smith, who once held the NBA record for consecutive games played, died at the age of 60. Smith had appeared in 906 straight games during the 1970's and early 1980's, a mark that stood until A. C. Green broke it in 1997.

On Feb. 26, 2009, Johnny "Red" Kerr, the first coach in Chicago Bulls history and Coach of the Year for the 1966-1967 season, died at age 76. Earlier that day, former Bulls star guard Norm Van Lier was found dead in his Chicago home at age 61.   ■ Michael Kates

Belarus. See Europe.

Belgium. The coalition government led by Prime Minister Herman Van Rompuy remained stable in 2009. It consisted of the Flemish (Dutch-speaking) and *francophone* (French-speaking) Christian Democrats and Liberals and the franco-phone Socialists. Van Rompuy became prime minister on Dec. 30, 2008, after King Albert II accepted the resignation of Yves Leterme and asked Van Rompuy to form a new government. However, the change in leadership did little to resolve Flemish demands for greater power for the regions.

Negotiations on the issue were deadlocked in early 2009, as politicians prepared for parliamentary elections in Belgium's three regions of Brussels, Flanders, and Wallonia in June. The Green Party and two right-wing Flemish parties were the big winners in these elections. After the elections, the government focused on the economic crisis.

In November, Van Rompuy was elected president of the European Council, the executive branch of the European Union (EU). The new position was established by the Lisbon Treaty, which came into force on December 1. King Albert nominated Yves Leterme to serve as prime minister and asked former Prime Minister Jean-Luc Dehaene to propose solutions to Belgium's political divisions before the next federal election in 2011.

Economy. Belgium responded to the global economic crisis with governmental support for several national banks and calls for greater oversight. The government also implemented a stimulus program to boost consumer confidence, reduce unemployment, and increase public investment in infrastructure projects. As a result, Belgium's deficit in 2009 rose to 5.9 percent of GDP, above the 3 percent permitted for EU members using the euro. (GDP—gross domestic product—is the value of all goods and services produced in a country in a year.) According to EU economists, Belgium's economy contracted by 2.9 percent in 2009. Unemployment rose to 8.2 percent from 7.0 in 2008.

Immigration. In July 2009, Van Rompuy announced an amnesty program for illegal migrants that would run from September 15 to December 15. About 25,000 people would be allowed to legalize their status if they could show that they had already integrated into Belgian society. The measure angered right-wing parties.

Foreign policy. In January, Belgium took steps to normalize relations with Congo (Kinshasa), its former colony, after having broken off ties in 2008. The government also announced its willingness to participate in the EU-led peacekeeping mission there. ■ Jeffrey Kopstein

See also **Europe; People in the news (**Herman Van Rompuy).

Belize. See Latin America.
Benin. See Africa.
Bhutan. See Asia.

Biology. Scientists found more evidence in 2009 that life can survive in even the harshest conditions. An April 17 report in the journal *Science* described bacteria living in a pond trapped under 1,300 feet (400 meters) of Antarctic glacier ice. The pond is four times as salty as the ocean, which prevents it from freezing, even though the temperature is only 23 °F (–5 °C). Bacteria in the pond are cut off from oxygen, sunlight, and outside nutrients. Yet, the bacteria thrive.

A team led by scientists at Harvard University in Cambridge, Massachusetts, found that the bacteria produce energy through chemical reactions involving iron and sulfur. In fact, the pond water contains so much iron that it turns red with rust when exposed to air. This water has created a frozen waterfall called "Blood Falls" at the glacier surface. By studying bacteria that flourish in dark, freezing, salty water, scientists hope to learn more about how alien life might survive similar conditions on other planets.

Heart of the comet. If life has developed on other planets, some of the ingredients may have arrived from space. In August, NASA scientists announced that they had found the amino acid glycine in samples taken from the comet Wild 2. (Amino acids are the building blocks of proteins, which are essential to life on Earth.) The samples were collected by the Stardust spacecraft when it passed by the comet in 2004. The material later dropped to Earth's surface by parachute.

Decoding a killer. For the first time, scientists have described the entire genetic code of HIV, the virus that causes AIDS. Researchers at the University of North Carolina at Chapel Hill published their findings in an August 2009 issue of the journal *Nature*. Scientists hope that a better understanding of HIV's genes will help them to develop new approaches to killing the virus.

Plant gatekeepers. Proteins that serve as gatekeepers can lock out bacteria that infect a plant's leaves, according to a report in the June 29 issue of the journal *Public Library of Science Biology*. Researchers at the University of California, Davis, found proteins that help the plant's immune system recognize invaders. The proteins then close tiny openings in leaves called *stomata* to lock out the invaders. Scientists hope that a better understanding of the proteins may lead to new ways to protect crops.

Second thoughts. Macaque monkeys weigh the consequences of their choices, according to a May report in the journal *Science*. Scientists at Duke University in Durham, North Carolina, presented the monkeys with eight squares representing various rewards. After the monkeys chose a square, scientists revealed the rewards the monkeys could have won had they chosen differently. The research showed that an area of the brain involved in measuring the consequences of actions had a higher response to more desirable rewards. The area also became active when considering rewards that were missed. Scientists said the study provides evidence that monkeys are able to second-guess their decisions.

Planning ahead. A report published in March offered dramatic evidence that apes can plan ahead. In the journal *Current Biology,* researchers described a male chimpanzee at Sweden's Furuvik Zoo that becomes agitated by zoo visitors. The chimp, named Santino, throws chunks of concrete when visitors appear. To stockpile ammunition, Santino gathers stones before the zoo opens, storing them near the area where visitors appear. Scientists once thought the ability to formulate plans was unique to human beings. Fortunately, chimps have poor aim, and Santino has never actually hit anyone.

Scientists at Israel's Weizmann Institute of Science have found that even bacteria are able to anticipate the future. Bacteria in the gut are frequently exposed to the sugar lactose, which is followed by the sugar maltose. In research published in June in the journal *Nature,* scientists found that when bacteria are exposed to lactose, genes needed to digest maltose are partially activated as well. However, maltose does not activate genes needed to digest lactose. Through adaptation, bacteria have become conditioned to prepare for maltose when lactose appears. In this way, even single-celled organisms may anticipate changing environmental conditions.

Of mice and men. Brain cells called *astrocytes* may represent a fundamental difference between the brains of mice and human beings. Astrocytes were long thought to be passive support cells to the neurons that generate electrical activity in the brain. Writing in the March 11 *Journal of Neuroscience,* scientists at the University of Rochester Medical Center in Rochester, New York, found that astrocytes are full partners in the work of the brain, communicating with neurons and each other. Moreover, human astrocytes are much larger than those in mice, with as many as 10 times the number of connections to other cells. Although the brains of human beings are larger than those of mice, little was thought to distinguish them at the cellular level. The complexity of our astrocytes may account for some of the remarkable power of the human brain.

Giant rats, fanged frogs. An international team of scientists exploring a remote volcanic crater in Papua New Guinea uncovered a treasure trove of new species in September. Among other creatures, they found a giant, woolly rat nearly as large as a cat. The expedition also discovered a fanged frog and many other species of amphibians, fish, reptiles, insects, and spiders.

Name and number. The number of species catalogued by scientists has risen to 1.9 million, according to a report prepared for the Australian government in September. The tally is 6 percent higher than the number reached in 2006. It is still only a fraction of the 11 million species the report estimates live on our planet altogether.

Antsy. Australian scientists may have found a new weapon in their fight against the cane toad. A native of Central and South America, the cane toad was introduced to Australia in 1935 to help control beetles that attack sugar cane. It soon escaped and has steadily advanced across regions of tropical Australia. Because the cane toad's skin contains poisonous glands, it has killed large numbers of Australian animals that have tried to eat it. More than half the crocodiles in some rivers have died from eating cane toads. Efforts to stop cane toads from spreading have failed.

In March 2009, a report in the journal *Functional Ecology* found that meat ants may help to control the cane toad. Meat ants are insects native to Australia, and they are known to feed on young frogs. In experiments, meat ants suffered no ill effects from eating cane toads. In fact, scientists found that cane toads are far more vulnerable to meat ants than are native frogs and are active during the day, when meat ants feed. By using meat ants to control cane toads, Australia can avoid importing another predator.

Vegetarian spiders. Scientists have found the only spider known to feed mainly on plant matter rather than insects. The spider lives on the acacia shrub of Central America, which is known for its relationship with ants. The ants drive off animals that might feed on the acacia. In return, the shrub provides the ants with nectar and nutritious leaf-tips. The spiders also feed on these acacia treats, along with small amounts of ant young. Scientists at Villanova University in Villanova, Pennsylvania, and Brandeis University in Waltham, Massachusetts, described the spider in an October issue of the journal *Current Biology.*

Mirror, mirror. A deep-sea fish found near New Zealand may be the only animal with a backbone that uses mirrors to see. The eyes of the four-eyed spookfish are divided into halves. The top half works much like an ordinary eye, using a lens to focus light from above. The bottom half uses a mirror to focus light from below. Many animals of the deep sea produce their own light through bioluminescence. Mirrors are better able to gather this faint light, giving the fish an advantage in spotting animals in the gloomy depths. The research, from scientists at the University of Bristol in England, was published in January 2009 in the journal *Current Biology.*

■ Edward Ricciuti

See also **AIDS; Conservation; Ocean; Zoos.**

The Swedish boat *Ericsson 4* captures the 37,000-nautical-mile Volvo Ocean Race on June 27, 2009, with Torben Grael of Brazil as the skipper. Grael's boat finished the 10-leg race in St. Petersburg, Russia, in 127 days, 7 hours, 46 minutes, and 21 seconds.

Boating. Brazil's Torben Grael captured the 37,000-nautical-mile Volvo Ocean Race in 2009, locking up the title with a third-place finish on June 16 in the ninth leg that ended in Stockholm. Grael, a five-time Olympic medalist, won five of the first nine legs aboard the Swedish boat *Ericsson 4.* The race started in Alicante, Spain, in October 2008, and for the first time featured stops in Asia. The 10th and final leg ended in St. Petersburg, Russia, on June 27, 2009. Grael's boat finished in 127 days, 7 hours, 46 minutes, and 21 seconds, and he accrued 114.5 points. The lone American entry, PUMA Ocean Racing, finished second with 105.5 points.

Around-the-world. Seventeen-year-old Cali-fornian Zac Sunderland, aboard a 36-foot (11-meter) sailboat, became the youngest person to sail solo around the globe when he finished his trip on July 16. Sunderland's claim did not last long. British sailor Mike Perham, a few months younger, finished his journey on a 50-foot (15-meter) racing yacht on August 27.

ISAF. France's Damien Iehl and Claire Leroy won the Open and Women's divisions in the Nations Cup at Porto Alegre, Brazil, on March 28. The International Sailing Federation (ISAF) Sailing World Cup ended September 19 in Weymouth, United Kingdom. Ivan Gaspic of Croatia won the Finn; Nathan Outteridge (helm) and Iain Jensen (crew) of Australia, the 49er; Nic Asher (helm) and

Elliot Willis (crew) of the United Kingdom, the Men's 470; Lisa Westerhof (helm) and Lobke Berkhout (crew) of the Netherlands, the Women's 470; Tom Slingsby of Australia, the Laser; Sari Multala of Finland, the Laser Radial; Ricardo Santos of Brazil, the Men's RS:X; Blanca Manchon of Spain, the Women's RS:X; Iain Percy (helm) and Andrew Simpson (crew) of the United Kingdom, the Star; Thierry Schmitter of the Netherlands, the 2.4 Meter; Renee Groeneveld of the Netherlands, the Women's Match Race; Scott Whitman (helm) and Julia Dorsett (crew) of the United States, the SKUD-18; and Rick Doerr (helm) and Hugh Freund (crew) of the United States, the Sonar.

America's Cup. A New York Supreme Court justice upheld a lower court ruling that BMW Oracle Racing was the legitimate challenger to Alinghi, setting the stage for the 33rd America's Cup races beginning on Feb. 8, 2010, at Ras al Khaymah, United Arab Emirates. After winning in July 2007, Alinghi had tried to install Spanish syndicate Desafío Español as the challenger. BMW Oracle sued and won, but legal wrangling over boat specifications continued even after the appeal was upheld.

Powerboats. Dave Villwock captured his seventh APBA Gold Cup in Detroit, piloting his Unlimited Hydroplane, *U-16 Elam Plus*, to victory on July 12, 2009.   ■ Michael Kates

Bolivia. On Dec. 6, 2009, Evo Morales Ayma easily won a second five-year term as president of Bolivia, taking more than 60 percent of the vote. "This process of change has prevailed," Morales told a cheering crowd from the balcony of the presidential palace in La Paz, Bolivia's administrative capital. The *indigenous* (native) president's Movement Toward Socialism party also took control of the upper house of Congress, clearing the way for further social reform in the poor Latin American country.

In January, Bolivians had narrowly approved a new Constitution that allows Morales to run for reelection. It also provided for the election of judges to Bolivia's Supreme Court of Justice rather than their appointment by the president. It specified separation of church and state, prohibited discrimination based on sexual orientation, recognized the right to self-determination of 36 distinct Indian groups, and authorized eastern lowland states to create semiautonomous assemblies to decide most local issues.

Lithium. Per the provision of the new Constitution giving the government control over all mineral and energy resources, Bolivia planned to exploit valuable lithium resources in the remote, treeless Salar de Uyuni. There, at a shallow depth, the salt flats hold an estimated one-half of the world's total supply of lithium, the

lightest of metals and a vital component of laptop, cell phone, and iPod batteries. Lithium is also crucial to the development of electric and hybrid vehicles.

In Paris in early 2009, President Morales called lithium "the hope not just for Bolivia but for all inhabitants of the planet." Morales was in France for a meeting with French industrialist Vincent Bolloré, a leader in the development of electric batteries and vehicles. During the year, Japanese conglomerates Mitsubishi and Sumitomo both vied for a chance to mine Bolivia's lithium. In September, Morales noted that Bolivia had still not decided on a partner to help exploit its lithium. However, he encouraged European companies to develop ways to manufacture lithium batteries and automotive parts in Bolivia.

Bicentennial. On July 16, Venezuelan President Hugo Chávez joined President Morales to celebrate the 200th anniversary of the beginning of the Bolivian war of independence. The ceremonies in La Paz marked the onset of the struggle that culminated in the birth of the Republic of Bolivia in 1825, which was named in honor of the Venezuelan-born liberator, Simón Bolívar.

■ Nathan A. Haverstock

See also **Latin America.**

Books. See Literature; Literature for children; Poetry.

Bosnia-Herzegovina. Ethnic tensions continued to dominate political life in Bosnia-Herzegovina in 2009, as efforts to reform central institutions failed repeatedly. Internationally sponsored talks among the three main ethnic groups—the Croats, the Muslim Bosnians (Bosniaks), and the Bosnian Serbs—failed in February and again in November to produce agreement on constitutional issues. After the November talks, Bosnian Serb leaders declared that they would boycott further negotiations unless the other parties accepted their right to secede.

At issue was the roadmap for Bosnia, set out in the 1995 Dayton Accords, which ended the Bosnian war. The roadmap called for two constituent states—the Muslim-Croat Federation (MCF) and the Republika Srpska (RS)—which were duly created. These entities were to have overarching national institutions, including a parliament, a tripartite presidency, and a justice system. Some of these institutions were created but had been hampered by lack of cooperation and consensus; others, such as a unified military, have never been implemented.

In 2009, as Bosnian politicians contemplated writing a permanent constitution, a majority of MCF political leaders advocated reforms to strengthen central institutions. However, RS Prime Minister Milorad Dodik and other Bosnian

Serb politicians proposed weakening central institutions to give the RS greater autonomy.

Officials of the European Union (EU) advocated strengthening Bosnia's central institutions to ensure the viability of the Bosnian nation and enhance stability in the western Balkans region. Bosnian leaders had in 2008 signed an agreement to begin EU membership talks, but EU officials repeatedly warned that Bosnia would make little progress until it enacted constitutional reforms.

Veto controversy. In June 2009, High Representative in Bosnia Valentin Inzko vetoed legislation passed by the RS parliament. The legislation prohibited any further transfer of authority to Bosnia's central government. The Dayton Accords empower the United Nations-appointed high representative to intervene in Bosnian institutions to enforce adherence to that agreement. Leaders of the RS protested the veto, labeling it "antidemocratic." Backed by allies Serbia and Russia, the RS leaders demanded the dissolution of the Office of the High Representative.

Economic growth slowed in Bosnia in 2009, as in most of the rest of Europe. Economists forecast that the Bosnian economy would contract by 3.8 percent in 2009 and then expand by 1 percent in 2010. ■ Sharon L. Wolchik

See also **Europe.**

Botswana. See Africa.

Bowling. Wes Malott, of Pflugerville, Texas, in 2009 captured his first Player of the Year award for his performances during the 2008-2009 season, finishing with 74 points to Norm Duke's 70. The race came down to the final match of the season on April 5 at the U.S. Open.

Duke, of Clermont, Florida, led the tour in winnings with $199,630 and was 13th in average. Malott, who won events in Vernon Hills, Illinois; Medford, Oregon; and Indianapolis, led the tour with a 222.98 average. He also had two second-place and three third-place finishes.

In the first major of the 2008-2009 season, Duke became the first player to win three straight major titles. He had won the final two the previous season. Duke beat Chris Barnes of Double Oak, Texas, 259-189, on Oct. 26, 2008, in Wichita, Kansas, in the Professional Bowlers Association (PBA) World Championship.

Patrick Allen, of Wesley Chapel, Florida, edged Rhino Page, 267-263, at the Tournament of Champions on Jan. 25, 2009, in Las Vegas for his second career major. John Nolen, of Waterford, Michigan, won his first title, and first major, with a 202-193 victory over Danny Wiseman of Baltimore on February 15 in Las Vegas to capture the United States Bowling Congress (USBC) Masters.

In the final major of the season, Mike Scroggins of Amarillo, Texas, won his second career major with a 191-173 victory over Duke on April 5 at the U.S. Open in North Brunswick, New Jersey.

2009 PBA World Championships. Men, women, and senior men shared the stage at the 2009 World Championships in Allen Park, Michigan, with a major title and a berth in the 2010 Tournament of Champions going to each winner. Kelly Kulick of Union, New Jersey, won the 2009 women's title, 219-204, over Shannon Pluhowsky, her first on the PBA women's series. Harry Sullins beat Hugh Miller, 222-192, for his first senior title. Tom Smallwood of Saginaw, Michigan, took the men's title with a 244-228 win over Wes Malott.

Seniors. Ron Mohr of Eagle River, Alaska, won three times in 12 Senior Tour events and was selected as PBA Senior Tour Player of the Year. The 53-year-old finished second in winnings with $41,600 and led the full-time touring seniors with a 223.14 average. Wayne Webb of Sacramento, California, defeated Brian Voss, 214-188, in Las Vegas on June 5 to win his second consecutive Senior U.S. Open. Dale Traber of Cedarburg, Wisconsin, won the other senior major, the USBC Senior Masters in Las Vegas on June 12, beating Ross Packard, 720-691 and 673-622.

Women. Tammy Boomershine of North Ogden, Utah, defeated Carolyn Dorin-Ballard, 269-225, on August 9 to win the U.S. Women's Open in Henderson, Nevada. ■ Michael Kates

Boxing. American welterweight Floyd Mayweather, Jr., came out of retirement after more than 21 months away from the ring with a dominating victory over a smaller Juan Manuel Marquez on Sept. 20, 2009, in Las Vegas. After the fight, Mayweather's record stood at 40-0 with 25 knockouts (KO's). Despite a large payday for the fight, Mayweather was hit with a $600,000 penalty for being too heavy at the prefight weigh-in.

Other notable fights. Manny Pacquiao, considered by many to be the best pound-for-pound fighter in the world, scored an impressive second-round knockout of Ricky Hatton on May 2 in Las Vegas to keep his super lightweight title. Puerto Rican fighter Miguel Cotto retained his World Boxing Organization (WBO) welterweight title with a gripping split decision over Joshua Clottey in New York City on June 13. Roy Jones, Jr., retained his North American Boxing Organization (NABO) light heavyweight title with a technical knockout of Jeff Lacy on August 15 in Biloxi, Mississippi.

World championships. Russia captured a pair of gold medals and four silver medals on September 12 in Milan, Italy. Russian Artur Beterbiev won the light heavyweight title and Egor Mekhontsev captured the heavyweight gold. Italian lightweight Domenico Valentino and super heavyweight Roberto Cammarelle won for Italy. Only one American made the finals, light welterweight Frankie Gomez. He lost to Cuba's Roniel Iglesias Sotolongo. Other champions included Ukraine's Vasyl Lomachenko (featherweight), Mongolia's Serdamba Purevdorj (light flyweight), Puerto Rico's McWilliams Arroyo (flyweight), Germany's Jack Culcay-Keth (welterweight), Uzbekistan's Abbos Atoev (middleweight), and Bulgaria's Detelin Dalaklie (bantamweight),

Boxers' deaths. Former champion Arturo Gatti, 37, was found dead at a seaside resort in northeast Brazil on July 11. Police originally said that the Canadian fighter's 23-year-old wife strangled him with her purse strap. However, she was released from jail after his death was ruled a suicide. Police revealed that he was found hanged. A second autopsy, this one in Canada, confirmed that he had died by hanging, but further investigation was to follow in late 2009.

American Vernon Forrest, 38, a three-time champion and first fighter to defeat "Sugar" Shane Mosley, was shot and killed by attackers during an apparent robbery in Atlanta in late July. Alexis Arguello, 57, who won at three different weight divisions, was found dead at his Nicaraguan home in early July. Olympic bronze medalist Darren Sutherland, 27, of Ireland was found hanged at his home in mid-September. Police were not treating the cause of death as suspicious.   ■ Michael Kates

WORLD CHAMPION BOXERS

WORLD BOXING ASSOCIATION

Division	Champion	Country	Date won
Heavyweight	David Haye	United Kingdom	11/09
Light heavyweight	Gabriel Campillo	Spain	6/09
Middleweight	Felix Sturm	Germany	4/07
Welterweight	Shane Mosley	United States	1/09
Lightweight	Juan Manuel Marquez	Mexico	2/09
Featherweight	Chris John	Indonesia	9/03
Bantamweight	Anselmo Moreno	Panama	5/08
Flyweight	Denkaosan Kaowichit	Thailand	12/08
Minimum	Roman Gonzalez	Nicaragua	9/08

WORLD BOXING COUNCIL

Division	Champion	Country	Date won
Heavyweight	Vitaly Klitschko	Ukraine	10/08
Light heavyweight	Jean Pascal	Haiti/Canada	6/09
Middleweight	Kelly Pavlik	United States	9/07
Welterweight	Andre Berto	United States	6/08
Lightweight	Edwin Valero	Venezuela	4/09
Featherweight	Elio Rojas	Dominican Republic	7/09
Bantamweight	Hozumi Hasegawa	Japan	4/05
Flyweight	Koki Kameda	Japan	11/09
Strawweight	Oleydong Sithsanerchai	Thailand	11/07

Brazil underwent important rites of passage in 2009, becoming the first major country to emerge from the global economic downturn and the first South American nation selected to host the Olympics. On October 2, Rio de Janeiro was chosen as the site of the 2016 Summer Olympic Games. Thousands of jubilant Brazilians watched the voting by the International Olympic Committee (IOC) on huge video screens set up on Copacabana beach. "Today we're getting the respect that Brazil has been deserving," said a happy President Luiz Inácio Lula da Silva. During 2009, da Silva, whose approval rating stood at 80 percent in Latin America, continued to draw on his popularity by promoting investment in Brazil and Brazilian trade abroad. Since taking office in 2003, da Silva had made official visits to 75 countries, opened 33 new Brazilian embassies overseas, and participated in global economic forums from which Brazil was previously excluded.

Business mergers. In September 2009, JBS of São Paulo merged with Bertin, a Brazilian competitor, and bought a majority stake in an American company, Pilgrims Pride of Texas. The new company, JBS-Bertin, became the world's largest meat producer. In March, the Banco Itaú of São Paulo became Latin America's largest bank. Following its acquisition of Unibanco, also in São Paulo, Itaú had a market value of $28 billion, making it one of the 20 largest banks in the world.

Flex-fuel cars. Thanks to help from foreign companies, Brazil continued to exert leadership in the manufacture of vehicles using alternative fuels. The Prisma, a flex-fuel vehicle—one that can be powered by either ethanol or gasoline—rolled off the assembly line in 2009. The Prisma was developed by the research center of Detroit-based General Motors (GM) near São Paulo. Although financially stressed at home, GM continued to make sizable investments in Brazil, where its operations had proved profitable in recent years, earning as much as $800 million annually. The bulk of GM's $1.5-billion Brazilian investment in 2009 was for the completion of a flex-fuel engine plant in the southern state of Santa Caterina.

Brazil-China relations. China replaced the United States as Brazil's leading trade partner in the first quarter of 2009. In April, China and Brazil traded $10 billion of their respective currencies (the yuan and the real), in a step toward replacing the weakening U.S. dollar to settle some of their future commercial debts.

Free press. On April 30, Brazil's Supreme Court ruled unconstitutional a 1967 press law on grounds that it violated guarantees of free expression. The law, enacted under military rule, had imposed harsh penalties on journalists for stories critical of the government.

Deforestation. In November 2009, data from

Brazil's National Institute for Space Research indicated a drop of nearly 46 percent in the rate of deforestation in the Brazilian Amazon from August 2008 to July 2009. The decline was the greatest since the government first began monitoring deforestation in 1988.

Itaipú power. In July 2009, President Lula da Silva, in a gesture of good will, approved a modification of an agreement with Paraguay that had governed that country's sale of power to Brazil from the hydroelectric plant at Itaipú on their shared border. In line with the change, Paraguay was to sell excess power to Brazil at market, rather than fixed low rates—thereby tripling Paraguay's income from the plant to an estimated $240 million annually.

Blackout. On November 10, Brazilians in 18 states lost electric power due to three downed transmission lines from Itaipú. The blackout caused chaos in such major cities as São Paulo, where it took all night to remedy the situation. Hapless passengers were forced to exit subways in the darkness and walk along the tracks to the nearest stations. ■ Nathan A. Haverstock

See also **Latin America.**

Britain. See United Kingdom.

British Columbia. See Canadian provinces.

Brunei. See Asia.

Building and construction. The 600-

seat Dee and Charles Wyly Theatre in Dallas opened in October 2009 to great fanfare. The 132-foot (40.2-meter) building is part of the new $354-million Dallas Center for the Performing Arts and features a radical architectural framework. A unique curtainwall system with 90-foot (27.4-meter) vertical aluminum shafts seems to hang in midair without exterior bracing. Designed by architects Joshua Prince-Ramus and Rem Koolhaas, the theater's outer "bird cage" is suspended on concrete stilts. The most demanding phase of construction involved lifting the shafts and securing them on the building's elaborate shell structure.

Much like certain truss bridge designs, the Wyly Theatre was structurally unsound until it was completed. Six perimeter columns and a perimeter wall form the basis of the shell, with a series of belt trusses forming the frame for the aluminum tube shafts. The columns are not located near the corners and are able to distribute the load on the belt trusses. The result is a "belt-and-suspenders" load design that can accommodate the aluminum tube shafts, which appear to float weightlessly on the exterior of the theater.

Chicago skyscraper breaks the mold. The 82-story residential Aqua building in Chicago was completed in late 2009. The 2.2-million-square-foot (204,400-square-meter) building features a wavy design, with concrete floor panels shaped into undulating curved forms, giving it a distinctive organic look when compared with the sheer lines of most glass-walled skyscrapers. The concrete balconies around the building jut out in unique curving shapes, without the aid of visible reinforcement or pillars.

The architect, Jeanne Gang, was inspired by the layered topography of limestone outcroppings along the Great Lakes. The complex, precise curves of the building's concrete balconies were made possible through the use of custom-made flexible steel forms, which allowed for the concrete to be cured into the odd, nonlinear shapes. The exacting dimensions of the concrete's edges were achieved through the use of electronic surveying technology called robotic total stations. These instruments are on-site surveying computers that employ laser measurement and calibration to ensure millimeter precision. This allows for each floor to follow its own contour, where no shape seems to repeat. The Aqua building has space for residential condominiums and apartments, and there are plans for a hotel to occupy the lower floors.

Las Vegas development. CityCenter, an $8.5-billion private development project on the famous Strip in Las Vegas, began opening in 2009. Despite several scaled-back design choices during construction, it remained one of the largest such projects ever undertaken.

Often cited as the largest private construction project in American history, the CityCenter is an 18-million-square-foot (1.67-million-square-meter) mixed-use complex consisting of hotels, condominiums, casinos, entertainment spaces, parking spaces, and related infrastructure. At its height, it was one of the busiest construction sites in the United States.

Conceived and begun at a time when Las Vegas was the center of a construction boom, CityCenter was to be the centerpiece of the new Las Vegas. A nationwide slowdown in construction and the global credit crisis hit CityCenter, which struggled briefly with funding issues and disagreements among its developers. The construction effort was also overshadowed by six worker deaths during 2007 and 2008, resulting in government-mandated safety training at the site.

Russian flood barrier. A massive, $3-billion project to build a series of dams and sluice gates to hold back the waters of the Gulf of Finland from Saint Petersburg, Russia, finally approached completion in late 2009. The St. Petersburg Flood Prevention Facility Complex, known locally as "the dam," spans the Gulf of

Two ends of a bridge over the Colorado River at Hoover Dam in Nevada near completion in June. One of the largest concrete bridges in the world, the structure is part of the Hoover Dam by-pass in the Lake Mead National Recreation Area.

Finland, with the island of Kotlin in the middle of the barrier. The current construction effort dates back decades and had until recently progressed only in fits and starts since the collapse of the Soviet Union. More than 270 large-scale floods have struck St. Petersburg since the city was founded in 1703, but it was not until 1978 that a flood protection plan was approved.

The project consists of an embankment that is 15.8 miles (25.4 kilometers) long and 16.4 feet (5 meters) high. It includes a pair of 400-foot- (122-meter-) long pivoting, wedge-shaped gates that can swing to close the 656-foot- (200-meter-) wide channel. The dam will prevent rising waters from flooding the Neva River estuary on which the city is located. The steel gates are designed to sit in dry dock when not in use and are then flooded and allowed to float into position during closing. A six-lane highway runs along the embankment, passing through a tunnel 56.7 feet (17 meters) beneath the southern main channel.

Construction began in 1980, but work was halted in 1986 with the project approximately 65 percent complete. The effort remained stalled until 2001 due to a lack of funds and coordination. Fresh design work began in 2003 and construction resumed in 2007. The barrier system is designed to withstand a massive flood and has an estimated functional life span of 100 years.

■ Jeffrey Rubenstone

See also **Architecture**.

Bulgaria. Parliamentary elections in July 2009 toppled the Socialist-led government and brought the center-right Citizens for the European Government of Bulgaria to power, with Boiko Borisov as the new prime minister. Borisov's government set out to combat corruption, responding, in part, to demands from European Union (EU) officials for effective anticrime measures. During 2008, the EU suspended more than $1.2 billion in aid earmarked for Bulgaria in response to allegations that EU funds had been routinely diverted into corrupt channels. Bulgaria joined the EU in January 2007.

In September 2009, the Borisov government announced sweeping reforms of its customs agency to combat smuggling. In October, the justice minister unveiled a detailed plan to reform Bulgaria's justice system.

Bulgaria's economy, responding to global economic conditions, contracted by 5.3 percent in 2009. For 2010, economists forecast expansion of 1.0 percent. ■ Sharon L. Wolchik
See also **Europe.**

Burkina Faso. See **Africa.**
Burma. See **Myanmar.**
Burundi. See **Africa.**
Business. See **Bank; Economics, U.S.; Economics, U.S.: A Special Report; Economics, World; International trade; Labor and employment.**

Cabinet, U.S. The United States Senate confirmed President Barack Obama's Cabinet in 2009.

State. Hillary Rodham Clinton, who had been Obama's chief rival for the 2008 Democratic presidential nomination, was confirmed as secretary of state on Jan. 21, 2009, by a 94-2 vote. The first lady from 1993 to 2001, Clinton had served as a U.S. senator (D., New York) since 2001.

Treasury. On Jan. 26, 2009, the Senate voted 60-34 to confirm Timothy Geithner as secretary of the treasury. He had been president of the Federal Reserve Bank of New York since 2003. His confirmation process was tainted by a flap over his failure to pay $34,000 in payroll taxes in the early 2000's. He finished paying the taxes in late 2008.

Defense. Robert Gates was retained as secretary of defense after President Obama took office in 2009. Gates had been appointed to the post in 2006 by President George W. Bush.

Justice. On Feb. 2, 2009, Eric Holder was confirmed as attorney general, 75-21. He became the first African American to hold the post. He had been deputy attorney general from 1997 to 2001.

Health and human services. The Senate voted 65-31 on April 28, 2009, to confirm Kansas Governor Kathleen Sebelius as secretary of health and human services. President Obama had previously nominated former U.S. Senator Tom Daschle (D., South Dakota). But Daschle withdrew his candidacy after it was revealed that he had failed to pay $128,000 in income taxes for the years 2005-2007. He paid the taxes in early 2009.

Commerce. Former Washington Governor Gary Locke was unanimously confirmed as secretary of commerce on March 24. The president had previously chosen New Mexico Governor Bill Richardson and U.S. Senator Judd Gregg (R., New Hampshire), but both men later withdrew.

Labor. On February 24, U.S. Representative Hilda Solis (D., California) was confirmed as secretary of labor, 80-17. She became the first Hispanic woman to serve in a Cabinet.

Other posts. In January, the Senate unanimously confirmed former Iowa Governor Tom Vilsack as agriculture secretary; Arne Duncan, chief executive officer of Chicago Public Schools, as education secretary; Steven Chu, a physicist and Nobel laureate, as energy secretary; Arizona Governor Janet Napolitano as homeland security secretary; Shaun Donovan, New York City's housing commissioner, as housing and urban development secretary; U.S. Senator Ken Salazar (D., Colorado) as interior secretary; former U.S. Representative Ray LaHood (R., Illinois) as transportation secretary; and retired Army General Eric Shinseki as veterans affairs secretary. ■ Mike Lewis
See also **People in the news; United States, Government of the.**

Cambodia. The first trial of a member of the Communist Khmer Rouge (KR) regime began on Feb. 17, 2009. The KR was responsible for the deaths of more than 1.5 million people during its rule of Cambodia from 1975 to 1979. A special UN-backed court was established to try KR members. The government of Prime Minister Hun Sen, himself a former KR officer, had resisted holding trials and sought to limit the number of people tried.

Kaing Guek Eav, known as Duch, was the first to be tried. Duch ran the Tuol Sleng prison, where an estimated 17,000 men, women, and children died. In March 2009, Duch admitted his responsibility for the torture and execution of prisoners at Tuol Sleng. Evidence indicated that most of the victims were innocent of any crimes. In December, the court charged former KR leaders Ieng Sary and Nuon Chea with genocide.

On June 12, the United States government removed Cambodia from its trade blacklist, noting that it had "ceased to be a Marxist-Leninist country." The move made Cambodia eligible for loans from the U.S. Export-Import Bank, a government agency that lends money to promote the export of U.S. goods and services.
■ Henry S. Bradsher
See also **Asia; Disasters; Thailand.**
Cameroon. See **Africa.**

Conservative Prime Minister Stephen Harper's minority government began 2009 by promising an extensive fiscal stimulus package designed to combat the global economic recession's effects on the Canadian economy. The announcement of the stimulus package followed a period of constitutional crisis in late 2008 during which the opposition Liberal, New Democratic, and Bloc Québécois parties in the Parliament threatened to vote no confidence in the young Conservative government. If Parliament passes a vote of no confidence in the government, the prime minister must resign or request that the governor general call a general election. The opposition parties proposed creating a Liberal-New Democratic coalition government with support from the Bloc Québécois on confidence matters instead of making voters return to the polls. Governor General Michaëlle Jean agreed to Harper's unprecedented request to adjourn Parliament until January 2009, thus enabling the Conservatives to avoid a risky confidence vote.

Speech from the Throne and budget. On January 26, Jean read the government's new Speech from the Throne, which lasted only eight minutes. The speech, designed to highlight the government's legislative agenda at the start of a new session of Parliament, revealed a six-point economic stimulus plan that would be fully revealed in a budget to be *tabled* (proposed) the next day. The plan included a combination of public and private investment; new commitments to infrastructure spending; aid for low-income and unemployed Canadians and indigenous people; and support for the ailing auto and forestry sectors.

On January 27, Finance Minister Jim Flaherty presented a budget that included the first federal deficit since the 1997-1998 fiscal year. The budget projected a string of deficits over several years: $33.7 billion for the 2009-2010 fiscal year; $29.8 billion for 2010-2011; $13 billion for 2011-2012; and $7.3 billion for 2012-2013 (all amounts in Canadian dollars). Much of the shortfall was expected to come from a massive injection of new spending intended to minimize the financial strain caused by the global credit crisis and job losses due to the ensuing economic recession. The new spending included funding for infrastructure projects, worker retraining programs, and enhanced employment insurance benefits.

The government also announced personal income-tax cuts worth nearly $4 billion over two years, as well as individual home-renovation tax credits worth up to $1,350, to encourage retail spending and construction projects. The finance minister said that Canadians likely would feel some benefits of the budget within 6 to 12 months; He also said that, although the government regretted running deficits, they were temporarily necessary during such a difficult economic period. The Liberal Party agreed to support the Speech from the Throne and the budget—both matters of confidence—in exchange for periodic reports detailing the implementation of the budget and ongoing fiscal updates.

On September 11, Flaherty presented a revised budget forecast that included a $56-billion deficit for 2009-2010, but which suggested that the deficit eventually would be eliminated without tax increases. Flaherty also stated that, despite the ballooning deficit, Canada was in the best financial situation of any of the major industrialized countries in the Group of Seven (Canada, France, Germany, Italy, Japan, the United Kingdom, and the United States).

Economy. From October 2008 to August 2009, Canadians lost 387,000 jobs. Personal bankruptcies increased by one-third in the first quarter of 2009, compared with the same period the previous year, and most major population centers experienced a depressed housing market during the year. However, Canada's banking system weathered the 2008 credit crisis extremely well. Because of a risk-averse fiscal culture and certain strict banking regulations, the banking sector did not require the extensive government bailouts and credit guarantees that were common in the United States and other industrialized countries. Third-quarter earning reports released in August 2009 from Canada's five major banks revealed combined earnings of $4.4 billion, up from $3.9 billion one year earlier.

On June 1, 2009, Prime Minister Stephen Harper and Ontario Premier Dalton McGuinty announced that their governments would buy a 12-percent stake in the newly restructured General Motors (GM) Company for $10.5 billion. The bailout deal enabled GM to avoid filing for bankruptcy in Canada, as it had done in the United States. Harper said that the two governments would have risked the future of Canada's auto industry, largely centered in Ontario, if they had not taken part in the U.S. government's plans to restructure the auto sector with public money. Ontario's government speculated that the province could have lost 85,000 jobs if GM had been allowed to fail.

Foreign affairs. On May 5, in protest against an annual hunt that legislators decried as cruel, the European Parliament voted resoundingly in favor

of a ban on the marketing of seal products in European Union (EU) countries. On July 27, the European Council of Ministers approved the ban without debate. The Canadian government said that it would challenge the ban, which did include some exemptions for Inuit communities, at the World Trade Organization (WTO). Government ministers contended that Canada's seal hunt was humane, sustainable, and essential to the livelihood of many people living in poor, isolated communities. Hunters kill about 300,000 harp seals each year on Canada's eastern coast. In 2008, the hunt supplied about $2.5 million worth of exports to EU countries.

On May 6, 2009, at the Canada-European Union Summit in Prague, Canadian and EU officials announced the launch of negotiations toward a Comprehensive Economic and Trade Agreement (CETA). The negotiations, which could last up to two years, were expected to focus on enhancing investment services and government procurement and on facilitating freer trade of agricultural goods. The proposed pact also would allow for the temporary movement of workers between Canada and EU countries for the first time; and for efforts to coordinate regulations on intellectual property protection, animal safety, and other issues. Canadian proponents of closer economic ties between Canada and Europe argued that a new trade deal would protect and create jobs and reduce Canadian dependence on trade with the United States, Canada's largest trading partner. The EU is Canada's second largest trading partner, but Canada is only the 11th largest trading partner of the EU. The first meeting on the trade agreement took place on June 10 in Montreal.

On September 4, a spokesperson for Jason Kenney, minister of citizenship, immigration and multiculturalism, announced that the government would appeal a controversial ruling that drew outrage from the government of South Africa. In the ruling, the Immigration and Refugee Board of Canada granted refugee status to a white South African who had been living illegally in Canada after he argued that he had been the victim of violence and racial discrimination by South Africa's black majority. South Africa's government condemned the ruling as one that would "only serve to perpetuate racism" and stated that it was fighting against violent crime by all people, regardless of color or creed. Kenney's spokesperson noted that the Immigration and Refugee Board was quasijudicial and independent from the government. The government planned to ask federal courts to overturn the decision.

Medical isotope crisis. Medical experts called the unplanned shutdown in mid-May of a Canadian nuclear reactor known as the NRU a "catastrophe." The reactor had provided a large percentage of the world's medical isotopes, which are inexpensive and effective tools for diagnosing cancer. The 52-year-old NRU at Chalk River, Ontario, shut down because of a heavy-water leak. (Heavy water is radioactive water that contains the hydrogen isotope deuterium.) Officials initially estimated that reactor repairs would take

at least a month, but later estimates pushed the completion of repairs into early 2010.

Although there are alternatives to some tests that use medical isotopes, they are not always available or ideal. The reactor shutdown led to the cancellation or postponement of medical tests for many people. Experts suggested that Canada's reputation as a safe and dependable supplier of medical-grade isotopes had been compromised badly and that such major importers as the United States likely would explore the possibility of manufacturing their own isotopes.

On June 10, 2009, Prime Minister Harper announced that the government would eventually be getting out of the medical isotope business by splitting up and selling off the Crown corporation Atomic Energy of Canada Limited (AECL). Harper's announcement followed an AECL decision to abandon development of two newer reactors, known as MAPLE I and MAPLE II, at Chalk River. At its annual meeting in August, the Canadian Medical Association (CMA) called on the government to reconsider pulling out of the isotope-production

FEDERAL SPENDING IN CANADA
Estimated budget for fiscal 2009-2010*

Department or agency	Millions of dollars[†]
Agriculture and agri-food	3,321
Atlantic Canada opportunities agency	341
Canada revenue agency	4,388
Canadian heritage	3,141
Citizenship and immigration	1,472
Economic development agency of Canada for the regions of Quebec	287
Environment	1,649
Finance	83,087
Fisheries and oceans	1,642
Foreign affairs and international trade	5,421
Governor general	19
Health	4,968
Human resources and skills development	43,651
Indian affairs and northern development	6,883
Industry	4,419
Justice	1,416
National defence	19,253
Natural resources	4,009
Parliament	565
Privy Council	308
Public safety and emergency preparedness	7,309
Public works and government services	2,387
Transport	6,642
Treasury board	7,951
Veterans affairs	3,364
Western economic diversification	242
Total	**218,046**

*April 1, 2009, to March 31, 2010.
[†]Rounded in Canadian dollars; $1 = U.S. $1.10 as of Sept. 30, 2009.

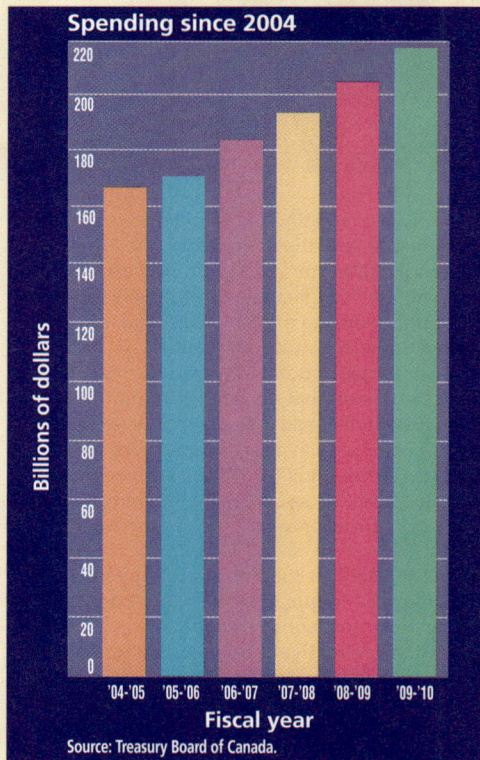

Spending since 2004

Billions of dollars

Fiscal year: '04-'05, '05-'06, '06-'07, '07-'08, '08-'09, '09-'10

Source: Treasury Board of Canada.

business. Robert Ouellet, president of the CMA, accused the government of putting finances ahead of patient care when it made its decision.

In early June, Minister of Natural Resources Lisa Raitt faced intense pressure to resign following the discovery that Raitt or one of her aides accidentally had left behind sensitive documents at a CTV News bureau in Ottawa. The documents contained information about funding for Atomic Energy of Canada Limited and the closed NRU nuclear reactor. Prime Minister Harper refused to accept Raitt's resignation. However, Raitt did accept the resignation of Jasmine MacDonnell, the aide who had handled the documents.

Raitt faced additional embarrassment in June after the *Halifax Chronicle-Herald* reported details from an audiotape on which Raitt had spoken candidly about an earlier isotope shortage and several Cabinet colleagues. Nova Scotia Supreme Court Justice Gerald Moir refused to block the release of the tape's contents, arguing that they were of public interest. On the tape, recorded in January, Raitt described the news value of a story involving radiation leaks and cancer as "sexy." She also questioned the ability of Minister of Health Leona Aglukkaq to respond to opposition attacks involving "hot" issues. Raitt initially rebuffed demands by opposition critics and cancer-survivor groups that she apologize for her comments, which many deemed disrespectful of cancer victims. However, she relented and apologized publicly on June 10.

H1N1 flu pandemic. Aboriginal leaders in Manitoba became incensed in September when they received shipments that included body bags from Health Canada. The federal agency had included the body bags with materials sent to First Nations communities in preparation for an H1N1 flu pandemic. Some aboriginal cultures view death preparations as an invitation to death. Health Canada later apologized and explained that the body bag shipment was part of a routine restocking for isolated communities and that the bags had not been intended to be part of the flu kits. Aboriginal leaders also expressed anger in June, when news emerged that Health Canada had delayed shipments of alcohol-based hand sanitizers to First Nations reserves affected by H1N1 flu because of worries that the residents would drink the sanitizer.

On September 19, Health Minister Aglukkaq unveiled a flu communications strategy for aboriginal communities. It was designed to give First Nations groups a conduit to discuss preparations for a second, expected wave of H1N1. Early research showed remote aboriginal communities to be disproportionately affected by the first wave of the virus, during the spring and summer. These communities' susceptibility to the flu likely was due in part to poor living conditions on native reserves.

Domestic politics. Former academic Michael

2009 CANADIAN POPULATION ESTIMATES

PROVINCE AND TERRITORY POPULATIONS

Alberta	3,660,400
British Columbia	4,456,100
Manitoba	1,222,500
New Brunswick	749,500
Newfoundland and Labrador	509,400
Northwest Territories	43,000
Nova Scotia	940,200
Nunavut	31,600
Ontario	13,071,200
Prince Edward Island	141,500
Quebec	7,812,500
Saskatchewan	1,032,300
Yukon	33,700
Canada	33,703,900

CITY AND METROPOLITAN AREA POPULATIONS

	Metropolitan area	City
Toronto, Ont.	5,632,100	2,516,500
Montreal, Que.	3,783,800	1,643,600
Vancouver, B.C.	2,313,300	598,800
Ottawa-Gatineau	1,213,900	
Ottawa, Ont.		836,300
Gatineau, Que.		252,100
Calgary, Alta.	1,213,200	1,063,700
Edmonton, Alta.	1,150,600	773,500
Quebec, Que.	746,300	500,400
Winnipeg, Man.	740,900	642,100
Hamilton, Ont.	737,400	513,500
London, Ont.	489,100	362,500
Kitchener, Ont.	487,800	214,000
St. Catharines-Niagara	403,500	
St. Catharines, Ont.		133,800
Niagara Falls, Ont.		84,300
Halifax, N.S.	399,600	381,200
Oshawa, Ont.	363,000	143,100
Victoria, B.C.	352,500	80,500
Windsor, Ont.	332,400	221,000
Saskatoon, Sask.	255,600	205,700
Regina, Sask.	210,100	179,900
Sherbrooke, Que.	192,800	152,600
Barrie, Ont.	190,400	147,700
Kelowna, B.C.	187,100	113,800
St. John's, Nfld. Lab.	186,900	101,500
Abbotsford-Mission, B.C.	174,000	
Abbotsford, B.C.		129,300
Mission, B.C.		36,600
Greater Sudbury/Grand Sudbury, Ont.	165,100	159,400
Kingston, Ont.	159,200	119,000
Saguenay, Que.	153,700	141,600
Trois-Rivieres, Que.	145,700	128,700
Brantford, Ont.	137,200	92,600
Guelph, Ont.	135,100	120,700
Moncton, N.B.	133,600	66,200
Saint John, N.B.	126,200	67,100
Thunder Bay, Ont.	123,400	109,200
Peterborough, Ont.	121,000	77,000

Source: World Book estimates based on data from Statistics Canada.

MEMBERS OF THE CANADIAN HOUSE OF COMMONS

The House of Commons of the second session of the 40th Parliament convened on Jan. 26, 2009. As of Dec. 1, 2009, the House of Commons consisted of the following members: 145 Conservative Party of Canada, 77 Liberal Party, 48 Bloc Québécois, 37 New Democratic Party, and 1 Independent. This table shows each legislator and party affiliation. An asterisk (*) denotes those who served in the 39th Parliament.

Alberta
Diane Ablonczy, C.P.C.*
Rona Ambrose, C.P.C.*
Rob Anders, C.P.C.*
Leon E. Benoit, C.P.C.*
Blaine Calkins, C.P.C.*
Rick Casson, C.P.C.*
Earl Dreeshen, C.P.C.
Linda Duncan, N.D.P.
Peter Goldring, C.P.C.*
Stephen Harper, C.P.C.*
Laurie Hawn, C.P.C.*
Brian Jean, C.P.C.*
Jason Kenney, C.P.C.*
Mike Lake, C.P.C.*
Ted Menzies, C.P.C.*
Rob Merrifield, C.P.C.*
Deepak Obhrai, C.P.C.*
LaVar Payne, C.P.C.
Jim Prentice, C.P.C.*
James Rajotte, C.P.C.*
Brent Rathgeber, C.P.C.
Blake Richards, C.P.C.
Lee Richardson, C.P.C.*
Devinder Shory, C.P.C.
Kevin Sorenson, C.P.C.*
Brian Storseth, C.P.C.*
Tim Uppal, C.P.C.
Chris Warkentin, C.P.C.*

British Columbia
Jim Abbott, C.P.C.*
Alex Atamanenko, N.D.P.*
Dona Cadman, C.P.C.
Ron Cannan, C.P.C.*
Jean Crowder, N.D.P.*
Nathan Cullen, N.D.P.*
John Cummins, C.P.C.*
Don Davies, N.D.P.
Libby Davies, N.D.P.*
Stockwell Day, C.P.C.*
Sukh Dhaliwal, Lib.*
Fin Donnelly, N.D.P.
Ujjal Dosanjh, Lib.*
John Duncan, C.P.C.
Ed Fast, C.P.C.*
Hedy Fry, Lib.*
Nina Grewal, C.P.C.*
Richard Harris, C.P.C.*
Russ Hiebert, C.P.C.*
Jay Hill, C.P.C.*
Peter Julian, N.D.P.*
Randy Kamp, C.P.C.*
Gary Lunn, C.P.C.*
James Lunney, C.P.C.*
Keith Martin, Lib.*
Colin Mayes, C.P.C.*
Cathy McLeod, C.P.C.
James Moore, C.P.C.*
Joyce Murray, Lib.
Denise Savoie, N.D.P.*
Andrew Saxton, C.P.C.
Bill Siksay, N.D.P.*
Chuck Strahl, C.P.C.*
Mark Warawa, C.P.C.*
Alice Wong, C.P.C.

Manitoba
Niki Ashton, N.D.P.
James Bezan, C.P.C.*
Rod Bruinooge, C.P.C.*
Steven Fletcher, C.P.C.*
Shelly Glover, C.P.C.
Candice Hoeppner, C.P.C.
Jim Maloway, N.D.P.
Inky Mark, C.P.C.*
Pat Martin, N.D.P.*
Anita Neville, Lib.*
Joy Smith, C.P.C.*
Vic Toews, C.P.C.*
Mervin Tweed, C.P.C.*
Judy Wasylycia-Leis, N.D.P.*

New Brunswick
Mike Allen, C.P.C.*
Keith Ashfield, C.P.C.
Jean-Claude D'Amours, Lib.*
Yvon Godin, N.D.P.*
Dominic LeBlanc, Lib.*
Rob Moore, C.P.C.*
Brian Murphy, Lib.*
Tilly O'Neill-Gordon, C.P.C.
Greg Thompson, C.P.C.*
Rodney Weston, C.P.C.

Newfoundland and Labrador
Scott Andrews, Lib.
Gerry Byrne, Lib.*
Siobhan Coady, Lib.
Judy Foote, Lib.
Jack Harris, N.D.P.
Todd Russell, Lib.*
Scott Simms, Lib.*

Northwest Territories
Dennis Bevington, N.D.P.*

Nova Scotia
Scott Armstrong, C.P.C.
Scott Brison, Lib.*
Rodger Cuzner, Lib.*
Mark Eyking, Lib.*
Gerald Keddy, C.P.C.*
Greg Kerr, C.P.C.
Megan Leslie, N.D.P.
Peter MacKay, C.P.C.*
Geoff Regan, Lib.*
Michael Savage, Lib.*
Peter Stoffer, N.D.P.*

Nunavut
Leona Aglukkaq, C.P.C.

Ontario
Harold Albrecht, C.P.C.*
Malcolm Allen, N.D.P.
Dean Allison, C.P.C.*
Charlie Angus, N.D.P.*
Navdeep Bains, Lib.*
John Baird, C.P.C.*
Mauril Bélanger, Lib.*
Carolyn Bennett, Lib.*
Maurizio Bevilacqua, Lib.*

Peter Braid, C.P.C.
Gordon Brown, C.P.C.*
Lois Brown, C.P.C.
Patrick Brown, C.P.C.*
Paul Calandra, C.P.C.
John Cannis, Lib.*
Colin Carrie, C.P.C.*
Chris Charlton, N.D.P.*
Michael Chong, C.P.C.*
Olivia Chow, N.D.P.*
David Christopherson, N.D.P.*
Tony Clement, C.P.C.*
Joe Comartin, N.D.P.*
Bonnie Crombie, Lib.
Patricia Davidson, C.P.C.*
Bob Dechert, C.P.C.
Dean Del Mastro, C.P.C.*
Barry Devolin, C.P.C.*
Paul Dewar, N.D.P.*
Ruby Dhalla, Lib.*
Ken Dryden, Lib.*
Kirsty Duncan, Lib.
Rick Dykstra, C.P.C.*
Diane Finley, C.P.C.*
Jim Flaherty, C.P.C.*
Royal Galipeau, C.P.C.*
Cheryl Gallant, C.P.C.*
Gary Goodyear, C.P.C.*
Claude Gravelle, N.D.P.
Albina Guarnieri, Lib.*
Helena Guergis, C.P.C.*
Martha Hall Findlay, Lib.
Ed Holder, C.P.C.
Mark Holland, Lib.*
Carol Hughes, N.D.P.
Bruce Hyer, N.D.P.
Michael Ignatieff, Lib.*
Andrew Kania, Lib.
Jim Karygiannis, Lib.*
Gerard Kennedy, Lib.
Peter Kent, C.P.C.
Daryl Kramp, C.P.C.*
Guy Lauzon, C.P.C.*
Jack Layton, N.D.P.*
Derek Lee, Lib.*
Pierre Lemieux, C.P.C.*
Ben Lobb, C.P.C.
Dave MacKenzie, C.P.C.*
Gurbax Malhi, Lib.*
Wayne Marston, N.D.P.*
Tony Martin, N.D.P.*
Brian Masse, N.D.P.*
Irene Mathyssen, N.D.P.*
John McCallum, Lib.*
Phil McColeman, C.P.C.
David McGuinty, Lib.*
John McKay, Lib.*
Dan McTeague, Lib.*
Larry Miller, C.P.C.*
Peter Milliken, Lib.*
Maria Minna, Lib.*
Rob Nicholson, C.P.C.*
Rick Norlock, C.P.C.*
Gordon O'Connor, C.P.C.*
Bev Oda, C.P.C.*
Robert Oliphant, Lib.

Glen Pearson, Lib.*
Pierre Poilievre, C.P.C.*
Joe Preston, C.P.C.*
Rob Rae, Lib.
John Rafferty, N.D.P.
Lisa Raitt, C.P.C.
Yasmin Ratansi, Lib.*
Scott Reid, C.P.C.*
Greg Rickford, C.P.C.
Anthony Rota, Lib.*
Gary Schellenberger, C.P.C.*
Judy Sgro, Lib.*
Bev Shipley, C.P.C.*
Mario Silva, Lib.*
Michelle Simson, Lib.
Bruce Stanton, C.P.C.
David Sweet, C.P.C.*
Paul Szabo, Lib.*
Glenn Thibeault, N.D.P.
David Tilson, C.P.C.*
Alan Tonks, Lib.*
Francis Valeriote, Lib.
Dave Van Kesteren, C.P.C.*
Peter Van Loan, C.P.C.*
Joseph Volpe, Lib.*
Mike Wallace, C.P.C.*
Jeff Watson, C.P.C.*
Bryon Wilfert, Lib.*
Stephen Woodworth, C.P.C.
Borys Wrzesnewskyj, Lib.*
Terence Young, C.P.C.

Prince Edward Island
Wayne Easter, Lib.*
Lawrence MacAulay, Lib.*
Shawn Murphy, Lib.*
Gail Shea, C.P.C.

Quebec
Guy André, B.Q.*
André Arthur, Ind.*
Gérard Asselin, B.Q.*
Claude Bachand, B.Q.*
Josée Beaudin, B.Q.
André Bellavance, B.Q.*
Maxime Bernier, C.P.C.*
Bernard Bigras, B.Q.*
Jean-Pierre Blackburn, C.P.C.*
Raynald Blais, B.Q.*
Steven Blaney, C.P.C.*
France Bonsant, B.Q.*
Robert Bouchard, B.Q.*
Sylvie Boucher, C.P.C.*
Diane Bourgeois, B.Q.*
Paule Brunelle, B.Q.*
Lawrence Cannon, C.P.C.*
Serge Cardin, B.Q.*
Robert Carrier, B.Q.*
Denis Coderre, Lib.*
Irwin Cotler, Lib.*
Claude DeBellefeuille, B.Q.*
Nicole Demers, B.Q.*
Johanne Deschamps, B.Q.*
Luc Desnoyers, B.Q.
Stéphane Dion, Lib.*
Jean Dorion, B.Q.
Gilles Duceppe, B.Q.*

Nicolas Dufour, B.Q.
Meili Faille, B.Q.*
Raymonde Folco, Lib.*
Carole Freeman, B.Q.*
Christiane Gagnon, B.Q.*
Marc Garneau, Lib.
Roger Gaudet, B.Q.*
Bernard Généreux, C.P.C.
Jacques Gourde, C.P.C.*
Monique Guay, B.Q.*
Claude Guimond, B.Q.
Michel Guimond, B.Q.*
Marlene Jennings, Lib.*
Jean-Yves Laforest, B.Q.*
Mario Laframboise, B.Q.*
Francine Lalonde, B.Q.*
Carole Lavallée, B.Q.*
Denis Lebel, C.P.C.*
Marc Lemay, B.Q.*
Yves Lessard, B.Q.*
Yvon Lévesque, B.Q.*
Luc Malo, B.Q.*
Serge Ménard, B.Q.*
Alexandra Mendes, Lib.
Maria Mourani, B.Q.*
Thomas Mulcair, N.D.P.*
Richard Nadeau, B.Q.*
Christian Ouellet, B.Q.*
Massimo Pacetti, Lib.*
Daniel Paillé, B.Q.
Pascal-Pierre Paillé, B.Q.
Pierre Paquette, B.Q.*
Christian Paradis, C.P.C.*
Bernard Patry, Lib.*
Daniel Petit, C.P.C.*
Louis Plamondon, B.Q.*
Roger Pomerleau, B.Q.
Marcel Proulx, Lib.*
Pablo Rodriguez, Lib.*
Jean-Yves Roy, B.Q.*
Francis Scarpaleggia, Lib.*
Thierry St.-Cyr, B.Q.*
Ève-Mary Thai Thi Lac, B.Q.*
Justin Trudeau, Lib.
Josée Verner, C.P.C.*
Robert Vincent, B.Q.*
Lise Zarac, Lib.

Saskatchewan
David Anderson, C.P.C.*
Kelly Block, C.P.C.
Ray Broughen, C.P.C.
Garry Breitkreuz, C.P.C.*
Rob Clarke, C.P.C.
Ralph E. Goodale, Lib.*
Randy Hoback, C.P.C.
Ed Komarnicki, C.P.C.*
Tom Lukiwski, C.P.C.*
Gerry Ritz, C.P.C.*
Andrew Scheer, C.P.C.*
Bradley Trost, C.P.C.*
Maurice Vellacott, C.P.C.*
Lynne Yelich, C.P.C.*

Yukon
Larry Bagnell, Lib.*

Ignatieff became interim Liberal Party leader on Dec. 10, 2008, after Stéphane Dion resigned from the position. Initially, Dion stated that he would remain Liberal leader until a formal leadership vote at the party's next convention on May 2, 2009. However, with a general election or a Liberal-New Democratic coalition looming as possibilities after the governor general *prorogued* Parliament (discontinued for a time) in December 2008, the Liberals decided they needed to choose a more permanent leader before Parliament reconvened on Jan. 26, 2009. Dominic LeBlanc and Bob Rae, two contenders for the Liberal leadership, announced that they would withdraw from the race, leaving Ignatieff unchallenged. At the May 2 Liberal convention, Ignatieff won 97 percent of delegates' votes for the party leadership. The Liberals also voted to adopt a one-member, one-vote electoral system for future leadership conventions, to replace its representative delegate system. The Liberals were the last national political party in Canada to adopt this kind of leadership vote.

During his victory speech, Ignatieff spoke about Liberal priorities, including early childhood care and learning, wage equity for women, protecting funding for scientific research, advancements in aboriginal education, and a national standard of eligibility for *employment insurance* (EI)—that is, unemployment benefits. In mid-June, with Liberals threatening to withdraw support for the Conservative government in an upcoming confidence vote, Harper and Ignatieff agreed to establish a two-party, six-member panel to review the employment insurance program.

In a September 1 speech at the Liberals' national caucus meeting in Sudbury, Ontario, Ignatieff said that the Conservatives had failed to protect the most vulnerable Canadians, to create jobs, to defend health care, and to restore public finances. Ignatieff went on to address the prime minister, saying: "Mr. Harper, your time is up. The Liberal Party cannot support this government any further. We will hold it to account. We will oppose it in Parliament."

Ignatieff's words appeared to set the stage for an imminent election. However, the New Democratic Party (NDP), which had opposed the government vocally in earlier confidence votes, and the Bloc Québécois both signaled that they would support the government temporarily. On September 18, the Conservatives survived a confidence vote when both the Bloc and the NDP supported a budget motion that included a popular home-renovation tax credit. NDP leader Jack Layton said his party would support the government until a proposed $1-billion increase in employment insurance funding became law. On October 1, the NDP abstained from voting on a nonconfidence motion introduced by the Liberals in Parliament, thus

ensuring the Conservative government's survival again. Commentators suggested that the NDP, which had criticized previous Liberal abstentions from confidence votes, found itself in the uncomfortable position of supporting the government because its own finances and approval ratings made an election undesirable.

Residential schools. On April 29, nearly one year after Canada's government formally apologized to aboriginal residential school survivors, Pope Benedict XVI expressed sorrow and apologized for the "deplorable conduct" of some Roman Catholics at state-funded residential schools run by the church. Catholic missionaries oversaw nearly three-fourths of the 130 residential schools that operated in Canada from the 1800's to the late 1900's. More than 150,000 First Nations children were forced to attend the schools, which were designed to help the government assimilate them into mainstream Christian society. Many students suffered from emotional, physical, psychological, and sexual abuse at these institutions. Phil Fontaine, then national chief of the Assembly of First Nations, had sought and accepted the pope's apology. The Anglican, Presbyterian, and United churches, which also oversaw some residential schools, previously had apologized for their part in the abuse.

■ William Stos

Canada, Prime Minister of. Con-

servative Prime Minister Stephen Harper appointed nine members to Canada's Senate on Aug. 27, 2009, including several former Conservative Party officials. Harper, who had long supported the election of senators, had vowed not to appoint any, but rather to wait for the provinces to establish a procedure for upper chamber elections. Harper defended his actions by stating that he had appointed only senators who would help advance his goal of an elected Senate. His appointees all pledged to pass legislation as soon as possible limiting Senate terms to eight years.

On November 18, Canadian diplomat Richard Colvin testified that Harper had falsely denied the torture of Afghan detainees turned over to Afghanistan's National Directorate of Security (NDS) by Canada. Colvin said that though he had warned the government beginning in 2006 that transferred prisoners were being tortured in Afghan jails, Harper denied there was evidence of abuse and the government continued transferring detainees to the NDS. A former official of the North Atlantic Treaty Organization (NATO) anonymously informed the media that the prime minister's office had directed NATO to deny prisoner-abuse allegations, despite their possible truth.   ■ William Stos

See also **Canada.**

Canadian provinces. Following a year in which every Canadian province forecast a balanced budget, a number of provincial budgets dropped into deficit spending in 2009. Some notable political incidents also occurred in 2009, including the resignation of Canada's longest-serving premier and the surprise victory of an upstart political party in an Alberta by-election.

Alberta, once Canada's economic engine, faced an unprecedented downturn in its fortunes because of a global economic recession. On April 7, Finance Minister Iris Evans predicted a historically high $4.7-billion deficit for the 2009-2010 fiscal year and a cumulative deficit of $10.3 billion over the next four years (all amounts in Canadian dollars). Alberta also expected to post a $1.4-billion deficit for 2008-2009, despite an initially balanced budget.

A sharp decrease in energy prices, falling corporate investments, and a slumping stock market reduced anticipated revenue for Alberta's government in 2009. Finance Minister Evans revealed that the province had no immediate plans to cut corporate taxes or spend more on infrastructure projects, because Alberta already had spent nearly twice as much as any other province on new infrastructure. Revenue from nonrenewable resources was projected to fall by 52 percent—one of the largest decreases on record—in 2009.

On August 26, Evans issued a revised budget forecast. It projected a $7-billion deficit for 2009-2010 and warned that this number could rise if energy prices remained depressed. In November, however, the government raised its revenue estimate by $3 billion and forecast a smaller deficit of $4.3 billion. Corporate income taxes, higher oil prices, and investments accounted for the predicted revenue increase.

In response to population growth and inflation, Alberta announced spending increases for more than half its government departments. The province also had to change an existing law requiring that budgets be balanced.

On September 14, the Progressive Conservative (PC) party suffered a stunning defeat in a by-election in the Calgary-Glenmore *riding* (electoral district). The party had held the riding since 1969 and has governed Alberta since 1971. Diane Colley-Urquhart, the PC candidate, finished a distant third behind the right-wing Wildrose Alliance and the center-left Liberal Party. Most commentators suggested that the loss offered a rebuke to PC Premier Ed Stelmach. Other experts suggested that the Wildrose victory could signal the Alberta voters' desire for a dramatic change in government.

British Columbia voters went to the polls on May 12, 2009, and reelected the center-right Liberals to a third straight majority government, with 49 seats in the Legislative Assembly. The election campaign contrasted the image of incumbent Premier Gordon Campbell as a strong leader with a call for change from the center-left New Democrats, who won 35 seats.

The first post-election Speech from the Throne, delivered by Lieutenant Governor Steven Point on August 25, warned that the global economic crisis likely would force the government to cut spending and grants, lay off public employees, and freeze public sector wages. In the speech, the government shared plans to review spending and forecast a higher deficit than had been projected in a preelection budget.

Lieutenant Governor Point also announced that $1.6 billion in federal inducements to institute a proposed 12-percent harmonized sales tax (HST) would be used to protect health and education programs. An HST combines the federal and provincial sales taxes into one tax. Opposition to the HST, which would save businesses millions of dollars but tax consumers on previously exempt goods and services, spurred more than a dozen rallies on September 19.

On September 1, Finance Minister Colin Hansen updated his estimate for the 2009-2010 budget deficit from $495 million to $2.8 billion. Hansen said the higher deficit was necessary to accommodate a sustained economic downturn.

The government ministry Fisheries and Oceans Canada reported a catastrophic decline in the Fraser River's sockeye salmon populations in August 2009. Although about 10.6 million salmon had been expected to return to the river to spawn, estimates suggested that fewer than 1 million were present in the river system. The federal government responded by closing commercial and recreational sockeye fishing for the third year in a row. Observers suggested a number of possible causes for the decline, including climate change and disease from nearby fish farms. Healthy numbers of fish migrating out of the Fraser suggested that the fish were dying in the Pacific Ocean and not in the river system itself.

Manitoba. On March 25, then-Finance Minister Greg Selinger *tabled* (proposed) a balanced budget that projected a modest $48-million surplus. The $12.7-billion budget raised tobacco taxes and user fees collected from tobacco companies to pay for new spending initiatives. It also drew $110 million from the provincial rainy-day fund to prevent cutbacks to education, health, and training programs. Infrastructure projects worth $1.6 billion were expected to create about 10,000 jobs. However, the provincial economy was expected to contract by about 0.2 percent.

On August 27, after 10 years as premier and more than 20 years as New Democratic Party (NDP) leader, Gary Doer announced plans to resign from both posts. The next day, the federal

A wildfire blazes in the Okanagan Valley in southern British Columbia at dawn on July 19. Several fires in and around the community of West Kelowna forced the evacuation of more than 10,000 residents from the area.

government announced that Doer would become Canadian ambassador to the United States. The NDP chose Greg Selinger as its new leader on October 17. Two days later, Doer and Selinger assumed their new roles.

New Brunswick. Graydon Nicholas, a former judge, became the province's first aboriginal lieutenant governor in a September 30 ceremony at Government House in Fredericton. During the ceremony, Nicholas also was inducted into the Order of New Brunswick, an honor awarded for contributions to the province's cultural, economic, or social well-being.

On March 17, Liberal Finance Minister Victor Boudreau tabled a budget that included a four-year plan to cut corporate taxes to the lowest in Canada, reduce income tax rates, and merge four income tax brackets into two. The budget predicted a $741-million deficit and estimated that the economy would shrink by 0.3 percent in the 2009-2010 fiscal year. The planned tax cuts and a $1.2-billion, two-year capital spending plan were aimed at making the province less dependent on federal transfer payments.

Newfoundland and Labrador. A judicial inquiry into how hundreds of breast cancer patients received erroneous test results from 1997 to 2005 uncovered failure at all levels of Newfoundland and Labrador's largest health authority, Eastern Health. The tests were intended to determine which treatments patients should receive. As a result of the testing errors, some patients did not receive the most appropriate treatments. On March 3, 2009, provincial

Supreme Court Justice Margaret Cameron reported that poor-quality laboratory work and "practically nonexistent" quality controls had failed patients. In October, victims of the botched lab work settled a class-action lawsuit, initiated in 2006 against Eastern Health, for $17.5 million.

On March 26, 2009, the Progressive Conservative government presented a budget that forecast a $750-million deficit to avoid public-sector job losses and stimulate the economy. Finance Minister Jerome Kennedy said that he expected balanced budgets to return shortly, despite lower royalties from offshore oil drilling. The budget contained a record $6.7 billion in spending, including a $519-million increase across government programs and a previously announced $800 million for investments in provincial infrastructure, including public housing, transportation infrastructure, educational facilities, and health care facilities and equipment.

Nova Scotia voters made history on June 9 when they elected the province's first New Democratic government. The center-left party won a majority government with 31 of 52 seats in the House of Assembly. The Liberals won 11 seats, and the incumbent Progressive Conservatives, who had governed for 10 years, won 10. The new premier, Darrell Dexter, campaigned to keep emergency rooms open, repair rural roads, and remove the *harmonized sales tax* (combined provincial and general sales tax) from electric power bills.

On September 24, Finance Minister Graham Steele tabled the new government's first budget.

Steele said that the fiscal plan, similar to one presented by the Conservatives before the election, would reveal the true state of provincial finances. In contrast with the Conservatives, who forecast a $4-million surplus, the New Democrats projected a $592-million deficit for 2009-2010. The government committed to fulfilling $31 million worth of financial commitments made during the election campaign without increasing the projected deficit.

Ontario. On March 26, 2009, Finance Minister Dwight Duncan presented a budget with a projected $14.1-billion deficit, the largest deficit in Ontario's history. Major budget line items included $32.5 billion over two years for infrastructure projects, $1.2 billion over two years for the creation and renovation of social housing, and Corporate Income Tax cuts for the manufacturing and processing sector.

The budget also included plans to institute a harmonized sales tax by July 1, 2010. The 13-percent HST would reduce businesses' expenses but increase costs to consumers. The government planned to offset the HST with tax relief payments for lower-income households. A fiscal review released on Oct. 22, 2009, revealed that the deficit was expected to reach $24.7 billion.

Ontario Progressive Conservative (PC) leader John Tory suffered a stunning defeat in a March 5 by-election in the traditionally Conservative riding of Haliburton-Kawartha Lakes-Brock. Tory had not held a seat in the provincial legislature since 2007, when he failed to win a seat in a Toronto-area riding. Conservative member of the provincial parliament Laurie Scott agreed to step aside to allow Tory to run for the Haliburton seat in 2009. Following Tory's defeat, commentators suggested that voters in the Haliburton riding had chosen the Liberal candidate, Rick Johnson, because he was local. Tory resigned as PC leader after the by-election. Former Ontario Cabinet Minister Tim Hudak won the PC leadership in a June 27 vote.

Ontario's Liberal government faced a series of spending scandals at public agencies and Crown corporations during the spring and summer. The government agency eHealth Ontario, charged with the task of creating electronic health records for Ontarians, was reported to have spent tens of millions of dollars on contracts closed to outside bidding. These included a $30-million contract awarded to International Business Machines Corporation (IBM) of Armonk, New York, for electronic health record management.

High-priced consultants for eHealth and executives of the Ontario Lottery and Gaming Corporation (OLG) also came under fire for some items that they had charged to their expense accounts. In September, Premier Dalton McGuinty announced new measures to increase accountability for, and transparency of, expense claims. The measures included mandatory online expense-claim training for the 22 largest public agencies in the province.

Prince Edward Island. On April 16, Treasurer Wesley Sheridan tabled a budget that projected increased revenues and spending and an $85-million deficit for the 2009-2010 fiscal year. The budget set aside $28 million for the provincial Department of Health, which planned to establish a new stroke care program at Queen Elizabeth Hospital in Charlottetown. Previously, specialized treatment for stroke patients had not been available in the province. Sheridan also earmarked $17 million for a new wind farm in Summerside and a conference and convention center in Charlottetown.

Quebec. On Feb. 17, 2009, Canada's National Battlefields Commission cancelled a reenactment of the 1759 Battle of the Plains of Abraham. The reenactment, scheduled to take place in Quebec City in August 2009, was intended to commemorate the pivotal battle's 250th anniversary. It was called off after Quebec sovereigntists threatened to hold protests at the event. The sovereigntists, who want Quebec to become independent from Canada, argued that the reenactment would be an insult to their French ancestors. The French lost the 1759 battle to the British, enabling Britain to take much of France's Canadian territory in North America.

On September 12 and 13, 2009, more than 140 people participated in another event in Quebec City to mark the historic Battle of the Plains of Abraham. The event, called "Moulin à paroles," meaning *chatterbox* or *windbag,* featured the reading of creative writing and historical documents related to Quebec's history. The Liberal government of Quebec refused to contribute funding for the event, because it included the reading of the manifesto of the Quebec Liberation Front (Front de libération du Québec, or FLQ), a separatist group that conducted kidnappings and fire bombings in the 1960's and 1970's. In 1970, the FLQ captured and murdered Quebec's then-labor minister, Pierre Laporte. The event's organizers said they wanted to celebrate the history of the French in North America.

On March 19, 2009, then-Finance Minister

Monique Jérôme-Forget tabled a budget that forecast a $3.9-billion deficit for the 2009-2010 fiscal year and three more consecutive years of deficits. The budget included several measures to be implemented on Jan. 1, 2011, including a 1-percent increase in the Quebec Sales Tax and plans to crack down on tax evasion schemes and to adjust user fees for certain government services. An update delivered by Finance Minister Raymond Bachand on Oct. 27, 2009, increased the deficit to $4.7 billion and estimated the economy would contract by 1.5 percent in 2009-2010.

Saskatchewan. On March 18, 2009, conservative Finance Minister Rod Gantefoer presented a balanced budget that included the largest property tax reduction in Saskatchewan history. The budget decreased the amount of taxes that property owners paid for education in the province. Other major line items included $1 billion for building provincial infrastructure, $200 million over two years for a new children's hospital in Saskatoon, and an additional $108.1 million to stabilize farm incomes. A fiscal update on August 14 revealed a dip in projected revenues. However, it also included plans to defer some capital projects and to find other ways to prevent a budget deficit.   ■ William Stos

See also **Canada; Canadian territories; Montreal; Toronto.**

Canadian territories. Canadian
sovereignty in the Arctic was a key priority for Prime Minister Stephen Harper's federal Conservative government in 2009. On August 18, the first full day of his annual Arctic tour, Harper announced the creation of a long-awaited northern development agency. The new Canadian Northern Economic Development Agency (CanNor) was designed to administer federal initiatives and infrastructure programs in the Canadian territories. Based in Iqaluit, Nunavut, and with additional regional offices in Yellowknife, Northwest Territories, and Whitehorse, Yukon, CanNor received a budget of $50 million (all amounts in Canadian dollars) for its first five years. Harper said the agency would help to "unleash the North's true potential."

Harper's five-day tour was intended to show international observers that Canada was serious about protecting its Arctic sovereignty in the face of increased shipping traffic and oil and gas exploration in the region. In the early 2000's, Canada, the United States, Russia, Denmark, and other nations competed for rights to Arctic mineral resources, which included an estimated 90 billion barrels of oil. Access to the Arctic shipping route known as the Northwest Passage, part of which Canada claimed as its internal waters, also was contested.

On Aug. 19, 2009, Harper observed Operation Nanook, a series of exercises asserting Canadian authority in the Baffin Island area. About 700 personnel participated in Nanook 2009, the largest such "sovereignty operation" to date. Nanook included surveillance patrols in the Hudson and Davis straits and a joint military exercise that included all branches of the Canadian Armed Forces, as well as the Canadian Coast Guard. The large scale of the operation was in part a response to recent Russian military flights near Canada's northern border.

Northwest Territories. On February 5, territorial Minister of Finance Michael Miltenberger presented a budget with $246 million earmarked for infrastructure spending. Miltenberger argued that spending on infrastructure would stimulate the territory's economy and help put it on a sound footing. The budget contained some environmentally friendly initiatives, including a new 25-cent tax on plastic grocery bags, increased funding for *hydro* (water) and wind power projects, and new money to make government buildings energy-efficient.

Dozens of senior citizens and their supporters demonstrated outside the Legislative Assembly building in Yellowknife on the day the budget was delivered to protest proposed changes to senior health care coverage. Under proposed changes, nonaboriginal people over 60 years old would lose coverage on prescriptions, dental work, and eyeglasses if their incomes were above a certain level.

Hearings in a conflict-of-interest inquiry involving Premier Floyd Roland ended on October 9. The inquiry involved suspicions that Roland's lover had shared confidential information with him. Roland had had an affair with a Legislative Assembly clerk who attended confidential committee meetings of legislators.

Previously, on February 6, Roland and his Cabinet had narrowly survived a confidence vote. It was the first time that regular members of the government had tried to unseat the premier and the entire Cabinet. The lawmakers who voted "no confidence" said the premier and the Cabinet had not communicated with them regarding controversial policy and spending decisions, including changes to health benefits, a $34-million loan to an aviation company, a $165-million bridge project, and the merging of school and public service boards into regional authorities.

Nunavut Minister of Finance Keith Peterson on June 4 tabled a $1.25-billion "transition budget" intended to provide economic stability. The financial plan contained no tax increases or public-sector job cuts, but included a $29.1-million deficit. The budget, which was the first under Premier Eva Aariak, provided $8.6 million for the implementation of a new Education Act and Official Languages Act, as well as legislation to protect the Inuit languages of Inuktitut and Inuinaqtun. The Official Languages Act, passed by Canada's Senate on June 11, added Inuit languages to Nunavut's other official languages, English and French. The budget also included $300 million for infrastructure projects and funding to create a territorywide recycling program.

Yukon Premier and Minister of Finance Dennis Fentie on March 19 presented a $1-billion budget that maintained a surplus for the seventh straight year while increasing government spending to stimulate the economy. The budget, which contained no new tax increases, included a 13.8-percent increase in transportation infrastructure spending, $21.6 million for a new territorial jail, and $20 million for Yukon's health care system.

On August 21, the final day of Stephen Harper's Arctic tour, the prime minister announced that his government would contribute $71 million to the Yukon Energy Corporation to help it upgrade a hydroelectric dam near the community of Mayo. Up to 300 people were expected to begin work on the project, which included plans to connect Yukon's northern and southern energy grids, resulting in a more stable power system.   ■ William Stos

See also **Canada.**

Cape Verde. See Africa.

Census. The United States Census Bureau estimated that the nation's total population on Jan. 1, 2009, was 305,529,237—an increase of 0.9 percent from Jan. 1, 2008. Throughout 2009, the bureau released data on recent demographic and social changes, several of which were attributed to the country's economic slump.

Income and poverty. From 2007 to 2008, real median household income in the United States fell 3.6 percent, from $52,163 to $50,303, according to a report released on Sept. 10, 2009. This decline offset the income increases of the previous three years. The number of U.S. residents in poverty rose significantly from 2007 to 2008, going from 37.3 million (12.5 percent of the population) to 39.8 million (13.2 percent). The number of U.S. residents without health insurance rose from 45.7 million (15.3 percent of the population) to 46.3 million (15.4 percent).

Mobility. From March 2007 to March 2008, 35.2 million people (11.9 percent of the population) moved to a new residence, according to data released on April 22, 2009. This was the smallest number of movers since 1962 and the lowest mover rate since the bureau began tracking mover data in 1948.

Population profile. On Sept. 21, 2009, the bureau released a variety of data for 2008 as part of its annual American Community Survey. For the first time since at least 1970, the number of foreign-born U.S. residents declined. There were about 38 million such residents in 2008 (12.5 percent of the population), down slightly from 38.1 million in 2007. The median value of a home fell to $197,600 in 2008 after rising steadily since 2000, and the homeownership rate fell to 66.6 percent in 2008, down from 67.2 percent in 2007. Also, from 2007 to 2008, the percentage of workers who drove alone to work fell slightly, to 75.5 percent, and the percentage of carpoolers and public transportation users rose slightly, to 10.7 percent and 5 percent, respectively.

Minorities. The United States continued to become more racially and ethnically diverse from 2007 to 2008. The minority population—including Hispanics, blacks, Asians, American Indians, Alaska Natives, Native Hawaiians, and other Pacific Islanders—reached 104.6 million on July 1, 2008, the bureau reported on May 14, 2009. This figure was 34 percent of the total population. The 199.5 million non-Hispanic, single-race whites made up the other 66 percent. Hispanics were the largest and fastest-growing minority group.

Age. The population also continued to get older from 2007 to 2008. The median age was 36.8 on July 1, 2008, up from 36.7 in 2007 and 35.4 in 2000, the bureau reported on May 14, 2009. There were 38.9 million people 65 or older (12.8 percent of the population) in 2008, as well as 191.2 million working-age (18-64) adults (62.9 percent) and 73.9 million children (24.3 percent).

Fastest-growing areas. In late 2008 and in 2009, the bureau announced which U.S. areas had the fastest population growth rates from July 1, 2007, to July 1, 2008. Utah was the fastest-growing state, with a 2.5-percent increase, and Arizona was second (2.3 percent). The Raleigh-Cary area of North Carolina grew by 4.3 percent, the fastest rate among metropolitan areas, and Austin-Round Rock, Texas, was second (3.8 percent). Among cities with 100,000 people or more, New Orleans grew 8.2 percent, as did Round Rock, Texas. New Orleans's 2008 population of 311,853 was still well below its 2005 population of 455,046 before Hurricane Katrina struck.

Preparations for the 2010 census were in full swing in 2009. Census officials announced that, unlike in previous censuses, there would be no "long form" questionnaire sent to a subset of people, but only a 10-question "short form" sent to every U.S. residence. Officials also announced that, for the first time, the census would record and release counts of same-sex couples who self-identify as husbands or wives.   ■ Mike Lewis

See also **City; Immigration; Population; State government.**

Central African Republic. See Africa.
Chad. See Africa.

Chemistry. A new way to fight the most challenging infections—using a chemical compound derived from a sea sponge—was announced in February 2009 by chemist Peter D. R. Moeller of the National Oceanic and Atmospheric Administration's Hollings Marine Laboratory in Charleston, South Carolina. Moeller and his team reported that they had isolated a ringed *organic* (carbon-based) compound from a hardy sponge capable of surviving in unfavorable environmental conditions. In laboratory experiments, the scientists found that the compound, named ageliferin, makes disease-causing, antibiotic-resistant microbes vulnerable to antibiotics again.

Moeller explained that ageliferin makes the "superbugs" susceptible to antibiotics by breaking down tough clusters they form, called biofilms, which normally provide a protective layer against antibiotics. Moeller's team demonstrated in the laboratory that antibiotic-resistant bacteria that cause ear infections, food poisoning, septicemia, and whooping cough can be destroyed by antibiotics if they are first exposed to ageliferin. Even methicillin-resistant *Staphylococcus aureus*, a bacterium notorious for killing thousands of people each year in the United States, was "tamed" with ageliferin.

Moeller noted that further research was needed before drugs containing ageliferin or ageliferinlike compounds become available as antibiotic "helpers."

Insect antenna jamming. The carbon dioxide that you exhale serves as a beacon that attracts mosquitoes in search of a blood meal. For hundreds of millions of people, a mosquito bite can cause infection that results in serious illness, such as elephantiasis, malaria, or sleeping sickness, as well as encephalitis, coma, or death from West Nile virus. *Entomologist* (insect expert) Anandasankar Ray and biochemist Stephanie Turner, both of the University of California at Riverside, reported in August that they had discovered a way to prevent mosquitoes from sensing carbon dioxide—potentially making human beings less visible to the pesky insects.

The scientists made the discovery while investigating why fruit flies—which emit carbon dioxide when under stress and, thus, associate it with danger—fly toward fruit that gives off that gas. Ray and Turner found that the fruit emits organic compounds that "jam" the nerve cell sensors on antennae that detect carbon dioxide.

Further investigation showed that these same organic compounds, including butanol and hexanol, also jam the antennae carbon dioxide sensors of mosquitoes in the genus *Culex*, the group of mosquitoes that spread elephantiasis and West Nile virus. The researchers found that the compounds have a long-lasting effect in insect repel-

lents at lower concentrations than the leading repellent, DEET. In addition, the investigators reported that the compounds can be easily and inexpensively produced in the laboratory.

Ray and Turner noted that before repellents and masking agents containing the compounds become available, the compounds have to be evaluated for safety for people and the environment. The scientists were also testing the best methods of application—such as aerosol versus lotion—and evaluating the compounds for effectiveness against other disease-carrying insect pests, including other kinds of mosquitoes and tsetse flies.

Tiny ribbons. A method of creating tiny carbon-based "ribbons" that might be used to replace silicon in microelectronic components was published in April by a team of researchers at Stanford University in California led by chemist Hongjie Dai. The method was based on nanotechnology, the manipulation of individual atoms and molecules to create larger structures.

Scientists have pursued the creation of carbon-based electronic devices, including so-called graphene nanoribbons, since the 1980's. Scientists had expected that such devices could function as *semiconductors*, materials that conduct electric current better than insulators but not as well as conductors. However, previous attempts at producing these items had been unsuccessful in creating nanoribbons of sufficient quality and in sufficient quantity.

Dai's team achieved success by splicing, or unzipping, *nanotubes*, tiny tubular structures made of carbon atoms. The researchers first placed nanotubes on a *substrate* (base) and coated them with a film of *polymers* (chainlike compounds made of two or more simple molecules). The film covered the surface of each nanotube, except for a thin strip where the tube contacted the substrate.

When the researchers peeled off the polymer film, the nanotubes came off with it—exposing the thin polymer-free strip on each tube. The scientists then used a chemical etching process to slice open each nanotube along the polymer-free strip. The team next removed the polymer from the rest of the split nanotubes, leaving behind well-defined graphene nanoribbons.

Using this method, according to Dai, tens of thousands of nanoribbons can be made efficiently and simultaneously. Dai's team also confirmed that the nanoribbons worked as semiconductors at room temperature. Dai noted that more research was needed to increase yields and to improve the quality of the nanoribbons—as well as to compare the advantages and disadvantages of the graphene nanoribbon semiconductors versus traditional silicon semiconductors.

■ Peter Andrews

Chess. In one of the greatest chess tournament performances ever by a teenager, 18-year-old Magnus Carlsen of Norway won the Nanjing Pearl Spring tournament in China in October 2009. At the tournament's end, Carlsen was well ahead of a field that included the world's top-rated player at the time, Veselin Topalov of Bulgaria. Carlsen continued to play well in November at the Tal Memorial tournament in Moscow—one of the strongest of invitational tournaments. He came in a close second to former world champion Vladimir Kramnik of Russia. The points earned in this tournament allowed Carlsen to overtake Topalov as top-rated player in the world. Carlsen became the fifth player in history, and the youngest ever, to reach a World Chess Federation rating of more than 2800.

United States tournaments. In May, Hikaru Nakamura won the U.S. Chess Championship, at which both men and women competed. The tournament was held at the Chess Club and Scholastic Center of Saint Louis. Rising star Robert Hess, 17—who has qualified for the highest title in chess, grandmaster—came in second by one-half point, the narrowest possible margin. At the same location in October, Anna Zatonskih dominated the U.S. Women's Championship, winning it for the third time. In August, Dmitry Gurevich captured his third U.S. Open title by winning the playoff for the 110th annual U.S. Open Championship, held in Indianapolis.

Young American champions. Every four years, the United States Chess Federation (USCF), which sanctions all official events in the United States, combines its annual high school, middle school, and elementary school championships into a "Supernational." In April 2009, more than 5,000 students from around the nation gathered in Nashville for the fourth such event. Former world champion—and one-time candidate for president of Russia—Garry Kasparov, women's world champion Alexandra Kosteniuk of Russia, and U.S. astronaut Greg Chamitoff gave presentations to the participants. Stuyvesant High School of New York City won the K-12 team championship. Solomon Schechter School of Westchester of Hartsdale, New York, won the K-9 team title. Mission San Jose Elementary School of Fremont, California, won the K-6 team championship.

In July, 14-year-old Andrew Ng won the Cadet Championship of the U.S. Chess Federation in Crossville, Tennessee. The tournament is limited to the top eight players under age 16. Ray Robson won the U.S. Junior Closed Championship, limited to the top eight players under age 21, in Milwaukee in July. At 14, Robson was the youngest player to compete in the tournament.

■ Al Lawrence

Chicago suffered a painful defeat in October 2009 when the city became the first of four "candidate cities" to be eliminated from a competition to host the 2016 Olympic Games. The International Olympic Committee (IOC) chose Rio de Janeiro, Brazil, to host the first Games in South America. Chicago's early loss was all the more galling after United States President Barack Obama, a long-time Chicago resident, stumped for the city at the IOC meeting in Copenhagen, Denmark. Rio's winning bid also came at the expense of Madrid, Spain, and Tokyo, Japan.

New Cubs owner. The Chicago Cubs of baseball's National League finalized a deal on Oct. 27, 2009, to sell the franchise to the family of billionaire businessman Joe Ricketts at a cost of $845 million. Tom Ricketts, a son, became the controlling owner of the team. The Cubs had filed for bankruptcy on October 12 as part of a move to protect the baseball club's assets from creditors of its parent, Tribune Company. The Tribune Company had filed for bankruptcy in December 2008 but had exempted the team and its assets from that deal.

New name for iconic building. On July 16, 2009, the Sears Tower, the tallest building in the United States, was officially renamed the Willis Tower. London-based insurance broker Willis Group Holdings, Ltd., gained naming rights to the 1,450-foot (442-meter) skyscraper as part of a lease agreement. Two weeks earlier, the tower had opened new glass-enclosed viewing boxes that extend from its Skydeck observation floor, offering visitors the opportunity to take in the view more than 1,300 feet (396 meters) below their feet.

A modern classic. The new Modern Wing at the Art Institute of Chicago opened on May 16. The $300-million, 264,000-square-foot (24,500-square-meter) addition by Italian architect Renzo Piano is linked by footbridge to the city's celebrated Millennium Park.

Airport deal axed. A $2.5-billion deal to lease Midway International Airport to a group of private investors fell through in April after the group failed to raise the necessary funds. The lease deal had been approved by the Chicago City Council in 2008.

Newspaper sold. On Oct. 8, 2009, a federal bankruptcy court judge approved the sale of the Chicago Sun-Times Media Group to a group led by local businessman Jim Tyree. Tyree's group paid $5 million for the Sun-Times and its affiliated publications and took on about $20 million of the Media Group's debts. The Media Group had filed for bankruptcy protection in March.

School violence. In September, the video-

More than 20,000 Oprah fans gather on Chicago's Michigan Avenue on September 8 to kick off the 24th season of "The Oprah Winfrey Show." The season premiere shut down Michigan Avenue for 2 1/2 days, rerouted traffic throughout the downtown, and ran up $54,832 worth of city services, for which the talk-show queen quickly reimbursed Chicago taxpayers.

taped beating death of 16-year-old student Derrion Albert highlighted the rise in violent deaths among school-age children in Chicago. In the period from September 2008 to September 2009, nearly 400 Chicago students were shot, according to a spokesperson from the Chicago Public Schools (CPS).

Albert, a sophomore honor roll student at Christian Fenger Academy High School on Chicago's South Side, was beaten to death seven blocks from the school after being swept into a street fight.

United States Attorney General Eric Holder and U.S. Secretary of Education Arne Duncan held a press conference on Oct. 7, 2009, to bring national attention to the problem of youth violence. They announced a $500,000 federal grant to help

Fenger-area students. Chicago schools chief Ron Huberman also announced a $30-million safety plan that targets high school students at risk of becoming victims of violence.

Corruption. Al Sanchez of the Hispanic Democratic Organization (HDO) was convicted on March 23 of four counts of mail fraud. In December, a federal judge overturned the conviction and ordered a new trial on the grounds that prosecutors did not disclose the criminal past of a key witness. In 2007, federal prosecutors indicted the former top Daley aide on charges of favoring HDO campaign workers with jobs, promotions, and raises.   ■ Ken Shenkman

See also **Art: A Special Report; News bytes. Children's books.** See **Literature for children.**

Chile. On Dec. 13, 2009, former senator Sebastián Piñera of the right-wing National Renewal Party won the first round in Chile's presidential election. Piñera was to face Eduardo Frei of the incumbent, center-left Concertación (Convergence) coalition in a runoff election scheduled for Jan. 17, 2010.

To minimize the impact of the global downturn, President Michelle Bachelet on Jan. 6, 2009, drew on Chilean reserves to mount a $4-billion stimulus package—the largest in the country's history. The funds were meant to create 100,000 jobs and provide Chileans with tax relief. To offset declining revenues from copper, the major source of Chile's export earnings, the stimulus included $1 billion in capital for Codelco, the state-owned copper company.

In September, Chilean judge Victor Montiglio issued warrants for the arrest of 129 former security officers. The officers, who had worked for the Dina secret police agency, were tied to the disappearances of leftists and the killing of Communist party leaders during the dictatorship of General Augusto Pinochet from 1973 to 1990.

◼ Nathan A. Haverstock

See also **Latin America.**

China celebrated the 60th anniversary of the establishment of its Communist government on Oct. 1, 2009. Under firm control of a Communist Party that increasingly applied capitalist economics, its economic output in 2009 surpassed that of Germany, according to figures from China's National Bureau of Statistics. China's economy became the world's third largest, behind only those of the United States and Japan.

Foreign economists expected China's overall output to surpass Japan's in a few years, but noted that more than 100 other countries still had higher incomes per person than China. The incomes of China's 1.3 billion people averaged less than $3,000 a year, with a wide gap between urban incomes and much lower rural ones.

The anniversary was marked by the country's largest-ever parade, in Beijing's Tiananmen Square. The parade was, however, closed to the general public. Hu Jintao, China's president and the Communist

Party's general secretary, told invited viewers that China had "realized the goal of the great rejuvenation of the Chinese nation." Its economic output had grown drastically since reforms in 1979 began moving China away from policies of the Communist state's founder, Mao Zedong.

Slowdown. Economic growth slowed in late 2008 and early 2009, mainly as a result of the global economic downturn. Foreign demand for China's exports fell, and an agriculture ministry survey released in February 2009 found that more than 20 million migrant workers from rural inland China had lost their jobs in the coastal factory towns that had boomed on export orders. By April, exports were 22.6 percent lower than a year earlier.

Hu's government introduced an economic stimulus package equivalent to $586 billion on Nov. 9, 2008. Many local governments were unable to match funds from Beijing, the state auditor reported on May 18, 2009. This limited the government's plan to increase employment for stimulus-funded infrastructure and public works projects.

Nevertheless, the stimulus plan began to show results. With the government providing huge tax breaks and other help to exporters, many factories had reopened by September. China's government-controlled banks provided $1.2 trillion in extra lending to consumers and businesses. Auto sales in August jumped 82 percent higher than a year earlier.

China's overall economy surged back above its long-term annual growth rate of more than

United States President Barack Obama tours parts of the Great Wall of China during his November visit. In China, Obama met with Premier Wen Jiabao to discuss trade, climate change, and international security.

Chinese sailors march in Beijing's Tiananmen Square during the celebration of the 60th anniversary of the establishment of China's Communist government. The parade, the largest ever mounted in China, was closed to the general public, but televised.

8 percent. Although Premier Wen Jiabao warned in a September 10 speech to the World Economic Forum that "China's economic rebound is unstable, unbalanced, and not yet solid," by late September the government began to slow down investment in six industries, including aluminum, steel, and cement. With the country already building the world's largest wind and solar power projects, the government also restricted manufacturing of equipment for such energy fields. Chinese economists worried that too-rapid expansion in these sectors could cause a boom-and-bust cycle.

Drought. The worst drought in 50 years hurt China's economy regionally in 2009. The government announced on August 21 that 4.61 million people were short of water in the north, and central areas were also threatened. After 2008's bumper corn crop, 2009 yields were expected to be down by 9.7 percent.

Military. The 60th anniversary parade marked China's increasing world importance in military as well as economic areas. The country had depended for years on high-tech weaponry bought from Russia, but the parade featured missiles and tanks, plus jet fighters overhead, that had all been built in China. Chinese com-

mentaries on the parade stressed the nation's commitment to peace.

With China's military spending growing at well over 10 percent a year for many years, it had developed modern armed forces able to project power well beyond its borders. In January, Chinese naval vessels arrived in the Gulf of Aden, off Africa's eastern coast, to protect Chinese merchant ships against pirates based in Somalia. The navy deployment was the first beyond China's home waters in modern history.

In March, a United States Navy surveillance ship was harassed by Chinese vessels in international waters 75 miles (120 kilometers) south of China's submarine base on Hainan Island. After military talks by the two countries on maritime safety, China called for a halt to U.S. offshore surveillance operations.

Pollution, a long-standing problem from China's headlong industrial growth, remained troublesome in 2009. In August, officials said that more than 1,300 children living near a manganese processing plant in Hunan Province had lead poisoning. By October, officials counted more than 3,000 children nationwide with memory loss and other ill effects of lead pollution.

China passed the United States in 2007 as the world's leading emitter of greenhouse gases, which many scientists believe contribute to global warming. Building coal-powered generating plants at a rapid rate to meet growing demand for electricity, China was on track to emit more such gases in the next 30 years than the United States had in its history, U.S. Energy Secretary Steven Chu warned on July 15, 2009. In September, Chinese economists estimated a cost of $438 billion a year to cut China's emissions significantly and called upon Western nations to help fund projects to reach this goal. The International Energy Agency announced on September 20 that Chinese targets for reducing emissions could make the country a world leader in combating climate change.

Foreign business. Abroad, government-owned enterprises bought companies, technology, and resources in 2009. In February, China made $25 billion in loans to Russia for promises of 300,000 barrels of oil a day for 20 years. China made a similar deal with Brazil in May, and another with Venezuela in September.

Efforts to guarantee Chinese iron ore supplies by buying an Australian mining company, Rio Tinto, were rebuffed, however. In August, four Rio Tinto negotiators working toward new trade contracts were arrested in Shanghai on suspicion of commercial bribery and stealing trade secrets. Foreign businessmen said the case could scare off foreign investment in China and limit countries' willingness to have Chinese investment.

Companies in India complained in June that China was hurting their businesses by selling products there below cost. They asked the Indian government to impose tougher safety and quality checks on Chinese imports. In response to these complaints, India's government imposed quality restrictions on mobile phones, toys, dairy products, and other goods.

Xinjiang Province in western China was torn in July by the country's worst ethnic unrest in decades. The government had since 1949 been settling ethnic Han Chinese people in the historic land of Turkic-speaking, Sunni Muslim Uygur (also spelled Uighur) people. Settlers raised the Han minority in Xinjiang to about 40 percent of the population. With Beijing's backing, they came to dominate political, economic, and cultural life. The provincial capital, Urümqi, became a predominantly Han city. Uygur resentment flared sporadically in protests, riots, and bombings.

Trouble began after two Uygur workers were killed in a fight with Han Chinese in Guangdong Province on June 25, 2009. On July 5, Uygurs demonstrated in Urümqi to demand an investigation into the incident. When police tried to break up the demonstration, violence erupted and many people were killed. Chinese officials said most of the deaths that day were of ethnic Han, but Uygurs claimed that the official reports were inaccurate and that the majority of the dead were Uygurs. Over several days of continued violence between Uygurs and Han Chinese, officials said 197 people were killed and more than 1,700 others were injured. Police detained more than 1,500 people across the province in connection with the riots.

In late August and early September, rumors spread in Urümqi that Uygurs were sticking Han with hypodermic needles containing poisons,

radioactive substances, or HIV. Some 530 people reported such attacks, but officials said none of the victims exhibited signs of poisonous, viral, or radioactive substances.

The government blamed the trouble on foreign-based Uygurs seeking independence for their homeland. Local Uygurs and foreign political observers felt, however, that the trouble was a local reaction to domination by the Han. On November 9, the government announced that it had executed nine people for their roles in the riots. The government did not provide specifics, but international affairs experts believed that the dead consisted of eight Uygurs and one Han. In December, more people believed to be Uygurs were sentenced to death.

Executions. After executing far more prisoners in 2008 than any other nation—1,718 by one estimate—China announced in July 2009 that it would change criminal laws and issue more suspended death sentences. The change would reduce executions to "an extremely small number," according to the government.

The vice minister of health, Huang Jiefu, said in August that most organs used in Chinese medical transplants had come from executed prisoners. He announced a voluntary organ donor program.

■ Henry S. Bradsher

See also **Asia; Australia; Disasters; Economics, World; International trade; Pacific Islands; Taiwan.**

City. Mayors from around the United States gathered in Providence, Rhode Island, from June 12 to June 16, 2009, for the 77th annual meeting of the United States Conference of Mayors (USCM). The Washington, D.C.-based USCM is a *nonpartisan* (politically unaffiliated) organization made up of mayors of cities with populations of at least 30,000. Among the many topics addressed by the municipal leaders were budget shortfalls, funding for infrastructure improvement, energy efficiency, and programs for helping released prisoners reenter communities.

Budget shortfalls. Many large cities in the United States faced budget shortfalls in excess of $100 million, and most cities of all sizes had shortfalls representing substantial portions of their total budgets. Tom Cochran, chief executive officer and executive director of the USCM, presented that information to the USCM meeting in a report on the budgets of 94 cities. Cochran noted that the budget shortfalls were related to the nationwide economic recession.

According to the report, the recession reduced city funds in several ways, such as through cuts in state financial aid, less tax revenue as a result of declining property values, and less sales tax and income tax revenue. City leaders took various actions in 2009 to address the bud-

50 LARGEST CITIES IN THE UNITED STATES

Rank	City	Population*
1.	New York, NY	8,414,579
2.	Los Angeles, CA	3,841,900
3.	Chicago, IL	2,858,583
4.	Houston, TX	2,301,952
5.	Phoenix, AZ	1,604,514
6.	Philadelphia, PA	1,444,165
7.	San Antonio, TX	1,383,818
8.	Dallas, TX	1,291,572
9.	San Diego, CA	1,287,578
10.	San Jose, CA	962,684
11.	Detroit, MI	909,218
12.	San Francisco, CA	820,213
13.	Jacksonville, FL	815,114
14.	Indianapolis, IN	801,865
15.	Austin, TX	778,575
16.	Columbus, OH	761,029
17.	Fort Worth, TX	734,219
18.	Charlotte, NC	707,895
19.	Memphis, TN	667,657
20.	Baltimore, MD	635,876
21.	El Paso, TX	621,542
22.	Boston, MA	613,237
23.	Denver, CO	611,231
24.	Seattle, WA	607,327
25.	Milwaukee, WI	605,410
26.	Nashville, TN	602,197
27.	Washington, DC	595,149
28.	Portland, OR	565,567
29.	Las Vegas, NV	563,639
30.	Oklahoma City, OK	558,721
31.	Atlanta, GA	558,317
32.	Louisville, KY	557,434
33.	Tucson, AZ	547,938
34.	Albuquerque, NM	531,293
35.	Fresno, CA	482,271
36.	Sacramento, CA	468,559
37.	Mesa, AZ	468,294
38.	Long Beach, CA	461,812
39.	Kansas City, MO	454,427
40.	Omaha, NE	443,963
41.	Virginia Beach, VA	432,476
42.	Cleveland, OH	428,728
43.	Miami, FL	424,459
44.	Raleigh, NC	409,455
45.	Oakland, CA	408,036
46.	Tulsa, OK	387,327
47.	Minneapolis, MN	384,733
48.	Colorado Springs, CO	383,530
49.	Arlington, TX	378,978
50.	Honolulu, HI	374,622

*2009 World Book estimates based on data from the U.S. Census Bureau.

50 LARGEST METROPOLITAN AREAS IN THE UNITED STATES

Rank	Metropolitan area*	Population†
1.	New York–Northern New Jersey–Long Island, NY-NJ-PA	19,072,390
2.	Los Angeles–Long Beach–Santa Ana, CA	12,892,048
3.	Chicago–Naperville–Joliet, IL-IN-WI	9,630,405
4.	Dallas–Fort Worth–Arlington, TX	6,474,104
5.	Houston–Sugar Land–Baytown, TX	5,881,254
6.	Philadelphia–Camden–Wilmington, PA-NJ-DE-MD	5,855,904
7.	Atlanta–Sandy Springs–Marietta, GA	5,532,281
8.	Miami–Fort Lauderdale–Pompano Beach, FL	5,427,989
9.	Washington–Arlington–Alexandria, DC-VA-MD-WV	5,404,727
10.	Boston–Cambridge–Quincy, MA-NH	4,545,836
11.	Phoenix–Mesa–Scottsdale, AZ	4,432,424
12.	Detroit–Warren–Livonia, MI	4,401,698
13.	San Francisco–Oakland–Fremont, CA	4,314,603
14.	Riverside–San Bernardino–Ontario, CA	4,202,435
15.	Seattle–Tacoma–Bellevue, WA	3,396,227
16.	Minneapolis–St. Paul–Bloomington, MN-WI	3,263,654
17.	San Diego–Carlsbad–San Marcos, CA	3,024,747
18.	St. Louis, MO–IL	2,831,456
19.	Tampa–St. Petersburg–Clearwater, FL	2,767,185
20.	Baltimore–Towson, MD	2,673,877
21.	Denver–Aurora, CO	2,559,189
22.	Pittsburgh, PA	2,344,200
23.	Portland–Vancouver–Beaverton, OR-WA	2,249,909
24.	Cincinnati–Middletown, OH-KY-IN	2,173,572
25.	Sacramento–Arden-Arcade–Roseville, CA	2,136,631
26.	Orlando–Kissimmee, FL	2,096,706
27.	San Antonio, TX	2,086,332
28.	Cleveland–Elyria–Mentor, OH	2,079,077
29.	Kansas City, MO-KS	2,024,316
30.	Las Vegas–Paradise, NV	1,925,196
31.	San Jose–Sunnyvale–Santa Clara, CA	1,845,750
32.	Columbus, OH	1,794,132
33.	Charlotte–Gastonia–Concord, NC–SC	1,770,279
34.	Indianapolis–Carmel, IN	1,740,651
35.	Austin–Round Rock, TX	1,723,329
36.	Virginia Beach–Norfolk–Newport News, VA-NC	1,661,271
37.	Providence–New Bedford–Fall River, RI-MA	1,592,205
38.	Nashville-Davidson–Murfreesboro–Franklin, TN	1,586,871
39.	Milwaukee–Waukesha–West Allis, WI	1,554,407
40.	Jacksonville, FL	1,336,183
41.	Memphis, TN-MS-AR	1,297,003
42.	Louisville/Jefferson County, KY–IN	1,257,578
43.	Richmond, VA	1,243,922
44.	Oklahoma City, OK	1,224,131
45.	Hartford–West Hartford–East Hartford, CT	1,194,451
46.	New Orleans–Metairie–Kenner, LA	1,159,193
47.	Salt Lake City, UT	1,140,506
48.	Raleigh–Cary, NC	1,140,427
49.	Birmingham–Hoover, AL	1,127,639
50.	Buffalo–Niagara Falls, NY	1,119,051

*The U.S. Census Bureau defines a metropolitan area as a large population nucleus with adjacent communities having a high degree of economic and social integration.

†2009 World Book estimates based on data from the U.S. Census Bureau and other sources.

get shortfalls. Among these actions were hiring freezes, elimination of positions, wage and benefit cuts, cancellation of projects, increases in fees and fines, and cuts in services (including code enforcement, landscaping, and street repairs).

Short-changing infrastructure. Major metropolitan areas did not receive their fair share of federal funds for infrastructure improvement under the so-called "economic stimulus" plan (the American Recovery and Reinvestment Act of 2009). That conclusion was contained in an economic report presented at the USCM meeting. The term "infrastructure" refers to such facilities as bridges, roads, hospitals, and schools. The report blamed the problem on the state governors and highway departments in charge of distributing the funds.

The report noted that the 85 largest metropolitan areas in the United States accounted for 73 percent of the U.S. *gross domestic product* (value of all goods and services produced in a given period). Despite their importance to the nation's economy, these metropolitan areas received only 48 percent of the "stimulus" funds. The report also concluded that large cities did not receive enough federal funds for projects to relieve traffic congestion.

Energy-efficiency opportunities. An opinion survey of 140 mayors in 40 states released at the USCM conference revealed several problems—as well as opportunities—related to urban infrastructure. Approximately half of the surveyed mayors agreed that the recession was an obstacle to their efforts to improve energy efficiency and fight climate change. Nevertheless, two-thirds of the mayors viewed technological innovations for addressing energy and environmental problems as an "enormous" economic opportunity for cities.

Among the technologies favored by the mayors were energy-efficient lighting, renewable energy sources (such as solar and wind power), and "smart grids" for distributing electricity. Smart grids are computerized electricity networks designed to save energy, reduce costs, and increase reliability. In addition, three-fourths of the mayors of large cities favored the expansion of public mass transit systems.

Helping released prisoners. A special task force reported at the USCM meeting that the recession caused local governments to reduce spending on services designed to help released prisoners reenter communities. The report was based on a survey of officials in 79 cities of various sizes.

The task force described a general lack of funding for reentry services, including the two "most essential" services—helping ex-prisoners find jobs and homes. The task force noted that

50 LARGEST URBAN CENTERS IN THE WORLD

Rank	Urban center*	Population
1.	Tokyo, Japan	35,983,000
2.	Mumbai, India	19,729,000
3.	São Paulo, Brazil	19,346,000
4.	Mexico City, Mexico	19,330,000
5.	New York City, U.S.	19,323,000
6.	Delhi, India	16,716,000
7.	Shanghai, China	15,501,000
8.	Kolkata, India	15,306,000
9.	Dhaka, Bangladesh	14,376,000
10.	Buenos Aires, Argentina	13,011,000
11.	Karachi, Pakistan	12,729,000
12.	Los Angeles, U.S.	12,686,000
13.	Cairo, Egypt	12,301,000
14.	Rio de Janeiro, Brazil	12,029,000
15.	Beijing, China	11,514,000
16.	Manila, Philippines	11,460,000
17.	Osaka, Japan	11,326,000
18.	Moscow, Russia	10,483,000
19.	Istanbul, Turkey	10,390,000
20.	Lagos, Nigeria	10,187,000
21.	Paris, France	9,946,000
22.	Seoul, South Korea	9,771,000
23.	Jakarta, Indonesia	9,468,000
24.	Guangzhou, China	9,238,000
25.	Chicago, U.S.	9,147,000
26.	Kinshasa, Congo	8,621,000
27.	London, U.K.	8,608,000
28.	Lima, Peru	8,264,000
29.	Bogotá, Colombia	8,161,000
30.	Tehran, Iran	8,100,000
31.	Shenzhen, China	7,934,000
32.	Wuhan, China	7,422,000
33.	Chennai, India	7,419,000
34.	Hong Kong, China	7,351,000
35.	Tianjin, China	7,350,000
36.	Bengaluru, India	7,094,000
37.	Lahore, Pakistan	6,910,000
38.	Bangkok, Thailand	6,837,000
39.	Taipei, Taiwan	6,825,000
40.	Hyderabad, India	6,634,000
41.	Chongqing, China	6,591,000
42.	Santiago, Chile	5,833,000
43.	Belo Horizonte, Brazil	5,831,000
44.	Miami, U.S.	5,712,000
45.	Madrid, Spain	5,707,000
46.	Ahmadabad, India	5,617,000
47.	Philadelphia, U.S.	5,586,000
48.	Ho Chi Minh City, Vietnam	5,573,000
49.	Toronto, Canada	5,378,000
50.	Baghdad, Iraq	5,259,000

Source: 2009 estimates based on data from the United Nations and other official government sources.

*The United Nations defines an urban center as a city surrounded by a continuous built-up area having a high population density.

these services were crucial for keeping ex-prisoners from returning to criminal activities.

City livability awards. Mayors Joseph O. Riley, Jr., of Charleston, South Carolina, and Kevin C. Foy, of Chapel Hill, North Carolina, were awarded first-place honors in the 2009 City Livability Awards Program in June. The awards, sponsored by the USCM and Waste Management, Inc., of Houston, recognize outstanding mayoral leadership in implementing programs that improve quality of life in cities.

Mayor Riley was honored for the "Palmetto Artisan Program," which helped youth who were selling artificial roses made of palmetto fronds learn how to become legitimate business vendors. The youth, many of whom had generated complaints from the public because of their overly aggressive behavior, were taught business, customer service, and social skills in the program. Mayor Foy was honored for his role in creating the Chapel Hill Transit fare-free system, one of the largest fare-free transit systems in the United States. The system, which is free for anyone in Chapel Hill, resulted in an increase in transit ridership of more than 130 percent.

Panhandler clampdown. As noted in an article in *USA Today* in June, city officials across the United States increasingly cracked down on panhandlers (beggars) in 2009. Among the measures being taken were the enactment of ordinances banning individuals from sitting on sidewalks during the daytime, banning "aggressive" panhandling, and banning all panhandling from certain sections of cities.

The new laws were designed to address a number of problems, including complaints by members of the public of being harassed and feeling unsafe because of panhandlers. In addition, law enforcement officials warned that many panhandlers engaged in shoplifting and soliciting of money to purchase illegal drugs and alcohol. However, critics of the crackdowns argued that the new laws were inhumane and that cities would benefit by providing more job training and public housing for people living on the streets.

National mover rate. In 2008, the percentage of people changing residences in the United States—the so-called "national mover rate"—declined to the lowest level since the U.S. Census Bureau began tracking the rate in 1948. The Census Bureau reported in April 2009 that the national mover rate declined to 11.9 percent in 2008, compared with 13.2 percent in 2007. A total of 35.2 million people moved between March 2007 and March 2008—the lowest number of movers since 1962. Experts attributed the reduced mover rate to the economic recession and the banking and mortage crisis.

According to the Census Bureau, major U.S. cities lost approximately 2 million residents from 2007 to 2008, while suburbs gained more than 2 million residents. Renters were five times as likely as homeowners to move. Sixty-five percent of movers switched homes within the same county, 18 percent moved to a different county in the same state, and 13 percent moved to a different state. Among racial/ethnic groups, blacks—with a mover rate of 16 percent—were the most likely to move, followed by Hispanics (15 percent), Asians (13 percent), and whites (10 percent).

2016 Summer Olympic shocker. In a vote that came as a shock to many people in the United States, the International Olympic Committee (IOC) voted in October 2009 to award the 2016 Summer Olympic Games to Rio de Janeiro rather than Chicago. The Brazilian capital also beat Tokyo and Madrid, Spain, for the honors.

Many Chicagoans and other Americans had been confident that the "Windy City" would win the prestigious games. This confidence rose after U.S. President Barack Obama, First Lady Michelle Obama, and popular television personality Oprah Winfrey made personal appeals before the IOC on Chicago's behalf. Despite these appeals, however, Chicago received fewer IOC votes than any of the other three finalist cities.   ■ Alfred J. Smuskiewicz

See also **Chicago; Dallas; Houston; Los Angeles; New York City; Philadelphia; Washington, D.C.**

Civil rights. See **Human rights.**

Performers, including baritone George Gagnidze (below, left), rehearse Swedish director Luc Bondy's new minimalist production of Giacomo Puccini's *Tosca* at the Metropolitan Opera in New York City. The unusual and stark staging of the opera drew loud boos from the Met audience at the close of the premier performance in September.

Classical music. In a venture sponsored by the popular online video community YouTube, in collaboration with the London Symphony Orchestra, 35 musicians from the United States joined 61 other musicians from 29 countries in 2009 to create the YouTube Symphony Orchestra—the first orchestra formed entirely through auditions submitted over the Internet. The YouTube community and conductor Michael Tilson Thomas selected the musicians from the submitted auditions. The new orchestra convened for a public concert, which was streamed live over the World Wide Web, on April 15 at Carnegie Hall in New York City. This concert included the premiere of Chinese composer Tan Dun's *Internet Symphony No. 1, Eroica*.

Musical discoveries. The International Mozarteum Foundation, based in Salzburg, Austria, announced in July that it had identified two fragmentary works for piano written by the great Austrian composer Wolfgang Amadeus Mozart. The works dated to 1763 or 1764, when Mozart was only 7 or 8 years old.

Also in July 2009, U.S. pianist Frederick Moyer and his uncle Paul Green announced that they had identified a seven-minute fragment of a piano sonata written by the German Romantic composer Robert Schumann. Moyer made his performance of the piece available on his Web site.

New maestros. American conductor Alan Gilbert's first concert as music director of the New York Philharmonic was performed in September in Avery Fisher Hall in New York City. The concert included the premiere of the 10-minute *EXPO*, composed by Magnus Lindberg. Venezuelan-born Gustavo Dudamel also made his debut as music director of a major U.S. orchestra. He led his Los Angeles Philharmonic in the world premiere of *City Noir*, by John Adams, in October.

New operas. *Brief Encounter*, with a score by U.S. composer and conductor André Previn and libretto by British director John Caird, had its world premiere in May by the Houston Grand Opera. Based on the play *Still Life* and the screenplay to the 1945 motion picture *Brief Encounter*, both by playwright Noel Coward, the opera is a compassionate look at emotional infidelity. Patrick Summers conducted.

In July 2009, Summers conducted the Santa Fe Opera in New Mexico in the premiere of another opera based partly on a well-known film. *The Letter*, with music by Paul Moravec and libretto by author Terry Teachout, was based on both W. Somerset Maugham's play of the same name and director William Wyler's 1940 film noir version.

New orchestral and choral works. Dutch composer Louis Andriessen's *The Hague Hacking*, a double piano concerto written for pianists Katia and Marielle Labeque, had its world premiere in Los Angeles in January 2009. Esa-Pekka Salonen conducted the Los Angeles Philharmonic. Salonen's own *Violin Concerto*, written for and performed by Leila Josefowicz, received its world premiere by the Los Angeles Philharmonic in April.

In January, conductor Hans Graf and the

Houston Symphony presented the premiere of a double concerto for soprano and harp by U.S. composer Augusta Read Thomas. *Absolute Ocean* was performed by soprano Twyla Robinson and harpist Paula Page at Houston's Jones Hall.

The 80th birthday of André Previn was celebrated in April when his *Trio for Piano, Violin and Cello* had its premiere at Carnegie Hall in New York City. Previn at the piano was accompanied by violinist Anne-Sophie Mutter and cellist Lynn Harrell. Four days later, a Carnegie Hall audience heard a second Previn world premiere—his *Concerto for Violin, Viola and Orchestra.* Mutter and violist Yuri Bashmet were soloists, with Previn conducting the Orchestra of St. Luke's.

American composer Jennifer Higdon was on hand in February when the Indianapolis Symphony Orchestra, under conductor Mario Venzago, presented her *Violin Concerto.* Hilary Hahn was soloist. Composer Christopher Rouse attended the world premiere of his *Oboe Concerto* in February in Minneapolis. The Minnesota Orchestra's principal oboist, Basil Reeve, performed with the orchestra under conductor Osmo Vanska.

Also in February—in honor of the 200th anniversary of the birth of U.S. President Abraham Lincoln—baritone Thomas Hampson and the Spokane (Washington) Symphony Orchestra performed American composer Michael Daugherty's song cycle *Letters from Lincoln.*

Marking the 70th birthday of American composer Ellen Taaffe Zwilich in April, the Kalichstein-Laredo-Robinson Trio and Miami String Quartet presented the first performance of her *Septet for Piano Trio and String Quartet* in New York City. Peter Lieberson's cantata *The World in Flower* received its premiere in May by mezzo-soprano Joyce DiDonato, baritone Russell Braun, the New York Choral Artists, and the New York Philharmonic under the baton of Alan Gilbert.

The world premiere of American composer Michael Torke's *Plans,* for vocal soloists, chorus, and orchestra, was performed in Chicago in June by the Grant Park Orchestra and Chorus with Carlos Kalmar conducting. The piece was commissioned in honor of the centennial of architect Daniel Burnham's plans for the layout of Chicago.

An audience attending the Tanglewood Festival of Contemporary Music in Lenox, Massachusetts, in August heard the world premieres of British composer Helen Grime's *Clarinet Concerto* and American composer Elliott Carter's *Poems of Louis Zukofsky.* Gergely Madaras led the Tanglewood Music Center Orchestra in both performances.

Music director James Levine and the Boston Symphony Orchestra (BSO) presented the world premiere of American composer Gunther Schuller's *Where the Word Ends* in February.

Levine also conducted the BSO in the September premiere of *On Willows and Birches, Concerto for Harp,* by famed Hollywood film composer John Williams. Ann Hobson Pilot was soloist.

Deaths. Alicia de Larrocha, the Spanish pianist who was celebrated for her performances of works by Spanish composers and her elegant readings of Mozart, died in September at age 86. Hildegard Behrens, a German soprano famed for the dramatic intensity she brought to such leading operatic roles as Richard Wagner's Brunnhilde, died in August at age 72.

Leon Kirchner, the eminent American composer and teacher, passed away in September at age 90. The distinguished American composer, conductor, and pianist Lukas Foss died in February at age 86. George Perle, a Pulitzer Prize-winning U.S. composer, author, theorist, and teacher, died in January at age 93.   ■ John von Rhein

See also **Popular music.**
Clothing. See Fashion.
Coal. See Energy supply.

GRAMMY AWARD WINNERS IN 2009

Classical Album, *Weill: Rise and Fall of the City of Mahagonny;* Los Angeles Opera Chorus and Orchestra; James Conlon, conductor; Fred Vogler, producer

Orchestral Performance, *Shostakovich: Symphony No. 4;* Chicago Symphony Orchestra; Bernard Haitink, conductor

Opera Recording, *Weill: Rise and Fall of the City of Mahagonny;* Los Angeles Opera Chorus and Orchestra; James Conlon, conductor; Anthony Dean Griffey, Patti LuPone, and Audra McDonald, soloists; Fred Vogler, producer

Choral Performance, *Stravinsky: Symphony of Psalms;* Rundfunkchor Berlin and Berliner Philharmoniker; Simon Halsey, chorus master; Simon Rattle, conductor

Instrumental Soloist with Orchestra, *Schoenberg/Sibelius: Violin Concertos;* Swedish Radio Symphony Orchestra; Esa-Pekka Salonen, conductor; Hilary Hahn, violin

Instrumental Soloist without Orchestra, *Piano Music of Salonen, Stucky, and Lutoslawski;* Gloria Cheng, piano

Chamber Music Performance, *Carter, Elliott: String Quartets Nos. 1 and 5;* Pacifica Quartet

Small Ensemble Performance, *Spotless Rose: Hymns to the Virgin Mary;* Phoenix Chorale; Charles Bruffy, conductor

Classical Vocal Performance, *Corigliano: Mr. Tambourine Man: Seven Poems of Bob Dylan;* Hila Plitmann, soprano

Classical Contemporary Composition, *Corigliano: Mr. Tambourine Man: Seven Poems of Bob Dylan;* John Corigliano, composer

Classical Crossover Album, *Simple Gifts;* The King's Singers

Colombia. In 2009, the Colombian government, helped by the United States miliary, claimed steady progress in its long-running war against the combined forces of drug traffickers and insurrectionists. Fewer terrorist attacks against foreign-owned oil installations helped boost oil exports to an average of 650,000 barrels a day.

Despite an otherwise lackluster economy and an annual growth rate of less than 1 percent, President Álvaro Uribe remained popular with most Colombians for having diminished the level of violence, especially in urban areas. In September, the Congress authorized a national referendum that, if approved, would allow him to run for an unprecedented third term in 2010.

More U.S. troops. During 2009, the United States unveiled a controversial plan to increase its military presence in Colombia. Under the new agreement, the United States was to station 1,400 military personnel at seven Colombian bases for a period of 10 years. The plan sparked anti-American protests and placed Uribe at odds with neighboring governments, who feared further American influence in the area.

Rebel hostages released. In February, the Revolutionary Armed Forces of Colombia (FARC), a rebel group long at war with the Colombian government, released several high-profile hostages. Among them was a former provincial governor held captive since 2001. In March 2009, a Swedish hostage, Erik Roland Larsson, 69, was released after almost two years in captivity. The Swedish engineer had worked on a hydroelectric project in northeastern Colombia. President Uribe offered to host peace talks with FARC, who still held more than 20 Colombian police officers and soldiers and hundreds of other Colombians.

Tent city. For more than four decades, the violence in rural areas had led to the displacement of as many as 3 million Colombians, according to a June 2009 study by the United Nations. In March, more than 2,000 of these *desplazados* (displaced refugees) erected a sprawling "tent city" on the green hillocks and red-brick squares of the Third Millennium Park in Bogotá, the capital. The refugees demanded that their government honor a 1997 law guaranteeing such basic needs as food, education, and jobs to victims of forced displacement.

■ Nathan A. Haverstock

See also **Latin America**.

Commonwealth of Independent States. See Armenia; Azerbaijan; Kyrgyzstan; Moldova; Russia; Turkmenistan; Ukraine; Uzbekistan.

Comoros. See Africa.

Computer. Popular new forms of computers—from small, inexpensive "netbook" laptops to Internet-equipped mobile phones—increasingly challenged the dominance of the "personal computer" in 2009. Part of this shift came as computer users increasingly relied on Web sites for work and entertainment, rather than on programs installed on their own computers. Demand for efficient, portable computers and cell phones that acted as quick gateways to Web sites and e-mail increased dramatically.

New operating systems in 2009 included streamlined updates of Cupertino, California-based Apple's OS X and Redmond, Washington-based Microsoft's Windows. Operating systems (OS's) are programs that control the most fundamental functions of a computer.

Apple's new OS, called Snow Leopard and released in August, ran faster and more efficiently than previous Apple OS's but otherwise displayed few noticeable changes.

Microsoft released Windows 7 in October, replacing its poorly received Vista OS. Windows 7, like Snow Leopard, was designed for speed and efficiency without a clutter of new features.

Jack of all chips. Santa Clara, California-based computer chip maker Intel, at a September conference, showcased new chips that could perform more specialized tasks than ever before. Computer chips carry out instructions that make up software programs or store memory. Most computers require several specialized chips, such as chips dedicated to graphics or sound—which take up more space than a single chip. Intel's new chips could, thus, help further shrink computers.

One new Intel chip, the CE 4100, combined graphics, video, networking, data transfer, and other functions with a main computer processor. Intel also showed the first laptop computer chip that combined a graphics processor with the central processor, which could increase laptop energy efficiency and battery life.

Netflix prize. Netflix, a video rental service based in Los Gatos, California, announced the winner of its $1-million computer programming "Netflix prize" in September. A seven-person team won the contest, which rewarded computer programmers who could best improve Netflix's automatic movie recommendation system.

When the contest was first announced in 2006, it attracted many talented computer programmers around the world; many formed into teams and alliances to combine their resources. The highly advanced programming and data analysis techniques developed during the competition had many potential uses beyond recommending movies.

■ Daniel Kenis

See also **Electronics; Internet**.

Congo (Brazzaville). See Africa.

Congo (Kinshasa). The killing of innocent civilians in the Democratic Republic of the Congo (DRC) continued throughout 2009 as President Joseph Kabila's government forces and rival rebel groups struggled for supremacy.

Joint operation. From January 20 to February 25, thousands of Rwandan troops joined Congolese soldiers in the DRC to hunt down members of a Rwandan rebel group, the Rwandan Liberation Democratic Forces (FDLR). The FDLR consists mostly of Hutus, many of whom fled to the DRC after the 1994 slaughter of Tutsis in Rwanda. Since then, FDLR fighters have waged a terror campaign against Tutsis in the DRC.

The United Nations Organization Mission in the Democratic Republic of the Congo, a 17,000-strong peacekeeping force known as MONUC, called the joint raid only a limited success. It failed to kill significant numbers of Hutu fighters, who simply disappeared into the bush. Congolese officials, in turn, accused MONUC of doing too little to protect civilians.

President Kabila's decision to allow Rwandan soldiers into the DRC put him under intense public pressure in 2009. His critics accused him of permitting Rwanda—the DRC's former enemy—to "invade" Congo. A Rwandan invasion in 1998 had helped spark Congo's 1998-2002 civil war. Since then, Rwandan troops have crossed the border on many occasions to pursue FDLR rebels.

Rebel officer seized. On Jan. 22, 2009, Rwandan forces arrested Laurent Nkunda, a former Congolese general, fleeing into Rwanda. Nkunda led Tutsi rebels in the eastern DRC who opposed the Congolese army. He claimed that he needed to protect Congo's Tutsis from Rwandan Hutus because, in his view, Congo's army could not.

LRA attacks. A Ugandan rebel group, the Lord's Resistance Army (LRA), increased its attacks on civilians in northern Congo in 2009. Uganda had expelled the LRA in 2008 after the group terrorized northern Uganda for over two decades. Humanitarian groups—including Human Rights Watch, based in New York City, and Doctors Without Borders, based in Geneva, Switzerland—said the LRA had carried out thousands of murders, rapes, and child kidnappings.

War crimes. On Jan. 26, 2009, the Congolese rebel leader Thomas Lubanga was put on trial at the International Criminal Court in The Hague, the Netherlands. Prosecutors accused him of forcibly recruiting child soldiers in the DRC's eastern Ituri region from September 2002 to August 2003. It was the first time that an African rebel leader had faced justice on charges of using child soldiers. In 2009, however, rebels continued to kidnap children in the DRC.   ■ Simon Baynham

See also **Africa; Belgium; Disasters; Uganda.**

Congress of the United States. Health care and the economy were the dominant issues in Congress in 2009. Both houses of Congress passed major health care reform bills late in the year, and a final compromise bill appeared headed for approval in early 2010. In February 2009, Congress enacted one of the largest economic rescue packages since President Franklin D. Roosevelt's New Deal of the 1930's.

When the 111th Congress convened on Jan. 6, 2009, the 435-seat House of Representatives consisted of 257 seats under Democratic control and 178 seats under Republican control. The 100-seat Senate consisted of 56 Democratic seats, 2 seats held by independents who caucused with the Democrats, 41 Republican seats, and a vacant seat for Minnesota, where a November 2008 Senate election was still in dispute. On April 28, 2009, Senator Arlen Specter of Pennsylvania switched his party affiliation from Republican to Democrat, giving the Senate Democratic Caucus its 59th member. On June 30, the Minnesota Supreme Court finally decided the disputed Senate election, ruling that the Democrat—comedian and liberal political commentator Al Franken—had defeated the Republican incumbent, Norm Coleman, by 312 votes out of about 2.9 million cast. This decision gave Senate Democrats the 60-seat supermajority needed to block Republican filibusters. In the House, one seat for northern New York shifted from Republican to Democratic after a November 3 special election, and Representative Parker Griffith (D., Alabama) switched his party affiliation to Republican on December 22.

Health care reform was Democratic President Barack Obama's chief legislative priority in 2009. His efforts to establish a universal health care system engendered a great deal of congressional and public debate as well as heavy media coverage throughout the summer and fall. On November 7, the House narrowly approved a $1.1-trillion bill that would extend health insurance to nearly all Americans. On December 24, the Senate approved a similar, $871-billion health reform bill on a party-line vote.

Cost and the role of government were the most contentious issues in the reform debate. Nearly all Republicans and some fiscally conservative Democrats attacked the reform proposals put forward by Democratic leaders as too costly and as an unacceptable expansion of government control over health care. Dissent was especially strong over whether to create a government-run insurance plan, or "public option," that would compete with private insurance plans.

The vote on the House bill was 220-215, with only one Republican (Anh "Joseph" Cao of Louisiana) in support and 39 Democrats opposed. The vote on the Senate bill was 60-39, with all 60

MEMBERS OF THE UNITED STATES SENATE

The Senate of the second session of the 111th Congress consisted of 58 Democrats, 40 Republicans, and 2 Independents when it convened on Jan. 5, 2010. The first date in each listing shows when the senator's term began. The second date shows when the senator's term expires.

STATE	TERM
Alabama	
Richard C. Shelby, R.	1987-2011
Jeff Sessions, R.	1997-2015
Alaska	
Mark Begich, D.	2009-2015
Lisa Murkowski, R.	2002-2011
Arizona	
John McCain III, R.	1987-2011
Jon Kyl, R.	1995-2013
Arkansas	
Blanche Lambert Lincoln, D.	1999-2011
Mark Pryor, D.	2003-2015
California	
Dianne Feinstein, D.	1992-2013
Barbara Boxer, D.	1993-2011
Colorado	
Mark Udall, D.	2009-2015
Michael F. Bennet, D.	2009-2011
Connecticut	
Christopher J. Dodd, D.	1981-2011
Joseph I. Lieberman, I.	1989-2013
Delaware	
Ted Kaufman, D.	2009-2010
Thomas Carper, D.	2001-2013
Florida	
Bill Nelson, D.	2001-2013
George S. LeMieux, R.	2009-2011
Georgia	
Saxby Chambliss, R.	2003-2015
Johnny Isakson, R.	2005-2011
Hawaii	
Daniel K. Inouye, D.	1963-2011
Daniel K. Akaka, D.	1990-2013
Idaho	
Jim Risch, R.	2009-2015
Mike Crapo, R.	1999-2011
Illinois	
Richard J. Durbin, D.	1997-2015
Roland W. Burris, D.	2009-2011
Indiana	
Richard G. Lugar, R.	1977-2013
Evan Bayh, D.	1999-2011
Iowa	
Charles E. Grassley, R.	1981-2011
Tom Harkin, D.	1985-2015
Kansas	
Sam Brownback, R.	1996-2011
Pat Roberts, R.	1997-2015
Kentucky	
Mitch McConnell, R.	1985-2015
Jim Bunning, R.	1999-2011

STATE	TERM
Louisiana	
Mary L. Landrieu, D.	1997-2015
David Vitter, R.	2005-2011
Maine	
Olympia Snowe, R.	1995-2013
Susan M. Collins, R.	1997-2015
Maryland	
Benjamin L. Cardin, D.	2007-2013
Barbara A. Mikulski, D.	1987-2011
Massachusetts	
Paul G. Kirk, Jr., D.	2009-2010
John F. Kerry, D.	1985-2015
Michigan	
Carl Levin, D.	1979-2015
Debbie Stabenow, D.	2001-2013
Minnesota	
Amy Klobuchar, D.	2007-2013
Al Franken, D.	2009-2015
Mississippi	
Thad Cochran, R.	1978-2015
Roger Wicker, R.	2007-2013
Missouri	
Christopher S. (Kit) Bond, R.	1987-2011
Claire C. McCaskill, D.	2007-2013
Montana	
Max Baucus, D.	1978-2015
Jon Tester, D.	2007-2013
Nebraska	
Mike Johanns, R.	2009-2015
Ben Nelson, D.	2001-2013
Nevada	
Harry M. Reid, D.	1987-2011
John Ensign, R.	2001-2013
New Hampshire	
Judd Gregg, R.	1993-2011
Jeanne Shaheen, D.	2009-2015
New Jersey	
Robert Menendez, D.	2006-2013
Frank R. Lautenberg, D.	2003-2015
New Mexico	
Tom Udall, D.	2009-2015
Jeff Bingaman, D.	1983-2013
New York	
Charles E. Schumer, D.	1999-2011
Kirsten E. Gillibrand, D.	2009-2011
North Carolina	
Kay Hagan, D.	2009-2015
Richard Burr, R.	2005-2011
North Dakota	
Kent Conrad, D.	1987-2013
Byron L. Dorgan, D.	1992-2011

STATE	TERM
Ohio	
Sherrod Brown, D.	2007-2013
George V. Voinovich, R.	1999-2011
Oklahoma	
James M. Inhofe, R.	1994-2015
Tom Coburn, R.	2005-2011
Oregon	
Ron Wyden, D.	1996-2011
Jeff Merkley, D.	2009-2015
Pennsylvania	
Arlen Specter, D.	1981-2011
Bob Casey, Jr., D.	2007-2013
Rhode Island	
Jack Reed, D.	1997-2015
Sheldon Whitehouse, D.	2007-2013
South Carolina	
Lindsey Graham, R.	2003-2015
Jim DeMint, R.	2005-2011
South Dakota	
Tim Johnson, D.	1997-2015
John Thune, R.	2005-2011
Tennessee	
Bob Corker, R.	2007-2013
Lamar Alexander, R.	2003-2015
Texas	
Kay Bailey Hutchison, R.	1993-2013
John Cornyn, R.	2003-2015
Utah	
Orrin G. Hatch, R.	1977-2013
Robert F. Bennett, R.	1993-2011
Vermont	
Patrick J. Leahy, D.	1975-2011
Bernie Sanders, I.	2007-2013
Virginia	
Mark Warner, D.	2009-2015
Jim Webb, D.	2007-2013
Washington	
Patty Murray, D.	1993-2011
Maria Cantwell, D.	2001-2013
West Virginia	
Robert C. Byrd, D.	1959-2013
John D. Rockefeller IV, D.	1985-2015
Wisconsin	
Herbert Kohl, D.	1989-2013
Russell D. Feingold, D.	1993-2011
Wyoming	
John Barrasso, R.	2007-2013
Mike Enzi, R.	1997-2015

MEMBERS OF THE UNITED STATES HOUSE OF REPRESENTATIVES

The House of Representatives of the second session of the 111th Congress consisted of 256 Democrats, 178 Republicans, and 1 vacancy (not including representatives from American Samoa, the District of Columbia, Guam, the Northern Mariana Islands, Puerto Rico, and the Virgin Islands) when it convened on Jan. 5, 2010. This table shows congressional district, legislator, and party affiliation. Asterisk (*) denotes those who served in the 110th Congress; dagger (†) denotes "at large."

Alabama
1. Jo Bonner, R.*
2. Bobby Bright, D.
3. Mike Rogers, R.*
4. Robert Aderholt, R.*
5. Parker Griffith, R.
6. Spencer Bachus, R.*
7. Artur Davis, D.*

Alaska
†Donald E. Young, R.*

Arizona
1. Ann Kirkpatrick, D.
2. Trent Franks, R.*
3. John Shadegg, R.*
4. Ed Pastor, D.*
5. Harry Mitchell, D.*
6. Jeff Flake, R.*
7. Raúl Grijalva, D.*
8. Gabrielle Giffords, D.*

Arkansas
1. Marion Berry, D.*
2. Vic Snyder, D.*
3. John Boozman, R.*
4. Mike Ross, D.*

California
1. Mike Thompson, D.*
2. Wally Herger, R.*
3. Dan Lungren, R.*
4. Tom McClintock, R.
5. Doris Matsui, D.*
6. Lynn Woolsey, D.*
7. George Miller, D.*
8. Nancy Pelosi, D.*
9. Barbara Lee, D.*
10. John Garamendi, D.
11. Jerry McNerney, D.*
12. Jackie Speier, D.*
13. Pete Stark, D.*
14. Anna Eshoo, D.*
15. Mike Honda, D.*
16. Zoe Lofgren, D.*
17. Sam Farr, D.*
18. Dennis Cardoza, D.*
19. George Radanovich, R.*
20. Jim Costa, D.*
21. Devin Nunes, R.*
22. Kevin McCarthy, R.*
23. Lois Capps, D.*
24. Elton Gallegly, R.*
25. Howard McKeon, R.*
26. David Dreier, R.*
27. Brad Sherman, D.*
28. Howard Berman, D.*
29. Adam Schiff, D.*
30. Henry Waxman, D.*
31. Xavier Becerra, D.*
32. Judy Chu, D.
33. Diane Watson, D.*
34. Lucille Roybal-Allard, D.*
35. Maxine Waters, D.*
36. Jane Harman, D.*
37. Laura Richardson, D.*
38. Grace Napolitano, D.*
39. Linda Sánchez, D.*
40. Ed Royce, R.*
41. Jerry Lewis, R.*
42. Gary Miller, R.*
43. Joe Baca, D.*
44. Ken Calvert, R.*
45. Mary Bono Mack, R.*
46. Dana Rohrabacher, R.*
47. Loretta Sanchez, D.*
48. John Campbell, R.*
49. Darrell Issa, R.*
50. Brian Bilbray, R.*
51. Bob Filner, D.*
52. Duncan Hunter, R.
53. Susan Davis, D.*

Colorado
1. Diana DeGette, D.*
2. Jared Polis, D.
3. John Salazar, D.*
4. Betsy Markey, D.
5. Doug Lamborn, R.*
6. Mike Coffman, R.
7. Ed Perlmutter, D.*

Connecticut
1. John Larson, D.*
2. Joe Courtney, D.*
3. Rosa DeLauro, D.*
4. Jim Himes, D.
5. Christopher Murphy, D.*

Delaware
†Michael Castle, R.*

Florida
1. Jeff Miller, R.*
2. Allen Boyd, D.*
3. Corrine Brown, D.*
4. Ander Crenshaw, R.*
5. Ginny Brown-Waite, R.*
6. Clifford Stearns, R.*
7. John Mica, R.*
8. Alan Grayson, D.
9. Gus Bilirakis, R.*
10. C. W. Bill Young, R.*
11. Kathy Castor, D.*
12. Adam Putnam, R.*
13. Vern Buchanan, R.*
14. Connie Mack, R.*
15. Bill Posey, R.
16. Tom Rooney, R.
17. Kendrick Meek, D.*
18. Ileana Ros-Lehtinen, R.*
19. Robert Wexler, D.*††
20. Debbie Wasserman Schultz, D.*
21. Lincoln Diaz-Balart, R.*
22. Ron Klein, D.*
23. Alcee Hastings, D.*
24. Suzanne Kosmas, D.
25. Mario Diaz-Balart, R.*

Georgia
1. Jack Kingston, R.*
2. Sanford Bishop, Jr., D.*
3. Lynn Westmoreland, R.*
4. Hank Johnson, Jr., D.*
5. John Lewis, D.*
6. Tom Price, R.*
7. John Linder, R.*
8. Jim Marshall, D.*
9. Nathan Deal, R.*
10. Paul Broun, R.*
11. Phil Gingrey, R.*
12. John Barrow, D.*
13. David Scott, D.*

Hawaii
1. Neil Abercrombie, D.*
2. Mazie K. Hirono, D.*

Idaho
1. Walt Minnick, D.
2. Mike Simpson, R.*

Illinois
1. Bobby Rush, D.*
2. Jesse Jackson, Jr., D.*
3. Daniel Lipinski, D.*
4. Luis Gutierrez, D.*
5. Mike Quigley, D.
6. Peter J. Roskam, R.*
7. Danny Davis, D.*
8. Melissa Bean, D.*
9. Jan Schakowsky, D.*
10. Mark Kirk, R.*
11. Debbie Halvorson, D.
12. Jerry Costello, D.*
13. Judy Biggert, R.*
14. Bill Foster, D.*
15. Timothy Johnson, R.*
16. Donald Manzullo, R.*
17. Phil Hare, D.*
18. Aaron Schock, R.
19. John Shimkus, R.*

Indiana
1. Peter Visclosky, D.*
2. Joe Donnelly, D.*
3. Mark Souder, R.*
4. Steve Buyer, R.*
5. Dan Burton, R.*
6. Mike Pence, R.*
7. André Carson, D.*
8. Brad Ellsworth, D.*
9. Baron P. Hill, D.*

Iowa
1. Bruce Braley, D.*
2. David Loebsack, D.*
3. Leonard Boswell, D.*
4. Thomas Latham, R.*
5. Steve King, R.*

Kansas
1. Jerry Moran, R.*
2. Lynn Jenkins, R.
3. Dennis Moore, D.*
4. Todd Tiahrt, R.*

Kentucky
1. Edward Whitfield, R.*
2. Brett Guthrie, R.
3. John Yarmuth, D.*
4. Geoff Davis, R.*
5. Harold (Hal) Rogers, R.*
6. Ben Chandler, D.*

Louisiana
1. Steve Scalise, R.*
2. Anh "Joseph" Cao, R.
3. Charles Melancon, D.*
4. John Fleming, R.
5. Rodney Alexander, R.*
6. Bill Cassidy, R.
7. Charles Boustany, Jr., R.*

Maine
1. Chellie Pingree, D.
2. Michael Michaud, D.*

Maryland
1. Frank Kratovil, Jr., D.
2. C. A. Ruppersberger, D.*
3. John Sarbanes, D.*
4. Donna Edwards, D.*
5. Steny Hoyer, D.*
6. Roscoe Bartlett, R.*
7. Elijah Cummings, D.*
8. Chris Van Hollen, D.*

Massachusetts
1. John Olver, D.*
2. Richard Neal, D.*
3. James McGovern, D.*
4. Barney Frank, D.*
5. Niki Tsongas, D.*
6. John Tierney, D.*
7. Edward Markey, D.*
8. Michael Capuano, D.*
9. Stephen Lynch, D.*
10. William Delahunt, D.*

Michigan
1. Bart Stupak, D.*
2. Peter Hoekstra, R.*
3. Vernon Ehlers, R.*
4. Dave Camp, R.*
5. Dale Kildee, D.*
6. Fred Upton, R.*
7. Mark Schauer, D.
8. Mike Rogers, R.*
9. Gary Peters, D.
10. Candice Miller, R.*
11. Thaddeus McCotter, R.*
12. Sander Levin, D.*
13. Carolyn Cheeks Kilpatrick, D.*
14. John Conyers, Jr., D.*
15. John Dingell, D.*

Minnesota
1. Timothy Walz, D.*
2. John Kline, R.*

†† vacant seat as of Jan. 3, 2010.

3. Eric Paulsen, R.
4. Betty McCollum, D.*
5. Keith Ellison, D.*
6. Michele Bachmann, R.*
7. Collin Peterson, D.*
8. James Oberstar, D.*

Mississippi
1. Travis Childers, D.*
2. Bennie Thompson, D.*
3. Gregg Harper, R.
4. Gene Taylor, D.*

Missouri
1. William Clay, D.*
2. Todd Akin, R.*
3. Russ Carnahan, D.*
4. Ike Skelton, D.*
5. Emanuel Cleaver II, D.*
6. Samuel Graves, R.*
7. Roy Blunt, R.*
8. Jo Ann Emerson, R.*
9. Blaine Luetkemeyer, R.

Montana
†Dennis Rehberg, R.*

Nebraska
1. Jeff Fortenberry, R.*
2. Lee Terry, R.*
3. Adrian Smith, R.*

Nevada
1. Shelley Berkley, D.*
2. Dean Heller, R.*
3. Dina Titus, D.

New Hampshire
1. Carol Shea-Porter, D.*
2. Paul Hodes, D.*

New Jersey
1. Robert Andrews, D.*
2. Frank LoBiondo, R.*
3. John Adler, D.
4. Christopher Smith, R.*
5. Scott Garrett, R.*
6. Frank Pallone, Jr., D.*
7. Leonard Lance, R.
8. William Pascrell, Jr., D.*
9. Steven Rothman, D.*
10. Donald Payne, D.*
11. Rodney Frelinghuysen, R.*
12. Rush Holt, D.*
13. Albio Sires, D.*

New Mexico
1. Martin Heinrich, D.
2. Harry Teague, D.
3. Ben Luján, D.

New York
1. Tim Bishop, D.*
2. Steve Israel, D.*
3. Peter King, R.*
4. Carolyn McCarthy, D.*
5. Gary Ackerman, D.*
6. Gregory Meeks, D.*
7. Joseph Crowley, D.*
8. Jerrold Nadler, D.*
9. Anthony Weiner, D.*
10. Edolphus Towns, D.*
11. Yvette Clarke, D.*
12. Nydia Velázquez, D.*
13. Michael McMahon, D.

14. Carolyn Maloney, D.*
15. Charles Rangel, D.*
16. José Serrano, D.*
17. Eliot Engel, D.*
18. Nita Lowey, D.*
19. John Hall, D.*
20. Scott Murphy, D.
21. Paul Tonko, D.
22. Maurice Hinchey, D.*
23. Bill Owens, D.
24. Michael Arcuri, D.*
25. Daniel Maffei, D.
26. Christopher Lee, R.
27. Brian Higgins, D.*
28. Louise McIntosh
    Slaughter, D.*
29. Eric Massa, D.

North Carolina
1. G. K. Butterfield, D.*
2. Bob Etheridge, D.*
3. Walter Jones, Jr., R.*
4. David Price, D.*
5. Virginia Foxx, R.*
6. Howard Coble, R.*
7. Mike McIntyre, D.*
8. Larry Kissell, D.
9. Sue Myrick, R.*
10. Patrick McHenry, R.*
11. Heath Shuler, D.*
12. Melvin Watt, D.*
13. Brad Miller, D.*

North Dakota
†Earl Pomeroy, D.*

Ohio
1. Steve Driehaus, D.
2. Jean Schmidt, R.*
3. Michael Turner, R.*
4. Jim Jordan, R.*
5. Robert Latta, R.*
6. Charles Wilson, D.*
7. Steve Austria, R.
8. John Boehner, R.*
9. Marcy Kaptur, D.*
10. Dennis Kucinich, D.*
11. Marcia Fudge, D.*
12. Pat Tiberi, R.*
13. Betty Sutton, D.*
14. Steven LaTourette, R.*
15. Mary Jo Kilroy, D.
16. John Boccieri, D.
17. Timothy Ryan, D.*
18. Zachary Space, D.*

Oklahoma
1. John Sullivan, R.*
2. Dan Boren, D.*
3. Frank Lucas, R.*
4. Tom Cole, R.*
5. Mary Fallin, R.*

Oregon
1. David Wu, D.*
2. Greg Walden, R.*
3. Earl Blumenauer, D.*
4. Peter DeFazio, D.*
5. Kurt Schrader, D.

Pennsylvania
1. Robert Brady, D.*

2. Chaka Fattah, D.*
3. Kathy Dahlkemper, D.
4. Jason Altmire, D.*
5. Glenn Thompson, R.
6. Jim Gerlach, R.*
7. Joe Sestak, D.*
8. Patrick Murphy, D.*
9. Bill Shuster, R.*
10. Christopher Carney, D.*
11. Paul Kanjorski, D.*
12. John Murtha, D.*
13. Allyson Schwartz, D.*
14. Michael Doyle, D.*
15. Charles Dent, R.*
16. Joseph Pitts, R.*
17. Tim Holden, D.*
18. Tim Murphy, R.*
19. Todd Platts, R.*

Rhode Island
1. Patrick Kennedy, D.*
2. James Langevin, D.*

South Carolina
1. Henry Brown, Jr., R.*
2. Joe Wilson, R.*
3. J. Gresham Barrett, R.*
4. Bob Inglis, R.*
5. John Spratt, Jr., D.*
6. James Clyburn, D.*

South Dakota
†Stephanie Herseth
  Sandlin, D.*

Tennessee
1. David Roe, R.
2. John J. Duncan, Jr., R.*
3. Zach Wamp, R.*
4. Lincoln Davis, D.*
5. Jim Cooper, D.*
6. Bart Gordon, D.*
7. Marsha Blackburn, R.*
8. John Tanner, D.*
9. Steve Cohen, D.*

Texas
1. Louis Gohmert, R.*
2. Ted Poe, R.*
3. Sam Johnson, R.*
4. Ralph M. Hall, R.*
5. Jeb Hensarling, R.*
6. Joe Barton, R.*
7. John Culberson, R.*
8. Kevin Brady, R.*
9. Al Green, D.*
10. Michael McCaul, R.*
11. K. Michael Conaway, R.*
12. Kay Granger, R.*
13. Mac Thornberry, R.*
14. Ron Paul, R.*
15. Rubén Hinojosa, D.*
16. Silvestre Reyes, D.*
17. Chet Edwards, D.*
18. Sheila Jackson-Lee, D.*
19. Randy Neugebauer, R.*
20. Charlie Gonzalez, D.*
21. Lamar Smith, R.*
22. Pete Olson, R.
23. Ciro Rodriguez, D.*
24. Kenny Marchant, R.*

25. Lloyd Doggett, D.*
26. Michael Burgess, R.*
27. Solomon Ortiz, D.*
28. Henry Cuellar, D.*
29. Gene Green, D.*
30. Eddie Bernice Johnson, D.*
31. John Carter, R.*
32. Pete Sessions, R.*

Utah
1. Rob Bishop, R.*
2. Jim Matheson, D.*
3. Jason Chaffetz, R.

Vermont
†Peter Welch, D.*

Virginia
1. Robert Wittman, R.*
2. Glenn Nye, D.
3. Robert Scott, D.*
4. J. Randy Forbes, R.*
5. Tom Perriello, D.
6. Robert Goodlatte, R.*
7. Eric Cantor, R.*
8. Jim Moran, D.*
9. Rick Boucher, D.*
10. Frank Wolf, R.*
11. Gerry Connolly, D.

Washington
1. Jay Inslee, D.*
2. Rick Larsen, D.*
3. Brian Baird, D.*
4. Doc Hastings, R.*
5. Cathy McMorris Rodgers, R.*
6. Norman Dicks, D.*
7. Jim McDermott, D.*
8. Dave Reichert, R.*
9. Adam Smith, D.*

West Virginia
1. Alan Mollohan, D.*
2. Shelley Moore Capito, R.*
3. Nick Rahall II, D.*

Wisconsin
1. Paul Ryan, R.*
2. Tammy Baldwin, D.*
3. Ron Kind, D.*
4. Gwen Moore, D.*
5. James Sensenbrenner, Jr., R.*
6. Thomas Petri, R.*
7. David Obey, D.*
8. Steve Kagen, D.*

Wyoming
†Cynthia Lummis, R.

Nonvoting representatives
American Samoa
Eni F. H. Faleomavaega, D.*

District of Columbia
Eleanor Holmes Norton, D.*

Guam
Madeleine Bordallo, D.*

Northern Mariana Islands
Gregorio "Kilili" Camacho Sablan, I.

Puerto Rico
Pedro Pierluisi, D.

Virgin Islands
Donna Christensen, D.*

Democratic Caucus members voting "yes" and 39 Republicans voting "no."

Under both bills, more people would be eligible for the Medicaid health care program for the poor. Almost everyone would be legally obligated to buy health insurance if they did not get it from their employer. Insurance "exchanges" would be created in which individuals and small businesses could shop for coverage. People with low or moderate incomes could get government subsidies to help them buy insurance. Insurance firms could no longer turn away people with preexisting medical conditions or cancel a policy because of expensive claims. Both bills would bar the use of federal funds to pay for abortion coverage.

The House bill would create a public option that would compete with private plans in the exchanges. The Senate bill would not establish a public option. Instead, the U.S. Office of Personnel Management, which oversees health coverage for federal employees, would contract with private insurers to offer plans in the exchanges.

Under the House bill, employers with annual payrolls over $500,000 would have to provide insurance to employees or pay a fine. The Senate bill would not require employers to offer insurance, but firms with more than 50 employees would have to pay a fine if any employee qualified for a federal subsidy to help buy coverage.

The House bill would be funded by cutting provider payments under Medicare insurance plans and imposing a 5.4-percent tax on individuals making over $500,000 annually and couples making over $1 million. The Senate bill would be funded by cuts in Medicare payments, a tax of 40 percent on high-cost health insurance plans, and extra Medicare payroll taxes on individuals making over $200,000 annually and couples making over $250,000.

Early in 2009, Congress passed a bill to provide $33 billion in additional funds for the State Children's Health Insurance Program (SCHIP), which provides insurance for children whose families earn too much to qualify for Medicaid but not enough to afford private coverage. Tobacco taxes were increased to pay for the SCHIP expansion. The president signed this bill on February 4.

Stimulus bill. On February 17, President Obama signed a huge $787-billion package of tax cuts and spending measures intended to stimulate the nation's struggling economy. Both houses of Congress had approved the final version of the bill on February 13 with almost no Republican support. In the House, the vote was 246-183, and in the Senate, 60-38. No House Republicans voted for the bill, and only three Senate Republicans—Susan Collins of Maine, Olympia Snowe of Maine, and Arlen Specter of Pennsylvania—supported it. Seven House Democrats voted against the bill.

The bill, known as the American Recovery and Reinvestment Act, included $212 billion in tax cuts for individuals and businesses and $575 billion in spending on education, health care, energy, transportation infrastructure, and aid to the needy, according to the Congressional Budget Office. Democrats claimed that the legislation would create or save 3 ½ million jobs and spur long-term economic growth. Republicans argued that the bill had too much wasteful spending and would fail to jump-start the economy.

Tax cuts in the bill included a "Making Work Pay" income tax credit, for both 2009 and 2010, of up to $400 for an individual or up to $800 for a couple; a provision to shield millions of middle-income people from the alternative minimum tax in 2009; an extension and expansion of a tax credit for first-time home buyers that had been set to expire in mid-2009; and an expansion of the refundable child tax credit. The bill provided financial aid to prevent teacher layoffs, modernize school buildings, expand Pell Grants for university students, and pay for special education programs and programs for disadvantaged students. Funding for Medicaid was increased; subsidies were provided for laid-off workers' health insurance premiums under the Consolidated Omnibus Budget Reconciliation Act (COBRA); and money was set aside for computerization of medical records. The bill expanded unemployment insurance benefits, boosted food stamp payments, and gave one-time $250 payments to people receiving Social Security or veterans' benefits. Funds were provided to encourage alternative energy development; improve the U.S. electricity grid; improve the energy efficiency of buildings; and build and maintain roads, railroads, and mass transit systems. Also, the bill put caps on bonuses for executives at banks that had gotten federal aid from the Troubled Asset Relief Program (TARP), a bailout fund created during the 2008 financial crisis.

In early November 2009, Congress passed a bill to further extend unemployment insurance benefits and the tax credit for home buyers. President Obama signed this bill on November 6.

Other economic legislation. In May, Congress passed a bill to restrict the ability of credit card companies to raise interest rates and impose fees on their customers. President Obama signed the bill on May 22. The restrictions were scheduled to take effect in February 2010.

In June 2009, Congress created an auto sales incentive program that was popularly called "cash for clunkers." President Obama signed the legislation for the program on June 24. It offered credits of $3,500 to $4,500 to people who traded in an old vehicle for one with better fuel economy. Many consumers took advantage of the program, causing its initial $1-billion appropriation to be used up just one week after the program's launch in July. Congress then passed a bill to add another $2 billion, and the president signed it on August 7. The program ended on August 24.

On December 11, the House voted 223-202 for a far-reaching bill that would increase the government's regulatory power over the financial system and create a new consumer financial protection agency. On December 16, the House voted 217-212 for legislation intended to create and preserve jobs by channeling funds to infrastructure projects and to state and local governments facing budget shortfalls. No Republicans voted for either measure, and there were several Democratic votes against both measures. The Senate did not pass financial reform or jobs legislation in 2009.

Global warming. The House on June 26 passed a bill that would place caps on emissions of man-made greenhouse gases and create a market in which companies could trade emissions permits. Greenhouse gases, such as carbon dioxide, are a chief cause of global warming. It was the first greenhouse gas restriction ever approved by either house of Congress. The vote was 219-212, with 44 Democrats opposing the bill and only 8 Republicans supporting it. Climate change legislation stalled in the Senate in 2009.

Other enacted bills. An omnibus spending bill for the remainder of the 2009 fiscal year (Oct. 1, 2008, to Sept. 30, 2009) was enacted in March, and a supplemental spending bill for the Iraq and Afghanistan wars was enacted in June. In late 2009, Congress passed all of its spending bills for the 2010 fiscal year (Oct. 1, 2009, to Sept. 30, 2010). Congress also passed legislation in 2009 that made it easier for workers to file claims of pay discrimination based on gender or race; allowed people to carry firearms in national parks and wildlife refuges; gave the Food and Drug Administration wide-ranging regulatory power over tobacco products; designated 2 million acres (810,000 hectares) of land in nine states as protected wilderness; expanded AmeriCorps and other national service programs; and broadened the definition of federal hate crimes to include crimes motivated by the victim's gender, sexual orientation, gender identity, or disability.

Kennedy death. A long-time titan of Democratic politics, Senator Edward M. (Ted) Kennedy of Massachusetts, died on August 25 at age 77 after battling brain cancer for over a year. Kennedy—the youngest brother of former President John F. Kennedy and former Senator Robert F. Kennedy—had served in the Senate since 1962. He had become known as that body's "liberal lion," forcefully championing national health insurance and greater spending on social programs.

Wilson outburst. Representative Joe Wilson

(R., South Carolina) gained notoriety on Sept. 9, 2009, when he shouted "You lie!" at President Obama during the president's address on health care reform before a joint session of Congress. The outburst came in response to a statement by the president that his health care plan would not apply to illegal immigrants. Later that evening, Wilson issued a statement apologizing to the president for the lack of civility. On September 15, the House voted 240-179, mostly along party lines, to formally rebuke Wilson for the outburst.

Longevity. On November 18, Senator Robert C. Byrd (D., West Virginia)—who had served in the House from 1953 to 1959 before joining the Senate in 1959—became the longest-serving member of Congress in history. Byrd surpassed the record of Carl Hayden (D., Arizona), who had served from 1912 to 1969, a total of 56 years, 319 days. Byrd had already held the status of longest-serving senator. Earlier, on Feb. 11, 2009, Representative John Dingell (D., Michigan), who had joined the House in 1955, became the longest-serving House member in history, eclipsing the 53-year-and-60-day tenure of Jamie L. Whitten (D., Mississippi, 1941-1995). ■ Mike Lewis

See also **Deaths: A Special Report; Democratic Party; Elections; Health care issues; People in the news; Republican Party; Taxation; Transportation; United States, Government of the.**

Conservation.

Afghanistan established its first national park in April 2009, despite growing violence between international forces and insurgents. The park, called Band-e-Amir, is high in the Hindu Kush mountains of central Afghanistan. It consists of six deep-blue lakes separated by natural walls of *travertine,* a rock similar to limestone. Assistance in planning and funding for the park were provided by the New York City-based Wildlife Conservation Society (WCS) and the United States Agency for International Development. Although the endangered snow leopard has vanished from the park, the area still provides a home for wild goats, sheep, wolves, and many other animals.

Several snow leopards were photographed in June by WCS researchers and Afghan game rangers in the Wakhan Corridor, a narrow finger of Afghanistan that extends into Pakistan. As many as 100 of the cats remain in the country.

Snow leopards were among the 32 species of animals and plants that the Afghan National Environment Protection Agency placed on its first list of protected species, issued in June. Wolves and brown bears were also on the list.

New parklands. Wilderness areas in the United States got their largest expansion in a generation in March. The Omnibus Public Land Management Act of 2009 extended federal pro-

The International Union for Conservation of Nature (IUCN) warned of an "extinction crisis" in 2009. IUCN's Red List of Threatened Species grew to include 17,291 species. At least 1,895 species of amphibians (far right) are threatened, along with 1,677 species of reptiles (below). Even insects are threatened, with 261 dragonfly species (right) endangered.

The giant jewel dragonfly

Panay monitor lizard

tection to more than 2 million acres (800,000 hectares) in nine states. Wilderness areas were extended by more than 250,000 acres (100,000 hectares) in the Rocky Mountain National Park area of Colorado and by more than 700,000 acres (275,000 hectares) in three areas in California. The largest single parcel was in southwestern Idaho, where about 500,000 acres (200,000 hectares) were protected. The act also banned oil and gas leasing on 1.2 million acres (500,000 hectares). Thousands of miles of trails were added to the National Trails System.

Arctic sanctuaries. Russia established a 3.7-million acre (1.5-million hectare) national park on the Arctic island of Novaya Zemlya in June. The island, which was used by the Soviet Union to test nuclear weapons, lies in the Arctic Ocean, north of Asia. The park will provide protection to polar bears, walruses, reindeer, and sea birds.

In October, the U.S. Department of the Interior (USDI) proposed designating more than 200,000 square miles (500,000 square kilometers) along the northern coast of Alaska as critical habitat for polar bears. The area would be the largest single area of protected habitat inside the United States. The USDI, which found that polar bears were

threatened with extinction in May 2008, estimated that roughly 3,500 bears depend on the area. Under the designation, oil and gas exploration could continue. However, companies would have to show that their activities would not harm polar bears or their habitat.

Saving wetlands. More than 300,000 acres (120,000 hectares) of wetlands in the Mississippi floodplain were declared wetlands of international importance in June 2009. The wetlands were already protected by state and federal law, but the new designation offered international recognition of their importance.

In September, the USDI announced it was spending $41 million to purchase and conserve more than 190,000 acres (75,000 hectares) of wetlands. About $8 million of the spending came from federal duck stamps, which must be purchased by hunters of waterfowl and other migratory birds.

Birds in peril. About one-third of U.S. bird species are threatened with extinction, according to the first comprehensive survey by the USDI. The March report found that over the last 40 years, ocean birds have declined by 39 percent, grassland birds by 40 percent, and birds that live in deserts and other arid areas by 30 percent. The worst news came from Hawaii, where nearly all native birds are in danger of extinction. More

Rabbs fringe-limbed treefrog

than 70 species of Hawaiian birds had died out since human beings colonized the islands, and at least 10 had disappeared in the last 40 years.

The report did include some positive notes. Efforts to protect wetlands had enabled dramatic recovery among ducks, pelicans, and other waterfowl. The report argued that such successes demonstrated the power of conservation to reverse declines among threatened species.

Saving whales. In May, scientists with the National Oceanic and Atmospheric Administration (NOAA) observed blue whales migrating from the California coast to waters off British Columbia and the Gulf of Alaska for the first time since the end of commercial whaling in 1965. Only 6,000 to 12,000 blue whales survive of an original population of about 200,000.

A rule banning krill fishing in waters off the west coast of North America may aid the recovery of blue whales. Krill are tiny shrimplike animals that are eaten by whales and many other creatures. Increasing numbers of krill are harvested for use in dietary supplements and as fish-farm food. The NOAA rule took effect in August 2009.

Wolverines return. In June, WCS reported the return of the wolverine to Colorado for the first time in 90 years. Scientists used a radio collar to track a wolverine as it journeyed from Wyoming to Colorado. Wolverines have nearly vanished from the continental United States but remain common in Canada.

New whoopers. For only the second time in a century, a naturally produced whooping crane chick hatched in the wild in the American Midwest. The chick was spotted in a nest in June by biologists at the Necedah National Wildlife Refuge in Wisconsin. Another chick hatched that same month from an egg that was produced in captivity and placed in a wild nest. About 360 whooping cranes survive in the wild.

Wolf wars. In June, the U.S. Fish and Wildlife Service (FWS) agreed to restore federal protection to wolves in the upper Great Lakes region. The court-ordered settlement came after a lawsuit challenged the government's decision to remove federal protection from the wolves in April, leaving wolf management up to the states. The settlement faulted the FWS for making its April decision without public notice. The FWS agreed to provide 60 days of notice on any future decision to remove protection from the wolves.

Meanwhile, in September, hunting of wolves began in Idaho and Montana after a federal court rejected a suit to restore federal protection to the Northern Rocky Mountain wolf population. Protection continued in Wyoming after the FWS determined that the state's wolf management plan was too weak. Wolf numbers in the area have climbed to about 1,600 since the animals were reintroduced in the 1990's. Conservationists worried that allowing hunters to shoot as many as 295 wolves would undermine the long and costly recovery effort. ■ Edward Ricciuti

See also **Biology; Environmental pollution; Ocean; Zoos.**

Costa Rica. See Latin America.
Côte d'Ivoire. See Africa.

Courts in 2009 convicted a New York City financier of carrying out a massive fraud, threw out the conviction of a former United States senator, and legalized same-sex marriage in Iowa.

Bernard Madoff, in a New York City federal court on March 12, pleaded guilty to bilking thousands of investors out of some $65 billion in one of history's largest frauds. As the head of Bernard L. Madoff Investment Securities, he had masterminded a Ponzi scheme in which investors were paid from the principal contributed by later investors rather than from returns on investments. The scheme unraveled in 2008, when an economic recession prompted investors to withdraw money faster than new principal could be brought in. Madoff pleaded guilty to 11 felony counts, including fraud, money laundering, perjury, and theft. On June 29, 2009, U.S. District Judge Denny Chin sentenced Madoff to 150 years in prison—one of the most severe white-collar sentences ever.

Meanwhile, civil or criminal charges were brought against a number of suspected participants in the scheme. On August 11, Madoff's top financial aide, Frank DiPascali, pleaded guilty to 10 felony charges in connection with the scandal. On November 3, long-time Madoff auditor David Friehling pleaded guilty to nine criminal counts.

Ted Stevens, a U.S. senator (R., Alaska) from 1968 to 2009, had his October 2008 corruption conviction overturned by U.S. District Judge Emmet Sullivan on April 7, 2009, in Washington, D.C. Sullivan also ordered a criminal probe into whether Stevens's prosecutors should themselves be prosecuted for misconduct. Attorney General Eric Holder had asked that the charges against Stevens be dropped after concluding that the prosecutors had withheld too much information from defense lawyers. Stevens had been found guilty of making false statements on Senate financial disclosure forms. His conviction contributed to his defeat in the November 2008 election.

Same-sex marriage. On April 3, 2009, the Iowa Supreme Court legalized same-sex marriage in the state when it struck down a 1998 state law that defined marriage as a union between a man and a woman. The court ruled that the law violated the Iowa Constitution's equal protection clause. Local officials in Iowa began issuing marriage licenses to same-sex couples on April 27, 2009.

On May 26, the California Supreme Court upheld Proposition 8, a ballot initiative that had amended the state Constitution to recognize only marriage between a man and a woman. But the court let stand same-sex marriages that had taken place prior to Proposition 8's passage. In May 2008, the court ruled that the state Constitution guaranteed same-sex couples the right to marry, but Proposition 8, passed in November 2008, voided that ruling. From June to November 2008, about 18,000 same-sex couples had wed in California.

Hurricane Katrina victims—four residents and one business in the New Orleans area—were awarded $719,698 in damages on Nov. 19, 2009, by U.S. District Judge Stanwood Duval in New Orleans. Duval ruled that the U.S. Army Corps of Engineers had failed to properly maintain the Mississippi River-Gulf Outlet, a canal linking the Gulf of Mexico and New Orleans, and that this failure had led to major flooding in the wake of Katrina, which struck in August 2005. The U.S. government was expected to appeal the ruling. Legal experts noted that the ruling, if upheld, could make the government liable for tens of thousands of similar claims worth billions of dollars.

William Jefferson, a U.S. representative (D., Louisiana) from 1991 to 2009, was convicted on Aug. 5, 2009, of 11 felony charges, including solicitation of bribes, money laundering, and racketeering, by a federal jury in Alexandria, Virginia. Prosecutors said that Jefferson had collected hundreds of thousands of dollars in bribes from 2001 to 2005 in exchange for using his influence to promote business deals in West Africa. On Nov. 13, 2009, U.S. District Judge T. S. Ellis III sentenced Jefferson to 13 years in prison.

Ali Saleh Kahlah al-Marri, a U.S. resident from Qatar, pleaded guilty in an Illinois federal court on April 30 to providing material support to terrorists. He admitted having been involved with the terrorist network al-Qa`ida. On October 29, U.S. District Judge Michael Mihm sentenced Marri to eight years and four months in prison. Prior to being charged on February 26 and transported to Illinois on March 20, Marri had been designated an "enemy combatant" by the U.S. government and detained since 2003, without charge, in a U.S. military prison in South Carolina. The U.S. Fourth Circuit Court of Appeals had, in 2008, upheld the government's authority to hold Marri indefinitely without charge. However, on March 6, 2009, the U.S. Supreme Court vacated this decision.

Samuel Kent, a U.S. district judge who had been facing sex-crime charges, pleaded guilty on February 23 in a Houston federal court to one count of obstruction of justice. The plea was part of an agreement in which prosecutors dropped five sexual abuse charges against Kent. As part of the plea deal, Kent admitted that his advances toward two female employees had not been invited. On May 11, Senior U.S. District Judge Roger Vinson sentenced Kent to 33 months in prison. In response to Kent's refusal to immediately resign as a judge, the U.S. House of Representatives impeached him on June 19. Kent then resigned on June 30, and the U.S. Senate agreed to call off his impeachment trial.   ■ Mike Lewis

See also **Crime; Supreme Court of the U.S.**

Cricket. The Indian Premier League (IPL) enhanced its status in 2009, as IPL commissioner Lalit Modi worked to make the glitzy Twenty20 competition a global brand. England's Kevin Pietersen and Andrew Flintoff were high-profile new recruits joining the IPL megastar circus, earning a combined total of more than $3 million for 3 weeks' play in the eight-team tournament. Following security concerns in India because of general elections taking place there at the same time, the April 2009 IPL series was relocated to South Africa, where Deccan Chargers of Hyderabad beat Royal Challengers Bangalore in the final on May 24.

A new Twenty20 venture was the Champions League for regional teams, such as counties and states. Hosted in India, the inaugural winners in October were Australia's New South Wales Blues over Trinidad and Tobago from the Caribbean.

Test cricket. Australia lost its top ranking to South Africa in test matches in 2009. Captain Ricky Ponting's team was beaten 1-2 by South Africa early in the year but returned with a 2-0 win in April. Australia and England fought for the Ashes in midsummer in the United Kingdom. England's 2-1 win was a boost for new captain Andrew Strauss and coach Andy Flower, who replaced Kevin Pietersen and Peter Moores, respectively.

England's tour of the West Indies in early 2009 started disastrously, when England scored only 51 runs in one inning. The second test in Antigua was abandoned because of an unplayable pitch. West Indies ran out 1-0 series winners but played poorly in England a couple of months later, losing 2-0. West Indies' best players then went on strike. A second-string West Indies team lost 0-2 to Bangladesh in July.

In New Zealand in April, India performed well and won 0-1. As 2009 closed, India took on Sri Lanka, New Zealand hosted Pakistan, Australia played West Indies, and South Africa met England. During New Zealand's 0-2 series loss in Sri Lanka in August, Black Caps captain Daniel Vettori became only the eighth player in internationals to take 300 wickets and score 3,000 runs.

In March, terrorists in Lahore, Pakistan, opened fire on a bus carrying the Sri Lankan team. Several Sri Lankans were wounded and the tour was abandoned. Pakistan visited Sri Lanka in July, losing 0-2. Ongoing security problems meant Pakistan was restricted to games overseas, playing Australia and New Zealand in the United Arab Emirates (UAE).

World records. The canceled series between Pakistan and Sri Lanka included a record 437-run partnership, the best for a 4th-wicket in tests, between Sri Lanka's Mahela Jayawardene (240 runs) and Thilan Samaraweera (231). They beat a record set in 1957 by England's Peter May and Colin Cowdrey (411 against West Indies). India's Rahul Dravid set a career record for test catches by an outfielder (182) and on Nov. 16, 2009, became the fifth player to pass 11,000 test runs.

One Day Internationals (ODI's). The major ODI tournament in 2009 was the eight-team International Cricket Council (ICC) Champions Trophy in South Africa held in September and October. In the final, Australia beat New Zealand. (ODI matches, introduced in the 1970's, are played on a 50-overs each innings format.)

In other ODI series, at the start of 2009 India defeated Sri Lanka 4-1. South Africa won 1-4 in Australia in January and again, 3-2, several months later. Australia finished 2-2 against New Zealand. England won 2-3 against West Indies in March and again, 2-0, in May but crashed 1-6 against Australia. Sri Lanka beat Pakistan 3-1, and Bangladesh beat Zimbabwe 5-1. Australia beat India 4-2 to clinch their top ODI ranking in October and November.

Lesser names also made their mark in 2009. Afghanistan defeated Netherlands in an ODI and beat the UAE to win the Asian Cricket Council Twenty20 Cup in November.

In Twenty20 cricket, which takes little more time than a soccer or baseball game, with 20 overs (120 balls) bowled each innings, teams increasingly chose specialist Twenty20 players. The Twenty20 World Cup in England in June featured the top squads plus such emerging teams as Ireland and Scotland. Winners Pakistan beat Sri Lanka in an exciting final at Lord's, in London.

Domestic cricket. Durham won their second successive English county title. English Twenty20 champions were Sussex, who also won the Pro40 competition. Hampshire won the 50-over Friends Provident Trophy. In Australia, Victoria's Bushrangers were 2008-2009 Sheffield Shield winners.

Women's World Cup. Staged in March in Australia, the ICC Women's World Cup brought together Australia, New Zealand, West Indies, and South Africa (in preliminary group 1); and England, India, Pakistan, and Sri Lanka (in group 2). The matches were played in a 50-overs ODI format. The final on March 22 saw New Zealand score 166 all out in 47.2 overs, a score England overhauled with 4 wickets and 23 balls to spare. India came third, and Australia, fourth. England batter Claire Taylor's 324 runs won her the player of the tournament award. In the women's Twenty20 World Cup in London in June, England beat New Zealand in the final. England also beat Australia in a one-match "women's Ashes" in July.

Deaths. Renowned statistician Bill Frindall, who worked on the BBC Test Match Special radio team from 1966, died in January. The death of world-respected English umpire David Shepherd came in October. He had officiated in 92 test matches.   ■ Brian Williams

Crime. The Federal Bureau of Investigation (FBI) reported in September 2009 that the number of violent crimes in the United States had decreased in 2008 for the second year in a row. The FBI's annual "Crime in the United States" report includes data from nearly 17,800 U.S. law enforcement agencies on the violent crimes of murder, nonnegligent manslaughter, forcible rape, robbery, and aggravated assault, as well as the property crimes of burglary, larceny-theft, motor vehicle theft, and arson.

According to the FBI report, the 1.38 million violent crimes in 2008 represented a decline of 1.9 percent compared with 2007. All four violent crime categories in the report decreased in number—murders and nonnegligent manslaughters by 3.9 percent; aggravated assaults by 2.5 percent; forcible rape by 1.6 percent; and robberies by 0.7 percent.

The FBI report noted that 9.77 million property crimes occurred in the United States in 2008—a decrease of 0.8 percent compared with 2007. This was the sixth straight year of property crime decreases. The number of motor vehicle thefts decreased by 12.7 percent; burglaries, by 2.0 percent; and larceny-thefts, by 0.3 percent.

The FBI estimated that law enforcement agencies across the United States made 14 million arrests in 2008, excluding arrests for traffic offenses. This number compared with 14.2 million arrests in 2007.

"Suicide by cop," in which an individual causes real or apparent danger to others in an attempt to get himself or herself killed by police officers, is more common than previously believed. That was the conclusion of a study reported in February 2009 by a team of researchers led by forensic psychologist Kris Mohandie of the Los Angeles Police Department.

Mohandie's team examined more than 700 police-related shootings that occurred in North America from 1998 to 2006. The team assessed the behaviors and backgrounds—including police reports, witness statements, and criminal histories—of individuals who died in the shootings to determine if they had suicidal motives. The researchers categorized 36 percent of the shootings as suicide by cop.

The findings verified not only the high rate of suicide by cop, but also the fact that suicidal individuals often injure or kill other people in their quest for death. In about a third of the examined incidents, other people were harmed or killed.

Forensic science flaws. The system of forensic science in the United States has serious flaws, according to a February 2009 report by the National Research Council (NRC), a Washington, D.C.-based scientific research organization that advises the federal government. The NRC reported that forensic science, the science of crime solving, lacks mandatory certification programs for scientists, strong standards for analyzing evidence, and adequate government funding.

The NRC also noted that few peer-reviewed studies have been published on the reliability of forensic methods other than DNA analysis. As a result, the reliability of such methods as bite-mark, fiber, fingerprint, and microscopic hair analysis was called into question.

The NRC recommended a number of reforms, as well as more research, for the forensic science system. Among these recommendations was the establishment of a National Institute of Forensic Science to develop and enforce standards and to lead research efforts.

Parole system problems. A bizarre case of kidnapping shed light on problems in the U.S. parole system in 2009. In August, San Francisco-area police arrested Phillip and Nancy Garrido for the kidnapping and rape of Jaycee Dugard, who was abducted outside her home in South Lake Tahoe, California, in 1991, when she was age 11. According to investigators, the husband-and-wife crime team kidnapped Dugard and held her hostage for 18 years in ramshackle tents and sheds hidden among trees on their property. Police said that Phillip fathered two daughters with Jaycee during that time.

Phillip had been convicted of the kidnapping

The police force of Oakland, California, attends a public memorial service at Oracle Arena for four officers slain on March 21. According to police, Lovelle Mixon shot and killed two officers during a routine traffic stop and then fled to an apartment complex, where he shot two other officers in a gunfight before being brought down by a S.W.A.T. team.

and rape of another woman in 1976, but he was paroled from prison after serving only about 10 years of his 50-year sentence. Despite numerous visits to the Garrido home since 1991, parole officers failed to notice Dugard in the home or the unusual tent/shed complex in the backyard. The officers also apparently ignored complaints from neighbors about Garrido's "psychotic" behavior.

The fact that Jaycee was still alive came to light after police at the University of California at Berkeley noticed Phillip and two young girls (Jaycee's daughters) distributing religious literature. Campus police learned Garrido was a sex offender when they ran a background check on him, and they then contacted his parole officer. After the parole officer summoned Garrido, he reported to the parole office with the 29-year-old Dugard, who was finally identified and rescued.

Phil Spector, a legendary rock music producer, was sentenced to 19 years in prison in May 2009 for the shooting and murder in 2003 of Lana Clarkson, a struggling actress, at his mansion in a Los Angeles suburb. A number of witnesses in the case testified that Spector had a history of threatening women with guns. Spector was famous for producing songs by some of the greatest rock artists of the 1960's and 1970's, including the Beatles and Rolling Stones.   ■ Alfred J. Smuskiewicz

See also **Courts; Terrorism.**

Croatia. Prime Minister Ivo Sanader unexpectedly resigned in July 2009, halfway through his second term in office. To replace him, the ruling right-of-center Croatian Democratic Union (HDZ) selected Deputy Prime Minister Jadranka Kosor. Subsequently confirmed by parliament, Kosor became Croatia's first female prime minister.

Ivo Sanader had led Croatia for six years, a period during which the small Balkan country recovered from the 1990's wars caused by the breakup of the former Yugoslavia, surged economically, and began membership talks with the European Union (EU). Sanader had inherited his political mantle from Franjo Tudjman, a hardline nationalist who created the HDZ and led Croatia through much of the 1990's. Tudjman died in 1999, and the HDZ's virtual monopoly on power ended following democratic elections in January 2000. Sanader subsequently transformed the HDZ into a mainstream, center-right party.

The new government headed by Kosor faced a number of challenges in 2009. Croatia's steady progress in EU accession talks bogged down after late 2008, when the country's northern neighbor, Slovenia, an EU member, blocked the process. Slovenia's grievance was a border dispute with Croatia centering on the two countries' Adriatic coastline. Slovenian leaders demanded settlement of the dispute as a

condition for Croatia's admission to the EU.

Talks between Kosor and Slovenian Prime Minister Borut Pahor in September led to an agreement to have the border dispute settled by arbitration. Slovenia subsequently yielded on Croatia's EU candidacy, and EU officials resumed accession talks with Croatian leaders. In late 2009, EU officials still held out hope that Croatia could become the 28th EU member nation in 2011.

Economy. Croatia went into negative growth in 2009, as the global recession stifled demand for exports. Receipts from tourism declined as well. Economists estimate that tourism accounts for more than one-fifth of Croatia's gross domestic product (GDP)—the total value of goods and services produced in a country in a year.

According to the Croatian Statistics Office, the country's GDP contracted by an annual rate of more than 6 percent in the first half of 2009. In November, EU economists forecast that Croatia would experience flat economic growth in 2010 and some recovery in 2011.

NATO membership. On April 1, 2009, Croatia joined the North Atlantic Treaty Organization (NATO). "The Republic of Croatia has fulfilled one of its two foreign policy targets: to join the European Union and NATO," declared Croatian President Stipe Mesic.   ■ Sharon L. Wolchik

See also **Europe.**

Cuba. In 2009, President Raúl Castro made increasing agricultural production Cuba's number one priority. In a speech on July 26—Revolution Day—Castro blamed decades of mismanagement by the Cuban government for worsening food shortages and a 33-percent decline in the area of cultivated land from 1997 to 2008.

In an effort to reverse the trend, Castro said, authorities had leased more than 1.7 million acres (690,000 hectares) of unused government-owned land in 2008 to some 82,000 private farmers and cooperatives. Still, food production fell by 7.3 percent in the first quarter of 2009 over the previous year, with meat output dropping by 14.7 percent. On August 1, Castro urged farmers to make greater use of the estimated 265,000 oxen in Cuba to increase production. The use of oxen would help conserve energy, he told parliament, while reducing the rising costs of food and fuel imports.

OAS OK. In June, the Organization of American States (OAS) voted to lift a ban on Cuba's membership in the regional association dating from 1962, when Cuba aligned itself with the Communist bloc. The United States accepted the move but insisted that Cuba take steps to restore democracy and guarantee human rights before being formally welcomed back. Cuba declined to rejoin.

In April 2009, the U.S. Congress eased restrictions on travel to Cuba by Cuban-Americans and allowed them to send more money back to friends and family. But it kept in place a long-standing trade embargo against Cuba, despite an October vote in the United Nations General Assembly. Only Israel and the Pacific Island nation of Palau joined the United States in supporting the embargo.

Oil exploration. In November, Cuban and Russian officials signed contracts that will permit Zarubezeneft, a Russian oil company, to help develop oil reserves in central and western Cuba. The reserves were near Ciego de Ávila, Matanzas, Sancti Spíritus, and Villa Clara.

Energy program. In May, the Cuban government ordered severe energy conservation measures to trim the cost of petroleum imports and the national budget. Lights and air conditioners were turned off at stores, banks, and government institutions during the summer months. State-run businesses and factories were ordered to shut down early to conserve electric power.

Peace concert. On September 20, more than 1 million Cubans—most dressed in white to symbolize peace—jammed Havana's Revolution Plaza for a "Peace Concert" headlined by Colombian rocker Juanes. It was the biggest crowd for a visitor to Cuba since Pope John Paul II arrived in 1998.   ◾ Nathan A. Haverstock

See also **Latin America.**

Cyprus. See Middle East.

Czech Republic. The center-right government of Prime Minister Mirek Topolánek fell in March 2009 following a no-confidence vote in parliament. President Václav Klaus subsequently appointed Jan Fischer, a government economist, to head an interim caretaker government. The change in government occurred while the Czech Republic was holding the rotating presidency of the European Union (EU). According to analysts, the governmental instability in Prague, the capital, hampered some EU diplomatic initiatives.

Prime Minister Fischer was to govern only until elections could be held in October. However, a constitutional challenge to the calling of early elections resulted in delay of the elections until June 2010.

In 2009, the export-dependent Czech economy suffered from the global economic crisis, which reduced international demand for Czech goods. Economists forecast that the Czech economy would contract by 4.3 percent in 2009, then expand by a meager 0.3 percent in 2010.

On Nov. 3, 2009, President Klaus signed the Lisbon Treaty, the blueprint for revamping the EU's executive arm and establishing a permanent office of president. President Klaus's assent provided the final formal approval necessary for ratification.   ◾ Sharon L. Wolchik

See also **Europe.**

Dallas. Cowboys Stadium, the largest domed stadium in the world and the new home of football's Dallas Cowboys, opened in Arlington, a Dallas suburb, on May 29, 2009. The $1.2-billion facility, which is used for a wide variety of sporting and entertainment events in addition to Cowboys games, also boasts the world's largest video screen. The city of Arlington committed $325 million in tax funds to the stadium project. On September 20, the Cowboys' opening game with the New York Giants attracted a crowd of 105,121, the largest ever to attend a National Football League game. The Cowboys lost, 33 to 31.

Terrorist plot alleged. On September 24, agents with the Federal Bureau of Investigation (FBI) arrested a 19-year-old Jordanian after he was accused of attempting to detonate a vehicle filled with explosives under a downtown Dallas skyscraper. Investigators said Hosam Smadi, who was in the United States illegally, planned to set off explosives in the garage beneath Fountain Place. An undercover FBI agent monitoring an extremist Web site said he discovered Smadi making terrorist threats against the United States six months earlier. Smadi was arrested after he allegedly dialed his cell phone, thinking it would detonate explosives in a sport utility vehicle parked beneath Fountain Place. The bomb, given to Smadi by undercover FBI agents posing as members of an al-Qa`ida sleeper cell, was a fake.

In October, a federal grand jury charged Smadi with attempting to use a weapon of mass destruction and trying to bomb a place of public use.

Former city official convicted. Former Dallas Mayor Pro Tem Don Hill was found guilty on October 5 of bribery and extortion charges stemming from a federal investigation into alleged misconduct by Hill, his wife, and three other defendants. In 2007, federal prosecutors had charged Hill and his codefendants with seeking hundreds of thousands of dollars in cash and contracts from affordable housing developers in return for supporting their development projects. Sentencing was scheduled for early 2010.

Arts center opens. The $354-million AT&T Performing Arts Center opened on Oct. 12, 2009, in the downtown Dallas Arts District, following the largest private fund-raising campaign for an arts facility in U.S. history.

Formerly known as the Dallas Center for the Performing Arts, the venue includes the Winspear Opera House, the Wyly Theatre, the Annette Strauss Artist Square, and the 10-acre (4-hectare) Sammons Park. Construction of a city performance hall will complete the center. More than 130 individuals and families donated at least $1 million apiece to the arts center project. With the opening, Dallas now has the nation's largest arts district, spanning 68 acres

(28 hectares) and 19 city blocks.

Rail line expanded. On September 12, Dallas Area Rapid Transit (DART) opened the first 3 miles (5 kilometers) and four new stations of its light rail system Green Line, with service from downtown Dallas to Fair Park in South Dallas. The rest of the 28-mile (45-kilometer) line, from Pleasant Grove in Southeast Dallas to Farmers Branch northwest of Dallas, was scheduled to open in 2010.

Championship forfeited. South Oak Cliff High School, winner of four consecutive state basketball titles, forfeited its 2005 championship in February 2009 after an investigation disclosed that grades for three players were improperly changed from failing to passing so they would be eligible for the tournament. The forfeiture marked the second time the Dallas high school was stripped of a championship. In June 2008, South Oak Cliff had to give up its 2006 title when state education officials discovered improper grade changing.

Park over downtown freeway. Construction began in October 2009 on a 5.2-acre (2.1-hectare) park that will span Woodall Rodgers Freeway and link downtown Dallas to the popular Uptown neighborhood. The $105-million project will feature a restaurant, performance pavilion, and dog park. The park project, financed with federal, state, city, and private funds, is slated to be finished in 2012. ■ Henry K. Tatum

Dance. Merce Cunningham was the dominant figure in dance in 2009. His creative output had not flagged; as his 90th birthday approached he was choreographing a new two-act work to mark the occasion. *Nearly Ninety* (a reference to both his years and the work's duration in minutes) had a gala premiere at the Brooklyn Academy of Music on Cunningham's birthday, April 16. In early June, the New York City-based Merce Cunningham Foundation made a sobering and unusual announcement, outlining its "Legacy Plan," the vision for Cunningham's dances and company beyond his lifetime. Part of the plan entailed digitizing and documenting Cunningham's dances to preserve them for future generations of dancers and scholars. Cunningham died on July 26.

Pina Bausch. The June 30 death of Pina Bausch, the German choreographer who had directed the celebrated Tanztheater Wuppertal since 1973, marked the sudden end of another influential career. Her theatrically daring works had a large following worldwide. Her distinctive synthesis of self-revelation, movement, and speech inspired many choreographers to incorporate more theatrical elements and approaches in their work. Her company, for which she had created new works almost annually, planned to continue performing and touring.

Ratmansky. The most creatively significant news in ballet in 2009 was the arrival in January of Alexei Ratmansky, former artistic director of Moscow's Bolshoi Ballet, as artist in residence of American Ballet Theatre (ABT) in New York City. He created two important new works for ABT that were performed in 2009: *On the Dnieper,* set to a little-known score by Russian composer Sergei Prokofiev, debuted in June; and *Seven Sonatas,* to the music of the Italian composer Domenico Scarlatti, debuted in October. Ratmansky also choreographed *Waltz Masquerade,* an affectionate gala *pièce d'occasion* for ABT ballerina Nina Ananiashvili. ABT announced in November that Ratmansky would create a new *Nutcracker* production that would have its premiere in 2010. Also active as a free-lancer, he created a new production of *Scuola di Ballo* ("School of Dance") for the Australian Ballet that premiered in August 2009.

Twyla Tharp assembled a group of dancers—many of them long-time and expert exponents of her choreography—to create *Come Fly with Me,* a program of dances set to Frank Sinatra songs. The show opened on September 23 at the Alliance Theater in Atlanta, where it ran for one month and attracted national press attention. The two-act production, which featured 4 lead couples and an ensemble of 12 dancers, marked a return to the music of Sinatra for Tharp. She had choreographed a duet for herself and Mikhail Baryshnikov—*Once More Frank,* in 1976, and then created her enduring masterwork *Nine Sinatra Songs* for her company in 1982. In *Come Fly with Me,* a live orchestra accompanied vintage recorded vocals of Sinatra, as Tharp evoked an evening of romance, conflict, exuberance, and regret through a mature and expansive series of dances. The show was expected to arrive on Broadway in 2010.

Ballets Russes. The 2009 centennial of the Ballets Russes, the company of primarily Russian dancers led by Serge Diaghilev, which blazed a path into the 1900's for ballet, was marked by many ballet companies, museums, and academic institutions. The Ballets Russes debut in May 1909 took Paris by storm. The company launched the careers of several seminal choreographers, including Mikhail Fokine, Leonide Massine, Bronislava Nijinska, and George Balanchine. It was also where Vaslav Nijinsky made his short-lived but historic impact—both as a remarkably exciting, technical, and accomplished dancer and as an experimental, controversial choreographer. During 2009, exhibitions at Boston's Harvard Theater Collection and New York City's Library for the Performing Arts captured the creativity and excitement of the Ballets Russes. Many companies programmed performances of the landmark bal-

Merce Cunningham
Lord of the Dance

Merce Cunningham—who died on July 26, 2009, at the age of 90—was one of the most inventive, challenging, and unpredictable creators of modern dance in the 1900's. His method of using chance to *choreograph* (create) dances became famous. To choreograph a piece, Cunningham would select a movement, a dancer, a length of time, and a space on the stage. He would then toss dice, flip a coin, or dip into a grab bag to decide which dancer would do what movement for how long and where. This use of chance led him to discover possibilities beyond his imagination. In 1989, he began to compose dances on a computer. In the 1990's, he developed a computer program called *LifeForms* (later renamed *DanceForms)* to create dances.

Cunningham was a superb dancer himself, famous for his strength and soaring leaps. Until the age of 70, he appeared in every performance given by his company, the New York City-based Merce Cunningham Dance Company. In 1999, at the age of 80, he danced a duet with the great Russian-born ballet dancer Mikhail Baryshnikov.

Cunningham often created dances without knowing the music that would accompany them. Dancers practiced the steps in silence. The choreography, musical score, set design, and costumes came together only at the first performance. If the parts fit together, that was lucky. If they did not fit, he considered it unimportant. He had little patience for people who insisted on meaning in art. Asked what one dance was about, he answered, "It's about 40 minutes."

Mercier Philip Cunningham was born in Centralia, Washington, on April 16, 1919. He began his dance career in 1939 with the Martha Graham company.

As a teenager, Cunningham had enrolled in a music class taught by the composer John Cage. The two became life partners. In 1944, they gave their first joint concert in New York City. In 1953, they formed the Merce Cunningham Dance Company with Cage as musical director and Cunningham as artistic director and choreographer. They lived and worked together for more than 40 years, until Cage died in 1992.

For many years, Cunningham's dances puzzled audiences and critics. On the company's first international tour in 1964, one audience threw tomatoes and eggs. However, the company also received rave reviews on that tour, and critics soon hailed Cunningham as a pioneer. His company performed to sold-out crowds. His ideas and methods influenced a generation of dancers and choreographers, including Karol Armitage, Mark Morris, Paul Taylor, and Twyla Tharp.

Cunningham created some 200 dance works. His final work, *Nearly Ninety*, premiered in April 2009 to mark his 90th birthday.

"You have to love dancing to stick to it," Cunningham once wrote. "It gives you nothing back, no manuscripts to store away, no paintings to show on walls … nothing but that single fleeting moment when you feel alive." Cunningham loved dancing and stuck to it. He gave his audiences, and himself, many moments of feeling alive.

■ Sara Dreyfuss

lets from its repertory that have survived. Ballet West, in Salt Lake City, offered "The Treasures of the Ballets Russes" in March and April, and the Boston Ballet's May performances, "Diaghilev's Ballets Russes Centennial Celebration," included three historic works. It also contained Jorma Elo's new interpretation of Igor Stravinsky's *Le Sacre du Printemps (The Rite of Spring),* which had originally been choreographed by Nijinsky for the Diaghilev company in 1913.

The School of American Ballet (SAB), founded by Balanchine and Lincoln Kirstein in 1934 and closely affiliated with New York City Ballet (NYCB), marked its 75th anniversary in 2009 with deserved pride in its accomplishments. On January 14, a special NYCB gala evening featured guest performances by school alumni who had gone on to become principal dancers with major companies.

Alvin Ailey American Dance Theater in New York City segued from its 50th-anniversary festivities in 2008 to a 2009 season celebrating Judith Jamison's 20th anniversary as the company's dynamic artistic director. Jamison, who had announced that she would retire from her position in 2011, became the company's director shortly after Ailey's death in 1989. For her anniversary season, she choreographed *Among Us: Public Spaces, Private Places,* to a commissioned score by Eric Lewis, first performed on December 4. Ronald K. Brown created a new work for the company, *Dancing Spirit,* which premiered December 11 and paid tribute to Jamison.

Retirements. Several ballerinas with exemplary careers lasting more than two decades retired with deserved fanfare during 2009. Nina Ananiashvili, an international star who started her career with the Bolshoi Ballet, had found a second home with American Ballet Theatre, dancing there since 1993. Ananiashvili gave her farewell performance with ABT in *Swan Lake* on June 27, 2009, at New York City's Metropolitan Opera House. She planned to continue working in ballet as artistic director of the State Ballet of Georgia, her native land.

On May 9, San Francisco Ballet bid a celebratory farewell to Tina LeBlanc, whose 25-year career began as a leading light of the Joffrey Ballet during the 1980's before she went on to explore more varied repertory and achieve new depth in San Francisco.

Louise Nadeau, a versatile and eloquent ballerina with Pacific Northwest Ballet in Seattle, danced her last performance on June 7 in a special program in her honor. All three women demonstrated that ballerinas can continue performing at peak level well into their 40's.

■ Susan Reiter

DEATHS

in 2009 included those listed below, who were Americans unless otherwise indicated.

Allingham, Henry (1896–July 18), supercentenarian who was one of the last surviving British veterans of World War I and, at 113, the United Kingdom's oldest man.

Allwine, Wayne (1947–May 18), award-winning Disney sound effects editor who was the voice of Mickey Mouse for more than 30 years.

Anderson, Robert (1917–February 9), playwright who had six plays on Broadway from 1953 to 1971, including *Tea and Sympathy* (1953) and *I Never Sang for My Father* (1968).

Annenberg, Leonore (Leonore Cohn) (1918–March 12), socialite and philanthropist who with her late husband Walter Annenberg gave $4 billion to cultural, educational, and medical institutions.

Aquino, Corazon (1933–August 1), president of the Philippines (1986–1992) who had been thrust into the role of leader of the opposition to President Ferdinand Marcos following the murder of her husband, a prominent senator.

Archerd, Army (Armand Andre Archerd) (1922–September 8), Hollywood reporter whose "Just for Variety" column was a nearly daily feature of *Variety* for more than 50 years.

Arneson, Dave (1947–April 7), co-creator with Gary Gygax of the fantasy game Dungeons & Dragons who developed many of the fundamental ideas of role-playing games.

Arthur, Bea (Bernice Frankel) (1922–April 25), husky-voiced actress who won a Tony Award in 1966 for the original Broadway production of *Mame* and Emmy awards for both "Maude" and "The Golden Girls."

Barry, Gene (Eugene Klass) (1919–December 9), actor who starred in the TV series "Bat Masterson" and "Burke's Law" and the Broadway musical *La Cage aux Folles.*

Bea Arthur, actress

Bausch, Pina (1940–June 30), German choreographer whose powerfully dramatic but dreamlike works influenced generations of dancers and choreographers.

Bee, Molly (Mollie Gene Beachboard) (1939–February 7), country music singer whose 1952 hit "I Saw Mommy Kissing Santa Claus" propelled her onto television's "Tennessee Ernie Ford Show."

Behrens, Hildegard (1937–August 18), German soprano who sang 171 performances, most notably as Brünnhilde, at New York City's Metropolitan Opera.

Bell, Griffin B. (1918–January 5), lawyer and judge who served as attorney general through much of the Jimmy Carter administration.

Bellson, Louie (1924–February 14), jazz drummer who played with Count Basie, Duke Ellington, Benny Goodman, and other band leaders and was his wife Pearl Bailey's music director.

Bennett, Estelle (1941–February 11?), member of the Rock and Roll Hall of Fame singing trio The Ronettes, whose 1960's hits included "Be My Baby" and "Walkin' in the Rain."

Blanchard, Johnny (1933–March 25), outfielder and catcher who played in five consecutive World Series for the New York Yankees in the early 1960's, hitting two homers and batting .400 in the 1961 series.

Bogle, Bob (1934–June 14), a founding member of the Ventures, who scored six Top 40 hits through the 1960's, including "Walk—Don't Run," which sold 2 million singles.

Bohr, Aage (1922–September 8), Danish nuclear physicist and son of Nobel laureate Niels Bohr. Aage Bohr shared the 1975 Nobel Prize in physics for his explanation of how the rotational motion of protons and neutrons inside the nucleus of an atom could distort the shape of the nucleus.

Bongo, Omar (1935–June 8), authoritarian leader who controlled Gabon and its vast oil resources from 1967 until his death.

Borlaug, Norman (1914–September 12), agronomist who, as the father of the "Green Revolution," is credited with saving more than 1 billion lives. See **Portrait** at **Agriculture.**

Braden, Tom (1917–April 3), newspaper editor and CIA officer who wrote *Eight Is Enough* and helped create CNN's "Crossfire."

Brady, James (1928–January 26), novelist and *Parade* magazine celebrity columnist who served as publisher for both *Harper's Bazaar* and *Women's Wear Daily* and created Page Six, the *New York Post's* famous gossip section.

Brinker, Norman (1931–June 9), restaurateur who created the salad bar, turned Jack-in-the-Box into a national brand, founded Bennigan's, and transformed Chili's into an international brand.

Brown, Anne (1912–March 13), soprano whose voice inspired George Gershwin to enlarge the part of Bess, which Brown sang in the original 1935 Broadway production of *Porgy and Bess.*

Browne, Ray (1922–October 22), Bowling Green State professor who founded the academic discipline of popular-culture studies and is credited with popularizing the term "popular culture."

Johnny Blanchard, outfielder

Burke, Paul (1926–September 13), actor noted for his roles in the 1960's TV series "Naked City" and "12 O'Clock High" and in the films *Valley of the Dolls* (1967) and *The Thomas Crown Affair* (1968).

Calisher, Hortense (1911–January 13), writer of highly diverse, stylistically and intellectually challenging novels and short stories.

Cardiff, Jack (1914–April 22), English cinematographer and director who received a lifetime-achievement Academy Award for filming such classics as *The Red Shoes* (1948), *The African Queen* (1951), and *War and Peace* (1956).

Carey, Philip (Eugene Joseph Carey) (1925–February 6), ruggedly handsome actor who starred in the "Laredo" TV series (1965-1967) and played the patriarch on the soap opera "One Life to Live" from 1980 to 2007.

Carradine, David (John Arthur Carradine) (1936–June 3), actor who starred in the 1970's TV series "Kung Fu" and appeared in more than 100 films, including Quentin Tarantino's *Kill Bill* films.

Carroll, Jim (1949–September 11), poet and punk rocker whose *The Basketball Diaries,* an account of his descent from high school sports star to drug addict, won him a cult following.

Carroll, Mickey (Michael Finocchiaro) (1919–May 7), actor and vaudevillian who was one of the last surviving Munchkins from the 1939 classic *The Wizard of Oz.*

Carter, Johnny (1934–August 21), singer who was twice inducted into the Rock and Roll Hall of Fame for his membership in two doo-wop groups, the Flamingos and the Dells.

Chaplin, Sydney (1926–March 3), actor (and son of Charlie Chaplin) who won a Tony Award in 1957 for the Broadway musical *Bells Are Ringing* and starred opposite Barbra Streisand in the original production of *Funny Girl* (1964).

Cifelli, Gus (1925–March 26), star tackle who helped Notre Dame win three national championships and the Detroit Lions win the National Football League title in 1952.

Cintrón, Conchita (1922–February 17), Chilean-Peruvian matador who was perhaps the most accomplished *torera* in the history of bullfighting.

Close, William T. (1924–January 15), personal physician to Zaire President Mobutu Sese Seko and father of actress Glenn Close. Doctor Close played a pivotal role in preventing the spread of the deadly Ebola virus in Zaire, now Congo (Kinshasa).

Cohn, Sam (1929–May 6), New York-based talent agent whose client list—ranging from Paul Newman, Meryl Streep, and Liza Minnelli to Woody Allen, Mike Nichols, and E. L. Doctorow—and skill at arranging deals made him the most powerful talent broker in the American theater and Hollywood in the 1970's and 1980's.

Cowles, Fleur (Florence Friedman) (1908–June 5), socialite, writer, and artist who most famously edited the influential magazine *Flair.*

Cronkite, Walter (1916–July 17), broadcast journalist. See **Portrait** at **Television.**

Cunningham, Merce (1919–July 26), dancer whom many critics considered the most talented, inventive, and influential choreographer of the second half of the 20th century. See **Portrait** at **Dance.**

Daly, Chuck (1930–May 9), basketball coach who guided the Detroit Pistons to two consecutive NBA titles in 1989 and 1990 and led the original Olympic basketball "dream team" in 1992.

Dausset, Jean (1916–June 6), French immunologist who shared the 1980 Nobel Prize in physiology or medicine for discoveries about the human immune system.

Davis, Glenn (1934–January 28), hurdler and sprinter who won a total of three gold medals at the Melbourne Olympics in 1956 and at the Rome Olympics in 1960.

Dean, Millvina (1912–May 31), British nonagenarian who was the last living survivor of the 1912 *Titanic* disaster.

Dearie, Blossom (1924–February 7), jazz and cabaret singer and songwriter who developed a cult following for her unique voice, innovative piano stylings, and subtle interpretations.

DeCarava, Roy (1919–October 27), photographer known for his images of both jazz greats and the ordinary people of New York City's Harlem and Bedford-Stuyvesant neighborhoods.

DeLuise, Dom (1933–May 4), mirthful comic actor and chef who was a regular on "The Dean Martin Show" and appeared in six of Mel Brooks's comedies, including *Blazing Saddles* (1974).

Des Forges, Alison (Alison Liebhafsky) (1942–February 12), human rights activist and historian who wrote what is considered to be the definitive work on the genocide in Rwanda in 1994.

Devi, Gayatri (1919–July 29), the last maharani of Jaipur. She served as a member of India's Parliament in the 1960's and was often described as one of the world's most beautiful women.

Digges, Deborah (Deborah Sugarbaker) (1950–April 10), award-winning poet whose works, including *Vesper Sparrows* (1986) and *Rough Music* (1995), were described as "among the most beautiful and moving of any being written by a poet of her generation."

DiMaggio, Dominic (1917–May 8), All-Star center fielder and Joe DiMaggio's younger brother and holder of the record for the longest consecutive game hitting streak in Red Sox history—34 consecutive games in 1949.

Donald, David Herbert (1920–May 17), Pulitzer Prize-winning Abraham Lincoln scholar and historian whose 1995 *Lincoln* is considered one of the greatest biographies of that president.

Downes, Sir Edward (1924–July 10), British conductor who led the BBC Philharmonic, the Royal Opera House, and Opera Australia. Nearly blind and growing deaf, Downes took his own life in tandem with his terminally ill wife of 54 years.

Dreyfus, Jack (1913–March 27), financier who founded the Dreyfus Fund, one of the first widely marketed mutual funds.

Druon, Maurice (1918–April 14), French novelist and minister of culture whose *Les Grandes Familles* won the 1948 Prix Goncourt. Druon wrote the lyrics to the World War II anthem "Chant des Partisans."

Dunne, Dominick (1925–August 26), producer and writer who chronicled the lives and misdeeds of the rich, famous, and infamous in his *Vanity Fair* column and in such novels as *The Two Mrs. Grenvilles* (1985) and *An Inconvenient Woman* (1990).

Eckert, Beverly (1951–February 12), woman who lost her husband in the New York City terrorist attacks on Sept. 11, 2001, and who went on to become a spokesperson for victims' families and an antiterrorist activist.

Erickson, Arthur (1924–May 20), Canadian architect whose modernist glass-and-concrete structures won gold medals from the American and Canadian institutes of architecture and from the French Academy of Architecture.

Evdokimova, Eva (1948–April 3), Swiss-born ballerina who was known for the delicacy of her movement and purity of form. She danced regularly opposite Rudolf Nureyev, whom she cited as a major inspiration.

Farmer, Philip José (1918–February 25), prolific, award-winning author who wrote more than 75 science fiction and fantasy novels, including the "Riverworld" and the "World of Tiers" series.

Fawcett, Farrah (1947–June 25), actress who rose above the fame of her bathing-suit posters, trend-setting hairstyle, and "Charlie's Angels" TV stardom with such critically acclaimed made-for-TV movies as *The Burning Bed* and *Small Sacrifices*.

Ferrante, Arthur (1921–September 19), one-half of the piano duo Ferrante and Teicher, whose lush orchestral recordings of movie themes sold some 90 million records.

Fidrych, Mark (1954–April 13), Detroit Tigers pitcher known as "Bird," who electrified baseball in 1976 with a 19-9 record, an earned run average of 2.34, and 97 strikeouts.

Farrah Fawcett, actress

Fisher, Don (1928–September 27), San Francisco businessman who with his wife, Doris, opened a blue jeans store that proliferated into Gap Inc., which in turn branched into Baby Gap, Gap Kids, Old Navy, and Banana Republic.

FitzGerald, Jerri Nielsen (1952–June 23), physician who in 1999 diagnosed and treated her own breast cancer while on an expedition at the Amundsen-Scott South Pole Station in 1999.

Flanagan, Barry (1941–August 31), British sculptor whose mature work consisted of oversized bronze representations of exuberantly athletic hares.

Foote, Horton (1916–March 4), celebrated playwright whose plays—*The Trip to Bountiful, The Orphans' Home Cycle* (a nine-play cycle), *Dividing the Estate,* and *The Young Man from Atlanta*—gently capture the angst and humor of small-town life in 20th century America. Foote won two Academy Awards for best screenplay—for *To Kill a Mockingbird* (1962) and *Tender Mercies (1983).*

Forrest, Vernon (1971–July 25), boxer who won the World Boxing Council (WBC) welterweight championship in 2002 and the WBC light-middleweight title in 2007.

Foss, Lukas (Lukas Fuchs) (1922–February 1), German-born composer, pianist, and conductor who explored and interwove a wide range of musical styles from Baroque to Minimalism, serialism, and improvisation.

Franklin, John Hope (1915–March 25), historian and scholar of the African American experience. See **Portrait** at **Education**.

French, Marilyn (1929–May 2), writer and activist whose 1977 novel *The Women's Room* propelled her into the front ranks of the feminist movement.

Freud, Sir Clement (1924–April 15), German-born English restaurateur, chef and food expert, writer, former member of Parliament, and radio wit and raconteur who was the grandson of Sigmund Freud and the brother of artist Lucian Freud.

Fuller, Millard (1935–February 3), Habitat for Humanity founder who was responsible for 300,000 new homes that housed at least 1 million people in more than 180 countries.

Furchgott, Robert (1916–May 19), pharmacologist who shared the 1998 Nobel Prize in physiology or medicine for his research on how the gas nitric oxide regulates important body functions.

Gelbart, Larry (1928–September 11), comedy writer who at age 16 was hired by Danny Thomas and went on to write the book for the musical *A Funny Thing Happened on the Way to the Forum* (1962), the screenplay for *Tootsie* (1982), and 97 episodes of "M*A*S*H."

Gibson, Henry (James Bateman) (1935–September 14), character actor and comic who most famously portrayed a cloying poet on the "Rowan & Martin's Laugh-in" TV series and a country music singer in Robert Altman's *Nashville* (1975).

Ginty, Robert (1948–September 21), film producer, director, and actor who starred in *The Exterminator* (1980) and other action movies.

Goldsmith, Thomas, Jr., (1910–March 5), physicist and engineer who with Allen B. DuMont perfected the cathode ray tube and turned oscilloscopes into full television displays.

Horton Foote, playwright

Gosdin, Vern (1934–April 28), country music singer known as "the voice" whose hits included "Set 'Em Up Joe," "I Can Tell by the Way You Dance," "I'm Still Crazy," and "Chiseled in Stone," which was named the 1989 song of the year by the Country Music Association.

Granger, Sir Clive W. J. (1934–May 27), British economist who shared the 2003 Nobel Prize in economics for proving that many of the standard formulas employed by economists to predict the future were outmoded.

Millard Fuller, humanitarian

Paul Harvey, radio personality

Greenwich, Ellie (1940–August 26), songwriter who with collaborator Jeff Barry wrote such early 1960's hits as "Be My Baby," "Da Doo Ron Ron," "Hanky Panky," "Leader of the Pack," and "Then He Kissed Me."

Hale, Monte (Buren Ely) (1919–March 29), Hollywood's last "singing cowboy" who appeared in a number of B-Westerns for Republic Pictures in the late 1940's and early 1950's.

Halprin, Lawrence (1916–October 25), landscape architect whose many prominent projects include Nicollet Mall in Minneapolis and the Franklin Delano Roosevelt Memorial in Washington, D.C.

Hamrol, Herbert (1903–February 4), last known survivor of the 1906 San Francisco earthquake and fire. Hamrol was also the city's oldest grocery clerk, working up to one week before he died.

Harris, E. Lynn (1955–July 23), best-selling writer whose novels explored the lives of African American men with sexual identity conflicts.

Harvey, Paul (Paul Harvey Aurandt) (1918–February 28), legendary radio broadcaster whose signature "Hello America," conservative take on the news, human interest stories, pregnant pauses, and "Good day" sign-off were cherished by millions of fans for more than 57 years.

Helgason, Sigurdur (1921–February 8), Icelandic aviation executive whose pioneering low-cost Icelandic Airlines made it possible for a generation of young Americans to travel to Europe.

Hewitt, Don (1922–August 19), CBS television producer who oversaw the Kennedy-Nixon debate in 1960 and who invented the "news magazine" with "60 Minutes," a Sunday fixture since 1968.

Hingle, Pat (1924–January 3), versatile character actor who appeared in the original Broadway productions of *Cat on a Hot Tin Roof* (1955) and *The Dark at the Top of the Stairs* (1957) and in such films as *On the Waterfront* (1954) and *Splendor in the Grass* (1961).

Hoagland, Mahlon (1921–September 18), scientist who was the codiscoverer of transfer RNA, a molecule that is essential to the process of making proteins. The discovery revolutionized biochemistry.

Holdridge, Cheryl (1944–January 6), child actress and performer who was one of the original mouseketeers on "The Mickey Mouse Club."

Houghtaling, John (1916–June 17), inventor who in 1958 clipped a vibrating device to a set of box springs, creating "Magic Fingers," a coin-operated staple of motels in the 1960's and 1970's.

Hoving, Thomas (1931–December 10), art historian who led New York City's Metropolitan Museum of Art into an era of expansion, major acquisitions, and blockbuster exhibitions, including the King Tut exhibit, which Hoving organized.

Hughes, John (1950–August 6), film writer, director, and producer who forged a new genre—the disaffected but good-at-heart teenager in conflict with authority. See **Portrait** at **Motion pictures**.

Jackson, Michael (1958–June 25), phenomenally successful singer, dancer, and entertainer whose private life was as colorful as his stage productions. See **Portrait** at **Popular music.**

Jacobi, Lou (Louis Harold Jacobovitch) (1913–October 23), Canadian-born character actor who appeared on Broadway in *The Diary of Anne Frank* (1955) and in such films as *The Diary of Anne Frank* (1959), *Arthur* (1981), and *Avalon* (1990).

Jameson, Betty (1919–February 7), Hall of Fame golfer who was one of the original founders in 1950 of the Ladies Professional Golf Association.

Jansen, Larry (1920–October 10), pitcher whose 23 victories, including the famous game on Oct. 3, 1951, featuring the "Shot Heard 'Round the World," helped the New York Giants win the 1951 National League championship.

Jarre, Maurice (1924–March 28), French composer who won Academy Awards for the scores of three David Lean films—*Lawrence of Arabia* (1962), *Dr. Zhivago* (1965), and *A Passage to India* (1984).

Jeanne-Claude (Jeanne-Claude Denat de Guillebon) (1935–November 18), French-American artist who with her husband, Christo, executed such art installations as wrapping the Reichstag in Berlin in fabric and positioning thousands of yellow and blue umbrellas across miles of inland valleys in California and Japan.

Johansson, Ingemar (1932–January 30), Swedish boxer who in 1959 knocked out Floyd Patterson to win the world heavyweight boxing title and then lost to Patterson in knockout bouts in 1960 and 1961.

Claude Lévi-Strauss, philosopher

Karl Malden, actor

Jones, Jennifer (Phylis Isley) (1919–December 17), movie actress who won the 1943 Academy Award for best actress for *The Song of Bernadette.*

Justice, William Wayne (1920–October 13), federal judge whose rulings, admired and detested, compelled Texas to integrate schools, educate illegal immigrants, and institute various other reforms.

Kaminsky, Stuart M. (1934–October 9), film scholar and author of more than 60 crime and detective novels who was named Grand Master of the Mystery Writers of America in 2006.

Kell, George (1922–March 24), Hall of Fame third baseman who captured the 1949 American League batting title while playing for the Detroit Tigers and later returned to Detroit to become a long-time broadcaster for the team.

Kemp, Jack (1935–May 2), Buffalo Bills quarterback and congressman (R., New York) who was a leading promoter of supply-side economics and tax cuts as economic stimulants. Kemp served as secretary of housing and urban development in the administration of President George H. W. Bush and ran for vice president in 1996.

Kennedy, Edward M. (1932–August 25), liberal politician and scion of one of the most famous American political families who represented Massachusetts in the U.S. Senate for nearly 47 years.

Khan, Ali Akbar (1922–June 18), Indian musician and sarod virtuoso who, with his brother-in-law Ravi Shankar, introduced the classical music of North India to the West.

Kim Dae-jung (1924?–August 18), former president of South Korea (1998-2003) who was awarded the Nobel Peace Prize in 2000 for his efforts to improve relations with North Korea.

Kinnard, Harry W. O. (1915–January 5), U.S. Army lieutenant general who uttered the famous "nuts" response to the German army's surrender ultimatum during the Battle of the Bulge in 1944 during World War II.

Kirchner, Leon (1919–September 17), composer, conductor, and teacher who brought a variety of styles to his orchestral works, piano concertos, and numerous chamber works.

Knopf, Alfred A., Jr., (1918–February 14), editor who left the publishing company founded by his parents, Alfred A. and Blanche Wolf Knopf, to cofound Atheneum Publishers in 1959.

Kolff, Willem (1911–February 11), Dutch-born physician who invented both the first artificial kidney and the first artificial heart, which Kolff named for an associate, Robert Jarvik, who had designed the device's multilayer diaphragm.

Kool, Molly (Myrtle Kool) (1916–February 25), Canadian-born woman who at age 23 in 1939 became the world's first merchant marine ship's captain and was thereafter known as "Captain Molly."

Krebs, Edwin G. (1918–December 21), pharmacologist who shared the 1992 Nobel Prize for discovering physical proces that helps govern cell division and muscle movement.

Kristol, Irving (1920–September 18), political commentator and "godfather of neoconservatism" who with William F. Buckley defined modern conservatism and helped revive the Republican Party in the 1960's and early 1970's.

Kunzel, Erich (1935–September 1), engaging conductor of the Cincinnati Pops who often led the National Symphony in Memorial Day and July 4 concerts on the National Mall.

La Rue, Danny (Daniel Patrick Carroll) (1927–May 31), Irish-born female impersonator who became a star in London's cabaret and music hall scene in the 1960's.

Lavelli, Dante (1923–January 20), Hall of Fame receiver, called "Gluefingers," who was one of the original Cleveland Browns players that in the 1940's and 1950's won four All-America Football Conference championships and three National Football League championships.

Lawrence, Andrea Mead (1932–March 30), Alpine racer who was the only U.S. skier to win two gold medals in a single Olympics, the 1952 Games.

Lawrence, Jack (Jack Lawrence Schwartz) (1912–March 15), popular song lyricist whose hits include the Ink Spots' 1939 recording of "If I Didn't Care," Frank Sinatra's 1943 recording of "All or Nothing at All," Sarah Vaughan's 1947 recording of "Tenderly," and Bobby Darin's 1959 smash recording of "Beyond the Sea."

Leonard, Hugh (John Keyes Byrne) (1926–February 12), Irish playwright and commentator who gained international stature when his play *Da* won the Tony Award in 1978 and ran for two years on Broadway.

Levine, David (1926–December 29), cartoonist whose big headed, rarely flattering caricatures of intellectuals and politicians provided *The New York Review of Books* with its characteristic look for half a century.

Levine, Irving R. (1922–March 27), bespectacled, bow-tied newsman who pioneered television coverage of economic issues during his 40-year career as an NBC correspondent.

Lévi-Strauss, Claude (1908–November 1), French anthropologist of international eminence who, with Jean-Paul Sartre and André Malraux, was considered one of the foremost French intellectuals of the 20th century.

Levitt, Helen (1913–March 29), one of the giants of 20th-century photography whose spare, often mysterious images of life, particularly children, on the streets of New York City captured a now-vanished era.

Lloyd, David (1934–November 10), Emmy Award-winning TV comedy writer who penned episodes of "Cheers," "Taxi," "Rhoda," "Frasier," and "The Mary Tyler Moore Show," including the classic "Chuckles Bites the Dust" episode.

Locklin, Hank (1918–March 8), country singer and 47-year veteran of the Grand Ole Opry who helped usher in the "Nashville sound" with such hits as "Send Me the Pillow You Dream On" and

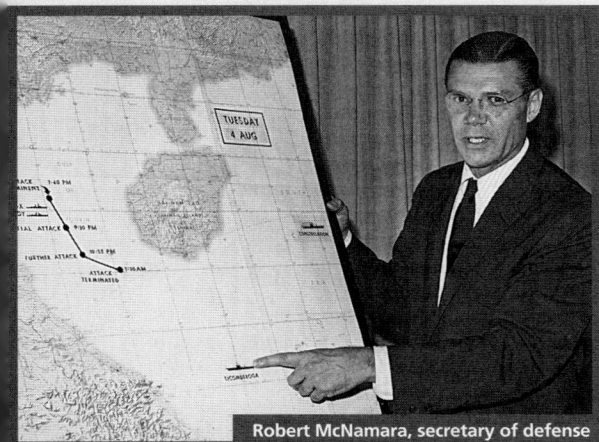
Robert McNamara, secretary of defense

"Please Help Me I'm Falling."

Long, Huey (1904–June 10), jazz guitarist who over 80 years was one of the Ink Spots and played with Texas Guinan, Fletcher Henderson, Earl Hines, Dizzy Gillespie, and Charlie Parker.

Low, Frank J. (1933–June 11), physicist whose research into infrared, or "heat," radiation from stars helped astronomers revolutionize the study of planets, stars, and galaxies.

Maddox, Sir John (1925–April 12), British editor who transformed the journal *Nature* into an internationally recognized authoritative source of the latest developments in scientific research.

Malden, Karl (Mladen Sekulovich) (1912–July 1), character actor who appeared in the productions of Arthur Miller's *All My Sons* (1947) and Tennessee Williams's *A Streetcar Named Desire* (1947); won an Academy Award for the 1951 film version of *Streetcar;* appeared with Marlon Brando in *On the Waterfront* (1954); and starred in "The Streets of San Francisco."

Martino, Al (Jasper Cini) (1927–October 13), baritone who had a string of hits—"Here Is My Heart" and "Spanish Eyes"—in the 1950's and played Johnny Fontane, the Sinatra-like singer, in *The Godfather* (1972).

Maw, Nicholas (1935–May 19), British classical music composer who is best known for his "Violin Concerto" (1993) and the *Odyssey symphony* (1987).

Maximova, Ekaterina (1939?–April 28), Russian ballerina and coach who was one of the great stars of the Bolshoi Theatre in the 1960's the 1970's.

Mays, Billy (William Darrell Mays, Jr.) (1958–June 28), boisterous, bearded TV pitchman of OxiClean and countless other products.

McCourt, Frank (1930–July 19), writer whose memoir of his wretched childhood in Ireland, *Angela's Ashes*, became a best seller and won the 1997 Pulitzer Prize for biography and the 1996 National Book Critics Circle Award.

McFarlane, Rodger (1955–May 15), gay rights advocate who served as the first executive director of the Gay Men's Health Crisis; executive director of Broadway Cares/Equity Fights AIDS; and president of Bailey House, for homeless people with AIDS.

McGoohan, Patrick (1928–January 13), actor who found fame in the 1960's on the British television series "Danger Man," then as No. 6 in the cult series "The Prisoner," which has been called "television's first masterpiece."

McMahon, Ed (1923–June 23), announcer who served as Johnny Carson's "second banana" from 1957 to 1992, first on the game show "Who Do You Trust?" and then on "The Tonight Show."

McNamara, Robert S. (1916–July 6), a former president of the Ford Motor Company who joined the Kennedy administration as secretary of defense and who became the architect and a political casualty of the Vietnam War.

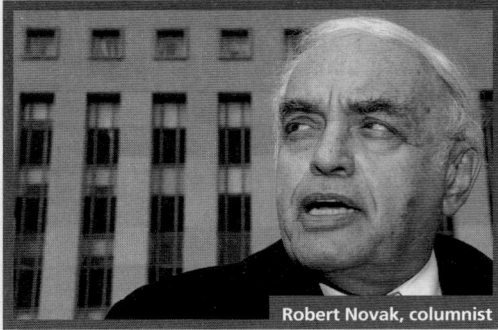
Robert Novak, columnist

Les Paul, musician and inventor

Melnick, Daniel (1932–October 13), Hollywood producer who made such films as *Network* (1976), *The China Syndrome* (1979), *All That Jazz* (1979), and *Roxanne* (1987).

Mikhalkov, Sergei V. (1913–August 27), Russian poet who was commissioned by Joseph Stalin to write the lyrics to the Soviet national anthem and by Russian President Vladimir Putin to rewrite them.

Millett, Lewis (1920–November 14), Army colonel who fought in World War II, the Korean War, and the Vietnam War and who was awarded the Medal of Honor for leading a bayonet charge up a heavily defended hill in Korea.

Mitchell, John F. (1928–June 11), engineer—and eventual president and chief operating officer of Motorola—who in 1973 invented the DynaTAC, prototype of the cellular phone.

Mizzy, Vic (1916–October 17), television and film composer who wrote the infernally catchy theme songs for the 1960's sitcoms "Green Acres" and "The Addams Family."

Montalbán, Ricardo (Ricardo Gonzalo Petro Montalbán y Merino) (1920–January 14), Mexican-born actor who played a Latin lover in dozens of films and hundreds of TV episodes, most famously as the debonair Mr. Roarke on "Fantasy Island."

Montgomery, Buddy (Charles Montgomery) (1930–May 14), jazz pianist and vibraphonist who most famously played in groups with his brothers Wes and Monk.

Mortimer, Sir John (1923–January 16), English barrister, free speech advocate, playwright, and novelist who created Horace Rumpole, the rumpled but brilliant defender of the British criminal classes.

Nelson, Jack (1929–October 21), Pulitzer Prize-winning investigative journalist whose aggressive coverage of the civil rights movement and the Watergate scandal helped make the previously provincial *Los Angeles Times* into a newspaper of national stature.

Noon, Carole C. (1949–May 2), primatologist whose interest in, and compassion for, chimpanzees led her to found Save the Chimps, the organization that funds and oversees the world's largest sanctuary for captive chimpanzees.

Novak, Robert (1931–August 18), political columnist and TV "talking head" whose exposure of Valerie Plame as a CIA operative set off a political firestorm for the George W. Bush administration.

Parker, Barbara (1946–March 7), best-selling author of the "Suspicion" mystery series.

Parker, Milton (1919–January 30), partner in New York City's famous Carnegie Deli, where he developed the five-inch-high, "much too large for human consumption" pastrami sandwich.

Patch, Harry (1898–July 25), supercentenarian who was the last British survivor of World War I trench warfare. (A British World War I sailor living in Australia survives Patch.)

Paul, Les (Lester William Polsfuss) (1915–August 12), guitarist and singer whose invention of the solid-body electric guitar and studio innovations—overdubbing and multitrack recording—formed the foundation for rock 'n' roll, changing the course of popular music in the 1900's.

Pell, Claiborne (1918–January 1), former U.S. senator (D., Rhode Island) who created the college grant program that bears his name and who crafted the legislation that produced the National Endowment for the Arts and the National Endowment for the Humanities.

Penn, Irving (1917–October 7), photographer whose elegant fashion images and penetrating portraits of celebrities made his work as recognizable to museumgoers as to readers of *Vogue*, to which he contributed for some 50 years.

Phair, Venetia (Venetia Burney) (1918–April 30), Englishwoman who in 1930 proposed the name Pluto for a newly discovered planet (now a dwarf planet). Her grandfather, Falconer Madan, took the idea to an Oxford astronomy professor who successfully proposed the name to the Royal Astronomical Society.

Poirier, Richard (1925–August 15), literary and cultural critic and man of letters who published the literary journal *Raritan: A Quarterly Review* and who was a founder of Library of America, the nonprofit publisher of American classics.

Powell, Jody (1943–September 14), political organizer who helped Jimmy Carter win the Georgia governorship and the presidency and who served Carter as press secretary and close adviser.

Presnell, Harve (1933–June 30), singer and actor who originated the role of Johnny Brown in the 1960 musical *The Unsinkable Molly Brown*, reprised the role in the 1964 movie, and played the cheap father-in-law in *Fargo* (1996).

Printz, Mary (1923–February 21), owner-operator of the Belles Celebrity Answering Service, upon whom Adolph Green and Betty Comden modeled the Judy Holliday character in the 1956 hit musical *Bells Are Ringing*. Printz's pampered clientele ranged from Noël Coward and Tennessee Williams to Woody Allen and the rock band Kiss.

Purdy, James (1914–March 13), author of nearly 20 novels—including *Malcolm* (1959) and *The Nephew* (1961)—many short stories, and plays.

Randolph, Jane (1915–May 4), 1940's B-movie actress who most famously played a young woman terrorized during a nocturnal swim in the 1942 noir classic *Cat People*.

Reed-Amini, Alaina (1946–Dec. 24), actress whose best-known characters lived on two of TV's most famous addresses, "Sesame Street" and "227."

Reid, Whitelaw (1913–April 18), war correspondent and editor, president, and chairman of the now-defunct *New York Herald Tribune*. Reid—grandson of Whitelaw Reid, who took over the *Herald Tribune* from Horace Greeley—was also president of the Fresh Air Fund, which provided inner-city children with country vacations.

Reimers, Ed (1912–August 16), announcer for such TV programs as "Maverick" and "Who Do You Trust?" who most famously assured TV viewers, "You're in good hands with Allstate."

Reverend Ike (Frederick Joseph Eikerenkoetter II) (1935–July 28), minister who preached the blessings of material success from his United Church Science of Living Institute in Harlem.

Richard, Wendy (Wendy Emerton) (1943–February 26), British actress who appeared in several "Carry On" film comedies, played Miss Brahms in the British TV comedy "Are You Being Served?" and portrayed the put-upon matriarch Pauline Fowler in the British soap opera "EastEnders."

Richardson, Natasha (1963–March 18), British-born actress who won a Tony for her role as Sally Bowles in the 1998 revival of *Cabaret*. Daughter of Vanessa Redgrave and director Tony Richardson and granddaughter of actor Sir Michael Redgrave and actress Rachel Kempson, Richardson was married to Irish actor Liam Neeson.

Rickert, Shirley Jean (1926–February 6), child actress who appeared in "Our Gang" and "Mickey McGuire" comedy shorts and later performed in burlesque as "Gilda and Her Crowning Glory," in reference to her waist-length blond hair.

Roberts, Oral (1918–December 15), televangelist and faith healer who founded Oral Roberts University in Tulsa, Oklahoma.

Rosburg, Bob (1926–May 14), golfer who won the 1959 PGA Championship and who become known as "Rossie," the long-time ABC-TV golf analyst.

Rostova, Mira (1909–January 28), Russian-born drama teacher who taught such actors as Alec Baldwin, Jessica Lange, Jerry Orbach, and her closest protégé, Montgomery Clift.

Ruby, Karine (1978–May 29), French Olympic snowboarding champion who died in a fall on Mont Blanc while training to be a mountain guide.

Ruby, Lloyd (1928–March 23), race car driver who competed in 18 consecutive Indianapolis 500 races—1960 to 1977. Mario Andretti called him "the greatest driver never to win the Indy."

Saban, Lou (1921–March 29), pro football player and coach who led the Boston Patriots, Buffalo Bills, and Denver Broncos; switched to college football at Miami, Army, and Central Florida; served as president of the New York Yankees under George Steinbrenner; and on retiring, coached high school football in South Carolina.

Safire, William (1929–September 27), Pulitzer Prize-winning journalist who for more than 30 years wrote Op-Ed pieces and "On Language" columns for *The New York Times*. As a Nixon administration speechwriter, Safire supplied Vice President Spiro Agnew with the famous "nattering nabobs of negativism."

Sailer, Toni (1935–August 24), Austrian skier who in 1956 became the first skier to win three Alpine gold medals at a Winter Olympics. A national hero, Sailer was awarded the Olympic Order in 1985 and named Austria's sportsman of the century in 1999.

Sales, Soupy (Milton Supman) (1926–October 22), TV comedian whose "Soupy Sales Show" was popular with kids in the 1960's and who graduated in the 1970's into game show panelist and host of a syndicated revival of "What's My Line?"

Samuelson, Paul (1915–December 13), author of the classic college textbook *Economics: An Introductory Analysis* and the first American to be awarded the Nobel Prize in economics.

San Juan, Olga (1927–January 3), singer and dancer known as the "Puerto Rican Pepperpot" who appeared opposite the likes of Bing Crosby and Fred Astaire in a number of '40's movie musicals.

Schulberg, Budd (1914–August 5), writer who received an Academy Award for the screenplay of *On the Waterfront* (1954) and whose 1941 novel *What Makes Sammy Run?* is a classic insider's account of Hollywood.

Naomi Sims, model

Mary Travers, singer

Schur, Sylvia (1917–September 9), food editor and consultant who is credited with inventing the corn dog, developed Metrecal and Clamato and Cran-Apple juices, wrote cookbooks for Campbell's Soup and other companies, and helped conceive the menu for New York City's famed Four Seasons restaurant.

Seeger, Mike (1933–August 7), folk musician (and brother of Pete Seeger) who played a major role in the folk music revival of the 1950's and 1960's.

Shneidman, Edwin (1918–May 15), psychologist and suicide authority who was founder of the first suicide prevention center.

Shriver, Eunice Kennedy (1921–August 11), founder of the Special Olympics. See **Portrait** at **Disability.**

Shulman, Julius (1910–July 16), photographer whose black-and-white prints of mid-20th century buildings, especially the works of Richard Neutra and R. M. Schindler, defined public perception of modern architecture and the California lifestyle.

Silver, Ron (1946–March 15), Tony Award-winning actor and activist who appeared in the original Broadway cast of David Mamet's *Speed the Plow*, (1988), portrayed Alan M. Dershowitz in the 1990 movie *Reversal of Fortune,* and played a campaign adviser on "The West Wing" TV series.

Sims, Naomi (1948–August 1), breakthrough African American supermodel who launched her own beauty empire, Naomi Sims Beauty Products.

Snodgrass, W. D. (1926–January 13), Pulitzer Prize-winning poet who was the founder of the "confessional" school of poetry and who became a major influence on Sylvia Plath and Anne Sexton.

Sosa, Mercedes (1935–October 4), Argentine folk singer who became world famous as the "voice of Latin America" and the voice of opposition to Argentina's military regime in the 1970's.

Stang, Arnold (1918–December 20), comic character actor who was voice of "Top Cat" and appeared regularly on such early TV programs as "The Milton Berle Show."

Sutton, Crystal Lee (1940–September 11), textile mill employee whose struggles to unionize the plant inspired the 1979 film *Norma Rae,* for which actress Sally Field won an Academy Award.

Suzman, Helen (1917–January 1), South African social activist who used her immunity as a member of the South African Parliament to speak out against the injustices of apartheid.

Swayze, Patrick (1952–September 14), actor and dancer who shot to fame as the romantic lead in *Dirty Dancing* (1987) and starred in such hits as *Ghost* (1990) and *Point Break* (1991).

Swett, James (1920–January 18), World War II Marine pilot who was awarded the Medal of Honor for shooting down seven Japanese dive bombers in the Solomon Islands in 15 minutes during his first combat operation.

Syms, Sy (Seymour Merinsky) (1926–November 17), retailer who built up the Syms chain of 52 off-price clothing stores from a single store in Manhattan's Financial District, using the slogan "An educated consumer is our best customer."

Taylor, Koko (Cora Walton Taylor) (1928–June 3), Chicago blues singer who, like Bessie Smith before her, was called "Queen of the Blues." Taylor's career was launched with the 1965 hit "Wang Dang Doodle," her signature song.

Tiller, George (1941–May 31), Kansas-based late-term abortion provider who was murdered by an antiabortion activist as Tiller served as an usher during the Sunday morning service at his church.

Tisdale, Wayman (1964–May 15), Olympic athlete and 12-year veteran of the National Basketball Association who, upon retiring from sports, became a noted jazz musician.

Todd, Richard (1919–December 3), Irish-born British actor who was nominated for an Academy Award for *The Hasty Heart* (1949) and appeared in such films as Alfred Hitchcock's *Stage Fright* (1950), *A Man Called Peter* (1955), and *The Longest Day* (1962).

Toler, Burl (1928–August 16), member of the legendary 1951 University of San Francisco football team who went on to become the first African American on-field official in the NFL.

Travers, Mary (1936–September 16), enigmatic singer with Peter, Paul, and Mary, the venerable folk group that won five Grammys and produced six Top 10 hits, including "If I Had a Hammer" (1962); "Puff (The Magic Dragon)" (1963), and "Leaving on a Jet Plane" (1969).

Trova, Ernest (1927–March 8), artist whose armless, featureless figure—the "Falling Man"—in a series of 1960's paintings and sculptures became a symbol of humanity, imperfect and defaced.

Updike, John (1932–January 27), poet, man of letters, and novelist who was among the first rank of writers of post-World War II America. See **Portrait** at **Literature**.

Van Bruggen, Coosje (1942–January 10), Dutch artist, art critic, and art historian who with her husband, Claes Oldenburg, created a series of giant, highly distinctive pop art sculptures.

Van Lier, Norm (1947–February 26), three-time National Basketball Association All-Star guard and defense player for the Chicago Bulls.

Vierny, Dina (Dina Aibinder) (1919–January 20), French art collector and museum director who modeled for Henri Matisse, Raoul Dufy, and Pierre Bonnard and was French sculptor Aristide Maillol's model, muse, and companion until his death in 1944.

Wallace, Cornelia (1939–January 8), former first lady of Alabama who most famously threw herself over her husband, Governor George Wallace, during a 1972 assassination attempt that left his legs paralyzed.

Wasserstein, Bruce (1947–October 14), chairman and chief executive officer of the investment bank Lazard Group LLC who reshaped how mergers and acquisitions are carried out worldwide.

Waterhouse, Keith (1929–September 4), British novelist, playwright, screenwriter, and columnist who wrote the novel *Billy Liar* (1959) and contributed to the 1960's satirical TV series "That Was the Week That Was."

Weisman, Joel (1943–July 18), Los Angeles physician who in 1981 was among the first physicians to detect among seriously ill gay patients a constellation of symptoms that would eventually be named acquired immuno-deficiency syndrome (AIDS).

Werber, Bill (1908–January 22), Yankee infielder who was a teammate of Babe Ruth and Lou Gehrig and who, at the time of his death, was the world's oldest former Major League Baseball player.

Wexler, Anne (1930–August 7), political operative and adviser who served as a top political aide in the administration of President Jimmy Carter.

As chief of the lobbyist firm Wexler & Walker, she was considered one of the most influential women in Washington.

Whitmore, James (1921–February 6), stage, screen, and TV character actor who appeared in hundreds of TV dramas during the so-called "golden age" of the 1950's and who appeared on Broadway in three one-man shows: *Will Rogers' USA* (1974); *Give 'Em Hell, Harry!* (1975) portraying Harry Truman; and *Bully* (1977) as Theodore Roosevelt.

Wilson, Margaret Bush (1919–August 11), civil rights lawyer who was part of the legal team that in 1948 challenged a restrictive covenant that barred black home-buyers from certain white-only neighborhoods and who was the first African American woman to chair the national NAACP board of directors.

Woodward, Edward (1930–November 16), British actor who is best known for playing Robert McCall on the television series "The Equalizer."

Wyeth, Andrew (1917–January 16), painter of enigmatic scenes of life in rural Pennsylvania and Maine whose *Christina's World* made him at age 31 one of America's most famous artists. He was the son of master illustrator N. C. Wyeth and the father of painter Jamie Wyeth.

York, Herbert (1921–May 19), Manhattan Project physicist and top Defense Department scientist during the administration of President Dwight D. Eisenhower and who later became a major advocate for nuclear disarmament.

Yow, Kay (1942–January 24), Hall of Fame college basketball coach who led her North Carolina State women's team to 737 victories, making her number six on the career victory list for both men's and women's coaches.

Zamecnik, Paul (1912–October 27), molecular biologist who was awarded the National Medal of Science and the Albert Lasker Award for Special Achievement in Medical Science for his codiscovery of transfer RNA, a molecule that is essential to the process of making proteins.

Andrew Wyeth, artist

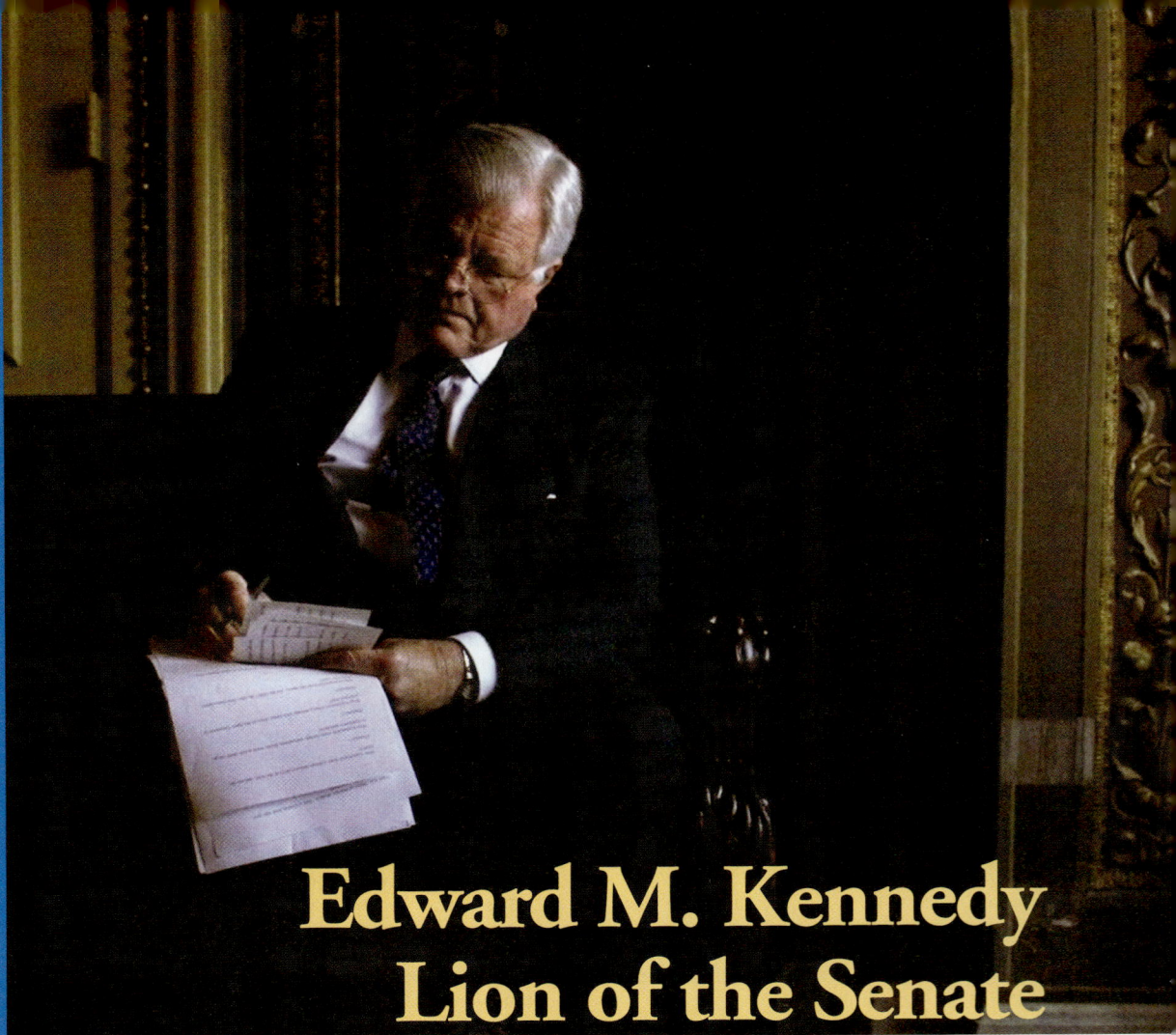

Edward M. Kennedy
Lion of the Senate

By Robert Knight

Edward M. Kennedy, who represented Massachusetts in the United States Senate for nearly 47 years, came from one of the most politically influential families in American history. One brother, John F. Kennedy, was president of the United States; another brother, Robert F. Kennedy, was U.S. attorney general, a U.S. senator, and candidate for president in 1968. Both men were assassinated, and both of their deaths rocked the nation. Voters of Massachusetts elected Edward Kennedy to the Senate nine times—a record matched by only one other senator, Robert Byrd. At the time of his death, he was the second most senior member of the Senate, and the third-longest-serving senator in U.S. history. (Robert Byrd [D., West Virginia] and Strom Thurmond [R., South Carolina] served longer.) Edward Kennedy died on Aug. 25, 2009, at the age of 77. Only one of his eight siblings survived him.

Edward Kennedy entered the U.S. Senate in 1962, eclipsed by his elder brothers and perceived by critics as a lightweight. By the time of his death, Kennedy was widely respected in the corridors of Congress and loved by many in its chambers. Although often a controversial figure in the public arena and an unapologetic champion of liberal causes, Kennedy had many admirers, particularly among his constituents in his home state of Massachusetts. For two days after Kennedy's death, thousands stood in line for hours at the John F. Kennedy Presidential Library in Boston to pay their respects.

Edward Moore Kennedy was born on Feb. 22, 1932, in Boston, the youngest of Joseph P. and Rose Fitzgerald Kennedy's children. She was the daughter of John "Honey Fitz" Fitzgerald, a Democratic mayor of Boston who had also served in Congress. Joseph Kennedy was a millionaire entrepreneur whom President Franklin D. Roosevelt would appoint the first chairman of the U.S. Securities and Exchange Commission and ambassador to the Court of St. James (United Kingdom).

Although privileged, the Kennedy children were brought up in an atmosphere of intense physical and intellectual competition. Joseph Kennedy wanted one of his four sons to be president of the United States, a position he could not attain. That ambition first fell on Joseph P. Kennedy, Jr., who died in a bombing mission during World War II (1939–1945); the father's ambition subsequently centered on the second oldest son, John F. Kennedy.

Following in his brothers' footsteps, "Teddy" enrolled in Harvard University in Cambridge, Massachusetts, in 1950. In his freshman year, he persuaded another student to take a Spanish exam for him, got caught, and was expelled. Kennedy then enlisted in the army and was posted to NATO headquarters in Paris. He was discharged in 1953 and reenrolled in Harvard, graduating in 1956. He graduated from the University of Virginia School of Law in Charlottesville in 1959.

Political life

In 1958, Edward ran his brother John's campaign for reelection to the U.S. Senate in Massachusetts, an experience he later described as an "internship" for politics and public service. He also married in 1958, to Joan Bennett of Bronxville, New York. They had three children: Kara Anne, Edward Jr., and Patrick. After his brothers' deaths in 1963 and 1968, Edward took on the role of surrogate father for John's 2 children and Robert's 11 children. The couple filed for divorce in 1982.

When John F. Kennedy won election as president of the United States in November 1960, Joseph Kennedy arranged to have a family ally fill the president-elect's vacated Senate seat for two years; son Teddy would not reach the constitutionally required minimum age for Senate service until 1962. In the interim, Ted Kennedy served as an assistant district attorney in Suffolk County, Massachusetts. He won the special election for the Senate seat and began his long tenure in the nation's highest legislative chamber. By most accounts, the young senator did his homework and worked effectively with other senators. Kennedy also proved an adept politician, establishing a lifelong rapport with Massachusetts voters. In 1964, he won reelection to the Senate from Massachusetts in the first of many victories.

While campaigning, Kennedy had a near brush with death in an airplane crash, suffering a broken back that kept him hospitalized for

The author:
Robert Knight is a free-lance writer.

Edward M. Kennedy with his brothers, John F. Kennedy and Robert F. Kennedy, in July 1960. Edward Kennedy was elected to the U.S. Senate in 1962 when John Kennedy was president and Robert Kennedy was attorney general.

almost six months. He made a full recovery and returned to the Senate, but back pain plagued him for the rest of his life.

On June 5, 1968, Robert F. Kennedy was shot in a Los Angeles hotel, having just won the California presidential primary. He died the next day. The mantle of Kennedy political leadership fell to Edward. Many political experts predicted that he would run for president at the earliest opportunity. Unforeseen events intervened.

Late on the night of July 18, 1969, Kennedy accidentally drove his car off a bridge into a pond on Chappaquiddick Island off the Massachusetts resort Martha's Vineyard. He was accompanied by Mary Jo Kopechne, a former secretary to Robert F. Kennedy. Edward Kennedy managed to escape but was not able to rescue Kopechne from the car, submerged in 8 feet (2.4 meters) of water. The senator left the scene of the accident and then waited about 10 hours to inform the authorities. Publicity surrounding the incident dogged Kennedy for years and effectively ruined his chances to ever become president of the United States.

Nevertheless, Kennedy challenged President Jimmy Carter during the Democratic primary season of 1980. Kennedy's campaign to wrest the Democratic nomination from President Carter fizzled, however, and Carter himself went down to defeat by Republican Ronald Reagan in November 1980. With any presidential ambitions effectively buried, Edward Kennedy rededicated himself to service in the Senate and transformed himself into what some colleagues described as "one of the most affective senators in U.S. history."

Senate career

Throughout his career, Ted Kennedy pressed for liberal causes. During political eras in which ideas of big government were out of fashion, he forged coalitions with Republicans and other Democrats to achieve incremental reforms in women's issues, social justice, and disability laws.

Kennedy long advocated reforms of the nation's health care system leading to universal coverage. He cosponsored several important incremental health care reforms passed by Congress, including the Health Insurance Portability and Accountability Act (1996), which he cosponsored with then Senator Nancy Kassebaum (R., Kansas). The "Kassebaum-Kennedy Act" enabled workers changing jobs to retain insurance coverage from the previous job for an extended period of time. Kennedy also cosponsored, with Senator Orrin Hatch (R., Utah), the Children's Health Insurance Program (CHIP), which became law in 1997. CHIP provides funding to help states expand health insurance coverage for children.

Senator Kennedy was also a staunch supporter of civil rights. He participated in congressional passage of the great civil rights reforms of the 1960's—the Civil Rights Act of 1964, the Voting Rights Act of 1965, and the Fair Housing Act of 1968. In 1982, he led a successful effort to renew the Voting Rights Act for 25 years and to strengthen certain provisions.

Last years

In 1992, Ted Kennedy married Victoria Reggie, a Washington, D.C., lawyer originally from Louisiana. By all accounts, Kennedy's second marriage was a happy one.

In May 2008, physicians diagnosed a malignant brain tumor after Kennedy suffered a seizure. Faced with a bleak prognosis, Kennedy underwent surgery and chemotherapy. He endorsed Barack Obama for the presidency at a critical moment in the 2008 presidential primaries, and in August, while still undergoing cancer treatment, he managed to travel to Denver and deliver a speech at the Democratic National Convention. He made his final public speaking appearance on April 21, 2009, in Washington, D.C., at a presidential signing ceremony of the Edward M. Kennedy Serve America Act.

When Kennedy's death on August 25 was announced, tributes poured in from Senate colleagues on both sides of the aisle. Vice President Joe Biden, who had represented Delaware in the Senate, stated: "He's left a great void in our public life and a hole in the hearts of millions of Americans and hundreds of us who were affected by his personal touch throughout our lives." Republican Orrin Hatch wrote, "Today America lost a great elder statesman, a committed public servant, and leader of the Senate. And today I lost a treasured friend. Ted Kennedy was an iconic, larger than life United States Senator whose influence cannot be overstated. Many have come before, and many will come after, but Ted Kennedy's name will always be remembered as someone who lived and breathed the United States Senate and the work completed within its chamber."

Edward Kennedy is about to escort his niece, Caroline Kennedy, down the aisle on her wedding day, July 19, 1986. Senator Kennedy acted as a surrogate father for John Kennedy's 2 children and Robert Kennedy's 11 children.

Democratic Party. The Democrats dominated United States politics in 2009, thanks to their strong performance in the 2008 elections. Democratic President Barack Obama was inaugurated on Jan. 20, 2009, succeeding Republican President George W. Bush. When the 111th Congress convened on January 6, Democrats controlled 257 seats in the 435-seat House of Representatives (up from 236 at the end of the 110th Congress) and 58 seats in the 100-seat Senate (up from 51). The Senate total included 2 independent senators who caucused with the Democrats. Later in 2009, 2 more Senate seats came under the Democrats' control, giving them the 60-seat supermajority needed to block Republican filibusters. Finally, throughout most of 2009, Democrats held 28 of the 50 state governorships.

Congress kicked off 2009 with a brouhaha over the Senate seat vacated by Obama after he won the presidency. On Dec. 30, 2008, Rod Blagojevich, the Democratic governor of Illinois, named Roland Burris, a former Illinois attorney general, as Obama's replacement. Earlier that month, federal corruption charges had been filed against Blagojevich, including an allegation that he had tried to sell or trade the Senate seat for personal gain. The scandal prompted Senate Democrats to initially block Burris from being seated, but they later relented and allowed him to be sworn in on Jan. 15, 2009. Burris, who at first testified that he had not discussed doing favors for Blagojevich, later admitted that he had discussed the possibility of raising funds for the governor. This admission prompted the Senate Ethics Committee and an Illinois state prosecutor to open investigations of Burris on February 17. The prosecutor announced on June 19 that there was insufficient evidence to charge Burris with perjury, but the Ethics Committee formally admonished him on November 20.

The Senate Democratic Caucus gained its 59th member on April 28 when Senator Arlen Specter of Pennsylvania announced that he was switching his party affiliation from Republican to Democrat. Specter, a moderate who had served in the Senate since 1981, said that his views had become more in line with those of Democrats. He also had concluded that he would be unlikely to win his state's Republican primary for the Senate seat in 2010.

The 60th Democratic senator, Al Franken of Minnesota, was sworn in on July 7, 2009. A week earlier, on June 30, the Minnesota Supreme Court had ruled that Franken had won the state's November 2008 Senate election. Later that day, the Republican incumbent, Norm Coleman, finally conceded the race. The election had been extremely close, with only a few hundred votes separating Franken—a former writer and performer for TV's "Saturday Night Live"—and Coleman. Following a statewide recount, there had been

months of legal wrangling over whether certain ballots should have been counted or rejected.

Congress lost a Democratic titan in 2009. Senator Edward M. (Ted) Kennedy of Massachusetts died on August 25 after battling brain cancer for more than a year. Kennedy—the youngest brother of former President John F. Kennedy and former Senator Robert F. Kennedy—had served in the Senate since 1962. He had become known as that body's "liberal lion," forcefully championing national health insurance and greater spending on social programs. President Obama called him "one of the most accomplished Americans ever to serve our democracy." On Sept. 24, 2009, Massachusetts Governor Deval Patrick (D.) appointed Paul G. Kirk, Jr., a former Democratic National Committee chairman, to temporarily fill Kennedy's seat until a special election in January 2010.

Governors. Blagojevich's corruption scandal led to the first impeachment of a governor in Illinois history and the nation's first gubernatorial impeachment since 1988. On Jan. 9, 2009, the Illinois House of Representatives voted 114-1 to impeach Blagojevich on grounds that he had abused his power as chief executive. On January 29, after a brief trial, the Illinois Senate voted 59-0 to remove him from office and permanently bar him from holding public office in the state. Lieutenant Governor Pat Quinn replaced Blagojevich as governor. On April 2, a federal grand jury indicted Blagojevich on 16 felony corruption counts. He pleaded not guilty to the charges on April 14.

Gubernatorial elections were held in two states on November 3, and the Democratic candidates lost both contests. In New Jersey, the Republican candidate, former U.S. Attorney Chris Christie, ousted incumbent Governor Jon Corzine. In Virginia, the Republican candidate, former State Attorney General Bob McDonnell, defeated State Senator Creigh Deeds in the race to succeed term-limited Governor Tim Kaine (D.).

Party leadership and fund-raising. The Democratic National Committee (DNC) voted to approve Kaine, the Virginia governor, as DNC chairman on Jan. 21, 2009. President Obama had tapped Kaine for the post on January 8.

In the first six months of 2009, Democratic Party committees—including the DNC, the Democratic Congressional Campaign Committee, the Democratic Senatorial Campaign Committee, and state and local committees—raised $109.8 million and spent $82.8 million, according to the Federal Election Commission. Their Republican counterparts raised $104.8 million and spent $82.1 million during the same period.   ■ Mike Lewis

See also **Cabinet; Congress; Deaths: A Special Report; Elections; People in the news; Republican Party; State government; United States, Government of the; United States, President of the.**

Denmark. In April 2009, Prime Minister Anders Fogh Rasmussen resigned to become the secretary-general of NATO. Queen Margrethe II chose Lars Løkke Rasmussen (no relation), a former finance minister, to replace him. Rasmussen continued to head a minority government of the Liberal Party and the Conservative People's Party, which rely on the support of the Danish People's Party to pass legislation. Both prime ministers faced increasing opposition from center-left and left-wing parties in 2009, especially after the global economic crisis resulted in a severe recession. Elections to the European Parliament in June demonstrated strong gains for the left-wing Socialist People's Party and the right-wing populist Danish People's Party.

Economic crisis. In early 2009, the government and opposition parties agreed on a rescue package for Danish banks. The measures provided $18 billion in loans to ensure sufficient funds for lending and restricted executive pay and stock dividends. Parliament also agreed on measures to boost employment, infrastructure spending, and consumer confidence and to restructure the tax system. European Union (EU) economists forecast that Denmark's economy would contract by 4.5 percent in 2009. Unemployment was expected to rise to 4.5 percent from 3.3 percent in 2008.

International affairs. Despite Anders Fogh Rasmussen's new position as secretary-general of NATO, Danes remained divided in 2009 over the participation of additional Danish troops in the NATO mission in Afghanistan. By November, 28 Danish troops had been killed since Denmark joined the United States-led coalition, one of the highest per-capita death rates among NATO forces.

Danes also remained divided about adopting the euro. Economists noted that Denmark's failure to participate in the common currency made the nation more vulnerable during the global financial meltdown. Surveys showed that a slight majority of Danes favored adopting the euro. However, politicians were reluctant to call for a referendum on the question while the economy remained unstable.

Greenland, a territory of Denmark, on June 21 officially adopted self-rule, a step toward independence. Voters in a referendum in November 2008 had overwhelmingly supported the move. Greenland's new status allowed it to adopt Kalaallisut, an Inuit dialect, as its official language and to take control of the police force and courts. Denmark retained control of defense and foreign policy.

Royal succession. In a referendum held in June 2009, Danes supported a constitutional change that allows the monarch's first-born child to take the throne, regardless of gender. Previously, a male child succeeded, even if he was a younger sibling.   ■ Jeffrey Kopstein

See also **Europe.**

Dinosaur. See Paleontology.

Disability. A divided United States Supreme Court ruled in 2009 that parents of students with learning disabilities may receive government reimbursement for their child's private school tuition even if the child has never received special education services at a public school. The ruling was issued on June 22 under a 1997 amendment to the Individuals with Disabilities Education Act (IDEA).

IDEA specifies that parents may be reimbursed for private school tuition for a child with learning disabilities if a public school is not able to provide a free, appropriate education. In the case before the court, a high school student called T. A. was evaluated for learning disabilities while attending a public school and found ineligible for special education classes. When he was enrolled in a private school and tested again, he was diagnosed with attention deficit hyperactivity and other disorders. In a 6-to-3 decision, the judges ruled that a previous attempt to provide special education services in a public school is not a prerequisite for private school reimbursement for a child with learning disabilities.

EEOC case. The largest disability-related case ever brought before the Equal Employment Opportunity Commission (EEOC) was settled in September 2009. The EEOC is an agency of the U.S. government that enforces laws that prohibit job discrimination because of race, religion, sex, national origin, age, or disability.

The case was brought before the EEOC in November 2004 by an employee of Sears, Roebuck and Co., one of the largest retail companies in the United States, headquartered in Hoffman Estates, Illinois. The employee was injured on the job and, after taking workers' compensation leave, tried to return to work with disabilities from his injuries. According to the employee, Sears denied his requests for accommodation for his disabilities and fired him when his leave ran out. As the EEOC prepared to bring the case to trial, the agency's attorneys found that at least 100 other former Sears employees had similarly lost their jobs after workplace injuries. A class-action suit was filed on their behalf.

Although Sears denied that the company has refused to provide reasonable accommodations for disabled employees, the firm agreed on Sept. 29, 2009, to settle the lawsuit in the amount of $6.2 million.

UN convention on disability rights. On July 31, the United States became the 143rd nation to sign the United Nations Convention on the Rights of Persons with Disabilities. The convention was adopted in 2006 and went into effect in 2008, after 20 signatory nations ratified the agreement. The convention provides a legal—rather than a strictly moral—basis for the rights of people with disabilities.   ■ Kristina Vaicikonis

Eunice Kennedy Shriver
A Special Friend

Eunice Kennedy Shriver never held public office. Yet upon her death on Aug. 11, 2009, many people believed that the transformation she brought about in the lives of people with disabilities was as significant as the legacies of her brothers—United States President John F. Kennedy and Senators Robert F. Kennedy and Edward M. Kennedy.

Eunice Mary Kennedy was born on July 10, 1921, in Brookline, Massachusetts. She was the fifth of the nine children of wealthy financier Joseph P. Kennedy, Sr., and Rose (Fitzgerald) Kennedy. From a young age, Eunice took to heart two of her parents' most passionate beliefs: in every endeavor, it was important to win; and of those to whom much is given, much is expected. She quickly became aware that one of her older sisters, Rosemary, who was intellectually challenged, was at a disadvantage among the fiercely competitive Kennedy clan. Eunice ensured that Rosemary was included in all the family's activities. The understanding that Eunice developed about the abilities of people with intellectual and physical challenges led to her life's work.

Eunice earned a degree in sociology from Stanford University in California in 1943. Her earliest jobs included working with a juvenile delinquency project and as a social worker at a penitentiary for women. In 1951, Eunice moved to Chicago to work at a shelter for women and at a juvenile court. In Chicago, she met her future husband, Robert Sargent Shriver, Jr., who would later become the first director of the Peace Corps, a U.S. ambassador to France, and a vice presidential candidate. The couple married in 1953.

In 1957, while starting a family that would include five children, Eunice became the executive vice president of the Joseph P. Kennedy, Jr., Foundation. Her father had established the organization in honor of her oldest brother, Joseph P. Kennedy, Jr., a U.S. Navy pilot who was killed during World War II (1939-1945). Under Eunice's leadership, the foundation funded research into the prevention of mental retardation and the study of bioethics.

When her brother John became president of the United States, Eunice made public what had been a closely guarded family secret. In an article for *The Saturday Evening Post,* she disclosed that a member of the Kennedy family, Rosemary, was mentally retarded. Until then, society generally treated mental retardation as a source of shame, and family members with intellectual disabilities were often isolated in institutions. The revelation did much to change public attitudes toward people with disabilities.

Even more revolutionary was Eunice's work with the Special Olympics, a program that she helped found. The first event was launched in Chicago in 1968, just six weeks after the assassination of her brother Robert. The Special Olympics, which provides year-round training and competition for intellectually challenged athletes, created opportunities for mentally challenged people to achieve in a world in which they previously were not allowed to compete. Under Eunice's leadership, the Special Olympics grew to include more than 1 million athletes in more than 160 countries. In 1984, President Ronald Reagan presented her with the Presidential Medal of Freedom, the nation's highest civilian honor. For Eunice Kennedy Shriver, the "most precious prize" was one she received from working with her "special friends": "faith in the unlimited possibilities of the human spirit." ■ Kristina Vaicikonis

Disasters. The deadliest disaster of 2009 was an earthquake that killed more than 1,100 people in Indonesia on September 30. Disasters that resulted in major loss of life include the following:

Aircraft crashes

February 12—United States. A commuter plane en route from Newark, New Jersey, to Buffalo, New York, crashes into a house outside Buffalo. All 49 passengers and crew members, as well as a resident in the house, are killed. Investigators suspect icing on the wings may have contributed to the crash.

May 20—Indonesia. A military transport plane crashes as it prepares to land at a base in Magetan, East Java, killing 101 people, including 2 people on the ground. The plane is carrying 112 passengers and crew members, most of them soldiers and their families, from Jakarta to the base.

June 1—Brazil. An Air France Airbus 330-200 en route from Rio de Janeiro to Paris carrying 228 passengers and crew members vanishes over the Atlantic Ocean. The flight encountered turbulence some time after taking off the night of May 31 and may have experienced mechanical failures, causing it to break apart. All aboard are lost.

June 30—Comoros. A Yemenia Airbus 310-300 jet en route from Sanaa, the capital of Yemen, to Comoros crashes into the Indian Ocean as it attempts a landing during strong winds. A 12-year-old passenger survives; 152 other passengers and crew members are killed.

July 15—Iran. All 168 passengers and crew members are killed when a Caspian Airlines flight drops from the sky and explodes on impact in Jannatabad, northern Iran, 16 minutes after take-off from Tehran, the capital. The flight was bound for Yerevan, Armenia.

Earthquakes

April 6—Italy. Nearly 300 people are killed and more than 65,000 others are left homeless when an earthquake of 6.3 magnitude strikes Italy's central Abruzzo region. Most of the deaths occur in L'Aquila, a medieval college city about 75 miles (120 kilometers) northeast of Rome, the capital.

September 2—Indonesia. An earthquake of 7.0 magnitude strikes the island of Java in Indonesia, causing landslides that kill at least 79 people and injure dozens of others. The quake's epicenter is in the Indian Ocean, about 120 miles (190 kilometers) southeast of Jakarta, the capital.

September 29—Samoa, American Samoa, Tonga. An earthquake of magnitude 8.0 strikes near the Samoan Islands in the South Pacific Ocean, causing a tsunami that floods Samoa, American Samoa, and Tonga. At least 186 people are killed as entire villages are washed away.

September 30—Indonesia. More than 1,100 people are killed and hundreds of others are injured when an earthquake of 7.6 magnitude strikes 38 miles (60 kilometers) from Padang, the capital of West Sumatra province. A second quake, of 6.6 magnitude, strikes the next day, hindering rescue efforts.

Explosions and fires

January 1—Thailand. A fire in a Bangkok nightclub, started by exploding fireworks during a New Year's celebration, leaves 66 people dead and some 200 others injured. Many of the victims die underfoot as the crowd stampedes toward the single exit.

January 31—Kenya. At least 113 people are killed and more than 175 others are injured when an overturned tanker truck explodes in Molo, about 105 miles (169 kilometers) northwest of Nairobi, the capital. The victims were siphoning gas into jerry cans as it spilled from the truck.

February 7—Australia. The worst wildfires ever to strike Australia burn across about 1 million acres (430,000 hectares) in the southeastern state of Victoria. The fires completely destroy the towns of Marysville and Kinglake and leave 173 people dead and thousands of others homeless.

June 5—Mexico. Forty-nine children are killed as fire engulfs a day care center for toddlers in Hermosillo, the capital of Mexico's northwestern Sonora state. Officials believe the fire started in a neighboring warehouse.

June 17—Russia. Seventy-five workers at the Sayano-Shushenskaya power plant in Siberia drown when a turbine explodes, causing water pipes to burst in the turbine hall. The power station, Russia's largest hydroelectric power plant, stands below an 800-foot (245-meter) dam on the Yenisei River in Siberia's Khakassia region.

December 5—Russia. At least 118 people are killed and some 130 others are injured as a fireworks display triggers a fire at a nightclub in Perm, about 870 miles (1,400 kilometers) east of Moscow, the capital.

Mine disasters

February 22—China. An explosion in one of the largest coal mines in China kills at least 78 men and leaves some 114 others injured. The accident takes place outside Taiyuan, the capital of Shanxi province, in northern China.

May 31—South Africa. At least 82 people are killed when fire breaks out in an unused shaft of a gold mine in central Free State, South Africa. The miners were in the shaft illegally.

November 21—China. A gas explosion in a coal mine in the city of Hegang, in northeasern Heilongjiang province, leaves 108 miners dead in the worst Chinese coal mine accident since 2007.

Shipwrecks

January 11—Indonesia. At least 311 passengers and crew members are killed when a ferry sinks about 31 miles (50 kilometers) off the west coast of Sulawesi Island in a storm. About 35 people survive.

January 25—Vietnam. Forty-two people are killed when a ferry overloaded with shoppers for Tet (Lunar New Year) festivities sinks in the Gianh River in Quang Binh province, central Vietnam.

March 29—Libya. At least 230 migrants drown when the boat with which they are trying to reach Italy capsizes in heavy winds and rain about 30 miles (48 kilometers) off the shore of Libya. Twenty-three passengers survive.

July 27—Turks and Caicos Islands. At least 85 migrants drown when the boat with which they left Haiti capsizes near the British territory of the Turks and Caicos Islands; 118 people survive.

August 5—Tonga. Seventy-five people drown when a ferry capsizes off the coast of Tonga, about 56 miles (90 kilometers) northwest of Nuku'alofa, the capital. The ferry's condition was so poor, it had been dubbed a floating death trap.

September 8—Sierra Leone. Thirty-four people are known dead, about 40 survive, and more than 220 others are missing and presumed dead after a ferry carrying traders, fishermen, and schoolchildren capsizes in the Atlantic Ocean during a storm. The boat was traveling from the town of Shenge to Tombo, near Freetown, the capital.

November 25—Congo (Kinshasa). At least 90 people are killed and an unknown number remain missing as a logging vessel illegally transporting passengers capsizes in bad weather in west Congo's Lake Mai Ndombe.

November 27—Bangladesh. At least 83 people are killed and dozens of others are missing as an overloaded ferry capsizes in the Tetulia River in southern Bangladesh. The passengers were traveling from Dhaka, the capital, to Bhola.

Storms and floods

January 28—United States. A storm that began in the southern Plains on January 26 and swept across the central and northeastern United States leaves 55 people dead. Sleet and freezing rain crippled areas of Texas, Arkansas, Kentucky, Indiana, and Ohio as some 1.3 million people lost electric power. The storm then dumped some 10 inches (25 centimeters) of snow on the Northeast.

February 10—United States. At least 15 people are killed and dozens of others are injured as several unusual February tornadoes sweep through central Oklahoma. Most of the deaths occur in Lone Grove, a town 90 miles (145 kilometers) south of Oklahoma City, the state capital.

May 26—Bangladesh and India. Cyclone Aila leaves more than 300 people dead and half a million others homeless in southern Bangladesh and eastern India. Heavy rains triggered mudslides in

Divers recover debris from Air France Flight 447, which disappeared over the Atlantic Ocean the night of May 31. All 228 passengers and crew members perished, as the craft encountered turbulence off the coast of Brazil. The flight was en route from Rio de Janeiro to Paris.

India's Darjeeling tea district and, in Bangladesh, acres of cropland were flooded with seawater.

August 5—Philippines. Typhoon Morakot (locally known as Typhoon Kiko) sweeps past the northern Philippines, amplifying monsoon rains. By August 10, at least 24 people have been killed, including a group of tourists who die in floods on the volcano Mount Pinatubo and miners caught in landslides at several makeshift camps.

August 7—Taiwan. Typhoon Morakot makes landfall in eastern Hualien county, bringing at least 83 inches (211 centimeters) of rain to parts of the island and the worst flooding in some 50 years. At least 700 people are killed as mudslides bury several villages in the mountains of southern Taiwan.

August 9—China. Typhoon Morakot reaches the east coast of mainland China with winds of 74 miles (119 kilometers) per hour, covering an area about 1,000 miles (1,600 kilometers) wide. The storm brings flooding and mudslides, displacing 1 million people and causing the deaths of 12 others.

September 9—Turkey. At least 36 people are killed when flash floods triggered by two days of rain sweep through the provinces of Istanbul and Tekirdag in northwest Turkey.

September 26—Philippines. More than 16 inches (40 centimeters) of rain in 12 hours from Tropical Storm Ketsana leaves 80 percent of Manila, capital of the Philippines, flooded. At least 420 people are killed and more than 300,000 others are left homeless by the storm.

September 29—Vietnam, Cambodia, and Laos. Tropical Storm Ketsana picks up strength as it crosses the China Sea and becomes a typhoon before striking central Vietnam and Cambodia. It weakens to a tropical depression before hitting Laos. At least 162 people in Vietnam, 17 people in Cambodia, and 24 people in Laos are killed as the storm causes landslides and floods.

October 3—Philippines. About 500 people die in floods and landslides as Typhoon Parma strikes the Philippines, just days after Tropical Storm Ketsana brought the worst flooding the island has experienced in 42 years.

October 9—India. At least 300 people are killed in flooding caused by days of incessant rain. Most of the deaths occur in the neighboring states of Karnataka, Andhra Pradesh, and Maharashtra in southern India.

October 31—Philippines. Typhoon Mirinae, packing winds of up to 115 miles (185 kilometers) per hour, strikes the Philippines, bringing more floods. At least 27 people are killed.

November 2—Vietnam. Mirinae is downgraded to a tropical depression before hitting Vietnam. At least 116 people are killed as floodwaters engulf the central provinces.

November 8—El Salvador. At least 140 people are killed as three days of rain cause floods and mudslides in the eastern part of the country. In San Salvador, the capital, entire roads are washed away.

November 25—Saudi Arabia. A rare, heavy storm brings more than 3.5 inches (90 millimeters) of rain and causes flash floods in western Saudi Arabia. At least 137 people are killed, primarily in the port city of Jeddah, where poor sewage infrastructure is blamed for the flooding.

Train wrecks

October 24—Egypt. At least 50 pasengers are killed and more than 30 others are injured when a speeding train hits the back of a standing train just outside of Cairo. The first train had stopped after hitting a cow.

Other disasters

January 5—Guatemala. At least 38 people are killed and some 30 others are missing when a landslide buries a road 124 miles (200 kilometers) north of Guatemala City, the capital. The victims were day laborers who had left their cars because the road was blocked by a previous landslide.

■ Kristina Vaicikonis

See also **Asia; India; Philippines; Weather.**

Djibouti. See Africa.

Dominica. See Latin America; West Indies.

Dominican Republic. See Latin America; West Indies.

Drought. See Weather.

Drug abuse. An estimated 20.1 million Americans aged 12 or older were *current* (within the past month) users of illegal drugs, 129 million were current drinkers of alcohol, and 70.9 million were current users of tobacco in 2008, according to the National Survey on Drug Use and Health (NSDUH) released in September 2009. The NSDUH is an annual survey by the United States Substance Abuse and Mental Health Services Administration.

Illegal drugs. The 8-percent rate of current overall illegal drug use reported in the 2008 NSDUH was similar to the rates reported each year since 2002. In addition, marijuana was once again the most commonly used illegal drug, with 6.1 percent of Americans using it in 2008.

The 2008 NSDUH also indicated that the decline in illegal drug use observed among youth since 2002 continued. For Americans between the ages of 12 and 17, current illegal drug use fell from a rate of 11.6 percent in 2002 to 9.3 percent in 2008. This decrease included reductions in the use of nearly all types of illegal drugs.

Current illegal drug use was higher among young adults between the ages of 18 and 25 (19.6 percent) than among younger or older age groups. From 2002 to 2008, significant increases in nonmedical use of prescription pain relievers and the hallucinogen LSD occurred among young adults.

Among unemployed adults in the United States, 19.6 percent were current users of illegal drugs in 2008. This percent was more than double the 8-percent rate of current illegal drug use among full-time employees. More than 10 percent of part-time employees used illegal drugs.

Alcohol. The 2008 NSDUH showed that 51.6 percent of Americans were current drinkers of alcohol, similar to the 51.1 percent reported for 2007. The rate of Americans participating in *binge drinking* (having five or more drinks on the same occasion) during the past month was 23.3 percent in 2008; the rate of Americans who were *heavy drinkers* (having five or more drinks on the same occasion on five or more days) during the past month was 6.9 percent. These rates were identical to those reported for 2007. However, the rate of current alcohol use among Americans between the ages of 12 and 17 decreased from 15.9 percent in 2007 to 14.6 percent in 2008.

Tobacco. According to the 2008 NSDUH, 28.4 percent of Americans were current users of a tobacco product (cigarettes, smokeless tobacco, cigars, or pipe tobacco)—compared with 30.4 percent in 2002. Among Americans aged 12 to 17, the rate of current cigarette use continued to decline—from 13 percent in 2002 to 9.1 percent in 2008. ■ Alfred J. Smuskiewicz

See also **Drugs.**

Drugs. The United States Food and Drug Administration (FDA) should reduce the maximum allowable doses of over-the-counter acetaminophen, recommended an FDA advisory panel in June 2009. Acetaminophen is the key ingredient in such popular pain-relieving medications as Tylenol and Excedrin.

The panel's recommendation was prompted by a May FDA report that attributed many cases of liver damage—including some deaths—to patients ingesting higher-than-recommended doses of acetaminophen. The panel urged the FDA to lower both the allowable total daily dose and the dose per pill of acetaminophen as a way to help reduce the risk of overdosing. Although the FDA is not obligated to follow advisory panel recommendations, it typically does so.

"Black box" warning for Darvon. Pain-killing drugs containing propoxyphene, sold primarily as Darvon, must carry a special "black box" warning emphasizing the dangers of overdose. The FDA announced that requirement in July after reviewing records of numerous deaths—from both accidental overdoses and suicides—linked to propoxyphene. Clinical evidence showed that some of these deaths were the result of *arrhythmias* (abnormal heart rhythms).

In June, the European Union's European Medicines Agency ordered the phase-out of propoxyphene because of the drug's risk of adverse health effects.

Morning-after pill easier to get. In April, the FDA eased access to the emergency contraceptive pill known as Plan B, or the "morning-after" pill, by allowing 17-year-old girls to obtain the drug over the counter without a prescription. The announcement came in response to a March ruling by a federal court that the FDA's decision in 2006 to restrict nonprescription access of Plan B to women aged 18 years and older was based on political considerations rather than science.

When taken within 72 hours of sexual intercourse, Plan B substantially reduces the chance of pregnancy. Plan B pills contain high doses of progesterone, a female sex hormone that hinders the release of eggs from the ovaries.

Some critics argued that 17-year-old girls should not be allowed to obtain Plan B so easily—potentially without parental consent. By contrast, other observers urged the FDA to further ease access to Plan B by allowing off-the-shelf sales of the drug with no age restrictions.

Tobacco regulated like a drug. United States President Barack Obama signed legislation in June 2009 regulating the manufacturing and marketing of cigarettes and other tobacco products. The law gave the FDA regulatory authority over tobacco similar to the authority the agency has long had over prescription drugs.

Health experts blame smoking for hundreds of thousands of deaths each year in the United States. The new law required larger and more strongly worded warnings about the dangers of smoking to be posted on cigarette packs. The legislation also restricted cigarette advertising, banned cigarette flavors, and required the FDA to approve any proposed new tobacco products.

Promising new drugs for diabetes. Studies reported in June at the American Diabetes Association conference in New Orleans indicated that certain medications under development were better than available drugs at helping patients with Type 2 diabetes mellitus (T2DM) control their *glucose* (blood sugar) levels and weight. The medications, known as glucagon-like peptide-1 (GLP-1) analogs (also called incretin mimetics), stimulate production of insulin in the body. Insulin, a substance that regulates the body's use of sugars, is not produced in sufficient quantities in patients with T2DM.

In one of the most promising reported studies, led by physician John Buse of the University of North Carolina School of Medicine at Chapel Hill, patients given a GLP-1 analog called liraglutide achieved lower glucose levels and lost more weight than patients given exenatide. Exenatide was the only FDA-approved GLP-1 analog on the market in 2009. In April, an FDA advisory panel reached a split decision regarding whether liraglutide should be approved. Some panelists expressed concern that the drug had been linked to thyroid tumors in laboratory rodents.

Antibiotics from ants. Bacteria living on the bodies of ants that cultivate fungus "gardens" have the potential to be used in the production of antibiotic drugs, according to a March report by a team of biologists led by Cameron Currie of the University of Wisconsin at Madison. The so-called leaf-cutter ants grow fungi on pieces of leaves that they cut from plants. The ants use the fungi as food for themselves and their *larvae* (immature ants). Colonies of actinomycete bacteria on the ant's bodies secrete antibiotic substances into the fungus gardens that protect the gardens against harmful, parasitic fungi.

Currie's team analyzed one of these bacterial antibiotics, named dentigerumycin, in the laboratory. In experiments, dentigerumycin slowed the growth of a drug-resistant strain of *Candida albicans*, a fungus that causes yeast infection in people. The biologists said that further research of antibiotics produced by bacteria living on leaf-cutter ants could help scientists develop more effective antibiotics to fight drug-resistant germs.

■ Alfred J. Smuskiewicz

See also **AIDS; Drug abuse; Health care issues; Medicine; Mental health; Public health.**

East Timor. See Asia.

Eastern Orthodox Churches.

Metropolitan Kirill of Smolensk and Kaliningrad was elected patriarch of the Russian Orthodox Church on Jan. 27, 2009. He succeeded Patriarch Alexy II of Moscow and All Russia, who had died on Dec. 5, 2008. On July 4 and 5, 2009, Patriarch Kirill visited the Ecumenical Patriarchate in Istanbul, Turkey. Kirill and Ecumenical Patriarch Bartholomew of Constantinople celebrated the Divine Liturgy together and discussed the state of the worldwide Orthodox Church. On July 27, Kirill visited Ukraine and urged the end of church divisions there. Since the Soviet Union dissolved in 1991, some Orthodox Ukrainians have called for independence from the Russian church.

Ecumenical Patriarch Bartholomew met with secular and religious leaders in 2009 to address the issues of religious and minority rights and the environment. On April 7, he received United States President Barack Obama in Istanbul. The leaders talked about religious liberty and the Turkish government's refusal to date to permit the reopening of the historic Orthodox Theological School on the island of Heybeliada (also called Halki). The government closed the school in 1971, after it passed a law prohibiting private institutions of higher learning.

On Aug. 15, 2009, Ecumenical Patriarch Bartholomew met Turkish Prime Minister Recep Tayyip Erdogan to discuss religious freedom and the rights of non-Muslim minorities in Turkey. He presented Erdogan with a report on the problems of religious minorities. Minority rights have proven to be a stumbling block for Turkey in its attempt to gain European Union membership.

From October 20 to 25, Ecumenical Patriarch Bartholomew visited New Orleans, where he led an environmental symposium about the Mississippi River. Bartholomew often is called the "Green Patriarch" because of his environmental awareness. On October 27, he received an honorary doctor of law degree from Fordham University in New York City.

Episcopal Assemblies. Representatives of the 14 *autocephalous* (independent) Orthodox churches attended the Fourth Pre-Conciliar Pan-Orthodox Conference in Chambésy, Switzerland, from June 6 to 12. They approved the establishment of Orthodox bishops' conferences, called Episcopal Assemblies, for Orthodox Diaspora communities. The Diaspora consists of Orthodox people living outside the jurisdiction of their regional churches. The decision reached by the conference paved the way for greater unification of the Orthodox Church. In September, the Standing Conference of the Canonical Orthodox Bishops in the Americas scheduled the first Episcopal Assembly for May 2010.   ■ Thomas FitzGerald

See also **Turkey.**

Economics, United States. Battered by one of the sharpest contractions in commercial activity since the 1930's, as well as by chaos in the banking system, the U.S. economy in early 2009 appeared to bottom out in its long, steep decline. Then, in the second half of the year, the economy began a tentative, fragile recovery.

As the economic storm was breaking in 2008, many economists had urged the federal government to take extraordinary actions to prop up the banking system, teetering from the cascading effect of overdependence on mortgage-based securities of uncertain value. Both the administration of President George W. Bush and that of Barack Obama, who became president on Jan. 20, 2009, responded to the urgings of these economists. Together with the Federal Reserve System (the Fed), which manages the nation's money supply, both administrations intervened in the private capital system to an unprecedented degree.

The federal government took over some major financial institutions outright, controlled others with a high degree of federal oversight, and injected huge amounts of money directly into banks through the U.S. Department of the Treasury and the Fed. The Fed set interest rates at historically low levels and adopted a number of measures to create new money and inject it into credit markets. Beyond the banking sector, the Obama administration forced the bankruptcies and reorganization in spring 2009 of the giant U.S. automobile manufacturers General Motors (GM) Corporation of Detroit and Chrysler LLC of Auburn Hills, Michigan, after investing large sums to keep them afloat.

Stimulus package. Obama, even before taking office, urged Congress to develop legislation authorizing massive spending programs and tax cuts to help stabilize and then revive the economy. On February 17, he signed the $787-billion American Recovery and Reinvestment Act, which emerged from intense negotiations in Congress. The law, unofficially known as "the stimulus package," represented the centerpiece of the Obama administration's recovery plan.

During the spring, economic conditions appeared to worsen. Although the massive stimulus package had become law, economists cautioned that the stimulative effects of its appropriations would be felt only over an extended period of time. Stock markets, meanwhile, hit new lows, with the Dow Jones Industrial Average dipping below 7,000 on March 2 for the first time since 1997. (In late 2007, the Dow had climbed to a peak of 14,000.) Jobs, moreover, were being shed at an alarming rate in early 2009. The U.S. Department of Labor reported that the national unemployment rate in the second quarter of 2009 spiked above 9 percent, compared with a rate of just under 5.5 percent for the same period one year earlier.

By early summer, however, stock market averages were inching upward again, initial stimulus funds began reaching consumers, and the downturn was finally bumping along its bottom. Prices of many commodities and goods, which had been tumbling in a deflationary spiral, were starting to firm again. Later in the year, other small but persistent signs hinted that business conditions were improving, with measures of factory activity and international trade suggesting recovery.

The "Great Recession." As the economic crisis unfolded in 2008, the collapse or purchase under duress of a number of U.S. financial firms revealed the vulnerability of the entire banking system, evoking comparison with the Great Depression of the 1930's, when the banking system had failed. Commentators soon introduced the term "the Great Recession" into public discourse.

Gross domestic product (GDP)—the total value of goods and services produced in a country in a year—shrank in the third and fourth quarters of 2008 as the financial crisis deepened. A steep slide of 5.4 percent in GDP in the fourth quarter of 2008 was followed by a plunge of 6.4 percent in the first quarter of 2009. However, the downturn braked to only a 0.7-percent drop in the second quarter, and third-quarter measurements showed a 2.2-percent expansion of GDP.

By July 2009, the recession had lasted at least 18 months, according to economists, making it the longest-lasting period of contraction since the Great Depression, which started in 1929 and lasted for years. The National Bureau of Economic Research (NBER), an organization specializing in the study of economics, pegged the start of the current recession in December 2007. NBER economists were not expected to announce an end date for the recession until some months after indicators showed unequivocal recovery.

Back from the brink, slowly. Many economists cautioned that the glimmers of growth seen in the second half of 2009 were too unsteady to enable them to predict a sustained recovery. The summer rebound continued into autumn but was heavily linked to government spending and the Fed's expansive creation of new credit made available to banks and other financial institutions. The Obama administration's late-summer stimulus program of payments to buyers of new automobiles if they traded in old vehicles to be scrapped proved highly popular. Dubbed "cash for clunkers," the program stimulated so much car buying that manufacturers restarted some idled assembly lines.

As the impact of the "cash for clunkers" program faded in autumn, analysts observed that the episode underlined the ongoing dependence of the private sector on government-supplied aid. Until the economy could sustain solid growth without massive government rescue efforts, economists said, the nation could face a prolonged period of slow or flat growth.

Economists with the International Monetary Fund (IMF), a United Nations affiliate that lends to member nations and advises on economic policies, estimated in October 2009 that the U.S. economy would shrink by 2.7 percent in calendar 2009. Looking ahead, the IMF forecast sluggish U.S. economic growth of 1.5 percent in 2010.

Pain for jobseekers. The U.S. economy shed jobs throughout 2009, as it did for most of 2008. The unemployment rate surged from 5.0 percent in December 2007 to 10.2 percent in October 2009, according to the Department of Labor, with the number of unemployed individuals jumping from 7.6 million to 15.7 million during that period. As signs of stabilization and recovery became apparent in the second half of 2009, economists warned that job creation was likely to lag well behind other areas of economic expansion.

Manufacturing upturn. The Institute for Supply Management—a Tempe, Arizona-based professional organization of U.S. purchasing managers—reported that its index of factory activity hit a recession low of 32.9 in December 2008. That figure was far below the 50-point threshold that represents the boundary between contraction and expansion. By August 2009, the index had climbed to 52.9, indicating expansion for the first time since January 2008. However, in September 2009 the index dipped to 52.6.

Spending by U.S. consumers declined or stagnated through much of 2008 and 2009, reflecting worries about the economy. Monthly declines in personal consumption expenditures (the money consumers spend on a wide range of goods and services) began to show up in 2008, leading to a one-month decline in December of 0.7 percent—an annualized rate of over 8 percent. Declines in early 2009 were followed by modest increases midyear, then a jump in spending of 0.9 percent in August, attributed, in part, to the "cash for clunkers" program. However, spending fell again slightly in September.

Fed leadership retained. On August 25, President Obama announced that he would reappoint Ben S. Bernanke to a new four-year term as Fed chairman, to begin in February 2010. The president praised Bernanke, an appointee of former President George W. Bush, crediting the Fed chief with decisive action that helped prevent a second Great Depression.   ■ John D. Boyd

See also **Bank; Economics, World; Stocks and bonds.**

SELECTED KEY U.S. ECONOMIC INDICATORS

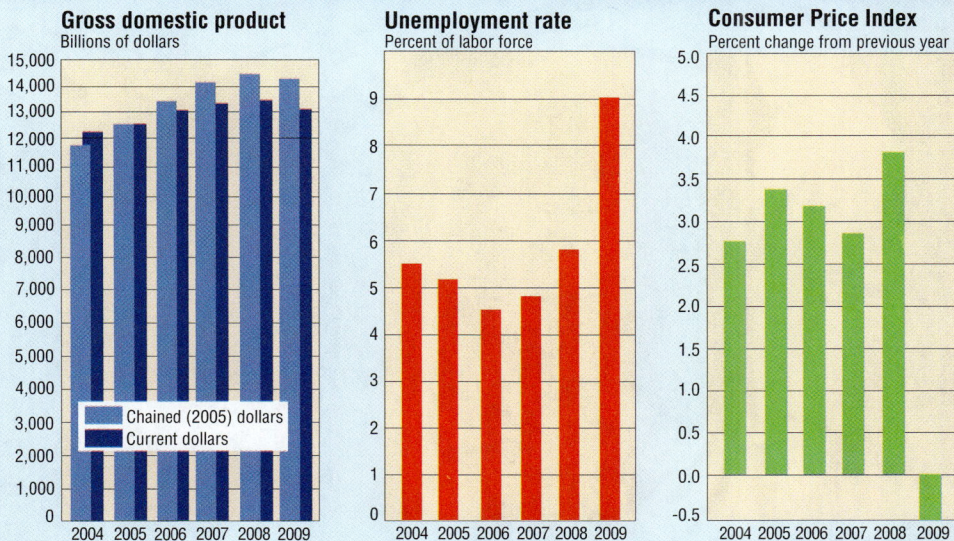

Gross domestic product
Billions of dollars

Chained (2005) dollars
Current dollars

2004 2005 2006 2007 2008 2009

Unemployment rate
Percent of labor force

2004 2005 2006 2007 2008 2009

Consumer Price Index
Percent change from previous year

2004 2005 2006 2007 2008 2009

Sources: U.S. Department of Commerce and U.S. Department of Labor, except 2009 figures, which are estimates from The Conference Board.

The gross domestic product (GDP) measures the value in current prices of all goods and services produced within a country in a year. Many economists believe the GDP is an accurate measure of the nation's total economic performance. Chained dollars show the amount adjusted for inflation. The unemployment rate is the percentage of the total labor force that is unemployed and actively seeking work. The Consumer Price Index measures inflation by showing the change in prices of selected goods and services consumed by urban families and individuals.

ECONOMIC CRISES
THEN AND NOW

By John D. Boyd

I t took a year after the September 2008 financial collapse for markets in the United States to stabilize and credit to slowly thaw. While some Wall Street banks and financial institutions returned to profitability by mid-2009, the U.S. economy eliminated another 263,000 jobs in September, pushing the unemployment rate up to 9.8 percent. First-time claims for unemployment insurance rose to a seasonally adjusted 551,000 during the last full week of September. Economists interpreted the rise as a troubling sign for the job market, which showed little sign of recovery. Yet debate continued to rage in the United States about how government officials responded to this Great Recession and what, or if, new government regulations were needed to prevent a recurrence.

FREE SOUP &

By September, many economists and government leaders agreed that the causes of the financial collapse were remarkably similar to those that triggered the October 1929 stock market crash and subsequent Great Depression—the worldwide economic slump of the 1930's. However, they also noted dramatic differences between the current downturn and the Depression. Unlike 1929, the U.S. government acted quickly in 2008 and 2009 to prop up the collapsing financial sector.

Fed action in 2008

Ben S. Bernanke, chairman of the Federal Reserve (Fed)—the U.S. central bank—guided the early response and the financial sector recovery. The Fed has dual roles: Injecting money into the economy to fuel growth and draining money to stem inflation; and regulating large bank holding companies whose operations can have an outsized impact on the money supply and the credit system that is the lifeblood of commerce.

Congress established the Fed in 1913. In 1929, no precedent yet existed to lower interest rates when a financial disaster seemed

A look at today's Great Recession in the mirror of the Great Depression.

likely. By the time of the 2008 financial collapse, the Fed's power to spur or constrain growth was fully established, and its chairman understood the danger of letting a new depression take root.

Bernanke argued in his doctoral thesis that the Fed did not cut rates fast enough after the '29 crash. Faced with a similar collapse, he oversaw a huge expansion of Fed powers. The Fed created trillions of dollars from 2007 into 2009 to back commercial activity as private bank credit withered. Many economists believed that Bernanke's actions were crucial to reviving the credit system and credited Fed-supplied liquidity with spurring commerce into growth by mid-2009.

However, Bernanke's prompt response also drew sharp criticism, from both the left and the right. Some liberals in Congress accused the Fed, under Bernanke, and under his predecessor, Alan Greenspan, of having failed to properly regulate the financial sector before the collapse. Many conservatives opposed the Fed's expanded powers and opposed the enormous deficit spending, fearing that the massive monetary build-up would eventually unleash inflation.

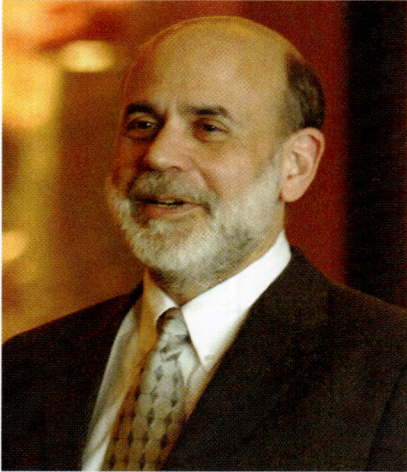

Former academic economist Ben S. Bernanke, chairman of the Federal Reserve, guided the federal government's early response to the 2008 financial crisis. His doctoral thesis had been on the Federal Reserve's failure to react effectively to the Great Depression of the 1930's.

Pre-Depression conditions

The 1920's had been a period of unsustainable "bubbles" in a number of markets, including stocks and real estate. Both the executive and legislative branches of government were controlled by conservatives, who had a hands-off attitude about intervening in markets or regulating private business. Tax cuts that favored those who controlled capital widened income disparity. The Revenue Act of 1926 and other tax cuts reduced federal income and inheritance taxes dramatically. Federal taxes on a $1-million annual income were reduced from $600,000 to $200,000. By 1929, the top 0.1 percent had a combined income equal to the bottom 42 percent and controlled 34 percent of all savings.

Most U.S. farmers did not prosper as the economy recovered from World War I (1914-1918). Hoping that the high prices and expanded production during the war would continue, many American farmers borrowed heavily to buy land. However, a worldwide increase in agricultural production drove down prices of farm products by about 40 percent in 1920 and 1921, and they remained low throughout the decade. Faced with falling commodity prices, many farmers could not pay their mortgages and lost their land. While the average per capita income in 1929 was $750 a year for all Americans, the average annual income for agricultural workers was $273.

Bank failures increased, primarily in agricultural areas because farmers experienced such poor conditions. More than 5,000 U.S. banks went out of business from 1921 to 1929.

Between 1923 and 1929, average output per worker increased 32 percent in manufacturing, while average wages in manufacturing rose only 8 percent. Corporations, not workers, were the beneficiaries of increased productivity. Between 1923 and 1929, corporate profits rose 62 percent.

The author:
John D. Boyd is associate editor for *The Journal of Commerce.*

A woman from Oklahoma and her children live as migratory farm workers in California in 1937. In the mid-1930's, many people, especially from the Dust Bowl region on the lower Great Plains, migrated to California in the hope of making a better life. As in the current recession, people unable to pay mortgages lost their property to foreclosure and ended up homeless.

At the same time, labor unions came under sharp attack, amid fears of spreading Communist influence.

With wealth divided so unevenly, many did not have enough money to satisfy needs. The solution was credit. New tools to expand credit—from installment payments for goods to speculating in stock with small margin deposits—put the decade's expansion on an ever more rickety foundation. Outstanding installment credit more than doubled between 1925 and 1929, from $1.3 billion to $3 billion.

At the same time, speculation drove the stock market. From early 1928 to September 1929, the Dow Jones Industrial Average rose from 191 to 381, and stock prices became divorced from earnings. The price of a share of the RCA Corporation climbed from $85 to $420 in 1928, without the corporation paying a single dividend. RCA stock, like many others of the period, was actually driven to dizzying heights by syndicates of Wall Street traders who would buy large numbers of shares until the rapid rise in value attracted other investors, which would further push up the price. At a certain point, the syndicate would dump its shares, taking a huge profit and ruinously driving down the stock's price.

Pre-Recession conditions

Many of the pre-Depression social and economic conditions were mirrored in the decade that began in 2000. While some trends, for example, deregulation of business, began in the 1980's and gathered strength in the 1990's, the administration of President George W. Bush, who took office in 2001, aggressively reined in a federal regulatory system it often regarded as an unwarranted threat to private enterprise.

The large tax cuts passed by Congress in 2001, 2002, and 2003 were signature items in President Bush's fiscal policy. Critics claimed the tax cuts were regressive; that is, they conferred greater benefits on high-income taxpayers. Under the tax rates, after-tax income increased by more than 6 percent for households in the top 1 percent of income distribution; 2 percent for households in the middle 60 percent; and 0.3 percent for households in the bottom 20 percent.

More than 2 million homes were foreclosed on in the United States in 2009—nearly 1 million in the third quarter alone. The housing boom, which began to deflate in 2007, collapsed in 2008. Between May 2007 and May 2008, property values in the United States fell by 15 percent. If homeowners had an adjustable rate mortgage and the interest on their loan rose, their monthly payments increased as the value of the property decreased. *Defaults* (failure to make payments) ballooned, leading to foreclosure.

Union membership weakened in the 1980's through the 2000's, and union leaders, who usually backed Democrats, found their policy influence sharply diminished with Republicans in the White House and in control of both houses of Congress. President Ronald Reagan's firing of striking federal air traffic controllers in 1981 sent a clear message that the influence of labor was waning. After the 2001 terrorist attacks, President Bush demanded that the Department of Homeland Security be established without certain union-friendly civil service and employee labor protec-tions, and 180,000 government employees were stripped of union rights.

Wages of average workers increased slowly through the 2000's, and wages of low earners actually declined when adjusted for inflation. Congress refused to increase the minimum wage until Democrats gained control in the 2006 elections. As a result, income disparity grew far beyond levels that had prevailed since World War II (1939–1945). During the 1940's, the income share held by the top 10 percent fell to around 35 percent, and it stayed there until the 1980's. By 2007, the income share controlled by the top 10 percent climbed to 50 percent of the total. As middle-class income flattened, personal debt expanded. Overall credit card debt grew in the United States by 315 percent from 1989 to 2006.

As in the pre-Depression era, the period before the current recession was characterized by widespread speculation and economic "bubbles." The 2008 collapse was triggered by a mortgage crisis that began in the United States in 2007. That crisis—largely brought on by mortgages going into default as a wild real estate bubble burst—had its roots in an era of deregulation. Fostered by the banking industry and by the Fed, Congress partially deregulated banking in the late 1990's and early 2000's.

Under intense pressure from the banking industry, Congress repealed the Glass-Steagall Act in 1999. Passed in 1933 to protect the savings of small investors from the riskier environment of investment banking, Glass-Steagall kept commercial and investment banking and the insurance industry separate. Its repeal allowed commercial banks and insurance companies to maintain in-house trading departments and invest in mortgage-backed securities. (A security is a corporate- or government-issued investment instrument that provides evidence of debt or equity.)

Like investment banks, the new "mixed-type" banks attempted to enlarge profits by speculating with their own money in such high-risk securities as *derivatives* (financial instruments whose values derive from the value of an underlying asset, such as a bond). Because derivatives were completely unregulated, no government agency required sellers—primarily banks, hedge funds, and insurance corporations—to hold reserves to back them. The seller of a derivative was, in effect, betting that the underlying asset would not default, allowing the financial institution to annually collect a percentage of the value of an asset it did not own. When large numbers of mortgages went into default, mortgage-backed securities lost much of their value. Without reserves, the sellers of derivatives derived from mortgage-backed securities were unable to pay, and the derivatives became worthless. Economists suggest that one reason for the freeze in credit was that banks—unsure of how many derivatives remained valuable, how much was owed, and the financial conditions of other banks—became unwilling to lend money for fear they would not be repaid—a situation that exactly mirrored the Great Depression.

Social conditions, then and now

The 1929 crisis hit eight months after the inauguration of Herbert C. Hoover, who combined an activist nature with a Republican philosophy of limited government. A wealthy engineer and businessman, Hoover had been known as the "Great Humanitarian" for his skill in organizing food relief in Europe after World War I. He burnished that image by commanding government and private rescue efforts for thousands trapped by

Herbert Hoover was the first president to use the power of the federal government to fight a depression. Nevertheless, he was blamed for the economic downturn of the 1930's. In New York City (left), and elsewhere around the country, shanty towns filled with homeless men were called Hoovervilles.

President Franklin D. Roosevelt sponsored "New Deal" legislation that established the Federal Deposit Insurance Corporation and such programs as Social Security, unemployment insurance, and the minimum wage—Great Depression legacies that helped moderate the effects of the current recession.

the massive Mississippi River flood of 1927. In 1928, he won the presidency in a landslide. He took office assuring the public that it was possible to continue an era of prosperity that could end American poverty. The financial collapse of 1929 threatened that vision.

Most political leaders in the 1920's, including Hoover, resisted making direct government relief payments to individuals, a practice they regarded as a socialist philosophy at odds with the American experience of individual initiative and responsibility. In the United States, Depression-era policymakers took years to agree on the need for a broad social safety net of support programs for the elderly, the poor, the unemployed, and others caught in the downward economic spiral. Relief efforts for the needy were left largely to private groups. With one out of every four working men out of work in many cities in the early 1930's, private charities and local governments were overwhelmed by long lines of hungry and homeless people.

In the modern era, government has an ongoing range of tools to support those in economic need: a national minimum wage law; state programs for employer-financed unemployment insurance; farm price supports; worker compensation funds for injuries; and Social Security payments to the aged and infirm. Many of these were put into place under "New Deal" legislation sponsored by President Franklin D. Roosevelt, who had defeated Hoover in 1932. In the modern era, such long-established programs—with timely injections of extra funds— helped moderate the effects of the current recession.

Economic recovery, then and now

Hoover is sometimes blamed for being too slow to respond after the stock market crash threatened to kill off economic growth. The reality is that Hoover responded fast and energetically. However, the severity of the collapse overwhelmed his efforts, and a deep-seated belief in the limits of government, both by him and by Congress, blocked further action.

When financial disaster struck, Hoover sprang into action with an emergency response plan that he had devised in 1921. As secretary of commerce under President Warren G. Harding, Hoover led a major economic conference to counterattack the effects of a sharp, postwar recession, or "panic," as such episodes were then known. The conference of business, labor, and government officials agreed that the best way to keep a panic from spreading was to prime the economic pump through aggressive spending by state and local governments on public works and by major private industries on capital improvements.

Just two weeks after the 1929 crash, Hoover hosted top railroad executives, the first of a furious round of meetings with business groups. He sought and won pledges from industries to go forward with capital

projects and avoid layoffs and wage cuts. He pressed states to maintain or speed up road projects and sought more federal infrastructure.

By spring 1930, the strategy of coordinated actions by the federal government, states, and private industry appeared to be working, but it was a false hope. Soon, bank failures spread, businesses cut back, and unemployment soared as the country fell into the grips of full-scaled depression. Over time, Hoover became an object of scorn, and the homeless who built shanty villages dubbed them "Hoovervilles."

The president continued to implement new policies to battle the downturn, but he resisted direct relief to the people. In the summer of 1932, thousands of World War I veterans—many of whom were destitute after losing their jobs and homes—marched on Washington, D.C., to lobby for early payment of a military service bonus due in 1945. Hoover eventually ordered the Army to forcefully disperse them, an action that solidified public sentiment against him.

After taking office in 1933, Franklin Roosevelt's first order of business was to stabilize a reeling banking system in which institutions were operating with a portfolio of worthless assets, leaving customers unsure if deposits were safe. He briefly shut down all banks to sort out which ones were solid enough to reopen. As part of Roosevelt's "first 100 days," Congress passed legislation creating the Federal Deposit Insurance Corporation (FDIC), an independent government agency that insures deposits at almost all U.S. banks and pays off the accounts of failed banks. This effectively stopped the banking panic. Because the FDIC continued to function effectively in the current recession, there have been few bank "runs," or panics, over the loss of bank accounts.

Roosevelt attempted to pull the economy out of the Depression and help the needy with a number of programs: work camps for veterans, indigents, and young men; farm supports; and a program for voluntary wage and price controls by industry. Social Security and unemployment insurance went into effect in 1937. Federal minimum wage legislation became law in 1938. It all helped, but it did not fix the economy. Most economists agree that the Great Depression in the United States ended

One of the New Deal's most successful programs, the Civilian Conservation Corps (CCC), was designed to provide work for unemployed, single men, who were typically 18 to 25 years of age. The CCC, in which more than 2 million served, conserved and developed natural resources by such activities as planting trees, building dams, and fighting forest fires. The public continues to enjoy national and state park facilities created by the CCC.

Treasury employees remove files from a Florida bank after a 2009 raid by the Troubled Asset Relief Program. Although more than 100 U.S. banks failed in 2009, the Federal Deposit Insurance Corporation, established during the Great Depression, continued to function effectively. With all bank deposits insured, there were no panic-driven "runs" on banks in 2009, as often happened in the Depression.

when the nation's economy was placed on a war footing after the country entered World War II.

Lessons of the Depression

Acting on the lessons of the Depression, the Fed in 2008 aggressively dropped short-term interest rates; created new accounts to back more types of finance; and put up money to facilitate the fire sale in March 2008 of a major investment bank that had run out of money. Congress and President Bush also agreed early in the year on a $350-billion tax rebate program to spur the economy. Days after the September financial meltdown, Bernanke and Bush Treasury Secretary Henry Paulson asked Congress for emergency powers and an immediate $700-billion financial industry rescue package. Action slowed, however, after the November election. President Bush was reluctant to back a proposed public works stimulus or rescue the failing giant auto makers General Motors Company (GM) and Chrysler Corporation, whose collapse would throw thousands out of work.

Before taking office, President Barack Obama asked Congress to pass a huge economic stimulus package. Critics on the right called him a socialist and said he was running up the national debt to dangerously high levels. Critics on the left accused him of not doing enough.

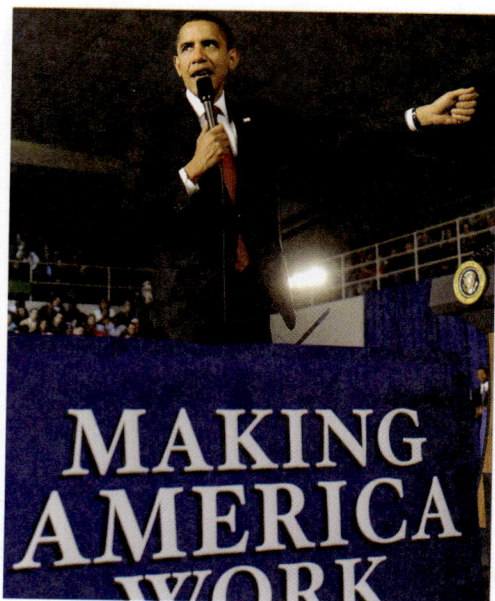

Before taking office in January 2009, Barack Obama asked Congress to approve what became a $787-billion stimulus package; it combined payroll tax cuts with infrastructure improvement programs and direct relief payments over two years. His administration got congressional funding to restructure GM and Chrysler, which went through rapid bankruptcies in the spring. By midyear, some auto plants reopened, and tax incentives for a "cash for clunkers" program spurred auto sales, at least temporarily. According to some economists, the slow-building stimulus package and extended unemployment benefits were, indeed, quietly but continuously pouring money into the economy; and credit markets, with Fed backing, were tight but functioning.

Even as the crisis seemed to ease by mid-2009, a national debate raged over whether Obama and the Democratic Congress were moving the United States toward a socialist government. Many Republicans criticized the government's interventions in the financial system, the auto industry, and in a planned overhaul of the health-care system.

Many liberals, including some leading economists, accused the Obama administration of being too timid. They suggested that the stimulus program was too small to be effective and pointed to governments in Europe and Asia whose stronger stimulus efforts were paying off with faster economic rebounds. They also accused the administration of not being tough enough with the banking industry and demanded tighter government regulations to curb Wall Street excesses.

On September 15, Fed Chairman Bernanke proclaimed a type of victory, stating that the recession was "very likely over." Speaking at a Washington think tank on the first anniversary of the collapse of the Lehman Brothers investment bank, Bernanke acknowledged no missteps in managing the worst economic crisis since the Great Depression. He did, however, concede that while the financial system had stabilized, credit remained tight and the economy had yet to generate new jobs. "It is still going to feel like a very weak economy for some time as many people still find their job security and their employment status is not what they wish it was," he noted. It took more than a decade and a world war for the country to dig itself out of the Great Depression. At the end of 2009, economists and ordinary Americans alike remained worried about how long it would take the economy to regenerate the millions of jobs lost to the Great Recession.

President Barack Obama's stimulus package—the $787-billion American Recovery and Reinvestment Act—combined infrastructure improvements, such as road building, with payroll tax cuts and direct relief payments.

Economics, World. As 2009 began, many of the world's economies were in recession and still contracting, as credit sources dried up and as domestic demand and international trade dwindled. By the second half of the year, however, the economies of major industrial nations were growing again, though few economists expected a strong recovery in 2010.

Economists with the International Monetary Fund (IMF), a United Nations affiliate that provides loans to member nations, summed up prospects for 2010 and beyond. Reporting in the organization's October 2009 World Economic Report, they observed, "The recovery has started, and the challenge is to sustain it."

The financial system underpinning the global economy appeared, in late 2008, to be in danger of collapsing. Banks and other financial institutions had invested in risky securities—particularly those based on mortgages in the overheated U.S. housing market—and found themselves dangerously exposed when the U.S. housing boom collapsed. In the global economy of the 2000's, these risks became widely distributed. A number of financial institutions failed; others were rescued by government bailouts or take-overs.

As the economic downturn spread globally, many central banks aggressively cut interest rates. In December 2008, the Federal Reserve System (the Fed), the central bank of the United States, cut the federal funds rate to a range of between 0 and 0.25 percent—a historic low. Throughout 2009, the Fed refrained from hiking interest rates. The European Central Bank and the Bank of England also kept interest rates historically low throughout 2009. Among major economies, only the central bank of Australia bucked the trend, notching its key interest rate upward several times in the autumn. Analysts speculated that the Australian action might put pressure on other central banks to hike interest rates in 2010.

Global statistics. IMF economists estimated that the global economy would shrink by 1.1 percent in 2009, then expand by 3.1 percent in 2010. They noted, however, that "it will take some time . . . until the outlook for unemployment improves significantly," and they projected that global growth rates would remain for some time below the pace experienced in 2007, when worldwide output rose 5.7 percent.

In the developing nations of Asia, a region that includes China and India, growth slowed substantially in 2009, but the region's more dynamic economies did not go into recession. China's government injected money into its economy with a huge stimulus package of public works projects. China and India also carried over such strong momentum from recent years that even though the global downturn slowed them, their economies managed still-impressive rates of growth. China's 2009 increase of 8.9 percent was well below the 13-percent growth rate it experienced in 2007, but it stood out as the strongest for a major nation. India followed with an estimated 5.4 percent growth rate, half of its 2007 pace. Together, they led developing Asia toward growth estimated at 6.2 percent for 2009. For the region, economists projected a 7.3-percent rate of growth in 2010.

The advanced economies. The traditional powerhouses of commerce—advanced economies including the United States, Japan, Canada, the United Kingdom, and the largest European nations of Germany, France, and Italy—shuddered to a halt in late 2008 as the global financial system unraveled. The economies of these major nations collectively shrank by 3.4 percent in 2009, according to IMF estimates.

These nations had collectively registered growth of 2.7 percent in 2007 and a mere 0.6 percent in 2008, when the global financial crisis broke. IMF economists predicted that, taken as a whole, these advanced economies would experience growth of only 1.3 percent in 2010.

Russia was also hard-hit by the global economic downturn, with economic output falling an estimated 7.5 percent in 2009. In 2008, Russia's economy had, by contrast, expanded by 5.6 percent. In late 2009, IMF economists predicted a slow recovery, with projected growth in 2010 of just 1.5 percent.

The economies of Latin America, closely tied to demand in the United States and Canada, collectively declined about 2.5 percent in 2009 after growing 4.2 percent in 2008. Economists predicted recovery to 2.9-percent expansion in 2010, led by stronger rebounds in the economies of Mexico and Brazil.

Economies in other regions managed to continue growing despite the global crunch. Growth in the small but dynamic economies of the Middle East, centered on petroleum exporting, slowed to 2 percent in 2008 after expanding by 5.4 percent in 2007. Economists

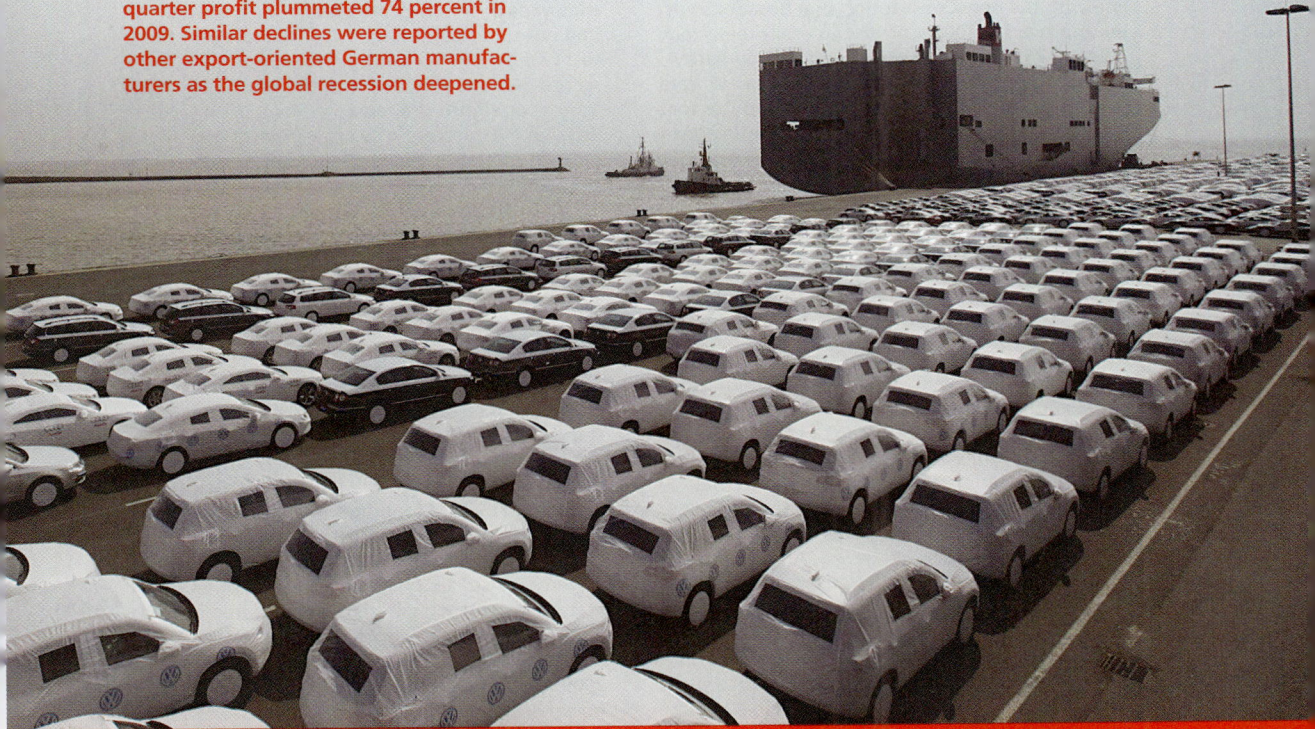

New Volkswagen vehicles, sheathed in white protective covers, wait dockside at a German port in April for shipment to international destinations. Volkswagen officials reported that the company's first-quarter profit plummeted 74 percent in 2009. Similar declines were reported by other export-oriented German manufacturers as the global recession deepened.

projected 4.2-percent growth for these economies in 2010.

The economies of Africa also had enough momentum to avoid continentwide recession, but nevertheless slowed in 2009 to an estimated 1.7-percent rate of growth—less than a third of the 2008 rate of growth. Economists at the World Bank, a United Nations affiliate, projected growth for Africa at 4 percent in 2010.

Trade in commodities, as well as commodity prices, fluctuated wildly in 2008 and 2009. (Commodities are basic unprocessed goods such as metal ores, bulk grains, coal, and oil.) Prices soared to record highs by mid-2008, only to plummet in late 2008 and early 2009 as fears of a 1930's-style depression took hold. In mid-2009, however, signs of a bottom to the recession for industrial nations, along with continuing growth in many developing economies, triggered a moderate increase in demand that lifted commodity prices off their lows.

An uncertain outlook. By the autumn of 2009, many economists judged that the global recession was ending. Nevertheless, some warned that the recovery could be fragile for some years to come.

In late 2009, many private banks in countries with developed economies kept a tight rein on lending to avert risk. The still-tight credit market spurred warnings from economists that true recovery might take many years, much like that during the Great Depression of the 1930's, when the economy recovered fully only in the 1940's because of wartime demand and production.

Tentative or uncertain recovery in the advanced industrialized economies continued to reverberate globally. IMF economists forecast growth of less than 1.0 percent in Europe's advanced economies in 2010. They said the U.S. economy might expand by 1.5 percent and Japan's by 1.7 percent. Slack consumer demand in those countries prompted developing countries to rely less on exports to the giant consumer nations and more on trade with each other or on growth in their own internal consumer markets.

■ John D. Boyd

See also **Bank; Economics, United States; Economics, U.S.: A Special Report; International trade.**

Ecuador. On Aug. 10, 2009, Rafael Correa, 47, leader of the Fatherland Alliance Party (PAIS Alliance), was sworn in for his second term as president. His first term was shortened to two years in line with the new Constitution that Ecuador's voters approved in 2008. Correa was easily reelected on April 26, 2009, after enhancing his popularity by tripling spending on education and health care despite a growing deficit due to falling prices for Ecuador's oil exports. He also raised monthly payments to poor single mothers to $30 and launched programs of subsidies for small-scale farmers and people building their own homes.

To fund these programs, Ecuador defaulted in March 2009 on foreign bonds totaling $3.2 billion. These debts were incurred by previous administrations, which, Correa argued, were "illegitimate and illegal." Subsequently, Ecuador bought most of the bonds back for about one-third of their face value, leading to a sharp drop in the country's international credit rating.

In February, the Ecuadorean government expelled two United States diplomats, accusing them of interfering with the country's internal affairs. The U.S. government denied the charges. In July, Ecuador refused to renew the lease on an air base at Manta used by the U.S. Air Force for antinarcotics operations. ■ Nathan A. Haverstock

See also **Latin America.**

Education. More than 55.6 million students were enrolled in prekindergarten, elementary, and secondary schools in the United States in 2009, according to projections by the U.S. Department of Education. Public schools accounted for nearly 49.8 million of the total. Some 5.8 million students attended private schools in 2009, continuing a decline that began in 2002.

The nation's colleges and universities enrolled more than 19 million students in 2009, according to government estimates, marking a nearly 30-percent increase over the previous decade. About 12 million students attended four-year institutions; nearly 7 million went to two-year colleges. Some 60 percent of the students took a full-time course load. Women made up more than 55 percent of full-time and nearly 60 percent of part-time undergraduates.

Student achievement at the nation's elementary and secondary public schools continued to be the primary challenge for educators in 2009, despite the passage of the No Child Left Behind Act (NCLB) in 2001. The law, formally called the Elementary and Secondary Education Act, focused attention on achievement gaps between students from different racial, ethnic, and socioeconomic groups, as well as those in special education programs, and sought to have 100 percent of students performing at a "proficient" level in reading and mathematics by 2014.

In October 2009, results on the National Assessment of Educational Progress in mathematics (the Nation's Report Card) proved disappointing. Results for fourth- and eighth-graders indicated that gaps between white and minority students had not diminished since 2007 (the last year the test was given). On average, fourth-graders scored 240 out of 500 points, the same as in 2007. Scores for eighth-graders rose from 281 in 2007 to 283. Only 39 percent of fourth-graders and 34 percent of eighth-graders scored at or above proficient in 2009.

National standards. Concern about student achievement renewed discussions in 2009 about the need for national academic standards. Each state currently sets academic guidelines for schools and uses its own test to determine student proficiency in core subjects. The meaning of proficiency, however, varies greatly from state to state. In October, a study released by federal researchers showed that one-third of states had lowered their academic standards since the passage of NCLB.

For the first time since the United States tried to develop national standards in the 1990's, an effort was begun in 2008 to define "common core" state standards—uniform expectations for what students should know in key subject areas. The National Governors Association and the Council of Chief State School Officers, both headquartered in Washington, D.C., led the effort. All states except Alaska and Texas took part in the project. In September 2009, the groups jointly released draft guidelines for determining "college and career readiness" in math and English/language arts. A committee was to review public comments on them, and the two organizations were to begin writing the standards.

Adoption of common standards and assessments would give states an edge toward securing some of the $4 billion in competitive grants from the new federal Race to the Top fund, according to regulations issued by the Education Department in November. The fund will be split between states for "plans for implementing coherent, compelling, and comprehensive education reform." The program also encourages states to focus on data systems for analyzing student achievement, effective teaching, and improving low-performing schools. State applications were due in January 2010, with funds to be distributed by September.

Graduation rates. More than 3.3 million students earned a high school diploma in 2009, a slight decrease from 2008, according to federal projections. Over 73 percent of ninth-graders completed high school within four years, according to data from the 2005-2006 school year (latest available).

NCLB requires states to report their high school graduation rates annually, but each state determines how the rate is calculated, making it difficult to compare results. Under a 2008 federal mandate,

John Hope Franklin
Mirror to America

For John Hope Franklin, an African American who overcame the obstacles of growing up in the segregated South to become a distinguished American historian and help shape American history, *hope* was more than a middle name .

Franklin was the author of several widely acclaimed histories of blacks in America, including the seminal *From Slavery to Freedom* (1947), published in an eighth edition in 2000. He was also part of the team of scholars who assisted Thurgood Marshall, the chief lawyer of the National Association for the Advancement of Colored People (NAACP), to win *Brown v. Board of Education of Topeka,* the landmark 1954 case in which the Supreme Court of the United States declared racial segregation in public schools to be unconstitutional.

Franklin died on March 25, 2009, in Durham, North Carolina, of congestive heart failure. He was 94 years old. His many other books include *The Free Negro in North Carolina* (1943), *The Militant South* (1956), *Reconstruction After the Civil War* (1961), *The Emancipation Proclamation* (1963), *Race and History: Selected Essays 1938-1988* (1990), and *The Color Line: Legacy for the Twenty-first Century* (1993). He also co-wrote a junior high school textbook, *Land of the Free* (1966).

Although Franklin wrote about African Americans, his work transcended race. "The tragedy is that black scholars so often have their specialties forced on them," Franklin told a *New York Times Book Review* contributor in 1990. "My specialty is the history of the South, and that means I teach the history of blacks and whites."

Franklin was born on Jan. 2, 1915, in Rentiesville, a small, all-black town in Oklahoma. His father practiced law and his mother taught elementary school. Franklin earned a bachelor's degree at Fisk University in Nashville and master's degree and doctorate from Harvard University in Cambridge, Massachusetts. He taught at a number of universities, including Howard University in Washington, D.C.; the University of Chicago; and Duke University in Durham, North Carolina. Franklin also served on many national delegations and presidential commissions.

In 1995, Franklin was awarded the Spingarn Medal for his achievements in the field of history. The medal is awarded annually by the NAACP to an outstanding African American. Franklin was also awarded the Presidential Medal of Freedom, the nation's highest honor for civilians, in 1995. At the ceremony, President Bill Clinton called Franklin "a moral compass for America, always pointing us in the direction of truth." In addition to his many awards, Franklin received honorary degrees from more than 100 colleges and universities. In 2000, the John Hope Franklin Center for Interdisciplinary and International Studies at Duke University opened in his honor.

Franklin's autobiography, *Mirror to America,* was published in 2005, when he was 90 years old. In it, he wrote of the pain and indignity of prejudice and discrimination that he had experienced firsthand throughout his life. On Jan. 20, 2009, just a few weeks after his 94th birthday, Franklin witnessed the swearing in of Barack Obama as the first African American president. Franklin described Obama's historic nomination as "an indication of the willingness as well as the ability of this country to turn a significant corner toward full political equality."

Franklin once said: "One lives by hope. I do. It's not merely my middle name, it's my life. I live by hope." Just as Obama emphasized a message of hope for America during his presidential campaign, John Hope Franklin, through his lifetime of contributions, inspired his own kind of hope in many Americans. ■ Shawn Brennan

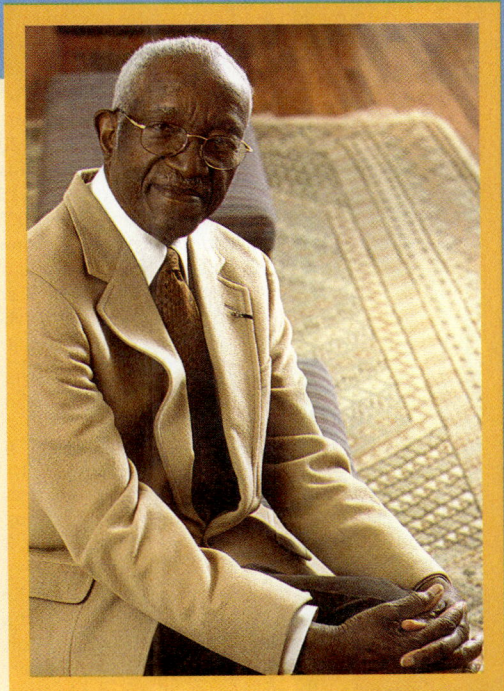

states were to begin using a standard formula for determining graduation rates beginning in the 2010-2011 school year.

SAT/ACT scores. Over 1.5 million students took the SAT college admission test in 2009. According to the New York City-based College Board, which owns the program, scores on the test in 2009 remained the same or dropped slightly from 2008. In mathematics, the average score was 515 on the 200-to-800-point scale, the same as in 2008. Scores for reading and writing each dropped one point in 2009, to 501 and 493 points, respectively.

On the ACT college admission test, scores held steady in 2009 for the 1.48 million test takers. Average scores remained the same as in 2008 (on a 36-point scale) in English (20.6), math (21.0), and reading (21.4) and rose slightly in science (20.9, up from 20.8 in 2008). The average score on the writing portion of the test dropped from 7.3 in 2008 to 7.2 on a 2- to 12-point scale. According to Iowa City, Iowa-based ACT Inc., which administers the test, fewer than one-fourth of the test takers met college-readiness benchmarks in English, algebra, biology, and social science.

Paying for college. In October 2009, the College Board reported that the cost of going to college has risen significantly, despite a decline in the Consumer Price Index. Tuition and fees at four-year public colleges rose by 6.5 percent in 2008; at private colleges, by 4.4 percent.

The rate of defaults on federal student loans grew as well, according to statistics released by the Education Department in September 2009. The rate of student-loan defaults among borrowers whose payments came due in fiscal year 2007 increased to 6.7 percent, up from 5.2 percent in 2006 (latest available data). A bill that would scrap the federal student-loan program and replace subsidies to private lenders with a direct-lending program through the U.S. Treasury was approved by the House of Representatives in September 2009. The Senate was to issue its own bill similar to the House version.

Admissions scandal. In May, a report by the *Chicago Tribune* alleged patronage in the admissions process at the University of Illinois at Urbana-Champaign, the state's flagship university. Six of the university's nine trustees, the university's chancellor, and the president resigned. According to the report, university administrators used a secret "clout list" to give special consideration in admissions decisions to underqualified applicants with connections to politicians or university donors. A commission appointed by Illinois Governor Patrick J. Quinn reported that the practice had existed for at least a decade and that it was "perhaps unparalleled among universities in its level of formality and structure."   ■ Kathleen Kennedy Manzo

See also **Disability; Supreme Court of the United States.**

Egypt. During an address from Cairo University in Egypt's capital on June 4, 2009, United States President Barack Obama called for a new beginning in the relationship between the United States and the Islamic world "based on mutual interest and mutual respect." President Obama maintained that the United States and Muslims around the world have common ideals, including "the principles of justice and progress, tolerance, and the dignity of all human beings." Egyptian President Hosni Mubarak praised the speech, saying that he appreciated the new approach to U.S.-Islamic relations.

Washington meeting and peace process. President Mubarak met with President Obama at the White House in Washington, D.C., in August to discuss the Israeli-Palestinian peace process, as well as conditions in Iran and Somalia and domestic reforms in Egypt. The meeting represented President Mubarak's first visit to Washington in five years.

To further facilitate the peace process, President Mubarak in 2009 sought to reconcile leaders of Hamas, the radical Palestinian organization controlling the Gaza Strip, with the more moderate Palestinian Authority, headed by Palestinian President Mahmoud Abbas.

Opposition leader released, attacked. Ayman Nour, a leading prodemocracy opposition politician, was released from prison in February. He had spent more than three years in prison on charges widely believed to be concocted by the government after challenging President Mubarak in the 2005 presidential election. In May 2009, Nour announced that he intended to be a candidate in the presidential election of 2011—despite being barred from running by the government.

A day after Nour's announcement, an assailant on a motorcycle attacked him by throwing flammable liquid on his face and igniting it. The attack left Nour with first-degree burns.

Escalating attacks on Copts. On Sept. 16, 2009, a militant Muslim riding a motorcycle stabbed to death—and reportedly beheaded—a 63-year-old Copt in the village of Bagour. Copts are Christians who trace their lineage to ancient Egyptians. The militant then stabbed three other Copts in two nearby villages.

The government explained these attacks as isolated incidents resulting from a dispute between the assailant and the victims. However, Coptic clergymen discounted this explanation, noting that the attacks were part of an escalating campaign of violence by Muslims against Christians. A son of one of the Copt victims accused the Egyptian government of appeasing the militants and giving them "a green light to do as they please with the Copts."   ■ Marius Deeb

See also **Disasters; Islam; Israel; Middle East.**

Elections. A limited number of elections took place in the United States in 2009. There were gubernatorial elections in two states, mayoral elections in a number of cities, and five special elections to fill congressional vacancies. In addition, a close 2008 U.S. senatorial election in Minnesota was finally resolved in 2009.

The Minnesota U.S. Senate election in November 2008 was one of the closest in the history of Congress. Only a few hundred votes out of about 2.9 million votes cast separated the top two finishers. The initial count gave the Republican candidate, incumbent Senator Norm Coleman, a 206-vote lead over his Democratic-Farmer-Labor (DFL) challenger, comedian and liberal political commentator Al Franken. (Minnesota's DFL Party is affiliated with the national Democratic Party.) This razor-thin margin triggered an automatic statewide manual recount, which shifted the result to a 225-vote lead for Franken. The State Canvassing Board certified this result on Jan. 5, 2009, prompting Coleman to challenge the result in court the following day.

There followed months of legal wrangling over whether certain ballots should have been counted or rejected. During this process, additional absentee ballots were counted, producing a new result in which Franken held a 312-vote lead. On June 30, the Minnesota Supreme Court unanimously upheld this result and declared Franken the winner of the election. Coleman conceded later that day.

Gubernatorial elections were held on November 3 in New Jersey and Virginia, with the Republican candidates winning both contests. In New Jersey, Republican Chris Christie, a former U.S. attorney, defeated incumbent Democratic Governor Jon Corzine, independent candidate Chris Daggett, and several minor candidates. In Virginia, the Republican, former State Attorney General Bob McDonnell, easily beat his Democratic opponent, State Senator Creigh Deeds, in the race to succeed term-limited Democratic Governor Tim Kaine. Deeds had defeated a high-profile rival, former Democratic National Committee Chairman Terry McAuliffe, in the June 9 Democratic primary.

Mayoral elections took place in several U.S. cities in 2009, including the two largest, New York City and Los Angeles. Antonio Villaraigosa, the Democratic mayor of Los Angeles, easily won a second term on March 3, defeating nine little-known rivals in a contest with an 18-percent voter turnout. In New York City on November 3, Michael Bloomberg, an independent who had left the Republican Party in 2008, won a third term as mayor by an unexpectedly narrow margin over Democratic City Comptroller Bill Thompson. Bloomberg contributed around $100 million of his own money to his campaign, bringing his total spending on his three mayoral races to well over $250 million—the largest personal expenditure of any office-seeker in U.S. history.

Special congressional elections were held to fill five vacant seats in the U.S. House of Representatives in 2009. The special election that drew the most attention was in New York's 23rd district, which included much of the northern part of the state. The vacancy had been created on September 21 when Republican Representative John McHugh resigned to become U.S. secretary of the Army. Three candidates—attorney Bill Owens, a Democrat; State Assembly member Dede Scozzafava, a Republican; and accountant Doug Hoffman of the Conservative Party of New York—were nominated by their parties to run for the seat.

During the campaign, several nationally prominent conservative Republicans, including former Alaska Governor Sarah Palin and Minnesota Governor Tim Pawlenty, endorsed Hoffman instead of the more moderate Scozzafava. Just days before the November 3 election, in the face of sagging poll numbers, Scozzafava dropped out of the race and endorsed Owens. Owens went on to defeat Hoffman, 49 percent to 46 percent, making him the first Democrat to represent that area of New York since the mid-1800's.

Other special elections in 2009 took place in New York's 20th district on March 31, Illinois's 5th district on April 7, California's 32nd district on July 14, and California's 10th district on November 3. The winners of these elections, all Democrats, were Scott Murphy, Michael Quigley, Judy Chu, and John Garamendi, respectively. Chu became the first Chinese American woman ever elected to Congress.

Ballot issues. In the highest-profile ballot question of 2009, Maine voters on November 3 repealed a law that had authorized same-sex marriage in the state. The vote in the referendum was 53 percent to 47 percent in favor of repeal. The Maine Legislature had passed the law on May 6, but it never went into effect. Also on November 3, voters in Maine approved an initiative to allow state-licensed medical marijuana dispensaries, and they rejected an initiative that would have limited the growth of state and local government spending.

Gay rights and government spending were also on the ballot in Washington state on November 3. There, voters upheld a state law that gave same-sex domestic partners rights that had previously been extended only to married spouses, and they rejected an initiative to cap the growth of government expenditures. ■ Mike Lewis

See also **Democratic Party; Houston; Los Angeles; New York City; People in the news** (Al Franken); **Republican Party; State government.**

Electric power. See Energy supply.

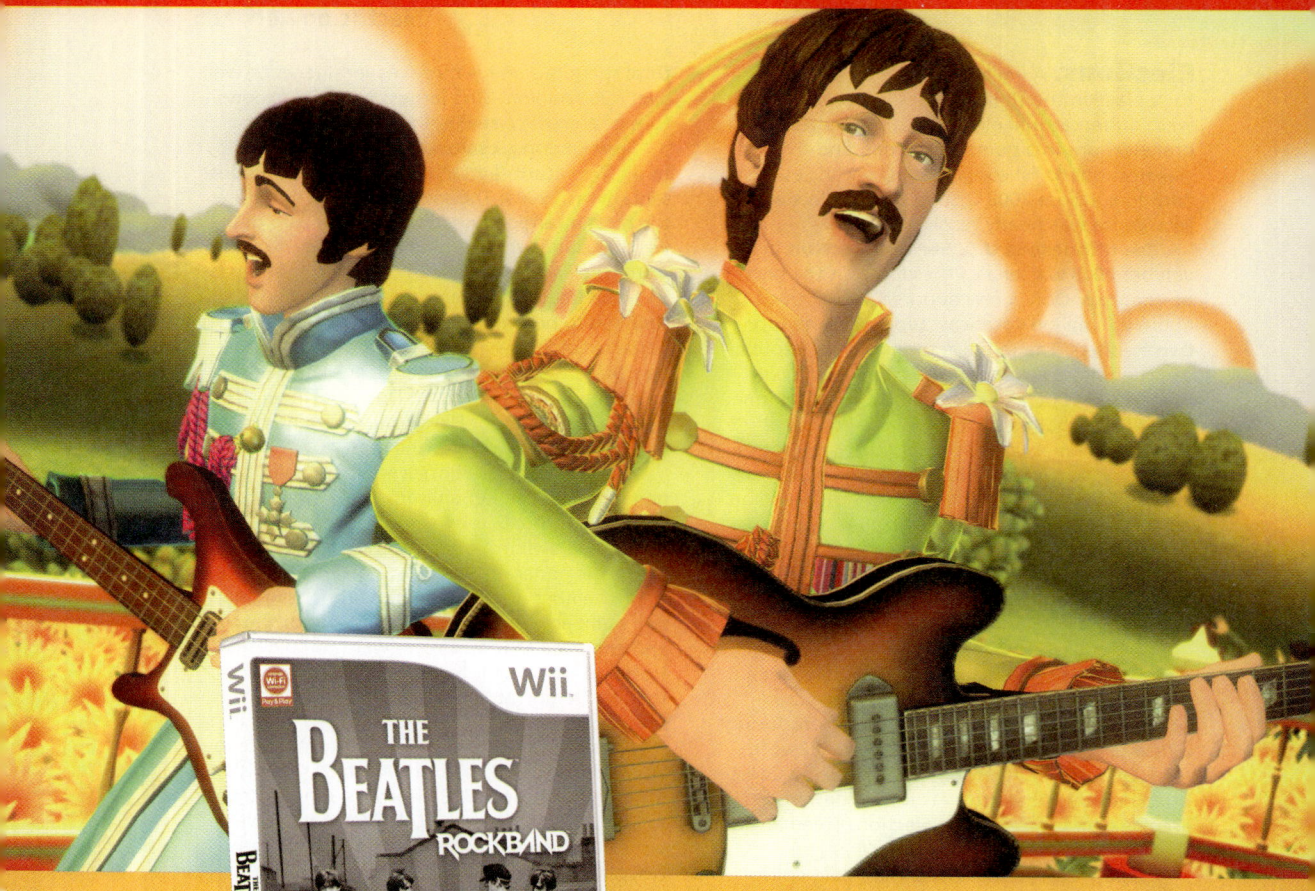

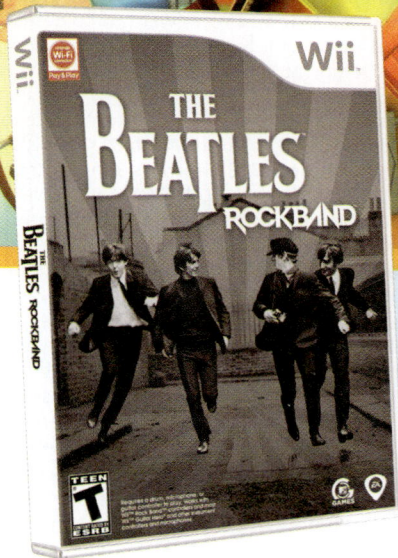

Graphics in the 2009 electronic game *Beatles: Rock Band* evoke the Beatles' likenesses in imagery of the late 1960's. Players perform the iconic songs with plastic instruments.

Electronic games. The prices of all three major game consoles dropped in 2009. The main versions of Redmond, Washington-based Microsoft's Xbox 360 and Tokyo-based Sony's PlayStation 3 (PS3) each cost $300—$100 less than previous versions—as of August. In September, Japan-based Nintendo dropped the Wii's price from $250 to $200. Small and independent games, distributed over the Internet, flourished on mobile phones.

Wii Sports Resort. In June and July, Nintendo released a sequel to its popular *Wii Sports* game called *Wii Sports Resort*. The new game, like its predecessor, allows players to act out various sports by swinging and tilting the Wii's wandlike controller. Sports in *Resort* include swordfighting, wakeboarding, and archery.

Wii Sports Resort came bundled with an add-on to the Wii controller called the MotionPlus. The small device plugs into the bottom of the controller and increases its sensitivity.

The Beatles are back. Cambridge, Massachusetts-based game company Harmonix released *The Beatles: Rock Band* on September 9, the same date on which new remasters of all the Beatles' albums were released. Like the other *Rock Band* games, *Beatles* players use plastic guitars and drum kits to play along with songs. The game also features karaoke gameplay for singers. It was released on the 360, the Wii, and the PS3.

While other *Rock Band* and *Guitar Hero* games offer songs from dozens of bands, *The Beatles: Rock Band* focuses only on the Beatles and traces their history as a band. Trippy, 1960's-inspired graphics and virtual band members accompany the music on-screen. Paul McCartney and Ringo Starr, the two surviving members of the Beatles, worked with Harmonix during development.

Action games in 2009 included several inventive titles acclaimed by critics. *Batman: Arkham Asylum,* released in August for the 360 and PS3, won praise for its tense, realistic gameplay. As Batman, the human comic-book hero, players are forced to rely on stealth, intelligence, and technology instead of brute force or superpowers.

Borderlands, released for the 360, PS3, and Windows systems in October, combines fast-paced, first-person shooting with complex, role-playing gameplay. Set in an alien world reminiscent of the American frontier, the game won praise for its stylized, cartoonish art design.

Brütal Legend, released in October for the 360 and PS3, takes place in a demonic fantasy realm inspired by the lyrics and imagery of heavy metal music. Players control a roadie, voiced by Jack Black and armed with a battle-ax and magical guitar, as he battles rival armies in a blend of action and strategy gameplay. ■ Daniel Kenis

See also **Toys and games.**

Electronics. In 2009, more electronic devices had computerlike functions and Internet access. Costa Mesa, California-based Vizio demonstrated a high-definition television, called Connected TV, capable of accessing Facebook, Flickr, and Netflix's online video collection using a keyboard-equipped remote. Palo Alto, California-based Hewlett-Packard released a digital photo frame that could also download weather information, stream Internet radio stations, and connect to Facebook.

New music and video players released in 2009 included many advanced features. In July, Tokyo-based Sony entered the touchscreen-equipped digital player fray with its new Walkman X-series. They featured a detailed organic light-emitting diode (OLED) screen, a built-in Internet radio program, advanced audio options—and a higher price tag than similar devices.

Redmond, Washington-based Microsoft released an update to its Zune series of portable players in September, called the Zune HD. The device has an OLED touchscreen and features a Web browser and wireless Internet access. Unlike the iPod, produced by Apple Inc. of Cupertino, California, the Zune HD can hook up to a television to display stored videos in high-definition. It also displays facts and images about whatever band or song is currently playing on the device.

Also in September, Apple released a new iPod Nano with a video camera, a robotic voice that speaks song information, and an FM radio tuner capable of briefly "pausing" radio stations and tagging songs for later purchase. Apple also released new versions of its other iPods.

Battle of the e-books. Online retailer Amazon, based in Seattle, released an updated version of its Kindle electronic reader in February 2009. In June, it released the Kindle DX, with a screen about 2 ½ times as large as the regular Kindle. The devices allowed users to purchase and wirelessly download books from Amazon's store, with the DX optimized for larger textbook pages. Like the original Kindle, both devices have "electronic paper" screens that remain clearly visible in bright light, like normal paper does.

In October, Barnes & Noble, based in New York City, unveiled its own electronic reader, called the Nook. Like the Kindle, the Nook features a paper-like screen and the ability to wirelessly download books. It also has the ability to "lend" books to friends for 14 days. Barnes and Noble planned to offer about 500,000 public domain books for free, based on a collection scanned by Mountain View, California-based Google. ■ Daniel Kenis

See also **Computer; Internet.**

El Salvador. On June 1, 2009, Carlos Mauricio Funes Cartagena, 49, of the Farabundo Martí National Liberation Front party, was sworn in for a five-year term as president. Elected by a narrow margin in March, Funes pledged to govern through consensus, preserve El Salvador's market economy, and safeguard individual property rights. Funes, a former television journalist, became his country's first elected leftist chief executive. Right-wing Nationalist Republican Alliance candidates had won the four previous presidential elections.

On his first day in office, Funes named his wife, Vanda Guiomar Pignato, to the post of minister of social inclusion to oversee programs benefiting the poor. Pignato, a Brazilian by birth and founder of the Workers Party of Brazil, headed the Brazilian Cultural Center in San Salvador before marrying Funes in 2006 and becoming a naturalized Salvadoran citizen.

In late June, Funes announced plans to invest $587 million to stimulate the Salvadoran economy, which fell into recession as part of the worldwide economic downturn in 2008. The money was to pay for low-income housing, the distribution of seeds and fertilizer to poor farmers, and additional police officers to curb an increase in crime. ■ Nathan A. Haverstock

See also **Disasters; Latin America.**

Employment. See Economics, United States; Economics, World; Labor and employment.

Energy supply. The global economic recession sharply depressed energy demand in 2009. World supplies of energy were abundant, and fuel prices were generally lower, some for the first time in years. Late in 2009, however, evidence of economic recovery brought signs of a possible upturn in energy demand for 2010.

Oil and gasoline. In its Short-Term Energy Outlook released in November 2009, the United States Energy Information Administration (EIA) estimated that the world would use nearly 1.3 million barrels more petroleum per day in 2010 than in 2009. "Sustained economic growth in China and other Asian countries is contributing to the beginning of a rebound in world oil consumption," reported the EIA, which is the statistical arm of the U.S. Department of Energy.

In its November 2009 Oil Market Report, the Paris-based International Energy Agency (IEA) estimated that global demand for oil, slightly less than 85 million barrels per day in 2009, would average 86.2 million barrels per day in 2010. An oil barrel holds 42 gallons (159 liters).

The IEA, which monitors world energy development for the industrial nations, also warned against global climate change. In its November 2009 World Energy Outlook, the IEA projected that although world energy use fell in 2009 as a consequence of the financial crisis, "it will soon resume its upward trend if government policies don't change."

Fossil fuels, such as petroleum and coal, "continue to dominate the energy mix, accounting for more than three-quarters of incremental demand," the IEA noted. Carbon dioxide emissions from the burning of fossil fuels are among the greenhouse gases that contribute to global warming. "The time has come to make the hard choices needed to combat climate change and enhance global energy security," the IEA said.

Partly because of the sluggish demand in 2009, petroleum supplies were more than ample. Some 40 percent of the world's oil is produced by the members of the Organization of the Petroleum Exporting Countries (OPEC), and changes in its policies can have a sharp impact on petroleum markets. In 2009, the 12-nation OPEC averaged some 29 million barrels a day for much of the year, down from the 2008 output because of the reduced demand. But OPEC was able to build up its spare producing capacity, and the oil industry expected its output to rise gradually in 2010 to meet the world's anticipated need for more oil.

Prices of crude oil peaked at $147 per barrel at mid-2008 and plunged in the second half of that year as the global recession took hold. By early 2009, the price of petroleum had dropped to one-fourth the peak level. However, outside investors poured money into oil markets in 2009, propping up prices. Also, much of the world's oil is priced in U.S. dollars, and the cost often rises if the currency weakens as it did in 2009. The cost of crude oil ranged between $40 and $80 per barrel for much of 2009.

The EIA estimated an average of $77 per barrel for West Texas Intermediate (WTI), the U.S. benchmark crude, over the 2009-2010 winter. This is a $26-increase over the prior winter. "The forecast for monthly average WTI prices rises to about $81 per barrel by December 2010, assuming U.S. and world economic conditions continue to improve," the EIA said.

Per-gallon costs of gasoline and heating oil generally reflect price patterns of crude. These fuels were cheaper in 2009, with gasoline at the pump priced well below the record $4 level reached in July 2008. For 2010, the EIA projected that gasoline prices will average $2.81 per gallon ($0.74 per liter), 45 cents higher than the 2009 level. Home heating oil prices were projected to be slightly less than those for gasoline.

Coal. According to the EIA, coal production for the first six months of 2009 fell by 5 percent in response to lower U.S. coal consumption, fewer exports, and higher inventories. Traditionally, coal is used to generate nearly one-half of the nation's electric power. "Lower total electricity generation combined with increases in generation from natural gas, nuclear, hydropower, and wind led to an 11-percent decline in coal consumption by the electric power sector in the first half of 2009," the EIA reported in its Short-Term Energy Outlook.

Natural gas. Consumption of natural gas, the third major fossil fuel, declined by nearly 2 percent in 2009. The EIA forecast a further decline of slightly more than 1 percent in 2010. Prices of natural gas fell, too. In addition to the reduced demand, there was a record amount of gas in above ground storage.

By September 2009, prices of natural gas had dropped to less than $2 per Mcf (thousand cubic feet [28.3 cubic meters]). "High storage levels and resilient domestic production are expected to keep prices around $5 per Mcf in the coming months, even as space-heating demand increases and economic conditions improve," the EIA Short-Term Energy Outlook reported. The role of natural gas expanded in 2009 due largely to its promise of being a less-polluting fuel and the availability of supplies from new fields.   ■ James Tanner

See also **Economics, United States; Economics, World.**

Engineering. See Building and construction.

England. See United Kingdom.

Environmental pollution. One of the largest cleanup efforts in history began on the Hudson River in New York in May 2009. About 200 miles (322 kilometers) of the river were contaminated by chemicals called PCB's, which were banned by the Environmental Protection Agency (EPA) in 1977. Research has shown that PCB's can cause cancer in human beings and wildlife. The river became contaminated when two factories owned by New York City-based General Electric (GE) released an estimated 1.3 million pounds (590,000 kilograms) of PCB's into the river in the 30 years before they were banned. The cleanup effort involves dredging the river and replacing the contaminated mud with clean soil and rocks. The toxic mud is transported by barge to a processing facility, where it is loaded onto trains and taken to a waste disposal facility in Texas. By October 2009, when work stopped for the winter, the effort had removed about 237,000 cubic yards (181,000 cubic meters) of material. Under federal law, GE is required to pay for the cleanup effort, which will cost at least $750 million. The effort will last through 2015.

Greenhouse gas pollution. On Dec. 7, 2009, the EPA determined that greenhouse gases are pollutants subject to regulation under the Clean Air Act. The decision covers six gases, including the carbon dioxide given off by burning such fossil fuels as coal. Such gases are called greenhouse gases because most scientists believe that they contribute to global warming, or the gradual increase in average world temperatures.

The EPA reported that concentrations of greenhouse gases had risen to levels unprecedented in human history. The agency found that the gases contribute to increased drought, heavier rainfall and flooding, more frequent heat waves and wildfires, and rising sea levels. The EPA, which described the science supporting its decision as "overwhelming," determined that global warming would harm agriculture, wildlife, and human health.

The EPA decision came in response to a 2007 order from the U.S. Supreme Court to determine whether greenhouse gases harm public health and the environment. If Congress does not enact laws regulating such gases, the EPA is required to set regulations under the Clean Air Act.

New fuel standards. On Sept. 15, 2009, the EPA and the National Highway Traffic Safety Administration issued new fuel efficiency standards for automobiles. Under the rules, new cars will have to achieve at least 35.5 miles per gallon (15 kilometers per liter) by 2016. The agencies claimed that the new standards would reduce oil consumption by 1.8 billion barrels (160 billion liters) over the lifetime of vehicles sold in a four-year period. For the first time, the standards set federal limits on tailpipe emissions, requiring cars to release no more than 9 ounces (250 grams) of carbon dioxide per 1 mile (1.6 kilometers) driven. The agencies reported that the new standards would reduce greenhouse gas emissions by nearly 1.1 billion tons (1 billion metric tons).

Walk the walk. The Obama administration issued an order in October 2009 that requires federal agencies to develop plans for reducing their emissions of greenhouse gases. The agencies are required to report targets by June 2010. The order also requires that agencies conserve water, reduce waste, and consume less petroleum.

Oil spills. A large oil spill on March 11, 2009, polluted beaches in Queensland, Australia, prompting the government to declare a state of emergency. The freighter M.V *Pacific Adventurer* spilled at least 230 tons (209 metric tons) of oil while approaching the Port of Brisbane. The freighter was damaged when it tried to navigate through a severe storm. The storm stripped 31 shipping containers from the freighter's deck. The containers, which were carrying 620 tons (562 metric tons) of the fertilizer ammonium nitrate, punctured the ship's hull, allowing the oil to leak. The spill polluted 37 miles (60 kilometers) of coastline. After it docked, the damaged freighter created an oil slick 1,600 feet (500 meters) long on the Brisbane River. The captain faces criminal charges. The freighter's owner, Swire Shipping, agreed to pay 25 million Australian dollars toward cleanup costs.

In Ecuador, a leak in an oil pipeline spilled 14,000 barrels (2.2 million liters) of crude oil into the Amazonian jungle on February 25. The pipeline pumps 130,000 barrels (20.7 million liters) of oil per day from wells in the Amazon to the Pacific port of Esmeraldas. The oil reportedly spilled into the Santa Rosa and Quijos rivers. The leak was apparently caused by an earthquake.

Schoolhouse peril. American schoolchildren may be exposed to toxic PCB's in caulk around windows and doors, according to a September report from the EPA. The agency found that hundreds of school buildings constructed before PCB's were banned used the caulk. The EPA recommends that schools test aging caulk to determine whether it is contaminated and take precautions to protect children.

An investigation by the Associated Press found unsafe drinking water at thousands of American schools in September. Schools that get their water from wells had the worst problems, with one in five reporting water contamination. The leading contaminant was bacteria, followed by lead and other toxic metals. Water in more than 2,000 schools from all 50 states showed such contamination. The investigation analyzed data gathered by the EPA from 1998 to 2008.

Coal ash anxiety. On June 29, 2009, the EPA

identified 44 sites in 10 states where coal ash impoundments pose a "high hazard potential" to life and property should the impoundments fail. Coal ash is a by-product of coal burned in power plants. More than 1 billion gallons (3.8 billion liters) of coal ash spilled from an impoundment in Kingston, Tennessee, on Dec. 22, 2008, when an earthen dike failed. The EPA generated the list of hazardous sites as part of an effort to develop new regulations for the impoundments.

Dirty air. An April 2009 report from the American Lung Association found that 186 million Americans live in areas with dangerous levels of air pollution. That number is equivalent to about 6 in 10 Americans. The figures are much higher than those in the previous year's report, which found that 125 million Americans lived in areas with dangerous levels of air pollution.

Heavy-metal fish. In August, the U.S. Geological Survey reported that every single fish it had sampled from 291 streams tested positive for mercury contamination. More than a quarter of those fish contained concentrations of mercury that exceeded safety limits set by the EPA. More than two-thirds exceeded the EPA's "level of concern" for fish-eating mammals. The study, which was conducted from 1998 to 2005, was the first comprehensive survey of mercury contamination in American streams and rivers. An average of five fish were taken from each waterway.

Mercury is a heavy metal that can harm the brain, heart, kidneys, lungs, and immune system. Infants and children are especially vulnerable to the effects of mercury, which interferes with the proper development of the brain and nervous system. Most mercury enters the environment in the form of air pollution, which falls from the sky with rain. The EPA has found that the largest source of atmospheric mercury is emissions from coal-fired power plants. The agency announced it would issue new rules under the Clean Air Act to limit mercury emissions from power plants.

Flame retardants. In April 2009, the National Oceanic and Atmospheric Administration announced that it had found toxic flame retardants in all U.S. coastal waters and the Great Lakes. Flame retardants are chemicals that resist fire. Since the 1970's, they have been added to such products as furnishings and clothing. Research has shown that these chemicals may cause a variety of health problems, including diseases of the liver, thyroid gland, and nervous system. Earlier studies found only limited contamination by flame retardants.   ■ Brian Johnson

See also **Conservation; Global warming.**

Equatorial Guinea. See Africa.
Eritrea. See Africa.
Estonia. See Europe.
Ethiopia. See Africa.

EUROPE

The Treaty of Lisbon, a constitution for the 27-member European Union (EU), went into force on Dec. 1, 2009. The charter brought to fruition a long series of attempts to reform EU institutions. An earlier attempt to ratify a constitution failed when French and Dutch voters rejected the document in referendums in 2005. In 2007, under the leadership of German Chancellor Angela Merkel, European leaders signed a simplified version of the constitution, renamed a treaty, in Lisbon.

The purpose of the treaty was to streamline decision-making in the organization, bring a greater measure of democracy and accountability to the EU's legislative process, and, perhaps most importantly, enhance the EU's profile abroad. Most European leaders felt that reform was essential, because the EU had grown from a small organization of 6 wealthy countries in 1958 to an unwieldy group of 27 nations by 2009.

The EU's predecessor—the European Community—led by a politically powerful France and an economically powerful Germany, concentrated primarily on trade. By 2007, the EU stretched from Spain to Bulgaria, included more than 500 million people, and shared a common currency—the euro—which was used by most member nations. Yet the group's decision-making process still required all members to agree unanimously on most important changes in policies, ranging from environmental regulations to consumer protection, the transport of farm animals, and judicial standards. Furthermore, though European citizens had expressed a desire for a common foreign policy, politicians in the United States and other nations continued to be confused about where the real power in Europe lies—in Brussels, Belgium, where the EU's headquarters is located, or in the national capitals of the more powerful member nations.

Changes. The most important changes introduced by the treaty included an increased use of qualified majority voting in the Council of Ministers, a body made up of cabinet ministers of the member nations. (Qualified majority voting takes into account the demographic "weight" of each member nation, so that the vote of a large, populous country such as Germany, for example, carries more weight than the vote of smaller countries with fewer inhabitants, such as Cyprus or Malta.) The method ensures that legislation cannot be blocked by a single country. Under the new constitution, the European Parliament, which is made

up of representatives elected by citizens of all member nations, will also have increased powers in approving legislation.

To increase continuity in the EU's agenda and raise its profile abroad, the treaty created two new offices, a president of the European Council and a high representative of the EU for foreign affairs and security policy. Under previous arrangements, the presidency of the EU rotated every six months to a different member nation. Although the rotating collective presidency will be retained, the new position of president of the European Council will serve over the course of several member nation presidencies. The high representative for foreign affairs, also known as the EU's foreign minister, will have a new diplomatic service drawn from existing EU diplomats and others appointed by the member nations.

Drama over ratification. The ratification of the new treaty did not go smoothly, and the date for the treaty's going into force—originally set for Jan. 1, 2009—had to be delayed. After passing through several member nations' legislatures, the process hit a snag in Ireland. Irish voters rejected the agreement in a referendum in 2008, after a lackluster campaign by its proponents. In a second referendum, held in October 2009, Irish voters approved the measure.

Poland's president, Lech Kaczyński, delayed signing the treaty, even after his parliament approved it. He maintained that it made no sense to sign until Ireland's voters had approved the agreement. A challenge to the treaty in Germany's Constitutional Court was overcome in June.

The Czech Republic's president, Václav Klaus, a well known skeptic of European integration, held out the longest. He signed the document only after the Czech Constitutional Court ruled that the treaty did not violate the Czech Constitution and after other member nations agreed that the Czech Republic be allowed to opt out of the treaty's Charter of Fundamental Rights and Freedoms. Klaus maintained that under the charter, Germans and Hungarians expelled from Czechoslovakia after World War II (1939-1945) could demand compensation or a return of their property. Klaus signed off on the document on Nov. 3, 2009.

The treaty's critics. The Treaty of Lisbon quickly came up against two different kinds of criticisms. One group of critics maintained that the treaty will undermine the sovereignty of democratically elected national governments and create an undemocratic European super state with an unaccountable bureaucracy. Most surveys show that Europeans do not fully understand who controls the European Union, and they tend to view its bureaucracy in Brussels, called the European Commission, as distant and unac-

FACTS IN BRIEF ON EUROPEAN COUNTRIES

Country	Population	Government	Monetary unit[†]	Foreign trade (million U.S.$)	
				Exports[††]	Imports[††]
Albania	3,245,000	President Bamir Topi; Prime Minister Sali Berisha	lek (91.95 = $1)	1,345	4,898
Andorra	84,000	Co-sovereigns bishop of Urgel, Spain, and the president of France; Head of Government Jaume Bartumeu Cassany	euro (0.70 = $1)	117	1,789
Austria	8,406,000	President Heinz Fischer; Chancellor Werner Faymann	euro (0.70 = $1)	163,600	168,900
Belarus	9,577,000	President Aleksandr Lukashenko; Prime Minister Sergei Sidorsky	ruble (2,840.00 = $1)	33,040	39,160
Belgium	10,520,000	King Albert II; Prime Minister Yves Leterme	euro (0.70 = $1)	371,500	387,700
Bosnia-Herzegovina	3,968,000	Chairman of the Presidency Željko Komšić; Prime Minister Nikola Spiric	marka (1.36 = $1)	5,177	12,270
Bulgaria	7,503,000	President Georgi Parvanov; Prime Minister Boiko Borisov	lev (1.36 = $1)	22,510	34,880
Croatia	4,440,000	President Stjepan Mesic*; Prime Minister Jadranka Kosor	kuna (5.00 = $1)	14,690	30,740
Czech Republic	10,202,000	President Václav Klaus; Prime Minister Jan Fischer	koruna (17.43 = $1)	145,700	139,400
Denmark	5,476,000	Queen Margrethe II; Prime Minister Lars Løkke Rasmussen	krone (5.18 = $1)	114,900	116,400
Estonia	1,321,000	President Toomas Hendrik Ilves; Prime Minister Andrus Ansip	kroon (10.90 = $1)	12,580	15,290
Finland	5,323,000	President Tarja Halonen; Prime Minister Matti Vanhanen	euro (0.70 = $1)	96,620	87,510
France	62,558,000	President Nicolas Sarkozy; Prime Minister François Fillon	euro (0.70 = $1)	601,900	692,000
Germany	82,327,000	President Horst Köhler; Chancellor Angela Merkel	euro (0.70 = $1)	1,498,000	1,232,000
Greece	11,197,000	President Carolos Papoulias; Prime Minister George Papandreou	euro (0.70 = $1)	29,140	93,910
Hungary	9,970,000	President László Sólyom; Prime Minister Gordon Bajnai	forint (189.44 = $1)	106,600	106,500
Iceland	314,000	President Ólafur Ragnar Grímsson; Prime Minister Jóhanna Sigurdardóttir	krona (124.69 = $1)	5,692	5,782
Ireland	4,458,000	President Mary McAleese; Prime Minister Brian Cowen	euro (0.70 = $1)	119,600	80,940
Italy	59,107,000	President Giorgio Napolitano; Prime Minister Silvio Berlusconi	euro (0.70 = $1)	546,900	546,900
Kosovo	2,262,000	President Fatmir Sejdiu; Prime Minister Hashim Thaçi	euro (0.70 = $1)	527	2,600
Latvia	2,242,000	President Valdis Zatlers; Prime Minister Valdis Dombrovskis	lat (0.49 = $1)	9,559	15,340
Liechtenstein	36,000	Prince Hans-Adam II; Prime Minister Klaus Tschütscher	Swiss franc (1.03 = $1)	2,470	917

*Mesic was to be replaced after a run-off election scheduled for Jan. 10, 2010.

[†]Exchange rates as of Sept. 30, 2009.
[††]Latest available data.

countable. The treaty did little to reduce what was often termed the "democratic deficit."

A second and perhaps larger group of critics argued that the provisions of the treaty were not powerful enough to deal with the significant challenges that the bloc confronts. The president of the European Council, though serving for 2 1/2 years, will compete with the president of the European Commission, as well as a rotating six-month presidency. Which of these three "presidents" will be more powerful remains an open question.

Furthermore, though Europe's new foreign minister will have a new diplomatic corps, the office will have responsibilities both in the European Council (made up of all EU heads of state or government) and the European Commission (made up

Country	Population	Government	Monetary unit*	Foreign trade (million U.S.$)	
				Exports[†]	Imports[†]
Lithuania	3,349,000	President Dalia Grybauskaitė; Prime Minister Andrius Kubilius	litas (2.40 = $1)	23,740	29,300
Luxembourg	495,000	Grand Duke Henri; Prime Minister Jean-Claude Juncker	euro (0.70 = $1)	21,430	27,730
Macedonia	2,057,000	President Gjorge Ivanov; Prime Minister Nikola Gruevski	denar (42.50 = $1)	3,970	6,522
Malta	412,000	President George Abela; Prime Minister Lawrence Gonzi	euro (0.70 = $1)	3,060	4,832
Moldova	3,784,000	Acting President Mihai Ghimpu; Prime Minister Vlad Filat	leu (11.17 = $1)	1,647	4,870
Monaco	33,000	Prince Albert II; Minister of State Jean-Paul Proust	euro (0.70 = $1)	716	916
Montenegro	612,000	President Filip Vujanovic; Prime Minister Milo Djukanovic	euro (0.70 = $1)	171	602
Netherlands	16,567,000	Queen Beatrix; Prime Minister Jan Peter Balkenende	euro (0.70 = $1)	533,200	475,900
Norway	4,786,000	King Harald V; Prime Minister Jens Stoltenberg	krone (6.01 = $1)	168,800	85,990
Poland	38,025,000	President Lech Kaczyński; Prime Minister Donald Tusk	zloty (2.85 = $1)	175,300	199,000
Portugal	10,221,000	President Aníbal Cavaco Silva; Prime Minister José Sócrates	euro (0.70 = $1)	56,420	87,830
Romania	21,150,000	President Traian Basescu; Acting Prime Minister Emil Boc	new leu (2.94 = $1)	49,410	76,170
Russia	140,542,000	President Dmitry Medvedev; Prime Minister Vladimir Putin	ruble (31.77 = $1)	471,600	302,000
San Marino	32,000	2 captains-regent appointed by Grand Council every 6 months	euro (0.70 = $1)	4,628	3,744
Serbia	7,377,000	President Boris Tadic; Prime Minister Mirko Cvetkovic	new dinar (65.15 = $1)	8,824	18,350
Slovakia	5,406,000	President Ivan Gasparovic; Prime Minister Robert Fico	euro (0.70 = $1)	72,570	73,620
Slovenia	2,008,000	President Danilo Türk; Prime Minister Borut Pahor	euro (0.70 = $1)	29,590	33,430
Spain	45,898,000	King Juan Carlos I; Prime Minister José Luis Rodríguez Zapatero	euro (0.70 = $1)	285,400	414,500
Sweden	9,243,000	King Carl XVI Gustaf; Prime Minister Fredrik Reinfeldt	krona (7.11 = $1)	183,100	165,300
Switzerland	7,595,000	President Doris Leuthard	franc (1.06 = $1)	233,100	213,000
Turkey	76,606,000	President Abdullah Gül; Prime Minister Recep Tayyip Erdogan	new lira (1.50 = $1)	140,800	193,900
Ukraine	45,378,000	President Viktor Yushchenko; Prime Minister Yulia Tymoshenko	hryvnia (8.47 = $1)	67,720	84,650
United Kingdom	61,489,000	Queen Elizabeth II; Prime Minister Gordon Brown	pound (0.61 = $1)	464,900	636,000

of representatives of all 27 member nations who perform the day-to-day functions of the EU). Foreign policy itself will still remain mostly in the hands of the member states.

New leaders. On November 19, after much negotiation and backroom dealing among Europe's leaders, Herman Van Rompuy was chosen as the EU's president, and Catherine Ashton, its foreign minister. Van Rompuy was Belgium's prime minister, and Lady Ashton—formerly a British politician in the Labour Party—was serving as the EU's commissioner for trade, a post she had held since 2008.

Both were regarded as competent—but not exciting—choices, and the overall process was seen as deeply political. Former British Prime Minister Tony Blair, who had expressed interest in the position and appeared earlier to have the support of French President Nicholas Sarkozy, was passed over. Ultimately, however, Blair was considered too pro-American, too much a British Labor Party politician, and too independent of the other national governments in Europe.

The choice of a Belgian from a center-right party for president constituted a compromise that suited both France and Germany, because Belgium is not considered a major power; the choice of a British citizen from a center-left party as foreign minister played to Britain's strengths and concerns that its traditional foreign policy independence not be disturbed. Critics maintained that neither had the experience or clout to project Europe's voice on the world stage. The fact that neither would have the stature or charisma to challenge the powerful elected leaders of national governments, such as German Chancellor Merkel or French President Sarkozy, and that both had reputations primarily as negotiators and deal makers, suggested that both would preside over rather than initiate or direct Europe's foreign policy.

Elections and a new commission. Elections to the European Parliament (the EU's only directly elected institution) were held in all member nations in June. The results marked a victory for the center-right European People's Party, a collection of center-right parties from the member countries, which won 265 of the 736 seats. The next-largest party bloc was the Party of European Socialists, comprised primarily of center-left parties, which won 184 seats. Because the European Parliament is not as powerful as the parliament of a democratic nation, voter turnout tends to be low, and the vote itself is largely an evaluation of a member's local national politics rather than a measure of public opinion on Europe-wide issues. In 2009, only 43 percent of eligible voters went to the polls, down from 45.5 percent in 2004 and the lowest turnout in 30 years.

One area in which the European Parliament does have power is in its right to approve the president of the European Commission (who is chosen by the European Council) and the European Commissioners, which together make up the EU's executive branch and head its bureaucracy. In June 2009, Commission President José Manuel Barroso was nominated by the European Council to a second five-year term, and in September he was reelected by the Parliament. Although Barroso's first term was not without controversy, he was credited with working hard for the passage of the Lisbon Treaty by national parliaments and referendums. In November, Barroso announced the 27 new commissioners (one for each member nation) who would oversee a large range of portfolios. They were expected to be approved by the Parliament in 2010.

Response to economic crisis. In late 2008 and early 2009, the EU faced criticism for failing to coordinate members' responses to the global economic crisis. Some nations intervened heavily in their banking sectors, while others merely provided guarantees. Still others supported failing industries, stretching the limits of EU law, which restricts government subsidies to industry to create a level playing field throughout Europe. In autumn, EU economists forecast that the bloc's economy would contract by 4.1 percent during 2009.

In December 2008, the European Council approved a modest, coordinated response to the economic downturn. The measures included a stimulus under the European Economic Recovery Plan of 1.5 percent of the EU's *gross domestic product* (GDP—the value of all goods and services produced in a year). The package amounted to about 200 billion euros ($260 billion) and was made up of funds contributed by both the EU and individual nations. The EU also, in effect, suspended sanctions for members who use the euro and whose deficits exceeded the 3 percent of GDP limit imposed by the bloc's stability and growth pact.

Long-term responses to the crisis were more difficult to formulate. French President Sarkozy called for global controls on the financial system, but progress was slow. In December 2009, the EU began negotiations with member countries aimed at regulating hedge funds, which were seen as having contributed to the severity of the economic crisis. No agreement was reached as members argued over which funds would be covered by new regulations, limits on borrowing, and rules on pay and disclosure for managers.

Foreign policy. The question of expansion remained on hold in 2009, as the EU concentrated on absorbing its most recent new members and ratifying the Lisbon Treaty, which was deemed essential for further enlargement. Turkey's chances for admission seemed to dim when it was revealed that new EU President Van Rompuy had once said that Turkey will never be admitted. Disputes with Greece and Cyprus over airspace during the summer also called into question Turkey's readiness to join the bloc. Macedonia's admission continued to be blocked by Greece, which objects to the country's name because of the belief that it represents a claim upon northern Greece, which is also called Macedonia. Slovenia, which had earlier blocked Croatia's negotiations because of a border dispute, declared in September that it would no longer let the dispute stand in the way of Croatia's accession.

■ Jeffrey Kopstein

See also various European country articles; **People in the news** (Herman Van Rompuy).

European Union. See Europe.

Explosion. See Disasters.

Farm and farming. See Agriculture.

Fashion reflected the economic realities of 2009, a year of mortgage defaults, unemployment, bankruptcies, and bank failures. The most obvious signs of the "Great Recession" in fashion were seen in store closings and the disappearance of well-known brands. Even the president of the United States was affected. Hartmarx, a Chicago-based company that owned the men's suit maker Hart Schaffner & Marx, filed for bankruptcy in January 2009. It was President Barack Obama's preferred suit brand. In November, a private equity firm purchased the company.

For the first time in years, people in the United States were saving their disposable income instead of spending it, and an industry built around luxury consumption had to change. Instead of imaginative clothing, some designers worked to create items that would be long-lived and suitable for various times and places.

Ralph Lauren's design house reduced costs by substituting the December runway fashion show for Lauren's collegiate line with a virtual fashion show. Models walked on a treadmill and were shown against a superimposed backdrop on Lauren's Web site. The virtual show cost less than $100,000 to produce, whereas the runway show would have cost around $1.5 million.

Credit crunch couture. In 2009, the collection shown in Paris during fashion week in October by the house Viktor & Rolf to an extent celebrated the economic climate. The high-concept Dutch designers Viktor Horsting and Rolf Snoeren referred to their collection as "credit crunch couture" and stated that they "cut the tulle from their ballgowns to make more tailored tulle gowns." This implied the gowns had been made with an attempt at cutting costs and recycling used fabric. In reality, the gowns were carefully tailored pieces that featured multiple layers of tulle—a type of net fabric—shirred and shaved into geometric shapes or with missing sections.

Photoshop controversy. A heavily altered photo of a Ralph Lauren model caused comment in the blogosphere in October. A photo of model Filippa Hamilton—at 5 feet 10 inches (178 centimeters) and 120 pounds (54 kilograms)—was digitally altered to make Hamilton appear yet thinner. The blog "Photoshop Disasters" showed the image, in which the model's head appeared larger than her waist. Lauren's company took legal action, claiming the photo's use was a copyright infringement. Soon after, however, the company apologized, agreeing that the photo had indeed been altered and that "... going forward [we] will take every precaution to ensure that the caliber of our artwork represents our brand appropriately."   ■ Bernadine Morris

Fiji. See **Pacific Islands**.

During the Paris fashion week in October, a model wears a gown of shaved tulle from the Viktor & Rolf collection, which the Dutch designers dubbed "credit crunch couture," an expression of the hard economic times.

Finland. Finland's center-right coalition government, led by Prime Minister Matti Vanhanen, remained in power in 2009, despite several setbacks. The coalition consisted of the Center Party, the conservative National Coalition Party, and two smaller parties, the Green Party and the Swedish People's Party.

During elections for the European Parliament in June, the popularity of Vanhanen's Center Party declined. The right-wing, anti-immigrant, anti-European Union (EU) True Finns party, led by charismatic Timo Soini, posted large gains as its share of the vote increased from 0.5 percent in 2004 to 9.8 percent in 2009. In October, opposition parties called for a no-confidence vote of the government. The opposition alleged that the Center Party had accepted questionable contributions from businesses, trade unions, and foundations during its 2007 election campaign. The governing coalition easily won the vote. However, Vanhanen remained embroiled in controversy amid allegations that he had accepted free building materials for his house. A TNT Gallup poll revealed in October 2009 that only 45 percent of Finns believed the government could continue to function.

Economic crisis. Buoyed by years of budget surpluses, Finland enjoyed a favorable position as the global economic crisis worsened in late 2008 and early 2009. However, later in 2009, its export-dependent economy was hit hard by the decline in international demand for its goods. The government instituted several waves of increased spending and tax cuts to boost employment, sustain consumer confidence, and stem the tide of the downturn. Nevertheless, EU economists forecast that Finland's economy would shrink by 7 percent in 2009 and show only modest growth of 0.9 percent in 2010. Unemployment was forecast to rise to 8.5 percent in 2009 from 6.4 percent in 2008.

Nuclear power stirred controversy in 2009 as construction of Finland's fifth power plant fell behind schedule and costs soared 50 percent over the amount budgeted when construction began in 2005. Being built by French and German contractors on Olkiluoto island in western Finland, the nuclear power plant is the first constructed in Europe in more than a decade. Thousands of defects pushed completion of the project from summer 2009 to 2012.

Internet access. In October 2009, Finland became the first nation to mandate broadband Internet access for all its citizens. According to the new law, telecommunications providers must connect all of the country's 5.3 million people to broadband lines with a minimum speed of 1 megabit per second by July 2010.　　■ Jeffrey Kopstein

See also **Europe.**

Fire. See **Disasters.**

Flood. See **Disasters.**

Food. Early in 2009, newly elected President Barack Obama vowed to make the United States food supply safer. In March, President Obama formally named Margaret A. Hamburg as the new commissioner of the Food and Drug Administration (FDA). Hamburg, a physician and bioterrorism expert, formerly served as New York City's health chief and as an assistant health secretary in the administration of President Bill Clinton. President Obama also appointed a Food Safety Working Group to modernize the nation's food safety laws.

In July, Vice President Joe Biden announced several steps recommended by the working group. The group suggested toughening standards to prevent the contamination of eggs, poultry, and turkey with *Salmonella* bacteria; stronger enforcement and increased guidance in preventing *Escherichia coli* contamination of beef, leafy greens, melons, and tomatoes; the creation of a tracking and consumer information system to deal with outbreaks of foodborne illnesses; and the creation of a new position at the FDA to handle food safety. The administration acted on the recommendations by delegating each to an agency for implementation and creating the new position of deputy commissioner in the Office of Foods.

Peanut butter recall. Problems with contamination of peanut butter led to the largest food recall in U.S. history in 2009. In January, the Peanut Corporation of America, based in Lynchburg, Virginia, recalled peanut butter contaminated with *Salmonella* bacteria. The product had been sold to such institutions as schools and nursing homes, where it sickened nearly 700 people in 46 states. Most people became ill from Oct. 1 to Dec. 31, 2008, and 9 people died of their illness.

Later in January 2009, manufacturers who used Peanut Corporation's peanut paste to make such products as peanut butter crackers, cookies, ice cream, and dog treats recalled their products, though no illnesses from eating those products were reported. Peanut butter sold directly to consumers was not affected. Nevertheless, consumer purchases of peanut butter fell by 25 percent.

On January 9, health inspectors confirmed that Peanut Corporation's Blakely, Georgia, plant was the source of the contamination and cited widespread unsanitary conditions. Such conditions were also found at the company's Plainview, Texas, plant. All products made at the company's Georgia facility since January 2007 and all those manufactured at the Texas plant since it opened in 2005 were recalled. In February 2009, the company filed for bankruptcy and ceased operations.

Other recalls. On April 6, Setton Pistachio of Terra Bella, California, the second-largest producer of pistachios in the United States, recalled its entire 2008 crop, though no illnesses had been reported from eating the nuts. An inspection of the company's plant revealed contamination with *Salmonella* bacteria.

A different type of bacteria, *E. coli*, was responsible for a recall of Nestlé USA's Toll House cookie dough in June 2009. Reports of illnesses began in March, and on June 29, federal investigators confirmed the presence of *E. coli* at the company's Danville, Virginia, plant. Eighty people in 31 states became ill after eating the raw cookie dough, though no one died of their illness.

Food costs. Despite the struggling economy, the Economic Research Service (ERS), an agency of the U.S. Department of Agriculture, projected in September that the cost of food would increase by only 2 to 3 percent during the year. That estimate was based on the Consumer Price Index (CPI), which shows the change in prices of selected goods and services consumed by urban families and individuals. In 2008, the CPI for all food increased 5.5 percent over 2007, the highest increase since 1990. According to the ERS, the estimated total cost for all food consumed in the United States in 2008 was $1.6 trillion. Of this amount, $599.9 billion (51.5 percent) was spent on food eaten at home and $565 billion (48.5 percent) was spent on food eaten away from home.

■ Kristina Vaicikonis

See also **Public health; Safety; United States, Government of the: A Special Report.**

Football.

The University of Alabama Crimson Tide defeated the University of Texas Longhorns 37-21 at the Rose Bowl in Pasadena, California, on Jan. 7, 2010, in the National Collegiate Athletic Association (NCAA) Bowl Championship Series (BCS) national championship game. Texas kept the game close, trailing 24-21 with three minutes remaining. Alabama, however, forced a fumble and clinched the game with two late scores. The national title was Alabama's first since 1992. It was also the fourth consecutive year that a Southeastern Conference (SEC) team won the BCS title.

The BCS title game pitted two unbeaten teams—SEC champion Alabama against Big 12 Conference powerhouse Texas—but not everyone was happy with the final match-up. Alabama's appearance in the game was undisputed after the team defeated the top-ranked Florida Gators in a 32-13 rout on Dec. 5, 2009, in Atlanta.

Texas's path to the title game was more controversial. In the Big 12 Championship game on December 5 in Arlington, Texas, the Longhorns struggled on offense and trailed Nebraska 12-10 as time appeared to run out. However, game officials examined the last play of the game and ruled that the final second of regulation play had not expired when Texas quarterback Colt McCoy threw an incomplete pass. Officials ruled that one second remained on the game clock, which

Texas then used to kick a game-winning field goal.

Three other unbeaten teams—Texas Christian (TCU), Boise State, and Cincinnati—were left out of BCS Championship contention. This was especially hard for TCU, which was ranked right behind Texas in the polls. TCU and Boise State faced each other in the BCS Fiesta Bowl, and Cincinnati faced Florida in the BCS Sugar Bowl.

In the National Football League (NFL), the Pittsburgh Steelers won Super Bowl XLIII, defeating the Arizona Cardinals 27-23 in the final minute of the game on Feb. 1, 2009, in Tampa. The Cardinals were denied their first championship since 1947 as the Steelers captured a record sixth Super Bowl trophy. Pittsburgh wide receiver Santonio Holmes, who caught the winning touchdown with 35 seconds left in the game, was named Super Bowl Most Valuable Player (MVP).

2009 Bowl Championship Series. In the other 2009 BCS bowls, Ohio State University defeated Oregon 26-17 in the Rose Bowl on Jan. 1, 2010, in Pasadena. The Florida Gators, with past Heisman-winning quarterback Tim Tebow in his final college game, crushed Cincinnati 51-24 in the Sugar Bowl on January 1 in New Orleans. On January 4, unbeaten Boise State faced unbeaten TCU in the Fiesta Bowl in Glendale, Arizona. Boise State won 17-10 to finish with a perfect 14-0 record. The University of Iowa won 24-14 over Georgia Tech on January 5 in the Orange Bowl in Miami.

The 2009-2010 NFL season. Quarterback Michael Vick, who had been out of the NFL since 2006, signed with the Philadelphia Eagles in August 2009. Vick had served 23 months in federal prison for his role in a dogfighting ring and was subsequently suspended from the NFL in 2007. In 2009, he gained full NFL reinstatement after the first two games of the regular season and served mainly as a backup to Eagles starting quarterback, Donovan McNabb. But in a dramatic appearance against the Atlanta Falcons, where he was a star prior to his legal troubles, Vick threw for one touchdown and ran for another. These scores were his first with the NFL in almost three years.

Quarterback Brett Favre retired from his one-year stint with the New York Jets—and then unretired in the off-season, returning to lead the Minnesota Vikings to the National Football Conference (NFC) play-offs. Favre, who turned 40 in November, threw 24 touchdown passes through his first 11 games as the Vikings started the season at 10-1. They finished the regular season at 12-4.

Super Bowl XLIII. The Pittsburgh Steelers made a dramatic comeback against the Arizona Cardinals on Feb. 1, 2009, to win their second Super Bowl championship in four seasons. Trailing 20-7 in the fourth quarter, Arizona scored 16 unanswered points. The Cardinals then took a 23-20 lead on

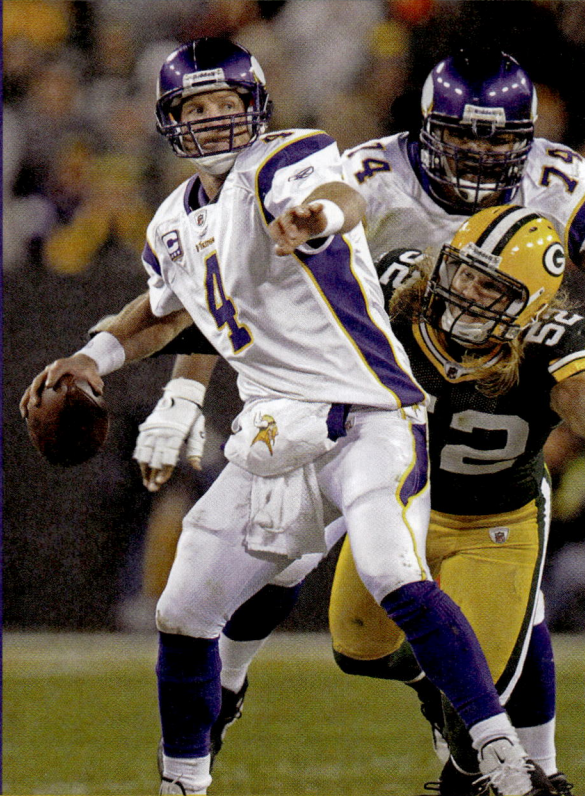

January 3 in Glendale, Arizona, and the sixth-seeded Philadelphia Eagles upset the Minnesota Vikings 26-14 on January 4 in Minneapolis. In Charlotte, North Carolina, the Cardinals beat the Carolina Panthers 33-13 on January 10, and the visiting Eagles crushed the defending champion New York Giants, on January 11. That set up a title game between two teams—the Cardinals (9-7) and the Eagles (9-6-1)—that had just barely made the play-offs. The Cardinals held on for a 32-25 victory on January 18 at home to become the first 9-7 team to make the Super Bowl since the Los Angeles Rams in 1979.

Off-field problems involving NFL players marred the 2009 season. In July 2009, former NFL star quarterback Steve McNair was shot and killed in a Nashville condominium by a girlfriend who then took her own life.

In June, Cleveland Browns wide receiver Donte Stallworth began serving a 30-day jail sentence after pleading guilty to manslaughter. He was charged for killing a pedestrian while driving intoxicated in Florida in March. The NFL suspended Stallworth without pay for a year.

Former New York Giants wide receiver Plaxico Burress accepted a plea bargain and a two-year prison sentence in August on charges of illegally possessing a firearm. Burress was charged after he accidentally shot himself in the leg in November 2008 at a New York City nightclub. The NFL suspended him indefinitely.

Cincinnati Bengals wide receiver Chris Henry was killed in December 2009 when he fell out of a moving pickup truck following a domestic dispute with his fiancée. Henry, who had a history of off-field problems and arrests, was on injured reserve with a broken arm when the accident happened. However, teammates said that the talented 26-year-old was successfully turning his life around before he was tragically killed.

Heisman Trophy. Running back Mark Ingram of the University of Alabama was awarded the 75th annual Heisman Memorial Trophy as the best player in college football on December 12. Ingram rushed 249 times for a school single-season-record 1,542 yards in 2009. He scored 15 rushing touchdowns and caught 30 passes for 322 yards and an additional 3 touchdowns.

College retirement. Florida State coach Bobby Bowden, the second winningest coach in NCAA Division I history, announced that the Gator Bowl on Jan. 1, 2010, would be the final game of his coaching career. Florida State's 33-21 victory over West Virginia in the Gator Bowl maintained the school's long winning streak. Florida has not had a

quarterback Kurt Warner's 64-yard touchdown pass to wide receiver Larry Fitzgerald with 2 minutes and 37 seconds left in the game. But Pittsburgh quarterback Ben Roethlisberger led a 78-yard touchdown drive for the victory. Steelers linebacker James Harrison returned an interception 100 yards for a score—the longest play in Super Bowl history.

2008-2009 NFL play-offs. In the American Football Conference (AFC) wild-card play-offs, the San Diego Chargers defeated the Indianapolis Colts 23-17 in overtime on Jan. 3, 2009, in San Diego. The Baltimore Ravens crushed the hosting Miami Dolphins 27-9 on January 4. The Ravens then took down the top-seeded Tennessee Titans, 13-10, on January 10 in Nashville to advance to the AFC title game. The Pittsburgh Steelers beat the Chargers 35-24 in Pittsburgh on January 11, then stopped the visiting Ravens 23-14 on January 18 in the AFC title game. In the NFC wild-card play-offs, the Arizona Cardinals defeated the Atlanta Falcons 30-24 on

2009-2010 NFL FINAL STANDINGS

AMERICAN CONFERENCE

North Division

	W.	L.	T.	Pct.
Cincinnati Bengals*	10	6	0	.625
Baltimore Ravens*	9	7	0	.562
Pittsburgh Steelers	9	7	0	.562
Cleveland Browns	5	11	0	.312

East Division

	W.	L.	T.	Pct.
New England Patriots*	10	6	0	.625
New York Jets*	9	7	0	.562
Miami Dolphins	7	9	0	.438
Buffalo Bills	6	10	0	.375

South Division

	W.	L.	T.	Pct.
Indianapolis Colts*	14	2	0	.875
Houston Texans	9	7	0	.562
Tennessee Titans	8	8	0	.500
Jacksonville Jaguars	7	9	0	.438

West Division

	W.	L.	T.	Pct.
San Diego Chargers*	13	3	0	.812
Denver Broncos	8	8	0	.500
Oakland Raiders	5	11	0	.313
Kansas City Chiefs	2	12	0	.250

*Made play-offs

TEAM STATISTICS

Leading offenses	Avg. points/game	Yards per game
New England	26.7	397.3
Houston	24.3	383.1
Pittsburgh	23.0	371.3
Indianapolis	26.0	363.1
San Diego	28.4	360.1

Leading defenses	Avg. points against	Yards per game
New York Jets	14.8	252.3
Baltimore	16.3	300.5
Cincinnati	18.2	310.4
Pittsburgh	20.3	305.3
Denver	20.3	315.0

INDIVIDUAL STATISTICS

Leading scorers, TD's	TD's	Rush	Rec.	Ret.
Maurice Jones-Drew, Jacksonville	16	15	1	0
Chris Johnson, Tennessee	16	14	2	0
Thomas Jones, New York	14	14	0	0
Willis McGahee, Baltimore	14	12	2	0

Leading kickers	XPA/XPM	FGA/FGM	Long	Pts.
Nate Kaeding, San Diego	50/51	32/35	55	146
Jay Feely, New York	32/32	30/36	55	122
Matt Prater, Denver	32/32	30/35	51	122
Rian Lindell, Buffalo	24/24	28/33	56	108

Leading quarterbacks	Att.	Comp.	Yds.	TD's	Ints.
Matt Schaub, Houston	583	396	4,770	29	15
Peyton Manning, Indianapolis	571	393	4,500	33	16
Tom Brady, New England	565	371	4.398	28	13
Ben Rothlisberger, Pittsburgh	506	337	4,328	26	12
Philip Rivers, San Diego	486	317	4,254	28	9

Leading receivers	Passes caught	Rec. yards	Avg. gain	TD's
Andre Johnson, Houston	101	1,569	15.5	9
Wes Welker, New England	123	1,348	11.0	4
Randy Moss, New England	83	1,264	15.2	13
Reggie Wayne, Indianapolis	100	1,264	12.6	10

Leading rushers	Rushes	Yards	Avg.	TD's
Chris Johnson, Tennessee	358	2,006	5.6	14
Thomas Jones, New York	331	1,402	4.2	14
Maurice Jones-Drew, Jacksonville	312	1,391	4.5	15
Ray Rice, Baltimore	254	1,339	5.3	7

Leading punters	Punts	Yards	Avg.	Long
Shane Lechler, Oakland	96	4,909	51.1	70
Dustin Colquitt, Kansas City	96	4,361	45.4	70
Brian Moorman, Buffalo	90	4,192	46.6	73
Kevin Huber, cincinnati	86	3,713	43.2	61

NATIONAL CONFERENCE

North Division

	W.	L.	T.	Pct.
Minnesota Vikings*	12	4	0	.750
Green Bay Packers*	11	5	0	.688
Chicago Bears	7	9	0	.438
Detroit Lions	2	14	0	.125

East Division

	W.	L.	T.	Pct.
Dallas Cowboys*	11	5	0	.688
Philadelphia Eagles*	11	5	0	.688
New York Giants	8	8	0	.500
Washington Redskins	4	12	0	.250

South Division

	W.	L.	T.	Pct.
New Orleans Saints*	13	3	0	.812
Atlanta Falcons	9	7	0	.562
Carolina Panthers	8	8	0	.500
Tampa Bay Buccaneers	3	13	0	.188

West Division

	W.	L.	T.	Pct.
Arizona Cardinals*	10	6	0	.625
San Francisco 49ers	8	8	0	.500
Seattle Seahawks	5	11	0	.312
St. Louis Rams	1	15	0	.062

*Made play-offs

TEAM STATISTICS

Leading offenses	Avg. points/game	Yards per game
New Orleans	31.9	403.8
Dallas	22.6	399.4
Minnesota	29.4	379.6
Green Bay	28.8	379.1
New York	25.1	366.0

Leading defenses	Avg. points against	Yards per game
Green Bay	18.1	274.3
Minnesota	18.5	288.8
Carolina	18.4	292.0
Dallas	20.8	292.4
Washington	22.8	294.3

INDIVIDUAL STATISTICS

Leading scorers, TD's	TD's	Rush	Rec.	Ret.
Adrian Peterson, Minnesota	18	18	0	0
Larry Fitzgerald, Arizona	13	0	13	0
Frank Gore, San Francisco	13	10	3	0
Vernon Davis, San Francisco	13	0	13	0

Leading kickers	XPA/XPM	FGA/FGM	Long	Pts.
David Akers, Philadelphia	43/45	32/37	52	139
Lawrence Tynes, New York	45/45	27/32	52	126
Mason Crosby, Green Bay	48/49	27/36	52	129
Ryan Longwell, Minnesota	54/55	26/28	52	132

Leading quarterbacks	Att.	Comp.	Yds.	TD's	Ints.
Tony Romo, Dallas	550	347	4,483	26	9
Aaron Rodgers, Green Bay	541	350	4,434	30	7
Drew Brees, New Orleans	514	363	4,388	34	11
Brett Favre, Minnesota	531	363	4,202	33	7
Eli Manning, New York	509	317	4,021	27	14

Leading receivers	Passes caught	Rec. yards	Avg. gain	TD's
Miles Austin, Dallas	81	1,320	16.3	11
Sidney Rice, Minnesota	83	1,312	15.8	8
Steve Smith, New York	107	1,220	11.4	7
DeSean Jackson, Philadelphia	63	1,167	18.5	9

Leading rushers	Rushes	Yards	Avg.	TD's
Steve Jackson, St. Louis	324	1,416	4.4	4
Adrian Peterson, Minnesota	314	1,383	4.4	18
Ryan Grant, Green Bay	282	1,253	4.4	11
Jonathan Stewart, Carolina	221	1,133	5.1	10

Leading punters	Punts	Yards	Avg.	Long
Andy Lee, San Francisco	99	4,711	47.6	64
Donnie Jones, St. Louis	90	4,212	46.8	63
Jon Ryan, Seattle	88	4,068	46.2	70
Ben Graham, Arizona	86	4,045	47.0	64

THE 2009 COLLEGE FOOTBALL SEASON

NATIONAL CHAMPIONS

NCAA BCS	Alabama	37	Texas	21
NCAA FCS	Villanova	23	Montana	21
NCAA Div. II	N.W. Missouri St.	30	Grand Valley State	23
NCAA Div. III	Wisc. (Whitewater)	38	Mount Union	28
NAIA	Sioux Falls (S.D.)	25	Lindenwood	22

BOWL CHAMPIONSHIP SERIES (BCS) GAMES

BOWL	RESULT			
Rose	Ohio State	26	Oregon	17
Orange	Iowa	24	Georgia Tech	14
Fiesta	Boise State	17	Texas Christian	10
Sugar	Florida	51	Cincinnati	24

OTHER BOWL GAMES

BOWL	RESULT			
Alamo	Texas Tech	41	Michigan State	31
Armed Forces	Air Force	47	Houston	20
Capital One	Penn State	19	Louisiana State	17
Car Care	Pittsburgh	19	North Carolina	17
Champs Sports	Wisconsin	20	Miami	14
Chick-fil-A	Virginia Tech	37	Tennessee	14
Cotton	Mississippi	21	Oklahoma State	7
EagleBank	UCLA	30	Temple	21
Emerald	Southern California	24	Boston College	13
GMAC	Central Michigan	44	Troy	41
Gator	Florida State	33	West Virginia	21
Hawaii	So. Methodist	45	Nevada	10
Holiday	Nebraska	33	Arizona	0
Humanitarian	Idaho	43	Bowling Green	43
Independence	Georgia	44	Texas A&M	20
Insight	Iowa State	14	Minnestoa	13
International	South Florida	27	Northern Illinois	3
Las Vegas	Brigham Young	44	Oregon State	20
Liberty	Arkansas	20	East Carolina	17
Little Caesar's	Marshall	21	Ohio	17
Music City	Clemson	21	Kentucky	13
New Mexico	Wyoming	35	Fresno State	28
New Orleans	Mid. Tennessee St	42	Southern Miss.	32
Outback	Auburn	38	Northwestern	35
Papa Johns.com	Connecticut	20	South Carolina	7
Poinsettia	Utah	37	California	27
St. Petersburg	Rutgers	45	Central Florida	24
Sun	Oklahoma	31	Stanford	27
Texas	Navy	35	Missouri	13

CONFERENCE CHAMPIONS

NCAA FOOTBALL BOWL SUBDIVISION (FBS)

CONFERENCE	SCHOOL
Atlantic Coast	Georgia Tech
Big 12	Texas
Big East	Cincinnati
Big Ten	Ohio State
Conference USA	East Carolina
Independents	Navy
Mid-American	Central Michigan
Mountain West	Texas Christian University (TCU)
Pacific 10	Oregon
Southeastern	Alabama
Sun Belt	Troy
Western Athletic	Boise State

NCAA FOOTBALL CHAMPIONSHIP SUBDIVISION (FCS)

CONFERENCE	SCHOOL
Big Sky	Montana
Big South	Liberty and Stony Brook (Tie)
Colonial	Villanova
Great West	University of California Davis
Independents	Marist
Ivy League	Pennsylvania
Mid-Eastern	South Carolina State
Missouri Valley	Southern Illinois
Northeast	Central Connecticut State
Ohio Valley	Jacksonville State
Patriot	Holy Cross
Pioneer	Butler and Dayton (Tie)
Southern	Appalachian State
Southland	Stephen F. Austin and McNeese St. (Tie)
Southwestern	Prairie View A&M

ALL-AMERICAN TEAM (FBS)

(as chosen by the Associated Press)

OFFENSE

Quarterback—Colt McCoy, Texas
Running backs—Toby Gerhart, Stanford; Mark Ingram, Alabama
Wide receivers—Golden Tate, Notre Dame; Jordan Shipley, Texas
Tight end—Aaron Hernandez, Florida
Center—J.D. Walton, Baylor
Other linemen—Russell Okung, Oklahoma State; Trent Williams, Oklahoma; Michael Johnson, Alabama; Mike Lupati, Idaho
Place-kicker—Leigh Tiffin, Alabama
All purpose player—C.J. Spiller, Clemson

DEFENSE

Linemen—Jerry Hughes, TCU; Derrick Morgan, Georgia Tech; Ndamuknog Suh, Nebraska; Terrence Cody, Alabama
Linebackers—Rolando McClain, Alabama; Greg Jones, Michigan State; Eric Norwood, South Carolina
Backs—Joe Haden, Florida; Javier Arenas, Alabama; Eric Berry, Tennessee; Earl Thomas, Texas
Punter—Drew Butler, Georgia

PLAYER AWARDS

Heisman Trophy (best player)—Mark Ingram, Alabama
Bednarik Trophy (best defensive player)—Ndamuknog Suh, Nebraska

losing team since 1976, the year Bowden took over. Bowden finished with a lifetime record of 389-129-4.

On Dec. 26, 2009, Head Coach Urban Meyer, who led the Florida Gators to BCS national championships in 2006 and 2008, abruptly announced that he would resign following the BCS Sugar Bowl on Jan. 1, 2010, for family and health reasons. However, the next day he announced he would take a leave of absence instead and would return to coach the Gators in the 2010 season.

Canadian Football League. The Montreal Alouettes defeated the Saskatchewan Roughriders 28-27 to win the Grey Cup on Nov. 29, 2009, in Calgary, Alberta. Montreal won the game with a 33-yard field goal as time expired to earn its sixth Grey Cup title.

■ Michael Kates

France.

France. President Nicolas Sarkozy's greatest challenge in 2009 was guiding the French economy through the global economic crisis. Sarkozy, head of the center-right Union for a Popular Movement (UMP), was elected in May 2007 to a five-year term. He benefited from a financial system that was much less tied to global markets than other large European economies and, therefore, was less vulnerable to a decline in international lending. In addition, Sarkozy was aided by the fact that the opposition Socialist Party, led by Martine Aubry, was in disarray. That Sarkozy's strong interventionist response to the financial meltdown included many traditionally Socialist elements was particularly damaging to the Socialists.

In European parliamentary elections in June 2009, the UMP scored a huge win of 28 percent. The Socialist Party captured only 17 percent of the vote. Sarkozy's popularity declined later in the year, as many of his reforms proved unpopular. His administration was also touched by scandal.

Economic policy. To combat the global economic downturn, Sarkozy announced a $35-billion economic stimulus package in December 2008. He followed up in early 2009 with tax cuts for low wage earners, a huge rise in work contracts subsidized by government contributions, and a subsidy for scrapping old cars and replacing them with new ones—a French "cash for clunkers."

In June, Sarkozy announced a huge series of public investments, which he planned to finance with a new government bond in 2010. He also supported the few national banks that required help and backed loans for French car manufacturers on the condition that they not close their factories in France, a policy that appeared to contradict European Union (EU) rules on unfair competition. In addition, Sarkozy called for eliminating the local business tax (to encourage French industries to keep production in France) and replacing it with a carbon tax—a tax on oil, gas, and coal for homes and businesses—to help fight global warming. The tax moves were criticized as aiding businesses at the expense of the poor and the middle class.

In July 2009, Sarkozy's plans for a major reform of the pension system and local government raised an uproar in Parliament, even within his own party. The reforms included raising the retirement age from 60 to 67 and cutting the number of local elected officials from 6,000 to 3,000.

Declining tax receipts and an ambitious program of public investment and generous payments for unemployed workers increased the budget deficit. It rose to 8.3 percent, above the EU limit of 3 percent of *gross domestic product* (GDP—the value of all goods and services produced in a year).

In September, Sarkozy argued against excessive bonuses for bankers. He also called repeatedly during the year for reforming the institutions of global capitalism, which he considered far too close to the American model, in which markets are loosely regu-

French Republican Guards salute President Nicolas Sarkozy as he enters the Palace of Versailles in June to address a joint session of Parliament. Sarkozy—the first French president to appear before Parliament since 1873—spoke on the economy and the wearing of traditional Islamic garments.

lated. EU economists forecast that the French economy would contract by 2.2 percent in 2009 and that unemployment would rise to 9.5 percent.

International relations. In March, Sarkozy announced that France would reintegrate into the military command structure of NATO. Although the nation had been a founding member of NATO in 1949, in 1966 President Charles de Gaulle decided that France would remain in the alliance but would remove its forces from NATO's military command to preserve French sovereignty. In subsequent years, France selectively contributed troops to NATO operations. However, French forces were not subordinated to the alliance's command structures. Sarkozy argued that full membership in NATO was important, so that France would have a voice in strategic decisions. He faced criticism for the move and submitted it to Parliament for debate, though it was not required by law. Parliament approved the plan.

Sarkozy also sought in 2009 to enhance France's role in the Middle East by improving relations with Syria; to intensify energy relations with other Middle Eastern countries; and to foster trade and economic development with North Africa. Although France maintained its commitment to the NATO-led mission in Afghanistan, it refused to send more troops, as requested by newly elected United States President Barack Obama. Sarkozy took a hard line on Iran in the fall, accusing the regime of secretly attempting to build nuclear weapons.

Scandal. In late 2009, political scandals plagued Sarkozy's administration. In October, amid talks with Thailand over ways to end sex tourism, both the extreme right and the left called for the resignation of Culture Minister Frédéric Mitterrand, a nephew of the late former President François Mitterrand. Frédéric Mitterrand had written a semi-autobiographical book in which he seemed to admit to paying young Asian boys for sex.

Also in October, Sarkozy's son, a 23-year-old student, was elected to head an agency that oversees the administration of La Defense, a neighborhood west of Paris that is the largest business district in Europe. After critics cried favoritism, Jean Sarkozy withdrew his bid. He was later appointed to a seat on the board of the organization.

Former President Jacques Chirac faced scandals of his own in October, when he became the first French head of state ordered to stand trial. Chirac was charged with corruption for allegedly paying campaign workers with city funds while he was mayor of Paris from 1977 to 1995. He denied the charges. ■ Jeffrey Kopstein

See also **Europe.**

Gabon. See Africa.

Gambia. See Africa.

Gas and gasoline. See Energy supply.

Genetic engineering. See Biology; Medicine.

Geology. A series of large earthquakes rocked the southwest region of the Pacific Ocean in late September and early October 2009, generating a devastating *tsunami* (series of huge, powerful ocean waves). The quakes and waves destroyed hundreds of buildings and roads and killed more than 1,100 people in Indonesia and other countries in the region.

The United States Geological Survey (USGS) measured the first earthquake, on September 29, at a magnitude of 8.0. That quake was centered in the Samoa Islands along the Pacific-Australian subduction plate boundary. A subduction plate boundary is where two *tectonic plates*—large, slow-moving slabs of Earth's crust—collide, with the edge of one plate pushing beneath the edge of the other plate. The second earthquake, on September 30, had a magnitude of 7.6 and was centered in southern Sumatra along the Australian-Sunda subduction plate boundary. On October 1, a 6.6-magnitude earthquake occurred in southern Sumatra within the Sunda Plate along a *strike-slip fault,* a deep fracture in which blocks of rock slide past each other. The USGS measured another 6.6-magnitude earthquake on October 4, in the Philippines.

Alaskan volcano awakes. After approximately 20 years of dormancy, Mount Redoubt in southern Alaska rumbled to life with a steam explosion on March 15. Between March 22 and April 4, Mount Redoubt unleashed numerous explosions of ash and gas as high as 65,000 feet (19,800 meters) into the atmosphere, dispersing ash over communities on the Kenai Peninsula and causing problems for commercial aircraft. Subsequently, a new lava dome developed at the volcano's summit, replacing the dome that had formed in 1990. The new lava dome reached a volume of more than 90 million cubic yards (68.8 million cubic meters).

The volcano's seismic activity and gas emissions decreased over the summer months. By late 2009, all signs suggested that Mount Redoubt had returned to a state of dormancy.

Ground water feeds life in Great Lakes. Limestone sinkholes, submerged vents from which ground water is discharged, are pouring sulfate-rich waters into deep regions of Lake Huron, creating unique hot spots of biogeochemical activity. That conclusion was reported in February by scientists at the National Oceanic and Atmospheric Administration's (NOAA's) Great Lakes Environmental Research Laboratory in Ann Arbor, Michigan. The researchers said that these deep sinkholes—where there is little sunlight or dissolved oxygen—are hostile to animal life, but they support diverse bottom-dwelling communities of bacteria, colorful cyanobacteria, and archaea. Archaea are single-celled microbes distinct from bacteria.

Investigators discovered the deep sinkholes of Lake Huron in 2002. The NOAA team found that—

like vents along deep-sea ocean ridges and in ice-covered Antarctic subglacial lakes—the vents in Lake Huron harbor microbial communities based on chemosynthesis rather than photosynthesis. In chemosynthesis, microbes create *carbohydrates* (nutritious compounds containing carbon, hydrogen, and oxygen) from carbon dioxide and water by using energy obtained from chemical oxidation. Oxidation involves the combination of a chemical substance with oxygen. In photosynthesis, by contrast, carbohydrates are created by using energy obtained from sunlight.

According to the NOAA scientists, some bacteria in the Lake Huron sinkhole communities consume sulfate from the discharged ground water, producing sulfide as a waste product. Other bacteria, as well as cyanobacteria and archaea, consume the sulfide. The cyanobacteria produce more sulfate, and the archaea produce methane. Still other bacteria consume the methane.

Scientists noted that the discovery of microbial communities in the deep, dark, oxygen-poor environment of Lake Huron added to the list of known extremophiles, organisms that live in extreme environmental conditions.

Deepest well yields big oil discovery. The deepest well ever drilled led to the discovery of a vast oil field in the Gulf of Mexico approximately 250 miles (402 kilometers) southeast of Houston. The announcement of this discovery was made in September 2009 by BP, an international oil company based in London, in conjunction with ConocoPhillips of Houston and Petrobras of Brazil.

Workers drilled the so-called Tiber well from the Deepwater Horizon oil rig, which floats in water about 4,100 feet (1,250 meters) above the gulf sea floor. The well was drilled to a depth of more than 31,000 feet (9,450 meters) below the gulf bottom, in geological formations that were between about 65 million and 38 million years old. These rocks dated from early in the Tertiary Period (65 million to 1.8 million years ago).

BP geologists expected the Tiber well to yield as much as 300,000 barrels of oil per day, and they estimated that the well may hold as much as 3 billion barrels of oil. Some 25 percent of domestic oil production in the United States is based in the Gulf of Mexico, and the BP team speculated that the deep gulf was probably the most promising part of the United States to make additional oil discoveries. Despite this major discovery, however, the well's estimated daily production capacity represented only a fraction of the roughly 84 million barrels of oil that the world consumes every day.

■ Henry T. Mullins

See also **Biology; Disasters; Indonesia; Ocean.**

Georgia. President Mikheil Saakashvili faced large-scale protests in 2009. Georgian opposition leaders accused him of mishandling an armed conflict with Russia over the breakaway South Ossetia region in August 2008, of responding poorly to the global financial crisis, and of exhibiting increasingly authoritarian tendencies.

Opposition action began on Jan. 29, 2009, when 12 parties signed a declaration demanding Saakashvili's resignation. Opposition parties then planned mass demonstrations in the capital, Tbilisi. On April 9, some 60,000 protesters took to the streets to call for Saakashvili's resignation. Demonstrations continued throughout April and May, as protesters blocked the main street of Tbilisi and set up mock jail cells throughout the city. Saakashvili refused to step down and accused Russian leaders of provoking the crisis. Although scuffles between police and demonstrators occurred, the government avoided a large-scale crackdown as had happened in November 2007, when riot police violently dispersed demonstrators.

The opposition protests culminated in a rally on May 26, 2009, that filled the 60,000-seat national football stadium to capacity. The rally represented the high point of the protests, as splits within the opposition movement grew. Some leaders were willing to engage in talks with the government; others advocated radical pressure tactics to force Saakashvili's resignation.

Saakashvili responded by pressing for legislation that would make protest marches more difficult and by offering limited concessions to the opposition. The legislation gave additional powers to the police, banned the use of street-blocking tactics, and increased the punishment for resisting the police from 30 to 90 days in custody. Parliament approved the legislation on July 17. In a speech to parliament on July 20, Saakashvili called for early local elections and the direct election of mayors, in addition to a range of other minor concessions and a call for nationwide talks on government priorities. Saakashvili's concessions increased the division among the opposition, and, as a result, mass protest activities began to dwindle.

Relations with Russia. Relations between the Georgian and Russian governments remained tense in 2009 as the two sides continued to spar over the fate of the breakaway Georgian regions of Abkhazia and South Ossetia. Following the military confrontation with Georgia in 2008, Russia recognized the two regions' independence. A European Union investigating commission added fuel to the diplomatic fire by releasing a controversial report in October 2009 that blamed Georgia for starting the conflict, though it noted that Russia had provoked the country for months.

■ Juliet Johnson

See also **Asia; Russia.**

Germany. Chancellor Angela Merkel was reelected to a second term in 2009, following a national election on September 27. Nevertheless, her victory was less than complete. In the formal parliamentary vote, nine members of Merkel's bloc did not vote for her. Analysts considered the result a sign of protest over some of her policies.

Merkel's center-right Christian Democratic Union (CDU) and its Bavarian sister party, the Christian Social Union (CSU), won 33.8 percent of the vote, a drop of 1.4 percent from the 2005 election. The CDU's partner in the previous "grand coalition" of the two largest parties, the Social Democratic Party (SPD), received only 23 percent of the vote, a drop of 11 percent from 2005 and the party's worst showing since the 1930's. The SPD went into opposition and, in November 2009, chose a new party leader, Sigmar Gabriel.

Smaller parties gained votes at the expense of the larger parties. The Free Democratic Party (FDP) won 14.6 percent and reentered the government as the junior coalition partner. The Left Party, consisting of former East German Communists and disaffected West German former Social Democrats, garnered 11.9 percent of the total. The Greens increased their support to 10.7 percent, their best performance ever.

Most analysts forecast that the demise of the grand coalition of main center-right and center-left parties would lead to a more conflict-prone political scene, as the SPD would attempt to win votes from the Left Party, the Greens, and non-voters by striking a harder oppositional tone in parliament. The government, on the other hand, was expected to be more stable, both because the CDU and FDP agreed on most issues and because the balance of power between the coalition parties clearly favored Merkel's Christian Democrats. From 2005 to 2009, the numbers of seats held by the CDU/CSU and the SPD were relatively equal. However, the results of the 2009 election left the CDU/CSU with a clear majority of 239 seats, versus the FDP's 93 seats.

Economic crisis. Germany's export-dependent economy was hit hard by the global economic downturn. The government responded with tax cuts and investments in mid-January totaling 50 billion euros ($67 billion), to be spent in 2009 and 2010. The package included a car-scrapping program, a version of America's "cash for clunkers." New car registrations hit an all-time high in February 2009, an increase of 22 percent over 2008.

The government also provided its largest banks with financial support. In January 2009, Germany's second-largest bank, Commerzbank, received the second in a series of cash infusions totaling 10 billion euros ($14.7 billion), in addition to the 8 billion euros ($11.8 billion) it received in 2008. In April 2009, the Hypo Real Estate bank was nation-

"Large" and "small" giant marionettes, suspended from cranes, are reunited during a street performance to symbolize the reunification of Germany. The performance took place during a celebration in October of the 20th anniversary of the fall of the Berlin Wall. It culminated before Berlin's Brandenburg Gate, which was itself once divided and a symbol of the infamous wall.

alized as it teetered on the brink of insolvency. It was the first German bank to be nationalized since the 1930's. A plan for removing worthless or highly discounted assets from troubled banks was unveiled in mid-May 2009.

In midyear, the government resisted calls for further stimulus programs and tax cuts. As a result, the government's debt, which had been estimated by European Union (EU) economists at 3.4 percent of *gross domestic product* (GDP), remained well below that of the United States, the United Kingdom, and other larger EU members. (GDP is the value of all goods and services produced in a year.) Even so, the deficit, which ran counter to Germany's conservative fiscal traditions, undermined the FDP's plans for tax cuts, because the economic downturn had greatly reduced government revenue. Unemployment rose from 7.3 percent in 2008 to 7.7 percent in 2009.

Foreign policy. Since World War II (1939-1945), German governments have been reluctant to use military power for other than self-defense. Although about 4,300 German troops continued to participate in the NATO-led mission in Afghanistan in 2009, the German parliament restricted their activities to peacekeeping and reconstruction. The troops were stationed in Afghanistan's relatively peaceful north. However, during the year, the situation deteriorated. On September 4, the German forces called in a NATO air strike that caused the deaths of at least 90 people, including some civilians. General Wolfgang Schneiderhan, the army chief of staff, and Labor Minister (formerly Defense Minister) Josef Jung resigned over the incident, and Chancellor Merkel faced intense criticism. In December, a parliamentary investigation sought to determine whether the government had deliberately withheld details of the incident because of the upcoming election.

In July, Merkel awarded four soldiers a newly designed medal for bravery called the Bundeswehr Cross. The cross was the first medal for acts of valor given to German troops since World War II.

In June, Germany's high court cleared the way for passage of the Lisbon Treaty, an agreement that seeks to make EU decision-making more efficient. Parliament ratified the treaty in September.

School shooting. Despite strict gun laws, Germans were horrified in March when a teen-aged gunman opened fire in a school in Winnenden, near Stuttgart, killing nine students and three teachers. He killed an additional three people as he fled, before taking his own life in a shoot-out with police. Germany had toughened its laws in 2002, after a school shooting in Erfurt, eastern Germany. ■ Jeffrey Kopstein

See also **Automobile; Europe.**

Ghana. See Africa.

Global warming. The United States Environmental Protection Agency (EPA) in 2009 found that greenhouse gases are pollutants subject to regulation under the Clean Air Act. The December decision covered six gases, including the carbon dioxide given off by burning fossil fuels. The EPA reported that concentrations of greenhouse gases had risen to levels unprecedented in human history. The agency found that the gases contribute to increased drought, heavier rainfall and flooding, more frequent heat waves and wildfires, and rising sea levels. The EPA determined that global warming is a threat to agriculture, wildlife, and human health. The agency said scientific evidence for its decision was "overwhelming."

The finding came in response to a 2007 order from the U.S. Supreme Court to determine whether greenhouse gases harm public health and the environment. If Congress does not enact laws regulating such gases, the EPA is required to set regulations under the Clean Air Act.

Cap and trade. The U.S. House of Representatives narrowly passed legislation on June 26, 2009, that would regulate greenhouse gases. The American Clean Energy and Security Act of 2009 would require a 17-percent reduction in greenhouse gas emissions by 2020 and an 83-percent reduction by 2050. The legislation would establish a cap and trade system, in which the government sets a total limit on greenhouse gas emissions. Companies would then buy or sell permits to emit the gases.

The U.S. Senate took up similar legislation in October 2009. Two committees approved the legislation, but it did not come before the full Senate for a final vote. The Senate was expected to take up the legislation again in 2010.

New fuel standards. On Sept. 15, 2009, the EPA and the National Highway Traffic Safety Administration issued new fuel efficiency standards for cars. For the first time, the standards set limits on tailpipe carbon emissions—no more than 9 ounces (250 grams) of carbon dioxide per 1 mile (1.6 kilometers) driven. The agencies reported that the new standards would reduce greenhouse gas emissions by nearly 1.1 billion tons (1 billion metric tons) over the lifetime of vehicles sold in a four-year period. Under the rules, new cars will also have to achieve at least 35.5 miles per gallon (15 kilometers per liter) by 2016.

G-8 pledge. On July 9, 2009, leaders of the world's eight major industrialized countries, called the G-8, set global warming goals at their summit in L'Aquila, Italy. The G-8 nations agreed to limit global warming to 3.6 Fahrenheit degrees (2 Celsius degrees) overall. To meet this goal, they agreed to cut carbon emissions by 80 percent by 2050. United Nations Secretary-General Ban Ki-moon criticized the extended deadline and urged the setting of more immediate goals.

Copenhagen. In December 2009, representatives of 192 countries met in Copenhagen, Denmark, to negotiate a new global warming treaty. Negotiators were unable to reach a final agreement, but about 30 countries signed a nonbinding accord. The countries committed to limit global warming to no more than 2 Celsius degrees by 2050. For the first time, such developing countries as China and India committed to emissions reductions that would be subject to international confirmation. Also, wealthier countries set aside $30 billion in clean-energy assistance for developing nations. Those countries pledged to provide $100 billion of assistance annually by 2020. Negotiations on a binding treaty were set to resume in 2010.

Carbon drop. Carbon emissions were projected to drop about 3 percent in 2009, according to an October report from the Paris-based International Energy Agency, a policy adviser to 28 member nations. The drop, the largest in the last 40 years, was attributed mainly to the global economic downturn. Except for three years, carbon emissions have increased by about 3 percent annually for the last 50 years.

Global temperature tie. The year 2008 tied with 2001 as the eighth warmest on record, according to a January 2009 analysis by the National Oceanic and Atmospheric Administration's National Climatic Data Center (NCDC). The analysis is based on records dating back to 1880.

Warmest seas. Global sea surface temperatures set a record high in August 2009, according to a September report from the NCDC. Also, average temperatures from June to August were the highest recorded since 1880.

Meltdown. NASA satellites revealed that ice sheets in Greenland and Antarctica are shrinking faster than scientists expected, according to a study published in the journal *Nature* in September 2009. The study, which was conducted by scientists with the British Antarctic Survey and the University of Bristol in the United Kingdom, found that ice is thinning across Greenland and that melting has intensified on key Antarctic coastlines. In parts of Antarctica, the yearly rate of ice thinning was 50 percent higher from 2003 to 2007 than it was from 1995 to 2003.

Arctic sea ice reached its third-lowest yearly minimum in September 2009, according to the University of Colorado at Boulder's National Snow and Ice Data Center (NSIDC). Although sea ice covered more area than it had the previous two summers, it remained about 649,000 square miles (1.7 million square kilometers) below its average minimum from 1979 to 2000. "We are still seeing a downward trend that appears to be heading toward ice-free Arctic summers," said NSIDC scientist Walt Meier.   ■ Brian Johnson

See also **Environmental pollution.**

Golf. Tiger Woods announced on Dec. 11, 2009, that he was taking an "indefinite" leave from professional golf to focus on his family. A minor, late-night car accident on November 27 led to revelations of multiple marital infidelities, which cost Woods commercial endorsements worth an estimated $100 million a year.

Woods had successfully returned to professional golf earlier in 2009 after recovering from a knee injury but suffered two major disappointments. On July 17, he failed to make the cut at the British Open. It was just the second time in his professional career (after the 2006 U.S. Open) that he did not qualify for weekend play at a major. Then, on Aug. 16, 2009, at the Professional Golfers' Association (PGA) championship, Woods appeared poised to win his first major of the year, leading by two strokes entering the final day. But he lost to the 110th-ranked player in the world, Y. E. Yang, a South Korean who became the first Asian-born player to win a major on the PGA Tour. Woods had never lost a major when he led entering the final round. He came in first in the point standings to win the FedEx Cup and a $10-million prize.

In women's golf, four different women won majors again in 2009; in all, 17 women have won the last 18 majors. The United States captured the Solheim Cup, which pits the best women golfers from the United States against the best of Europe. The U.S. women scored 16 points to 12 for the Europeans.

PGA. Angel Cabrera of Argentina won a three-man play-off, finishing off Chad Campbell and Kenny Perry on the second extra hole to capture the Masters on April 12 in Augusta, Georgia. Unheralded Lucas Glover began a run of three unlikely champions on the men's tour, winning a rain-delayed U.S. Open on June 22 that stretched into a fifth day. Phil Mickelson, the crowd favorite in Farmingdale, New York, was playing just months after his wife was diagnosed with breast cancer. Mickelson made a charge in the final round to tie Glover but faded and finished in a three-way tie for second, two shots behind Glover, who finished with a 4-under 276.

With Woods out of the British Open at Turnberry, Scotland, Tom Watson stole the show, and the 59-year-old nearly became the oldest major champion in history on July 19. But Watson missed an 8-foot putt on 18, then fell apart in the four-hole play-off with Stewart Cink and lost by six shots. They had finished tied at 2-under 278 in regulation. Woods seemed poised to win the final major of the year, the PGA Championship, on August 16 in Chaska, Minnesota, but Yang kept making his shots and Woods kept missing his. Yang, who finished at 8-under for a three-shot victory, rallied from two strokes down and

led by a shot on the final hole. He hit a brilliant second shot and birdied while Woods landed in the rough and bogeyed.

LPGA. Brittany Lincicome eagled the final hole on April 5 to capture the Kraft Nabisco Championship in Rancho Mirage, California, by one stroke. Swedish rookie Anna Nordqvist finished with a 15-under 273 to capture the McDonald's Ladies Professional Golf Association Championship (LPGA) on June 14 in Havre de Grace, Maryland, by four shots. South Korean Eun Hee Ji shot an even par 71 on the final day to finish at even for the tournament and win the U.S. Women's Open on July 12 in Bethlehem, Pennsylvania, by one shot. Scotland's Catriona Matthew won the women's British Open in Lytham St. Annes, England, on August 2 by three shots. finishing at 3 under par.

Champions Tour. Michael Allen won his first big tournament in two decades with a two-shot victory at the Senior PGA Championship—the tour for men over age 50— in Beachwood, Ohio, on May 24. Loren Roberts claimed his second Senior British Open championship, defeating Ireland's Mark McNulty on the third play-off hole in Sunningdale, United Kingdom, on July 26. Fred Funk set a U.S. Senior Open record with his 20-under-par finish on August 2 in Carmel, Indiana, winning by six shots. Mike Reid won The Tradition on August 23 in Sunriver, Oregon, with a birdie on the first play-off hole after finishing tied with John Cook at 16-under 272. Jay Haas won the final major of 2009, the Senior Players Championship in Timonium, Maryland, on October 4, beating Tom Watson by one stroke.   ■ Michael Kates

Great Britain. See **United Kingdom.**

Greece. On Oct. 4, 2009, the Panhellenic Socialist Movement (PASOK), led by George Papandreou, defeated the ruling center-right New Democracy Party in national elections. Prime Minister Kostas Karamanlis had called elections halfway through his term to win a clear mandate as he dealt with the global economic crisis.

PASOK took 44 percent of the vote to New Democracy's 34 percent, giving PASOK a majority of 160 seats in the 300-seat parliament. The result was the worst performance in New Democracy's history. The party had grown unpopular because of corruption scandals and poor performance during the economic crisis. Papandreou, the son and grandson of former prime ministers, became prime minister. He immediately reduced the number of government ministries, enacted measures to reduce corruption and increase transparency, and implemented a $4.4-billion stimulus plan.

Nevertheless, the country's budget deficit soared to 12.7 percent during 2009, and Greece's debt—of about $440 billion—threatened to send the country into default. In December, Papan-

Caryatids (columns carved in the form of a female figure) from the Caryatid Porch of the Erechtheum Temple on the Acropolis stand bathed in natural light on the first floor of the new museum.

Greece's new Acropolis Museum, built at the foot of the Acropolis in Athens, opened to the public in June 2009. It was built to house the treasures of ancient Greece, including treasures still held by other countries.

Walls of high-tech glass on the top floor of the new museum allow visitors to view the structures of the Acropolis (upper right) while examining the artifacts within the museum. A digital animated display of artifacts is projected on the lower wall of the museum during the opening ceremony.

In a first-floor gallery (right), hundreds of marble statues from the Archaic and Classical eras are displayed amid structural columns, placing the works in an architectural context not unlike the columned interior of an ancient Greek temple.

The Parthenon Gallery (left) houses sculptures from the Parthenon that remain in Greece. It was designed to also house the Parthenon sculptures not in Greece, known as the Elgin Marbles. In 1801, pieces from the pediments and frieze were removed by Lord Elgin and taken to Britain. They are now in the British Museum. Greece demands that they be returned and reunited with the rest of the sculpture in this space.

dreou announced that he would cut government spending by 10 percent, crack down on tax evasion, reduce bureaucracy, and introduce a new progressive tax scale to bring down the debt.

Foreign policy. Greece and Turkey continued to disagree in 2009 over territorial boundaries. Low-level flights of Turkish planes over Greek territory intensified during the summer, endangering Turkey's candidacy for membership in the European Union (EU). At the same time, Greece continued to block the entry of the Republic of Macedonia into the EU and NATO because of the former Yugoslav republic's choice of name. Greece considers the name an explicit claim upon the northern region of Greece, also called Macedonia.

Crime, strikes, and urban unrest. In early 2009, farmers, civil servants, and doctors staged strikes that temporarily disrupted traffic in response to government austerity measures. Urban unrest erupted in December around the anniversary of a deadly police shooting in 2008 of a 15-year-old boy. ■ Jeffrey Kopstein

See also **Europe; Macedonia; People in the news** (George Papandreou).

Grenada. See **Latin America; West Indies.**
Guatemala. See **Latin America.**
Guinea. See **Africa.**
Guinea-Bissau. See **Africa.**
Guyana. See **Latin America.**

Haiti. On Nov. 11, 2009, Jean-Max Bellerive, 51, became the sixth person to hold the post of prime minister in Haiti since 2004. An experienced civil servant, Bellerive replaced Michèle Pierre-Louis, who was removed by Haiti's senate for her poor performance in promoting Haiti's recovery following hurricane-caused devastation. In the government of President Réné Préval, Bellerive had previously helped coordinate investment and foreign aid for Haiti.

Several prominent individuals visited Haiti in 2009, calling for increased international economic assistance. In March, United Nations (UN) Secretary General Ban Ki-moon stressed that the impoverished Caribbean nation stood at a crossroads between salvation and "the darkness." Rap artist and native Haitian Wyclef Jean joined former United States President Bill Clinton and U.S. philanthropist George Soros in making high-profile visits. In 2005, Jean founded Yéle Haiti, a charity that promotes education in the destitute nation.

On Oct. 9, 2009, six Uruguayan and five Jordanian peacekeepers were killed when their surveillance plane crashed into a mountain near the Dominican Republic border. They were part of the 9,000-member UN military force in Haiti to keep order and reduce crime. ■ Nathan A. Haverstock

See also **Latin America.**
Harness racing. See **Horse racing.**

Health care issues. Early in 2009, United States President Barack Obama declared that instituting major changes in U.S. health care would be his highest domestic priority. He outlined eight principles he favored: protecting families' finances; making coverage affordable; creating "a clear path to cover all Americans"; allowing people to keep coverage when they change jobs; guaranteeing choice of plans; placing a focus on wellness; improving quality of care; and laying the groundwork for the program's long-term financial stability. He left it up to Congress to draft the legislation.

The debate. The congressional debate was affected by political shifts. In April, Senator Arlen Specter (R., Pennsylvania) switched parties and became a Democrat; in July, Democrat Al Franken was seated as the junior senator from Minnesota, replacing Republican Norm Coleman after a very close election. As a result, Democrats had the minimum number of votes necessary to avoid a filibuster and pass health care reform, as long as Independent Senators Bernard Sanders of Vermont and Joseph Lieberman of Connecticut voted with them. Senate Republicans were unanimously opposed to the health care reform package proposed by the Democrats.

In the House. The Democratic majority was greater in the House than the Senate, but certain issues proved troublesome: coverage of abortion services; the so-called "public option," a government-operated plan that would compete with private insurance; and how the reform program would be funded. After much compromise, the House of Representatives passed the bill on November 7 by a vote of 220 to 215.

The focus shifted to the Senate, where Senate Majority Leader Harry Reid (D., Nevada) combined two competing bills. A number of conservative Democrats disliked some aspects of the new bill, and compromises had to be made to appease them, including restricting abortion services and eliminating the public option. On December 24, the Senate approved the legislation by a vote of 60-39, with all Republicans opposing it.

The drafting of the bills and their slow passage through Congress occurred in a highly charged, controversial atmosphere, with many advocacy groups in support or opposition. When politicians held "town meetings" about the issue, they were often met with vocal protests. Initially, private insurers supported reform, then announced their opposition. Hospitals and other providers agreed to payment cuts of $155 billion over 10 years, but began to reconsider their position in light of proposed cuts that were much higher.

Key provisions. The two bills shared many provisions: a requirement that most legal U.S. residents acquire insurance, with subsidies for lower-income people; a mandate that most employers

offer coverage to employees or else pay a fee to the federal government, with subsidies for smaller employers; "insurance exchanges" through which individuals and employers could shop for coverage; limitations on such private insurance practices as refusing to cover sick people, dropping coverage because of preexisting conditions, or charging older people higher premiums; and an expansion of the public Medicaid program for lower-income people.

The coming debate. The bills passed by the House and the Senate in 2009 differed in major areas, including abortion coverage, the government-operated public plan, eligibility for assistance, and funding, among other issues. Representatives of the House and Senate were scheduled to begin in January 2010 the process of reconciling the two bills into one that can be passed by both houses.

Other legislation. In February 2009, President Obama signed the Children's Health Insurance Program Reauthorization Act, which extended federally subsidized health care for many low-income children though 2013. In June 2009, he signed the Family Smoking Prevention and Tobacco Control Act, which expanded federal regulation of tobacco products.

Number of uninsured rises. In September, the Census Bureau reported that 46.3 million Americans lacked health insurance in 2008, a minor increase over 2007. Texas had the highest rate of uninsured individuals (25.1 percent); Massachusetts had the lowest (5.5 percent).

Mammogram controversy. In November 2009, a federal panel advised that most women under 50 do not need annual mammograms, a screening procedure for breast cancer. The advisory triggered a storm of controversy, with women's groups and cancer activists protesting the recommendation. Insurers and federal officials responded that they would not change policies covering the procedure for younger women.

Appointments. The Obama administration made the following appointments in 2009: Kansas Governor Kathleen Sebelius was named secretary of the Department of Health and Human Services; Regina Benjamin was appointed U.S. surgeon general; Francis Collins was named director of the National Institutes of Health, the federal government's main medical research agency; Margaret Hamburg was made commissioner of the Food and Drug Administration; and Thomas Frieden was named director of the Centers for Disease Control and Prevention. ■ Emily Friedman

See also **Congress of the United States; People in the news** (Kathleen Sebelius); **State government; United States, Government of the: A Special Report.**

Hobbies. See **Toys and games.**

NATIONAL HOCKEY LEAGUE STANDINGS

WESTERN CONFERENCE

Central Division	W.	L.	OT.†	Pts.
Detroit Red Wings*	51	21	10	112
Chicago Blackhawks*	46	24	12	104
St. Louis Blues*	41	31	10	92
Columbus Blue Jackets*	41	31	10	92
Nashville Predators	40	34	8	88

Northwest Division				
Vancouver Canucks*	45	27	10	100
Calgary Flames*	46	30	6	98
Minnesota Wild	40	33	9	89
Edmonton Oilers	38	35	9	85
Colorado Avalanche	32	45	5	69

Pacific Division				
San Jose Sharks*	53	18	11	117
Anaheim Ducks*	42	33	7	91
Dallas Stars	36	35	11	83
Phoenix Coyotes	36	39	7	79
Los Angeles Kings	34	37	11	79

EASTERN CONFERENCE

Northeast Division	W.	L.	OT.	Pts.
Boston Bruins*	53	19	10	116
Montreal Canadiens*	41	30	11	93
Buffalo Sabres	41	32	9	91
Ottawa Senators	36	35	11	83
Toronto Maple Leafs	34	35	13	81

Atlantic Division				
New Jersey Devils*	51	27	4	106
Pittsburgh Penguins*	45	28	9	99
Philadelphia Flyers*	44	27	11	99
New York Rangers*	43	30	9	95
New York Islanders	26	47	9	61

Southeast Division				
Washington Capitals*	50	24	8	108
Carolina Hurricanes*	45	30	7	97
Florida Panthers	41	30	11	93
Atlanta Thrashers	35	41	6	76
Tampa Bay Lightning	24	40	18	66

*Made play-offs   †Overtime/shoot-out losses

STANLEY CUP CHAMPIONS—Pittsburgh Penguins
(defeated Detroit Red Wings, 4 games to 3)

LEADING SCORERS	Games	Goals	Assists	Pts.
Evgeni Malkin, Pittsburgh	82	35	78	113
Alex Ovechkin, Washington	79	56	54	110
Sidney Crosby, Pittsburgh	77	33	70	103
Pavel Datsyuk, Detroit	81	32	65	97
Zach Parise, New Jersey	82	45	49	94

LEADING GOALIES (25 or more games)	Games	Goals against	Avg.
Tim Thomas, Boston	54	114	2.10
Steve Mason, Columbus	61	140	2.29
Niklas Backstrom, Minnesota	71	159	2.33
Nikolai Khabibulin, Chicago	42	96	2.33
Roberto Luongo, Vancouver	54	124	2.34

AWARDS

Adams Award (coach of the year)—Claude Julien, Boston

Calder Trophy (best rookie)—Steve Mason, Columbus

Conn Smythe Trophy (Most Valuable Player in Stanley Cup)—Evgeni Malkin, Pittsburgh

Hart Trophy (Most Valuable Player)—Alex Ovechkin, Washington

Jennings Trophy (goalkeeper[s] for team with fewest goals against)—Tim Thomas and Manny Fernandez, Boston

King Clancy Trophy (leadership)—Ethan Moreau, Edmonton

Lady Byng Trophy (sportsmanship)—Pavel Datsyuk, Detroit

Masterton Trophy (perseverance, dedication to hockey)—Steve Sullivan, Nashville

Norris Trophy (best defenseman)—Zdeno Chara, Boston

Pearson Award (best player as voted by NHL players)—Alex Ovechkin, Washington

Richard Trophy (most goals scored)—Alex Ovechkin, Washington

Ross Trophy (most points scored)—Evgeni Malkin, Pittsburgh

Selke Trophy (best defensive forward)—Pavel Datsyuk, Detroit

Vezina Trophy (best goalkeeper)—Tim Thomas, Boston

Hockey. The Pittsburgh Penguins won the Stanley Cup as champions of the National Hockey League (NHL) in 2009, stunning the defending champion Detroit Red Wings with a 2-1 victory in Game 7 on June 12, 2009. Pittsburgh center Evgeni Malkin won the Conn Smythe Trophy as the play-off's Most Valuable Player, scoring 36 points.

Play-offs. Pittsburgh, which was in 10th place in February when it fired its coach and replaced him with Dan Bylsma, made it to the Stanley Cup finals by sweeping the Carolina Hurricanes in four straight games in the Eastern Conference finals. The fourth-seeded Penguins had upset the Washington Capitals in the conference semifinals with a road victory in Game 7 and won their first-round series over the Philadelphia Flyers, four games to two. In the Western Conference final, the Red Wings won 4 games to 1, beating back the upstart Chicago Blackhawks in their first play-offs in seven seasons after replacing the team's coach just four games into the season. The second-seeded Wings needed seven games to eliminate the Anaheim Ducks in the conference semifinals and swept the Columbus Blue Jackets in the first round.

In the Stanley Cup Finals, Detroit appeared to seize control by winning Game 5 at home 5-0. But Pittsburgh goaltender Marc-Andre Fleury contributed brilliant performances in the next two games, making 25 saves in a 2-1 victory on June 9 in Pittsburgh to force a Game 7, and then 23 stops—including an amazing save in the closing seconds—for a 2-1 victory in the finale.

Regular season. The Boston Bruins enjoyed a momentous turnaround during the 2008-2009 season, rising from an eighth seed the previous season to the best record in the East. Boston won 53 games and finished with 116 points atop the Northeast Division. But the Bruins were upset by Carolina in the semifinals. In the Western Conference, the San Jose Sharks posted the best record in the NHL with 117 points, also on 53 wins. New Jersey goaltender Martin Brodeur set the NHL's all-time record for victories with his 552nd triumph on March 17, 2009, a 3-2 victory over the Blackhawks.

World championships. Russia held onto the men's championship, beating Canada 2-1 on May 10 in Bern, Switzerland, in a rematch of the 2008

title game. Sweden beat the U.S. men for the bronze. Also in a rematch of the 2008 title game, the U.S. women won their second straight championship on April 12, 2009 in Hämeenlinna, Finland, beating Canada 4-1.

Colleges. Boston University scored two goals in the final minute to force overtime, then defeated Miami of Ohio 4-3 on April 11 in Washington, D.C., for its fifth men's National Collegiate Athletic Association (NCAA) title. The University of Wisconsin (Madison) won its third women's title in four years with a 5-0 rout of Mercyhurst on March 22 in Boston. ■ Michael Kates

Honduras. Following five months of political turmoil, Porfirio Lobo Sosa, 62, of the center-right National Party was elected president of Honduras on Nov. 29, 2009. He was to take office in early 2010. Lobo, a career politician from a wealthy farm family, pledged to work hard to win back international recognition. The Honduran government came under serious criticism after the man Sosa succeeded, Roberto Micheletti Baín, was installed as the country's de facto president following the ouster of President Manuel Zelaya in a military *coup* (overthrow) on June 28, 2009.

This unconstitutional action led to a drying up of foreign investment and prompted the United States and some European countries to cut off economic assistance to impoverished Honduras. To further exacerbate the situation, remittances sent home by some 1 million Hondurans working abroad fell by 12 percent in 2009. This dropoff contributed to the shrinking of the national economy by 4.5 percent. Former tourism minister Ricardo Martínez reported that tourist arrivals to Honduras dropped by 70 percent following Zelaya's forced removal.
■ Nathan A. Haverstock
See also **Latin America.**

Horse racing. Jockey Calvin Borel, who won the first two races of the Triple Crown in 2009 on two different horses, failed in his attempt to be the first jockey to win a personal Triple Crown when his mount, Mine That Bird, was upset by 11-to-1-shot Summer Bird at the Belmont Stakes on June 6.

On November 7, Zenyatta became the first mare to win the Breeders' Cup Classic, coming from behind to beat 11 male horses, including Mine That Bird and Summer Bird. The five-year-old finished her career at 14-0.

Sea the Stars, one of the greatest race

MAJOR HORSE RACES OF 2009

THOROUGHBRED RACING

RACE	WINNER	VALUE TO WINNER
American Triple Crown		
Belmont Stakes	Summer Bird	$600,000
Kentucky Derby	Mine That Bird	$1,417,200
Preakness Stakes	Rachel Alexandra	$660,000
United Kingdom Triple Crown		
Epsom Derby	Sea the Stars	£709,625
St. Leger Stakes	Mastery	£306,580
Two Thousand Guineas	Sea the Stars	£241,840
Breeders' Cup races		
Breeders' Cup Classic	Zenyatta	$2,700,000
Breeders' Cup Ladies' Classic	Life Is Sweet	$1,080,000
Breeders' Cup Mile	Goldikova	$1,080,000
Breeders' Cup Dirt Mile	Furthest Land	$540,000
Breeders' Cup Sprint	Dancing in Silks	$1,080,000
Breeders' Cup Turf	Conduit	$1,620,000
Breeders' Cup Turf Sprint	California Flag	$540,000
Breeders' Cup Marathon	Man of Iron	$270,000
Breeders' Cup Filly & Mare Sprint	Informed Decision	$540,000
Breeders' Cup Filly & Mare Turf	Midday	$1,080,000
Breeders' Cup Fillies Turf	Tapitsfly	$540,000
Breeders' Cup Juvenile	Vale of York	$1,080,000
Breeders' Cup Juvenile Fillies	She Be Wild	$1,080,000
Breeders' Cup Juvenile Turf	Pounced	$540,000
Other major races		
Blue Grass Stakes	General Quarters	$465,000
Canadian International Stakes	Champs Elysees	$1,200,000
		(Canadian dollars)
Dubai World Cup (United Arab Emirates)	Well Armed	$3,600,000
Haskell Invitational Stakes	Rachel Alexandra	$700,000
Hollywood Gold Cup Stakes	Rail Trip	$420,000
Irish Derby (Ireland)	Fame and Glory	£843,000
Jockey Club Gold Cup	Summer Bird	$450,000
Kentucky Oaks	Rachel Alexandra	$336,914
King George VI and Queen Elizabeth Diamond Stakes (United Kingdom)	Conduit	£567,700
Lane's End Stakes	Hold Me Back	$282,000
Melbourne Cup	Shocking	$3,390,000
		(Australian dollars)
Oaklawn Handicap	Runforthedoe	$300,000
Pacific Classic Stakes	Richard's Kid	$600,000
Prix de l'Arc de Triomphe (France)	Sea the Stars	€2,285,600
Santa Anita Derby	Pioneerof the Nile	$450,000
Santa Anita Handicap	Einstein	$600,000
Stephen Foster Handicap	Macho Again	$396,924
Travers Stakes	Summer Bird	$600,000
Woodbine Mile (Canada)	Ventura	$600,000
		(Canadian dollars)

HARNESS RACING

RACE	WINNER	VALUE TO WINNER
Trotting Triple Crown		
Hambletonian	Muscle Hill	$760,167
Kentucky Futurity	Muscle Hill	$300,000
Yonkers Trot	Judge Joe	$355,387
Pacing Triple Crown		
Cane Pace	Vintage Master	$162,500
Little Brown Jug	Well Said	$297,265
Messenger Stakes	If I Can Dream	$271,030
Other major races		
Meadowlands Pace	Well Said	$500,000
Woodrow Wilson	Windfall Blue Chip	$222,700

€ = euro (European Union dollar)

horses in European racing history, retired in 2009 after a 15-month career. From May through October, he won six major races.

Three-year-olds. On May 2, Borel captured the Kentucky Derby aboard Mine That Bird, the only gelding in the race, surging from the back of the 19-horse field to win by 6 ¾ lengths. Set off at 50-1 odds, Mine That Bird paid $103.20 on a $2 bet, the second-highest return in the 135-year history of the race. (Donerail paid $184.90 in 1913.) Borel then rode Rachel Alexandra, a 9-5 favorite, to a one-length triumph at the Preakness Stakes on May 16, 2009. Rachel Alexandra became the first filly since 1924 to win the Preakness. With the filly sitting out the Belmont Stakes on June 6, Borel was back aboard Mine That Bird, who could not hold off a charging Summer Bird and faded to third place, behind Dunkirk.

International racing. Well Armed broke quickly from the gate and cruised to a 14-length victory in the $6-million Dubai World Cup on March 28 in Dubai, United Arab Emirates. Eastern Anthem captured the $5-million Dubai Sheema Classic in a three-horse photo finish, and Gladiatorus easily captured the $5-million Dubai Duty Free.

Sea the Stars won the Epsom Derby on June 6, becoming the first horse in 20 years to win the race after capturing the Two Thousand Guineas. Sea the Stars beat favorite Fame and Glory by 1 ¾ lengths. With Sea the Stars not running, Fame and Glory won the Irish Derby on June 28 by a convincing five lengths. On October 4 in Paris, Sea the Stars captured the Prix de l'Arc de Triomphe.

Shocking captured the prestigious Melbourne Cup on November 3 in Melbourne, Australia.

Harness. Muscle Hill, who retired in late 2009 after winning his 20th straight race in 21 starts, captured the first leg of the trotting Triple Crown, the $1.5-million Hambletonian, on August 8 by 6 lengths. Muscle Hill skipped the second leg, the Yonkers Trot, on August 29, which was won by Judge Joe. Muscle Hill captured the final leg, the Kentucky Futurity, on October 3 by 2 ½ lengths. In the pacing Triple Crown, Vintage Master captured the Cane Pace on September 7; Well Said took the Little Brown Jug on September 24; and If I Can Dream won the Messenger Stakes on November 7.

■ Michael Kates

Hospital. See **Health care issues.**
Housing. See **Building and construction.**

Houston. The Houston region in 2009 took significant steps toward recovering from Hurricane Ike, which hit nearby Galveston on Sept. 13, 2008. The hurricane was one of the most damaging tropical systems in United States history, with an estimated $32 billion in losses. Galveston lies about 45 miles (72 kilometers) southeast from Houston on the Gulf Coast.

For Galveston Island, the most significant recovery was the reemergence in 2009 of its largest employer, the University of Texas Medical Branch at Galveston (UTMB). The storm shut down the hospital's emergency department until August 1. Shortly after the storm, hospital officials publicly wondered whether the institution would ever again have 300 beds. By late 2009, its total bed count had already risen to 400.

In addition, UTMB embarked upon an ambitious $667-million construction program that included new clinics and the remodeling of the medical school's John Sealy Hospital, the Blocker Burn Unit, and the labor and delivery unit. The hospital received the funds from the Federal Emergency Management Agency, the state of Texas, and private insurance.

Hurricane Ike, which delivered a 12- to 15-foot (3.6- to 4.6-meter) surge of water atop normal tides, also spurred governments in the Houston region to consider how best to mitigate similarly destructive storm-surge events in the future.

William Merrell, a marine sciences professor at Texas A&M University at Galveston, proposed building the "Ike Dike"—a multibillion-dollar series of walls, dikes, and gates that would block Galveston Island, Bolivar Peninsula, and Galveston Bay from storm surges. The plan would protect populated areas on Galveston Island and along Galveston Bay, as well as the Johnson Space Center and heavy industries along the Houston Ship Channel. The idea gained traction with some public officials, and the state of Texas directed six coastal counties, including Harris and Galveston, to create an intergovernmental corporation to study storm-surge suppression systems and propose a solution.

City budget and economy. The global recession made its presence felt in the city of Houston, where predicted declines in revenue from property and sales taxes forced Mayor Bill White and the City Council to strip $50 million from their annual budget in September. To cover the shortfall, the city cut funding for some departments and identified new sources of funds, including money from hurricane-related reimbursements. The city also considered selling real estate and delaying expenditures on new technology and purchases of new helicopters for the police department. White, who was serving his final year in office, urged his successor to hold the line on new spending, as tax receipts for 2010 were projected to continue upon a flat or downward trend.

Earlier in 2009, in an annual survey of Harris County residents conducted by sociologist Stephen Klineberg of Rice University in Houston, the economic downturn jumped past crime and traffic to become the region's overwhelming concern. The 2009 Houston Area Survey found that 44 percent of respondents said the economy was the Houston area's most serious problem, up from just 15 percent in 2008. The rise was the sharpest increase in economic jitters since the depths of the city's oil bust in 1987.

Mayoral election. City Controller Annise Parker defeated former City Attorney Gene Locke in a runoff election on Dec. 12, 2009, becoming the first openly gay woman elected mayor of a major American city. Parker and Locke had received the most votes among a group of four major mayoral candidates on November 3, but neither topped 50 percent, forcing the runoff.

New schools chief. The Houston Independent School District hired a new superintendent from the San Diego Unified School District in August. Terry Grier replaced Abelardo Saavedra and faced the difficult choice of how to balance resources for highly regarded, popular magnet schools while ensuring that neighborhood schools also provide quality education.   ■ Eric Berger

See also **City.**

Human rights. An arrest warrant was issued for Sudanese President Umar al-Bashir on March 4, 2009, by the International Criminal Court (ICC) in The Hague, the Netherlands. Bashir—the first sitting head of state to be targeted by the ICC—was charged with war crimes and crimes against humanity. He was believed to have masterminded a campaign of murder, forcible transfer, torture, and rape of civilians in Sudan's Darfur region. Rebels in Darfur had been fighting government forces and government-backed militias since 2003. The ongoing violence had killed over 200,000 people and displaced more than 2 ½ million others.

In response to the ICC action, Bashir's government ordered several foreign aid agencies to leave the country. On July 3, 2009, delegates to an African Union (AU) summit in Libya adopted a resolution stating that AU member nations would refuse to cooperate with the ICC regarding the arrest warrant. Bashir remained at large at the end of 2009.

The first-ever ICC trial began on Jan. 26, 2009, in The Hague. (The ICC had been created in 2002.) The defendant was Thomas Lubanga, a former militia leader from Congo (Kinshasa) who was accused of using children under age 15 as soldiers in an ethnic conflict in eastern Congo in 2002 and 2003. Lubanga pleaded not guilty.

Fujimori in Peru. Former Peruvian President Alberto Fujimori was convicted of crimes against humanity by a three-judge panel of Peru's Supreme Court on April 7, 2009, in Lima. He received a 25-year prison sentence. Fujimori was found guilty of backing two massacres by military death squads in 1991 and 1992 and of authorizing two kidnappings in 1992. The massacres, which killed 25 people, had been part of a counterinsurgency campaign against guerrilla groups in Peru. The verdict marked the first time that an elected head of state was convicted of human rights abuses by a court in his own country.

Khmer Rouge. The first trial of a member of Cambodia's brutal Khmer Rouge movement began on Feb. 17, 2009, in Phnom Penh before a joint tribunal of Cambodia and the United Nations. The Khmer Rouge had ruled Cambodia from 1975 to 1979 and had been responsible for over 1 ½ million deaths. The defendant was Kaing Guek Eav (also known as Comrade Duch). He ran the Tuol Sleng prison, where over 15,000 people had died from execution, torture, and poor conditions. Duch admitted responsibility for the crimes and apologized for them. He claimed that he had been ordered to carry them out by senior Khmer Rouge leaders and that he did not dare disobey the orders for fear of being killed himself.   ■ Mike Lewis

See also **Africa; Sudan; United Nations.**

Hungary. In a surprise move, Prime Minister Ferenc Gyurcsány resigned in March 2009, admitting that he had been unsuccessful at implementing measures to trim Hungary's budget deficit. Such measures were deemed necessary to enable Hungary to conform to targets set by the European Union (EU), of which Hungary is a member. Gyurcsány, of the ruling Socialist Party, was replaced in April by Gordon Bajnai, a political independent who received support from the ruling Socialists as well as their former coalition partner, the Free Democrats.

Hungary, one of the European nations hardest hit by the worldwide economic crisis of 2008-2009, received a $25-billion assistance package arranged in October 2008 by the International Monetary Fund (IMF)—a United Nations organization that provides short-term credit to member nations. The loan was designed to stave off collapse of the country's currency and banking system. Economists projected that Hungary's gross domestic product (GDP)—the total value of goods and services produced in a country in a year—would contract by 6.5 percent in 2009.

Elections to the European Parliament in June gave Hungary's main opposition party, Fidesz, a landslide victory. The center-right party, led by Victor Orbán, took 14 of Hungary's 22 allocated seats. In an upset, the extremist right-wing party Jobbik took three seats, nearly reaching par with the ruling Socialists, who took only four. Opposition members of the Hungarian parliament in Budapest called for the Socialist-led government, in power since 2002, to resign, but Socialist leaders rejected their demands.

Relations with neighboring Slovakia deteriorated in 2009. On August 21, Slovak officials prevented László Sólyom, the president of Hungary, from entering Slovakia to attend a ceremony in a predominantly Hungarian town. Slovak authorities alleged that Sólyom intended to evoke Hungary's historic claims to southern Slovakia, and they objected to the timing of the visit—the anniversary of the 1968 Warsaw Pact invasion of Czechoslovakia, when Soviet, Hungarian, and other Eastern European troops had suppressed democratic reforms in the country.

Hungarian officials took issue with a new language law enacted by Slovakia's parliament in 2009. The law limits use of Hungarian in schools and in official transactions and imposes fines for violations. Political leaders in Hungary regard the law as a serious liability for the 500,000 ethnic Hungarians who reside in southern Slovakia. In September, Prime Minister Bajnai and Slovak Prime Minister Robert Fico met to discuss ways to defuse the crisis.   ■ Sharon L. Wolchik

See also **Europe; Slovakia.**

Ice skating. Kim Yu-Na became the first South Korean to win a world figure skating title with her record-setting performance at the 2009 World Figure Skating Championships. Evan Lysacek became the first man from the United States to win the title in 13 years.

World championships. In Los Angeles, Kim won the title on March 28, 2009, despite botching one jump and receiving no points on her final spin. Kim still managed 207.71 points to break the mark set in 2007 by Japan's Mao Asada and win over Canadian Joannie Rochette by 16 points. Rochette's silver was the first won by a Canadian woman in 21 years. Japan's Miki Ando was third. Lysacek, second to France's Brian Joubert after the short program, electrified the crowd on March 26 to win the free skate and the title with 242.23 points, edging out Canada's Patrick Chan. Joubert took the bronze.

Russians Oksana Domnina and Maxim Shabalin captured the ice dancing title, denying Tanith Belbin and Benjamin Agosto's attempt to become the first duo from the United States to claim that discipline. The German tandem of Aliona Savchenko and Robin Szolkowy repeated in the pairs competition.

U.S. championships. In Cleveland in late January 2009, Alissa Czisny won her first national title a year after finishing ninth. Czisny, who at

21 was much older than most of her competition, finished about 6 points ahead of Rachael Flatt, who took the silver, and Caroline Zhang, who finished third. Lysacek, a two-time defending champion, finished a surprisingly low third in the men's competition, struggling through his free skate. Jeremy Abbott captured the title with 241.89 points, more than 12 points ahead of Brandon Mroz, with whom he trains in Colorado Springs, Colorado.

In ice dancing, Belbin and Agosto skipped the nationals while Agosto recovered from a back injury. Meryl Davis and Charlie White captured the title. Keauna McLaughlin and Rockne Brubaker were the pairs winners.

European championships. In Helsinki in late January, Laura Lepistö became the first Finnish woman to win a European championship despite losing the free skate to two-time defending cham-

pion Carolina Kostner of Italy, who took the silver. Finland's Susanna Pöykiö finished third. In the men's competition, France's Joubert won his third title, finishing well ahead of Italy's Samuel Contesti (silver) and Belgium's Kevin Van Der Perren (bronze). Savchenko and Szolkowy captured the pairs championship for the third year in a row, and Russia's Jana Khokhlova and Sergei Novitski won their first ice dancing title.   ■ Michael Kates

Iceland. See Europe; People in the news (Jóhanna Sigurdardóttir).

Immigration. The administration of United States President Barack Obama made adjustments in U.S. immigration law enforcement policy in 2009. However, neither the president nor Congress undertook major immigration reform.

Enforcement. On October 16, officials of U.S. Immigration and Customs Enforcement (ICE), an agency of the Department of Homeland Security (DHS), announced that new agreements had been reached with 67 state and local law enforcement agencies under a program that enlists those agencies' help in enforcing federal immigration laws. ICE officials pledged to more closely oversee the program—known as 287(g) for the section of the 1996 law that authorized it—and to have local police focus mainly on dangerous criminal immigrants. Critics of 287(g) had accused police of engaging in racial profiling and of too often targeting immigrants who commit such minor offenses as traffic violations. A major focus of both praise and criticism had been Sheriff Joe Arpaio of Maricopa County, Arizona, whose large, high-profile crackdown on illegal immigrants had drawn national attention. In March 2009, the U.S. Department of Justice began a civil rights investigation of Arpaio's agency, and in October, ICE took away his deputies' authority to arrest immigrants in the field, allowing the deputies only to check the immigration status of already-jailed inmates. However, Arpaio vowed to continue his agency's immigration sweeps and field arrests.

On April 30, the DHS issued new guidelines for cracking down on employment of illegal immigrants. The guidelines directed ICE agents to focus more on employers and less on workers and to limit the use of workplace raids, which had been

Evan Lysacek waves to the crowd after taking the gold medal in the men's competition in the World Figure Skating Championships in Los Angeles on March 26, 2009. Lysacek became the first United States man to win the world championship since Todd Eldredge skated to the title in 1996.

A stretch of fencing along the U.S.-Mexico border in the desert spanning Arizona and California is part of more than 600 miles (965 kilometers) of barrier erected by the end of 2009 to deter illegal immigration.

common under the administration of President George W. Bush. Such raids had led to the arrests of thousands of illegal workers but relatively few employers. ICE agents were told to step up efforts to build criminal cases against employers who knowingly hire illegal immigrants. ICE also intensified its efforts in 2009 to force businesses to dismiss illegal employees. One high-profile business targeted by ICE was the Los Angeles-based American Apparel, which fired about 1,800 immigrant employees in the fall of 2009 at the behest of ICE.

On August 6, ICE officials announced plans to overhaul the ICE detention system for illegal immigrants. The system consisted of about 350 local, state, and private jails and prisons, holding, at any one time, tens of thousands of immigrants awaiting legal proceedings. Many of the facilities had been criticized for poor conditions and substandard medical care. The plans included creating new oversight offices within the DHS to investigate detainee complaints and inspect and redesign detention facilities. Also, ICE officials announced that immigrant families would no longer be sent to the T. Don Hutto Residential Center in Taylor, Texas. This facility had drawn criticism in 2006 and 2007 in response to reports that chil-

dren were receiving little schooling there and were being held in family cells with open toilets.

State laws. As of Nov. 20, 2009, state legislatures had passed 353 immigration-related measures in 48 states in 2009, including 222 laws and 131 resolutions, according to the National Conference of State Legislatures. The 2009 total far exceeded the 206 measures passed in 41 states in 2008. Many of the 2009 laws set eligibility requirements, based on immigration status, for driver's licenses, health benefits, or education benefits. Other laws dealt with employment or law enforcement issues.

Census data. In 2008, the U.S. immigrant population declined for the first time since at least 1970, according to U.S. census data released on Sept. 21, 2009. There were about 38 million foreign-born U.S. residents in 2008 (12.5 percent of the population), down slightly from about 38.1 million in 2007. Mexicans were by far the largest foreign-born group. *The New York Times* reported on May 15, 2009, that 25 percent fewer Mexicans immigrated to other countries (mainly the United States) during the year that ended in August 2008 than during the prior year, according to Mexico census data. ■ Mike Lewis

Income tax. See Taxation.

India. The Congress Party won a decisive victory in parliamentary elections in April and May 2009. The party had led India to independence in 1947 and governed it for much of the time since. The result retained Manmohan Singh for a second five-year term as prime minister, strengthened Sonia Gandhi's role as party president, and enhanced prospects for her son, Rahul, to become India's future leader. Sonia Gandhi is the widow of assassinated Prime Minister Rajiv Gandhi; their son Rahul is the grandson of Prime Minister Indira Gandhi and the great-grandson of India's first prime minister, Jawaharlal Nehru. Sonia Gandhi became the Congress Party's president in 1998 and was credited with rebuilding the organization.

Politics. After the Hindu-nationalist Bharatiya Janata Party (BJP) had ruled India for six years, Congress won an upset victory in 2004 and formed a coalition government. Communist members of the coalition, however, opposed many of the reforms advocated by Singh, an economist turned politician. Sonia Gandhi formed a new coalition without them in 2008.

The 2009 voting was held on six days over the course of April and May to allow 6.5 million election workers and security personnel to move around among 828,804 polling centers. Voter turnout was reported at around 60 percent of those eligible, or roughly 420 million people. Congress won 206 seats. Its allies won another 56 seats, enabling the party to pick up enough other support to give Singh a majority in the Lok Sabha, the lower house of India's parliament. The BJP-led coalition dropped from 185 seats in 2004 to 158.

Singh had served as finance minister from 1991 to 1996 and was credited with reforms that helped promote India's economic growth. As prime minister, he launched several welfare programs and a massive write-off of small farmers' debts. These measures won broad support for Congress, which also benefited from unprecedentedly high economic growth in recent years.

The Congress Party's 2009 election manifesto promised to expand rural welfare programs and distribute cheap food to the poor. Some 70 percent of India's 1.2 billion people live in rural areas, and 27.5 percent live in poverty, according to the United Nations Development Programme. A national budget introduced after the election expanded a rural program to guarantee 100 days of work a year to each impoverished family.

The election result made Singh the first prime minister to win a second term since Indira Gandhi, who was prime minister from 1966 to 1977 and from 1980 until her assassination in 1984. Although Congress in 2009 achieved its best election

People line up to vote in parliamentary elections near Srinagar in the Indian state of Jammu and Kashmir in May. On six days over the course of a month, approximately 420 million Indians, 60 percent of eligible voters, cast ballots.

results since 1991, the party remained a collection of factions held together mainly by the Nehru-Gandhi heritage.

Rahul Gandhi campaigned nationally before enthusiastic crowds in the 2009 elections and won reelection to parliament. He was widely seen as a fourth-generation Nehru-Gandhi heir to power. With Singh in frail health at the age of 76, political observers believed Rahul might succeed him as prime minister within a few years.

Economics. Singh's new government faced severe economic problems. After several years of 9-percent growth, the economy slowed in 2009. Exports fell and industrial output shrank, partly as a result of the international economic downturn. However, India was one of the world's few large economies to continue some growth through the downturn.

Agriculture, the backbone of India's economy, was hard hit by below-average monsoon rainfalls. By the end of monsoon season in late September, the nation's rainfall was 23 percent below average—India's worst drought since 1972. Government officials announced that there were sufficient stockpiles of food to avoid widespread hunger. The drought caused a drop in agricultural output, and the prices of some staple foods rose. State governments raided dealers who were believed to be hoarding food.

After drought came floods that destroyed farms and crops. In early October, several days of rain in southern India triggered floods that killed at least 300 people and left some 1.5 million others homeless.

Maoist rebels ravaged rural parts of central and eastern India during 2009, continuing guerrilla attacks on officials, police, and landowners. Hundreds of police, soldiers, and civilians had been killed annually for years in skirmishes in several states. India's government banned the Maoist Communist political party in June and began a broad offensive against rebels who claimed to fight for landless peasants and workers.

Foreign relations. Prime Minister Singh met with Prime Minister Yousaf Raza Gilani of Pakistan in Egypt in July to discuss resuming efforts to improve relations between the two countries. The two nations had long disputed the ownership of the state of Jammu and Kashmir. Efforts had been disrupted by a November 2008 terrorist attack on the Indian port city of Mumbai. The attackers were based in Pakistan, which heightened the tension between the countries. Pakistan promised it would begin prosecuting the Mumbai attack's organizers, though in October 2009 a Pakistani court dropped charges against the leader of the group believed to be responsible.

■ Henry S. Bradsher

See also **Asia; Disasters; Pakistan; Terrorism.**

Indian, American. The largest class-action lawsuit ever brought against the United States government came close to resolution in 2009. The suit had been brought by Elouise Cobell of the Montana Blackfeet Nation in 1996, on behalf of more than 300,000 Indians. Cobell charged the Interior Department with mishandling billions of dollars in department-administered trust funds for individual Indians since 1887 and demanded an accounting of the missing funds. The accounts contain royalties from leasing rights for mining, oil and gas extraction, timber, and grazing on Indian lands. Since 1996, two secretaries of the Interior Department had been held in contempt of court in the case.

The department, which conducted a partial accounting of the funds, claimed that only a small percentage of the accounts contain errors and that the amounts of the errors are, in most cases, less than $10. In addition, the department maintained that an accounting is an extremely complicated task because of the beneficiary structure of the funds. About 300,000 owners hold some 4 million interests (fractions of ownership) in more than 56 million acres (23 million hectares) of allotted lands.

The lawsuit originally claimed that more than $100 billion were owed to individual trust account owners. In 2007, a Senate committee briefly considered proposing to settle the case for $7 billion. During a trial in 2008, Cobell stated that, based on new evidence brought forth during the trial, $48 billion had been lost due to mismanagement. In August, Judge James Robertson of the U.S. District Court for the District of Columbia ruled that because records pertaining to the accounts had been destroyed, no true accounting is possible and that the government is liable for $455.6 million. Both parties rejected the amount and appealed the ruling.

In a hearing before the U.S. Court of Appeals for the D.C. Circuit on May 11, 2009, the government argued that the accounts had been administered fairly and that the Indians were due nothing. The Indians maintained that the accounts had never been audited and that because of the missing records, the funds in the accounts could not be considered complete. The three-judge panel on July 24 upheld the Indians and reversed the court's setting of $455.6 million in restitution. On December 8, the two sides agreed on $3.4 billion to settle the case; $1.4 billion would be divided among the plantiffs, and $2 billion would be used to buy fractions of land and place them under tribal control, consolidating the holdings. At the end of 2009, the agreement awaited congressional approval.

New head for Bureau of Indian Affairs. On May 19, the U.S. Senate confirmed the nomination of Larry EchoHawk as the Interior Department's assistant secretary for Indian affairs and head of the Bureau of Indian Affairs. He was sworn in on May 22. EchoHawk, a member of the Pawnee Nation of

Oklahoma, had previously served as attorney general of Idaho, the only American Indian elected to such a position in any state.

Domestic Policy Council. In June, U.S. President Barack Obama created the position of senior policy adviser for Native American affairs on the Domestic Policy Council. The council advises the president on domestic policy and oversees its implementation. President Obama appointed Kimberly Teehee of the Cherokee Nation to the post.

White House Tribal Nations Conference. In November, President Obama met with the leaders of 386 tribes to discuss the problems and priorities of Native Americans. The leaders of all 564 federally recognized tribes had been invited. President Obama acknowledged the broken promises and treaties of the past and the social and health problems of the present. He promised federal aid and the beginning of a new relationship between the U.S. government and the tribal nations.

The Presidential Medal of Freedom, the nation's highest civilian honor, was bestowed by President Obama upon Joe Medicine Crow-High Bird on July 30. Medicine Crow, the last living Plains Indian war chief, an anthropologist, author, and lecturer, was honored for his "contributions to the preservation of the culture and history of the First Americans" and for his importance as a role model to young Indians. ■ Kristina Vaicikonis

Indonesia. President Susilo Bambang Yudhoyono won reelection on July 8, 2009, taking 60.8 percent of the vote. The runner-up, with 26.8 percent, was former President Megawati Sukarnoputri, whom Yudhoyono had defeated in 2004 in Indonesia's first direct election for president. Yusuf Kalla, who had served as Yudhoyono's vice president but who ran against him in the election, received only 12.4 percent of the vote. Yudhoyono's new vice president was a Western-educated central banker, Boediono, who had no political ties.

Some 38 political parties contested seats in parliamentary elections held on April 9, 2009. Yudhoyono's Democratic Party won 20.85 percent of the votes, a result that was triple its showing in 2004 and better than any other party's. This gave the president stronger support in the 560-seat parliament than in his first term, though he still needed coalition backing to get legislation passed.

Economics. Yudhoyono's political successes reflected an improved economic situation in Indonesia, which is Southeast Asia's most populous nation and has the region's largest economy. After decades of having to import rice, a staple of Indonesian diets, the country achieved self-sufficiency in 2008. The worldwide economic decline in 2008 and 2009 hit Indonesia less hard than nearby nations, and in 2009, Indonesia's economy recovered.

When world oil prices soared in 2008, Yudhoyono made the unpopular move of raising the government-subsidized domestic price for fuel. As world oil prices fell in 2009, he cut fuel prices.

Earthquakes with magnitudes of 7.6 and 6.6 shook the western coast of the Indonesian island of Sumatra on September 30 and October 1. Padang, a port city of 900,000 people, was badly damaged, and nearby villages on volcanic slopes were buried by landslides. Amid slow, poorly coordinated relief efforts, officials estimated that some 1,100 people had died following the quakes.

Terrorism. On July 17, coordinated suicide attacks inside two luxury hotels in the capital, Jakarta, killed 9 people and wounded at least 50 others. One of the hotels had been attacked previously, in 2003. Since then, improved police work had broken up some terrorist organizations. Noordin Mohammed Top, the presumed mastermind of the July 2009 attacks and numerous other bombings, was killed by police on September 17.

Death. Former President Abdurrahman Wahid, also known as Gus Dur, died in Jakarta on Dec. 30, 2009. He had defeated Megawati Sukarnoputri, the daughter of Indonesia's founding president, Sukarno, in presidential elections in 1999. Wahid quickly lost popularity and was ousted by parliament in 2001. ■ Henry S. Bradsher

See also **Asia; Disasters; Terrorism.**

International trade. Commerce in goods and services among nations declined sharply in 2009, as severe economic recession in most of the world's advanced industrial economies bottomed out in the first half of the year. The recession struck the United States and other major economic regions in the second half of 2008 in response to a global financial crisis triggered by the collapse of the mortgage market in the United States. The crisis crippled the global banking system, freezing the credit on which international trade depends. Some analysts speculated that disruptions in trade patterns could reshape long-established trends in international trade.

Prior to the economic crisis, such wealthy consumer nations as the United States, Canada, Japan, and Europe's more advanced economies had stimulated world economic growth by importing heavily from producers in such developing nations as China, India, and Mexico. As residents of the consumer nations curbed their purchases, demand for goods from these developing nations weakened. As a result, economic growth slowed markedly worldwide.

Ebbing trade. The International Monetary Fund (IMF)—a United Nations organization that provides short-term credit to member nations—projected in October 2009 that the value of global trade would decline 11.9 percent for the year. In

2008, international trade had grown by a mere 3 percent; by contrast, trade in 2007 had surged by 7.3 percent.

Impact on developing nations. Analysts noted that many developing nations had experienced shallower economic downturns or even avoided outright recession and anticipated stronger rebounds than advanced economies. However, IMF economists warned that "poverty could increase significantly in a number of developing economies." Demand in industrial nations for imports would continue to be weak, the economists noted, and constraints on credit in the impaired global financial system could persist, limiting cross-border trade growth.

Economists also noted that the value of the U.S. dollar—which serves as a global currency in trade—fell steadily against other major world currencies in 2009. This development made U.S. exports cheaper and those of many U.S. competitors relatively more expensive. The falling dollar, therefore, reduced demand in the enormous U.S. market for goods of many developing countries. On the other hand, U.S. producers had to pay more with their weaker dollars for commodities—unprocessed basic goods—in effect boosting revenues for commodity producers, many of which are in developing nations.

The changed U.S. market. The massive U.S. economy traditionally acts as a locomotive for world growth by pulling in much more of the world's output than it sells in goods and services abroad. Trade statistics amassed in 2009, however, prompted some economists to wonder if a long-term shift in trading patterns might be taking place. For decades, the U.S. trade deficit—the shortfall between goods and services exported and those imported—had been growing steadily. During the first eight months of 2009, however, the U.S. trade deficit shrank by more than half.

The U.S. Department of Commerce in October reported that the U.S. trade deficit for January through August amounted to $238 billion, down from $491 billion for the same period in 2008. During the first eight months of 2009, U.S. consumers slashed their import purchases 29.2 percent; U.S. exports declined by 20.3 percent in the same period, resulting in a net shift away from imports in the trade balance.

Canada ranked first among U.S. trading partners in 2009, as in the previous year; China ranked second. Mexico ranked third; Japan, a distant fourth; and Germany, fifth. The United States shrank its trade deficit with all five nations. The U.S. shortfall with Canada in the period from January to August fell to $12 billion from $59 billion for the same period in 2008; the shortfall with Mexico slimmed to $28 billion from $47 billion a year earlier. With China, the U.S. trade deficit fell to $144 billion from $168 billion.

Sparks over trade. Trade tensions intensified between the United States and China after U.S. President Barack Obama imposed a tariff on Chinese-made automobile tires in September 2009. The tariff imposed taxes ranging from 25 to 35 percent on Chinese tire imports over a three-year period.

President Obama acted in response to a complaint by the United Steelworkers union that Chinese exports of tires to the United States, which tripled from 2004 to 2008, were endangering jobs in U.S. tire factories. The president invoked a technical provision in the agreement that China had signed with the World Trade Organization (WTO) upon that Asian nation's entry in 2001 into the Geneva, Switzerland-based body that oversees international trade.

New trading bloc. On Oct. 15, 2009, officials of the European Union (EU) and South Korea signed an agreement to remove tariffs between the association of European nations and the East Asian nation. Key provisions of the pact were to be enacted over five years. Analysts noted that the new free-trade bloc was the largest created since the North American Free Trade Agreement (NAFTA) of Canada, Mexico, and the United States came into effect in 1994.   ■ John D. Boyd

See also **Bank; China; Economics, United States; Economics, World.**

Internet. The Internet continued to extend its reach throughout the world in 2009. For the first time, more Americans got their news from Internet sources than from such printed sources, as newspapers. The number of Chinese Internet users also continued to skyrocket in 2009, nearly equaling the total population of the United States.

Google Books, the project to make the world's libraries available online, ran into stiff opposition and legal trouble throughout 2009. Google, Inc., based in Mountain View, California, had reached a settlement with authors and publishers in October 2008, addressing their concerns over the project's potential copyright violations. Google agreed to pay $125 million to help ensure that authors and publishers were fairly paid for work accessed on Google's site.

However, various individuals, nonprofit groups, and library associations accused the settlement of potentially creating an anticompetitive environment for online books. Together, the individuals and groups formed the Open Book Alliance. In August 2009, three other large Internet companies joined the Open Book Alliance against Google's settlement: Redmond, California-based Microsoft; Sunnyvale, California-based Yahoo!; and Seattle-based Amazon.

The Alliance urged the U.S. Justice Department

to investigate Google's settlement for violations of antitrust laws, which promote fair competition. In September, a federal judge concluded that the settlement was not acceptable. However, the judge noted the potential social benefits of Google Books and allowed Google time to modify the settlement to address the concerns raised.

Conficker lurks. Throughout 2009, a malicious computer program called Conficker remained active on the Internet. The program, which first appeared in November 2008, eventually spread to millions of computers in more than 200 countries. Similar in nature to a computer virus, Conficker exploited loopholes in Windows security systems. It also updated its code several times, using sophisticated programming techniques to evade detection and deletion.

Conficker also made it possible to link together the infected computers, forming a powerful system known as a botnet. Experts worried that there were criminals behind the program who could use this botnet to conduct various illegal activities, from generating huge amounts of *spam* (unsolicited e-mail) to stealing credit card information and passwords. Experts also noted the use of botnets in full-scale cyberwarfare between countries—such as when Russia attacked Estonia's computer infrastructure in 2007—and wondered whether a state government was behind Conficker.

Conficker's scale and effectiveness prompted various computer experts to begin working together, seeking to halt its spread and figure out who was behind it. The group of experts kept a close watch on Conficker throughout 2009. They could not, however, trace the program back to a human source. Although Conficker's botnet remained a potential threat, it was not used in any major criminal operation.

Microsoft's search. In May 2009, Microsoft released a search engine called Bing. Search engines, one of the main ways people navigate the Internet, respond to keywords typed in by users with a list of relevant Web sites.

Microsoft's new search engine was widely seen as a challenge to Google, which owns the most popular search engine. Bing offers similar features to Google's search engines. Unlike Google's sparse white background, Bing features a rotating assortment of striking photographs.

Companies make money from search engines by selling ads that run alongside the list of search results. Microsoft, which makes most of its money selling software programs that run on computers, had failed for years to make inroads into the search advertisement market dominated by Google. Microsoft had tried to purchase Yahoo!, which runs another popular search engine, to better compete on Google's turf.

The next wave. In September, Google released a preliminary version of a new form of Internet communication called Google Wave. A wave is a shared space that a number of users can access from their Web browsers. They can use a wave to type e-mail-like messages to one another or—if they are online at the same time—to have real-time conversations similar to instant messages. A wave can also function as a document or photo collection that several users can edit at once.

Google hoped that waves would replace e-mails as the central form of online communication, arguing that the concept of e-mail was built around now-outdated technology. Google released the code for Wave as open source— that is, anyone is allowed to view or modify it. The company sought to establish Wave as a "protocol," allowing other companies to provide their own wave services that nevertheless all work together—much the same way e-mails can be sent to and from different providers.

Net neutrality. In September, the United States Federal Communications Commission (FCC) proposed a new governing principle for Internet providers that prohibits blocking or charging extra for Internet traffic based on its content. This principle, often called net neutrality, was meant to ensure that the Internet remains a "democratic" place where all bits of information are treated equally. The main Internet service providers (ISP's) are such large telecommunications companies as AT&T and Comcast.

The FCC had previously adopted four principles related to net neutrality, which gave consumers the right to use Internet content and devices of their choosing. The principles also intended to promote competition between ISP's. The latest proposal would go further, ensuring that an ISP, for example, could not charge extra for access to a competitor's Internet content.

"Three strikes" antipiracy laws met with opposition in Europe and New Zealand throughout 2009, but were successfully adopted in France in October. The laws were so named because they proposed to disconnect Internet access for people guilty of three copyright violations, such as illegal file-sharing.

The French law, called Hadopi, gave a judge authority to disconnect Internet access, similar to the way traffic courts restrict drivers' licenses. Critics worried such laws would be used as blunt instruments, arguing that Internet access is a fundamental right, similar to such other utilities as water and electricity. In November, countries in the European Union (EU) agreed to a broad framework, outlawing cuts to Internet access without legal review. ■ Daniel Kenis

See also **Computer; Telecommunications.**

Constant Comments:
What's All the Twitter About?

Bystanders capture images of demonstrations that erupted in Iran following the highly contested presidential election in June 2009. Despite government attempts to restrict journalists from reporting the turmoil, people managed to evade the censors by downloading cell phone images of the violence on social networking sites.

By Cassie Mayer

On June 12, 2009, the supreme leader of Iran, Ayatollah Ali Khamenei, acknowledged incumbent President Mahmoud Ahmadinejad the winner of the presidential election. The announcement was made only hours after voting stations closed, despite the fact that the record 39 million ballots cast required manual counting. Outraged by the presumed rigging of the election, hundreds of thousands of supporters of reformist candidate Mir Hussein Moussavi and other candidates took to the streets in protest. Clashes soon erupted between government forces and citizens during massive demonstrations in cities throughout Iran.

The Iranian government, which prior to the election had blocked access to some Web sites, quickly responded to the protests by restricting text-messaging services on cell phones to prevent opposition forces from organizing. In addition, the regime banned international journalists from reporting and threatened to retaliate against protesters with brute force. Yet some Iranians, with the help of sympathizers outside Iran, were able to work around such censorship measures. Armed with cell phones or other mobile devices, they sent text messages, photographs, and videos documenting the brutality of the regime's crackdown against people on the streets.

Home   Profile   Friends   Inbox

Social media tools allow people to connect in ways previously unimaginable, but at what price?

One such video graphically showed the death of a young woman, later identified as Neda Agha-Soltan, who was hit by a stray bullet. The video circulated over the Internet through social networking sites and *blogs* (Web sites on which an author posts written entries) and was reported on by major international news organizations. It was also posted on YouTube, a free video-sharing site. Agha-Soltan quickly became a symbol of the Iranian protests, helping to rally opposition forces against the ruling clerics.

Before the early 2000's, no such video would likely have been seen outside Iran. But the proliferation of mobile devices with text, photo, and video capabilities, combined with the widespread use of social networking sites on which users can instantly post and share information and media, have produced scores of "citizen journalists" who are not easily contained by even the most sophisticated censorship apparatuses.

As the world witnessed during the Iranian protest movement, a new, tech-savvy generation has expanded the uses of social media tools in ways the developers of such tools never imagined. Such Web sites as Facebook, Twitter, YouTube, and others demonstrate how social media allow the world to share information today.

By 2009, a variety of social networking Web sites had created thousands of virtual communities, where users may keep in touch with friends or connect with people who share common interests. On many social networking Web sites, members create a personal profile, which may include biographical information, lists of likes and dislikes (such as favorite movies, books, and music), photographs, and other media. The site allows users to find others with similar profiles, creating links between users.

spinescape

music

presentation

pictures

msc

swatches

work

styles

☺friendster.

Though social networking Web sites were first developed in the mid-1990's, it was not until the launch of Friendster in March 2003 that the sites became widely popular. Developed by a California-based computer programmer as a way for users to meet new people and connect with friends, Friendster signed up 3 million registered users within six months of its launch. Members could search through the site's database to find people to whom they could send friend requests. When two people confirmed that they were friends, they could view each other's list of friends. From there, a user could send additional friend requests and make new connections.

Friendster, launched in March 2003, was the first social networking site to gain widespread popularity. It allowed members to establish connections by "friending" each other and each other's friends.

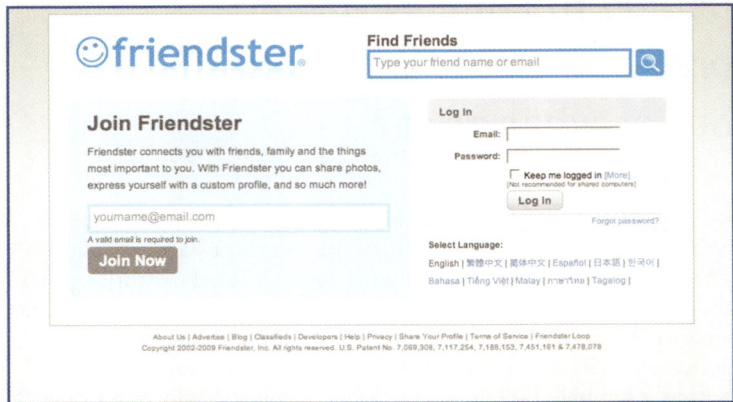

Friendster set the template for the basic features of many social networking sites that came into use in the early 2000's. Members of Friendster each had a profile page, where they could display such personal information as city of residence, birthday, and activities and write a short autobiography. Profile pages also contained "testimonials"—statements or anecdotes written by friends about the person.

In 2009, Friendster reported more than 110 million members worldwide—the majority of them in Asia. The site continued to add new features and applications to compete with other social networking sites. However, technological problems early in the site's history, such as the slow downloading of pages, allowed other social networking sites to eclipse Friendster in popularity in the United States.

👥myspace.

The author:
Cassie Mayer is associate manager of World Book Supplementary Publications.

MySpace, the first serious rival to Friendster, was launched in August 2003 and contained features similar to Friendster. However, MySpace allowed open access to member profiles, whereas Friendster limited profile access to people within one's own network. Thus, it was easier for members on MySpace to make connections with people they didn't already know. In addition, MySpace allowed users to customize the design of their profile page and to add such features as music clips, embedded video, or a personal blog. By 2009, MySpace, which reported 130 million members worldwide, had become a popular forum for bands to connect with fans—or for new bands to establish a fan base—and to advertise upcoming shows and new music.

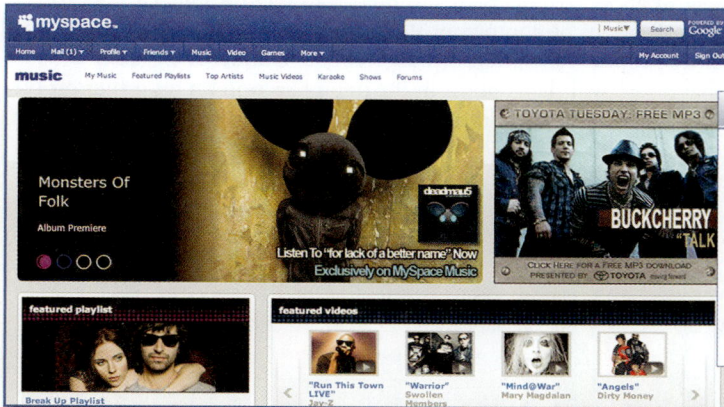

MySpace, launched in August 2003, gave members the opportunity to personalize their pages to a greater degree than Friendster. Users can add music clips, embedded video, and other features.

In 2004, as MySpace continued to expand its membership, several Harvard undergraduates developed a Web site that allowed students at Harvard—and, later, at universities across the United States and around the world—to connect online. They named it Facebook, a nickname for the book containing student photographs and personal information commonly distributed to college freshmen at private colleges. By late 2006, Facebook had opened its membership to anyone 13 years old or older.

In 2009, Facebook was the most popular social networking site in many countries of the world. In July, the company reported about 250 million users. By mid-September, that number had reached 300 million. Although Facebook, MySpace, and Friendster all have the same basic features, some users find Facebook easier to navigate than MySpace and more engaging than Friendster. Facebook has attracted a wide range of age groups, moving beyond the teen and 20-something set and quickly gaining a fan base among middle-aged users. Facebook also has a large international membership, with more than 70 percent of its users residing outside the United States.

Facebook is organized around status updates—brief comments that are often used to describe a person's mood or what they are currently doing. When members log into Facebook, they are taken to their home page, which contains a feed of status updates from their friends.

Friends can write comments in response to a person's status update, which are then displayed within the feed. The home page also includes sections that show recent requests from friends, such as invitations to social events or suggestions for organizations the member may wish to join.

Each member also has a profile page, which contains such personal information as relationship status, religious views, place of work, and a list of fan pages for authors, musicians, or certain organizations to which the member subscribes. Members can also upload to their profile page photo "albums" (collections of photographs), and add captions and tags (labels) that identify people in the photo. (If a Facebook member is tagged in a photo, that photo will then appear in the photos section on his or her profile page.) Friends can also add comments to photos, regardless of whether they appear in the photo.

The main feature of the profile page is the Wall—a mini-feed that displays the person's recent Facebook activity, such as status updates, photo

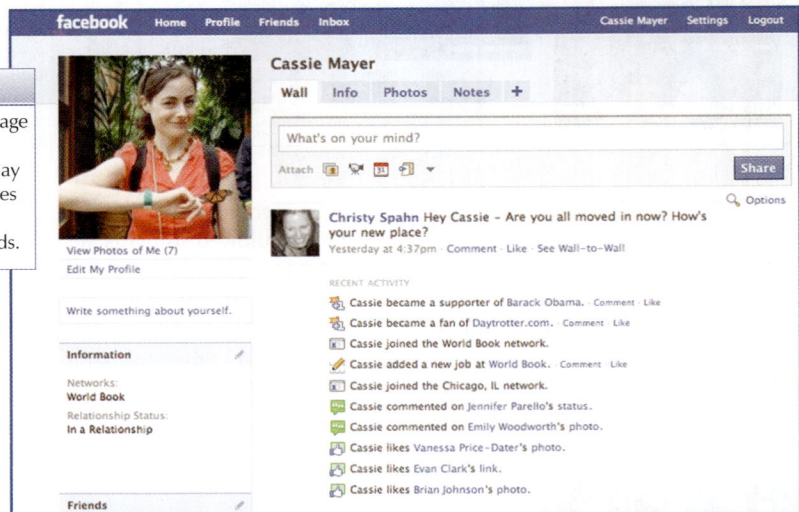

A user's Facebook page includes a feature called the Wall. It may contain status updates and photos and messages from friends.

uploads, changes to personal information, and messages from friends. (In Facebook jargon, people "write" on each other's Walls. Their messages can then be viewed by anyone who visits the person's profile page.)

In addition to the Wall, Facebook offers a variety of ways for users to keep in touch with one another, such as e-mail and instant messaging (IM), where users can send messages in real time. Users can also "poke" one another, which is akin to a virtual shoulder tap; use the "like" feature (a thumb's up icon) to show that they like a friend's status update; or purchase and send "gifts"—virtual greeting cards. Facebook has numerous other features and applications, including games and a Notes section on the profile page, which allows users to post text and images in a blog format.

Although members may use Facebook primarily to keep up with friends, there are many features that allow users to connect with people who share common interests. Users may join networks, which are often based around city of residence, school affiliation, or employer. People within the same network can view each other's profiles and write comments on the network's home page. Members can also join and form groups, where people who share similar interests can connect. Many groups feature favorite authors, musicians, or hobbies, or serve as professional networking sites. In addition, users may subscribe to any number of fan pages, which range from professional pages designed to advertise for companies or television shows, to silly, free-form message boards where subscribers can commiserate on their love for—or hatred of—a particular theme or topic (for example, "I Hate Mosquitoes").

Posting personal information on such semi-public forums as Facebook or MySpace is not without its risks. A disparaging remark about a colleague, friend, or employer may eventually be seen by the wrong person. Potential employers have used such sites to get a sense of a job candidate's personality and judgment. In some cases, photos revealing inappropriate behavior have cost potential employees a job.

A Tech-savvy
President

During the heated 2008 primary for the nomination of the Democratic presidential candidate, United States Senator Barack Obama's campaign recruited an army of supporters via e-mail, text messages, and social networking sites. The Obama campaign even announced Obama's selection of Joe Biden as the vice presidential candidate via Twitter. The candidate himself, rarely seen without his Blackberry, seemed to embody a new generation of innovative and technologically savvy citizens.

Since President Obama took office in January 2009, his media staff has continued to use social technologies to inform citizens about the administration's agenda. The White House's official Web site, Whitehouse.gov, includes a blog, videos, and links to official Obama-related media on such Web sites as Facebook, Twitter, MySpace, and YouTube. President Obama's media team also uploads photographs of the president and his family to Flickr, a free photo-sharing site. The White House has its own YouTube channel, where users may view professionally filmed videos of the president's weekly addresses to the nation, speeches, and other official appearances. Such items are also available as audio and video files on iTunes.

The Obama administration has also tracked how social media tools are affecting politics outside the United States. During the Iranian protests in June 2009, members of the Obama administration recognized the key role that Twitter was playing as a communication tool for protesters. A State Department official contacted Twitter and asked the company to delay scheduled maintenance of the site, so that Iranians could continue to share information with each other and the world about the protests in Tehran. Twitter complied with the request.

twitter

One of the most talked-about social networking sites in 2009 was Twitter, a free microblogging service launched in July 2006 that took the concept of the status update and made it the main feature. Often described as a "one-to-many" network, Twitter allows users to send short messages—called tweets—in real time to hundreds, thousands, or even millions of users at once. Messages are limited to 140 characters and may be sent or received via computer, cell phone, or other mobile device.

The social networking site Twitter is based on tweets, messages limited to 140 characters. Users can tweet each other or follow the tweets of celebrities, politicians, and organizations.

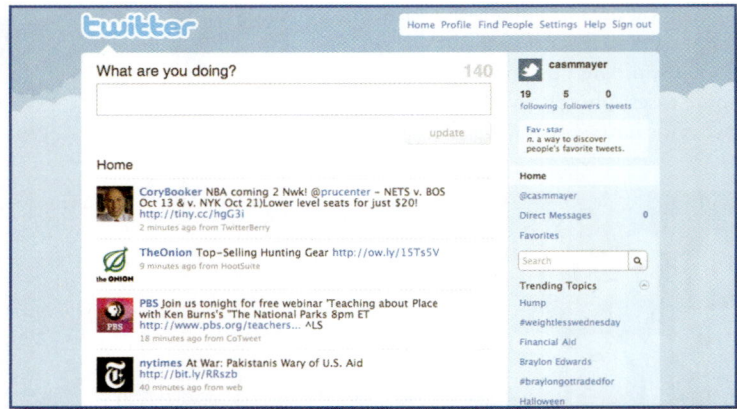

Users may search Twitter's database to find any number of individuals, organizations, celebrities, and politicians whose tweets they wish to follow. (Some of the most-followed Twitter feeds in mid-2009 included the Cable News Network [CNN], U.S. President Barack Obama, the actor Ashton Kutcher, *The New York Times,* and the band Coldplay.) Users may also sign up to receive a feed of Twitter postings related to a certain topic, such as a headline news story. Tweets from selected individuals or organizations automatically feed into a user's Twitter account.

Because of the 140-character limit, Twitterers may choose not to use punctuation and often use abbreviations and symbols instead of words. For example, many Twitterers use the + sign instead of "and." Another key symbol is the hashtag. (Hash refers to the hash mark, which is the symbol #; tag is a virtual label.) Hashtags allow people to tag tweets that pertain to a particular event or topic. Those tweets can then be grouped together by using the search.twitter.com feature. For example, at a conference event that included a Twitter feed, the presenter could assign the event a name to use as a hashtag (such as #wb233), so that both attendees and people not able to attend could share their notes and follow one another's tweets.

Among regular Twitter users, a unique culture and code of conduct has developed. Most Twitterers are happy to have others repost their tweets. However, it is considered common courtesy to retweet (RT)—

that is, to credit the person by posting his or her name in the tweet and linking to the original Twitterer's account. Twitter fans have also formed Tweetups—social gatherings (in the physical world) of people who had previously only known each other through Twitter. Such events have become popular in numerous cities.

Although some critics have questioned Twitter's usefulness, the immediacy of Twitter feeds has numerous applications. Twitter can be used to instantly relay public safety alerts during such emergencies as fires and earthquakes and to broadcast real-time news developments. Some politicians use Twitter to inform constituents about the day-to-day dealings of government or to rally support for their causes. In addition, businesses can use the service to communicate with customers, to find out what people think of their brand or products, to suggest products that may be useful to a particular customer, or to offer discounts or special promotions.

You Tube ™

Anyone who has been sent videos via e-mail or viewed them online has likely used YouTube, a video-sharing Web site launched in 2005. On the site, users may view, upload (post), and download video. YouTube's content is as diverse as its users. Individuals can post such personal expressions as video diaries (vlogs), comedy sketches, or footage of their favorite bands. Commonly watched videos include clips from old TV shows, homemade how-to videos, and films by aspiring and professional artists.

Although YouTube is not considered a social networking site, it contains several features similar to other online communities. Users may post comments and rate the videos they watch, organize their favorite videos using tags, create playlists, save videos to their favorites list, and e-mail video links to friends. In addition, they can post videos onto other Web pages, such as a blog or social networking site. Although most videos are accessible to anyone, users may adjust the settings so that the videos they post may only be viewed by members who have been invited to see them.

YouTube has many tools that facilitate content searches. A user may type a keyword into the search box, such as "Muppet Show." The page will then list all Muppet Show-themed videos on the site. There is also a "related videos" window, which displays links to videos with similar content to ones previously watched by the viewer. Users may also search by channel—individuals or organizations that post public videos.

Because of YouTube's immediacy and accessibility, some videos have generated instant news stories that otherwise would have gone unnoticed. In 2005, video footage of a virtuoso guitarist playing a rock version of German composer and organist Johann Pachelbel's *Canon*

A rendition of Canon Rock posted on YouTube in 2005 became an instant hit as viewers marveled over the virtuoso performance of an unknown guitarist who called himself Funtwo. By mid-2009, the clip had been viewed more than 63 million times.

(published in the late 1600's) began to circulate on the Internet; by mid-2009, the performance of Canon Rock by Funtwo had been viewed more than 63 million times. The musician was later identified as Lim Jeong-Hyun, a South Korean university student. On April 11, an unknown Scottish singer, Susan Boyle, performed "I Dreamed a Dream" on the television show *Britain's Got Talent.* Boyle's powerful voice, in contrast with her plain appearance, created such a sensation that videos of her audition posted on YouTube resulted in a record 100 million hits in nine days. Her unpublished album became a best seller in pre-sales on the Internet retail site Amazon.com.

Although YouTube has brought fame to some individuals, it has also been the cause of peril for others, such as politicians who make gaffes that, pre-YouTube, likely would not have become news stories. In 2006, Senator George Allen (R., Virginia), while campaigning for the position of governor of Virginia, called an audience member of Indian descent a "macaca." The meaning of the term is controversial, but in some cultures, it is considered a racial slur. Although Allen denied such allegations, he lost the election to Democratic candidate Jim Webb, despite having had a double-digit lead in the polls prior to the incident.

The ease with which people may now create and publish videos has spawned new genres of video. One of the earliest YouTube phenomena was the mash-up, where users respond to a video by adding to it or creating their own version. Newer YouTube-spawned genres include "fail" videos—videos that show failed attempts at such tasks as parking, driving, and dancing, or general moments of embarrassment—and "haul" videos, in which people show off new purchases.

In November 2006, less than a year after the site's launch, YouTube was purchased by Google Inc. of Mountain View, California. By late 2006, the number of visitors to the site had grown so numerous that mainstream television networks were seeking ways to promote programs by making clips of shows available on the site. By 2009, YouTube had deals with CBS, the BBC, Universal Music Group, Sony Music Group, Warner Music Group, the NBA, and the Sundance Channel, among other organizations.

New uses and growing concern

As social networking sites grow in popularity, many have become more customized to better accommodate users' needs and interests. On LinkedIn, a professional networking site, members create a professional profile, where they can list their work experience, education, and professional recommendations, among other information. The site also has a search bar, where people can search by name, keyword, industry, company name, or location for companies and professionals. By mid-2009, LinkedIn had more than 45 million members worldwide.

Businesses large and small are beginning to use social networking sites to create online communities centered around their company or products. By forming fan pages or developing Twitter followers, businesses can create advertisements that often have a more personalized, casual feel than traditional print or TV ads. A restaurant may have its head chef tweet about a special fish he or she purchased for the evening's menu. Such advertisements give users the feeling of connection to the business. This form of advertising has been a boon to small businesses that may not be able to pay for advertising and that can benefit from Twitter's word-of-mouth. Businesses can also use Twitter to research customers' preferences. A business could do a search of their company to see what messages people have posted about their brand or product.

On Facebook, businesses target their ads to a specific audience using such filters as location, age, sex, keywords, education, relationship status, and languages. They also create "engagement" ads, which ask users to become fans of their product or company. If a Facebook user became a fan of the television show "Mad Men," he or she would receive promotional messages, such as information about the next week's episode, which can then be viewed by friends within their network.

As more people use social technologies to post personal information, and as businesses look for ways to capitalize on the data on social networking sites, the question of who owns such data has become a growing concern. In early 2009, Facebook announced new service terms that many felt gave the company too much commercial control over the site's content. Facebook later revised the terms, but it maintains the right to license, copy, and distribute members' content.

In September 2009, Facebook settled a class-action lawsuit over its use of an advertising system that tracked users' activities on partner Web sites, such as Blockbuster and Overstock.com. The system fed information about users' purchases into their Facebook feed. Facebook executives said the system was meant to serve as yet another way for friends to see each other's actions. However, many Facebook users disliked having their off-site activities monitored and published. In the settlement, Facebook agreed to dismantle the system and paid $9.5 million to establish a foundation that will promote online privacy and security.

Despite such privacy concerns, users of such tools as Twitter are moving social technologies toward public access of personal information. In the years to come, people may find there is a lot more at stake when they "reach out and touch someone"—and a myriad of ways to do it.

Iran. International tension continued in 2009 regarding Iran's program to enrich uranium for use as nuclear fuel. Officials with the United Nations (UN)—concerned that Iran might use the fuel to build nuclear weapons—sought to pressure Iran to halt all enrichment activities. Iranian officials resisted this pressure by insisting that they wished to enrich uranium only for the generation of electric power.

In September, Iranian officials revealed the existence of a previously secret site for uranium enrichment at the base of a mountain near the city of Qom. A report by the UN's International Atomic Energy Agency (IAEA) responded to this disclosure with the statement, "Iran's declaration of the new facility reduces the level of confidence in the absence of other [undeclared] nuclear facilities under construction."

In November, Iranian President Mahmoud Ahmadinejad announced plans to construct 10 new uranium enrichment plants. However, the Iranian president said details of the plants would remain secret. The announcement came after IAEA Director General Mohamed ElBaradei censured Iran for not cooperating with the agency.

Iranian officials also rejected an IAEA plan—supported by the United States and its allies—to ship some of Iran's enriched uranium abroad to be reprocessed into fuel for a medical research reactor in Iran. The Iranian officials demanded "objective guarantees" that Iran would receive the refined fuel for research at the reactor.

Election results rock Iran. Results of the June presidential election, as announced by the Iranian Ministry of Interior, gave President Ahmadinejad 62.6 percent of the vote and former Prime Minister Mir Hussein Moussavi, his main challenger, 33.7 percent of the vote. Moussavi, who had been leading in preelection public opinion votes, was an opponent of the strict enforcement of Islamic attire and social conduct imposed by the ruling regime.

Moussavi's supporters and other opponents of President Ahmadinejad staged massive demonstrations in Tehran, Iran's capital, and other cities after the announcement of the election results, which were widely viewed as fraudulent. On June 15, Moussavi and almost 1 million other people attended a rally in Tehran—making the gathering the largest demonstration in Iran since the 1979 Islamic Revolution.

A video showing the shooting and killing of a young woman at a demonstration on June 20, 2009, rallied Iranian and international opposition to the Iranian regime after it was posted on the Internet. Demonstrations continued throughout the rest of 2009. ■ Marius Deeb

See also **Disasters; Internet: A Special Report; Middle East: A Special Report; United Nations.**

Iraq. Terrorists staged numerous bombings and other attacks in Iraq in 2009, many of which appeared to be of a *sectarian* (affiliated with a sect) nature. In February, a female suicide bomber blew herself up south of Baghdad, the Iraqi capital, killing about 40 Shi`ite pilgrims who were walking in an annual procession toward the holy city of Karbala. The bombing was the deadliest of several attacks against Shi`ite pilgrims in 2009.

Two separate suicide bombings took place on April 23. The first occurred in Baghdad at a humanitarian aid distribution point, where police were distributing Iraqi Red Crescent food parcels to mainly Shi`ite residents. The attack killed about 20 people. The second suicide bombing took place at a crowded restaurant north of Baghdad, in Diyala province, killing about 55 people. The following day, suicide bombings killed about 70 people outside the most important Shi`ite shrine in Baghdad—that of Imam Musa al-Kazim. Among the dead were 25 Iranian pilgrims. In June, a series of terrorist bombings and other attacks left more than 430 Iraqis dead—the highest monthly death toll in almost a year.

A number of bombings in 2009 targeted Iraqi government institutions and buildings. In August, on the sixth anniversary of the bombing of the United Nations headquarters in Baghdad, three simultaneous, coordinated car bombings and mortar strikes took place in the Iraqi capital, killing some 130 people. Investigators noted that the bombings appeared to be aimed at the ministries of foreign affairs and finance. In October, two synchronized car bombings damaged government buildings in the capital, including the justice ministry and the provincial council complexes. At least 150 people were killed. Coordinated blasts on December 8 at several government sites in Baghdad left more than 125 people dead.

The terrorist bombings of 2009 were widely seen as attempts to undermine the power of Iraqi Prime Minister Nouri Kamel al-Maliki by showing that he was not in control of the country. The prime minister had tried to portray Iraq as having "turned the corner" on the internal violence that wracked the country in 2006 and 2007, and he had even ordered the removal of protective blast walls from many streets in Baghdad.

Elections. Provincial elections were held in January 2009 in 14 of Iraq's 18 *governorates* (provinces). For the first time since the United States-led invasion of Iraq in 2003, international election observers were present in all 712 constituencies. According to these observers, the elections were fair and took place in a relatively peaceful atmosphere. More than 14,000 candidates representing some 400 political parties—three-quarters of which were newly created—competed for 444 local and provincial offices.

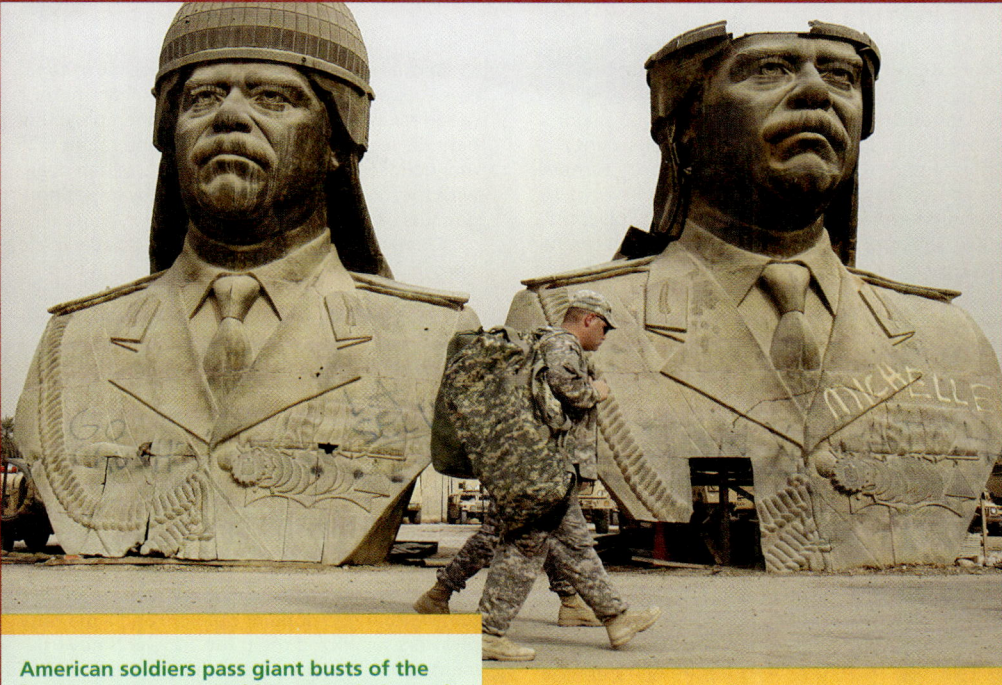

American soldiers pass giant busts of the former Iraqi tyrant Saddam Hussein in Baghdad's Green Zone in March. The U.S. military handed over control of the Green Zone—site of Iraqi government offices—to Iraqi authorities in January and pulled out of Baghdad and other major cities in June.

Prime Minister Maliki was the principal victor in the elections. His State of Law coalition captured a 38-percent majority of the vote in Baghdad and 37 percent of the vote in Basra, the second largest city in Iraq. The coalition's members ran on a platform of restoring law and order, rather than focusing on religious themes. Although Prime Minister Maliki's government in 2008 cracked down on the forces of Muqtada al-Sadr, an influential radical Shi`ite cleric, the prime minister's coalition allied itself with al-Sadr during the 2009 elections. Experts noted that the purpose of this alliance was to prevent another party, Al-Mihrab Martyr List, from retaining control of nine Shi`ite provinces in southern Iraq and challenging the power of the central government. Al-Mihrab Martyr List represented the Shi`ite Supreme Islamic Iraqi Council (SIIC).

The SIIC, which had entered the 2009 elections with the greatest number of seats in the Iraqi parliament and control of the southern Shi`ite provinces, did not win a single province in the 2009 elections. However, because the Iraqi electoral system requires proportional representation, the SIIC continued to be represented in the southern provinces—though it held fewer seats than the State of Law coalition.

2010 election legislation. In November, Iraqi Vice President Tariq al-Hashemi vetoed legislation required to hold national elections in January 2010. The vice president argued that the legislation would have *disenfranchised* (taken representation away from) Iraqi *refugees* (those living abroad), most of whom were Sunni Muslims.

In December 2009, Iraqi lawmakers agreed on a formula for religious and ethnic representation in a new parliament—clearing the way for elections in early 2010. New legislation increased the total number of parliamentary seats from 275 to 325, allowing for more Sunni representation without decreasing the number of Kurdish seats. Kurds are an ethnic group living in a mountainous region of southwest Asia. The legislation also allowed votes of Iraqis abroad to be counted as being from their provinces of origin.

U.S.-Iraq relations. A new U.S. embassy opened in Baghdad in January 2009. The structure, the largest embassy in the world, cost more than $700 million and occupied a vast swath of real estate in the heart of the Iraqi capital. Since 2004, the U.S. embassy staff had occupied one of the Baghdad palaces of deposed President Saddam Hussein. The palace was turned over to the Iraqis when the new U.S. embassy was completed. At a ceremony to inaugurate the new embassy complex, U.S. Deputy Secretary of State John Negroponte spoke of a "partnership for generations" between the United States and Iraq.

United States troops pulled out of 15 major Iraqi cities in June 2009, handing over security enforcement to Iraqi forces. The security turnover was based on the Status of Forces Agreement reached between Iraq and the United States in 2008. The agreement also set a goal of December 2011 for U.S. forces to pull out of Iraq.

To mark the June 2009 milestone, the Iraqi government declared a national holiday. Celebrations included parades and fireworks in Baghdad and other Iraqi cities.

Water shortage. Iraqis in the southern part of the country struggled with a severe water shortage in 2009. The shortage was caused by unusually scarce rainfall during the previous two years and disruptions in water distribution stemming from the war. The water shortage—and resulting low water levels in the Euphrates River—affected not only drinking and agricultural supplies but also electric power in the region, which depends on hydroelectric dams on the river. The water supply of the Euphrates River in Iraq was also depleted by the building of new dams and reservoirs on and along the river in Iran, Syria, and Turkey.   ■ Mary-Jane Deeb

See also **Armed forces; Middle East; Syria; Terrorism.**

Ireland. Events in the Republic of Ireland in 2009 were dominated by the worldwide economic downturn and by a second referendum on the Lisbon Treaty, an agreement to reform the structure of the European Union (EU). Prime Minister Brian Cowen's coalition government—made up of his Fianna Fáil party, the Green Party, and the Progressive Democrats—became increasingly unpopular because of the recession. Cowen had become prime minister *(taoiseach)* in 2008, taking over from Fianna Fáil's Bertie Ahern, who had led the country since 1997.

Ireland's economy had moved into recession in September 2008, partly because of the global financial crisis but also because of a decline in homebuilding and sales and consumer spending and investment. The impact of the recession was particularly dramatic because of the prosperity the "Celtic Tiger" had enjoyed over the previous 15 years. EU economists forecast that unemployment would rise to 11.7 percent in 2009 from 6 percent in 2008. The economy was expected to contract by 7.5 percent in 2009, after a 3-percent drop in 2008.

In January 2009, the government nationalized the Anglo-Irish Bank to secure its deposits. It rescued the Bank of Ireland in February. In September, the state-run National Asset Management Agency helped stabilize the nation's banks by buying bad debts of 77 billion euros ($115 billion).

Because the recession led to a decline in tax revenues, Finance Minister Brian Lenihan in April raised taxes, cut spending, halved unemployment benefits for people under age 20, and raised taxes on public sector pay. In December, Lenihan dealt with the 12-percent budget deficit by imposing pay cuts on public sector workers.

Elections. The government fared badly in elections in June. In local elections, the opposition party Fine Gael won the most votes. Fianna Fáil lost one of its seats in elections to the European Parliament and also did badly in two parliamentary by-elections. Fine Gael initiated a parliamentary vote of no confidence in the government, which the ruling coalition narrowly survived.

Lisbon Treaty. In 2008, voters rejected the Lisbon Treaty in a referendum required by Ireland's Constitution. The vote created a political crisis in Europe. After securing assurances from the EU about the protection of Irish sovereignty—a key voter concern—Cowen held a second referendum in October 2009. Economic concerns seemed to have changed popular opinion, and a majority of voters supported the treaty. Cowen's government nearly collapsed afterward, as the Green Party debated whether to remain in the coalition. The party voted to support the government in return for concessions.   ■ Rohan McWilliam

See also **Europe; Northern Ireland.**

Islam. On Nov. 29, 2009, a Swiss referendum resulted in a ban on *minarets* (towers attached to mosques) in Switzerland. The ban, which won 58 percent of the vote, will be added to Switzerland's Constitution, which also guarantees freedom of religion. The Swiss government said it would respect the referendum, though it had opposed the initiative, sponsored by conservative political parties.

Niqab controversy. In early October, rector Muhammad Tantawi of Egypt's Al-Azhar University ruled that the *niqab* (full-face covering) was unnecessary for women and was an exaggeration of more appropriate modesty requirements. The niqab was banned in female dormitories and all-female classrooms at the university. The Supreme Council of Al-Azhar University confirmed Tantawi's opinion, saying that it did not oppose the niqab, but it opposed "imprinting it on the minds of girls."

The government ministries of Pious Endowments and of Health also criticized the niqab. Their position met with an immediate response from the former head of Egypt's Fatwa Council and others. Technically, the issue was whether a practice that was "permitted" or even "encouraged" could be banned. Abdalhamid al-Atrash, a researcher at the Islamic Studies Institute in Cairo, said that the veil had been abused by activists.

"There have even been instances of men entering [schools for girls] under cover. So there is no reason why a ruling that benefits the people and the nation cannot be issued," al-Atrash said.

**Sunni-Shi`ite relations.** Throughout the summer of 2009, relations between Shi`ite and Sunni Muslims in various Muslim countries took a turn for the worse. In recent years, even followers of the hyper-rigorous Wahhabi sect in Saudi Arabia had worked toward a kind of Muslim *ecumenism* (movement for unity), and pressure on Shi`ites in Saudi Arabia, Kuwait, and Bahrain had lessened. But in February 2009, Saudi Shi`ite boys practicing mourning rituals in Medina's al-Baqui cemetery, where a number of early Shi`ite figures are buried, ran afoul of the Wahhabi religious police. The Wahhabis forbid any veneration of gravesites, considering it a form of idolatry.

This incident led to demonstrations in Saudi Arabia, Kuwait, and London. A group called Free Men of Qatif issued statements of defiance, and the Shi`ite Sheik Nimr al-Nimr gave a scathing sermon known as "the dignity speech," which circulated throughout the world on the Internet.

In Yemen in 2009, the Zaydi school of Shi`ah, whose leader had ruled northern Yemen for much of the last 1,000 years, continued its rebellion against President Ali Abdullah Saleh. Saleh has had the support of southern Yemeni Sunnis and, more recently, of Saudi Arabians and their Yemeni ideological compatriots, known as "al-Islah." The Zaydi Shi`ite leaders of what is known as the al-Huthi rebellion claim the right to be led religiously and politically by an imam of their own school. In 2009, Yemen also battled al-Qa`ida, whose ideology is close to al-Islah's.

Islamist movements in Nigeria, Somalia, and Indonesia sought to transform the social landscape in 2009. In late July, the Nigerian military raided and closed down the headquarters of the Islamist movement Boko Haram and arrested its leader, Muhammed Yusuf, who was later shot and killed while in custody. The government claimed that Boko Haram was a militant sect planning a military movement. Boko Haram asserted that it was not a political movement, but rather aimed at removing corrupt features of Western education from Muslim life. In August, Nigerian authorities raided the headquarters of another Shari`ah-oriented movement, Darul Islam, in Mokwa.

In Somalia, the al-Shabab (Youths) movement, which modeled itself on the Taliban in Afghanistan and formally had offered allegiance to Osama bin Laden, was increasingly successful in seizing urban areas and imposing Shari`ah (Islamic law) there. Although somewhat weakened by a feud with another Islamist group, Hizbul Islam, al-Shabab managed to take the port

city of Kismayo in October and impose its version of Shari`ah on its inhabitants.

Throughout 2009, in Aceh, Indonesia, Islamists pursued their agenda much more peacefully, using the political process to create an environment shaped by the norms of Shari`ah.

Islam in America. A survey published in August 2009 by the Pew Research Center, a Washington, D.C.-based nonpartisan public opinion organization, showed that of about 4,000 Americans polled, those most familiar with Islam had more favorable views of the religion. However, 38 percent of interviewees said that Islam, more than other faiths, encouraged violence.

A report on Muslim Americans published in 2009 by the Washington, D.C.-based Gallup Center for Muslim Studies indicated that Muslim Americans were the most racially diverse religious group in the United States. A majority of those surveyed labeled themselves as politically moderate or liberal. Muslim Americans had a higher degree of economic gender *parity* (equity) than other religious groups in the United States, but they were less likely than other groups to describe themselves as "thriving." However, compared with Muslims in other Western nations and predominantly Muslim countries, a higher percentage (41 percent) said they were "thriving."

■ A. Kevin Reinhart

Israel. Fighting between Israel and Hamas, a Palestinian militant organization that gained control of the Gaza Strip in 2007, continued in 2009. In December 2008, Hamas had declared that it would not renew its six-month cease-fire with Israel, and the organization began a series of rocket attacks on Israeli civilian centers. Israel responded with a military offensive dubbed Operation Cast Lead, which included air attacks on Hamas targets in Gaza.

In early January 2009, Israel launched a multipronged attack with three brigades—each supported by a squadron of unmanned aerial vehicles—entering the Gaza Strip and surrounding the strip's principal city, Gaza City. Battles raged between Israeli forces and Palestinian militants until mid-January, when a new cease-fire brokered by Egypt came into effect. Deaths resulting from Operation Cast Lead included 10 Israeli soldiers, 3 Israeli civilians, and more than 1,000 Palestinian combatants and civilians.

In September, the United Nations (UN) Fact-Finding Mission on the Gaza Conflict issued a lengthy report on the matter. Investigators analyzed numerous controversial incidents, including the firing by Israeli forces of white phosphorus shells (smoke-producing incendiary devices) and the alleged shooting by Israeli soldiers of civilians carrying white flags. The UN

Plumes of smoke rise from Israeli military strikes on Palestinian militants with the group Hamas in the Gaza Strip in January. Israeli forces staged a major offensive—involving artillery, helicopters, and tanks—in an unsuccessful attempt to crush Hamas, which had launched numerous rocket attacks against Israel.

commission concluded that both the Israeli forces and the Palestinian militants had committed "war crimes" during the fighting in Gaza.

Parliamentary elections. Some analysts of Israeli political affairs noted that Israel's military response to Hamas's provocations in Gaza in late 2008 was likely motivated by desires of Foreign Minister Tzipi Livni (leader of the Kadima Party) and Defense Minister Ehud Barak (leader of the Labor Party) to improve their parties' standings in public opinion polls ahead of February 2009 parliamentary elections. The election results, however, were most favorable to parties more closely associated with hard-line stances against Palestinian militants.

In the elections, the Kadima Party decreased its representation in the Knesset (Israeli parliament) from 29 to 28 seats, while the Labor Party decreased its representation from 19 to 13 seats. By contrast, the hard-line Likud Party, led by Benjamin Netanyahu, increased its representation in the Knesset from 12 to 27 seats, and the strongly nationalist Yisrael Beiteinu (Our Home

Israel) Party, led by Avigdor Lieberman, increased its representation from 11 to 15 seats.

Netanyahu's Cabinet. Because the Kadima Party maintained the largest number of seats in the Knesset, Israeli President Shimon Peres asked its leader, Foreign Minister Livni, to form a new Cabinet. However, political difficulties prevented her from doing so. Consequently, President Peres asked Likud Party leader Netanyahu to form the Cabinet, thereby designating Netanyahu as the new prime minister.

In April, Netanyahu announced that his Cabinet would comprise 15 ministers from Likud, 5 from Labor, 5 from Yisrael Beiteinu, and 5 from the ultra-Orthodox Shas Party. Labor Party leader Barak was given the defense portfolio, and Yisrael Beiteinu leader Lieberman was given the foreign affairs portfolio.

No progress on peace process. The administration of United States President Barack Obama attempted unsuccessfully to revive dormant Israeli-Palestinian peace negotiations in 2009. Former Senator George Mitchell, President

Obama's envoy for Arab-Israeli peace talks, made numerous visits to the Middle East, meeting with both Prime Minister Netanyahu and Palestinian President Mahmoud Abbas.

The Obama administration repeatedly pressured Prime Minister Netanyahu to freeze the construction of Israeli settlements in the West Bank and East Jerusalem, areas claimed by Palestinians. Prime Minister Netanyahu initially refused to comply with any part of President Obama's request—and even unveiled plans to build 900 new housing units in East Jerusalem. In late November, however, the Netanyahu administration announced a 10-month moratorium on approvals for new homes for Jews in the West Bank. Palestinians condemned the moratorium because it did not include East Jerusalem.

In addition, Prime Minister Netanyahu continued unsuccessfully to demand that Palestinian leaders recognize Israel as a "Jewish state." Such recognition would preempt efforts by Palestinians to exercise what they considered their "right of return"—that is, the right of Palestinian refugees from earlier wars with Israel (and their descendants) to move back to Israel.

Weapons shipment intercepted. The Israeli Navy intercepted the *Francop*, an Antigua-flagged cargo ship, off the coast of Cyprus in November. Upon inspection, Navy commandos discovered that the ship carried more than 3,000 rockets and munitions that Iran was sending to Hezbollah, a militant Islamic group supported by Iran and Syria and based in southern Lebanon. According to Israeli authorities, the shipment was destined for the Syrian port of Latakia, and from there it was to be transferred to Hezbollah.

The *Francop* shipment was a violation of UN Security Council Resolution 1701, which banned the transfer of any weapons to Hezbollah. The Security Council had passed that resolution after the end of the Hezbollah-Israel conflict of July-August 2006. ■ Marius Deeb

See also **Judaism; Middle East; Syria; United Nations.**

Italy. Prime Minister Silvio Berlusconi faced a cascade of personal and political scandals in 2009. Although his approval rating fell during the year, he and his center-right coalition government—made up of Berlusconi's People of Freedom party and the Northern League—continued to enjoy broad popular support.

Berlusconi's wife announced in May that she was seeking a divorce, after a long series of very public spats. Accusations that the prime minister had spent a night with a prostitute appeared in newspapers throughout the summer. Continued allegations of an improper relationship with an aspiring model led to a ruling by the Constitutional Court in October. The judges determined that a law passed by Berlusconi's government in 2008, granting the prime minister and other high government officials immunity from prosecution while in office, was unconstitutional.

The invalidation of the law reopened several trials implicating Berlusconi. He was accused of bribing a lawyer to give false testimony; charged with tax fraud in connection with one of his companies; and charged with attempting to bribe members of Parliament to join his coalition. Berlusconi proclaimed his innocence, arguing that the charges were politically motivated. His party's coalition partner, the Northern League, continued to support him, despite disagreements over policy.

In European parliamentary elections in June, Berlusconi's People of Freedom party won 35 percent of the vote, compared with 26 percent for the opposition center-left Democratic Party. Analysts observed that the prime minister's popularity remained high in part because of the disarray among Italy's left-of-center parties. Nevertheless, opposition leaders expressed concern that Berlusconi's legal troubles may hamper the government's ability to deal with the economic crisis. The Democratic Party faced its own scandal in October, when a founding member was blackmailed after being filmed in an encounter with an alleged prostitute.

The media. Berlusconi's critics charged that his popularity remained high in the face of continuing scandals because of his control over much of Italy's broadcast media. In 2009, his Fininvest company's holdings included three national television channels, Italy's largest publishing house, and an advertising agency. Berlusconi's brother Paolo owned controlling interest in a daily newspaper. In addition, as prime minister, Berlusconi had influence over the state broadcasting network, RAI.

In October, after Berlusconi sued several newspapers for negative coverage of the allegations regarding his personal life, some 300,000 people throughout Italy protested over what they considered threats to freedom of the press. Berlusconi's supporters pointed out that one of the three state television channels was highly critical of him.

Economic crisis. Italy's banks appeared to be in better shape than many of their European counterparts at the beginning of the global economic crisis. However, it soon became clear that they were significantly exposed to risk through their investments in several banks in Eastern Europe. In January, the Cabinet approved a decree providing $17.8 billion to increase the supply of the banks' capital, should it become necessary.

At the same time, Italy's large public debt prevented it from introducing a stimulus package on the scale of several of its European partners. Italy's projected budget deficit for 2009 of 5.3 percent of GDP was low relative to other European Union members. (GDP—gross domestic product—is the value of all goods and services produced in a country in a year.) However, Italy had run large budget deficits for several years. Unemployment was forecast to rise to 7.8 percent from 6.8 percent in 2008.

In October 2009, Parliament approved a measure aimed at encouraging Italians who had avoided taxes by depositing undeclared funds abroad to repatriate their money to Italian banks. Anyone who did so by December and paid a tax would not be penalized. Critics argued that the measure—the third such amnesty in nine years—benefited organized crime and encouraged tax evasion. The government stated that the program would raise funds to offset the public debt.

Foreign policy. In September, six Italian soldiers were killed by a roadside bomb in Afghanistan. Berlusconi called for the withdrawal of all international troops from the conflict, but stated he would not withdraw the 3,200 Italian troops serving there without consulting his NATO partners.

Berlusconi continued a foreign policy friendly to Russia, from which Italy imports most of its natural gas. In October, he attended a private birthday party for Prime Minister Vladimir Putin, the only serving Western head of government to do so.

Disasters. On April 6, nearly 300 people were killed and over 65,000 others were left homeless when an earthquake hit Italy's Abruzzo region. To help draw relief efforts to the area, the prime minister moved the G-8 meeting of industrialized nations from the island of La Maddalena to L'Aquila, a city that was hit hard by the earthquake. The summit, held in July, was considered a success.

On October 1, torrential rains caused flash floods and landslides that swept away roads and caused buildings to collapse in the town of Messina in northeastern Sicily. At least 35 people were killed. A government official blamed illegal construction in an area with poor drainage for the tragedy. ■ Jeffrey Kopstein

See also **Disasters; Europe.**

Ivory Coast. See Côte d'Ivoire in **Africa.**
Jamaica. See **Latin America; West Indies.**

The coffins of more than 200 victims of an earthquake that struck Italy on April 6 lie in the town square of L'Aquila during a memorial service. Nearly 300 people died in the quake, most of them in L'Aquila, a medieval college city northeast of Rome.

Japan underwent a ballot-box revolution in 2009. In an election for the lower house of parliament on August 30, voters crushed the Liberal Democratic Party (LDP), which had governed the nation almost continuously since 1955. They gave power to the Democratic Party of Japan (DPJ). Its leader, Yukio Hatoyama, became prime minister on September 16, succeeding the LDP's Taro Aso.

The election was hailed by political observers as a likely beginning of two-party politics that might offer policy choices to voters. They noted that this could end years of unelected bureaucrats formulating government policies to suit LDP members' ties to big business interests. The DPJ said it would make political decisions favoring consumers over industrial conglomerates, with bureaucrats simply implementing them.

LDP rule had favored the industries that rebuilt Japan's economy after its ruin in World War II (1939-1945). Economic growth slowed by 1990, however, leading to long periods of stagnation. The LDP's failure to make enough reforms to stimulate the economy was a primary reason for its defeat, noted political experts.

Hatoyama's and Aso's grandfathers formed the LDP in 1955 by merging their two parties. Aso's grandfather had been prime minister, and Hatoyama's grandfather succeeded him after the merger. A split in the LDP, engineered mainly by Ichiro Ozawa, caused it to lose power in 1993. After 11 months, the new ruling coalition collapsed, and the LDP regained control.

The LDP continued its system of patronage politics as leaders of different factions fought over top jobs. When Aso became prime minister on Sept. 24, 2008, he was the fourth LDP leader to hold the post in two years. He quickly became the least popular.

Ozawa became a leader of what in 1998 became the DPJ. The party was a left-center collection of former socialists and disaffected LDP conservatives. Ozawa was credited with guiding the DPJ to victory in July 2007 elections for the less-powerful upper house of parliament, where the party could delay but not block legislation from the LDP-dominated lower house. However, Ozawa was forced to resign the party's presidency on May 11, 2009, after unsuccessfully attempting to distance himself from a scandal involving an aide accused of accepting illegal donations.

The DPJ presidency was taken by Hatoyama, an heir to both political prominence and an industrial fortune, with a doctorate in engineering from Stanford University in Stanford, California. He led the party to power after an unpopular Aso called parliamentary elections following an LDP defeat in July municipal elections in the capital, Tokyo.

DPJ victory. Ozawa, who was long known as a backroom manipulator, was again seen as the DPJ's mastermind for organizing the party's 2009 victory. The party won 308 of the 480 seats in the lower house, up from the 113 seats it had won in the previous election, in 2005. Two parties allied with the DPJ, the Social Democratic Party and the People's New Party, won another 10 seats. The LDP fell from 296 seats in 2005 to 119 in 2009. Aso resigned as LDP leader and was succeeded by former finance minister Sadakazu Tanigaki.

Previous political campaigns had been muddled, but in 2009 the DPJ issued a manifesto of its plans. It promised a better welfare system at a time of high unemployment and more retirees, plus generous child allowances to encourage families to have more children to offset a rapidly aging, dwindling population. With a national debt nearing twice the amount of Japan's gross domestic product, however, the party did not give details of how it proposed to pay for such programs. (Gross domestic product, or GDP, is the value of goods and services produced in a country in a given year.)

New leadership. Hatoyama named two former DPJ presidents to key cabinet posts. Katsuya Okada became foreign minister. Naoto Kan became deputy prime minister and head of a new agency intended to take decision making away from the bureaucracy. The agency, the National Strategy Bureau, would set budget guidelines and oversee policy actions. Ozawa became the party's secretary general, and political observers saw him as a key power behind Hatoyama's government.

Foreign relations. During the election campaign, the DPJ raised questions about Japan's dependence on the United States for security since the end of World War II. Hatoyama moved quickly after the election to reassure the U.S. government that he would not challenge the alliance. Despite this, the DPJ sought changes to defense agreements that kept some 50,000 American troops stationed in Japan. They had been considered indispensable during tensions with China and the former Soviet Union, but now Japan sought improved relations with its big neighbors. Japan continued to worry, however, about hostility from nearby, nuclear-armed North Korea.

As foreign minister, Okada ordered a probe into alleged secret security agreements with the United States. He said the Cold War-era agreements permitted nuclear-armed U.S. warships to use Japanese ports and allowed the United States to put nuclear weapons in Japan in emergencies. He also sought to revise an agreement on relocating a U.S. military base on Japan's island of Okinawa.

Some DPJ members suggested withdrawing Japanese support for U.S. military activity in Afghanistan. They suggested that Japan should only back military actions led by the United Nations.

Economy. In July 2009, Japan's unemployment

rate reached a record 5.7 percent, but late in the year, signs indicated that the country's deepest recession since World War II was ending. The country's economic strength had been built on exports of cars, electronics, and other manufactured goods. Exports plunged in February 2009 to only half their level a year earlier as the worldwide economic downturn cut demand. After three decades of exporting goods of more value than imports, the country fell into a trade deficit.

In the first quarter of 2009, Japan's GDP shrank at a record annualized rate of 14.2 percent. To encourage recovery, Prime Minister Aso in April announced an additional $154-billion stimulus package, the government's third such plan in a year.

A rise in exports and greater economic output in general by the third quarter of 2009 broke 12 months of decline. However, in November, the government announced that the economy was in a state of *deflation* (falling prices) for the first time since 2006. On Dec. 8, 2009, Prime Minister Yukio Hatoyama announced an additional $81-billion stimulus package to further protect Japan from slipping into a recession.

■ Henry S. Bradsher
See also **Asia; People in the news** (Yukio Hatoyama).

Jordan. King Abdullah II of Jordan in 2009 became the first Arab leader to have a summit with United States President Barack Obama. The two leaders met in Washington, D.C., in April. King Abdullah thanked President Obama for reaching out to Arabs and Muslims. Both leaders called for a comprehensive Middle East peace agreement, and they endorsed a two-state solution for the Israeli-Palestinian conflict.

Reports indicated that from January to late September, at least 12 Jordanian women were killed by their relatives for alleged immoral behavior and for consequently "dishonoring" the reputation of their families. Queen Rania of Jordan condemned these so-called "honor killings" as a violation of women's human rights and as "non-Islamic." The queen called for education to promote changes in public perceptions of the place and the value of women in society. She also called for stronger penalties in the law for individuals who commit these kinds of crimes against women.

Pope Benedict XVI visited Jordan in May as part of a pilgrimage to the Holy Land. The pope praised King Abdullah for allowing religious freedom in Jordan and for being at the forefront of promoting interfaith dialogue between Muslims and Christians. ■ Marius Deeb

See also **Israel; Middle East.**

Judaism. The global recession dominated headlines in 2009. Tough economic times necessitated strategic conversations regarding the future of Jewish organizations worldwide.

United States. The deepening recession and financial scandals dramatically impacted American Jewish nonprofit organizations. Estimates placed their monetary losses at 20 to 30 percent. The scandals led to calls for higher ethical standards and greater transparency in Jewish philanthropy. Some Jewish nonprofits shut down, while others adopted new strategies, including merging with their non-Jewish counterparts, attracting new donors, and focusing on volunteerism. The New York City-based umbrella organization known as the United Jewish Communities hired a new executive director and changed its name to the Jewish Federations of North America.

Financial scandals involving Jewish defendants sparked fears of anti-Semitism in 2009. Jewish businessman Bernard Madoff was indicted and found guilty in 2009 of defrauding thousands of investors, including Jewish foundations, of billions of dollars in a giant Ponzi scheme. A Ponzi scheme uses incoming investments to pay "profits" to earlier investors. In July 2009, a corruption scandal erupted in New Jersey involving some rabbis and members of the Syrian Jewish community in Brooklyn, New York.

On taking office, U.S. President Barack Obama articulated a new vision for peace between Israel and Palestinians. In May, the Obama administration advocated a freeze on Israeli settlement construction in the West Bank as an important step toward resuming Arab-Israeli peace talks, which broke down in 2003. In response, Israeli Prime Minister Benjamin Netanyahu proposed a 10-month moratorium on approvals for new homes for Jews in the West Bank. In November 2009, the Obama administration praised Israel's "unprecedented" gesture and urged the Palestinian Authority to return to the negotiating table.

Noteworthy ritual moments occurred in 2009. On April 8, Jews from all branches of Judaism throughout the United States recited the *Birkat Hachamah,* a blessing over the sun that is recited every 28 years. On April 9, President Obama hosted the White House's first Seder, a ceremonial meal commemorating the Passover holiday, for a small group of family, friends, and staff.

Israel. Israel's military campaign in the Gaza Strip, Operation Cast Lead, lasted from Dec. 27, 2008, to Jan. 17, 2009, when the government declared a cease-fire. Jewish communities around the world rallied to support this Israeli campaign to stop the firing of Qassam rockets into Israel by Palestinian militants. On September 15, a United Nations (UN) report authored by former South African judge Richard Goldstone accused both

Israel and the Palestinian group Hamas of committing war crimes during Operation Cast Lead. The report was particularly critical of Israel, which had refused to cooperate with a UN investigative body. The report created international controversy.

Israeli parliamentary elections on February 10 gave the Kadima party, led by Tzipi Livni, the most votes. But Benjamin Netanyahu's Likud party headed an alliance with the most combined seats in the legislature. For this reason, President Shimon Peres asked Netanyahu to form a government. Political pundits deemed Avigdor Lieberman's right-wing Yisrael Beiteinu party, which placed third, the big winner in the election. Lieberman became Netanyahu's foreign minister.

In a June 14 speech, Netanyahu publicly endorsed for the first time a two-state solution to the Arab-Israeli conflict. Netanyahu's solution included creating a demilitarized Palestinian state. In a September 24 speech delivered at the UN, Netanyahu responded to charges by Iranian President Mahmoud Ahmadinejad that the Holocaust, the Nazis' systematic genocide of Jews during World War II (1939-1945), was a fabrication. Netanyahu presented historical evidence of the Holocaust and pleaded that the international community confront Iran's nuclear threat.

■ Jonathan D. Sarna and Jonathan J. Golden
See also **Israel; Middle East; United Nations.**

Kenya.
Kenya. During 2009, Kenya's power-sharing government teetered on the brink of collapse. Rival politicians from President Mwai Kibaki's Party of National Unity and Prime Minister Raila Odinga's Orange Democratic Movement clashed repeatedly. The political infighting virtually paralyzed the government and raised the possibility of renewed instability and political violence.

The *coalition* (partnership) government had come into being on April 12, 2008. Earlier that year, ethnic clashes had erupted following the elections of 2007, which were widely regarded as rigged. About 1,500 people had died, and hundreds of thousands of others were forced from their homes. Most of the fighting involved the Kikuyu and the Luo, two of Kenya's largest ethnic groups. Kibaki is Kikuyu, and Odinga is Luo.

The lack of unity ensured that Kibaki and Odinga made little headway in 2009 to deal with long-neglected national issues. The most pressing problems included land reform, poverty, and the need for a new constitution. The next presidential and parliamentary polls were due in 2012.

Minister quits. Martha Karua—Kenya's minister for justice, national cohesion, and constitutional affairs—resigned from the coalition government on April 6, 2009. Karua claimed that coalition squabbling had hindered her program of reform and that President Kibaki had under-

mined her. Earlier that month, Kibaki had appointed five new judges and promoted two others without consulting her. Kibaki appointed Mutula Kilonzo to replace Karua.

Officials accused. On July 17, 2009, the state-run Kenya National Commission on Human Rights accused 219 civilians and security officials of causing the post-election violence in 2008. The suspects included Cabinet ministers and members of Parliament from both sides of the coalition government. However, the Cabinet ignored calls from within Kenya and from other countries to try the suspects at the International Criminal Court (ICC) in the Netherlands. Parliament also failed in its attempts to set up a special Kenyan court to try the suspects. Because Kenya had signed the ICC's founding charter, however, the ICC could force the government to send ministers, and even its president, to the ICC.

Fire deaths. At least 113 people died after an overturned oil tanker exploded and caught fire on January 31 near Molo in western Kenya. People had gathered to collect the fuel gushing out onto the road. Three days earlier, a fire at a Nairobi supermarket had killed up to 40 people. Newspapers criticized emergency services for responding slowly to the two tragedies.   ■ Simon Baynham
See also **Africa; Disasters.**

Kiribati.
Kiribati. See **Pacific Islands.**

Korea, North.
Korea, North. The government of North Korean leader Kim Jong-il caused international concern in 2009 by conducting missile tests and a nuclear weapons test. But later in the year, it seemed willing to return to international talks.

Tension. On January 30, the North announced that it would no longer honor political and military agreements with South Korea. On April 5, North Korea launched a missile that it claimed put a communications satellite into orbit. Western experts believed it was a failed test of a military missile and that it did not launch a satellite. The United Nations (UN), which had warned Kim's government against missile tests, tightened economic and financial sanctions on North Korea. The North then expelled UN nuclear monitors, said it had restarted its nuclear program, and quit international disarmament talks. In May, North Korea conducted another nuclear test and test-fired three missiles, further inflaming tensions.

Softening. Two American journalists working on a documentary about refugees fleeing North Korea were arrested on March 17 for violating the North's border with China. They were each sentenced to 12 years' hard labor. On August 4, former United States President Bill Clinton met Kim in Pyongyang, North Korea's capital, and secured the journalists' release. Soon after this meeting, relations between North and South Korea eased.

Former U.S. President Bill Clinton poses with North Korean leader Kim Jong-il (front right) in August, after Clinton secured the release of two American journalists who had been condemned to years of hard labor for crossing into North Korea from China.

Kim sent a delegation to the August 23 funeral of former South Korean President Kim Dae-jung, who had sought to improve relations between North and South. The delegates gave South Korea's president, Lee Myung-bak, a message that Kim wanted to improve ties with the South.

On September 1, the two countries resumed regular train service across their joint border for workers in the Kaesong industrial park, where South Korean businesses own factories that employ both North and South Korean workers. The head of one of those businesses met with Kim later that month to secure the release of an employee who had been detained for denouncing the North's government. Also in September, the Red Cross was allowed to resume a program that arranges reunions of families separated after the division of the Korean peninsula following the Korean War (1950-1953). The program, which was initiated in 2000, had been halted amid rising tensions in 2007.

Currency. In December 2009, North Korea's government *revaluated* (changed the value of) the country's currency, the won, to 1/1000 of its previous value. The government also limited the amount of old won each citizen could exchange for new won. The measure was intended to curb inflation and counteract a growing black market for currency.   ■ Henry S. Bradsher

See also **Asia; Korea, South; United Nations.**

Korea, South. Polling in 2009 showed public opinion turning against both South Korea's governing Grand National Party (GNP) and the opposition Democratic Party (DP). As members of parliament quarreled, public patience wore thin.

Politics. On January 6, opposition members of parliament called off a sit-in that had blocked GNP legislation since both parties' members battled with fire extinguishers and sledgehammers three weeks earlier. The DP fought against a free-trade agreement with the United States that it argued could harm South Korean farmers. DP members resumed obstructive tactics several months later, which led to new violence in parliament on July 22. Lawmakers screamed and wrestled as the DP tried to keep GNP members from getting into the National Assembly to pass legislation relaxing restrictions on ownership of television stations.

President Lee Myung-bak replaced Prime Minister Han Seung-soo on September 3 with an American-educated economist, Chung Un-chan. Lee also replaced his defense minister, with whom he had a public falling-out over military spending.

The economy in 2009 underwent one of the world's fastest and strongest recoveries from the international economic downturn. In the third quarter, South Korea's economy grew faster than it had in 7 ½ years. Finance minister Yoon Jeung-hyun introduced a supplementary budget with

$20.9 billion to stimulate business activity.

Kim Dae-jung, who had been South Korea's president from 1998 to 2003, died on August 18. An opponent of South Korea's military dictatorships in the 1960's and 1970's, Kim was the first opposition leader elected president.

In 2000, Kim met in North Korea with leader Kim Jong-il in an effort to ease hostilities between the Communist North and the democratic South. The meeting was the first ever between the leaders of the two countries, and Kim Dae-jung won the Nobel Peace Prize for his efforts to ease the rift. The achievement was later clouded by the revelation that some $500 million had been channeled to the North in dubious business deals that apparently bought Kim Jong-il's approval of the meeting. The North sent a delegation to Kim Dae-jung's funeral in Seoul, South Korea's capital, as part of a more conciliatory policy after years of Northern hostility.

Roh Moo-hyun, who had narrowly won election as president in 2003 and served until 2008, killed himself by jumping off a cliff on May 23, 2009. Roh had lost public support in office during continual labor unrest, accusations of incompetence, and personal conflicts with opponents and the media. He was under investigation for corruption when he died. ■ Henry S. Bradsher

See also **Asia; Korea, North.**

Kosovo. In November 2009, voters went to the polls to choose local officials. Observers reported that voting in Kosovo's first elections since independence was orderly and peaceful.

Kosovo declared independence from Serbia in February 2008, despite Serbia's strenuous objections. From 1999 to 2008, Kosovo, a nominal province of Serbia, had been administered by United Nations (UN)-appointed officials assisted by NATO peacekeeping troops. NATO troops remained in Kosovo in late 2009.

Serbian officials, who do not recognize Kosovo, declared the November elections illegal and urged ethnic Serbs in Kosovo to boycott the polls. However, turnout reached 45 percent and, according to election officials, included some Kosovar Serbs, though a minority. Ethnic Albanians comprise nearly 90 percent of Kosovo's population; about 7 percent are ethnic Serbs.

In the elections, the ruling coalition of Prime Minister Hashim Thaçi won the majority of local offices. However, the candidate of the chief opposition party won the mayor's office in Pristina, the capital.

Legislators in Kosovo, under the guidance of European Union (EU) advisers, continued setting up government institutions in 2009. The EU officials were part of a civilian mission called EULEX, which went into operation in December 2008. In May 2009, Kosovo's parliament appointed judges to the new nation's highest court, rounding out the judicial system.

Tensions remained high within Kosovo in 2009, particularly in predominantly Serb communities. Violence flared sporadically in Mitrovica, a predominantly ethnic Serb town in northern Kosovo. In January, the bombing of the home of ethnic Albanians in Mitrovica prompted EULEX representatives to emphasize the right of displaced persons to return to their homes.

Economists forecast that Kosovo's economy would expand by 3.8 percent in 2009 and 4.3 percent in 2010. However, unemployment hovered around 45 percent, the highest in Europe.

Border settlement. In October 2009, officials of Kosovo and Macedonia resolved a dispute over their mutual border. Macedonia then extended full diplomatic recognition to Kosovo.

The European Commission, the EU's executive agency, issued a report on Kosovo in October. The report proposed measures to assist Kosovo in developing a market economy and combating organized crime. It also recommended eliminating visa requirements for Kosovo citizens traveling to EU member nations. ■ Sharon L. Wolchik

See also **Europe; Macedonia; Serbia; United Nations.**

Kuwait. See Middle East.

Kyrgyzstan. Incumbent President Kurmanbek Bakiev was reelected on July 23, 2009. Bakiev, who became president after an uprising in 2005, had since steadily consolidated his political power. Bakiev's main challenger, former ally Almazbek Atambaev, withdrew his candidacy during the polling process, claiming massive voter fraud. The Kyrgyz Central Election Commission announced that Bakiev won the election with 76.1 percent of the vote, compared with Atambaev's 8.4 percent. Election monitors from the Organization for Security and Co-operation in Europe condemned the vote as "marred by many problems and irregularities."

In October 2009, Bakiev further strengthened his rule by demanding the resignation of the government and ushering in new measures to broaden presidential powers. Bakiev named his chief of staff, Daniyar Usenov, to the position of prime minister on October 21, after Prime Minister Igor Chudinov resigned in protest over Bakiev's changes. Parliament voted on October 22 to place security services and foreign policy under direct presidential control. Bakiev continued the government shakeup by appointing his son, Maksim Bakiev, as director of the newly created Central Agency for Development, Investment, and Innovation on October 30. ■ Juliet Johnson

See also **Asia.**

Labor and employment. Fears that chaos in the financial markets and the global economic downturn in late 2008 might develop into a second Great Depression eased as the United States economy showed tentative signs of recovery in the second half of 2009. Nevertheless, the "Great Recession," as the slump came to be known, rivaled the severe recession of 1980–1983 in terms of job loss, and a steady hemorrhaging of jobs continued throughout 2009.

In October, total U.S. employment stood at 138.3 million, according to the U.S. Bureau of Labor Statistics (BLS), an agency of the Department of Labor (DOL); at the end of 2008, BLS had reported total employment of 143.3 million. BLS data show that the U.S. unemployment rate rose from 7.2 percent in late 2008 to 10.2 percent in October 2009.

Among men, the jobless rate rose from 6.3 percent at the start of 2009 to 10.7 percent in October; among women, from 5.3 percent to 8.1 percent during the same period; and among teenagers, from 20.6 percent to 27.6 percent.

The unemployment rate of white workers was 6.0 percent at the start of 2009; by October, it stood at 9.5 percent. African American workers' jobless rate was 11.3 at the start of the year and 15.7 percent in October. For Hispanic workers, the jobless rate ranged from 8.8 percent at the beginning of 2009 to 13.1 percent in October; and for Asian American workers, it rose from 3.8 percent to 7.5 percent.

Automobile manufacturing. The U.S. automobile industry, which had employed 1.3 million workers in 1999, maintained only 664,000 workers on payrolls in late 2009. General Motors (GM) Corporation of Detroit—once the world's largest corporation—and Chrysler Corporation LLC of Auburn Hills, Michigan, declared bankruptcy in mid-2009. GM, with billions of dollars invested by the federal government, emerged from bankruptcy a slimmer company supposedly positioned for future growth. Chrysler was salvaged by purchase in June by Italian automaker Fiat SpA.

Ford Motor Company of Dearborn, Michigan, fared better than its two U.S. rivals and did not seek nor accept any direct federal help. In the third quarter of 2009, Ford reported nearly $1 billion in profits.

In 2007 and 2008, the United Automobile Workers (UAW) accepted pay and benefit changes to save GM, Chrysler, and Ford millions of dollars. However, UAW members in November 2009 rejected a contract with Ford that would have trimmed pay and benefits to bring them more in line with GM and Chrysler contracts.

Retail trade. One measure of the severity of the recession was the loss of employment in the retail trade industry, a sector of the economy that had fared relatively well in previous downturns. From the onset of the recession in December 2007 to October 2009, retail trade employment fell by more than 800,000 jobs.

A harbinger of what was to come was the announcement in January of the bankruptcy of Circuit City Corporation of Richmond, Virginia, a retail electronics outlet. Circuit City sought and received court approval for liquidation of its assets, leaving its 34,000 workers jobless.

Communications industry. In June, the United Parcel Service (UPS) and the Independent Pilots Association (IPA) announced an agreement to cut operational costs and thereby avoid the furloughing of 10 percent of UPS's pilot workforce. The agreement emerged from IPA efforts to identify savings through voluntary actions of its pilots, such as leaves of absence, job sharing, and early retirement. "This is a remarkable achievement," observed IPA president Bob Miller. "It shows tremendous solidarity [among] pilots."

UPS also negotiated a pact in June with the International Association of Machinists (IAM). The four-year agreement, which covered 3,200 employees, specified hourly wage hikes of 95 cents or less in each year of the contract.

During 2009, the Communications Workers of America (CWA) bargained with AT&T Inc. of Dallas on new contracts covering 120,000 employees in the five geographic regions of the company. CWA workers in the Midwest, West, and Southeast concluded contracts that contained wage increases of up to11.5 percent, pension improvements, and some job protections. In late 2009, CWA negotiators continued bargaining for new contracts in AT&T's East and Southeast regions.

In June, the Newspaper Writers Guild rejected a package of wage and benefit cuts proposed by the New York Times Company (NYTco), owner of *The Boston Globe,* to reduce annual costs for the hard-pressed newspaper by $10 million. Although some analysts speculated that NYTco might shut down the *Globe,* company officials imposed a unilateral 23-percent pay cut on the paper's staff and asserted their intention to keep the paper alive. NYTco and the Guild renegotiated the contract, still designed to cut costs by $10 million; in July, union members voted to approve it.

Entertainment industry. In April, the Screen Actors Guild and the American Federation of Radio and Television Artists approved a new three-year agreement with the Joint Policy Committee on Broadway Talent Union Relations, which represents broadcast media in the New York City area. The pact provided pay increases of 4.4 to 5.35 percent in the first year only.

In June, the 120,000-member Screen Actors Guild (SAG) ratified a three-year agreement with the Alliance of Motion Picture and Television

Tents and temporary shelters crowd the riverside in Sacramento, California, in early 2009. For several years the abode of homeless people, the tent city underwent a population boom in 2009 as joblessness in California soared. The city eventually moved the several hundred inhabitants onto the state fairgrounds.

Producers (AMPTP), the negotiating entity for the Hollywood studios. In February, AMPTP had presented the Guild with its "last, best, offer" to replace a contract that expired on June 30, 2008. The June 2009 contract provided no pay increase in the first year, 3 percent in the second year, and 3.5 percent in the third year.

Airlines. In February, Delta Airlines of Atlanta and Northwest Airlines, which merged in October 2008, began to integrate the two airlines' seniority lists for flight attendants. The process was complicated by the fact that the 7,000 Northwest flight attendants were members of the Association of Flight Attendants (AFA) union, and the 14,000 Delta flight attendants were non-union labor. A sticking point of the negotiations was the practice of Delta management in previous union elections of counting nonvoting as explicit "no" votes. In November 2009, the National Mediation Board (NMB), an independent federal agency that coordinates labor-management relations in the airline and railroad industries, recommended that only explicit votes be tabulated. Representatives of the flight attendants then petitioned Delta management to hold a union election for the merged workforce.

In March, the AFA ratified a two-year agreement with Alaska Airlines of Seattle covering 2,830 flight attendants. The pact provided incentive bonuses based on payscales and 1.5-percent pay increases in 2009 and 2010.

In May 2009, the Airline Pilots Association ratified a four-year agreement with Alaska Airlines. The pact provided pay increases, benefit expansions, and more flexible scheduling for 1,455 pilots.

In March, IAM, the machinists' union, and Hawaii Airlines of Honolulu reached agreement on a two-year contract. The pact included an immediate wage boost of 3 percent and a provision to freeze employee health care contributions.

In November, the Southwest Airline Pilots Association ratified a five-year contract with Southwest Airlines of Dallas that resulted from three years of negotiation. The contract provides job protections, pay increases, expanded retirement benefits, and scheduling improvements.

Aerospace. In March 2009, negotiators for engineers at a Wichita, Kansas, defense plant concluded a three-year contract with Chicago-based Boeing Company. The agreement, retroactive to Dec. 5, 2008, guaranteed each employee a pay increase of at least 3 percent for one year of the three-year contract period.

In June 2009, the UAW voted to strike Bell Helicopter Textron Inc., of Hurst, Texas, after rejecting a contract offer. The strike, at eight Texas plants, lasted six weeks. In July, UAW members voted to approve a four-year agreement offered by Bell. The contract boosted wages by 3 percent in the last three years of the contract and authorized signing bonuses of $3,500.

On October 28, Boeing officials announced that the company would build its second 787 Dreamliner factory not in Washington state, traditionally Boeing's production base, but in Charleston, South Carolina. A major factor in the decision, analysts said, was the desire to cut costs by engaging a nonunion workforce. In negotiations before the decision, Boeing officials asked for—but did not receive—a no-strike guarantee from IAM, the union representing most of Boeing's production-line employees. Elected officials in Washington state lamented the loss of Boeing production jobs and cited the need to be more aggressive in competing for Boeing facilities.

Government. In February 2009, Congress passed and President Barack Obama signed the $787-billion American Recovery and Reinvestment Act of 2009—the "stimulus package." Its purpose was to halt the steep job loss that began in late 2008 and to create new employment opportunities. Jobs to be saved, principally in fiscally strapped state and local governments, included police, firefighting, and teaching positions. Jobs to be created included hiring for "shovel-ready" construction projects such as road and bridge repair.

In November 2009, Congress passed and President Obama signed a measure to extend unemployment benefits. The legislation provided 14 additional weeks of benefits for all unemployed workers and 20 weeks for unemployed workers in states with the highest unemployment rates.

New labor secretary. In February, the U.S. Senate confirmed President Obama's pick for secretary of labor, Hilda L. Solis. A veteran of the U.S. House of Representatives and California Legislature, Solis had a reputation as an advocate for labor, particularly low-wage earners.

Unions. Union membership increased from 12.1 percent to 12.4 percent of U.S. workers during 2008, according to the most recent data from the BLS. Labor analysts said it was the most significant increase in union membership since 1983.

In March 2009, about one-third of the members of UNITE HERE, a union representing hotel and restaurant workers, withdrew and formed Workers United, which became affiliated with the Service Employees International Union. The split led to strife among union members and court battles over contested holdings of the two unions. In September, UNITE HERE reaffiliated with the AFL-CIO federation, from which the union had withdrawn in 2005 to join a competing federation.

In September, the AFL-CIO elected Richard L. Trumka, formerly AFL-CIO secretary-treasurer, as president of the federation. Also in September, the Screen Actors Guild (SAG) elected Ken Howard, a veteran actor, as its new president.

Legislation. In 2009, the principal national legislative goal of the labor movement was passage of the Employee Free Choice Act (EFCA). EFCA would permit unions to organize workers if a majority within a work facility fill out union cards. Unions have long complained that federal rules requiring the National Labor Relations Board to conduct elections for union representation give employers time to intimidate employees in various ways. In March, EFCA was introduced in both houses of Congress. The bill made little legislative progress in 2009, however, as Congress focused on other legislative priorities.

International unemployment. Joblessness in the 30 member countries of the Organisation for Economic Co-operation and Development (OECD), an association of nations that promotes economic and social welfare, rose from 6.5 percent at the end of 2008 to 8.8 percent by October 2009. Unemployment ranged from a low of 3.4 percent in South Korea to a high of 19.3 percent in Spain.   ■ Robert W. Fisher

See also **Economics, United States; Economics, United States: A Special Report; People in the news** (Hilda Solis).

Labrador. See Canadian provinces.
Laos. See Asia.

CHANGES IN THE UNITED STATES LABOR FORCE

	2008	2009*
Civilian labor force	154,329,000	154,423,000
Total employment	145,368,000	140,562,000
Unemployment	8,961,000	13,860,000
Unemployment rate	5.8%	9.0%

Change in weekly earnings of production and nonsupervisory workers (nonfarm business sector)

Current dollars	2.2%	0.7%
Constant (1982) dollars	2.9%	2.5%

Change in output per employee hour (nonfarm business sector)

	1.2%	4.3%

*All data represent averages for the year; the figures for 2009 are obtained from statistics for the first three quarters of the year.

Source: *World Book* estimates based on data from the U.S. Bureau of Labor Statistics.

Supporters of ousted President Manuel Zelaya clash with police on the streets of Tegucigalpa, capital of Honduras, on June 29. After Zelaya had tried to amend the Constitution in an attempt to remain in office, the Honduras military staged a *coup* (overthrow) on June 28 and escorted him out of the country.

Political leaders from Israel, Palestine, China, and Iran, among others, paid official visits to the Brazilian capital, Brasília, in 2009, to curry favor with a nation long known for its reluctance to become involved in the affairs of others. The visits were accompanied by several other signs of Brazil's growing prominence on the world stage. One was the October 2 decision by the International Olympic Committee (IOC) to designate Rio de Janeiro—*a cidade maravilhosa* ("the marvelous city")—as the site of the 2016 Summer Olympic Games. Brazil, already the designated host for the 2014 World Cup soccer matches, was the first South American nation so honored by the IOC.

On the economic front, in 2009, Brazil became the first Latin American nation to be invited to the councils of the world's major

FACTS IN BRIEF ON LATIN AMERICA

Country	Population	Government	Monetary unit[†]	Foreign trade (million U.S.$) Exports[††]	Imports[††]
Antigua and Barbuda	88,000	Governor General Dame Louisse Lake-Tack; Prime Minister Baldwin Spencer	XCD dollar (2.70 = $1)	84	523
Argentina	40,519,000	President Cristina Fernández de Kirchner	peso (3.85 = $1)	70,590	54,550
Bahamas	342,000	Governor General Arthur Hanna; Prime Minister Hubert Ingraham	dollar (1.00 = $1)	674	2,401
Barbados	284,000	Governor General Sir Clifford Straughn Husbands; Prime Minister David Thompson	dollar (2.02 = $1)	385	1,586
Belize	315,000	Governor General Sir Colville Young, Sr.; Prime Minister Dean Barrow	dollar (2.00 = $1)	458	740
Bolivia	10,040,000	President Evo Morales	boliviano (6.97 = $1)	6,494	4,674
Brazil	199,132,000	President Luiz Inácio Lula da Silva	real (1.87 = $1)	197,900	173,100
Chile	17,088,000	President Michelle Bachelet	peso (553.10 = $1)	66,460	57,610
Colombia	46,271,000	President Álvaro Uribe Vélez	peso (2,056.80 = $1)	38,550	37,560
Costa Rica	4,672,000	President Óscar Arias Sánchez	colón (583.70 = $1)	9,738	14,550
Cuba	11,265,000	President Raúl Castro	peso (0.93 = $1)	3,780	14,500
Dominica	73,000	President Nicholas Liverpool; Prime Minister Roosevelt Skerrit	XCD dollar (2.70 = $1)	94	296
Dominican Republic	9,884,000	President Leonel Fernández Reyna	peso (35.92 = $1)	6,949	16,080
Ecuador	14,012,000	President Rafael Correa	U.S. dollar	19,150	17,790
El Salvador	7,191,000	President Mauricio Funes Cartagena	colón (8.75 = $1) U.S. dollar	4,611	9,003
Grenada	110,000	Governor General Sir Carlyle Arnold Glean; Prime Minister Tillman Thomas	XCD dollar (2.70 = $1)	38	343
Guatemala	14,368,000	President Álvaro Colom	quetzal (8.24 = $1)	7,862	13,380
Guyana	757,000	President Bharrat Jagdeo; Prime Minister Samuel Hinds	dollar (200.34 = $1)	800	1,299
Haiti	9,723,000	President Réne Préval; Prime Minister Jean-Max Bellerive	gourde (40.75 = $1)	490	2,107
Honduras	7,737,000	President Porfirio Lobo Sosa*	lempira (18.90 = $1)	6,046	10,390
Jamaica	2,758,000	Governor General Patrick Allen; Prime Minister Bruce Golding	dollar (83.30 = $1)	2,602	7,185
Mexico	110,155,000	President Felipe Calderón Hinojosa	peso (13.33 = $1)	291,300	308,600
Nicaragua	5,916,000	President Daniel Ortega	gold cordoba (20.50 = $1)	2,922	5,042
Panama	3,511,000	President Ricardo Martinelli	balboa (1.00 = $1)	10,290	15,000
Paraguay	6,502,000	President Fernando Lugo Méndez	guaraní (4,920.00 = $1)	8,152	9,172
Peru	28,971,000	President Alan García Pérez	new sol (2.94 = $1)	31,530	28,440
Puerto Rico	4,000,000	Governor Luis G. Fortuño	U.S. dollar	46,900	29,100
St. Kitts and Nevis	51,000	Governor General Sir Cuthbert Montraville Sebastian; Prime Minister Denzil Douglas	XCD dollar (2.70 = $1)	84	383
St. Lucia	171,000	Governor General Dame Pearlette Louisy; Prime Minister Stephenson King	XCD dollar (2.70 = $1)	288	791
St. Vincent and the Grenadines	122,000	Governor General Sir Frederick Nathaniel Ballantyne; Prime Minister Ralph E. Gonsalves	XCD dollar (2.70 = $1)	193	578
Suriname	466,000	President Runaldo Ronald Venetiaan	dollar (2.75 = $1)	1,391	1,297
Trinidad and Tobago	1,345,000	President George Maxwell Richards; Prime Minister Patrick Manning	dollar (6.18 = $1)	15,900	9,843
Uruguay	3,360,000	President Tabaré Ramón Vázquez Rosas**	peso (22.45 = $1)	7,100	8,654
Venezuela	28,920,000	President Hugo Chávez Frías	new bolívar (2.15 = $1)	93,540	48,100

*Scheduled to take office Jan. 27, 2010.
[†]Exchange rates as of Sept. 30, 2009.
**Scheduled to be replaced by José Mujica on March 1, 2010.
[††]Latest available data.

industrialized powers. These included the first summit of the four largest "emerging markets"—countries that will together account for most of the growth in the global economy in the next half-century. At the June meeting in Russia, Brazil declared its solidarity with China, India, and Russia in the creation of a more diverse global monetary system. This was a matter of urgency in the wake of the financial crisis that had originated in the United States in 2008 and was still hurting Latin America in 2009. Especially hard-hit were Mexico and more than a dozen smaller nations closely tied to the U.S. economy. By contrast, Brazil had survived the global downturn largely unscathed thanks to a sharp growth in Brazilian consumers and the opening up of new markets for the country's exports in Africa and Asia.

As the leader of the first large nation to emerge from the global recession, President Luiz Inácio Lula da Silva spoke at meetings of major industrialized nations in Italy, the United Kingdom, and the United States. He argued for a restructuring of the international monetary system to prevent the recurrence of such crises. The proposal included reforming the International Monetary Fund, a United Nations affiliate, to provide poor nations with more voting power in its decisions, and a greater role for currencies other than the U.S. dollar. During 2009, Argentina, Brazil, and Venezuela all swapped more than $10 billion of their respective national currencies for the yuan of China, thereby creating an alternative to the dollar, if necessary, to finance a portion of their mutual trade. Brazil and Argentina entered into a similar arrangement worth $1.5 billion.

Expanded China trade. In the first quarter of 2009, China replaced the United States as Brazil's leading trade partner and was second-ranked in its trade with the entire Latin American region. China continued to use its financial clout to lock in future access to food supplies and raw materials vital to its own growth and industrialization. In line with this, China loaned Petrobras, Brazil's state-run petroleum company, $10 billion in 2009. The Asian nation also doubled the size of its development fund in Venezuela to $12 billion and provided Argentina with a $10 billion line of credit.

New constitutions. Several Latin American nations put into effect or approved new constitutions in 2009. They commonly allowed second and even third terms for incumbent presidents, enhanced the powers of the presidency, and contained articles that tightened state control over such nonrenewable resources as minerals, natural gas, and petroleum. The new constitutions also provided for greater transparency of

how national governments spend the revenues from resource exploitation and safeguard people and communities from environmental damage.

The chief proponents and beneficiaries of the new political charters were popular leaders who sought to keep themselves in power. In Venezuela, voters approved a referendum on February 15 that will enable President Hugo Chávez to stay in office indefinitely. In Ecuador, President Rafael Correa, whose first term was shortened by a new constitution, easily won re-election to a second term on April 26 and became eligible for a third. In Bolivia, President Evo Morales, following the approval of a new constitution January 26, won a landslide victory for a second consecutive term on December 6.

In Colombia, President Álvaro Uribe became eligible to run for an unprecedented third term in 2010, following the approval by the Colombian Congress of a change in the Constitution in September 2009. Uribe was credited with having restored tranquility to the country's cities during his first two terms thanks to large-scale financial and military assistance from the United States.

In Nicaragua, President Daniel Ortega on July 19 proposed a national referendum on a new constitution that would remove term limits. The occasion was a celebration of the 30th anniversary of the Sandinista revolution, which was the genesis of his political party.

On November 25, voters of St. Vincent and the Grenadines overwhelmingly rejected a referendum that would have largely dissolved ties with the United Kingdom and replaced the British queen as head of state in the island nation with a president chosen by parliament.

Military coup. On June 28, Honduran President Manuel Zelaya was forcibly removed from office in a military coup that drew universal condemnation. There followed five months of ineffectual regional diplomacy aimed at restoring him to power. For much of this period Zelaya pleaded his case from the Brazilian embassy in Tegucigalpa, the Honduran capital, where he had sought refuge after sneaking back into the country.

In the meantime, Honduras was ruled by a de facto interim government that oversaw scheduled national elections on November 29. The winner was Porfirio Lobo Sosa, a wealthy rancher and career politician of the center-right National Party, who was to be sworn in as president in early 2010.

Elections. Elsewhere in Latin America, the political process unfolded in a more conventional and democratic fashion. On March 12, Prime Minister Baldwin Spencer, 60, of the United Progressive Party, survived the fallout from the biggest financial scandal in the history of Antigua and Barbuda to win another term. On October 24, Prime Minister Denzil L. Douglas, 56, of the Labour Party, easily won a third term as prime minister of St. Kitts and Nevis. On December 18, the people of Dominica reelected Prime Minister Roosevelt Skerrit, 37, of the Dominica Labour Party to a second term.

On March 15, the people of El Salvador elected Mauricio Funes Cartegena, of the Farabundo Martí Liberation Front, as president. The popular former television personality became his country's first left-wing leader. In a run-off election on November 25, José Mujica of the incumbent Broad Front coalition became Uruguay's second leftist president. Mujica, a Socialist, was imprisoned for more than a decade for terrorist activities under military rule. On May 3, Panamanians turned to the right in electing conservative Ricardo Martinelli, the wealthy owner of a chain of supermarkets, as their new president. On December 13, Sebastián Piñera of the right-wing National Renewal Party won the first round in Chile's presidential election. Piñera was to face Eduardo Frei in a runoff election scheduled for Jan. 17, 2010.

Economic losses. A slump in oil prices and a failure to invest in new technology to boost production negatively impacted the oil industries of Venezuela and Mexico in 2009. In response, Venezuela was forced to cut back drastically the generous foreign aid program mounted by President Chávez as a means of enhancing his influence abroad.

In Mexico, continuing violence associated with drug trafficking and an outbreak of the H1N1 flu virus endangered tourism, the country's second most important source of earnings. In Argentina, the worst drought in more than half a century caused widespread losses of crops and cattle. Around 1.5 million livestock died of hunger and the heat, according to authorities.

U.S. relations. Latin Americans across the political spectrum from right to left welcomed the inauguration of U.S. President Barack Obama. On Obama's first birthday in office, August 4, Antigua rechristened its highest peak "Mount Obama" in his honor. For his part, President Obama brought a new tone to relations in the Western Hemisphere. He admitted in meeting Latin American leaders that the United States was not doing as much as it should to curb the consumption of narcotic drugs by Americans and to stem the flow of arms south across the U.S. border. Both shortcomings continued to fuel increased violence in several nations, especially Mexico, where a virtual war involving drug traffickers continued to rage in 2009.

U.S. military in Colombia. At the same time, many Latin Americans viewed an increase in the U.S military presence in Colombia with skepticism and alarm. Under a 2009 agreement, the United States was to lease seven Colombian military bases for a period of 10 years. These were to accommodate 1,400 Americans in uniform, plus an unspecified number of contractors involved in the fight against drug trafficking. The Colombian government welcomed the increased U.S. assistance in a year with fairly frequent attacks by the Revolutionary Armed Forces of Colombia (FARC) against its military. In November, FARC rebels killed nine Colombian soldiers and wounded four in the southwestern department of Cauca.

OAS ends Cuba's exclusion. On June 3, the Organization of American States (OAS) voted to end Cuba's 47-year exclusion from the regional body at its meeting in San Pedro Sula, Honduras. At that time, the United States was the only Western Hemisphere nation without bilateral diplomatic relations with Cuba. The United States continued to insist that before reinstatement Cuba would have to affirm its commitment to the democratic values of the OAS charter. For its part, Cuba seemed less interested in OAS membership than in ending the nearly half-century-old U.S. trade embargo, and it declined to rejoin the organization.

Conservation. International donors lent financial support in 2009 to South American countries to help save their dwindling rain forests. Norway pledged $1 billion over a period of several years to Brazil's Amazon Fund. The Japanese government agreed to lend Peru $120 million to protect 212,000 square miles (549,000 square kilometers) of Amazonian rain forest.

Censorship. In April, Brazil's Supreme Court struck down a dictatorship-era law imposing harsh penalties for slander and libel. However, throughout much of Latin America—including Brazil—blatant censorship continued despite the promises of new leaders and governments. In July, a federal judge in Brasília, the capital, ordered a newspaper to stop publishing reports of alleged government corruption. In Venezuela, the government shut down 34 privately owned radio stations on August 1. An additional 208 stations were at risk of being shut down for violating new official regulations. Bolivian President Evo Morales called the press the main enemy of the government. Nicaraguan President Daniel Ortega described the media as CIA-financed "children of [Nazi propagandist Joseph] Goebbels." Journalists critical of their governments were discredited by officials in Argentina, Colombia, and Ecuador as well.

Overall, Latin governments moved toward the relaxation of censorship in 2009, according to

Human Rights Watch, an international nongovernmental organization that defends human rights. Venezuela was the "notable exception," it said.

Blackout. On the night of November 10, a severe storm caused widespread electric power outages in Brazil and Paraguay. Strong winds, heavy rain, and lightning brought down lines that cut power from the Itaipú hydroelectric dam on the Brazil-Paraguay border. Nearly all of Paraguay went dark, and around one-fifth of Brazil—including São Paulo, Rio de Janeiro, and Espírito Santowas—was plunged into darkness. In all, around 50 million people were affected. Some areas remained without power for more than five hours, creating chaos as subway and traffic systems shut down.

The blackout raised doubts about the reliability of Brazil's energy infrastructure ahead of its dates to host the 2014 World Cup and the 2016 Olympics. Adriano Pires, director of the Brazilian Center for Infrastructure Studies, said Brazil's transmission lines were very badly maintained. "This shows that Brazil is very vulnerable," he added. The last such Brazilian power outage occurred in 1999 when a lightening bolt struck a transmission line in São Paulo state.

■ Nathan A. Haverstock

See also **West Indies;** various Latin American country articles.

Latvia was hit hard by the global financial crisis in 2009. It experienced the European Union's deepest recession, with unemployment rising from 8.3 percent in January to 18.3 percent in August.

Some 10,000 Latvians demonstrated against the government's handling of the crisis on January 13 in Riga, the capital. The protests escalated into a violent riot, and more than 100 people were arrested. The four-party ruling coalition of Prime Minister Ivars Godmanis collapsed on February 20, and President Valdis Zatlers invited former Finance Minister Valdis Dombrovskis of the center-right New Era party to form a government.

Parliament approved Dombrovskis's five-party coalition on March 12. The new government announced harsh budget cuts to meet the demands of international creditors. The revised 2009 budget included drastic cuts in public sector wages and pensions. Thousands of people protested against the government in the following months, blaming it for mismanaging the country's finances. Under pressure from the European Union and the International Monetary Fund, a United Nations affiliate, the Latvian government on December 1 approved a strict budget for 2010 that further cut public services and introduced new taxes.

■ Juliet Johnson

See also **Europe.**

Law. See **Congress; Courts; Crime; Prisons.**

Lebanon. Nationwide parliamentary elections were held in Lebanon on June 7, 2009—marking the first time that such elections were held throughout the country on the same day. All 128 seats in the National Assembly (parliament) were up for election, with the seats constitutionally mandated to be divided equally between Christians and Muslims. The distribution of parliamentary seats was based on a division of Lebanon into 25 electoral constituencies that varied in size from 2 seats to 10 seats.

The elections gave the anti-Syria Cedar Revolution a majority. The Cedar Revolution first achieved majority status in parliamentary elections held after the evacuation of the Syrian army from Lebanon in April 2005. In the 2009 elections, Cedar Revolution members won 71 seats in the National Assembly, and minority parties won 57 seats. The minority seats included those won by staunchly pro-Syria organizations, such as the Shi`ite parties of Hezbollah and Amal, and seats won by followers of General Michel Awn. Awn had previously been part of the Cedar Revolution, but in 2006, he allied his political movement with pro-Syria forces.

International observers who monitored the parliamentary elections of 2009 reported that the elections were basically free and fair.

Complicated Cabinet formation. After consulting the various parliamentary blocs, Lebanese President Michel Suleiman asked the leader of the majority, Saad al-Hariri, to form the new Cabinet. However, because of obstacles put into place by Syria through its allies in Lebanon, it took al-Hariri unusually long—135 days—to put the Cabinet together. Analysts of Lebanese affairs noted that the "national unity" Cabinet had to include pro-Syria elements because Hezbollah, known to be Syria's terrorist proxy, was heavily armed and had used its military might against Cedar Revolution strongholds in Mount Lebanon and Beirut, the Lebanese capital, in May 2008.

Analysts further pointed out that pro-Syria leaders wanted to be part of the Cabinet so that they would be in position to try to thwart efforts of an international tribunal established by the United Nations (UN) to investigate the assassinations of several prominent Lebanese journalists, army officers, and political figures, including Saad al-Hariri's father, Rafik. According to these experts, pro-Syria forces feared that the tribunal would conclude that Hezbollah and its Syrian master were responsible for the assassinations.

The formation of the new Cabinet, with Saad al-Hariri as prime minister, was completed in early November 2009. Its 30 members were equally divided between Christians and Muslims. The Cedar Revolution had 15 Cabinet ministers, and Hezbollah and its allies had 10 ministers. The remaining five ministers were chosen by President Suleiman to act as arbitrators between these majority and minority factions.

Weapons cache explosions. On July 14, a huge explosion rocked the village of Khirbet Slim in southern Lebanon, causing great panic among residents. Another explosion, on October 12 in the southern Lebanese village of Tayr Filsi, caused the deaths of at least five people.

Both explosions took place in facilities used by Hezbollah to store arms and munitions. Experts noted that these weapons caches were in violation of UN Resolution 1701, which barred the shipment and storage of weapons in the region of Lebanon south of the Litani River.

Russian MiG-29's to Lebanon. A military delegation from Russia visited Lebanon in November to inspect air bases at three airports. The inspections were conducted in preparation for the delivery of 10 MiG-29 fighter aircraft, which Russia was donating to Lebanon. The Russian delegation also reportedly inspected Lebanese army units and military academies and met with senior Lebanese military officers.

◾ Marius Deeb

See also **Middle East; Syria.**

Lesotho. See Africa.

Liberia. See Africa.

Library. Loss of government funding plagued public libraries in the United States in 2009, many to the point of crisis. For the first time since 2005, attention shifted from devastation caused by hurricanes and floods to threats of library closures and cuts in services. Due to the recession, many cities and states struggled to continue paying for libraries and other public services.

Budget cuts. Officials in several of the nation's urban areas announced that, due to financial difficulties, they would have to close library branches. Within days of hearing about closures in suburban Atlanta; Providence, Rhode Island; Omaha, Nebraska; Denver; Philadelphia; and Pittsburgh, residents began to protest.

Angry citizens in suburban Atlanta's Gwinnett County petitioned to have the library's director and board of directors fired for trying to close, or reduce to computer labs, branches in three lower-income communities. In response, the county commissioner proposed increasing property taxes to raise the funds needed to keep the branches open. In Providence, a private citizens' group made a deal with those in charge of the library system—a foundation and the city government—to let the citizens' group run all the branch libraries and raise money to pay the bills. After protests in Omaha, Denver, and Philadelphia, government officials took a second look at their cities' spend-

ing priorities and found ways to keep their libraries open. Under public pressure, the mayor of Pittsburgh asked library officials there to rethink their plan to close 4 of the city's 19 branches.

Public libraries also faced funding cuts at the state level in Connecticut, Hawaii, Michigan, Ohio, and Pennsylvania. There, too, citizens rallied to stop the threats and sent e-mail messages and letters to elected officials. In Ohio, protesters swamped the governor's Facebook page with pleas to leave libraries alone. The protests were somewhat successful. Lawmakers agreed that libraries were very important and reduced the spending cuts.

Popularity. Ironically, the funding cuts forced libraries to reduce the number of hours they were open each week just as the number of people using them rose dramatically. A 2008-2009 survey conducted by the American Library Association (ALA) showed that the number of libraries in which adults used free Internet access to fill out unemployment forms, search for jobs, and post job applications online increased nearly 25 percent over the number reported in the ALA's 2006-2007 survey.

Freedom to read. Another ALA report stated that, by mid-2009, more than 500 challenges against specific books in library collections had been raised by people who objected to the books' contents. In an unusual case in June, four men sought permission from a town north of Milwaukee to publicly burn the library's copy of a young-adult novel that contains sexual themes. They also filed a lawsuit and threatened to have the town mayor fired for allowing the library to openly display the novel. None of these actions actually materialized.

Digitization. In April, the United Nations Educational, Social, and Cultural Organization; the U.S. Library of Congress; and the national libraries of 31 other countries launched the World Digital Library—a collection of primary documents from cultures around the world. The library's Web site comprises rare books and manuscripts, maps, prints, photographs, films, and sound recordings in seven languages.

A four-year battle between Google Inc., the Internet search-engine giant based in Mountain View, California, and librarians, authors, and publishers continued in 2009. One of the controversies involves copyright issues with Google Book Search, a project that gives Internet access to the contents of more than 10 million books, many of which are still protected by copyright. Google offered to create a Book Rights Registry, in which copyright holders can resolve their claims and receive a portion of Google's revenue.

◾ Beverly Goldberg

See also **Internet.**

Libya. On Sept. 23, 2009, Libyan leader Mu'ammar al-Qadhafi addressed the United Nations (UN) General Assembly in New York City for the first time. Although speakers before the General Assembly are expected to limit the length of their talks to 15 minutes, Qadhafi spoke for more than 1 ½ hours. The Libyan leader praised United States President Barack Obama as "a son of Africa" and as "the beginning of change." Qadhafi then proceeded to call the UN Security Council the "terror council" and tore up a copy of the UN Charter.

Lockerbie bomber released. In August, the Scottish government released convicted terrorist Abdel Basset al-Megrahi from prison and allowed him to return to Libya. Megrahi had been convicted of participating in the bombing of Pan Am Flight 103 over Lockerbie, Scotland, in 1988. The bombing killed 270 people, including 189 Americans. The Scottish government's official justification for the release was that it was part of a prisoner transfer agreement between the United Kingdom (UK) and Libya in which prisoners could serve out their sentences in their home countries. Scottish authorities also argued that Megrahi was eligible for release on "compassionate grounds" because he had terminal prostate cancer.

Some observers of international affairs speculated that Megrahi's release was related to a multibillion-dollar oil and natural gas exploration deal between Libya and BP, a London-based oil company. Libya's ratification of the BP deal reportedly happened only after UK authorities privately agreed to release Megrahi. However, this account of Megrahi's release was denied by both Libyan and UK officials.

Officials in the United States strongly objected to the transfer of Megrahi to Libya, and they had urged Scottish authorities not to release him. On the eve of Qadhafi's arrival in New York City for his UN address, the U.S. Senate unanimously passed a resolution calling on the Libyan government to apologize for the welcome ceremony the state provided for Megrahi upon his return to Libya. Libyan officials ignored the resolution.

Human Rights Watch, a human rights organization based in New York City, issued a report in September 2009 condemning Libya and Italy for working together to capture "boat people" (migrants traveling by sea) fleeing North Africa for *asylum* (refuge from political persecution) in Europe. According to the report, the captured migrants were taken to Libya (though few of them were Libyans), where many were detained in overcrowded, unsanitary conditions and brutally mistreated. ■ Mary-Jane Deeb

See also **Africa; Disasters; United Kingdom; United Nations.**

Liechtenstein. See Europe.

Literature. The world of American letters was shaken in 2009 by the passing of John Updike in January, at age 76. He was the author of seemingly countless novels, stories, essays, critical reviews, and volumes of poetry. One of his most memorable characters, Harry "Rabbit" Angstrom, was an ordinary, small-town businessman featured in four of Updike's novels *Rabbit Run* (1960), *Rabbit Redux* (1971), *Rabbit Is Rich* (1981), and *Rabbit at Rest* (1990); and one novella, "Rabbit Remembered" (2000). Updike was twice awarded the Pulitzer Prize for Fiction, in 1982 and 1991; won two National Book Awards, in 1964 and 1982; and received a National Humanities Medal, in 2003. After Updike's death, Philip Roth stated in *The New York Times* that Updike "...is and always will be no less a national treasure than his 19th-century precursor, Nathaniel Hawthorne...." Critic Brooke Allen wrote in *The Wall Street Journal* that "Updike's precise, elastic prose, its joy, its unexpectedly baroque adjectives yoked with the most banal objects and images, turn the ordinary into the extravagantly artful...."

J. G. Ballard, born James Graham Ballard, the celebrated Chinese-born British novelist and memoirist, died in April at age 78. Ballard, who called his work "apocalyptic" rather than "science fiction," may be best known for his autobiographical novel, *Empire of the Sun* (1984), about his childhood experience in a Japanese internment camp in Shanghai during World War II (1939-1945). The book was short-listed for the Man Booker Prize and also made into a successful motion picture in 1987 by Steven Spielberg. An obituary in *The Daily Telegraph* noted that Ballard's many "novels and short stories were marked by the same dark, surreal landscapes, and all described a future in which his characters had abandoned themselves to personal obsessions."

Nobel Prize in Literature. The 2009 Nobel Prize in Literature was awarded to a Romanian-born German novelist and poet, Herta Müller. The Nobel committee described Müller as an author "...who, with the concentration of poetry and the frankness of prose, depicts the landscape of the dispossessed." Müller had emigrated to Germany from Romania because many of her works in her native country had been censored or banned. Her better-known novels include *Herztier* (1994), published in English translation as *The Land of Green Plums* (1996); and *Atemschaukel* (2009), to be published in English as *Everything I Possess I Carry With Me.* Both novels explore the lives of German-speaking Romanians under harsh political conditions.

Pulitzer Prize for fiction. The 2009 Pulitzer Prize for fiction was awarded to Elizabeth Strout for *Olive Kitteridge* (2009), a collection of 13

John Updike
American Man of Letters

John Updike was that rarity in American literature, a true man of letters. During his 50-year career, he wrote novels, short stories, poetry, literary criticism, art criticism, autobiography, and personal essays. Updike composed elegant, sophisticated prose that made him one of the most recognizable literary stylists of his day. He died on Jan. 27, 2009, at the age of 76.

Updike was the laureate of middle-class life and America's shifting moral and political attitudes during the second half of the 1900's. His fiction explored the frustrations and tensions among the Protestant middle class in small towns and suburbia. He wrote with sensitivity and realism about love and marriage, with many of those marriages beginning happily and ending in adultery and divorce.

Updike is best known for his four "Rabbit" novels that center on the life of Harry "Rabbit" Angstrom, a small-town Pennsylvania man struggling to find a satisfying life. The novels take Rabbit through a series of personal and marital crises and involve him in some of the turbulent events that rocked American society in the 1960's. The series consists of *Rabbit, Run* (1960), *Rabbit Redux* (1971), *Rabbit Is Rich* (1981), and *Rabbit at Rest* (1990). The last two books each won a Pulitzer Prize for fiction.

Updike's early writings dealt largely with childhood, adolescence, and conflicts between parents and their offspring. Beginning with the novel *Couples* (1968), he turned to examining tensions, both sexual and spiritual, among suburban American families in the eastern United States. Updike probed these tensions in the later Rabbit novels and in the trilogy consisting of *A Month of Sundays* (1975), *Roger's Version* (1986), and *S.* (1988). He also won praise for a series of stories about Henry Bech, an American writer who is a stand-in for Updike. Through Bech, Updike wryly commented on writing and the writer's life in the United States. Bech appears in *Bech: A Book* (1970), *Bech Is Back* (1982), and *Bech at Bay* (1998).

John Hoyer Updike was born on March 18, 1932, in Shillington, Pennsylvania. Many of his early short stories are set in a fictional town based on Shillington. At the age of 18, Updike won a scholarship to Harvard University, where he studied literature. He graduated in 1954 and joined *The New Yorker* magazine in 1955 as a staff editor. Updike remained at *The New Yorker* for only two years, but he published short stories, poems, reviews, and essays in the magazine for the rest of his life, becoming closely identified with *The New Yorker*'s sophisticated style.

Updike published his first book in 1958, a collection of light verse called *The Carpentered Hen*. He established himself on the American literary scene the next year with a collection of short stories, *The Same Door*, and his first novel, *The Poorhouse Fair*. But it was the publication of *Rabbit, Run* that earned Updike recognition as a major American writer. At his death, Updike had published about 50 books that constitute one of the great bodies of work in American literature in their variety, their distinctive style, and in their penetrating examinations of American society.   ■ Dan Zeff

linked short stories set in coastal Maine. The recurring title character is a schoolteacher, the brusque and unhappy Olive, but the stories also feature others in her geographical and personal milieu. *Olive Kitteridge* is Strout's third book, following the novels *Amy and Isabelle* (1998) and *Abide with Me* (2006).

The finalists for the prize were Louise Erdrich for *The Plague of Doves* (2008) and Christine Schutt for *All Souls* (2008). Erdrich's novel is a multigenerational murder mystery set on and around an Ojibwe (Chippewa) reservation in North Dakota; it is as much an investigation of racial tension as of the aftershocks of a horrific crime. *All Souls,* Schutt's experimental novel, chronicles the effects of a young girl's illness on her peers at an elite Manhattan prep school.

PEN/Faulkner award. Joseph O'Neill won the 2009 PEN/Faulkner award for fiction for his 2008 novel *Netherland*. The finalists for the prize were Sarah Shun-Lien Bynum for *Ms. Hempel Chronicles*, Susan Choi for *A Person of Interest*, Richard Price for *Lush Life*, and Ron Rash for *Serena*, all published in 2008.

Genius grants. The Chicago-based John D. and Catherine T. MacArthur Foundation awarded two of its 2009 "genius" fellowships—a "no strings attached" $500,000 grant—to fiction writers. One went to Deborah Eisenberg, a short story writer. Eisenberg's most recent work is *Twilight of the Superheroes* (2006), a collection of six stories on issues of identity, emotional life, and mental health. One story focuses on a group of young friends who witness the World Trade Center attacks of Sept. 11, 2001, at close range. The book, which enjoyed almost unanimous acclaim, followed three other collections of work the foundation praised as "elegant explorations of the human psyche in tales of increasing complexity, fluency, and moral depth."

The other MacArthur grant for a fiction writer was given to Haitian-born American novelist Edwidge Danticat. Danticat's 2007 memoir, *Brother, I'm Dying,* about her family's often tragic immigrant experience, won that year's National Book Critics Circle Award for Autobiography. Her 2004 novel-in-stories, *The Dew Breaker,* explored the lives affected by one of the torturers who worked for François Duvalier (the president of Haiti from 1957 to 1971). *The Washington Post* said of this work that by "reconstructing such specific and personal memories of a brutal political past, Danticat awakens us to the beauty and terror that can exist in everyday life in Haiti...." She is the author of two other novels, *Breath, Eyes, Memory* (1994) and *The Farming of Bones* (1998); a story collection called *Krik? Krak!* (1995); and the memoir *After the Dance: A Walk Through Carnival in Jacmel, Haiti* (2002).

A literary event. *The Original of Laura*, Vladimir Nabokov's final novel, which remained unfinished at his death in 1977, was published in 2009. The ultimate fate of the manuscript, which was preserved by family members despite Nabokov's wish that it be burned, had been hotly debated. The journalist Ron Rosenbaum of *Slate* played a major role in persuading Nabokov's son to publish it. The manuscript, written on 138 index cards, had been secreted in a vault in a Swiss bank for decades. Alfred A. Knopf, Inc., published the book in an unusual format. The publisher created facsimiles of each index card onto a page with perforations, allowing readers to remove the cards and reorder them.

Bolaño awarded. In 2009, the late Chilean novelist Roberto Bolaño was posthumously awarded the National Book Critics Circle award for his epic *2666*. The book was published in Spanish in 2004 and in translation to English in 2008 to an outpouring of critical admiration. A translation of Bolaño's *The Skating Rink* was released in 2009. A reviewer for *The New York Times* remarked that this earlier work "could seem, in thumbnail, little more than a modest whodunit..." but that it was in fact "exquisite..." and "another unlikely masterpiece...."

Fiction in 2009. Philip Roth published *The Humbling* in 2009. The book's protagonist is a has-been stage actor in his 60's. As in *Everyman* from 2006, Roth explores the themes of old age and death, as well as the nature of a fulfilling and successful life. John Irving's novel, *Last Night in Twisted River,* follows a father and son forced to go on the lam after an accident in their New Hampshire logging camp.

E. L. Doctorow, whose past historical novels have drawn from such events as the 1951 treason trial of Julius and Ethel Rosenberg (*The Book of Daniel,* 1971) and Sherman's March during the Civil War (*The March,* 2005), turns his sights in *Homer & Langley* on the infamous Collyer brothers, reclusive hoarders who died, trapped in their Harlem brownstone by the old newspapers and junk collected over a lifetime. In *The Washington Post,* critic Michael Dirda wrote that it "provides a...Platonic overview of American life in the twentieth century, touching on familiar and perennial American obsessions, including xenophobia, racism, criminality, imperialism and religion."

Thomas Pynchon released a new novel, *Inherent Vice,* a noir mystery. The book features a hippie private eye, Larry "Doc" Sportello, working a surfing community in 1970's Southern California. The book received a mixed critical response, with *Publishers Weekly* judging it "a tad slight" and a *New York* magazine reviewer calling it "manically incoherent." Jonathan Lethem's novel *Chronic City* unfolds in an imaginatively exaggerated New York City, which Lethem uses to "...[explore] the disconnections among art, government, space travel and parallel realities..." according to *Kirkus Reviews.* Kazuo Ishiguro's short-story collection *Nocturnes: Five Stories of Music and Nightfall,* a critical sensation in the United Kingdom, was hailed as a "real demonstration of virtuosity" by Adam Kirsch in the *Barnes & Noble Review.*

Paul Auster's novel *Invisible* boasts three narrators, three settings—New York City, Paris, and the Caribbean—and a time span from 1967 to 2007. Joyce Carol Oates's *Little Bird of Heaven* is a tale of squalor and murder in blue-collar Sparta, New York. *The Washington Post* noted "its mixture of the Gothic and the fatalistic" and praised Oates as "lyrical, moral, unforgiving." Richard Russo, himself known for tales of industrial New York's decay and decline, made a departure from this subject matter in *That Old Cape Magic,* about a man grappling with middle age and family turmoil while visiting Cape Cod in Massachusetts.

Jay McInerney, whose *Bright Lights, Big City* (1984) depicted the hedonism of 1980's Manhattan, released *How It Ended,* a collection of new and selected stories spanning his entire career. His gift for capturing time and place earned him comparisons to such writers as F. Scott Fitzgerald and John O'Hara. Colson Whitehead published his fourth novel, a gentle, humorous coming-of-age story—at least partly autobiographical—called *Sag Harbor.* The book was warmly received by critics despite representing a departure from Whitehead's previous, more fantastical works.

Library of America. The Library of America (LoA) released a number of editions in 2009. One of the publishing events of the year was the release of John Cheever's complete works in two volumes: *Collected Stories and Other Writings* and *Complete Novels,* the latter made up of *The Wapshot Chronicle* (1957), *The Wapshot Scandal* (1964), *Bullet Park* (1969), *Falconer* (1977), and *Oh What a Paradise It Seems* (1982). Cheever, often called "the Chekhov of the suburbs" for his tales of middle-class life in suburban New York, was also the subject of a biography by Blake Bailey that was released in 2009. Bailey was the editor of the Cheever editions issued by LoA. Other 2009 Library of America releases included Raymond Carver's *Collected Stories;* a collection of Thornton Wilder's writings, *The Bridge of San Luis Rey and Other Novels 1926-1948;* an anthology of Lafacadio Hearn's work, *American Writings;* and *VALIS and Other Novels,* a third and final volume of the work of science-fiction writer Philip K. Dick.   ■ Stefan Beck

See also **Literature for children; Nobel Prizes; Poetry; Pulitzer Prizes.**

Literature for children. Fiction for readers ages 10 to 14 was especially strong in 2009, as were informational books for all ages of young readers. Some of the outstanding books of the year included the following:

Picture books. *Hello Baby!* by Mem Fox, illustrated by Steve Jenkins (Beach Lane Books). The narrator asks, "Who are you?" Possible answers are the baby animals pictured in Jenkins's signature torn-paper collages. The answer is revealed when the narrator's hands reach out to meet a baby's. Ages 2 to 5.

Birds, by Kevin Henkes, illustrated by Laura Dronzek (Greenwillow). A little girl watching birds through her window sees so much—single birds, the sudden arrival of many birds on a telephone line, and that moment when a flock of birds leaves a tree all at once. Ages 3 to 5.

The Snow Day, by Komako Sakai (Arthur A. Levine Books). A big snow overnight means no kindergarten for the little bunny, no errands to run with his mother, and his father's plane home is canceled. A quiet, gentle story that shows how different the world can look when there is time to really see it. Ages 3 to 5.

All the World, by Liz Garton Scanlon, illustrated by Marla Frazee (Beach Lane Books). The book focuses on one family at the beach and follows them throughout the day, from farmers' market to living room, while revealing the larger worlds around them. Ages 4 to 7.

Duck! Rabbit! by Amy Krouse Rosenthal and Tom Lichtenheld (Chronicle). Unseen speakers argue about what they see in lines on a page— a rabbit's ears or a duck's bill? Wittily, the text shows how hard it is to let go of what we are absolutely sure we see. Ages 4 to 7.

Fiction. *A Season of Gifts,* by Richard Peck (Dial). Bob Barnhart, a "preacher's kid" newly moved to a small town in downstate Illinois in 1958, cannot see much good in their eccentric elderly neighbor, Grandma Dowdel. But Grandma D has powerful and comic methods for social change, and all the Barnhart kids need help—with friends, with bullies, even with Elvis. Ages 9 to 12.

The Evolution of Calpurnia Tate, by Jacqueline Kelly (Holt). It's 1899, and for Calpurnia, 11, being the only girl with six brothers is not easy. She would rather work with her grandfather, who reads Darwin (and shares the book with her) and gathers specimens, but her mother is trying to direct her evolution into thimbles and tatting. Ages 10 to 14.

Also Known as Harper, by Ann Haywood Leal (Holt). Fifth-grader Harper, named after the author of *To Kill a Mockingbird,* writes poetry and dreams of winning a school contest. When her mother loses her job and the family is evicted, Harper discovers that homes, landlords, families, and writing are more complicated than she knew. Ages 10 to 14.

Marcelo in the Real World, by Francisco Stork (Arthur A. Levine Books). Marcelo, 17, does not label himself with Asperger syndrome ("I perceive reality just fine"). He agrees to take a summer job in the mailroom at his father's law firm. If successful there, he can choose between remaining, for his senior year, in a special school or going to a public high school. Marcelo learns about office politics, flirting, bad decisions, good friends, and how differences can be strengths. Ages 14 to 17.

Fantasy. *The Magician's Elephant,* by Kate DiCamillo (Candlewick). More than 100 years ago, in the dreary country of Baltese, a magician tries to conjure up a bouquet of lilies but brings an elephant crashing through the ceiling instead. His failed illusion sparks new realities for young orphan Peter and all the other inhabitants of Baltese. Ages 9 to 12.

When You Reach Me, by Rebecca Stead (Wendy Lamb Books). In a puzzle mystery that is all about time, it is the 1978-1979 school year for sixth-grader Miranda, a latch-key child of a single mother on Manhattan's Upper West Side. Small things start going wrong: An old friend becomes standoffish; a "crazy guy" shows up on a nearby corner; and someone is leaving her notes that mysteriously predict her future. Ages 11 to 14.

Fire, by Kristin Cashore (Dial). A prequel to Cashore's popular debut novel, *Graceling,* the novel explores a nearby kingdom, where human beings and monsters of exceptional beauty do battle. Fire is a rarity, the last human-monster hybrid, trying to find her place in a world part Machiavelli, part *Wuthering Heights.* Ages 13 to 16.

Catching Fire, by Suzanne Collins (Scholastic). Volume 2 in *The Hunger Games* continues the story of Katnis and Peeta, who survived the horrific games by forcing a draw. As they are dragged on a triumphal tour of the Districts for political purposes, a rebellion against the totalitarian government smolders and cliff-hanger endings abound. Ages 13 to 16.

Poetry. *Red Sings from Treetops: A Year in Colors,* by Joyce Sidman, illustrated by Pamela Zagarenski (Houghton Mifflin). Colors encourage a different way of seeing—much as poetry does—as the seasons change. Spring's red is a cardinal on a bare branch but in summer, red marks a hummingbird's throat. Ages 4 to 8.

A Whiff of Pine, A Hint of Skunk: A Forest of Poems, by Deborah Ruddell, illustrated by Joan Rankin (Margaret K. McElderry). Twenty-three poems provide a wonderful range of voices, as when a wild turkey speaks indignantly about how much the standard preschool turkey pictures—outline your hand—fall short. Ages 5 to 9.

Informational books. *One Beetle Too Many: The Extraordinary Adventures of Charles Darwin,* by Kathryn Lasky, illustrated by Matthew Trueman

(Candlewick). The book examines Darwin's active curiosity and collecting, from an early age through the more adventurous land explorations of the Beagle voyage. Ages 7 to 9.

Moonshot: The Flight of Apollo 11, by Brian Floca (Richard Jackson Books). Floca's subtle watercolors and poetic text recreate the historic flight: the moment of the launch; the angle of the cars parked at Cocoa Beach; a head-on view level with the launch pad; the sounds and special silences of the voyage; and finally, families on Earth, in very 1969 rooms, watching. Ages 6 to 10.

The Frog Scientist, by Pamela S. Turner, illustrated by Andy Comins (Houghton Mifflin). Amazing photographs of frogs entice the reader, but the focus is on the scientist, Dr. Tyrone Hayes. Following his childhood fascination with amphibians through his Berkeley lab and field work in Wyoming, the book provides a study of a life lived in science and will make young readers want to join up. Ages 9 to 12.

A Savage Thunder: Antietam and the Bloody Road to Freedom, by Jim Murphy (Margaret K. McElderry). Murphy moves past Antietam's status as America's single bloodiest day of battle to bring personalities, geography, and chronology to life. Central to his argument is the connection of this battle with Lincoln's Emancipation Proclamation, a controversial document for both North and South. Includes period photos, maps, and drawings and quotations from participants. Ages 12 to 15.

Claudette Colvin: Twice Toward Justice, by Phillip Hoose (Farrar, Straus and Giroux). Colvin, a 15-year-old girl arrested before Rosa Parks, did not become the familiar name associated with the Montgomery bus boycott. Hoose helps us understand what was so brave about her, and her family, and why the popular history constructed around the event left her behind. Ages 12 to 15.

Marching for Freedom: Walk Together, Children, and Don't You Grow Weary, by Elizabeth Partridge (Viking). Partridge focuses on the march from Selma to Montgomery, Alabama, in the spring of 1965, and explains—with interviews, photographs, and convincing detail—why children and teens were so essential. Ages 12 to 15.

Awards. The 2009 Newbery Medal was awarded to Neil Gaiman for *The Graveyard Book.* The award is given by the American Library Association (ALA) for the "most distinguished contribution to American literature for children" published the previous year. The ALA's Caldecott Medal for "the most distinguished American picture book" was awarded to *The House in the Night,* illustrated by Beth Krommes and written by Susan Marie Swanson. The Michael L. Printz Award, for excellence in young adult literature, went to *Jellicoe Road* by Melina Marchetta. ■ Mary Harris Russell

See also **Literature.**

Lithuania. European Union Budget Commissioner Dalia Grybauskaitė won the Lithuanian presidential election on May 17, 2009, becoming Lithuania's first female president. Grybauskaitė, who ran as an independent, took 69.1 percent of the vote to defeat runner-up Algirdas Butkevicius of the Social Democratic Party. Grybauskaitė replaced outgoing President Valdas Adamkus, who had served two five-year terms, the most allowed by the Constitution. Voter turnout was 51 percent, just over the 50 percent required for the poll to be considered valid. The Lithuanian president's powers include implementing foreign and defense policies as well as the ability to veto the nation's budget. Grybauskaitė, a former finance minister, swept to victory amid deep public discontent over Lithuania's deteriorating economic situation.

On June 7, Lithuania's disgraced former President Rolandas Paksas made a political comeback by winning a seat in the European Parliament. In 2004, Lithuania's parliament had removed Paksas from office after he was charged with corruption. Parliament barred him from holding government offices in the future, but the ban did not apply to the European Parliament. Paksas's Order and Justice Party came in third in the 2009 poll, winning 2 of Lithuania's 12 seats in the 736-seat European Parliament. ■ Juliet Johnson

See also **Europe.**

Los Angeles. The recession took its toll on Southern California in 2009, hitting construction, manufacturing, trade, education, health care, and local government. During the summer, unemployment rates exceeded 11 percent in the region, which includes Los Angeles, Orange, Riverside, San Bernardino, and Ventura counties. Forecasts by the Los Angeles Economic Development Corporation predicted slow growth until 2011 but indicated that transportation needs and "green" industries could stimulate jobs growth.

The University of California at Los Angeles (UCLA) Anderson Forecast noted that some of Southern California's difficulties were made worse by state regulatory laws, which made it costly to do business, and higher education cutbacks, which could affect the area's long-term competitiveness. A report by the Milken Institute, a Santa Monica think tank, also blamed the state's high taxes for sending business elsewhere.

Government. Los Angeles Mayor Antonio Villaraigosa, who was reelected on March 3, 2009, and began his second and final term on July 1, worked with the City Council to close a $530-million shortfall in a $7-billion budget. Cuts included summer school classes, court closings, hiring freezes, and furloughs or layoffs. Cuts also were made to the $22.8-billion Los Angeles County budget, though layoffs and program cuts generally were averted.

On July 17, United States District Court Judge Gary Feess terminated the consent decree federal officials had imposed on the Los Angeles Police Department (LAPD) in 2001 after a corruption scandal involving the LAPD's Rampart Division. He said the LAPD had reformed significantly.

On Aug. 5, 2009, popular Police Chief William J. Bratton announced his resignation, effective October 31, to join an international private security firm in New York City. Deputy Chief Charlie Beck, a 32-year veteran of the LAPD, was named Bratton's replacement on November 3.

Sports. The Los Angeles Lakers defeated the Orlando Magic in the National Basketball Association finals on June 14 to win the national championship for the 15th time in franchise history. In baseball, both the Los Angeles Dodgers of the National League and the American League's Los Angeles Angels of Anaheim advanced to the second round of league play-offs.

Gustavo Dudamel, who gained international acclaim as the director of the Ibero-American Youth Orchestra, took over as music director of the Los Angeles Philharmonic in 2009. The young Venezuelan director succeeded Finnish maestro Esa-Pekka Salonen.

Arts. After a yearlong dispute over pay raises and *residuals* (payments) for shows viewed online, the 110,000-member Screen Actors Guild ratified a two-year contract in June.

In October, Venezuelan conductor Gustavo Dudamel, 28, made his debut as music director of the Los Angeles Philharmonic. He succeeded Esa-Pekka Salonen, who moved to London.

Millions of fans mourned the death of Michael Jackson, the "King of Pop," after the 50-year-old entertainer died on June 25. More than 20,000 people attended a memorial at the Staples Center on July 7.

Trade. The Ports of Los Angeles and Long Beach, traditionally the nation's busiest container ports, showed steep declines in imports and exports in 2009 as traffic from Asia and Europe dropped during the worldwide recession. In the first six months of 2009, imports to the Port of Los Angeles were down 17.7 percent, and exports fell 15.5 percent, compared with the same period in 2008. At Long Beach, container imports fell 27.4 percent, and exports were down 29.3 percent.

Fire. The Station Fire burned across 160,000 acres (65,000 hectares) of Angeles National Forest north of Los Angeles from late August to mid-October 2009. Police and fire authorities said that arson was the cause of the blaze, the largest fire in the history of Los Angeles County.

Transportation. Los Angeles's famous "freeway" system may become history by late 2010 or early 2011, as new efforts to raise money and ease traffic congestion take hold. In July 2009, the Metropolitan Transit Authority set tolls that will allow solo motorists to drive in carpool lanes on the 10 Freeway east of downtown and the 110 Freeway south of downtown. ■ Margaret Kilgore

See also **City; Popular music: Michael Jackson Portrait.**

Luxembourg. See Europe.

Macedonia. The ruling VMRO-DPMNE, a center-right coalition, held on to its popular mandate in 2009. In April polling, Macedonian voters elected Gjorge Ivanov of the VMRO-DPMNE as president. The party also fared well in local elections conducted in April.

Macedonia's leaders continued in 2009 to press for European Union (EU) and NATO membership. Greece opposes both memberships because of Macedonia's name. Greeks insist that Macedonia is a historic region in Greece and that other countries are not entitled to use the name in an official capacity.

In September, President Ivanov invited Greek President Carolos Papoulias to Skopje, Macedonia's capital, for direct talks on the name issue. Resolution of the controversy assumed urgent importance for Macedonia in October, when EU officials announced they were ready to begin membership talks with Macedonia. According to EU rules, Greece could block the talks.

Macedonia's economy, affected by the global recession, contracted by 3 percent in 2009. Economists forecast an expansion of 1 percent in 2010. Unemployment in Macedonia remained above 30 percent throughout 2009. ■ Sharon L. Wolchik

See also **Europe; Greece.**

Madagascar. See Africa.

The venerable *Reader's Digest* announced in August 2009 that it would file for bankruptcy. *Reader's Digest* was one of many respected publications that struggled to survive during 2009, a year of declining print advertising revenues for nearly all types of periodicals.

Magazine. The collapse of print advertising during the economic downturn that continued in 2009 sent shock waves through the already-troubled magazine industry. Spending on magazine advertisements had been in a decline for the last five years. Such spending dropped further, by around 28 percent for the first half of 2009 compared with the first half of 2008. For the first time in years, the fall fashion magazines shrank. *Vogue,* for example, which usually featured a September fall fashion issue at around 800 pages, was cut to 584 pages for September 2009.

Closures. The list of magazines that closed in 2009 was extensive. In shelter magazines, the Iowa-based Meredith Corporation closed *Country Home* with its March 2009 issue. New York City-based Condé Nast's *Domino* also published its last issue in March.

Business and finance magazines fell as well. Condé Nast closed *Portfolio,* with its final issue in May. Condé Nast had spent around $100 million on the magazine since its launch in 2007. Foodies were stunned when Condé Nast announced that its iconic cooking and travel magazine, *Gourmet,* published since 1941, would cease publication after the November 2009 issue.

Music magazines had an especially difficult year in 2009. Alpha Media Group closed the print operation of *Blender* with its last issue in April. *Vibe,* a hip-hop magazine founded by famed music producer Quincy Jones, closed in June. The magazine was bought in August by a private equity firm. The new owner planned on relaunching *Vibe* with a stronger focus on the magazine's online edition.

For sale? The iconic African American magazine *Ebony* was reported to be on the auction block. In September, *Newsweek* reported that the publisher, Chicago-based Johnson Publishing Co., was looking for a buyer or investor for the financially troubled publication.

Reader's Digest, first published in 1922, announced in August that it would file for Chapter 11 bankruptcy for its U.S. operations. The magazine fell into difficulties maintaining the debt it absorbed when a private equity firm, Ripplewood, purchased it in 2007.

Video advertising. *Entertainment Weekly* (*EW*) featured a new ad format in its Sept. 18, 2009, issue. A pliable, thin, battery-powered LCD screen was inserted into the magazine for readers in selected areas. When readers opened that page in *EW,* the screen, which could hold up to 40 minutes of content, displayed video advertisements for television programs and soft drinks. ■ Christine Sullivan

Malawi. See Africa.

Malaysia. Najib Razak became prime minister of Malaysia on April 3, 2009. He succeeded Abdullah bin Ahmad Badawi, who had resigned the previous day. In 2008, under Abdullah, the United Malays National Organization (UMNO) lost its two-thirds majority in parliament for the first time since Malaysia became independent in 1957.

Najib introduced economic reforms to try to end Malaysia's recession, which was linked to the worldwide financial downturn. He altered a policy introduced in 1971 by his father, Prime Minister Abdul Razak, that required companies to reserve 30 percent of their shares for ethnic Malays. The policy was intended to overcome economic dominance by ethnic Chinese and Indians. It led to financial success for some UMNO leaders but left many Malays still impoverished. Najib's change was intended to attract foreign investment.

Najib also promised to respect civil liberties and soften repressive laws. However, on Aug. 1, 2009, police broke up a rally in Kuala Lumpur, the capital, and arrested some 600 people. The protesters were calling for the repeal of a law that allowed critics of the government to be jailed indefinitely without charge. ■ Henry S. Bradsher

See also **Asia.**

Manitoba. See **Canadian provinces.**
Marshall Islands. See **Pacific Islands.**
Mauritius. See **Africa.**

Medicine. Approximately 10.2 million surgical and nonsurgical cosmetic procedures were performed in the United States in 2008—a 12-percent decrease compared with 2007—the American Society for Aesthetic Plastic Surgery reported in March 2009. The society, based in Garden Grove, California, speculated that the decrease was caused by the economic downturn.

The report also noted that, since 1997, nonsurgical cosmetic procedures had increased by more than 230 percent—driven mainly by the popularity of Botox (botulinum toxin) injections. Botox injections, used to reduce wrinkle-causing muscle activity, were the most common cosmetic technique in 2008.

The use of liposuction, the surgical removal of fat, decreased in number in 2008 by 25 percent compared with 2007. Breast augmentation—though down in number by 11 percent compared with a year earlier—supplanted liposuction in 2008 as the most common surgical cosmetic procedure.

Gene-silencing side effects. A "gene-silencing" technique under investigation as treatment for *macular degeneration* (a vision disorder), viral infections, and other conditions can lead to more harmful side effects than previously believed. These findings were reported in April 2009 by *ophthalmologist* (eye-disease specialist) Jayakrishna Ambati of the University of Kentucky

in Lexington. The experimental treatment, involving injections of siRNA's (small-interfering ribonucleic acids), was designed to block the activity of disease-causing genes by preventing the assembly of proteins coded by the genes.

In experiments with laboratory animals, Ambati's team found that siRNA's killed cells lining blood vessels and lymph vessels, causing vascular system abnormalities. Nevertheless, the team also reported that siRNA's might be useful in cases in which physicians wish to hinder vascular growth, such as in cornea transplants.

No Alzheimer's inflammation. An international team of investigators reported in June that, contrary to claims of many scientists, inflammation of brain cells does not contribute to the *dementia* (deterioration of mind) common in patients with Alzheimer's disease. Researchers at the McKnight Brain Institute of the University of Florida in Gainesville and colleagues in Germany used high-resolution microscopy to analyze brain tissue from patients with Alzheimer's disease. They found no evidence that cells called microglia were *inflamed* (of abnormally large size) in the tissue. Rather, the microglia were dead and broken into pieces.

The researchers noted that their finding suggested that anti-inflammatory drugs would not be effective in Alzheimer's treatment. Instead, they urged research into drugs that would keep microglia alive and strong.

Controversial cancer guidelines. The U.S. Preventive Services Task Force recommended in November that most women begin screening for breast cancer at age 50. The task force is an independent panel of experts in preventive and primary care appointed by the Department of Health and Human Services.

The new recommendations were controversial because they were at odds with guidelines from several other professional and advisory organizations, which urged breast cancer screening beginning at age 40. In addition, the task force's new recommendations reversed its own previous screening guidelines, which had also recommended breast cancer screening at age 40.

New prostate cancer test. A study of more than 10,000 men with prostate cancer indicated that a new test for such patients, conducted at time of diagnosis, allows for a more accurate evaluation of the likely course of the disease. A team at the University of California at San Francisco reported in June that the test, called Cancer of the Prostate Risk Assessment (CAPRA), is highly accurate regarding predictions for cancer *metastasis* (spread) and patient *mortality* (death).

■ Alfred J. Smuskiewicz

See also **AIDS; Drugs; Health care issues; Mental health; Public health.**

Mental health. More and more people in the United States are using prescription drugs as treatment for mental illness, according to a study released in May 2009 by a team of researchers led by Sherry A. Glied, professor of health policy at Columbia University in New York City. After examining data from several large U.S. public surveys of health, the researchers reported that 73 percent more adults and 50 percent more children were using prescription *psychotropic drugs* in 2006 than in 1996. Psychotropic drugs affect the mind, emotions, and behavior. Among adults older than age 65, the use of such medications doubled from 1996 to 2006.

Glied's group attributed the increased use of psychotropic drugs to several factors, including greater awareness among physicians about drugs for managing such conditions as depression, schizophrenia, and Alzheimer's disease. The researchers also noted that expanded coverage of psychotropic drugs by government insurance programs made them affordable for more people.

Pill for bad memories. A pill that seems to erase unpleasant memories was described in February 2009 by scientists in the Netherlands led by psychologist Merel Kindt of Amsterdam University. The researchers said the pill might help people who have recurring memories of traumatic events (such as in cases of post-traumatic stress disorder), as well as people with excessive anxieties, phobias, or obsessions.

The drug developed by Kindt's team was a type of beta-blocker, a class of drugs that block certain substances in the nervous system. The researchers said their beta-blocker interfered with chemical activities in the brain that create and re-create stressful memories. They demonstrated the drug's effectiveness by giving it to volunteers who had previously been conditioned to associate pictures of spiders with feelings of discomfort and fear. After taking the drug, the volunteers showed measurably weaker startle responses to the spider pictures, suggesting that they no longer made the unpleasant association.

Kindt said that clinical trials would be needed to confirm the drug's effectiveness. However, some other scientists raised questions about the ethical implications of a "memory-erasing" drug.

Depression diagnoses. Unintended changes in the way that physicians diagnose and treat cases of depression resulted from a 2003 warning by the U.S. Food and Drug Administration (FDA) about the increased risk of suicide in children given antidepression medications. That was the conclusion of a study reported in June 2009 by a team of investigators led by psychiatrist Anne M. Libby of the University of Colorado Denver School of Medicine in Aurora. The team reported that the FDA warning seemed to cause physicians to become reluctant to diagnose depression in both children and adults.

Libby's group reached its conclusion after analyzing a large database of managed care insurance claims in the United States dating from 1999 to 2007. The analysis revealed a sudden drop-off in childrens' and adults' claims related to depression after 2004—following several years of steadily rising depression-related claims. The investigators attributed this drop-off to fewer people being diagnosed with depression after the 2003 FDA warning. As a result, they added, many people were likely not receiving the treatment they needed to manage their depression.

Internet therapy effective. Internet-based therapy for depression may be as effective as face-to-face therapy, according to a June 2009 report by a team of scientists led by psychiatrist Gavin Andrews of the University of New South Wales in Australia. In a study of 45 people with depression, the team found that patients who exchanged e-mails with clinicians and participated in other online therapy activities for eight weeks had rates of recovery similar to patients who met clinicians in face-to-face sessions. In addition, the Internet-based therapy involved much less patient time than traditional therapy for depression.   ■ Alfred J. Smuskiewicz

See also **Drugs; Medicine.**

Mexico. On Sept. 2, 2009, President Felipe Calderón offered Mexicans little to cheer about in his annual state of the union address. The global economic crisis, a swine flu outbreak, drug violence, drought, and drops in oil prices and production, he said, had conspired to cast a shadow over the country halfway through his six-year term. As he spoke, forecasters were predicting that Mexico's economy would contract by as much as 8 percent in 2009 and shed 1 million jobs.

Midterm election defeat. Despite Calderón's approval rating of nearly 70 percent, his National Action Party (PAN) lost badly in mid-term elections on July 5. The old-line Institutional Revolutionary Party (PRI) won control of the lower house of Congress and many of Mexico's city governments. They also won most of the state races for governor. The PRI had lost control of the government in 2000 after nearly 71 years of rule.

Calderón therefore faced a Congress dominated by his political opponents for the rest of his term. Despite this setback, he pressed ahead with all-out war against drug trafficking, which had corrupted Mexico's government and law enforcement forces at all levels. The main theater of the fight continued to be northern Mexico along the border with the United States. More than 13,500 people had died in drug-related violence since Calderón took office in 2006.

Drug battles. In 2009, drug traffickers fought among themselves and retaliated against federal and local officials participating in the crackdown. On July 11, Arnoldo Rueda Medina, a leading figure in a drug cartel called La Familia ("The Family"), was arrested in Morelia, capital of the president's home state of Michoacán. Minutes later, his confederates launched an unsuccessful attack to free him—throwing hand grenades and firing high-powered weapons at the police post where he was held. Five federal officers and soldiers were killed and 18 others were wounded.

On September 4, 18 people were murdered and 2 wounded at a drug treatment center in Ciudad Juárez. In the week before the attack, 75 people were killed in drug-related violence in the city. Over the previous 12 months, four other rehabilitation clinics—some suspected of operating as fronts for drug traffickers—in Ciudad Juárez had been attacked. Mexican army troops had entered the city in March 2009 to try to contain the violence.

Decriminalizing drugs. On August 21, the Mexican Congress decriminalized the possession of small amounts of marijuana, cocaine, and heroin. Officials denied that the controversial law legalized drugs, saying it was a realistic way to reduce drug-related violence and crime. In the previous three years, authorities noted, they had detained some 95,000 Mexicans on minor drug offenses—few of whom were charged with a crime.

Drought losses. A persistent, countrywide drought caused the loss of more than $1 billion in spring barley, beans, corn, sorghum, and livestock. In 2009, municipal authorities imposed water rationing on millions of people living in Mexico City's metropolitan area, as reservoirs serving the area hit 16-year lows. The drought was the worst in Mexico in 69 years.

Swine flu response. In late April 2009, the Mexican government shut down schools and prohibited public gatherings for two weeks after more than 80 people died from swine flu. Although the measure won praise from international health authorities for helping contain the spread of the flu, it cost Mexico $3.5 billion in lost revenues and led to a steep drop in tourism.

National identity cards. In late July, President Calderón announced that Mexico would issue national identity cards to help streamline social welfare claims and fight organized crime. By 2012, all Mexicans were to have cards, each with a photo of the bearer, fingerprints, and facial and iris scans on a magnetic strip.   ■ Nathan A. Haverstock

See also **Crime; Disasters; Drug abuse; Latin America.**

Micronesia, Federated States of.

See **Pacific Islands.**

Events in the Middle East in 2009 painted a mixed picture of democratic progress and continued conflict. United States President Barack Obama addressed Muslims around the world with two major speeches in the Middle East. Conflict in the Gaza Strip between Israel and the Palestinian militant organization Hamas led to many civilian deaths. Israeli elections resulted in the formation of a hard-line Cabinet presided over by Prime Minister Benjamin Netanyahu, and attempts by the administration of President Obama to revive the Israeli-Palestinian peace process were unsuccessful.

The democratic alliance of the Cedar Revolution won parliamentary elections in Lebanon. A presidential election in Iran was widely seen as rigged, leading to mass protests. Iraqis prepared for parliamentary elections scheduled for early 2010 despite continued violence by terrorist organizations in 2009. A near economic meltdown in Dubai threatened the global economy.

Obama addresses Islamic world. President Obama traveled to Turkey in April to deliver his first speech intended for Muslims throughout the world. In his speech before the Turkish parliament, which was broadcast worldwide, President Obama stated, "The United States is not, and will never be, at war with Islam." He added that relations between the United States and the Islamic world should not be viewed from the perspective of war against the Islamic terrorist organization al-Qa'ida, but should be based on common interests. Turkey was chosen as the site for this speech because it was the Muslim nation with closest relations to the United States.

President Obama's second speech to Muslims was delivered in June at Cairo University in the capital of Egypt. In the speech, President Obama again maintained that relations between the United States and the Islamic world should be "based on mutual interest and mutual respect." Egypt was chosen as the site for this speech because it was the closest Arab ally of the United States and the first Arab country to reach a peace agreement with Israel.

Conflict in Gaza. On Jan. 3, 2009, three Israeli brigades—each supported by helicopters and a squadron of unpiloted aerial vehicles—attacked Hamas sites in the Gaza Strip and encircled Gaza City. The military offensive, dubbed Operation Cast Lead, was staged in response to a series of rocket attacks that Hamas initiated against Israeli settlements in December 2008.

Battles between Hamas fighters and Israeli forces continued unabated until Jan. 18, 2009, when a cease-fire arranged by Egypt took hold. The Gaza conflict resulted in the deaths of approximately 1,400 Palestinians and the destruction of much infrastructure, including buildings and roads, in the Gaza Strip.

After six months of investigation, the United Nations (UN) Fact-Finding Mission on the Gaza Conflict, headed by South African jurist Richard Goldstone, issued a lengthy report. The UN commission concluded that both the Israeli forces

Kadima leader Tzipi Livni to form a new Cabinet were unsuccessful, Israeli President Shimon Peres tapped Netanyahu to form the Cabinet and to again become prime minister. In April, Prime Minister Netanyahu announced the formation of his Cabinet, with 15 ministers from his Likud Party and the remaining 15 ministers evenly divided among the other three major parties.

and the Hamas fighters had committed war crimes during the conflict in Gaza by targeting civilians. The Israeli government and Hamas each rejected the conclusions of the report.

Israeli parliamentary elections. In elections for the Knesset (Israeli parliament) in February, parties known for their hard-line stances against Palestinian militants were victorious. Former Prime Minister Netanyahu's Likud Party won 15 additional seats in the Knesset, increasing its parliamentary representation to a total of 27 seats. The strongly nationalist Yisrael Beiteinu (Our Home Israel) Party, headed by Avigdor Lieberman, added 4 seats to increase its parliamentary total to 15 seats.

The Kadima Party lost one seat but retained its majority in the Knesset. After attempts by

Attempts to revive peace process. President Obama's special envoy for Arab-Israeli peace talks, former U.S. Senator George Mitchell, made numerous visits to the Middle East in 2009. Mitchell met with both Prime Minister Netanyahu and Palestinian President Mahmoud Abbas.

Despite these visits, many obstacles for reviving the peace process remained. Prime Minister Netanhayu asked that Palestinian leaders recognize Israel "as a Jewish state," but they refused to do so. President Obama asked Prime Minister Netanyahu to freeze the building of Israeli settlements in the West Bank and East Jerusalem. Although the Israeli prime minister in November declared a temporary halt to the building of settlements in the West Bank, he refused to do the same in East Jerusalem, where the

FACTS IN BRIEF ON MIDDLE EASTERN COUNTRIES

Country	Population	Government	Monetary unit*	Foreign trade (million U.S.$)	
				Exports[†]	Imports[†]
Bahrain	794,000	King Hamad bin Isa Al-Khalifa; Prime Minister Khalifa bin Salman Al-Khalifa	dinar (0.38 = $1)	17,490	14,250
Cyprus	812,000	President Demetris Christofias; (Turkish Republic of Northern Cyprus: President Mehmet Ali Talat)	euro (0.70 = $1)	1,689 (includes Northern Cyprus)	9,876
Egypt	81,495,000	President Mohammed Hosni Mubarak; Prime Minister Ahmed Nazif	pound (5.53 = $1)	29,850	56,620
Iran	74,131,000	Supreme Leader Ayatollah Ali Khamenei; President Mahmoud Ahmadinejad	rial (8,229.00 = $1)	95,090	67,250
Iraq	30,623,000	President Jalal Talabani; Prime Minister Nouri Kamel al-Maliki	dinar (1,150.00 = $1)	66,100	43,500
Israel	7,279,000	President Shimon Peres; Prime Minister Benjamin Netanyahu	shekel (3.79 = $1)	56,640	64,310
Jordan	6,361,000	King Abdullah II; Prime Minister Samir Rifai	dinar (0.70 = $1)	7,783	15,030
Kuwait	2,919,000	Emir Sabah al-Ahmad al-Jabir al-Sabah; Prime Minister Nasser Muhammad al-Ahmad al-Sabah	dinar (0.29 = $1)	89,400	24,910
Lebanon	4,236,000	President Michel Suleiman; Prime Minister Saad al-Hariri	pound (1,500.00 = $1)	5,035	16,250
Oman	2,815,000	Sultan and Prime Minister Qaboos bin Said	rial (0.39 = $1)	37,710	16,660
Qatar	895,000	Emir Hamad bin Khalifa al-Thani; Prime Minister Hamad bin Jassim bin Jabr al-Thani	riyal (3.64 = $1)	55,060	21,160
Saudi Arabia	26,551,000	King and Prime Minister Abdullah ibn Abd al-Aziz Al Saud	riyal (3.75 = $1)	309,800	108,300
Sudan	41,186,000	President Umar Hassan Ahmad al-Bashir	pound (2.45 = $1)	12,150	9,339
Syria	21,399,000	President Bashar al-Assad; Prime Minister Mohammed Naji al-Otari	pound (45.95 = $1)	12,780	14,490
Turkey	76,606,000	President Abdullah Gül; Prime Minister Recep Tayyip Erdogan	new lira (1.50 = $1)	140,800	193,900
United Arab Emirates	4,765,000	President Khalifa bin Zayed al-Nahyan; Prime Minister Mohammad bin Rashid al-Maktum	dirham (3.67 = $1)	210,500	145,800
Yemen	24,536,000	President Ali Abdullah Saleh; Prime Minister Ali Muhammad Mujawwar	rial (204.00 = $1)	8,977	8,829

*Exchange rates as of Sept. 30, 2009.　　　　　　[†]Latest available data.

construction of at least 900 new housing units was projected. Palestinian President Abbas condemned this freeze because of the exclusion of East Jerusalem.

Cedar Revolution victory. Lebanese parliamentary elections in June were seen by many observers of Middle East affairs to be of utmost importance not only for Lebanon but also for the region as a whole. The elections pitted the

anti-Syria, prodemocracy Cedar Revolution coalition against a coalition of parties led by the militant organization Hezbollah, which has ties to the two leading state sponsors of terrorism in the Middle East—Syria and Iran. The results of the elections were a victory for the Cedar Revolution, which won 71 of the 128 seats in the parliament.

The Cedar Revolution won a clear mandate to rule Lebanon. However, the fact that Hezbollah was heavily armed and had used its military might against Cedar Revolution strongholds in May 2008 meant that the so-called "national unity" Cabinet had to include pro-Syria elements. In November 2009, a 30-member Cabinet was formed, with 15 seats representing the Cedar Revolution majority, 10 seats representing the pro-Syria minority, and 5 seats chosen by Lebanese President Michel Suleiman to act as arbitrators between these two opposing factions.

Rigged election in Iran. The election in June for president of Iran involved two leading candidates—the *incumbent* (ruling) President Mahmoud Ahmadinejad and the reformist former Prime Minister Mir Hussein Moussavi. In his campaign, Moussavi criticized President Ahmadinejad for isolating Iran by denying the Holocaust (the systematic extermination of Jews by Nazi Germany) and by making anti-Western speeches. Moussavi called for private ownership of the media and opposed the strict enforcement of Islamic attire and social conduct imposed by the ruling regime— a message that appealed to many women and young people.

Despite pre-election public opinion polls showing Moussavi in the lead, results of the election announced by the Iranian Ministry of Interior gave President Ahmadinejad about 63 percent of the vote and Moussavi about 34 percent of the vote. Moussavi 's followers protested against these results—which were widely viewed as fraudulent—with massive demonstrations in the streets of Tehran, the capital, and in many other major Iranian cities.

Iranian authorities, headed by Supreme Leader Ayatollah Ali Khamenei, responded to these demonstrations with violence. Analysts of Iranian affairs noted that this violent reaction by the government was prompted by fears that the mass movement would lead to a revolution that could topple the regime.

Uranium enrichment. In September, the Iranian government revealed the existence of a secret plant for uranium enrichment at a mountain site near the city of Qom. The location of the site was revealed by Iranian officials after it became known to Western intelligence services.

A report by the UN's International Atomic Energy Agency stated that "Iran's declaration of the new facility reduces the level of confidence in the absence of other nuclear facilities under construction." The UN agency was concerned that Iran might use enriched uranium to build nuclear weapons, though Iranian officials maintained that the uranium would be used only for peaceful purposes.

Terrorist attacks continue in Iraq. Iraqis continued to experience major terrorist bombings and other attacks during 2009. Some attacks targeted Shi`ite Muslims and their shrines. Among the deadliest of these attacks were bombings in February and April that killed scores of people, including 25 Iranian Shi`ite pilgrims. In June, a series of bombings and other attacks killed more than 430 Iraqis—the highest monthly death toll in Iraq in 11 months.

Other terrorist attacks targeted government institutions. In August, three coordinated car bombings and mortar strikes against the ministries of foreign affairs and finance in Baghdad, the Iraqi capital, killed some 130 people and wounded hundreds more. In October, two synchronized car bombings in Baghdad severely damaged the ministry of justice and provincial council complexes, killing at least 150 people and wounding hundreds of others. In early December, coordinated blasts at several government sites left more than 125 people dead.

Iraqi election legislation. After much debate, Iraqi parliamentarians reached agreement in December to increase the number of seats in the parliament from 275 to 325, including increased numbers of seats for Sunni Muslims and ethnic minorities. The legislation also allowed Iraqis living abroad to have their votes counted as being from their provinces of origin. The passage of this legislation was necessary to hold parliamentary elections in early 2010.

Dubai economic scare. In December 2009, the government of Dubai, the largest city in the United Arab Emirates (UAE), received $10 billion from Abu Dhabi, the UAE capital, to help Dubai pay its debts. The crisis began on November 25 when Dubai asked to delay payment on billions of dollars of debt issued by Dubai World, a government-associated conglomerate, and Nakheel, Dubai World's primary real estate subsidiary. In response, investors around the world dumped stocks, especially stocks in banks holding Dubai debt, and moved into assets regarded as safe, gold and the U.S. dollar. Many economists feared that a default could drag down the fragile global economic recovery.

In the face of a possible default, the central bank of the UAE announced in November that it would provide Dubai's banks with extra liquidity to forestall sudden massive withdrawals of cash from the banks. Much of the $10-billion infusion in December went to keep Dubai World and Nakheel from bankruptcy. ■ Marius Deeb

See also **Armed forces; Economics, World; Middle East: A Special Report; Terrorism; United Nations; United States, President of the;** various Middle East country articles.

Mining. See Energy supply.

IRAN'S LONG, HOT SUMMER

By Christine Moss Helms

Iran has been through two transformational periods in its modern history. The first—the 1979 Islamic Revolution—overthrew the regime of Mohammad Reza Pahlavi, who had ruled Iran as *shah* (king) since 1941. The revolution ultimately produced an Islamic *theocracy* (government headed by religious authorities) that soon flexed its revolutionary and Islamic credentials around the world. Thirty years later, Iran's contested June 12, 2009, presidential election left the legitimacy of that theocracy—including those who claimed to be its spiritual guardians—challenged both at home and abroad.

Neighboring Arab governments, wary of provoking Islamist sympathies, watched the election and its aftermath in silence. Leaders in the West were divided. Some, outraged by the apparent election fraud, condemned the Iranian government. Others cautioned that involvement could result in a backlash, strengthening the regime by inciting anti-Western feelings.

In the aftermath of the election and subsequent violence, little

Fiery election protests in the summer of 2009 rocked Iran's regime to its foundations.

appeared to change in Iran, at least on the surface. The two top leaders—President Mahmoud Ahmadinejad *(ah MAH dih nee ZHAHD)* and Ayatollah Ali Khamenei *(kah MAY nee)*—remained in power. Both were considered "hard-liners"—that is, rigidly conservative leaders who were reluctant to compromise. Despite their unyielding stance, they have not been able to extinguish the opposition movement.

Election surprise

No one predicted an election surprise. Ahmadinejad, the current officeholder, held a 2-to-1 lead just three weeks prior to the election. He had strong support in rural areas and among the urban poor due to government *subsidies* (grants of money) and price supports. Although one poll showed that 80 percent of Iranians wanted "change," there were few clear differences between Ahmadinejad and his three rivals: Mir Hussein Moussavi *(moo sah VEE)*; Mehdi Karroubi *(kah roo BEE)*; and Mohsen Rezai *(reh zah EE)*. Political parties, as known in the West, do

Defeated presidential candidate Mir Hussein Moussavi (standing with his arms raised) appears at a demonstration in Tehran, Iran, on June 15, 2009. Moussavi's supporters held mass rallies to protest what they charged was election fraud by the government.

not exist in Iran. All Iranian political candidates must receive the approval of the Guardian Council, a 12-man group half appointed by Khamenei and half chosen by parliament from a list approved by the judiciary. The council can disqualify any candidate it views as disloyal to the theocracy. All three rival candidates had held key positions in Iran's government. Moussavi had served as prime minister. Karroubi, himself a cleric, had twice been the speaker of parliament. Rezai had commanded the Revolutionary Guards, an armed force established after the revolution to protect the theocracy from both internal and external threats.

Ahmadinejad, confident of victory, agreed to Iran's first-ever televised presidential debates. It was a fateful decision. The debates, which ran from June 2 to 8, electrified support for Moussavi, especially among Iran's increasingly young, urban, and educated population. Young city dwellers were a significant group given the massive population changes that had transformed Iran since the 1979 revolution. The population had doubled to 73 million. One-third of the people were between the ages of 15 and 29. Nearly 70 percent of the population lived in urban areas due to massive emigration from rural areas. Many had access to international news via the Internet and television.

The debates backfired for the government. Ahmadinejad lashed out against Moussavi, even attacking his wife, a university administrator named Zahra Rahnavard. Ahmadinejad also criticized two influential religious conservatives, former presidents Mohammad Khatami *(kah TAH mee)* and Akbar Hashemi Rafsanjani *(ruhf sehn JAN ee)*. Ahmadinejad also hinted at corruption by Rafsanjani's family. Moussavi, on the other hand, focused on the country's economic problems. The problems included a 25 percent inflation rate; declining investment in

The author:
Christine Moss Helms is a writer and consultant who has traveled extensively in the Middle East and written several books about the region.

the energy sector, which is the main source of government revenues; and high unemployment. Although the government pegs the unemployment rate at 10 percent, unofficial estimates suggest it could be at least double that number among young people. Moussavi supported Iran's nuclear research program but called for a less defiant stance to the West. His arguments found sympathetic listeners among young people and those with business interests.

In the short countdown to the election, many were stunned when large and growing crowds took to the streets in the capital, Tehran, and other major cities in support of Moussavi. Many Moussavi supporters wore green, a symbol of his campaign and the traditional color of Islam. At times, the size of the crowds rivaled that of the protests against the shah during the late 1970's. Zahra Rahnavard campaigned for her husband. Herself a professional, she energized another group—young and increasingly educated women trying to enter the work force.

On election day, Iranians turned out to vote in numbers seldom seen before. Voter turnout was estimated to be 80 percent, a huge increase over approximately 50 percent in the 2005 presidential elections. Turnout was especially high among young people and in urban areas.

Less than a day after the election, the government announced that Ahmadinejad had won by a wide margin, 63 percent of the vote over Moussavi's 34 percent. The remaining two candidates each received only about 1 percent. Moussavi's supporters and other "reformists," a term loosely applied to government opponents who criticize some aspects of government policy, condemned the "stolen" elections. Aside from the speed of the count and the wide margin of victory, critics pointed out

Iran's President Mahmoud Ahmadinejad (left) appears with opposition presidential candidate Mir Hussein Moussavi (right) in Iran's first-ever televised presidential debates, just days before the election on June 12, 2009.

Presidential candidate Mehdi Karroubi, an Islamic clergyman, speaks at a rally in Tehran in February 2009. After the election, Karroubi charged Iranian officials with mistreating protesters who were being held in government custody.

that Ahmadinejad had won in areas unlikely to support him—his rivals' home districts and discontented minority regions, such as Kurdistan.

Ten days of violence

Demonstrations erupted in major cities. Some were spontaneous and peaceful. Others, especially in Tehran, turned violent as crowds mushroomed into tens of thousands. Security forces, chiefly a civilian militia called the Basij, tried to stop the demonstrations. The Basij, which reports to Khamenei and the Revolutionary Guards, protects the theocracy from domestic threats. Instead of quieting the protests, however, the harsh tactics by the security forces ignited a cycle of violence that escalated rapidly. Hundreds of demonstrators were arrested daily. The government later admitted that 30 people had died, though protesters claimed at least 70 had been killed.

Government censors attempted to block unfavorable stories in the Iranian press. The government restricted Internet access and satellite television and arrested foreign reporters. Even so, Iranian citizens posted descriptions and images of the protests on social networking Web sites, such as Facebook and YouTube.

On June 17, 2009, about 2 million people marched silently through Tehran to protest their "lost votes." Three days later, a young woman—Neda Agha-Soltan—was killed during demonstrations. Her dying moments, posted on the Internet, became a rallying cry for protesters. They defied Khamenei, who reaffirmed his support for the election results. On June 22, 10 days after the election, security forces warned that dissent would no longer be tolerated.

Iran's feared security forces

The government's threat ended the demonstrations and for a good reason. Khamenei and Ahmadinejad controlled the government's most feared security forces, the Revolutionary Guards and the Basij. Both organizations had an interest in the government's survival. Ayatollah Khomeini had created both after the 1979 revolution, and both now reported to Khamenei. The Revolutionary Guards, originally organized to balance the power of Iran's military, had developed into a powerful institution in its own right. Government subsidies and profitable contracts fueled its growth. Members of the Basij, who at first served as enforcers of moral behavior, had also expanded their role. During daily patrols of neighborhoods, Basij members gathered a wealth of information about possible threats to the government.

Ahmadinejad, a former member of the Revolutionary Guards, strengthened both organizations after becoming president in 2005. Some people believe he funneled money to his supporters in the two organizations, creating secret factions more loyal to him than to Khamenei. To further strengthen his hold on power, Ahmadinejad appointed loyal Revolutionary Guards commanders to key positions in the military and the intelligence service. He had also appointed political allies to government posts.

Charges of torture

In July 2009, the families of some prisoners arrested during the demonstrations charged that their relatives had been beaten and raped.

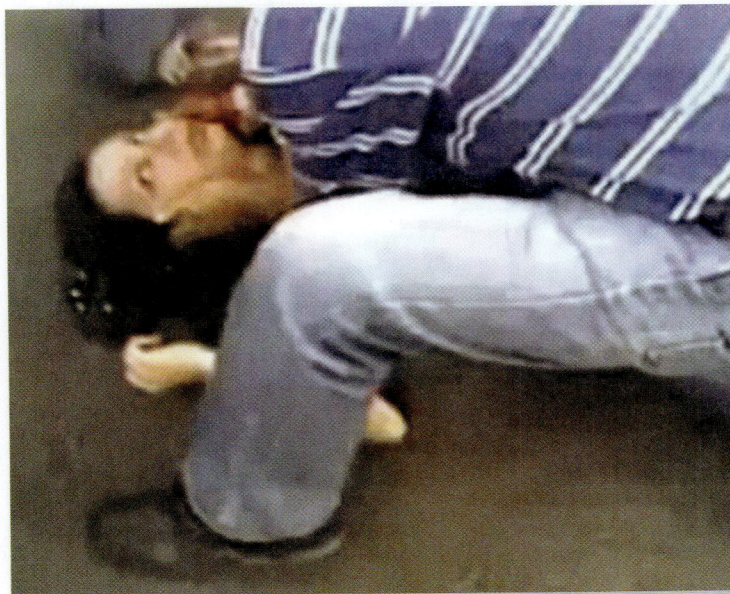

A young bystander, Neda Agha-Soltan, lies dying on a Tehran street on June 20, 2009, after being shot. Amateurs took videos of her death and broadcast them over the Internet. The opposition called Agha-Soltan the "Angel of Freedom."

Rumors circulated that at least three prisoners had died in custody. Karroubi, one of the defeated presidential candidates, assembled evidence of the mistreatment of prisoners. He offered to present the evidence in a public forum, but the government seized his files.

The rumors kept discontent at a quiet boil. Charges of torture and deaths awakened memories of the 1979 revolution, when Islamic leaders had leveled similar charges against the shah. His secret police force, the SAVAK, had used torture and imprisonment to crush opposition to his rule. The idea that Iran's theocracy had committed such abuses cast doubt on its claim to be the guardian of Islamic justice and democracy.

At first, the government denied the charges and questioned the loyalty of those making the accusations. In late July 2009, Khamenei suddenly ordered the closing of Kahrizak, a Tehran detention center that had held many political prisoners after the election. Later reports linked the closing to the death of a young man arrested in the protests, Mohsen Ruholamini. He reportedly had died of abuse in Kahrizak. Ruholamini was the son of a key aide to presidential candidate Rezai. The death drew particular attention, even among hard-line conserv-

Ayatollah Ali Khamenei (bottom), Iran's supreme leader, leads Friday prayers at the University of Tehran on June 19, 2009, a week after the disputed election. President Mahmoud Ahmadinejad (wearing a light-colored jacket) kneels in prayer behind him. Khamenei's sermon after the prayers denied any election fraud. The sermon also confirmed Ahmadinejad's victory and demanded an end to demonstrations.

atives, because Rezai had been a Revolutionary Guards commander.

The closing of Kahrizak did little to ease concerns. Iran's prosecutor general, the head of the court system, acknowledged in August that 200 people remained in Evin prison in Tehran. The Revolutionary Guards and Basij also continued to arrest dozens of people daily. The Justice Ministry, which did not control the security forces, struggled to cope with the flood of prisoners now charged with political crimes.

In early August, the government began weekly televised "show trials"—public trials conducted chiefly for propaganda purposes. Some 140 political prisoners stood trial for a range of national security offenses. One group included opposition politicians, journalists, lawyers, and student activists. Another group of defendants, including a French researcher and several Iranian workers employed by the British and French embassies, were charged with spying. Guards paraded the defendants before TV cameras, where the prisoners confessed to crimes against the state. The opposition charged that the government had used torture to extract confessions. The trials disturbed many Iranians, including prominent religious conservatives.

Khamenei's image tarnished

The contested election and its aftermath tarnished the reputation of a person previously thought untouchable—Ayatollah Khamenei. He was only the second person to hold the post of Iran's supreme spiritual

A police officer sprays tear gas at a protester who is attacking him with a steel bar during demonstrations on June 13, 2009, in Tehran. Although some demonstrations were peaceful, others turned violent. The government admitted that 30 people had died, but the opposition claimed at least 70 had been killed.

Ayatollah Ali Khamenei (left) hands a presidential decree to President Ahmadinejad (right) at a ceremony in Tehran on Aug. 3, 2009. Major religious and political leaders stayed away from the ceremony, in which the ayatollah gave an Islamic blessing to the president.

leader. His primary role was to protect the theocracy by playing the part of a just, neutral authority while protecting the government's interests. But his early support for Ahmadinejad undermined his neutrality.

That the election and its aftermath diminished Khamenei's image became apparent in August. On the 3rd of August, Khamenei conducted an Islamic blessing of Ahmadinejad and, on the 5th, he officiated at the president's *secular* (nonreligious) swearing-in ceremony. Major religious and political leaders skipped one or both ceremonies, a major breach of protocol. The absentees included Ahmadinejad's three presidential rivals, members of parliament, and two former presidents, Rafsanjani and Mohammad Khatami. Even a grandson of Khomeini reportedly failed to attend the religious ceremony. Some people questioned whether Khamenei, then 79 years old, had lost touch with Iran's increasingly young, educated, and global-minded population.

Mixed messages

Khamenei delivered a number of mixed messages that left Iranians baffled. He alternated firm declarations of hard-line Islamist ideals with gestures of good will toward the West and toward Iranian critics. In August, he said that he did not believe that the West had stirred up Iran's election protests. Some people saw that statement as a sign that Khamenei opposed demands by Ahmadinejad and other hard-liners to punish opposition leaders. Then, in September, Khamenei urged "ardent defenders of Islam" to review the teaching in Iran's universities of the humanities and liberal arts, subjects he called "un-Islamic." The message, along with reports that security groups had made lists of suspect students and teachers, frightened many. Khamenei also issued stern warnings to the opposition in September. "Confronting the system, confronting the tenets of the system, standing up to and drawing a sword against the system will get a harsh response," he stated.

At the same time, Khamenei apparently tried to restrain Ahmadinejad. In September, the ayatollah reportedly told the president to listen to "benevolent criticism." Khamenei's office also released a letter from influential clerics asking the government to focus on "solving people's problems and the country's economic woes and social challenges."

Ahmadinejad defiant

Many critics doubted that Khamenei could control Ahmadinejad even if he wished to do so. In July, Ahmadinejad appointed his daughter-in-law's father as Iran's first vice president. The first vice president leads Cabinet meetings in the absence of the president and is considered the most important of Iran's several vice presidents. Khamenei ordered Ahmadinejad to withdraw the appointment. Ahmadinejad obeyed, but only after a week. He then appointed the daughter-in-law's father as a key personal aide.

Questions about an "unholy alliance" between Khamenei and Ahmadinejad arose again after the president submitted a controversial list of 21 Cabinet nominees to parliament in August. Some lawmakers had previously criticized Ahmadinejad for replacing qualified administrators with political appointees. Many legislators, even conservatives, objected to the new list of Cabinet choices. Ultimately, all but three were approved, but only after the intervention of Khamenei, who stressed the need for unity. Although conservatives controlled at least two-thirds of the parliamentary seats, many of Ahmadinejad's nominees were approved by narrow margins. The close votes indicated dissent among the conservatives.

Only three nominees—all candidates for positions related to national security—won strong approval. All three new Cabinet members—the ministers of the interior, of intelligence and security, and of defense—had links to the Basij or the Revolutionary Guards. The appointments further aroused international anger. Interpol, an

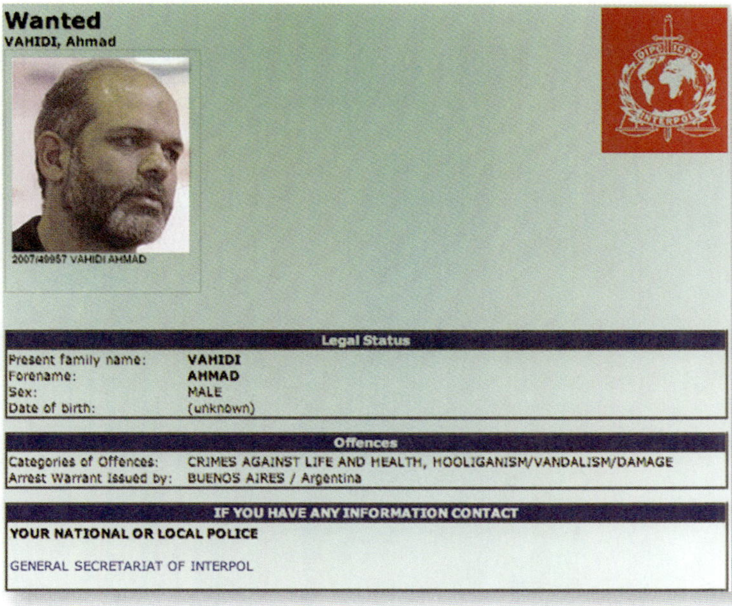

Wanted
VAHIDI, Ahmad

2007/49957 VAHIDI AHMAD

Legal Status	
Present family name:	**VAHIDI**
Forename:	**AHMAD**
Sex:	MALE
Date of birth:	(unknown)

Offences	
Categories of Offences:	CRIMES AGAINST LIFE AND HEALTH, HOOLIGANISM/VANDALISM/DAMAGE
Arrest Warrant Issued by:	BUENOS AIRES / Argentina

IF YOU HAVE ANY INFORMATION CONTACT
YOUR NATIONAL OR LOCAL POLICE

GENERAL SECRETARIAT OF INTERPOL

A wanted poster circulated by the international police organization Interpol describes the charges against Ahmad Vahidi, Ahmadinejad's choice for defense minister. The warrant accuses Vahidi of planning a 1994 bombing in Buenos Aires, Argentina, that killed 85 people.

international organization of police forces from many countries, had an arrest warrant for Ahmad Vahidi *(vah hee DEE),* the new defense minister. The warrant called for Vahidi's arrest for his alleged role in a 1994 bombing that killed 85 people at an Argentine Jewish center.

International reactions

Many Arab leaders privately took comfort in Iran's contested elections. They had long resented Iran's claims to be the standard-bearer of Islam and of Islamic democracy. They viewed Iran as an outsider because Iranians are Persian, not Arab. They were angered that Iran reportedly supported Arab groups, such as radical Palestinian groups and Hezbollah in Lebanon. Some suspected Iran had supported armed groups in Iraq and a rebel group in Yemen. They argued that Iran's interference threatened the stability of Arab states and fractured Arab unity. Arab opposition groups, who had clamored for greater freedom, went largely silent after Iran's postelection turmoil. There was one exception, however—Arab women who admired the prominent role of their Persian counterparts in both the election and the protests that followed.

The West's reaction to the election was muted. Many leaders had hoped that strong election results, especially if Ahmadinejad won, would enable Iran's government to reconcile with the West. Their hopes grew after Barack Obama, the new president of the United States, offered a "dialogue" to defuse tensions between Islamic nations and the West. For some strategists, the key issue was Iran's enrichment of uranium, one of the steps involved in preparing uranium for use as a nuclear fuel and in nuclear weapons. Others argued that the international *sanctions* (penalties) imposed after the 1979 revolution had isolated Iran, making its behavior dangerous and unpredictable.

President Ahmadinejad answers questions during a news conference in New York City on Sept. 25, 2009. He stated that the United Kingdom, the United States, and France would "regret" accusing Iran of hiding an underground plant to make nuclear fuel. Ahmadinejad denied that the nuclear plant was a secret.

Discussions between Iran and Western nations about Iran's nuclear development program ended with no conclusion in the autumn of 2009. Some analysts believed that Ahmadinejad, weakened by the election, no longer had sufficient power to agree to a compromise.

Dangerous times

Iran's present government bore little resemblance to Khomeini's postrevolutionary Iran and its stated ideals of Islamic justice and democracy. Now entrenched, the theocracy wielded powerful political and security forces, not unlike those of the shah. By some estimates, the Revolutionary Guards and other groups linked to the theocracy controlled more than 30 percent of the economy.

At year's end, the government remained in control. There was no unified opposition and no clear leader. Moussavi's call for "change" triggered a large, rapid shift in public opinion. In the fall, however, he warned of "dangerous" times and largely disappeared from the scene. He had reason to fear. Ahmadinejad and his supporters demanded that the government deal harshly with opponents, including Moussavi, Karroubi, and Khatami. Security forces reportedly arrested relatives of conservative critics; and authorities sentenced at least five protesters to death for their role in the June demonstrations and announced a special investigation of Karroubi.

Even so, Iran's opposition remained defiant. In mid-December, Khamenei accused the opposition of breaking the law by insulting the founder of the Islamic Republic, Ayatollah Khomeini. State television showed someone tearing up a poster of Khomeini during a demonstration. Moussavi and Karroubi said that the government faked the incident to tarnish the opposition. Reformists again clashed with police on December 21 in the holy city of Qom after the funeral of the dissident cleric Grand Ayatollah Hoseyn Ali Montazeri. Clashes between security forces and opposition protesters in Tehran on December 27 resulted in the deaths of at least eight people, including Moussavi's nephew. The government's use of deadly force on Ashura, one of the holiest of Shi`ite holidays, deeply shocked many Iranians. Authorities subsequently arrested Moussavi's top aids and other opposition figures.

By year's end, the Iranian opposition, Iran's Arab neighbors, and the West found themselves trapped in a complex, dangerous dance with the new government. Ahmadinejad's aims remained unclear. He continued to defy Khamenei and to strengthen his own power at key ministries. The role of Khamenei, once considered the voice of neutrality who could settle disputes, was now questioned.

One thing was clear. Iran's theocracy was under great stress. The election had deepened a divide within Iran's population, of whom about 70 percent were born after the revolution. The government's response to the election deepened splits and created new ones, even among Islamic conservatives. The regime also faced a silent enemy. In 2009, roughly half of the population was under the age of 15. Each year, unemployment among young people grows. If Iran's theocracy survives, it will soon be forced to deal with that economic reality.

Moldova. Two sets of parliamentary elections in Moldova in 2009 failed to produce a coalition large enough to choose a new president. In the April 5 election, President Vladimir Voronin's long-ruling Communist Party won 60 seats in the 101-seat parliament—one less than the three-fifths required to elect a president. Some 10,000 demonstrators marched in the capital of Chisinau, alleging vote-rigging by the ruling Communists. Clashes with police led to widespread arrests.

The Communist Party put Prime Minister Zinaida Greceanii forward as its presidential candidate, but she twice failed to garner the 61 parliamentary votes necessary for election. According to the Moldovan Constitution, a second failure automatically results in parliament's dissolution.

In the resulting July 29 parliamentary elections, the Communist Party won only 48 seats. Four pro-Western parties formed a coalition and elected Liberal Democratic Party head Vlad Filat as prime minister on September 25. However, Communist walkouts prevented the election of the coalition's presidential candidate, Marian Lupu, in votes held on November 10 and December 7. A further parliamentary election was expected for 2010.
　　　　　　　　　　　　　　 ■ Juliet Johnson
　　See also **Europe.**

Monaco. See Europe.

Mongolia. See Asia.

Montenegro. Prime Minister Milo Djukanovic and his ruling European Montenegro coalition retained a firm hold on power in Montenegro after parliamentary elections in March 2009. The elections, called 18 months early, delivered 48 parliamentary seats to Djukanovic's coalition and only 31 to opposition parties. Opposition politicians accused Djukanovic of calling elections early to avoid having to campaign later, after the effects of the global economic downturn fully set in. Djukanovic, who has dominated Montenegrin politics since the 1990's, led Montenegro in June 2006 to independence from a union with Serbia.

The worldwide economic downturn reversed a trend of strong economic growth in Montenegro in recent years. Economists projected that the country's gross domestic product (GDP)—the value of all goods and services produced in a year—would shrink by 5 percent in 2009. In 2008, GDP had expanded by 7.5 percent.

In April 2009, the member nations of the European Union (EU) referred Montenegro's application for EU candidacy, submitted in December 2008, to the European Commission, the EU's executive arm. Approval of the application would set the stage for negotiations toward eventual EU membership.　　 ■ Sharon L. Wolchik
　　See also **Europe; Serbia.**

Montreal residents rose to great heights in 2009 as a trio of the city's astronauts made news: one as Canada's first space tourist; another on her second NASA mission; and the third selected to join the Canadian Space Agency's national program from among more than 5,000 applicants.

Guy Laliberté, the 50-year-old billionaire philanthropist and founder of the Cirque du Soleil, paid approximately $35 million (U.S.) to join Russian cosmonaut Maksim Surayev and NASA astronaut Jeffrey Williams for a ride aboard a Russian Soyuz spacecraft to the International Space Station. The 11-day trip began on September 30.

Julie Payette made her second trip to the space station in July as the flight engineer aboard the space shuttle Endeavour. The 45-year-old helped complete a 16-day mission to finish construction of Japan's orbital laboratory. Payette had made her first voyage on the shuttle Discovery in May 1999. She was the first Canadian to board the space station and participate in an assembly mission on it.

David Saint-Jacques, an astrophysicist and physician who works as a clinical faculty lecturer at Montreal's McGill University, was one of the country's two newest astronauts announced by the Canadian Space Agency on May 13, 2009. Canadian Air Force Captain Jeremy Hansen, a fighter pilot from Ontario, was also selected.

Bicycle sharing. Back on Earth, Bixi, the City of Montreal's award-winning public bicycle rental system, was launched in May and quickly became an international hit. The innovative bike-sharing program—an abbreviation of the words *bicyclette* and *taxi*—is being adopted by a growing number of cities, including Ottawa, Boston, and London. Created by employees of the municipal parking authority, the service's self-service rental stations are solar powered, enabled through Wi-Fi (wireless Internet access), and accessible by credit card.

Mayoral election. In elections on November 1, Mayor Gérald Tremblay defeated his main rival, former provincial politician Louise Harel, to win a third term. He won 37 percent of the vote, compared with Harel's 33 percent.

Port expansion. The Montreal Port Authority, operator of the world's largest inland port, announced plans in January to build a $500-million (U.S.) container facility to further expand into United States markets. The 50th anniversary of the opening of the St. Lawrence Seaway, which allowed Montreal's port to flourish, was celebrated on June 26.

Sports. The Montreal Canadiens of the National Hockey League marked the team's 100th anniversary with a host of celebrations during the 2008-2009 season. The team also experienced a change in both ownership and coaching staff. On June 1, management named Jacques Martin the 29th head coach in team history. On June 20, owner George Gillett, Jr., announced he was selling the team to a group led by three brothers from the beer-brewing Molson family. Members of the Molson family owned the team from 1957 to 1971 and from 1978 to 2001, when Molson, Inc., sold a majority stake of the team to Gillett.

Bed-in anniversary. Forty years after the historic May 1969 John Lennon and Yoko Ono bed-in at Montreal's Queen Elizabeth Hotel, the Montreal Museum of Fine Arts hosted the free exhibition *Imagine: The Peace Ballad of John & Yoko,* from April 2 to June 21, 2009. The couple recorded the song "Give Peace a Chance" at the hotel. Endorsed by Ono, the exhibition featured memorabilia, lectures, and films. Ono even recorded a message of peace that was broadcast throughout the Métro subway system for the duration of the show.

World Wide Web-slinger. John Philip Neufeld, a 21-year-old music major at Montreal's Concordia University, was credited by police in the United Kingdom with thwarting a planned March 17 firebombing of a British high school. Neufeld spotted the plot in an Internet posting and notified the Norfolk police via a phone call over the Internet. Half an hour later, a 16-year-old boy was arrested outside the school. He was carrying a jug of fuel, matches, and a knife.   ■ Mike King

See also **Canada; Canadian provinces; City.**

Morocco. See **Africa.**

Motion pictures. Despite the struggling economy, Hollywood set a box-office record in 2009 with annual ticket sales of over $10 billion in the United States. A surprising number of hits were features without big-name superstars. The science-fiction action sequel *Transformers: Revenge of the Fallen* was the year's top-grossing film, earning nearly $109 million in its opening weekend in June. Its "stars" were Shia LaBeouf and Megan Fox. Other high-performing summer films without big stars included *Star Trek,* based on the original television series; *G.I. Joe: The Rise of Cobra,* based on the American action figure; the latest J. K. Rowling installment, *Harry Potter and the Half-Blood Prince;* the buddy comedy *The Hangover;* the Pixar animated adventure *Up;* the 3-D animated adventure sequel *Ice Age: Dawn of the Dinosaurs;* the romantic comedy *(500) Days of Summer;* and the South African science-fiction film *District 9.* These films outperformed 2009 films featuring such A-listers as Russell Crowe, Will Ferrell, Tom Hanks, Eddie Murphy, Julia Roberts, Adam Sandler, John Travolta, and Denzel Washington. Even megastar Johnny Depp, who starred as the American gangster John Dillinger in the much-hyped crime drama *Public Enemies,* delivered disappointing box-office sales.

Glorious summer. One A-list star who did not fail to deliver at the summer box office was Brad Pitt in the R-rated Nazi thriller *Inglourious Basterds,* directed by Quentin Tarantino. The acclaimed film, described by the director as a "spaghetti western with World War II iconography," brought in $38 million in its first weekend in August—Tarantino's best opening yet. The few other big stars who managed to win summer box-office glory included Hugh Jackman in the superhero action film *X-Men Origins: Wolverine,* based on the Marvel Comics fictional character; and Ben Stiller, Owen Wilson, and Robin Williams in the family adventure film *Night at the Museum: Battle of the Smithsonian.*

The "Twitter" effect. Early filmgoers had the power to make or break films in 2009, using instant messaging (IM) via social networking sites Twitter and Facebook. Industry observers noted that negative reactions expressed via IM doomed Sacha Baron Cohen's much-hyped mockumentary *Brüno,* while positive IM buzz made the low-budget horror film *Paranormal Activity* a hit. Without stars or a large marketing campaign, *Paranormal Activity* started out in late September as a midnight-only release in 13 cities. Paramount expanded the film's markets and showtimes based on the online community's requests. By its fourth week, it was number one at the box office. *Paranormal Activity* was compared by many to *The Blair Witch Project* (1999), which caused a sensation with its spooky, cinéma vérité approach.

Family fare. Several notable family-friendly 2009 features were adaptations of famous children's books. The animated fantasy-horror *Coraline* was based on the 2002 book by Neil Gaiman. *Cloudy with a Chance of Meatballs* was an animated version of the 1978 book by Judi Barrett and Ron Barrett. The live-action, animatronic *Where the Wild Things Are,* based on the 1964 book by Maurice Sendak and directed by Spike Jonze, was a big hit with adult audiences. *Fantastic Mr. Fox,* a stop-motion animated version of the 1970 Roald Dahl classic, was directed by Wes Anderson and featured the voices of Jason Schwartzman, George Clooney, and Meryl Streep. The award-winning *Ponyo,* by the Japanese anime master Hayao Miyazaki and presented by Walt Disney Pictures, was based on the Hans Christian Andersen fairy tale "The Little Mermaid" (1837). *The Princess and the Frog,* a retelling of the Grimm's fairy tale "The Frog Prince," featured traditional Disney animation. It was Disney's first animated feature with an African American heroine. *Disney's A Christmas Carol* featured the voice of Jim Carrey as Ebenezer Scrooge in a motion-capture animated reimagining of the Charles Dickens 1843 classic.

The Iraq War and U.S. involvement in Afghanistan were common themes in several notable 2009 films. *The Hurt Locker,* directed by Kathryn Bigelow, followed a U.S. Army bomb disposal unit as it contends with the threat of insurgency in Baghdad during the Iraq War in 2004. Shot

Kate Winslet (above) won the Academy Award as best actress for her performance as a former Nazi concentration camp guard who has an affair with a teenager (David Kross) in *The Reader.*

A biographical picture, a World War II romantic drama, and a rags-to-riches tale thrilled audiences and won Academy Awards in 2009.

Sean Penn received the Academy Award for best actor for his performance in *Milk*. Penn portrayed the openly gay politician Harvey Milk, the San Francisco supervisor who was assassinated along with San Francisco Mayor George Moscone in 1978.

ACADEMY AWARD WINNERS IN 2009

The following winners of the 2008 Academy Awards were announced in February 2009:

Best Picture: *Slumdog Millionaire*

Best Actor: Sean Penn, *Milk*

Best Actress: Kate Winslet, *The Reader*

Best Supporting Actor: Heath Ledger, *The Dark Knight*

Best Supporting Actress: Penélope Cruz, *Vicky Cristina Barcelona*

Best Director: Danny Boyle, *Slumdog Millionaire*

Best Original Screenplay: Dustin Lance Black, *Milk*

Best Screenplay Adaptation: Simon Beaufoy, *Slumdog Millionaire*

Best Animated Feature: *WALL·E*

Best Cinematography: Anthony Dod Mantle, *Slumdog Millionaire*

Best Film Editing: Chris Dickens, *Slumdog Millionaire*

Best Original Score: A. R. Rahman, *Slumdog Millionaire*

Best Original Song: "Jai Ho" from *Slumdog Millionaire*

Best Foreign-Language Film: *Departures* (Japan)

Best Art Direction: Donald Graham Burt and Victor J. Zolfo, *The Curious Case of Benjamin Button*

Best Costume Design: Michael O'Connor, *The Duchess*

Best Sound Mixing: Ian Tapp, Richard Pryke, and Resul Pookutty, *Slumdog Millionaire*

Best Sound Editing: Richard King, *The Dark Knight*

Best Makeup: Greg Cannom, *The Curious Case of Benjamin Button*

Best Visual Effects: Eric Barba, Steve Preeg, Burt Dalton, and Craig Barron, *The Curious Case of Benjamin Button*

Best Animated Short Film: *La Maison en Petits Cubes (The House of Small Cubes)*

Best Live-Action Short Film: *Spielzeugland (Toyland)*

Best Feature Documentary: *Man on Wire*

Best Short Subject Documentary: *Smile Pinki*

Dev Patel (left) and Freida Pinto embrace in *Slumdog Millionaire*, about an orphaned teenager from the slums of Mumbai, India, who becomes a contestant on an Indian version of the television game show "Who Wants to Be a Millionaire?" The film won eight Academy Awards, including best picture.

in the Middle East, the film earned numerous awards at festivals. *The Messenger* starred Ben Foster and Woody Harrelson as Iraq War veterans whose job is informing families that their sons and daughters have died during combat. *Brothers,* starring Natalie Portman, Tobey Maguire, and Jake Gyllenhaal, told the story of a young man who comforts his older brother's wife and children after the brother goes missing in Afghanistan. The dark comedy *The Men Who Stare at Goats,* based on the 2004 best seller by Jon Ronson, starred George Clooney as a U.S. operative who joins a reporter in Iraq to find the founder of a secret, telepathic military unit. The film also starred Ewan McGregor, Jeff Bridges, and Kevin Spacey.

Biopics. In addition to the John Dillinger film *Public Enemies,* several other biographical pictures attracted the attention of audiences and critics in 2009. Meryl Streep received rave reviews for her portrayal of American chef Julia Child in the summer hit *Julie & Julia,* written and directed by Nora Ephron. The film contrasts the early years of Child's culinary career with the life of blogger Julie Powell (Amy Adams), who in 2002 aspired to cook all 524 recipes from Child's first cookbook, *Mastering the Art of French Cooking* (1961), in one year.

Invictus, directed by Clint Eastwood, starred Morgan Freeman as South Africa's first black president, Nelson Mandela, when he campaigned to host the 1995 Rugby World Cup. Hilary Swank starred as American aviator Amelia Earhart in *Amelia.* Emily Blunt and Rupert Friend were lauded for their portrayals of the young Queen Victoria and Prince Albert in *The Young Victoria.* Other notable biographical pictures included *Bright Star,* directed by Jane Campion, about the romance between 19th-century English poet John Keats and Fanny Brawne; and *Coco Before Chanel,* starring Audrey Tautou as the French designer Coco Chanel.

Documentaries. The sudden death of Michael Jackson on June 25, 2009, prompted the release in October of *This Is It.* The film documented the singer's last rehearsals for a concert series that had been scheduled for later in the year. It became the highest grossing concert film ever, earning more than $100 million worldwide in its opening weekend.

Another popular documentary was Michael Moore's *Capitalism: A Love Story,* which examined the impact of capitalism on Americans' lives. The acclaimed *More than a Game* followed National Basketball Association (NBA) phenomenon LeBron James and four of his former teammates through the trials and tribulations of high school basketball in Akron, Ohio, to James's journey to NBA fame. *The Providence Effect* told the story of a blacklisted civil rights activist who set up an academically distinguished school in an impoverished, high-crime Chicago neighborhood.

Vampires, zombies, and aliens. One of 2009's most anticipated films, the *Twilight* teen vampire movie sequel *The Twilight Saga: New Moon, was* based on the best-selling series of novels by Stephenie Meyer. The film earned nearly $73 million at the box office when it was released in November, setting a one-day box-office record.

Director Sam Raimi's summer horror gross-out, *Drag Me to Hell,* about a cursed young woman who is tormented by the vengeful spirit of a dead Gypsy, was a box-office hit in May. The R-rated horror-comedy *Zombieland,* starring Woody Harrelson as a Twinkie-obsessed zombie killer, debuted at number one at its October release.

The South African film *District 9,* about extraterrestrials forced to live in a militarized Johannesburg ghetto, became a surprise hit in August. It attracted interest in part due to a clever marketing campaign in various cities that featured "humans only" signs advertising the film in public places such as bus stops. The much-hyped 3-D special-effects blockbuster *Avatar,* directed by James Cameron, was a predictable year-end hit. The film revolves around a band of humans who are pitted in a battle against a distant planet's indigenous population. The film helped break a weekend box-office record of $278 million in December, along with *Sherlock Holmes, Alvin and the Chipmunks: The Squeakquel,* and *It's Complicated.*

Other notable fall and late-2009 films included director Steven Soderbergh's dark political comedy *The Informant!* Based on a true story, the film starred Matt Damon as a bipolar agribusiness whistleblower who becomes a spy for the Federal Bureau of Investigation. The acclaimed British film *An Education,* set in 1961, told the story of a 16-year-old schoolgirl (Carey Mulligan) who is seduced by a 35-year-old playboy con artist (Peter Sarsgaard). The Coen brothers' black comedy *A Serious Man,* set in 1967, told the story of a physics professor whose life unravels when his wife tells him she is leaving him. Drew Barrymore made a strong directorial debut with *Whip It,* about a teenaged girl (Ellen Page) who runs away to join a roller derby league. The painful *Precious,* directed by Lee Daniels, starred newcomer Gabourey Sidibe as an abused, illiterate, obese teenager who struggles to find hope in her despair-filled life. *Up in the Air,* starring George Clooney as a traveling contractor who fires people for a living, was named best picture by the National Board of Review (NBR). The board named the romantic comedy *It's Complicated,* starring Meryl Streep, Alec Baldwin, Steve Martin, and John Krasinski, as best ensemble film. Nicolas Cage won acclaim for his performance in director Werner Herzog's crime drama *Bad Lieutenant: Port of Call New Orleans.* Jeff Bridges was lauded for his portrayal of an aging, alcoholic country music singer in *Crazy Heart. Nine,* based

John Hughes
"Philosopher of adolescence"

John Hughes has been called "the philosopher of adolescence" for writing and directing several popular motion-picture comedies about teenage life in the mid-1980's. In such movies as *Sixteen Candles* (1984) and *The Breakfast Club* (1985), he combined lighthearted comedy with a sincere concern for the problems of young people. His best films captured both the popular culture of the 1980's and the timeless awkwardness of growing up. Hughes died on Aug. 6, 2009.

John Wilden Hughes, Jr., was born on Feb. 18, 1950, in Lansing, Michigan. When he was 13, his family moved to the Chicago area, where Hughes would later set and film his best-known works. Hughes attended high school in the Chicago suburb of Northbrook. Many of his films are set in Shermer, Illinois—a fictional reimagining of Northbrook as the all-American, upper-middle-class everytown.

After dropping out of college, Hughes worked as an advertising copywriter in Chicago. He also sold jokes to professional comedians and wrote for the humor magazine *National Lampoon*. His career in film began as a screenwriter, with early successes including the 1983 hit comedies *Mr. Mom* and *National Lampoon's Vacation*.

Hughes's most iconic works are the series of high school movies that he wrote and directed in the mid-1980's. *Sixteen Candles* introduced the actress Molly Ringwald as an awkward and sensitive teenager whose family forgets her birthday. In *The Breakfast Club,* five high-schoolers from different social cliques spend the day together in detention. Separated from the social conventions that alienate them, they find that they have much in common, in what remains Hughes's most sober and touching study of adolescence. *Weird Science* (1985) is the story of two nerdy teenage boys who create the perfect artificial woman. In *Ferris Bueller's Day Off* (1986), a boy and his friends skip school to spend the day in Chicago. The film is memorable for Matthew Broderick's portrayal of the wily Ferris and for its use of Chicago landmarks such as the Art Institute, Sears (now Willis) Tower, and the baseball stadium Wrigley Field. *Pretty in Pink* (1986), a high school movie written but not directed by Hughes, is often ranked with these works.

Hughes eventually moved on to more adult and family-oriented fare. He traded the vulnerability of his teenage protagonists for the boisterousness of the late comic veteran John Candy in *Planes, Trains, and Automobiles* (1987) and *Uncle Buck* (1989). The latter stood out for Candy's performance as the lovable ne'er-do-well Buck Russell and for the introduction of child actor Macaulay Culkin. Culkin would star in Hughes's most commercially successful movie, *Home Alone* (1990). The film, written and produced by Hughes, is a vicious slapstick comedy in which a young boy defends his home from burglars.

Hughes's career faded with the passing of the 1980's. After the flop *Curly Sue* (1991), he retired from directing and from public life, moving to a farm in Harvard, Illinois. He continued to write, however, turning out scripts for more than a dozen movies before his death. His influence can be seen in the work of a younger generation of filmmakers who grew up with his movies, including Wes Anderson, Judd Apatow, and Kevin Smith. ■ Jeff De La Rosa

on the 1982 Broadway musical inspired by the Federico Fellini film *8 ½,* starred Daniel Day-Lewis as a film director who has trouble completing his ninth film. The star-studded musical also featured Penélope Cruz, Judi Dench, Nicole Kidman, Sophia Loren, and Marion Cotillard. The action-charged mystery *Sherlock Holmes,* directed by Guy Ritchie, starred Robert Downey, Jr., in a bohemian take on the famous detective . Post-apocalyptic films included the blockbuster *2012,* starring John Cusack, and *The Road,* based on the 2006 novel by Cormac McCarthy, starring Viggo Mortensen, Charlize Theron, and Robert Duvall.

Twice the best pics picks. The Academy of Motion Picture Arts and Sciences announced that it would double the number of best picture Oscar nominees to 10, beginning with the 82nd Academy Awards in 2010. The best picture would be selected by a preferential voting system, rather than the single-choice voting used in other categories. In the single-choice system, voters make their selections for best picture and the film with the most votes wins. In the preferential system, voters rank their best picture choices. Preferential voting helps choose the candidate with the strongest support of a majority of the electorate. ■ Shawn Brennan

See also **People in the news** (Kate Winslet).

Mozambique. See Africa.

Music. See Classical music; Popular music.

Myanmar in 2009 extended the house arrest of human rights activist Aung San Suu Kyi after an event involving a man who entered her residence unannounced. Myanmar's ruling *junta* (military government) had kept her under house arrest for about 14 of the past 20 years. During that time, she supported economic sanctions by the United States and other countries intended to pressure the junta into restoring democracy.

On May 3, 2009, an American named John Yettaw swam across a lake to avoid guards and sneaked into Suu Kyi's house. He claimed to have been sent by God to warn Suu Kyi of an assassination attempt. Yettaw was arrested on May 6 as he attempted to swim away.

Both Suu Kyi and Yettaw stood trial for violating the terms of her house arrest. On August 11, Suu Kyi was sentenced to three years' hard labor, which was commuted to an additional 18 months' house arrest. The sentence would keep her out of parliamentary elections scheduled for 2010. Yettaw was sentenced to seven years in prison, including four years' hard labor. On Aug. 15, 2009, U.S. Senator Jim Webb (D., Virginia) met with junta leader Than Shwe and secured Yettaw's release.

On September 25, Suu Kyi wrote a letter to the junta indicating that she was willing to assist them in getting the sanctions lifted. She was allowed to meet with a government minister and

The collapse of a 2,300-year-old Buddhist temple in Yangon, Myanmar's largest city, just three weeks after the wife of the ruling junta's top general had rededicated it, was widely interpreted as a very bad omen. Myanmar has been called the most superstitious country in Asia.

then with Western diplomats in Myanmar.

Economy. In 2009, economists cited an unreleased report by the United Nations-affiliated International Monetary Fund that painted a bleak picture of Myanmar's economy. Government-controlled oil and gas exports had helped bolster the economy. However, critics noted that despite large foreign reserves, money was spent on political vanity projects and military development rather than rebuilding Myanmar after a 2008 cyclone that left almost 140,000 people dead or missing.

Fighting. In 2009, Myanmar's military, mostly made up of members of the ethnic Burmese majority, launched attacks on ethnic groups living in the country's eastern highland border regions. Many members of these minority groups had long resisted government rule, and the new offensive aimed to secure government control over the country's entire territory. In June, some 4,000 members of the Karen ethnic group fled across Myanmar's border into Thailand. In August, some 30,000 people fled into China from the ethnically Chinese Kokang region. The army also targeted other ethnic areas.

■ Henry S. Bradsher

See also **Asia.**

Namibia. See **Africa.**

Nauru. See **Pacific Islands.**

Nepal. Pushpa Kamal Dahal resigned as prime minister on May 4, 2009, after a power struggle over his attempt to dismiss the chief of Nepal's army. He was succeeded on May 23 by Madhav Kumar Nepal, a moderate Communist.

Background. Dahal, using the name Prachanda ("the fierce one"), led a 10-year guerrilla war by self-styled Maoists to overthrow Nepal's monarchy. The war, which raged from 1996 to 2006, left more than 16,000 people dead. The United Nations (UN) brokered a truce between the government and the Maoists in 2006, and in 2008 the Maoists won 220 out of 601 seats in national assembly elections. The assembly abolished the monarchy and named Dahal as prime minister.

The truce agreement provided for some 19,000 former Maoist guerrillas to be held in UN-supervised camps until they could be integrated into Nepal's army. The army chief, General Rookmangud Katawal, a monarchist who had fought the Maoists, resisted the planned integration.

Dahal fired Katawal on May 3, 2009. President Ram Baran Yadav argued that the dismissal was unconstitutional and ordered Katawal to remain as head of the army. The Communist Party of Nepal (United Marxist-Leninist) withdrew from the ruling coalition to protest Dahal's effort to oust Katawal. Dahal then quit, announcing that he was stepping down to "create a positive

environment for salvaging democracy, nationalism, and the peace process." Communist Party head Madhav Kumar Nepal took over as the head of an unstable 22-party coalition government.

The political struggle hampered work on writing a new constitution. The assembly had been elected to complete one by May 2010 that would establish a more representative political system in a nation long dominated by upper-caste Hindus.

One sensitive constitutional issue involved official languages. Nepali, the mother tongue of about half of the country's 29.9 million people, had been the language of official communication. Some assembly members wanted to give 11 other languages the same status.

Inequality. A report prepared jointly by Nepal's government and the UN Development Programme warned in August 2009 of profound inequalities in Nepali society. The report's authors wrote that the underlying causes of the Maoist guerrilla war, including poverty and discrimination on the basis of gender and ethnic group, had not improved. They warned that failure to deliver better social services and provide greater opportunities for such groups as Muslims, low-caste Hindus, and women could lead to mass unrest.

■ Henry S. Bradsher

See also **Asia.**

Netherlands. Prime Minister Jan Balkenende's government—consisting of the Christian Democratic Appeal, the Labor Party, and the Christian Union—remained stable during 2009. In June, however, the far-right Freedom Party, led by Geert Wilders, took second place in elections to the European Parliament, after Balkenende's center-right Christian Democrats but ahead of the center-left Labor Party. In May, the Dutch Supreme Court had cleared the way for prosecuting Wilders for inciting hatred against Muslims, a move that only seemed to increase his popularity. The trial was scheduled for January 2010. Observers maintained that the growing popularity of the Freedom Party made its participation in future governments more likely.

Economic crisis. In response to the global economic crisis, the government took over and pledged financial participation in many large and medium-sized Dutch financial institutions in late 2008 and throughout 2009. In March, the coalition announced an agreement on a fiscal stimulus package totaling 6 billion euros ($9 billion). The move increased funding for infrastructure and was expected to lead to large increases in public debt.

In addition, the government proposed a number of austerity measures. Part of the plan was an increase in the age at which workers can receive state pensions from 65 to 67. The policy change, which was enacted by the Cabinet and sent to Parliament for approval, resulted in bitter opposition by unions and political parties on both the left and the far right. Because of the stimulus package, the budget of the Netherlands fell from a surplus of 0.7 percent in 2008 to a deficit of 4.7 percent in 2009. At 3.4 percent, the unemployment rate remained well below the 9.1-percent average for other European Union nations.

Foreign policy. The Netherlands continued to be a strong supporter of United States foreign policy during 2009, including providing about 1,400 troops for the NATO-led mission in Afghanistan. Dutch troops served in areas of the country where the most intense fighting occurred and were committed to remain there until mid-2010.

In February 2009, Balkenende, after resisting previous calls, approved the creation of a parliamentary commission to investigate the legality of the Dutch government's support for the United States in the run-up to the war in Iraq in spring 2003. The report was to be released in 2010.

Queen Beatrix and her family escaped harm when the driver of a car tried to crash into the open-air bus in which they were riding during Queen's Day celebrations April 30, 2009. Six onlookers were killed, as well as the driver, whose motive remained unclear.　　■ Jeffrey Kopstein

See also **Europe.**

New Brunswick. See Canadian provinces.

New York City. Mayor Michael R.
Bloomberg won a close election on Nov. 3, 2009, for a third four-year term. In 2008, he worked to bypass a City Charter law he once supported that limited incumbents to two terms. The billionaire mayor—whose $16-billion net worth makes him the richest person in New York—reached into his own deep pockets to spend more than $100 million on his reelection. In total, he has spent more than $250 million running for office since 2001.

Bloomberg, a political moderate running as a Republican and Independent, defeated Comptroller William C. Thompson, a Democrat who had the lukewarm support of President Barack Obama. Bloomberg, 67, became the fourth mayor elected to three terms, joining Fiorello H. La Guardia, Robert F. Wagner, and Edward I. Koch.

Councilman John C. Liu, 42, who immigrated to America from Taiwan at age 5, became in 2009 the first Asian American to hold citywide office by decisively winning the comptroller's post. When Liu was a child, his parents changed his first name from Chun in honor of President John F. Kennedy.

End of an era. The election also closed out the legendary public service career of Robert Morgenthau. The 90-year-old New York County (Manhattan) district attorney announced on February 27 that he would not seek reelection after 34 years as the city's top prosecutor and eight years as U.S.

attorney for the Southern District of New York.

Morgenthau is a member of one of America's most distinguished families—his father was Henry Morgenthau, Jr., President Franklin D. Roosevelt's treasury secretary, and his grandfather was U.S ambassador to the Ottoman Empire during World War I (1914-1918). Robert Morgenthau gained a reputation for prosecuting high-profile corruption, organized crime, and white-collar crime.

Among the people prosecuted by his office were Mark David Chapman, who pleaded guilty to killing Beatle John Lennon; Bernie Goetz, the "subway vigilante"; and Tyco executive Dennis Kozlowski. Morgenthau was also a mentor to many assistant district attorneys who went on to prominent careers, including Supreme Court Justice Sonia Sotomayor and former Governor Eliot Spitzer.

Morgenthau's hand-picked successor, former assistant Cyrus R. Vance, Jr., won a spirited Democratic primary on September 15 and went on to win the election on November 3. Vance, whose father served as President Jimmy Carter's secretary of state, became only the fourth elected Manhattan district attorney since 1937.

Sports. Plans for a massive high-rise development in downtown Brooklyn, including a soaring sports arena, took a strange turn on Sept. 24, 2009, when Mikhail Prokhorov, reputedly Russia's richest man, announced that he was buying the New Jersey Nets of the National Basketball Association.

The 6-foot 9-inch (206-centimeter) Prokhorov, a basketball aficionado, bought an 80-percent controlling interest in the Nets from developer Bruce Ratner, who intended to move the team from its Meadowlands home in New Jersey to anchor Atlantic Yards, his proposed Brooklyn complex. The deal also called for Prokhorov to take a 45-percent interest in the arena, if it is ever built. Frank Gehry, the arena's original architect, said on June 4 that he had been removed from the project to save money.

A new Yankee Stadium opened in the Bronx in 2009 as the club with baseball's highest payroll made its first World Series appearance in six years against the Philadelphia Phillies. The Yankees won the series, four games to two.

The Mets' new home, Citi Field, in Queens, also opened in 2009 for what turned out to be a disastrous first season. The Mets finished the year with a 70-92 record.

Hero pilot. Pilot Chesley "Sully" Sullenberger became a national hero on January 15 after he landed his sputtering plane in the frigid Hudson River in the "Miracle on the Hudson." All 155 passengers and crew members were safely rescued by ferry boats and fireboats. Sullenberger's US Airways Flight 1549 lost power when it hit a flock of geese moments after his plane left LaGuardia Airport.
　　■ Owen Moritz

See also **Aviation; City.**

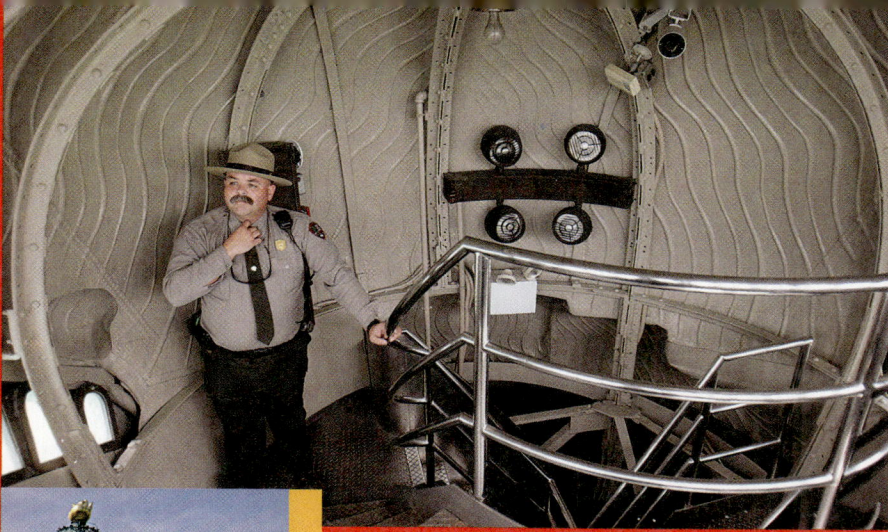

A National Park Service ranger surveys the crown observation deck from inside the Statue of Liberty's skull in anticipation of the reopening. The Park Service initially reopened the statue in 2004, but visitors were only allowed into the pedestal and the observation deck at the base of the statue.

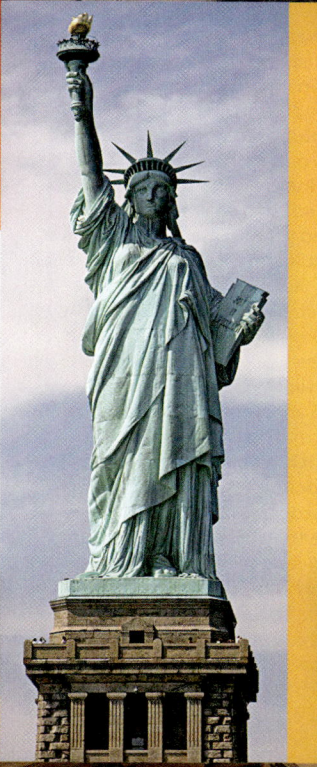

The interior of the Statue of Liberty, including the crown observation deck, reopened in 2009, nearly eight years after its closure following the Sept. 11, 2001, terrorist attacks.

A National Park Service police officer checks out the staircase before the statue's interior reopened on July 4, 2009. Only 30 visitors per hour—10 at a time—are allowed to climb the 168-step spiral staircase to the crown. The arm and torch have been closed to the public since 1916.

New Zealand in 2009 showed early signs of recovering from the global economic downturn. Government accounts for the year to June showed a deficit of $10.5 billion, compared with a surplus of $2.4 billion only a year earlier. (All amounts are in New Zealand dollars.) Unemployment reached a nine-year high of 6.5 percent in September, and a sharp drop in tax revenue forced the government into heavy borrowing, which economists predicted would be required for much of the next decade.

However, in the second quarter the economy began to show minor growth—0.2 percent—after five quarters of contraction. Higher prices for dairy products and demand from China for more forestry products suggested a recovery in the market was underway. Sales in two-thirds of retail industries rose in August. In October, the median sale price of houses exceeded the 2007 level after a sharp dip in 2008.

Tighter bank lending regulations in New Zealand had prevented subprime property collapses such as those experienced in the United States and the United Kingdom, and there had been no retail bank failures as a result of the recession. However, from 2007 through 2009, some 30 finance companies collapsed. They had been subject to less stringent controls than retail banks, and criminal investigations were launched in relation to a number of the failures.

Government. In October, the government announced that referendums would be held in 2011 and 2014 to decide whether the mixed member proportional (MMP) representation form of voting should be changed. Introduced in 1996, the MMP system determines parliamentary seats through combined candidate/party votes and has led to a succession of coalition governments.

In April 2009, the government announced plans to merge the eight local authorities that govern Auckland, the largest city in New Zealand. The "super city" plan, which generated considerable controversy over issues of representation and function, was to be formed in time for elections in October 2010.

Crime. For the first time in New Zealand history, a former member of parliament (MP) was jailed on charges of bribery, corruption, and perverting the course of justice. Taito Philip Field had been a Labour Party MP and government minister when allegations arose in 2005 that he had expedited a man's immigration application in return for work on his house. In August 2009, Field was found guilty on 26 of the 35 charges he faced and was sentenced to six years' imprisonment.

■ Gavin Ellis

See also **Pacific Islands.**

Newfoundland and Labrador.

See **Canadian provinces.**

NEWS BYTES

Selected news from 2009:

Oldest English words. In February 2009, a researcher at the University of Reading in the United Kingdom detailed how he used a supercomputer—the fastest type of mainframe computer—to find some of the oldest words in the English language. Evolutionary biologist Mark Pagel determined that words that are used more frequently are less likely to change over time than words that are used less frequently. Pagel began with lists of words in related languages that stem from a common "ancestral word." He then used a supercomputer to create a model of the evolution of words in English and other *Indo-European languages* (languages primarily based in India and Europe).

Pagel determined that the words "I," "we," "two," "three," and "thou" are among the oldest English words still in use. According to Pagel, those words are at least 10,000 years old. Pagel's model also predicted words that, because they are developing rapidly across the Indo-European language family, are likely to die out sooner. According to the model, such words as "dirty," "guts," "squeeze," and "stick" are more likely to disappear than other words.

Famed lost British ship found. In February 2009, an international team of explorers announced the discovery of a warship that had been lost for more than 250 years. In October 1744, the H.M.S. *Victory*, flagship of the Channel Fleet and the predecessor to the ship of the same name commanded by Admiral Horatio Nelson, sank in the English Channel during a storm. About 1,000 men went down with the ship, which was reportedly carrying some 100,000 gold coins now valued at roughly $1 billion. Also on board were approximately 40 bronze cannons emblazoned with the seal of King George I. The high cost of making bronze cannons led to them being replaced by iron cannons on later ships.

Odyssey Marine Exploration, a team of researchers, scientists, and archaeologists based in Tampa, first located the wreck of the *Victory* in April 2008. They used sonar to scan an area of the English Channel some 60 miles (100 kilometers) from the spot where historians believed the *Victory* went down. The team found signs of metal on the sea floor and explored the area using an underwater robot. The robot recorded footage of the remains of a shipwreck, including bronze cannons and parts of the hull. They raised two cannons, but left the rest of the wreck intact. By studying the cannons, the researchers were able to determine where and when they were made. This made it possible to positively identify the wreck as the *Victory*. Odyssey Marine Exploration worked together with the British Ministry of Defence, which gave the company permission to continue salvaging the wreck. Although the ship was found in international waters, its contents belong to the British government because it is a military wreck.

Funerals for Poe. American poet and short-story writer Edgar Allan Poe was memorialized with a pair of funerals in 2009. In recognition of the bicentennial of Poe's birth (Jan. 19, 1809), the city of Baltimore held a public celebration of his life that included a wake, funeral procession, and funeral ceremony. Although Poe had connections to several East Coast cities during his lifetime, it was in Baltimore that he died under unexplained circumstances on Oct. 7, 1849. He was buried there the following day. Although Poe was famous as the author of such poems as

"The Raven" and such short stories as "The Fall of the House of Usher," fewer than 10 people attended his three-minute funeral service in 1849.

Baltimore began its ceremonies on Oct. 7, 2009, the 160th anniversary of the death, with a public viewing of a mannequin representing Poe in a replica casket. Over the following days, a number of events celebrated the life and works of Poe, who is often seen as influential for his works in detective and horror fiction. On October 11, following a funeral procession, actor John Astin presided over a funeral service that featured actors and other speakers offering tributes to Poe. Astin, a Baltimore native, is best remembered for his portrayal of Gomez Addams on the 1960's television show "The Addams Family." More recently, he depicted

The U.S.S. *New York* cruises under the Verrazano Narrows Bridge as it arrives in New York Harbor on its maiden voyage in November 2009. The navy warship, which was built in New Orleans by Northrop Grumman Ship Systems, contains 7.5 tons (6.8 metric tons) of steel from New York City's World Trade Center in her bow. The ship, announced in September 2002, serves as a memorial to the people who died in the Sept. 11, 2001, terrorist attacks on the Trade Center.

As part of a documentary on Hitler for the Discovery Channel, a cable television network, archaeologist Nick Bellantoni from the University of Connecticut in Storrs traveled to Moscow to study the skull. Although it had been damaged by fire and stored under less-than-ideal conditions, Bellantoni was able to obtain a DNA sample. On his return to Storrs, he and a team of other researchers subjected the sample to a series of tests. The DNA revealed that the skull was that of a female, probably between the ages of 20 and 40. Another of the researchers, geneticist Linda Strausbaugh, emphasized that the results of the test prove nothing about Hitler's fate, merely that the skull was not his.

Poe in a one-man theatrical show titled *Edgar Allan Poe: Once Upon a Midnight.* A second service was performed to accommodate hundreds of Poe fans who had flocked to Baltimore for the memorial.

Skull not Hitler's, say scientists. A team of American researchers in 2009 announced that a skull that had long been thought to be that of Adolf Hitler was actually that of an unknown woman. Historians generally agree that Hitler died in Berlin in 1945, toward the end of World War II. Most accounts state that Hitler committed suicide by taking cyanide before shooting himself in the head. However, some historians doubted that Hitler shot himself, believing that detail to have been added by his supporters to make him seem heroic. After the war, Soviet troops kept a jawbone and skull fragment they believed to be Hitler's. The skull, which has a bullet hole and, therefore, seemed to prove that Hitler had shot himself, was put on display in Moscow in 2000.

At auction in 2009: On November 14, a charred bottle of Lowenbrau became the most expensive bottle of beer ever auctioned, selling for more than $16,000. The bottle had been taken from the wreckage of the *Hindenburg,* a German airship that burst into flame in New Jersey on May 6, 1937, killing 35 people. A firefighter at the now-famous disaster scene recovered six bottles of Lowenbrau and a milk pitcher. He buried them for safekeeping and eventually passed them along to a family member.

The chess set featured in the classic Ingmar Bergman film *The Seventh Seal* sold for $143,000 on Sept. 28,

fashion designer Yves Saint Laurent sold for more than $484 million at Christie's in Paris. The auction of 773 pieces collected by Saint Laurent, who died in 2008, and his partner was controversial for its inclusion of two bronze sculptures that had disappeared from China in 1860. China's State Administration of Cultural Heritage was unsuccessful in its attempts to reclaim the sculptures or stop the auction. Other pieces at the auction included a pair of Louis XV velvet couches and paintings by Piet Mondrian and Henri Matisse.

The Olivetti Lettera typewriter used by American novelist Cormac McCarthy to write more than a dozen novels since the 1960's sold at Christie's in New York City for $254,500 on Dec. 4, 2009. McCarthy is the author of *All the Pretty Horses, No Country for Old Men*, and the Pulitzer Prize-winning *The Road*. He purchased the typewriter at a pawnshop in the early 1960's for $50 and had used it to compose all of his novels as well as short stories, plays, and letters. He finally agreed to part with the machine after a friend bought him another Lettera in better condition.

■ S. Thomas Richardson

2009. In the iconic 1957 motion picture, a knight returning from the Crusades plays a game of chess with Death in hopes that his life will be spared from a deadly plague. The set was among more than 300 of Bergman's possessions auctioned off. The Swedish director died in 2007.

The manuscript of a speech written by President Abraham Lincoln shortly after his 1864 reelection sold for $3.44 million on Feb. 12, 2009. The Southworth Library Association in Dryden, New York, had owned the document since 1926. The library planned to use the money realized by the auction to build a new wing.

Over three days in late February 2009, a collection of art treasures owned by the late

Newspaper. The year 2009 was financially challenging for newspapers in the United States. A sharp decrease in readers and advertising revenue forced many papers to stop publishing or printing.

Newspapers that closed in 2009 included, in February, the *Rocky Mountain News,* a daily published out of Denver since 1859. Other papers stopped their print editions and began publishing only online. The *Seattle Post-Intelligencer,* which began in 1863, stopped printing and became an online newspaper in March 2009. *The Christian Science Monitor,* founded in 1908, became an online-only publication also in March. In May, the *Tucson Citizen,* an Arizona newspaper published since 1870, suspended print for online. In November, Window Media and United Media closed down. These parent companies owned a number of papers across the United States that catered to the lesbian, gay, bisexual, and transgender (LGBT) communities, including the *Southern Voice* and the *Washington Blade.* The *Washington Blade* was the oldest LGBT newspaper in the United States and was regarded by many as the newspaper of record for that community.

A number of major newspapers were still printing but in financial difficulty in 2009. The owners of the *Chicago Sun-Times,* first published in 1948, filed for bankruptcy in March 2009. The *Sun-Times* was purchased by an investment group in October. The city's other major daily, the *Chicago Tribune,* founded in 1847, had filed for bankruptcy in December 2008. Early in 2009, the New York Times Co., which owned *The Boston Globe,* threatened to sell or close that paper. Founded in 1872, the *Globe* was projected to lose $85 million in 2009, until cost-cutting measures were introduced. Even the venerable *New York Times* was forced to sell its new headquarters building in Manhattan to cut costs.

Why print newspapers faltered. The problems in the industry went beyond and predated the advent of the Internet. One factor was based in demography. Newspapers are more successful in urban areas with dense populations, where readers can buy a paper on every street corner without the need for delivery or subscriptions. But, after World War II (1939-1945), many people in the United States began to migrate from big cities to suburban areas. People in distant suburbs often felt less connection to their city newspaper and quit reading a paper. However, because the population of the United States was quickly increasing, publishers still sold large numbers of newspapers, and the impact of this demographic change was blunted. Nevertheless, according to data from *Editor & Publisher,* in 1940, the number of households in the United

States was 40 million, and daily circulation—the number of papers distributed in a day—was 35 million. By 2000, there were around 105 million households in the United States, but daily circulation was under 60 million.

Not all of this decrease was demographic. The decrease in the percentage of people who read newspapers can also be attributed to television news. Television became the dominant news source for Americans in the 1960's, during the heyday of network nightly news programs. While viewership of the national news began dropping in the 1980's, local news, morning news programs, and cable news caused the number of people who got their news from TV to keep growing.

In addition to reducing newspaper readership, TV hurt newspaper advertising. Companies that advertised nationally, such as automobile manufacturers, found it easier to organize ad campaigns with TV networks, as opposed to advertising in many individual newspapers.

In the 2000's, these long-time problems were compounded by the Internet. In 1995, *USA Today* became one of the first major daily newspapers with an online edition. According to surveys by the Pew Research Center, a Washington, D.C.-based think tank, around 70 percent of the people in the United States in 1995 regularly read a daily print newspaper. By 2002, that number had dropped to around 62 percent. By 2008, when the Internet had truly emerged as a news source, the number had dropped to 34 percent. Growing online readership, however, could not substitute for lost print readers. Revenues from online advertising were much smaller than from print.

Even fewer ads were purchased in newspapers in the troubled business climate of 2009. Ad revenues for newspapers in the United States dropped 28 percent in the first quarter and 29 percent in the second.

Looking for new revenue. Only a small number of papers, such as *The Wall Street Journal* and the London-based *Financial Times,* charged for access to even some of their online content in 2009. In May, a "summit" of sorts with some two dozen newspaper executives was held in Chicago to debate how best to charge for Internet content.

Another hope for getting readers to pay for content was seen in the sale of electronic editions designed to be read on such devices as smartphones and Amazon's e-book reader, the Kindle. *The New York Times* charged around $50 per month for a print subscription and $13.99 for a Kindle subscription in 2009. Therefore, *The Times* needed three and one-half Kindle subscribers to make up for each print reader lost.

■ Christine Sullivan

Nicaragua. In 2009, the suspension of international aid owing to credible corruption allegations pushed Nicaragua into a deepening recession. An April report by the Nicaraguan Foundation for Economic and Social Development predicted increasing poverty and the loss of 30,000 to 50,000 more jobs by year's end. Increasingly authoritarian actions by President Daniel Ortega prompted the United States government to cancel the remaining $62 million of a $175-million program to help Nicaragua fight poverty.

In January, Nicaragua's Supreme Court overturned corruption charges against former President Arnoldo Alemán. Alemán had been convicted in 2003 of stealing millions of dollars in public funds while in office (1997-2002). Opposition lawmakers suspected a deal between Alemán and the Sandinista government. After his release, Alemán's supporters in the Liberal Constitutionalist Party came to an agreement with the Sandinista Party, giving Ortega control of the National Assembly.

On July 1, 2009, Alexis Argüello, mayor of the capital city of Managua, was found dead, an apparent suicide. Argüello, 57, a former world champion boxer and national celebrity, was elected mayor in November 2008.

■ Nathan A. Haverstock

See also **Latin America.**

Niger. See **Africa.**

Nigeria. In 2009, Nigerian President Umaru Yar'Adua's government faced a new threat from Muslim rebels in northern Nigeria. The rebels sought to establish Shari`ah (Islamic law) throughout the country. About half the people of Nigeria are Muslims. They make up the majority of the population in the north. Nearly 40 percent of the people are Christians. They live mainly in southern and central parts of Nigeria. The two religious groups have clashed repeatedly since the late 1990's.

The Muslim rebels were called Boko Haram, meaning "Western civilization is forbidden" in the Hausa language of northern Nigeria. They were also called Nigeria's Taliban. But analysts said the rebels had no links to the conservative Islamic group believed to be centered in Afghanistan and Pakistan.

Boko Haram attacked churches, police stations, prisons, and government buildings in several northern states during July, leaving more than 700 people dead. The violence centered on Maiduguri, the capital of Nigeria's Borno state. Mohammed Yusuf, the founder and spiritual leader of the group, died in police custody on July 30. Officials said he was shot while trying to escape.

Oil rebels. Another rebel group, the Movement for the Emancipation of the Niger Delta (MEND), stepped up its armed campaign against foreign oil companies in Nigeria in 2009. The rebels claimed to be fighting for a fairer share of the oil revenues for the people of the Niger Delta, the site of almost all of Nigeria's oil reserves.

On June 9, MEND set fire to a pumping station owned by Chevron Corporation, a United States company that ranks as one of the world's largest petroleum companies. In July, the group bombed a Chevron pipeline for the second time after it had been repaired after a MEND attack in June. The group also set fire in June and July to several pipelines owned by Royal Dutch/Shell Group, a Netherlands-based petroleum company.

On July 12, MEND carried out its first attack outside of the Niger Delta. The group struck a government-owned oil terminal in Lagos in southwestern Nigeria. MEND fighters attacked the terminal and set fire to a fuel depot and tankers. Formal peace talks between MEND and the government began in November, bringing some hope of an end to the violence in the Niger Delta

Child poisonings. In February 2009, the country's Ministry of Health announced that at least 84 Nigerian children had died since November 2008 from drinking a tainted syrup. The syrup, given for teething pain, contained diethylene glycol, a poisonous substance normally found in antifreeze and brake fluid.

■ Simon Baynham

See also **Africa.**

Nobel Prizes in literature, peace, economics, and the sciences were awarded in October 2009 by the Norwegian Storting (parliament) in Oslo and by the Karolinska Institute, the Royal Swedish Academy of Sciences, and the Swedish Academy of Literature, all in Stockholm. Each prize was worth about $1.4 million.

The 2009 Nobel Prize in literature was won by Romanian-born German novelist and essayist Herta Müller. Müller's work, which describes the brutal oppression of people living under a totalitarian regime in spare, poetic prose, is relatively unknown outside of Germany. She has written about 20 books, 6 of which have been translated into English. Her first work, a collection of short stories about life in a Romanian village, was censored by Romanian authorities. Her later works—*The Land of Green Plums* (1996) and *The Appointment* (2001)—are haunting depictions of life in Romania under Nicolae Ceausescu.

The 2009 Nobel Peace Prize was awarded to United States President Barack Obama. The Nobel committee chose Obama for "extraordinary efforts to strengthen international diplomacy and cooperation between peoples." Obama accepted the honor as a "call to action, a call for all nations to confront the challenges of the 21st century."

The 2009 Nobel Prize in economics was shared by two Americans, Elinor Ostrom at Indiana

University in Bloomington and Oliver E. Williamson at the University of California, Berkeley. The prize was awarded for their independent work on how local communities can reduce conflict.

Ostrom showed that such communities as those that harvest lumber in the undeveloped countries that she studied can often monitor and limit each other's use of shared resources (called "the commons") better than can such outside authorities as governments or corporate hierarchies. Williamson studied corporations and showed that they arise not only to make profits, but also because they often reduce the cost and complexity of doing business, thus eliminating conflicts.

The 2009 Nobel Prize in physiology or medicine was shared equally by three American biologists—Australian-born Elizabeth H. Blackburn, English-born Jack W. Szostak, and Carol W. Greider—for their discoveries about cell structures that play critical roles in cancer and aging. The structures, called telomeres, are found on the ends of chromosomes, the threadlike parts in cells that carry genes, which determine hereditary characteristics. Genes are long sequences of DNA (deoxyribonucleic acid) molecules that contain the chemical instructions that determine the form and function of each cell in an organism.

Blackburn discovered that the end of each chromosome in a single-celled organism called *Tetrahymena* contains a highly repetitive sequence of DNA and specialized proteins that form the telomere. Szostak detected telomeres in yeast and also found that DNA degrades rapidly when inserted into dividing yeast cells. Together, Blackburn and Szostak determined that telomeres form a protective "cap" at the ends of chromosomes that prevents damage to DNA. Greider, as a graduate student in Blackburn's laboratory, found that an enzyme was necessary in the formation of telomeres. Scientists have learned that cancer and other diseases associated with aging involve chromosome damage. By protecting chromosomes, telomeres play a role in preventing such disease.

The 2009 Nobel Prize in physics was shared by three scientists: British and American electrical engineer Charles K. Kao; and Canadian and American physicist Willard S. Boyle and American physicist George E. Smith, both of Bell Labs in Murray Hill, New Jersey. In the 1960's, Kao discovered how light travels through glass fibers. His research is considered a turning point in the development of fiber optics, a technology critical for the high-speed transfer of computer data in such fields as communication and medicine.

Boyle and Smith in 1969 invented the charge-coupled device (CCD), a light-sensitive device that captures light and converts it into an electrical signal. The development of CCD's provided a breakthrough in digital photography. CCD's are the primary element in consumer digital cameras and are used in such astronomic instruments as the Hubble Space Telescope and the Mars rovers.

The 2009 Nobel Prize in chemistry was shared equally by three scientists who independently described the structure of the ribosome and explained how it functions at the atomic level. Ribosomes are the parts of a cell that assemble proteins, molecules that build, maintain, and repair body tissues.

Indian-born American biochemist Venkatraman Ramakrishnan of the Medical Research Council Laboratory in Cambridge, England, and Israeli crystallographer Ada Yonath were the first to produce images of one part of the ribosome—the small subunit—in 2000, revealing the individual atoms within. American biochemist Thomas Steitz of Yale University in New Haven, Connecticut, produced an image, also in 2000, of the second part of the ribosome—the large subunit—including its atomic structure. Ramakrishnan and Steitz later determined how the ribosome "reads" strands of RNA (ribonucleic acid) that serve as instructions for assembling the proteins. Their work has important applications in antibiotic, medical, and pharmaceutical research.

■ Kristina Vaicikonis

See also **Literature; Physics; United States, President of the.**

Northern Ireland. The peace between Roman Catholics and Protestants held firm in 2009, despite some acts of violence. Northern Ireland was formed as a province of the United Kingdom (U.K.) from the six counties of Ulster in 1920. The rest of Ireland gained independence from the U.K. in 1921. In Northern Ireland, the Roman Catholic minority accused the Protestant majority of denying Catholics their civil rights and excluding them from political power. Sinn Féin, the nationalist political organization that drew support from some Catholics, demanded the incorporation of the province into the Republic of Ireland. The Protestant population, however, wished to maintain the union with the U.K.

An upsurge in violence between Catholics and Protestants in 1969 led the British government to send troops to the province to keep the peace. The so-called "troubles" came to an end in 1998, when then-British Prime Minister Tony Blair negotiated a cease-fire between Sinn Féin and the Ulster Unionists. The pact led to the *decommissioning* (putting beyond use) of weapons by the Irish Republican Army (IRA), the military wing of Sinn Féin; the withdrawal of most British troops; and the reorganization of the police force, which the Catholic community distrusted. A power-sharing assembly at Stormont in which parties on both sides of the religious divide participate was created in 2007. In

2008, Peter Robinson, leader of the Democratic Unionist Party (DUP), took over as first minister for Northern Ireland from Ian Paisley, a Protestant clergyman. Martin McGuinness of Sinn Féin was deputy first minister. Concern remained, however, about dissident nationalist and loyalist groups that refused to accept the peace process.

Violence. In March 2009, the Real IRA, a nationalist group opposed to the peace process, took responsibility for the murder of two off-duty soldiers, who were killed near their barracks in County Antrim. The soldiers—the first troops to be killed in Northern Ireland since the peace process began—were preparing for deployment to Afghanistan. Two days later, a similar group, the Continuity IRA, took responsibility for shooting a Catholic policeman in County Armagh. The killing was in protest against Catholics joining the new Police Service of Northern Ireland, whose predecessor organization had favored Protestants. Protestant and Catholic politicians denounced the murders.

Violence continued in the fall. In May, loyalists killed a Catholic community worker during disturbances following a soccer match. In July, riots between Catholic and Protestant groups broke out in Belfast. In October, dissident republicans set two bombs in Belfast, and masked supporters of the Real IRA fired handguns during the funeral of a member. No one was killed in any of the incidents.

Ethnic attacks. About 40 Poles living in Belfast fled their homes after attacks following a soccer match in March 2009 between Northern Ireland and Poland. Loyalist paramilitary groups blamed local Poles after Polish football fans caused violence and disorder. In June, ethnic attacks by Loyalists on more than 100 Romanians in South Belfast forced the Romanians to take shelter in a church. Many of those attacked subsequently chose to return to Romania under a program funded by the Northern Ireland government.

Decommissioning. In June, the peace process continued when three Loyalist groups—the Ulster Volunteer Force, the Ulster Defence Association, and the Red Hand Commandos—began to decommission their weapons. Canadian General John de Chastelain, who had overseen the decommissioning of weapons by the IRA, oversaw the process.

Devolution. In October, British Prime Minister Gordon Brown announced the final stage in the devolution process by promising funds to transfer justice and policing powers to the Northern Ireland Assembly. The aim was to create a new justice ministry at Stormont, though some members of the DUP felt the proposal was a concession to Sinn Féin.   ■ Rohan McWilliam

See also **Ireland; United Kingdom.**

Northwest Territories. See Canadian territories.

Norway. Prime Minister Jens Stoltenberg retained his position after parliamentary elections held on Sept. 14, 2009. His three-party, center-left coalition was elected with a narrow majority to a second, four-year term. The largest coalition member, the Labor Party, increased its share of the vote; the Center Party's share remained unchanged; and the Socialist Left Party's declined. Observers credited the coalition's reelection to Stoltenberg's popularity and the inability of the fragmented center-right parties to field an effective candidate.

In October, the coalition partners presented a new governmental platform called Soria Moria II, after the agreement developed following the 2005 election. The plan called for increased spending in health care, education, and environmental protection. The election also led to a Cabinet reshuffle, with fully half the positions being filled by women for the first time. Leader of the Socialist Left Party Kristin Halvorsen gave up her position as finance minister to become minister of education, a position that was expected to strengthen her party's profile, as education was a coalition priority.

Foreign policy. The ruling coalition continued to face internal disagreements over potential membership in NATO, which the Socialist Left Party opposed. Even so, in 2009 Norway contributed 700 troops to the NATO-led International Security Assistance Force in Afghanistan.

While Norway continued to remain outside the European Union (EU) in 2009, its economic and social standards almost completely conformed to EU standards. Soria Moria II stipulated that in cases where Norwegian and EU law disagree, the government will follow the course that best promotes Norway's interests. The addition of two EU laws to Norwegian legislation came into question in 2009. The first concerned the government's postal monopoly; the second, the EU directive calling for the government to store electronic communications for 6 to 24 months, so that they can be used in criminal investigations. Norwegian trade unions criticized the former law as a vehicle for reducing wages and job security in the public sector. The latter was considered by some coalition members a violation of individual privacy.

Economy. Norway's significant North Sea oil and gas reserves largely shielded the country from the worst effects of the global economic downturn. Nevertheless, the nation's finance department forecast in May that Norway's economy would contract by 1.9 percent in 2009. Unemployment was expected to be 3.75 percent in 2009, among the lowest in Europe.   ■ Jeffrey Kopstein

See also **Europe.**

Nova Scotia. See Canadian provinces.

Nuclear energy. See Energy supply.

Nunavut. See Canadian territories.

Nutrition. See Food.

Ocean. Scientists described seven new species of deep-sea bamboo corals in research published by the National Oceanic and Atmospheric Administration on March 6, 2009. The corals were found in an area northwest of Hawaii, in the Papahanaumokuakea Marine National Monument, at depths reaching 5,745 feet (1,750 meters). Six of the corals represent new *genera* (groups) of species. The research team also found a giant sponge approximately 3 feet (1 meter) across.

Green bombers. Researchers with the University of California at San Diego described a unique group of deep-sea worms in the August 21 issue of the journal *Science.* The seven new species live at depths between 5,900 and 12,140 feet (1,800 and 3,700 meters). Scientists dubbed the worms "green bombers" because, when threatened, the animals release body parts that produce a brilliant green light. This light is thought to help the worms escape predators.

Benthic explorer. A new deep-sea robot explored the muddy ocean bottom off the coast of California in July. The robot, called the *Benthic Rover,* has the size and weight of a compact car. Unlike other submersibles, the rover slowly rolls across the ocean floor on tracks. Every 10 to 16 feet (3 to 5 meters), the rover stops to measure the activity of microbes living in the sediment. Among other goals, scientists hope to learn how the rich microbial life of the ocean floor survives on only tiny amounts of food.

Ocean acidification. In January, more than 150 leading scientists from 26 countries signed a declaration warning that the increasing acidity of the oceans could devastate marine life. Ocean acidification is caused by the increase in atmospheric carbon dioxide, which results from people burning such fossil fuels as coal. The oceans absorb about one-third of the additional carbon dioxide, causing ocean water to become more acidic. Research has shown that ocean acidification is especially threatening to corals and shellfish because it interferes with their ability to build shells and other body structures. The Monaco Declaration urged countries to reduce carbon dioxide emissions before ocean acidification causes irreversible damage.

Corals may be a canary in the coal mine when it comes to ocean acidification. In September, French researchers published a study in the journal *Biogeosciences* showing that ocean acidification could cut the growth rate of deep-sea corals in half by 2100. A separate study warned that coral reefs may actually begin to dissolve if ocean water becomes too acidic. Scientists with the Carnegie Institution in Washington, D.C., and Hebrew University of Jerusalem found that coral reefs may disappear altogether if atmospheric carbon dioxide doubles in concentration, com-

pared with 200 years ago. Carbon dioxide could reach such concentrations in as little as 50 years. The March 2009 study was published in the journal *Geophysical Research Letters.*

Researchers with the Woods Hole Oceanographic Institution in Maryland warned that ocean acidification could cause painful economic consequences. The scientists predicted that harvests of *molluscs* (shellfish) in the United States will decline by 10 to 25 percent over the next 50 years. That decline could cause a $1.4-billion drop in sales by 2060. The research was published in the June 2009 *Environmental Research Letters.*

Put on the red light. Researchers from Oregon State University at Corvallis succeeded in analyzing the activity of plankton by measuring the light they produce. Plankton that get their energy from sunlight produce a dim red light called *fluorescence.* Using the Aqua satellite, scientists were able to measure this fluorescence from space, allowing them to evaluate the health of plankton around the world. Such plankton are at the base of nearly all food chains in the oceans. By measuring the activity of plankton, researchers can evaluate the overall health of the oceans. The new method was described in a June issue of *Biogeosciences.* ■ Brian Johnson

See also **Conservation; Global warming.**

Olympic Games. The International Olympic Committee (IOC) on Oct. 2, 2009, awarded the 2016 Summer Olympics to Rio de Janeiro, Brazil, marking the first time a South American city had been chosen to host any Olympic Games competition. Chicago, considered by many observers at the very least a cofavorite to land the games, suffered a stunning first-round defeat. Chicago's poor showing--it got just 18 votes in the first round compared with 22 for Tokyo, 26 for Rio, and 28 for Madrid—was blamed in part on problems at the United States Olympic Committee (USOC), but also on a flat presentation and not enough IOC voters from North America. About half of the IOC's 106 members are European.

The USOC acting chief executive officer, Stephanie Streeter, announced less than a week after Chicago's failed bid that she would step down in March 2010. Streeter had taken over in March 2009 after Jim Scherr was forced to resign after six years. Streeter came under fire almost immediately, in part for her lack of experience with international sports and her inability to get enough sponsors for a television network that the USOC had been planning. ■ Michael Kates

Oman. See Middle East.
Ontario. See Canadian provinces.
Opera. See Classical music.

FACTS IN BRIEF ON PACIFIC ISLAND COUNTRIES

Country	Population	Government	Monetary unit*	Foreign trade (million U.S.$) Exports[†]	Imports[†]
Fiji	877,000	President Ratu Epeli Nailatikau; Interim Prime Minister Frank Bainimarama	dollar (1.96 = $1)	1,202	3.120
Kiribati	105,000	President Anote Tong	Australian dollar (1.18 = $1)	17	62
Marshall Islands	67,000	President Jurelang Zedkaia	U.S. dollar	19	79
Micronesia, Federated States of	113,000	President Emanuel Mori	U.S. dollar	14	133
Nauru	11,000	President Marcus Stephen	Australian dollar (1.18 = $1)	0.06	20
New Zealand	4,293,000	Governor General Sir Anand Satyanand; Prime Minister John Key	dollar (1.46 = $1)	30,800	32,450
Palau	20,000	President Johnson Toribiong	U.S. dollar	6	107
Papua New Guinea	6,719,000	Governor General Sir Paulius Matane; Prime Minister Sir Michael Somare	kina (2.54 = $1)	5,719	3,124
Samoa	192,000	Head of State Tuiatua Tupua Tamasese Efi; Prime Minister Tuila'epa Sailele Malielegaoi	tala (2.50 = $1)	131	324
Solomon Islands	533,000	Governor General Sir Frank Kabui; Prime Minister Derek Sikua	dollar (7.47 = $1)	237	256
Tonga	104,000	King George Tupou V; Prime Minister Feleti Sevele	pa'anga (1.91 = $1)	22	139
Tuvalu	12,000	Governor General Sir Filoimea Telito; Prime Minister Apisai Ielemia	Australian dollar (1.18 = $1)	1	13
Vanuatu	236,000	President Iolu Johnson Abil; Prime Minister Edward Natapei	vatu (99.70 = $1)	40	156

*Exchange rates as of Sept. 30, 2009.   [†]Latest available data.

Pacific Islands. In 2009, Fiji was suspended from the Pacific Islands Forum as well as the Commonwealth of Nations after it failed to hold elections. A series of powerful tsunami waves battered Samoa, American Samoa, and Tonga, leaving about 190 people dead. A tragic ferry accident in Tonga left 74 people dead. The governments of both the Marshall Islands and Vanuatu chose new presidents. Palau agreed to house Chinese Muslims after they were released from United States custody.

Fiji. On May 1, the Pacific Islands Forum suspended Fiji's membership after the country failed to hold elections. The Forum comprised 16 Pacific countries or territories, including Australia and New Zealand. The latter two countries led the move for suspension on the grounds that Fiji's Interim Prime Minister Frank Bainimarama failed to live up to earlier promises to restore democracy to the nation. Bainimarama, a military leader, overthrew the government in 2006. He promised to revise Fiji's Constitution and hold national elections in 2014.

In September 2009, Fiji was suspended from the Commonwealth of Nations, which is made up of the United Kingdom, its dependencies, and former British colonies. The Commonwealth had demanded that Bainimarama commit to holding elections in 2010, but he refused to do so.

Tsunamis. On Sept. 29, 2009, an 8.0-magnitude undersea earthquake about 120 miles (190 kilometers) east of Apia, the capital of Samoa, generated tsunami waves up to 15 feet (4.5 meters) high. The waves left about 190 people dead in American Samoa, Samoa, and Tonga. The worst damage was in Samoa, where waves swept away entire villages. Australia, the European Union, New Zealand, and the United States all pledged relief assistance.

Palau. The government of Palau in June 2009 confirmed that it would temporarily house several Uygurs after they were released from the Guantánamo Bay prison camp in Cuba. A group of 22 Uygurs (Chinese Muslims) had been living in self-imposed exile in Afghanistan prior to the Sept. 11, 2001, terrorist attacks on the United States. They were detained by the United States after the invasion of Afghanistan and were transferred to Guantánamo Bay. Although they were officially cleared of wrongdoing, U.S. government officials refused to send the Uygurs to China out of concern for their safety. Although Palau has no Uygur population, it does have a small Muslim community. In late October 2009, lawyers confirmed that six Uygurs had arrived in Palau.

Marshall Islands President Litokwa Tomeing was ousted in a parliamentary vote of no confidence on October 21. It was the third parliamentary attempt in 12 months to remove Tomeing from office, and the motion passed by a single vote. Opposition had grown against Tomeing after he fired Cabinet ministers from his own party and replaced them with opposition members from a party to which he had once belonged. On October 26, Parliament elected its speaker, Jurelang Zedkaia, to succeed Tomeing.

Tonga. Late on August 5, Tonga's inter-island ferry, *Princess Ashika,* sank in waters near the Ha'apai group of islands, some 55 miles (90 kilometers) northwest of Tonga's capital, Nuku'alofa. Of the 128 people on board, 54 survived. Only two bodies were recovered—the rest of the passengers, mostly women and children, presumably drowned. Tonga's minister of transport, Paul Karakus, said the ship had recently been inspected and pronounced seaworthy. He resigned on August 11.

Vanuatu. On September 1, Vanuatu's electoral college met to choose a new president after the term of President Kalkot Mataskelekele ended. The electoral college consists of the 52 members of Parliament plus the presidents of the six provincial governments; a two-thirds majority is required for election. Three ballots were necessary before a candidate, Iolu Johnson Abil, captured a majority. Abil had previously served as a Cabinet minister in Vanuatu's government shortly after it gained independence in 1980. ■ Eugene Ogan

See also **China; Disasters.**

Painting. See Art.

Pakistan. Terrorist bombings rocked Pakistan repeatedly in 2009 as Islamic militants fought to bring down the civilian government. Pakistan's army had only limited success in offensives against militant strongholds.

Terrorism. Interior Minister Rehman Malik said in March that Pakistan was "in a state of war." After terrorists attacked government facilities, Malik stated on October 15 that an alliance of militant groups sought to destabilize the country and wanted to see "Pakistan as a failed state."

The Pakistani Taliban (PT), allied with the Afghan Taliban, was in 2009 based in the mountainous Federally Administered Tribal Areas (FATA) along Pakistan's Afghanistan border. Malik also named several banned groups based in Pakistan's Punjab province as well as the international organization al-Qa`ida. Some reports suggested the Punjab groups had been aided by Pakistani military intelligence, the Directorate for Inter-Services Intelligence (ISI). The ISI was also known to have supported the Afghan Taliban.

Attacks against civilians early in 2009 included the March 3 ambush in Lahore of a cricket team from Sri Lanka. The attack left six police officers and a driver dead; eight cricketers were injured. On March 27, a suicide bombing during prayers at a mosque near Peshawar in northwestern Pakistan left some 70 people dead. The PT took credit for a March 30 attack on a police academy near Lahore that left eight people dead and more than 100 others wounded.

A suicide bomber killed 14 police recruits on August 30 in the northwestern Swat Valley. In an attempt to drive foreign aid workers out of Pakistan, the PT bombed offices of the United Nations (UN) World Food Programme in the capital, Islamabad, on October 5, killing five people. On October 9, some 49 people died in the bombing of a Peshawar market. Pakistani schools closed temporarily to reinforce security after an October 20 suicide attack on an Islamic university in Islamabad killed eight people. Another Peshawar market bombing on October 28 killed at least 118 people, mostly women and children. These and other attacks weakened public confidence in the government.

Many attacks targeted Pakistan's armed forces as the army stepped up offensives on militant strongholds. On October 10, militants shot their way into the army's headquarters in Rawalpindi, near Islamabad. In a 20-hour siege, 23 people were killed, including 9 attackers. An army brigadier was assassinated in Islamabad on October 22, and the next day a suicide bomber killed six people at a nearby air force facility.

Army offensives. The attacks on Pakistan's armed forces appeared to be retaliation for army offensives against militant strongholds in the

The explosion of an enormous car bomb in Peshawar, Pakistan, on October 28 killed more than 100 people, most of them women and children. Peshawar is the gateway to South Waziristan, where the Pakistani army was engaged in an offensive against Taliban militants.

North-West Frontier Province (NWFP) and FATA. In February, the army urged the NWFP government to arrange a cease-fire with Taliban militants who had terrorized the Swat Valley. In early April, the Taliban violated the cease-fire by advancing into the Buner valley, some 60 miles (100 kilometers) from Islamabad. In late April, the army launched a drive that reestablished government authority in the area as millions of people fled.

A key PT leader, Baitullah Mehsud, was killed by a missile fired from a United States *drone* (remotely controlled aircraft) on August 5. He had claimed responsibility for dozens of attacks across Pakistan. The army estimated that 80 percent of the suicide bombings in the previous three years had been launched from his territory in FATA's rugged South Waziristan, which was also known for harboring members of the Afghan Taliban.

On October 17, Pakistan's army launched a large-scale campaign against the PT and al-Qa`ida in FATA. Some 28,000 soldiers, supported by aerial bombardments, sought to reclaim control of South Waziristan from an estimated 10,000 PT militants. The militants resorted to guerrilla harassment of the soldiers.

The United States, which had given more than $12 billion in aid to Pakistan since 2001, encouraged the country's efforts to destroy PT safe havens along the Afghan border. Relations were tense, however, because of U.S. suspicions that much of the aid intended to fight the PT was used for Pakistan's armed confrontation with India; that ISI was sheltering al-Qa`ida in FATA mountains; and that ISI was aiding the Taliban in Afghanistan. On a visit to Pakistan, U.S. Secretary of State Hillary Clinton said on October 29 that she found it "hard to believe" that Pakistan's government did not know where al-Qa`ida leaders were hiding and could not "get them if they really wanted to."

On October 15, U.S. President Barack Obama signed a bill tripling American nonmilitary aid to Pakistan to $7.5 billion over five years. Reflecting U.S. concern over instability and corruption in Pakistan, the bill required the Obama administration to report to Congress on Pakistan's progress in fighting militants and the extent of civilian control over the Pakistani armed forces. It urged Pakistan not to support militants based there.

The bill added tension to the difficult relationship between American officials and the Pakistani military, which had run Pakistan for much of its history and had seldom been under control of elected civilian governments. Some critics accused the U.S. government of trying to assert too much control over Pakistan, and international affairs experts noted growing anti-American sentiment within Pakistan.   ■ Henry S. Bradsher

See also **Asia; India; Terrorism.**

Paleontology. On May 19, 2009, an international team led by Norwegian paleontologist Jørn Hurum of the University of Oslo Natural History Museum described a remarkably well preserved, virtually complete fossil skeleton of an early primate in the Public Library of Science online journal *PLoS ONE*. The squirrel-sized fossil of *Darwinius massilae*, nicknamed "Ida," was discovered at the Messel Shale, an Eocene-age lake bed about 47 million years old, near Darmstadt, Germany. Such a stunningly complete fossil is rare and offers great insight into the life of an extinct primate species. The published description occurred along with a press conference, a book, a television special, and a major display at the American Museum of Natural History in New York City, where Ida was touted as the key "missing link" in the evolution of human beings.

The fossil specimen was originally discovered in 1987 and sold in two pieces. The left side was sold to a museum in Wyoming. The more complete right side was purchased by the Oslo Museum. Eventually, the Oslo museum purchased the other half of the fossil, and Hurum's published description is the first available look at the entire fossil specimen. Ida is a nearly complete skeleton of a young female, perhaps only 9 months old, who was a tree-dwelling primate, with nails on her fingers and a long tail. The fossil also preserves an outline of the soft body parts, including the skin and fur of the animal, and even remnants of a last meal of leaves and fruit in the shadowy outline of the animal's digestive tract.

Hurum and his group argue that Ida is an important missing link that bridges the evolutionary gap between the *higher primates* (monkeys, apes, and human beings) and their more distant relatives, such as the primitive lemurs, found today only on the island of Madagascar. However, other paleontologists suggest that other features show that Ida is more likely a member of an extinct group of lemur-like primates called adapids and not the sensational missing link as advertised. Most paleontologists believe that a group of ancient primates called omomyids are the ancestors of

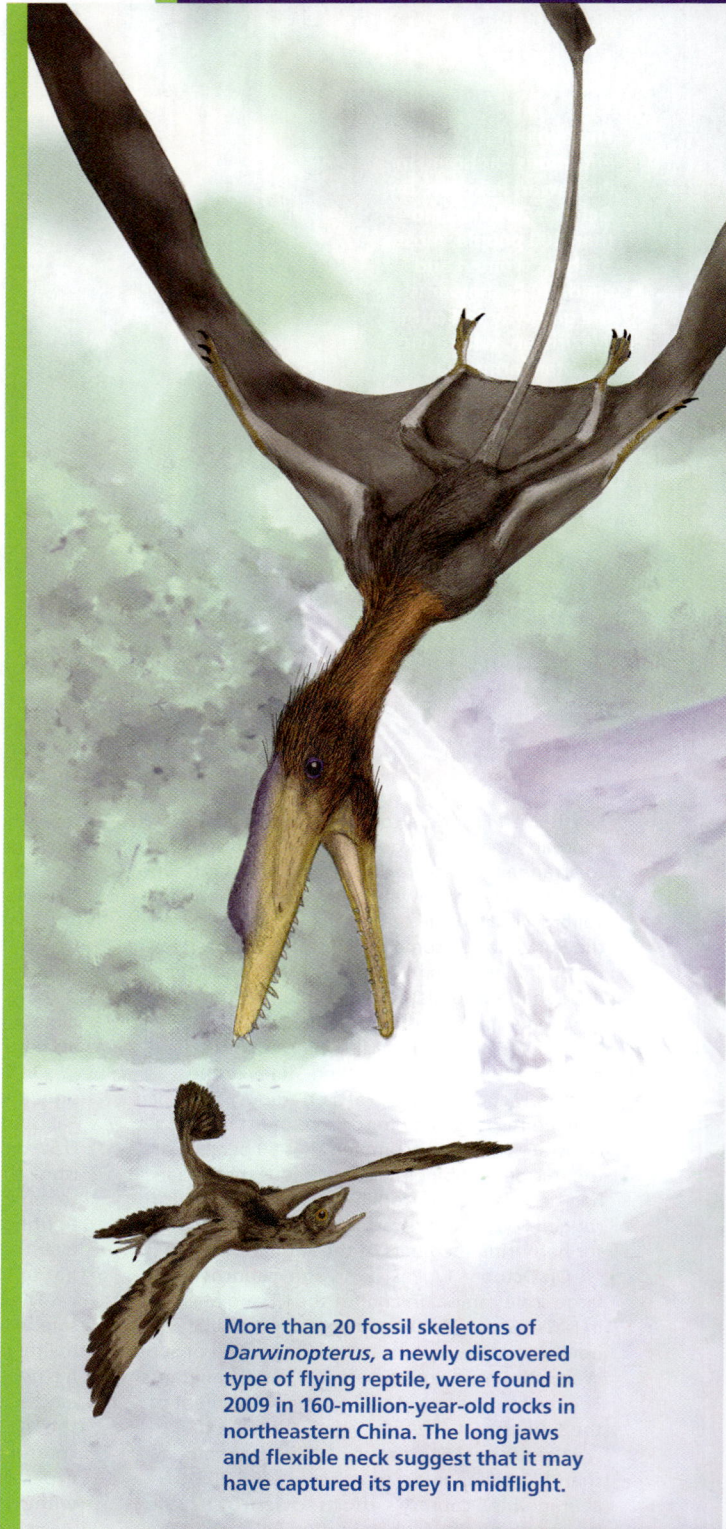

More than 20 fossil skeletons of *Darwinopterus*, a newly discovered type of flying reptile, were found in 2009 in 160-million-year-old rocks in northeastern China. The long jaws and flexible neck suggest that it may have captured its prey in midflight.

the higher primates, while the adapids, including Ida, are related to lemurs. Some scientists were also irritated by the publicity that surrounded Ida, which they felt oversold the significance of the fossil.

Earliest jaws. Paleontologist Min Zhu and colleagues of the Institute of Vertebrate Paleontology and Paleo-anthropology in Beijing, described a new and exceptionally well preserved fossil fish in the March 26, 2009, issue of *Nature*. The fossil provides a clearer picture of evolution in the earliest jawed fishes, known as *gnathostomes*. The fossil fish, classified in the genus *Guiyu*, was found in Upper Silurian limestone deposits dating to 419 million years ago in Yunnan in southern China. It is the oldest well preserved fossil of a jawed *vertebrate* (animal with a backbone). Unlike most Silurian fossil fish that have been discovered, this specimen clearly displays a bony skeleton. The anatomy of the fish shows characteristics that link it to the *lobe-finned fishes,* a group that includes modern lungfish, the *coela-canth* (a primitive fish found in the Indian Ocean), and the earliest *tetrapods,* the ancestors of all land-dwelling vertebrates, including amphibians, reptiles, and mammals.

Paleontologists have long understood that lobe-fins and the more numerous ray-finned fishes must have shared a common ancestor. Together, the two groups form the class Osteichthyes, fishes with bony skeletons. The fossil specimen extends the span of lobe-finned fish in the fossil record back more than 20 million years. This indicates that such a common ancestor lived far earlier than paleontologists had previously thought.

Ancient relative of seals. In April 2009, paleontologists Natalia Rybczynski of the Canadian Museum of Nature in Ottawa; Mary Dawson of the Carnegie Museum in Pittsburgh; and Richard Tedford of the American Museum of Natural History in New York City reported the discovery of a new fossil mammal, *Puijila darwini,* that appears to be an early relative of modern seals. Unlike whales, whose ancestry is now well understood by paleontologists, the evolution of *pinnipeds* (seals, sea lions, and walruses) has been poorly understood

due to the lack of a good fossil record. *Puijila* was discovered in Lower Miocene lake deposits, about 24 to 25 million years old, on Devon Island, Nunavut, in the Canadian Arctic. The nearly complete skeleton retains a long tail. The limbs are shaped like those of modern land-dwelling carnivores. Although *Puijila* walked on dry land, its feet were webbed, and it had a long, streamlined body that allowed it to move through water with the agility and speed of an otter. The skull, however, shows several anatomical features characteristic of seals.

Puijila resembles other, less complete fossils from deposits in Europe and Asia and does not appear to be on the direct line leading to modern pinnipeds. The discoverers argue that *Puijila* is an early, intermediate form along a multi-branched evolutionary journey from land to sea. However, *Puijila* indicates that this journey most likely originated in freshwater Arctic lakes. Eventually, these mammals extended their range to the seashore, where they would have further adapted to life in the water. Today, pinnipeds live mainly in the polar oceans or inland seas, though a few species have returned to live in freshwater lakes.   ■ Carlton E. Brett

Panama. On July 1, 2009, Ricardo Alberto Martinelli Berrocal, 57, of the Democratic Change party, began his four-year term as Panama's new president. In the May general election, Martinelli easily defeated Balbina Herrera of the Democratic Revolutionary Party. Martinelli was the wealthy owner of Panama's largest supermarket chain and spent millions of dollars of his own money on his campaign. Martinelli pledged to reduce political corruption and violent crime and to improve the country's education, health, and transportation systems.

On July 8, the Panama Canal Authority (ACP) announced that a group led by Sacyr Vallehermoso S.A. of Madrid, Spain, had won the job of designing and building a new set of locks for the Panama Canal expansion. Sacyr's winning bid of $3.12 billion was $300 million less than the ACP had budgeted for this phase of the project. The Sacyr-led group includes construction companies from Belgium, Italy, the Netherlands, Panama, and the United States. The expansion, scheduled for completion by 2014, will double the capacity of the canal and allow larger ships to use it.

On Aug. 11, 2009, Canadian Prime Minister Stephen Harper signed a free trade agreement between Canada and Panama.
               ■ Nathan A. Haverstock

See also **Latin America.**

Papua New Guinea. See **Pacific Islands.**
Paraguay. See **Latin America.**

in 2009 included those listed below, who were from the United States unless otherwise indicated.

Bryan, Bob, and Bryan, Mike

(1978-), won the doubles competition of the Australian Open, one of the four "grand slam" tournaments of tennis, in Melbourne in January 2009. Bob Bryan, teamed with South African tennis pro Liezel Huber, won the mixed doubles crown at the French Open in Paris in June. The Bryan twins, from California, have dominated doubles tennis for much of the decade of the 2000's, winning a total of seven grand-slam events beginning in 2003 and earning the title of ATP Doubles Team four times. (The ATP, or Association of Tennis Professionals, organizes the men's professional tennis tour.) In December 2007, the Bryan twins clinched the final match of the Davis Cup competition in Portland, Oregon, bringing the prize home to the United States team.

Bob Bryan and Mike Bryan

Robert Charles Bryan and Michael Carl Bryan were born two minutes apart on April 29, 1978. Their parents, both professional athletes, taught tennis in Camarillo, California, where the twins grew up. The twins' mother, Kathy Blake Bryan, competed in tennis at Wimbledon in the United Kingdom.

Bob and Mike nabbed their first tennis trophy, in a southern California novice tournament, at the age of 6. They entered Stanford University in Stanford, California, in 1996 and in 1998 won the National Collegiate Athletic Association (NCAA) doubles tennis title. Bob also won the NCAA singles title in 1998. Following their sophomore year, the twins turned pro and left Stanford.

Bob and Mike Bryan won their first grand slam competition, the French Open, in 2003. They have since competed as doubles partners in most grand slam and men's professional tennis tour events. In the 2008 Beijing Summer Olympics, the Bryans won bronze in tennis doubles competition.

Chu, Steven

(1948-), became secretary of the U.S. Department of Energy in January 2009 following confirmation by the Senate. President-elect Obama had nominated Chu, a Nobel prizewinner in physics, on Dec. 15, 2008, declaring that he wanted to "send a signal to all that my administration will value science."

Along with scientists Claude Cohen-Tannoudji and William Daniel Phillips, Steven Chu developed a technique for trapping atoms—that is, greatly slowing down atoms so they can be more easily

studied. The three scientists shared the 1997 Nobel Prize in physics.

Chu's career has included teaching physics at Stanford University in Stanford, California, and at the University of California at Berkeley; conducting applied research at Bell Laboratories (now part of Alcatel-Lucent) in New Jersey; and directing the Lawrence Berkeley National Laboratory in Berkeley, California, which conducts research for the U.S. Department of Energy. In this latter role, Chu, beginning in 2004, promoted development of such alternative energy technologies as solar electric generation and biofuels.

Steven Chu was born on Feb. 28, 1948, in St. Louis but grew up in Garden City, New York. His parents had come to the United States from China to attend American universities; they opted to settle in the United States permanently in the late 1940's as civil war in China resulted in a Communist take-over.

Steven Chu attended the University of Rochester in New York, where he obtained bachelor's degrees both in mathematics and in physics. In 1976, he received a doctorate in physics from the University of California at Berkeley.

Collins, Susan

(1952-), a Republican member of the U.S. Senate from Maine, played a key role in achieving legislative consensus in the Senate on President Barack Obama's proposals for a so-called stimulus package, a massive funding program to stimulate the U.S. economy in severe recession. Senator Collins's negotiations with majority Democrats resulted in a $100-billion reduction in the bill's price tag and several other changes. Collins joined her fellow Maine Republican, Senator Olympia Snowe, in voting for the final version of the American Recovery and Reinvestment Act in February 2009, ensuring its passage in the Senate. President Obama signed the bill into law on February 17.

Susan Margaret Collins was born on Dec. 7, 1952, in Caribou, one of Maine's northernmost towns. Her family has, for generations, run a lumber business in the Caribou area. Both of her parents served as mayor of Caribou, and her father served in the Maine Senate. Susan Collins attended college at St. Lawrence University in Bronxville, New York, where she received a bachelor of arts degree in 1975.

From 1975 to 1987, Collins worked as a staff member for William Cohen, a Republican member of the U.S. Senate from Maine. From 1987 to 1992, she served as commissioner of professional and financial regulation in Maine's state government. In 1992, Collins accepted an appointment to be New England regional administrator of the Small Business Administration, an independent agency of the U.S. government that promotes and protects small business companies. A run for the governorship of Maine in 1994 fell short, but Collins won election to the U.S. Senate in 1996, replacing William Cohen, who was retiring. She was reelected to the Senate in 2002 and 2008.

Donovan, Shaun (1966-), was sworn in as secretary of the U.S. Department of Housing and Urban Development (HUD) on Jan. 26, 2009, following his nomination by President Barack Obama and confirmation by the Senate. Donovan had previously headed New York City's Department of Housing Preservation and Development (HPD), a municipal agency that works to preserve and develop affordable housing for New York City residents. During the 2008 U.S. presidential campaign, Donovan took a leave of absence to work on the Obama campaign.

Shaun L. Donovan was born in New York City on Jan. 24, 1966. He attended Harvard University in Cambridge, Massachusetts, and received a bachelor's degree in engineering in 1987. Donovan later returned to Harvard for graduate study. In 1995, he received a master's degree in architecture from Harvard and a master's degree in public policy from the Kennedy School of Government at Harvard. Donovan worked as an architect for several years.

During the administration of President Bill Clinton, Donovan served as HUD's deputy assistant secretary for multifamily housing, a position in which he administered federal programs that help families access affordable housing. From 2000 to 2001, Donovan served as head of the Federal Housing Administration (FHA), the federal agency (also within HUD) that insures home mortgages and provides other housing services. As New York City's HPD commissioner (2004-2008), Donovan created and implemented a plan to build and preserve 165,000 affordable homes.

Duffy, Carol Ann (1955-), became the first female poet laureate of the United Kingdom in May 2009. According to British literary tradition, King James I appointed Ben Jonson as the first poet laureate in 1616, mainly to compose verse for royal celebrations. In modern times, the position entails a 10-year tenure and a modest stipend, with no compulsory duties. British poet laureates have included such literary notables as John Dryden, Robert Southey, William Wordsworth, and Alfred, Lord Tennyson.

Carol Ann Duffy has published several books of poetry. Literary critics note that her poems are often suffused with irony, humor, and realism. Much of her writing gives voice to culturally alienated outsiders. One of her most celebrated collections, *The World's Wife* (1999), presents imagined monologues by the wives of famous or infamous men of history or cultural tradition, ranging from Mrs. Aesop (spouse of the writer of fables) to Queen Herod, wife of Herod the Great, the Biblical figure who ordered all first-born Jewish sons put to the sword.

Carol Ann Duffy was born in Glasgow, Scotland, but grew up in Stafford, England. She attended Liverpool University, earning a bachelor's

Carol Ann Duffy

degree in philosophy in 1977. In 1999, Duffy began teaching in the Department of English at Manchester Metropolitan University. Duffy received the Somerset Maugham Award in 1988 and the Dylan Thomas Award in 1990. In 1999, she was appointed a fellow of the Royal Society of Literature, London.

Duncan, Arne

(1964-), was confirmed as secretary of the U.S. Department of Education by the Senate on Jan. 20, 2009, following his nomination for the post by President-elect Barack Obama. Since 2001, Duncan had held the position of chief executive officer of Chicago Public Schools (CPS), the third largest U.S. school system. Friends since the 1990's, Arne Duncan and Obama occasionally played "pickup" (informal games of) basketball.

Duncan has spent much of his career working in education in Chicago, from tutoring inner-city children and youth to administering the city's school system. Education analysts note that under Duncan's leadership, the CPS student body achieved an increase in overall math and verbal standardized test scores. Some critics, however, faulted Duncan for closing poorly performing public schools.

Arne Duncan was born on Nov. 6, 1964, in Chicago. His father was a professor at the University of Chicago. His mother, also an educator, has run a tutoring program for inner-city children on Chicago's South Side since the early 1960's. Duncan attended Harvard University in Cambridge, Massachusetts, becoming co-captain of the basketball team and earning a bachelor of arts degree in sociology in 1987.

From 1987 to 1991, he played professional basketball in Australia. Duncan returned to Chicago in 1992 and spent several years working for the Ariel Education Initiative, a nonprofit foundation promoting higher education among poor inner-city youth. In 1999, Duncan was hired as deputy chief of staff to the CPS's top administrator. Chicago Mayor Richard M. Daley appointed Duncan head of the CPS in June 2001.

Franken, Al

(1951-), won election to the U.S. Senate as a Democrat from Minnesota on Nov. 4, 2008, but was not admitted until July 2009. The result of the election between Franken and incum-

Al Franken

bent Norm Coleman was so close that state law mandated a recount. Coleman rejected the result of the recount, which gave Franken a razor-thin lead, and appealed the decision in court. Subsequent recounts confirmed Franken's lead, and on June 30, the Minnesota Supreme Court declared Franken the winner.

Al Franken became nationally known in the 1970's as a writer and performer on the TV show "Saturday Night Live." He went on to write screenplays for several films and later became known as a political satirist.

Alan Stuart Franken was born on May 21, 1951, in New York City. The Franken family moved to Albert Lea, Minnesota, when Al was four years old and later to St. Louis Park, a suburb of Minneapolis. After high school, he enrolled in Harvard University in Cambridge, Massachusetts, and was awarded a bachelor of arts degree in 1973.

After graduation from Harvard, Franken went to New York City to pursue a writing career in the entertainment industry. During this period, he married Franni Bryson. The Frankens moved back to Minneapolis in 2005 in preparation for Al Franken's run for the U.S. Senate in 2008.

Geithner, Timothy

(1961-), became secretary of the U.S. Department of the Treasury in January 2009 following his confirmation by the Senate. President-elect Obama tapped Geithner for the post shortly after his election in November 2008.

Geithner came to the top U.S. Treasury position from the New York Federal Reserve Bank, where he had served as president since 2003. (The New York Federal Reserve is one of 12 regional banks in the Federal Reserve System, which oversees the nation's banking system.) As the New York Fed president, Geithner played a major role in 2008 in arranging multibillion-dollar loans from the federal government to failing financial institutions, such as New York City-based Bear Stearns and others. These "bailouts," as the financial rescue plans came to be known, generated controversy around Geithner's nomination and tenure as Treasury secretary. Geithner asserted, however, that without these financial interventions, the entire financial sector of the economy might have collapsed during the global financial crisis of late 2008 and 2009.

Timothy Franz Geithner was born on Aug. 18, 1961, in New York City. Geithner's father, Peter F.

Geithner, worked for international development agencies, and the family lived abroad, in various countries of Africa and Asia, through much of Geithner's childhood.

Geithner attended Dartmouth College in Hanover, New Hampshire, earning a bachelor's degree in government and Asian studies in 1983. In 1985, he earned a master's degree in economics and Asian studies from Johns Hopkins University in Baltimore. Geithner studied Mandarin Chinese in his degree programs, and when he visited China as secretary of the treasury 25 years later, he delighted Chinese audiences by including phrases in Chinese in his speeches.

Before his 2003 appointment to the New York Fed, Geithner worked for a Washington, D.C.-based international consulting company and in several positions in the Treasury Department. From 2001 to 2003, Geithner worked for the International Monetary Fund, a United Nations affiliate that provides short-term credit to member nations.

Hatoyama, Yukio (1947-), became prime minister of Japan on Sept. 16, 2009, following a historic landslide in parliamentary elections by his Democratic Party of Japan (DPJ). In elections on August 30, voters trimmed the electoral bloc of the Liberal Democratic Party (LDP) in the dominant lower house of Japan's parliament from 300 to 119, out of a total 480 seats, while the opposition DPJ won a commanding majority of 308 seats. The election marked the first time that the LDP had been ousted from power since its creation after World War II (1939-1945).

Prime Minister Hatoyama pledged to break the so-called "iron triangle" in Japanese society and government. The phrase refers to the close relationships that exist among politicians, career bureaucrats, and powerful business interests in Japan. According to political analysts, such relationships enabled the LDP to dominate Japanese politics and government for more than 50 years. Hatoyama also signaled a shift in foreign policy by pledging that he would not visit a controversial shrine in Tokyo at which high-ranking members of Japan's militaristic World War II regime are buried. Analysts noted that such a decision was likely to be well received by Chinese leaders in Beijing.

Yukio Hatoyama, born in Tokyo on Feb. 11, 1947, comes from a wealthy, politically connected family that is sometimes likened to the American Kennedy family. Hatoyama's paternal grandfather was the first LDP prime minister after the party's formation in 1955; his father served as foreign minister; and his brother Kunio served as a minister in the outgoing LDP government. Hatoyama's maternal grandfather founded the Bridgestone Corporation, a manufacturer of tires. Yukio Hatoyama studied engineering at the University of Tokyo and at Stanford University in Stanford, California. He taught at Tokyo's Senshu University before entering politics in 1983.

Yukio Hatoyama

Holder, Eric (1951-), became attorney general of the United States on Feb. 3, 2009, following his nomination by President-elect Barack Obama and his confirmation by the Senate. Holder is the first African American to serve as the nation's top law enforcement officer.

Eric Holder has spent much of his career working in the U.S. Department of Justice or the federal court system. Following graduation from law school in 1976, he worked as a prosecutor in the Public Integrity Section of the Justice Department. In that position, he investigated and prosecuted corrupt public officials. In 1988, President Ronald Reagan appointed Holder an associate judge for the District of Columbia Superior Court. In 1993, President Bill Clinton appointed Holder U.S. attorney for the District of Columbia; in 1997, the president tapped Holder as deputy attorney general. During much of the 2000's, Holder worked in a private law firm in Washington, D.C.

As attorney general, Holder found himself in 2009 at the center of a controversy over whether the Justice Department should conduct a criminal investigation into the conduct of U.S. intelligence agents who interrogated terror suspects after the Sept. 11, 2001, terrorist attacks on the United States. Demands for an investigation mounted as allegations surfaced of detainee abuse, including treatment that might be construed as torture. On Aug. 25, 2009, Attorney General Holder appointed John D. Durham, a former U.S. attorney, as a special prosecutor to further investigate such allegations.

Eric Himpton Holder, Jr., was born on Jan. 21, 1951, in New York City and was raised in the borough of Queens. He attended New York City's Columbia University, obtaining a bachelor of arts degree in 1973. In 1976, he received a law degree from Columbia's law school.

LaHood, Ray (1945-), was sworn in as secretary of the U.S. Department of Transportation on Jan. 23, 2009, following his nomination by President Barack Obama and confirmation by the U.S. Senate. Analysts noted that the transportation secretary would play a major role in administering transportation infrastructure projects funded by the Obama administration's $787-billion stimulus and recovery program, which Congress approved in February.

LaHood, a native of Illinois, had represented the state's 18th Congressional District in the U.S. House of Representatives since 1995. Tense partisan divisions characterized much of LaHood's tenure in the House, but the Illinois Republican earned a reputation for working with Democrats. When President-elect Obama nominated LaHood in December 2008, he noted that "Ray's appointment reflects [the] bipartisan spirit."

Ray LaHood was born on Dec. 6, 1945, in Peoria, Illinois. His grandfather had immigrated to the United States from Lebanon. LaHood worked his way through college, earning a bachelor's degree from Peoria's Bradley University, after which he taught at area junior and senior high schools. LaHood entered the political arena by becoming a precinct committeeman in Peoria. He worked for several state agencies and then accepted a job as an assistant to Republican Tom Railsback, a U.S. House member representing western Illinois. In 1983, LaHood went to work for Bob Michels, then

Eric Holder

U.S. House member for the Illinois 18th Congressional District, which includes Peoria. When Michels retired in 1994, LaHood ran for, and won, Michels's House seat.

Locke, Gary (1950-), was confirmed as secretary of the U.S. Department of Commerce by the Senate on March 24, 2009, following his nomination for the post by President Barack Obama. In 1997, Locke became the first Chinese American chief executive of a U.S. state when he took office as governor of Washington. Locke, a Democrat, served two terms as governor, from 1997 to 2005.

Locke strengthened commercial ties between Washington state and the People's Republic of China during his tenure as governor, a period when the state's exports to China doubled. Drawing on his personal cultural and linguistic heritage, Locke forged strong ties with Chinese leaders, particularly President Hu Jintao, who visited Locke in Seattle on his 2006 state visit to the United States. Between 2005 and Locke's confirmation as secretary of commerce in 2009, the former Washington governor worked as a China-trade specialist for a law firm in Seattle.

Gary Faye Locke was born on Jan. 21, 1950, in Seattle, of second-generation Chinese Americans. The Locke family lived in public housing but eventually saved enough money to start a grocery store, which grew into a successful small business. Gary won a scholarship to Yale University in New Haven, Connecticut, graduating in 1972 with a bachelor's degree in political science. He then attended law school at Boston University in Massachusetts, earning a law degree in 1975.

Locke returned to Washington state and in 1983 entered the state's House of Representatives. From 1994 to 1997, he served as chief executive of King County, Washington's most populous county.

Napolitano, Janet (1957-), was sworn in as secretary of the U.S. Department of Homeland Security on Jan. 21, 2009, following her nomination by President Barack Obama and confirmation by the Senate. The previous day, Napolitano had resigned as governor of Arizona, the position she had held since 2003.

Janet Napolitano was first elected governor of Arizona in November 2002; she won reelection in 2006. In November 2005, *Time* magazine named

Napolitano as one of the nation's five best governors. Analysts credit her, in cooperation with state legislators, with retiring a $1-billion deficit during her first term. Education experts gave Napolitano high marks for sponsoring legislation in 2004 to provide full-day universal kindergarten in Arizona public schools.

Janet Ann Napolitano was born on Nov. 29, 1957, in New York City but grew up in Albuquerque, New Mexico. Napolitano attended Santa Clara University in Santa Clara, California, earning a Bachelor of Science degree in 1979. In 1983, she received a law degree from the University of Virginia in Charlottesville. Napolitano subsequently made her home in Arizona, working for a Phoenix law firm.

In 1991, Napolitano served as an attorney for Anita Hill, who testified in U.S. Senate hearings that Clarence Thomas, then a nominee for the Supreme Court, had sexually harassed her. The case attracted intense publicity, though Hill's allegations remained unproven and Thomas was eventually confirmed by the Senate.

In 1993, President Bill Clinton appointed Janet Napolitano as the U.S. attorney for the District of Arizona. In 1998, Napolitano won election to a four-year term as Arizona's attorney general.

Papandreou, George (1952-), became

prime minister of Greece on Oct. 6, 2009, following the victory of his party, the Panhellenic Socialist Movement (PASOK), in parliamentary elections on October 4. Papandreou, the son and grandson of Greek prime ministers, succeeded Kostas Karamanlis of the center-right New Democracy Party, who is the nephew of a former prime minister.

Papandreou pledged to work with parliament to pass a stimulus package of spending projects to jump-start the Greek economy, hard-hit by the global recession in 2009. In addition to the prime minister's post, he took over the foreign ministry portfolio, promising an emphasis on diplomacy. In the late 1990's, Papandreou had, as foreign minister, achieved a thawing of relations with Turkey, Greece's historic adversary. Papandreou also appointed five women to ministerial posts in his government and created a new ministry for the environment.

George Andreas Papandreou was born on June 16, 1952, in St. Paul, Minnesota, where his father, Andreas Papandreou, held a post on the University of Minnesota faculty. The elder Papandreou had gone into voluntary exile from Greece in 1940 and settled in the United States. In 1951, he married Margaret Chant, an American, who gave birth to George and three other children.

The 1960's and early 1970's were a volatile time in Greece, with a military junta mounting a successful *coup* (take-over) in 1967 and holding

power until 1974. The Papandreou family spent various years of this period in Canada and Sweden. The elder Papandreou returned to Greece in 1974 and organized PASOK; he became prime minister in 1981. George Papandreou won election to the Greek parliament in 1981. He held several ministerial posts in his father's administration and later served in subsequent PASOK governments. George Papandreou was elected leader of PASOK in 2004.

Salazar, Ken (1955-), was confirmed as

secretary of the U.S. Department of the Interior by the Senate on Jan. 20, 2009, following his nomination for the post by President-elect Barack Obama. Salazar resigned in January from the U.S. Senate, where he had been serving as a Democratic member from Colorado since 2005.

Ken Salazar was born on March 2, 1955, in Alamosa, Colorado. The Salazar family descend from early Spanish settlers of the region that was later to become New Mexico and Colorado.

Ken Salazar attended Colorado College in Colorado Springs, where he earned a bachelor's degree in political science in 1977. Salazar studied law at the University of Michigan at Ann Arbor, obtaining a law degree in 1981.

Afterward, Salazar farmed and ranched for several years on family land in south-central Colorado near the New Mexico border and also began building a law practice. In the late 1980's, he served as chief legal counsel to Colorado Governor Roy Romer, a Democrat. From 1990 to 1994, Salazar was director of the state's Department of Natural Resources. During his tenure, Salazar led an initiative that created the Great Outdoors Colorado Board (GOCO), a trust fund devoted to conservation activities and programs.

Salazar was elected attorney general of Colorado in 1998 and served in that position from 1999 to 2005. Salazar's brother, John Salazar, has represented Colorado's third district in the U.S. House of Representatives since 2004.

Sebelius, Kathleen Gilligan (1948-),

was sworn in as secretary of the U.S. Department of Health and Human Services (HHS) on April 28, 2009, following her confirmation by the Senate. President Barack Obama nominated Sebelius in March after his previous nominee for the post, former U.S. Senator Tom Daschle, withdrew from consideration following the revelation that he had filed amended income tax returns with payment of more than $128,000 in back taxes.

When nominated as HHS secretary, Kathleen Sebelius, a Democrat, was in her second term as governor of Kansas. Sebelius was first elected to the Kansas governorship in 2003 and reelected in 2006. In November 2005, *Time* magazine named Sebelius as one of the nation's five best governors.

Sebelius is credited with reducing waste in state government and overseeing reforms to public school funding.

From 1995 to 2003, Sebelius served as the insurance commissioner of Kansas, a statewide elective office. In 2002, she successfully blocked a take-over of Blue Cross and Blue Shield of Kansas by an out-of-state health care conglomerate, winning praise nationally from advocates of health insurance reform.

Kathleen Gilligan was born in Cincinnati on May 15, 1948. Her father, John Gilligan, entered politics in the early 1950's; in 1970, he won election as governor of Ohio. John Gilligan and Kathleen Sebelius are the first father-and-daughter governors in U.S. history.

Kathleen Gilligan earned a Bachelor of Arts degree from Trinity College (now Trinity Washington University) in Washington, D.C., in 1974. That same year, she married Gary Sebelius, the son of a Republican Kansas congressman. Later, Sebelius earned a Master of Public Administration degree from the University of Kansas at Lawrence. Sebelius began her career in politics with her election in 1986 to the Kansas House of Representatives.

Sigurdardóttir, Jóhanna (1942-),

became prime minister of Iceland in a caretaker government on Feb. 1, 2009, upon the resignation of Prime Minister Geir Haarde. On April 26, Sigurdardóttir's Social Democratic-Green Party coalition swept parliamentary elections, and she was con-

firmed as prime minister of the new government. Jóhanna Sigurdardóttir is the first female prime minister of Iceland, a small island nation in the North Atlantic with slightly more than 300,000 residents. She is also the first openly lesbian leader of a nation in modern history. Sigurdardóttir married and had two children as a young adult before the marriage ended in divorce. In 2002, she entered a civil union with her same-sex partner, Jónína Leósdóttir, a journalist and author.

The rise of a left-of-center government in Iceland followed the collapse of Iceland's economy in autumn 2008 as Iceland's three major banks, virtually unregulated and highly overextended, failed. Prior to the economic crisis, conservative, market-oriented coalitions had ruled Iceland for more than a decade.

Jóhanna Sigurdardóttir was born on Oct. 4, 1942, in Reykjavík, the capital. After graduating from a vocational high school in 1960, she began working as an airline flight attendant with the Icelandic national airline. Eventually, she became a leader of the airline's employee union. Sigurdardóttir first won election to the Althing, Iceland's parliament, in 1978. As of 2009, she was the longest-serving member of that body.

Snowe, Olympia (1947-), a Republican

member of the United States Senate from Maine, provided key bipartisan support on several major initiatives by the Democratic administration of President Barack Obama in 2009. Snowe, along with her Maine Republican colleague, Senator Susan Collins, voted for the Obama administration's stimulus package in February, ensuring its passage in the Senate. In October, Senator Snowe was the only Republican on the Senate Finance Committee to vote for proposed health care reform legislation sponsored by Senator Max Baucus (D., Montana). The key committee vote cleared the way for health care legislation to move to the full Senate.

Snowe was born Olympia Jean Bouchles on Feb. 21, 1947, in Augusta, Maine. Her parents were immigrants from Greece. She earned a bachelor's degree in political science from the University of Maine at Orono in 1969.

After graduation from college, Olympia Bouchles married Peter Snowe, a Maine politician serving in the state's House of Representatives. In 1973, Peter Snowe was killed in an automobile accident. Olympia Snowe, then active in state politics, ran for the vacant legislative seat in a special election and won. Snowe later married John McKernan, Jr., a Maine politician who has served as governor of the state and as a member of the U.S. House of Representatives. Olympia Snowe served in Maine's legislature for five years. In 1978, she won election to the U.S. House of Repre-

Jóhanna Sigurdardóttir

Olympia Snowe

been diagnosed with juvenile diabetes and began taking insulin injections. Sotomayor's mother, Celina, raised Sonia and a brother, Juan, in public housing on a nurse's salary.

In 1972, Sotomayor enrolled in Princeton University in Princeton, New Jersey. She graduated in 1976 and went on to Yale Law School in New Haven, Connecticut. In her final year of law school, she served as editor of the Yale University Law Review. Sotomayor obtained her law degree from Yale in 1979.

Sotomayor joined the office of the district attorney, county of New York, as an assistant district attorney in 1979. In 1984, she went into private practice with a New York City law firm.

In 1992, President George H. W. Bush appointed Sotomayor as a U.S. district court judge for the Southern District of New York. While on that bench, Sotomayor issued a ruling in 1995 that settled a strike by major league baseball players and enabled teams to resume the disrupted baseball season. Sotomayor was appointed in 1998 to the U.S. Court of Appeals (second circuit) in New York City, the judgeship she held until her elevation in 2009 to the Supreme Court.

Van Rompuy, Herman *(ROM pow)* (1947-), was selected to be the first president of the European Council by leaders of the 27 member states of the European Union (EU) in November

sentatives from Maine's Second District. In 1994, Snowe won election to the U.S. Senate; she was reelected in 2000 and 2006.

Solis, Hilda (1957-), was confirmed by the U.S. Senate as secretary of the Department of Labor on Feb. 24, 2009. Solis was serving in her fifth term as a member of the U.S. House of Representatives from California when she was nominated for labor secretary by President Obama.

Hilda Lucia Solis was born on Oct. 20, 1957, in Los Angeles. Her mother was an immigrant from Nicaragua, and her father was from Mexico. They both worked and belonged to labor unions.

In 1979, Hilda Solis became the first member of her family to graduate from college, with a bachelor's degree in political science from California State Polytechnic University in Pomona. Solis worked in the administration of President Jimmy Carter (1977-1981), first in the Office of Hispanic Affairs and then in the Office of Management and Budget.

In 1992, Solis was elected to the California state Assembly and, in 1994, to the state Senate. In the Senate, she campaigned successfully to have the minimum wage raised and wrote laws to combat domestic violence. Solis won election to the U.S. House of Representatives in 2000.

Sotomayor, Sonia (1954-), was sworn in on Aug. 8, 2009, as the first Hispanic and only the third woman justice to serve on the U.S. Supreme Court. Nominated by President Barack Obama, she was confirmed by the Senate on August 6.

Sonia Sotomayor was born in the Bronx, New York City, on June 25, 1954. Her parents had moved to the United States from Puerto Rico. Sonia's father, Juan Sotomayor, died when she was 9 years old; a few months earlier, she had

Sonia Sotomayor

2009. The council is the supreme political body of the EU.

Van Rompuy was born on Oct. 31, 1947, in Etterbeek, the central municipality of Brussels, Belgium. At Catholic University of Leuven, he earned a bachelor's degree in philosophy in 1968 and a master's degree in applied economics in 1971.

Van Rompuy served as chairman of the Flemish Christian Democratic Party from 1988 to 1993 and as Belgium's deputy prime minister and minister of the budget from 1993 to 1999. In 2004, he became minister of state.

When the previous government collapsed in December 2008 amid economic crisis and political controversies, King Albert II of Belgium asked Van Rompuy, who was then speaker of the Chamber of Representatives, to become prime minister. During his long political career, Van Rompuy developed a reputation for integrity, high ethics, and modesty.

Herman Van Rompuy

Vilsack, Tom (1950-), was confirmed as secretary of the U.S. Department of Agriculture by the Senate on Jan. 21, 2009. A Democrat, Vilsack served as governor of Iowa from 1999 to 2007. He entered the 2008 presidential campaign but later withdrew, eventually throwing his support to Barack Obama.

Vilsack was born on Dec. 31, 1950, in Pittsburgh and placed in an orphanage. He was adopted by Bud and Dolly Vilsack of Pittsburgh.

Vilsack earned a bachelor's degree in history from Hamilton College in Clinton, New York, in 1972. While in college, he met Ann Christine Bell; they married in 1973. In 1975, Vilsack received a law degree from Albany Law School in New York. The Vilsacks then moved to Christine's home state of Iowa. He began his political career in 1987 as mayor of Mount Pleasant, Iowa. He was elected to the state Senate in 1993 and became governor in 1998. As governor, Vilsack signed legislation to create the Grow Iowa Values Fund, an initiative to attract new businesses to the state, and Vision Iowa, a program to fund construction of projects for recreational and cultural venues. Energy analysts credited Vilsack with

encouraging development of such alternative energy sources as ethanol, biodiesel, and wind power.

Winslet, Kate (1975-), received the Academy Award for best actress on Feb. 22, 2009, for her portrayal of a complex woman with a Nazi past in the 2008 film *The Reader.* Winslet had previously received five Academy Award nominations.

Kate Elizabeth Winslet was born on Oct. 5, 1975, in Reading, United Kingdom, into an acting family. Her grandparents founded the Reading Repertory Theatre, and her father and mother were both actors.

Winslet made her motion-picture debut in the 1994 film *Heavenly Creatures,* in which she played a teenager involved in a murder. One of Winslet's most memorable movie roles was as the doomed romantic heroine in *Titanic* (1997), one of the most popular films of all time. Kate Winslet and husband Sam Mendes divide their time between homes in New York City and London. Mendes, a Hollywood director, directed Winslet in the leading female role in the 2008 feature film *Revolutionary Road.*   ■ Robert Knight

See also **Cabinet, U.S.; Democratic Party; Elections; Europe; Motion pictures; Supreme Court of the United States.**

Kate Winslet

Peru. Wounded by corruption scandals and charges that his administration was favoring foreign investors over the Peruvian people, Peruvian President Alan García's approval rating dropped to 20 percent in 2009. The focus of public outrage were proinvestor decrees that García issued under special legislative powers granted him by Congress to bring Peru into compliance with a free trade agreement with the United States. The decrees opened up vast areas of Peru's Amazonian lowlands to exploitation by private agricultural, energy, and mineral developers. In April protests, Indians of the Awajún tribe, wearing warpaint and armed with spears, overran roads and rivers in this region, disrupting oil production and halting flights at remote airports.

Indigenous violence and unrest. On June 5, violence erupted between the indigenous protesters and security forces near the oil town of Bagua. More than 30 people were killed, including 11 police officers. Peru's Congress then repealed several of the most controversial land laws. Emboldened by this rare victory, some 300,000 Peruvian Indians from more than 50 indigenous groups began organizing to stand up for their rights. The Indians occupied resource-rich lands accounting for nearly two-thirds of Peru's territory. With outside help, the indigenous groups demanded schools, health clinics, and representation within the government bodies that allocate profits from oil and natural gas reserves taken from their traditional lands.

Cabinet shuffle. In response to the increasing militancy and nationwide protests, Prime Minister Yehude Simon resigned, replaced on July 12 by the president of Congress, Javier Velásquez Quesquén. The change was part of an effort by President García to revamp his Cabinet and restore public confidence in the government. Seven other ministers were also replaced.

Former president convicted. On April 7, a panel of three Supreme Court judges convicted former President Alberto K. Fujimori of human rights abuses and sentenced him to 25 years in prison. In defense, Fujimori argued that some excesses were necessary to win the war against Peru's Maoist Shining Path terrorists. Fujimori served as the president of Peru from 1990 to 2000.

Shining Path. In September 2009, Shining Path guerrilla fighters shot down an air force helicopter in the Apurímac and Ene River Valley, a remote coca-growing region. Violence in the area had increased following an August offensive by the Peruvian army to eliminate drug trafficking and the illicit cocaine trade, which was fueling a resurgence of the terrorist group.

■ Nathan A. Haverstock

See also **Human rights; Latin America.**

Petroleum and gas. See Energy supply.

Philadelphia. Former Pennsylvania state Senator Vincent J. Fumo, a Philadelphia Democrat with a wide network of appointees and a reputation as a powerful deal maker, was sentenced on July 14, 2009, to serve 55 months in prison on corruption charges. Fumo began serving time on August 31 at the Federal Correctional Institution in Ashland, Kentucky. Federal prosecutors, who had urged that Fumo be given a 15-year sentence in the $3.5-million-plus fraud case, said they were disappointed with U.S. District Judge Ronald L. Buckwalter's sentence. Philadelphia Mayor Michael Nutter joined with those who protested the sentence, calling it "absurdly low."

Fumo, 66, was a long-time fixture in Philadelphia politics. He was convicted on March 16 of 137 counts of conspiracy, mail and wire fraud, obstruction of justice, and tax offenses. The case against him centered on allegations that he skimmed money from the state Senate, the city's Independence Seaport Museum, and a nonprofit South Philadelphia community improvement group called Citizens' Alliance for Better Neighborhoods.

The Federal Bureau of Investigation investigated Fumo for about four years, raiding his legislative office in South Philadelphia in 2005 and seizing computers and his e-mail server in Harrisburg, the state capital. The grand jury transcript in the case totaled almost 7,000 pages.

A codefendant, Ruth Arnao, 52, who had worked for Fumo for more than two decades and headed the Citizens' Alliance, was also found guilty of 45 counts of conspiracy, fraud, and obstruction of justice. Judge Buckwalter sentenced her on July 21, 2009, to a year and a day in prison.

Approval for new museum. The Philadelphia Arts Commission on October 7 approved a design for the city's newest museum, the Barnes Foundation, to be built on the Benjamin Franklin Parkway downtown, alongside several of the city's key museums. The $200-million building will house artworks currently shown at a gallery in Merion, a suburb just outside the city.

The arts commission's approval marked the end of a long battle over whether to move the huge collection of Impressionist and early-modern paintings, plus African, Asian, and other art, collected by the late Albert C. Barnes. Barnes, a patent medicine inventor, had dictated in his will that the works stay as he arranged them in the Merion museum. However, the $10-million endowment he left upon his death in 1951 failed to generate income in the last decade, and the foundation's trustees said that a move downtown was necessary to attract prospective donors.

The new building, scheduled to open in 2012, will hold his 181 works by Pierre-Auguste Renoir, 69 by Paul Cézanne, 59 by Henri Matisse, 46 by Pablo Picasso, and many other works.

Venerable law firm closes. Wolf, Block, Schorr & Solis-Cohen, a 106-year-old law firm that had been prominent in city affairs for much of its history, dissolved after its partners voted to discontinue the firm on March 23, 2009. The firm cited a difficult credit market, declining profits, and defections of lawyers as reasons for closing.

World Series. Baseball's Philadelphia Phillies failed to win a second consecutive World Series in 2009, losing four games to two to the New York Yankees. The Yankees won the sixth and deciding game, 7-3, on November 4.

A transit strike that shut down subway and bus travel in the city for six days was resolved on November 9, after the Southeastern Pennsylvania Transportation Authority (SEPTA) and the transit system's largest union reached an agreement. Transport Workers Union Local 234, which represents more than 5,000 SEPTA drivers, mechanics, and operators, had sought concessions from SEPTA on health care, pension, and salary issues.

Cell phone ban. On April 6, SEPTA banned cell phone use on one car of most rush-hour trains. Conductors on the "Quiet Ride" car of each train also discouraged loud conversations.

Weather. On December 19, Philadelphia was hit by 23.2 inches (59 centimeters) of snow, the city's second largest snowfall since record keeping began in 1884.   ■ Howard S. Shapiro

Philippines. A politically motivated massacre in the southern province of Maguindanao shocked Philippine officials in late 2009. On November 23, 57 people, including supporters and family members of provincial gubernatorial candidate Esmael Mangudadatu, were murdered in an ambush as they attempted to file Mangudadatu's candidacy papers for the 2010 election.

Some 24 people were charged, including several members of the powerful Ampatuan family, which had long controlled Maguindanao. Mangudadatu claimed that Andal Ampatuan, Jr., a small-town mayor who police believed organized the attack, had threatened to kill him if he ran for office. Mangudadatu sent female family members to file for him, thinking that they would not be harmed. Regarding the situation, a local journalist called it "an undying fact that [the] Philippines is still ruled by clans and warlords." In early December 2009, President Gloria Macapagal-Arroyo briefly imposed martial law in Maguindanao to restore order.

Economics and politics. In a state-of-the-nation speech on July 27, Macapagal-Arroyo detailed the country's uninterrupted economic growth since she took office in 2001. She said gross domestic product (GDP) had expanded from $76 billion to $186 billion and that average inflation was the lowest since 1966. (GDP is the total value of goods and services produced in a country during a

People wade in chest-deep floodwater in Cainta, a Manila suburb, after Tropical Storm Ketsana dropped more than 16 inches (40 centimeters) of rain on the Philippines island of Luzon on September 26. A typhoon struck the island later in the same week. The two storms left more than 920 people dead.

given year.) Under Macapagal-Arroyo, foreign debt dropped from 73 to 32 percent of GDP. Macapagal-Arroyo, who was not eligible for re-election when her term ended in May 2010, said she would run for Congress, as did former First Lady Imelda Marcos.

Insurgents clashed with government troops in the south in 2009. On August 12, the army raided the Basilan Island training camp of Abu Sayyaf, a militant Islamic group believed to be linked to the terrorist organization al-Qa`ida. The clashes left 23 soldiers and at least 31 guerrillas dead. Government troops captured Abu Sayyaf's main camp on Jolo Island on September 21. The Moro Islamic Liberation Front, another Islamic separatist group, may have supported Abu Sayyaf in this fighting.

Storms. Two storms battered the island of Luzon within a week of each other in late 2009. The storms caused flooding and landslides that killed more than 920 people and left hundreds of thousands homeless. On September 26, Tropical Storm Ketsana dumped more than 16 inches (40 centimeters) of rain on the area around Manila, the capital. The floodwaters receded slowly, and critics accused the government of slow, inadequate relief efforts. The second storm, Typhoon Parma, hit provinces northeast of Manila on October 3. Parma caused flooding and landslides, and standing water furthered the spread of disease. ■ Henry S. Bradsher

See also **Asia; Disasters; Terrorism.**

Physics.
Scientists analyzing data from NASA's Gravity Probe B (GP-B) spacecraft reported in February 2009 the first precise measurements of an effect predicted in 1916 by German-born physicist Albert Einstein. The GP-B results were described by the project's principal investigator, physicist Francis Everitt of Stanford University in California.

GP-B, placed into orbit in 2004, had four highly precise *gyroscopes* (spherical devices that use rotation to produce stable direction in space). According to Einstein's theory of gravity, known as the general theory of relativity, the axes of these gyroscopes should slowly drift because of two effects—the geodetic effect and the frame-dragging effect.

In the geodetic effect, a large mass, such as Earth, distorts space-time, the combined entity of space and time that Einstein said permeates the universe. This effect would shift the gyroscope axes by about two-thousandths of a degree per year. In frame-dragging, Earth's rotation partially drags the distortions of space-time with it, resulting in an additional shift, at right angles to the geodetic shift and 170 times smaller.

Everitt's team used magnetic sensors on GP-B to track the movement of the gyroscope axes. By 2007, analysis of the data had confirmed the geodetic shift to within 1 percent. However, the

much smaller frame-dragging effect required more analysis. Everitt reported that GP-B's measurements confirmed the frame-dragging effect to within 15 percent—further confirmation that Einstein's general theory of relativity is correct. He added that continued analysis was likely to improve the precision of these measurements.

Quark-antiquark masses equal. One of the best-established "rules" in particle physics holds that any particle of matter must have an antimatter counterpart of exactly equal mass. Antimatter resembles ordinary matter but with reversed properties, such as electric charge. The matter-antimatter "rule" had previously been verified to high precision with stable subatomic particles, such as the electron and proton. However, it had not been tested with unstable particles, such as quarks, which are the "building blocks" of particles in the atom's *nucleus* (center). In June 2009, physicists at the Fermi National Accelerator Laboratory (Fermilab) near Batavia, Illinois, reported results of such an analysis.

Making direct measurements of quark masses is difficult because when a quark is produced, it does not remain alone for long. Within 10-billion-trillionths of a second, the quark "dresses" itself in other quarks, antiquarks, and particles called gluons. However, the heaviest quark—the so-called top quark—remains undressed for an extremely brief time before breaking up into lighter particles. This brief time provides scientists with an opportunity to measure and compare the masses of "clean" quarks and antiquarks.

The Fermilab scientists analyzed several years of data generated by the DZero detector of the lab's Tevatron particle accelerator, focusing on 220 clean examples of top quark-antiquark pairs produced in collisions of protons with antiprotons. Analysis of each example provided a precise measurement of the masses of both quark and antiquark—proving that these masses are equal.

Large Hadron Collider. In November—after a series of technical problems—crucial tests were performed to resume operations of the Large Hadron Collider (LHC) at the CERN laboratory near Geneva, Switzerland. The tests came after a shutdown of 14 months to repair the technical problems, which began only a few days after the device was first turned on. The LHC is the world's most powerful particle accelerator, a device that speeds up subatomic particles to high energies and collides them to reveal information about properties of matter.

Physicists hoped the LHC would eventually enable them to solve several mysteries of the subatomic world, including the source of mass, which is believed to involve an undiscovered particle called the Higgs boson. ■ Robert H. March

See also **Nobel Prizes.**

Poetry. Incoming United States President Barack Obama selected poet Elizabeth Alexander to read at his presidential inauguration on Jan. 20, 2009. Alexander was born in New York City's Harlem neighborhood in 1962 and raised in Washington, D.C. She teaches in the African American Studies Department at Yale University in New Haven, Connecticut. Alexander's poems cover a range of subjects and tones, from public to private, playful to political.

The type of poem recited at an inauguration is what is known as an "occasional" poem—that is, a poem written to commemorate a specific event or person. Including Alexander, four poets have written and read commemorative works for an inauguration. The first was Robert Frost at John F. Kennedy's inauguration in 1961. Momentarily dazzled by sun and wind, the 86-year-old Frost could not make out the poem he had written for the occasion, "Dedication." Instead, he recited from memory an earlier creation, "The Gift Outright," which begins with the line, "The land was ours before we were the land's."

Bill Clinton also selected a poet to read at his presidential inaugurations. In 1993, Maya Angelou's "Inaugural Poem" possessed a visionary sweep: "Yet, today I call you to my riverside,/ If you will study war no more. Come,// Clad in peace and I will sing the songs/ The Creator gave to me when I and the/ Tree and the stone were one." Miller Williams, a poet from Arkansas, in 1997 recited his poem "Of History and Hope" at Clinton's second inauguration.

"Praise Song for the Day" is the title of Alexander's poem for the 2009 inauguration. The "praise song" is a common poetic form in the African tradition, which incorporates a string of commendatory attributes that lavishes honor on the object of praise. Alexander ends her poem with a celebration of love: "Love beyond marital, filial, national,/ love that casts a widening pool of light,/ love with no need to pre-empt grievance.// In today's sharp sparkle, this winter air,/ any thing can be made, any sentence begun./ On the brink, on the brim, on the cusp,/ praise song for walking forward in that light."

A new poet laureate. In May 2009, Carol Ann Duffy was appointed poet laureate of the United Kingdom, the first woman to hold the position in its 400-year (or more) history. She succeeds the poet Andrew Motion, who, during his 10-year stint as laureate, wrote a number of occasional poems to commemorate events in the United Kingdom. These included a poem for the 80th birthday of Queen Elizabeth; for the death of Queen Elizabeth, the Queen Mother; on the marriage of Prince Charles to Camilla Parker Bowles; and a "rap" poem for Prince William's

birthday. Until recently, the position of British poet laureate was typically held for life. However, beginning with Andrew Motion in 1999, the appointment was limited to a term of 10 years.

On Duffy, Alison Flood, writing in *The Guardian* newspaper, noted that she is "one of the bestselling poets in the UK, [and] has managed to combine critical acclaim with popularity: a rare feat in the poetry world." She came to popularity in 1999 with her poetry collection *The World's Wife*, a series of lyrics in the voices of the wives of historical figures and characters from literature, such as Mrs. Tiresias, Mrs. Faust, Mrs. Quasimodo, Mrs. Aesop, and Queen Herod. Duffy was made an Officer of the Order of the British Empire (OBE) in 1995 and a Commander of the Order of the British Empire (CBE) in 2002.

Her other honors include the Somerset Maugham Award (1988), the Forward Poetry Prize for best collection of poetry (1993), the Lannan Literary Award for Poetry (1995), and the T. S. Eliot Prize (2005). Duffy, born in 1955, has written several collections of poetry for adults, as well as poetry and picture books for children. She lives in Manchester and directs the writing program at Manchester Metropolitan University.

■ David Yezzi

See also **Literature; Literature for children; People in the news** (Carol Ann Duffy).

Poland. Scandal led to the resignation in October 2009 of five ministers from Prime Minister Donald Tusk's government. The scandal, dubbed "Gamble Gate" by the press, involved allegations that some high-ranking members of the government—including the leader of the ruling party, Civic Platform, and the minister for sports—had attempted to strip a gaming tax provision from legislation in response to urgings from casino owners. Some of the politicians had been recorded on phone wiretaps in compromising conversations. Opinion polls published in Poland in mid-October registered a sharp drop in support for Civic Platform.

Economy. Poland, despite the ongoing worldwide recession, continued to experience some economic expansion in 2009. Economists forecast that the economy would grow by 1.3 percent in 2009 and 1.8 percent in 2010. Although far below the country's 5.3-percent rate of growth in 2008, Poland's 1.3-percent advance in 2009 was considerably better than the negative growth rates in other Central and East European economies.

Foreign relations. In September, United States officials announced the cancellation of plans for a controversial missile defense system to be based partly in Poland and the Czech Republic. The plan, put forth by the administration of U.S. President George W. Bush, proposed basing interceptor missiles in Poland, allegedly as a deterrent to a nuclear strike by a prospective nuclear-armed Iran. Based on unproven technology, interceptor missiles are designed to knock incoming offensive missiles out of the sky.

Some Polish politicians expressed displeasure with the decision and suggested that it sent the wrong signal to Russian leaders, who had strongly opposed the plan. In October, U.S. Vice President Joe Biden met with Polish leaders in Warsaw, the Polish capital, to offer alternative defense strategies.

Lisbon Treaty. Poland's president, Lech Kaczynski, signed the Lisbon Treaty of the European Union (EU) on October 10 after the treaty won overwhelming approval in a closely watched referendum in Ireland. With Kaczynski's assent, the treaty awaited approval only by Czech Republic President Václav Klaus, who signed on November 3. Kaczynski and Klaus both have reputations as "Euroskeptics"—politicians opposed to expansion of EU institutions.

The Lisbon Treaty streamlines the decision-making processes of the EU. It also creates the offices of president of the Executive Council and high representative for foreign and security policy, or foreign minister. ■ Sharon L. Wolchik

See also **Czech Republic; Europe; Russia.**

Pollution. See **Environmental pollution.**

Popular music. As digital sales stagnated and CD sales continued to decline in 2009, sales of vinyl records continued an upward trend, doubling last year's sales. Nielsen SoundScan, which monitors album sales at point of purchase in the United States, predicted vinyl sales would reach 2.8 million units by the end of the year, a record since the service began tracking sales data in 1991. However, vinyl sales make up less than 1 percent of overall album sales. Album sales were 309.5 million by the end of November 2009, down 13 percent from the same period in 2008.

The "King of Pop" is dead. Michael Jackson died at his Los Angeles home on June 25, 2009, from an accidental overdose of the anesthetic propofol administered by his physician to treat his insomnia. Within minutes of media reports announcing Jackson's death, the Seattle-based Internet dealer Amazon.com was sold out of its supply of Michael Jackson and Jackson Five CD's and DVD's. Radio play of Jackson's songs immediately spiked, and his albums again set sales records. For six nonconsecutive weeks after his death, Jackson's *Number Ones* (2003) greatest hits compilation was the biggest-selling album in the country.

Jackson's memorial service was broadcast live around the world, attracting a global audience of up to 1 billion people. In August 2009, Jackson's death was ruled a homicide by the Los Angeles

Scottish singer Susan Boyle performs on the TV show "America's Got Talent" in September. The singing sensation, who emerged from obscurity in 2009 on "Britain's Got Talent," enjoyed the largest-ever album sales for a debut female artist.

County coroner. Jackson was 50 years old.

Jackson's *This Is It,* a two-CD soundtrack of the music documentary of the same name, was released in October. The film documented Jackson's last rehearsals for a concert series that had been scheduled to begin later in the year. The film and soundtrack both topped sales in their first week of release.

The voice of a young Jackson was also featured on the October release *I Want You Back! Unreleased Masters,* which included previously unheard music by the Jackson Five. The album's release marked the 40th anniversary of the original Motown release of the group's hit debut single, "I Want You Back."

The Beatles also hit the music charts—nearly

four decades after the group broke up. Remastered CD's of the 12 original Beatles albums were released in September. Stereo versions were available both individually and as a boxed set, and a second collection comprised all mono titles along with the original stereo mixes of *Help!* and *Rubber Soul.* During the first five days of release, U.S. consumers purchased more than 1 million copies of remastered Beatles titles, and the individual CD and boxed sets debuted strongly across several Billboard charts. *The Beatles: Rock Band*, a video game in the style of *Rock Band* and based on the Beatles, was released the same day as the remastered albums.

Country's finest. The "King of Country," George Strait, dethroned the "King of Pop" in August when Strait's 26th studio album, *Twang,* replaced Jackson's *Number Ones* as the top album on the Billboard 200. It was Strait's fifth number-one album. The singer was named the Academy of Country Music's (ACM) artist of the decade in April.

Country duo Brooks & Dunn—the biggest-selling duo in any genre—announced in August that they would be breaking up after a farewell tour in 2010. Their two-disc compilation, *#1s and Then Some,* featuring 28 hits and 2 new songs, was released in September 2009.

Country superstar Garth Brooks, who had said in 2000 that he was retiring from music, announced in October 2009 that he was coming out of retirement to begin a concert engagement in Las Vegas.

Carrie Underwood's third album, *Play On,* reached number one after it was released in November. The 2005 "American Idol" winner was named ACM's entertainer of the year in April.

In November, Taylor Swift, 19, won four Country Music Association awards, including entertainer of the year. She was the youngest artist to win that award. Swift's second album, *Fearless,* released in 2008, was the best-selling album of 2009.

A bad rap. Rapper Kanye West attracted attention in September when he disrupted a live telecast of the 26th annual MTV Video Music Awards. As Taylor Swift was accepting her award for best female video for "You Belong with Me," West ran onto the stage and grabbed the microphone from Swift to proclaim that Beyoncé's video for "Single Ladies (Put a Ring on It)," nominated for the same award, was "one of the best videos of all time." West was booed and removed from the show. Later that evening, when Beyoncé won the award for best video of the year for "Single Ladies," she invited Swift to the stage to finish her acceptance speech. Swift was the first country music artist to win an MTV Video Music Award (VMA). West later apologized to Swift.

Going Gaga. Several weeks after the VMA incident, West canceled his "Fame Kills" tour with pop sensation Lady Gaga. Lady Gaga announced that she would begin her own tour in November. The singer and songwriter attracted attention in 2009 for her hits "Just Dance" and "Poker Face" and for her bizarre outfits and live performances.

Blueprint for success. As music sales declined overall, rap and hip-hop artists continued to hold strong on the charts. Jay-Z's 11th studio album, *The Blueprint 3,* released in September, became the rapper's 11th album to reach number one on the Billboard 200, surpassing the record held by Elvis Presley. Eminem's sixth studio album, *Relapse,* was 2009's second-highest-selling album for a sales week. Other number-one rap and hip-hop albums included Rick Ross's third studio album, *Deeper Than Rap;* the Black Eyed Peas's fifth studio album, *The E.N.D.;* and Fabolous's fifth studio album, *Loso's Way.*

She dreamed a dream. Susan Boyle, whom critics described as a frumpy, middle-aged, Scottish woman with the voice of an angel, became a worldwide sensation after her April performance on the singing competition TV show "Britain's Got Talent." The 47-year-old contestant stunned the show's judges and studio audience with her moving performance of "I Dreamed a Dream" from the musical *Les Misérables.* Days after the show aired, a clip of Boyle's performance set a record as the most-watched video on the Internet. Boyle was signed to a recording contract by judge Simon Cowell. Her album, *I Dreamed a Dream*—though not released until November—hit number one on Amazon's Best Sellers in Music list in September. By the time of its release, Boyle's album had become the most pre-ordered CD in the online retailer's history. It was 2009's highest-selling album for a sales week and the best-selling debut for a female artist in Soundscan history. In the United Kingdom, *I Dreamed a Dream* became the best-selling album of 2009 in just four weeks.

Whitney Houston looked for a comeback in 2009. Her first album in seven years, *I Look to You,* was released in August. The album entered the Billboard 200 at number one with the best opening-week sales of Houston's career. In September, Houston gave a highly publicized interview on "The Oprah Winfrey Show"—her first interview in seven years—in which she openly discussed her years of cocaine addiction and the disintegration of her troubled marriage to singer Bobby Brown. Houston struggled with her voice in a much-hyped comeback concert in New York City's Central Park, which aired on "Good Morning America" in September.

Mariah Carey's 12th studio album, *Memoirs of an Imperfect Angel*, released in September, met with mixed reviews. The slickly produced album included a 34-page *Elle* "mini-magazine"—complete with upscale fashion, jewelry, champagne, and tourism ads—covering Carey's life and career. "Obsessed" debuted at number 11, Carey's highest-ranking single since 1998's "My All."

Michael Jackson
King of Pop

From pop prodigy to international superstar, from eccentric Peter Pan to drug casualty, Michael Jackson was a magnetic presence who grew up, lived, and died in the public spotlight. Following news of his sudden death on June 25, 2009, radio play of Jackson's songs immediately spiked and his albums again set sales records. Jackson's memorial service was broadcast live around the world, attracting a global audience of up to 1 billion people. Many predicted that Jackson's popularity after death would rise to the almost legendary status attained by Elvis Presley.

Like Presley, the "King of Rock and Roll," Jackson, the "King of Pop," became one of the best-selling artists in popular music. And like Presley, Jackson's thrilling dance moves galvanized audiences into a frenzy. Jackson's music videos for "Billie Jean," "Beat It," and "Thriller" helped define the music video form in the mid-1980's. The album *Thriller* (1982) remains the world's best-selling album.

Michael Joseph Jackson was born on Aug. 29, 1958, in Gary, Indiana. He began performing locally at the age of 5 with his brothers Jackie, Tito, Jermaine, and Marlon. In 1968, the brothers signed with Motown Records as the Jackson Five, with 10-year-old Michael as the lead singer and dancer. The group became a sensation with such hits as "I Want You Back" (1969); "ABC," "I'll Be There," and "The Love You Save" (all 1970); "Never Can Say Goodbye" (1971); and "Dancing Machine" (1974). Michael also had a series of solo hit singles in 1971 that included "Got to Be There," "Rockin' Robin," and "Ben." The Jackson Five moved to Epic Records in 1976 and reformed as the Jacksons, recording such hits as "Enjoy Yourself" (1976), "Shake Your Body (Down to the Ground)" (1978), and "Lovely One" (1980). Michael began a series of successful solo albums with *Off the Wall* (1979). After the huge success of *Thriller,* he released the hit albums *Bad* (1987) and *Dangerous* (1991). Jackson was inducted into the Rock and Roll Hall of Fame in 1997 as a member of the Jackson Five and in 2001 as a solo performer.

As Jackson's wealth increased, his controversial private life made him a focus of national attention. He radically altered his appearance through a series of plastic surgeries. His California home, known as Neverland Valley Ranch, included an amusement park and zoo. In 1993, Jackson was accused of child sexual abuse, but no charges were brought. From 1994 to 1995, Jackson was married to Presley's daughter, Lisa Marie. From 1996 to 1999, he was married to Debbie Rowe, a nurse. They had two children of whom Jackson was granted custody. Jackson also had a third child, but the mother's identity was kept secret. In 2003 and 2004, Jackson was charged with sexual abuse of a minor. Jackson denied any wrongdoing, and after a highly publicized trial in 2005, a jury acquitted him of all charges.

Jackson was rehearsing for a series of comeback concerts scheduled for later in 2009 when he died at his Los Angeles home at age 50 from an accidental overdose of a sleeping medication administered by his physician. In August, Jackson's death was ruled a homicide by the Los Angeles County coroner.

■ Shawn Brennan

Sticky & bittersweet. Madonna wrapped up her record-breaking "Sticky & Sweet Tour" in September 2009 in Tel Aviv, Israel. The tour, which began in August 2008, drew more than 3.5 million fans at 85 concerts in 32 countries and grossed $408 million, making it the most successful tour by a solo artist. However, the tour met with controversy and tragedy. In July 2009, 2 people were killed and 36 were injured when a stage collapsed at a concert in Marseille, France. Most of the victims were stage technicians. In August, during a concert in Bucharest, Romania, thousands of fans booed Madonna after she spoke out against discrimination against Roma (Gypsies) in Eastern Europe. *Celebration,* Madonna's third greatest-hits album, was released in September. It contained 34 hits spanning the singer's career plus 2 new songs.

Divas. Barbra Streisand knocked fellow divas Carey and Madonna out of the top slot in October with the release of her collection of jazz standards, *Love Is the Answer.* Streisand promoted the album with an interview on "The Oprah Winfrey Show" and a rare performance at the Village Vanguard in New York City. The album was produced by Canadian jazz pianist and singer Diana Krall.

Bob Dylan had two albums released in 2009. *Together Through Life,* Dylan's 33rd studio album, reached number one on the Billboard 200 in its first week of release in April. The holiday album *Christmas in the Heart* was released in October. Dylan said he would donate proceeds from the release to charities that feed the needy. ■ Shawn Brennan

See also **Classical music; Electronic games; Radio; Television.**

GRAMMY AWARD WINNERS IN 2009

Record of the Year: "Please Read the Letter," Robert Plant and Alison Krauss

Album of the Year: *Raising Sand,* Robert Plant and Alison Krauss

Song of the Year: "Viva la Vida," Guy Berryman, Johnny Buckland, Will Champion, and Chris Martin

New Artist: Adele

Pop Vocal Album: *Rockferry,* Duffy

Pop Vocal Performance, Female: "Chasing Pavements," Adele

Pop Vocal Performance, Male: "Say," John Mayer

Pop Instrumental Album: *Jingle All the Way,* Béla Fleck and the Flecktones

Pop Instrumental Performance: "I Dreamed There Was No War," Eagles

Pop Performance by a Duo or Group with Vocals: "Viva la Vida," Coldplay

Pop Collaboration with Vocals: "Rich Woman," Robert Plant and Alison Krauss

Traditional Pop Vocal Album: *Still Unforgettable,* Natalie Cole

Solo Rock Vocal Performance: "Gravity," John Mayer

Rock Performance by a Duo or Group with Vocals: "Sex on Fire," Kings of Leon

Hard Rock Performance: "Wax Simulacra," The Mars Volta

Metal Performance: "My Apocalypse," Metallica

Rock Song: "Girls in Their Summer Clothes," Bruce Springsteen

Rock Album: *Viva la Vida or Death and All His Friends,* Coldplay

Alternative Music Album: *In Rainbows,* Radiohead

Rhythm-and-Blues Vocal Performance, Female: "Superwoman," Alicia Keys

Rhythm-and-Blues Vocal Performance, Male: "Miss Independent," Ne-Yo

Rhythm-and-Blues Performance by a Duo or Group with Vocals: "Stay with Me (by the Sea)," Al Green, featuring John Legend

Rhythm-and-Blues Song: "Miss Independent," Mikkel S. Eriksen, T. E. Hermansen, and S. Smith

Rhythm-and-Blues Album: *Jennifer Hudson,* Jennifer Hudson

Traditional Rhythm-and-Blues Vocal Performance: "You've Got the Love I Need," Al Green, featuring Anthony Hamilton

Contemporary Rhythm-and-Blues Album: *Growing Pains,* Mary J. Blige

Traditional Blues Album: *One Kind Favor,* B. B. King

Contemporary Blues Album: *City that Care Forgot,* Dr. John and the Lower 911

Rap Solo Performance: "A Milli," Lil Wayne

Rap Performance by a Duo or Group: "Swagga Like Us," Jay-Z and T. I., featuring Kanye West and Lil Wayne

Rap Album: *Tha Carter III,* Lil Wayne

Rap Song: "Lollipop," D. Carter, S. Garrett, D. Harrison, J. Scheffer, and R. Zamor

Contemporary Jazz Album: *Randy in Brasil,* Randy Brecker

Jazz Vocal Album: *Loverly,* Cassandra Wilson

Jazz Instrumental, Solo: "Be-Bop," Terence Blanchard

Jazz Instrumental Album, Individual or Group: *The New Crystal Silence,* Chick Corea and Gary Burton

Large Jazz Ensemble Album: *Monday Night Live at the Village Vanguard,* The Vanguard Jazz Orchestra

Country Album: *Troubadour,* George Strait

Country Song: "Stay," Jennifer Nettles

Country Vocal Performance, Female: "Last Name," Carrie Underwood

Country Vocal Performance, Male: "Letter to Me," Brad Paisley

Country Performance by a Duo or Group with Vocals: "Stay," Sugarland

Country Vocal Collaboration: "Killing the Blues," Robert Plant and Alison Krauss

Country Instrumental Performance: "Cluster Pluck," Brad Paisley, James Burton, Vince Gill, John Jorgenson, Albert Lee, Brent Mason, Redd Volkaert, and Steve Wariner

Gospel Performance: "Get Up," Mary Mary

Gospel Song: "Help Me Believe," Kirk Franklin

Traditional Folk Album: *At 89,* Pete Seeger

Contemporary Folk/Americana Album: *Raising Sand,* Robert Plant and Alison Krauss

Population. The population of the world was expected to reach 6.8 billion in July 2009, according to an annual revised projection issued by the United Nations (UN) Population Division in March. The 2009 estimate reflected an increase of 313 million people since 2005, an annual gain of 78 million people. The division projected that the world population would reach 7 billion by 2012 and 9 billion by 2050.

"Future population growth is highly dependent on the path that future fertility takes," the UN division indicated in presenting its figures. If future population growth follows the agency's medium variant, fertility rates will decline from 2.56 children per woman in the 2005 to 2010 period to 2.02 children in 2045 to 2050. If fertility rates remain slightly above the medium variant, the population will grow to 10.5 billion by 2050. At slightly below the medium variant, the population will be 8 billion by 2050.

According to the UN, population growth is expected to continue in the world's most populous nations. Nine countries were expected to account for half of the projected world population growth from 2010 to 2050 (in descending order of population increase): India, Pakistan, Nigeria, Ethiopia, the United States, Congo (Kinshasa), Tanzania, China, and Bangladesh.

As has been the constant projection in demographic studies, most of the 2.3 billion additional people by 2012 will be in developing nations, where people of working age and those aged 60 and over are expected to increase. Developing countries in 2009 made up 5.6 billion of the total 6.8 billion world population.

An aging world. According to the UN report, the number of people aged 60 and over is increasing rapidly in both developed and developing nations. That number is expected to grow from 739 million in 2009 to 2 billion by 2050. Up to 79 percent of people over 60 are expected to be living in developing nations by 2050.

In 2009, however, the number of children and young people in developing regions of the world was at an all-time high. Providing education or employment for such numbers posed a major challenge for those nations as the world struggled to recover from an economic and financial crisis. UN Secretary-General Ban Ki-moon reported in November that 17,000 children a day die of hunger.

In more developed countries, the number of children under 15 was projected to remain stable, and the number of youths ages 15 to 24 was expected to decrease. Most developed countries have had below replacement fertility—fewer than 2.1 children per woman—since the 1970's, the UN said.   ◼ J. Tuyet Nguyen

See also **Census.**

Portugal. In the general election held on Sept. 27, 2009, the Socialist Party (PS) government of Prime Minister José Sócrates was reelected for a second four-year term. However, the PS lost its parliamentary majority, forcing it to rule as a minority government in which legislation could be passed only by forming ad hoc coalitions with other parties.

The PS won 37 percent of the vote, a decline from 45 percent in the 2005 election. The opposition Social Democratic Party (PSD) also lost votes, receiving only 29 percent. The result surprised analysts, because the PSD outperformed the PS in elections to the European Parliament in June 2009. The parties that benefited from the decline of the PS and the PSD were two far-left parties—the Left Bloc and the Portuguese Communist Party—and the center-right Popular Party. The Left Bloc received 9.8 percent of the vote; the Communists, 7.9 percent; and the Popular Party, 10.5 percent.

The government and the president. Relations between the PS government and President Aníbal Cavaco Silva deteriorated significantly during the campaign. The governing party accused the president of campaigning for the opposition PSD, even though he is supposed to remain above partisan politics. In turn, two journalists revealed concerns from the president's staff that the government had electronically eavesdropped on the president's office. These tensions began in 2008 when the government passed a bill allowing greater independence for the Azores—islands controlled by Portugal—a policy shift with which the president did not agree.

Economic crisis. Portugal was ill-positioned for the global economic downturn in 2009. The nation had been plagued by weak economic growth, low productivity, and high unemployment throughout the 2000's.

During the election campaign, the PS promised to continue an aggressive public works program to counter the crisis, even though European Union (EU) economists forecast that Portugal's budget deficit would grow to a record 8 percent of GDP in 2009. (GDP—gross domestic product—is the value of all goods and services produced in a country in a year.) The government provided extra credit to small and medium-sized firms and also introduced a program to support mortgage payers who had fallen behind in their payments. In March, 200,000 workers protested in Lisbon, the capital, against the government's policies. EU economists forecast that Portugal's economy would contract by 2.9 percent in 2009.   ◼ Jeffrey Kopstein

See also **Europe.**

President of the United States. See **United States, President of the.**

Prince Edward Island. See **Canadian provinces.**

Prisons. Statistics released by the United States Department of Justice (DOJ) in December 2009 revealed that the number of adults in U.S. state or federal prisons, in local jails, or on probation or parole was 7.3 million at the end of 2008. This number, which was 0.5 percent greater than that recorded a year earlier, represented the smallest annual increase in the population under correctional supervision since 2000.

The DOJ report also noted that prison populations decreased in 20 states during 2008, led by New York, Georgia, and Michigan. The decreases or slowed increases in prison populations were partly the result of a decrease in the number of African Americans who were sentenced to prison, according to the report.

Prisoner sexual abuse. The National Prison Rape Elimination Commission (NPREC), which was established by the U.S. Congress in 2003, released its final report in June 2009. The report contained proposed standards to prevent, detect, monitor, and respond to sexual abuse of inmates in U.S. prisons, jails, and other detention facilities. The NPREC noted that tens of thousands of inmates are raped each year by other inmates or by facility staff because of a lack of basic protection measures.

The NPREC standards addressed special vulnerabilities of certain inmates, including those who are homosexual, transgendered, slight of stature, young, and new to the prison or jail system. The report urged facility officials to place greater emphasis on screening inmates for such vulnerabilities, as well as to improve medical and mental health services, internal investigations, and staff training.

Private prisons profit. In February, The GEO Group Inc., a private company paid by the U.S. government to detain illegal immigrants and other federal prisoners, reported that its income increased to $61 million in 2008 from $38 million the year before. The Nashville-based firm also expanded the inmate capacities of its several U.S. facilities, which contain more than 62,000 beds. Another private prison firm, Corrections Corporation of America, based in Boca Raton, Florida, expanded the capacity of its facilities beyond 87,000 beds in 2009.

Experts noted that private prisons were expanding in the United States in 2009 for a number of reasons, including an increase in the prosecution of illegal immigrants and the economic recession, forcing the government to cut costs in its overcrowded prison system. Private prisons housed roughly 7.5 percent of imprisoned adults in the United States in 2009.

■ Alfred J. Smuskiewicz

See also **Crime; Immigration; State government.**

Prizes. See Nobel Prizes; Pulitzer Prizes.

Protestantism. Protestant institutions in the United States suffered economic setbacks in 2009, the second year of a recession. Many churches and theological schools had to cut budgets and reduce staffs. Many evangelical Christian elementary schools also lacked essential funding. The Association of Christian Schools International, which usually reports about 150 member schools closing annually, had more than 200 schools close from January to August 2009.

Declining membership figures. According to a new American Religious Identification Survey (ARIS), released in March 2009, membership in *mainline* (moderate) Protestant churches was declining, and an increasing number of people identified themselves as "nondenominational Christians." Between 1990 and 2008, the percentage of Americans who identified themselves as mainline Christians fell from 18.7 to 12.9 percent. In June 2009, the Presbyterian Church (U.S.A.) announced that its membership had shrunk more in 2008 than in any single year since 1983. The ARIS also reported a significant decline in the percentage of Americans who identified themselves as Christian and a sharp increase in the percentage who were not religious at all.

Conservative as well as mainline Protestant denominations suffered declining memberships in 2009. The Presbyterian Church in America reported that in 2008 it had experienced the first membership decline in its 36-year history. A study presented at a June 2009 meeting of the Southern Baptist Convention, the largest Protestant denomination in the United States, predicted that membership could drop by half by 2050.

Controversies. Two issues dominated debate within Protestant churches in 2009—abortion and homosexuality. On May 31, a *pro-life* (antiabortion) activist entered the Reformation Lutheran Church in Wichita, Kansas, and shot and killed parishioner George Tiller. Tiller was a physician who had performed controversial late-term abortions, which are carried out during the later stages of pregnancy. Leaders of the pro-life movement condemned Tiller's murder.

The second major debate within Protestant churches in 2009 centered on policies concerning homosexuals. In April, the Judicial Council of the United Methodist Church ruled that pastors may not perform same-sex marriages and that to do so was a chargeable offense. Also in April, regional districts of the Presbyterian Church (U.S.A.) voted against changing a rule that required clergy to live either within a heterosexual marriage or to refrain from sexual activity. However, the vote was closer than 1997 and 2001 votes on the same issue.

In August 2009, the Churchwide Assembly of the Evangelical Lutheran Church in America voted to permit the ordination of people in committed, long-term, same-sex relationships. It also voted to respect the conscience of dissenters.

The Episcopal Church, part of the worldwide Anglican Communion, voted in July 2009 to lift a ban on consecrating gay bishops and to allow bishops to bless same-sex unions. These developments led Archbishop of Canterbury Rowan Williams, head of the Communion, to suggest the possibility of a "two-tier" or "two-track" structure that could allow churches with conflicting beliefs to coexist within the Communion.

A number of Episcopal dioceses and congregations left the Episcopal Church in 2009. They nurtured ties to conservative African Anglican churches, which generally opposed the ordination of homosexuals. Some congregations that left the Episcopal Church initiated legal battles to retain church property.

On October 20, Roman Catholic Church officials unexpectedly announced measures that would make it easier for Anglicans, including married priests, to convert to Catholicism while keeping some of their religious traditions. Some people were irritated by what they saw as an effort to lure conservative Anglicans opposed to the ordination of women and gays and the blessing of same-sex unions.   ■ Martin E. Marty

Psychology. See Mental health.

Public health. On June 11, 2009, the World Health Organization (WHO), a United Nations (UN) agency based in Geneva, Switzerland, declared swine flu to be a *pandemic* (an outbreak of disease in many parts of the world). The declaration of a pandemic was the first since the 1968-1969 Hong Kong flu, which caused the deaths of 700,000 people around the world.

Swine flu, caused by the novel influenza A (H1N1) virus, originated in swine and first led to human illness in March 2009 in Mexico. Spreading mainly through coughs and sneezes, H1N1 had caused more than 28,000 confirmed cases of infection, with more than 140 deaths, in 74 countries by the time of the June WHO declaration. More than 13,000 cases, with at least 27 deaths, had occurred in the United States by June. The number of worldwide deaths from H1N1 increased to more than 10,000 by December 2009.

The WHO increased the availability of antiviral drugs in developing countries to relieve swine flu symptoms. In addition, vaccines were available to prevent H1N1 infection. In many parts of the United States and other countries, however, vaccine demand exceeded supply in late 2009.

UN program results unclear. In two studies published in June in the British medical journal *The Lancet*, investigators reported that UN public health programs spent more than $196 billion

since 1990 to improve health in poor countries. Despite this great expenditure, the researchers found little evidence that the UN programs were responsible for progress in public health in those countries.

In one study, WHO researchers reported that—though such advances as higher vaccination rates and improved diagnoses happened in some countries given UN funds—UN health programs led to disruptions in basic health services and cuts in government health spending in several nations. Furthermore, the researchers could not determine if UN health programs addressed the most pressing needs of nations.

In the other study, researchers concluded that those countries in greatest need of public health donations did not necessarily receive more UN funds than countries with lesser needs. Health economist Christopher Murray of the University of Washington in Seattle led that study.

New malaria guidelines. New guidelines for fighting malaria—with the goal of global eradication of the disease—were unveiled in April 2009. The guidelines were developed by the Malaria Elimination Group, an international team of researchers, policy experts, and program managers convened by the Global Health Group of the University of California at San Francisco.

Malaria kills nearly 1 million people every year, according to the WHO. The new guidelines covered various operational, technical, and financial matters related to malaria control, elimination, and research investment. The UN's special envoy for malaria called for increased political and financial support to implement the guidelines.

Phthalates and birth defects. Chemical compounds called phthalates may not be responsible for *urogenital* (urinary and reproductive organ) abnormalities in male infants, according to results of a study published in June. This conclusion contradicted previous reports that had blamed a supposed increase in urogenital abnormalities, such as *hypospadias* (defects in the penis present at birth), on phthalates in the environment. Phthalates are used to make certain plastic products, shampoos, pesticides, and other items.

After reexamining data from 1992 to 2005, a research team based at New York-Presbyterian Hospital/Columbia University Medical Center in New York City and Children's Hospital of Philadelphia found that there had been no increase in the rate of hypospadias in New York state. Furthermore, the researchers noted that similar findings had been made in other states. They concluded that these and other findings "break the link" between phthalates and urogenital abnormalities.   ■ Alfred J. Smuskiewicz

See also **AIDS; Drugs; Food; Medicine; Public Health: A Special Report; Safety.**

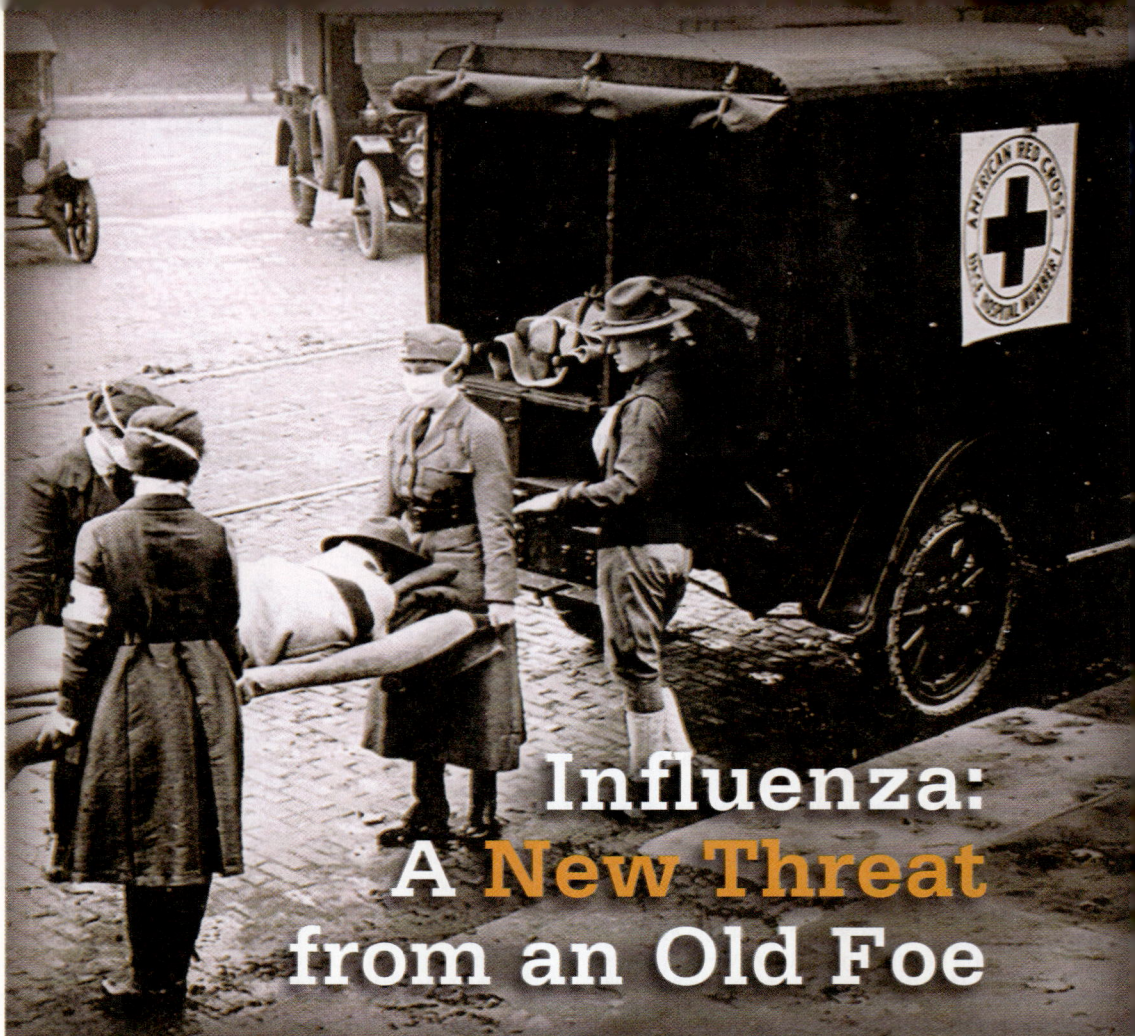

Influenza:
A New Threat
from an Old Foe

By Edward Ricciuti

In early 2009, hundreds of people in the Mexican state of Veracruz suddenly developed the chest congestion, coughs, and fever of severe respiratory infections. The abruptness and scope of the outbreak prompted health officials to begin searching for its cause. What came to be known as the swine flu epidemic of 2009 had begun.

"Swine flu," public health officials eventually learned, was a misnomer. The scientific name for the virus is H1N1, a subtype of a variety called type A influenza that has been around for decades. Pigs experience a respiratory illness caused by H1N1 called swine flu, and they can transmit it to human beings. Birds get a version of H1N1 called avian flu. Avian H1N1 can also be transmitted to people. Human beings have their own version of H1N1, which they can transmit to pigs.

The 2009 type of flu was a new strain, a mongrelized virus that is a mix of swine, bird, and human H1N1 genes. Such a mixture is not particularly unusual. New types of flu viruses, many of them combinations, continually appear. It is the nature of viruses to *mutate* (change genetically) by incorporating new genes. The United States Centers for Disease Control and Prevention in Atlanta (CDC) called the new strain "novel H1N1 virus."

The 2009 flu spread so quickly and infected so many people that public health officials feared it might become as severe as the 1918 Spanish flu.

Because the flu virus spreading throughout Mexico contained some swine flu genes, Veracruz seemed to be a logical place for it to have originated. Not only did the first known cases appear there, but Veracruz is near a pig breeding center, where the animals are mass-produced on factory farms. However, no pigs examined at the breeding center tested positive for the new flu virus (though the virus might have disappeared from the animals before they were tested). As late as June 2009, the new virus had not been found in any North American pigs except for a Canadian herd—and those pigs were known to have been infected by a human being. Research indicated, however, that the new 2009 swine flu (as it continued to be commonly called) evolved at least partly from flu viruses in American and Eurasian pigs.

American Red Cross workers (opposite) transport a victim who has died of the flu in St. Louis, Missouri, in October 1918. Paramedics in Mexico (above) prepare for duty during the flu outbreak in spring 2009.

Colleges and universities throughout the United States prepared for an epidemic of swine flu as students returned to campus in fall 2009. The new strain of H1N1 caused more illness and death in young people under the age of 25 than it did among older people.

The author:
Edward Ricciuti is a free-lance writer.

Wherever it started, the 2009 H1N1 flu quickly broke out all over the world. It advanced not like a wave, but in scatter-shot fashion. Individual eruptions popped up here and there, in country after country, with seemingly no organized pattern. The United States had the first major outbreaks outside of Mexico, presumably carried by travelers from south of the border. One of the earliest outbreaks was among students of a New York City prep school who sickened in April after returning from a spring break trip to Mexico.

By early summer, H1N1 was reported in about 100 countries. On June 11, the World Health Organization (WHO), an agency of the United Nations headquartered in Geneva, Switzerland, declared the outbreak a pandemic, a generalized term for a global illness that occurs in major portions of populations at roughly the same time. Three flu pandemics occurred during the 1900's, all of them influenzas that infected both human beings and animals and were transmitted between them: the Spanish flu of 1918, the Asian flu of 1957, and the Hong Kong flu of 1968. In addition, there were such potential pandemics as the avian flu threat of 1997. The novel H1N1 flu is the first pandemic of the 2000's.

Public health experts believe the H1N1 flu of 2009 may have begun to spread by air travel. A study of air travel patterns from Mexico released in late June by the CDC shows a distinct similarity to the pattern of the spread of H1N1 flu. Scientists say that air travel is undoubtedly a major distributor of the flu virus once it begins. An infected person spreads the virus through coughing or sneezing. People can become infected by touching a surface contaminated by the virus and then transferring it to their mouth, nose, or eyes.

Although typical flu subsides during the summer, swine flu showed no signs of slowing down in the Northern Hemisphere. Meanwhile, the winter flu season had begun south of the equator, and the flu spread rapidly there. Argentina, which was hit particularly hard, closed its schools in July for a longer-than-usual winter break.

At a WHO forum on swine flu in Mexico in July, the director-general of the group, physician Margaret Chan, described the international spread of the swine flu as "unstoppable" but added that the pandemic is of only "moderate severity." By then, the number of reported confirmed swine flu cases worldwide hit 70,000, with more than 300 deaths. Countless other cases were assumed to be unreported. Public health officials in the United Kingdom predicted 100,000 new cases daily by summer's end, and in July, the CDC estimated that 1 million people in the United States had been infected with the virus since the outbreak began.

The Spanish flu

While stressing that swine flu was a serious problem, health officials warned against panic. Even so, the fear of a terrifying pandemic similar to one that occurred almost a century ago—the so-called Spanish flu of 1918-1919—lurked in the background. The Spanish flu swept the world, killing more people than any other single event in history, including major wars and plagues. Scientists estimate that more people died in one year of the Spanish flu than did during the years of the European bubonic plague—the Black Death (1347-1351).

The flu pandemic of 1918-1919 impacted the final year of World War I (1914-1918), and the war, in turn, was a factor in the spread of the flu and the mystery that surrounds it. The flu sickened so many combatants that it held up the plans of generals for certain attacks and, in one case, kept the British fleet from sailing for three weeks. Immense numbers of troops on the move spread the flu more rapidly than might have been the case in peacetime. Crowded camps housing thousands of military recruits in the United States became fertile breeding grounds for the flu. Rallies in the United States supporting the war and war bonds brought masses of people into close contact and helped spread the disease. The chaos caused by the war and news censorship imposed by warring nations helped obscure the flu's beginnings and, for a time, masked the danger it posed. To this day, scientists are unsure of how or where the 1918 flu began, or even when the first cases appeared. "Its origin remains puzzling," according to Jeffery K. Taubenberger of the Armed Forces Institute of Pathology in Rockville, Maryland, a molecular pathologist and one of the world's top flu experts. One fact is certain: It began as a typical, not especially dangerous, flu, then suddenly changed into a terribly lethal form.

The name often applied to it—Spanish flu—was a poor choice. The disease did not originate in Spain. However, it was more intensely reported there because Spain was neutral during the war and the press was not censored. The outbreak in Spain was part of the first of three waves of the flu, which began in March 1918 and spread across the United States, Europe, and parts of Asia. Millions of people were sickened, including the kings of Spain and the United Kingdom. President Woodrow Wilson of the United States also became ill, while involved in international negotiations to end the war. Even so, the first wave was the mildest, if not in terms of the number of cases, then in the number of deaths, which was not abnormal. A real crisis seemed to have been averted when the flu disappeared.

But the flu returned, and not just in a few places, but around the world from Alaska to New Zealand. The second wave, which started in the fall, and the third, which spanned the winter, were deadly. The one, two, three punch of flu waves was extraordinary, and scientists still do not know whether the virus remained the same in all three waves or changed with time. If it changed significantly, it did so much more rapidly than usual.

The mild form of the 1918 flu was fairly typical: chills, fever, coughs, aches, and after a week or so, recovery in most cases. Severe symptoms were uncommon in the first wave. Their frequency skyrocketed in the two waves that followed: burning fever, difficulty breathing, and blood hemorrhaging from the nose and ears, and in mucus coughed up from fluid-filled lungs. The faces of victims who died often turned bluish-brown as they struggled to breathe. Death could come within hours after symptoms appeared, as a case involving four Yale University students demonstrates. After leaving campus and boarding a train in New Haven, Connecticut, the students became ill, so when the train stopped at Hartford, about 35 miles (56 kilometers) away, they walked to Hartford Hospital. Within 24 hours of arriving there, they died, despite efforts by physicians to save them.

Many historians believe that the first wave of flu emerged in the United States, at Camp Funston, a training camp at Fort Reilly, Kansas, in March 1918. (Some historians suggest that soldiers from Haskell County, Kansas, carried the virus to the base in February.) All agree that the disease spread to other military bases from Camp Funston. Most victims recovered after some discomfort and went back to their duties. Because most infections were not serious, little attention was paid to the outbreak outside of the military. That spring, when some 200,000 American soldiers shipped out for Europe, they carried the flu with them. It then spread to the general European population, though still in its mild form. When troops returned to the United States at the end of summer, they brought the flu back with them. However, by then it had become much more lethal.

Emerging in waves

The second wave appeared first in Boston where, in late August, dozens, then hundreds, of returning sailors and dockworkers reported in sick. Within days, the flu cropped up at other military installations around Massachusetts. Sailors sickened at the Navy Radio School at Harvard University in Cambridge. The 50,000 soldiers packed into barracks at Camp Devens, near Boston, were decimated, with about 100 deaths daily. Rumors spread that the Germans were waging germ warfare against the American populace.

Soldiers ill with the flu fill an emergency hospital at Camp Funston in Fort Riley, Kansas, in spring 1918. Epidemiologists believe that the movement and concentration of troops during World War I contributed to the spread of the disease.

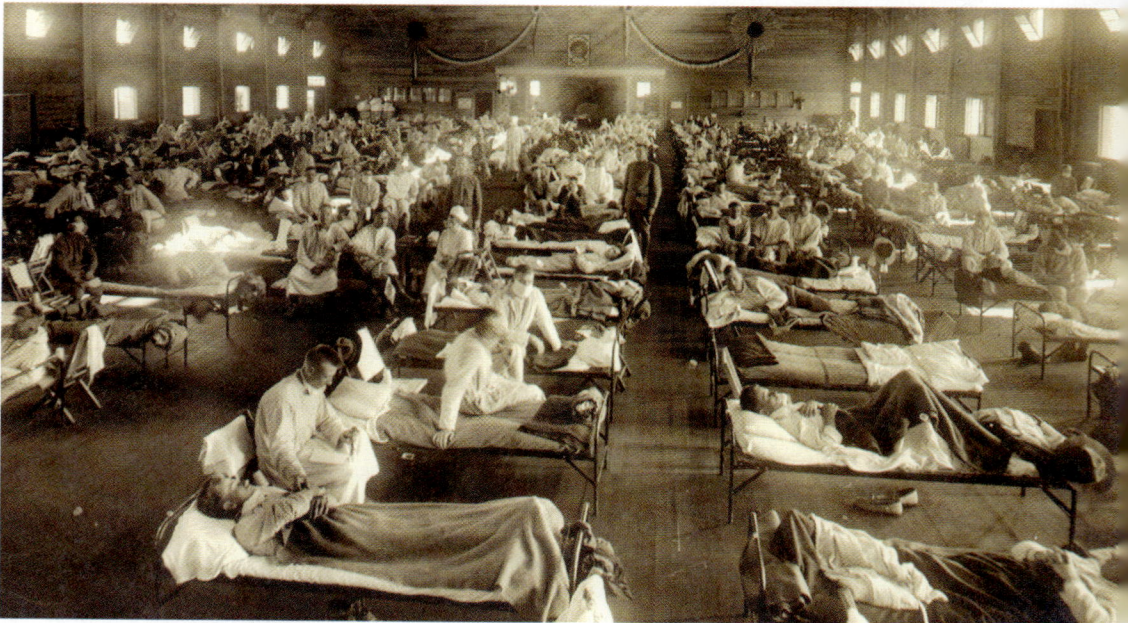

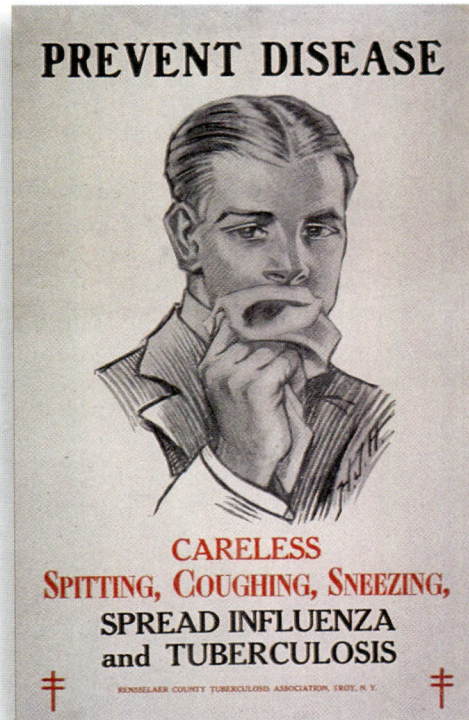

PREVENT DISEASE

CARELESS
Spitting, Coughing, Sneezing,
**SPREAD INFLUENZA
and TUBERCULOSIS**

RENSSELAER COUNTY TUBERCULOSIS ASSOCIATION, TROY, N.Y.

It took only a few weeks for the flu to cross the country to the West Coast. In the month of October alone, 195,000 Americans died. More than 850 New Yorkers and 200 Bostonians died on single days. As autumn passed, the outbreak continued, with 5,000 cases reported in San Francisco in December. Out of the population of 105 million Americans, one-fourth were infected and 675,000 died from September 1918 to April 1919. According to the CDC, during a typical flu season of October to May, about 5 to 20 percent of Americans get the flu; more than 200,000 people are hospitalized; and about 36,000 die from flu-related causes.

In many cities, patients overwhelmed the capacity of hospitals, and temporary hospitals were set up in community centers, schools, fraternity houses, children's homes, and other buildings. In Connecticut, the exclusive Hartford Golf Club became an emergency hospital. A woman in nearby New Britain offered her 10-room house for the same purpose.

Funerals often were limited to 15 minutes, and sometimes services were held outside in hopes of preventing the spread of flu. Funeral parlors, morgues—and even cold-storage facilities, which had been pressed into emergency use—ran out of space to hold bodies. A nurse at a U.S. Naval Hospital in Illinois described how the hospital morgue dealt with the overwhelming number of deaths: bodies were stacked one atop the other almost to the ceiling. Corpses piled up in hallways, and in Philadelphia, one of the hardest-hit cities, on porches and in the streets. Volunteers drove by in wagons, calling for people to bring out their dead. So many children were orphaned in Philadelphia that authorities could not care for

People using public transportation in Seattle (above, left) during the second wave of the flu in fall 1918 were required by law to wear gauze masks. Public health officials thought that such a precaution might help prevent the spread of the disease. A poster of the time (above) encouraged people to cover their mouths while coughing and sneezing, a practice that was also urged in 2009.

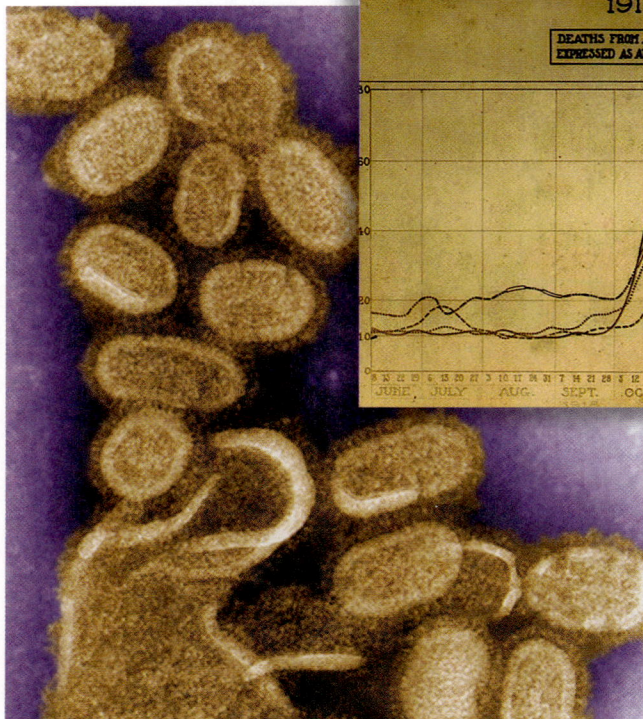

INFLUENZA PANDEMIC
MORTALITY IN AMERICA AND EUROPE DURING 1918 AND 1919

DEATHS FROM ALL CAUSES EACH WEEK EXPRESSED AS AN ANNUAL RATE PER 1000

NEW YORK
LONDON
PARIS
BERLIN
BERLIN RATES MISSING FOR AUG. 17, 31, OCT. 19, 1918.

Source: Armed Forces Institute of Pathology, National Museum of Health and Medicine, Washington, D.C.

A period graph (above) plots the number of deaths caused by the Spanish flu each week in 1918 and 1919 in several major cities throughout the world. In 2005, researchers re-created the virus that caused the 1918 epidemic (left), to gain a better understanding of why the microorganism was so deadly.

all of them. Funeral homes ran out of caskets, and dead family members were often buried together. In Alaska, the dead were buried in mass graves in permafrost.

In October, the U.S. Congress authorized $1 million for the Public Health Service to pay for additional physicians and nurses. Many medical personnel, however, were abroad with the troops. Because of their constant exposure to victims, health workers were especially vulnerable, and many caught the flu themselves. Physicians had to be brought out of retirement, and medical and nursing students were called into service. Many cities, including Phoenix, San Francisco, and Seattle, passed laws mandating that gauze masks be worn in public, a controversial measure because scientists are still unsure whether the masks prevent infection (viruses are so small that they pass through gauze). People were advised not to spit in public or to kiss. Schools, theaters, and churches were shut down.

The exact toll taken by the 1918-1919 flu worldwide will never be known. Even in the United States, influenza was not a reportable disease during those years. By best estimates, about 500 million people—one-third of the world's population at the time—were stricken. Perhaps 50 million victims died, though some scientists suspect the number may have been twice that figure.

During the winter of 1918-1919, the flu disappeared in many places, quite suddenly in some instances. Thousands of people had died during October 1918 in Philadelphia, for example, but by the middle of November—when armistice brought an end to the Great War—the city was almost flu-free. In many nations, a third wave of the flu, weaker than the second, returned in early 1919. It is possible that the virus mutated quickly into a type that was not as deadly and then faded away. It has not returned since, but the legacy of the 1918-1919 flu virus remains.

Re-creating the 1918 flu virus

Smaller than a bacterium, a virus is an infectious organism consisting of genes surrounded by a coat of proteins. The proteins attach to living cells, enabling the virus to enter a cell and take it over, the only way the virus can grow and reproduce.

Flu viruses were first isolated and identified in 1933, but the type that caused the Spanish flu disappeared from the earth with the last of its victims. For decades, researchers tried to reconstruct the Spanish flu virus to determine its nature and why it was so deadly. In 2005, scientists led by Taubenberger, with the permission of the CDC, accomplished the task by sequencing the virus's genome, figuring out the genes of which it is made. The researchers analyzed tiny, fragile fragments of viral genes in tissue from victims of the second wave of flu. The best samples came from the lungs of an Inuit woman whose body, buried in November 1918 in a grave with 71 other victims, had been preserved by freezing under 6 feet (1.8 meters) of Alaskan permafrost. She apparently had been obese, and her body fat helped insulate the viral remains during periodic thaws. The woman's body was disinterred by Swedish-American pathologist Johan Hultin, who had hoped, in vain, to find the living virus in permafrost burials.

The other samples came from the lungs of two soldiers. The samples had been preserved in formaldehyde and placed in wax cubes, then stored in a government warehouse in Washington, D.C. The live virus was long

In 1998, pathologist Johan Hultin exhumed the body of a victim of the 1918 flu from the frozen tundra in Brevig, Alaska. The victim's lungs still contained fragments of genes from the 1918 flu. Scientists later reconstructed the virus from those fragments.

gone, but from its genetic fragments, the researchers were able to determine the eight genes that made it unique.

Deadly secrets

Since then, researchers have used the reconstructed virus to try to learn why the 1918-1919 flu was so deadly. When scientists infected mice and monkeys, the virus triggered an uncontrolled immune response, killing the animals more quickly than any other human flu virus. *Antibodies* (proteins that attack foreign invaders in the body) that normally fight disease stormed the lungs, inflaming them so badly that the lungs stopped functioning. This may be why young adults, who have strong immune systems, seemed especially vulnerable to the Spanish flu, as they have been to the 2009 novel H1N1 flu. About half the deaths in 1918-1919 were among people 20 to 40 years of age, which has not been the case in pandemics before or since. As if the direct effects of the flu were not bad enough, many—perhaps most—of the deaths stemmed not from the flu itself (which usually affects only the upper respiratory system), but from bacteria that invaded the lungs of weakened patients and caused pneumonia.

As the second wave of flu developed in the American Midwest in late 1918, millions of pigs there were also infected, apparently by human beings. Since then, forms of swine flu have survived in pigs and have periodically appeared in people, as occurred in 2009. Taubenberger and his team proposed that the 1918 flu virus was avianlike but that its eight genes teamed up in a combination that adapted it to infect and spread among people and then pigs. In April 2009, researchers led by microbiologist Juergen A. Richt of Kansas State University's College of Veterinary Medicine found that the reconstructed virus can infect pigs but does not kill them. Previous research had shown, on the other hand, that it kills such animals as monkeys and mice, as well as human beings.

In June, immunologists Anthony S. Fauci and David M. Morens of the U.S. National Institute of Allergy and Infectious Diseases (NIAID), along with Taubenberger, described the 1918 virus as the founder of a "dynasty" of viruses, a family of flu strains that includes the 2009 H1N1 virus. According to the researchers, all human type A influenza viruses today are descendants of the 1918 virus. Since 1918, the scientist argued, we have lived in an "influenza pandemic era," with the 1918 flu as "the mother of all pandemics." The descendants of the 1918 flu virus, which have circulated the globe for almost a century, are responsible for all pandemic flu and, indeed, seasonal flu outbreaks. The only exceptions are certain types of bird flu.

If the 1918 virus were to erupt again, scientists might be able to develop a vaccine against it, based on their reconstruction of the virus. Understanding the traits that made the 1918 virus so deadly would help health authorities assess the risk of future pandemics and perhaps moderate their impact. Scientists studying the 1918 flu are trying to determine why it spread so readily from person to person and why it attacked the lungs so savagely. They have found that the protein in the outer coat of the virus, with which it attaches to cells in the respiratory system, was particularly good at its job.

Microbiologist Terrence Tumpey of the U.S. Centers for Disease Control and Prevention in Atlanta wears a respirator as he works in 2005 to re-create the 1918 influenza virus. Researchers hoped that a greater under-standing of the deadly virus would help them develop vaccines and treatments to fight future, similar epidemics.

In July 2009, researchers at the Massachusetts Institute of Technology in Cambridge and the CDC found that, in ferrets, the protein that attaches the 2009 swine flu virus does so much less effectively than other seasonal flu strains do, perhaps limiting the ability of novel H1N1 to spread, as well as its severity. However, Dutch researchers also working with ferrets reported the opposite: In their experiments, novel H1N1 was just as efficient in attaching to cells in the respiratory system as seasonal strains are, indicating that it can spread rapidly. Further work will need to be done to determine exactly which conclusion is the right one.

By mid-September, the U.S. Food and Drug Administration had approved a vaccine against novel H1N1, and patients began receiving the vaccine in October. Because of the rapidity with which viruses mutate, however, public health officials remained concerned that the 2009 virus could adapt before the flu season ended in the Northern Hemisphere, making it more deadly. Scientists speculate that since the 1918 pandemic, the human immune system and the flu viruses have been involved in an endless dance, with each trying to take the lead. New viruses continually appear and the body tries to develop defenses against them. The viruses, in turn, try to adapt to the body's defenses. The human body's successful adaptation to the virus dynasty may account, in part, for the fact that pandemics since 1918 have not been as severe, according to researchers. Human adaptation could also enable viruses to develop new pathways of infection.

Given the right conditions, say Taubenberger and Morens, a killer pandemic could occur again. Even with modern drugs and vaccines, they add, a virus as lethal as that of 1918 could kill 100 million people. Deadly or not, more flu pandemics will occur. The more scientists learn about the 1918 flu and its descendants, the better prepared we will be to cope with them.

Puerto Rico. On Jan. 2, 2009, Luis Guillermo Fortuño Burset, 48, was sworn in for a four-year term as governor of the Commonwealth of Puerto Rico. Fortuño is a Republican and leader of the pro-statehood New Progressive Party. In his inaugural address, he noted, "It's time to control government spending" in confronting a projected 2009 budget deficit of $3.2 billion.

In March, Fortuño unveiled a plan to cut more than 30,000 jobs from the commonwealth's 218,000-member work force for an annual savings of about $2 billion. Fortuño promised that those laid off would receive health insurance coverage for six months. They were also eligible for a one-time payment of $5,000 to go back to school or start a new business, or $2,500 in relocation costs.

For further savings, the personally wealthy governor reduced his annual salary of $70,000 by 10 percent for two years and that of his Cabinet members by 5 percent. He also pledged to raise the taxes of those earning more than $100,000 annually by 5 percent over this period.

Sonia Sotomayor. Puerto Ricans celebrated the confirmation and August 8 swearing-in of Sonia Sotomayor, 55, as a justice of the United States Supreme Court. Sotomayor was the first Hispanic and third woman to hold that post. The story of her rise from an early childhood in a public housing project in New York City resonated with people in Puerto Rico at a time when their own economy was mired in recession and unemployment topped 15 percent.

Former governor cleared. On March 20, a 12-person jury found former Puerto Rican Governor Aníbal Acevedo Vilá not guilty on nine counts of conspiracy, money laundering, and lying to federal authorities. The acquittal, after only four hours of deliberation, was a blow to former U.S. Justice Department officials who had served in the George W. Bush administration. Their decision to prosecute Acevedo Vilá prior to the 2008 elections had contributed to his defeat in a bid for a second term and left him with more than $1 million of unpaid legal bills. Acevedo Vilá was governor of Puerto Rico from 2005 to 2008.

Vieques munitions. In 2009, the U.S. Navy continued its cleanup of hazardous materials on a former training and live-fire base on the island of Vieques, about 7 miles (11.3 kilometers) east of the Puerto Rican mainland. Nearly 19,000 rounds of unexploded ordnance have been located on former Navy land, about one-third of which has been detonated. The U.S. Environmental Protection Agency was overseeing the project. The base, once the largest training area for the U.S. Atlantic Fleet Forces, closed in 2003.

■ Nathan A. Haverstock

See also **Latin America; People in the news** (Sotomayor, Sonia).

Pulitzer Prizes in journalism, letters, drama, and music were announced on May 28, 2009, by Columbia University in New York City on the recommendation of the Pulitzer Prize Board.

Journalism. The public service prize went to the *Las Vegas Sun* for exposing the high death rate among construction workers on the Las Vegas Strip. The prize for breaking news reporting went to *The New York Times* for its coverage of a sex scandal that resulted in the resignation of New York Governor Eliot Spitzer. The investigative reporting prize went to David Barstow of *The New York Times* for his story about retired United States generals, many with undisclosed ties to military contractors, being used by the Department of Defense to provide public support for the Iraq war.

Bettina Boxall and Julie Cart of the *Los Angeles Times* shared the explanatory reporting prize for their exploration of the cost and effectiveness of fighting wildfires in the western United States. The prize for local reporting was shared by the staff of the *Detroit Free Press* for its expose of a pattern of lies by Detroit Mayor Kwame Kilpatrick surrounding an affair with his chief of staff. The prize also went to Ryan Gabrielson and Paul Giblin of the *East Valley Tribune,* Mesa, Arizona, for reporting on how a sheriff's focus on immigration enforcement endangered investigation of violent crime. The staff of the *St. Petersburg Times* shared the national reporting award for its fact-checking of political claims during the 2008 presidential campaign. The international reporting prize was shared by the staff of *The New York Times* for its coverage of U.S. military and political challenges in Afghanistan and Pakistan.

Lane DeGregory of the *St. Petersburg Times* won the feature-writing prize for her story of a severely neglected girl who was adopted by a nurturing family. Eugene Robinson of *The Washington Post* won the commentary award. Holland Cotter of *The New York Times* won for art criticism. Mark Mahoney of *The Post-Star,* Glens Falls, New York, won for editorial writing. Steve Breen of *The San Diego Union-Tribune* won for editorial cartooning. Patrick Farrell of *The Miami Herald* won for breaking news photography. Damon Winter of *The New York Times* won the feature photography prize.

Letters, drama, and music. Elizabeth Strout won the fiction prize for *Olive Kitteridge.* Lynn Nottage won the drama prize for *Ruined.* Annette Gordon-Reed won the history award for *The Hemingses of Monticello: An American Family.* Jon Meacham's *American Lion: Andrew Jackson in the White House* won for biography. W. S. Merwin won the poetry prize for *The Shadow of Sirius.* Douglas A. Blackmon won the nonfiction prize for *Slavery by Another Name: The Re-Enslavement of Black Americans from the Civil War to World War II.* Steve Reich's *Double Sextet* won for music. ■ Shawn Brennan

Quebec. See **Canadian provinces.**

Radio. As radio struggled to survive in 2009, technology continued to shift the definitions and boundaries of the medium. Digital wireless reception and Internet streaming combined to allow almost any radio station to be heard anywhere in the world from *smartphones* (devices that combine the features of a cell phone and handheld computer).

Citadel Broadcasting Corporation, the third-largest radio broadcasting company in the United States, filed for bankruptcy protection in December in order to shed $1.4 billion of debt. The Las Vegas-based company owns and operates 224 radio stations and produces news and talk radio programming for thousands of affiliates.

Sirius XM, based in New York City, narrowly escaped filing for bankruptcy in February when Liberty Media Corporation of Meridian, Colorado, agreed to invest $530 million in the struggling satellite radio broadcaster. The move rescued Sirius XM from default or a possible take-over by the satellite television company Dish Network Corp., headquartered in Englewood, Colorado. Declining auto sales have slowed the growth of Sirius XM, which had deals with all the major carmakers for preinstalled satellite radios in their vehicles.

Beginning in June, Sirius XM subscribers were able to download software that allowed programming play on Cupertino, California-based Apple Inc.'s iPhone or iPod Touch. The service was free for Sirius XM customers who subscribed to its Internet option. Others had to pay about $3 per month for the service.

Internet radio. In July, after a two-year battle, Internet radio stations and record labels agreed on new royalty rates that cover music streaming. Internet radio services—from small podcasters to the popular music site Pandora—were on the verge of collapse due to the high royalty rates. The new agreement treats services according to their size and business model. The agreement covers the period from 2006 through 2014 for small Web sites and from 2006 though 2015 for large sites. Webcasters agreed to provide detailed information about the songs they play and how many people listened to them to SoundExchange, the organization that collects and distributes royalties on behalf of artists and labels.

Low-power radio stations also hoped to get a boost from the Local Community Radio Act of 2009, introduced in Congress in February and passed by the House of Representatives in December. The measure would allow the Federal Communications Commission to license thousands of low-power FM community radio stations in the United States. This would double the number of such stations from 800 to 1,600 or more and allow them to compete with the world's largest stations.

Rush to judgment. Conservative talk radio show host Rush Limbaugh sparked controversy throughout 2009 for comments he made about President Barack Obama. On January 16, four days before Obama was inaugurated, Limbaugh announced on his radio show that he "hopes [Obama] fails." Limbaugh later clarified the statement by saying that he meant that he wanted to see Obama's policies fail, not the man himself.

Limbaugh became the target of additional scrutiny in March when White House Chief of Staff Rahm Emanuel, on the CBS political interview show "Face the Nation," said that he regarded Limbaugh as the spokesman for the Republican Party. Republican Party Chairman Michael Steele countered that Limbaugh was an "entertainer" whose rhetoric was "incendiary" and "ugly." Steele apologized to Limbaugh the next day.

Paul Harvey . . . good-bye. American radio broadcasting pioneer Paul Harvey died on February 28 at the age of 90. His "Paul Harvey News and Comment" and "The Rest of the Story" radio segments were heard by tens of millions of listeners daily. Harvey began broadcasting at ABC Radio Networks in 1951. ■ Shawn Brennan

Railroad. See Transportation.
Religion. See Eastern Orthodox Churches; Islam; Judaism; Protestantism; Roman Catholic Church.

Republican Party. Republicans in 2009 found themselves relegated to subordinate status throughout United States elective politics for the first time since 1994. They lost control of the federal executive branch on Jan. 20, 2009, when Democratic President Barack Obama succeeded Republican President George W. Bush. When the 111th Congress convened on January 6, Republicans controlled only 178 seats in the 435-seat House of Representatives (down from 199 at the end of the 110th Congress) and only 41 seats in the 100-seat Senate (down from 49). One Republican senator switched parties in the spring of 2009, reducing the Senate Republican count to 40. Finally, throughout most of 2009, Republicans held only 22 of the 50 state governorships.

Congress. On April 28, Senator Arlen Specter of Pennsylvania announced that he was switching his party affiliation from Republican to Democrat. Specter, a moderate who had served in the Senate since 1981, said that his views had become more in line with those of the Democrats. He also had concluded that he would be unlikely to win his state's Republican primary for the Senate seat in 2010.

On June 16, 2009, Senator John Ensign (R., Nevada) admitted that in 2007 and 2008 he had had an extramarital affair with a woman on his campaign staff, Cynthia Hampton, who was married to one of his Senate aides, Douglas Hampton. The next day, Ensign—who had been touted as a potential 2012 presidential candidate—resigned as chairman of the Republican Policy Committee, the party's fourth-ranking Senate post. In October 2009, the Senate Ethics Committee began investigating whether Ensign had violated federal law or ethics rules by arranging lobbying work for Douglas Hampton and helping Hampton's clients deal with federal agencies. Ensign apparently had taken these steps to try to placate Douglas Hampton.

Yet another blow to Senate Republicans occurred on June 30, 2009, when the Minnesota Supreme Court ruled that Democratic candidate Al Franken had won the state's November 2008 Senate election. Later that day, the Republican incumbent, Norm Coleman, conceded. The election had been extremely close, with only a few hundred votes separating Franken and Coleman. After a statewide recount, there had been months of legal wrangling over whether certain ballots should have been counted or rejected. Franken's win gave the Senate Democratic Caucus its coveted 60th vote, enough to block Republican filibusters.

Representative Joe Wilson (R., South Carolina) gained instant notoriety on Sept. 9, 2009, when he shouted "You lie!" at President Obama during Obama's address on health care reform before a joint session of Congress. Later that evening, Wilson issued a statement apologizing to the president for the lack of civility. On September 15, the House voted 240-179, mostly along party lines, to formally rebuke Wilson for the outburst.

Governors. Mark Sanford, the Republican governor of South Carolina, admitted on June 24—after having been out of the state since June 18 with his whereabouts unknown—that he had been having an extramarital affair with a woman in Argentina. Sanford's disappearance had caused significant controversy because state security officials, as well as Sanford's own staff, had been unable to contact him. On June 22, a Sanford aide told reporters that the governor was hiking the Appalachian Trail. But Sanford confessed on June 24 that he had lied to his staff and had actually gone to Argentina. Sanford—who, like Ensign, had been seen as a 2012 presidential contender—refused to resign as governor over the scandal. In November 2009, the State Ethics Commission accused Sanford of 37 ethics law violations from 2005 to 2009 relating to airplane travel and use of campaign funds. In December 2009, a state legislative panel rejected a bid to impeach Sanford, instead endorsing a resolution to censure him.

On July 3, 2009, Sarah Palin, the Republican governor of Alaska, announced that she was resigning as governor, effective July 26. Palin had been the 2008 Republican nominee for vice president. Her resignation, 18 months before the end of her term, surprised many observers, and her motivations for resigning were unclear. In November 2009, Palin drew widespread media attention with the release of her memoir, *Going Rogue: An American Life.* The book became a best seller.

A bright day for Republicans in 2009 was November 3, when Republican candidates won two gubernatorial elections. In New Jersey, former U.S. Attorney Chris Christie ousted incumbent Democratic Governor Jon Corzine. In Virginia, former State Attorney General Bob McDonnell defeated Democratic state Senator Creigh Deeds in the race to succeed term-limited Governor Tim Kaine (D.).

Party leadership and fund-raising. On Jan. 30, 2009, the Republican National Committee (RNC) elected former Maryland Lieutenant Governor Michael Steele as RNC chairman. Steele became the first African American to hold the post.

In the first six months of 2009, Republican Party committees—including the RNC, the National Republican Congressional Committee, the National Republican Senatorial Committee, and state and local committees—raised $104.8 million and spent $82.1 million, according to the Federal Election Commission. Their Democratic counterparts raised $109.8 million and spent $82.8 million during the same period.   ■ Mike Lewis

See also **Congress; Democratic Party; Elections; People in the news; Radio; State government; United States, Government of the.**

Roman Catholic Church officials

announced measures on Oct. 20, 2009, that would allow entire congregations of Anglicans to convert to Catholicism while retaining many of their traditions. Officials planned to create new church structures called personal ordinariates administered by former Anglican clergy in the Catholic Church. The ordinariates would operate under Catholic dioceses. During the early 2000's, Anglicans intensely debated homosexuality and same-sex marriage. Some congregations left the Episcopal Church, a part of the Anglican Communion that allowed the ordination of female and gay clergy and the blessing of same-sex unions.

Ongoing investigations of women's religious orders in the United States were conducted by the Vatican in 2009. Religious orders are communities of monks or nuns dedicated to God. Officials voiced concern over the adherence of women's congregations to church doctrine and their efforts to develop and retain their membership, which had fallen steeply since the 1960's.

The Vatican department that deals with religious life initiated the first investigation on Dec. 22, 2008. Officials said the investigation was meant to determine certain congregations' "quality of life" and their fidelity to their orders' and the church's guidelines for religious life.

In a letter dated Feb. 20, 2009, Cardinal

William Levada, head of the Congregation for the Doctrine of the Faith, informed the Leadership Conference of Women Religious (LCWR) of a second investigation. The LCWR's 1,500 members represent about 95 percent of the approximately 68,000 American women in religious orders.

Levada expressed concern about the LCWR's initiatives to promote church teachings on homosexuality and ordination. The church teaches that only celibate men may be ordained and forbids homosexual activity. Some women in religious orders have advocated the ordination of women and greater acceptance of homosexuals.

Excommunications reversed. On January 24, Pope Benedict XVI lifted the excommunication of four bishops ordained without Vatican approval in 1988. One had denied details of the Holocaust, the Nazis' effort to eliminate the Jews during World War II (1939-1945). The reversal angered Jews and also Catholics concerned about the legacy of Vatican Council II, a 1960's convocation of bishops that liberalized the church and condemned anti-Semitism. The four bishops were followers of the late Archbishop Marcel Lefebvre, who had denounced the council's reforms.

Conservative voice lost. Conservative American Catholics lost a powerful advocate with the death of Father Richard John Neuhaus, age 72, on Jan. 8, 2009. The former liberal Lutheran minister converted to Catholicism in 1990 after becoming disenchanted with the political left. Neuhaus founded the journal *First Things,* an influential publication among the religious right.

Notre Dame controversy. A furor erupted after Notre Dame University, a leading Catholic institution located in South Bend, Indiana, invited U.S. President Barack Obama to speak at its May 17, 2009, graduation ceremony and to receive an honorary degree. Dozens of bishops loudly criticized the invitation, because of Obama's liberal stance on abortion and embryonic stem cell research. However, the Vatican newspaper, *L'Osservatore Romano,* gave Obama's administration positive reviews, and Pope Benedict XVI received the president warmly on July 10 in Rome.

Saint Damien of Molokai. On October 11, Pope Benedict XVI canonized five new saints, among them Jozef De Veuster, a Belgian-born priest known as Father Damien. From 1873 to 1889, Father Damien worked on the island of Molokai, Hawaii, with victims of leprosy (also known as Hansen's disease). He was stricken with the disease in 1885 and died of it in 1889.

▪ Thomas W. Roberts

Romania. Political instability in late 2009 hindered Romania's progress on reforms mandated by the European Union (EU) and the country's ability to respond to a severe economic recession. The coalition government of Prime Minister Emil Boc fell on October 13. Efforts by President Traian Basescu to appoint a new prime minister failed to meet with parliament's approval.

Basescu himself was in a tight race for reelection against Social Democratic leader Mircea Geoana. Basescu won the first round of voting in November. However, neither candidate garnered more than 50 percent of the vote, and so they were forced to compete in a runoff election. In the runoff in December, Basescu won 50.33 percent of the vote to Geoana's 49.6 percent. Geoana protested to the Constitutional Court that the runoff had been riddled with fraud. On December 14, the court confirmed Basescu's reelection.

Romania's economy, hard hit by the global economic downturn, contracted by 8 percent in 2009. Unemployment rose to over 7 percent. In November, the International Monetary Fund and the EU withheld installments on loans to Romania, pending resolution of its political stalemate. The loans were contingent on reduction of government spending. ■ Sharon L. Wolchik

See also **Europe**.

Rowing. See Sports.

Russia faced disputed regional elections, turmoil in the Northern Caucasus, legal controversies, and economic woes in 2009. These domestic difficulties led President Dmitry Medvedev to assume an increasingly independent and critical stance in Russian politics. Observers disagreed on whether or not this reflected underlying tensions between the president and his prime minister, former two-term President Vladimir Putin.

Elections. Putin's ruling United Russia party dominated mayoral, regional, and district elections held in 75 of Russia's 83 regions on October 11. The Communist Party, the pro-Kremlin Just Russia party, and the nationalist Liberal Democratic Party each gained only a handful of positions; liberal parties Yabloko and Right Cause were shut out entirely. This mirrored the results of similar elections in nine regions on March 1.

Claiming widespread electoral fraud, 135 members of the 450-seat State Duma (the lower house of parliament) walked out of the October 14 session. Representatives of the Communist Party, Just Russia, and the Liberal Democratic Party all participated in the unprecedented protest. After President Medvedev agreed to meet with the dissatisfied representatives, Just Russia and Liberal Democratic Party members returned to the Duma. The Communist Party maintained its defiant stance, holding a 1,500-person demonstration in central Moscow on October 22 protesting the alleged vote rigging. In his meeting with opposition leaders on October 24, Medvedev defended the results of the elections while acknowledging the need for greater fairness and transparency in the electoral process.

Northern Caucasus. Violence pervaded the Russian republics of Chechnya, Ingushetia, and Dagestan in 2009, despite the Russian government's April 16 decision to end decade long counterterrorism operations in Chechnya. Medvedev's order to begin troop withdrawals increased the authority of controversial strongman and Kremlin-backed Chechen President Ramzan Kadyrov.

Human rights organizations have accused Kadyrov's militia of systematic repression. The prominent human rights group Memorial blamed Kadyrov for the July 15 murder of rights campaigner Natalya Estemirova after she was abducted in Groznyy, the Chechen capital. Kadyrov denied the charges and successfully sued Memorial's director for slander.

Islamist militant attacks on local administrators and security officers took place in the region with stunning regularity in 2009. On June 5, Dagestan's interior minister, Adilgerei Magomedtagirov, was shot to death at a wedding. Yunus-Bek Yevkurov, the leader of Ingushetia, was seriously injured in a June 22 suicide car bomb attack. Some 20 people died and more than 130 others were wounded after a suicide truck bomber rammed a police station in Ingushetia on August 17. On December 8, Russian Federal Security Services head Aleksandr Bortnikov reported that government forces had detained nearly 800 militants in the Northern Caucasus in 2009, seizing 1,600 firearms and 490 homemade bombs.

Terrorism. Islamist militants killed at least 26 people and injured more than 90 others in a bomb blast that derailed a luxury train running from Moscow to St. Petersburg on November 27. It was the deadliest Russian terrorist attack outside the Northern Caucasus since suicide bombers downed two planes in 2004.

Law and order. On Feb. 19, 2009, a Moscow court acquitted three men accused of helping to murder journalist Anna Politkovskaya in October 2006. On June 25, the Russian Supreme Court annulled the verdict and ordered a new trial of the suspects. Politkovskaya's relatives protested the decision, arguing that the case required a new investigation rather than another trial.

On July 20, Medvedev signed legislation easing restrictions on the activities of nongovernmental organizations (NGO's) in Russia. The original 2006 law passed under President Putin imposed heavy paperwork on NGO's operating in Russia, forcing many to curtail their activities or

edly of inhumane conditions and that his captors had withheld medical treatment. The cause of his death was determined to be toxic shock and heart failure. In December, Medvedev fired more than 20 prison officials by presidential decree following an investigation into Magnitsky's death.

On November 19, the Russian Constitutional Court indefinitely extended a ban on the use of the death penalty in Russia. In February 1999, the court had ruled that the death penalty could not be used until jury trials were available in every region of Russia. In the current ruling, the court declared that the impending introduction of jury trials in Chechnya (the last region to introduce trial by jury) on Jan. 1, 2010, "does not open the way for the possible use of the death penalty."

Economy. After several years of impressive growth, Russian gross domestic product (GDP) shrank by 10 percent in the first three quarters of 2009. (GDP is the value of goods and services pro-

close down. Medvedev called these regulations a "burden" when proposing the revisions to the Duma earlier in 2009.

Sergei Magnitsky, a lawyer for embattled investment fund Hermitage Capital Management, died in prison on November 17 at the age of 37. Imprisoned since November 2008, Magnitsky had been diagnosed with pancreatitis and gallbladder disease in June 2009. He had complained repeat-

duced in a country in a given year.) Unemployment peaked in February at 9.5 percent while the ruble continued its slide against the U.S. dollar in the beginning of the year. Several Russian cities hit hard by the downturn experienced protest demonstrations that worried top government officials. However, the economy began to rebound in the third quarter on the back of rising oil prices.

President Medvedev sharply criticized Russian conditions in three key statements in late 2009. On September 10, his article "Go Russia!" identified dependence on raw materials exports, pervasive corruption, and an overreliance on the government to solve problems as "persistent social ills." On October 30, Russia's Day of Remembrance for victims of political repression, Medvedev denounced the crimes of former Soviet dictator Joseph Stalin, saying that "there can be no excuse for repressions." Medvedev's statement implicitly rebuked the steady efforts to rehabilitate Stalin's reputation since Putin's rise to power in 2000.

Medvedev reiterated these themes in his state-of-the-nation address on Nov. 12, 2009, promising to "create a new economy instead of a primitive resource-oriented economy" and to introduce reforms to improve the quality of Russian democracy. Some observers saw Medvedev's statements as heralding a split with Putin, but others viewed them as a political ploy to defuse criticism of the regime. Putin himself stirred the pot further on December 3 by declaring during a four-hour live television appearance that he would consider running for president again when Medvedev's term ends in 2012. The Russian Constitution prohibits a president from serving more than two consecutive terms but places no limit on the total number.

U.S. relations. United States Vice President Joseph Biden declared on Feb. 7, 2009, that the Obama administration would "press the reset button" in relations with Moscow. The U.S. and Russian governments were often at odds under the outgoing administration of President George W. Bush. On September 17, President Obama announced that he was canceling Bush administration plans to establish land-based missile defense sites in Eastern Europe. United States and Russian officials failed to complete negotiations on a new arms control treaty to replace the 1991 Strategic Arms Reduction Treaty (START), which expired on Dec. 5, 2009. The countries agreed to continue to observe the old treaty.

Death. Economist and politician Yegor Gaidar died in his residence near Moscow on December 16. Gaidar was one of the primary architects of the economic transition away from Communism that took place in Russia after the collapse of the Soviet Union in 1991. ■ Juliet Johnson

See also **Disasters; Europe; Georgia; Ukraine.**

Rwanda. See Africa.

Safety. Plans to refocus federal safety standards from reactions to outbreaks of food-borne illness to prevention were announced in July 2009 by the administration of United States President Barack Obama. Among the many tougher regulations planned for the food industry was one aimed at reducing intestinal infections caused by eating foods contaminated with *Salmonella* bacteria.

The announcement came after a series of outbreaks and recalls associated with tainted peanuts, hot peppers, beef, and other foods. From September 2008 to April 2009, health authorities attributed more than 700 illnesses—and 8 deaths—in 46 states to eating peanut products contaminated with *S. typhimurium.*

Bottled water contaminants. In a report released in July, the Government Accountability Office (GAO) urged the U.S. Food and Drug Administration (FDA) to require manufacturers to disclose more information about test results for contaminants in bottled water. The GAO is a federal agency that reviews operations of other federal agencies. Experts said that the report was prompted by several recent recalls of bottled water that was tainted with bacteria, arsenic, cleaning compounds, and other contaminants.

The FDA's principal deputy commissioner testified before the U.S. Congress in July that the FDA would, by late 2009, require bottlers to report test results indicative of serious health threats. However, the commissioner noted that Congress would need to grant the FDA additional funding and regulatory power to fully implement the GAO's recommendations.

Teflon guidelines. The U.S. Environmental Protection Agency (EPA) issued guidelines in January recommending that public water supplies contain no more than 0.4 parts per billion of perfluorooctanoic acid (PFOA). This toxic chemical, used to make the nonstick coating Teflon, was linked to cancer, liver damage, and other health problems in laboratory animals. Some public health experts called for even lower PFOA limits in water supplies. In 2006, several companies had agreed to phase out the manufacture of PFOA and to eliminate its release into the environment by 2015. ■ Alfred J. Smuskiewicz

See also **Disasters; Food; Public health; Toys and games; United States, Government of the: A Special Report.**

Sailing. See Boating.

Saint Kitts & Nevis. See Latin America; West Indies.

Saint Lucia. See Latin America; West Indies.

Saint Vincent & the Grenadines. See Latin America; West Indies.

Samoa. See Pacific Islands.

São Tomé and Príncipe. See Africa.

Saskatchewan. See Canadian provinces.

Saudi Arabia. King Abdullah University for Science and Technology opened in September 2009 in Thuwal, on the Red Sea coast, with inaugural ceremonies that were attended by numerous heads of state and other prominent individuals from around the world. The university was the brainchild of Saudi King Abdullah, who invested more than $10 billion to establish it as a center for international scientific research.

Teaching at the university is conducted in English, and the campus is coeducational—a first in Saudi Arabia. The campus houses one of the world's fastest supercomputers, and the school's electric power is partially provided by solar energy. Much of the university's research is to focus on renewable energy and water resources.

World economic crisis. Saudi Arabia's *gross domestic product* (the value of all goods and services produced during a year) was projected to grow at a rate of only 2.1 percent in 2009—half the rate in 2008. This projection was made by Business Monitor International, a London-based business consulting firm.

For the first time since the collapse of the Soviet Union in 1991, Russia's oil exports surpassed those of Saudi Arabia in the second quarter of 2009. Exports of Russian crude oil and refined oil products topped 7.4 million barrels a day in that quarter, compared with Saudi exports of 7 million barrels a day. Industry analysts attributed the decline in Saudi oil output partly to the decision of the Organization of the Petroleum Exporting Countries to cut output after oil prices plunged to $32 a barrel in January.

Assassination attempt. In August, Abdullah Hassan al-Assiri—one of Saudi Arabia's most wanted men and a senior member of the Islamist terrorist organization al-Qa`ida—attempted to assassinate Prince Muhammad bin Nayif, head of Saudi Arabia's counterterrorism operations. Assiri entered the prince's palace with explosives and a detonator hidden in a body cavity. He asked to see the prince, claiming that he and other senior members of al-Qa`ida wanted to surrender. During the meeting, a signal sent over a cell phone detonated the explosives, killing Assiri and wounding the prince.

Amnesty International, a London-based human rights organization, in a July report criticized antiterrorism measures taken by the Saudi state since 2001. The report described numerous human rights violations, including tortures, killings, secret arrests, and convictions based on closed trials. Most of the arrested individuals were suspected of supporting radical Islamist groups, including al-Qa`ida.   ■ Mary-Jane Deeb

See also **Energy supply; Middle East; Terrorism.**

School. See Education.

Senegal. See Africa.

Serbia. Videos broadcast on Sarajevo (Bosnia) Federation TV (SFTV) in June 2009 showed Ratko Mladic, the alleged war criminal from the Bosnian War (1992-1995), enjoying his retirement at various Serbian locales. SFTV commentators claimed that the videos provided proof that Mladic was living freely in Serbia, but Serbian officials said the videos predated the July 2008 formation of Prime Minister Mirko Cvetkovic's pro-Western government. The officials—in sensitive negotiations with European Union (EU) officials regarding Serbia's possible membership in the EU—insisted that Serbia was actively searching for Mladic and intended to turn him over to the International Criminal Court (ICC) in The Hague, Netherlands, for trial.

During the Bosnian War, Mladic led a Bosnian Serb army in a four-year siege of the Bosnian capital, Sarajevo, resulting in the deaths of at least 10,000 civilians. Mladic is also implicated in the massacre of thousands of Muslim men and boys in Srebrenica, Bosnia, in 1995. The ICC indicted Mladic in 1995 for genocide and crimes against humanity.

On Dec. 22, 2009, Prime Minister Cvetkovic and President Boris Tadic formally applied for membership in the EU. Serbian officials in 2008 had signed a stabilization and association agreement with EU officials, the first step toward membership. However, several EU member states, particularly the Netherlands, blocked progress on Serbia's candidacy until such time as Serbia delivered key war criminals to The Hague.

During 2009, the trial of Radovan Karadzic, Mladic's co-indictee for the Srebrenica massacre, proceeded slowly in The Hague. Serbian officials turned Karadzic in to the tribunal in July 2008.

United States Vice President Joe Biden met with Serbian leaders in Belgrade, the Serbian capital, in May 2009. Biden, the highest-level U.S. official to visit Serbia since President Jimmy Carter in 1980, said that Serbian officials would not be expected to formally recognize the independence of Kosovo, as long as they cooperate with the international community in improving living conditions there. Kosovo, formerly a province of Serbia, unilaterally declared independence in February 2008. Serbian leaders regard the action as illegal, but many nations, including the United States, recognized Kosovo's independence.

Economic growth in Serbia, hard-hit by the global economic downturn, moved into negative growth in 2009. Economists predicted that the economy would contract by 4 percent in 2009, then grow only 1 percent in 2010. During 2009, unemployment in Serbia increased from about 18 percent to 23 percent.   ■ Sharon L. Wolchik

See also **Europe; Kosovo; United Nations.**

Seychelles. See Africa.

Sierra Leone. See Africa.

Lindsey Vonn of the United States reacts with glee upon winning the women's downhill competition at the World Alpine Ski Championships on Feb. 9, 2009, in Val d'Isère, France. Vonn also won the women's super G event at the world championships on February 3.

Singapore in 2009 suffered its worst recession since independence in 1965. Its economy contracted by 11.5 percent in the first three months of 2009, compared with the same period in 2008. By the end of 2009, the economy was recovering, though economists predicted an overall annual decline of from 2 to 2.5 percent.

Dependent on trade, and having to import all its food and fuel, the island state had been hit by the worldwide economic downturn and inflationary pressures. Prime Minister Lee Hsien Loong introduced measures to cushion the blow of the economic downturn, including using reserves to fund plans to save jobs. In his annual National Day address on August 8, Lee credited this and other measures with helping stabilize the country, though he cautioned that challenges still lay ahead.

The government tightened controls of public gatherings in a law passed on April 13, after riots disrupted an international meeting in Thailand. The Public Order Act required a police permit for any kind of public gathering. Although the law was intended to protect against riots and terrorist attacks, an opposition member of parliament said such "draconian laws" limited citizens' rights.

■ Henry S. Bradsher

See also **Asia; Thailand.**

Skating. See **Hockey; Ice skating; Sports.**

Skiing. American Lindsey Vonn and Norwegian Aksel Lund Svindal each captured their second World Cup overall world titles, Vonn in convincing fashion and Svindal in the closest finish in World Cup history.

Vonn wrapped up her second straight crown—the most by an American woman—by capturing the final downhill race of the season on March 11, 2009, in Åre, Sweden. She finished with 1,788 points, 364 points more than Germany's Maria Riesch. Vonn also won the downhill and super giant slalom championships and captured two gold medals at the world championships in early February.

Svindal, who also won the super G discipline title, took the overall title by two points on March 14 when Austrian Benjamin Raich, the runner-up, straddled a gate in the final race of the season during a slalom in Åre. Svindal's 1,009 points was the lowest winning total in history.

Swiss skier Daniel Albrecht resumed training in May, about five months after a devastating wreck left him in an induced coma for three weeks.

World championships. In Val D'Isère, France, Vonn captured her first gold medal in either the Olympics or the world championships with her triumph in the super G on February 3. She followed that up with the downhill gold on February 9. Austria's Kathrin Zettel captured the super-combined gold on February 6; Kathrin Hoelzl of Germany won the giant slalom on February 12; and Riesch took the slalom gold on February 14.

Switzerland's Didier Cuche won his first world championships gold medal with a victory on February 4 in the super G. Canada's John Kucera captured the downhill gold on February 7; Svindal captured gold in the super-combined on February 9; Switzerland's Carlo Janka won the giant slalom on February 13; and Austria's Manfred Pranger took the slalom for his country's only men's gold in the final event on February 15.

World Cup. Svindal's second-place finish in the final super G of the season, in Åre, on March 12 clinched that discipline title. He took the lead in the overall chase a day earlier with his win in the downhill and then sweated out Raich's run in the final slalom three days later. Austria's Michael Walchhofer took the downhill discipline title; France's Jean-Baptiste Grange won the slalom title; Cuche took the giant slalom title; and Janka won the super-combined crown. Joining Vonn as discipline winners were Finland's Tanja Poutiainen in the giant slalom, Riesch in the slalom, and Sweden's Anja Paerson in the super-combined. Italy won the mixed team event on March 15 to end the season.   ■ Michael Kates

See also **Sports.**

Slovakia. Tensions with Hungary and between the Slovak government and Slovakia's Hungarian minority escalated in 2009. On August 21, Slovak officials prevented László Sólyom, the president of Hungary, from entering Slovakia to dedicate a statue of Hungary's first king in a predominantly Hungarian town. Slovak authorities alleged that Sólyom intended to evoke Hungary's historic claims to southern Slovakia.

Ethnic and cross-border tensions were further fueled by a language law passed by Slovakia's parliament in 2009. The law limited the use of Hungarian in official transactions and in schools and imposed fines for violations. Slovakia has a Hungarian minority of approximately 500,000 people.

Slovakia's previously fast-growing economy experienced a sharp setback in 2009 in response to the worldwide economic crisis and a slump in exports to Germany, its chief trading partner. Economists estimated that the Slovakian economy would contract by 6.0 percent in 2009. Unemployment rose from 9.0 percent in October 2008 to 12.0 percent in September 2009.

On January 1, Slovakia adopted the euro as its currency. Economists observed that the country experienced a smooth transition to the new currency.   ■ Sharon L. Wolchik

See also **Europe; Hungary.**

Slovenia. See **Europe.**

Soccer. In 2009, soccer fans and teams focused their attention on qualifying matches for the 2010 World Cup in South Africa. The interest of fans was also aroused by the great sums of money made available to top soccer clubs and star players.

In January 2009, Cristiano Ronaldo of Portugal was named World Player of the Year by FIFA (the Fédération Internationale de Football Association, the governing body for international soccer). In second place in the 2009 player of the year list was Barcelona's Lionel Messi (Argentina), with Liverpool's Fernando Torres (Spain) coming in third.

In June, Ronaldo, 24, was transferred from English Premier League champions Manchester United to Real Madrid of Spain for a record fee of $132 million. In February, the Deloitte ratings ranked Real Madrid as the world's wealthiest soccer club, with an annual revenue of $414 million. Next came Manchester United, Barcelona (Spain), Bayern Munich (Germany), and Chelsea, Arsenal, and Liverpool (all England).

Unstable coaching positions. Veteran Coach Sir Alex Ferguson enjoyed continued success at Manchester United in the English Premier League in 2009. However, Chelsea's Brazilian coach, Luiz Felipe Scolari, was dismissed in February, after spending only seven months as coach. Dutchman Guus Hiddink, coach to the Russian national squad, took temporary charge at Chelsea before Carlo Ancelotti arrived from AC Milan (Italy) to take over. In April 2009, Bayern Munich's Jürgen Klinsmann also left his post, paying the penalty for not securing the top spot in the German national league or in the European Champions League.

U.K. soccer. The 2008-2009 season ended with Manchester United again becoming Premier League champions, with Liverpool as the runners-up. Chelsea took the Football Association (FA) Cup with a 2-1 win over Everton. In Scotland, Glasgow Rangers won both the Scottish Cup and the Scottish Premier League, their first championship since 2005.

European soccer. Barcelona of Spain were the European club champions in 2009. Matched against world club champions Manchester United, Barcelona triumphed, 2-0, in the European Champions League final in Rome on May 27 through goals from Samuel Eto'o and Lionel Messi. Coached by Pep Guardiola, Barcelona also won the Spanish league and cup, to complete a remarkable triple of national trophies. On August 28, Barcelona beat Shaktar Donetsk (Ukraine) 1-0 to win the European Super Cup.

In Italy, Josè Mourinho led Inter Milan to the Serie A league title in his debut season as coach. German Bundesliga champions were VfL

Wolfsburg; French champions, Bordeaux; Turkish champions, Besiktas; and Dutch champions, AZ Alkmaar.

In 2009, the UEFA (Union of European Football Associations) inaugurated a new club competition, the Europa League. It replaced the UEFA Cup. The last UEFA Cup winners, on May 20, were Shaktar Donetsk (Ukraine), who won 2-1 over Werder Bremen (Germany). For the new Europa League, UEFA experimented with a fourth official behind the goal. UEFA President Michel Platini resisted suggestions that it was time to introduce electronic goal-line technology to rule on disputed or doubtful "goals." Never shy of controversy, Platini also expressed his personal preference for national teams to be coached by a countryman (England's national coach, Fabio Capello, is Italian) and for more opportunities for home-grown youth players at top clubs. He commented that "99 percent of people" did not understand any player being valued as highly as Ronaldo ($132 million).

The globalization of soccer was highlighted in November, when English Premier League club Manchester City flew midseason to the United Arab Emirates (UAE) to play the UAE national team. The English team also tried out a winter training facility funded by billionaire owner Sheik Mansour bin Zayed Al Nahyan.

Major League Soccer (MLS). The 2009 play-off schedule brought together the top two teams from the Eastern and Western conferences, as well as the next four in the standings. The MLS final on November 22 matched Real Salt Lake and the Los Angeles Galaxy, which Real Salt Lake won 5-4 in a penalty shootout following a 1-1 full-time score.

The Seattle Sounders won their first major trophy, the Lamar Hunt U.S. Open Cup, played on September 2, with a 2-1 win over 2008 cup winners DC United at RFK Stadium in Washington, D.C. MLS planned to expand to 16 teams in 2010 and to 20 by 2012.

LA Galaxy's veteran English international (and marketing) icon David Beckham secured a

loan to AC Milan of Italy in a "club-share" deal, purportedly to further his hopes of impressing England coach Fabio Capello and securing a squad slot for the 2010 World Cup. Beckham was hoping to overtake the English record of 125 international appearances, held by goalkeeper Peter Shilton. Galaxy Coach Bruce Arena also allowed star striker Landon Donovan to go, on loan, to Bayern Munich in Germany.

World soccer. Qualifying rounds for the 2010 World Cup were played on a zonal basis. Among the first countries to secure finals places in South Africa were England, Germany, Brazil, the United States, and Mexico. Other early qualifiers included Ghana, Japan, North Korea (the country's first World Cup qualification since 1966), South Korea, and Australia. Argentina, coached by erratic former playing legend Diego Maradona, nearly failed to make it but scraped through to the 2010 finals after reducing their fans to nervous exhaustion.

As a warm-up for the 2010 matches, South Africa hosted the FIFA Confederations Cup, from

Fans welcome Cristiano Ronaldo to Santiago Bernabeu Stadium in Madrid, Spain, in July after he transferred from the Manchester United club to Real Madrid. In the most expensive deal in soccer history, Real Madrid paid £80 million ($132 million) for the winger.

June 14 to 28, 2009. The competition featured eight national teams from the major world soccer federations. In the final, Brazil defeated the United States 3-2, the best-ever finish by the U.S. team in a major international competition.

For the CONCACAF (Confederation of North, Central American and Caribbean Association Football) Gold Cup hosted by the United States (July 3 to 26), U.S. Coach Bob Bradley introduced several untried players. The U.S. team did well to reach the final (July 25) at the Giants' Izod Stadium in East Rutherford, New Jersey, but lost 0-5 to Mexico. For 2009-2010, the CONCACAF Champions League replaced the Champions Cup (which ran from 1962 to 2008), with eight teams from regional nations taking part. The winners in 2009 were Atlante (Mexico), who beat Cruz Azul (also Mexico).

The 2009 Superliga tournament, hosted by the United States, also brought together eight teams, four from the MLS and four from the Primera División de México. The final (on August 5) at Toyota Park in Bridgeview, Illinois, saw Tigres UANL of Mexico beat the Chicago Fire 4-3 on penalty kicks, after a 1-1 full-time score.

The Asian Football Confederation (AFC) Champions League, in Tokyo on November 7, was won by the Pohang Steelers (South Korea), who beat Al-Ittihad (Saudi Arabia) 2-1. In South America's Copa Libertadores, Estudiantes of Argentina beat Cruzeiro of Brazil by an aggregate score of 2 goals to 1—the first win by Estudiantes in South America's premier cup competition since 1970.

In Africa's major club competition, the CAF (Confederation of African Football) Champions League, TP Mazembe (Congo [Kinshasa]) won against Heartland (Nigeria) in the final (November 8), on the away goals rule (aggregate score 2-2).

2012 Olympics. With the 2012 Olympic Games scheduled for London, a deal was struck in May 2009 for an all-English team to compete under the Team GB banner in London. The four U.K. "home nations"—England, Scotland, Wales, and Northern Ireland—have their own football associations and compete separately in international tournaments. Earlier objections to entering a combined Olympic team were motivated by fears that such a move might threaten this historic arrangement within FIFA.

Women's soccer. Germany won the European Championship in Helsinki, Finland, defeating England in the final (Sept. 11, 2009) by 6 goals to 2. Twice World Cup winners, the impressive German women's squad secured their fifth European title.   ■ Brian Williams

See also **Sports.**

Social Security. The Social Security Administration announced on Oct. 15, 2009, that, because of deflation (a decline in the general level of prices in an economy), there would be no cost-of-living adjustment (COLA) in monthly Social Security and Supplemental Security Income benefits in 2010. That would make 2010 the first year without a COLA since 1975, when benefit increases were first tied to cost-of-living increases. (Prior to 1975, benefit increases were set by legislation.) Federal forecasts indicated that a COLA was also unlikely in 2011. The 2009 COLA was 5.8 percent.

The Social Security and Medicare trustees released their 2009 reports on May 12, projecting that, without reforms, both programs would run out of money earlier than previously predicted. The financial outlook for Medicare continued to be especially bad. According to the reports, the Social Security trust fund would be exhausted by 2037, four years earlier than the trustees had projected in 2008, and the Medicare hospital insurance trust fund would be exhausted by 2017, two years earlier than the 2008 projection. Social Security payments were expected to begin exceeding tax receipts in 2016. Medicare hospital payments began exceeding tax and other revenues in 2008. The deficits were being made up by dipping into trust fund reserves.   ■ Mike Lewis

Solomon Islands. See Pacific Islands.

South Africa. On April 22, 2009, South Africa's ruling African National Congress (ANC) overwhelmingly won parliamentary elections with 65.9 percent of the vote, taking 264 seats in the 400-member National Assembly. The mainly white Democratic Alliance came in second with 16.7 percent, winning 67 seats. The Congress of the People, a group that had broken away from the ANC, won 7.4 percent and 30 seats. Most Congress of the People members left the ANC in December 2008 out of loyalty to former President Thabo Mbeki, who had resigned in September. Ten other parties divided the remaining 39 seats in the 2009 elections.

The ANC also won clear majorities in eight of South Africa's nine provincial legislatures on April 22. However, the Democratic Alliance toppled the ANC from power in the Western Cape Provincial Parliament, where it won a majority.

As expected, on May 6, the South African Parliament formally elected Jacob Zuma as president. Zuma became the country's fourth head of state since the fall of apartheid, the system of racial segregation that ended in the early 1990's.

Criminal charges dropped. Before the election, the National Prosecuting Authority of South Africa announced on April 6, 2009, that it would drop criminal charges against Zuma. The National Prosecuting Authority is the government body with power to begin criminal proceedings.

The crimes of which Zuma was accused related to a multimillion-dollar arms deal in 1999. The charges included corruption, fraud, *money laundering* (disguising illegally obtained money as legal income), *racketeering* (forming or running an organization engaged in criminal activities), and tax evasion. Zuma denied wrongdoing. A judge had dismissed the charges in September 2008, but South Africa's Supreme Court of Appeal reinstated them on Jan. 12, 2009.

Dropping the charges closed a long chapter in South African politics and cleared the way for Zuma to become president. Opposition politicians claimed that the charges had been dropped on a technicality and that Zuma would always be regarded with suspicion because he had not cleared his name in court. Democratic Alliance leader Helen Zille said that the National Prosecuting Authority had caved in to ANC pressure and "thrown the law book out of the window."

Cabinet changes. Zuma announced his first Cabinet on May 10, 2009. Analysts said that the appointments indicated no major shifts in policy. Zuma named former interim president Kgalema Motlanthe as deputy president. Motlanthe had taken the interim position following the resignation of President Mbeki in 2008.

The most notable Cabinet change in 2009 was the transfer of the country's widely admired

minister of finance, Trevor Manuel, to head a powerful new government agency. The agency, the National Planning Commission, will plan for South Africa's economic development. Pravin Gordhan replaced Manuel as minister of finance. Gordhan previously headed the South African Revenue Service, the government agency responsible for collecting taxes.

Other key Cabinet posts went to a labor leader, Ebrahim Patel, and to the leader of the South African Communist Party, Blade Nzimande. Patel became minister of economic development, and Nzimande was named minister of higher education and training. Patel and Nzimande had supported Zuma during the election.

A surprise Cabinet appointment was that of Pieter Mulder, who became deputy minister of agriculture, forestry, and fisheries. Mulder heads Freedom Front Plus, a political party that represents South Africa's Afrikaners. Most Afrikaners are of Dutch descent, and many supported the policy of apartheid.

Zuma delivered his first State of the Nation address on June 3, 2009. He promised that his government would create 500,000 new jobs by the end of the year. Zuma also said that 4 million new jobs would be created by 2014. He promised better health and education services, as well as measures to combat crime. South Africa had announced in May that its economy had gone into a recession for the first time since 1992.

In July 2009, just weeks after Zuma's speech, rioting erupted in townships across the country. The rioters were poverty-stricken South Africans demanding better housing and basic services, such as water and sanitation.

Police scandal. On Oct. 5, 2009, South Africa's national police chief, Jackie Selebi, went on trial on corruption charges at the High Court in Johannesburg. He was charged with taking money and gifts from a convicted gangster, Glenn Agliotti. Selebi was also accused of "defeating the ends of justice." Selebi pleaded not guilty to the corruption charges. His trial was expected to take months.

The indictment against Selebi painted a dismaying picture of corruption at the highest levels of law enforcement. South Africa has one of the highest crime rates in the world. The case touched a nerve at a time when crime-plagued South Africa was trying to assure foreign tourists that it had crime under control.

Soldiers clash with police. Police used rubber bullets and tear gas to scatter troops from the South African National Defence Force, the country's armed forces, on Aug. 26, 2009. Up to 3,000 military personnel had marched on the Union Buildings, the administrative headquarters of South Africa's government in Pretoria. The marchers demanded a 30-percent pay increase

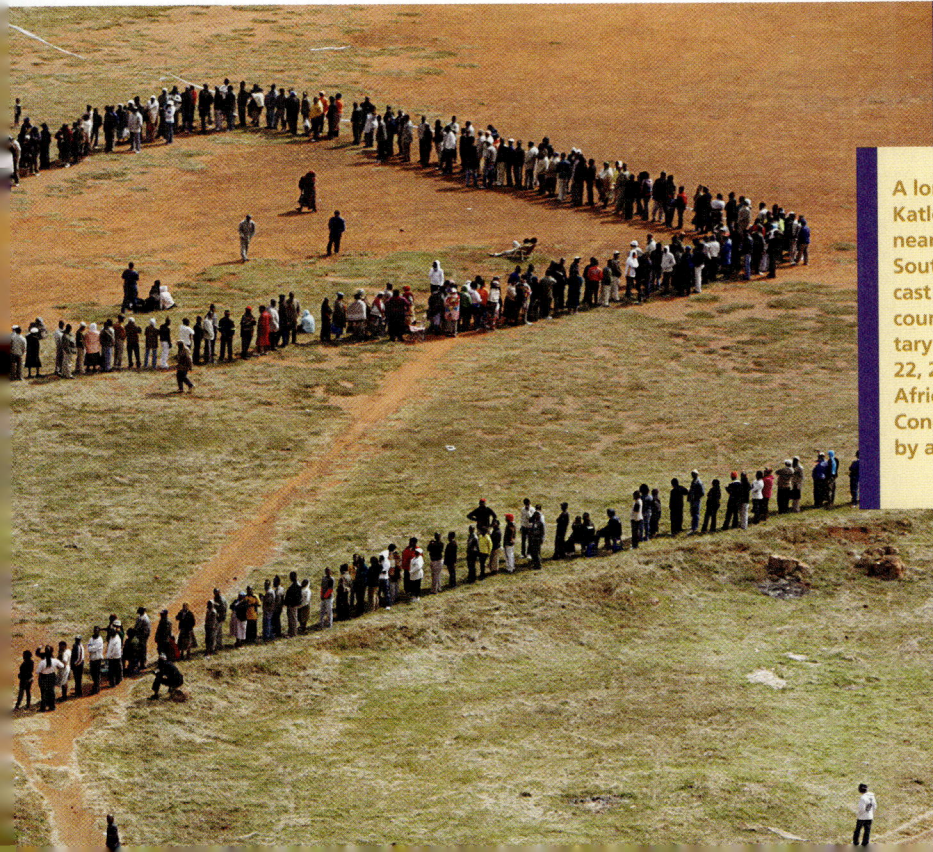

A long line of voters in Katlehong township near Johannesburg, South Africa, wait to cast ballots in the country's parliamentary election on April 22, 2009. The ruling African National Congress (ANC) won by a large majority.

and better employment conditions. More than 20 soldiers were injured. Following the protest, nearly 700 soldiers received letters of dismissal.

The violent protest was the latest in a series of rallies and disputes over military pay and working conditions. Defence and Military Veterans Minister Lindiwe Sisulu condemned the soldiers' actions as the "severest form of criminality in a democracy." Military analysts said that the protests could threaten national security.

HIV/AIDS. In a speech to Parliament on October 29, President Zuma acknowledged that a virus caused AIDS and called for better preventive measures to deal with the global epidemic of the disease. In a national address on December 1, Zuma promised to expand drug treatment for women and babies infected with HIV, the virus that causes AIDS. Health experts noted that Zuma's position departed sharply from that of former President Mbeki. Mbeki had questioned whether HIV causes AIDS and said it was "irresponsible" for the state to hand out *antiviral drugs.* Such drugs interfere with the reproduction of HIV. In 2009, South Africa had 5.7 million HIV-infected citizens, more than any country in the world.   ■ Simon Baynham

See also **Africa; Disasters.**

South America. See Latin America;
various Latin America country articles.

Space exploration. Full-time human
presence in space doubled in 2009, when the crew of the International Space Station (ISS) grew from three to six. As the larger team of astronauts and cosmonauts picked up the pace of scientific research in the orbiting laboratory, scientists on the ground used the remote sensors on new space probes to study Earth's changing climate, its neighbors in the solar system, our moon, and planets orbiting distant stars.

The space shuttle Atlantis reached the Hubble Space Telescope in May to perform the last servicing mission on the telescope. Astronauts used several spacewalks to add and repair instruments and install new batteries and gyroscopes. These improvements give the telescope the most advanced set of instruments in its history. The Hubble servicing mission helped show how space travelers will repair and upgrade machines when Earth is too far away for fast delivery of replacement parts. In July, one of the first Hubble observations after the repair was a close examination of a dark spot on Jupiter produced when a comet plunged into the planet.

The final mission of the shuttle is scheduled to lift off from the Kennedy Space Center in Florida by the end of 2010 or in early 2011. In 2009, engineers at NASA worked on the rocket and capsule that will replace the shuttle. The new spacecraft

will not be able to carry out complex servicing missions such as the one to Hubble. Instead, they are being designed to deliver crews to the space station and to other vehicles that will take them farther from Earth. A pair of tests in 2009 of the new Ares I-X gathered data for the final design of the Ares I crew launcher and also tested its powerful solid-fuel motor on the ground. However, amid concerns that there may not be enough money to finish building the new rocket, NASA began looking for a less expensive launcher.

Until the United States has a replacement for the space shuttle, the only way for astronauts and cosmonauts to get to the space station will be in a Russian Soyuz three-seat capsule. Also, unless Russia builds more of the capsules, there will not be room for any more space tourists. Cirque de Soleil founder Guy Laliberté of Canada, a circus clown, flew aboard a Soyuz capsule to the ISS on a mission that lasted from September 30 to October 11. During his flight, he donned a red clown nose as part of a multimedia show to teach people about the fragility of Earth's supply of fresh water.

The International Space Station looked very different at the end of 2009 than it did at the beginning. During the year, shuttle astronauts added the fourth and final solar array. The solar panels measure 240 feet (73 meters) and will generate more electricity for the science labs and life support systems. Astronauts also completed Japan's laboratory module, named Kibo, by attaching a "porch" (outside platform). Scientists can now more easily expose experiments to the vacuum and temperature extremes of open space. The lab has its own airlock and robotic arm to move scientific equipment around the new platform.

Once the exposed facility was in place, Japan used an H-II rocket to launch its first H-II Transfer Vehicle (HTV) to the space station. In a demonstration of international cooperation, NASA astronaut Nicole Stott used the station's Canadian-built robotic arm to snare the Japanese cargo vehicle and plug it into the Harmony pressurized node, which was built in Italy. Helping her were astronauts from Belgium and Canada, all under the command of Russian cosmonaut Gennady Padalka.

Twice during 2009, when shuttles visited the ISS, a record total of 13 space travelers were aboard the station, representing all five of the space agencies that make up the station partnership. To keep the ISS crew healthy, shuttle crews delivered new oxygen generators, carbon dioxide scrubbers, and a state-of-the-art wastewater recycling system.

The new water system will become especially useful after the shuttles, the main source of water for the space station, stop flying. Although Japan's HTV, the Automated Transfer Vehicle (ATV) operated by the European Space Agency, and the Progress cargo-carriers launched by Russia can also

The space shuttle Atlantis flies in silhouette before the sun after taking off for a servicing mission to the Hubble Space Telescope on May 12. The crew of the shuttle performed major repairs and upgrades to the telescope.

carry water, recycling will stretch the supply for the new, larger crew.

The United States may add its own commercial cargo carriers to the station resupply chain. NASA's Ares I could be adapted to this type of mission. But the U.S. space agency may switch to an upgrade of the long-flying Atlas or Delta rockets, or perhaps a new vehicle like the privately built SpaceX Falcon 9 or Orbital Science's Taurus II, as a cost-saving way to deliver crews and cargo.

Robotic probes continued to send back results from beyond the atmosphere. To monitor Earth's climate, Japan launched its Greenhouse Gases Observing SATellite, or GOSAT, in January. Nicknamed Ibuki, or "breath" in Japanese, GOSAT measures, at 56,000 points around Earth every three days, the carbon dioxide that warms the atmosphere by trapping solar energy. Unfortunately, a similar NASA satellite, the Orbiting Carbon Observatory (OCO), crashed into the ocean near Antarctica in February when the shroud that protected it during launch failed to come off, making the satellite too heavy to reach orbit.

To study the moon, NASA launched its Lunar Reconnaissance Orbiter (LRO) in June. Riding along was a small satellite called the Lunar Crater Observation and Sensing Satellite (LCROSS). LCROSS guided the mission's upper stage to a carefully targeted impact in the crater Cabeus at the moon's south pole. Telescopes in space and on Earth focused on the barely visible plume of debris kicked up by the crash to see if it contained water ice left over from comets that hit the lunar surface. Analysis of the observations later confirmed a large abundence of water ice in the plume. Two other spacecraft, Japan's Selene and China's Chang'e-1, also crashed into the moon in 2009 at the end of their missions, which like LRO mapped the terrain and minerals in great detail.

NASA's Messenger probe flew close to Mercury once again, using the planet's gravity to pull it toward becoming the first spacecraft to orbit the planet closest to the sun. Robots in orbit and on the surface of Mars found new evidence of water, some of which may be liquid.

Farther afield, the Kepler probe, which NASA launched in March, continued the search for extrasolar planets orbiting other stars. The probe observed a section of space, using super-sensitive light meters, to detect the extremely faint flicker that occurs when a planet passes in front of a star and blocks some of its light. Hundreds of extrasolar planets have been found, but most are more like Jupiter than Earth. Scientists believe the Kepler spacecraft will help them detect planets with Earth-like characteristics that could support life.   ■ Frank Morring, Jr.

See also **Astronomy.**

SPACE EXPLORATION

Neil Armstrong speaks at the Apollo 40th anniversary celebration at the National Air and Space Museum on July 20, 2009, in Washington, D.C. Armstrong, the Apollo 11 mission commander, was the first person to set foot on the moon.

NASA and the nation celebrated the 40th anniversary of the Apollo 11 moon landing in July 2009.

Buzz Aldrin salutes the United States flag planted on the surface of the moon during the Apollo 11 mission. Apollo 11 launched from Earth on July 16, 1969. The first two people to walk on the moon, Neil Armstrong and Buzz Aldrin, reached the surface on July 20. The astronauts spent about 2 ½ hours outside the lunar lander.

In one of a series of photographs taken by the Apollo 11 crew, the astronauts capture an "Earthrise" —the Earth coming into view after being hidden behind the moon—as their spacecraft rounds the far side of the moon. Apollo 11 was the first of six Apollo missions to successfully land people on the moon.

Buzz Aldrin conducts a solar wind experiment while standing in front of the lunar module *Eagle*. During the time Armstrong and Aldrin were on the lunar surface, the third member of the Apollo 11 mission, Michael Collins, remained in the command module in orbit around the moon. The crew safely returned to Earth on July 24, 1969.

Spain. Prime Minister José Luiz Rodríguez Zapatero's Spanish Socialist Workers' Party (PSOE) lost popularity during 2009 because of poor economic performance, a growing centralization of power in the prime minister's office, and a sense of loss of direction in government policy. The party had defeated the conservative People's Party (PP) in national elections in 2008. However, the PSOE remained seven seats short of a majority, requiring the cooperation of several smaller regional parties to pass legislation through parliament.

Attempting to stem the tide of increasing criticism, Zapatero announced a major Cabinet reshuffle in April 2009. He replaced a veteran minister of the economy with a lesser known and more compliant politician, Elena Salgado. Nevertheless, in the June election to the European Parliament, the opposition PP won a larger share of votes than the PSOE. At the same time, the PP remained deeply divided and scandal-ridden, amid allegations of illicit financial dealings between business and senior PP politicians and internal party spying.

Regional politics. Terrorism in the Basque region of northern Spain spiked in 2009 in the run-

up to the 50th anniversary of the founding of the main separatist organization, ETA. (The group's initials stand for Basque Homeland and Freedom in the Basque language; ETA seeks to create an independent nation from the three Basque provinces of Spain and part of southwestern France.) Overall, however, the fortunes of separatist politicians declined in 2009. In March elections, nationalist parties in the Basque region failed to attain a majority for the first time since democracy was restored in Spain in 1980.

In July 2009, the PSOE announced an agreement on a reform of the law governing financing for Spain's regions. The agreement, which allows the regions greater financial autonomy, awaited parliamentary approval.

Foreign policy. In a move criticized by many of its allies, Spain in September became the first country to pull its troops out of the NATO-led peacekeeping mission in Kosovo. Spain had contributed troops despite its refusal to recognize Kosovo's independence. In November, however, Spain began increasing the number of its troops serving in the NATO-led mission in Afghanistan.

Economy. Spain's budget deficit soared in 2009 as its economy contracted by 3.7 percent, following a growth rate of 0.9 percent in 2008. Unemployment rose from 11.3 percent in 2008 to 17.9 percent in 2009. Analysts noted that, unlike the economies of many other European nations, Spain's economy was not likely to recover quickly, because its previous growth was based on a housing construction and lending boom that could not be sustained. ■ Jeffrey Kopstein

See also **Europe.**

Crowds gather in Madrid's Plaza de Cibeles in October to protest a government proposal to allow abortions upon request to any woman—including those as young as 16 without parental consent—during the first 14 weeks of pregnancy. Nevertheless, the lower house of parliament approved the measure in December.

Sports. Tiger Woods, one of the most recognized athletes in the world and the top golfer in the Professional Golfers Association (PGA) of America, took an indefinite leave of absence from the sport in late 2009 after his personal life erupted in scandal. The headline-grabbing story began in late November after Woods had an early morning automobile accident while pulling out of his driveway. Reports focused on a domestic dispute with his wife, Elin. Several women soon came forward to say they had sexual relations with Woods while he was married. Woods, in announcing his leave from golf, admitted to infidelity and said he wanted to work on his marriage. But by late 2009, it appeared that his wife and their two children had moved out of their home and that his wife was filing for divorce.

Spanish cyclist Alberto Contador won his second Tour de France, capturing the 2009 race in part by holding off American Lance Armstrong. Armstrong, Contador's teammate and seven-time Tour champion, was making a comeback after a 3 ½-year retirement. After years of numerous doping scandals, only one positive test was reported after the 21-stage race through Monaco, Spain, Andorra, and France was held from July 4 to 26. However, officials from France's antidoping agency cautioned that testing on riders' blood samples would not be completed for months.

In professional team sports, the Los Angeles Lakers captured their 15th title in the National Basketball Association (NBA). In the National Hockey League (NHL), the Pittsburgh Penguins won their third Stanley Cup, capturing Game 7 on the road, the first NHL team to take a title that way in 38 years. In the National Football League (NFL), the Pittsburgh Steelers won a record-setting sixth Super Bowl and their second in the last four seasons. The New York Yankees captured Major League Baseball's World Series.

In men's tennis, Switzerland's Roger Federer established a new record for major titles at 15 with a thrilling five-set marathon victory at Wimbledon in England. He also finished 2009 by winning two of the four Grand Slam events, including his first French Open title.

Tour de France. Contador, who also won the race in 2007, captured the critical Stage 18 time-trial to open up a sizable lead on Armstrong and Andy Schleck of Luxembourg, who finished second at 4 minutes and 11 seconds behind. Armstrong, 37, became the second-oldest rider to finish in the top three at 5 minutes and 24 seconds behind Contador. (France's Raymond Poulidor was 40 when he finished third in 1976.) Armstrong formed a new team for 2010 in an attempt to win the race for the eighth time.

The United Kingdom's Mark Cavendish became the first rider to win six stages in a sprint but was no match for Contador in the mountains. Contador covered the 2,175 miles (3,500 kilometers) in 85 hours, 48 minutes, and 35 seconds.

Awards. Olympic gymnast Shawn Johnson won the 79th Amateur Athletic Union (AAU) Sullivan Award, which is presented to the top amateur athlete in the United States. She is the first woman gymnast to win the award. At the 2008 Summer Olympics, Johnson took the gold medal in the women's balance beam and silver medals in the all-around, team, and floor exercise.

Biathlon. In the World Championships, held in February 2009, Norway's Ole Einar Bjorndalen captured three individual gold medals. The most accomplished biathlete in history, Bjorndalen won the 10-kilometer sprint, 12.5-kilometer pursuit, and 20-kilometer individual and a relay gold (4 x 7.5 kilometers) to bring his world championship record haul to 14 golds. Austria's Dominik Landertinger captured the other men's race, the 15-kilometer mass start. In the women's competition, Germany's Kati Wilhelm captured two golds (7.5-kilometer sprint and 15-kilometer individual), Sweden's Helena Jonsson won the 10-kilometer pursuit, Russian Olga Zaitseva won the 12.5-kilometer mass start, and Russia won the 4 x 6-kilometer relay. France captured the mixed relay.

Bobsled and skeleton. At the World Championships, held from February 20 to March 1 at Lake Placid, New York, Americans captured the four-man bobsled competition for the first time in 50 years. Driver Steve Holcomb and his team of Justin Olsen, Steve Mesler, and Curt Tomasevicz won by nearly a full second. The United Kingdom's Nicola Minichiello and braker Gillian Cooke won the women's title; Switzerland's Ivo Rueegg and braker Cedric Grand won the two-man gold; Germany won the team title. In skeleton, Germany's Marion Trott won the women's title, and Switzerland's Gregor Staehli won the men's title.

Gymnastics. Winners of the World Championships in October in London were: men's individual all-around, Kohei Uchimura, Japan; men's floor, Marian Dragulescu, Romania; men's pommel horse, Zhang Hongtao, China; men's rings, Yan Mingyong, China; men's vault, Marian Dragulescu, Romania; men's parallel bars, Wang Guanyin, China; men's high bar, Zou Kai, China; women's individual all-around, Bridget Sloan, United States; women's vault, Kayla Williams, United States; women's uneven bars, He Kexin, China; women's beam, Deng Linlin, China; women's floor, Elizabeth Tweddle, United Kingdom.

Judo. At the world championships held from August 26 to 30 in Rotterdam, the Netherlands, Japan's men's team failed to win a gold medal for the first time in 59 years. France's Teddy Riner repeated as men's heavyweight champion, and China's Tong Wen won her fourth straight women's heavyweight title.

Luge. American Erin Hamlin stunned the luge world by capturing the women's gold medal at the World Championships in Lake Placid, held from February 6 to 8. Hamlin's triumph ended a streak of 99 straight victories by German women dating back to 1997. Italians Gerhard Plankensteiner and Oswald Haselrieder won the men's doubles; German Felix Loch took the men's singles title; and Germany took the team relay.

Marathon running. Kenya's Salina Kosgei won the closest women's race in the 113-year history of the Boston Marathon. She took first place on April 20, 2009, by 1 second over defending champion Dire Tune of Ethiopia. Kosgei finished in 2 hours, 32 minutes, and 16 seconds, the slowest time since 1985. Ethiopian Deriba Merga won the men's race in 2 hours, 8 minutes, and 42 seconds. American runners took third place in both races, the best U.S. finish in 24 years.

Nordic combined. At the World Championships, held February 19 to March 1 in Liberec, Czech Republic, the United States had its greatest showing ever at an Olympics or World Championship. American skiers won four gold medals and six total medals. Norway finished on top with 12 medals. American Lindsey Van captured the first-ever women's ski jumping title, and Todd Lodwick won the 10-kilometer normal hill and 10-kilometer mass start/ski jumping normal hill. The fourth U.S. gold came from Bill Demong in the 10-kilometer/large hill. Other individual winners were Finland's Aino Kaisa Saarinen (women's 10-kilometer classic), Estonia's Andrus Veerpalu (men's 15-kilometer classic), Poland's Justyna Kowalczyk (women's 15-kilometer pursuit, 30-kilometer mass start), Austria's Wolfgang Loitzl (men's ski jumping normal hill), Norway's Petter Northug (men's 30-kilometer pursuit, 50-kilometer mass start), Norway's Ola Vigen Hattestad (men's 1.6-kilometer sprint), Italy's Arianna Follis (women's 1.3-kilometer sprint), and Switzerland's Andreas Kuettel (men's ski jumping large hill).

Rodeo. Trevor Brazile of Decatur, Texas, won a record-tying seventh All-Around World Champion Cowboy title in the National Finals Rodeo on December 12 in Las Vegas.

Rowing. A team from Brown University captured the Ladies' Challenge Plate for intermediate eights on July 5 at the Henley Royal Regatta in Henley-on-Thames, England. Brown beat a team from England's Leander and Molesey clubs by half a length. Also on July 5, a team from Leander and Molesey clubs beat a team from Princeton and the California Racing Club by half a length to win the Grand Challenge Cup in international men's eights.

At the World Championships, held on August 29 in Poznan, Poland, New Zealand's Mahe Drysdale won his fourth consecutive men's single sculls title. Ekaterina Karsten-Khodotovitch of Belarus successfully defended her women's singles sculls title, and Duncan Grant of New Zealand won his third consecutive men's lightweight single sculls.

Sled-dog racing. Lance Mackey, a cancer survivor from Fairbanks, Alaska, became the third musher in the 37-year history of the Iditarod Trail Sled Dog Race to win three straight titles. He completed the 1,131-mile (1,820-kilometer) race from Anchorage to Nome on March 18 more than six hours ahead of his nearest competitor.

Soap Box Derby. Girls won four of six titles at the 72nd All-American Soap Box Derby on July 25 in Akron, Ohio. A 10-year-old, Sarah Whitaker of Norton, Ohio, was the 15th member of her family to participate in the event and captured the Stock division. Other girls to win titles were Megan Thornton, of Cleveland, in the Masters Division; Maija Liimatainen, of Madison, Wisconsin, in Super Stock; and Megan Hydutsky, of Pottstown, Pennsylvania, in the Rally Masters.

Speed skating. American speed skater Shani Davis captured the men's overall title and China's Wang Beixing won the women's overall title at the World Sprint Speed Skating Championships in Moscow on January 18.

At the World Allround Speed Skating Championships in Hamar, Norway, Dutch skater Sven Kramer won his third straight title on February 8, while Czech Martina Sablikova won her first women's gold medal. Davis, who set world records in the 1,000 meters and 1,500 meters in a World Cup meet on March 6 to 8, captured the 1,500-meter event at the World Single Distance Speed Skating Championships on March 12 in Richmond, British Columbia. But Davis was stunned a day later in the 1,000-meter by American teenager Trevor Marsicano, who became the youngest gold medal winner in the event. Later that day, Marsicano took the bronze in the 5,000-meter, won by Kramer for a third straight time. Kramer added the 10,000-meter title on March 14. On the final day of competition, Germany's Jenny Wolf won the women's 500-meter gold and South Korea's Lee Kang-Seok won the men's 500-meter. Canada won the women's pursuit; the Netherlands won the men's pursuit.

Triathlon. Australia's Emma Moffatt won the International Triathlon Union World Championship Grand Finale in Gold Coast, Australia, to secure the women's overall title. England's Alistair Brownlee won the men's race on September 12 to take the men's overall title.

Other champions

Archery. World Target Championships gold medalists: women's individual compound, Albina Loginova, Russia; women's individual recurve, Joo Hyun-Jung, South Korea; women's team compound, Russia; women's team recurve, Korea; men's individual compound, Reo Wilde, United States; men's individual recurve, Lee Chang-Hwan, South Korea; men's team compound, United States; men's team recurve, South Korea.

Badminton. World champions: men's singles, Lin Dan, China; women's singles, Lu Lan, China; men's doubles, Cai Yun and Fu Haifeng, China; women's doubles, Zhang Yawen and Zhao Tingting, China; mixed doubles, Thomas Laybourn and Kamilla Rytter Juhl, Denmark.

Curling. World champions: men, Scotland; women, China.

Equestrian. 2009 World Cup Final individual show jumping champion: Meredith Michaels-Beerbaum, Germany; dressage champion: Steffen Peters, United States.

Field hockey. Champions Trophy gold medal: men, Australia; women, Argentina.

Lacrosse. Men's NCAA champion: Syracuse University; women's NCAA champion: Northwestern University.

Modern pentathlon. World champions: men, Adam Marosi, Hungary; women, Chen Qian, China; men's and women's relays, Czech Republic.

Motorcycle racing. FIM Grand Prix 500-cc champion: Valentino Rossi, Italy.

Table tennis. World champions: men's singles, Wang Hao, China; women's singles, Zhang Yining, China; men's doubles, Chen Qi/Wang Hao, China; women's doubles, Guo Yue/Li Xiaoxia, China; mixed doubles, Li Ping/Cao Zhen, China.

Taekwondo. World champions: men, South Korea; women, China.

Team handball. World champions: men, France; women, Russia.

Water polo. World champions: men, Serbia; women, United States.

Weightlifting. Women's 165-pound (75-kilogram) champion, Svetlana Podobedova, Kazakhstan; men's 231-pound (105-kilogram) champion, An Yong-Kwon, South Korea. ■ Michael Kates

See also **Australian rules football; Automobile racing; Baseball; Basketball; Boating; Bowling; Boxing; Cricket; Football; Golf; Hockey; Horse racing; Ice skating; Olympic Games; Skiing; Soccer; Swimming; Tennis; Track and field.**

Sri Lanka. A civil war that had raged in Sri Lanka for 26 years came to an end in May 2009. According to the United Nations, from 80,000 to 100,000 people died in the conflict. The war was followed by accusations of human rights violations and uncertain prospects for reconciliation between the two sides.

The civil war was between the government of the island, 74 percent of whose population are ethnic Sinhalese Buddhists, and rebels from the ethnic Tamil Hindu minority. The rebels, the Liberation Tigers of Tamil Eelam (LTTE), fought a guerrilla war for a separate Tamil state in northern and eastern Sri Lanka. Their leader, Velupillai Prabhakaran, had sent many suicide bombers to kill government leaders over the course of the conflict.

A 2005 election, boycotted by the LTTE, brought Mahinda Rajapakse to the presidency. He and his government were determined to crush the rebels and launched a major offensive in January 2008. By 2009, the army had driven LTTE fighters into a small area in the north that was home to an estimated 250,000 Tamil civilians. Sri Lanka accused the LTTE of holding the civilians hostage.

Western aid agencies were denied access to the area and accused both sides of a "wanton disregard for human life" as civilians came under intense fire. The United Nations estimated that 7,000 civilians had been killed by late April but noted that the number of civilian deaths skyrocketed in the final weeks of the conflict.

The war ends. Rajapakse announced victory over the LTTE on May 19. Prabhakaran's body was discovered on the battlefield where the fighting ended. In late July, LTTE representatives in hiding abroad announced that they had selected international arms smuggler Selvarasa Pathmanathan as their next leader. Pathmanathan was captured in Southeast Asia in August and was flown to Sri Lanka for questioning.

After the fighting ended, international aid groups accused Sri Lanka's government of holding up to 300,000 people in refugee camps with limited access to food or medicine. To international complaints of continuing human rights violations, the government said the detainees needed to be screened to find LTTE fighters hiding among civilians. In addition, many people could not return home until land mines had been cleared. On December 1, the government announced that the 130,000 people remaining in the camps could leave and that all the camps would close by the end of January 2010.

In August 2009, a prominent Tamil journalist was sentenced to 20 years in prison for allegedly supporting terrorism. A number of other Sri Lankan journalists who criticized the government's conduct of the war were murdered, kidnapped, or assaulted in what critics said was a government campaign to silence dissent.

■ Henry S. Bradsher

See also **Asia; Terrorism.**

Sri Lankan soldiers carry the body of rebel leader Velupillai Prabhakaran in May 2009. Prabhakaran had led the Liberation Tigers of Tamil Eelam in a 26-year civil war against the Sri Lankan government. After killing Prabhakaran in combat, the government declared victory over the Tamil Tigers, ending the war.

State government. Most states in the United States faced huge budget shortfalls in 2009 and responded by slashing public services and raising taxes. Only federal economic stimulus funds to states helped maintain health care and education spending. Two states chose new governors in off-year elections, and new governors succeeded to vacated offices in five other states.

Governors. Republicans won the two gubernatorial elections on November 3. Robert F. McDonnell became the new governor of Virginia, defeating Democrat R. Creigh Deeds, a state senator. In New Jersey, Chris Christie unseated one-term Democratic Governor Jon Corzine.

Five governors' offices changed hands without elections. Alaska Governor Sarah Palin, the 2008 Republican vice presidential candidate, stepped down in July 2009 and was replaced by Lieutenant Governor Sean Parnell, a fellow Republican.

Illinois Governor Rod Blagojevich, a Democrat, lost his battle to keep his office following his arrest on federal corruption charges in December 2008. He was accused of trying to sell the United States Senate seat vacated by President-elect Barack Obama. After the Illinois House of Representatives impeached Blagojevich, the state Senate removed him from office on Jan. 29, 2009. Lieutenant Governor Pat Quinn, a Democrat, was then sworn in as governor.

President Obama appointed three sitting governors to federal offices in early 2009. After Arizona Governor Janet Napolitano, a Democrat, became the new head of the U.S. Department of Homeland Security, she was succeeded by Republican Lieutenant Governor Jan Brewer. Democratic Kansas Governor Kathleen Sebelius, the new head of the U.S. Department of Health and Human Services, was replaced by Lieutenant Governor Mark Parkinson, a former Republican turned Democrat. Utah Governor Jon Huntsman, Jr., a Republican, became the U.S. ambassador to China, and Lieutenant Governor Gary Herbert, a fellow Republican, succeeded him. After the changes, the gubernatorial split was expected to stand at 26 Democrats and 24 Republicans as of Jan. 20, 2010.

South Carolina Governor Mark Sanford, once touted as a Republican presidential hopeful for 2012, made national news in June 2009 when he confessed, after a mysterious disappearance, that he had flown to Argentina to visit his mistress. Sanford subsequently refused to leave office, and his wife moved out of the governor's mansion with the couple's children. In November, the State Ethics Commission released a report accusing Sanford of 37 ethics violations, including the use of state aircraft for personal and political purposes. The ethics panel was scheduled to hold a hearing into the charges in early 2010.

Legislatures. New York Democrats lost control of the state Senate to Republicans for a month when two Democratic senators switched parties in June 2009. Governor David Paterson, a Democrat, responded by appointing Richard Ravitch as lieutenant governor to break tie votes before one senator rejoined the Democrats.

The speakers of the state houses of representatives in both Florida and Massachusetts resigned their posts and later were indicted in 2009. Glenn Richardson, the Republican speaker of the Georgia House of Representatives, resigned in December following a suicide attempt weeks earlier.

Revenue and budget. Nearly all states cut public services, including health, education, aid for the elderly and disabled, criminal justice, and state work forces. The cuts came to avoid collective deficits for fiscal 2009-2010 estimated from $200 billion to as much as $350 billion, according to various calculations by the National Governors Association and the nonprofit Center on Budget and Policy Priorities, both in Washington, D.C.

State and local governments in 2008 and 2009 experienced the biggest decline in tax revenues in decades, according to figures from the U.S. Census Bureau. Sales tax revenues and personal incomes plunged. The collapse of the housing market also hit some areas hard. At the same time, states faced increased demand for such services as unemployment benefits, food stamps, and health care. At least 20 states ran out of money for unemployment trust funds and had to borrow billions from the federal government to pay jobless workers.

In response to declining state revenues, many states hiked taxes or ordered workers to take unpaid leave. Federal stimulus money helped maintain state services. States divided 60 percent of stimulus funds between health care and education and spent 16 percent on transportation and 10 percent on income security. Republican governors Sarah Palin of Alaska and Mark Sanford of South Carolina both failed to convince their legislatures to refuse federal stimulus money.

Education. About one-third of the federal stimulus money to states went to education. However, more than half the states still cut public education funding, with big reductions in California, Florida, Mississippi, and South Carolina. In addition, 35 states reduced aid to public higher education or raised tuition, according to the American Council on Education, an association of higher education officials.

Health. As people lost their jobs and health insurance, more turned to the state-federal Medicaid program. More than 50 million poor Americans rely on Medicaid to cover health care costs. Enrollment in Medicaid stood at a six-year high in 2009, according to a 50-state survey by the Kaiser Family Foundation's Commission on Medicaid and the Uninsured, a nonprofit foundation based in

SELECTED STATISTICS ON STATE GOVERNMENTS

State	Resident population*	Governor†	Legislature† House (D)	House (R)	Senate (D)	Senate (R)	State tax revenue‡	Tax revenue per capita‡
Alabama	4,661,900	Bob Riley (R)	§60	44	21	14	$ 9,071,000,000	$ 1,950
Alaska	686,293	Sean Parnell (R)	18	22	10	10	8,425,000,000	12,280
Arizona	6,500,180	Jan Brewer (R)	25	35	12	18	13,706,000,000	2,110
Arkansas	2,855,390	Mike Beebe (D)	#71	28	27	8	7,531,000,000	2,640
California	36,756,666	Arnold Schwarzenegger (R)	**50	28	25	15	117,362,000,000	3,190
Colorado	4,939,456	Bill Ritter (D)	38	27	21	14	9,625,000,000	1,950
Connecticut	3,501,252	M. Jodi Rell (R)	114	37	24	12	13,368,000,000	3,820
Delaware	873,092	Jack Markell (D)	24	17	16	5	2,931,000,000	3,360
Florida	18,328,340	Charlie Crist (R)	44	76	14	26	35,850,000,000	1,960
Georgia	9,685,744	Sonny Perdue (R)	††72	103	22	34	18,183,000,000	1,880
Hawaii	1,288,198	Linda Lingle (R)	45	6	23	2	5,147,000,000	4,000
Idaho	1,523,816	C. L. "Butch" Otter (R)	18	52	7	28	3,652,000,000	2,400
Illinois	12,901,563	Pat Quinn (D)	70	48	37	22	31,891,000,000	2,470
Indiana	6,376,792	Mitch Daniels (R)	52	48	17	33	14,916,000,000	2,340
Iowa	3,002,555	Chet Culver (D)	56	44	32	18	6,892,000,000	2,300
Kansas	2,802,134	Mark Parkinson (D)	49	76	9	31	7,160,000,000	2,560
Kentucky	4,269,245	Steve Beshear (D)	§64	35	**17	19	10,056,000,000	2,360
Louisiana	4,410,796	Bobby Jindal (R)	‡‡52	50	23	16	11,004,000,000	2,490
Maine	1,316,456	John Baldacci (D)	95	56	20	15	3,682,000,000	2,800
Maryland	5,633,597	Martin O'Malley (D)	§§104	36	33	14	16,606,000,000	2,950
Massachusetts	6,497,967	Deval Patrick (D)	144	16	35	5	21,836,000,000	3,360
Michigan	10,003,422	Jennifer Granholm (D)	67	43	§16	21	24,782,000,000	2,480
Minnesota	5,220,393	Tim Pawlenty (R)	87	47	46	21	18,321,000,000	3,510
Mississippi	2,938,618	Haley Barbour (R)	74	48	27	25	6,618,000,000	2,250
Missouri	5,911,605	Jay Nixon (D)	##71	88	§10	23	10,965,000,000	1,850
Montana	967,440	Brian Schweitzer (D)	50	50	23	27	2,458,000,000	2,540
Nebraska	1,783,432	Dave Heineman (R)	unicameral (49 nonpartisan)				4,175,000,000	2,340
Nevada	2,600,167	Jim Gibbons (R)	28	14	12	9	6,116,000,000	2,350
New Hampshire	1,315,809	John Lynch (D)	223	177	14	10	2,251,000,000	1,710
New Jersey	8,682,661	Chris Christie (R)	48	32	23	17	30,617,000,000	3,530
New Mexico	1,984,356	Bill Richardson (D)	45	25	27	15	5,675,000,000	2,860
New York	19,490,297	David Paterson (D)	109	41	32	30	65,400,000,000	3,360
North Carolina	9,222,414	Bev Perdue (D)	68	52	§29	20	22,781,000,000	2,470
North Dakota	641,481	John Hoeven (R)	§35	58	21	26	2,312,000,000	3,600
Ohio	11,485,910	Ted Strickland (D)	53	46	12	21	26,374,000,000	2,300
Oklahoma	3,642,361	Brad Henry (D)	39	62	22	26	8,484,000,000	2,330
Oregon	3,790,060	Ted Kulongoski (D)	36	24	18	12	7,250,000,000	1,910
Pennsylvania	12,448,279	Ed Rendell (D)	§104	98	20	30	32,124,000,000	2,580
Rhode Island	1,050,788	Don Carcieri (R)	69	6	§§33	4	2,761,000,000	2,630
South Carolina	4,479,800	Mark Sanford (R)	§51	72	19	27	8,455,000,000	1,890
South Dakota	804,194	Mike Rounds (R)	24	46	14	21	1,321,000,000	1,640
Tennessee	6,214,888	Phil Bredesen (D)	48	51	14	19	11,538,000,000	1,860
Texas	24,326,974	Rick Perry (R)	74	76	12	19	44,676,000,000	1,840
Utah	2,736,424	Gary Herbert (R)	22	53	8	21	5,945,000,000	2,170
Vermont	621,270	Jim Douglas (R)	***94	48	23	7	2,544,000,000	4,090
Virginia	7,769,089	Robert McDonnell (R)	†††39	59	21	19	18,408,000,000	2,370
Washington	6,549,224	Christine Gregoire (D)	62	36	31	18	17,945,000,000	2,740
West Virginia	1,814,468	Joe Manchin III (D)	71	29	28	6	4,879,000,000	2,690
Wisconsin	5,627,967	Jim Doyle (D)	§§52	46	18	15	15,089,000,000	2,680
Wyoming	532,668	Dave Freudenthal (D)	19	41	7	23	2,168,000,000	4,070

*July 1, 2008, estimates. Source: U.S. Census Bureau.
†As of January 2010. Source: National Governors' Association; National Conference of State Legislatures; state government officials.
‡2008 figures. Source: U.S. Census Bureau.
§One vacant at press time.
#One Green Party.
**One independent, one vacant at press time.

††Five vacant at press time.
‡‡Three independents.
§§One independent.
##Four vacant at press time.
***Five Progressive Party, three independents.
†††Two independents.

Illinois Governor Rod Blagojevich defends himself before the state Senate during his impeachment trial on January 29. Federal prosecutors had accused Blagojevich of abusing the power of his office by attempting to sell the U.S. Senate seat vacated by President Barack Obama. State senators voted 59-0 to remove Blagojevich from office.

Menlo Park, California. Total Medicaid spending grew by an average of nearly 8 percent in the 2009-2010 fiscal year. Some 30 percent of federal stimulus funds to states went to prop up Medicaid.

On the bright side, 14 states expanded children's health insurance as permitted by a decision by President Obama to reverse restrictions enacted during the administration of President George W. Bush. Among the bolder moves to expand health care, Connecticut legislators overrode a gubernatorial veto to establish a state program of expanded coverage, including a public option—that is, a nonprofit insurance plan set up by the government—by 2012. Maine, Massachusetts, and Vermont all have programs underway to achieve universal coverage.

Medical marijuana gained a higher profile in October 2009 when the U.S. Department of Justice announced that it would not prosecute people who use the drug for medical purposes in states where it is legal. Medical use is legal in Alaska, California, Colorado, Hawaii, Maine, Michigan, Montana, Nevada, New Mexico, Oregon, Rhode Island, Vermont, and Washington. Maine voters on November 3 approved a ballot measure expanding its law allowing state-regulated dispensaries to grow and sell the drug to patients.

Crime, corrections. In bids to save money, at least nine states closed some prisons, including Colorado, Kansas, Michigan, New Hampshire, New Jersey, New York, North Carolina, Tennessee, and Washington. In addition, various states began releasing prisoners early.

Arizona moved to privatize its entire prison system, including death row, seeking bids from private companies for 9 of the state's 10 prisons, housing roughly 40,000 inmates. Arizona would be the first state to contract out its entire system. To help reduce its budget deficit, California moved to reduce spending on corrections by $1 billion.

New York eased its tough drug-sentencing laws to give judges more leeway to send offenders to rehabilitation instead of jail. Nevada and Illinois established special courts to handle veterans of the U.S. military who commit crimes.

Capital punishment. In 2009, New Mexico became the 15th state to eliminate the death penalty, replacing it with a sentence of life without possibility of parole.

Social issues. Legislatures in Maine, New Hampshire, and Vermont sanctioned marriage by same-sex couples in 2009. Maine's new law was, however, repealed by voters on November 3. Also on November 3, Washington state voters approved a law expanding state legal protections to same-sex partners. In California, the state Supreme Court on May 26 upheld the November 2008 voter ban on gay marriage (Proposition 8). However, the court also upheld same-sex marriages that occurred before the ban took effect. ■ Elaine Stuart McDonald

See also **Courts; Democratic Party; Elections; Immigration; Republican Party.**

STOCK MARKET RISES IN 2009

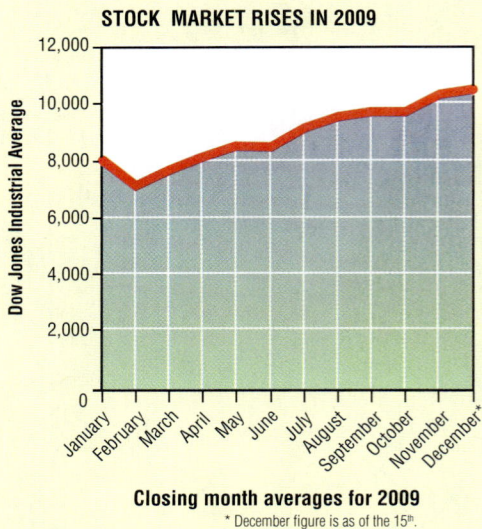

Dow Jones Industrial Average (y-axis: 0; 2,000; 4,000; 6,000; 8,000; 10,000; 12,000)

Months (x-axis): January, February, March, April, May, June, July, August, September, October, November, December*

Closing month averages for 2009
* December figure is as of the 15th.

In the first months of 2009, stock prices fell 25 percent after having already declined by 40 percent in 2008. Then, in a historic rally over the next nine months, Dow Jones Industrial Average stocks surged by nearly 60 percent.

Stocks and bonds.

Investors underwent both fear and relief in 2009 as the stock market early on continued the worst decline since the Great Depression of the 1930's, then shocked investors with one of the most powerful rallies in United States history. Investors faced January in a panicky mood, fearing a worldwide economic catastrophe. After stock market prices had already declined 40 percent in 2008, they fell another 25 percent by early March 2009. But by year-end, stock market prices had climbed 23.5 percent.

As banks continued to face financial troubles caused by a history of mortgage failures and lax lending practices, the U.S. government bailed them out with its $700-billion Troubled Asset Relief Program (TARP). In addition, changes in accounting rules made banks appear less distressed. After the market fell from its peak on Oct. 9, 2007, to its lowest point on March 9, 2009, the historic rally carried the stocks of the Dow Jones Industrial Average (an index of the stock prices of 30 major companies) up nearly 60 percent during the last nine months of the year. The rally restored about $5.2 trillion of the money investors had lost in the market since October 2007. Yet, the devastation was so great that, as the year came to a close, investors still had not recovered $5.7 trillion—a loss of 30 percent from the peak.

Analysts have described 2000-2009 as a "lost decade," because investors lost more than 10 percent in the stock market during the 10 years. The shock left many wondering if the risk of investing in stocks was worth it. The few investors who bought stocks during the March lows, however, described them later as "deals of a lifetime." As bargain buying gradually caught on, more investors joined their peers. Growing confidence powered the rally higher and generated faith in government programs to stimulate hiring.

By the end of 2009, investors were, however, beginning to worry about the impact the nation's 10-percent unemployment rate would have on corporate profits and the stock market, and the rally slowed. Although 25 percent of companies had record profits in the third quarter, most profits were gained by sharp cost-cutting. As consumers struggled with debts and job losses, corporate sales stagnated. At the same time, the crush of the recession made investors worry about the ability of such states as California and Illinois, such countries as Greece and Spain, and the *emirate* (state) of Dubai to repay their bond investors.

Winners and losers. Amid fear early in the year, investors clung to companies with little or no debt, which they expected would survive a severe recession. Stock in Cupertino, California-based Apple Inc., maker of computers and iPhones, climbed 22 percent in the first quarter. The stock of Mountain View, California-based Google Inc., the Internet search engine giant, climbed 11 percent during the same period.

On the downside in 2009, government attention focused on bailing out Detroit-based automaker General Motors Corp., hurt badly by the credit crisis. Despite $19.4 billion in aid, the company went bankrupt and stockholders lost everything. The company then reorganized under a new name, General Motors Company (GM). The U.S. government's loans to GM translated into a 61-percent ownership. The remaining 39 percent went to the Canadian and Ontario governments, a health care trust for the United Auto Workers union, and bondholders.

As the market gained strength, investors turned to financial stocks and real estate funds, which were cheap. Stock prices for New York City-based American Express, a lending institution, plunged 30 percent in the first quarter to under $10, then rose to over $40 in the fourth quarter. Stock prices for San Francisco-based Wells Fargo, a bank company, dropped 54 percent between January and March, then rebounded to January's highest price in October. The Dow Jones Total Stock Market Index climbed 43 percent in 2009. The Dow Jones U.S. Automobile and Parts Index rose 86 percent, due largely to a government program that provided cash to people who turned in "clunkers" and bought new cars.

As the economies of such countries as China and Brazil continued to expand, the demand for basic materials strengthened and the Dow Jones Basic Resources Index climbed 66 percent. The greatest laggard of the year was the Dow Jones U.S. Bank Index, which included small banks struggling without the aid the government had provided the largest banks.

Bonds. Early in 2009, investors were unwilling to take a chance on anything but safe U.S. government bonds, such as Treasury bonds. They bought the bonds despite almost no return as the Federal Reserve (the nation's central bank) tried to spur the economy by keeping the federal funds rate at 0 to 0.25 percent. With a yield of 3.2 percent on 10-year Treasury bonds, the value declined 5.4 percent as investors moved money to higher-yielding, yet higher-risk, corporate bonds.

Quality corporate bonds climbed 10.5 percent for the year, and the riskiest bonds, known as high-yield bonds, climbed 53.7 percent, despite ongoing concerns about bankruptcies as the economy remained weak.

While risk-taking increased throughout the year, individual investors remained leery of stocks and poured a record $340 billion into mutual funds that invest in bonds. ■ Gail MarksJarvis

See also **Bank; Economics, United States; Economics, U.S.: A Special Report; Economics, World.**

Sudan. In March 2009, the International Criminal Court (ICC), at The Hague in the Netherlands, issued a warrant of arrest for Sudanese President Umar Hassan al-Bashir on charges of war crimes and crimes against humanity. The warrant stated that Bashir was suspected of being responsible "for murdering, exterminating, raping, torturing, and forcibly transferring large numbers of civilians, and pillaging their property." The arrest warrant marked the first such action taken against a sitting head of state by the ICC.

At a July meeting in Libya of the African Union (an organization working to achieve cooperation among African nations), other African leaders denounced the ICC's action. The leaders declared that they would not cooperate with the ICC and that they would refuse to turn President Bashir over to the international court.

Widespread arrests. Throughout 2009, the Sudanese National Intelligence and Security Services arrested and detained numerous individuals perceived to be threats to the government—though critics referred to many of the arrests as arbitrary. The arrested individuals included lawyers who had been active in human rights programs, other human rights activists, opposition political leaders, and leaders of rebel groups. In addition, Sudanese authorities closed three human rights organizations and expelled 13 international aid organizations from Darfur, a western province where government forces and rebel groups were fighting.

Some of the detained individuals remained in custody without access to lawyers and without being charged with any crime. Human Rights Watch, an international organization based in New York City, reported that the true scale of arbitrary arrests in Sudan was unknown because of restrictions on freedom of speech and freedom of assembly.

Census results questioned. In April, government officials announced preliminary results of Sudan's fifth population and household census. The census had been conducted to categorize electoral constituencies for parliamentary and presidential elections scheduled for 2010. Sudan's minister for presidential affairs stated that the census placed the country's population at 39.15 million. The regional population breakdown—leaked to the public by an independent newspaper—showed more than 5 million people in Khartoum, the capital; about 7.5 million people in Darfur; and no more than 8.2 million people in southern Sudan.

Many opposition political leaders and other Sudanese questioned the accuracy of the reported census results. Salva Kiir Mayardit, president of *semiautonomous* (partially self-governing) southern Sudan, declared that the census figures had been "deflated in some regions and inflated in others" for political reasons.

Calls for reform. At a meeting in southern Sudan in September 2009, leaders of 20 political parties threatened to boycott the 2010 elections unless the Sudanese government implemented reforms "of all laws related to freedom and democratic transformations." The party leaders claimed that many existing laws were in breach of the interim constitution approved by the National Assembly (parliament) in 2005. The leaders also demanded that agreement be reached on the disputed census results and that the conflict in Darfur be brought to an end.

Revised U.S. policy. In October 2009, the administration of United States President Barack Obama announced a new U.S. policy toward Sudan. The revised policy was aimed at ending the conflict in Darfur; at implementing terms of the Comprehensive Peace Agreement, signed by the government and southern rebels in 2005; and at preventing Sudan from providing safe haven to international terrorists. Under the new policy, the U.S. administration also proposed unspecified "incentives and disincentives" for pressuring Sudanese authorities to respect human rights in Darfur and other regions of conflict in Sudan.

■ Mary-Jane Deeb

See also **Africa; Human rights; United Nations.**

Supreme Court of the United States.
Sonia Sotomayor was sworn in as the 111th justice of the Supreme Court on Aug. 8, 2009, replacing retiring Justice David Souter. She became the first Hispanic and the third woman to join the court in its history. Earlier, during its 2008-2009 term, the court decided 79 cases, including a few notable civil rights cases late in the term.

Souter and Sotomayor. Souter announced on May 1, 2009, that he would retire from the Supreme Court at the end of the term. He had been appointed to the court in 1990 by President George H. W. Bush, a Republican. However, Souter had gone on to disappoint conservatives by usually voting with the more liberal side of the bench.

President Barack Obama, a Democrat, nominated Sotomayor, a Bronx native of Puerto Rican descent, to the court on May 26, 2009. She had been a member of the U.S. Second Circuit Court of Appeals in New York City since 1998 and a federal judge since 1992. On Aug. 6, 2009, the U.S. Senate voted 68-31 to confirm Sotomayor to the Supreme Court. She was backed by 9 of the Senate's 40 Republicans as well as all 59 members of the Senate Democratic Caucus who were present for the vote.

Job discrimination. In a 5-to-4 decision on June 29, the court held that the city of New Haven, Connecticut, had discriminated against a group of mostly white firefighters by throwing out the results of examinations used to decide promotions to lieutenant and captain rank. The highest scorers on the tests included 17 whites, 2 Hispanics, and no blacks. At issue in the case was Title VII of the Civil Rights Act of 1964, which prohibits *disparate treatment* (intentional discrimination) based on race, as well as practices having a *disparate impact* (unintentional adverse effect) on racial minorities.

City officials had chosen not to certify the exam results because they feared that the city would be sued for an employment practice having a disparate impact on minorities. The high-scoring firefighters responded by filing a lawsuit claiming disparate treatment based on race. The Supreme Court ruled that the city's rejection of the exam results constituted disparate treatment and that the city did not have a "strong basis in evidence" to conclude that its action was necessary to avoid disparate-impact liability. Voting in the majority in the case were the court's conservatives—Chief Justice John Roberts and Justices Samuel Alito, Antonin Scalia, and Clarence Thomas—and the court's centrist swing voter, Justice Anthony Kennedy. The court's liberals—Justices Stephen Breyer, Ruth Bader Ginsburg, David Souter, and John Paul Stevens—dissented.

Voting rights. The court issued a decision on June 22, 2009, that sidestepped the question of whether Section 5 of the Voting Rights Act of 1965 is constitutional. Many observers had expected the court to strike down the provision.

The Voting Rights Act prohibits states and their political subdivisions from imposing measures that cause voting rights to be denied or limited on account of race. Prior to the act, many places, especially in the South, had used literacy tests, poll taxes, and other measures to prevent blacks from voting. Section 5 requires political subdivisions in areas with a history of voting discrimination to gain preclearance from the federal government before changing election procedures. Exemptions from Section 5 may be granted if certain conditions are met. Critics have argued that Section 5 is no longer needed to protect racial minorities' voting rights and is, therefore, an unconstitutional federal intrusion into state and local affairs.

A utility district in Texas had sought a Section 5 exemption, but a lower court had ruled that the district was ineligible for exemption because it did not register its own voters. In its appeal, the district had challenged the constitutionality of Section 5. The Supreme Court reversed the lower court decision, ruling that all political subdivisions, including the district, may try to gain a Section 5 exemption. However, the Supreme Court opted to let Section 5 stand, despite the misgivings of some justices about its constitutionality. The vote in the case was 8 to 1, with Thomas, the dissenter, arguing that Section 5 should be declared unconstitutional.

Strip search. On June 25, 2009, the court ruled, 8 to 1, that a strip search of a 13-year-old girl in 2003 by school officials in Safford, Arizona, had violated her Fourth Amendment right against unreasonable searches and seizures. The officials had suspected that the girl might have brought pain-relief pills to school without the school's permission. They found no pills. A strip search had not been warranted, the court ruled, because the pills would not have posed a danger to students and because there had been no reason to suppose that pills were hidden in her underwear. However, the court also ruled that the officials who ordered and conducted the strip search could not be sued for damages because the law had not, at the time, clearly established that the search was illegal. Thomas cast the dissenting vote in the case.

Detainee lawsuit. In a 5-to-4 decision on May 18, 2009, the court ruled against a Pakistani Muslim man, Javaid Iqbal, who had tried to sue former Attorney General John Ashcroft and Federal Bureau of Investigation Director Robert Mueller. Iqbal had been arrested on immigration fraud charges shortly after the terrorist attacks of Sept. 11, 2001, and had been detained under maximum-security conditions. He alleged that he had been beaten and abused while in detention, and that Ashcroft and Mueller had knowingly perpetrated policies that allowed such abuse to occur solely on the basis of the detainees' race, religion, or national origin. The court ruled that Iqbal had failed to provide sufficient factual evidence to proceed with his claim of purposeful discrimination. Kennedy joined the four conservative justices to form the majority. Many observers suggested that the most significant effect of this decision was to make it easier for judges to dismiss civil lawsuits right after they are filed, if the judges view the claims as implausible.

Campaign donations to judges. On June 8, 2009, the court decided, 5 to 4, that a state judge should have recused himself from a case that involved his biggest campaign contributor. Brent Benjamin had been elected in 2004 as a justice of West Virginia's Supreme Court of Appeals with the help of $3 million in spending by Don Blankenship, the head of Massey Energy, a large coal company. A state jury in 2002 had ordered Massey to pay $50 million in damages to a smaller coal company in a fraud case. From 2006 to 2008, Benjamin denied, during appeal proceedings in the state Supreme Court, repeated motions to recuse himself from the case, and the court issued two rulings to overturn the $50-million verdict. The U.S. Supreme Court ruled that Benjamin's refusal to recuse himself violated the 14th Amendment's due process clause, because Blankenship's unusually large campaign donations created too high a probability of bias. Kennedy and the four liberal justices made up the majority in the ruling.

Drug company liability. In a 6-to-3 ruling on March 4, 2009, the court held that Wyeth, a major pharmaceutical company, could not avoid being sued in state court for harm done by a drug with a federally approved warning label. A Vermont resident, Diana Levine, had had the antinausea drug Phenergan injected directly into her vein, after which she had developed gangrene and had to have her forearm amputated. She had sued Wyeth, Phenergan's manufacturer, in state court, claiming that the company had failed to provide adequate warning of the dangers of directly injecting the drug. The Vermont jury decided the case in Levine's favor and awarded her damages. Wyeth had appealed the verdict, arguing that Levine's claims were preempted by federal law because the drug's label had been approved by the U.S. Food and Drug Administration. The U.S. Supreme Court rejected Wyeth's argument, ruling that it was not impossible for the company to comply with both state laws and federal regulations. Alito, Roberts, and Scalia cast the dissenting votes in the ruling. ■ Mike Lewis

See also **Courts; Disability; People in the news** (Sonia Sotomayor).

Surgery. See **Medicine.**
Suriname. See **Latin America.**
Swaziland. See **Africa.**

Sweden. Prime Minister Fredrik Reinfeldt's center-right coalition government—made up of Reinfeldt's Moderate Party, the Center Party, the Liberal Party, and the Christian Democratic Party—remained stable in 2009, and most observers forecast that it would remain so until the next general election in September 2010. According to opinion polls held in mid-2009, the government and the opposition were roughly equally popular. Two opposition parties, the Social Democrats and the Greens, presented themselves as viable alternatives to the ruling coalition. However, they were unable to present a unified front on such issues as the government's 2010 budget.

Economic crisis. In 2009, global financial instability caused large swings in the value of the Swedish currency, the krona, and led to renewed debate on adoption of the euro as the country's currency. (Although Sweden is a member of the European Union [EU], Swedes rejected adoption of the common currency in a 2003 referendum.) Reinfeldt determined not to hold a referendum on the issue during his current term in office.

The global economic crisis had a particularly strong effect on Sweden's export-dependent economy in 2009, resulting in the nation's weakest single-year economic performance since World War II (1939-1945). In response, the government included a 32-billion krona ($4.6-billion) stimulus package in its 2010 budget. The plan included tax cuts for businesses to encourage hiring and expansion; investment in infrastructure; and increases in funds for social welfare services. The government also passed a financial package to insure bank deposits and provide money to Swedish banks, many of which were exposed to losses through subsidiaries in the Baltic nations.

Despite government efforts, the unemployment rate rose from 6.2 percent in 2008 to 8.5 percent in 2009, according to forecasts by EU economists. Sweden's budget fell from a surplus of 2.5 percent in 2008 to a deficit of 2.1 percent in 2009.

In November, an agreement by Swedish-based Koenigsegg Group to purchase troubled automaker Saab from its United States parent, General Motors (GM) of Detroit, fell through. The future of Saab remained uncertain as GM considered offers from other potential buyers.

International relations. Sweden held the rotating EU presidency in the second half of 2009. In this role, Reinfeldt shepherded the Lisbon Treaty through the final stages of ratification. The agreement is designed to streamline decision-making and create new offices of president and foreign minister for the EU. Sweden also engaged in negotiations on Europe's behalf in the run-up to the international climate summit held in Copenhagen in December. ■ Jeffrey Kopstein

See also **Europe.**

Swimming. American swimmer Michael Phelps provided major news in 2009, in and out of the pool. Controversial high-tech swimming suits also garnered headlines.

World championships. Phelps captured five gold medals and set four world records in the 2009 world championships in Rome but lost an individual race for the first time in four years. Full-body, high-tech polyurethane swimsuits contributed to most of the 43 world records set during the eight-day meet in late July and early August. The suit enables the swimmer to glide on top of the water with far less resistance and has been banned by FINA, swimming's governing body, effective Jan. 1, 2010.

Phelps did not use the full-body suit. But he said he was also rusty, having missed six months of training and competition.

The United States finished atop the medals table, but its 22 medals (10 golds, 6 silvers, 6 bronzes) were its fewest since 1994, when the Americans won just 21 medals.

Phelps and the U.S. 4-x-100-meter medley relay team set the final record of the meet on Aug. 2, 2009, shattering their own record by more than 2 seconds and finishing in 3 minutes, 27.28 seconds. Germany's Paul Biedermann handed Phelps his only silver medal and took nearly a second off the American's world record, winning the 200 freestyle in 1 minute, 42 seconds on July 28. Two days earlier, Biedermann topped Ian Thorpe's 2002 record in the 400 freestyle by .01 second, winning in 3 minutes, 40.07 seconds.

Inge de Bruijn's 2000 record set in the 100 women's butterfly was the other long-standing mark to fall. Sweden's Sarah Sjostrom swam 56.44 to beat the mark by .17 second on July 26.

American Ryan Lochte made a strong showing. He captured four gold medals and a bronze medal and broke two world records, one with Phelps in the 4-x-200 freestyle relay and the other in the 200 individual medley.

Phelps's trouble. In early February 2009, a British tabloid printed a picture of Phelps inhaling from a marijuana pipe, reportedly at a party in South Carolina in November 2008, while the swimmer was taking a break from training. Phelps did not deny the authenticity of the photo and apologized. The incident cost him a major sponsor, cereal and snack maker Kellogg Co., and USA Swimming suspended him for three months.

Other records. Two world marks set earlier in 2009 were not broken in Rome. France's Frédérick Bousquet swam the 50 freestyle in 20.94 seconds at the French Championships in April. Aaron Peirsol set a new standard in the 100 backstroke with a time of 51.94 at the U.S. Championships in early July.   ■ Michael Kates

Switzerland. The Federal Council—Switzerland's governing body, made up of representatives of the four largest parties—was more stable in 2009 than in recent years. The Swiss People's Party (SVP) returned from opposition in late 2008, bringing about the broad consensus needed to pass legislation. In December 2009, the Federal Assembly elected Doris Leuthard of the Christian Democratic Party as president for 2010. The presidency rotates among the members of the council. Leuthard's election marked the first time that women headed all three branches of the government.

Economic crisis. The government spent much of 2009 mitigating the effects of the 2008 global economic crisis, providing stimulus packages several times during the year. Switzerland was vulnerable both as a major banking center and as an export-driven economy. The country's two largest banks, UBS and Credit Suisse, came under pressure because of bad loans and exposure to losses among subsidiaries in Eastern Europe. In midyear, the government lowered its economic forecast for the second time, indicating that Switzerland's *gross domestic product* (GDP—the value of all goods and services produced in a year) would fall by 2.7 percent, the largest drop in some 30 years.

Bank secrecy. In March 2009, Switzerland escaped being put on the 30-nation Organisation for Economic Co-operation and Development's so-called blacklist of countries whose secrecy laws enable the illegal avoidance of taxes. The Swiss Bankers Association agreed to comply with global regulatory norms and weaken its rules on secrecy. The changes were followed by agreements with several European countries to avoid double taxation. Some partners, however, demanded even greater transparency. Relations with Italy deteriorated in November when Italian police raided Swiss bank branches in Italy over capital hidden by Italian citizens. In response, the Swiss government postponed negotiations with Italy on a new taxation treaty.

In August, the governments of Switzerland and the United States settled a pending lawsuit by the U.S. Internal Revenue Service that would have forced Switzerland's largest bank, UBS, to break Swiss banking secrecy laws by transferring data on 52,000 client accounts to the U.S. government. Swiss lawmakers worried that a change in the secrecy laws and greater transparency would lead to a decrease in the size of one of the most important sectors of the Swiss economy.

Minarets. In a referendum sponsored by right-wing parties in November, voters ignored government and church leaders and approved a ban on the building of *minarets* (towers attached to mosques). The ban sent a hostile signal to Switzerland's rising Muslim minority.   ■ Jeffrey Kopstein

See also **Economics, World; Europe; Islam.**

Syria. Syrian President Bashar al-Assad attended the Arab Economic Summit in Kuwait in January 2009 and called for the punishment of Israel for its actions in the conflict in the Gaza Strip. That conflict lasted from late December 2008 to mid-January 2009, resulting in the deaths of more than 1,400 Palestinians and about 13 Israelis. Experts in Middle Eastern affairs noted that the violence was provoked by the militant Palestinian organization Hamas, with support from Syria and Iran.

Arab League Summit. President Assad also attended the Arab League Summit in Qatar in March. Hosni Mubarak, the pro-Western president of Egypt, chose to not attend the summit because of Syria's continued support of both Hamas and the controversial regime in Iran.

U.S. ambassador returns. In June, the administration of United States President Barack Obama revealed that it would return the U.S. ambassador to Syria after an absence of four years. Administration officials said they hoped the policy change would prompt Syria to support peace and stability in the Middle East. However, that outcome did not occur. Instead, experts noted that Syria continued to block—through its terrorist proxy organization Hezbollah—the formation of a new Cabinet in Lebanon. Middle East experts believed that Syria also continued to dispatch Arab terrorists to Iraq.

Syrian-Saudi summit. King Abdullah of Saudi Arabia visited Syria in October, signifying the normalization of Syrian-Saudi relations. These relations had deteriorated as a result of the assassination of former Lebanese Prime Minister Rafik al-Hariri by Syrian proxies in February 2005.

Iraq accuses Syria. Iraqi Prime Minister Nouri al-Maliki accused Syria of harboring Iraqi Baathists who were responsible for two bombings that took place in Baghdad, the Iraqi capital, on Aug. 19, 2009. (Baathists are Arab nationalists.) The bombings killed some 130 people. The Iraqi prime minister also claimed that 90 percent of Arab terrorists in Iraq entered the country through Syria, where they received training. President Assad denied these accusations and claimed that Syria had played a humanitarian role by accepting 1.2 million Iraqi refugees.

Syrian-Turkish relations improved in 2009. Leaders from both countries exchanged a number of visits, and in September, Syria and Turkey agreed to establish the Syrian-Turkish Strategic Cooperation Council. In October, the foreign ministers of Syria and Turkey signed an agreement to eliminate visa requirements for traveling between the nations. Joint Syrian-Turkish military exercises were also held in 2009. ■ Marius Deeb

See also **Iraq; Israel; Lebanon; Middle East; Saudi Arabia; Turkey.**

Taiwan. Typhoon Morakot dumped at least 83 inches (211 centimeters) of rain on southern Taiwan from Aug. 7 to Aug. 9, 2009. The storm triggered the island's worst flooding and mudslides in 50 years. Morakot left at least 700 people dead or missing as villages were buried in mud and roads and bridges were washed away. Some 38,000 soldiers worked with thousands of volunteers to help those still stranded in the mountains after the storm. President Ma Ying-jeou was strongly criticized for failing to evacuate people from vulnerable areas, for responding slowly, and for only belatedly accepting foreign aid.

The Dalai Lama, the exiled Tibetan Buddhist leader, visited Taiwan to console disaster survivors. Ma reportedly agreed to the visit only reluctantly because of intense hostility toward the Dalai Lama by China, which claims both Tibet and Taiwan.

Premier Liu Chao-shiuan resigned on September 7, saying "someone must take responsibility" for the slow response to the disaster. Wu Den-yih, the general secretary of Ma's Kuomintang party, became premier on September 10.

Taiwan's relations with China improved in 2009, despite Chinese denunciations of the Dalai Lama's visit. On April 26, representatives of the two nations signed agreements for increased financial cooperation and air travel. China also lifted its long blockade of Taiwan's participation in international organizations. On May 18, Taiwan's health minister became an observer at a meeting of the United Nations World Health Assembly.

On July 27, 2009, Hu Jintao, general secretary of the Chinese Communist Party and China's president, sent Ma a congratulatory message after Ma was elected chairman of the Kuomintang party. This was the first direct communication between presidents of the two often-confrontational states. Although China insists that Ma is not the president of a sovereign nation, international observers suggested that Ma and Hu might meet as party chiefs.

Taiwan's economy contracted in 2009 as part of the worldwide financial downturn, but in August, officials announced that the country was coming out of recession. They expected gross domestic product (GDP) output to return to prerecession levels before the beginning of 2010. (GDP is the value of goods and services produced in a country in a given year.)

Former president sentenced. Former Taiwanese President Chen Shui-bian was sentenced to life in prison on Sept. 11, 2009, for embezzlement, taking bribes, and laundering money while he was in office from 2000 to 2008. Chen's wife, Wu Shu-chen, was also sentenced to life in prison on similar charges. ■ Henry S. Bradsher

See also **Asia; China; Disasters.**

Tajikistan. See Asia.

Tanzania. See Africa.

Taxation. A $787-billion economic stimulus bill was passed by the U.S. Congress on Feb. 13, 2009, and signed by President Barack Obama on February 17. The bill included dozens of individual and business tax breaks costing $212 billion, according to the Congressional Budget Office.

Stimulus bill tax provisions. The bill established a new "Making Work Pay" refundable income tax credit, for both 2009 and 2010, of up to $400 for an individual or up to $800 for a married couple. Most people making under $75,000 a year ($150,000 for couples) were made eligible for the full credit. People making above those amounts but not more than $100,000 ($200,000 for couples) were allowed a partial credit.

A fix was implemented in the alternative minimum tax (AMT) to keep millions of people from becoming subject to it in 2009. The AMT had been created in 1969 with the intent of preventing wealthy people from using deductions to reduce their taxable income to little or nothing. However, the AMT was never indexed for inflation, putting many middle-class taxpayers at risk of being ensnared by it each year.

A refundable tax credit originally enacted in 2008 for first-time home buyers was prolonged and increased in 2009. The maximum credit was raised from $7,500 to $8,000 for first-time buyers who purchased homes between Jan. 1 and Dec. 1, 2009. In addition, the requirement that the credit be paid back was eliminated, essentially converting the credit from a loan into a grant, so long as the buyers kept the home for at least three years. On November 6, shortly before the credit was to expire, President Obama signed a bill to extend it for first-time buyers entering into a contract before May 1, 2010, and closing on it before July 1.

The stimulus bill also made more poor families eligible for the refundable child tax credit; enhanced the credit for college tuition, fees, and expenses and made the credit partially refundable; boosted the earned income tax credit for working families with three or more children; exempted $2,400 of a worker's 2009 unemployment compensation from federal income tax; allowed taxpayers who bought new cars between Feb. 17, 2009, and Feb. 17, 2010, to deduct sales and excise taxes paid on those cars when calculating income taxes; and extended certain 2008 business tax breaks to the end of 2009, including a provision allowing businesses to write off a large portion of the cost of new equipment in the year it is purchased.

Cigarette taxes. On Feb. 4, 2009, President Obama signed a bill to expand funding for the State Children's Health Insurance Program by $33 billion over five years. To pay for the expansion, the federal cigarette tax was raised from 39 cents per pack to $1.01 per pack. Other tobacco taxes were also increased.   ■ Mike Lewis

Telecommunications increasingly centered on Internet use and access in 2009. In April, Dallas-based AT&T offered customers in Atlanta a netbook, a type of small, inexpensive laptop computer, for just $50—if they also signed up for an Internet plan. Meanwhile, computerlike cell phones, called smartphones, gobbled up wireless bandwidth as their users accessed more and more Internet data.

The iPhone 3GS, released in June by Cupertino, California-based Apple Inc., dominated telecom news in 2009. The new iPhone, like previous versions, featured a touchscreen, Internet browsing, and a music and video player. Upgrades included a digital compass, a video camera, and faster hardware.

Other smartphones in 2009 offered similar hardware features, but the iPhone's main advantage over its competition was its large stable of downloadable software programs, called apps. Since the first iPhone's release in 2007, programmers have created tens of thousands of apps, most of which are only available on the iPhone.

Enter the Pre. In June 2009, Sunnyvale, California-based Palm Inc. released a touchscreen-equipped smartphone called the Pre. The phone featured Internet access, a GPS (global positioning system) receiver, a camera, and the ability to play music and videos. It also featured a plastic keyboard with physical keys, unlike the iPhone's touchscreen-based keyboard. However, only a few dozen apps were available for the Pre in 2009.

A social phone. Motorola, based in Schaumburg, Illinois, released a phone called Cliq in October. The phone had similar hardware features as the iPhone and the Pre, using Mountain View, California-based Google's Android operating software. The Cliq differentiated itself from competitors by featuring functions from such social networking Web sites as Facebook and Twitter. Apps on the phone downloaded information from the Web sites automatically and constantly showed status updates from friends.

One charger for all. In October, the International Telecommunications Union (ITU) of the United Nations approved a technology standard for a universal cell phone charger. The proposed technology, based on a Universal Serial Bus (USB), was similar to the plugs used by digital cameras and could also connect to computers.

The ITU hoped the new standard would reduce the need for specialized chargers for each individual phone, helping cell phone users avoid clutter and confusion. Although cell phone manufacturers would not be legally required to adopt the charger standard, the ITU expected most manufacturers to comply.   ■ Daniel Kenis

See also **Computer; Internet.**

Television. On June 12, 2009, all full-power analog television broadcasting came to an end in the United States. Under the Digital Television Transition and Public Safety Act of 2005, all U.S. full-power broadcast television stations were to stop broadcasting on analog airwaves and begin broadcasting only in digital signals on Feb. 17, 2009. The act also established a federally sponsored digital television (DTV) converter set-top box coupon program. The program allowed each U.S. household to receive two $40 coupons to be used toward the purchase of converter boxes. President Barack Obama signed a law to change the mandatory analog cutoff date to June 12 to allow more time for the conversion.

Comcast to buy NBC Universal. General Electric and Comcast, the largest U.S. cable company, announced in December a joint venture—worth a combined $37.25 billion—that includes the sale of 51 percent of NBC Universal to Comcast. Although the deal values NBC Universal at $30 billion, neither the NBC television network nor the Universal film studio was very successful in the

PRIMETIME EMMY AWARD WINNERS IN 2009

COMEDY

Best Series: "30 Rock"
Lead Actress: Toni Collette, "United States of Tara"
Lead Actor: Alec Baldwin, "30 Rock"
Supporting Actress: Kristin Chenoweth, "Pushing Daisies"
Supporting Actor: Jon Cryer, "Two and a Half Men"

DRAMA

Best Series: "Mad Men"
Lead Actress: Glenn Close, "Damages"
Lead Actor: Bryan Cranston, "Breaking Bad"
Supporting Actress: Cherry Jones, "24"
Supporting Actor: Michael Emerson, "Lost"

OTHER AWARDS

Miniseries: "Little Dorrit"

Reality/Competition Series: "The Amazing Race"

Variety, Music, or Comedy Series: "The Daily Show with Jon Stewart"

Made for Television Movie: "Grey Gardens"

Lead Actress in a Miniseries or Movie: Jessica Lange, "Grey Gardens"

Lead Actor in a Miniseries or Movie: Brendan Gleeson, "Into the Storm"

Supporting Actress in a Miniseries or Movie: Shohreh Aghdashloo, "House of Saddam"

Supporting Actor in a Miniseries or Movie: Ken Howard, "Grey Gardens"

early 2000's. According to industry analysts, the deal, which is subject to regulatory approval, reshapes the nation's entertainment industry, giving Comcast a huge portfolio of new content.

TV and politics. President Obama was a frequent and popular figure on television in 2009. Nearly 38 million Americans watched coverage of Obama's inauguration on January 20. It was the most watched inauguration day on television since Ronald Reagan took office in 1981. On Sept. 20, 2009, Obama gave five back-to-back television interviews broadcast on CNN, NBC, ABC, CBS, and Univision focusing on health care reform. No other president had been a guest on so many Sunday talk shows at once. The following day, Obama was a guest on the "Late Show with David Letterman." It was the first time that a sitting president appeared on the show and only the second time that a sitting president appeared on a late-night talk show.

Criticism of Obama by Fox News Channel's Glenn Beck led to a boycott organized by the grass-roots group Color of Change that resulted in 80 advertisers withdrawing their commercials from "The Glenn Beck Program" by October. The controversial political commentator came under fire for calling Obama a racist during an appearance on "Fox & Friends" in July. In October, then-White House Communications Director Anita Dunn attracted controversy when she said that Fox News was a "wing of the Republican Party" and not a legitimate news organization.

David Letterman had his share of controversy in 2009. In June, the talk show host drew criticism from former Alaska governor and vice presidential candidate Sarah Palin after he made a joke about her daughter during his monologue on the "Late Show." He apologized twice on the show.

In October, Letterman revealed on his show that he was the victim of an alleged $2-million extortion attempt and had to give grand jury testimony as part of a sting operation. The blackmailer, a CBS News producer, had threatened to disclose Letterman's sexual relationships with female staff members. Letterman admitted to the relationships. The revelation gave the show a 36-percent boost in ratings. An estimated 5.7 million viewers tuned in to watch the next show as Letterman apologized to his wife and staff and joked about his situation. The National Organization for Women accused Letterman of promoting a hostile work environment.

Late-night shuffle. In May, Conan O'Brien became the host of "The Tonight Show" after the departure of host Jay Leno. O'Brien had hosted "Late Night" since 1993. Jimmy Fallon took over O'Brien's spot as host of "Late Night."

In September 2009, Leno began hosting the prime-time "Jay Leno Show." Leno had been the host of "The Tonight Show" since 1992, when he took over from Johnny Carson. "The Jay Leno Show" premiered to almost 18 million viewers, but ratings declined by the second week.

"American Idol," the country's top-rated TV show, experienced several changes to its panel of judges during its eighth season. In January 2009, singer, songwriter, and record producer Kara Dio-Guardi became the panel's fourth judge, joining judges Paula Abdul, Simon Cowell, and Randy Jackson. In August, Abdul announced that she would not be returning for the show's ninth season. In September, comedian and daytime talk show host Ellen DeGeneres was named as Abdul's replacement for the ninth season, beginning in January 2010. DeGeneres assured her studio audience that she would not be quitting "her day job." Abdul had been a judge on "American Idol" since the show's first season in 2002.

"Britain's Got Talent." Susan Boyle, a 47-year-old Scottish woman, became a worldwide sensation after her April 2009 performance on the singing competition TV show "Britain's Got Talent." The show's judges and studio audience initially snick-

TOP-RATED U.S. TELEVISION PROGRAMS

The following were the most-watched television programs for the 2008-2009 regular prime-time season, which ran from Sept. 22, 2008, to May 22, 2009.

1. "American Idol" (Wednesday) (FOX)
2. "American Idol" (Tuesday) (FOX)
3. "NBC Sunday Night Football" (NBC)
4. "Desperate Housewives" (ABC)
5. "Grey's Anatomy" (ABC)
6. "Two and a Half Men" (CBS)
7. "House" (FOX)
8. "Dancing with the Stars" (ABC)
9. "CSI" (CBS)
10. "The OT" (FOX)
11. "Lost" (ABC)
12. "Sunday Night NFL Pre-Kick" (NBC)
13. "Survivor: Gabon" (CBS)
14. "Office" (NBC)
15. "The Bachelor" (ABC)
16. "Rules of Engagement" (CBS)
17. "Survivor: Tocantins" (CBS)
18. "Biggest Loser 7" (NBC)
19. "Dancing with the Stars: Results" (ABC)
20. "CSI: Miami" (CBS)

Copyright – Nielsen Media Research, 2009.

Walter Cronkite
The Voice of the News

Walter Cronkite, the "CBS Evening News" anchor from 1962 until 1981, died in New York City on July 17, 2009. To many Americans living through the turbulent 1960's and 1970's, Cronkite was the human face of the news media. His signature sign-off, "And that's the way it is," punctuated the rhythm of daily life for millions.

Cronkite's authoritative but kindly demeanor and his confident, serene delivery put TV audiences at ease and earned their trust. When the news was bad—as in the horrific news bulletin on the afternoon of Nov. 22, 1963, that President John F. Kennedy was dead of gunshot wounds in Dallas—Cronkite spoke with quiet, authoritative dignity. To viewers, it made a difference: hearing the unthinkable from Walter Cronkite was more like getting bad news from a friend than from a stranger.

Cronkite was born on Nov. 4, 1916, in St. Joseph, Missouri. He began his journalism career by reporting for Scripps-Howard Newspapers while attending the University of Texas at Austin from 1933 to 1935. During his long career, he also worked as a newspaper correspondent both in the United States and abroad and as a radio broadcaster.

Cronkite intersected with history on many occasions. He was there—sometimes with giddy enthusiasm—for the historic early missions of NASA. When Apollo 11 astronaut Neil Armstrong first set foot on the moon on July 20, 1969, Cronkite effused, "Oh boy!" Along with the American public, he looked on as the administration of President Lyndon B. Johnson conducted a massive build-up of United States troops in the Vietnam War. Cronkite's urging of a negotiated solution in 1968, in fact, convinced President Lyndon B. Johnson that his administration had lost the public's support for the war effort.

Cronkite was at front and center in the tumultuous events of 1968—antiwar demonstrations; riots; the assassinations of civil rights leader Martin Luther King, Jr., and Democratic presidential candidate Robert F. Kennedy; the chaotic Democratic nominating convention that year in Chicago; and the historic election victory in November of Richard M. Nixon over Democratic candidate Hubert H. Humphrey and Independent candidate George C. Wallace.

Again, in the mid-1970's, Cronkite played a pivotal role in the political life of the nation by allotting unprecedented air time to the unraveling Watergate scandal. In the end, Watergate—the bungled 1972 burglary by Nixon administration operatives of Democratic campaign headquarters and its subsequent cover-up—forced Nixon's resignation on Aug. 9, 1974.

Through all of the epochal events he covered, Walter Cronkite never lost his audience and never forfeited their trust. Long after his retirement in 1981, polls continued to rank him as "the most trusted man in America."

■ Robert N. Knight

ered at the middle-aged contestant's plain looks, but all were stunned by her moving performance of "I Dreamed a Dream" from the musical *Les Misérables.* Boyle received a standing ovation from the audience and unanimous praise from the judges. Days after the show aired, a clip of Boyle's performance set a record as the most-watched video on the Internet. Although Boyle finished in second place for the series' season, she was signed to a recording contract by judge Simon Cowell. Her debut album *I Dreamed a Dream,* released in November, was 2009's top seller for a sales week.

"Jon & Kate Plus 8" minus Jon. In June, Jon and Kate Gosselin, the parents of eight children with whom they starred on the popular TLC reality show "Jon & Kate Plus 8," announced on their show that they were separating. The show was the most-watched in the network's history, with 10.6 million viewers. In October, TLC filed suit against Jon for allegedly violating his contract by making other TV appearances. He filed a counter lawsuit against the network, claiming television producers violated Pennsylvania's child labor laws in filming the show and were preventing him from working. In November, the show's title was changed to "Kate Plus Eight" and began focusing on Kate as the single mother of twins and sextuplets.

Celebreality TV. Farrah Fawcett, star of the 1970's hit "Charlie's Angels," attracted nearly 9 million viewers in May 2009 with "Farrah's Story," which she partially shot, documenting her battle with cancer. The actress died on June 25.

In September, former U.S. House Majority Leader Tom DeLay competed on "Dancing with the Stars." The indicted former congressman tied or finished in last or second-to-last place among the 16 competing couples.

Anchors away. Lou Dobbs, one of CNN's founding anchors, abruptly quit the cable network in November. Media commentators speculated that the network clashed with Dobbs over his controversial political views. The anchor said he planned to seek a political activist role. Dobbs was replaced by veteran CNN journalist John King. ABC "World News" anchor Charles Gibson retired from ABC News at the end of the year. "Good Morning America" anchor Diane Sawyer was scheduled to replace Gibson, 66, in January 2010. Gibson had been with ABC News for almost 35 years.

A "king's" farewell. A global audience of up to 1 billion people watched "King of Pop" Michael Jackson's star-studded memorial service on July 7, 2009. Jackson died on June 25 at age 50, from an accidental overdose of anesthesia administered by his physician as a sleeping medication.

Oprah Winfrey announced in November that she would end "The Oprah Winfrey Show" in September 2011, after its 25th season. Winfrey said she wanted to concentrate on her cable channel,

OWN: Oprah Winfrey Network, to launch in 2011.

Turning out the "Light." "Guiding Light," the longest-running television drama, was canceled by CBS in September due to low ratings. It began airing on the network in 1952. CBS also announced in December 2009 that its daytime drama "As the World Turns" would also be canceled due to low ratings, in September 2010. It began airing in 1956. NBC's acclaimed medical drama "ER" ended in April 2009. It won 23 Emmy Awards in its 15 seasons.

New shows. CBS hoped to fill the "ER" void with the medical drama "Three Rivers," about organ transplants as seen through the three experiences of physician, donor, and recipient. The show debuted in the fall to strong reviews. The ABC "mockumentary" situation comedy "Modern Family," about three interrelated families, also debuted in the fall to critical acclaim. Two ABC sci-fi series, "V" and "FlashForward," were two other popular fall premieres. The CW cashed in on the vampire craze with "The Vampire Diaries," which also debuted in the fall. The show was based on the book series of the same name by L. J. Smith, which began in 1991. The hit Fox musical comedy-drama "Glee," about a high school show choir, premiered in spring 2009. It was compared to the highly successful TV film franchise *High School Musical,* which began in 2006.   ■ Shawn Brennan

See also **Chicago; Popular music.**

Tennis.
Roger Federer of Switzerland won both the Championships (Wimbledon) and the French Open in 2009 to establish a new men's record of 15 Grand Slam titles. Federer reached the final in both other major events—suffering a stunning upset at the United States Open—and competed in 17 of the last 18 Grand Slam finals.

In women's tennis, American Serena Williams captured two majors, the Australian Open and Wimbledon, to bring her career total to 11 grand slam titles. Kim Clijsters of Belgium won the U.S. Open in only her third tournament back after a 2½-year retirement. Clijsters became just the third mother to win a major and the first since Evonne Goolagong Cawley of Australia in 1980. Clijsters had previously won the U.S. Open in 2005.

Australian Open. Rafael Nadal captured the first five-set men's final in 21 years, topping Federer 7-5, 3-6, 7-6 (3), 3-6, 6-2 on Feb. 1, 2009, in Melbourne. It was Nadal's first Australian Open championship. Serena Williams won her 10th career Grand Slam title with a 6-0, 6-3 demolition of Dinara Safina of Russia on January 31. The twin brothers Bob and Mike Bryan of the United States won the men's double title, sisters Serena and Venus Williams won women's doubles, and India's Sania Mirza and Mahesh Bhupathi took mixed doubles.

French Open. Federer matched American Pete Sampras's record of 14 Grand Slam titles, winning his first French Open on June 7 in Paris. Federer rolled Sweden's Robin Soderling 6-1, 7-6 (1), 6-4. Soderling had stunned Nadal, the four-time defending champion, in the fourth round. In the women's final on June 6, Russian Svetlana Kuznetsova beat Safina, who double-faulted seven times, 6-4, 6-2. Lukas Dlouhy of the Czech Republic and India's Leander Paes won the men's doubles title; Spain's Anabel Medina Garrigues and Virginia Ruano Pascual took the women's doubles title; and Americans Liezel Huber and Bob Bryan captured mixed doubles.

Wimbledon. Federer broke Sampras's record in a final Wimbledon match for the ages, outlasting American Andy Roddick in an exciting five-set final on July 5, 5-7, 7-6 (6), 7-6 (5), 3-6, 16-14. Federer served 50 aces, a career best, and the 77-game match was the longest in Grand Slam final history, topping the previous mark of 71 in the 1927 Australian Open. In an all-Williams sister final on July 4, Serena won 7-6 (3), 6-2. Canada's Daniel Nestor and Serbia's Nenad Zimonjic captured the men's doubles title; the Williams sisters took the women's doubles title; and Anna-Lena Groenefeld of Germany and Mark Knowles of the Bahamas won mixed doubles.

U.S. Open. Unheralded Juan Martín del Potro shocked the tennis world by upsetting Federer on September 14 in the U.S. Open in New York City. Del Potro, of Argentina, trailed 2 sets to 1 and was two points from defeat before rallying for a 3-6, 7-6 (5), 4-6, 7-6 (4), 6-2 victory. Federer, who was trying to become the first man in eight decades to win six straight U.S. Opens, had won 40 straight tournament matches since 2003.

In the women's final, unseeded Kim Clijsters captured her second title, the last being in 2005, with a 7-5, 6-3 victory over ninth-seeded Caroline Wozniacki of Denmark on September 13. Clijsters had upset second-seeded Serena Williams in the semifinals after Williams was penalized a point on match point for verbal abuse of a lines-woman. It was her second code violation of the match. Williams was upset with a double fault call a point earlier that gave Clijsters match point. Dlouhy and

Roger Federer of Switzerland leaps for joy after defeating Andy Roddick of the United States to win the men's singles title at Wimbledon in a classic five-set match on July 5, 2009. The victory gave Federer his 15th career grand slam singles title, breaking the record of 14 championships held by Pete Sampras of the United States.

Paes won the men's doubles, the Williams sisters won the women's doubles, and Americans Carly Gullickson and Travis Parrott won mixed doubles.

Davis Cup. Spain repeated as Davis Cup champion, defeating the Czech Republic 5-0 at Barcelona, Spain, on December 4-6. It was Spain's fourth cup victory since 2000. Nadal and David Ferrer each won two singles matches. Feliciano Lopez and Fernando Verdasco won the doubles match. Beginning in 1999, Spain has won 18 consecutive Davis Cup matches at home.

■ Michael Kates

See also **People in the news** (Bob and Mike Bryan).

Terrorism. A number of significant changes in terrorist activities occurred in 2009. Much of South Asia experienced sharp increases in the number of attacks and fatalities. In Sri Lanka, however, an insurgency that had lasted for almost three decades ended when the government announced a military defeat of the Liberation Tigers of Tamil Eelam (known as the Tamil Tigers). Violent incidents declined in East Africa and the Middle East, except in Iraq, where bombings and other acts of terrorism continued at about the same level, and in Somalia and Yemen, where terrorist and counterterrorist attacks escalated.

South Asia. Pakistan remained a terrorist battleground with a steady increase in suicide attacks. Suicide bombers targeted crowded areas in the streets, bazaars, universities, mosques, and hotels. Many of the assaults were attributed to the Pakistani Taliban and other militant Islamist groups. One of the most deadly attacks occurred on March 27 in a mosque in the town of Jamrud, where about 50 worshipers were killed and more than 100 others were wounded.

Violence surged in April, when Pakistani forces launched a counterinsurgency campaign against militants in the Swat district of the North-West Frontier Province. However, October and November were Pakistan's deadliest months, with 15 incidents that resulted in the deaths of more than 400 people. On October 9, a suicide terrorist detonated his explosive-filled minibus in Peshawar, killing over 50 people. In two other attacks, one in the Swat district on October 12 and the other at the International Islamic University in Islamabad on October 20, suicide terrorists killed 47 people. The worst attack in Peshawar took place on October 28, when a car bomb ravaged a busy market, leaving more than 100 people dead and about 200 injured. Terrorists attacked Rawalpindi's high-security zone on October 30, November 2, and November 27, killing a total of 82 people and injuring more than 160 others.

Violence escalated in eastern India, where Maoist guerrillas known as Naxalites have battled the government since the late 1960's. The Maoists have gained support in 20 states among poor tribal peoples who fear losing their land to developers. According to the Indian government, some 1,400 rebel attacks were responsible for more than 600 deaths in 2009. In India's easternmost state of Assam, the United Liberation Front of Asom (ULFA), a separatist group, was believed to be responsible for several attacks.

Sri Lanka experienced a series of terrorist attacks from January to May, when the government took control of the entire island and killed the leader of the Tamil Tigers. On January 2, a suicide bomber killed 3 people and wounded 37 others in Colombo. Sri Lankan soldiers were attacked twice in early February, when a bomb on a bus carrying soldiers was detonated in Colombo and when a female suicide bomber detonated her belt in Vishvamadu. About 30 people were killed and more than 100 others were injured. On March 10, 14 people were killed and 41 others were wounded in a suicide attack in southern Sri Lanka.

Southeast Asia. Three southern provinces in Thailand underwent a spike in insurgency in 2009. On March 19, a roadside bomb believed to have been placed by a Muslim insurgent group killed four soldiers in Pattani. Six soldiers were injured a week later in an explosion in Yala. On June 8, 10 worshipers were killed and a dozen injured in a mosque in Narathwat.

In the Philippines, clashes between terrorists and government forces continued on the island of Mindanao, where an Islamic-based insurgency has long sought independence. On August 12, at least 31 suspected terrorists and 23 soldiers were killed when government troops stormed the training camps of the militant group Abu Sayyaf. Ten members of the Moro Islamic Liberation Front, a larger, somewhat more moderate group, were among the terrorists killed in the assault.

Africa. Somalia continued to be wracked by violence between the Somali government, an Islamist group called al-Shabab, and Ethiopian troops called in to aid the government. On January 24, a car bomb killed 15 civilians and a police officer in the capital, Mogadishu. In the same city on May 24, seven people, including six police officers, died when a suicide terrorist detonated his car near a police station. Another suicide attack on June 18 in Beled Weyne killed Somalia's minister of security, Colonel Umar Hashi Adan, as well as 19 other victims. The al-Shabab group claimed responsibility for the attack.

Middle East. Civil strife in Yemen has made that country increasingly vulnerable to terrorist activities. Militants of al-Qa`ida have allegedly been using Yemen as a new base for recruitment and training. On March 15 near Shibam, a suicide bomber killed five people, including four South Korean tourists, and injured four more. Another terrorist attack in Sanaa three days later targeted South Korean officials who were investigating the previous attack. No injuries were reported.

Christmas attack. On December 25, a Nigerian man attempted to detonate an explosive aboard a transatlantic Northwest Airlines flight as the plane prepared to land in Detroit. The device, which the man had sneaked onto the aircraft, failed to go off properly, and none of the 278 people aboard were seriously hurt, except the attacker. ■ Richard E. Rubenstein

See also **Afghanistan; Aviation; India; Iraq; Pakistan; Philippines; Russia; Sri Lanka.**

Thailand. Supporters of former Prime Minister Thaksin Shinawatra calling themselves the United Front for Democracy Against Dictatorship (UDD) demonstrated against Thailand's government in 2009. The UDD accused Prime Minister Abhisit Vejjajiva of being controlled by the country's military and demanded that he step down.

The protests began in late March in the capital, Bangkok. Abhisit's office was blockaded for three weeks by tens of thousands of UDD protesters. Ousted by the army in 2006, Thaksin lived abroad to avoid a jail sentence for corruption. He called in 2009 for "a people's revolution."

On April 11, UDD protesters pushed past military and police personnel and forced their way into a convention center at Pattaya, a Thai beach resort. Abhisit was forced to cancel a summit meeting of the Association of Southeast Asian Nations (ASEAN) being held at the resort. ASEAN leaders had gathered to discuss the regional impact of global economic problems. They were forced to flee the meeting site by helicopter and boat.

The next day, Abhisit declared a state of emergency. The army moved in to end the demonstrations, sparking clashes that left 2 people dead and more than 100 others injured. Thaksin urged a peaceful end to the protests, and protest leaders told people to go home. The demonstrations ended on April 14, but tensions remained high between bureaucratic and business elites in Bangkok and Thaksin's rural and lower-class supporters.

Separatist violence flared again in 2009 in four provinces at the southern tip of Thailand. Ethnic Malay Muslims there sought autonomy from the ethnic Thai Buddhist majority. Since the Thai army began fighting insurgents in 2004, more than 3,000 people had died in the region. A January 2009 report by the London-based human rights organization Amnesty International alleged that security forces "systematically engage in torture" in seeking information about insurgents.

A group known as the National Revolutionary Front-Coordinate was reported to have drawn students from Islamic schools in the south to develop a force estimated at 1,800 to 3,000 fighters facing 60,000 soldiers, police, and militia. The fighters targeted symbols of Thai authority, killing Buddhist schoolteachers and government officials, as well as Muslims thought to be government spies. After an army crackdown appeared to have reduced violence, each side blamed the other for a June 8 mosque shooting that left at least 10 people dead and at least 12 others wounded.   ■ Henry S. Bradsher

See also **Asia; Disasters; Myanmar; Terrorism.**

Protesters in Bangkok attack a car carrying Prime Minister Abhisit Vejjajiva on April 12, 2009. The protesters called for Abhisit to step down, alleging that his government was under the control of the country's military.

Theater. Many theaters in the United States, Canada, and the United Kingdom showed signs of financial recovery during 2009. The improvement was a welcome relief from the steep economic downturn that began in late 2008 and caused a number of shows and resident theater companies to close their doors.

According to Patrick Healy of *The New York Times,* Broadway enjoyed its strongest fall season in recent years, due in large part to the success of three hit plays. Two of the three—*God of Carnage* by Yasmina Reza and *A Steady Rain* by Keith Huff—broke box-office records in October 2009 with weekly grosses of $1 million apiece. Exceptionally high grosses are usually associated with such big-budget Broadway musicals as *Billy Elliot,* which received the 2009 Tony Award for best musical, and the long-running *The Lion King,* directed by Julie Taymor. The third play to generate such robust figures was *Hamlet,* starring Jude Law as the melancholy Danish prince. By mid-October, the production had generated receipts totaling more than $20 million.

The National Theatre in London enjoyed its highest attendance figures in seven years, according to a report by Louise Jury in the *London Evening Standard.* More than 800,000 ticket buyers attended the National's 25 productions. *War Horse,* which is adapted from the novel by the English children's author Michael Morpurgo, earned £2.7 million at the box office and played to 99-percent capacity.

War Horse, which takes place during World War I (1914-1918), tells the story of Albert, the son of an English farmer, whose horse is sold to the cavalry and shipped to the battlefields of France. Albert risks his life in the trenches to find the horse and bring him home. The Olivier Award-winning production featured life-sized puppets created by the Handspring Puppet Company. The surplus generated by the National's successful season will be used to develop an educational center at the theater.

Stratford. In Canada, the renowned Stratford Shakespeare Festival also reported rebounding sales, which it described as a "dramatic turnaround." In April 2009, the theater announced that it was putting 30 performances on hold due to fears about the weakened economy, but those performances were subsequently reinstated in the wake of more promising sales. Although sales were stronger than expected, they were still roughly 25,000 tickets short of the previous year's figure of 534,000 tickets sold. In addition to improved sales by the end of the season in early November, the company's fiscal concerns were further allayed by provincial and federal government subsidies to the festival totaling $3.5 million to support marketing at the festival.

Doors closed. Not all theaters fared as well. The critically acclaimed Catalyst Theater Company in Washington, D.C., which, according to its mission statement, produced "plays that reflect a moment of remarkable change in the world view of the culture from which they were written," was forced to disband due to financial troubles. The theater's move from a 50-seat facility into a larger venue in late 2008 strained the company's budget and caused it to fold. At the end of 2009, the company was attempting to raise money to settle $20,000 in outstanding debts.

God of Carnage. In addition to its box office success, *God of Carnage,* at the Bernard Jacobs Theater on Broadway, garnered widespread critical acclaim and received the 2009 Tony Award for best play. *God of Carnage,* translated from the French by Christopher Hampton, examines the tensions and violent emotions that lurk just beneath the surface of civilized social interactions.

As Ben Brantley wrote in his review of the show in *The New York Times,* "Examined coldly, this 90-minute play about two couples who meet to discuss a playground fight between two of their children isn't much more than a sustained Punch and Judy show, dressed to impress with sociological accessories. But there's a reason that Punch and Judy's avatars have fascinated audiences for so many centuries." Brantley likened the eruptive drama to Edward Albee's now-classic 1962 drama of warring married couples, *Who's Afraid of Virginia Woolf?*

On Broadway, the four-character play starred James Gandolfini, Hope Davis, Jeff Daniels, and Marcia Gay Harden, who won the 2009 Tony for best performance by a leading actress. The play was first performed in English at the Gielgud Theatre in London, with Ralph Fiennes, Tamsin Greig, Janet McTeer, and Ken Stott. That production won the 2009 Olivier Award for best new comedy. In November 2009, the original cast of the Broadway production, directed by Matthew Warchus, was replaced by Jimmy Smits, Annie Potts, Christine Lahti, and Stott.

The author, Yasmina Reza, is a French playwright, actress, novelist, and screenwriter, whose work has appeared to wide acclaim previously on Broadway. Her other plays include *Life x 3* (performed on Broadway in 2003) and the Tony Award-winning *Art* (1998).

Hollywood on Broadway. Gandolfini received enthusiastic notices for his performance in *God of Carnage,* despite being more widely known as a television and film actor than as a stage actor. As Peter Marks pointed out in *The Washington Post,* Broadway plays in 2009 were increasingly populated by star actors from Hollywood. "More and more," Marks wrote, "actors who have made their names in TV and movies turn up—maybe to prove their suc-

cess is not a function of crafty camera work. Or because producers know their fame translates into dollars."

The lineup of celebrated film actors who appeared on Broadway in 2009 included Jane Fonda *(33 Variations),* Joan Allen and Jeremy Irons *(Impressionism),* Geoffrey Rush and Susan Sarandon *(Exit the King),* Daniel Craig and Hugh Jackman *(A Steady Rain),* Rupert Everett and Angela Lansbury *(Blithe Spirit),* and Catherine

Rupert Everett and Angela Lansbury take a bow following the opening-night performance of Noel Coward's *Blithe Spirit* on March 15, 2009. The 83-year-old Lansbury picked up her fifth Tony Award for her portrayal of Madame Arcati.

Zeta-Jones (*A Little Night Music*). Although many of these stars have distinguished themselves as stage actors as well, their box-office draw derives in large part from the fame they have achieved though major roles on the big screen.

A long road to the stage for Spider-Man. Further evidence of the important role played by Hollywood in the commercial theater in 2009 was the ill-fated production of *Spider-Man: Turn Off the Dark,* based on the three Sony motion pictures about the superhero, starring Toby McGuire as the web-slinging Spider-Man. One of the most anticipated productions of spring 2010, *Spider-Man* was reportedly the most expensive production in Broadway history, with a budget of $52 million. The show was scheduled to begin previews in February 2010, but a number of delays left the fate of the production uncertain. According to John Horn, writing in the *Los Angeles Times,* the musical needed to raise $24 million to meet its initial costs, which included the renovation and restoration of the Hilton Theatre on Broadway.

The artistic team included the director Julie Taymor, whose imaginative production of *The Lion King* has grossed $3.6 billion worldwide since it opened in 1997. The music was in the hands of Bono and guitarist the Edge (David Howell Evans), both members of the Irish rock group U2, whose worldwide record sales total 145 million copies.

The story begins with New York City in ruins, as Spider-Man (whose real name is Peter Parker, a high school student) battles a villain named Arachne. One of the most striking effects planned for the production featured Spider-Man swinging out over the audience as he battles a host of criminals. Signed on to the cast by December 2009 were Reeve Carney as Spider-Man; Evan Rachel Wood as Mary Jane, Peter Parker's romantic interest; and Alan Cumming as Spider-Man's enemy Green Goblin.

The longest-running show. *The Phantom of the Opera,* which has run longer than any other show in Broadway history, reached a new milestone on September 17—its 9,000th performance at the Majestic Theatre. The original production opened at Her Majesty's Theatre in London on Oct. 9, 1986. *Phantom* features a score by Andrew Lloyd Webber. The show, based on the 1910 French novel *Le Fantôme de l'Opéra* by Gaston Leroux, has grossed more than $740 million, another Broadway record. In 2009, there were 10 productions of the musical playing throughout the world, from Hungary and Japan to Argentina and South Korea. More than 100 million people have attended a production of the show in 144 cities and 27 countries. Only *Les Misérables* has run longer in London's West End. ■ David Yezzi

Togo. See Africa.

Tonga. See Pacific Islands.

Toronto. Rising unemployment and sluggish home sales showed in January 2009 just how hard the worldwide recession had hit Toronto over the previous year. The city's 7.8-percent unemployment rate was almost 2 percentage points higher than January 2008 figures. In the region's normally bustling real estate market, January 2009 housing sales fell to 2,670, compared with 5,075 in January 2008; and the average house price fell to about $344,000, compared with $374,000 a year earlier (all figures are in Canadian dollars). Toronto economists consider the housing trade a reliable indicator of the health of the area's overall economy.

The real estate market appeared to be recovering by October 2009. Home prices rebounded, and sales were up 34 percent compared with October 2008. With unemployment still hovering around 8 percent, however, the city's financial picture remained uncertain.

Transit progress. On April 1, 2009, Ontario Premier Dalton McGuinty announced that the province would provide $9 billion for the construction of new transit facilities in Toronto and in the suburban York region to the north of the city. McGuinty's announcement had been preceded by years of haggling over the amount each level of government—municipal, provincial, and federal—should contribute to new transit lines. McGuinty committed the province to paying almost the full cost of four new transit facilities and two-thirds of the cost of a fifth. The new facilities are a part of Toronto's comprehensive Transit City plan and the regional transit program developed by Metrolinx, a provincial agency. Toronto officials said they hoped the plan would promote investment and reduce traffic and pollution.

Strike. On June 22, unions representing 30,000 inside and outside civic workers went on strike. The strikers' main concerns were job security and the city's insistence on a reduction in sick-pay benefits. Toronto residents began depositing uncollected garbage in public parks and scrambling to make alternative arrangements for day care and summer recreational programs. McGuinty refused to order the strikers back to work, as he had with earlier strikes in basic services, and Mayor David Miller chose not to order binding arbitration, which would have imposed a settlement on both sides. The strike dragged on for 39 days before a negotiated settlement was reached.

On September 25, Mayor Miller, who had been actively assembling a campaign team for the civic election in 2010, announced that he would not seek a third term.

Flu outbreak. The H1N1 flu pandemic started mildly in Toronto in 2009, with 313 cases being reported through May—none of them fatal. But on October 26, Evan Frustaglio, a 13-year-old boy, collapsed and died less than 48 hours after he first complained of a sore throat. Health officials attributed his death to the H1N1, or swine flu, virus.

Earlier in October, Toronto public health authorities decided to establish vaccination clinics that could accommodate large numbers of people, rather than attempt to distribute vials of serum to thousands of physicians around the region. Following Frustaglio's death, long lines formed at the clinics. By October 29, the clinics had been overwhelmed and began to run short of vaccine. Authorities issued an advisory that only members of priority groups—primarily pregnant women and small children—should get the shots.

By early November, the city's clinics were functioning effectively. In December, officials reported that more than 1,200 H1N1 cases, and 19 deaths, had been confirmed in Toronto since August.

Film festival home. On September 9, ceremonies were held to mark the completion of the first stage of the Bell Lightbox, a building that will become the permanent headquarters for the prestigious Toronto International Film Festival. Festival officials predicted that their new headquarters—a glass-covered 5-story building with five state-of-the-art theaters, topped by a 41-story condominium tower—would be finished by late 2010 or early 2011. ■ David Lewis Stein

See also **City; Public Health: A Special Report.**

Toys and games. Toy manufacturers and retailers continued to focus in 2009 on assuring the safety of children's toys and games. After an apparent lapse in monitoring adherence to United States toy safety standards allowed some noncompliant toys to be sold in 2007, the industry took steps to restore consumer confidence. In February 2009, the Consumer Product Safety Improvement Act went into effect, strengthening the U.S. toy safety system. Toy makers in 2009 continued to capture key youth lifestyle trends and translate them into toys.

Hot hamsters and exploding spheres. One of the hottest toy lines of the holiday season was Zhu Zhu Pets, made by St. Louis-based Cepia LLC. The battery-operated hamsters squeak, coo, and scurry about. In December, a consumer Web site reported that one of the toys—Mister Squiggles—had a slightly higher level of the heavy metal antimony than that approved by the U.S. Consumer Product Safety Commission (CPSC). The CPSC reaffirmed that the toy met federal safety standards, noting that it did not recognize the test used by the Web site to determine chemical levels.

Bakugan Battle Brawlers, sold by Spin Master of Toronto in 2008, were back with new accessories. The game involves cards and action figures that children love to collect. The toys' name comes from the Japanese words *baku* (to explode) and *gan* (sphere), in which the figures are hidden.

Move your feet. Elmo's Tickle Hands, by the Fisher-Price division of Mattel, Inc., in El Segundo, California, encourages children to "get up and move." When a child puts on the fuzzy red hands, presses Elmo's nose, and touches any surface, the hands start to "tickle" (vibrate). Elmo also sings a song to go with the "Tickle Hand Groove" dance. A DVD shows all the moves.

Smart Fit Park, also by Fisher-Price, has been compared to a Wii Fit for kids. A play mat plugs into a home television set and provides learning games and races. Children can run and jump in place while they learn letters, shapes, and colors.

Virtual worlds. Toys tied to child-safe virtual worlds continued to be popular in 2009. The Dora Links doll by Mattel, an older version of Dora the Explorer, connects to a computer for online play. As a child changes Dora's features online, the doll's features change, too: her hair grows and her eyes change color. Dora and her friends share adventures in their virtual Puerto Verde world.

Spin Master introduced the Liv line of dolls in July. Four teenagers come with interchangeable wigs and accessories. A code provided with purchase gives online access to the dolls' personalities, life stories, diaries, and virtual closets.

Make it yourself. Printies Design Studio, by Hong Kong-based Techno Source, allows kids to make their own stuffed toys. Children can use their home computer to design, color, and size a stuffed toy online. They print it on special fabric sheets using an inkjet printer and stuff it to make their own toy sea creatures, jungle animals, and pets.

Children who love to build can make and fix things with Fisher-Price's Handy Manny's Repair Shop, based on the "Handy Manny" television show. Kids can slide a project into the diagnostic center and hear instructions for completing more than 20 projects. Tools and parts are reusable.

Science. Ever-popular dinosaurs continued in 2009 to encourage children to learn about science firsthand. Xtractaurs by Mattel features dinosaur action figures with specific attributes. A child can "extract" a dinosaur's DNA to a home computer and manipulate it to create hybrid dinosaurs that can be used in online games.

Many classic toys and games made a comeback in 2009, often coinciding with a movie release. A new generation discovered *Where the Wild Things Are* and the Transformers in films, toys, and other products. Both Barbie and the Little People toy lines turned 50; G.I. Joe returned to fight Cobra at 45; and the Mighty Morphin Power Rangers marked their 25th anniversary with new and retro figures. In 2009, children rediscovered classic games, but with a twist. Clue by Hasbro, Incorporated, of Pawtucket, Rhode Island, provided clues that arrived via text messages. ■ Adrienne Citrin

See also **Electronic games.**

Usain Bolt of Jamaica wins the 200-meter race at the World Athletics Championships on Aug. 20, 2009, in Berlin, setting a world record of 19.19 seconds. Earlier in the meet, Bolt had set another world record by winning the 100-meter race in 9.58 seconds on August 16.

WORLD TRACK AND FIELD RECORDS ESTABLISHED IN 2009

Event	Holder	Country	Where set	Date	Record
WOMEN INDOOR					
5,000 meters	Meseret Defar	Ethiopia	Stockholm, Sweden	February 18	14:24.37
Pole vault	Yelena Isinbayeva	Russia	Donetsk, Ukraine	February 15	5.0 m
MEN OUTDOOR					
100 meters	Usain Bolt	Jamaica	Berlin, Germany	August 16	9.58
200 meters	Usain Bolt	Jamaica	Berlin, Germany	August 20	19.19
10 kilometers	Micah Kipkemboi Kogo	Kenya	Brunssum, Netherlands	March 29	27:01
15 kilometers	Deriba Merga	Ethiopia	Ras al Khaymah, United Arab Emirates	February 20	*41:29
30 kilometers	Haile Gebrselassie	Ethiopia	Berlin, Germany	September 20	†1:27:49
	Samuel Kiplimo Kosgei	Kenya	Berlin, Germany	September 20	†1:27:49
4X1,500-meter relay	Kenya	Kenya	Brussels, Belgium	September 4	†14:36.23
WOMEN OUTDOOR					
Pole vault	Yelena Isinbayeva	Russia	Zurich, Switzerland	August 28	†5.06 m
Hammer throw	Anita Wlodarczyk	Poland	Berlin, Germany	August 22	77.96 m

m = meters
* = tied existing world record
† = not yet ratified   Source: International Association of Athletics Federations (IAAF).

Track and field. Sprinter Usain Bolt of Jamaica shattered his own world records in both the 100-meter and 200-meter sprints during the 2009 season. The two records firmly established Bolt as the fastest man on the planet and led many veteran track observers to wonder just how much lower the man could move the marks.

World championships. In the 100-meter sprint at the World Championships in Berlin, Germany, on August 16, Bolt finished in 9.58 seconds, trimming 0.11 second off the mark he had established at the 2008 Beijing Olympic Games. The 0.11 second was one of the largest chunks of time ever shaved off the world record for this event.

Bolt lowered his 200-meter mark, also set in Beijing, by 0.11 second by running a time of 19.19 seconds on August 20, 2009. Bolt captured a third gold medal on August 22, running the third leg in the 4x100-meter relay. Jamaica failed to break the world record of 37.10 seconds also set by Jamaica in the 2008 Olympics but still won the event in 37.31 seconds.

Anita Wlodarczyk of Poland joined Bolt as the only athlete to set a world record in the world championships. Wlodarczyk set a new world mark in the women's hammer throw with a toss of 255 feet, 9 inches (77.96 meters) on August 22.

Other highlights of the championships, which ran from August 15 to August 23, included American runner Sanya Richards winning her first gold medals in a major meet (400 meters, 4x400-meter relay), and two gold medals each for Americans Allyson Felix (200 meters and 4x400-meter relay) and LaShawn Merritt (400 meters and 4x400-meter relay). Also, Bai Xue became the first Chinese woman to win the world championship in the marathon.

The United States topped the medal standings with 10 gold medals (22 medals overall). Jamaica finished second with 7 gold medals and 13 overall.

Simply Golden. Sanya Richards, Russian pole vaulter Yelena Isinbayeva, and Ethiopian distance runner Kenenisa Bekele split the $1-million Golden League jackpot by winning their events in all six of their European meets, concluding with the meet on September 4 at the Memorial Van Damme in Brussels, Belgium. Richards cruised to victory in the 400-meter run with a time of 48.83 seconds, more than 1.5 seconds ahead of her nearest competitor. Isinbayeva only needed a vault of 15 feet, 5 inches (4.7 meters) to beat Poland's Monika Pyrek. Bekele outkicked fellow Ethiopian Imane Merga to win the 5,000 meters.

Usain Bolt did not compete in every one of the Golden League meets. As a result, he was ineligible for the jackpot.

Other records. Isinbayeva established new pole vault records in both indoor and outdoor competition in 2009. She set the new outdoor mark of 16 feet, 7 1/4 inches (5.06 meters) on August 28 at a meet in Zurich, Switzerland. Isinbayeva set the new indoor mark of 16 feet, 4 3/4 inches (5.0 meters) on February 15 in Donetsk, Ukraine. Meseret Defar of Ethiopia broke the women's 5,000-meter indoor record on February 18 in Stockholm, Sweden, finishing with a time of 14 minutes 24.37 seconds.

Doping. Justin Gatlin, who received a four-year ban in 2008 for testing positive for stimulants in 2006, settled a civil suit against the U.S. Anti-Doping Agency, the U.S. Olympic Committee, USA Track and Field, and the International Association of Athletics Federations in February 2009. Gatlin sued, saying he was being discriminated against and claiming the positive test was the result of medication he took for attention deficit disorder. He can return to racing in July 2010.

Athanasia Tsoumeleka of Greece, the 2004 Olympic champion race walker, and Rashid Ramzi of Bahrain, the 2008 Olympic gold medalist in the 1,500 meters, awaited their fates in late 2009 after positive doping test results were revealed.   ■ Michael Kates

Transit. See Transportation.

Transportation. The economic recession that continued in the United States through 2009 had a positive effect on U.S. transportation spending.

The economic stimulus package. On Feb. 17, 2009, President Barack Obama signed the American Recovery and Reinvestment Act (ARRA). The bill was one of the largest economic recovery programs since President Franklin Roosevelt's New Deal in the 1930's.

The ARRA included an approximate total of $48 billion for infrastructure projects overseen by the U.S. Department of Transportation (DOT). Of that, around $27 billion was allotted for such projects as highways and bridges. The federal government wanted ARRA money to be spent quickly, to put as many unemployed workers as possible back on the job and to put money into the economy as quickly as possible. The government requested that priority be given to projects that were *shovel-ready*—that is, already planned and ready to begin. Much of the ARRA transportation money was, therefore, allocated to projects repairing infrastructure already in place.

According to the Internet site Pro Publica, as of September 2009, the DOT had spent around $3 billion, had allocated around $25 billion, and had approximately $20 billion left to spend of its ARRA money.

In addition to providing much-needed work for the construction industry, government money spent on transportation infrastructure was likely to give a good return on investment. An economist writing for Moody's Investment Services, which provides investment research and credit ratings, estimated the likely one-year contribution to gross domestic product (GDP) created by varying types of stimulus spending. The Moody's estimate was that such spending as a tax rebate would generate a boost to GDP of $1.22 for every $1.00 spent, whereas spending on infrastructure generated $1.59 for every $1.00 spent. (GDP is the value of all goods and services produced in a country during a given period.)

One troubling feature of the transportation stimulus spending was highlighted in *The New York Times* on July 8, 2009. According to the paper's analysis, a disproportionate amount of the money was being spent in rural areas. The 100 largest metropolitan areas in the United States contribute three-quarters of the nation's economic activity, yet less than half the transportation stimulus money was being spent in urban areas. Transportation stimulus money spent in areas where fewer people lived provided jobs, but the economic value of the infrastructure was lower.

High-speed rail. The stimulus package had $8 billion in transportation money for the wide-scale development of high-speed rail. President Obama promised to seek another $5 billion over the next five years, bringing the total amount being budgeted for high-speed rail to $13 billion.

The DOT defined high-speed rail as trains capable of traveling more than 110 miles (177 kilometers) per hour. Based on even this rather slow definition, the United States was far behind Europe and Japan in modern train service. Currently in the United States, only small sections of track on Amtrak's Acela lines in the densely populated Northeast corridor permit speeds of more than 100 miles (160 kilometers) per hour. The average speed on most Acela routes, however, is actually around 70 to 80 miles (112 to 129 kilometers) per hour due to track limitations. By comparison, Japan's Shinkansen high-speed trains are capable of traveling at speeds of up to 185 miles (300 kilometers) per hour over some 1,500 miles (2,400 kilometers) of rail lines.

The Obama administration had identified 10 corridors in the United States that held potential for high-speed rail projects: California (San Francisco to San Diego); Pacific Northwest (Vancouver, British Columbia, to Eugene, Oregon); South Central (Tulsa, Oklahoma, to San Antonio); Gulf Coast (Houston to Atlanta); the Chicago hub (Chicago to a number of cities, including Minneapolis; Kansas City, Kansas; and St. Louis); Florida (Orlando to Miami); Keystone (Philadelphia to Pittsburgh); Empire (New York City to Buffalo, New York); and Northern New England (Boston to Montreal, Canada). However, $13 billion was only a starting point for such projects in the United States. The cost of completing a line between San Francisco

and Los Angeles, for example, was estimated to be $30 billion to $40 billion.

The need for maintenance. The importance of maintaining transportation infrastructure was highlighted in a 2009 report published by the Transportation Research Board (TRB) of the National Academies. In its 2009 update to "Critical Issues in Transportation," the TRB stated, "to maintain for the next 20 years the condition and performance of the nation's huge inventory of roads and transit systems, given their current and projected use, would cost ... approximately $95 billion per year." The actual amount dedicated to infrastructure maintenance, however, was around $80 billion per year in the 2000's. Given the ongoing shortfall that had occurred in transportation spending, the nearly $50 billion allocated in 2009 was a helpful start on a major backlog of deferred maintenance.

■ Christine Sullivan

Trinibad and Tobago. See Latin America; West Indies.

Tunisia. See Africa.

Billionaire investor Warren E. Buffett (above) announced on November 3 that his investment company, Berkshire Hathaway, was buying the 77.4 percent of Burlington Northern Santa Fe (BNSF) Railroad that it did not already own. The price was $26 billion in cash and stock, the largest deal in Berkshire history. "It's an all-in wager on the economic future of the United States," Buffett declared.

Turkey. United States President Barack Obama visited Turkey in April 2009 to deliver his first speech addressing Muslims worldwide. In the Turkish Grand National Assembly (parliament), President Obama told his televised audience, "The United States is not, and will never be, at war with Islam." He emphasized that the U.S. relationship with the Muslim world would be based on "mutual interests and mutual respect."

President Obama stated that he would maintain U.S. support for Turkey's bid to become a member of the European Union (EU). He also raised the contentious issue of the killings of Armenians by Turkish soldiers in 1915, noting that "the United States strongly supports the full normalization of relations between Turkey and Armenia." The Armenian government claims that Turks purposely massacred more than 1 million Armenians in 1915, but Turkish officials maintain that the Armenians died as a result of civil strife.

Anger over Armenian statements. In late April 2009, the Turkish government complained to U.S. Ambassador James Jeffrey about comments made by President Obama in Washington, D.C. In the comments, President Obama referred to the 1915 Armenian killings as "one of the greatest atrocities of the 20th century."

Also in April 2009, the Turkish government recalled its ambassador to Canada to protest participation by Canadian officials in a ceremony commemorating the 1915 Armenian killings as *genocide* (systematic extermination of a cultural or racial group).

Turkey-Armenia protocols. In October 2009, the foreign ministers of Turkey and Armenia signed two protocols establishing diplomatic and bilateral relations. The ministers also pledged to establish a joint commission of historians to investigate the 1915 Armenian killings. After the signing, the protocols were submitted to the parliaments of both countries for ratification.

Other controversial issues arose between Turkey and the West in 2009. Turkish officials threatened to back out of the Nabucco pipeline project—scheduled to carry natural gas across Turkey from the Caspian Sea to Europe by 2014—if the EU did not make progress on Turkey's application for membership. Many Western governments expressed disappointment when Turkey congratulated Iranian President Mahmoud Ahmadinejad on his highly disputed victory in June 2009 presidential elections. However, Western officials applauded Turkey's success in persuading Iran to release five members of the British embassy staff in Iran who had been arrested and accused of playing a role in postelection unrest. ■ Mary-Jane Deeb

See also **Armenia; Europe; Iran; Islam.**

Turkmenistan. See Asia.

Tuvalu. See Pacific Islands.

Uganda. During 2009, the Ugandan government repeatedly ruled out further peace talks with the rebel Lord's Resistance Army (LRA). The government, headed by President Yoweri Museveni and his National Resistance Movement (NRM), said that it saw no point in renewing talks. The two sides had settled on the terms of a peace agreement to end more than 20 years of fighting. They were supposed to sign it in April 2008, but LRA leader Joseph Kony remained in hiding and did not sign. The International Criminal Court (ICC) in The Hague, the Netherlands, called for Kony's immediate arrest in July 2009, saying that he would never make peace.

Cross-border attack. On March 16, the Uganda People's Defence Force (UPDF), Uganda's armed forces, ended a three-month assault on LRA bases in neighboring Congo (Kinshasa). The operation disrupted the LRA command structure but failed to capture Kony. Congolese and Sudanese forces joined the UPDF in the attack, called Operation Lightning Thunder. LRA fighters had killed some 1,000 civilians, mostly Congolese, from September 2008 to March 2009. The UPDF had pushed the LRA out of most of northern Uganda in 2008. However, the rebels then set up new bases in southern Sudan and in Congo (Kinshasa), as well as farther away in the Central African Republic.

Anti-Museveni protests. On Aug. 18, 2009, Ugandan police arrested 10 members of the Forum for Democratic Change (FDC), Uganda's leading opposition party. The FDC members were arrested for protesting President Museveni's decision to reappoint the members of the nation's Electoral Commission ahead of the 2011 presidential elections. Opposition leaders said that the commission, which supervises elections in Uganda, was biased in favor of the National Resistance Movement. The NRM has governed Uganda under Museveni since it seized power in 1986.

Members of the Ganda, the country's largest ethnic group, clashed with the police in three days of riots starting on Sept. 10, 2009. The rioters burned vehicles and property near a police station in Kampala, the capital. Twenty-four people were killed in and around the city—most of them shot by the security forces. The rioters protested that security forces had blocked Kabaka Ronald Muwenda Mutebi II, the king of Buganda, from a planned visit to Kayunga District northeast of Kampala. Buganda is a region in south-central Uganda. At least 29 of the rioters were charged with terrorism relating to the violence. Successive Ugandan governments have tried to undermine the traditional authority of the kings of Uganda's major ethnic groups.

Simon Baynham

See also **Africa; Congo (Kinshasa).**

Ukraine. Gas-price disputes with Russia and political turmoil plagued Ukraine again in 2009. In addition, the country's struggling economy was hit hard by the global financial crisis.

Gas dispute. Russian state-run gas company Gazprom cut off gas supplies intended for the Ukrainian domestic market on January 1, after the two nations were unable to agree on a price for the gas. Gazprom stopped gas shipments to Ukraine entirely on January 7, accusing Ukraine's state-run gas company, Naftogaz, of siphoning off gas intended for Russia's European customers. The European Union, whose members rely heavily on Russian gas transported through Ukraine for heating each winter, pressured the two governments to resolve the crisis. On January 19, Russia and Ukraine signed a new 10-year supply agreement allowing preferential gas and transit fees in 2009 and a switch to world market prices in 2010.

Politics. The row indirectly led to parliament's dismissal of Foreign Minister Volodymyr Ohryzko on March 3, 2009. The pro-Russian Party of Regions initiated the vote after Ohryzko—an ally of the increasingly unpopular, pro-Western president Viktor Yushchenko—threatened to expel Russian Ambassador and former Gazprom head Viktor Chernomyrdin from Ukraine. Chernomyrdin had angered Ohryzko by making derogatory remarks about Ukraine's government.

On April 1, Ukraine's parliament voted overwhelmingly to schedule presidential elections for October 25. Ukraine's Supreme Court upheld Yushchenko's challenge to the decision, deeming the October poll date unconstitutional. The current Constitution calls for presidential elections to be held on the last Sunday of the president's fifth year in office, which will be Jan. 17, 2010. Parliament had argued that the rules of the former constitution, in place when Yushchenko was originally elected, should take precedence. Campaigning for the January 2010 presidential election began in October 2009, with 18 candidates registered.

Economy. Ongoing political infighting undermined efforts to deal with Ukraine's deep recession. In April, the World Bank, a United Nations (UN) affiliate, projected that Ukraine's economy would contract by 9 percent in 2009, but in July the organization revised this estimate to 15 percent. The UN-affiliated International Monetary Fund (IMF) delayed several credit payments because the Ukrainian government did not comply with IMF loan provisions. The IMF insisted that Yushchenko veto a parliamentary measure passed in October that raised the minimum wage by more than 20 percent. Yushchenko defied the IMF and signed the bill on October 30. ■ Juliet Johnson

See also **Europe.**

Unemployment. See Economics; Labor.

United Arab Emirates. See Middle East.

London's Westminster Palace, seat of the Houses of Parliament, lies under a blanket of snow on February 2, as the heaviest snowfall in 18 years brought traffic in the capital to a halt. At least 8 inches (20 centimeters) of snow fell in some areas, forcing the cancellation of bus routes, train lines, and air flights.

The popularity of the Labour Party government continued to decline during 2009, mainly because of the ongoing global financial downturn and its impact on the economy of the United Kingdom (U.K.). The government had been in power since 1997, originally under the leadership of Tony Blair. When Blair stepped down from office in 2007, he was replaced by Gordon Brown, who had served as chancellor of the exchequer (treasury minister) since 1997. Both Blair and Brown had defined themselves as "New Labour" in the 1990's, shifting the party from its socialist roots to the political center.

Recession. As chancellor of the exchequer, Brown had claimed credit for Britain's strong economic performance, characterized by relatively low levels of unemployment. Critics, however, claimed that Britain's economic success was too dependent on an overvalued housing market and on the financial sector based in the City of London (London's financial district). In 2008, the U.K. slid into recession because of the global financial crisis. The government intervened heavily to prevent the banking and financial sectors from collapsing.

The crisis continued in 2009. In January, the Royal Bank of Scotland revealed that it lost £28 billion ($41 billion) in 2008—the largest loss in British corporate history—because of investments in the United States home loan market. The government took a 58-percent share in the bank (effectively nationalizing it) to prevent

its collapse. Also in January 2009, Lloyds TSB merged with Halifax Bank of Scotland, creating the Lloyds Banking Group—the largest bank in the U.K. The merger required the government to take a 43-percent stake in the new bank.

Throughout 2009, investment and the construction industry declined, and the value of property fell. Unemployment increased to over 2 million people. Education Secretary Ed Balls declared in February that the U.K. was experiencing its worst recession in 100 years. In March, the Bank of England, which controls the money supply, cut interest rates to 0.5 percent, the lowest level since the bank's founding in 1694. When that move failed to quell the economic crisis, the bank introduced a policy of *quantitative easing* (printing money to expand the supply), despite the risk of inflation.

During 2009, the government developed a financial asset protection plan for British banks. As part of the plan, the Financial Services Authority, a nongovernmental regulatory agency, called for more regulation to eliminate dangerous risk-taking by banks and for limits on bankers' salaries. The reforms were introduced, in part, in response to public outcry early in the year, when it was discovered that Sir Fred Goodwin, former chief executive of the Royal Bank of Scotland, had received a generous severance package and a £700,000 ($1.16 million) annual pension, despite leading the bank into financial disaster. In June, Goodwin agreed to a reduction in the size of his pension.

Budget. In his April budget speech to the House of Commons, Chancellor of the Exchequer Alistair Darling laid out additional plans for dealing with the recession. He announced an increase in the tax rate from 40 percent to 50 percent for people earning over £150,000 ($249,000) annually—the top 1 to 2 percent of taxpayers—to begin in April 2010. The move was particularly significant because New Labour had long defined itself by its determination not to increase income tax. Darling also revealed plans for government spending to stimulate the economy, including a *scrappage* (turning in old cars for cash) program to increase car sales and measures to tackle youth unemployment, protect pensioners, and combat climate change. Although Darling asserted that "we are determined to continue building a fairer society," he projected severe cuts in public spending over the long term.

According to the government's calculations, to maintain spending on public services, the national debt would rise to 80 percent of *gross domestic product* (GDP—the value of all goods and services produced in a country in a year) by 2013—the highest level ever reached in peacetime. In December 2009, Darling projected that the U.K.'s GDP would decline by 4.75 percent in 2009 (the biggest fall since 1921). He announced a 0.5-percent increase in National Insurance and a two-year freeze on public sector pay from 2011. He also introduced a 50 percent tax on bankers' bonuses.

Parliamentary expenses. A political scandal over improper use of allowances by members of Parliament (MP's) dominated the news in 2009 and undermined popular faith in politicians as well as Parliament. London's *Daily Telegraph* began publishing details in May about expenses for which MP's had filed for reimbursement.

Much of the controversy centered on the "second homes allowance." (Most MP's work both in London and in their constituencies, requiring them to maintain two residences.) Although the allowance entitles MP's to reimbursement for the cost of maintaining a second home, the public was outraged upon learning the extent and nature of the requested reimbursements—by members of nearly all political parties—at a time of rising unemployment. One MP was reimbursed for the cleaning of the moat around his house; another received money for the construction of a floating duck house on a pond on his estate. Constituents were particularly angry over revelations about the practice of *flipping* (repeatedly changing the residence designated as a second home to maximize profits from tax and allowances).

After the expense records were revealed, some members of government were dismissed. One MP resigned from Parliament, and some chose not to contest their seats at the next election. In June, Brown announced the creation of an independent standards authority to oversee parliamentary matters. (MP's had traditionally policed themselves.) In addition, Brown appointed an independent panel in July to examine all claims under the second homes allowance from 2004 to 2008. In October 2009, the panel reported that more than 300 of 646 MP's had requested reimbursements to which they were not entitled. Many MP's quickly repaid the money claimed, including the leaders of the main parties—Brown; David Cameron of the opposition Conservative Party; and Nick Clegg of the Liberal Democrats.

Brown and the speaker of the House of Commons, Michael Martin, were criticized for not acting quickly enough on the crisis. In addition, Martin, in his role as speaker, had tried to use the 2005 Freedom of Information Act to prevent the disclosure of MP expenses. In May 2009, Martin was forced to resign, the first resignation of a speaker since 1695. In June 2009, MP's elected the Conservative MP John Bercow to be the new speaker. Bercow promised to restore the dignity of Parliament.

The Conservatives enjoyed leads of up to 20 percentage points in opinion polls during 2009, raising expectations of a win in the general election, which the prime minister is required to call by June 2010. In November 2009, however, the party's lead fell to 6

THE CABINET OF THE UNITED KINGDOM*

Gordon Brown—prime minister; first lord of the treasury; minister for the civil service

Alistair Darling—chancellor of the exchequer

David Miliband—secretary of state for foreign and Commonwealth affairs

Hilary Benn—secretary of state for environment, food, and rural affairs

Lord Adonis—secretary of state for transport

Andy Burnham—secretary of state for health

Shaun Woodward—secretary of state for Northern Ireland

Bob Ainsworth—secretary of state for defence

Jim Murphy—secretary of state for Scotland

Lord Mandelson—secretary of state for business, innovation, and skills; first secretary and lord president of the Council

Ben Bradshaw—secretary of state for culture, media, and sport

Alan Johnson—secretary of state for the home department

Liam Byrne—chief secretary to the treasury

Harriet Harman—leader of the House of Commons; lord privy seal

Ed Balls—secretary of state for children, schools, and families

Baroness Royall of Blaisdon—leader of the House of Lords; chancellor of the Duchy of Lancaster

Jack Straw—secretary of state for justice; lord chancellor

Douglas Alexander—secretary of state for international development

Yvette Cooper—secretary of state for work and pensions

Peter Hain—secretary of state for Wales

Tessa Jowell—minister for the Cabinet office and for the Olympics; paymaster general

Edward Miliband—secretary of state for energy and climate change

John Denham—secretary of state for communities and local government

*As of Dec. 1, 2009.

HOUSE OF COMMONS

Queen Elizabeth II opened the 2009-2010 session of Parliament on Nov. 18, 2009. As of that date, the House of Commons was made up of the following:

350	Labour Party
193	Conservative Party
63	Liberal Democrats
9	Democratic Unionist Party
7	Scottish National Party
5	Sinn Féin
3	Plaid Cymru
3	Social Democratic and Labour Party
5	Independent
1	Independent Conservative
1	Independent Labour
1	Respect
1	Ulster Unionist Party

In addition, the unaffiliated speaker and 3 deputies attend sessions but do not vote.

points, a development that analysts attributed to renewed public optimism about the economy.

With the prospect of a new Conservative government, there was a greater focus on the party's policies. The Conservatives, including Cameron, had moved in an increasingly *Eurosceptic* (critical of many aspects of the European Union [EU]) direction since the 1990's. Cameron had promised to hold a referendum on the Lisbon Treaty to reform the structure of the EU. He had also withdrawn the Conservatives from the center-right group in the European Parliament to create in 2009 a new, controversial grouping with Eurosceptic parliamentarians, some of whom were drawn from the far right. The ratification of the Lisbon Treaty in November led Cameron to back down on his "cast iron guarantee" of a referendum (which infuriated some supporters), though he promised to repatriate some powers from the EU.

Cameron received tremendous public sympathy in February when his 6-year-old son, Ivan, died. The child had cerebral palsy and a severe form of epilepsy from birth. As a mark of respect, Prime Minister's Questions (a weekly half-hour session in which MP's address questions directly to the prime minister) were canceled that week.

Elections. The Labour Party fared badly in the June local elections held in parts of the U.K. The Conservatives won 38 percent of the vote and the Liberal Democrats, 28 percent, with Labour trailing at 23 percent.

Labour also performed poorly in elections to the European Parliament held at the same time. The Conservatives took 27.7 percent of the vote; Labour, 15.7 percent; and the Liberal Democrats, 13.7 percent. The United Kingdom Independence Party (which supports withdrawal of the U.K. from the EU) achieved 16.5 percent of the vote and won 13 seats. The election was also noteworthy for the success of the far-right British National Party (BNP), which won 6.2 percent of the vote, entitling it for the first time to two representatives in the European Parliament.

Reshuffle. The June election results created problems for Brown, but the difficulties were overshadowed by a wave of Cabinet resignations. Jacqui Smith, the U.K.'s first female home secretary, told Brown before the elections that she wished to resign, after allegations about financial irregularities. Hazel Blears, the communities secretary, resigned two days before the elections, following criticism of her financial affairs. James Purnell, the work and pensions secretary, resigned as the elections ended, asking Brown to stand down as leader and claiming that Labour could not win a general election with Brown as prime minister. The next day, Caroline Flint resigned as minister for Europe, accusing Brown of failing to promote women in his Cabinet.

Brown reshuffled the Cabinet on June 5. Among other changes, Peter Hain, who had been forced to resign from the government in 2008, returned as Welsh secretary. Glenys Kinnock, wife of former Labour Party leader Neil Kinnock, became minister for Europe. Purnell's call for Brown to stand down as leader went unheeded. There were insufficient rebels to trigger a leadership contest, and surviving members of the Cabinet led by Lord Mandelson continued to support Brown.

In his speech to the Labour Party conference in September 2009, Brown promised to revive democracy by offering a referendum on the electoral system. Voters would be allowed to choose between the current "first-past-the-post" system (in which the candidate with the most votes wins) and a more proportional system based on the alternative vote, in which electors rank candidates and the person who gets over 50 percent wins.

A British Supreme Court was inaugurated on October 1 with the swearing in of justices. The court, which became the U.K.'s highest court of appeal, replaces the Law Lords, the House of Lords committee that had performed that function since 1876. The change was part of a reform process instituted by the Labour government under Tony Blair to more fully separate the judicial and legislative branches of government.

Security. The government continued in 2009 to support the United States in the so-called "war on terror" in Iraq and Afghanistan. However, early in the year, questions arose over the treatment of suspected terrorist Binyam Mohamed, an Ethiopian-born resident of the U.K. who had been arrested in Pakistan in 2002. He was held for a time in Morocco—where he claimed he was tortured with the knowledge of MI5, the branch of the British secret service concerned with internal security—before being taken to the U.S. prison camp at Guantánamo Bay, Cuba. Mohamed was returned to the U.K. in February 2009. Two British judges rejected a demand to publish U.S. evidence about Mohamed's treatment on the grounds that it threatened national security. In March, the attorney general ordered an investigation into claims that MI5 had been complicit in a process that involved torture.

In a raid in April, 12 Pakistani students were arrested on suspicion of organizing terrorist attacks. Two weeks later, however, all 12 were released by the police without charge. The same month, the second trial of three men accused of conspiring with the men who bombed London transport on July 7, 2005, killing 52 people, ended with their acquittal. Two were, however, imprisoned for the lesser charge of planning to attend a terrorist training camp in Pakistan.

In August 2009, the Scottish executive (which enjoys devolved powers and its own Parliament) made the controversial decision to release Libyan Abdel Basset al-Megrahi. Megrahi was in prison after being the only person convicted of the bombing of Pan Am Flight 103 over the Scottish town of Lockerbie in 1988. All 270 people aboard the plane were killed. Megrahi was terminally ill and was allowed to return to Libya on compassionate grounds. The U.S. government protested the release, as many Americans had died in the bombing. Many people were further outraged when Megrahi was treated to a hero's welcome upon his arrival in Tripoli, Libya's capital.

In September 2009, four men accused of planning to blow up several transatlantic planes in 2006 with liquid explosives smuggled aboard the flights were retried. They were found guilty of conspiracy to murder. The plot resulted in restrictions on the amount of liquids passengers are allowed to carry aboard planes.

Roman Catholic Church. In October 2009, Pope Benedict XVI created controversy by announcing that traditionalist members of the Church of England (Anglicans) unhappy with liberal reforms could be accepted into a special section of the Roman Catholic Church. Anglicans would be allowed to retain their liturgy and married priests, though those priests would not be allowed to become bishops. ■ Rohan McWilliam

See also **Europe; Iraq; Ireland; Northern Ireland.**

United Kingdom, Prime Minister of.

Prime Minister Gordon Brown experienced a difficult year in 2009. Brown became prime minister of the Labour Party government in 2007, after serving as chancellor of the exchequer (finance minister) under the previous Labour prime minister, Tony Blair. As the global economic crisis worsened in 2009, Brown was blamed for failing to secure the economy and to regulate the financial sector in the decade when he was chancellor.

Following Labour's poor performance in local and European elections in June, a group of Labour members of Parliament (MP's) attempted to oust him. However, he survived the confidence vote. Critics both outside and inside his party complained that Brown would not be able to win a general election, which was to be called by June 2010.

Brown won more respect on the world stage, where he played a major role in combating the financial crisis. In March 2009, he was the first European leader to meet with United States President Barack Obama after his inauguration. Brown also addressed a joint session of the U.S. Congress in which he urged greater international cooperation to fight the recession. In April, at the G-20 Summit (a forum of the world's largest economies) in London, he helped form an agreement on measures to deal with the crisis. ■ Rohan McWilliam

See also **United Kingdom.**

United Nations.

The United Nations (UN) General Assembly opened its 64th annual session on Sept. 15, 2009. On June 10, Ali Treki, a former foreign minister of Libya, had been chosen president of the assembly, a largely ceremonial post that rotates every year.

In 2009, five new members were elected to the UN Security Council for a two-year term beginning Jan. 1, 2010—Bosnia-Herzegovina, Brazil, Gabon, Lebanon, and Nigeria. They joined the five permanent members—China, France, Russia, the United Kingdom, and the United States—and five members completing a two-year term—Austria, Japan, Mexico, Turkey, and Uganda.

In September 2009, the United States attended a meeting of the UN Human Rights Council for the first time since the agency re-formed in 2006. The United States had opposed a previous UN human rights body because it included nations with poor human rights records.

Economic summit. The UN held a summit of world leaders in New York City from June 24 to June 26 to discuss the effects of the global economic crisis on developing countries. However, representatives of only 140 out of 192 member nations attended, including barely a dozen heads of state. Most delegates represented developing countries in Africa, Asia, and Latin America.

The representatives pointed out that though developing nations had not caused the economic downturn, their economies had been severely affected by it, as foreign direct investment dried up and income from exports fell. According to some estimates, 100 million people may be forced into extreme poverty (the equivalent of living on less than $1.25 a day) because of the crisis.

Summit delegates called for more than $1 trillion in stimulus money, including funds for debt relief, increased aid to poor nations, and reform of such institutions as the International Monetary Fund. (The fund is a UN-affiliated organization that provides short-term credit to member nations.) Critics pointed out that lack of support by Western nations made concrete results doubtful.

War crimes. On February 26, the International Criminal Tribunal for the Former Yugoslavia in The Hague, the Netherlands, found former Serbian President Milan Milutinovic not guilty of war crimes and crimes against humanity in Kosovo. Milutinovic was president from 1998 to 2002. Former Yugoslav and Serbian forces conducted a military campaign against Kosovo's independence-seeking ethnic Albanians in 1999, until a temporary UN government stopped the violence. The tribunal had previously found five other Serb officials guilty of all or some of the crimes. However, the judges found that Milutinovic did not have direct control of the army in 1999. Rather, then-Yugoslav President Slobodan Milosevic did. Milosevic died in 2006 during his trial for war crimes.

The International Criminal Court (ICC), established by the UN and also located at The Hague, on March 4, 2009, issued a warrant for the arrest of President Umar Hassan Ahmad al-Bashir of Sudan. He was charged with war crimes and crimes against humanity for his role in the ethnic war in Sudan's western region of Darfur. Al-Bashir became the first sitting president facing an ICC arrest warrant. He denied the charges.

Middle East conflict. A UN fact-finding mission investigating fighting in the Gaza Strip between Israel and Palestinian militant groups from December 2008 to January 2009 delivered its conclusion to the Human Rights Council on September 15. The mission reported that it had found evidence of war crimes and possibly crimes against humanity by both sides. About 1,400 civilians died in the fighting. The group suggested that the Security Council refer the case to the ICC if both parties do not investigate and prosecute those responsible. Israel and the United States rejected the mission's findings as deeply flawed. Nevertheless, in November the General Assembly voted to endorse the report and demanded that Israel and the Palestinians carry out investigations into the allegations within three months.

Nuclear crises. On May 25, North Korea exploded a nuclear device and then test-fired a series of ballistic missiles, raising global tensions. In response, the Security Council on June 12 unanimously adopted sanctions against North Korea. In an unprecedented move, the council called on member nations to board and search any North Korean vessel suspected of carrying arms.

In September, Iran shocked world leaders when it revealed that it was building a nuclear facility near Qom, southwest of Tehran. Although Iran claimed the installation was to produce energy for peaceful purposes, many nations were concerned that Iran may attempt to produce nuclear weapons. In October, Iran allowed the UN's nuclear "watchdog," the International Atomic Energy Agency (IAEA), to inspect the facility. The five permanent members of the Security Council and Germany also proposed a plan in which Iran would ship its enriched uranium to Russia for processing; Russia would return the material in a form usable only in a civilian nuclear facility. Iran refused to cooperate, and on November 27, the IAEA censured Iran and demanded that it stop construction of the plant. On November 29, Iran announced it was building 10 new sites to enrich uranium. In a rare show of unity, Russia and China endorsed the IAEA resolution, which the United States planned to bring before the Security Council to impose sanctions on Iran. ■ J. Tuyet Nguyen

See also **Economics, World; Global warming; Iran; Israel; Korea, North; Middle East; Sudan.**

United States, Government of the.

Barack Obama, a Democrat, was inaugurated as the 44th president of the United States on Jan. 20, 2009, succeeding George W. Bush, a Republican. The Obama administration spent much of 2009 trying to revive the nation's struggling economy, an effort that had begun under the Bush administration. President Obama shepherded a massive economic stimulus bill through Congress shortly after taking office. The Obama administration also made major interventions in the financial, real estate, and auto industries in an effort to prop them up. The U.S. *gross domestic product* (GDP, the total value of goods and services produced in the country in one year) grew in the third quarter of 2009 after having contracted for a year. However, the unemployment rate remained high, rising above 10 percent in October.

The Obama administration took steps to scale back the U.S. military effort in Iraq in 2009 while ramping up the U.S. military effort in Afghanistan. The administration also worked toward closure of the controversial U.S. military prison at Guantánamo Bay, Cuba, where hundreds of foreigners had been detained since 2001 after being captured during antiterrorism operations.

President Obama also lobbied hard in 2009 for comprehensive reform of the nation's health care system. Extensive congressional and public debate over health reform took place throughout the summer and fall, and both houses of Congress passed reform bills late in the year. But the bills were not reconciled before 2009 ended.

Stimulus package. On February 17, President Obama signed a $787-billion package of tax cuts and spending measures intended to stimulate the economy. The package, known as the American Recovery and Reinvestment Act (ARRA), included $212 billion in tax reductions for individuals and businesses and $575 billion in spending on education, health care, energy, transportation infrastructure, unemployment benefits, and aid to the needy, according to the Congressional Budget Office (CBO). By December, about 30 percent of the $787 billion had been distributed in the form of tax benefits; contracts, grants, and loans; and entitlements. The Obama administration reported that as of October 30, about 640,000 jobs had been created or saved as a result of ARRA funding. On November 30, the CBO estimated that in the third quarter of 2009, an additional 600,000 to 1.6 million people were employed, and real GDP was 1.2 percent to 3.2 percent higher, than would have been the case without ARRA funding.

Financial industry. The Treasury Department continued in 2009 to administer the $700-billion Troubled Asset Relief Program (TARP), which had been established in October 2008 to stabilize the faltering U.S. financial system. Half of the $700 billion was released for use by the Bush administration when TARP was first created. Most of this initial $350 billion was used to directly inject capital into hundreds of U.S. banks by buying stock in them. The second $350 billion was released in January 2009 for use by the Obama administration. The banks that received the most TARP aid were Bank of America, Citigroup, Goldman Sachs, JPMorgan Chase, Morgan Stanley, and Wells Fargo. All six of these banks, as well as many others, were allowed in 2009 to repay all or part of their TARP aid to the government after demonstrating sufficient financial strength. A few other major U.S. companies—including the insurer American International Group (AIG) and the automakers General Motors Company (GM) and Chrysler Corporation—also received TARP aid.

In early 2009, the Obama administration unveiled a major financial rescue plan, involving the potential injection of huge sums into the financial system by the Treasury Department, the Federal Reserve System (the Fed, the nation's central bank), the Federal Deposit Insurance Corporation (FDIC), and private investors. The plan's main component was creating public-private partnerships to buy toxic mortgage-backed assets from financial firms. Other components included making more capital available to ailing banks; expanding a Treasury-Fed program intended to stimulate student, auto, small business, and credit card lending; and providing aid to help homeowners refinance their mortgages or lower their monthly mortgage payments.

As part of the plan, the government conducted "stress tests" on 19 large U.S. banks. The test results, released on May 7, showed that 9 of the banks had enough capital to withstand losses and sustain lending if the economy deteriorated further. The other 10 banks were given six months to raise a combined $75 billion in capital. On November 9, the Fed reported that all but 1 of the 10 banks had raised the capital. The only bank that had failed to do so, GMAC, was expected to receive more TARP aid.

The Fed, which had cut interest rates several times in 2008 in an attempt to spur growth, left its benchmark interest rate at a record low of between zero and 0.25 percent throughout 2009. The Fed also continued to pump large amounts of money into the financial system in 2009. It purchased $300 billion in long-term U.S. Treasury securities, a departure from its usual practice of buying short-term debt. It also bought more than

FEDERAL SPENDING — United States budget for fiscal 2009*

Billions of dollars

National defense	662.8
International affairs	36.9
General science, space, technology	29.9
Energy	4.7
Natural resources and environment	45.8
Agriculture	14.0
Commerce and housing credit	292.8
Transportation	84.3
Community and regional development	26.3
Education, training, employment, and social services	78.2
Health	334.3
Social security	683.0
Medicare	430.1
Income security	533.9
Veterans' benefits and services	95.5
Administration of justice	53.8
General government	17.3
Interest	190.9
Undistributed offsetting receipts	-92.6
Total budget outlays	**3,521.7**

*Oct. 1, 2008, to Sept. 30, 2009.
Source: U.S. Department of the Treasury.

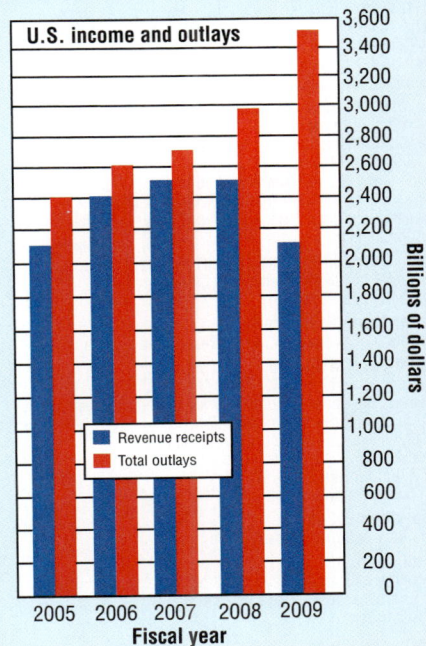

U.S. income and outlays

Revenue receipts
Total outlays

Billions of dollars

Fiscal year

SELECTED AGENCIES AND BUREAUS OF THE U.S. GOVERNMENT*

Executive Office of the President
President, Barack Obama
Vice President, Joe Biden
White House Chief of Staff, Rahm Emanuel
Presidential Press Secretary, Robert Gibbs
Domestic Policy Adviser, Melody Barnes
National Security Adviser, General James Jones
Office of Science and Technology Policy—
  John Holdren, Director
Council of Economic Advisers—
  Christina Romer, Chairwoman
Office of Management and Budget—
  Peter Orszag, Director
Office of National Drug Control Policy—
  R. Gil Kerlikowske, Director
U.S. Trade Representative—Ron Kirk, Ambassador

Department of Agriculture
Secretary of Agriculture, Thomas J. Vilsack

Department of Commerce
Secretary of Commerce, Gary F. Locke
  Bureau of Economic Analysis—
    J. Steven Landefeld, Director
  Bureau of the Census—Robert Groves, Director

Department of Defense
Secretary of Defense, Robert M. Gates
  Secretary of the Air Force, Michael B. Donley
  Secretary of the Army, John M. McHugh
  Secretary of the Navy, Ray Mabus
  Joint Chiefs of Staff—
    Admiral Michael G. Mullen, Chairman
    General James E. Cartwright, Vice Chairman
    General Norton A. Schwartz, Chief of Staff, Air Force
    General George W. Casey, Jr., Chief of Staff, Army
    Admiral Gary Roughead, Chief of Naval Operations
    General James T. Conway, Commandant, Marine Corps

Department of Education
Secretary of Education, Arne Duncan

Department of Energy
Secretary of Energy, Steven Chu

Department of Health and Human Services
Secretary of Health and Human Services, Kathleen Sebelius
  Centers for Disease Control and Prevention—
    Thomas R. Frieden, Director
  Food and Drug Administration—Margaret A. Hamburg,
    Commissioner
  National Institutes of Health—Francis S. Collins, Director
  Surgeon General of the United States, Regina Benjamin

Department of Homeland Security
Secretary of Homeland Security, Janet A. Napolitano
  U.S. Citizenship and Immigration Services—
    Alejandro Mayorkas, Director
  U.S. Coast Guard—Admiral Thad W. Allen, Commandant
  U.S. Secret Service—Mark J. Sullivan, Director
  Federal Emergency Management Agency—W. Craig Fugate,
    Administrator

Department of Housing and Urban Development
Secretary of Housing and Urban Development,
  Shaun L. S. Donovan

Department of the Interior
Secretary of the Interior, Kenneth L. Salazar

Department of Justice
Attorney General, Eric H. Holder, Jr.
  Federal Bureau of Prisons—Harley G. Lappin, Director
  Drug Enforcement Administration—
    Michele Leonhart, Acting Administrator
  Federal Bureau of Investigation—
    Robert S. Mueller III, Director
  Solicitor General, Elena Kagan

Department of Labor
Secretary of Labor, Hilda L. Solis

Department of State
Secretary of State, Hillary Rodham Clinton
  U.S. Ambassador to the United Nations,
    Susan Rice

Department of Transportation
Secretary of Transportation, Raymond H. LaHood
  Federal Aviation Administration—J. Randolph Babbitt, Administrator

Department of the Treasury
Secretary of the Treasury, Timothy F. Geithner
  Internal Revenue Service—Douglas Shulman, Commissioner
  Treasurer of the United States, Rosie Rios
  Office of Thrift Supervision—John E. Bowman, Acting Director

Department of Veterans Affairs
Secretary of Veterans Affairs, Eric K. Shinseki

Supreme Court of the United States
Chief Justice of the United States, John G. Roberts, Jr.
  Associate Justices—
    John Paul Stevens   Ruth Bader Ginsburg
    Antonin Scalia   Stephen G. Breyer
    Anthony M. Kennedy   Samuel Anthony Alito, Jr.
    Clarence Thomas   Sonia Sotomayor

Congressional officials
  President of the Senate pro tempore, Robert C. Byrd
  Senate Majority Leader, Harry Reid
  Senate Minority Leader, Mitch McConnell
  Speaker of the House, Nancy Pelosi
  House Majority Leader, Steny H. Hoyer
  House Minority Leader, John Boehner
  Congressional Budget Office—Douglas W. Elmendorf, Director
  Government Accountability Office—Gene Dodaro, Acting
    Comptroller General of the United States
  Library of Congress—James H. Billington, Librarian of Congress

Independent agencies
Central Intelligence Agency—Leon E. Panetta, Director
Commission of Fine Arts—Earl A. Powell III, Chairman
Commission on Civil Rights—Gerald A. Reynolds, Chairman
Consumer Product Safety Commission—
  Inez Moore Tenenbaum, Chairwoman
Corporation for National and Community Service—
  Nicola Goren, Acting CEO
Environmental Protection Agency—Lisa P. Jackson, Administrator
Equal Employment Opportunity Commission—
  Stuart J. Ishimaru, Acting Chairman
Federal Communications Commission—Julius Genachowski, Chairman
Federal Deposit Insurance Corporation—
  Sheila C. Bair, Chairwoman
Federal Election Commission—Steven T. Walther, Chairman
Federal Reserve System Board of Governors—
  Ben S. Bernanke, Chairman
Federal Trade Commission—Jon Leibowitz, Chairman
General Services Administration—
  Stephen R. Leeds, Acting Administrator
National Aeronautics and Space Administration—
  Charles F. Bolden, Jr., Administrator
National Endowment for the Arts—Rocco Landesman, Chairman
National Endowment for the Humanities—Jim Leach, Chairman
National Labor Relations Board—Wilma B. Liebman, Chairwoman
National Railroad Passenger Corporation (Amtrak)—
  Joseph H. Boardman, President and CEO
National Science Foundation—Arden L. Bement, Jr., Director
National Transportation Safety Board—
  Deborah A. P. Hersman, Chairwoman
Nuclear Regulatory Commission—Gregory B. Jaczko, Chairman
Office of the Director of National Intelligence—
  Dennis C. Blair, Director
Peace Corps—Aaron S. Williams, Director
Securities and Exchange Commission—
  Mary L. Schapiro, Chairwoman
Selective Service System—Lawrence G. Romo, Director
Small Business Administration—Karen G. Mills, Administrator
Smithsonian Institution—G. Wayne Clough, Secretary
Social Security Administration—Michael J. Astrue, Commissioner
U.S. Postal Service—John E. Potter, Postmaster General

*As of Dec. 31, 2009.

$1 trillion in mortgage-backed securities.

The Obama administration urged Congress in 2009 to overhaul the nation's financial regulatory system. Administration officials proposed increasing the government's power to supervise—and if necessary, seize and dismantle—any financial firm that posed a risk to the financial system as a whole if the firm were to fail. They also proposed creating a new agency to regulate mortgages, credit cards, and other consumer debt products. Late in 2009, the president unveiled a number of proposals to encourage job creation and economic growth, including using TARP funds to boost lending to small businesses and investing more federal funds in infrastructure improvements. Congress did not enact final legislation for any of these initiatives before the end of 2009.

The FDIC seized and sold about 140 failed banks in 2009. At the end of the third quarter, the agency's deposit insurance fund fell into the red. To replenish the fund, the FDIC on November 12 implemented a plan to raise $45 billion by requiring banks to prepay three years of fees to the fund at the end of 2009.

Auto industry. At the behest of the Obama administration, both GM and Chrysler underwent bankruptcy restructuring in 2009. The two automakers, faced with falling sales, had been given TARP aid in late 2008 and, as a condition of receiving the aid, had prepared reorganization plans in early 2009. But on March 30, the administration rejected the plans and outlined further steps that the companies needed to take. Neither company was able to secure sufficient concessions from investors to meet the administration's demands. Chrysler filed for bankruptcy on April 30, and GM filed for bankruptcy on June 1. Both automakers raced through the restructuring process. On June 10, Chrysler finalized an alliance with the Italian automaker Fiat and emerged from bankruptcy as a smaller company called Chrysler Group LLC. GM emerged from bankruptcy on July 10 as a smaller company focused on four core brands—Buick, Cadillac, Chevrolet, and GMC. The U.S. government took a 61-percent stake in GM and a 10-percent stake in Chrysler.

In June, Congress created an auto sales incentive program that was popularly called "cash for clunkers." It offered credits of $3,500 to $4,500 to people who traded in an old vehicle for one with better fuel economy. Under the $3-billion program, which ran from July 24 through August 24, nearly 700,000 vehicle trades took place.

Pay limits. The government took several steps in 2009 to limit executive pay at companies that had received federal bailouts, in an effort to discourage excessive risk-taking by executives. In February, President Obama announced that executive salaries would be capped at these compa-

nies. Later that month, a provision was added to the Recovery Act to cap executive bonuses at banks that had gotten TARP aid. In March, a public outcry erupted in response to news that AIG—the recipient of $180 billion in loans and other aid from the Fed and from TARP—was paying $165 million in bonuses to employees. On June 10, the Treasury Department named lawyer Kenneth Feinberg to serve as its "pay czar" overseeing compensation for the highest earners at firms that had received exceptional TARP aid. On October 22, Feinberg ordered steep pay cuts for the 25 highest earners at each of those companies. The same day, the Fed announced that it would begin regulating pay packages at banks.

Terrorism detainees. The Bush administration often had been accused of violating human rights in its treatment of people detained in the "war on terrorism." On January 22, President Obama signed a series of executive orders relating to the detention and interrogation of terrorism suspects. The executive orders called for the Guantánamo Bay military prison—where more than 200 detainees were still being held—to be closed by January 2010; instructed the Central Intelligence Agency (CIA) to shut down its secret overseas prisons for detainees; and banned the use of harsh interrogation techniques by the CIA.

On Aug. 24, 2009, the Justice Department released a 2004 report by the CIA inspector general on the CIA's terrorism detention and interrogation program. The report had found that unauthorized and inhumane techniques had been used on detainees. Later that day, Attorney General Eric Holder appointed a special prosecutor, John Durham, to review several cases of alleged CIA mistreatment or abuse of detainees.

The Obama administration faced numerous legal, political, and logistical issues in its effort to close the Guantánamo prison, including where to transfer or release the remaining detainees, and whether, where, and how to prosecute them. On Nov. 13, 2009, Holder announced that five men accused of planning the Sept. 11, 2001, terrorist attacks on the United States—including Khalid Shaikh Mohammed, a Pakistani believed to have masterminded the attacks—would be prosecuted in a federal civilian court in New York City. On Nov. 18, 2009, President Obama acknowledged that the Guantánamo prison would not be closed by the January 2010 deadline. ■ Mike Lewis

See also **Armed forces; Automobile; Bank; Cabinet; Congress; Conservation; Courts; Drugs; Economics, U.S.; Environmental pollution; Global warming; Health care issues; Immigration; People in the news; Social Security; State government; Supreme Court; Taxation; Transportation; United States, Government of the: A Special Report; United States, President of the; Welfare.**

Food and Drug Safety and the

FDA

Can the Food and Drug Administration adequately safeguard food and drugs?

By Emily Friedman

Tainted peanut butter. Contaminated cookie dough. Pistachio nuts that can make you sick. Hamburgers that could kill you. Drugs recalled because of dire side effects. Tainted pharmaceutical ingredients that turned out to have been imported from China. Bottled water that might be less healthful than tap water. In 2009, Americans were confronted by two discomforting questions: Are prescription drugs and the food supply really safe in one of the wealthiest nations on Earth? Can the Food and Drug Administration (FDA) really protect us?

The crisis had been years in the making. Although problems had surfaced from time to time, a major scare erupted in 2006, when people started becoming ill from eating fresh spinach contaminated with *E. coli,* a bacterium that can cause severe disease and even death. More than 100 Americans were sickened, and at least 1 person died. In 2007, cats and dogs got sick and some died from eating a variety of pet foods, which the U.S. Department of Agriculture (USDA) later determined contained melamine. (Melamine is a substance that is normally used in farming but can be used to make it appear that there is more protein in a food than there actually is.) To increase profits, Chinese processors had added the melamine to wheat gluten which is widely used in the manufacture of pet food.

In the last three years, a number of foods and food products—including cookie dough, peppers, fish farmed in China, and spinach—were found to be contaminated with deadly bacteria or tainted with dangerous drugs.

TEN RISKIEST FOODS

The Center for Science in the Public Interest, a Washington, D.C.-based food safety and health advocacy group, issued a list in October 2009 of the 10 foods regulated by the U.S. Food and Drug Administration (FDA) that pose the greatest hazards for consumers. A study conducted by the group revealed that from 1990 to 2006, the following foods have caused 40 percent of all outbreaks of illness from such *pathogens* (disease-causing micro-organisms) as *E. coli, Norovirus,* and *Salmonella.*

leafy greens, including spinach and lettuce—363 outbreaks
eggs, usually when undercooked—352 outbreaks
tuna, both fresh and canned—268 outbreaks
oysters, especially when improperly washed—132 outbreaks
potatoes, usually in dishes that contain several ingredients—108 outbreaks
cheese, especially unpasteurized and soft cheeses—83 outbreaks
ice cream, especially soft-serve and homemade—74 outbreaks
tomatoes, raw—31 outbreaks
sprouts, raw and lightly cooked—31 outbreaks
berries, including strawberries, raspberries, and blackberries—25 outbreaks

In 2008, melamine was detected in infant formula in China; it caused widespread illness and some deaths. The source was Chinese milk, though melamine was also found in processed eggs, fish food, and other products. In November 2008, the United States barred importation of any Chinese products containing milk or milk products until they could be tested for melamine. Also in 2008, an outbreak of *Salmonella,* another bacterium that can cause illness and sometimes death, was linked to fresh tomatoes and jalapeño peppers grown in Mexico; more than 1,300 people were sickened.

Criticism of the main federal agency charged with ensuring the safety of the food supply and prescription drugs—the Food and Drug Administration—became widespread. "How many times does this have to happen before the FDA gets serious about food safety?" asked Sarah Klein, an attorney with the Center for Science in the Public Interest, an advocate for nutrition and health and food safety. In April 2008, a Harris Poll/ *Wall Street Journal* survey found that only 29 percent of Americans were very or somewhat confident in the safety of foods and drug ingredients produced in developing countries.

The flood of food safety crises crested in 2009. In January, a peanut processing facility in Georgia was found to have been shipping products that were contaminated with *Salmonella.* Initial tests had found contamination, though subsequent tests did not. Nonetheless, critics charged, none of the products should have been distributed.

The manufacturer originally ordered a recall of all products made since July 2008, then expanded the recall to include all products made since July 1, 2007. Its products were distributed so widely, and in so many forms, that it was impossible to determine how many people had been placed at risk. It is known that at least 650 people were sickened, and 9 deaths were believed to be associated with the contamination.

The author:
Emily Friedman is a health policy and ethics analyst.

In January 2009, the FDA launched a criminal investigation of the peanut processor and found that the plant had been shipping suspect products for years. Furthermore, a Texas plant owned by the same manufacturer did not have a license from the state health department. Sanitation violations at the plant had been observed as early as 2005. The Texas plant was closed in February 2009.

The list of food contaminations goes on and on. In April, pistachio nuts processed and sold by a California manufacturer were found to be contaminated with *Salmonella*. In June, a popular raw prepared cookie dough was recalled after it was linked to an *E. coli* outbreak. Five days later, a Colorado beef processor recalled 380,000 pounds (172,365 kilograms) of a product feared to be tainted with *E. coli*—a recall that was later expanded. In July, a popular hot breakfast cereal was recalled by its manufacturer because of possible *Salmonella* contamination. A few days later, a report by the Government Accountability Office (GAO) found that FDA standards for and regulation of bottled water—which is popularly viewed as healthier than tap water—were weaker than those for tap water. (The GAO is an independent agency in the legislative branch of the U.S. government that reviews the operations and programs of most federal government agencies.) On August 13, a California meat processor recalled from California and Arizona restaurants 3,516 pounds (1,595 kilograms) of hamburger patties suspected to be contaminated with *E. coli*.

In April 2009, the federal Centers for Disease Control and Prevention (CDC), an Atlanta-based federal agency that works to protect public health, issued a report stating that the safety of the U.S. food supply was not improving and that, in the case of *Salmonella* contamination, the situation was actually getting worse.

What about drug safety?

On Nov. 18, 2004, David Graham, associate director for science and medicine of the FDA Office of Drug Safety, bluntly testified before Congress that the FDA's drug safety program, administered by the FDA

Representative Gary Walden (R., Oregon), speaking at a congressional committee hearing, holds aloft a container of food items that were recalled due to the 2009 *Salmonella* outbreak in peanut products. At least 650 people were known to have been sickened by eating foods containing the contaminated peanut products.

Center for Drug Evaluation and Research (CDER), was "broken" and that Americans were "completely defenseless" in terms of the safety of the prescription drugs they take. His accusations stemmed from one of the worst drug safety failures in recent years: the FDA's 1999 approval of the painkiller Vioxx, which subsequently was linked to more than 27,000 heart attacks, strokes, and sudden deaths from 1999 through 2003. Graham testified that several studies released as early as the year 2000 had revealed that Vioxx was associated with fatal cardiac events, but the FDA failed to take action.

The manufacturer, Merck & Co. of Whitehouse Station, New Jersey, recalled Vioxx in 2004. In the face of many lawsuits, Merck set aside $4.85 billion in 2007 to settle future claims. In 2008, a study in a U.S. medical journal reported that Merck had prevented negative information about Vioxx from being released. At a congressional hearing in April 2008, Senator Charles Grassley (R., Iowa) stated that he was "deeply troubled" by Merck's actions.

Vioxx was not the only drug involved in controversial FDA actions. In 2008, the diabetes drug Avandia, approved in 2000, was subjected to scrutiny after its manufacturer was found to have failed to fully report to the FDA the results of early tests of the drug, which is required by law. Those results, which revealed a link to heart problems, might have influenced FDA approval. As early as 2000, physicians had tried to warn the FDA that Avandia could cause such problems. Although the FDA issued a strong warning about Avandia's dangers in 2007, the drug was still on the market in 2009.

In 2008, at least 81 deaths were associated with a blood-thinning drug, heparin. A key ingredient, manufactured in China, proved to be contaminated. In December of that year, two FDA officials warned of dangers associated with four asthma drugs—Advair, Symbicort, Serevent, and Foradi—but the drugs were not recalled.

Representative Bart Stupak (D., Michigan) greets Johanna Marie Staples and Leroy Hubley (center) prior to a 2008 House sub-committee hearing on the pharmaceutical heparin. Staples lost her husband and Hubley lost his wife and son after they took the blood-thinner containing a contaminated key ingredient manufactured in China.

In June 2009, an FDA panel recommended that the painkillers Vicodin and Percocet be banned because of possible liver damage. Also in June, the FDA warned against the use of Zicam, a prescription cold remedy, because it could destroy a person's sense of smell.

Fraud settlement

In September 2009, New York City-based pharmaceutical giant Pfizer Inc. agreed to pay $2.3 billion to settle various accusations of health care fraud. The settlement was the largest in U.S. history to resolve criminal and civil liability arising from the illegal promotion of certain

Associate Attorney General Tom Perrelli—flanked by Kathleen Sebelius, secretary of the Health and Human Services Department, and Tony West, assistant attorney general for the Civil Division—announce that Pfizer Inc. will pay a record $2.3 billion in damages and criminal penalties to settle federal charges of unlawful prescription drug promotions.

pharmaceutical products, including the painkiller Bextra. Pfizer had pulled Bextra from the market in 2005 after evidence surfaced that the drug might increase the risk of heart attack and stroke.

Nonprescription drugs

Nonprescription drugs also came in for increased FDA attention. In May 2009, the FDA requested and received a recall of the popular diet drug Hydroxycut, because of reports of liver damage and other negative side effects. An agency panel also recommended setting limits on how high a dose of Tylenol, a nonprescription painkiller, could be used safely. Similar problems were found with some approved medical devices: questionable data and clinical trials, dubious approvals, and negative side effects once the products reached the market.

These incidents, and others, led the FDA to begin to take more time for its review process of new drugs. Pharmaceutical companies complained that the process had slowed to the point that it was taking too long for products to be approved, cutting into profits.

Focus on the FDA

The string of highly publicized food and drug safety problems triggered increasing calls for improvements at the FDA, which faced internal challenges as well. In 2006, Lester M. Crawford, a veterinarian who had served as acting commissioner of the agency and was appointed commissioner by then-President George W. Bush, resigned two months after that appointment, giving no reason. However, he had been accused of lax oversight, foot-dragging on approval of a birth-control drug, and conflict of interest for owning stocks in firms that his agency oversaw. He pleaded guilty later that year to failing to report the stock ownership; he was sentenced to 3 years' probation and 90 hours of community service and required to pay a $90,000 fine.

In November 2008, eight FDA scientists wrote to members of Congress, complaining about misconduct at the agency, after a May

The Jungle, a 1906 novel by Upton Sinclair (below), described the unhealthful and inhumane conditions in Chicago's Union Stock Yards (right). The sensation caused by the novel led to the passage in 1906 of the Pure Food and Drug Act and the Meat Inspection Act.

2008 letter they had written to the latest commissioner, Andrew C. von Eschenbach, had gone unheeded. Their complaints centered on FDA approval of products the scientists deemed ineffective or unsafe.

Not a new issue

Food and drug safety is hardly a new issue in the United States. In 1906, Upton Sinclair's groundbreaking book *The Jungle*, which described horrible conditions in U.S. slaughterhouses and meat-packing plants, created a sensation that sparked the passage that same year by Congress of the Pure Food and Drug Act and the Meat Inspection Act.

Decades before, in 1862, President Abraham Lincoln had appointed a chemist, Charles M. Wetherill, to work on food safety within the USDA. Wetherill's appointment eventually led to the establishment of the USDA Bureau of Chemistry. When the Pure Food and Drug Act was passed in 1906, responsibility for enforcing it was assigned to the USDA. Those responsibilities were consolidated in the newly established FDA, which became a part of the USDA, in 1930. The FDA's scope of authority was greatly increased in 1938 by the passage of the Food, Drug, and Cosmetic Act, which was sparked by mass poisonings caused by tainted foods and beverages. In 1988, the FDA was transferred from the USDA to the U.S. Department of Health and Human Services.

Over the years, the FDA has had notable successes and equally notable failures, but the recent spate of scandals has put a spotlight on the agency and its problems. One issue is that its scope of power is limited and conflicted. The FDA is charged with ensuring the safety of food and drug products on the one hand and approving them for use on the other, often while being pressured by manufacturers. Also, if a product is found to be potentially dangerous, the FDA cannot order a recall; it can only request that the manufacturer initiate one. Furthermore, many FDA activities are funded by fees from manufacturers, which can and does produce conflicts of interest.

In addition, the agency is chronically underfunded. Its responsibilities have increased greatly while its funding has not kept pace. Indeed, in May 2008, von Eschenbach asked Congress for $275 million in emergency funding to meet several urgent needs, including opening overseas offices to inspect food and drug sources and ensure the safety of imported products and ingredients.

Also, the FDA does not have total responsibility for oversight of the food supply. The USDA has duties and obligations in that arena as well, especially for inspection and approval of farm and livestock products, and the two agencies have not always fully cooperated with each other. According to a former FDA deputy commissioner, Michael R. Taylor, in testimony before Congress in April 2009, the FDA oversees 80 percent of the U.S. food supply and has an annual budget of approximately $650 million. The USDA's food safety arm, the Food Safety and Inspection Service (FSIS), oversees 20 percent of the food supply with a $1-billion budget. Ten other federal agencies have some role in food safety oversight, and coordination among them has been lacking for years.

The FSIS has challenges of its own, including chronically insufficient staffing. Its employees are required to continually inspect the products of some 6,200 U.S. meat, poultry, and egg processing plants. Although the FSIS supposedly employs 7,800 inspectors, there are many vacancies; in 2007, the vacancy rate was 12.2 percent and in some areas was 15 percent or higher. An official of the union that represents the inspectors reported that the actual number of working inspectors in 2007 was approximately 6,500. Later that year, a long-time FSIS inspector told the *Chicago Tribune*, "We've been short the whole time I've been in." Given dramatic

An FDA inspector examines coffee beans being unloaded at the Baltimore docks. In 2008, 15 percent of the entire U.S. food supply was imported, from some 150 countries. The FDA and other federal agencies inspected less than 1 percent of it.

growth in the amount of food being produced, the inevitable result is that workloads have increased significantly.

Although inspectors are supposed to be on plant premises any time meat, poultry, or eggs are being processed, this is not always the case, which can allow contaminated products to go undetected. Even if an inspector is present, he or she may not have time to do the work thoroughly, especially in light of continued expansion in the food processing industry. In 1981, the year it was created, the FSIS spent $13.22 per thousand pounds of meat and poultry inspected; by 2007, the figure was $8.26. In 1981, the FSIS employed approximately 190 people per billion pounds of meat and poultry products inspected and approved; in 2007, the number had dropped to 85 workers.

Finally, the sources of the food supply are not just family farms in the heartland. The desire for a wide variety of foods available the year around has contributed to globalization of the food supply. According to David W. K. Acheson, associate FDA commissioner for foods, approximately 15 percent of all U.S.-consumed foods are imported—from 150 countries. Michael Doyle of the University of Georgia in Albany reported in 2008 that 80 percent of the fish and seafood consumed in the United States is imported.

According to Acheson, imported foods enter this country through more than 300 ports. Doyle reported in 2008 that less than 1 percent of these products are inspected. Approximately 200,000 foreign firms are registered with the FDA as supplying imported food products. Some of these products are unsafe because of unintentional tainting; others are contaminated for profit, as appears to have been the case with most of the melamine incidents.

FDA and drug safety

The FDA also has primary responsibility for ensuring the safety of drugs—both prescription and nonprescription—and of medical devices, and the agency faces the same problems in this arena that it has on the food safety side: insufficient funding, potential conflicts of interest, and politics. And entire classes of products are beyond the reach of FDA oversight, including dietary supplements such as vitamins. Furthermore, as is true with food products, the FDA cannot recall a drug that is thought to be dangerous. It can only request that the manufacturer do so or order that a stern warning (commonly called a "black box warning") be placed on the package.

The FDA faces another hurdle. To a high degree, its approval decisions are based on the results of clinical trials—tests of new drugs and devices—that are not conducted by the FDA, but rather by researchers who often have close ties to the manufacturers of the drugs. In some cases, researchers have direct financial relationships with drug manufacturers or may benefit financially if a drug they are testing is approved.

Sometimes these close relationships occur within the FDA. In March 2008, the Bush administration appointed veteran FDA official Janet Woodcock director of the Center of Drug Evaluation and Research; she had served as acting director of the center since October 2007. Although some critics charged that her appointment meant "business as usual," then-FDA director Andrew von Eschenbach described her as "a change agent." In August 2009, she was accused of improper professional contact with the president of a firm seeking approval for a drug. She had coauthored scientific journal articles with the executive and had appointed him to an FDA task force.

New initiatives

Congress began to pressure the FDA in 2008 to do more to protect U.S. residents from unsafe imported foods, drugs, and ingredients. The FDA announced that it would open offices in key foreign countries to work more closely with suppliers, conduct more inspections, and attempt to ensure that the entire chain of production, from beginning to end, was properly monitored. The FDA opened three offices in China in November 2008, two in India in early 2009, and one in Costa Rica in 2009. Offices were planned for other locations in Latin America, Europe, and the Middle East.

Other initiatives have been undertaken. Von Eschenbach resigned in January 2009 before Barack Obama assumed the presidency of the United States; in March, Margaret Hamburg, former health commissioner of New York City, was named as the new head of the FDA. Joshua Sharfstein, health commissioner of the city of Baltimore, was named principal deputy commissioner.

Also in March, President Obama established a Food Safety Working Group (FSWG), chaired by the secretaries of Health and Human Services and Agriculture, which suggested a closer working relationship between the two federal departments.

The mission of the FSWG included enhancing food safety systems; building collaborative partnerships with key stakeholders; increasing the "transparency" (that is, public visibility and understanding) of food safety activities; preventing contamination of foods by *Salmonella* and *E. coli*; building a national system that can trace foodborne disease outbreaks more quickly; improving the communication to the public of food safety risks; and better organization and coordination of federal food safety efforts.

At the same time, the Obama administration announced that it was closing a "loophole" that had allowed cattle that might have bovine spongiform encephalopathy (BSE), or "mad cow" disease, to come to market. No cattle that showed any symptoms of neurological disorders would be allowed into the food chain. Furthermore, the administration announced that it would seek greater funding for more food safety inspectors and modernization of food safety laboratories.

The new agency administrators also indicated that the FDA might crack down on misleading food advertising claims. The agency sent a

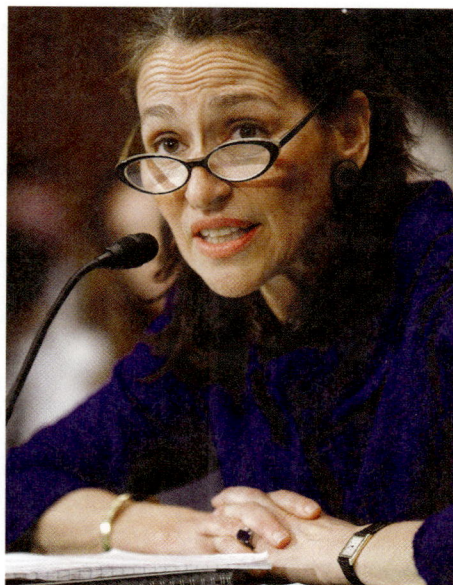

Margaret Hamburg testifies before the Senate Health, Education, Labor and Pensions Committee on May 7, 2009, on her nomination as director of the FDA. With Hamburg's nomination, President Barack Obama promised an overhaul of the troubled agency. As former New York City health commissioner, Hamburg was credited with substantially reducing tuberculosis rates and increasing childhood immunizations.

FDA and Health and Human Services officials open a U.S. food and drug inspection facility in Guangzhou, capital of south China's Guangdong province, in November 2008. The plant was opened after food and drug ingredients exported to the United States were found to be tainted. A contaminated key ingredient in the blood-thinning pharmaceutical heparin killed dozens of people in 2008.

letter in May to Minnesota-based General Mills, manufacturer of the popular breakfast cereal Cheerios, warning the firm that its claims that the cereal could lower blood cholesterol (a substance that has been linked to heart disease) might lead Cheerios to be classified as a drug, rather than a food, and that it thus might need to be approved as such. Given widespread marketing of some foods as having health-promoting properties, which had previously been allowed by the FDA, this was a notable change in direction.

In July, the FDA issued a new regulation that would, it was hoped, prevent 79,000 annual illnesses and 30 deaths from eggs contaminated with *Salmonella*. It requires more careful testing, monitoring, cleaning and disinfecting, and better refrigeration. The FDA also issued "guidances" regarding the production of tomatoes, leafy greens, and melons designed to minimize hazards associated with those foods.

In August, Director Hamburg announced a series of reforms in the FDA's regulatory and enforcement system, including tighter deadlines for producer responses to FDA inspection findings; a streamlined process for issuing warning letters to food suppliers; better coordination among the FDA and state and local agencies; and quicker FDA action on "significant public health concerns."

Congressional action

In 2009, the U.S. House considered several bills designed to strengthen both the FDA and food and drug safety overall, including H.R. 875, the Food Safety Modernization Act, and H.R. 2749, the Food Safety

Enhancement Act. Although both had supporters, H.R. 2749 had the stronger political base. Among other provisions, it would increase federal oversight and inspection of both foreign and domestic food production facilities; require that certain imported foods be certified as safe by the Department of Health and Human Services; and require labeling of foods by country of origin. Most importantly, the bill would allow the FDA, for the first time, to issue mandatory recalls of contaminated foods and to prevent the transportation of such foods.

Despite significant opposition from parties ranging from organic farmers to small food processors, the bill passed in the House in July. It was then sent to the Senate, where its fate was uncertain, especially because a competing bill, the Food Safety Modernization Act (S.B. 510), had significant support in the upper house.

In February 2008, the FDA announced a new program, "Safety First," intended to monitor the effects of drugs and devices after they have been marketed. In January 2009, the GAO reported that "the FDA faces challenges in postmarket surveillance of medical devices," noting that the number of negative events associated with such devices had increased markedly between 2000 and 2006.

In June 2009, following years of complaints that the FDA had withheld negative information about medical products, sometimes resulting in harm to patients, the new FDA commissioner, Margaret Hamburg, announced formation of a task force that would determine how information could be made available on a more timely basis. Health advocates hoped that this might allow the public to learn of potential dangers sooner than in the past.

On June 22, 2009, President Obama signed into law the Family Smoking Prevention and Tobacco Control Act, bringing tobacco products under FDA oversight for the first time. Antitobacco advocates had been seeking such authority for the agency for years. The act gave the FDA power to ban most flavored cigarettes (use of menthol was allowed for the time being); prohibit claims of low levels of tar; restrict tobacco advertising (including banning ads near schools); and empower the FDA to set standards for the level of nicotine in cigarettes. The FDA cannot, however, ban the sale of tobacco products.

What will the future hold?

Given the U.S. desire for a broad variety of affordable foods available at any time of the year, the growing globalization of the food supply, an increasingly complex food supply chain, and overburdened government agencies that cannot possibly cope with ever-increasing demands and dangers, it seems unlikely that a completely safe, thoroughly inspected, risk-free food supply will ever again be a feature of American life—if it ever was. However, the recent initiatives will make it less likely that grossly contaminated food products—domestic or foreign—will be widely distributed without public knowledge or warnings.

It remains to be seen how the FDA will handle its new drug-regulation responsibilities. Funding, staffing, and a supportive political environment will be very important. But for now, at least, it appears that a new day is dawning for the agency.

United States, President of the.

Barack Obama, a Democrat, was inaugurated on Jan. 20, 2009, as the 44th president of the United States, succeeding George W. Bush, a Republican. Obama made history by becoming the nation's first African American president. He spent much of his first year in office responding to an economic recession, lobbying for health care reform, and overseeing U.S. military efforts in Afghanistan, Pakistan, and Iraq. On October 9, President Obama was awarded the Nobel Peace Prize.

Economic policy. The president's chief domestic achievement in 2009 was shepherding a huge economic stimulus package through Congress. This legislation, which he signed on February 17, included $212 billion in tax cuts and $575 billion in spending on education, health care, energy, transportation infrastructure, and aid to the unemployed and needy. The Obama administration also launched efforts in early 2009 to stabilize the banking system, unfreeze credit markets, and help homeowners at risk of foreclosure. In June, the administration took a controlling interest in the U.S. automaker General Motors Company after forcing it to undergo bankruptcy restructuring. Later in 2009, the president urged Congress to increase the government's regulatory power over the financial system and to pass additional measures to encourage job creation. But Congress did not enact final legislation for these initiatives before the year ended.

Health care reform. President Obama made a major effort in 2009 to push for health care reform. He urged Congress to enact a bill that would extend health insurance coverage to all Americans and control the growth of health care costs. The House of Representatives passed a reform bill on November 7, and the Senate passed one on December 24. But the bills were not reconciled before the end of 2009. The bills received almost no support from Republicans.

Nobel Prize. The Norwegian Nobel Committee's decision to give the Peace Prize to President Obama came as a surprise to most observers. According to the committee, the prize was awarded "for his extraordinary efforts to strengthen international diplomacy and cooperation between peoples." The committee especially praised his vision of a world without nuclear weapons. A number of Americans and foreigners celebrated the committee's choice, but others suggested that President Obama did not yet deserve the honor after only nine months in office. Many people saw the prize as a denunciation of President Bush's foreign policy, which had been unpopular in much of Europe.

■ Mike Lewis

See also **Cabinet, U.S.; Congress of the United States; Nobel Prizes; Television; United States, Government of the.**

Throngs of people—over 1 million, by many estimates— gather on the National Mall in Washington, D.C., to witness the inauguration. The gathering may have been the largest Mall event in history.

President Barack Obama and First Lady Michelle Obama (left) parade down Pennsylvania Avenue after the swearing-in ceremony on January 20. The Obamas dance (below) at the Neighborhood Inaugural Ball, the first of 10 inaugural balls on their schedule that evening.

Barack Obama was inaugurated president of the United States on Jan. 20, 2009, the first African American president in U.S. history.

Chief Justice John Roberts administers the oath of office to President Obama again on January 21 because Roberts had stumbled over the words of the oath on the previous day.

Uruguay. On Nov. 29, 2009, José Mujica, 74, of the incumbent left-wing Broad Front coalition, was elected president of Uruguay. Mujica, a former minister of agriculture, had been serving as a Socialist Party senator. Tabaré Ramón Vázquez Rosas, the sitting president, enjoyed a successful term, finishing with approval ratings above 60 percent. Uruguay's Constitution, however, does not allow for reelection. Mujica was expected to continue many of his predecessor's popular economic policies. Mujica was imprisoned for more than 10 years for his political actions as a guerrilla fighter rebelling against the military dictatorship that ruled Uruguay from 1973 to 1985.

In September 2009, Uruguay became the first Latin American nation to allow gay couples to adopt children. Unmarried couples of any orientation were also given the right to adopt. Earlier, the Uruguayan congress legalized same-sex civil unions and gave homosexuals the right to openly serve in the armed forces.

In October, former President Gregorio Álvarez, 83, was sentenced to 25 years in prison for murder and human rights violations. A court in Montevideo, the capital, found Álvarez guilty of 37 murders committed while he was serving as head of the army in the 1970's and as president from 1981 to 1985.   ■ Nathan A. Haverstock

See also **Latin America.**

Uzbekistan. In a move widely criticized by international human rights groups, the European Union (EU) lifted its arms embargo on Uzbekistan on Oct. 27, 2009. The EU had imposed the sanctions after Uzbek government troops fired on hundreds of unarmed demonstrators in the eastern city of Andijon in 2005. Rights groups argued that the Uzbek government's conduct had not improved, as it continued to repress and imprison activists and opposition leaders. The EU said that it lifted the sanctions to encourage Uzbekistan to improve the human rights situation in the country.

Amendments to Uzbekistan's election laws passed in December 2008 expanded the size of the lower house of the Uzbek parliament, the Oliy Majlis, from 120 seats to 150 and reserved 15 seats for the Ecological Movement of Uzbekistan. In elections on Dec. 27, 2009, only 94 of the 135 contested seats were filled, prompting a runoff for the remaining seats. President Islam Karimov called the election the "first steps towards building a democratic society" in Uzbekistan. International election monitors, however, noted that all legal parties support Karimov's government and cited instances of ballot stuffing and other forms of voter fraud.   ■ Juliet Johnson

See also **Asia.**

Vanuatu. See **Pacific Islands.**

Venezuela. On Feb. 15, 2009, Venezuelan voters approved a referendum that abolished term limits on elected officials and allowed President Hugo Chávez to run for reelection in 2012. "Those who voted 'yes' today voted for socialism, for revolution!" Chávez thundered to thousands of supporters as fireworks lit up the skyline of Caracas, the capital.

Chávez visited dozens of countries in 2009 to promote his personal vision of a new world in which economic power was shared to replace a United States-dominated capitalistic one that, in his opinion, had failed. "The pure energy of the man is intoxicating," declared U.S. filmmaker Oliver Stone, who interviewed Chávez for a documentary about how leftist Latin American leaders were effecting their "liberation from the United States."

Uncertain oil markets. In early 2009, the plunging price of oil, which accounted for 94 percent of Venezuela's exports and nearly half of its federal budget, forced Chávez to scale back Venezuela's spending on foreign assistance. Previously announced plans to help build oil refineries in eight smaller, energy-short Latin American nations were put on hold, as was Chávez's proposal to construct a natural gas pipeline across the South American continent.

The cuts in total Venezuelan spending overseas for all purposes, including foreign aid, were huge, according to a May study by the Center of Economic Investigations in Caracas. The independent financial consulting firm estimated that Venezuela would spend about $6 billion abroad in 2009, compared with $79 billion in 2008.

Oil deals. In January 2009, senior officials of Petróleos de Venezuela—the state-run oil company—invited bids from international oil companies to develop the huge reserves in the Orinoco Belt. According to industry analysts, this would require more than $20 billion in investment, plus state-of-the-art technology to transform enough of the region's heavy crude deposits to produce 1.2 million barrels of oil per day.

In September, Chávez announced that some of this investment would come from China, which planned to invest $16 billion more over three years to increase the output of oil from the Orinoco Belt. A prior investment, similar in size, was secured by future shipments of oil to China. Also in September, Russia and Venezuela agreed on a $20-billion investment by Russian companies to boost production of the Junin 6 oil field in the Orinoco Belt.

Russian arms. In response to Colombia's decision to grant the United States access to Colombian military bases, Chávez reached an agreement to buy tanks and antiaircraft systems from Russia. The September deal, worth more than $2 billion, was intended to strengthen Venezuela's military defenses. "We have the largest petroleum reserves in the world," Chávez said. "The empire [Chávez's description of the United States] has set its sights on them."

Barinas crime. The western state of Barinas, stronghold of the Venezuelan president's family, was the scene of 66 kidnappings in the first six months of 2009. Adán Chávez, the president's brother and governor of the state, blamed the surge in crime on political opponents trying to destabilize the local economy. Others blamed corruption within the Chávez family, which had governed the state since the 1990's and profited from internal projects. The Chávez family—native to Barinas—controls the state, with family members in top government and business positions.

Radio silence. In what was widely viewed as a blatant attack on freedom of expression, the Venezuelan government closed 34 privately owned radio stations on Aug. 1, 2009. An additional 208 stations were at risk of being shut down for failing to comply with government regulations. Officials claimed they were attempting to "democratize" the airwaves.

■ Nathan A. Haverstock

See also **Colombia; Latin America.**

Vietnam. The strongest domestic challenge ever faced by Vietnam's Communist government developed in 2009 over its plan to allow a Chinese company to mine bauxite, the base material for aluminum, in the country's Central Highlands region. Some experts believe that Vietnam may have the world's third-largest reserves of bauxite.

Prime Minister Nguyen Tan Dung called the plan "a major policy of the [Communist] party and the state." Scientists and environmentalists campaigned against the plan, warning of pollution and the displacement of minority populations who live in the area. They also questioned the need for bringing Chinese laborers into Vietnam, which has high unemployment.

The Vietnamese government released more than 5,000 prisoners on September 2 as part of a National Day amnesty. Officials did not free Roman Catholic priest Nguyen Van Ly, who had spent 17 years in prison since the 1970's for advocating human rights. In 2007, he was sentenced to eight years in prison on a charge of spreading antigovernment propaganda after he attempted to start a prodemocracy political party. In July 2009, a group of 37 United States senators wrote to Vietnamese President Nguyen Minh Triet to request the priest's freedom. ■ Henry S. Bradsher

See also **Asia; Disasters.**

Vital statistics. See **Census; Population.**

Washington, D.C. A self-proclaimed white supremacist and anti-Semite allegedly shot and killed a security guard at the United States Holocaust Memorial Museum on June 10, 2009. The gunman had a history of Internet hate statements against African Americans and Jews.

James W. von Brunn, 88, was charged with the slaying. Reports from the scene said the guard, Stephen T. Johns, 39, was stationed just inside the museum when he held open the door for the elderly gunman. The man immediately lowered a rifle at Johns and fired at him at close range. Other security guards fired back, wounding the gunman. Johns, an African American who worked for the Wackenhut security agency, subsequently died of his wounds.

At a September 2 hearing in District of Columbia federal court, Assistant U.S. Attorney Nicole Waid said the murder was premeditated and that von Brunn was on a suicide mission to promote his belief that the Holocaust was a fabricated story. The Holocaust was the mass murder of Jews and other groups by the Nazis from 1933 to 1945. Von Brunn, a resident of Annapolis, Maryland, was indicted on seven counts that included first-degree murder and hate crimes. No one else was charged.

The area around the Holocaust Museum, heavy with tourists who flock there to visit Washington's most popular sites, was chaotic just after the shooting, with S.W.A.T. teams and emergency vehicles responding. Each year, about 2 million people visit the museum, which opened in 1993.

Deadly rail crash. Nine people were killed and more than 50 others were injured on June 22, 2009, when a southbound Metrorail train struck the rear end of a stopped train near the Fort Totten station on the city's north side. National Transportation Safety Board investigators said an automatic detection system did not identify the stopped train or send signals for the moving train to stop.

School layoffs. Michelle A. Rhee, the chancellor of the D.C. public schools, notified 388 school employees, including 229 teachers, on October 2 that their jobs were being terminated. The teachers composed about 6 percent of the District's public school classroom educators.

School officials said the layoffs reflected a steep enrollment decline over the past 10 years, to about 44,400 students. The officials hoped the cuts would help close a deficit of about $44 million in the school district's $760-million budget.

On October 16, D.C. Council Chairman Vincent C. Gray convened a hearing on the layoffs. More than 100 people testified during the hearing, which lasted 18 hours. Those testifying included teachers, students, and parents, almost all of whom were opposed to the cutbacks. The hearing ended just after 4 a.m. on October 17.

Gun ownership. In a bid to preserve some of its gun restrictions, the D.C. Council issued new regulations on June 19 that permitted residents to own about 1,000 new handgun models.

The Supreme Court of the United States had ruled in 2008 that a D.C. ban on handgun ownership, in effect since 1976, violated the constitutional rights of citizens. After the 2008 decision, Washington's police department began registering handguns, and the city began loosening its gun ownership requirements.

The new regulations drawn up in June 2009 were intended to head off challenges that the law still violated the Second Amendment to the Constitution of the United States. The amendment guarantees, in part, that "the right of the people to keep and bear arms shall not be infringed."

Same-sex marriage. The D.C. Council passed an ordinance in May that recognizes same-sex marriages performed in other states and countries as legal in the District. The decision, passed by a vote of 12-1, took effect on July 7.

The D.C. Council voted on December 15 to legalize same-sex marriage in the District. Following the vote, the measure was subject to a 30-day review period by the U.S. Congress before it could become law. ■ Howard S. Shapiro

Water. See **Environmental pollution.**

Weather. A deep winter chill gripped the midwestern and northeastern United States as 2009 began. On January 15, temperatures in Waterloo, Iowa, dropped to –34 °F (–36.7 °C), its lowest January temperature on record. The next day, Caribou, Maine, reached an all-time January low of –37 °F (–38.3 °C). A new state low was set in Maine when the temperature plummeted to –50 °F (–45.6 °C) at Big Black River on January 16. Later that month, severe ice storms struck the Southern Plains and Ohio Valley from January 26 to 28, resulting in 55 deaths. About 1.3 million people lost electric power due to downed lines.

In western Europe, a fierce storm with winds of about 120 miles (193 kilometers) per hour slammed southwestern France and northeastern Spain in January. Twenty-seven people were killed in the worst storm to hit the region in a decade.

In the Southern Hemisphere, intense heat gripped Australia in early 2009. On February 7, the hottest temperature ever recorded so far south in the world—120 °F (48.8 °C)—was reported at Hopetoun, Victoria. The heat sparked the worst wildfires in Australian history. In the hardest-hit state, Victoria, 173 people were killed as around 1 million acres (430,000 hectares) of brush were singed and 2,000 homes burned.

Early spring storms from March 25 to 28 pounded the central United States. Parts of north-

Washington, D.C., transit employees and firefighters work at the scene of a deadly rail crash on the city's north side. On June 22, a southbound Metrorail train struck the rear end of a stopped train, killing 9 people and injuring more than 50 others.

western Texas and western Oklahoma were buried by up to 2 feet (0.6 meter) of snow, while more than 60 tornadoes were counted farther east. On March 30 and 31, 1 to 2 feet (0.3 to 0.6 meter) of snow smothered areas from Colorado to the Northern Plains. Fargo, North Dakota, received 28.1 inches (71.4 centimeters) of snow in March, the city's largest total snowfall for that month on record. Heavy winter precipitation and snowmelt over the Northern Plains led to record flooding along parts of the Red and Missouri rivers. Ice jams caused the Missouri River at Bismarck, North Dakota, to flood for the first time since the 1950's. Farther east, a record crest of 40.8 feet (12.4 meters) was measured on the Red River at Fargo, just 9 inches (22.9 centimeters) below the highest levees in the city. Nearly 4,000 people were evacuated from around Fargo, and 2 people were killed.

Several episodes of severe weather struck across the upper South later in the spring. On April 9 and 10, 2009, 112 tornadoes were reported. A strong twister, with peak winds estimated at 265 miles (426 kilometers) per hour, tore a 15-mile (24-kilometer) path through Murfreesboro, Tennessee, killing a mother and her 9-week-old infant and causing $42 million in damages.

Record heat came to parts of the nation in late April and May. On April 28, the temperature in Portland, Maine, soared to 92 °F (33.3 °C), the city's hottest-ever April reading since record keeping began in 1871. Fairbanks, Alaska, also had its highest April temperature since record keeping began in 1904. On April 30, 2009, the mercury hit 76 °F (24.4 °C).

Wildfires plagued the Southern Plains, a result of the second-driest winter on record. Flames engulfed over 200 homes and led to 3 deaths in Oklahoma and Texas. Farther east, wildfires near Myrtle Beach, South Carolina, burned across nearly 20,000 acres (8,094 hectares) from April 22 to 24. The fires damaged or destroyed about 200 homes, forced the evacuation of 2,500 people, and caused an estimated $16 million in damages.

The spring tornado season was unusually quiet in 2009. The Storm Prediction Center in Norman, Oklahoma, issued no severe thunderstorm or tornado watches in the seven days ending on May 23. This was the first time since record keeping began in 1970 that no watches were issued during that week.

Unusual weather. May and June 2009 were marked by strong temperature and precipitation contrasts in the West. For the first time on record, the temperature in May at Phoenix reached 100 °F (37.8 °C) for 14 straight days. In June, the temperatures in Phoenix stayed below 100 °F (37.8 °C) for 15 days, the longest such cool period in June since 1913.

Beginning on May 22, downtown Los Angeles had 40 consecutive days with below-normal afternoon temperatures. The highest reading in June at Los Angeles International Airport was 71 °F (21.7 °C), the lowest maximum temperature for June since record keeping began in 1944. Seattle had its longest dry spell on record for May and June, with 30 consecutive days ending on June 19, 2009. Denver had its wettest June since 1882, and Salt Lake City set a record for its greatest number of days with rain—17 days in June 2009.

In Florida, Pensacola reached its highest June temperature on record with 102 °F (38.9 °C). New Orleans, with 101 °F (38.3 °C), and Houston, with 104 °F (40 °C), also had their highest temperature for any June day. July was marked by a recurrent summer chill in the Midwest and Northeast. Six states in a swath from Iowa to Pennsylvania recorded their coolest July since record keeping began in 1895. New York City marked its longest string of cool summer days since record keeping began in 1869. Temperatures remained below 85 °F (29.5 °C) for 46 consecutive days ending on July 16, 2009.

Hurricane activity. A pattern of diminished hurricane activity that began in 2007 continued in 2009. Through August, the amount of wind energy produced in a two-year period by tropical cyclones in the Northern Hemisphere reached its lowest value since continuous satellite coverage began in the 1970's. No hurricane made landfall in the United States in 2009. However, Hurricane Bill brushed Nova Scotia and Newfoundland and Labrador on August 22.

Typhoons in Asia. A series of tropical typhoons wreaked havoc over the western Pacific. Typhoon Morakot made landfall in Taiwan on August 7, bringing the worst flooding in 50 years. As much as 83 inches (211 centimeters) of rain fell over the mountains of the southern part of the island. In late September and October, the northern Philippines were lashed by three tropical cyclones. The first, Ketsana, triggered the worst flooding in four decades around the capital, Manila, as it crossed the island of Luzon on September 26. Ketsana then moved into Southeast Asia. The storm caused at least 600 deaths. During October, two more typhoons, Parma and Mirinae, struck the northern Philippines, bringing more rain that hampered recovery efforts from Ketsana and caused the deaths of about 500 people.

Repeated rain in September saturated the ground in parts of the southeastern United States, leading to exceptional flooding around Atlanta. Up to 17 inches (43 centimeters) of rain was reported over parts of the the city's northern suburbs in eight days ending on September 22. The floods caused nine deaths in Georgia

Typhoons triggered massive flooding in central and eastern Asia in 2009, leaving thousands dead and tens of thousands homeless.

A local man ferries two girls across a flooded street (below) in China's Wenzhou province in August 2009, after Typhoon Morakot moved over mainland China.

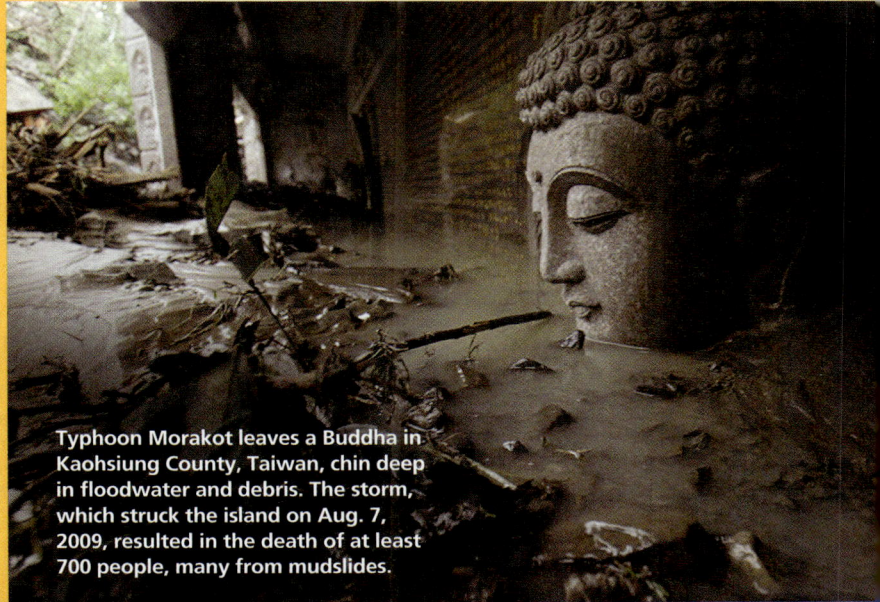

Typhoon Morakot leaves a Buddha in Kaohsiung County, Taiwan, chin deep in floodwater and debris. The storm, which struck the island on Aug. 7, 2009, resulted in the death of at least 700 people, many from mudslides.

Heavy monsoon rains flood the streets of Mumbai on Oct. 5, 2009, causing at least 300 deaths. Before the October rains, India's monsoon season from June to September had been the driest since 1972.

and more than $250 million in damages.

In October, chilly temperatures and a surge of moisture brought weather extremes to much of the nation. On October 10, the third game of the National League baseball divisional play-offs was postponed due to snow and temperatures in the lower 20's in Denver. Widespread inclement weather during the month led to the slowest corn harvest since 1992 and the slowest cotton harvest in the past 25 years. Averaged across the entire United States, it was the wettest and third-coldest October since record keeping began in 1895.

December storm. On Dec. 20 and 21, 2009, an enormous winter storm dumped record-breaking amounts of snow—30 inches (76 centimeters) in some areas—along the East Coast of the United States from Virginia to New England. Sixteen inches (40 centimeters) of snow, the most ever recorded for a single December day, crippled Washington D.C. Philadelphia had 23.2 inches (59 centimeters), the city's second largest snowfall since record keeping began in 1884. The storm disrupted transportation all along the coast, with thousands of travelers stranded in airports and train and bus stations. Hundreds of thousands of households were without electric power, and shopping malls were nearly empty on what is usually one of the busiest shopping days of the year. The deaths of at least five people, in traffic accidents and from exposure, were blamed on the storm. ■ Fred Gadomski and Todd Miner

Weightlifting. See Sports.

Welfare. Welfare rolls continued to rise in many parts of the United States in early 2009, according to data released by the U.S. Administration for Children and Families and a survey conducted by *The Wall Street Journal* and National Conference of State Legislatures in mid-2009. Nationwide, welfare rolls grew by about 3 percent in 2008 because of the recession that began in late 2007. This rise was the first in welfare numbers since welfare reform legislation was enacted in 1996. The number of families receiving cash aid under the Temporary Assistance for Needy Families (TANF) program rose from 1,643,136 in December 2007 to 1,691,695 in December 2008, and the number of individuals receiving aid during that period rose from 3,825,359 to 3,950,357. (These numbers were still far lower than the August 1996 numbers—4,408,508 families and 12,242,125 individuals.) TANF cash aid is provided, for up to five years, to needy families with dependent children, with the requirement that the parents must be working, training for work, or seeking work.

In 2009, the U.S. Food and Nutrition Service reported that in 2007, 26 million people participated in the Supplemental Nutrition Assistance Program (then called the Food Stamp Program)—66 percent of the 39 million who were eligible. The program provides benefits to low-income people to help them buy food. ■ Mike Lewis

West Indies. In April 2009, Caribbean leaders at the Fifth Summit of the Americas appealed to United States President Barack Obama for increased economic assistance to cope with the global economic downturn. The summit brought 34 chief executives from Western Hemisphere countries to Port-of-Spain, capital of Trinidad and Tobago. Obama pledged $30 million to strengthen the region's security system in the fight against drug trafficking and organized crime. He also promised to ask international financial agencies to help island nations that had experienced a 15- to 25-percent drop in tourism and high rates of unemployment.

International support. In July, the European Commission announced that it had set aside $56 million for Caribbean energy, transportation, and information technology projects. In September, the World Bank, a United Nations affiliate, entered into a "strategic alliance" that was expected to lead to as much as $500 million in support of the Dominican Republic from 2010 through 2013. The agreement was aimed at protecting the poor while enhancing the competitiveness of the Dominican economy. The World Bank also approved a $15-million loan to reduce poverty in rural areas of Jamaica in September 2009 by improving market access for small-scale farmers to tourist areas.

Stanford scandal. Many depositors of the Bank of Antigua withdrew their funds after the bank's owner, Texas property developer and banker Sir Allen Stanford, was charged with fraud on February 17. The U.S. Securities and Exchange Commission accused him of running an $8-billion fraudulent investment scheme. Stanford was a dual citizen of the United States and twin-island nation of Antigua and Barbuda. He had received a knighthood from the Antiguan government for his charitable work and cricket sponsorship.

Tax havens. During 2009, there was increasing scrutiny of banking operations in several Caribbean countries for allegedly failing to measure up to international standards in reporting taxable income. In September, the French banking giant BNP Paribas announced it would shut down its offices in the Bahamas because of concerns over the matter.

Death of a president. On March 28, former Guyanese President Janet Rosenberg Jagan died at age 88 in Georgetown, the capital. The Chicago-born Jagan moved to Guyana in 1943. She served as the country's first woman president from 1997 to 1999. ■ Nathan A. Haverstock

See also **Haiti; Latin America; Puerto Rico.**

Yemen. See **Middle East.**
Yukon. See **Canadian territories.**
Zambia. See **Africa.**

Zimbabwe. Confidence in Zimbabwe's unity government wavered throughout 2009. In September 2008, President Robert Mugabe and his Zimbabwe African National Union-Patriotic Front (ZANU-PF) had made a power-sharing agreement with Morgan Tsvangirai's opposition Movement for Democratic Change (MDC). However, a lack of cooperation and what the MDC charged was ZANU-PF persecution of its supporters made the agreement virtually unworkable. The political standstill stalled efforts to deal with a continuing economic crisis and a worsening cholera epidemic.

Unity deal. In accordance with the 2008 power-sharing deal, Tsvangirai finally took office as prime minister on Feb. 11, 2009. His appointment followed five months of wrangling over the relative powers of the two leaders and over the distribution of key Cabinet seats.

On February 13, a new unity Cabinet took office with 20 seats for each party. However, the future of the *coalition* (partnership) was immediately thrown into doubt by the arrest on the same day of Roy Bennett, a high-ranking MDC official who had been named deputy agriculture minister. Bennett pleaded not guilty to terrorism charges, and his trial began on November 16. Independent analysts said the charges against him were part of a ZANU-PF plot to discredit the MDC and undermine the coalition. Bennett's imprisonment led the MDC to "disengage"—but not officially withdraw—from the unity government from mid-October to early November.

Other analysts blamed *hard-liners*—rigid leaders who were reluctant to compromise—inside the powerful Joint Operations Command. The command, consisting of military and police commanders and other high-ranking officials who favored ZANU-PF, was believed to be angered by the MDC's participation in the government. Besides Bennett, a number of other MDC members of Parliament were arrested in 2009 on charges that the MDC called false.

International reactions. On September 9, the Southern African Development Community (SADC) called for the unconditional lifting of international *sanctions* (penalties) against Zimbabwe. The SADC, which brokered the 2008 power-sharing deal, is a group devoted to improving economic conditions and political cooperation among the nations of southern Africa. The European Union, the United States, and other Western governments refused to lift the sanctions, however, until the Zimbabwe government showed it was willing to make political and economic reforms. The sanctions included the withholding of billions of dollars in aid.

Cholera crisis spreads. The World Health Organization (WHO), a United Nations agency, said that the death toll from Zimbabwe's cholera epidemic had exceeded 4,200 by July 2009. WHO estimated that more than 100,000 others were infected with the disease. The epidemic, which had begun in August 2008, was one sign of the country's deepening economic crisis, which was marked by severe food shortages. Roughly half of all Zimbabweans needed food aid in 2009.

Child abuse. Tens of thousands of children in Zimbabwe suffer sexual abuse every year, according to a report on November 9 in the British newspaper *The Guardian.* The article noted that one clinic in the capital, Harare, had treated nearly 30,000 abused girls and boys over the previous four years—a rate of some 20 children per day. The Family Support Trust, a child welfare organization in Harare, said that the real number of children who had suffered rape or other forms of sexual abuse was likely double that reported.

Human rights activists said that the abuse statistics indicated a wider social and economic breakdown under Mugabe, who had led Zimbabwe's government since independence in 1980. During the Mugabe years, many children lost their parents to HIV/AIDS or were left in the care of other adults because their parents had become economic refugees, leaving the country to escape bad economic conditions. ■ Simon Baynham

See also **Africa.**

Zoology. See Biology; Conservation; Ocean.

Zoos. The economic recession hit zoos hard in 2009, as many zoos suffered severe budget cuts due to reduced public funding and charitable donations. Some zoos responded with warnings that they would have to shutter exhibits or even close altogether. In July, newspapers reported that the Franklin Park Zoo in Boston might euthanize as many as 20 percent of its animals due to budget cuts. In response, legislators restored much of the funding. In August, the Bronx Zoo announced that budget shortfalls would force it to close exhibits and relocate hundreds of animals. This move came even after a public campaign resulted in restored public funding. Among the exhibits shuttered was the World of Darkness, an exhibit for nocturnal animals.

On the bright side, zoo attendance increased in Baltimore, Cincinnati, St. Louis, and many other cities, according to the American Zoo and Aquarium Association. One major zoo even swam against the funding tide. In May, the Phoenix Zoo announced that it had raised half of the $20 million funding goal it announced in October 2008. The money is slated for new exhibits housing tigers, Komodo dragons, and orangutans.

Blockbuster exhibits. A $45-million exhibit that houses living relatives of prehistoric beasts opened in May 2009 at the San Diego Zoo. The Harry and Grace Steele Elephant Odyssey includes a 137,000-gallon (519,000-liter) pool that covers 7.5 acres (3 hectares). Billed as a "journey through time," the cornerstone of the exhibit is a herd of seven Asian elephants. These elephants are the closest living relatives to the Columbian mammoths that went extinct about 10,000 years ago in North America. The exhibit displays dozens of other animals that are endangered or related to creatures of the region's prehistoric past. Replicas of prehistoric animals are distributed throughout the exhibit. Living species shown include the California condor, tree sloth, jaguar, and pronghorn.

The Shedd Aquarium in Chicago completed a $50-million renovation of its Oceanarium in May. During remodeling, Shedd's seven beluga whales and four Pacific white-sided dolphins lived at the Mystic Aquarium in Connecticut. Among other improvements, Shedd visitors can now wade into a pool and touch the whales. In addition to the whales and dolphins, the exhibit features California sea lions, along with Magellanic and rockhopper penguins.

The Philadelphia Zoo opened its new McNeil Avian Center in May. The renovation to the original bird house took 10 years and cost $17.5 million. The new center houses more than 100 bird species, many of them endangered. The center simulates a variety of habitats, including the African savanna and the Pacific Islands.

After a 10-year absence, African lions returned to the Oregon Zoo in Portland in September. Three young lions joined cheetahs and African wild dogs in the Predators of the Serengeti exhibit. The exhibit, which occupies 2.5 acres (1 hectare) and cost $6.4 million, also houses red-billed hornbills, dwarf mongooses, and a huge African rock python.

Happy anniversary. The Fort Worth Zoo in Texas celebrated its 100th anniversary in 2009. The zoo opened with only one lion, two bear cubs, an alligator, a coyote, a peacock, and a few rabbits. Today, the zoo houses 5,000 animals and is visited by more than 1 million people a year.

Name game. A bevy of animals with unusual names reproduced at zoos in 2009. In June, an addax gave birth at the Brookfield Zoo in Illinois. The addax is a rare antelope with screwlike horns that lives in the Sahara. In May, four Tadjik markhors were born at the Los Angeles Zoo. These are wild sheep from Asia. A Chinese goral, a takin, and a Japanese serow also gave birth. All belong to a group loosely called "goat-antelopes." Other newborns included a gerenuk, which is an African antelope with a giraffelike neck, and two babirusas, which are wild Indonesian pigs.

A bongo gave birth at the Louisville Zoo in Kentucky in July. The bongo is an African forest antelope with lyre-shaped horns. Two Meller's ducklings, which are native to Madagascar, hatched that same month.

Rare and endangered. Zoos continued to breed endangered animals in 2009. The Henry Doorly Zoo in Omaha, Nebraska, welcomed a baby gorilla in July. A giant panda at the San Diego Zoo produced her fifth cub in August. An endangered Indian rhinoceros was born at the Lowry Park Zoo in Tampa in July. Only about 2,000 of the one-horned rhinos remain in the wild. In September, the Albuquerque Biological Park in New Mexico added an Asian elephant.

Red pandas are rare, so the Cleveland Metroparks Zoo was delighted to welcome red panda triplets in September. The National Zoo Conservation and Research Center in Front Royal, Virginia, celebrated the birth of its own red panda in July. The zoo also announced the birth of a clouded leopard. This native of Southeast Asia has unusually long canine teeth and a skull that somewhat resembles those of prehistoric saber-toothed cats.

Old-timer. In June, a female Japanese macaque affectionately known as "Baldy" turned 35 years old at the Blank Park Zoo in Des Moines, Iowa. Animal keepers celebrated Baldy's record-breaking birthday with a round of special monkey brownies and cookies for the 21 members of her troop.

■ Ed Ricciuti

Aurora, a 20-year-old beluga whale, swims with her newborn calf at the Vancouver Aquarium in British Columbia on June 7, 2009. Aurora delivered the calf after four hours of labor.

WORLD BOOK SUPPLEMENT

Four new or revised articles are reprinted from the 2010 edition of *The World Book Encyclopedia.*

Havana, on Cuba's northwest coast, is the country's capital and largest city. It has many government buildings, including the Ministry of the Interior building, shown in the foreground. A steel image of Che Guevara, a powerful member of the Cuban government under Fidel Castro, decorates the side of the building.

© Steven S. Miric, SuperStock

Cuba

Cuba, *KYOO buh,* is an island nation that is the only Communist state in the Americas. It lies about 90 miles (145 kilometers) south of Key West, Florida. Havana is Cuba's capital and largest city.

Cuba is the largest and one of the most beautiful of the islands in the West Indies. Towering mountains and rolling hills cover about a third of the island. The rest of Cuba consists mainly of gentle slopes and broad grasslands. Cuba has a magnificent coastline marked with deep bays, sandy beaches, and colorful coral reefs.

Cuba's location has greatly influenced its history. The island lies at the intersection of major sea routes between the Atlantic Ocean, the Caribbean Sea, and the Gulf of Mexico. The famous explorer Christopher Columbus, sailing in the service of Spain, landed in Cuba in 1492. The island later became strategically important in Spain's American empire.

In the late 1700's and early 1800's, sugar cane became Cuba's leading crop. Sugar-cane growers of European ancestry raised their crops on large plantations that depended heavily on human labor. To provide cheap labor, growers brought thousands of Africans to Cuba and forced them to work as slaves.

During the 1800's, many Cubans rebelled against Spanish rule. In 1898, the United States helped defeat Spain, which then gave up all claims to Cuba. A U.S. military government ruled Cuba from 1899 to 1902, when the island became a republic. However, the United

Facts in brief

Capital: Havana.
Official language: Spanish.
Official name: República de Cuba (Republic of Cuba).
Area: 42,427 mi² (109,886 km²). *Greatest distances*—northwest-southeast, 708 mi (1,139 km); north-south, 135 mi (217 km). *Coastline*—2,320 mi (3,735 km).
Elevation: *Highest*—Pico Turquino, 6,542 ft (1,994 m). *Lowest*—sea level.
Population: *Estimated 2010 population*—11,265,000; density, 266 per mi² (103 per km²); distribution, 76 percent urban, 24 percent rural. *2002 census*—11,177,743.
Chief products: *Agriculture*—coffee, fruits, sugar cane, tobacco, vegetables. *Manufacturing*—cement, cigars, fertilizers, food processing, leather goods, paper and wood products, refined petroleum, refined sugar, textiles. *Mining*—chromium, cobalt, copper, iron, manganese, nickel.
National anthem: "La Bayamesa" ("The Bayamo Song").
Money: *Basic units*—Cuban peso and Cuban convertible peso (also called chavito). One hundred centavos equal one peso. One hundred convertible centavos equal one convertible peso. See **Peso.**

States maintained close ties with Cuba and often intervened in the island's internal affairs. From 1934 to 1940 and from 1952 to 1959, Cuba was controlled by the dictator Fulgencio Batista y Zaldívar.

Fidel Castro led a revolution that overthrew Batista in 1959. Relations between Cuba and the United States became tense soon after the revolution. Castro set up a Communist government and developed close ties with the Soviet Union, then the main rival of the United States in a struggle for international power. In 1961, the United States ended diplomatic relations with Cuba and imposed strict *economic sanctions* on the island. Economic sanctions are actions that seek to limit or end economic relations with a target country.

Today, the government of Cuba is highly centralized. It provides many benefits for the people, including free medical care and free education. However, political and economic freedom are severely limited.

Outline

Government

According to the Cuban Constitution, adopted in 1976, Cuba is a socialist state. It is governed by a single political party—the Partido Comunista de Cuba (Communist Party of Cuba), also known as the PCC. The Constitution establishes the Communist Party as the leading authority in the government and society. The Party Congress, a gathering of delegates from throughout the country, officially meets every five years. However, these meetings have been irregular. The Central Committee, an administrative body elected by the Congress, is responsible for making the highest levels of policy, and it influences all government institutions. The Central Committee elects members of a smaller group called the Political Bureau, which handles day-to-day policy and decision making. Another small group, the Secretariat, handles daily administrative work.

Until the 1990's, membership in the PCC was highly restricted. For example, people who attended religious services could not join. In the 1990's, however, the party began to expand its membership and to include religious believers. The PCC also sought to attract greater numbers of young people and women.

National government. The National Assembly of People's Power has been Cuba's chief legislative body since 1976. The people elect the members of the Assembly to five-year terms. Citizens who are at least 16 years old may vote.

The National Assembly holds two regular sessions each year. Between sessions, the Assembly is represented by the Council of State and several standing commissions. Council members are elected by the National Assembly from among its members. The president of the council, who serves as both head of state and head of government, is the most powerful government official.

The president, with the approval of the Assembly, appoints a Council of Ministers, which in effect serves as a cabinet. This council enforces laws, directs government agencies, and conducts Cuba's foreign policy.

Provincial and local government. Cuba has a number of provinces, which are divided into municipalities for purposes of local government. Each province and municipality has an assembly. The people elect the members of each municipal assembly. The municipal assemblies of a province elect the members of the provin-

cial assembly. Cuba's largest offshore island, the Isla de la Juventud (Isle of Youth), does not belong to any province. It is ruled directly by the central government.

Municipal assemblies supervise and control local economic enterprises, including retail operations and factories that produce goods for the local market. Municipal assemblies also exercise some authority over schools, health services, cultural activities, sports facilities, and transportation.

Cuba's flag was officially adopted in 1902, shortly after Cuba became a republic. The star stands for independence.

Coat of arms. The key means Cuba is the key to the Gulf of Mexico. The stripes are taken from the nation's flag.

WORLD BOOK map

Cuba is an island country between the Caribbean Sea and the Atlantic Ocean, about 90 miles (145 kilometers) south of Florida.

Courts. The People's Supreme Court is Cuba's highest court. It consists of a president, a vice president, and the members of the court's five *chambers* (divisions). These chambers are civil and administrative, criminal, labor, military, and state security. Each chamber consists of a president, at least two other professional judges, and *lay judges.* Lay judges are citizens who hold their regular jobs while serving on the Supreme Court. The National Assembly elects the Supreme Court justices. The president and vice president of the court are nominated by the president of the Council of State and approved by the National Assembly. Cuba also has provincial and municipal courts throughout the island.

Armed forces. Cuba's armed forces have decreased in size since 1990, but they still rank as one of the largest military forces in Latin America. About 50,000 men and women serve on active duty in the Cuban air force, army, and navy. Approximately 40,000 men and women serve in an army reserve. Territorial militias, civilian groups with military training, also stand ready to defend their country. All Cuban men must serve two years of active duty after they turn 16.

People

Ancestry and language. Most Cubans are descendants of people who came to the island from Spain and Africa. About 30 to 40 percent of the people are white, and approximately 10 to 20 percent are black. Most of the rest are *mulattoes*—that is, people of mixed white and black ancestry. Cuba also has a small percentage of people of Chinese descent. The country's racial and social composition changed significantly between 1959

and 1980, when about 750,000 people emigrated. Most of them were white and middle-class. Spanish is Cuba's official language.

Way of life. The majority of Cuban people live in urban areas. Havana is Cuba's capital, largest city, and commercial and cultural center. Most people in the cities have jobs in government agencies or government-owned businesses and factories, but some run small private businesses. Cuba's cities have a serious housing shortage. Many buildings, neglected for several decades, are in need of repair.

Most of the people in rural areas work on farms. Some rural people live in traditional *bohíos,* which are thatch-roofed dwellings with dirt floors.

Before the 1959 revolution, many rural communities lacked health facilities, schools, adequate transportation and communication, and housing. Since 1959, however, the government has built hospitals, clinics, and schools in the countryside. It also has expanded transportation and communication facilities and increased housing construction. Nevertheless, many rural areas of Cuba continue to lack certain necessities.

Food and drink. Pork, chicken, beans, and rice are the most common Cuban foods. Rice is often served with various kinds of beans, or it is mixed with tomatoes, onions, green peppers, and chicken in a dish called *arroz con pollo.* Another popular dish is *picadillo,* which consists of ground beef, pork, or veal mixed with onions, garlic, tomatoes, and other ingredients. Corn meal is used in tamales and many other dishes. Coffee, rum, and beer are popular beverages.

In the early 1960's, the government organized a food

Cuba
political map

——	Provincial boundary
——	Road
——	Railroad
⊛	National capital
★	Provincial capital
•	Other city or town

WORLD BOOK map

rationing system to deal with the limited availability of scarce and imported foods. This system is designed to provide all households with minimum quantities of rice, beans, meat, chicken, eggs, sugar, milk, and coffee.

Recreation. Cubans are enthusiastic sports fans. Baseball arrived in Cuba from the United States in the late 1800's and quickly became the island's national pastime. Other popular sports include basketball, boxing, swimming, track and field, and volleyball. Soccer also has a growing national following.

Religion. About 40 percent of Cubans belong to the Roman Catholic Church. Many Cubans also believe in Santería, a religion that combines traditional African religious beliefs with Roman Catholic ceremonies. Protestant groups with widespread membership in Cuba include Methodists, Baptists, and Presbyterians. A small Jewish community is concentrated mostly in Havana.

Education. Cuba has one of the most extensive networks of schools in Latin America. All Cubans from the ages of 6 to 14 are required to attend school. Education is free. Nearly all Cuban adults can read and write.

Cuba has dozens of universities and university-level educational institutions. The most important educational institutions include the Central University "Marta Abreu" of Las Villas in Santa Clara, the University of Havana, the University of Oriente in Santiago de Cuba, and the Higher Institute of Art. In the early 2000's, the government began working on a plan to build a university branch in each municipality.

The arts. Cuba has a distinguished tradition in the arts. The Cuban government strongly supports the arts and sponsors free ballets, plays, and other cultural

© Pierre Logwin, Alamy Images

Santiago de Cuba is Cuba's second largest city. It lies at the foot of the Sierra Maestra mountains. A tower of the Cathedral of Our Lady of the Assumption can be seen rising above the buildings.

Provinces

Camagüey	789,883	..C	8
Ciego de Avila	410,701	..C	7
Cienfuegos	...396,691	..B	5
Ciudad de La Habana	..2,186,632	..A	4
Granma	832,644	..D	9
Guantánamo	..514,121	..E	11
Holguín	1,032,670	..D	10
Isla de la Juventud*	80,091	..C	3
La Habana	707,764	..A	4
Las Tunas	530,328	..D	9
Matanzas	661,901	..B	5
Pinar del Río	...737,342	..B	2
Sancti Spíritus	462,320	..C	7
Santiago de Cuba	...1,037,690	..E	10
Villa Clara	836,322	..B	6

Cities and towns†

Aguada de Pasajeros	30,983	..B	5
Artemisa	79,620	..B	3
Báguanos	54,912	..D	10
Banes	86,838	..D	11
Baracoa	81,191	..D	12
Bauta	42,873	..A	3
Bayamo‡	209,714	..D	9
Cabaiguán	67,380	..B	7
Caibarién	40,630	..B	7
Camagüey‡	322,815	..C	8
Camajuaní	64,150	..B	6
Campechuela	48,859	..E	9
Cárdenas	97,564	..A	5
Ciego de Avila‡	126,729	..C	7
Cienfuegos‡	...161,259	..B	6
Colón	69,317	..B	5
Consolación del Sur	87,067	..B	2
Contramaestre	103,314	..D	10
Cueto	37,521	..D	10
Florida	75,980	..C	8
Fomento	36,060	..B	7
Gibara	72,069	..C	10
Guáimaro	58,152	..E	9

Guantánamo‡	.249,850	..E	11
Güines	71,067	..A	4
Güira de Melena	37,181	..B	3
Havana (La Habana)	..2,186,632	..A	3
Holguín‡	309,371	..D	10
Jagüey Grande	57,409	..B	5
Jatibonico	43,066	..C	7
Jiguaní	59,763	..D	10
Jovellanos	56,144	..B	5
Las Tunas‡	...184,183	..D	9
Los Palacios	40,455	..B	3
Manicaragua	..78,494	..B	6
Manzanillo	...135,807	..D	9
Matanzas‡	...138,582	..A	5
Mayarí	108,534	..D	11
Moa	64,684	..D	11
Morón	61,944	..B	8
Niquero	41,606	..E	8
Nuevitas	44,881	..C	9
Palma Soriano	...125,514	..E	10
Pinar del Río‡	..188,091	..B	2
Placetas	73,842	..B	7
Puerto Padre	..92,518	..C	9
Ranchuelo	63,329	..B	6
Remedios	49,017	..B	6
Sagua de Tánamo	59,191	..D	11
Sagua la Grande	60,925	..B	6
San Antonio de los Baños	..43,191	..A	4
San Cristóbal	..69,750	..B	3
San José de las Lajas	64,877	..A	4
San Luis	89,136	..E	10
Sancti Spíritus‡	127,653	..C	7
Santa Clara‡	...230,631	..B	6
Santiago de Cuba‡	477,016	..E	10
Santo Domingo	55,702	..B	6
Trinidad	72,637	..C	6
Vertientes	53,434	..C	8
Yaguajay	60,295	..B	7
Yara	60,127	..E	9

*Municipality responsible to central government.
†Population of municipalities, which may include rural areas as well as the urban center.
‡Provincial capital.
Source: 2000 official estimates.

Map labels

9 10 11 12

75°
Long Island
BAHAMAS
Crooked Island
Acklins Island

A

B

Cayo Romano
Archipiélago de Camagüey

North Atlantic Ocean

Minas Nuevitas
Camagüey
Sibanicú Manatí
Puerto Padre Gibara
Guáimaro Las Tunas Jesús Menéndez
Colombia Jobabo Antilla Banes
Amancio Las Tunas Holguín Bahía de Nipe
Guayabal Báguanos Moa
Golfo de Cueto Mayarí Sagua de Tánamo
Guacanayabo Urbano Holguín
Manzanillo Bayamo Noris Baracoa
Jiguaní Mella Cabo
Campechuela Yara Contramaestre La Maya Guantánamo Maisí
Bartolomé Masó Palma Soriano San Luis Guantánamo
Niquero Santiago Caimanera
Pilón de Cuba Siboney
Cabo Santiago Guantánamo UNITED STATES
Cruz de Cuba Bay NAVAL BASE

North Latitude 21°

C

D

E

75°

400 Miles   500 Miles
600   700   800 Kilometers

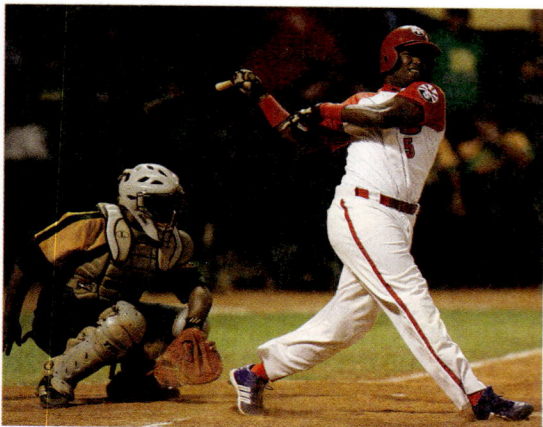

© Claudia Daut, Reuters/Landov

Baseball is extremely popular in Cuba. People play the sport in parks, stadiums, and playgrounds throughout the island. Baseball arrived in Cuba from the United States in the late 1800's.

events for Cubans. The work of the government-sponsored Cuban Institute of Cinematographic Art and Industry has made Cuba a center of the Latin American film industry. The Casa de las Américas (House of the Americas)—which supports the work of artists, writers, and musicians—is one of Latin America's most prestigious cultural institutions.

Cuban paintings are known primarily for their strong colors and portrayals of dramatic actions. Armando Menocal, who began painting in the late 1800's, became famous for his murals and depictions of historical events. Well-known Cuban painters of the 1900's include Amelia Peláez, René Portocarrero, and Wifredo Lam. Peláez pioneered the introduction of Modern art in Cuba. Portocarrero and Lam combined African and Cuban elements in their works.

The poet José Martí was the most famous Cuban writer of the 1800's. Martí wrote eloquently on political subjects. Beginning in the 1880's, he led Cuba's fight for independence from Spain. The most prominent Cuban novelists of the early and middle 1900's included Alejo

Carpentier and José Lezama Lima. Carpentier produced works in the style of *magic realism,* which blends dreams and magic with everyday reality. Lezama wrote poetry and literary reviews. Guillermo Cabrera Infante became one of Cuba's best-known novelists and short-story writers of the late 1900's. His innovative works of fiction are filled with many kinds of wordplay.

Cuban popular music has gained worldwide renown. This highly rhythmic music combines African and European, especially Spanish, traditions. Much Cuban music features guitars and such percussion instruments as castanets, maracas, and a variety of drums, including bongo drums. Cuban music has given rise to a number of dances, including the *cha-cha-cha, conga, Cuban bolero, mambo, rumba, son,* and *salsa.*

The land

Cuba consists of a main island (Cuba) surrounded by more than 1,600 smaller islands. The Cuban mainland extends about 710 miles (1,150 kilometers) from northwest to southeast. At its widest point, the island measures 135 miles (217 kilometers). At its narrowest point, it reaches only about 20 miles (32 kilometers).

Cuba consists mainly of three mountainous regions separated by gentle slopes, rolling plains, and wide, fertile farmlands. The three mountainous regions rise in the west, in south-central Cuba, and in the southeast.

The westernmost mountainous region of Cuba consists of two mountain ranges—the Sierra de los Órganos and the Sierra del Rosario. The south-central mountainous region is known as the Sierra de Escambray. It includes two ranges, the Sierra de Trinidad and the Sierra de Sancti Spiritus. The southeastern mountainous zone has several ranges. Among them is the Sierra Maestra, which rises abruptly from the southeastern coast. The highest point in Cuba, the Pico Turquino, stands 6,542 feet (1,994 meters) high in the Sierra Maestra.

Cuba has more than 200 rivers and streams. Most of them are short, narrow, and shallow. Few inland waterways on the island can be navigated for any great distances. The longest river, the Cauto, flows about 150 miles (240 kilometers) through southeastern Cuba. It is navigable for only about 40 miles (65 kilometers).

Marice Cohn Band, © *The Miami Herald*

The Sierra Maestra, *shown here,* is one of several mountain ranges in southeastern Cuba. The Sierra Maestra has played an important role in Cuba's history. It has served as a refuge for various rebel groups, including the one that brought Fidel Castro to power in the late 1950's.

Cuba terrain map

Numerous coral reefs and small islands form bays along the Cuban coast. Cuba also has many small rivers. Pico Turquino, the country's highest mountain, rises in the Sierra Maestra range.

WORLD BOOK map

Geographical Terms

Archipiélago..........................islands
Bahía.....................................bay
Cabo......................................cape
Golfo.....................................gulf
Pico......................................mountain
Río..river
Sierra....................mountain range

★ National capital
• Other city or town
+ Elevation above sea level
  Swamp

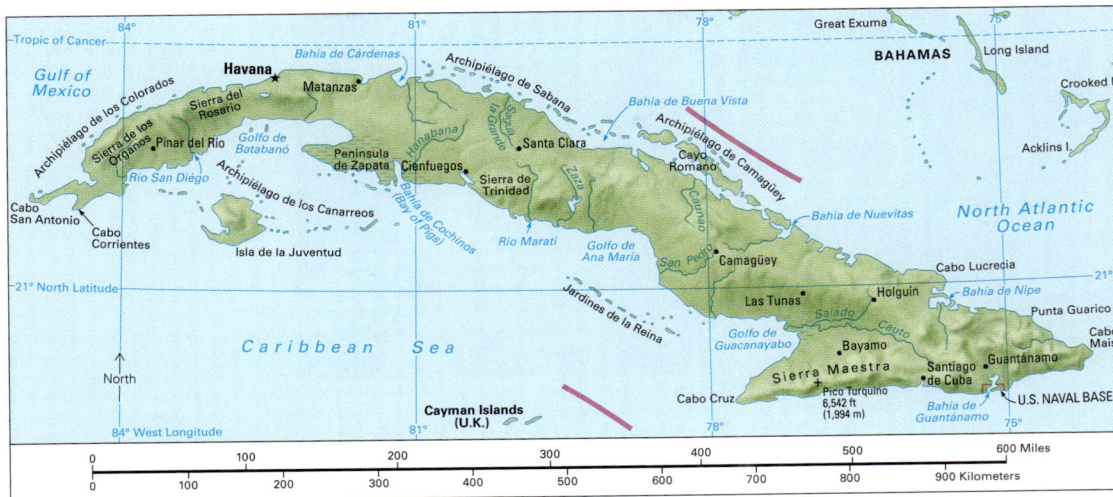

The coastline of Cuba is marked with deep bays and sandy beaches. Much of the southern shoreline of Cuba in the west consists of a band of low marshland that is broken up into hundreds of *coral keys* and *mangrove swamps.* Coral keys are low islands that form when coral growths build up above the water. Mangrove swamps are created when the spreading roots of mangrove trees catch and hold soil. West of Cienfuegos lies the Zapata Peninsula, a vast swampland.

Cuba has over 200 natural harbors along its shoreline. The larger harbors have narrow entrances, which protect the inner area against winds and waves. Important northern harbors include Antilla, Cabañas, Cárdenas, Gibara, Havana, Honda, Manatí, Mariel, Matanzas, Nuevitas, and Puerto Padre. The chief southern harbors include Cienfuegos, Guantánamo, and Santiago de Cuba.

Climate

Cuba lies within the northern tropics and has a semitropical climate. Cool ocean breezes during the summer and warm breezes in the winter give the island a mild climate throughout the year. Average daily temperatures in Cuba range from about 70 °F (21 °C) in winter to about 80 °F (27 °C) in summer. The interior has a greater temperature range than the coastal regions. Temperatures on the island rarely fall below 40 °F (4 °C) or rise above 100 °F (38 °C). Frosts sometimes occur in the mountains.

Cuba has dry and rainy seasons. The dry season lasts from November through April, and the rainy season runs from May through October. Cuba has an average annual rainfall of more than 50 inches (125 centimeters). Thunderstorms occur almost daily in the rainy season.

Hurricanes frequently strike the island, especially its eastern and western tips. Hurricane season lasts from June to November. The strong winds from hurricanes occasionally destroy buildings and crops and create high waves that flood the coastal lowlands. Earthquakes also occasionally hit Cuba. They occur most frequently and most severely along the southeastern coast.

Economy

Cuba has a *gross domestic product* (GDP) of about $50 billion. A country's GDP is the total value of all goods and services the country produces in a year.

From 1961 to the early 1990's, government planning dominated key economic decisions in Cuba. A U.S. trade embargo imposed in 1960 contributed to the stagnation of Cuba's economy during this period. As a result, Cuba relied heavily on aid from the Soviet Union and other Communist nations. Trade with the Soviet Union and the Communist countries of Eastern Europe was vital to Cuba's economy.

Communism collapsed in Eastern Europe during the late 1980's, and the Soviet Union broke apart in 1991. These political changes caused a loss of trade for Cuba. To combat the economic crisis brought on by this loss, the Cuban government loosened its control over the economy. Foreign investment, previously discouraged by the government, began to return to the island, mainly in the tourist industry. Beginning in 1993, Cuba gradually started to permit some private enterprise. Many Cubans opened small businesses, including restaurants.

Manufacturing traditionally centered on sugar production, but about half of Cuba's sugar mills closed in the early 2000's as a result of decreased sugar prices. The manufacture of cigars is also important. Cuba is famous for fine hand-rolled cigars made from high-quality tobacco. Most cigar factories are in Havana. Other important industrial products include agricultural machin-

Cigar manufacturing is an important industry in Cuba. Most cigar factories are in Havana. Skilled workers, *shown here,* roll the cigars by hand, the traditional method of making high-quality cigars.

© Alex Quesada, Matrix

ery, cement products, food and beverage products, petroleum and pharmaceutical products, and steel.

Agriculture. Sugar cane historically has been Cuba's most important crop. Although Cuba's sugar production has decreased significantly since the late 1900's, the country is still an important sugar producer. Coffee and tobacco are also important crops.

Through the years, the government has promoted attempts to grow other crops as a way for the country to supply more of its own food. As part of these efforts, the government has increased the production of bananas, citrus fruits, corn, potatoes, rice, and tomatoes. Livestock farming, particularly the raising of beef and dairy cattle, chickens, and hogs, is also important.

In the 1960's, about three-fourths of Cuba's farmland came under state control. Most farms were run as *state farms,* owned and operated by the government. Others were reorganized and operated as *farm cooperatives,* owned jointly by the government and groups of farmers. Some small farms remained under the control of individual owners, producing chiefly coffee and tobacco. In all cases, farmers were required to sell their products to the state at prices set by the government.

In the early 1990's, the government distributed more state lands to cooperatives and authorized farmers to sell their surplus production on the open market after certain quotas had been met. Soon, small farmers' markets sprang up across the island to sell a variety of products directly to the public. Cuba's armed forces also manage farms throughout the island and are a major producer of food.

Mining. Cuba's mines produce cement, cobalt, gold, iron ore, natural gas, nickel, and stone. Most of the nickel mines are on the eastern end of the island. Cuba also

© Marc Pokempner

Workers harvest sugar cane on a government-operated farm. Sugar cane historically has been Cuba's most important crop. However, sugar production has decreased significantly since the late 1900's.

Cuba's gross domestic product

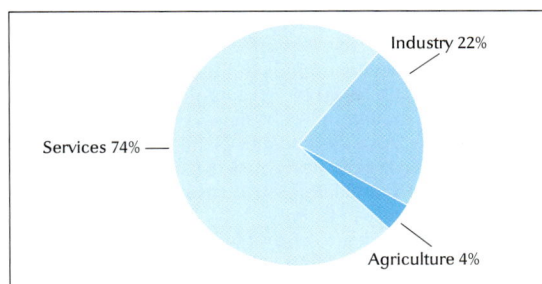

Industry 22%

Services 74%

Agriculture 4%

The gross domestic product (GDP) is the total value of goods and services produced within a country in a year. The GDP measures a nation's total economic performance and can be used to compare the economic output and growth of different countries. Cuba's GDP was $52,300,000,000 in 2007.

Production and workers by economic activities

| Economic activities | Percent of GDP produced | Employed workers | |
		Number of persons	Percent of total
Community, social, & personal services	36	2,063,400	42
Trade, restaurants, & hotels	26	613,600	13
Manufacturing	13	523,300	11
Transportation & communication	8	289,300	6
Construction	6	243,700	5
Finance, insurance, real estate, & business services	5	111,400	2
Agriculture	4	912,300	19
Utilities	2	85,000	2
Mining	2	25,700	1
Total*	100	4,867,700	100

*Figures do not add up to 100 percent due to rounding.
Figures are for 2007.
Source: Cuba's Office of National Statistics; United Nations.

produces small but growing quantities of petroleum, which accounts for much of its energy production.

Fishing industry. State-owned Cuban fishing fleets range over the Caribbean Sea and parts of the North Atlantic Ocean. The important catches include such shellfish as lobsters and shrimp. Caibarién, Cienfuegos, and Havana are important fishing ports.

Service industries produce services rather than manufactured goods or agricultural products. They include banking, education, and health care. One of Cuba's fastest-growing service industries is tourism. The Cuban government has formed joint ventures with foreign investors to build new hotels and to restore old ones. Tourists have arrived in growing numbers, mainly from Canada and Europe.

International trade. From about 1900 to 1960, Cuba's principal trading partner was the United States. Beginning in the early 1960's, especially after U.S. sanctions were imposed, Cuban trade shifted largely to the Soviet Union and the Communist countries of Eastern Europe. By the mid-1980's, about 85 percent of all Cuban trade was with these Communist nations. The collapse of Communism left Cuba in search of new trading part-

ners. Today, Cuba's chief trading partners are Brazil, Canada, China, Germany, Italy, Mexico, Russia, Spain, and Venezuela.

Cuban exports include citrus fruits, coffee, fish and shellfish, medical products, nickel, rum, sugar, and tobacco products. Among Cuba's chief imports are machinery, petroleum, and wheat and other food products.

Transportation and communication. About half of Cuba's roads are paved. The Central Highway extends between Pinar del Río, in the northwest, and Santiago de Cuba, in the southeast. However, gasoline rationing, problems in obtaining spare parts, and a scarcity of new vehicles often have made automobile transportation difficult. Railroads cross the island, but more people ride buses than trains. José Martí International Airport is the country's largest airport.

Cuba's principal newspaper is *Granma,* published by the Cuban Communist Party. The government or the Communist Party controls all newspapers, most magazines, and television and radio broadcasts.

History

Early years. The famous explorer Christopher Columbus landed in Cuba in 1492. At the time of Columbus's arrival, three groups of American Indians inhabited the island: the Guanahatabey, the Ciboney, and the Taino. Estimates of the size of the Indian population at the time of European arrival vary widely—from as few as 16,000 to as many as 600,000.

Spanish soldiers and priests arrived in Cuba in 1511. The Indians resisted the Spanish effort to take over the island but soon were defeated. The Spaniards then forced the Indians to work in agriculture and mining. Many Indians died from diseases and harsh treatment. By the mid-1500's, only a few thousand Indians remained. As the Indian population declined, the Spaniards brought Africans to Cuba to work as slaves. The trade in African slaves began in Cuba during the 1520's but remained relatively limited until the late 1700's.

The island became strategically important to the Spanish colonial system in the New World. Control of Cuba offered Spain command of sea routes to Mexico, the Gulf Coast, western Florida, and Central America, as well as control of the chief shipping lanes of the Caribbean Sea. In 1564, Spain officially introduced its *fleet system.* Under this system, merchant vessels carrying treasure from the New World sailed together in groups called *convoys,* which were protected by warships. Havana became the gathering place for the treasure ships before they set sail in convoys for Spain. Havana soon emerged as the island's political, administrative, economic, and cultural hub.

In 1762, the British seized Havana during the Seven Years' War, known in the United States as the French and Indian War. During their occupation, the British introduced reforms and established new trade ties between Cuba and the British colonies of North America, thus creating new, larger markets for Cuban sugar. The British also imported thousands of Africans to the island to work as slaves.

The British returned control of Havana to Spain in 1763. After the restoration of Spanish rule, Spain eased trade restrictions, abolished duties on Cuban imports, and opened Cuban ports to unlimited trade in slaves. These actions helped the Cuban economy flourish.

In the late 1700's, a rebellion of black slaves in the French colony of Saint-Domingue (now Haiti) destroyed the production of sugar and coffee there. About the same time, the world price of these products soared. In response, Cuban producers soon launched coffee production in eastern Cuba and expanded sugar cane cultivation throughout the island.

Through the years, sugar emerged as the most important Cuban export. Expanding sugar production led to the desire for more cheap labor. As a result, tens of thousands of Africans were brought to the island to work as slaves. Many owners treated their slaves brutally. In 1812, a group of slaves headed by José Antonio Aponte planned a revolt. The Spaniards discovered the plot and hanged Aponte and his followers.

Struggle against Spain. By the mid-1820's, nearly all of Spain's colonies in Latin America had won their independence. Various Cuban groups sought to end Spanish rule of their country as well. However, most of the island's white, sugar-growing elite preferred to remain under Spanish rule to guarantee their wealth and a supply of slaves.

During the mid-1800's, some Cubans and Americans supported a movement to *annex* (join) Cuba to the United States. The annexation movement received much support from Cuban and American slaveholders. Other groups in Cuba and the United States favored American control of the island for economic and military reasons. The United States made three offers to buy Cuba, but Spain rejected them.

Cuba's struggle against Spanish rule led to the start of the Ten Years' War in 1868. Carlos Manuel de Céspedes, a landowner, headed a revolutionary group made up largely of poor sugar planters, mulattoes, free blacks, and slaves. The rebels wanted independence from Spain, the founding of a republic, and the gradual freeing of slaves. Spain rejected these demands, and bitter fighting followed.

The Ten Years' War ended with the signing of the Pact of Zanjón in 1878. This treaty provided for political reforms and for the liberation of slaves who had joined the rebel army. A second unsuccessful rebellion against Spanish rule broke out in August 1879. Known as the Little War, it lasted until late 1880. A royal decree of 1886 finally ended slavery in Cuba.

In 1892, largely due to efforts by the exiled writer José Martí, the Cuban Revolutionary Party was organized. It united Cuban separatists in both Cuba and the United States. In 1895, these separatists launched a new war for Cuban independence.

President William McKinley of the United States claimed that the fighting in Cuba threatened American interests. He told Spain's government to either change its policy toward Cuba or give up the island completely. In February 1898, the U.S. battleship *Maine,* which had been sent to Havana to protect Americans in Cuba, exploded mysteriously. The United States blamed the Spaniards and, in April, declared war on Spain. This war became known in the United States as the Spanish-American War. In Cuba, the war that was fought from 1895 to 1898 is called the Spanish-Cuban-American War.

The U.S. intervention delivered the final blow to the Spanish army in Cuba. The Spaniards surrendered in July 1898, and an armistice in August ended the fighting. Under the Treaty of Paris, signed by the United States and Spain on December 10, Spain gave up all rights to the island. The United States then set up a military government in Cuba. Consequently, the Cubans did not achieve the independence they had hoped to gain.

The Platt Amendment. In 1901, Cuba adopted a con-

National Archives

The U.S. battleship *Maine* arrived in Havana in 1898 to protect Americans during Cuba's fight for freedom from Spain. The ship exploded mysteriously, triggering the Spanish-American War.

stitution. The United States insisted that the constitution include a set of provisions called the Platt Amendment. The amendment limited Cuban independence by permitting the United States to intervene militarily in Cuban affairs. It also limited the Cuban government's power to make treaties with other governments. The amendment required Cuba to allow the United States to buy or lease land for naval bases on the island. Under a 1903 treaty with Cuba, the United States received a permanent lease on Guantánamo Bay and built a large naval base there.

The government of Cuba from 1902 to 1934 sometimes is referred to as a *neocolony,* meaning *new colony.* This period was marked by political instability, public corruption, and popular protest. The United States gained increasing control over Cuba's economic affairs and began to dominate Cuban trade.

In 1901, the Cuban people elected Tomás Estrada Palma as the first president of the Republic of Cuba. American troops left the country. In 1906, violent protests broke out in Cuba over the disputed outcome of a presidential election. United States troops then returned to

Cuba under the terms of the Platt Amendment. A government headed by Charles E. Magoon of the United States ruled Cuba from 1906 to 1909, when the United States returned control of the country to the Cubans. American forces left the country, but the United States retained naval bases on the island.

An uprising broke out among black Cubans in 1912. The protesters objected to the lack of political opportunity and social advancement for black people in Cuba. In 1917, a revolt protesting electoral fraud erupted. During both uprisings, the United States sent military forces into the country.

Cuba suffered a severe economic collapse in 1920, when sugar prices rose rapidly, became overinflated, and then suddenly dropped. In 1924, still suffering from the economic collapse, Cubans elected Gerardo Machado president. During his campaign, Machado had attacked the Platt Amendment and promised reforms. But from 1927, he ruled as a dictator, provoking widespread unrest. In August 1933, a general strike and an army revolt forced Machado out of office. A month later, a group of army sergeants, corporals, and enlisted men led by Fulgencio Batista y Zaldívar and a group of university students and professors led a revolt that overthrew the new government. A five-man government briefly ruled the country, and then former university professor Ramón Grau San Martín became president.

The Grau government wanted to reduce U.S. influence in Cuba and make far-reaching changes. It passed a number of popular reforms, including laws that established an eight-hour workday and required all Cuban businesses to employ Cubans for at least half of their total work force. The United States refused to recognize the Grau government. Left-wing and right-wing groups in Cuba also actively opposed the government.

Important dates in Cuba

1492 Christopher Columbus landed in Cuba.

1520's The Spaniards began to import Africans to work as slaves in Cuba.

1762 The British seized Havana. They returned it to Spanish control in 1763.

1868-1878 Cuban revolutionaries fought Spanish rule in the Ten Years' War. Under the Pact of Zanjón, which ended the war, Spain promised reforms.

1886 Slavery was abolished in Cuba.

1895 A revolution, led by José Martí, broke out in Cuba against Spanish rule.

1898 The United States, supporting the Cuban rebels, defeated Spain in the Spanish-American War. Spain gave up all claims to Cuba.

1899-1902 A U.S. military government controlled Cuba.

1901 Cuba adopted a constitution that included a set of provisions called the Platt Amendment. The amendment allowed the United States to intervene in Cuban affairs.

1902 Tomás Estrada Palma became the first president of the Republic of Cuba.

1906-1909 United States forces again occupied Cuba.

1933 A revolutionary group led by Fulgencio Batista y Zaldívar took control of the government.

1934 The United States and Cuba signed a treaty that canceled the Platt Amendment.

1959 Fidel Castro's forces overthrew Batista's government, and Castro became ruler of the country.

1961 Cuban exiles sponsored by the U.S. Central Intelligence Agency (CIA) invaded Cuba at the Bay of Pigs and were quickly defeated by Castro's army.

1962 The Soviet Union agreed to U.S. demands that it remove its missiles from Cuba and dismantle the remaining missile bases on the island.

1976 Cuba adopted a new constitution declaring the Cuban Communist Party the leading authority in the government and society.

1991 The Soviet Union, which had been an important source of trade and economic support to Cuba, was dissolved.

1993 Cuba instituted economic reforms that allowed some workers to start private businesses.

2008 Fidel Castro stepped down as president of Cuba's Council of State, and his brother Raúl succeeded him.

United Press International
Fulgencio Batista, famous for his fiery speechmaking, ruled Cuba as dictator from 1934 to 1940, as an elected president from 1940 to 1944, and again as dictator from 1952 to 1959.

The Batista era. Batista forced Grau to resign from office in 1934. Until 1940, Batista ruled Cuba as a dictator through presidents who served in name only. The United States recognized and supported Batista's government. In 1934, the United States and Cuba signed a treaty that canceled the Platt Amendment, except for the Guantánamo Bay lease. United States investments in Cuba continued to expand during the 1940's and 1950's. American interests eventually controlled about 40 percent of Cuba's sugar production. The United States also continued to be Cuba's chief trading partner.

In 1940, Cubans adopted a new constitution and elected Batista president. The constitution prevented Batista from seeking reelection in 1944. Grau, then leader of the Authentic Cuban Revolutionary Party (also known as the Auténticos), was elected president. Another member of the Auténticos, Carlos Prío Socarrás, won the 1948 presidential election.

In 1952, Batista overthrew Prío's government and ruled Cuba as a dictator once again. Batista encouraged foreign companies, along with gambling and crime enterprises, to build businesses in Cuba. He also began to improve public works. But many Cubans remained unemployed and impoverished, and political conflict expanded across the island. Strikes and demonstrations became common.

The Castro revolution. On July 26, 1953, Fidel Castro, a young lawyer, tried to start a revolution against Batista by leading an attack on the Moncada army barracks in Santiago de Cuba. Fidel and his brother Raúl were captured and imprisoned. Many of their followers were either imprisoned or murdered.

The Castro brothers were released from prison in 1955. They then traveled to Mexico, where they met the Argentine revolutionary Ernesto "Che" Guevara. In 1956, while in Mexico, the brothers organized the 26th of July Movement, named for the date of their first revolt. The revolutionary forces landed in Oriente Province in late 1956. Most of the rebels were imprisoned or killed. However, the brothers and about a dozen of their followers escaped to the nearby Sierra Maestra.

In 1957, the rebel forces began to wage a guerrilla war against the Cuban government. The same year, university students stormed the presidential palace in an attempt to assassinate Batista. Attempts by the government to crush dissent increased the people's support of the rebels. Continued poor economic conditions also led to growing support for the rebels, particularly among workers, peasants, students, and the middle class. By mid-1958, Batista's government had lost the support of the United States and most Cubans.

On Jan. 1, 1959, Batista fled the country. The Castro rebel forces then took control of the government. Fidel Castro became prime minister of Cuba. He went on to lead the nation for nearly 50 years, first as prime minister, and later as president. Raúl served as Fidel's second-in-command, becoming defense minister and leader of Cuba's armed forces.

The revolutionary leaders did away with the political and military structure of Batista's government. Many former political officials and military officers were tried and executed. A large number of middle- and upper-class Cubans went into exile in Florida.

The new Cuban government quickly set out to change

© Claudia Daut, Reuters/Landov

Health care improved under Fidel Castro's revolutionary government. This photograph shows a therapist at a Havana hospital working with a child who has a hearing disability.

Cuban relations with the United States. In particular, it sought to reduce U.S. influence on Cuban national affairs. In 1959, for example, the Cuban government seized U.S.-owned sugar estates. As a result, U.S.-Cuba relations quickly became strained. As relations with the United States deteriorated, Cuba developed stronger economic ties with the Soviet Union. In 1960, Castro's government signed a broad trade pact with the Soviet Union.

In June 1960, the Castro government took over American and British oil refineries in Cuba after the refineries refused to process crude oil imported from the Soviet Union. The United States then stopped buying sugar from Cuba. Over the next few months, the Castro government took over all the remaining American businesses in Cuba and accepted Soviet offers to purchase Cuban sugar. In October 1960, the United States placed an economic embargo on Cuba that banned all U.S. exports except medicines and some food products. In January 1961, the United States ended diplomatic relations with Cuba.

The Bay of Pigs invasion. In April 1961, Cuban exiles sponsored by the United States Central Intelligence Agency (CIA) invaded Cuba at the Bay of Pigs on the south coast. Castro's forces crushed the invasion and captured most of the exiles. Castro later released many of the exiles to the United States in exchange for nonmilitary supplies. Shortly before the invasion, Castro had declared Cuba's revolution to be socialist. In the months after the invasion, Cuba's political system began to follow a Communist model. The political groups supporting Castro were combined and reorganized several times before the Cuban Communist Party that exists today was created in 1965.

The Cuban missile crisis. Cuban leaders feared another direct U.S. invasion. The Soviet Union offered military aid to Cuba, and Cuba agreed to let the Soviet Union send missiles and materials to build launch sites. In October 1962, the United States learned that Cuba had nuclear missiles in place that could be launched toward American cities. President John F. Kennedy ordered a naval blockade to halt the further shipment of arms. He demanded that the Soviet Union remove all missiles from the island and dismantle the remaining missile bases. For days, the world stood on the brink of nuclear war. Finally, the Soviet Union removed the weapons under protest from Castro. The Soviet action came after Kennedy privately agreed not to invade Cuba.

Social programs. The Castro government made many changes for the better. It built many new schools and improved old ones, and school enrollments and literacy rates increased dramatically. The government also improved medical and dental care facilities. The number of doctors and other health professionals increased. Health conditions improved, and life expectancy rose. Housing reforms, the introduction of food rationing, and a drive for greater equality led to more opportunities for minorities and the poor. Women began attending universities and joining the labor force in greater numbers. Blacks also received increased educational, employment, and political opportunities.

However, other changes were not as good. The government jailed many of its opponents. Critics charged that the Cuban people lacked many political and economic freedoms. Government-run companies had an equal-pay system that paid similar wages to many workers regardless of their position or experience level.

Foreign relations. In the 1960's, Castro and Che Guevara tried to spread revolution throughout Latin America, mainly by supplying military aid to guerrilla groups in several Latin American countries. In the 1970's, Cuba also sent troops and civilian military advisers to aid new governments in Angola and Ethiopia, in Africa. The Soviet Union eventually provided most of the military supplies for Cuba's African operations. Cuba withdrew its last troops from Africa in 1991.

Relations between Cuba and the United States remained strained, despite occasional signs of improvement. Partial diplomatic relations between the two countries were restored in 1977. The United States kept its trade embargo, imposed in 1960, in place. During the 1990's, the United States passed legislation, including the Helms-Burton Act of 1996, to broaden and tighten trade sanctions against Cuba. In 2000, however, the U.S. Congress passed legislation allowing cash sales of U.S. food and medicine to Cuba.

Another serious issue between Cuba and the United States involved the immigration of Cubans to the United States. During the first decade after the revolution, hundreds of thousands of Cubans left the country because they opposed Castro or were dissatisfied with their social and economic conditions. Most of these people settled in the United States. From 1966, the United States had a policy of giving political asylum to all Cubans who reached its shores.

Another wave of immigration took place in 1980, when more than 125,000 Cubans moved to the United States. Most of them came from the western port of Mariel. Following yet another wave of immigration, of about 35,000 people, in 1994, Cuba and the United States reached an immigration agreement. The United States consented to admit at least 20,000 new legal immigrants from Cuba annually and to return to Cuba any illegal migrants caught at sea. In return, Cuba pledged to do more to prevent illegal departures.

Economic troubles. In the late 1980's, non-Communist governments replaced Communist ones in most Eastern European nations. In 1991, the Soviet Union was dissolved and its Communist government was replaced. As a result, Cuba lost its most important source of trade and financial support, and the economy suffered. To ease the economic crisis, the Cuban government undertook limited reforms that loosened state control over parts of the economy. In an attempt to stimulate foreign investment in Cuba, the government also sought to improve relations with Canada and with European and Latin American nations.

Recent developments. In late 2000, relations between Cuba and the United States began to worsen. The United States again tightened its trade embargo in the early 2000's. In Cuba, the government began a so-called Battle of Ideas. This campaign sought to strengthen the commitment of Cuba's young people to their country's political system and introduced educational reforms. In 2002, former U.S. President Jimmy Carter traveled to Cuba in an attempt to improve relations between the two countries. Carter unsuccessfully urged the Cuban government to adopt democratic reforms and called on the United States to end its trade embargo.

In 2006, Fidel Castro became ill and temporarily gave control of the government to Raúl. In 2008, Fidel gave up the leadership of Cuba, and the National Assembly elected Raúl to succeed him. Raúl's government soon announced a number of economic reforms. For example, it lifted restrictions on consumer access to certain electronic goods, allowed farmers greater control of land use, and ended the equal-pay system, enabling workers to earn more for better performance.

In 2008, Hurricanes Gustav and Ike caused billions of dollars' worth of damage to Cuba. Hundreds of thousands of homes were destroyed or damaged, and many agricultural crops were devastated.   Antoni Kapcia

© Reuters/Landov

The Castro brothers have controlled Cuba's government since 1959. Raúl, *left,* succeeded Fidel, *right,* as the nation's leader in 2008. Raúl soon announced a number of economic reforms.

Additional resources

Base, Ron. *Cuba: Portrait of an Island.* Interlink Bks., 2005.
Dosal, Paul J. *Cuba Libre: A Brief History of Cuba.* Harlan Davidson, 2006.
Dubois, Muriel L. *Cuba.* Capstone Pr., 2005. Younger readers.
Pérez, Louis A., Jr. *Cuba: Between Reform and Revolution.* 3rd ed. Oxford, 2006.
Sheehan, Sean, and Jermyn, Leslie. *Cuba.* 2nd ed. Benchmark Bks., 2005. Younger readers.
Staten, Clifford L. *The History of Cuba.* Greenwood, 2003.

Kenya, *KEHN yuh,* is a country that extends from the east coast of Africa on the Indian Ocean into the interior of Africa. The equator runs through the center of Kenya.

Kenya's coastal area is hot and humid. Beautiful sandy beaches, lagoons, swamps, and patches of rain forest line the coast. Inland, a vast plains area stretches over about three-fourths of Kenya. Its extremely dry climate and generally poor soil support only scattered plant life. But a highland in the southwest receives more rainfall and has fertile soil to allow extensive farming. Most of Kenya's people live in the highland.

A spectacular variety of wild animals live in Kenya. This wildlife—which includes antelopes, elephants, giraffes, leopards, lions, rhinoceroses, and zebras—attracts thousands of tourists to Kenya each year.

Most of Kenya's people live in rural areas, farming and raising livestock for a living. But many people, especially young people, move to Kenya's cities and towns, which are growing rapidly. Nairobi is Kenya's capital and largest city. Mombasa, on the coast, is the country's second largest city and chief port.

The United Kingdom ruled Kenya from 1895 until it became an independent nation in 1963. During this period, the British influenced both the economic and cultural life of Kenya. Since independence, Kenyan leaders have emphasized the African heritage of the nation.

Government

Kenya is a republic. Its Constitution, adopted in 1963, grants the people such rights as freedom of speech and religion. Kenyan citizens 18 years of age or older may vote in elections.

National government. According to Kenya's Constitution, a president heads the country. The president selects a vice president and about 40 Cabinet ministers. Each Cabinet minister heads an executive department of the government. A National Assembly with 224 voting members makes Kenya's laws. A 2008 power-sharing agreement cre-

---

Carlene J. Edie, the contributor of this article, is Professor in the Department of Political Science at the University of Massachusetts, Amherst.

Facts in brief

Capital: Nairobi.
Languages: *Official*—English; *National*—Swahili (or Kiswahili).
Official name: Jamhuri ya Kenya (Republic of Kenya).
Area: 224,081 mi^2 (580,367 km^2). *Greatest distances*—north-south, 640 mi (1,030 km); east-west, 560 mi (901 km). *Coastline*—284 mi (457 km).
Elevation: *Highest*—Mount Kenya, 17,058 ft (5,199 m) above sea level. *Lowest*—sea level along the coast.
Population: *Estimated 2010 population*—40,602,000; density, 181 per mi^2 (70 per km^2); distribution, 79 percent rural, 21 percent urban. *1999 census*—28,686,607.
Chief products: *Agriculture*—bananas, beef, coffee, corn, milk, pineapples, potatoes, pyrethrum, sisal, sugar cane, tea, wheat. *Manufacturing*—brewing, cement, cigarettes, motor vehicle parts, petroleum products, processed foods, textiles.
Money: *Basic unit*—Kenyan shilling. One hundred cents equal one shilling.

---

ated the post of prime minister to head the National Assembly. The president appoints the prime minister and Cabinet members based on the relative strength of political parties in the Assembly.

Kenya's voters elect the president and 210 members of the National Assembly to five-year terms. Political parties nominate the other 14 Assembly members. Cabinet members are normally selected from among the members of the Assembly. Candidates for the presidency must run for

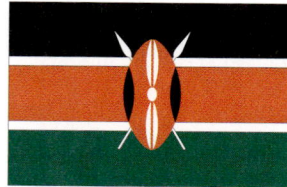

Kenya's flag and coat of arms were adopted in 1963. The flag's black stripe represents the Kenyan people, the red stripe their struggle for independence, and the green stripe agriculture. The shield and spears stand for the defense of freedom. The coat of arms bears the Kiswahili word for *pulling together.*

WORLD BOOK map

Kenya lies in eastern Africa. It borders the Indian Ocean. The equator runs through the middle of the country.

Mount Kenya, the highest mountain in Kenya, stands out against the central highland countryside. In Africa, only Mount Kilimanjaro in Tanzania is taller. Although Mount Kenya sits just south of the equator, it is capped by snow and has glaciers on its upper slopes. The mountain forms part of Mount Kenya National Park, home to a large variety of wild animals.

© Jon Arnold Images/SuperStock

a seat in the National Assembly at the same time as they run for the office of president. To become president, a candidate must win both elections.

Local government. Kenya is divided into eight provinces for purposes of local government. The provinces are divided into districts, and further divided into divisions. A commissioner, who is responsible to the president, heads each province. Local authorities, consisting of mayors and councils, help govern rural counties and cities and towns within Kenya's districts.

Politics. From 1982 to 1991, only one political party—the Kenya African National Union (KANU)—was allowed in Kenya. In late 1991, other political parties were legalized. KANU joined a group of parties called the Party of National Unity. Kenya's other parties include the Orange Democratic Movement and the Orange Democratic Movement-Kenya.

Courts. Kenya's highest courts are the Court of Appeal and the High Court. The High Court hears appeals from lower courts, and the Court of Appeal hears appeals from the High Court. Kenya's lower courts include resident magistrate courts and district magistrate courts.

Armed forces of Kenya include an army, an air force, and a small navy and coastal patrol. All military service is voluntary.

People

Population and ethnic groups. Kenya has a rapidly growing population. About 99 percent of the population is *indigenous* (native) African and consists of about 40 ethnic groups. The largest group, the Kikuyu, make up about 20 percent of the population. Four other ethnic groups—Kalenjin, Kamba, Luhya, and Luo—each make up between 10 and 15 percent of the population. Other population groups in Kenya include Arabs, South Asians, and Europeans, chiefly British.

Kenya's ethnic groups are divided by separate languages, and, in many areas, by differing ways of life. Differences in economic development and social factors have sometimes led to friction between groups. The Kenyan government has struggled to overcome ethnic divisions and provide a sense of national unity.

Languages. Most of Kenya's ethnic groups have their own local language or dialect. In addition to their ethnic language, most Kenyans also speak Swahili (which Africans call Kiswahili). Swahili, Kenya's national language, is widely used for communication between people of different ethnic groups. Many Kenyans also speak English, the other official language of the country.

Way of life. Most of Kenya's rural people live on small farm settlements and raise crops and livestock for a living. Most of these rural farm families produce enough food for their own use. Many grow enough that they can offer their extra produce for sale. Many Kenyan farmers hold part-time jobs to add to their income. Some work part time on large farm estates—especially coffee and tea plantations—that are owned by wealthy landowners.

About 3 percent of Kenya's people are *pastoralists,* who raise livestock for a living. These people move between locations in search of grazing land and water for their ani-

© Images of Africa Photobank/Alamy Images

Nairobi is the capital and largest city of Kenya. The city lies on a high plateau in south-central Kenya. The central area of Nairobi includes the parliament buildings and many hotels and commercial buildings. Nairobi is a center for banking, trade, and other commercial activities. Tourism is an important part of Nairobi's economy.

Kenya map index

Cities and towns

Physical features

*Does not appear on map; key
shows general location.
Source: 1999 census.

Kenya

- 🟩 National park (N.P.)
- ▬ International boundary
- ─ Road or trail
- ─ Railroad
- ⊛ National capital
- • Other city or town
- + Elevation above
  sea level

WORLD BOOK map

© Robert Frerck

Rural homesteads with thatch-roofed buildings, such as this
Kikuyu household, dot Kenya's countryside. Most Kenyans live in
rural areas, but many young people are moving to cities for jobs.

mals. They rely on their animals for food, and they judge a
person's wealth by the number of animals owned. The
best-known Kenyan pastoralists are the Maasai. The Maasai are famous for their traditional dress, including beaded
jewelry and vivid red fabrics.

Kenya's rural people value friendships in their communities. Although they must work hard to make a living,
most rural Kenyans find time for regular social visits with
their neighbors.

Many rural Kenyans move to cities and towns to find
jobs. Most of the country's urban people work in stores,
factories, or business or government offices. Kenyans who
move to cities and large towns find they must adjust to the
fast pace, regular work schedules, and impersonal relations that are typical of urban areas. But most urban
Kenyans keep close ties with their rural relatives.

Kenyans place much value on large families. Many
Kenyan families have six or more children, and so the
women are kept busy with child care. In addition, almost
all women of Kenya's rural regions take part in the planting
and harvesting of crops. Some also work part time on
large farm estates.

The government recognizes the equality of men and
women, and it encourages women to become educated

Kenyan schools in many rural areas are set up and operated by community groups and charities. These schools are called self-help, or *harambee,* schools. *Harambee* is a Swahili word that means *pulling together.* Harambee schools provide primary or secondary education for a small tuition. Government schools, which are free, also operate in many regions.

© Kirsty McLaren, Alamy Images

and achieve high-paying jobs. Some women have done so. But most Kenyan women are too busy with child care and farm work to advance to high positions.

Kenya's Arabs, Europeans, and South Asians live chiefly along the coast and in Nairobi. Most of them own businesses or hold professional jobs.

Housing. Most rural Kenyans live in small houses with thatched or tin roofs, walls made of mud or cement, and dirt floors. In the cities, such houses are usually found crowded together in slum areas. Kenya's cities have dwellings that range in style from simple, inexpensive units for working-class people to expensive, large houses and apartment buildings for the wealthy.

Clothing. Most Kenyans wear clothing like that worn in Europe and the Americas. Rural Kenyans may wear more traditional clothing. They may wrap a brightly colored one-piece cloth, called a *kanga,* around their bodies for clothing.

Food and drink. Corn (called *maize* in Kenya) is a basic food of the people. Kenyans often grind corn into a porridge and mix it with other vegetables to make stew. They add fish or meat to the stew when they can afford to do so. Beer is a popular beverage in Kenya.

Recreation. Dancing is a favorite form of recreation throughout Kenya. Most of the people enjoy both dancing and watching concerts and dance performances. Motion pictures are also popular in Kenyan cities.

Soccer ranks as Kenya's most popular sport. Children and adults throughout the country play the game for fun, and soccer matches between organized teams draw large crowds. Track and field is another favorite sport. Kenyan distance runners, especially marathon runners, have won many medals in international competition.

Religion. More than 75 percent of Kenya's people are Christians. About two-thirds of the Christians are Protestants, and about one-third are Roman Catholics. About 10 percent of Kenya's people are Muslims. Most live in Mombasa and the coastal regions. Nairobi also has several mosques and a sizable Muslim population. Many of the traditional African religions are no longer widely practiced. These faiths are based on the belief in one supreme being and many spirits that influence events.

Education. Elementary education is compulsory in Kenya. The government operates schools in most parts of

the country. In addition, community groups have set up schools in many places. These schools are called self-help, or *harambee,* schools. *Harambee* is a Swahili word that means *pulling together.* Government elementary schools are free. Students in high schools and all students in harambee schools must pay tuition.

Kenya has a number of public and private universities. Major public universities include the University of Nairobi and Kenyatta University in Nairobi, and Moi University in Eldoret. Kenya also has many public and private technical schools and training colleges.

The arts. Kenya has a rich artistic tradition. Carved statues, paintings, and jewelry are among the most popular art objects. Such items can be found for sale in cities and most towns. Kenyans enjoy highly artistic dances that are performed during such ceremonies as birth celebrations, marriages, and funerals. Such traditional dances are also part of national holiday celebrations.

Land and climate

Land regions. Kenya's land includes three distinct regions: (1) a tropical coastal area, (2) a dry plains area, and (3)

AP/Wide World

The Samburu are one of Kenya's *pastoralist* ethnic groups, who raise livestock for a living. Pastoralists, like these Samburu women, are known for their traditional dress and independent ways.

© Robert Frerck

Kenya's highland is a region of mountains, valleys, and plateaus in the southwestern part of the country. Its fertile soil and good climate make it Kenya's chief farming region. This man is working on a tea plantation in the highland.

a fertile highland. The coastal area is a narrow strip of land along the Indian Ocean. The region has beautiful beaches, lagoons, mangrove swamps where the roots of mangrove trees hold the soil, coconut palms, and a few small rain forests. The climate of the coastal area is hot and humid the year around. Temperatures average about 80 °F (27 °C). Rainfall totals about 40 inches (100 centimeters) annually. Much of the soil near the coast is suitable for farming, especially in the south. Mombasa, Kenya's second largest city and its chief port, lies along the coast.

The plains stretch inland from the coastal area and cover about three-fourths of Kenya. The plains form a series of plateaus, rising from near sea level at the coast to about 4,000 feet (1,200 meters) inland. Bushes, shrubs, and grasses grow on the plains. The area is the driest part of Kenya. Much of it receives only 10 to 30 inches (25 to 76 centimeters) of rain yearly. A large northern region is desertlike, receiving less than 10 inches (25 centimeters) of rain a year. Average temperatures vary with altitude, ranging from about 80 °F (27 °C) at low levels to about 60 °F (16 °C) at the highest levels. The plains area is the most thinly populated part of Kenya. It has no large towns or cities. Pastoralists move about the region in search of grazing land and water for their livestock. The soil is too dry for extensive farming.

The highland lies in southwestern Kenya. It covers a little less than one-fourth of the country. It is a region of mountains, valleys, and plateaus. Mount Kenya, at its eastern end, is the highest point in the country. It rises 17,058 feet (5,199 meters) above sea level. Only one African mountain—Kilimanjaro in Tanzania—is higher. Forests and grasslands cover much of the highland. The highland has fertile soil and a good climate for agriculture. It is Kenya's chief farming region. Temperatures average about 67 °F (19 °C), and yearly rainfall ranges from 40 to 50 inches (100 to 130 centimeters). About 75 percent of Kenya's people live in the highland. Nairobi, Kenya's largest city, is there.

The Great Rift Valley divides the highland into eastern and western sections. This deep valley, which cuts

through much of eastern Africa from north to south, has some of the continent's most fertile soil.

Rivers and lakes. The Athi and the Tana are Kenya's chief rivers. Both flow from the highland to the Indian Ocean. The eastern part of the Athi is called the Galana. Lake Turkana covers 2,473 square miles (6,405 square kilometers) in the far north. Its northern tip extends into Ethiopia. Lake Victoria, Africa's largest lake, lies at the western end of Kenya. Most of the lake is within Tanzania and Uganda. The lake covers 26,828 square miles (69,484 square kilometers), of which about 1,460 square miles (3,781 square kilometers) fall within Kenya.

Animal life. Kenya is world-famous for its wildlife. The country's plains and—to a lesser extent—its highland are the home of large numbers of fascinating animals. Antelope, buffaloes, cheetahs, elephants, giraffes, leopards, lions, rhinoceroses, and zebras roam open spaces. Crocodiles and hippopotamuses are found where water is plentiful. Numerous large birds, such as eagles, ostriches, and storks, and dozens of species of small, brightly colored birds also live in Kenya.

Through the years, hunters and *poachers* (people who hunt illegally) have killed large numbers of wild animals in Kenya. In the mid-1900's, Kenya's government established a number of national parks and game reserves to protect animals from poachers. In 1977, the government outlawed hunting altogether to protect the animals. Today, thousands of tourists visit the national parks and game reserves each year to see and photograph the wild animals that live there. However, poaching remains a problem in some regions.

Economy

Kenya's economy has made much progress since the nation became independent. However, it still faces major problems. Less than 10 percent of the land is high-quality farmland, and the population is growing at a rapid rate. Agriculture is the chief economic activity. It accounts for about a fourth of the country's economic production and employs about three-fourths of Kenya's people. But Kenya has greatly increased its industry and tourist trade to lessen its reliance on agriculture. Manufacturing and construction account for about a sixth of the economic production. Service industries, including government, real estate, tourism, and wholesale and retail trade, account for most of the rest. Kenya's economy operates as a free enterprise system, but the government places many regulations on businesses.

Agriculture. Agricultural activity in Kenya is divided about equally between the production of *cash crops* and *subsistence crops*. Cash crops are products raised for sale. Subsistence crops are those raised by farmers for their own use and for the use of their families.

Coffee and tea are Kenya's chief cash crops. Kenya is one of the world's largest producers and exporters of tea. Corn is the country's main subsistence crop. Farmers also grow bananas; beans; cashews; cotton; pineapples; potatoes; sugar cane; sweet potatoes; wheat; pyrethrum, which is used to make insecticide; and sisal, used to make fiber. Beef and dairy products are Kenya's most important livestock products. Other important livestock include sheep and poultry.

Most Kenyan farmers own the land they work or rent it from the government. The majority of farms are small. But Kenya has a number of large farm estates where cash crops—especially coffee and tea—are raised. Most Kenyan

Wildebeests run in front of a tourist van in the Maasai Mara Game Reserve. Thousands of people visit Kenya's national parks and game reserves each year to see and photograph the wide variety of wild animals that live there.

© Radu Sigheti, Reuters/Landov

farmers use traditional tools in their work. Large-scale farms, however, typically use more mechanical equipment.

Manufacturing. Nairobi and Mombasa are Kenya's most important industrial centers. Food processing is a major industrial activity in Kenya. Kenya produces a small but diverse amount of manufactured products, including beer and soft drinks, cement, ceramics, cigarettes, furniture, leather goods, machinery, motor vehicle parts, soap, and textiles. A petroleum refinery at Mombasa refines oil imported from other countries.

Tourism is vital to Kenya's economy. More than a million tourists visit Kenya annually to enjoy its scenic coastal area and to view and photograph its wildlife on safaris. Most tourists come from Europe, especially Germany and the United Kingdom. Many tourists also come from Asia and the United States. Tourism is a leading source of foreign income in Kenya.

Mining. Kenya has few valuable minerals. Mining centers on the production of fluorite, used in metalworking, and soda ash, used in glassmaking. Other mined products include cement, gemstones, gold, and salt.

International trade. Kenya exports less than it imports. Coffee, refined petroleum products, and tea are Kenya's main exports. Other exports include cement, flowers, fruits and vegetables, and sisal. Kenya imports industrial machinery, iron and steel, petroleum and petroleum products, and transportation equipment. Kenya's chief trading partners include Japan, the Netherlands, South Africa, Uganda, the United Arab Emirates, the United Kingdom, and the United States.

In 1999, Kenya, Tanzania, and Uganda signed a treaty to revive the East African Community (EAC), which aims to promote economic and political cooperation. This organization had originally been created in 1967 but collapsed in 1977 because of strained relations among the three member nations. The new EAC was formally launched in 2001. In 2007, Burundi and Rwanda joined.

Transportation and communication. Railroads and paved roads connect Kenya's major cities. But most of the country's roads are unpaved. Less than 1 percent of all Kenyans own an automobile. Many people travel in buses or in crowded taxis called *matatus*. International airports operate at Mombasa and Nairobi. Mombasa is the main seaport.

The Kenya Broadcasting Corporation, a government-owned network, broadcasts radio and television programs in local languages, Swahili, and English. Several daily newspapers are published in Swahili and English —all of them in Nairobi. The cost of computers has kept many Kenyans from using the Internet. However, Internet cafes provide access for many people in Nairobi and larger towns in Kenya.

History

Early days. Scientists have found some of the earliest-known remains of human beings in the Great Rift Valley of eastern Africa, including parts of Kenya. Fossil discoveries by the Leakeys—a family of anthropologists—and others show that human beings may have first lived there about 2 million years ago.

After about 2,000 years ago, various peoples from other parts of Africa began moving into the Kenya area. These groups became the ancestors of today's Kenyans. They included farmers, herders, and hunters.

Arab and Portuguese control. Kenya's location along the Indian Ocean made it a stopping place for many early seafaring peoples, including Greeks, Romans, and Arabs. Arabs began visiting the coast about 2,000 years ago. In the A.D. 700's, Arabs established coastal settlements. They soon gained control of the coastal area, and they traded extensively with the people of Kenya and other areas on the Indian Ocean.

In 1498, Vasco da Gama of Portugal reached the Kenyan coast after sailing around the Cape of Good Hope. The Portuguese took control of the coastal area from the Arabs by force in the early 1500's. They profited heavily from trade in Kenya. In the late 1600's, the Arabs defeated the Portuguese and regained control of the area. The Arabs and Portuguese seldom traveled inland. As a result, they had little direct influence over the people of the interior of Kenya.

British rule. In 1887, a private British business association leased a part of the Kenyan coast controlled by the sultan of Zanzibar. The association received a charter from the British government as the Imperial British East Africa Company in 1888. However, the association lacked the money needed to develop the area. In 1895, the British government took over the area. The United Kingdom soon extended its control to all of Kenya. Kenya became known as British East Africa.

In 1901, the United Kingdom completed a railroad between Mombasa and Lake Victoria. The United Kingdom encouraged British citizens and other Europeans to settle in Kenya. Before long, many Europeans had established large farms throughout the fertile highland region. They hired Africans to work for them. Many Kikuyu were displaced from their lands, which became known as the *White Highlands*. British officials ruled Kenya, and the Africans had no voice in the government.

Opposition to the British. During the 1940's, many Kenyan Africans began opposing British rule. The chief opposition came from Kikuyu people of central Kenya, many of whom lived in poverty under the British. In 1944, the Kikuyu and other Kenyans formed a political party called the Kenya African Union (KAU) to organize their opposition. Jomo Kenyatta, a Kikuyu, became the party's leader in 1947.

In the late 1940's, a rebel movement developed among Kikuyu members of the KAU. The movement sought greater unity among Kenyans and demanded new British policies designed to improve the lives of the Africans. The rebels called themselves the Land and Freedom Army. Europeans and some Africans called the movement the Mau Mau rebellion. The British government took military action against the movement in 1952 after the rebels began committing terrorist acts. The British jailed thousands of rebels in detention camps, and widespread fighting broke out between the government and the rebels. In 1953, Kenyatta was convicted of leading the Mau Mau uprising, although there was no direct evidence linking him to the movement. He was jailed in a remote part of Kenya. The fighting ended in 1956. It had killed over 13,000 people, mostly African fighters.

Although the Mau Mau uprising was defeated, it forced the United Kingdom into negotiations that led to Kenyan independence. In February 1961, elections were held to choose Africans for a new parliament. Kenyatta's political party, the Kenya African National Union (KANU), won the elections. But the party refused to take office unless the British released Kenyatta. They did not release him until August 1961. As a result, KANU's rival party, the Kenya African Democratic Union (KADU), formed a government.

Independence. Kenya gained independence from the United Kingdom on Dec. 12, 1963. Its new Constitution provided for a constitutional monarchy. KANU won elections that were held to choose a government for the new nation. Kenyatta became the country's prime minister. In 1964, Kenya became a republic, and Kenyatta's title was changed to president.

Building the new nation. Following independence, Kenya moved rapidly to replace the British colonial economic and cultural systems and to expand the public school system. It took over many farms and businesses owned by non-Africans, and it sold or rented them to Africans. Non-Africans who became Kenyan citizens were allowed to keep their property. The majority of Africans who benefited were Kikuyu.

At the time of independence, most Kenyans had more loyalty to their ethnic group than to the national government. Also, divisions existed between many ethnic groups, and some groups had been favored by British colonial rulers. Since independence, Kenya's government has had difficulty promoting national pride and reducing disunity.

Politically, Kenya became a one-party state in 1964, when the KADU members dissolved their party and joined KANU. A new party, the Kenya People's Union (KPU), was formed in 1966 by a group of former KANU members. But President Kenyatta dissolved it in 1969, after accusing many of its leaders of antigovernment activities. Kenya again became a one-party state. KANU governed without opposition from 1964 until 1991. Political power was concentrated in the hands of the president and his allies in the army and civil service. They formed a political elite consisting mostly of Kikuyus. Many public sector jobs were created for Kenyatta's political allies. Many of these people became wealthy in trade, transportation, and construction.

Kenyatta died in 1978, and Vice President Daniel T. arap Moi, a member of the Kalenjin ethnic group, succeeded him as president. Although KANU had been Kenya's only political party since the 1960's, others were not banned by law. Following an attempted coup by members of the Kenya Air Force in 1982, Kenya's leaders changed the Constitution to make KANU the only legal party.

Moi introduced the *mlolongo* (lining up) system of voting in the 1988 election. It required voters to line up behind the candidate they chose instead of using a secret ballot to vote. In 1990, domestic protests and international pressure forced Moi to abandon the lining-up system and to make other changes. In 1991, the Constitution was amended to allow for a multiparty system.

The first multiparty elections for the president and National Assembly were held in 1992. Moi won the presidential election, and KANU won the majority of seats in the Assembly. In the following years, protesters held many demonstrations calling for constitutional reforms to reduce the power of the presidency. But the government harassed activists supporting democratic reforms, and opposition parties remained weak and poorly organized. In 1997, Moi was reelected to another term.

Kenya's Constitution required Moi to step down as president at the end of his term in 2002. Elections were held in December of that year. In the presidential election, Mwai Kibaki—a Kikuyu and leader of the National Rainbow Coalition (NRC)—defeated the KANU candidate, Uhuru Kenyatta, a son of Jomo Kenyatta. Kibaki promised to end government corruption and ethnic favoritism and to improve the economy and living standards in Kenya. The NRC also won a majority in the National Assembly.

In 2003, the NRC enacted the Anti-Corruption and Economic Crimes Act and the Public Officer Ethics Act, both aimed at fighting corruption in government. Other reforms and laws helped increase international investment and foreign aid to Kenya. However, ethnic-based economic favoritism continued. The government often awarded land, contracts, and gifts to its ethnic allies. Economic inequality, government corruption, and political repression hampered Kenya's drive to become stable and prosperous. By 2005, public dissatisfaction with Kibaki was growing.

Recent developments. On Dec. 27, 2007, Kenya held elections. Kibaki ran for president as leader of the Party of National Unity. He was opposed by Raila Odinga of the Orange Democratic Movement. On December 30, Kibaki was announced as the winner of the election and quickly sworn in. However, his party suffered National Assembly losses in several regions of Kenya. Odinga accused Kibaki of election fraud and demanded a recount.

Riots broke out across the country. The riots soon escalated into fighting between ethnic groups, causing the deaths of about 1,500 people and displacing hundreds of thousands of others.

In 2008, former United Nations Secretary-General Kofi Annan held talks between Odinga and Kibaki. The Kenyans signed a power-sharing agreement under which Kibaki remained president. The pact created the post of prime minister. Odinga became prime minister with the power to coordinate government functions. The power-sharing agreement ended the violence and protests, but political infighting continued.　　　　Carlene J. Edie

The Battle of Lexington, 19th April 1775 (1910) oil on canvas by William Barnes Wollen; National Army Museum, London (© Bridgeman Art Library/Getty Images)

The American Revolution began in 1775 when colonial militias clashed with British redcoats at Lexington, Massachusetts. No one knows who fired the first shot. The conflict, which arose from colonial resistance to British tax laws, led to American self-government based on individual liberty.

Revolution, American

Revolution, American (1775-1783), led to the birth of a new nation—the United States. The revolution caused a military conflict called the Revolutionary War in America. The war was fought between Britain (now also called the United Kingdom) and its 13 colonies that lay along the Atlantic Ocean in North America. The war began on April 19, 1775, when British soldiers and American patriots clashed at Lexington, Massachusetts, and at nearby Concord. The war lasted eight years. On Sept. 3, 1783, Britain signed the Treaty of Paris, by which it recognized the independence of the United States. The revolution stood as an example to peoples in many lands who later fought to gain their freedom. In 1836, the American author Ralph Waldo Emerson referred to the first shot fired by the patriots at Concord as "the shot heard round the world."

Tension had been building between Britain and the American Colonies for more than 10 years before the Revolutionary War began. Starting in the mid-1760's, the British government passed a series of laws to increase its control over the colonies. Americans had grown used to a large measure of self-government. They strongly resisted the new laws, especially tax laws. Fierce debate developed over the British Parliament's right to tax the colonies without their consent.

The disobedience of the American Colonies angered the British government. In 1775, Britain's Parliament declared Massachusetts—the site of much protest—to be in rebellion. The British government ordered its troops in Boston to take swift action against the rebels. The Revolutionary War broke out soon afterward.

The American Colonies were unprepared for war. They lacked a central government, an army, and a navy. Delegates from the colonies formed the Continental Congress, which took on the duties of a national government. The Congress directed the war effort and voted to organize an army and a navy. It appointed George Washington commander in chief of the colonial army, called the Continental Army. Washington was a wealthy Virginia landowner and former militia officer. On July 4, 1776—more than a year after the beginning of the Revolutionary War in America—the Congress adopted the Declaration of Independence. In that document, the

British government to begin peace talks with the Americans. The Treaty of Paris formally ended the war in 1783.

This article will trace the background and causes of the American Revolution; the beginning of the Revolutionary War; the conduct of the war, including weapons and tactics and how the war was financed; the war in the North, West, and South; the end of the war; and the results of the revolution.

Massachusetts Historical Society

A tax stamp placed on certain items showed that colonists had paid taxes on them.

Background and causes of the revolution

Britain's power in North America was at its height in 1763, only 12 years before the Revolutionary War began. Britain had just defeated France in the French and Indian War (1754-1763). The treaty that ended the war gave Britain almost all of France's territory in North America. That territory stretched from the Appalachian Mountains in the east to the Mississippi River and included much of Canada. Most American colonists took pride in being part of the British Empire, which was then the world's most powerful empire.

Yet in 1775, the American Colonies rebelled against British authority. The dramatic turnabout resulted from disagreements over the proper relationship between Britain and its colonies. Britain expected the colonists to obey the British Parliament "in all cases whatsoever." The colonists, on the other hand, believed that there were limits to Parliament's power. They believed they had certain rights that Britain should respect. Each side refused to yield, which led to a military showdown.

Life in the American Colonies during the 1700's differed in important ways from life in the most advanced European nations. Well-to-do merchants and planters formed a small upper class, or *gentry,* in the seaboard colonies, but they lacked the wealth and power of the English aristocracy. A large middle class consisted mainly of farmers who owned their land, of shopkeepers, and of craftworkers. Unskilled workers and farmers who rented their land ranked among the poor, or "lower sort." In addition, by the mid-1700's, about 20 percent of the colonists were slaves of African descent. Slaves lived in all the mainland colonies, though they were most numerous in the South.

Farming was by far the main occupation in the American Colonies. It provided a living for nearly 90 percent of the people. Only about 10 percent of the colonists lived in towns or cities. Philadelphia, with about 40,000 people, was the largest American city in 1775. The next largest cities were New York City and Boston.

The opportunity to own land had drawn many settlers to the American Colonies. Owning property gave a person a chance to get ahead. It could also give men the right to vote, though some colonies denied that right to Roman Catholics and Jews. All colonies denied it to blacks and to most women. In each colony, voters elected representatives to a legislature. Colonial legislatures

colonies declared their freedom from British rule.

Britain launched a huge land and sea effort to crush the revolution. The British had a far larger and better-trained army than did the Americans. But Britain had to transport and supply its army across the Atlantic Ocean and pacify a vast territory. Although the British won many battles, they gained little from their victories. The American patriots were able to form new forces and fight on.

In 1777, the Americans won an important victory at Saratoga, New York. The victory convinced France that the Americans could win the war. As a result, France went to war against Britain, its long-time enemy. France provided the Americans with the money and military equipment they badly needed to fight the war.

In October 1781, a large British force surrendered to Washington at Yorktown, Virginia. That defeat led the

Important dates in the Revolutionary War

1775

April 19 Minutemen and redcoats clashed at Lexington and Concord.

June 15 The Congress named George Washington commander in chief of the Continental Army.

June 17 The British drove the Americans from Breed's Hill in the Battle of Bunker Hill.

1776

Feb. 27 The patriots defeated the Loyalists at Moore's Creek Bridge.

March 17 The British evacuated Boston.

July 4 The Declaration of Independence was adopted.

Aug. 27 The redcoats defeated the patriots on Long Island.

Sept. 15 The British occupied New York City.

Dec. 26 Washington mounted a surprise attack on Hessian troops at Trenton.

1777

Jan. 3 Washington gained a victory at Princeton.

Aug. 6 Loyalists and Indians forced the patriots back at Oriskany but then withdrew.

Aug. 16 The patriots crushed the Hessians near Bennington.

Sept. 11 The British won the Battle of Brandywine.

Sept. 19 Gates's forces checked Burgoyne's army in the First Battle of Freeman's Farm.

Sept. 26 The British occupied Philadelphia.

Oct. 4 Washington's forces met defeat in the Battle of Germantown.

Oct. 7 The patriots defeated the British in the Second Battle of Freeman's Farm.

Oct. 17 Burgoyne surrendered at Saratoga.

Dec. 19 Washington's army retired to winter quarters at Valley Forge.

1778

Feb. 6 The United States and France signed an alliance.

June 28 The Battle of Monmouth ended in a draw.

Dec. 29 The redcoats took Savannah.

1779

Feb. 25 British defenders of Vincennes surrendered to George Rogers Clark.

June 21 Spain declared war on Britain.

Sept. 23 John Paul Jones's ship, the *Bonhomme Richard*, captured the British ship *Serapis*.

1780

May 12 Charleston fell after a British siege.

Aug. 16 The British defeated the Americans at Camden.

Oct. 7 Americans stormed the Loyalist positions on Kings Mountain.

1781

Jan. 17 The patriots won a victory at Cowpens.

March 15 Cornwallis clashed with Greene at Guilford Courthouse.

Sept. 5 A French fleet inflicted great damage on a British naval force at Chesapeake Bay.

Oct. 19 Cornwallis's forces surrendered at Yorktown.

1782

March 20 King George's chief minister, Lord North, resigned.

Nov. 30 The Americans and British signed a preliminary peace treaty in Paris.

1783

April 15 Congress ratified the preliminary peace treaty.

Sept. 3 The United States and Britain signed the final peace treaty in Paris.

---

passed laws and could tax the people. But the governor of a colony could veto any laws passed by the legislature. The king appointed the governor in most colonies.

Britain expected the American Colonies to serve its economic interests, and it regulated colonial trade. In general, the colonists accepted British regulations. For example, they agreed not to manufacture goods that would compete with British products.

British policy changes. Britain had largely neglected the American Colonies while it fought France in a series of wars during the 1700's. But after the French and Indian War ended in 1763, the British government sought to tighten its control over the colonies. The war had drained Britain's treasury and left a huge debt. Most British leaders did not expect the colonists to help pay off the debt. However, Britain planned to station troops in America to defend the colonies' western frontier. It wanted the colonists to help pay for those troops.

Relations between the colonies and the mother country steadily worsened from 1763 to 1775. During that time, Parliament passed a number of laws to increase Britain's income from the colonies. The colonists reacted angrily. They lived far from Britain and had grown increasingly self-reliant. Many Americans believed that the new British policies threatened their freedom. In late 1774, Britain's King George III declared, "The die is now cast, the colonies must either submit or triumph." A few months later, the Revolutionary War broke out.

The Proclamation of 1763. Before the French and Indian War, France had helped prevent colonists from settling on Indian hunting lands west of the Appalachians. But settlers began crossing the frontier soon after Britain defeated France. In the spring of 1763, an Ottawa

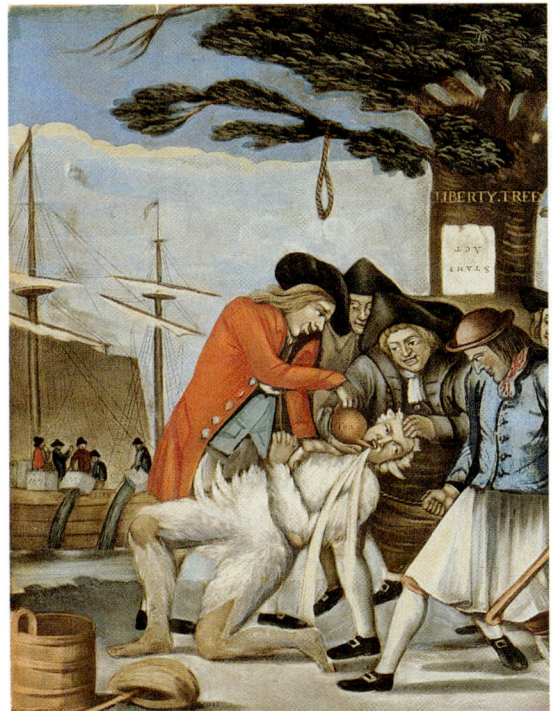

Detail of *The Bostonians Paying the Excise Man* (1774), a color engraving by an unknown artist; John Carter Brown Library at Brown University, Providence, Rhode Island

British propaganda showed unruly colonists forcing a tax collector they had tarred and feathered to drink scalding tea. The colonists in the background are dumping British tea overboard.

The Boston Massacre took place on March 5, 1770, when British soldiers fired into a mob, killing five Americans. Patriot propaganda like this engraving by Paul Revere called the incident a massacre to stir up feeling against the British government. Hundreds of British soldiers had come to Boston two years earlier to keep order and protect the city's customs collectors.

Detail of *The Boston Massacre, 5th March 1770* (1770) engraving by Paul Revere; Worcester Art Museum (© Bridgeman Art Library/SuperStock)

chief named Pontiac began an uprising in which tribes attacked many western forts the British had taken from the French. Hundreds of colonists along the western frontier were killed.

Britain feared a long and bloody Indian war, which it could not afford. To prevent future uprisings, King George issued the Proclamation of 1763. The document reserved lands west of the Appalachians for Indians and forbade white settlements there. Britain sent soldiers to guard the frontier and keep settlers out.

The Proclamation of 1763 angered many colonists. Some wealthy Americans hoped to profit from the purchase of Western lands. Poorer colonists saw the lands as an opportunity to escape poverty. Colonists living on the frontier, or the "backcountry," resisted British efforts to enforce the Proclamation of 1763.

The Sugar Act. George Grenville became King George's chief Cabinet minister in 1763. Grenville was determined to increase Britain's income from the American Colonies. At his urging, Parliament passed the Revenue Act of 1764, also known as the Sugar Act. The act placed a threepenny tax on each gallon (3.8 liters) of molasses entering the colonies from ports outside the British Empire. Several Northern colonies had thriving rum industries that depended on imported molasses. Rum distillers angrily protested that the tax would eat up their profits. In 1766, Parliament reduced the tax on molasses to a penny a gallon.

The Quartering and Stamp acts were passed by Parliament in 1765, again with Grenville's support. The laws were intended to make the colonists pay part of the cost of stationing British troops in America. The Quartering Act ordered the colonies to supply the soldiers with living quarters, fuel, candles, and cider or beer. The Stamp Act required the colonists to buy tax stamps for newspapers, playing cards, diplomas, and various legal documents.

Most colonies half-heartedly obeyed the Quartering Act, often providing fewer supplies than requested. But the Stamp Act resulted in riots. Angry colonists refused to allow the tax stamps to be sold. Merchants in port cities agreed not to order British goods until Parliament abolished the act.

In October 1765, delegates from nine colonies met in New York City and prepared a statement protesting the Stamp Act. The objections of that so-called Stamp Act Congress stemmed from the colonists' belief that the right of taxation belonged only to the people and their elected representatives. The delegates argued that Parliament had no power to tax the colonies because the colonies had no representatives in Parliament. The meeting of the Stamp Act Congress was the first united action by the colonies against an unpopular British law.

Parliament repealed the Stamp Act in 1766. But at the same time, it passed the Declaratory Act, which stated that the king and Parliament had full legislative authority over the colonies in all matters.

The Townshend Acts. Many members of the British government disliked giving in to the disobedient colonies over the Stamp Act. They included Chancellor of the Exchequer Charles Townshend, who developed a new plan for raising money from the colonies. Townshend convinced Parliament that the colonists would find a *duty* (tax on imported goods) more agreeable than the Stamp Act. Whereas the Stamp Act had taxed the colonists directly, the government would collect duties only from importers. In 1767, Parliament passed the Townshend Acts. One act placed duties on glass, lead, paint, paper, and tea imported into the colonies. Another act set up a customs agency in Boston to collect the duties efficiently.

The Townshend Acts led to renewed protests in the colonies. The colonists accepted Britain's right to regulate their trade. But they argued that the Townshend duties were taxes in disguise. To protest the duties, Americans stopped buying British goods. In 1770, Parliament withdrew all the Townshend duties except the one on tea. It kept the tea duty to demonstrate its right to tax the colonies.

Protests against what the colonists called "taxation without representation" were especially violent in Boston. In 1768, British officials sent soldiers to police Boston and to protect the city's customs collectors. Nearly 1,000 soldiers entered the city on October 1, and more soon followed. Sending the soldiers made matters worse. On March 5, 1770, soldiers and townspeople clashed in a street fight. During the fight, frightened British soldiers fired into a crowd of rioters. Five men died, including a black patriot named Crispus Attucks. Patriots called the killing of the five colonists "the Boston Massacre" and spread news of it to turn public opinion in America against Britain.

In 1772, Boston political leaders formed the Committee of Correspondence to explain to other communities by letters and other means how British actions threatened American liberties. Other committees of correspondence soon sprang up throughout the colonies. The committees helped unite the colonies in their growing struggle with the British government.

The Tea Act. To avoid paying the Townshend duty on tea, colonial merchants smuggled in tea from the Netherlands. A British trading company called the East India Company had been the chief source of tea for the colonies. The smuggling hurt the company financially, and it asked Parliament for help. In 1773, Parliament passed the Tea Act, which enabled the East India Company to sell its tea below the price of smuggled tea. Lord North, who had become the king's chief minister in 1770, believed that the colonists would buy the cheaper British tea and thereby acknowledge Parliament's right to tax them. In the process, the colonists would lose their argument against taxation without representation.

Samuel Adams, a Boston patriot, led the resistance to the Tea Act. On the evening of Dec. 16, 1773, Bostonians disguised as Indians raided British ships docked in Boston Harbor and dumped their cargoes of tea overboard. The so-called Boston Tea Party enraged King George and Lord North and the king's other ministers. They wanted the Bostonians punished as a warning to all colonists not to challenge British authority.

The Intolerable Acts. Britain responded to the Boston Tea Party in 1774 by passing several laws that became known in America as the Intolerable Acts. One law closed Boston Harbor and stated that it would reopen only after Bostonians paid for the tea and showed proper respect for British authority. Another law restricted the activities of the Massachusetts legislature and gave added powers to the governor of Massachusetts. Those powers in effect made him a dictator. King George named Lieutenant General Thomas Gage, the commander of British forces in North America, the new governor of Massachusetts. Gage was sent to Boston with troops.

Committees of correspondence throughout the colonies warned citizens that Britain could also disband their legislatures and take away their political rights. Several committees called for a convention of delegates from the colonies to organize resistance to the Intolerable Acts. The convention was later called the Continental Congress.

The First Continental Congress met in Philadelphia from Sept. 5 to Oct. 26, 1774, to protest the Intolerable Acts. Representatives attended from all the colonies except Georgia. The leaders included Samuel Adams and John Adams of Massachusetts and George Washington and Patrick Henry of Virginia. The Congress voted to cut off colonial trade with Britain unless Parliament abolished certain laws and taxes, including the Intolerable Acts. It also approved resolutions advising the colonies to begin training their citizens for war.

None of the delegates to the First Continental Congress called for independence from Britain. Instead, the delegates hoped that the colonies would regain the rights Parliament had taken away. The Congress agreed to hold another Continental Congress in May 1775 if Britain did not change its policies before that time.

The beginning of the war

Fighting broke out between American patriots and British soldiers in April 1775. The Americans were defended at first by the members of their citizen army, the *militia.* The militia came out to fight when the British neared their homes. The patriots soon established a regular military force known as the Continental Army. Britain depended chiefly on professional soldiers who had enlisted for long terms. The British soldiers were called *redcoats* because they wore bright red jackets.

The patriots won several victories in New England, the two Chesapeake colonies of Virginia and Maryland, and the Southern colonies during the early months of the Revolutionary War. As the fighting spread, many Americans became convinced of the need to cut their ties with Britain.

Lexington and Concord. In February 1775, Parliament declared that Massachusetts was in open rebellion. This declaration made it legal for British troops to treat troublesome colonists as rebels and shoot them on sight. The king and his ministers hoped to avoid a war by crushing the disorder in Boston. In April, General Gage received secret orders from the British govern-

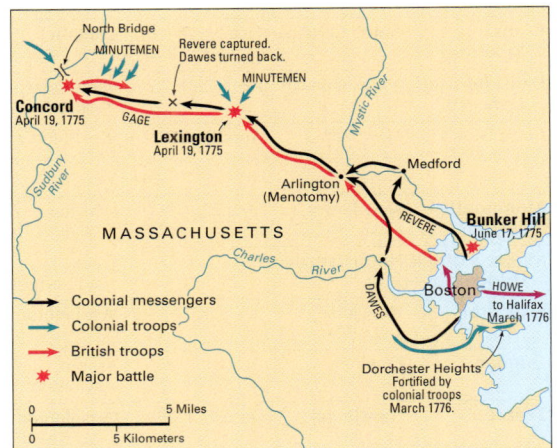

WORLD BOOK map

Clashes at Lexington and Concord opened the Revolutionary War. In March 1776, the British evacuated Boston. This map locates major battles and troop movements in and around Boston.

ment to take military action against the Massachusetts troublemakers and arrest their principal leaders.

Boston patriots learned about the secret orders before Gage did, and the leaders of the rebellion fled Boston to avoid arrest. Gage decided to capture or destroy arms and gunpowder stored by the patriots in the town of Concord, near Boston. On the night of April 18, 1775, about 700 British soldiers marched toward Concord. Joseph Warren, a Boston patriot, discovered that the British were on the march. He sent two couriers, William Dawes and Paul Revere, by separate routes to ride to Concord and warn the people about the coming redcoats. A third rider, Samuel Prescott, joined them on the road outside Lexington. Only he made it past British

patrols to warn the patriots at Concord.

The redcoats reached the town of Lexington, on the way to Concord, near dawn on April 19, 1775. Revere's ride had alerted American volunteer soldiers who were called *minutemen* because they were prepared to take up arms on a minute's notice. About 70 minutemen *mustered* (gathered) on the Lexington village green to watch the redcoats pass. Suddenly, shots were fired. No one knows who fired first. But 8 minutemen fell dead, and 10 more were wounded. One British soldier had been hurt.

The British force continued to Concord, where they searched for hidden arms. One group of redcoats met minutemen at North Bridge, just outside Concord. In a brief clash, three redcoats and two minutemen were

Major battles of the Revolutionary War

Name	Place	Date	Commander		Dead and wounded*		Results
			American	British	American	British	
Bennington	New York, near Bennington, Vermont	Aug. 16, 1777	Stark	Baum, Breymann	80	200	British defeat encouraged the patriots in their campaign against Burgoyne.
Brandywine	Pennsylvania	Sept. 11, 1777	Washington	Howe	700	540	An American retreat enabled the British to occupy Philadelphia.
Bunker Hill	Massachusetts	June 17, 1775	Prescott	Howe	400	1,000	The patriots were driven from their positions overlooking Boston.
Camden	South Carolina	Aug. 16, 1780	Gates	Cornwallis	1,000	300	The British crushed an American army.
Cowpens	South Carolina	Jan. 17, 1781	Morgan	Tarleton	70	330	Patriot victory encouraged Southern militias to come out and fight.
Freeman's Farm (First Battle)	New York	Sept. 19, 1777	Gates	Burgoyne	300	600	The British advance from Canada was halted.
Freeman's Farm (Second Battle)	New York	Oct. 7, 1777	Gates	Burgoyne	150	600	The patriots turned back a second attack.
Germantown	Pennsylvania	Oct. 4, 1777	Washington	Howe	650	550	An American attack turned into a loss and a retreat.
Guilford Courthouse	North Carolina	March 15, 1781	Greene	Cornwallis	250	650	The British decided to give up most of North Carolina.
Kings Mountain	South Carolina	Oct. 7, 1780	Campbell	Ferguson	100	300	The British advance into North Carolina was delayed.
Lexington and Concord	Massachusetts	April 19, 1775	Parker and others	Smith	90	250	The Revolutionary War in America began.
Long Island	New York	Aug. 27, 1776	Washington	Howe	250	400	The British forced the Americans from Long Island.
Monmouth	New Jersey	June 28, 1778	Washington	Clinton	250	400	A patriot attack ended in a draw.
Moore's Creek Bridge	North Carolina	Feb. 27, 1776	Caswell and others	McLeod	2	70	Lopsided patriot defeat of Loyalist militia.
Princeton	New Jersey	Jan. 3, 1777	Washington	Cornwallis	50	100	The British withdrew from western New Jersey.
Quebec	Quebec	Dec. 31, 1775	Arnold, Montgomery	Carleton	100	18	The Americans failed to seize the city of Quebec.
Trenton	New Jersey	Dec. 26, 1776	Washington	Rall	10	100	The patriots crushed the Hessians in a surprise assault.
Yorktown	Virginia	Oct. 6-19, 1781	Washington	Cornwallis	100	600	The British surrendered in the war's last major battle.

*Approximate totals. The figures listed are a compromise between several conflicting estimates.

Revolutionary War battles and campaigns

British strategy at first called for crushing the American Revolution in the North. After 1778, the fighting shifted to the South. In 1781, an American and French force defeated the British at Yorktown in the last major battle of the war. This map locates important battles and campaigns.

WORLD BOOK map

Colonial and allied campaign

British campaign

★ Major battle

The 13 colonies

Other British territories

Detail of an oil painting on canvas (1921), by J. L. G. Ferris; Archives of 76, Bay Village, Ohio

The Declaration of Independence was adopted on July 4, 1776. The statesmen shown working on a draft are, *from left to right*, Benjamin Franklin, John Adams, and Thomas Jefferson.

killed. The British then turned back to Boston. Along the way, militia fired at them from behind trees and stone fences. British dead and wounded for the day numbered about 250, and American losses came to about 90.

Word spread rapidly that fighting had broken out. Militias throughout New England took up arms and gathered outside Boston. The Americans prepared to pounce on Gage's troops if they marched out of Boston. Three British officers—Major Generals John Burgoyne, Henry Clinton, and William Howe—arrived in Boston with more troops in late May 1775.

Bunker Hill. The British and the Americans each hoped to gain an advantage by occupying hills overlooking Boston. The Americans moved first. They dug in on Breed's Hill, close to the city.

On June 17, 1775, British troops led by Howe attacked American positions on Breed's Hill. To save ammunition, American officers ordered the patriots: "Don't fire until you see the whites of their eyes." The Americans drove back two British charges before they ran out of ammunition. During a third charge, British bayonets forced the Americans to flee. The fighting, usually called the Battle of Bunker Hill, was the bloodiest battle of the entire war. More than 1,000 British soldiers and about 400 Americans were killed or wounded.

The Continental Army. The Second Continental Congress began meeting in Philadelphia in May 1775, soon after the battles at Lexington and Concord. Patriot leaders in Massachusetts urged the Congress to take charge of militia units outside Boston and raise an army strong enough to challenge the redcoats. On June 14, the Congress established the Continental Army. The next day, George Washington was made the Army's commander in chief. The Congress named 13 more generals soon afterward. It then had to figure out how to recruit troops, supply an army, and pay for a war.

Washington took command of the military camps near Boston on July 3, 1775. He immediately worked to establish order and discipline in the army. The militia units were poorly trained and lacked weapons and over-

all organization. Their camps were filthy. Most soldiers had volunteered for service to defend their families and farms. They expected to return home after a few months. Washington issued a flood of orders and dismissed junior officers who failed to enforce them. Soldiers who disobeyed were punished.

The evacuation of Boston. Soon after Washington took charge of the Continental Army, he sought to drive the British from Boston. To accomplish that task, the Americans needed artillery. In May 1775, Colonels Ethan Allen and Benedict Arnold had seized Fort Ticonderoga, a British post in the colony of New York. Shortly afterward, their troops captured another British post at nearby Crown Point. The two victories provided the Americans with much-needed artillery.

In November 1775, Colonel Henry Knox, Washington's chief of artillery, proposed a plan to move the heavy guns by sled from Ticonderoga across the snow-covered Berkshire Mountains to Boston. The guns reached Framingham, near Boston, by late January 1776.

The arrival of the artillery enabled the patriots to fortify a high ground south of Boston known as Dorchester Heights. They completed the work during the night of March 4, 1776. General Howe, who had taken command of the British army several months earlier, realized his soldiers could not hold Boston with American cannons pointed at them. By March 17, the British troops had boarded ships headed for Nova Scotia, a British colony in Canada. But the evacuation of British troops from Boston was only a temporary victory for the Americans. Howe and his troops landed at New York City in July.

The invasion of Canada. To prevent British forces from sweeping down from Canada into New York, the Continental Congress ordered an invasion of Canada.

The Noble Train of Artillery (1946) oil on canvas by Tom Lovell; Fort Ticonderoga Museum, NY (© SuperStock)

Colonel Henry Knox led an American expedition that moved captured cannons over snowy mountains to high ground near Boston, forcing the British to evacuate the city in March 1776.

British soldiers, commonly known as redcoats, lined up shoulder-to-shoulder in firing formation, as demonstrated in this battle reenactment. Soldiers fired in massed formations because of the musket's inaccuracy and limited range. The British fighting force was better trained and equipped than that of the Americans for much of the war.

AP Images

Some delegates also hoped that Canada might join the colonies in their rebellion against Britain.

In the fall of 1775, two American expeditions marched northward into Canada. Benedict Arnold led one force along rivers and over rugged terrain toward the city of Quebec. Disease and hunger caused many of his troops to turn back. The other expedition, under Brigadier General Richard Montgomery, headed toward Montreal. Montgomery captured Montreal on November 13. He then joined Arnold outside Quebec.

On Dec. 31, 1775, under cover of a blizzard, the Americans stormed Quebec, but they failed to take the city. Montgomery died in the attack, and Arnold was seriously wounded. Major General Guy Carleton, governor of the colony of Quebec, commanded the British forces in Canada. The Americans retreated to New York in the spring, after British reinforcements reached Canada. The invasion of Canada had ended in failure for the patriots.

Fighting in the Chesapeake and Southern colonies. Some planters in the Chesapeake and Southern colonies feared that a rebellion against Britain in the name of liberty might inspire black slaves to rise up against them. For that reason, Britain expected to restore its authority more easily in the Chesapeake and Southern colonies than in the North. However, the patriots had great success in the Chesapeake and South at the start of

The flintlock musket was the chief firearm of the Revolutionary War. Loading a musket required great care, as demonstrated by the Continental Army soldier *at left.* First, he bites open a paper cartridge to release the gunpowder. He next pours powder into the firing pan. More gunpowder and a lead ball are then rammed down the barrel. After the flintlock is cocked, the musket is ready to fire.

WORLD BOOK illustrations by David A. Cunningham

Artillery took part in attacks and defense. Cannons fired slowly because soldiers had to swab the barrel after each round, as these British gunners demonstrate.

A rifle fired more accurately than a musket, and many Americans on the frontier were good shots with rifles. This sharpshooter takes aim at a British officer.

A bayonet fastened to a musket was used in hand-to-hand combat. A German soldier hired by the British, *left,* clashes with an American infantryman, *right.*

A naval battle between the frigate *Bonhomme Richard,* commanded by Continental Navy Captain John Paul Jones, and the British warship *Serapis* took place off the coast of England in September 1779. The two ships were lashed together much of the time, and the crews fought in hand-to-hand combat. Jones captured the *Serapis* though his own ship was badly damaged.

Detail of an oil painting on canvas (1789) by William Elliott; U.S. Naval Academy Museum

the Revolutionary War. A few weeks before the battles of Lexington and Concord, Patrick Henry had urged his fellow Virginians to raise a militia and prepare for war. He declared, "I know not what course others may take, but as for me, give me liberty or give me death."

Many of Virginia's wealthiest slaveholders disagreed, urging patience and caution. In November 1775, the British governor of Virginia, Lord Dunmore, offered to free black slaves who took up arms on Britain's side. About 1,000 slaves joined Dunmore. This action angered many conservative slaveholders, who eventually came to support the patriots' military effort. In December, Virginia patriots defeated a force led by Dunmore at Great Bridge, south of Norfolk. Dunmore fled Virginia the following summer.

North Carolina's governor, Josiah Martin, also hoped to crush the rebellious colonists by force. He urged North Carolinians loyal to Britain to join him. More than 1,500 colonists answered Martin's call and marched toward the coast to join British troops arriving by sea. But on the way, these colonists took a beating from patriot forces at Moore's Creek Bridge, near Wilmington, North Carolina. British troops under General Clinton had sailed southward from Boston. However, they failed to arrive in time to prevent the defeat at Moore's Creek Bridge on Feb. 27, 1776.

The British warships continued on to Charleston, South Carolina, the chief port in the South. They opened fire on a fort outside the city on June 28, 1776. However, Clinton called off the attack later that day, after gunfire from the fort damaged several ships. Clinton soon rejoined British forces in the North.

The Declaration of Independence. When the Second Continental Congress opened in May 1775, few delegates wanted to break ties with the mother country. John Dickinson of Pennsylvania led the group that urged a peaceful settlement with Britain. Dickinson wrote the Olive Branch Petition, which the Congress approved in July 1775. The document declared that the colonists

were loyal to the king and urged him to remedy their complaints. However, George III ignored the petition. On August 23, he declared all the colonies to be in rebellion. In December, Parliament passed the Prohibitory Act, which closed all American ports to overseas trade. Those actions convinced many delegates that a peaceful settlement of differences with Britain was impossible.

Support for American independence continued to build early in 1776. In January, the political writer Thomas Paine issued a pamphlet titled *Common Sense.* Paine attacked George III as unjust, and he argued brilliantly for the complete independence of the American Colonies.

In June 1776, Richard Henry Lee of Virginia introduced the resolution in the Congress "That these United Colonies are, and of right ought to be, free and independent States.…" The Congress appointed a committee to draft a declaration of independence in case Lee's resolution was adopted. On July 2, the Congress approved Lee's resolution. It adopted the Declaration of Independence on July 4, and the United States of America was born.

Progress of the war

After the Americans declared their independence, they had to win it by force. The task proved difficult, partly because the people never fully united behind the war effort. A large number of colonists remained unconcerned about the outcome of the war and supported neither side. As many as a third of the people sympathized with Britain. They called themselves Loyalists. The patriots called those people Tories, after Britain's Tory Party, which strongly supported the king. Victory in the Revolutionary War depended on the patriots, who made up less than a third of the population.

Although the patriots formed a minority of the colonial population, they had many advantages over the British in the Revolutionary War. They had plenty of troop strength, if they could only persuade citizens to come out and fight. Unlike the British, they did not have

Detail of an oil painting on canvas (about 1790) by William Mercer; Historical Society of Pennsylvania, Philadelphia

The Battle of Princeton, which took place on Jan. 3, 1777, resulted in a major victory for the Americans. This painting shows George Washington, on horseback in the foreground, rallying his troops shortly before they drove the redcoats from the field. The patriot victories at Princeton and at Trenton a week earlier raised American morale and allowed Washington to rebuild his army.

to supply their army across an ocean. In addition, the patriots fought on familiar terrain and could retreat out of reach of the British. In time, Britain's chief rivals, France and Spain, joined the war. Their aid enabled the patriots to win independence.

The American patriots also benefited from British blunders. The British expected an easy victory. They thought that the patriots would turn and run at the sight of masses of redcoats. Yet British military leaders were cautious in their battle plans. American military leaders were less experienced than British officers, but they were more willing to take chances. In the long run, daring leadership gave the Americans an advantage.

The fighting forces. The American Colonies entered the Revolutionary War without an army or a navy. Their fighting forces consisted of militia units in the various colonies. The militias were made up of citizen-soldiers from 16 to 60 years old who were ready to defend their homes and families when danger threatened. The colonies could call up militias for periods of service ranging from a few days to a few months.

Britain had an army of well-trained and highly disciplined soldiers. Britain also hired professional German soldiers. Such soldiers were often called Hessians because most of them came from the German state of Hesse-Kassel. American Loyalists, escaped slaves, and Indians also joined British fighting forces during the war. At its peak, the British military force in North America numbered about 50,000.

Washington and other patriot leaders doubted that part-time militias could defeat the British in a long war. Therefore, Washington worked to build an army of disciplined soldiers who had enlisted for several years. However, recruitment for the Continental Army remained a constant problem. Most citizens preferred to serve in local militias and support the Continental Army when a major battle threatened nearby.

Washington rarely commanded as many as 15,000 soldiers at a time, and he frequently commanded far fewer.

Soldiers often went without pay, food, and proper clothing because the Continental Congress was so poor and transportation in the colonies was so bad. Yet many poor soldiers stayed in the army because they had been promised free land after the war. They fought as much for economic gain as for political liberty.

In time, most states permitted blacks to serve in the Continental Army. In all, about 5,000 African Americans fought on the patriot side in the war. Many were slaves who had been promised freedom in exchange for military service.

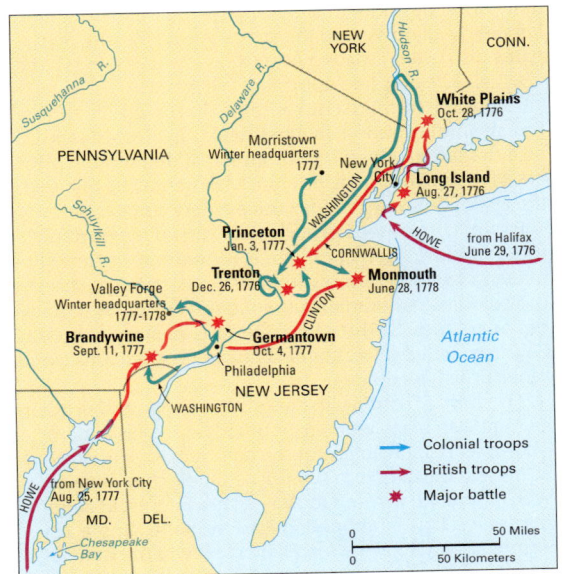

WORLD BOOK map

In the North, Washington and the redcoats fought a seesaw campaign. The patriots lost several battles but kept on fighting. British generals acted cautiously and failed to cooperate.

Weapons and tactics. The most important weapons of the war were the flintlock musket, the rifle, and the cannon. The musket discharged a large lead ball and could fire three or four rounds a minute. Rifles had much greater accuracy than muskets, but they took longer to reload, which made them less efficient in battle. Colonists from the western frontier improved the rifle's value by developing their skill at rapid loading. Cannons hurled shells long distances and blasted soldiers at closer range.

On the battlefield, soldiers lined up shoulder to shoulder, two or three rows deep. Their muskets had little accuracy beyond about 60 yards (55 meters). For that reason, the attackers advanced as far as possible before shooting. After firing several rounds, the two sides closed in for hand-to-hand combat with *bayonets* (knives that fit on the barrel of a gun). The battle ended when one side broke through enemy lines or forced the other side to retreat. In the early years of the war, the Americans had few bayonets, which gave the redcoats an enormous advantage.

Maritime forces. The Congress established the Continental Navy in 1775, but it was small and poorly equipped to challenge Britain's powerful Royal Navy. The British Navy loosely blockaded American ports and supported British military operations along the Atlantic coast. However, the Continental Navy sank or captured many smaller British vessels, especially cargo ships. Privately owned American vessels known as *privateers* also captured enemy cargo ships. The privateers then sold the stolen cargoes and divided the profits among investors, the ship captains, and the crews.

Patriot governments. The Continental Congress provided leadership for the 13 former colonies during most of the war. After the Declaration of Independence, each former colony called itself a state. The Congress drew up a plan called the Articles of Confederation to unify the states under a central government. The Articles left nearly all powers to the states because many delegates distrusted a strong central government. By March 1781, all 13 states had approved the Articles.

Each state formed a government to replace its former British administration. In most states, an elected legislature drafted a written constitution that defined the powers of the government. In 1780, Massachusetts became the last of the states to introduce a new constitution.

Patriot committees in each state stirred support for the war effort. Such committees tormented citizens suspected of sympathizing with Britain. Many Loyalists left the colonies rather than submit to the demands of patriot committees. By the end of the war, as many as 100,000 Loyalists had fled to Canada, England, the Bahamas, and other British territories.

The home front. With husbands, fathers, and brothers away at war, many women assumed new roles at home. They took responsibility for the daily functioning of family farms and businesses. They policed their communities with a watchful eye and took a greater interest in community issues. On a number of occasions, for example, city women rioted to force merchants to lower the price of grain and other items. Women also contributed directly to the war effort. In 1780, Esther De Berdt Reed helped to found the Philadelphia Ladies Association, which raised over $300,000 for the Continental Army.

Detail of an oil painting on canvas (1786), by John Trumbull; Yale University Art Gallery

The British surrender at Saratoga on Oct. 17, 1777, marked a turning point in the war. In this painting, defeated General John Burgoyne, *left,* offers his sword to General Horatio Gates.

Financing the war. The Continental Congress had to pay for the Revolutionary War, but it had no power to tax the people. Late in 1775, the Congress began to issue paper currency known as Continental dollars, or Continentals. However, it issued so many Continentals that they became nearly worthless. The Congress received some money from the states, but never enough. Loans and gifts of cash from other nations—especially from France, the Netherlands, and Spain—saved the patriots. The Congress also obtained loans from patriot merchants and other Americans who had cash or goods to spare. Those citizens received certificates that promised full repayment of their loans with interest.

Diplomacy. Vital support for the American cause came from France, Spain, and the Netherlands. Benjamin Franklin represented the Americans in France and helped win French support for the patriots.

Before the Revolutionary War began, French leaders had watched with interest the widening split between Britain and the American Colonies. France still smarted from its defeat by Britain in the French and Indian War. France's foreign minister, the Count de Vergennes, believed that a patriot victory would benefit France by weakening the mighty British Empire. France agreed to aid the patriots secretly. However, France refused to ally itself openly with the Americans before they had proved themselves in battle.

From 1776 to 1778, France gave the American government loans, gifts of money, and weapons. In 1778, treaties of alliance were signed, making France and America "good and faithful" allies. Thereafter, France also provided the patriots with troops and warships. Spain entered the war as an ally of France in 1779. The Netherlands joined the war in 1780.

The war in the North

The outcome of the battles in 1775 convinced the British that defeating the American Colonies required a major military effort and an effective strategy. As a result, Britain sent additional troops and a large naval force to America. The initial British strategy called for isolating and destroying the uprising in the North first. Once New England was knocked out, Britain expected resistance to crumble in the remaining colonies.

Britain nearly conquered the patriots several times during the fighting in the North, which lasted from 1775 to 1778. But British generals failed to carry out their strategy effectively.

The campaign in New York. After the British evacuated Boston in March 1776, General Howe began to plan his return to the American Colonies. In July, he landed on Staten Island in New York Harbor. Howe was joined by General Clinton's troops, following their defeat in South Carolina, and by Hessian soldiers from Europe. Howe commanded a total force of more than 45,000 experienced soldiers and sailors. They faced about 20,000 poorly trained and poorly equipped Americans.

Washington had shifted his forces to New York City after the redcoats withdrew from Boston. He did not expect to hold New York City, but he wanted to make the British fight for it. To defend the city, patriot troops fortified Brooklyn Heights, an area of high ground on the western tip of Long Island.

Howe saw an opportunity to trap patriot troops in Brooklyn. In August 1776, British troops landed on Long Island in front of the American lines. Howe surrounded the patriots' forward positions in the Battle of Long Island on August 27. However, the slow-moving Howe paused before attacking again, enabling the remainder of the Americans to escape. In September, Washington sent Captain Nathan Hale behind British lines to obtain information about British positions on Long Island. The British caught Hale and hanged him for spying. Before being hanged, he reportedly said, "I only regret that I have but one life to lose for my country."

By mid-September 1776, Howe had driven Washington's troops from New York City. Howe slowly pursued the Americans as they retreated toward White Plains, New York, but his hesitation cost the British a chance to crush Washington's army. Another patriot force remained on Manhattan Island to defend Fort Washing-

ton. The fort fell to Howe in November, and Britain captured nearly 3,000 Americans. New York City remained in British hands until the war ended.

During the summer and fall of 1776, General Carleton led a British force southward from Canada. British strategy called for Carleton to link up with Howe in the Hudson River Valley, thereby cutting New England off from the rest of the colonies. But Carleton met heavy resistance from patriot forces under Brigadier General Benedict Arnold in a naval battle near Valcour Island on Lake Champlain. In November, Carleton turned back to Canada for the winter.

Trenton and Princeton. The patriot situation appeared dark at the end of 1776. Washington's discouraged forces had withdrawn to New Jersey. In late November, British troops led by Major General Charles Cornwallis poured into New Jersey in pursuit of Washington. The patriots barely escaped to safety by crossing the Delaware River into Pennsylvania on December 7.

Washington's forces were near collapse, and the New Jersey militias failed to come to their aid. Yet Howe again missed an opportunity to destroy the Continental Army. He decided to wait until spring to attack and ordered his troops into winter quarters in Trenton, Princeton, and other New Jersey towns. Clinton was assigned to capture Newport, Rhode Island.

Howe believed he had broken the patriot rebellion, but he was mistaken. Although Washington had few troops, he decided to strike at Trenton. The town was defended by Hessians. On the stormy and bitterly cold night of Dec. 25, 1776, Washington and about 2,400 troops crossed the Delaware River. They landed 9 miles (14 kilometers) north of Trenton and marched through the night. The next morning, they surprised the Hessians and took more than 900 prisoners.

On Jan. 2, 1777, Cornwallis advanced toward Trenton. He planned to attack the Americans the next day. But during the night, Washington's troops silently stole away and marched past Cornwallis's army. The following morning, Washington attacked at Princeton. He won a brilliant victory over redcoats on their way to join

Detail of an oil painting on canvas (1883) by William B. Trego; Valley Forge Historical Society

A ragged and hungry Continental Army was reviewed by General Washington, mounted on the white horse, as it marched toward winter quarters at Valley Forge, Pennsylvania, in December 1777. The army suffered from a severe shortage of food, shoes, and warm clothing that winter, and many soldiers died or deserted as a result.

Colonel George Rogers Clark led a force of colonists from the western frontier across flooded countryside to recapture Fort Sackville at Vincennes in 1779. Clark's successful campaign in the Illinois country disrupted the flow of British supplies to allied western Indian tribes and helped to prevent Indian war leaders from coordinating attacks along the frontier.

Cornwallis. Washington then moved his troops northward to winter headquarters near Morristown, New Jersey. He soon began to rebuild his army.

The victories at Trenton and Princeton revived patriot hopes. The Continental Army had almost been destroyed, but it had kept going and regained most of New Jersey. Despite superior strength, the British had again failed to defeat the rebels.

Brandywine and Germantown. Washington's successful maneuvering at Trenton and Princeton had embarrassed Howe. In the spring of 1777, Howe sought to lure Washington into battle and destroy his army. After failing to draw Washington into battle in New Jersey, Howe set out to take Philadelphia, the patriot capital.

In the summer of 1777, Howe's redcoats sailed from New York City to the top of Chesapeake Bay, about 50 miles (80 kilometers) southwest of Philadelphia. Washington had rebuilt his army during the spring, and he had received weapons from France. He positioned his troops between Howe's forces and Philadelphia.

The opposing armies clashed on Sept. 11, 1777, at Brandywine Creek in southeastern Pennsylvania. One wing of the British army swung around the Americans and attacked from behind. The surprised patriots had to retreat. Howe skillfully moved his troops after the Battle of Brandywine and occupied Philadelphia on September 26. The Continental Congress had fled to York, Pennsylvania, where it continued to direct American affairs.

On Oct. 4, 1777, Washington struck back at British forces camping at Germantown, north of Philadelphia. However, his complicated battle plan created confusion. In a heavy fog, patriot forces fired on each other. The Americans again had to retreat.

Victory at Saratoga. While Howe won victories at Brandywine Creek and Germantown, another British force became stranded near Saratoga, New York. That force had advanced southward from Canada under Lieutenant General John Burgoyne.

Burgoyne had a successful start against the Americans. On July 6, 1777, he recaptured the British post of Fort Ticonderoga in New York from the Americans without a struggle. A second British expedition, led by Lieu-

tenant Colonel Barry St. Leger, marched up the Mohawk River Valley to meet Burgoyne. In August, St. Leger ambushed militias outside Oriskany, New York. In the bloody Battle of Oriskany, the British beat back patriot forces. General Arnold stopped St. Leger soon afterward. By then, conditions favored the patriots.

As Burgoyne advanced southward, patriot forces destroyed bridges and cut down trees to block his path. American rifles fired on the British from the woods, and Burgoyne ran short of food and other supplies. In August 1777, the Congress appointed Major General Horatio Gates to command the Northern Department of the Continental Army. Gates was popular with New England patriots, and they poured out to support him and his soldiers, called Continentals. On August 16, militias overwhelmed two groups of Hessians and Loyalists looking for horses and food in New York, just west of Bennington, Vermont.

Burgoyne trudged slowly through the wilderness along the Hudson River. His slowness gave the Americans time to fortify a wooded area along the Hudson about 40 miles (64 kilometers) north of Albany. On Sept. 19, 1777, British troops attacked the fortifications, but they were met by patriot forces in a clearing on a nearby farm. Nightfall and the bravery of Hessian soldiers saved Burgoyne's troops from destruction in what became known as the First Battle of Freeman's Farm.

Although the patriot forces greatly outnumbered his army, Burgoyne chose not to retreat toward Canada. On Oct. 7, 1777, he attacked again. Arnold's daring leadership won the Second Battle of Freeman's Farm for the patriots. Burgoyne finally began to retreat, but he soon found himself encircled by the Americans at Saratoga. On October 17, Burgoyne surrendered. The Americans took nearly 6,000 prisoners and large supplies of arms.

The victory at Saratoga marked a turning point in the Revolutionary War. It revealed the failure of British strategy. More importantly, the decisive victory at Saratoga helped convince France that it could safely enter the war on the American side.

Valley Forge. Washington's army of about 10,000 soldiers spent the winter camped at Valley Forge, about 20 miles (32 kilometers) northwest of Philadelphia. Many of the troops lacked shoes and other clothing. They also suffered from a severe shortage of food. By spring 1778, nearly a fourth of the soldiers had died of malnutrition, exposure to the cold, and such diseases as smallpox and typhoid fever. Many soldiers deserted because of the miserable conditions.

In February 1778, a Prussian officer called Baron Friedrich von Steuben arrived at Valley Forge. He convinced Washington that he could train the Continental Army in European military formations and bayonet charges. By late spring, Steuben had created a disciplined fighting force. The Marquis de Lafayette, a young French soldier, also spent part of the winter at Valley Forge. Fired with enthusiasm for the revolution, Lafayette had joined Washington's staff as a major general without pay.

France's entry into the Revolutionary War in 1778 forced Britain to defend the rest of its empire. The British expected to fight the French in the West Indies and elsewhere, and so they scattered their military resources. As a result, Britain no longer had a force strong enough to battle the Americans in the North.

In May 1778, General Clinton became commander in chief of British forces in North America. He replaced Howe, who had occupied Philadelphia since September 1777. Clinton received orders to abandon Philadelphia and move his army to New York City. He was also told to send troops to the West Indies and other areas.

Monmouth. Clinton left Philadelphia on June 18, 1778, and marched across New Jersey toward New York City. The Continental Army followed him. On June 28, the patriots attacked near Monmouth Court House, New Jersey. Clinton soon counterattacked. After early confusion, the Americans held their ground, and the battle ended in a draw. During the night, Clinton's exhausted forces limped off the battleground and continued the march toward New York. The Battle of Monmouth was the last major Revolutionary War battle in the North.

Stalemate in the North. Washington hoped to drive the British from New York City in a joint operation with the French. In July 1778, a fleet under the French admiral

Charles Hector, Comte d'Estaing, reached America. But a sandbar at the mouth of New York Harbor blocked the French warships. Later that summer, a combined French and American effort to take Newport, Rhode Island, also failed. In November, d'Estaing sailed south to protect the French West Indies from British attack.

The war in the West

When the Revolutionary War began, about 150,000 Native Americans lived in territory claimed by Britain. East of the Appalachian Mountains, native people lived mainly in separate communities surrounded by English-speaking colonists. The Indians participated in the colonial economy as whalers, agricultural laborers, and craftworkers. West of the Appalachians, they inhabited what was sometimes called "Indian country"—a patchwork of hundreds of villages belonging to a number of distinct Indian nations. Native people in this region lived by a combination of farming and hunting. They traded with American colonists for necessities they could not produce themselves, such as iron utensils, firearms, and ammunition. However, they guarded their land and welcomed British efforts to prevent the colonists from settling west of the Appalachian Mountains.

When the fighting began in 1775, Native Americans faced a difficult choice. Some native communities attempted to remain neutral in the conflict. Others, such as the Stockbridge and Mashpee Indians of Massachusetts and the Catawba Indians of South Carolina, contributed soldiers to the American war effort. In the West, however, most native communities allied with the British. They feared that an American victory would threaten their survival. American colonists had crossed the Appalachian Mountains and settled on Indian land, often in violation of British policy. During the Revolutionary War, Indians attacked and tried to disperse these settlements.

Invasion of the Iroquois country. Burgoyne's campaign in the Hudson Valley prompted four of the six Iroquois nations—the Mohawks, Senecas, Cayugas, and Onondagas—to enter the war as British allies. After Burgoyne's surrender at Saratoga in 1777, the Iroquois con-

Detail of an oil painting on canvas (about 1845) by William Ranney; State Capitol, Columbia, South Carolina (Victor Tutte)

The Battle of Cowpens was fought in a cattle-grazing area of South Carolina in January 1781. It ended in victory for the patriots. In the clash shown here, a young American bugler shoots a British officer who is trying to stab an American cavalry commander. The inability of the British to secure the Southern Colonies hindered their efforts to retake positions in the North.

General Cornwallis surrendered his army to George Washington at Yorktown, the site of the war's last major battle, on Oct. 19, 1781. This painting shows French and American officers, including Washington, lined up to receive the surrender. Britain began peace talks with the Americans several months after its defeat at Yorktown. The war officially ended with the signing of the Treaty of Paris on Sept. 3, 1783.

The Surrender of Lord Cornwallis at Yorktown (1817-1824), an oil painting by John Trumbull; Yale University Art Gallery

tinued to harass American settlements on the frontiers of New York and Pennsylvania. In 1779, Washington sought to remove the Iroquois from the war through "the total destruction and devastation of their settlements." Patriot troops commanded by General John Sullivan invaded the Iroquois country in the late summer and fall of that year. They burned 40 villages and destroyed crops ready for harvest. That winter, some Iroquois died of starvation. Several thousand fled as refugees to Fort Niagara, a British post on the southwestern shore of Lake Ontario. But Iroquois warriors continued to fight.

The Illinois campaign. Soon after the war began, some Native American war leaders in the West began raiding settlements to try to push settlers out of Kentucky and the Ohio River Valley. Colonel George Rogers Clark of Virginia executed a daring campaign in the Illinois country that disrupted the flow of British supplies to the western tribes and helped to prevent Native American war leaders from coordinating attacks along the frontier. In the summer of 1778, Clark captured several settlements in what are now southern Illinois and southern Indiana. The British recaptured the settlement at Vincennes in Indiana. Clark and his troops fought their way back to Vincennes across flooded countryside and took its British and Indian defenders by surprise in February 1779.

The war in the South

Britain changed its strategy after France entered the Revolutionary War. Rather than attack in the North, the British concentrated on conquering the colonies from the South. British leaders believed that most Southerners supported the king. Although the British failed to find as much Loyalist support as they expected, they defeated the Americans in several key battles. This strategy forced the patriots onto the defensive in the South.

Savannah and Charleston. The first stage of Britain's Southern strategy called for the capture of a major Southern port, such as Charleston, South Carolina, or Savannah, Georgia. Britain would then use the port as a base for rallying Southern Loyalists and for launching further military campaigns. After Britain's army moved on, the British expected Loyalists to keep control of the conquered areas. Britain assumed it could more easily retake the North after overcoming resistance in the South.

Britain's Southern campaign opened late in 1778. On December 29, a large British force that had sailed from New York City easily captured Savannah. Within a few months, the British controlled all of Georgia.

The Continental Congress named Major General Benjamin Lincoln commander of the Southern Department of the Continental Army. In October 1779, Lincoln and Comte d'Estaing tried to drive the British from Savannah but failed. Afterward, d'Estaing returned to France, and Lincoln retreated to Charleston.

Success at Savannah led the British to invade South Carolina. In February 1780, British forces commanded by General Clinton landed near Charleston. They slowly closed in on the city, trapping its defenders. On May 12, General Lincoln surrendered his force of over 5,000 soldiers—almost the entire Southern army. Clinton placed General Cornwallis in charge of British forces in the South and returned to New York City.

The loss of Charleston and Lincoln's army badly damaged American morale. However, the British victory had an unexpected result. Soon afterward, bands of South Carolina patriots began to roam the countryside, battling Loyalists and attacking British supply lines. The rebels made it risky for Loyalists to support Cornwallis. The chief rebel leaders included Francis Marion, Andrew Pickens, and Thomas Sumter.

Camden. In July 1780, the Continental Congress ordered General Gates, the victor at Saratoga, to form a new Southern army to replace the one lost at Charleston. Gates hastily assembled a force made up largely of untrained militias. The rest of his troops consisted of disciplined Continentals. He rushed to challenge Cornwallis at a British base in Camden, South Carolina.

On Aug. 16, 1780, the armies of Gates and Cornwallis met outside Camden and went into battle. The militias quickly panicked. Most of them turned and ran without firing a shot. The Continentals fought on until heavy casualties forced them to withdraw. The British had defeated a second American army in the South.

The disaster at Camden marked a low point for the patriots. They then received a further blow. In September 1780, the patriots discovered that General Arnold, who commanded a military post at West Point, New York, had joined the British side. The Americans learned of Arnold's treason just in time to stop him from turning West Point over to the enemy.

Kings Mountain. Cornwallis's victory at Camden in August 1780 led him to act more boldly. In September, he charged into North Carolina before the Loyalists had gained firm control of South Carolina. After Cornwallis's departure, rebels in South Carolina terrorized suspected Loyalists. In addition, colonists from the western frontier turned out to fight the British.

In October 1780, the patriots surrounded and captured the left wing of Cornwallis's army, which was made up of Loyalist troops, on Kings Mountain, just inside South Carolina. After the defeat at Kings Mountain, Cornwallis temporarily halted his Southern campaign and retreated into South Carolina.

Cowpens and Guilford Courthouse. In October 1780, the Continental Congress named Major General Nathanael Greene to replace Gates as commander of the Southern army. Greene was a superb choice because he knew how to accomplish much with few resources. Greene divided his troops into two small armies. He led one army and put Brigadier General Daniel Morgan in

charge of the other. Greene hoped to avoid battle with Cornwallis's far stronger force while he rebuilt the Southern army. Greene planned to let the British chase the Americans around the countryside.

Cornwallis set out to trap Morgan's army. Just before the British caught up with him, Morgan prepared for battle in a cattle-grazing area known as the Cowpens in northern South Carolina. On Jan. 17, 1781, Morgan's troops, armed with sharpshooting rifles, quickly killed or captured nearly all the attacking redcoats.

The patriot victory at Cowpens enraged Cornwallis, and he pursued Morgan with even greater determination. Greene rushed to join Morgan, hoping to crush Cornwallis's weakened force. On March 15, 1781, a bloody conflict occurred at Guilford Courthouse in North Carolina. Although Cornwallis drove Greene from the battlefield, the British took a battering. Cornwallis halted the chase after the Battle of Guilford Courthouse. He moved to Wilmington, North Carolina, where he gave his exhausted army a brief rest.

Greene challenged British posts in South Carolina during the spring of 1781. The patriots fought several small battles but failed to win clear victories. Yet the fact that a rebel army moved freely about the countryside proved that Britain did not control the Carolinas.

The end of the war

The fighting in the Revolutionary War centered in Virginia during 1781. In January, Benedict Arnold began conducting raids in Virginia for the British, who had made him a brigadier general. Arnold's troops set fire to crops, military supplies, and other patriot property. In response, Washington sent Lafayette with a force of Continentals to rally Virginia's militia and to go after Arnold. However, Lafayette had too few troops to stop Arnold.

Cornwallis rushed into Virginia in the spring of 1781 and made it his new base in the campaign to conquer the South. However, Cornwallis had departed from Britain's Southern strategy by failing to gain control of North and South Carolina before advancing northward. General Clinton believed that the Southern campaign was therefore doomed. He also feared an American attack on his base at New York City. Clinton ordered Cornwallis to adopt a defensive position along the Virginia coast and to prepare to send his troops north. Cornwallis moved to Yorktown, which lay along Chesapeake Bay.

Surrender at Yorktown. The last major battle of the Revolutionary War was fought at Yorktown. French and American forces cooperated to deliver a crushing defeat to British forces under Cornwallis.

About 5,500 French soldiers had reached America in July 1780. They were led by Lieutenant General Jean Rochambeau. Washington still hoped to drive the British from New York City in a combined operation with the French. In August 1781, however, Washington learned that a large French fleet under Admiral François de Grasse was headed toward Virginia. De Grasse planned to block Chesapeake Bay and prevent Cornwallis from escaping by sea. Washington and Rochambeau rushed their forces southward to trap Cornwallis on land. A British naval force sailed from New York City and battled de Grasse at the mouth of Chesapeake Bay in early September. But after several days, the British

The borders of the United States were set by the Treaty of Paris, which ended the Revolutionary War. The new nation extended from the Atlantic Ocean west to the Mississippi River.

ships returned to New York for repairs.

By late September 1781, Cornwallis knew that he was in trouble. A combined French and American force of about 18,000 soldiers and sailors surrounded him at Yorktown. The soldiers slowly and steadily closed in on the trapped British troops. Cornwallis made a desperate attempt to ferry his forces across the York River to safety on the night of October 16, but a storm drove them back. Cornwallis asked for surrender terms the next day.

The surrender at Yorktown took place on Oct. 19, 1781. More than 8,000 soldiers laid down their arms as a British band reportedly played a tune called "The World Turned Upside Down." They represented about a fourth of Britain's military force in America.

Britain's defeat at Yorktown did not end the Revolutionary War. The fighting dragged on in some areas for two more years. However, British leaders feared they might lose other parts of Britain's empire if they continued the war in America. Cornwallis's defeat at Yorktown brought a new group of British ministers to power early in 1782. They began peace talks with the Americans.

The Treaty of Paris. Peace discussions between the Americans and the British opened in Paris in April 1782. Richard Oswald, a wealthy merchant, represented the British government. The statesmen Benjamin Franklin, John Adams, and John Jay negotiated for the United States.

The Congress instructed the American delegates to consult with the French before they took any action. But the Americans disregarded the instructions and concluded a preliminary peace treaty with Britain on Nov. 30, 1782. The Congress approved the treaty on April 15, 1783, and the treaty was signed on Sept. 3, 1783.

The Treaty of Paris recognized the independence of the United States and established the new nation's borders. United States territory extended west to the Mississippi River, north to Canada, east to the Atlantic Ocean, and south to about Florida. Britain gave Florida to Spain. The treaty also granted the Americans fishing rights off Newfoundland and Nova Scotia. It also instructed the Congress to recommend that the states restore property taken from Loyalists during the war. The last British soldiers withdrew from New York City in November 1783.

Results of the revolution

As a result of the American Revolution, the Thirteen Colonies threw off royal rule. In its place, they established governments ruled by law and dedicated to the guarantee of certain basic rights, including life, liberty, and the pursuit of happiness. Admiration for the principles that guided the revolution led peoples elsewhere to demand political reforms. Thomas Paine declared that the American Revolution "contributed more to enlighten the world, and diffuse a spirit of freedom and liberality among mankind, than any human event … that ever preceded it."

War losses. Most historians estimate that about 7,200 Americans were killed in battle during the Revolutionary War. Approximately 8,200 more were wounded. About 10,000 others died in military camps from disease or exposure. Some 8,500 died in prison after being captured by the British. American military deaths from all causes during the war thus numbered about 25,700. In addition, approximately 1,400 soldiers were missing. British military deaths during the war totaled about 10,000.

Many soldiers in the Continental Army came out of the war penniless, as they had received little or no pay while they served. Soldiers who had enlisted for the entire war received certificates for Western land. But many veterans had to sell the certificates because they needed money before Western lands became available. In 1818, Congress agreed to pay pensions to needy veterans.

Costs of the war. The 13 states and the Congress went deeply into debt to finance the Revolutionary War. A new Constitution, approved in 1788, gave Congress the power of taxation. Largely through taxes, Congress paid off much of the war debt by the early 1800's.

The Revolutionary War severely strained Britain's economy. The king and Parliament feared the war might bankrupt the country. But after the war, greatly expanded trade with the United States helped the economy recover. Taxes on trade reduced Britain's debt.

Of all the warring nations, France could least afford its expenditures on the Revolutionary War. By 1788, the country was nearly bankrupt. France's financial troubles helped bring on the French Revolution in 1789.

Historical significance. The American Revolution fundamentally changed life in America. Above all, the revolution opened the doors that shut ordinary citizens out of the political process. Previously, the right to vote had been limited to adult white males who owned property. The property requirement was based on the idea that property owners had the strongest interest in good government and so were best qualified to make decisions. During and after the revolution, requirements for property ownership were reduced. By the 1830's, they were eliminated in nearly all the states. Black men and women of all races, however, did not gain the vote for many years.

Revolutionary ideals and the practical circumstances of the war also made it possible for African Americans, with others, to mount a challenge to slavery. In the Northern states, their efforts succeeded. Between 1777 and 1804, every state north of Maryland adopted a plan to end slavery within its boundaries. Meanwhile, in the South, slaveholders worked to shore up and preserve the institution of slavery. The American Revolution thus helped create a new division between free and slave states. This division laid the foundation for the American Civil War (1861-1865) and, with it, the ultimate end of slavery in the United States.   Nathaniel Sheidley

Additional resources

Level I
Bobrick, Benson. *Fight for Freedom: The American Revolutionary War.* Atheneum, 2004.
Rosen, Daniel. *Independence Now: The American Revolution, 1763-1783.* National Geographic Soc., 2004.
Schanzer, Rosalyn. *George vs. George: The American Revolution As Seen from Both Sides.* National Geographic Soc., 2004.

Level II
Fredriksen, John C. *Revolutionary War Almanac.* Facts on File, 2006.
Fremont-Barnes, Gregory, and others, eds. *The Encyclopedia of the American Revolutionary War.* 5 vols. ABC-CLIO, 2006.
Middlekauff, Robert. *The Glorious Cause: The American Revolution, 1763-1789.* Rev. ed. Oxford, 2005.
Savas, Theodore P., and Dameron, J. David. *A Guide to the Battles of the American Revolution.* Savas Beatie, 2006.
Selesky, Harold E., ed. *Encyclopedia of the American Revolution.* 2 vols. 2nd ed. Scribner, 2006.

A popular Shakespeare romantic comedy called *The Taming of the Shrew* takes place in Italy during the Renaissance of the 1400's and 1500's. Shakespeare's plays are performed throughout the world in front of audiences who attend performances in indoor theaters and at open-air festivals.

William Shakespeare

Shakespeare, William (1564-1616), was an English playwright, poet, and actor. Many people regard him as the world's greatest dramatist and the finest poet England has ever produced.

Shakespeare wrote at least 38 plays, two major narrative poems, a sequence of sonnets, and several short poems. Translators have put his works into a remarkable number of languages, and theaters throughout the world have performed his plays. Shakespeare's plays have formed a vital part of the theater in the Western world since he wrote them about 400 years ago. Through the years, most serious actors have considered the major roles of Shakespeare to be the supreme test of their art.

Shakespeare's plays have attracted large audiences in big, sophisticated cities and in small, rural towns. Theaters on the frontiers of Australia and New Zealand have performed his works. The plays made up part of the cultural life of the American Colonies and provided entertainment in the mining camps of the Old West. Today, theaters in many nations are dedicated to staging his works.

Shakespeare used language of startling originality to portray many-sided characters and tell fascinating stories. Critics and readers celebrate him as a great student of human nature. A remarkable group of vivid characters populate his plays. They include rogues and aristocrats, housewives and stuffy teachers, soldiers and generals, shepherds and philosophers. The most successful of these characters create an impression of psychological depth never before seen in English literature.

Shakespeare has had enormous influence on culture throughout the world. His works have helped shape the literature of all English-speaking countries. His work has also had an important effect on the literary cultures of such countries as Germany and Russia. In addition, his widespread presence in popular culture extends to motion pictures, television, cartoons, and even songs.

Shakespeare's characters, language, and stories are a source of inspiration, quotation, and imitation. Many words and phrases that first appeared in his plays and poems have become part of our everyday speech. Examples include such common words as *assassination, bump, eventful, go-between, gloomy,* and *lonely,* as well as such familiar phrases as *fair play, a forgone conclusion,* and *salad days.*

Shakespeare has so saturated modern culture that many people who have never read a line of his work or seen one of his plays performed can identify lines and passages as his. Examples include "To be, or not to be," "Friends, Romans, countrymen, lend me your ears," "Parting is such sweet sorrow," "A rose by any other name would smell as sweet," and "A horse! A horse! My kingdom for a horse!"

Shakespeare's poetry is full of vivid metaphors and brilliant images. His verbal skill also reveals itself in a tendency for word play and puns. Critics and readers acknowledge his superb way with words even when the richness of his language blurs what his text means.

Besides influencing language and literature, Shakespeare has affected other aspects of our culture. His plays and poems have long been a required part of a liberal ed-

Portrait of William Shakespeare (c.1610), oil on canvas painting attributed to John Taylor; National Portrait Gallery, London (Bridgeman Art Library)

This portrait of Shakespeare is generally considered the only likeness of him painted during his lifetime. The portrait is credited to the English artist John Taylor about 1610. It is called the Chandos portrait because the Duke of Chandos once owned it.

Outline

ucation. Generations of people have absorbed his ideas concerning heroism, romantic love, loyalty, and the nature of tragedy as well as his portraits of particular historical characters. To this day, most people imagine Julius Caesar, Mark Antony, Cleopatra, and Richard III as Shakespeare portrayed them.

Shakespeare's plays appeal to readers as well as to theatergoers. His plays—and his poems—have been reprinted and translated countless times. Indeed, a publishing industry flourishes around Shakespeare, as critics and scholars examine every aspect of the man, his writings, and his influence. Each year, hundreds of books and articles appear on Shakespearean subjects. Thousands of scholars from all over the world gather in dozens of meetings annually to discuss topics related to Shakespeare. Special libraries and library collections focus upon Shakespeare. Filmmakers have made numerous motion pictures of his plays. Composers have written operas, musical comedies, and instrumental works based on his stories and characters.

The world has admired and respected many great writers. But only Shakespeare has generated such varied and continuing interest—and such constant affection. The extent and durability of Shakespeare's reputation is without equal.

This article will discuss Shakespeare's life, the England of Shakespeare's day, the Elizabethan theater, Shakespeare's plays, Shakespeare's poems, and Shakespeare's style. A final section will discuss the history of Shakespeare publishing.

Shakespeare's life

During Shakespeare's time, the English cared little about keeping biographical information unrelated to affairs of the church or state. In addition, playwriting was not a highly regarded occupation, and so people saw little point in recording the lives of mere dramatists. However, a number of records exist that deal with Shakespeare's life. They include church registers and accounts of business dealings. Although these records are few and incomplete by modern standards, they provide much information. By relating these records to various aspects of English history and society, scholars have constructed a believable and largely comprehensive account of Shakespeare's life. However, gaps remain. Perhaps the most frustrating gap is the general absence of personal papers that might provide access to the playwright's thoughts and feelings. As a result, biographers almost always examine the plays and poems for autobiographical clues.

His life in Stratford. Shakespeare's parents belonged to what today would be called the middle class. John Shakespeare, William's father, was a glove maker who owned a shop in the town of Stratford-upon-Avon. Stratford is about 75 miles (120 kilometers) northwest of London in the county of Warwickshire. John Shakespeare was a respected man in the town and held several important positions in the local government.

William Shakespeare's mother was born Mary Arden. She was the daughter of a farmer but related to a family of considerable social standing in the county. John Shakespeare married Mary Arden about 1557. The Ardens were Roman Catholics. Mary may also have been a Catholic, but the Shakespeares publicly belonged to the Church of England, the state church.

Early years. William Shakespeare was born in the small market town of Stratford-upon-Avon in 1564, the third of eight children. The register of Holy Trinity, the parish church in Stratford, records his baptism on April 26. According to the custom at that time, infants were baptized about three days after their birth. Therefore, the generally accepted date for Shakespeare's birth is April 23.

The Shakespeares were a family of considerable local prominence. In 1565, John Shakespeare became an alderman. Three years later, he was elected *bailiff* (mayor), the highest civic honor that a Stratford resident could receive. Later, he held several other civic posts. But toward the end of his life, John Shakespeare had financial problems.

Beginning at about the age of 7, William probably attended the Stratford grammar school with other boys of his social class. The school's highly qualified teachers were graduates of Oxford University. Students spent about nine hours a day in school. They attended classes the year around, except for three brief holiday periods. The teachers enforced strict discipline and physically punished students who broke the rules. The students chiefly studied Latin, the language of ancient Rome. Knowledge of Latin was necessary for a career in medicine, law, or the church. In addition, the ability to read Latin was considered a sign of an educated person. Young Shakespeare may have read such outstanding ancient Roman authors as Cicero, Ovid, Plautus, Seneca, Terence, and Virgil.

Despite the long hours he spent in school, Shakespeare's boyhood was probably not all boring study. As a market center, Stratford was a lively town. Holidays provided popular pageants and shows, including plays about the legendary outlaw Robin Hood and his merry men. By 1569, traveling companies of professional actors were performing in Stratford. Stratford also held two large fairs each year, which attracted numerous visitors from other counties. For young Shakespeare, Stratford could thus have been an exciting place to live.

Stratford also offered other pleasures. The fields and woods surrounding the town provided opportunities to hunt and trap small game. The River Avon, which ran through the town, had fish to catch. Shakespeare's poems and plays show a love of nature and rural life. This display undoubtedly reflects Shakespeare's childhood experiences and his love of the Stratford countryside.

Marriage. On Nov. 27, 1582, Shakespeare received a license to marry Anne Hathaway, the daughter of a local farmer. The two families knew each other, but the details of the relationship between William and Anne have been a source of speculation. At the age of 18, William was young to marry, while Anne at 26 was of normal marrying age. The marriage appears to have been hurried, and the birth of their first child, Susanna, in May 1583 came only six months after marriage. Some scholars have suggested that William may have been forced to marry Anne because she was pregnant. However, birth and marriage records indicate that many women in England at that time were already pregnant before they married, and so Shakespeare's marriage was not unusual. Early in 1585, Anne gave birth to twins, Judith and Hamnet. The record of baptism marks the start of an important gap in the documentary evidence of Shakespeare's life.

The lost years. Scholars have referred to the period between 1585 and 1592, when Shakespeare was called an "upstart" by a London writer, as the "lost years." Scholars have proposed a number of theories about his activities during that time. But what is certain is that some time before 1592 Shakespeare arrived in London and began to work in the theater.

Early career in London. By 1592, Shakespeare apparently attracted the hostile attention of a jealous rival. Robert Greene was a university-trained writer who was among the first to attempt to make a career of writing for the stage and the commercial press. *Greene's Groats-Worth of Wit Bought with a Million of Repentance,* a pamphlet published after Greene's death in 1592, contains a harsh reference to Shakespeare. The English playwright Henry Chettle prepared the pamphlet for publication and may have been the true author. A passage in the pamphlet addressed to playwrights says:

> … an upstart Crow, beautified with our feathers, that with his *Tiger's heart wrapped in a Player's hide,* supposes he is as well able to bombast out a blank verse as the best of you: and being an absolute *Johannes fac totum* [Jack of all trades], is in his own conceit the only Shake-scene in a country.

The line "Tiger's heart wrapped in a Player's hide" echoes a line spoken by the Duke of York in Shakespeare's *Henry VI, Part III.* The line is "O tiger's heart wrapped in a woman's hide." The pun on Shakespeare's name makes the object of attack clear. Whether written by Greene or Chettle, this passage indicates that Shakespeare was in 1592 an actor who also wrote plays. He was successful enough to provoke the scorn and jealousy of competitors who considered themselves socially and culturally superior.

His work in theater companies. After arriving in London, Shakespeare began an association with one of the city's *repertory* theater companies. These companies consisted of a permanent cast of actors who presented a variety of plays week after week. The companies had aristocratic patrons, and the players were technically servants of the nobles who sponsored them. But the companies were commercial operations that depended on selling tickets to the general public for their income.

Scholars do not know which of the various companies first employed Shakespeare. Scholars have noted connections between Shakespeare's early plays and a number of plays that were performed by the Queen's Men, a company that played in Stratford in 1587. What is certain is that by 1594 Shakespeare was a *sharer* in the Lord Chamberlain's Men. As a sharer, Shakespeare was a stockholder in the company and entitled to a share in the company's profits.

The Lord Chamberlain's Men were one of the most popular companies in London. In large part because of Shakespeare's talents, they would go on to become the dominant company in England during the late 1500's and early 1600's. Shakespeare's position as sharer allowed him to achieve a level of financial success unmatched by other dramatists of the age, many of whom lived in poverty. Most playwrights were free-lancers who were paid a one-time fee for their plays and usually worked for several companies. After 1594, Shakespeare maintained a relationship with a single company.

His first poems. From mid-1592 to 1594, London authorities frequently closed the theaters because of repeated outbreaks of plague. Without the income provided by acting and playwriting, Shakespeare turned to poetry. In 1593, *Venus and Adonis* became the first of Shakespeare's

© Hideo Kurihara, Alamy Images

Shakespeare's birthplace was probably one of these two adjoining houses in Stratford. According to tradition, the playwright was born in the house on the left, called the Birthplace.

Peter Baker

A bedroom in the Birthplace is furnished in the style common among middle-class families of Shakespeare's day. Shakespeare may have been born in this room.

works to be published. The publisher was Richard Field, a native of Stratford who may have known Shakespeare in childhood. As was customary at the time, Shakespeare dedicated his volume to a noble patron, in this case Henry Wriothesley, the Earl of Southampton. *Venus and Adonis* proved to be extremely popular and was reprinted at least 15 times in Shakespeare's lifetime.

In 1594, Field printed Shakespeare's *The Rape of Lucrece.* The book's dedication to Southampton suggests a closer acquaintance between the writer and the aristocrat. The volume was not as popular as *Venus and Adonis,* but it still sold well. Seven editions had been published by 1632. Despite the commercial success of these early publications, Shakespeare made no effort to make a career of poetry. When the theaters reopened, he returned to acting and playwriting.

The years of fame. Throughout the 1590's, Shakespeare's reputation continued to grow. From 1594 to 1608, he was fully involved in the London theater world. In addition to his duties as a sharer and actor in the Lord Chamberlain's Men, he wrote an average of almost two plays a year for his company. During much of this period, Shakespeare ranked as London's most popular playwright, based on the number of times his plays were performed and published. But his reputation was largely that of a popular playwright, not of a writer of unequaled genius.

Few people gave Shakespeare the praise that later generations heaped on him. An exception was the English clergyman and schoolmaster Francis Meres. In 1598, Meres wrote *Palladis Tamia: Wit's Treasury,* a book that has become an important source of information about Shakespeare's career. In this book, Meres said of Shakespeare: "As *Plautus* and *Seneca* are accounted the best for Comedy and Tragedy among the Latins: so *Shakespeare* among the English is the most excellent in both kinds for the stage." Although Meres's praise did not represent everyone's opinion, it indicates that Shakespeare had become an established writer by at least the late 1590's.

Shakespeare's name did not appear on his earliest published plays, but the 1598 edition of *Love's Labour's Lost*

includes his name on the title page. Later editions prominently advertise his authorship, in some cases falsely. In 1599, a printer named William Jaggard published *The Passionate Pilgrim,* a collection of 20 poems supposedly written by Shakespeare. However, the volume offered only five sonnets by Shakespeare, three taken from *Love's Labour's Lost.* By the end of the 1590's, Shakespeare's reputation was being used to sell books. And he had not yet written most of his great tragedies, such as *Hamlet, Othello, King Lear,* and *Macbeth.*

By the late 1590's, Shakespeare not only had become an established writer but also had become prosperous. In October 1596, John Shakespeare was granted a coat of arms, an emblem symbolic of family history, about 25 years after his initial application. Most scholars have suggested that William Shakespeare renewed the application on his father's behalf and paid the necessary fees. To have

By permission of the Headmaster and Governors (Peter Baker)

The Stratford grammar school provided Shakespeare with all his formal education. He probably entered the school at about the age of 7. The school dates from 1295 and is still used.

a coat of arms was an important mark of social standing in England at that time. Certainly Shakespeare was eager to establish himself in Stratford. In May 1597, he purchased New Place, one of the town's two largest houses. Shakespeare obviously remained a Stratford man at heart in spite of his busy, successful life in London. Records of business dealings and of minor lawsuits reveal that he preferred to invest most of his money in Stratford rather than in London.

The Globe Theatre. As was customary, Shakespeare's company, the Lord Chamberlain's Men, rented performance space. For most of the 1590's, the Lord Chamberlain's Men performed in a building called the Theatre. The English actor and theatrical manager James Burbage had built the structure on leased land. Burbage was the father of the famous actor Richard Burbage, star of the Chamberlain's Men. After a disagreement with the landlord, the company was forced to find new accommodations. Richard Burbage and the Lord Chamberlain's Men dismantled the Theatre and moved it across the River Thames to a new site in Southwark. There they used the old timbers to erect a new theater called the Globe Theatre. The Globe could accommodate 3,000 spectators.

Shakespeare was one of six shareholders who signed the lease for the new site in 1599. He thus became part of the first group of actor-sharers to also be theater owners. Although this arrangement meant financial risk, it also promised to be profitable if the new theater was a success. The Globe proved to be a wise investment, and it remained a home to Shakespeare's acting company until the religious reformers known as Puritans closed the theaters in 1642, during the English Civil War.

The King's Men. In 1603, Queen Elizabeth I died and was succeeded by her cousin James VI of Scotland. As king of England, he became James I. James enjoyed and actively supported the theater. He issued a royal license to Shakespeare and his fellow players, which allowed the company to call itself the King's Men. In return for the license, the actors entertained the king at court on a more or less regular basis.

James's support came at a convenient time. An outbreak of plague in 1603 had closed the theaters for long periods, making theatrical life uncertain. In fact, James's entry into London as king had to be postponed until 1604 because of the plague. When James finally made his royal entry into London, the King's Men accompanied him. The members of the company were officially known as *grooms of the chamber.* In spite of this title and the name King's Men, the actors were not actually friends of the king. Their relationship to the royal court was simply that of professional entertainers.

The King's Men achieved unequaled success and became London's leading theatrical group. In 1608, the company leased the Blackfriars Theatre for 21 years. The theater stood in a heavily populated London district called Blackfriars. The Blackfriars Theatre had artificial lighting, mainly candles. The theater was probably heated and served as the winter playhouse for the company. The King's Men performed at the Globe Theatre during the summer.

The period from 1599 to 1608 was a time of extraordinary literary activity for Shakespeare. During these years, he wrote several comedies and almost all the tragedies that have made him famous. Shakespeare's masterpieces during this period include the comedies *Much Ado About Nothing* and *Twelfth Night;* the history *Henry V;* and the tragedies *Antony and Cleopatra, Hamlet, Julius Caesar, King Lear, Macbeth,* and *Othello.*

The sonnets. In 1609, a London publisher named Thomas Thorpe published a book called *Shakespeare's Sonnets.* The volume contained more than 150 sonnets that Shakespeare had written over the years. Scholars have long been curious about the book's puzzling dedication. It reads, in modernized spelling: "To the only begetter of these ensuing sonnets Mr. W. H." We do not know whether these are Shakespeare's or Thorpe's words, nor do we know the identity of the mysterious W. H. For additional information on the sonnets, see the section *Shakespeare's poems.*

His last years. During his last eight years, Shakespeare was the sole author of only three plays—*Cymbeline, The Tempest,* and *The Winter's Tale.* He collaborated with John Fletcher, another English dramatist, in writing three more plays. In the past, some scholars argued that *The Tempest,* written about 1610, was Shakespeare's last play. Such a theory was encouraged by the presence in the play of passages that sound like a farewell to the stage. However, in 1612 and 1613, Shakespeare worked closely with Fletcher, who replaced him as the chief dramatist for the King's Men, on *Cardenio* (now lost), *King Henry VIII,* and *Two Noble Kinsmen.* In addition, Shakespeare purchased a house in the Blackfriars district of London in 1613. The evidence thus suggests that Shakespeare gradually reduced his activity in London rather than ending it abruptly.

By 1612, Shakespeare had become England's most successful playwright. He apparently divided his time between Stratford and London. He had lodgings in London at least until 1604 and probably until 1611. Such family events as his daughter Susanna's marriage in 1607 and his mother's death in 1608 would likely have called him back to Stratford. By 1612, he may have spent much of his time in the comforts of New Place in Stratford.

On Feb. 10, 1616, Shakespeare's younger daughter, Judith, married Thomas Quiney, the son of his Stratford neighbor Richard Quiney. Six weeks later, Shakespeare revised his will. Within a month, he died. He was buried inside the Stratford parish church. His monument records the day of death as April 23, the generally accepted date of his birth.

Shakespeare's son, Hamnet, died in 1596 at the age of 11. The playwright's daughter Susanna had one child, Elizabeth, who bore no children. Shakespeare's daughter Judith gave birth to three boys, but they died before she did. Shakespeare's last direct descendant, his granddaughter Elizabeth, died in 1670.

England of Shakespeare's day

During most of Shakespeare's lifetime, England was ruled by Queen Elizabeth I. Her reign is often called the Elizabethan Age. Shakespeare's works reflect the cultural, social, and political conditions of the Elizabethan Age. Knowledge of these conditions can provide greater understanding of Shakespeare's plays and poems. For example, most Elizabethans believed in ghosts, witches, and magicians. No biographical evidence exists that Shakespeare held such beliefs, but he used them effectively in his works. Ghosts play an important part in *Hamlet, Julius Caesar, Macbeth,* and *Richard III.* Witches are major characters in *Macbeth.* Prospero, the hero of *The Tempest,* is a magician.

Shakespeare's London had grown from 120,000 inhabitants in 1550 to 200,000 by 1600. By 1650, London contained 375,000 people. This exceptional population growth is remarkable considering London's high mortality rate. The crowded and unsanitary city often experienced outbreaks of plague that regularly reduced the population. Sewage flowed in open ditches that drained into the Thames, and overbuilding led to slum conditions in many parts of the city. However, London continued to grow as the result of a massive flow of migrants, like Shakespeare himself, from the English countryside.

The crowded streets helped give London an air of bustling activity. But other factors also made London an exciting city. It was the commercial and banking center of England and one of the world's chief trading centers. London was also the capital of England. The queen and her court lived there for much of each year, adding to the color and excitement. The city's importance attracted people from throughout England and from other countries. Artists, teachers, musicians, students, and writers all flocked to London to seek advancement.

Although large for its day, London was still small enough so that a person could be close to its cultural and political life. The wide range of knowledge that Shakespeare showed in his plays has amazed many of his admirers. Yet much of this knowledge was the kind that could be absorbed by being in the company of informed people. The range of Shakespeare's learning and the variety of his characters owe something to his involvement in London life.

Elizabethan society. It was once common to claim that in the late 1500's, when Shakespeare first began to write his plays, the English people were experiencing a period of great optimism and patriotism. Under Elizabeth I, they enjoyed a long period of relative peace while continental Europe was burdened by war. In 1588, the English Navy defeated the Spanish Armada, an invasion fleet designed to return Protestant England to Catholicism. After this victory, many English writers declared that God had chosen England to play a special role in world history.

However, there were tensions beneath the surface in English life. England was still a Protestant country on the margins of a Europe dominated by Catholic forces. As the 1500's drew to a close, the aged and childless Elizabeth refused to name a successor, leading to uncertainty about what would follow her death. The possibility of a succession crisis leading to a foreign invasion or civil war disturbed both the political powers and the common people.

The peaceful accession of James I in 1603 eased these anxieties, but the enormous expectations put upon the new king soon led to disappointment. Although initially met with enthusiasm, James quickly made enemies of a number of important parts of English society. The early 1600's saw an increase in dramas portraying corrupt courts, though they were always represented as Italian. To many English people, the world appeared to be deteriorating and becoming, in Hamlet's words, "an unweeded garden/That grows to seed."

Certainly Shakespeare's plays reveal a shift from optimism to pessimism. All his early plays, even the histories and the tragedy *Romeo and Juliet,* have an exuberance

British Tourist Authority

A statue of Shakespeare stands in Stratford's Holy Trinity Church, where the playwright is buried. Scholars consider this statue to be one of the few authentic likenesses of Shakespeare.

that sets them apart from the later works. After 1600, Shakespeare's dramas show the confused, gloomy, and often bitter social attitudes of the time. During this period, he wrote his greatest tragedies. Even the comedies *Measure for Measure* and *All's Well That Ends Well* have a bitter quality not found in his earlier comedies. A character in the tragedy *King Lear* cries out in despair, "As flies to wanton boys are we to the gods./They kill us for their sport." These lines reflect the uncertainties of the time.

Elizabethans were keenly aware of death and the brevity of life. They lived in constant fear of plague. When an epidemic struck, they saw victims carted off to common graves. Yet death and violence also fascinated many Elizabethans. Londoners flocked to public beheadings of traitors, whose heads were exhibited on poles. They also watched as criminals were hanged, and they saw the corpses dangle from the gallows for days. Crowds also flocked to such bloodthirsty sports as bearbaiting and bullbaiting, in which dogs attacked a bear or bull tied to a post.

Elizabethan literature mirrored the violence and death so characteristic of English life. Shakespeare's tragedies, like other Elizabethan tragedies, involve the murder or suicide of many of the leading characters.

In spite of their tolerance of cruelty, Elizabethans were extremely sensitive to beauty and grace. They loved many forms of literature, including poetic drama, narrative and lyric poetry, prose fiction, and essays. People of all classes enjoyed music, and English composers rivaled the finest composers in all Europe.

Instrumental music, singing, and dancing are important

in Elizabethan drama. Some of Shakespeare's romantic comedies might almost be called "musical comedies." *Twelfth Night,* for example, includes instrumental serenades and rousing drinking songs as well as other songs ranging from sad to comic. Dances form part of the action in *The Tempest, The Winter's Tale,* and *Romeo and Juliet.*

The English ruler. Shakespeare's 10 history plays deal with English kings and nobility. Nine of the plays concern events from 1398 to the 1540's. A knowledge of these events and of the Elizabethans' attitude toward their own ruler can help a playgoer or reader understand Shakespeare's histories.

During the 100 years before Elizabeth I became queen, violent political and religious conflicts had weakened the throne. From 1455 to the 1480's, a series of particularly bitter civil wars tore England apart. The wars centered on the efforts of two rival families—the House of Lancaster and the House of York—to control the throne. The wars are called the Wars of the Roses because Lancaster's emblem was said to be a red rose and York's a white rose. Four of Shakespeare's historical plays deal with the Wars of the Roses. These plays, in historical order, are *Henry VI,* Parts I, II, and III; and *Richard III.* A second sequence of plays, *Richard II, Henry IV,* Parts I and II, and *Henry V,* deal with earlier events that led up to the Wars of the Roses. These eight plays together describe events leading up to the establishment of the Tudor *dynasty* (line of rulers) and

form an extended and sophisticated meditation on a long and turbulent period in English history.

Religion. The two history plays that are not part of the major sequence running from *Richard II* to *Richard III* are *King John* and *Henry VIII.* Both deal largely with the problem of religious conflict. King Henry VIII broke with the Roman Catholic Church and tentatively moved the English church toward Protestantism. His son, Edward IV, was fully committed to the Protestant cause and instituted sweeping reforms after he came to the throne in 1547. After Edward's early death, his sister Mary succeeded in 1553 and returned England to the Catholic faith. Mary's short reign was followed by the accession of Elizabeth, who reestablished Protestantism in 1558. Thus, from 1534, when Henry first declared independence from Rome, to 1558, when Elizabeth took the throne, every change in monarch was accompanied by a change in the official religion. A change in religion was always accompanied by attempts to suppress, often violently, those who remained loyal to the other faith.

As a result of the dynastic struggles of the 1400's and the religious conflicts of the 1500's, many Elizabethans came to believe that a strong but just ruler was necessary to keep social order. In seeing Shakespeare's history plays, they would have understood his treatment of royal responsibilities as well as royal privileges. Elizabethans would have been aware of the dangers of a weak king—

From *Memoirs of the Court of Queen Elizabeth* (1825) after an oil attributed to Robert Peake (c. 1600-1603); Sherborne Castle (The Stapleton Collection/Art Resource)

Queen Elizabeth I and her court lived in Shakespeare's London much of the time, adding color and excitement to the city's political and social life. This painting, completed about 1600 by an unknown artist, shows the queen and members of her court in a typical public appearance. Shakespeare's acting company performed many times before the queen and other nobles.

dangers that Shakespeare described in *Richard II.* They would also have been alert to the dangers of a cruel and unjust ruler, which Shakespeare portrayed in *Richard III.*

The Elizabethan theater

Shakespeare wrote his plays to suit the abilities of particular actors and the tastes of specific audiences. The physical structure of the theaters in which his works were presented also influenced his playwriting. He used many dramatic devices that were popular in the Elizabethan theater but are no longer widely used. Modern readers and theatergoers can enjoy Shakespeare's plays more fully if they know about the various theatrical influences that helped shape them.

Theater buildings. By the late 1500's, Elizabethan plays were being performed in two kinds of theater buildings—later called *public* and *private* theaters. Public theaters were larger than private ones and held at least 2,500 people. They were built around a courtyard that had no roof. Public theaters gave performances only during daylight hours because they had no artificial lights. Private theaters were smaller, roofed structures. They had candlelight for evening performances. Private theaters charged higher prices and were designed to attract a higher-class audience. The King's Men only acquired an indoor theater, the Blackfriars, in 1608 and began to perform there in 1609.

Most of Shakespeare's plays were written for the public theater. However, *The Winter's Tale, Cymbeline,* and *The Tempest* all take advantage of the different kinds of staging made possible by the Blackfriars. For example, these later plays used the more sophisticated stage machinery to represent flight. The more intimate space also allowed the inclusion of more musical interludes, both during the plays and during intermissions. Although the Blackfriars had an important impact on these later plays, what follows will focus chiefly on the design and structure of public theaters.

In 1576, James Burbage built England's first successful public theater, called simply the Theatre. It stood in a suburb north of London, outside the strict supervision of London government authorities. Soon other public theaters were built in the London suburbs. These theaters included the Curtain, the Rose, and the Swan. In 1599, Shakespeare and his associates built the Globe Theatre. Detailed evidence of how the Elizabethan public theaters looked is limited. But scholars have been able to reconstruct the general characteristics of a typical public theater.

The structure that enclosed the courtyard of a public theater was round, square, or many-sided. In most theaters, it probably consisted of three levels of galleries and stood about 32 feet (10 meters) high. The courtyard, called the *pit,* measured about 55 feet (17 meters) in diameter. The stage occupied one end of the pit. For the price of admission, the poorer spectators, called *groundlings,* could stand in the pit and watch the show. For an extra fee, wealthier patrons could sit on benches in the galleries.

The stage of a public theater was a large platform that projected into the pit. This arrangement allowed the audience to watch from the front and sides. The performers, nearly surrounded by spectators, thus had close contact with most of their audience.

Actors entered and left the stage through two or more doorways at the back of the stage. Behind the doorways were *tiring* (dressing) rooms. At the rear of the stage, there was a curtained *discovery* space. Scholars disagree about the details of this feature. But the space could be used to "discover"—that is, reveal—one or two characters by opening the curtains. Characters could also hide there or eavesdrop on conversations among characters up front on the main stage. The gallery that hung over the back of the main stage served as an upper stage. It could be used as a balcony or the top of a castle wall. The upper stage allowed Elizabethan dramatists to give their plays vertical action in addition to the usual horizontal movement. Some theaters may have had a small third-level room for musicians.

A half roof projected over the upper stage and the back part of the main stage. Atop the roof was a hut that contained machinery to produce sound effects and various special effects, such as the lowering of an actor playing a god. The underside of the hut was sometimes called the *heavens.* Two pillars supported the structure. The underside of the heavens was richly painted, and the interior of the theater undoubtedly

Woodcut (1578) by an unknown artist; Folger Shakespeare Library, Washington, D.C.

A belief in witches was common in Shakespeare's time. The playwright used witches as major characters in his tragedy *Macbeth.* This woodcut shows Macbeth and his friend Banquo meeting three witches on a lonely road. The illustration appeared in the *Chronicles* by the English historian Raphael Holinshed. Shakespeare used Holinshed's book as a basic source for *Macbeth* and many other plays.

had a number of other decorative features.

The main stage had a large trap door. Actors playing the parts of ghosts and spirits could rise and disappear through the door. The trap door, when opened, could also serve as a grave.

Scenic effects. Unlike most modern dramas, Elizabethan plays did not depend on scenery to indicate the *setting* (place) of the action. Generally, the setting was unknown to the audience until the characters identified it with a few lines of dialogue. In addition, the main stage had no curtain. One scene could follow another quickly because there was no curtain to close and open and no scenery to change. The lack of scenery also allowed the action to flow freely from place to place, as in modern motion pictures. The action of Shakespeare's *Antony and Cleopatra,* for example, shifts smoothly and easily back and forth between ancient Egypt and Rome.

Although the stage lacked scenery, the actors employed various *props* (objects used on stage), such as thrones, swords, rocks, trees, tables, and beds. *Richard III* calls for two tents, one at each end of the stage.

Costumes and sound effects. The absence of scenery did not result in dull or drab productions. Acting companies spent much money on colorful costumes, largely to produce visual splendor. Flashing swords and swirling banners also added color and excitement.

Sound effects had an important part in Elizabethan drama. Trumpet blasts and drum rolls were common. Sometimes unusual sounds were created, such as "the noise of a sea-fight" called for in *Antony and Cleopatra.* Music also played a vital role. Shakespeare filled *Twelfth Night* with songs. In *Antony and Cleopatra,* the playwright included mysterious-sounding chords to set the mood before a fatal battle.

Acting companies consisted of only men and boys because women did not perform on the Elizabethan stage. A typical acting company had 8 to 12 sharers, a number of salaried workers, and apprentices. The sharers were the company's leading actors as well as its stockholders. They had charge of the company's business activities. They bought plays and costumes, rented theaters, paid fees, and split the profits. The salaried workers, who were called *hirelings,* took minor roles in the plays, performed the music, served as prompters, and did odd jobs. The apprentices were boys who played the roles of women and children.

The acting companies operated under the sponsorship either of a member of the royal family or of an important noble. Most sponsorships were in name only and did not include financial support. From 1594 to 1603, Shakespeare's company was sponsored, in turn, by the first and second Lord Hunsdon, a father and son. The first Lord Hunsdon held the important court position of lord chamberlain until he died in 1596. In 1597, his son became lord chamberlain. Thus from 1594 to 1603, Shakespeare's company was mostly known as the Lord Chamberlain's Men. After James I became king of England in 1603, he singled out the company for royal favor. It then became known as the King's Men.

Shakespeare was unusual among Elizabethan playwrights. He not only wrote exclusively for his own company but also served as an actor and sharer in it. The close association between Shakespeare, his fellow actors, and the conditions of production had enormous influence on his dramas. Shakespeare wrote most of his plays with a particular theater building in mind and for performers whom he knew well. Each major actor in the company specialized in a certain type of role. For example, one actor played the leading tragic characters, and another played the main comic characters. Still another actor performed the roles of old men. Shakespeare wrote his plays to suit the talents of specific performers. He knew when he created a Hamlet, Othello, or King Lear that the character would be interpreted by Richard Burbage, the company's leading tragic actor.

Shakespeare's comedies reveal the influence that specific actors had on the creation of his plays. From 1594 to 1599, the company's leading comic actor was Will Kemp. During this time, many of the comedies seem designed to take advantage of Kemp's talents as a physical comedian who specialized in playing rustic characters. He was especially known for performing *jigs,* short pieces of song and dance with simple plots that were performed at the end of the main play. After Kemp left the company, Robert Armin took his place, and the style of Shakespeare's comedy shifted noticeably. The playwright skillfully used Armin's more sophisticated and intellectual comic talents in such lively but thoughtful comedies as *Twelfth Night* and *As You Like It.*

Elizabethan acting companies were eager to stage plays that had roles for all their major performers. This, in part, explains the appearance of comic characters—such as the first gravedigger in *Hamlet,* the porter in *Macbeth,* and the fool in *King Lear*—in even the most violent and severe of Shakespeare's tragedies.

The exact nature of Elizabethan acting style remains a puzzle. Parodies of acting—such as the "Pyramus and Thisbe" play in *A Midsummer Night's Dream* or the "Mousetrap" in *Hamlet*—provide some clues about what was considered good acting. Occasional comments on performance, such as Hamlet's famous advice to the players, provide another way in which scholars can reconstruct standards of performance. In addition, a consideration of the physical conditions of the theater allows for some conclusions. Most scholars agree that Elizabethan actors spoke their lines more rapidly than modern performers do. In addition, Elizabethan actors had an especially clear and musical speaking style. This method of speaking developed from years of acting experience and from the Elizabethan love for the musical possibilities of the English language.

Dramatic conventions. The writing and staging of Elizabethan plays were strongly influenced by various dramatic *conventions* of that time—customs that the audience accepted and did not take literally. The most widespread convention was the use of poetic dialogue. Although Shakespeare's plays contain prose and rhymed verse, he chiefly used an unrhymed, rhythmical form of poetry called *blank verse.*

Two common conventions that audiences expected were *soliloquies* and *asides.* In a soliloquy, an actor, who is alone on the stage, recites a speech directly to the audience. Or he speaks aloud to himself his thoughts and feelings. In an aside, a character speaks words that the other characters onstage are not supposed to hear. Audiences also liked and expected long lyrical speeches. Many of these speeches had little direct relation to the play's action. Mercutio's "Queen Mab" speech in *Romeo and Juliet* is a famous example.

The boy actors were thoroughly trained and highly skilled, but Shakespeare was always aware of the artificial nature of boys playing female roles. Frequently, the audience was reminded of this fact, as when Cleopatra worries that the victorious Romans will make her watch "Some squeaking Cleopatra boy my greatness." This forces the audience to recognize that the actor voicing this concern is himself a boy. At the same time, the fiction of Cleopatra's remarkable attractiveness succeeds largely on the strength of Shakespeare's poetry. The same is true of other beautiful women in the plays. "The Beauty too rich for use, for earth too dear" of Juliet lies more in Shakespeare's language than in the physical attractions of the performer.

Disguise played an important part in Elizabethan drama. Audiences enjoyed comic situations in which a boy played a girl character who disguised herself as a boy. Female characters masquerade as men in several of Shakespeare's plays, including *As You Like It, The Merchant of Venice,* and *Twelfth Night.* Social conditions also made disguise an effective theatrical device in Elizabethan times. The Elizabethans recognized sharp distinctions between social classes and between occupations. These distinctions were emphasized by striking differences in dress. People immediately recognized nobles by their clothing, as well as doctors, lawyers, merchants, or pages. Characters could thus easily disguise themselves by wearing the garments of a certain social class or occupation.

Another convention found in Shakespeare's plays is called the "bed trick" and is used in *All's Well That Ends Well* and *Measure for Measure.* In this convention, a male character is tricked into believing that he has had sexual relations with one woman when another has secretly substituted herself for the object of his desire.

Shakespeare's audiences. Shakespeare wrote most of his plays for audiences with a broad social background. To the Globe Theatre came a cross section of London society, ranging from apprentices skipping work to members of the nobility passing the time. But most of the Globe's audience consisted of prosperous citizens, such as merchants, craftworkers, and their wives, and members of the upper class. The theaters of London were an attraction, and visitors to the city were often part of the audience.

Shakespeare's plays were also produced at the royal court, in the houses of noble families, and sometimes in universities and law schools. For most of his career, he thus wrote plays that had to appeal to people of many backgrounds and tastes.

Shakespeare's plays

Scholars do not know exactly what Shakespeare wrote. With the possible exception of a short passage from *Sir Thomas More,* no manuscripts in Shakespeare's handwriting exist. Thus, editors have had to sort through the early printed documents to determine what was written by Shakespeare. Their labors have been greatly assisted by Shakespeare's *Comedies, Histories & Tragedies,* published in 1623. This volume, called the First Folio, was published by a group of publishers led by Isaac Jaggard and Edward Blount. The publishers were assisted by two leading members of the King's Men, John Heminge and Henry Condell, who were able to provide copies of the 18 plays that had not appeared before in print. Along with these 18 plays, the First Folio republished an additional 18 plays, making a total of 36.

The 36 plays in the First Folio form the basis of what has become known as Shakespeare's *canon* (accepted complete works). Although *attributed* (credited) to Shakespeare in versions published in 1609 and 1611, *Pericles* was not included in the First Folio. Most scholars accept the play as Shakespeare's, though many argue that it is a collaboration with the English dramatist George Wilkins.

More open to dispute is *The Two Noble Kinsmen,* thought to be a collaboration between Shakespeare and John Fletcher. Past scholars regularly excluded this play from the canon. Since the mid-1900's, however, most col-

Detail of *Long View of London* (1616), an engraving by Claes Jansz Visscher; British Museum, London

The Globe Theatre became the home of Shakespeare's acting company in 1599. It stood near the south bank of the River Thames in the London suburb of Southwark. The Globe is the many-sided building in the lower center of this illustration. A similar structure to the left is the Hope Theatre, sometimes called the Bear Garden.

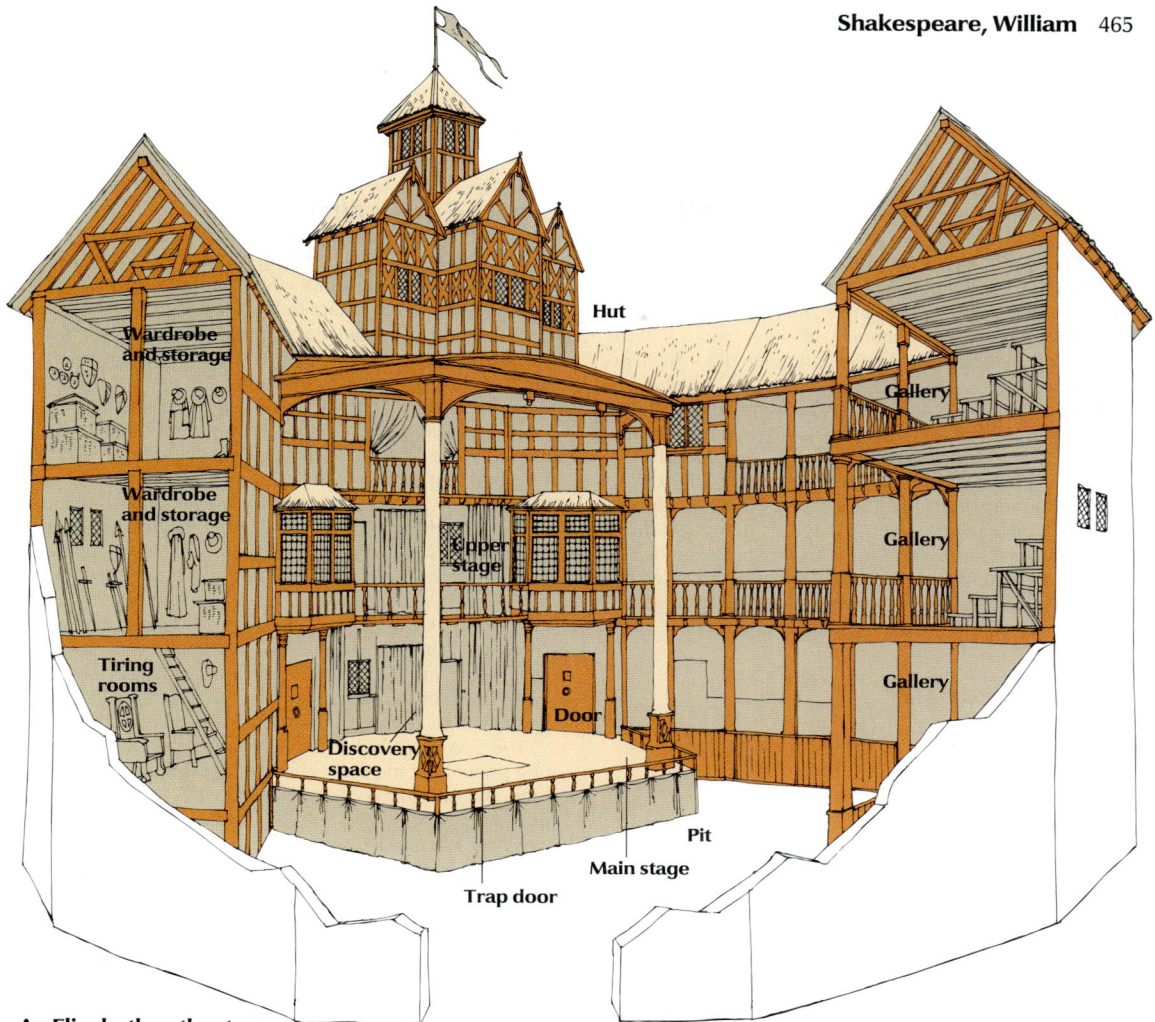

An Elizabethan theater

This illustration shows the general appearance of an Elizabethan public theater. The buildings were round, square, or many-sided. All were open at the top. Spectators stood in the pit or sat in the galleries. Actors performed on the main stage, in the discovery space, and on the upper stage. The hut atop the roof contained machinery to produce sound effects and various special effects.

WORLD BOOK illustration by Allan Phillips

lections of Shakespeare's works have included it, bringing the total number of plays to 38. Collaboration, which was common among playwrights of the period, is one of the complicating factors in determining what Shakespeare wrote. It is now generally accepted that several plays in the First Folio are not solely his work.

Further complicating the establishment of the canon is the existence of various *apocryphal plays*—that is, plays not now considered Shakespearean texts. However, *Edward III*, long considered an apocryphal play, has been included in a number of prestigious editions. There are also two lost plays, *Love's Labour's Won* and *Cardenio*, credited to Shakespeare in records of his day.

The Shakespeare canon is not permanently fixed. New attributions remain possible. But when considered as a whole, the body of work accepted as Shakespearean has remained remarkably stable over the last 300 years.

Much Shakespearean research has been devoted to determine the order in which Shakespeare's plays were written and first performed. The Elizabethans kept no records of play premieres, and no newspapers existed to provide opening-night reviews. The publication dates of the individual plays provide some help because plays were frequently performed before they were published. But because there was often a delay between performance and publication, the publication dates do not indicate exactly when a play was performed.

To establish the order in which Shakespeare's plays were probably written and first performed, scholars have relied on a variety of literary and historical evidence. This evidence includes records of performances, mention of Shakespeare's works by other Elizabethan writers, and references in Shakespeare's plays to events of the day. Scholars can also roughly date a play by Shakespeare's literary style. But for many of the plays, precise dates remain uncertain.

The First Folio divided the plays into three categories—comedies, histories, and tragedies. Modern scholars have added a fourth category, romance. At each stage of his career, Shakespeare tended to concentrate on a certain kind of drama, depending on the tastes of his audience at that time. For example, he wrote 9 of his 10 histories during a period when such plays were especially popular.

Shakespeare generally followed the Elizabethan custom of basing his plots on published historical and literary works. But he differed from most other dramatists in one important way. In retelling a story, Shakespeare shaped the borrowed material with such genius that he produced a work of art that was uniquely different from its source.

This section describes the plots and notable characteristics of the 38 existing plays that make up the generally accepted canon of Shakespeare's dramatic work. The plays have been divided into four periods, each of which reflects a general phase of Shakespeare's artistic development. Within each period, the plays are discussed in the order in which they were probably first performed.

For readers interested in a specific play, the following table lists the plays alphabetically and gives the period in which a description of each play may be found.

Play	Period
All's Well That Ends Well	Third
Antony and Cleopatra	Third
As You Like It	Second
Comedy of Errors, The	First
Coriolanus	Third
Cymbeline	Fourth
Hamlet	Third
Henry IV, Parts I and II	Second
Henry V	Second
Henry VI, Parts I, II, and III	First
Henry VII	Fourth
Julius Caesar	Second
King John	First
King Lear	Third
Love's Labour's Lost	Second
Macbeth	Third
Measure for Measure	Third
Merchant of Venice, The	Second
Merry Wives of Windsor, The	Second
Midsummer's Night Dream, A	Second
Much Ado About Nothing	Second
Othello	Third
Pericles	Third
Richard II	Second
Richard III	First
Romeo and Juliet	Second
Taming of the Shrew, The	First
Tempest, The	Fourth
Timon of Athens	Third
Titus Andronicus	First
Troilus and Cressida	Third
Twelfth Night	Second
Two Gentlemen of Verona, The	First
Two Noble Kinsmen, The	Fourth
Winter's Tale, The	Fourth

The first period (1590-1594). The plays of Shakespeare's first period have much in common, though they consist of comedies, histories, and a tragedy. The plots of these plays tend to follow their sources more closely than do the plots of Shakespeare's later works. The plots also tend to consist of a series of loosely related episodes, rather than a tightly integrated dramatic structure. In addition, the plays generally emphasize events more than the portrayal of character.

In his first period, Shakespeare's use of language indicates that he was still struggling to develop his own flexible poetic style. For example, Shakespeare's descriptive poetry in this period is apt to be flowery, rather than directly related to the development of the characters or the story. Speeches often use highly patterned schemes that involve word and sound repetitions.

The Comedy of Errors is a comedy chiefly based on the play *Menaechmi* by the Roman playwright Plautus. The play was first performed during the period from 1589 to 1594 and first published in 1623.

The action in *The Comedy of Errors* takes place in the ancient Greek city of Ephesus. The plot deals with identical twin brothers, both named Antipholus. Each brother has a servant named Dromio, who also happen to be twin brothers. The twins of each set were separated as children, and neither twin knows where his brother is living. One twin and his servant live in Ephesus. Their brothers live in Syracuse. After Antipholus and Dromio of Syracuse arrive in Ephesus, a series of mistaken identities and comical mix-ups develops before the twin brothers are reunited.

The Comedy of Errors has little character portrayal or fine poetry. But the play is filled with intrigue, broad humor, and physical comedy, which makes it highly effective theater.

Henry VI, Parts I, II, and III are three related histories partly based on *The Union of the Two Noble and Illustrious Families of Lancaster and York* (1548) by the English historian Edward Hall and on the *Chronicles of England, Scotland, and Ireland* (1577) by the English historian Raphael Holinshed, often called *Holinshed's Chronicles*. Each part was probably first performed during the period from 1589 to 1592. Part I was published in 1623, Part II in 1594, and Part III in 1595.

The three parts of *Henry VI* present a panoramic view of English history in the 1400's. The action begins with the death of King Henry V in 1422. It ends with the Battle of Tewkesbury in 1471. The plays vividly depict the Wars of the Roses—the series of bloody conflicts between the houses of York and Lancaster for control of the English throne. Part I deals largely with wars between England and France. But all three plays dramatize the plots and counterplots that marked the struggle between the two royal houses.

The *Henry VI* plays are confusing to read because of their large and shifting casts of characters. The plays are more successful on the stage. In performance, the constant action, exaggerated language, and flashes of brilliant characterization result in lively historical drama.

Richard III is a history partly based on Hall's 1548 *The Union of the Two Noble and Illustrious Families of Lancaster and York* and on *Holinshed's Chronicles* of 1577. The play was probably first performed from 1592 to 1594 and first published in 1597.

The play deals with the end of the Wars of the Roses. It opens with the hunchbacked Richard, Duke of Gloucester, confiding his villainous plans to the audience. He addresses the audience in a famous soliloquy that begins, "Now is the winter of our discontent/ Made glorious summer by this sun of York." Richard refers to the success of his brother Edward, Duke of York. Edward has overthrown Henry VI of the House of Lancaster and taken the English throne. Now weak and ill, he rules England as Edward IV. Richard wants to gain the crown for himself. He has his other brother, the Duke of Clarence, murdered. After King Edward dies, Richard sends the Prince of Wales, the dead king's son, and the prince's younger brother to the Tower of London. After seizing the throne as Richard III, he has the two boys murdered.

Before long, Richard's allies turn against him and join forces with the Earl of Richmond, a member of the House of Lancaster. Richmond's forces defeat Richard's army at the Battle of Bosworth Field. Richard utters the famous cry "A horse! a horse! my kingdom for a horse!" after his mount is slain during the battle. Richmond finally kills Richard and takes the throne as King Henry VII.

Richard is a superb theatrical portrait of evil. Although Richard is thoroughly wicked, his soliloquies give his character depth, and his frequent asides engage the audience. He pursues his schemes with such energy and resourcefulness that he wins the grudging admiration of the audience.

The Taming of the Shrew is a comedy possibly based on *The Taming of a Shrew* by an unknown English playwright and on *Supposes* (1566), a comedy by the English author George Gascoigne. Shakespeare's version was probably first performed in 1593 and first published in 1623.

This play dramatizes how Petruchio, an Italian gentleman, woos the beautiful but *shrewish* (bad-tempered) Katherine, whose biting tongue has discouraged other suitors. Petruchio marries her. But before and after the wedding, he systematically humiliates Katherine to cure her of her temper. After many comical clashes between the two, Petruchio's strategy succeeds and Katherine becomes an obedient wife. At this point, Petruchio reveals himself to be genuinely fond of Katherine.

The Taming of the Shrew is a broad and vigorous comedy that provides two outstanding roles in the characters of the battling lovers. The parts of Petruchio and Katherine have been a showcase for generations of gifted actors.

Titus Andronicus is a tragedy possibly based in part on *The History of Titus Andronicus,* a story by an unknown English author. The play was probably first performed about 1594 and first published in 1594. Some scholars believe the English dramatist George Peele wrote part of the play.

This play is a revenge tragedy, which was popular in the Elizabethan theater. The action takes place in and around ancient Rome and involves a succession of violent acts. The central conflict is between Tamora, the captured queen of the Goths, and Titus Andronicus, a Roman general. The exchange of insults and injuries reaches its climax at a feast in which Titus serves Tamora a pie containing the remains of two of her sons.

In spite of the play's emphasis on spectacular violence, it does have moments of highly charged and effective poetry. The most complex character is Aaron the Moor, Tamora's lover and a self-declared villain in the mold of Richard III. Aaron's plotting drives much of the action, but when the child he has fathered with Tamora is threatened with death, he displays an unexpected warmth and humanity.

The Two Gentlemen of Verona is a comedy partly based on *Diana* (about 1559), a story by the Spanish author Jorge de Montemayor, and on *The Book of the Governor* (1531), an educational work by the English author Sir Thomas Elyot. The play was probably first performed in 1594 and first published in 1623.

The play is a witty comedy of love and friendship set in Italy. Two friends from Verona, Valentine and Proteus, meet in Milan. They soon become rivals for the love of Silvia, the daughter of the Duke of Milan. Valentine discovers Proteus as his friend is about to force his attentions on Silvia. Proteus repents his action, and Valentine forgives him. Valentine then tells his friend that he can have Silvia. But Valentine's generosity becomes unnecessary. Proteus learns that Julia, his former mistress, has followed him to Milan disguised as a page. Proteus realizes that he really loves Julia. He marries her at the end of the play, and Valentine marries Silvia.

In *The Two Gentlemen of Verona,* Shakespeare introduced several features and devices that he later used effectively in the great romantic comedies of his second period. For example, he included beautiful songs, such as "Who Is Silvia?"; scenes in a peaceful, idealized forest; and a young woman, disguised as a page, braving the dangers of the world.

King John is a history primarily based on *The Troublesome Reign of John, King of England* (1591), a play by an unknown English author. *King John* also uses *Holinshed's Chronicles* and may draw on other historical sources as well. Shakespeare's play was probably first performed about 1594 and first published in 1623.

The story concerns the efforts of England's King John to defend his throne against the claims of his older brother's son, Arthur, the young Duke of Brittany. John defeats and captures Arthur, who is supported by the king of France. When the young prince dies under suspicious circumstances, many of John's nobles abandon him and join an invading French force. The rebellious English lords only return to John when they learn that the French, if victorious, will execute their English supporters. A long war is avoided by the intervention of Pandulph, the papal representative, just as King John dies either from poison or illness.

Although King John is on morally questionable ground, he is supported by Philip Faulconbridge, the illegitimate son of Richard I. Faulconbridge is arguably the moral center of the play. His sarcastic and witty comments on the action orient the audience's response to the play, which is deeply concerned with loyalty, allegiance, and legitimacy.

The second period (1595-1600). During his second period, Shakespeare brought historical drama and Elizabethan romantic comedy to near perfection. Particularly in his histories and comedies of this period, Shakespeare demonstrated his genius for weaving various dramatic actions into a unified plot, rather than writing a series of loosely connected episodes. Throughout the second period, Shakespeare steadily developed the matchless gift for characterization that marks the great tragedies he produced in the early 1600's.

A Midsummer Night's Dream is a comedy probably based on several sources, none of which was a chief source. The play was probably first performed in 1595 and first published in 1600.

The play begins in Athens, Greece, with preparations

for a wedding between Theseus, Duke of Athens, and Hippolyta, queen of the Amazons. But most of the action takes place in an enchanted forest outside Athens. In the forest, two young men, Lysander and Demetrius, and two young women, Hermia and Helena, wander about together after they become lost. Lysander and Demetrius both love Hermia and ignore Helena, who loves Demetrius. Oberon, king of the fairies, orders the mischievous elf Puck to anoint Demetrius's eyes with magic drops that will make him love Helena. However, Puck mistakenly anoints Lysander's eyes, creating much comic confusion. Puck finally straightens out the mix-up.

In a subplot, Oberon quarrels with Titania, his queen. He then anoints Titania's eyes with the magic drops while she sleeps so that when she awakens, she will love the first living thing she sees. At this time, Nick Bottom, a weaver, and his comical friends are rehearsing a play they plan to present at the duke's wedding. When Titania awakens, she sees Bottom and falls in love with him. To increase Titania's humiliation, Puck gives Bottom the head of a donkey. Aided by her fairy attendants, Titania woos Bottom until Oberon takes pity on her and has Puck remove the spell. The play ends with the duke's wedding. The two young couples—Lysander and Hermia and Demetrius and Helena—also marry during this ceremony. Bottom and his friends perform their hilariously silly play at the wedding celebration.

For *A Midsummer Night's Dream,* Shakespeare wrote some of his most richly lyrical poetry. Oberon tells Puck, "I know a bank where the wild thyme blows / Where oxlips and the nodding violet grows." The passage transports the audience in imagination to a magic wood where flowers bloom and fairies play. Shakespeare balanced this romantic fantasy with the rough humor of Bottom and his friends. The self-absorbed Bottom ranks as one of Shakespeare's finest comic figures. The comedy also has a serious side. Gaily but firmly, it makes fun of romantic love. As Puck comments, "Lord, what fools these mortals be!"

Richard II is a history partly based on *Holinshed's Chronicles.* The play was probably first performed in 1595 and first published in 1597.

As the play begins, King Richard exiles his cousin Bolingbroke from England. Later, Richard seizes Bolingbroke's property. While Richard fights rebels in Ireland, Bolingbroke returns to England and demands his property. After Richard learns of Bolingbroke's return, he hurries back to England to find his cousin leading a force of nobles who are discontented with Richard's rule. Instead of preparing the royal army to fight Bolingbroke, Richard wastes his time in outbursts of self-pity. He finally gives up his crown to Bolingbroke without a fight. Bolingbroke then orders Richard to prison.

After Bolingbroke is crowned Henry IV, the imprisoned Richard is killed by a knight who mistakenly believed that the new king wanted Richard murdered. At the end of the play, Henry vows to make a journey to the Holy Land to pay for Richard's death.

In *Richard II,* Shakespeare seriously explored for the first time the idea that a person's character determines his fate. The play is a study of a weak, self-centered man. Richard becomes so out of touch with reality that his only defense of his kingdom is the hope that his "master, God omnipotent, / Is mustering in his clouds on our behalf / Armies of pestilence." When he faces the certain loss of

his crown, Richard compares himself to Christ, who "in twelve, / Found truth in all but one; I, in twelve thousand none."

Love's Labour's Lost is a comedy probably based on several sources, none of which was a chief source. The play was probably first performed in 1596 and first published in 1598.

King Ferdinand of Navarre and his friends Berowne, Longaville, and Dumain vow to live in seclusion without the company of women for three years to pursue philosophical study. But the princess of France unexpectedly arrives at the king's court with three female companions. The comedy centers on the efforts of the men to woo the women while pretending to keep their vow. At the play's end, the men propose to their visitors, who promise to give their answer in a year and a day.

This witty comedy has more references to events of the day than do any of Shakespeare's other plays. Many of these references have lost their meaning for modern audiences, which makes numerous passages difficult to understand. In addition, much of the language is elaborate and artificial. But Shakespeare included two simple and lovely songs—"When Daisies Pied and Violets Blue" and "When Icicles Hang by the Wall." *Love's Labour's Lost* also has handsome scenes of spectacle and several entertaining comic characters.

Romeo and Juliet is a tragedy based on *The Tragicall Historye of Romeus and Juliet* (1562), a poem by the English author Arthur Brooke. The play was probably first performed in 1596 and first published in 1597.

Romeo and Juliet deals with two teenage lovers in Verona, Italy, who are caught in a bitter feud between their families, the Montagues and the Capulets. Romeo, a Montague, and his friends come uninvited to a masked ball given by the Capulets. At the ball, Romeo meets Juliet, a Capulet, and they fall in love. The next day, the couple are secretly married by Friar Laurence. Returning from the wedding, Romeo meets Juliet's cousin Tybalt, who tries to pick a fight with him. But Romeo refuses to fight his new relative. To defend the Montague honor, Romeo's friend Mercutio accepts Tybalt's challenge. As Romeo attempts to part the young men, Tybalt stabs and kills Mercutio. In revenge, Romeo kills Tybalt. As a result, Romeo is exiled from Verona.

Juliet's father, unaware that she is already married, tries to force her to marry a kinsman named Paris. To allow Juliet to escape from her father's demand, Friar Laurence gives Juliet a drug that puts her into a deathlike sleep for 42 hours. The friar sends a messenger to the exiled Romeo to tell him of the drug, but the messenger is delayed. Romeo hears that Juliet is dead and hurries to the tomb where she has been placed. There, he takes poison and dies by Juliet's side. Juliet awakens to find her husband dead and stabs herself. The discovery of the dead lovers convinces the two families that they must end their feud.

The popularity of *Romeo and Juliet* owes much to Shakespeare's sympathy for the young people in the play. Although the play does suggest that the boldness of young love is dangerous, Shakespeare does not present Romeo and Juliet as responsible for their fate. Instead, the play draws attention to the violence and aggressivenesss that shapes the adult world. The success of the play also comes from effective characterizations and intensely lyrical poetry. Shakespeare's language shows signs of the

Shakespeare, William 469

A Midsummer Night's Dream is a comedy that mixes realistic humor with scenes involving fairies and enchanted lovers. England's Royal Shakespeare Company gained acclaim for its imaginative interpretation of the play. This scene from the company's production shows fairies singing Titania, their queen, to sleep.

Holte Photographics

simpler, more direct style he would use in his later tragedies.

The Merchant of Venice is a comedy partly based on a story in *Il Pecorone,* a collection of tales written about 1378 by the Italian author Giovanni Fiorentino. The play was probably first performed in 1597 and first published in 1600.

Antonio, a merchant in Venice, Italy, borrows money from the Jewish moneylender Shylock to help his friend Bassanio. Antonio has promised Shylock a pound of his flesh if he does not repay the loan in three months. The three months pass, and Shylock demands his money. But Antonio cannot pay. Shylock then demands the pound of flesh.

Meanwhile, Bassanio has courted and married the beautiful and gifted heiress Portia. She has a plan to save Antonio from Shylock. Shylock goes to court to demand the flesh. Portia, disguised as a learned lawyer, asks him to reconsider in a famous speech that begins, "The quality of mercy is not strained." Shylock remains firm. Portia then explains that he can, according to the contract, take one pound of flesh but not a drop of blood. If Shylock spills any blood, he will not only forfeit his own property but his life as well. Shylock drops his demand, and Antonio is saved.

In *The Merchant of Venice,* Shakespeare combined comic intrigue with a vivid portrait of hatred and greed. Although the play ends happily for everyone except Shylock and the melancholy Bassanio, it is not a light-hearted comedy. In Shakespeare's time, both the church and the state considered moneylending at high interest a crime. Shylock was thus a natural object of scorn. On the surface, Shakespeare's view of him reflected the attitudes of the day. But the dramatist treated the moneylender as a human and even sympathetic person. For example, Shakespeare provided Shylock with an eloquent statement of how it feels to be part of a harshly treated minority: "If you prick us, do we not bleed? If you tickle us, do we not laugh? If you poison us, do we not die? And if you wrong us, shall we not revenge?"

Henry IV, Parts I and II, are two related histories based on *Holinshed's Chronicles* and on *The Famous Victories of*

Henry the Fifth, a play by an unknown English author. Part I was likely first performed in 1597 and first published in 1598. Part II was probably first performed in 1598 and first published in 1600.

The two parts of *Henry IV* dramatize events that follow the murder of England's King Richard II. In Part I, the guilt-ridden Henry IV wants to go to the Holy Land in repentance for Richard's death. But political unrest in England prevents him. At the same time, Prince Hal, his son, leads an apparently irresponsible life with his brawling friends, led by the fat, jolly knight Sir John Falstaff. Falstaff's clowning provides most of the play's humor. The king quarrels with Henry Percy, known as Hotspur, the fiery young son of the powerful Earl of Northumberland. As a result of the quarrel, the Percy family revolts. At the Battle of Shrewsbury, Hal reveals himself to be a brave warrior and kills Hotspur.

Part II of *Henry IV* also has many scenes of Falstaff's clowning. These scenes are set against the background of the continuing Percy rebellion and the approaching death of Henry IV, who is ill. Hal's brother, Prince John, finally defeats the rebels. The king dies, and Hal takes the throne as Henry V. He quickly reveals his royal qualities and rejects Falstaff and his friends, telling them to stay away until they have abandoned their wild living.

Of the two plays, Part I is more memorable. It introduces Falstaff, best characterized by his comment in Part II that "I am not only witty in myself, but the cause that wit is in other men." Falstaff is a bragging, lying, and thievish drunkard. But his faults are balanced by his clever sense of humor, his contagious love of life, and his refusal to take either himself or the world seriously. Falstaff is one of the great comic roles in the theater.

As You Like It is a comedy partly based on *Rosalynde* (1590), a novel by the English author Thomas Lodge. The play was probably first performed in 1599 and first published in 1623.

Rosalind and her cousin Celia leave the court of Celia's father, Duke Frederick, after he unjustly banishes Rosalind. Accompanied by Touchstone, the court jester, the two young women take refuge in the Forest of Arden. Also in the forest are Orlando, who loves Rosalind;

Jaques, a melancholy philosopher; Audrey, a goatherd; Silvius, a shepherd; and Phebe, a shepherdess. Duke Frederick's brother, who is Rosalind's father and the rightful ruler of the land, lives in the forest with a band of merry outlaws.

Rosalind, disguised as a young shepherd named Ganymede, meets Orlando in the forest. Not recognizing the young woman in disguise, Orlando agrees to pretend that Ganymede is Rosalind so he can practice his declarations of love. Rosalind finally reveals her identity and marries Orlando. Oliver, Orlando's formerly wicked brother, marries Celia, Touchstone marries Audrey, and Silvius marries Phebe. The news that Rosalind's father has been restored to his dukedom completes the comedy's happy ending.

Like many other Elizabethan romantic comedies, *As You Like It* concerns young lovers who pursue their happy destiny in a world seemingly far removed from reality. Although evil threatens, it never harms. Shakespeare enriched the play with beautiful poetry as well as several charming songs.

Shakespeare consistently balanced the merry laughter of *As You Like It* with seriousness and even sadness. Touchstone's wit and Jaques's remarks question the nature of love and the values of society. The play discusses the advantages and disadvantages of city and country life. Jaques adds a strong note of melancholy to the play with his famous description of the seven ages of man. At the end of the description, he claims that man's final fate is "second childishness and mere oblivion, / Sans [without] teeth, sans eyes, sans taste, sans everything."

Henry V is a history partly based on *Holinshed's Chronicles* and on *The Famous Victories of Henry the Fifth,* a play by an unknown English author. *Henry V* was probably first performed in 1599 and first published in 1600.

The play continues the action of *Henry IV, Part II,* and presents an idealized portrait of England's King Henry V. The king decides to press a claim he believes he has to the French throne. He heads an army that lands in France. Inspired by Henry's leadership, the outnumbered English

troops defeat the French at the town of Harfleur. The two armies then meet in battle near the village of Agincourt. Against overwhelming odds, the English win a great victory. The triumphant Henry is received at the French court. There he is promised the throne and the hand of Katherine, the French princess.

The play consists of loosely related episodes unified by the character of the brave but modest king. Shakespeare filled *Henry V* with patriotic passages, especially the king's famous address to his troops at Harfleur. It begins, "Once more unto the breach, dear friends, once more." The speech concludes, "The game's afoot! / Follow your spirit; and upon this charge / Cry 'God for Harry! England and Saint George!'"

Henry claims to hate war in general. Yet he finds himself carried away by the glamour and glory of the French campaign. Although the play occasionally seems to glorify war, Shakespeare sets the heroics against a background of political treachery and empty honor. Comic scenes mock the vanity of the royal court. These scenes remind audiences that monarchs and their councils plan wars, but ordinary people must fight and die in them.

Julius Caesar is a tragedy partly based on *Lives* by the ancient Greek biographer Plutarch, as translated by the English writer Sir Thomas North. The play was probably first performed in 1599 and first published in 1623.

The play takes place in ancient Rome and concerns events before and after the assassination of the Roman ruler Julius Caesar. In spite of its title, the play's central character is Brutus, a Roman senator and Caesar's best friend. Brutus reluctantly joins a plot to murder Caesar because he believes Rome's preservation requires Caesar's death. The conspirators attack Caesar in the Roman Capitol, and his final words are "Et tu, Brute? [You too, Brutus?] Then fall, Caesar!"

Brutus defends the assassination to a crowd of Romans. But he unwisely allows the clever and eloquent Mark Antony to deliver a funeral speech over Caesar's body. Antony tells the people, "I come to bury Caesar, not to praise him." He then describes the plotters with heavy sar-

Henry V is one of Shakespeare's most popular historical dramas. The play provides an idealized portrait of the real-life king who ruled England in the 1400's. The English actor Laurence Olivier, shown seated on a horse, played Henry in a popular motion-picture adaptation of the play in 1944. This scene shows Henry speaking to the English troops before their battle against the French army.

casm as "honorable men." At the same time, Antony points out Caesar's virtues and thus gradually turns the crowd into a mob ready to avenge Caesar's death. The conspirators are forced to flee Rome.

Mark Antony leads an army that defeats the conspirators at the Battle of Philippi. At the end of the battle, Brutus commits suicide. Over his corpse, Antony states, "This was the noblest Roman of them all." Antony says that the other plotters killed Caesar out of envy but only Brutus acted with "honest thought / And common good to all."

Julius Caesar has become a popular play because of its magnificent language and sharp character portraits. For example, Caesar describes the plotter Cassius as having a "lean and hungry look." But the real interest in *Julius Caesar* centers on the character of Brutus. A thoughtful, withdrawn man, he is torn between his affection for Caesar and his strong sense of duty to the Roman republic.

Much Ado About Nothing is a comedy partly based on *Orlando Furioso* (published in 1516, revised in 1521 and 1532), an epic poem by the Italian author Ludovico Ariosto, and on a story in *Novelle* (1554-1573), a collection of tales by the Italian author Matteo Bandello. The play was probably first performed in 1599 and first published in 1600.

This romantic comedy concerns the attempts by the villainous Don John to slander the virtue of Hero, the daughter of the governor of Messina, Italy. Hero is about to be married to Claudio, a young lord from Venice. Don John invents an accusation of infidelity that causes Claudio to jilt Hero at the altar. After much intrigue, Don John's plot is exposed and the couple happily marry. Much of the interest in the play centers on the relationship between Beatrice, Hero's cousin, and Benedick, a lord of Padua. These two characters trade insults for much of the play, but they come together in an attempt to restore Hero's damaged honor and soon realize they are themselves in love. This combination of sharp intelligence and lack of self-knowledge produces rich comedy. Broad humor is supplied by the talkative village constable, Dogberry, and his assistant, Verges.

Twelfth Night is a comedy partly based on a story in *Barnabe Riche: His Farewell to Military Profession* (1581), a collection of tales by the English author Barnabe Riche. Shakespeare's *Twelfth Night* was probably first performed in 1600 and first published in 1623.

Viola and Sebastian, who are twins, become separated during a shipwreck. Viola finds herself stranded in the country of Illyria. She disguises herself as Cesario, a page, and enters the service of Duke Orsino. The duke sends the page to woo Countess Olivia for him. But the countess falls in love with Cesario. Meanwhile, Viola complicates matters by falling in love with the duke.

The romantic action alternates with scenes of realistic comedy involving the fat knight Sir Toby Belch and his friends. One friend, Sir Andrew Aguecheek, fights Cesario in a comic duel. Maria, Countess Olivia's lady-in-waiting, tricks the countess's steward, Malvolio, into thinking that Olivia loves him. The plot becomes increasingly tangled when Sebastian, Viola's twin brother, appears and readily agrees to marry Olivia. In the final scene, Viola, still disguised, is confronted by Olivia, who is confused by the youth's refusal to acknowledge their recent marriage. Duke Orsino is enraged by the treachery of "Cesario" and threatens violence. But all is resolved when Sebastian reappears and Viola reveals her identity. Viola and Orsino then declare their mutual love, and the play concludes anticipating their marriage. Only Malvolio is left unhappy.

In *Twelfth Night,* Shakespeare created a perfect blend of sentiment and humor. In addition, he provided Feste, Olivia's clown, with witty comments on the foolish ways of people. Feste's songs contribute both gaiety and sadness to the mood of the play. In one famous song, he reminds the audience that they should enjoy the present because nobody can know what the future will bring:

> What is love? 'Tis not hereafter;
> Present mirth hath present laughter;
> What's to come is still unsure:
> In delay there lies no plenty;
> Then come kiss me, sweet and twenty!
> Youth's a stuff will not endure.

Liz Lauren, Chicago Shakespeare Theater

Much Ado About Nothing is a romantic comedy that centers on Beatrice and Benedick, two witty people who exchange insults until they finally recognize that they love each other. In this scene, Claudio, *far left,* Leonato, *seated,* and Don Pedro, *center,* discuss how much Beatrice loves Benedick, knowing that the concealed Benedick, *far right,* is eavesdropping on their conversation.

Only Malvolio, who thinks he is more moral than other people, spoils the gentle mood of the play. Sir Toby Belch angrily asks him, "Dost thou think, because thou art virtuous, there shall be no more cakes and ale?"

The Merry Wives of Windsor is a comedy possibly based on an unknown source or sources. The play was probably first performed in 1600 and first published in 1602.

According to a popular though unproven story, Queen Elizabeth requested the play. She so enjoyed the comic character Sir John Falstaff in the *Henry IV* plays that she asked Shakespeare to write a comedy portraying Falstaff in love. The comedy dramatizes Falstaff's efforts to make love to Mistress Ford and Mistress Page, two honest housewives in the town of Windsor. Instead of winning their love, Falstaff ends up the victim of a number of comical tricks invented by the women.

Although *The Merry Wives of Windsor* lacks the romantic poetry of most Shakespearean comedies, the play is highly entertaining. The Falstaff in this work has less imagination and wit than the Falstaff in the *Henry IV* plays. But the character remains theatrically effective, even though the audience laughs at him rather than with him, as in the earlier plays.

The third period (1601-1608). Shakespeare wrote his great tragedies during the third period of his artistic development. Except possibly for *Pericles,* every play of this period shows Shakespeare's awareness of the tragic side of life. Even the period's two comedies—*All's Well That Ends Well* and *Measure for Measure*—are more disturbing than amusing. For this reason, they are often called "problem" comedies or "bitter" comedies. *Pericles* represents Shakespeare's first *romance*—a drama that is generally serious in tone but with a happy ending.

During this period, Shakespeare's language shows remarkable variety and flexibility, moving easily back and forth between verse and prose. The verse shows an increasing tendency to allow sentences to extend past the end of the verse line. Shakespeare used a rhythmic pattern called *iambic pentameter* in most of his writing. This pattern, or meter, consists of 10 syllables alternately unaccented and accented in each line. In the third period, he shows a marked tendency to vary the standard iambic pentameter line, creating an overall effect of increased verbal fluidity. The writing of this period also is marked by especially dense descriptive language. Shakespeare's language becomes a flexible dramatic tool that makes possible the skillful psychological portraits that mark this period.

Hamlet is a tragedy partly based on *Hamlet,* a lost play by an unknown English author, and on a story in *Histoires Tragiques* (1559-1580), a collection of tales by the French author François de Belleforest. Shakespeare's *Hamlet* was probably first performed in 1601 and first published in 1603.

Prince Hamlet of Denmark deeply mourns the recent death of his father. He also resents his mother's remarriage to his uncle Claudius, who has become king. The ghost of Hamlet's father appears to the prince and tells him he was murdered by Claudius. The ghost demands that Hamlet take revenge on the king.

Hamlet broods about whether he should believe the ghost. In his soliloquies, he criticizes himself for not acting against his uncle. He also considers suicide. Hamlet decides to have a band of traveling actors perform "some-

Detail of an oil painting on canvas (1839) by Eugène Delacroix; the Louvre, Paris (Giraudon/Art Resource)

Hamlet is a tragedy about a sensitive young prince in Denmark who feels he must avenge his father's murder. When Hamlet sees that a gravedigger has unearthed the skull of his father's jester, Yorick, the prince begins to face the reality of death.

thing like the murder of my father" before the king to see if Claudius will show any guilt. The king's violent reaction convinces Hamlet that the ghost has told the truth. But Hamlet rejects a chance to kill Claudius while the king is on his knees in prayer.

Polonius, the king's adviser, decides to eavesdrop on Hamlet while the prince is visiting his mother in her sitting room. He hides behind a curtain, but Hamlet becomes aware that someone is there. Hamlet stabs Polonius through the curtain and kills him.

Claudius exiles Hamlet to England for killing Polonius. He also sends secret orders that the prince be executed after he arrives in England. But Hamlet intercepts the orders and returns to Denmark. He arrives in time to see the burial of Ophelia, the daughter of Polonius. The young woman, whom Hamlet had loved, had gone insane following her father's death and drowned in a river.

Laertes, Ophelia's brother, blames Hamlet for the deaths of his sister and father. He agrees to a plot suggested by Claudius to kill Hamlet with a poisoned sword in a fencing match. Laertes wounds Hamlet during the duel and, in turn, is wounded himself by the poisoned weapon. While watching the match, Hamlet's mother accidentally drinks from a cup of poisoned wine Claudius had prepared for Hamlet. Although dying from his wound, Hamlet kills Claudius. At the end of the play, Hamlet, his mother, Claudius, and Laertes all lie dead.

Shakespeare handled the complicated plot of *Hamlet* brilliantly. In this play, he also created perhaps his greatest gallery of characters. The role of Hamlet in particular is considered one of the theater's greatest acting challenges. Shakespeare focused the play on the deep conflict within the thoughtful and idealistic Hamlet as he is torn between the demands of his emotions and the hesitant skepticism of his mind. Hamlet reveals this conflict in several famous and eloquent soliloquies. The best known is the soliloquy that begins, "To be, or not to be."

Troilus and Cressida is a dark comedy based on several sources, none of which was a chief source. The play was probably first performed in 1602 and first published in 1609.

Troilus and Cressida takes place during the Trojan War, fought between ancient Greece and the city of Troy. It dramatizes the disastrous love affair between two Trojans, Troilus, one of the king's sons, and Cressida, a woman whose father has joined the Greeks. Cressida is sent to the Greek camp in exchange for a Trojan prisoner. Despite her promise to be faithful to Troilus, she accepts the love and protection of the Greek warrior Diomedes in the enemy camp. The play ends with the death of Troilus's brother, the great Trojan hero Hector.

In spite of its heroic setting, *Troilus and Cressida* is neither noble nor stirring. The play's satirical account of the heroic virtue associated with the epic tradition results in dark cynicism. Although the play has some splendid language, no single character provides an authoritative vision of the events shown. This atmosphere of moral confusion, along with the play's extreme shifts between sexual humor and psychological realism, have led many critics to classify it as one of Shakespeare's "problem plays" because it does not seem to fit neatly into any recognized dramatic category.

All's Well That Ends Well is a comedy partly based on a story in *The Palace of Pleasure* (1567, revised in 1575), a collection of tales by various European authors, translated by William Painter, an English author. The play was probably first performed in 1603 and first published in 1623.

This play takes place in France and Italy. Helena, the beautiful orphaned daughter of a physician, loves Bertram, a nobleman. In Paris, Helena cures the French king of an illness and wins Bertram as her husband in reward. But Bertram considers Helena beneath him socially and deserts her immediately after the wedding. He tells her in a letter that she can never call him husband unless she gets a ring from his finger and becomes pregnant by him. In Florence, Bertram attempts to seduce the young Diana. But Helena, having followed her husband, intervenes. She has Diana demand Bertram's ring in exchange for meeting him. Using the bed trick, Helena substitutes herself for Diana and makes love to Bertram. When Bertram finds that Helena has fulfilled both conditions, he is forced to accept her as his wife.

On the surface, *All's Well That Ends Well* resembles other Elizabethan comedies of romantic intrigue. But unlike Shakespeare's earlier comedies, it has little gaiety and romance. Helena has many of the virtuous traits found in other Shakespearean heroines, but her dogged pursuit of the unworthy Bertram puzzles some critics. Although the play does not emphasize character development, Helena's struggle to save Bertram from his own worst inclinations does present a complex vision of human nature. The play anticipates elements of the late romances in its use of such fairy-tale elements as miraculous cures and its emphasis on reconciliation.

Measure for Measure is a comedy partly based on *Promos and Cassandra* (1578), a play by the English author George Whetstone. Shakespeare's play was probably first performed in 1604 and first published in 1623.

Vincentio, Duke of Vienna, turns over the affairs of the city to Angelo, his stern deputy. The duke hopes Angelo will introduce needed moral reforms. In one of his first acts, Angelo sentences Claudio to death for making Juliet,

his fiancée, pregnant. Claudio's sister, Isabella, pleads with Angelo for Claudio's life. Overcome by her beauty, Angelo agrees to save Claudio if she will allow him to make love to her. Isabella refuses, preferring to let her brother die rather than yield her honor. After much intrigue and plotting, including a bed trick like the one in *All's Well*, Claudio is saved, Isabella keeps her virtue, and Angelo's wicked deeds are exposed.

Many critics have objected to the happy ending of *Measure for Measure*. They consider it false to the spirit of the play. The first part of the play is serious, almost tragic. The latter part becomes a typical romantic intrigue. This lack of artistic unity creates problems. The first part of the play, for example, raises serious questions about the nature of justice that remain unanswered at the play's end. Because of these perplexing moral entanglements, *Measure for Measure* is another play that critics have classed as a "problem play" that cannot easily be categorized.

In spite of its flaws, *Measure for Measure* has many excellent features. Shakespeare drew the characters of Angelo and Isabella with keen understanding. He also included much broad comedy that is highly effective. In addition, his dramatic poetry in *Measure for Measure* at times equals that of the best in his tragedies.

Othello is a tragedy partly based on a story in *Hecatommithi* (about 1565), a collection of tales by the Italian author Giambattista Giraldi, who wrote under the name Cinthio. The play was probably first performed in 1604 and first published in 1622.

Othello, a noble black Moor (North African), has spent his life as a soldier and become a general in the army of Venice, then a self-governing area called a *city-state,* ruled by nobles. Othello elopes with Desdemona, the beautiful daughter of a Venetian senator. Immediately after the marriage, Othello is ordered to Cyprus to defend against an expected attack from the Turks. Desdemona insists on accompanying her new husband. Iago, Othello's aide, declares his hatred of the Moor and begins to plot his downfall. The play's dramatic core consists of scenes in which Iago convinces Othello that Desdemona has been unfaithful to him with Michael Cassio, Othello's lieutenant. A master of psychological manipulation, Iago prefers insinuation to outright lying. He successfully exploits Othello's insecurity over his race, age, and lack of sophistication. Tormented by thoughts of Desdemona's infidelity, Othello murders her. After the Moor learns he has been tricked, he stabs himself and dies, describing himself as "one that loved not wisely, but too well."

Othello is one of Shakespeare's most powerful tragedies. The action moves rapidly without any unimportant plot developments. The language is also direct and forceful. Both Othello and Iago use especially vivid images, but when Othello is enraged, his language becomes fractured and incoherent. The play is centered on the impossibility of truly knowing the mind of another and insists on the fragility of human goodness and love.

King Lear is a tragedy partly based on *Holinshed's Chronicles;* on *The True Chronicle History of King Leir,* a play by an unknown English author; and on *Arcadia* (1590), a romance in prose and verse by the English author Sir Philip Sidney. *King Lear* was probably first performed in 1605 and first published in 1608.

The main plot concerns Lear, an aged king of ancient Britain. He prepares to divide his kingdom among his three daughters—Regan, Goneril, and Cordelia. Lear becomes angry when Cordelia, his youngest daughter, refuses to flatter him to gain her portion of the kingdom. Lear rashly disinherits her, but the king of France agrees to marry her even though she has no dowry. Lear also exiles his trusted adviser, Kent, for supporting Cordelia.

Regan and Goneril soon show their ingratitude. They deprive Lear of his servants and finally force him to spend a night outdoors during a storm accompanied only by his jester, called the Fool. Lear's mind begins to snap under the strain. But as he descends into madness, he finally sees his errors and selfishness. Cordelia returns from France leading an army and finds the king insane. Lear recovers his sanity and recognizes her. Armies raised by the wicked sisters capture Lear and Cordelia, who is put to death. Meanwhile, Goneril has poisoned Regan in a bitter quarrel over a man they both love and then killed herself. Order is finally restored in the kingdom. But Lear dies of a broken heart as he kneels over the body of Cordelia.

Shakespeare skillfully wove a subplot into the main story of Lear and his daughters. Gloucester, a nobleman in Lear's court, makes the mistake of banishing his faithful son, Edgar, and trusting his wicked son, Edmund. Edmund soon betrays his father, who is blinded by Regan's husband. Edgar, disguised as a beggar, discovers his blind father and comforts him. Having realized his error in rejecting Edgar, Gloucester wants only to commit suicide. Edgar remains in disguise and attempts to teach his father the importance of patience and optimism. But after the battle between Cordelia's forces and those of her sisters, Edgar reveals himself to his father, who dies overwhelmed by joy and grief.

In *King Lear,* Shakespeare created the brilliant characterizations that mark his dramas at their best. The characters realize their mistakes, which reflects Shakespeare's basic optimism. But they do so too late to prevent their destruction and that of the people around them. *Lear* is widely regarded as the bleakest of Shakespeare's tragedies.

Macbeth is a tragedy partly based on *Holinshed's Chronicles. Macbeth* was probably first performed in 1606 and first published in 1623.

This play is set in Scotland. Returning from battle with his companion Banquo, the nobleman Macbeth meets some witches. They predict that Macbeth will first become *thane* (baron) of Cawdor and then king of Scotland. After the first part of the witches' prophecy comes true, Macbeth begins to think that the second part may also come true. King Duncan visits the Macbeths. Encouraged by Lady Macbeth, Macbeth murders Duncan and throws suspicion on the king's two sons, Malcolm and Donalbain. The princes, fearing for their lives, flee, and Macbeth is crowned king of Scotland.

But Macbeth has no peace. Malcolm has escaped to England, where he seeks support against Macbeth. In addition, the witches had predicted that Banquo's descendants would be kings of Scotland. Macbeth therefore orders the murder of Banquo and his son, Fleance. Macbeth's men kill Banquo, but Fleance escapes. Macbeth is now hardened to killing. He orders the murder of the wife and children of his enemy Macduff, who has fled to England. Macduff joins Malcolm, who leads an army against Macbeth. By this time, Lady Macbeth, burdened with guilt over the murders, has become a sleepwalker. She finally dies. At the end of the play, Macduff kills Mac-

Peggy Ashcroft and Paul Robeson in a 1929 production; © Hulton Archive/Getty Images

Othello was written during Shakespeare's third period, when he created his greatest tragedies. It concerns Othello, a black Moorish general, who marries a younger woman, Desdemona. Tricked into believing she has been unfaithful, Othello kills her.

beth in battle. Duncan's son Malcolm is then proclaimed king of Scotland.

In *Macbeth,* Shakespeare wrote a tragedy of a man's conscience. During the course of the play, Macbeth changes from a person of strong but imperfect moral sense to a man who will stop at nothing to get and keep what he wants. By the play's end, he has lost all emotion. He cannot even react to his wife's death, except to conclude that life is only "a tale / Told by an idiot, full of sound and fury, / Signifying nothing." On the other hand, Lady Macbeth encourages murder in the beginning. But her conscience grows as her husband's lessens. In addition to its psychological insights, *Macbeth* has passages of great poetry. The play is also noted for its bitter humor, which reinforces the tragic action.

Timon of Athens is a tragedy partly based on Plutarch's *Lives* as translated by Sir Thomas North. The play was probably first performed in 1607 and first published in 1623. Some scholars believe that Thomas Middleton wrote part of the play.

Timon is a nobleman in ancient Athens. Surrounded by flatterers, he spends his money extravagantly. But after he becomes penniless, his friends desert him. Their ingratitude turns Timon into a bitter person who hates humanity. Timon leaves Athens and goes to live in a cave near the sea, where he finds a buried treasure. But his new-found wealth brings him no happiness. He dies, still bitter, in his cave.

Although *Timon of Athens* has flaws, it also has passages of great eloquence. Several such passages occur when Timon pours out his scorn for humanity. Throughout the play, Shakespeare portrays people at their worst, with few of the noble qualities that lighten the gloom in his great tragedies.

Pericles is a romance partly based on a story in *Confessio Amantis* (1390), a collection of European tales retold by the English poet John Gower. *Pericles* was probably first performed in 1607 and first published in 1609. Some scholars believe that George Wilkins wrote part of the play.

This play consists of many loosely related episodes and is uneven in quality. The action in *Pericles* covers many years and ranges over much of the ancient Mediterranean world. The plot deals with the adventures of Prince Pericles of Tyre. Upon discovering that the beautiful woman he has been courting is corrupt and vicious, Pericles flees, only to become shipwrecked. Poor and unknown, he comes ashore at Pentapolis. Despite his tattered appearance, the king's daughter, the virtuous Thaisa, recognizes his basic nobility, and they marry. They have a daughter, Marina, but soon the three family members are separated. The loss of his wife and daughter causes Pericles to fall into a deep melancholy from which he recovers only when reunited first with his daughter and then with his wife.

Pericles shares a number of qualities with the later romances *Cymbeline, The Winter's Tale,* and *The Tempest.* Character development is less important than a complex plot that threatens to end in tragedy only to come to an almost miraculous happy conclusion. Along the way, there is real suffering and even death, but all difficulties are redeemed by the joy of recovery and reunion. The two characters who are most fully portrayed are Pericles and Marina, whose radiant and saintly virtue protects her from the evils of the world.

Antony and Cleopatra is a tragedy partly based on Plutarch's *Lives* as translated by Sir Thomas North. The play was probably first performed in 1607 and first published in 1623.

Mark Antony shares the rule of the Roman Empire with Octavius Caesar and Lepidus. Antony lives in Roman-conquered Egypt, where he pursues a love affair with Cleopatra. Political problems in Rome and the death of his wife force Antony to leave his life of pleasure and return home. In Rome, he marries Octavius's sister Octavia for political reasons. But Antony soon returns to "his Egyptian dish." Octavius then prepares for war against him.

Antony decides unwisely to fight Octavius at sea. During the battle, Cleopatra's fleet deserts him, and Antony flees with the queen. After Cleopatra's ships desert him in a second battle, Antony finally realizes that he has lost everything. Cleopatra deceives him into thinking that she is dead, and Antony attempts suicide. But before he dies, he learns that Cleopatra is still alive. Antony returns to her and dies in her arms. Cleopatra is captured by Octavius, who plans to lead her in triumph through Rome. Although under guard, Cleopatra obtains poisonous snakes and uses them to commit suicide. She dies anticipating her reunion with Antony in the afterlife.

The dazzling poetry of *Antony and Cleopatra* is one of the play's most notable features. Early in the play, Enobarbus, one of Antony's officers, gives a famous description of Cleopatra that begins, "The barge she sat in, like a burnished throne, / Burned on the water." Cleopatra is a wonderfully complex character. She goes from playfulness to irritation, from sweet intimacy to fierce anger, all in an instant. At the same time, she shows courage and determination. As Enobarbus says, "Age cannot wither her, nor custom stale / Her infinite variety."

When Enobarbus becomes convinced that Antony has abandoned reason, he deserts him to join the realist Octavius. In a grand gesture, Antony sends Enobarbus the treasure he has left behind. Enobarbus, overwhelmed by his own disloyalty, dies of a broken heart.

Shakespeare's dramatic use of poetry creates portraits of the play's two main characters that are filled with ambiguity. From the perspective of the Romans especially, they appear to be nothing more than aging pleasure seekers. But the lovers describe themselves in lofty poetic language. The play suggests that there is something noble about them.

Coriolanus is a tragedy partly based on Plutarch's *Lives* as translated by Sir Thomas North. The play was probably first performed in 1608 and first published in 1623.

Caius Marcius, a general in ancient Rome, wins the name Coriolanus after he captures Corioli, the capital city of a people known as the Volscians. Coriolanus returns to Rome in triumph and is nominated for the important office of consul. But he cannot hide his scorn for the common people, whose support he needs to become consul. Coriolanus's superior attitude leads to his exile. He joins forces with his old enemy, the Volscian general Tullus Aufidius, and heads an army against Rome. Coriolanus's mother, wife, and young son meet him outside the city and beg him to spare it. Moved by their pleas, Coriolanus withdraws his troops. Aufidius denounces him as a traitor and has him murdered.

In *Coriolanus,* Shakespeare raised issues that remain particularly important today. The tragedy questions the values of personal popularity and political success. It also debates the conflicting interests of public and private life. Shakespeare's direct and dramatic verse contributes to the play's power.

The fourth period (1609-1614). During his final period, Shakespeare wrote five plays—four romances and a history. Scholars believe Shakespeare collaborated with John Fletcher, who took over for Shakespeare as the lead dramatist for the King's Men, on two of these plays—*Henry VIII* and *The Two Noble Kinsmen.*

The four romances are beautifully constructed, and their poetry ranks among Shakespeare's finest writing. But unlike his masterpieces of the third period, the romances seem detached from reality. Scholars disagree on the reason for this change in Shakespeare's works. Some claim he was calmly looking back on his life and philosophically summing up his career. Other scholars believe that the romances are a response to the growing popularity of plays that mixed comic and serious elements and that in writing them Shakespeare was adapting his work to the changing tastes of his audience. These claims are not, however, mutually exclusive. Throughout his career, Shakespeare was attentive to the desires of his audience. At the same time, his work never appears merely commercial.

Cymbeline is a romance partly based on several sources, none of which was a chief source. *Cymbeline* was probably first performed in 1609 and first published in 1623.

Cymbeline, king of Britain, angrily exiles the poor but honorable Posthumous after the young man marries Imogen, the king's daughter. The treacherous Iachimo bets Posthumous that Imogen is not virtuous. Iachimo then tries to seduce her. He fails but tricks Posthumous into believing that he has succeeded. Posthumous orders his wife killed, but she escapes disguised as a court page. After many adventures, Imogen and her husband are happily reunited. Iachimo, filled with regret, confesses his wickedness.

Cymbeline is a lively mix of historical elements. It includes portrayals of ancient Britons, classical Romans, and, in Iachimo, an Italian plotter who appears modern. Cymbeline's queen is the sort of wicked stepmother found in fairy tales. Her son, Cloten, is a cowardly clown. Posthumous is brave and virtuous, but the play's most appealing character is the loyal and resourceful Imogen.

The play includes a subplot that involves the recovery of Imogen's two brothers, who had been stolen in infancy. These elements unfold against the background of an international conflict between Britain and the Roman Empire. The resolution of all these conflicts allows the play to end in a celebration of global peace.

The Winter's Tale is a romance partly based on *Pandosto* (1588), a prose romance by the English author Robert Greene. The play was probably first performed in 1610 and first published in 1623.

Leontes, king of Sicilia, becomes uncontrollably jealous of his faithful wife, Hermione, and suspects her of sleeping with his boyhood friend Polixenes. Polixenes is now the king of Bohemia, and he has been visiting Sicilia for the past nine months. Leontes tries to have Polixenes murdered, but he escapes and returns to Bohemia. Leontes then orders his wife to prison, where she gives birth to their daughter, Perdita. Leontes declares the child illegitimate and orders that she be abandoned in a deserted place. Leontes sends agents to consult the oracle of Apollo and puts Hermione on trial for adultery. As the trial begins, a report arrives from the oracle declaring Hermione's innocence. But Leontes rejects the oracle and immediately learns that his young son has died of grief. At this news, Hermione falls into a deathlike faint. Suddenly convinced of his error, Leontes is left to mourn the loss of his wife, daughter, and son.

Meanwhile, Perdita has been saved by an old shepherd. She grows into a lovely young woman and wins the love of Florizel, prince of Bohemia. But Florizel's father, Polixenes, angrily disapproves of their romance, and the couple flee to Leontes's court for protection. There, Leontes discovers that Perdita is his daughter. The king's happiness is complete when he is also reunited with his wife, who was thought to be dead. Instead, with the help of a lady-in-waiting, she had been living in seclusion, hoping for Perdita's return.

Like *Cymbeline*, *The Winter's Tale* concerns exile, women suffering from male jealousy, and the reuniting of loved ones. Also like the earlier play, *The Winter's Tale* takes a potentially tragic situation and uses it to stress recovery rather than destruction. Still, there is loss. The young prince and the lord sent to dispose of Perdita are both dead. The play's conclusion includes a wonderful piece of theater in which a supposed statue of Hermione comes to life. The conclusion is finely balanced between the joy of reconciliation and the painful knowledge of loss.

The Tempest is a romance partly based on several sources, none of which was a chief source. *The Tempest*

was probably first performed in 1611 and first published in 1623.

Prospero, the wrongfully deposed Duke of Milan, Italy, lives on an enchanted island with his beautiful daughter, Miranda. The mischievous spirit Ariel and the monster Caliban serve Prospero, who is a skilled magician. Using magic, Prospero creates a *tempest* (storm) that causes a ship carrying his enemies to be wrecked on the island. The ship also carries the young prince Ferdinand. Miranda loves him at first sight and cries out, "O brave new world that hath such creatures in it." With his magic, Prospero brings Miranda and Ferdinand together and upsets plots laid against him by his shipwrecked enemies. Prospero appears before his enemies and forgives them. He decides to give up his magic and return to Italy, where Ferdinand and Miranda can marry.

Like *Cymbeline* and *The Winter's Tale*, *The Tempest* tells a story in which old injuries are forgiven and the characters begin a new and happier life. In *The Tempest*, Shakespeare blended spectacle, song, and dance with a romantic love story, beautiful poetry, and broad comedy. The result of this blending is a brilliant dramatic fantasy. In one of Shakespeare's most famous speeches, Prospero tells the audience:

> Our revels now are ended. These our actors,
> As I foretold you, were all spirits and
> Are melted into air, into thin air;
> And, like the baseless fabric of this vision,
> The cloud-capped tow'rs, the gorgeous palaces,
> The solemn temples, the great globe itself,
> Yea all which it inherit, shall dissolve,
> And, like this insubstantial pageant faded,
> Leave not a rack behind.

Many scholars have taken these lines to be Shakespeare's farewell to his profession. But no one knows if he intended the speech to be autobiographical.

Henry VIII is a history partly based on Holinshed's *Chronicles* and on *The Book of Martyrs* (1563), a religious work by the English author John Foxe. The play was probably first performed in 1613 and first published in 1623. Many scholars believe that John Fletcher wrote part of the play.

The play dramatizes the events that led to England's break with the Roman Catholic Church. It deals with King Henry VIII's *annulment* (cancellation) of his marriage to Catherine of Aragon (spelled Katherine in the play) and his marriage to Anne Boleyn. The play also covers the fall of Cardinal Thomas Wolsey as the king's adviser and the rise of Archbishop Thomas Cranmer as Wolsey's replacement. *Henry VIII* is a loosely constructed drama and better known for its pageantry than for its characterization. But the play attempts to move beyond the anger found in almost all the historical accounts of England's split from Catholicism available during Shakespeare's lifetime. The play's alternate title, *All Is True*, suggests a mildly ironic attempt to create an account of the country's recent past that covers all the major events and invites agreement among the various sides.

The Two Noble Kinsmen is a romance chiefly based on "The Knight's Tale" from Geoffrey Chaucer's *Canterbury Tales*. The play was probably first performed in 1613 or 1614 and first published in 1634. Most scholars believe Shakespeare wrote it with John Fletcher.

The play tells the story of two young aristocrats from Thebes, Palamon and Arcite. Although Thebes is ruled by the tyrant Creon, the two friends decide that loyalty requires them to help defend their city against the attack of Theseus, king of Athens. The two are captured in battle and taken to Athens. In prison, Palamon sees and falls in love with Emilia, the sister of Hippolyta, the wife of Theseus. Arcite, too, falls in love with Emilia.

The two friends argue bitterly over their claims to Emilia. Arcite is released from prison and exiled, but he remains in Athens in disguise. Palamon escapes from prison and encounters Arcite in the woods. The two are about to fight a duel over Emilia when they are discovered by Theseus, who condemns them to death. The king is talked into sparing the two on the condition that they return in a month to fight each other. The winner will marry Emilia, and the loser will be executed.

In preparation for the fight, Arcite prays to Mars, the god of war. Palamon prays to Venus, the goddess of love, and Emilia prays to Diana, the goddess of virginity. Arcite wins the fight but afterward is thrown from his horse and fatally injured. Palamon, on the verge of execution, is permitted a final interview with his dying friend, who confesses that he has wronged Palamon and urges him to take Emilia. Theseus spares Palamon and agrees to his marriage to Emilia.

The Two Noble Kinsmen, like other late romances, has an artificial quality and an improbable plot designed to highlight the guiding role of Providence in human affairs. Like *Henry VIII,* the play emphasizes courtly ceremony and pageantry. However, the play's central focus is on a friendship between two men that is jeopardized by their rivalry for the same woman. Some of the play's best dialogue concerns the qualities and claims of friendship.

Shakespeare's poems

Shakespeare wrote two long poems, *Venus and Adonis* and *The Rape of Lucrece.* Both are *narrative* poems—that is, they tell a story. Shakespeare also composed a sequence of 154 sonnets, which concludes with a short poem called "A Lover's Complaint." He contributed another short lyric, "The Phoenix and the Turtle," to an anthology of poetry titled *Love's Martyr* (1601).

The narrative poems. *Venus and Adonis* (1593) draws on the *Metamorphoses,* a collection of tales in verse by the ancient Roman poet Ovid. The poem tells how Venus, the goddess of love, tries to win the love of the handsome young mortal Adonis. He resists her and is finally killed by a wild boar while hunting.

Shakespeare wrote *Venus and Adonis* in six-line stanzas. Most of the lines are iambic pentameter. The lines of *Venus and Adonis* rhyme *ababcc,* which means the first and third lines rhyme, as do the second and fourth, and the fifth and sixth.

The poem is witty and filled with sexual references. But the work is most notable for its vivid settings and its formal and elaborate speeches. *Venus and Adonis* represents Shakespeare's successful attempt to write the kind of love poetry that was fashionable in court circles and enormously popular.

The Rape of Lucrece (1594) is also partly based on the works of Ovid, as well as on writings by other authors. The poem tells of Lucrece, the virtuous wife of a Roman nobleman. Raped by Sextus Tarquinius, son of the tyrant Roman king Lucius Tarquinius, Lucrece demands that her husband and his friends swear to revenge her ruined

honor. She then kills herself. Her supporters publicize the deed, and the people expel the Tarquins and establish the Roman Republic.

Shakespeare wrote *The Rape of Lucrece* in *rime royal,* which uses seven-line stanzas of iambic pentameter that are rhymed *ababbcc.* The poem is more serious in tone than *Venus and Adonis.* Although the poem describes a violent event that has enormous consequences, it mostly consists of elaborate speeches.

The sonnets. In the late 1500's, it was fashionable for English gentlemen authors to write sequences of sonnets. Some sonnet sequences followed a narrative pattern that was autobiographical in varying degrees. For this reason, scholars have tried to learn about Shakespeare's life from his sonnets. But Shakespeare scholars have reached no general agreement on autobiographical information that the poems might contain.

Scholars generally do agree, however, that Shakespeare addressed the first 126 sonnets to a young nobleman and that the next 26 concentrate on a woman. But they have not been able to identify either person. They have long debated over the nature of Shakespeare's relationship with the young man and have come to no general conclusion. A similar uncertainty surrounds the woman known as the "dark lady." The sexually charged sonnets concerning this figure reveal a mixture of desire and disgust. Attempts to identify the "dark lady" have been unconvincing.

In several of the first 126 sonnets, the speaker refers to another poet he considers a rival for his young friend's affection and support. Scholars have proposed many candidates for the role of the "rival poet," but no general agreement has emerged. Sonnets 153 and 154 are a notable departure from the preceding poems. Ultimately inspired by an epigram in Greek, both sonnets treat Cupid, the Roman god of love. This shift in subject matter has caused some scholars to question the authenticity of these last two sonnets. The volume concludes with "A Lover's Complaint," which tells the story of a jilted woman in 47 stanzas of rime royal.

Composition and publication. Shakespeare probably wrote the sonnets over several years, though their dates are not clear. He wrote the poems in three units of four lines each with a concluding *couplet* (two-line unit). Shakespeare's sonnets rhyme *abab cdcd efef gg.*

Two of the sonnets originally appeared in a book of poetry called *The Passionate Pilgrim* (1599). Thomas Thorpe published the sonnets as a collection in 1609. Thorpe dedicated the book to Mr. W. H., whom he called "the only begetter of these ensuing sonnets." Scholars do not know who Mr. W. H. was or even if he inspired the poems or merely collected them for the publisher. The individual poems have no titles. Scholars refer to them either by their first line or by the number Thorpe assigned to them. Because the volume was not clearly authorized by Shakespeare, scholars have raised questions about the order in which the poems appear.

Themes. In the sonnets to his aristocratic friend, Shakespeare treated a variety of subjects. "Shall I compare thee to a summer's day?" (sonnet 18) praises physical beauty. "When, in disgrace with Fortune and men's eyes" (sonnet 29) shows the power of friendship to cheer the poet. "Devouring time, blunt thou the lion's paws" (sonnet 19) tells of poetry's power to confer immortality.

The sonnets' most common themes concern the destructive effects of time, the quickness of physical decay, and the loss of beauty, vigor, and love. Although the poems celebrate life, it is with a keen awareness of death. This awareness of death is perhaps best expressed in "Poor soul, the center of my sinful earth" (sonnet 146).

A distrust of love and human nature runs through the "dark lady" sonnets. Sonnet 138, which appears below, reflects this attitude. The poem is also representative of the entire sequence in two ways. The sonnet tells of the poet's concern over the passing of time, and it shows his strong emotion controlled by his highly intellectual wit.

> When my love swears that she is made of truth
> I do believe her, though I know she lies,
> That she might think me some untutored youth,
> Unlearned in the world's false subtleties.
> Thus vainly thinking that she thinks me young,
> Although she knows my days are past the best,
> Simply I credit her false-speaking tongue:
> On both sides thus is simple truth suppressed.
> But wherefore says she not she is unjust?
> And wherefore say not I that I am old?
> O, love's best habit is in seeming trust,
> And age in love loves not to have years told.
>   Therefore I lie with her and she with me,
>   And in our faults by lies we flattered be.

"The Phoenix and the Turtle." This 67-line poem appeared in 1601 in the collection called *Love's Martyr*. In the poem, Shakespeare praises ideal love, using as symbols two birds, the phoenix and the turtledove. The poem has philosophical and symbolic qualities that have led to various biographical, political, and religious interpretations by critics.

Shakespeare's style

Writing at a time when early modern English was assuming its fully modern form, Shakespeare and other Elizabethan writers looked upon the English language as alive and changing. They did not consider it fixed for all time in a set of correct and unbreakable rules. Shakespeare, for example, used both *has* and its earlier form *hath*. In the same way, he used the pronouns *thee* and *thou* as well as their modern equivalent, *you*. Shakespeare experimented freely with sentence structure and vocabulary to create special effects. He also used various literary devices to present information and ideas in a dramatic and appealing way. But Shakespeare's style is perhaps best known for its brilliant use of language to create vivid pictures in the mind.

Shakespeare's style has helped shape the language of all English-speaking countries. This influence has chiefly been felt directly through his writings. But it has also been felt through the interest his work has aroused in the literature of the Elizabethan period in general. Many later writers in English have accepted the Elizabethan style as their model. As a result, much English and American literature reflects the highly individualized enthusiasm of most Elizabethan writing.

Vocabulary. Shakespeare's vocabulary of about 29,000 words is remarkably rich. Like his fellow writers, he put old words to new uses, borrowed from other languages, and invented new terms. What sets apart Shakespeare's verbal creativity is that so many of his innovations were adopted by English speakers. Thomas Nashe, a contemporary of Shakespeare's, also freely invented words, but most of them are now forgotten.

However, the richness of Shakespeare's vocabulary sometimes raises difficulties for modern readers. Not all the words and meanings used by Shakespeare remain current. Perhaps the trickiest are the class of words that look familiar and modern but carry changed meanings and associations. The adjective *silly* was beginning to carry the modern meaning of *foolish* or *stupid*, and Shakespeare uses it in this sense in *Love's Labours Lost* and *A Midsummer Night's Dream*. But the word was used in its earlier meaning of *helpless* when Queen Margaret describes herself as a "silly Woman" in *Henry VI, Part III*. Most editions of Shakespeare's plays include notes that define such unfamiliar uses of words.

Rhetoric. Shakespeare and other Elizabethan writers were trained in *rhetoric*—the art of using language to persuade. Based on classical and medieval models, Renaissance rhetoric was an established discipline offering a body of rules and techniques that could be studied, practiced, and absorbed. Rhetorical training was so central to Elizabethan culture that some critics, such as Sir Francis Bacon, began to worry that it promoted an interest in words at the expense of a knowledge of things. Traditionally, the discipline of rhetoric is divided into (1) invention, (2) arrangement, (3) style, (4) memory, and (5) delivery. Although Shakespeare was familiar with each of these parts, style is the most important category for the study of his work. Style includes *rhetorical figures*—devices or patterns in language that change or embellish meaning. These figures are conventionally divided into *tropes* and *schemes*. Tropes involve a change in a word's usual meaning. Schemes are verbal patterns that do not change the meaning of the words.

Classical rhetoric has an extensive classification of schemes, most of which involve word or sound repetition. For example, Shakespeare made frequent use of *anaphora*, the repetition of the same word or words at the beginning of successive clauses or lines of verse. In the opening of *Richard III*, the Duke of Gloucester says:

> Now are our brows bound with victorious wreaths,
> Our bruised arms hung up for monuments,
> Our stern alarums changed to merry meetings
> Our dreadful marches to delightful measures.

In addition, this passage uses *antithesis*, the joining of opposite ideas, to emphasize the contrast between past and present. When the anguished King Lear realizes he will never see his dear, dead daughter again, he laments "Never, never, never, never, never." This is an example of *epizeuxis*, the emphatic repetition of a word, and a perfect example of iambic pentameter. The line is also a powerful and entirely natural expression of loss.

The most important trope is *metaphor*—a figure of speech in which one thing is identified as another. For example, when Ophelia calls Hamlet "The expectancy and rose of the fair state," she is identifying him as a perfect example of young manhood. In *As You Like It*, Jaques begins a famous soliloquy with a metaphor:

>   All the world's a stage,
> And all the men and women merely players.
> They have their exits and their entrances,
> And one man in his time plays many parts,
> His acts being seven ages.

Shakespeare enjoyed using puns. When Claudius, who is both uncle and stepfather to Hamlet, addresses the prince as "son," Hamlet bitterly remarks "A little more than kin, and less than kind." This pun plays on the sense of *kind* as benevolent and as belonging to the natural order. Hamlet is suggesting that Claudius's marriage to Gertrude is both unnatural and malicious. Claudius then asks, "How is it that the clouds still hang upon you?" Hamlet replies, "Not so, my lord. I am too much in the sun." The *sun/son* pun refers back to Claudius's initial form of address. Such serious punning is an essential part of Hamlet's character. Elsewhere, Shakespeare's characters pun for the sheer fun of it.

Imagery. Shakespeare used rhetorical techniques to create rich imagery that gives his writing its unique style. A famous example of his brilliant imagery comes from *Macbeth*. Horrified by his murder of King Duncan, Macbeth looks at his bloodstained hands and says:

> What hands are here? Ha! They pluck out mine eyes!
> Will all great Neptune's ocean wash this blood
> Clean from my hand? No. This my hand will rather
> The multitudinous seas incarnadine,
> Making the green one red.

The image of Duncan's blood turning all the oceans *incarnadine* (blood-red) reveals the terrifying guilt Macbeth feels over committing the murder.

Another vivid example of Shakespeare's imagery appears in *Richard II*. Richard warns Bolingbroke that his rebellion against the king will bring the horrors of civil war to England:

>   He is come to open
> The purple testament of bleeding war.
> But ere the crown he looks for live in peace,
> Ten thousand bloody crowns of mothers' sons
> Shall ill become the flower of England's face,
> Change the complexion of her maid-pale peace
> To scarlet indignation, and bedew
> Her pastures' grass with faithful English blood.

Verse form. Shakespeare reinforced his imagery with the rhythm of his verse. He composed his plays largely in blank verse—that is, in lines of unrhymed iambic pentameter. In such a pattern, each line is divided into five units called *feet,* with the accent falling on every second syllable. Of all English metrical patterns, blank verse—particularly when occasionally varied—comes closest to the rhythms of everyday speech. In his earliest plays, much of Shakespeare's blank verse was highly regular and stopped or paused at the end of each line. In addition, plays from his first decade of work display a high percentage of rhymed lines, which make the verse more forced. But as his writing developed, Shakespeare's verse became increasingly flexible and natural sounding. Perhaps most significantly, verse dialogue in Shakespeare's later work increasingly tends to have a speaker end at midline with the next speaker completing the verse line.

While Shakespeare's verse becomes increasingly accomplished, his plays also employ prose in a sophisticated way. A number of early plays do not use prose, but most of the plays beginning with Shakespeare's second period exhibit some mixture of prose and verse. The two plays with the highest percentage of prose are *The Merry Wives of Windsor* and *Much Ado About Nothing*. In addition, most of the characters associated with prose, such as Falstaff, are notably comic and witty. Whether comic or serious, prose usually serves to mark a shift in tone.

Publishing history

No manuscripts of Shakespeare's plays exist. As a result, modern editions of the plays must be based on early published texts. There are two kinds of these texts, *quartos* and *folios*. A quarto is a small volume containing one Shakespeare play. A folio is a large volume of his collected plays. Twenty of Shakespeare's plays first appeared in quarto form. For his remaining 18 plays, the First Folio of 1623 is the only source.

The publishing history of Shakespeare's plays has been a story of constant attempts by editors to correct errors and deficiencies in the quartos and folios. Editors have also worked to make Shakespeare's text accessible to their readers by marking scene and act divisions, commenting on stage directions, and explaining difficult words and phrases.

Quartos have traditionally been classified as *good* or *bad*. The good quartos are thought to have been printed either from Shakespeare's own manuscripts or from accurate handwritten copies. Generally, the good quartos provide a clear and readable text, but they are not free from error. The bad quartos, in contrast, have some notable deficiencies, including textual errors and a tendency toward compression or abbreviation. Initially, five plays were identified as bad quartos, but soon an additional three plays were added. For a long time, scholars believed that the bad quartos were illegally produced by *memorial reconstruction*—a process in which an actor or actors who appeared in a play would recall the play's language for transcription and publication. Scholars are increasingly skeptical of whether the entire set of bad quartos can be explained as memorial reconstructions. Scholars now generally agree that the bad quartos contain valuable textual information.

Folios. Shakespeare did not live to supervise the publication of his own work. The first edition of his collected plays, known as the First Folio, was published in 1623, seven years after Shakespeare's death. It included 36 plays (*Pericles* and *The Two Noble Kinsmen* were excluded) arranged in three categories: comedies, histories, and tragedies. The two principal publishers, Isaac Jaggard and Edward Blount, formed a group that included William Jaggard (Isaac's father), John Smethwick, and William Aspley to share the costs of production and split the profits.

The initiative behind the First Folio probably came from John Heminge and Henry Condell, who had been shareholders with Shakespeare in the Lord Chamberlain's Men and later the King's Men. As long-time members of Shakespeare's company, Heminge and Condell presumably had access to unpublished manuscripts, and they gathered the texts that appeared in the First Folio. In their introduction, they boast, "As where (before) you were abused with diverse stolen, and surreptitious copies, maimed, and deformed by the frauds and stealths of injurious imposters, that exposed them: even those, are now offered to your view cured, and perfect in their limbs; and all the rest, absolute in their numbers, as he conceived them." Although the First Folio does not quite live up to this statement, it remains an outstanding publishing achievement for its time.

Heminge and Condell obtained the texts of the plays from various sources, including quartos and playhouse

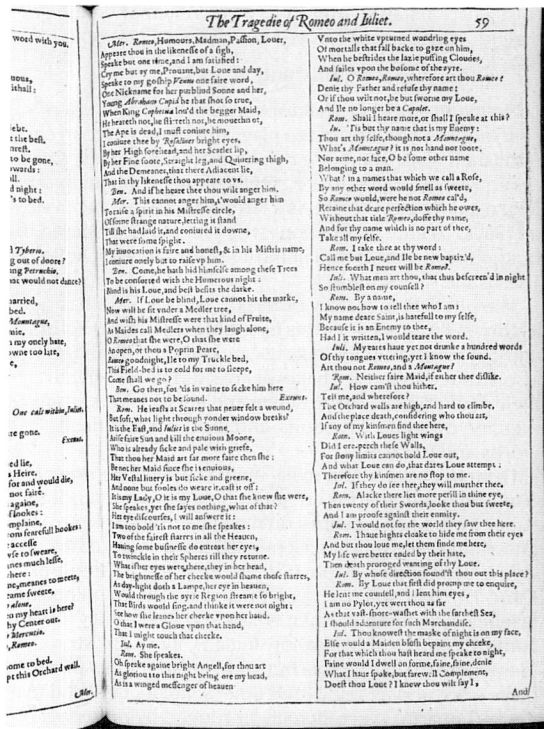

The Newberry Library, Chicago

The First Folio was the earliest edition of Shakespeare's collected plays. The book was published in London in 1623. A page from the tragedy *Romeo and Juliet* is reproduced here.

promptbooks. A promptbook was a copy of the script with detailed directions for performing the play. The First Folio was followed by the Second Folio (1632); the Third Folio (1663-1664), which added seven plays *(Pericles* and another six now referred to as the Shakespeare Apocrypha and not considered authentic); and the Fourth Folio (1685). The final three folios show attempts at editorial corrections, but since each successive folio is based on the preceding one, scholars do not consider these corrections to be authoritative.

Editions of the 1700's and 1800's. During the 1700's, the business of editing Shakespeare began seriously. In 1709, Nicholas Rowe produced an innovative multivolume edition that represented a profound departure from the earlier folios. Among Rowe's innovations were adding a short biography of Shakespeare, carefully observed scene and act divisions, elaborate stage directions that identify locations as well as actions, and illustrations that show dramatic moments in the plays.

Other notable editors of the 1700's, with the year in which their edition appeared, included Alexander Pope (1725), Lewis Theobald (1733), Samuel Johnson (1765), Edward Capell (1768), and Edmund Malone (1790). Theobald's edition is particularly important for its many corrections that try to restore the text to its original meaning. Johnson's edition is significant for its scholarly comments on the plays themselves. Malone's edition is notable for its commitment to authenticity. It is the first edition to include a scholarly description of the language and poetry of the Elizabethan Age, a rigorous examination of the many unverified facts included in Rowe's biography, a full chronology of the plays, and Shakespeare's sonnets.

The first *variorum* editions of the plays appeared in the 1800's. Variorum editions include notes by previous editors as well as alternate versions of disputed passages. The most elaborate is the *New Variorum* edited by H. H. Furness and others. The first volume was published in 1871. The project was later taken over by the Modern Language Association, a professional association for scholars of language and literature.

In the 1800's, the most important edition of the plays probably was the nine-volume *Cambridge Shakespeare* (1863-1866) edited by W. G. Clark, J. Glover, and W. Aldis Wright. In 1864, the edition was published in a single volume. Known as *The Globe Shakespeare,* it became the standard work for scholarly reference.

Modern Shakespeare editions reveal an increasing tendency toward specialized marketing. Editors and publishers concentrate on producing editions for a particular target audience. For example, the Folger Shakespeare Library and Barnes & Noble publish editions designed to make Shakespeare accessible to high school readers. Bantam Classics Shakespeare and the Penguin Group's Pelican Shakespeare and Signet Classics Shakespeare offer paperbacks with light annotations to appeal to both the college market and general readers. Oxford University Press, Cambridge University Press, and the Arden Shakespeare publish series of single volumes for the scholarly market. Editions of the complete works, with texts and reliable commentary, include *The Riverside Shakespeare* and *The Complete Works of Shakespeare* edited by David Bevington.   Jesse M. Lander

Additional resources

General

Andrews, John, F., ed. *Shakespeare's World and Work: An Encyclopedia for Students.* 3 vols. Scribner, 2001.

Dobson, Michael, and Wells, S. W., eds. *The Oxford Companion to Shakespeare.* Oxford, 2001.

Kastan, David S., ed. *A Companion to Shakespeare.* Blackwell, 1999.

Kermode, Frank. *The Age of Shakespeare.* Modern Library, 2004.

Shakespeare's life and times

Burgess, Anthony. *Shakespeare.* 1970. Reprint. Carroll & Graf, 2002.

Chrisp, Peter. *Shakespeare.* DK Pub., 2002. Younger readers.

Greenblatt, Stephen. *Will in the World: How Shakespeare Became Shakespeare.* W. W. Norton, 2004.

Honan, Park. *Shakespeare: A Life.* 1998. Reprint. Oxford, 2000.

Southworth, John. *Shakespeare, the Player: A Life in the Theatre.* Sutton, 2000.

Shakespeare's theater

Aliki. *William Shakespeare & the Globe.* HarperTrophy, 1999. Younger readers.

Barton, John. *Playing Shakespeare: An Actor's Guide.* Anchor Bks., 2001.

Fallon, Robert T. *A Theatergoer's Guide to Shakespeare.* Ivan R. Dee, 2001.

Gurr, Andrew. *The Shakespearean Stage, 1574-1642.* 3rd ed. Cambridge University Press, 1992.

Meagher, John C. *Shakespeare's Shakespeare: How the Plays Were Made.* Continuum, 1997.

Shakespearean criticism

Bevington, David. *Shakespeare.* Blackwell, 2002.

Kermode, Frank. *Shakespeare's Language.* Farrar, 2001.

Index

How to use the index

This index covers the contents of the 2008, 2009, and 2010 editions.

Each index entry gives the edition year and the page number or page numbers—for example, **Clean Air Act** (U.S.), **10:** 189. This means that information on this topic may be found on the page indicated in the 2010 edition.

The indications (il.) or (ils.) mean that the reference on this page is to an illustration or illustrations only, as in **Clinton, Bill,** in the 2010 edition.

The "see" and "see also" cross-references refer the reader to other entries in the index. For example, information on colleges and additional information related to computers will be found under articles indicated.

When there are many references to a topic, they are grouped alphabetically by clue words under the main topic. For example, the clue words under **Congress of the United States** group the references to that topic under several subtopics.

A page number in italic type means that there is an article on this topic on the page or pages indicated. For example, there is an Update article on **Courts** on pages 137-138 of the 2010 edition. The page numbers in roman type indicate additional references to this topic in other articles in the volumes covered.

An entry followed by *WBE* refers to a new or revised *World Book Encyclopedia* article in the supplement section, as in **Cuba.** This means that there is a *World Book Encyclopedia* article on pages 418-429 of the 2010 edition.

Acknowledgments

The publishers acknowledge the following sources for illustrations. Credits read from top to bottom, left to right, on their respective pages. All maps, charts, and diagrams were prepared by the staff unless otherwise noted.

8 © A. Coppel, Newspix/Rex USA
9 © Jason Reed, Reuters
10 © Behrouz Mehri, AFP/Getty
12 © Jason Reed, Reuters
15 © Chip Somodevilla, Getty
16 © Mario Anzuoni, Reuters/Landov
19 © Vincenzo Pinto, AFP/Getty
20 © Scott Olson, Getty
23 AP Images
24 © Robert Galbraith, Reuters/Landov
27 © Jonathan Ernst, Reuters
28 © Gene Blevins, Reuters
31 AP Images
32 © Lindsey Parnaby, epa/Corbis
35 U.S. Air Force/DoD
38 U.S. Marine Corps/U.S. Navy; © Oleg Popov, Reuters
39 © Robert Nickelsberg, Getty
41 U.S. Navy
46 WORLD BOOK photo
49 © J. H. Matternes
51 © Wathiq Khuzaie, Getty
52 © Stefan Falke, laif/Redux
55 © Win McNamee, Getty
58 *The Crucifixion of Saint Peter* (1550), fresco by Michelangelo; The Vatican Museums (Osservatore Romano, Reuters)
60 *Head* (1934), bronze by Alberto Giacometti and *Spoon Woman* (1926-27), bronze by Alberto Giacometti; Tom Evans (used with permission of Art Institute of Chicago)
61 Art Institute of Chicago
62 Andrew Campbell Photography/ Art Institute of Chicago; Charles G. Young, Interactive Design Architects/Art Institute of Chicago
64 Tom Evans (used with permission of Art Institute of Chicago)
65 Dave Jordano, Art Institute of Chicago
66 Charles G. Young, Interactive Design Architects/Art Institute of Chicago
67 Dave Jordano, Art Institute of Chicago; Untitled (Strange Music) (1993) by Félix González-Torres; Tom Evans (used with permission of Art Institute of Chicago)
68 © Prakash Mathema, AFP/Getty
73 NASA, ESA, SSC, CXC, and STScI
74 NASA/JPL; NASA/JPL/Space Science Institute
75 NASA/JPL-Caltech/Keck; NASA/JPL/Space Science Institute
76 © A. Coppel, Newspix/Rex USA
80 © Tim Wimborne, Reuters
84-85 © General Motors/Wieck Media Services
86 AP Images
92 © Shaun Best, Reuters
94-99 AP Images
104 © Ethan Miller, Getty
107 © David Boily, AFP/Getty
114 © Andy Clark, Reuters
120 AP Images
121 © Jason Reed, Reuters
122 © Feng Li, Getty
126 © Andrea Mohin, *The New York Times*/Redux
136 © Kai Schuette, IUCN; © Tim Laman, IUCN

137 © Brad Wilson, IUCN
140 © Michael Macor, Reuters
144 © CBS Photo Archive/Getty
145 AP Images
146 © Diamond Images/Getty
148 © ABC Photo Archives/Getty; © Laura Levine, Corbis
149 © Erik S. Lesser, Getty; © ABC/Getty
150 AP Images; © John Springer/Corbis
151 AP Images
152 © Jonathan Ernst, Reuters; © CBS/Getty
154 © Yale Joel, Time & Life Pictures/Getty; © Michael Ochs Archives/Getty
155 AP Images
162 Special Olympics
164 Força Aérea Brasileira
170 © Bettman/Corbis
171 © Andrew Lichtenstein, Corbis
172 © Matthew Staver, Bloomberg/Landov
173 AP Images
174 © Carlos Barria, Reuters/Landov
175 Library of Congress; © Everett Collection/Rex USA
176 © Phelan Ebenhack, ZUMA Press; © Marie Hansen, Time Life Pictures/ Getty
177 © Hulton Archive/Getty
178 © Tannen Maury, UPI/Landov
179 © Rick Wilking, Reuters/Landov
181 © Krafft Angerer, Getty
183 North Carolina Bookwatch/UNC-TV
186 Apple Corps, Ltd./MTV Games/Harmonix
191 © Sebastien Pirlet, Reuters
195 © Dominique Charriau, WireImage/Getty
198 © Tom Dahlin, Getty
201 © Benoit Tessier, Reuters
203 © Matangi Tonga Online/Reuters
205 AP Images
208 Nikos Daniilidis, Acropolis Museum
209 © Louisa Gouliamaki, AFP/Getty; Nikos Daniilidis, Acropolis Museum
211-217 AP Images
218 © David McNew, Getty
219 AP Images
224 © Reuters/Landov
229 © Charles Ommanney, Getty
235 AP Images
238 © Mohammed Salem, Reuters
240 AP Images
244 © KCNA/Reuters
247 © Justin Sullivan, Getty
249-256 AP Images
260 © Andre Kosters, EPA/Corbis
262 © Shannon Stapleton, Reuters
265 © Jorge Dan Lopez, Reuters
266 AP Images
270 © Behrouz Mehri, AFP/Getty
273 AP Images
274 © Scott Peterson, Getty
275 © DPA/ZUMA Press
276 © UPI/Landov
277 © Olivier Laban-Mattei, AFP/Getty
278 © UPI/Landov
279 Interpol
280 © Lucas Jackson, Reuters/Landov
284 © The Weinstein Company/ZUMA Press; © Fox Searchlight Pictures/ZUMA Press;
285 © Focus Features/ZUMA Press
287 © Paul Natkin, WireImage/Getty

288 AP Images
291 © Chris Hondros, Getty; © Paul Hakimata, Dreamstime; © Chris Hondros, Getty
293 © Timothy A. Clary, AFP/Getty
294 AP Images
295 *The Torment of Saint Anthony* (1487-1488), tempera and oil on panel by Michelangelo; Kimbell Art Museum; AP Images
303 AP Images
304 © Mark Witton
306 © Mick Tsikas, Reuters
307 AP Images
308 Office of Al Franken
309 © Kaori Nishida, World Economic Forum
310 U.S. Department of Justice
312 © Halldor Kolbeins, epa/Corbis
313 U.S. Senate; Stacey Ilyse Photography/ White House
314 © Belgian Federal Government; © Gary Hershorn, Reuters
316-319 AP Images
321 © Sankei Archive/Getty
326 © akg-images
327 © Jose Mendez, EPA/Corbis
328 © Dave Darnell, The Commercial Appeal
330 National Museum of Health and Medicine
331 © akg-images; National Library of Medicine
332 Cynthia Goldsmith, Centers for Disease Control and Prevention; National Museum of Health and Medicine
333 © MCT/Landov
335 James Gathany, Centers for Disease Control and Prevention
339 © Menahem Kahana, Reuters
341-344 AP Images
346 © Alejandro Gonzalez, Real Madrid/Getty
348 AP Images
351 NASA/Thierry Legault
352-353 NASA
354 © Hector Font, EPA/Corbis
358 © Reuters
361 © Scott Olson, Getty
369 © CBS
371 © CBS/Landov
373 © Simon Bruty, *Sports Illustrated*/Getty
375 © Reuters
377 © PA Photos/Landov
380 © Michael Dalder, Reuters
382 © Bloomberg/Getty
383 Berkshire Hathaway, Inc.
385 © Toby Melville, Reuters
386 © Peter Macdiarmid, Getty
395 © Richard Peterson, Shutterstock; © Donald Chan, Reuters/Landov; AP Images; © Tyler Olson, Shutterstock
396 © Shutterstock
397-399 AP Images
400 © North Wind Pictures/Alamy Images; © Everett Collection/Rex USA
401 © Martha Cooper from Peter Arnold
403 © Win McNamee, Getty
404 © Du Juan, Xinhua/Landov
406 © Emily Barnes, Getty
407 © Doug Mills, UPI Photo/Landov; U.S. Air Force/DoD; Pete Souza, White House
410 © Yuri Gripas, Reuters
412 AP Images; © Lang Lang, Reuters
413 AP Images; © Punit Paranjpe, Reuters
416 © Andy Clark, Reuters